Masterpieces of Painting

1(

n u

Front cover: details from pages 26, 266, 5, 574 (top), Paul Gauguin, *Nevermore* (1897, Courtauld Institute Galleries, London) and 733; half title page: Egon Schiele, *Female Nude with One Leg Raised* (see p. 729)

Library of Congress Control Number: 2001095248
Die Deutsche Bibliothek – CIP Einheitsaufnahme data is available

Visit our website www.prestel.com
Head Office: Mandlstrasse 26 · 80802 Munich
Tel. (089) 381709-0, Fax (089) 381709-35
e-mail: sales@prestel.de
Prestel London: 4 Bloomsbury Place · London WC1A 2QA
Tel. (020) 7323 5004, Fax (020) 7636 8004
e-mail: sales@prestel-uk.co.uk
Prestel New York: 175 Fifth Avenue, Suite 402, New York, NY 10010
Tel. (212) 995 27 20, Fax (212) 995 2733
e-mail: sales@prestel-usa.com

Concept and picture selection: Jordi Vigué
Editors: Jordi Vigué and Ramón de Jesús Rodríguez
Editorial direction: Miquel Ridola
Picture editor: Marta Vilà
Design: Paloma Nestares
Typesetting and production: Paloma Nestares and Noemi Blanco
Translation: Mark A. Lodge and Catalina Girona

Printed in Spain
ISBN 3-7913-2582-5

Masterpieces of Painting

1000
nudes

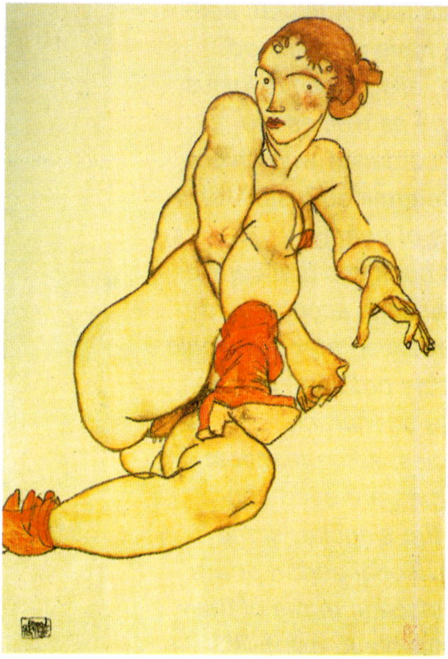

Prestel

From time immemorial, the representation of the nude has been omnipresent in the history of art, and especially in painting. The way in which this subject matter has been conceived and reflected provides an invaluable insight into the social reasoning of each period, and, throughout time, illustrates unequivocally the evolution and development of ideas, styles and, in short, society.

The main aim of this work is to illustrate how the nude has been manifested in Western painting.

Painters have always based their nudes on concepts or interests (sociocultural, aesthetic, erotic, etc.) that have conditioned the motif (mythological, allegorical, religious, historical, romantic, etc.) as well as the forms and styles, in accordance with given manners of thinking, determined tastes, or pre-established canons of beauty.

When compiling this book, we first considered presenting the paintings according to styles, but we quickly realized that this would give rise to an unsolvable problem: many works include elements or characteristics of widely varying tendencies; some manifest influences that sometimes are even contrasted, certain works are singular; some works belong to a transitional period or are chronologically out of place in terms of their style. Since it is not possible to establish a clear division between movements and styles, we finally opted to catalogue the works in chronological order, which not only illustrates everything we have just mentioned, but also gives the reader an overview

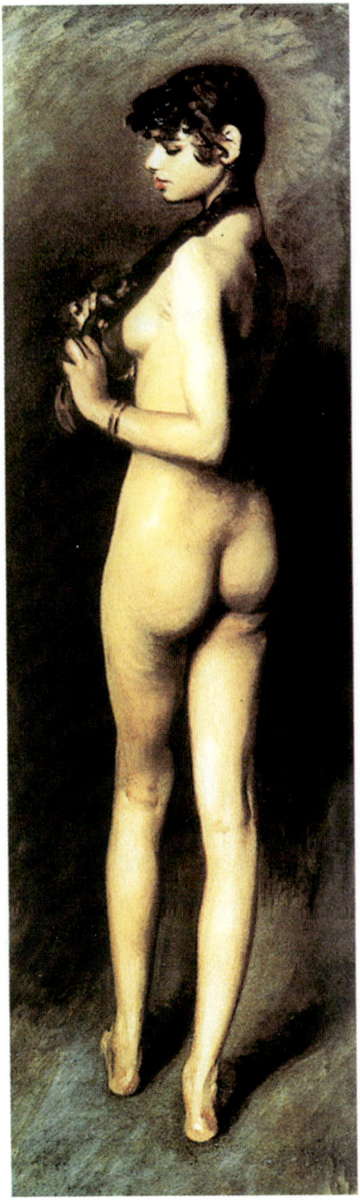

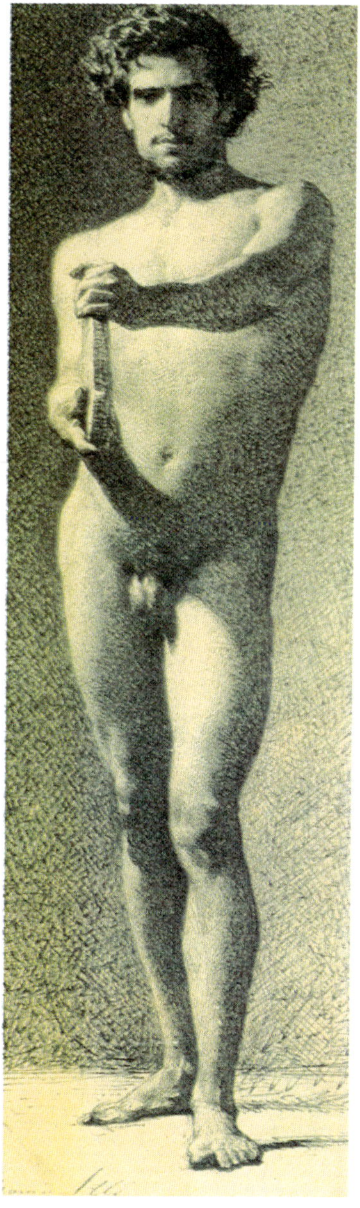

of the evolution of the genre and shows how completely different styles co-existed at the same time and in a specific geographical area. This approach also provides an explanation into the motive behind certain representations, or sociocultural circumstances that brought about gaps or limitations, and the reason that certain themes or scenes were prevalent.

Every effort has been made to ensure historical accuracy in terms of the dates of birth and death of certain artists, as well as the dates and measurements of certain works. Sometimes, such information is unavailable; in other cases, reference sources may contradict one another.

The choice of works could, of course, have been different. Whatever the case, following the work undertaken and the amount of materials studied, this volume fulfils satisfactorily the aim established at the outset: to provide an overview of the nude genre throughout the history of Western painting

If the reader learns something from this book, and/or enjoys browsing through it, then the team that put it together can consider the effort and enthusiasm they invested in this work to have been handsomely rewarded.

Jordi Vigué

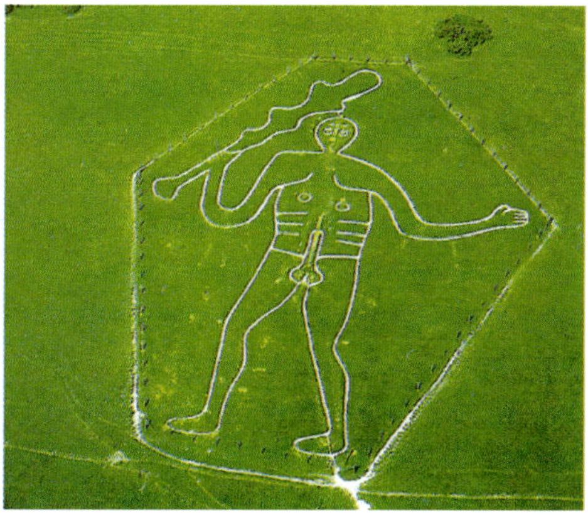

Cerne Abbas Giant

- date uncertain, possibly late century B.C.
- figure cut into the ground
- Cerne Abbas, near Dorchester

The origins of this, as of many other figures cut in the ground, are unknown. The dimensions of such figures suggest they were designed for some form of religious cult or celebration. This figure depicts a giant wielding a club, his erect member a symbol of power and fertility. Despite the figure's size, its line is clean and its curves perfectly executed, suggesting that those who fashioned this work must have had knowledge of geometry.

Paleolithic Hunter

- 15,000-10,000 B.C.
- cave painting
- Chimanimani Cave, Zimbabwe

Paleolithic paintings sought to reflect everyday reality, and a recurrent subject matter was therefore the existentially indispensable activity of hunting. The figures here are schematic to the point where they take on an almost calligraphic quality; they probably played a role in contexts of ritual and magic, possibly as an aid to optimizing the chances of success in a hunt—an interesting representation in the present case, the male organ clearly distinguishable and other anatomical features having been kept fairly realistic.

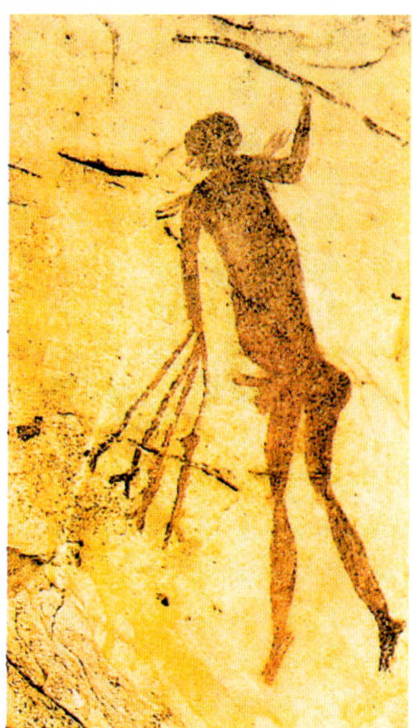

Hunting Wild Boar

- ca. 8000 B.C.
- prehistoric cave painting
- Cueva Remigia, Ares del Maestrat, Castellón de la Plana, Spain

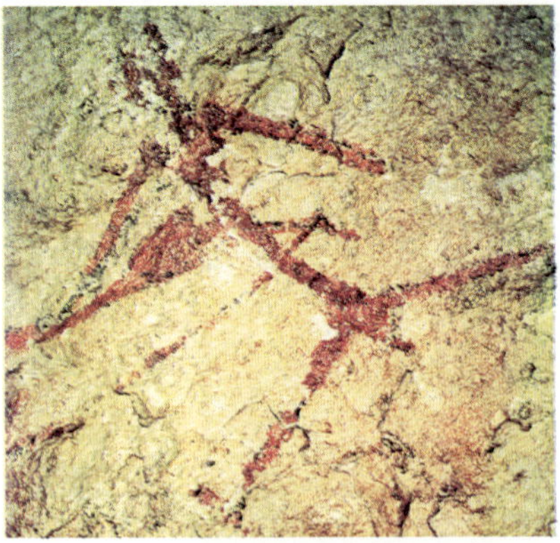

A male figure, bow in hand, legs wide apart, is pursuing a wild boar. The representation of human figures has evolved since earliest times, from a synthetic representation of the body in which the phallus seems to be the only graphic element determining and identifying its presence, as in this painting. The torso and light curvature of back lend the work great subtlety.

Ritual Scene from the Cave of Cogull

- ca. 12,000 B.C.
- prehistoric cave painting
- Cueva de los Moros, Lérida

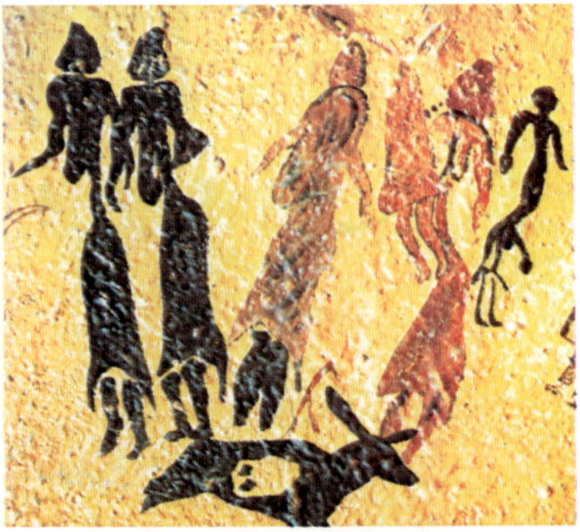

The series of over 45 Mesolithic paintings in this cave were discovered in 1907. In this ritual dance, possibly a fertility dance, large-breasted women are depicted near a man whose member is visible.

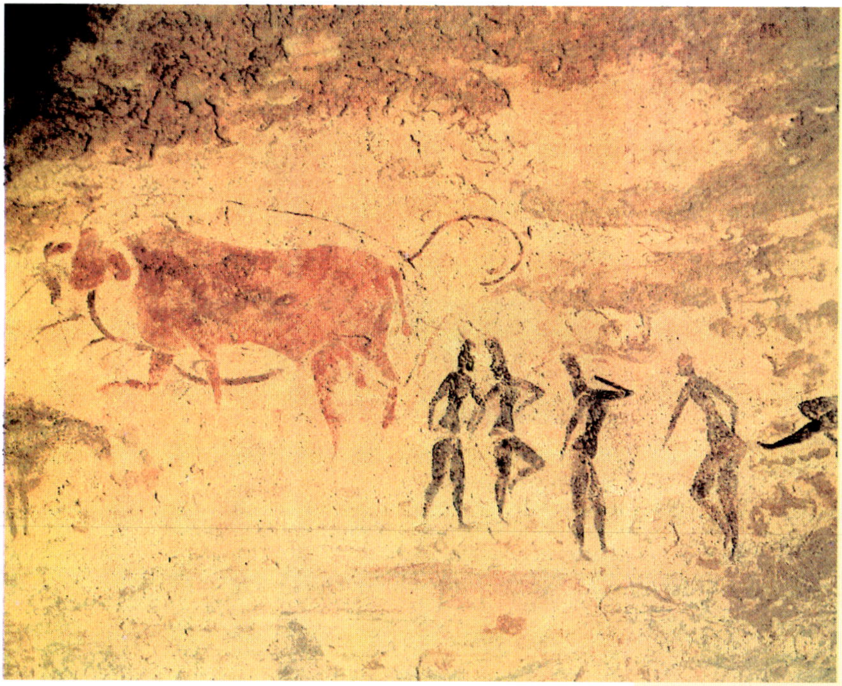

Scenes from Everyday Life

- cave painting
- Neolithic Period (ca. 4000 B.C.)
- Ahaggar Mountains, Algeria

During the Neolithic period, man moved away from subsistence through hunting, fishing and gathering, to the founding of villages based on the production and control of foodstuffs. This seems to be reflected in the present scene. We see slender-bodied figures, probably women, in sophisticated poses: relaxing, resting, conversing and walking with a bull and a cow that form part of their livestock. Despite the thousands of years separating us from them, the gestures, poses and attitudes of the figures are not so far from ours. Their attractive silhouettes and the rhythm of the group of bodies lend the scene great movement, freshness and spontaneity.

Ritual Scene

- rock drawing
- ca. 5000 B.C.
- Ti-n-Lalan, Fezzan, Libya

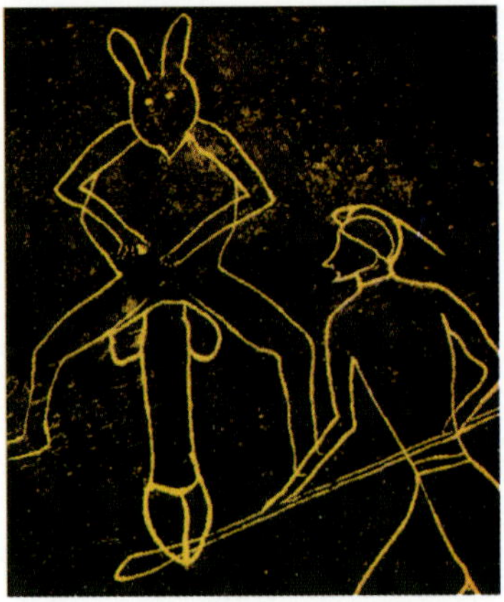

Prehistoric nudes often appear in depictions of rituals involving dances, allegories of fertility, anthropomorphic figures, hunting scenes and the like. This work appears to refer to fertility and hunting, two themes interlinked from both iconographical and magical points of view. A rabbit-like figure displays an enormous phallus, next to it a hunter with a spear; both nudes are linear, their anatomies rigidly defined; while the hunter has an athletic figure, the rabbit-figure's body, for whatever reason, is bloated.

Standard of Ur

- 1st Lagash Dynasty (ca. 2800-2470 B.C.)
- mosaic of ivory and lapis lazuli
- Lagash, Mesopotamia
- British Museum, London

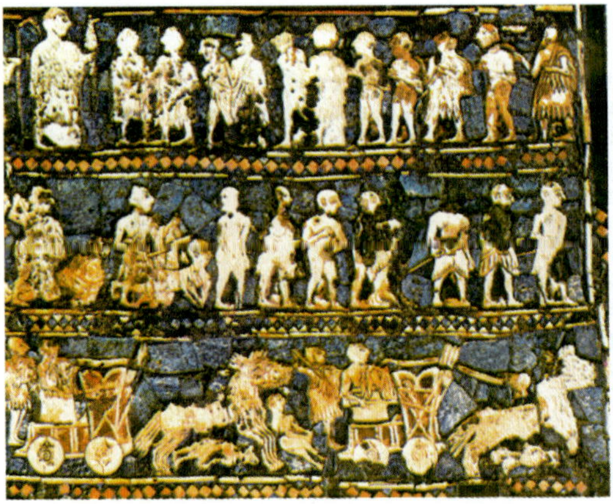

This fragment displays a facet in the life of Sumerian princes, namely war. It is an animated representation of combat involving chariots and nude prisoners that have been artistically executed in a highly naturalistic manner, the contours of their bodies defined through precise draftsmanship. The figures are depicted non-hieratically yet in a clearly-established lateral view, with hints of foreshortening in arms and shoulders.

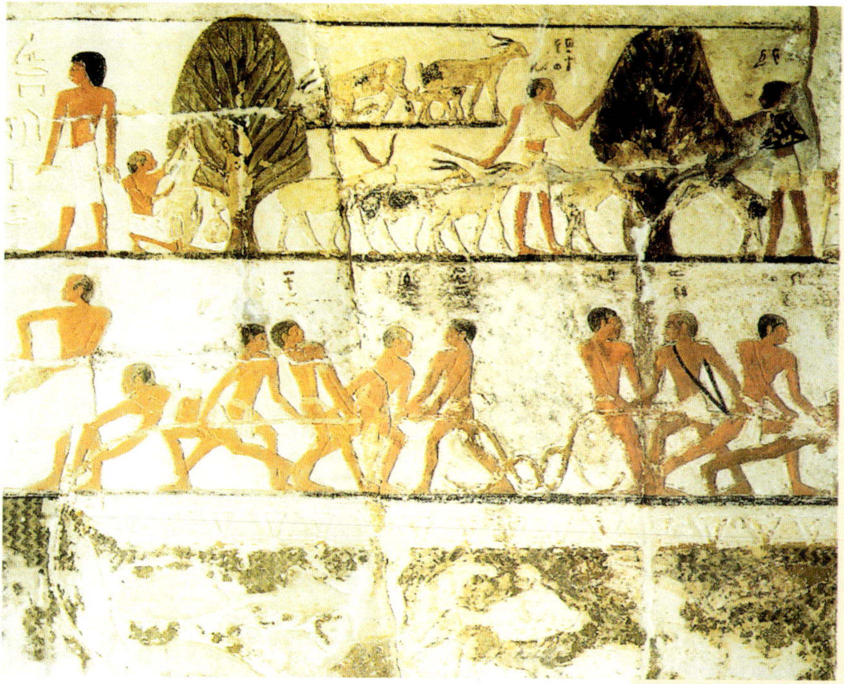

The manner in which human figures were depicted in Egyptian art remained virtually unchanged for thousands of years, the style having been passed on from one generation to the next. Tomb paintings constituted part of the funerary rites. They were a sort of codified reminder that, when leaving this life, the deceased took all their belongings and personal history with them. In the upper register goatherds are shown grazing their sheep among trees. In the middle, men can be seen fishing with a large net, while in the lower register, the net is shown full of fish. The nudes in this mural have dynamic, expressive bodies with tubular limbs. The torsos are rendered frontally while the heads, legs, feet and arms are seen in profile. The figures wear various types of garment to cover their genitalia.

Grazing Sheep and Net Fishing

- middle of the 5th Dynasty (ca. 2450 B.C.)
- eastern wall of the hypogeum of the singers of the Nefer and Kahay Court, Saqqara

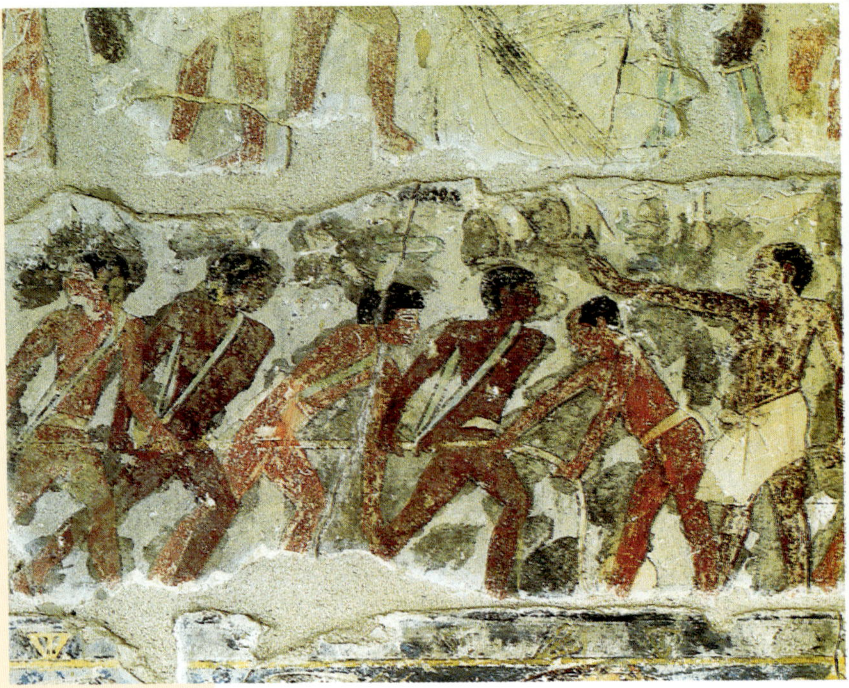

Fishing Scene

- 5th Dynasty, Old Kingdom (ca. 2380 B.C.)
- paint on limestone
- Tomb of Niankhkhnum, Saqqara

The figures represented in Egyptian mural paintings do not correspond to what today would be regarded as a portrait. Yet, if we learn to read these paintings, we soon discover that they provide a wealth of information on the deceased person's social, economic and personal background, even in the minutest details. This scene depicts an everyday activity in ancient Egypt, a group of fishermen who are being directed by an obese overseer as they pull a heavy net laden with fish from the water, no doubt a symbol of the fertile Nile River. Save their harnesses, the figures are completely nude. They are naturalistically depicted, with a careful rendering of the limbs and proportions.

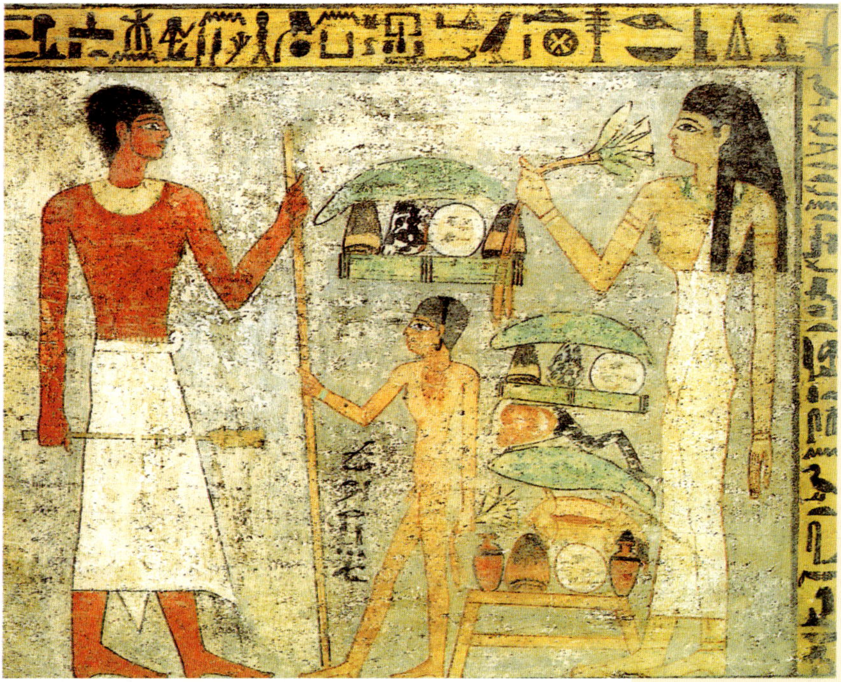

On the left of this funerary stele, the deceased, Heny, holds the cane of a venerable old man and a scepter symbolizing power. His neck is adorned with a broad necklace and he is wearing the customary skirt-like attire and revealing his bare torso. In the center, his son, Rehu, stands completely naked, and on the right is a stylized image of his daughter, It, who is wearing a long white dress that leaves one breast bare. Between the two children appear a series of offerings, several of which are stored in various receptacles. Although in Egyptian art nudity usually indicates a figure's lower social standing, Rehu's naked body here attests to his youth. He is portrayed in a more naturalistic manner than is often the case in Egyptian art, in which children are normally represented with the same features and proportions as adults, only smaller in size. The naturalism here can be observed in the child's build, whose thorax is disproportionately narrower than that of his father.

Stele of Heny and His Children

- Middle Kingdom, early 12th Dynasty (ca. 1920 B.C.)
- paint on limestone
- Glyptotheque Ny, Carlsberg, Copenhagen

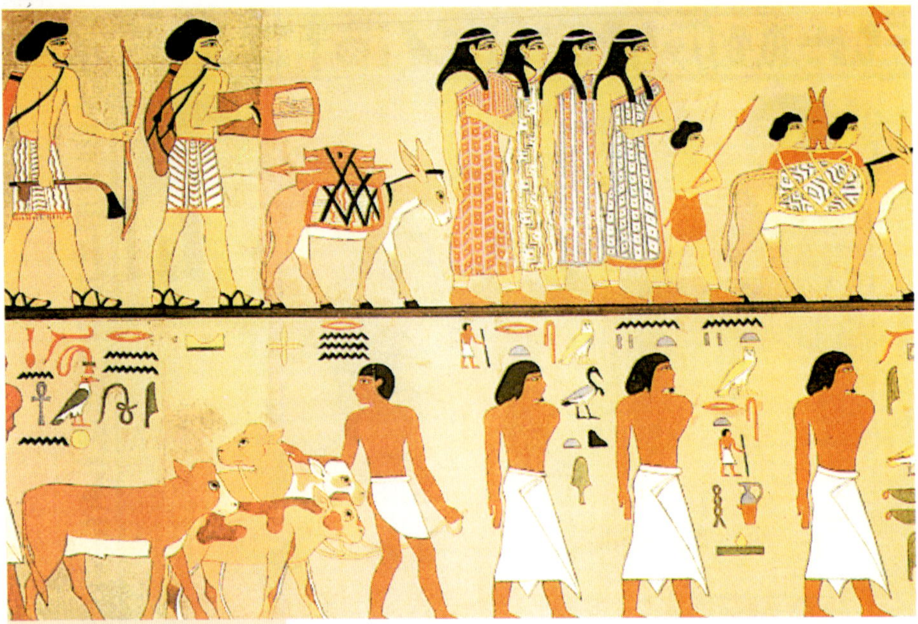

Semitic Tribe Entering Egypt

- ca. 1900 B.C.
- Tomb of Chnemhotep (No. 3), Beni Hasan

Egyptian paintings are usually either of a religious nature or they convey contemporary values, made explicit in the accompanying hieroglyphics. The type of image determined many aspects of the figures, such as their size, attire and placement in the scene. This painting depicts a group of Bedouins entering Egypt with their animals, arranged on two levels. The execution of the figures reveals how strictly prescribed the conventions of Egyptian art were: the feet are shown in profile, as are the heads, whereas the nude torsos are seen frontally, and nearly all the figures are looking in the same direction. They have no other function than to represent the witnesses of an event in which Chnemhotep had taken part. It was standard practice at the time for painters to depict on the walls of tombs the feats of the deceased, at once acknowledging their triumphs and providing a sort of votive offering, which was intended to accompany him on his long journey to the netherworld.

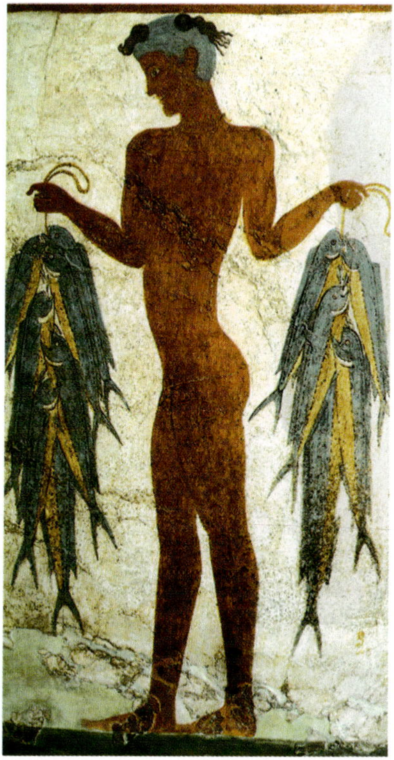

Artistic trends in Greece sprang up one after the other on account of the continual exchange of ideas that took place among the various city-states, or poleis. Numerous archaeological remains exist from the Mycenaean period, especially in the form of architecture and artifacts. This nude is a fine example of the paintings that graced the walls of Minoan buildings. The figure represented here, a simple fisherman proudly holding up his catch for all to see, displays harmonic proportions and a slender build, bearing witness to the Greeks' interest in the human body and the care they took in depicting it, down to the minutest details. The rhythmic, highly attractive figure is imbued with the sensuality inherent in painted Greek figures, despite their lack of volume.

Young Fisherman

- Mycenaean Period (1550–1500 B.C.)
- fresco from Thera, Santorini
- National Archaeological Museum, Athens

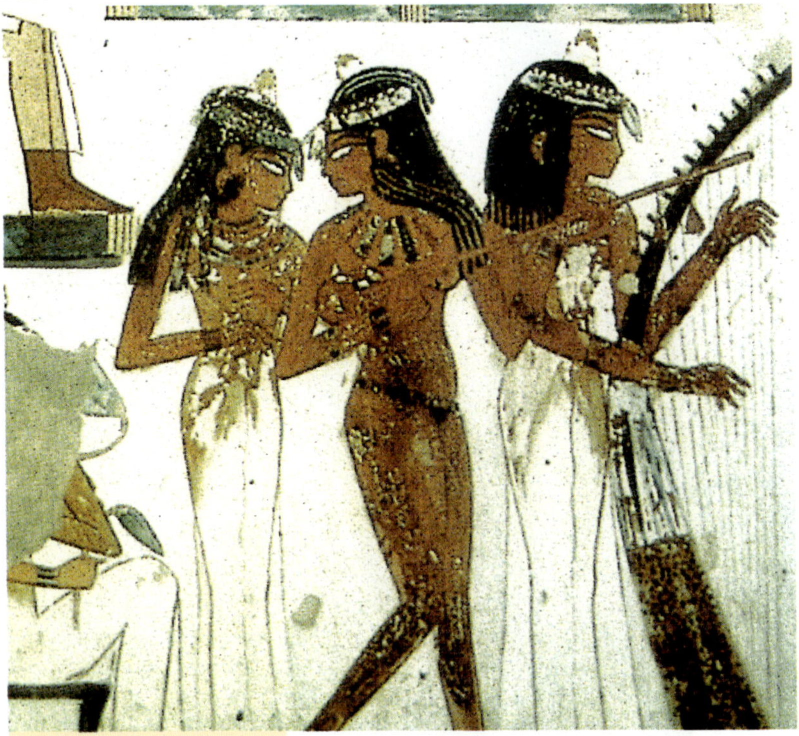

Group of Three Women Musicians

- 18th Dynasty, New Kingdom, reign of Tuthmosis IV (ca. 1422–1411 B.C.)
- paint on plaster
- Tomb of Nakht (No. 52), Thebes

This painting depicts scenes from the festival celebrating the coming of the god Amun of Karnak to beget a child with Hathor, the goddess of the Valley of the Desert, now called Deir el-Bahri. The festival was held there so that both the living and the dead could partake of it. The Thebans went to the tombs of their loved ones and played music there in their memory. This scene presents three women musicians playing various instruments—a flute, a mandola and a harp. The nude, central figure, who danced at certain points during the concert, is extremely elegant and sensual, owing to her feminine curves and the position of her legs. These young women are admirably individualized, each head being quite unlike the others, largely owing to their different postures and the movement of the tresses of hair. The expressive "language" here is centered on the hands, notably those of the girls in long, straight-falling garments.

Blonde Dancer

- 1420 B.C. (18th Dynasty, New Kingdom)
- wall painting
- tomb of Horemheb, Necropolis of Western Thebes (Luxor)

This depiction of a dancer from the period of the New Kingdom of Egypt (18th Dynasty), who performed at festivals in the court of the pharaohs, furnishes a good deal of factual information. The dancer's facial features and (bleached) hair suggest he is a Nubian, a negroid race from the south, who lived under Egyptian subjection on account of the rich supplies of gold found in their country. Great attention has been given to the dancer's gestures and costume.

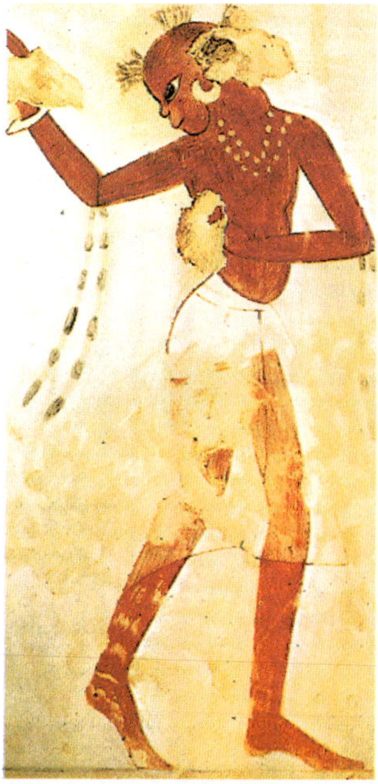

Carpenters

- 15th century B.C.
- mural painting
- Tomb of Rekhmire, Vizier of Tuthmosis III, Necropolis of West Thebes (Luxor)

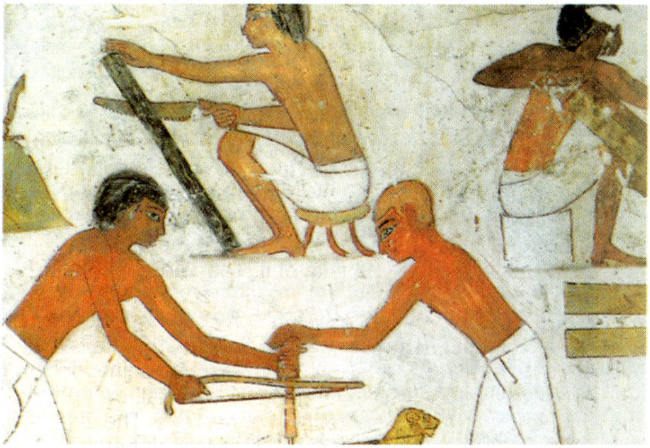

This decorative mural is of great historical interest. In it we see diverse carpentry operations being performed. The workers' hair colors differ, as do their skin colors. Wearing only short skirt-like cloths around their loins, their neat torsos are so delicate as almost to clash with the efforts they are making.

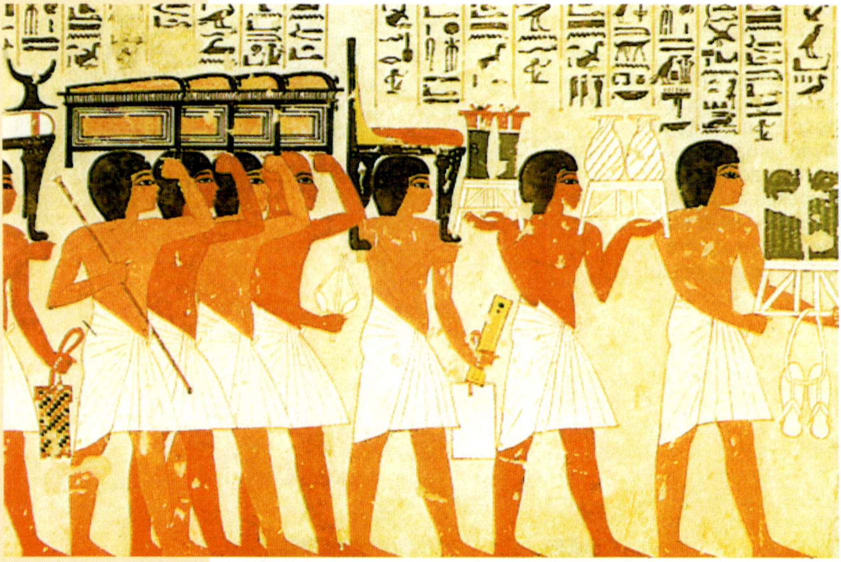

Funeral Procession

- end of the reign of Amenhotep III (18th Dynasty), 1411–1375 B.C.
- Tomb of Ramose (No. 55), Thebes

Most Egyptian art is invariably related to the worship of deities or the deceased, for whom scenes were painted, which related stories or depicted moments of everyday life, religious ceremonies or allegories. In this painting we see a procession of furniture-bearers accompanying a catafalque, being led by a bell-ringer. The hieroglyphics in the upper register summarize the life of the deceased and invoke the protection of the gods on his journey to the beyond. The figures, rendered with nude torsos, are portrayed according to established artistic canons, both in their typology and their poses. Their flat, masculine bodies, with crisp outlines and slender builds, are painted alternately in red ocher and brown, creating a sense of ordered diversity. The scene duly reflects the solemnity of the moment, conveying the profound respect the figures have for the body they are carrying to the grave.

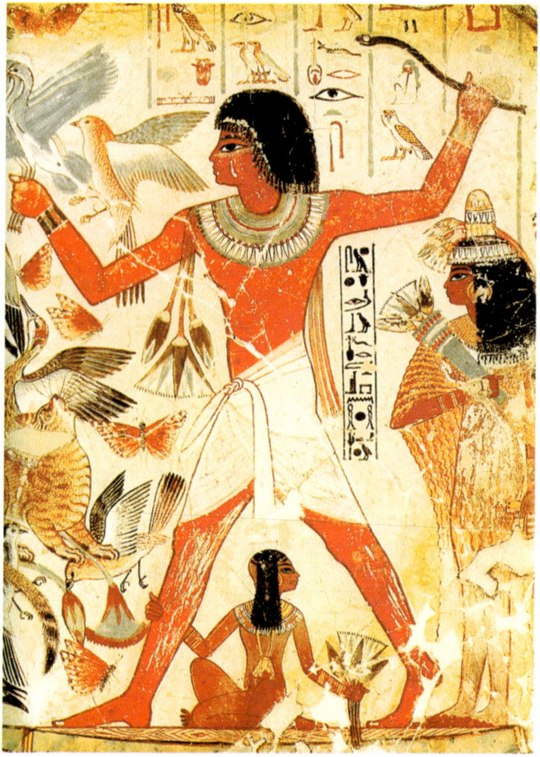

Nebamun, his beautifully-clothed wife right and a servant (naked, smaller, under her master) are depicted on a raft, surrounded by numerous birds and animals, an evident sign that this figure bore a significant relation to nature. The scene illustrates social hierarchies: the man is at the center, all-powerful. He is the most significant figure. Behind him is his wife, smaller, a background figure. The servant, a young, slender woman, appears totally submissive to her master who would yet seem to provide her with protection and security. Her gesture of holding on to one of his legs seems to indicate a certain tenderness between them, not just a cold and distant master-slave relationship.

Hunting in a Marsh

- ca. 1400 B.C. (18th Dynasty, New Kingdom)
- mural
- Tomb of Nebamun, Necropolis of West Thebes (Luxor)
- British Museum, London

Egyptian Dancers

- 1400 B.C. (18th Dynasty, New Kingdom)
- mural
- Tomb of Nebamun, Necropolis of West Thebes (Luxor)
- British Museum, London

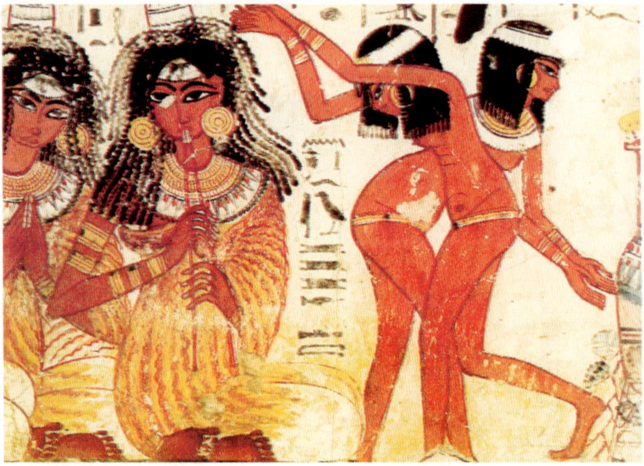

This painting illustrates the foundations of Egyptian art. Outlines have been limned with a brush using red paint, while for the skin a flat, yellowish ochre has been applied. There are neither highlights nor shading. The delicately sensual figures of the dancers nevertheless create a sense of three-dimensionality and movement, as well as of colorfulness and light.

The Daughters of Akhnaton

- ca. 1380 B.C. (18th Dynasty, New Kingdom)
- mural from the Royal Palace of Tell-el-Amarna
- Ashmolean Museum, Oxford

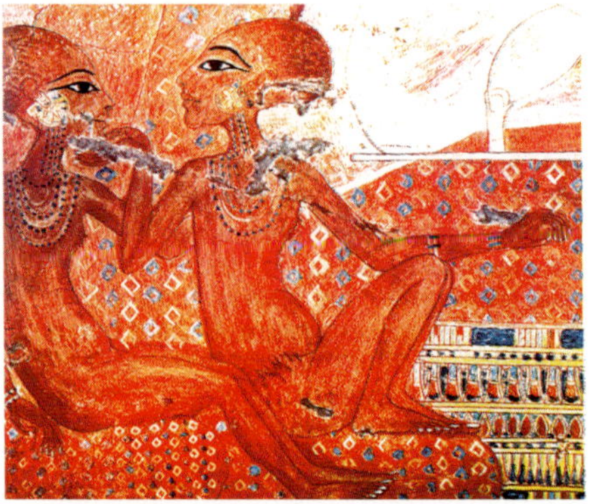

Depicted here are the youngest daughters of Akhnaton and Nefertiti, their nude bodies fragile and delicate, as befits their condition as children. This mural breaks with the tradition of representing children as having adult bodies only proportionately smaller: features and gestures are in keeping with their young age. The figures display a relatively naturalistic treatment that is characteristic of the period, utilizing strong lines and powerful red hues.

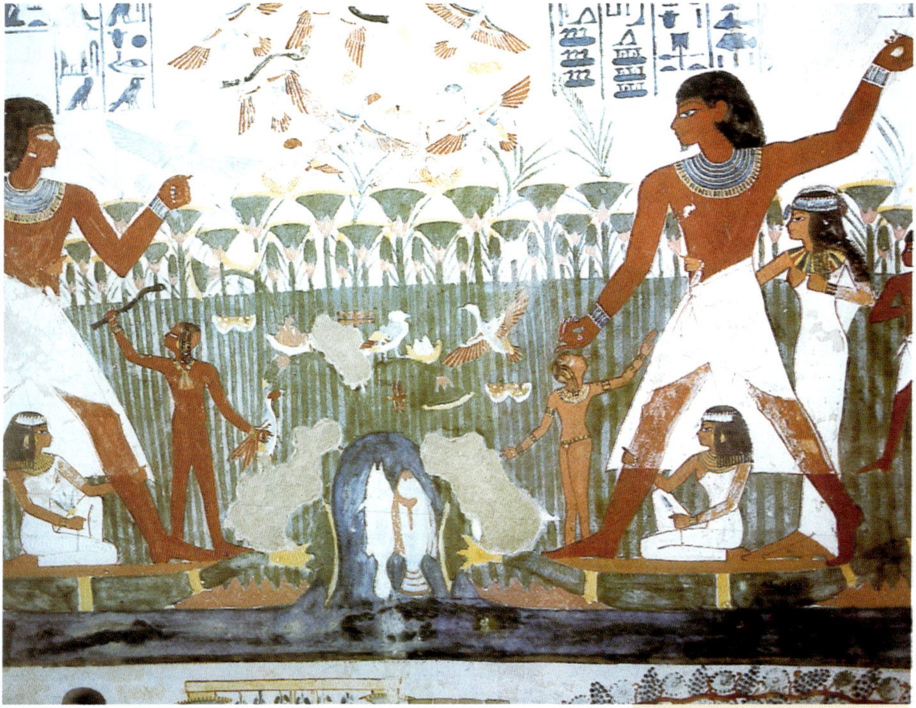

Fowling Scene in Papyrus Marshes

- 18th Dynasty, reign of Tuthmosis IV (ca. 1422–1411 B.C.)
- Tomb of Nakht (No. 52), Thebes

This scene shows the deceased hunting birds in papyrus marshes. He appears in the foreground twice, the large, symmetrical figures directly opposite each other, standing on a raft accompanied by his wife and children, all of whom are festively dressed. The size and placement of the figures in relation to that of the deceased indicate their relative importance. The concept of the nude in ancient Egypt has little in common with that in Western society. Eroticism does not lie so much in what is shown as in how it is shown. In everyday life the nude was commonplace (slaves were either totally or partly nude) and eroticism had a language of its own. Egyptians set great store by physical appearance, making frequent use of such accessories as wigs and makeup.

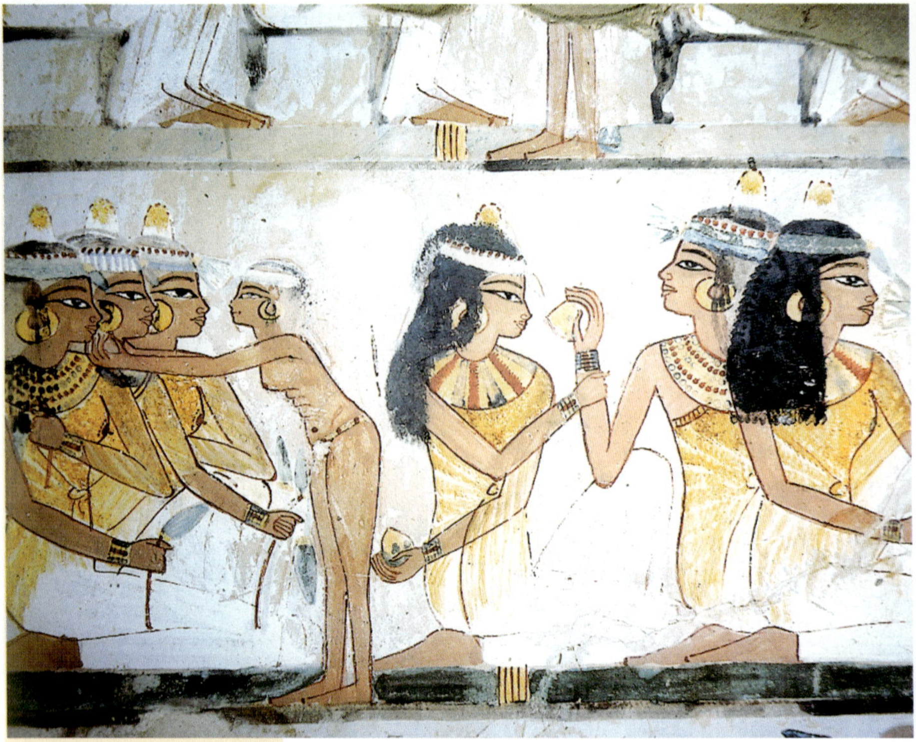

Banqueting Scene

- 18th Dynasty, New Kingdom, reign of Tuthmosis IV (ca. 1422–1411 B.C.)
- Tomb of Nakht (No. 52), Thebes

In this scene, two clearly distinguished groups of three women are depicted, sumptuously dressed and wearing headdresses. Whereas those on the left are bunched together in a sequence, partly covering the figures behind them, those on the right have much more space between them and each one is set in a different pose, including the central figure, whose twisted torso forms a clear contrast to that of her companions. In the central area and much smaller, as she belongs to a lower social class, appears a nude servant, who acts as a counterpoint in the composition. The naturalism with which she has been rendered reveals many characteristics of her attractive anatomy: she is young and well-proportioned, with firm breasts, visible ribs and strong thighs. The inclination of the body seems to be indicative of the submission that was expected of her before women of higher standing.

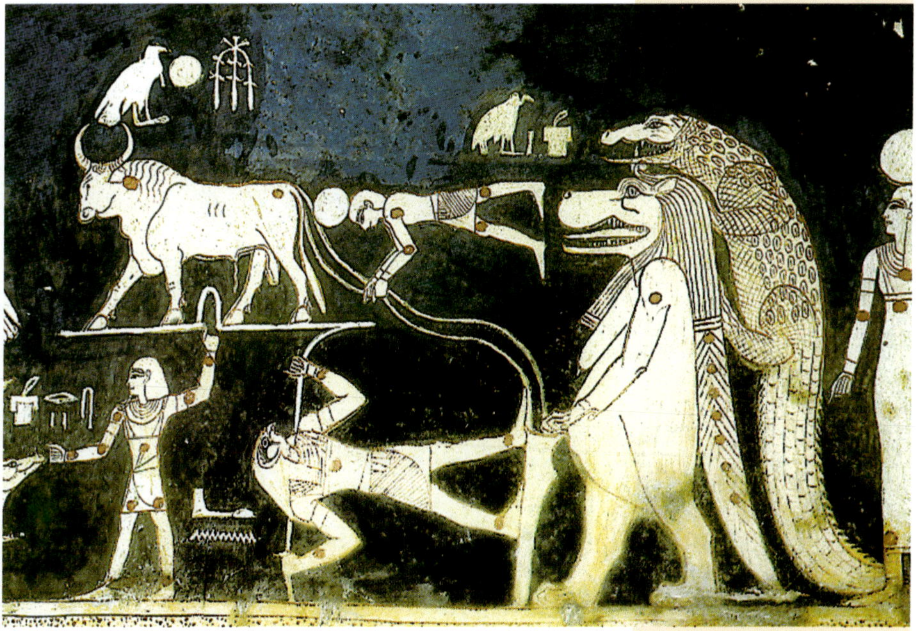

Scene from the Ceiling of the Burial Chamber of Seti I

- 19th Dynasty (ca.1280 B.C.)
- Tomb of Seti I, Valley of the Kings, Thebes

This scene presents Thoeris, the goddess of pregnancy, who appears on the right with the body of a hippopotamus and a large abdomen, as she herself is pregnant. The crocodile on her back symbolizes her ability to defend herself and the lion claws her ferociousness. In this image, the frontal torso has been replaced by a full profile. The body of the goddess is curious, belonging to a woman who has breast-fed many children. As this is a nocturnal scene the sky is dark and various stars and constellations (Orion, Sirius and Ursa Major) can be seen, represented here by their corresponding symbols. This iconography is probably based on the idea that the deceased cannot only look at the sky, but can also fly up into it in the form of a bird.

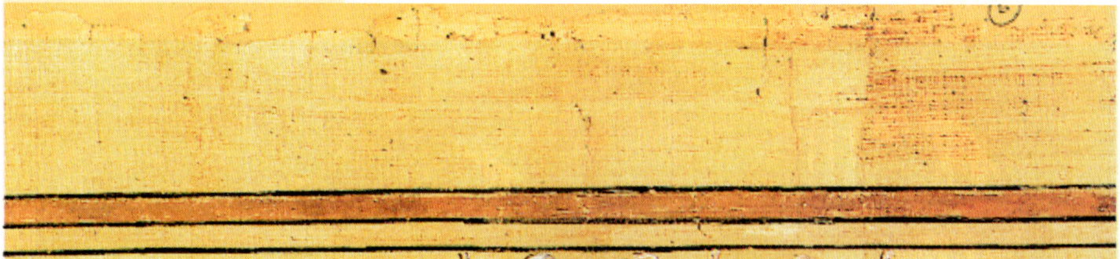

Funeral Procession

- New Kingdom (ca. 1250 B.C.)
- paint on papyrus
- Book of the Dead of Ani
- British Museum, London

The figures in this painting are part of a funeral procession, a group of mourners whose nude bodies are painted white and covered by mere transparent veils, giving expression to a refined sensuality that is heightened by their gestures, as well as a studied dramatization. Curiously, the iconography gives rise to a theatricality uncommon in Egyptian art, for the group conveys a dynamism that is accentuated by the movement of the arms, the direction in which the heads are facing and the position of the bodies.

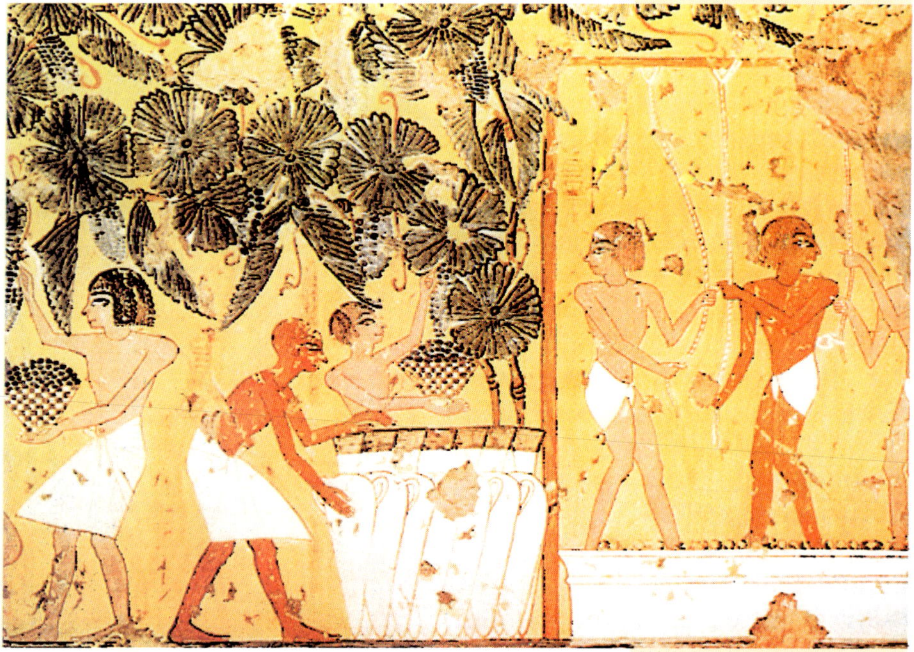

In this painting, two scenes illustrate different stages of the grape harvest. On the left, figures can be seen cutting large clusters of grapes from the grapevine above their heads. On the right, several workers tread on the grapes in an open vat to press the juice out of them. The scene contains the elements necessary for its comprehension, which are set against a bright ocher background to make them stand out. The realism of the scene, which can be observed in the figures' poses and different skin colors, is remarkable indeed. Following the turbulent reign of Amenhotep IV (1372–54 B.C.), Egyptian society underwent considerable changes. Consequently, the traditional artistic style gave way to a freer means of expression, to which the sense of movement conveyed by the figures in this painting attest.

Grape Harvest at the Ipy Vineyard

- 13th century B.C.
- Tomb of Ipy (No. 217), Thebes

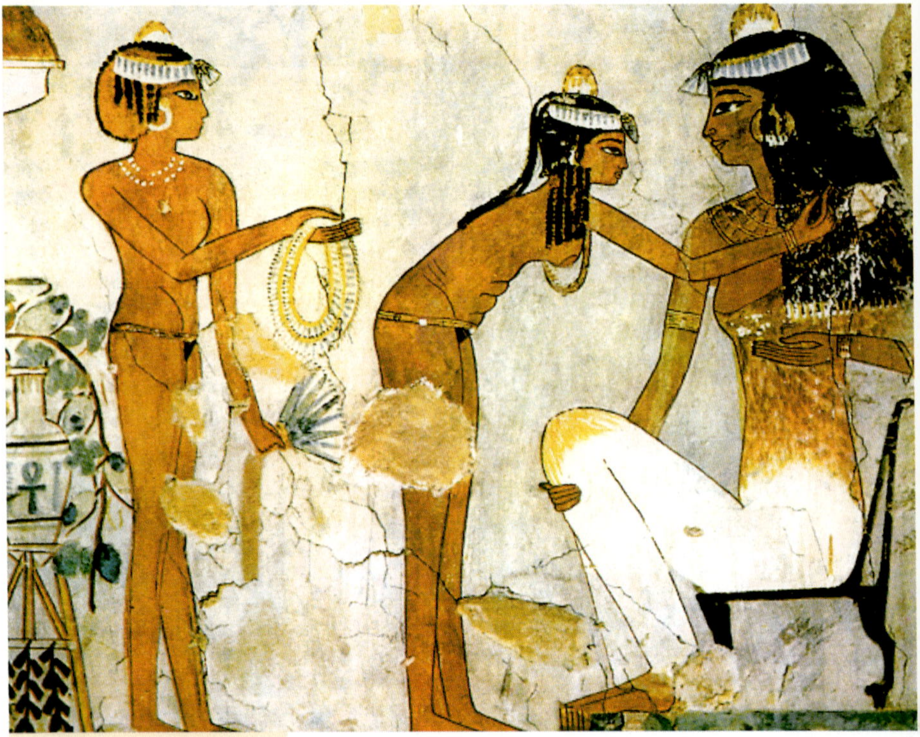

Woman at Her Toilet

- 15th century B.C.
- Tomb of Deserkarasonb (No. 38), Thebes

This painting shows a woman seated on a dais against a simple white background. Dressed and made up, the woman's coiffure is given some final touches by a servant while another waits to adorn her with a necklace. The figures of the servants, which are naked and smaller in size than the woman, are particularly interesting. They have slender bodies with long, fine legs, and their anatomical details, including some folds in the skin, are skillfully executed. They are exquisitely made up, wearing elegant bands around their heads, as well as necklaces and earrings. Curiously, whereas one of the servant's torsos is portrayed frontally, the entire body of the other servant is shown in profile. The manner in which they cover their genitals with a tiny cloth on a thin band is an interesting detail. Although it was certainly not the artist's intention, to modern viewers, these figures are extremely sensual.

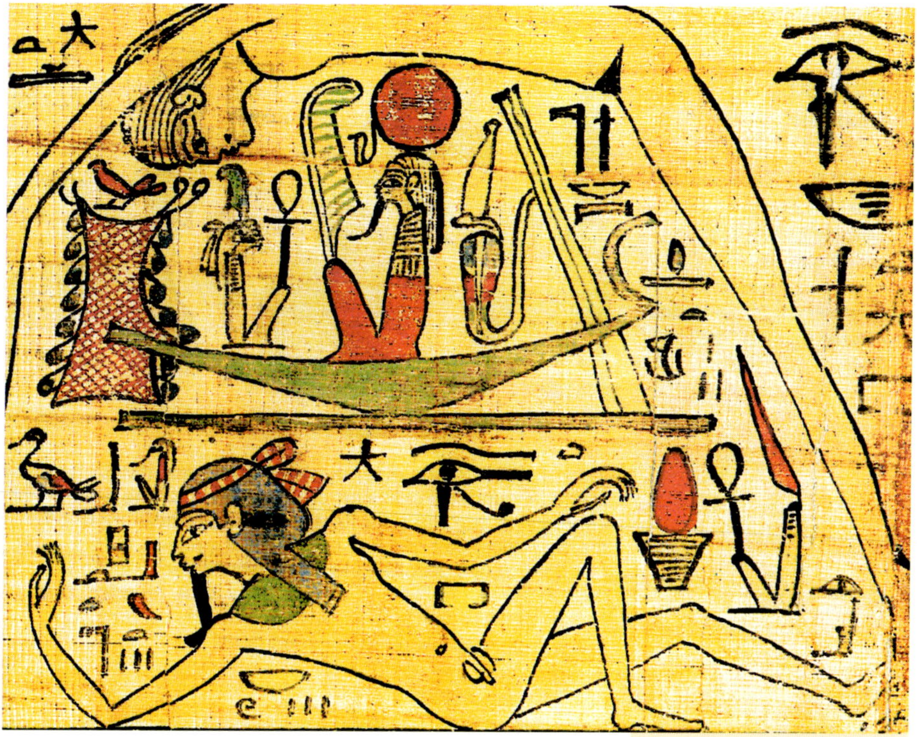

The Goddess Nut (the Sky) and the God Geb (the Earth) are shown separated. The space between them is occupied by Xu, the God of the Air, before whom the Goddess Maât sits, the image of balance in the universe. The painting illustrates Ancient Egyptian cosmology, according to which the world is full of gods and powers. Curiously, Nut and Geb are depicted completely nude, the Goddess displaying pubic hair and the God his genitals. Despite the proportions of the two gods being adapted to the space available, they have stylized, delicate and slender bodies. Of course, they are not warrior gods, but kind beings watching over humanity's most valued goods.

Nut and Geb as Heaven and Earth

- 11th century B.C.
- paint on papyrus from the Book of the Dead of Nes Pa Ka Xuti
- Musée du Louvre, Paris

Ostrakon of the Dancer

- ca. 1180 B.C. (Dynasty of the New Kingdom, beginning of the reign of Ramses III)
- paint on a fragment of pottery from Deir el-Medina
- Museo Egiziano, Turin

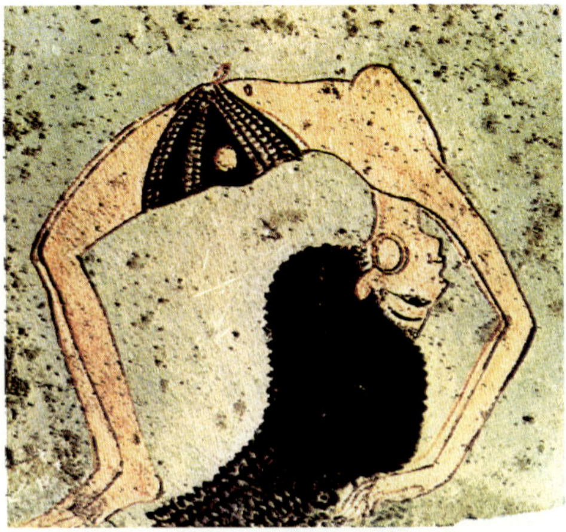

This depiction of a dancer displays anatomical details that are highly unusual in the art of Ancient Egypt. The representation is surprising for its dynamism, but even more so for the conception of a woman's body it evinces: for the breast is drawn according to anatomical criteria—pulled tight at the top while its base continues to be rounded, due to the woman's position. Her long spirals of hair brushing the ground is a singularly poignant detail.

Scene with figures

- ca. 1000 B.C.
- engraved in stone, painted with red ochre
- Tanum, Bohuslän, Sweden

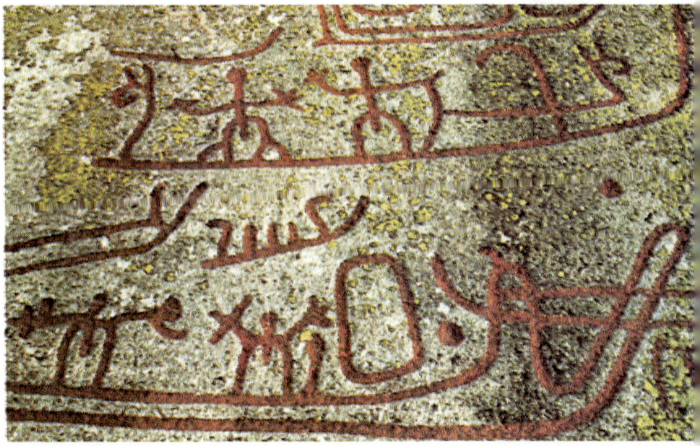

While in Egypt art was flourishing to great refinement, primitive tribes in Europe continued to make synthetic representations of the human figure in an almost calligraphic manner. In this cave engraving, the figures are highly schematic and frontal, which facilitates a direct conveyal of information. The figures are represented with arms extended, legs spread and sexual organs visible.

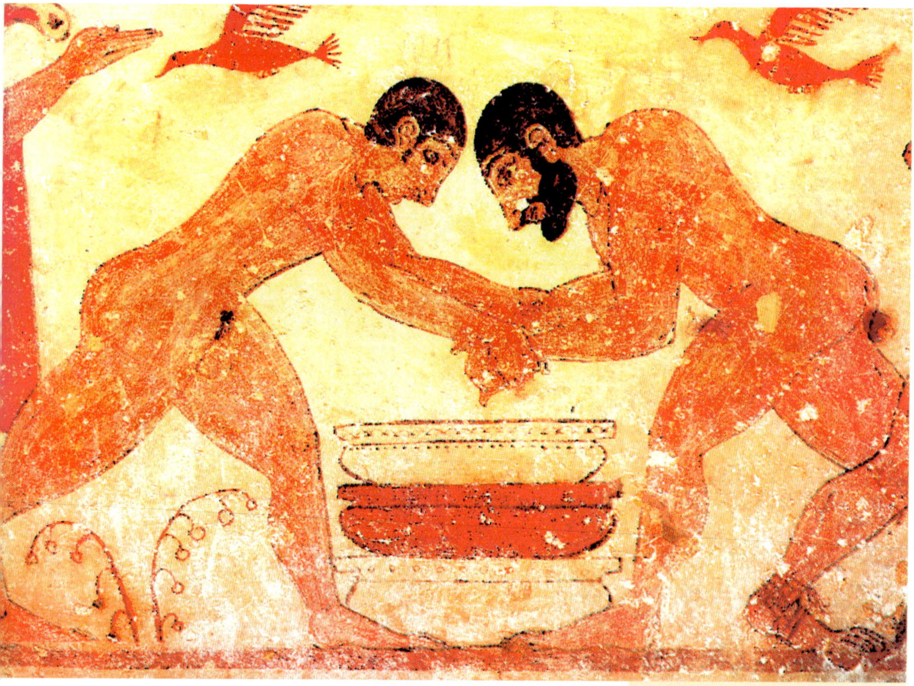

Two wrestlers perform the customary salute at the start of a bout. Athletes would wrestle naked and greased with oil or bitumen to make the contest more difficult. Combat was bloodless and usually ended when one of the opponents gave in or was immobilized. Both wrestlers here have large, robust and hairless bodies, their heads differentiated through facial features, hair-color and presence or absence of beard. A thin line demarcates each of their bodies the surfaces of which are a flat, reddish ochre. The plain lighter background makes the figures stand out. Despite the simplicity of draftsmanship and technique, the mural captures well the solemnity of the moment and the wrestlers' mutual respect.

Wrestlers

- ca. 550 B.C.
- mural painting
- Tomba degli Auguri, Tarquinia

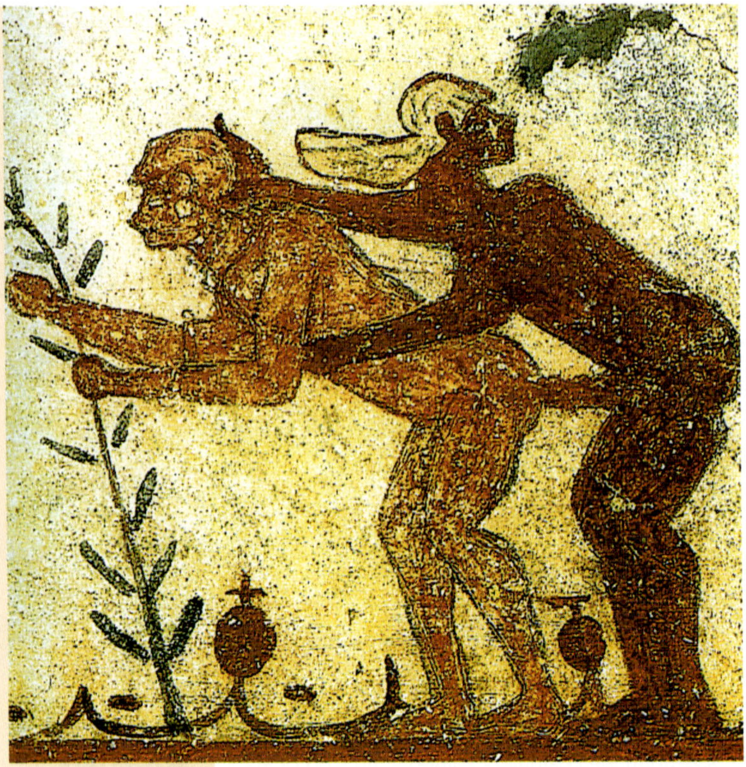

Homoerotic Scene

- 1st century
- fresco from the Tomba dei Tori, Tarquinia
- Museo Archeologico, Naples

Murals often provide insight into early sexual lifestyles, including the practice of homosexuality, which was accepted up to a certain age, a custom inherited from Greek culture. This mural illustrates two naked men engaged in sodomy. Whereas the figure on the right displays a large erect member, that of the figure on the left is limp. The depiction of the action is not only explicit but appears completely natural, right down to the detail of the figure holding onto a sapling to steady himself, while his partner holds and caresses him. Despite the archaic appearance of the figures, they have been drawn with a sinuous line and produce a harmonious composition.

The Etruscan art of Tarquinia is beautifully expressive. This well-built nude is depicted in a pose whose dynamism is far removed from the hieraticism characteristic of so many representations of the period. Even the expression on the dancer's face—a subtle smile—contributes a certain sense of drama. The dancer's muscular body combines a lateral view of the legs with a frontal view of the torso, which was not uncommon.

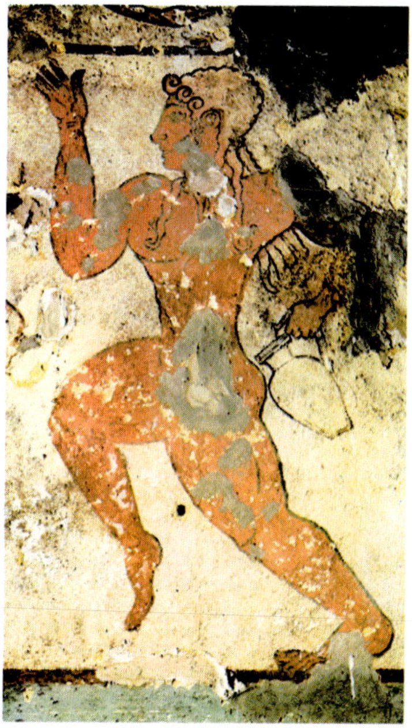

Ritual Dance

- ca. 520 B.C.
- fresco
- Tomb of the Lionesses, Tarquinia

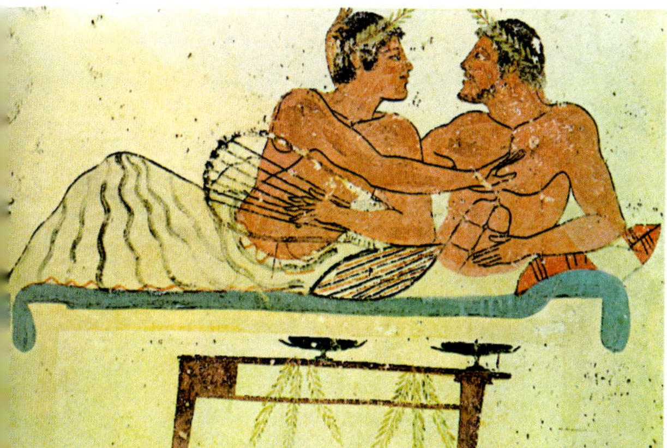

ʼhe sexual liberty prevailing in Greece at the time is evident
ı this depiction of an erotic relationship between two men.
Vhile the older of the two men caresses the younger one's
ıead and draws him closer, the younger man reaches out
ın arm. Both bodies are athletic, their muscles firm and their
ʼutlines clean. A highly elegant interpretation of the nude.

Funerary Banquet: Musicians

- ca. 480 B.C.
- fresco from the Tomb of the Diver
- Museo Archeologico, Paestum

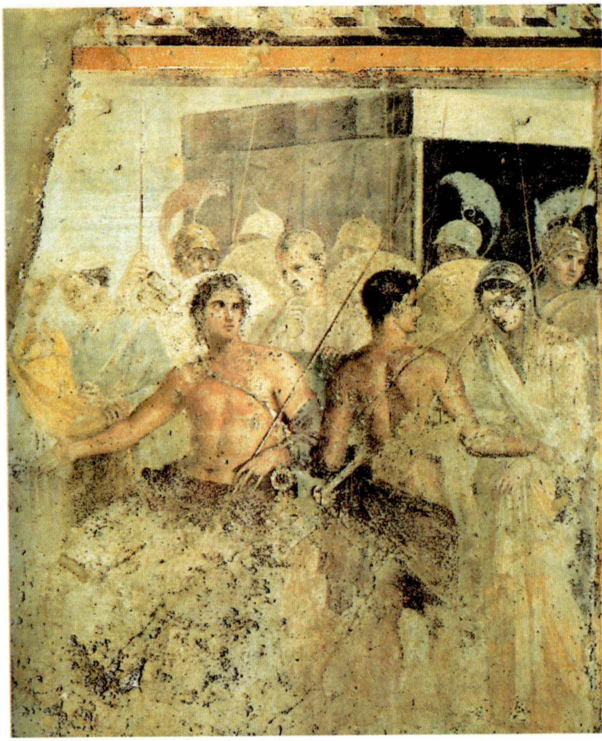

Achilles and Briseis

- ca. 330 B.C.
- mural from Pompeii
- Museo Archeologico, Naples

Despite the poor condition of this mural, the nude torsos of Achilles and Agamemnon still stand out, with their pleasingly sculptural treatment. The skin tones have been rendered with great attention to realistic detail. The poses are a little static and somewhat theatrical perhaps.

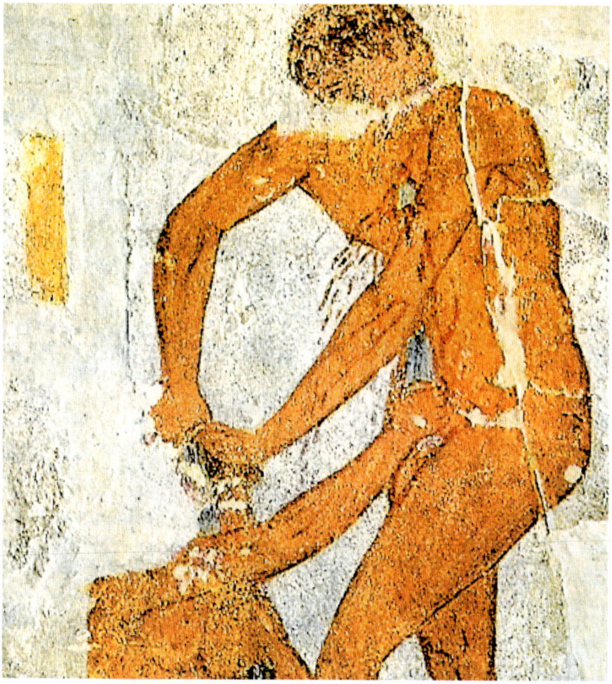

According to Greek, legend Eteoclus and Polynices were sons of Oedipus, King of Thebes, whom both were to succeed, reigning in alternating years. When his first-year term was over, Eteoclus refused to cede the throne to his brother, which caused a fierce fight in which they stabbed each other to death. With simple means the artist has brilliantly captured the drama of the incident, evoking powerful male bodies, with well-defined profiles and intense, ocher-colored skin, entangled in a violent struggle. The sense of movement and the poses of the figures have little in common with earlier Egyptian art. The painting combines elements of both Egyptian, Greek and Etruscan art, recalling the figures adorning Greek vases, both in its virtuoso use of line and in the freedom with which the figures are rendered.

Eteoclus and Polynices

- fresco
- 2nd century B.C.
- French tomb, Vulvi

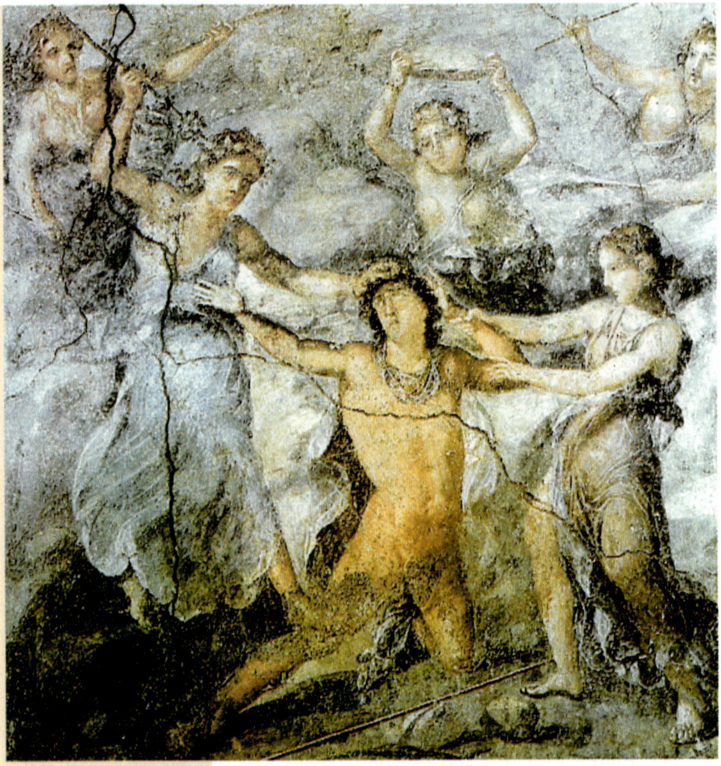

Pentheus Being Torn in Pieces

- 2nd century B.C.
- fresco
- Villa dei Vettii, Pompeii

When Pentheus, King of Thebes, refused to sanction the orgiastic veneration of Bacchus, his mother Agave and other followers of Bacchus tore the king to pieces. In the present scene, the unfortunate king has had his clothing stripped off by the maenads and is now totally naked, humiliated and defenseless. One maenad has her foot on the king's leg to immobilize him. The feelings of enraged fury of the figures come across well in their gestures and actions. The artist has achieved a harmonious and well-balanced composition. Forcefulness and dramatic interest distinguish this fresco.

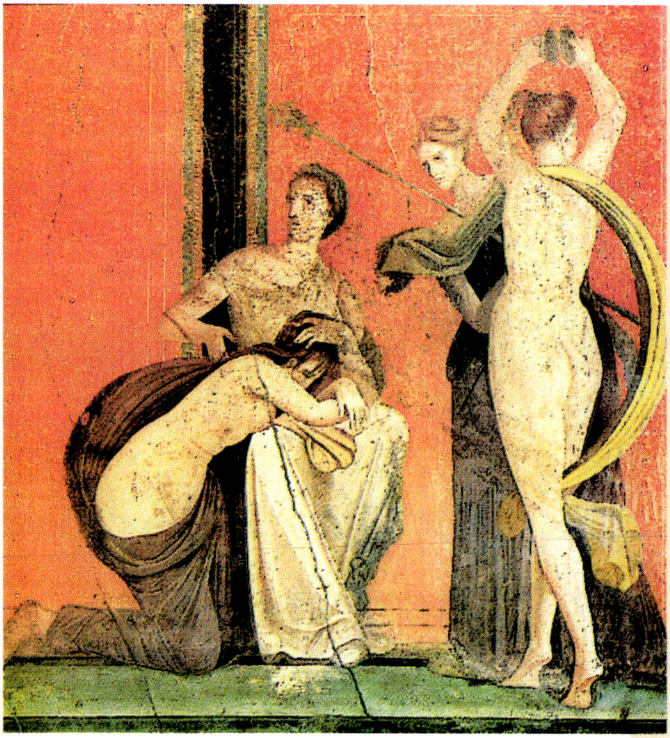

Works preserved in Pompeii testify not only to the eloquence of Greco-Roman painting, but to social conditions as well. The head of a house was master and absolute ruler. This scene depicts a Dionysian initiation ceremony involving, amongst other things, ritual punishment. The work is filled with a mixture of sadism and lasciviousness. The master, seated with a slave girl before him with her head in his lap, undresses the girl and strokes her hair. The lady of the house wields a rod that will be used to flog her, and a dancer stands by, ready to dance in rhythm to the blows. The nudes are expressive and have a thoroughly natural appearance. The slave girl seems to be relaxed under the circumstances, while the dancer is depicted standing on tiptoes and turning her head in what looks like a coordinated movement. Both nudes are well-built, with full hips and robust limbs. The handling of light on the bodies is superb, its effects brought out yet more by the red background.

Initiation Rites of a Mystery Cult

- 1st century B.C.
- fresco from Villa dei Misteri, Pompeii
- Museo Archeologico, Naples

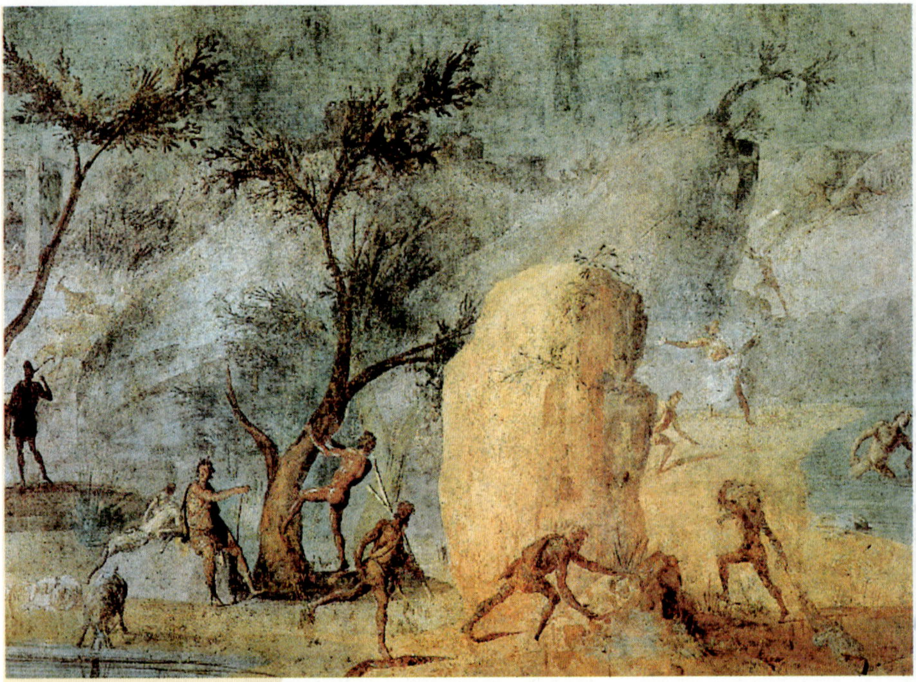

Ulysses in the Land of the Laestrygones

- 50-40 B.C.
- fresco from Casa di Esquilino
- Pinacoteca Vaticana, Vatican

After sailing for seven days, Ulysses reached a land of cannibal giants called the Laestrygones, and sent out three men to reconnoitre. They came to the dwelling of the giants' king, Antiphates, who devoured two of them, the others managing to escape and warn Ulysses of the danger. But too late. Many of the giants had already reached the cliffs, from which they hurled boulders down onto the ships and ate any men they captured. All ships except one were sunk, and by its means Ulysses and the few remaining men now made their escape. This fresco depicts several finely rendered nudes in a scene that is rich in diversified action. The proportions of the figures are dignified, and evince delicate foreshortening. The setting is at once bucolic and atmospheric.

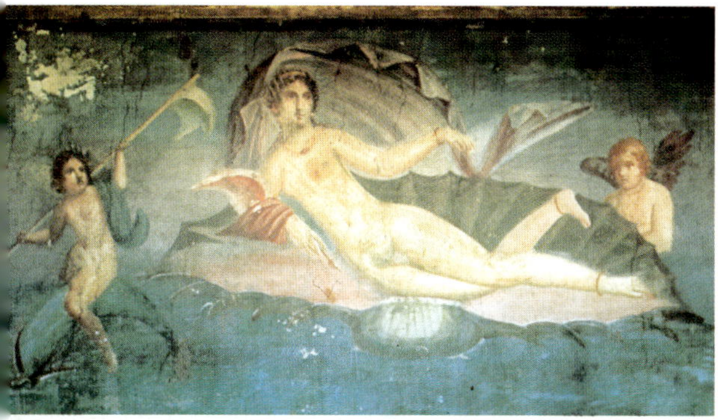

Venus and the Shell

- 1st century
- fresco
- Casa della Venere in Conchiglia, Pompeii

The delicacy of treatment accorded the human figure in Ancient Roman art was expressed in various manners, depending upon the artist. In this work, great skill is evinced in the treatment of the nude figure's modeling, as well as in the anatomical precision of the figure on the left, probably Aeolus. That the work has a definite sensual intention is evident in the goddess' facial expression, the smooth voluptuousness of her curves and in her physical delicateness.

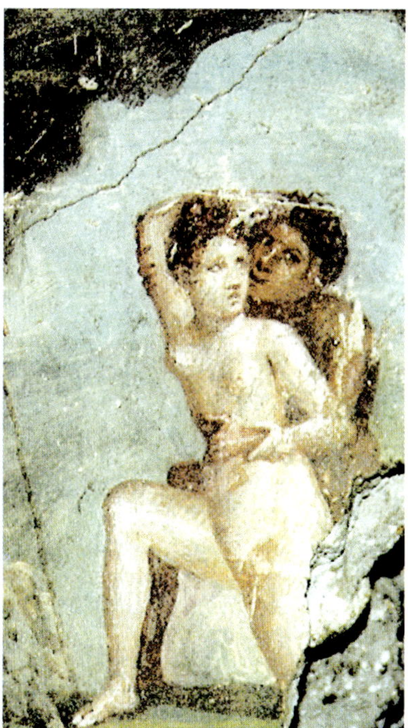

Satyr Embracing a Maenad

- 1st century
- fresco from Pompeii

The treatment of these figures is Classical, with particular focus on proportions, movement and anatomical rigor. A lover is embracing passionately a beautiful maenad, whose expression would seem to indicate aversion rather than the opposite. The three-dimensionality of her body has been successfully conveyed, despite its luminosity, the darker male body behind allowing it to stand out more clearly.

Polyphemus and Galatea

- 1st century
- fresco from Casa della Caccia Antica, Pompeii
- Museo Archeologico Nazionale, Naples

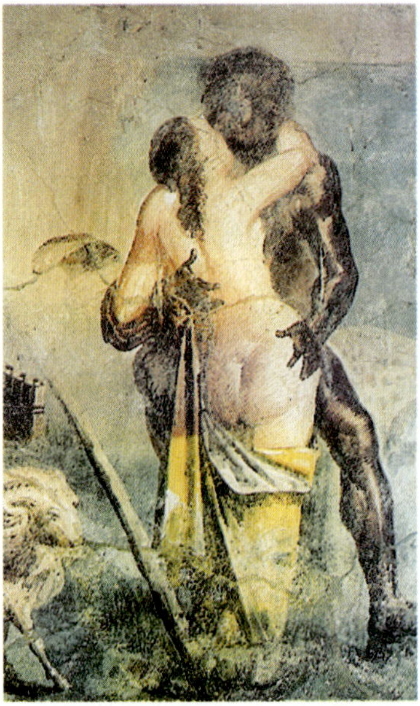

According to one version of the legend, Galatea, a beautiful, young, female inhabitant of the sea took Polyphemus, a savage, one-eyed giant, as her lover. The fresco depicts their passionate embrace. The two nude figures are boldly modeled by means of powerful tonal contrasts and gradations. Galatea, with rounded, sculptural forms, is abandoning herself to her lover, who is drawing her towards him. Awkward and muscular, his black skin gleans intensely.

Bacchanal

- 1st century
- fresco
- house of the Casti Amanti, Pompeii

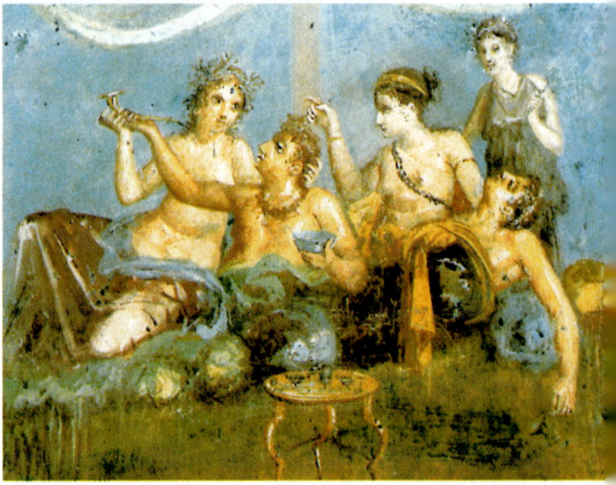

This extremely successful composition is yet further enhanced by the treatment the figures receive. Although they are closely grouped, contrasts have been sufficiently worked out—mainly by means of tonal differences in their complexions—to separate them spatially. The figures' expressions and gestures are telling: the women are professionals and remain sober, while the men are depicted in drunken surrender to the pleasures of sex and wine.

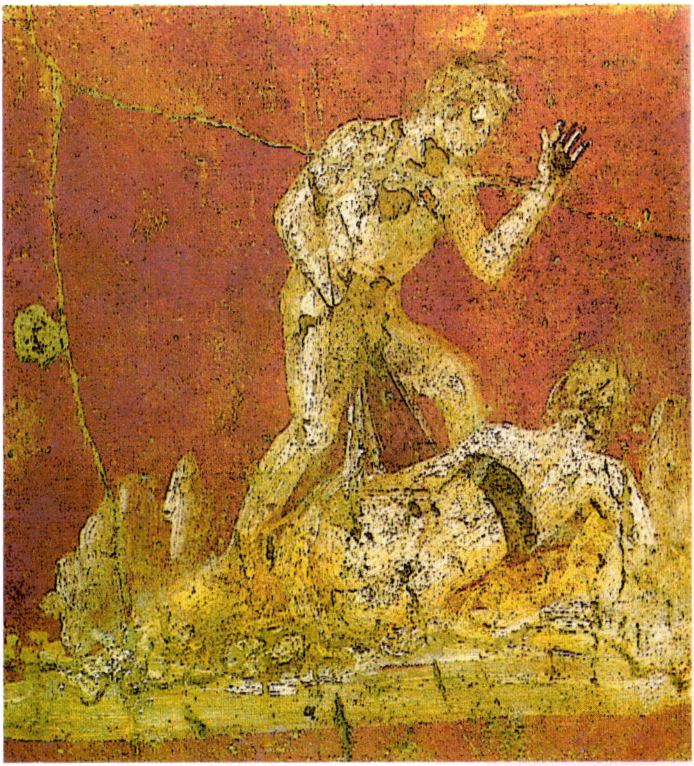

Man Removing a Veil Covering a Woman's Body

- 1st century
- fresco
- Pompeii

\ man brusquely removes the transparent veil covering the ›ody of a woman lying in bed while revealing his genitals to ıer. She is seen naked and from behind. Her boldly fore-hortened legs are flexed, perhaps indicating her willingness › fulfill the man's desires. Her anatomy is correctly execut-d and the bone structure well defined. The nude's forms re harmonious, and both the highlights and the shadows re rendered naturalistically. The volumes, achieved in the ubtle transitions between the light and dark areas, are rein-›rced by the atmospheric red background, which harmo-ıizes with the flesh tones of the figures.

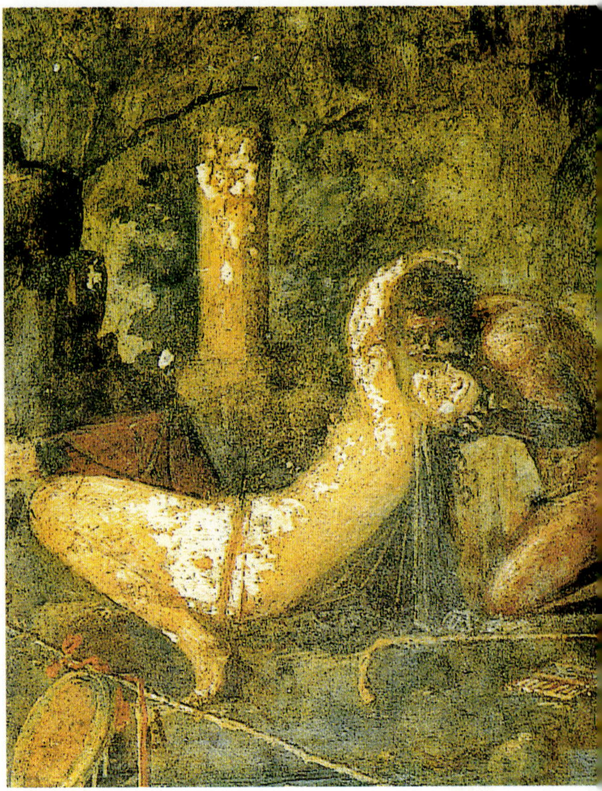

The Lovers' Kiss

- 1st century
- fresco
- Herculaneum

Many of the painters of Herculaneum's wall decorations were of Greek extraction, for, like its neighbor, Pompeii, the city had been founded by Etruscans. These early works are of a remarkably high quality. The most striking features of this painting are the masterly foreshortening and arrangement of the figures, who are shown making love. The woman, rendered with subtle curves, holds her lover's head in her hands, a gesture that is frozen in time. Her body is raised off the ground, supported only by the tips of her toes, as she offers herself to her lover. The naked man is shown giving her a passionate kiss, while caressing one of her breasts with his right hand. The tanned figure is highly naturalistic in style, which is achieved in part by means of an interplay of light and shade.

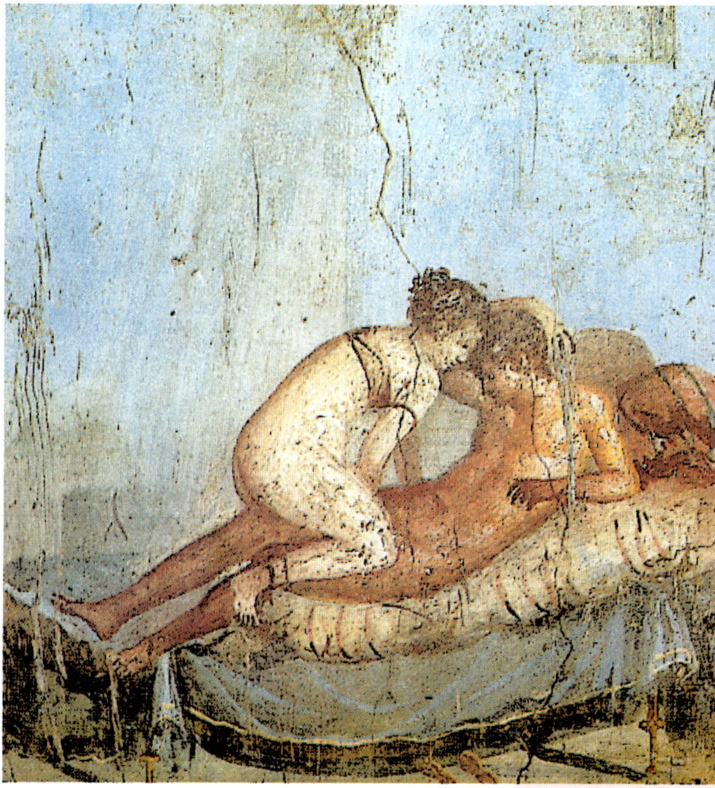

Lovers on a Bed

- 1st century
- fresco
- Villa del Centenario, Pompeii

his overtly erotic scene shows two lovers caught in the sexal act. The woman, shown crouching over her lover, suports her weight with her left hand, which is resting on the ed, while she uses the other to consummate their love. er lover looks on attentively, while he waits for her to make erself comfortable and continue. The two figures are perctly executed, each with its own skin color, which serve intensify the work's chromatism and model the anatomical olumes by means of highlights and shadows, with subtle hading that outlines the young woman's white skin and innse highlights that manifest the man's muscular abdomen.

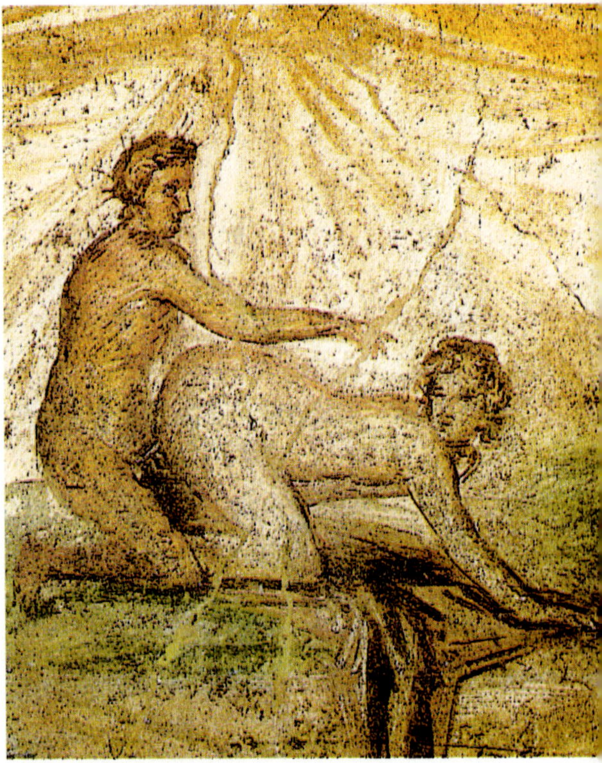

Erotic Scene

- 1st century
- fresco
- Villa dei Veti, Pompeii

This work shows two lovers engaged in the sexual act. The woman, bending forward on her knees, takes the erect penis of her lover behind her in her hand and inserts it into her vag na while he caresses her back. She is not wearing the sash customarily worn by women of the time as a sort of brassiere which both supported and accentuated their breasts. Unlike other paintings on the same theme, the lines of the prelimina drawing are clearly visible in certain areas, especially in the contours. Moreover, the volumes of both figures are skillfully modeled, with a subtle treatment of highlights and shadows and the employment of varying color intensities, resulting in a aesthetically pleasing and chromatically balanced work. One the most interesting aspects of this fresco is the luminous ar of the woman's body, which lends her three-dimensionality.

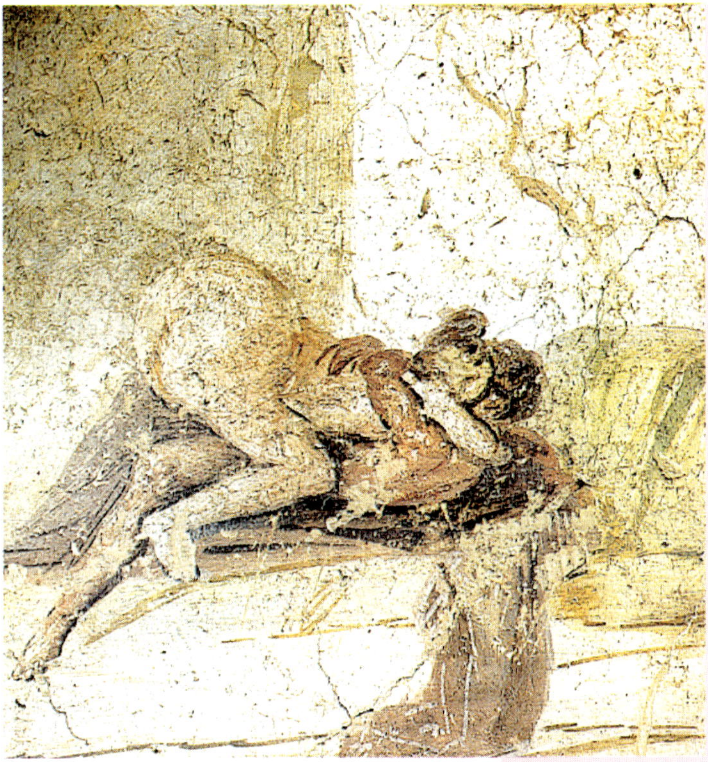

Two lovers are shown on a bed making love, the woman straddling and embracing the man. Certain physical characteristics of each figure can be discerned, highlighting the techniques employed in fresco painting of the period. The tanned, muscular body of the man is almost eclipsed by the woman's luminous, pale skin. The anatomical features are skillfully executed and could well represent the prevailing ideal of beauty of the day: a small and elongated torso, small breasts, a narrow waist and large buttocks giving rise to exaggeratedly broad hips. The passion of the moment is faithfully illustrated here, particularly in the poses adopted by the lovers, which the artist renders with extreme naturalism.

Erotic Scene

- 1st century
- fresco
- 41 x 41 cm
- Pompeii

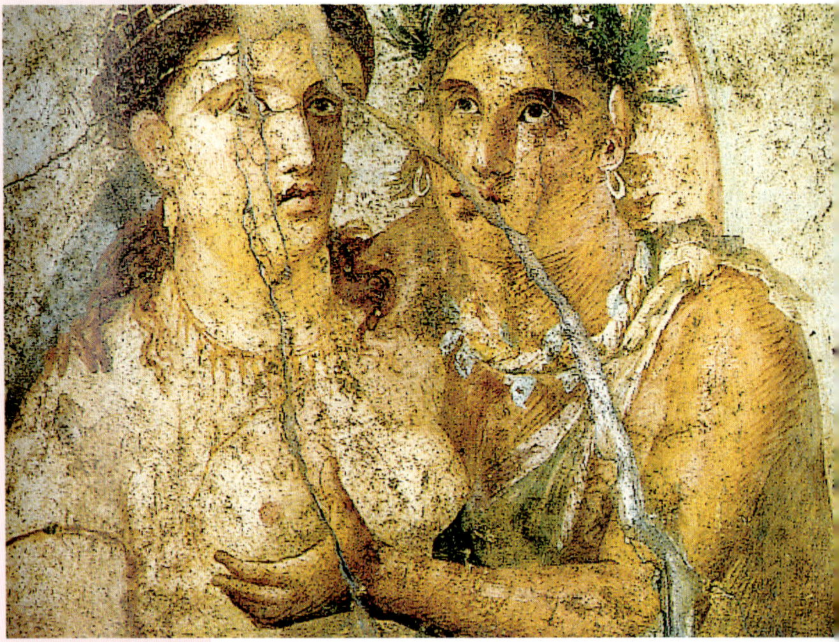

Young Woman Caressed by a Satyr

- 1st century
- mural from Villa de L. Caecilius Iucundus, Pompeii
- Museo Archeologico, Naples

The present erotic scene has been executed with all the delicacy characteristic of the art of Pompeii. A well-built young man is depicted with his mistress, whose right breast he is caressing. She appears to be well-disposed to these caresses in view of the fact that her arm is slung over his shoulder. She has been drawn with the utmost meticulousness, even her face could be a portrait. Her body's dimensions and size are well defined, and have been painted with subtle tones. The artist avoided in her breasts the harsh contrasts he had used for her face. The resulting effect heightens both the innocence of the scene and its potential impact, especially that due to the combined white breast and the tanned hand caressing it.

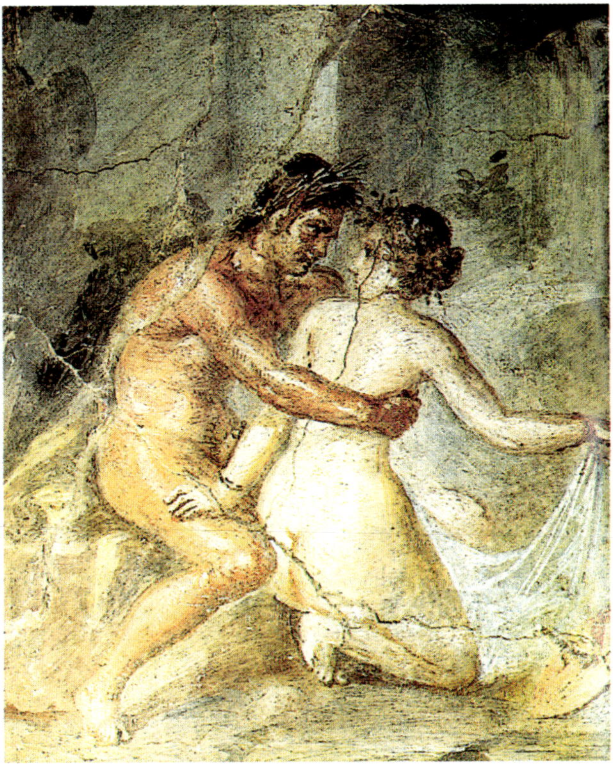

Satyr Seducing a Young Woman

- 1st century
- mural from Villa de L. Caecilius Iucundus, Pompeii
- Museo Archeologico, Naples

The young woman's innocent look contrasts sharply with the stern expression on the satyr's face. Tanned and with Apollonian yet muscular forms, he has been depicted with member erect. Despite her relative fragility, the woman does not appear to be rejecting the satyr's advances. On the contrary, she has a trusting, receptive air. These two nudes display a thorough grounding in draftsmanship and techniques of pictorial representation. The handling of lighting is also extremely impressive, and one can observe here how ideals of bodily beauty in ancient Rome and those of the Baroque were not so far removed from each other.

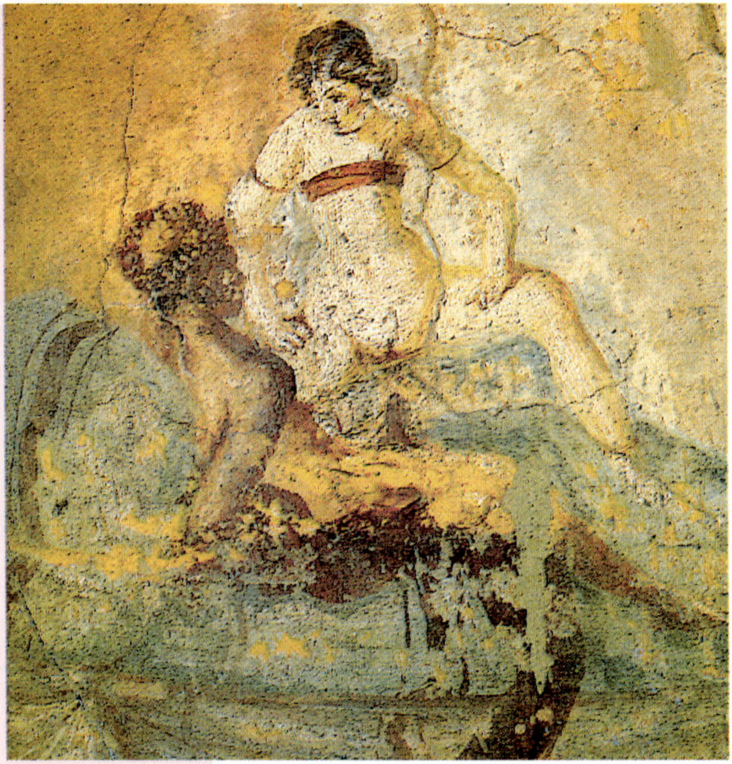

Satyr and Young Woman in Loveplay

- 1st century
- mural from Villa de L. Caecilius Iucundus, Pompeii
- Museo Archeologico, Naples

Brothel interiors were often decorated with erotic scenes of a highly explicit nature. This work depicts two subjects conversing on a couch. The man, recumbent, back to the spectator, has been drawn with strong foreshortening, his legs spread so as to display his private parts, while the woman, a little further off, does the same.

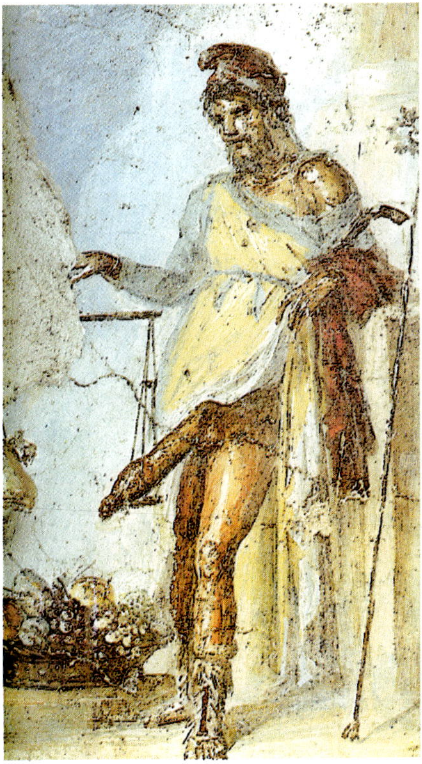

The ashes and lava from the volcanic eruptions at Pompeii and Herculaneum preserved a large number of paintings of nudes. Priapus was the god of fertility, gardens and flocks, hence his presence in this town where agriculture and livestock were abundant. Priapus is frequently depicted with a large if not erect male member, and in this scene he is shown weighing it. Worship of him centered on orgiastic rites, and spread from the Mediterranean as far afield as Britain. The god's stupendous organ is depicted here with notable realism, and without any sense of shame. Whether as instruments in fertility rites, or symbols of life and pleasure in life, works such as this were widely admired and might even become objects of worship. They possessed little or none of the pejorative associations they have in many contemporary cultures.

Priapus Weighing his Phallus

- 1st century
- fresco from Casa dei Vettii, Pompeii
- Museo Archeologico, Naples

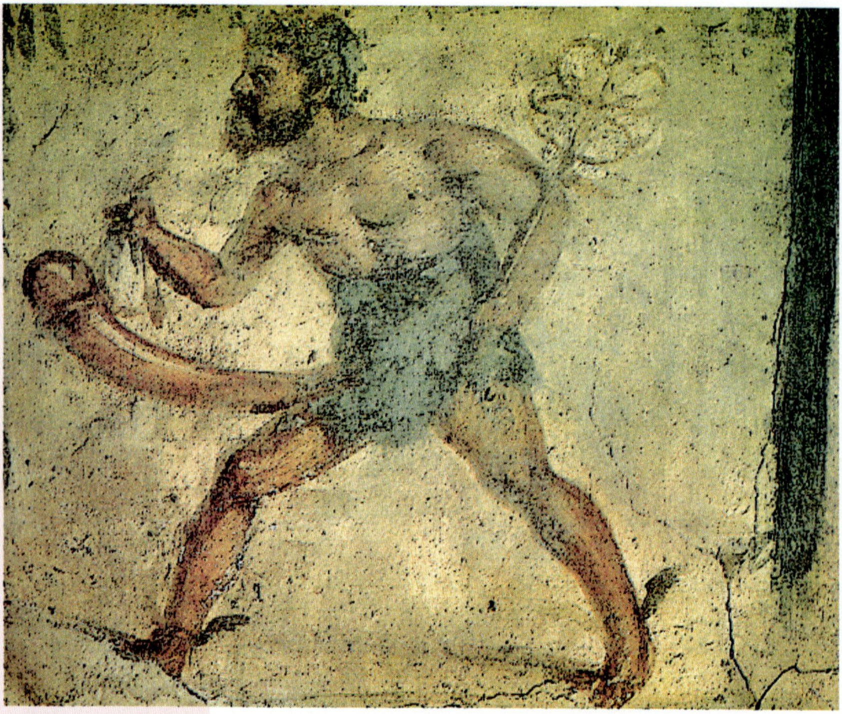

Phallic Deity

- 1st century
- fresco from Casa dei Vettii, Pompeii
- Museo Archeologico, Naples

The most explicit erotic art was not seldom used in humorous as well as religious contexts, and sometimes in both. In the present work, the Herculean subject is depicted in a walking pose. The figure displays numerous attributes: winged feet and caduceus, usually associated with Mercury, crown of vine leaves, associated with Bacchus, and a large, erect phallus, symbol of Priapus, regarded by the Romans as a kind of good-luck charm. The inclusion of all these elements suggests that the work alludes to all the divinities at once. Apart from the subject's male member, the study is natural; modeling is correct and gesture determined, a far remove from the hieratic style of other representations from antiquity. The skin tones are realistic and the artist clearly had a firm grounding in anatomy, something that Roman artists took over directly from the Greeks.

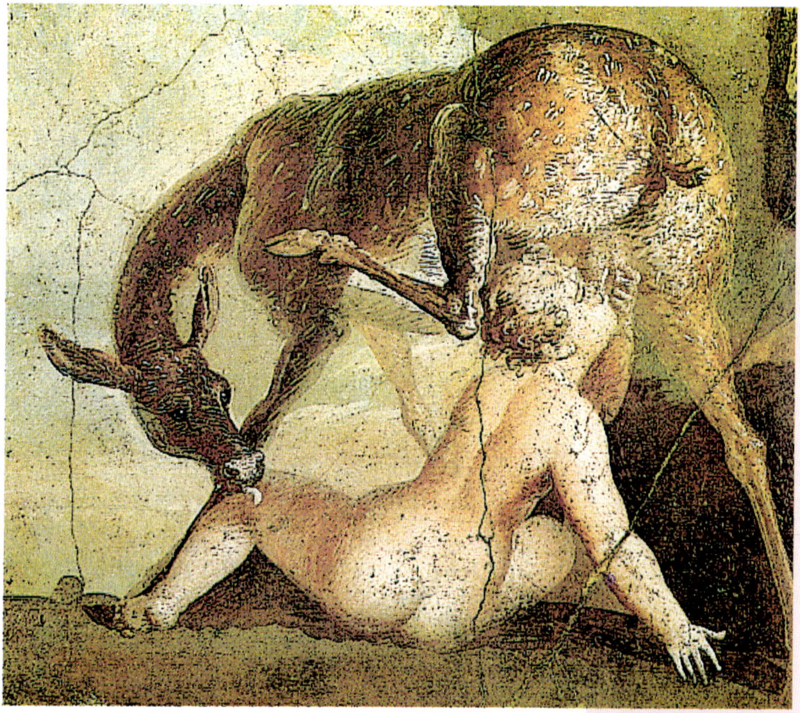

Both theme and execution indicate the artist's mastery of draftsmanship and human anatomy. The figure's shapeliness is sensual, its proportions realistic and far-removed from a merely idealized depiction. Remarkable is the treatment of light, which models a body of most delicate and nearly infantile forms. The figure's pose, which includes elements of foreshortening and perspective, is both complex and flawlessly executed, while its torsion lends the whole composition tremendous rhythm.

Telephus Suckling a Faun at the Parthenon

- 1st century
- fresco from Herculaneum
- Museo Archeologico, Naples

Young Man and Hetaera

- 1st century
- fresco from Herculaneum
- 59 x 53 cm
- Museo Archeologico, Naples

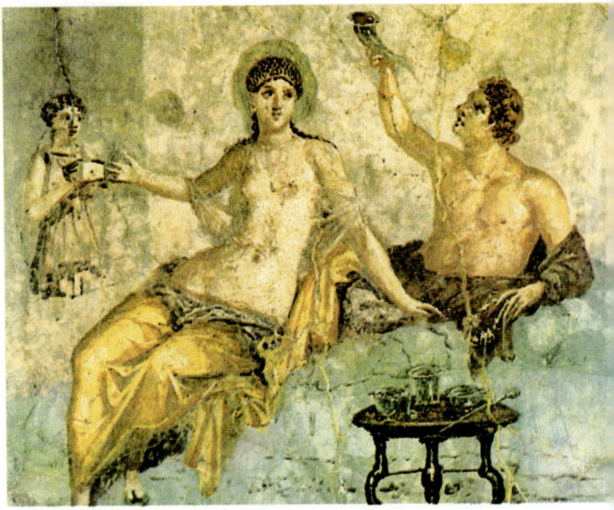

In Ancient Greece, the hetaeras were well-educated courtesans of high social standing who participated in festivals and banquets as luxury prostitutes. The treatment of the theme here is distinctly Roman in style, the taste of the period comin out both in the sculptural treatment of the woman and in the treatment of light that emphasizes her elegance and sensuality. Curvature of trunk and hips are particularly notable details.

Adam and Eve

- end of the 3rd century
- fresco
- Catacombs, Cemetery of St. Peter and Marcellinus, Rome

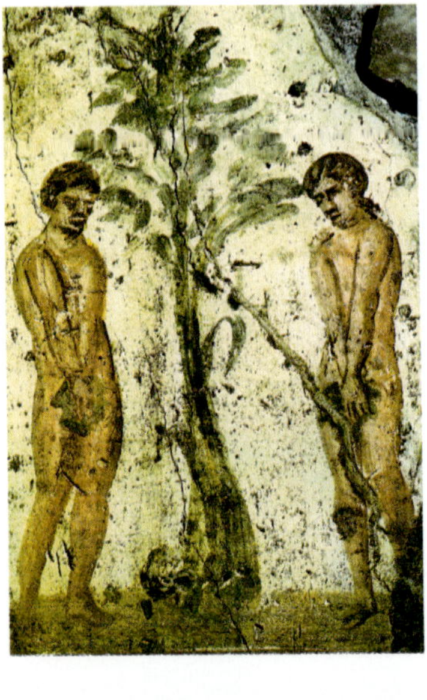

The motif of Adam and Eve effectively transformed Western art. The forebears of mankind are depicted here concealing their nakedness with fig leaves, between them the tree of good and evil. The figures display many characteristics that are typical of Roman painting, such as the clearly-drawn outlines, which serve to emphasize gender differences. The proportioning of Eve's limbs in particular is most interesting. The refined treatment of highlights and shadows is also noteworthy.

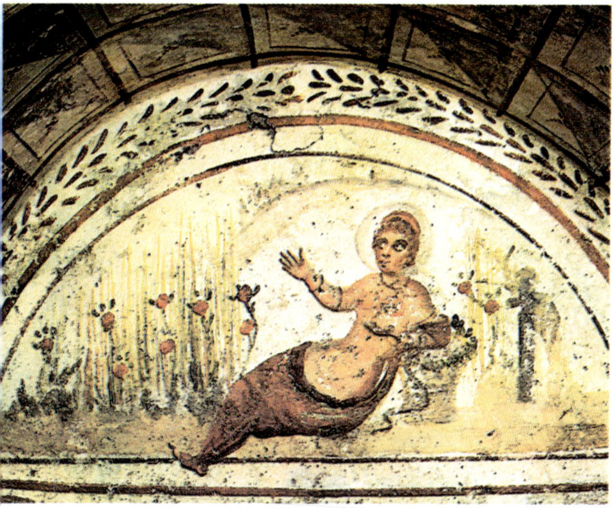

Cleopatra with the Asp in a Field of Wheat and Poppies

- second half of the 4th century
- fresco
- Via Latina Catacombs, Rome

This painting is an example of the so-called belle style: while the figure's forms are harmonious, they lack a sculptural dimension. From such representations it is but a short step to the icon that foregoes every form of ornamentation including the more detailed study of shadows. This Cleopatra is expressive and has the eroticism befitting her person. Pureness of line characterizes the work, as well as a more differentiating treatment of contours, for instance, in the hands.

Hercules Slaying the Hydra

- second half of the 4th century
- fresco
- Via Latina Catacombs, Rome

Following Hera's advice, Eurystheus enjoined twelve labours upon Hercules, hoping he might lose his life while undertaking them. One of the labours was the slaying of the Hydra, a many-headed water serpent, which Hercules slew by severing all its heads at a single stroke. This nude is beautifully proportioned and naturalistically depicted. The limbs display foreshortening, which introduces motion into the scene. The curvature of hip and torso, and the muscles of the abdomen brought out with highlights, increase the physical presence of this representation.

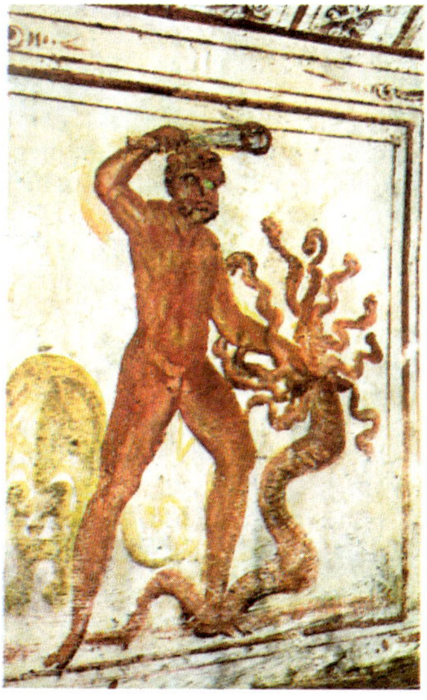

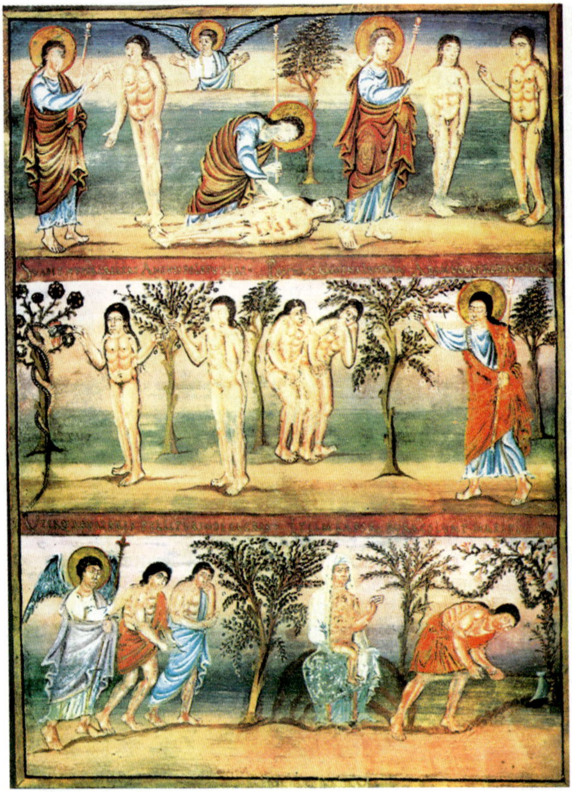

Scenes from the Book of Genesis

- ca. 850
- tempera on parchment
- Illumination from the Bible of Charles the Bald, Bibliothèque Nationale, Paris

This page, displaying great simplicity, had of course a didactic purpose. Its continuous narrative recounts the Creation of man and woman, the Temptation, the Fall, and the expulsion from the Garden of Eden. In terms of bodily shape and size, these nudes figures are all more or less identical: pectoral and abdominal muscles are prominent, and rib-cages tend to protrude considerably; bent at the abdomen, the puppet-like form gesticulate with their arms. Their placement on a slope shows that the artist had a rudimentary knowledge of perspective. We see this in particular in the way feet have been drawn. As in other biblical scenes, no attempt has been made to arouse the spectator sensually, an aspect the artist had little interest in, given the primarily didactic aim of the work. For this reason, the nudes are androgynous, lacking sexual attributes.

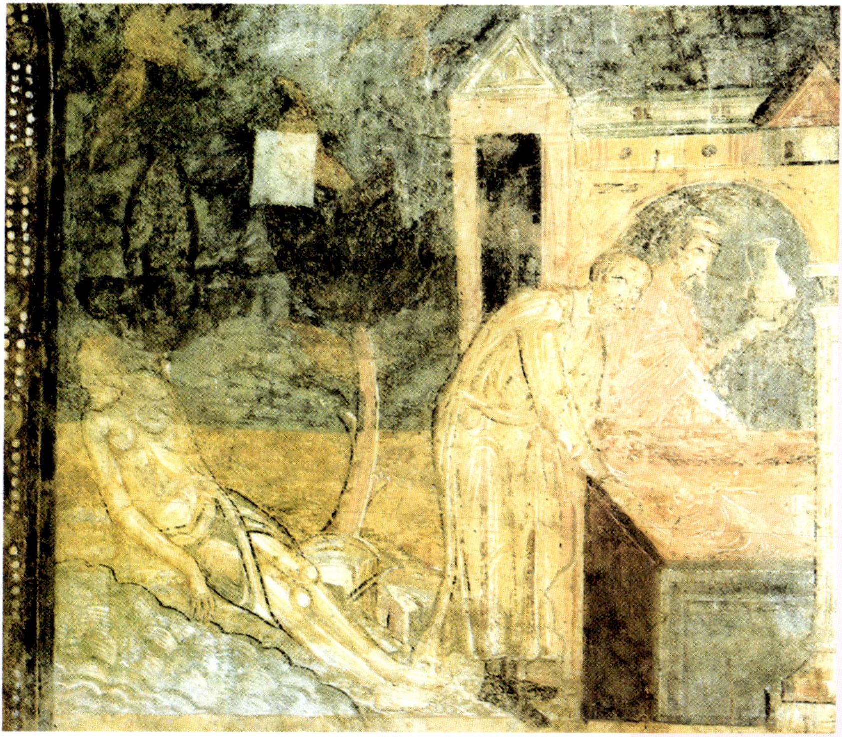

Nudes were uncommon in medieval art, figures generally being painted clothed, except in the case of Adam and Eve, or scenes from the life and crucifixion of Jesus Christ, or of certain saints. Interest in a figure's sensuality tended to be kept to a minimum, while bodily size and shape played a far greater role; a figure's expressivity would be heightened; there was often something synthetic in the manner, as these works were destined to bring the Holy Scriptures home to the masses. The nude figure in this scene is stylized to a degree in regard to its proportions, a device designed to convey spirituality, and the non-frontally positioned body is shown in somewhat indecisive foreshortening.

Scene from the Life of St. Vincent

- 1004-07
- fresco
- Church of San Vicente de Galliano, Cantu

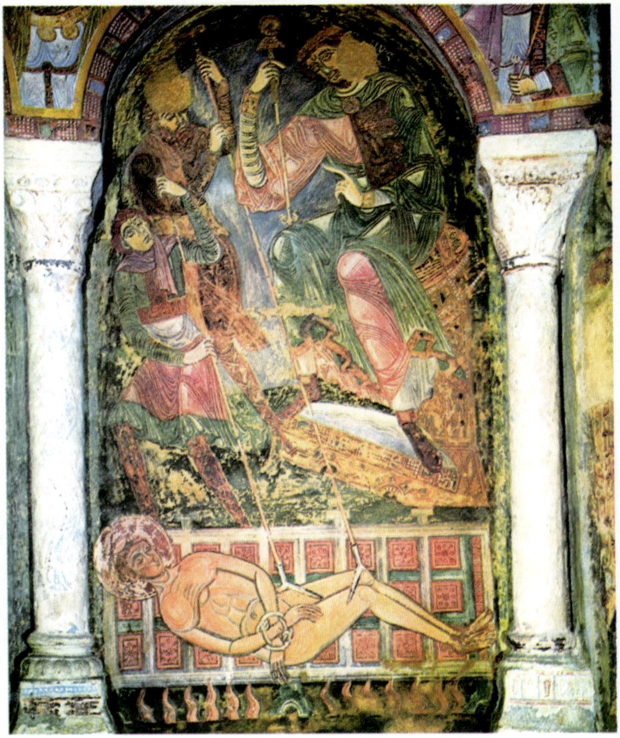

Martyrdom of St. Vincent

- ca. 1109
- fresco
- Church of Berzé-la-Ville, Cluny

St. Vincent was martyred by roasting on a grill. While a certain aesthetic intention is evident in this representation, proportions are inexact, for once again the work is primarily didactic. Line demarcates form, while the chief three-dimensional quantities are effected through concentric circles, mainly in chest and knees. Such renderings provided a viewer with ample information without distracting him with stylistic or aesthetic considerations. Nor is there any foreshortening, because it, too, perhaps, would further complicate an otherwise easily understood story. Simplicity, as well as contrast, were also essential for this type of depiction so that they could be made out in the dimly-lit Romanesque churches.

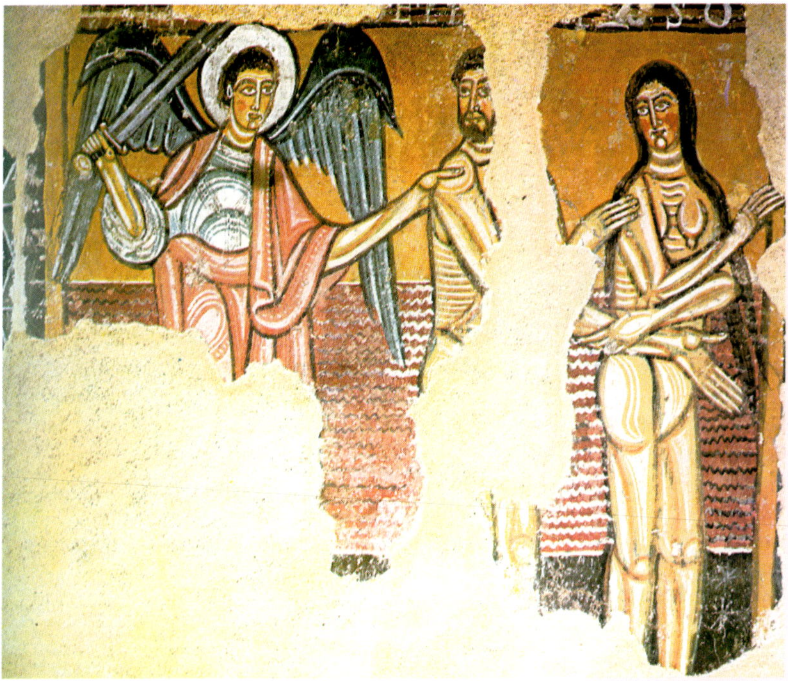

The Expulsion of Adam and Eve from Paradise

Anonymous

- 1100/30
- fresco
- 110 x 98 cm
- Museu Episcopal de Vic, Barcelona

This fresco depicts an angel dressed in a white tunic and red cloak, with large wings, wielding a sword, expelling Adam and Eve from Paradise. The two nude bodies are executed in a highly singular manner by means of a series of parallel strokes in different colors (white, ochre and green). Eve's body, being much better preserved, displays the artist's interest in geometry, compositional balance and formal aesthetics. The painter has depicted the woman's breasts in a manner that is at once naïve and descriptive.

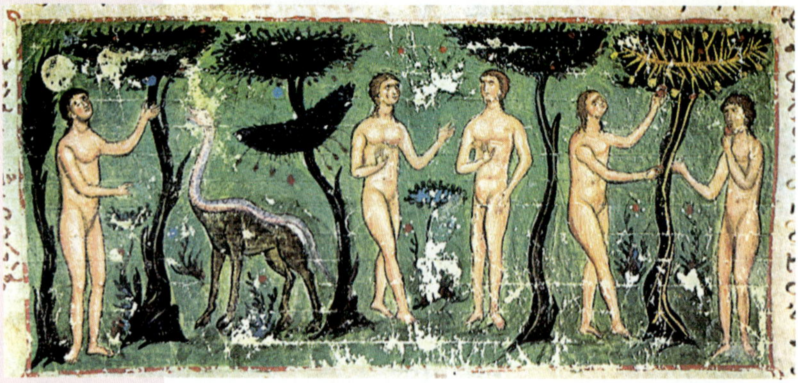

Adam and Eve in Paradise

- 12th century
- tempera on parchment
- miniature
- Topkapi Palace, Istanbul

The author of this miniature is unknown, although it is known that a son of Alejo Commeno (1081–1118) collaborated on it. We see the serpent, portrayed as a four-legged animal, tempting Eve, who then persuades Adam to taste the forbidden fruit. Both Adam and Eve are depicted androgynously, neither showing any sign of gender; Eve's body is formless.

Scene from The Book of Genesis

Anonymous

- first half of the 12th century
- fresco
- 285 cm high
- Museu Episcopal de Vic, Barcelona

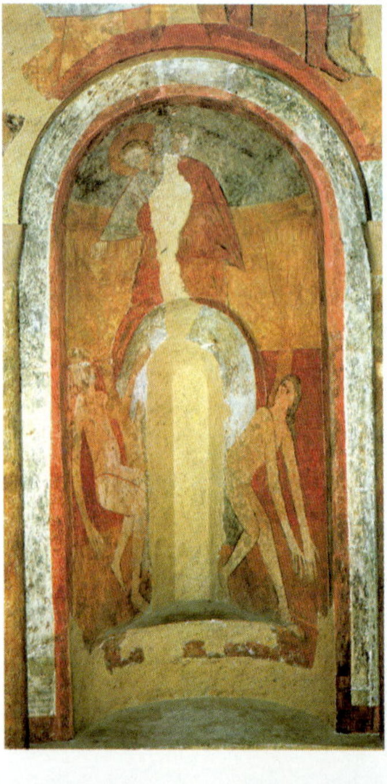

The Creator is depicted here, seated upon high and calling Adam and Eve below after they have eaten of the forbidden fruit. Adam is turning towards God, while Eve seems to be turning away in an attempt to hide. Despite the fact that the nude figures are very rudimentary, with simple outlines and only perfunctory reference to bodily shape and form, their respective attitudes find adequate expression.

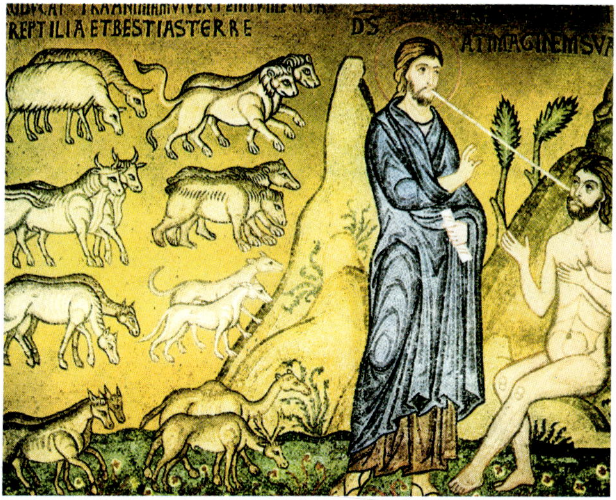

This mosaic depicts the creation of Adam. Naturalistic portrayal has been forfeited in the interest of religious instruction. The torso is represented frontally, with little or no foreshortening.

The Creation of Adam

- 12th century
- mosaic
- Cappella Palatina, Palermo

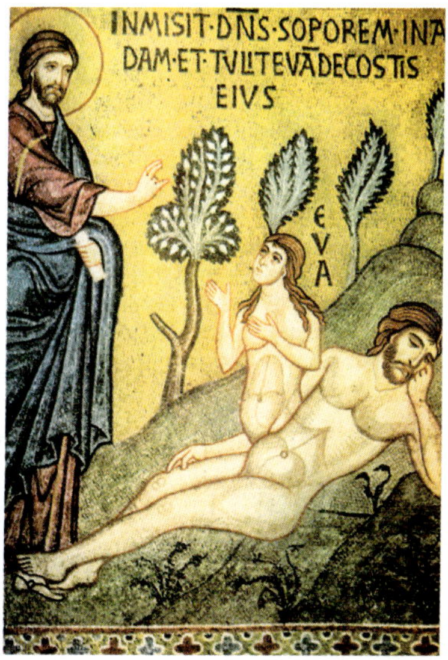

The scene evinces a marked interest in geometry and line. The draftsmanship is elegant without neglecting details such as the muscles of Adam's torso. There is even a certain degree of foreshortening in Adam's abdomen and in the arm he uses to support his head. Eve's treatment is more hieratic, despite her apparent rising movement.

The Creation of Eve

- 12th century
- mosaic
- Cappella Palatina, Palermo

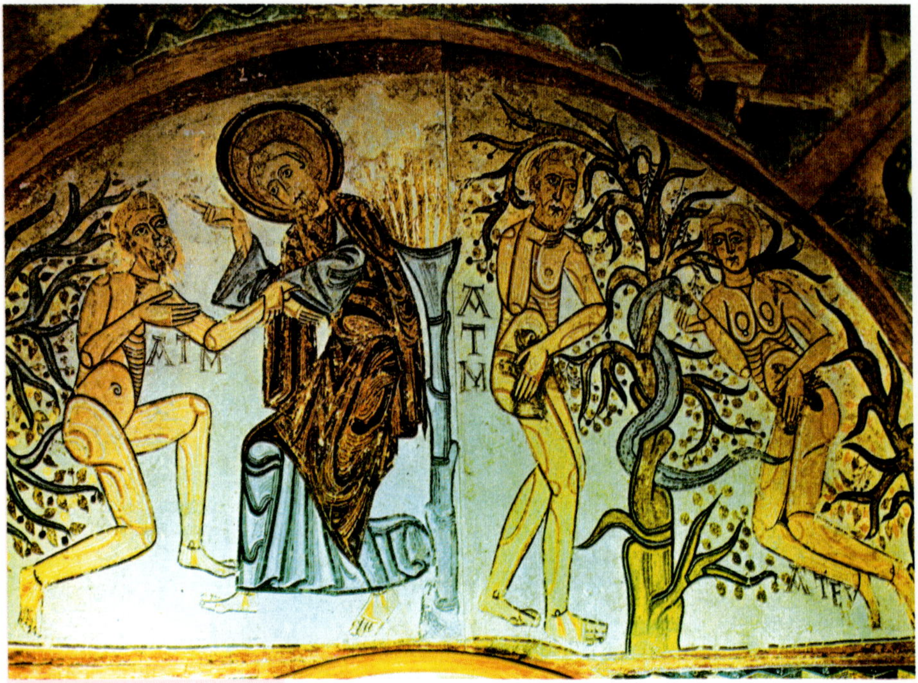

Fresco from the Santa Cruz Hermitage in Maderuelo, Spain

Anonymous
(Segovia, Spain)

- first half of 12th century
- fresco transferred to canvas
- Museo del Prado, Madrid

The scene shows two episodes from the Book of Genesis: the Creation of Adam and Eve on the left, and Adam and Eve after the Fall on the right. The contours of the stylized nudes are drawn in an almost calligraphic manner. The torsos and heads, which are composed of a variety of shapes, are shown frontally; the legs, on the other hand, are rendered in profile. Despite the illustrative intention of the artist, the figures cover their sexual organs with their hands because they are ashamed of the Original Sin that they have just committed. The calligraphic quality of these scenes, independent of the painter's taste and the scene's didactic value, can also be explained by the poor lighting conditions in the church. These nudes exhibit close stylistic affinities with the work of a Catalan painter found in the church of Santa Maria in Taüll.

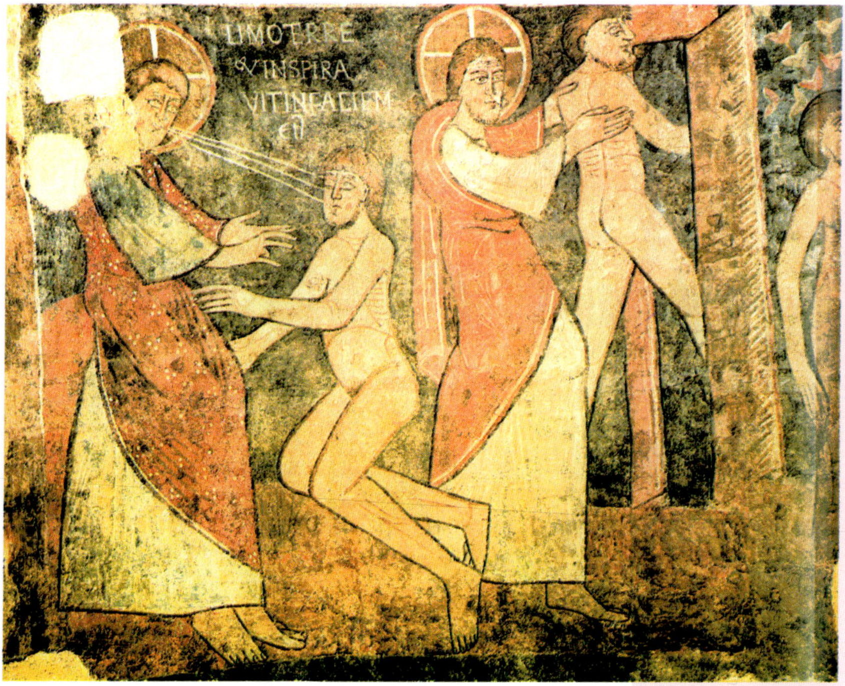

This fresco fragment depicts two episodes from the Book of Genesis: left, God is seen breathing life into Adam, while on the right, He is placing him in earthly paradise. The two scenes perfectly fulfil their didactic objectives. The painter expended great care in delineating the nudes, limning out their outlines with a black line, while principal anatomical features are defined by means of a brown line. In keeping with the bulk of the art of this period, the artist strove here to transmit biblical ideas through a language kept simple by using a minimal number of elements.

The Creation of Adam

Anonymous

- ca. 1125/50
- fresco
- 1.70 x 2.10 m
- Museu Episcopal de Vic, Barcelona

This mural decoration was taken from the apse of the Sant Sadurní d'Osormort church.

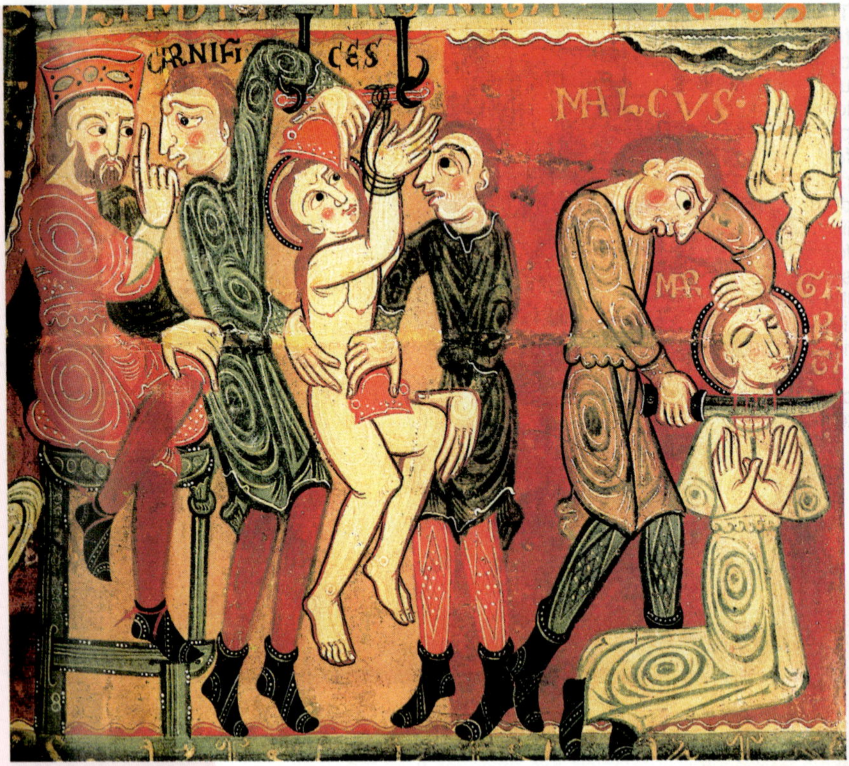

The Martyrdom of St. Margaret

- ca. 1180
- tempera on panel
- 32 x 45 cm
- Museu Episcopal de Vic, Barcelona

This panel was part of the main altar of the church of Santa Margarida in Vila-Seca, in Barcelona.

On the left, Olybrius, who has failed to persuade Margaret to renounce her faith and become his wife or concubine, sits watching as her executioners hang her by the hands and apply two plates of red-hot iron to her body. On the right, she is shown being beheaded. The nude figure here, conveniently outlined in brown, is interestingly modeled and delicately executed in curved or undulating lines of tenuous beige with a light skin coloration. As a result, the body is softly feminine, even somewhat sensual, a factor emphasized by the saint's drooping yet full breasts.

Pietà

- 1164
- fresco
- Hagios Pantaleon, Nerezi, Macedonia

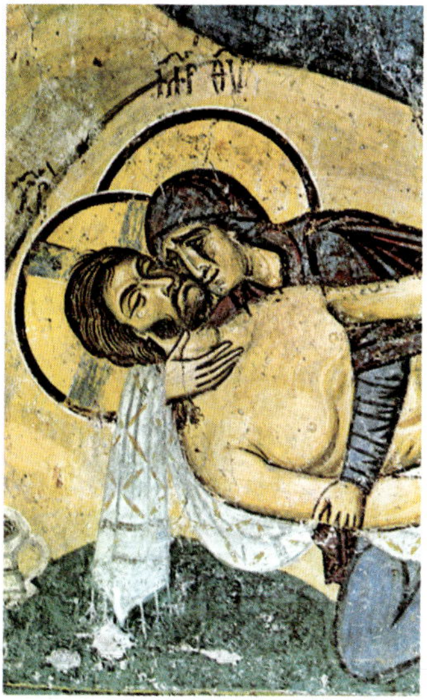

The work is one of several frescos discovered in the church in 1926. The figures have been meticulously executed, and the psychology displayed in features and gestures is profound. Naturalism and drama here are outstanding for their time, while foreshortening has been skilfully deployed. While the figure's shape is limned out with a dark line, the skin colors bring out the body's three-dimensionality, an unusual technique at that time.

Adam and Eve

- end of 12th century
- paint on panel
- Museu Diocesà i Comarcal de Solsona, Lérida

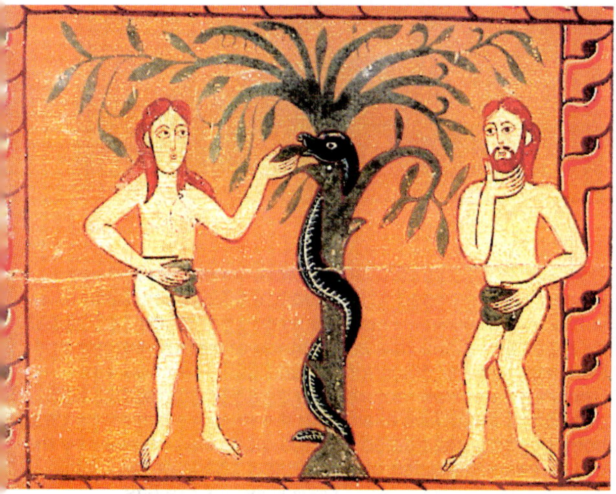

The tree of the knowledge of good and evil stands at the center of this panel, with a serpent entwined around it. It is the moment after Adam and Eve have eaten of the forbidden fruit, Adam holding a hand to his throat as a sign that he has just done so. Both figures are shown discreetly covering their loins. The panel has all the aesthetic and didactic components typical of Romanesque art.

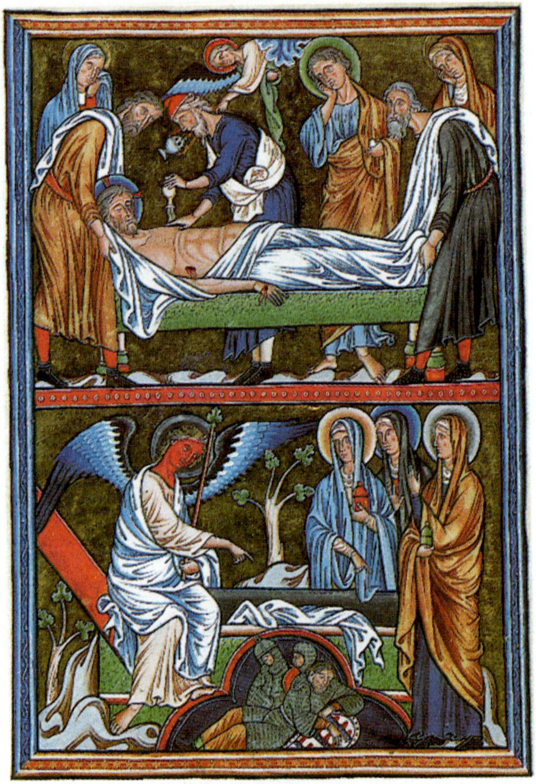

The Preparation for Christ's Entombment and the Three Marys at the Tomb

Anonymous (France)

- ca. 1213
- illuminated manuscript
- 30.4 x 20.4 cm
- Musée Condé, Chantilly

The Gothic iconography in this work is very rich indeed. Since it was intended to be readily intelligible to laymen, its subjects are explicit. Thus, the events portrayed here speak for themselves: the role and attitude of each character and their expressions of weariness and grief are apparent. Christ's anatomical features are as unrealistic as the composition of the scene itself, with the musculature of the dead body perfectly delineated and the modeling achieved by the use of various shades of pink. In this phase of the Gothic period it is no longer possible to speak of the flat colors of Romanesque miniatures, for this work reveals an attempt to produce volumes by means of blending simple tonal values. The body is no longer depicted frontally, but, instead, by means of a rather crude kind of foreshortening.

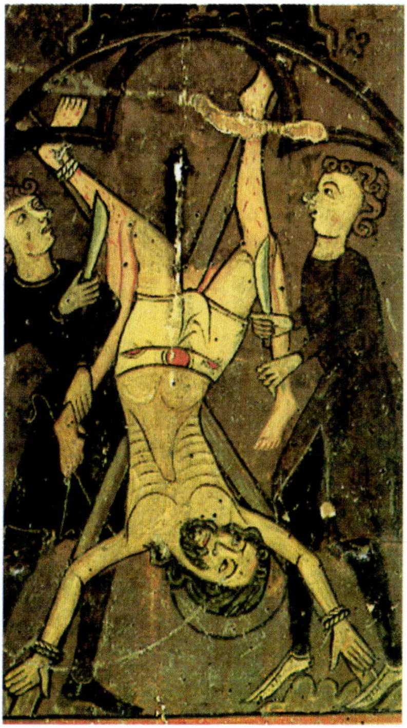

'he saint is depicted upside down, arms and legs tied
› a cross, while two executioners are flaying him alive.
leither blood nor the martyr's physical suffering play
ny role here, as the panel is designed to present a
eroic view: the saint is able to withstand his pain
hrough the strength he gains from his faith.

Martyrdom of St. Bartholomew

- ca. 1300
- paint on panel
- Museu Municipal d'Art, Terrassa, Barcelona

Part of the retable at the Carthusian Monastery of Vallparadís Castle (origin unknown).

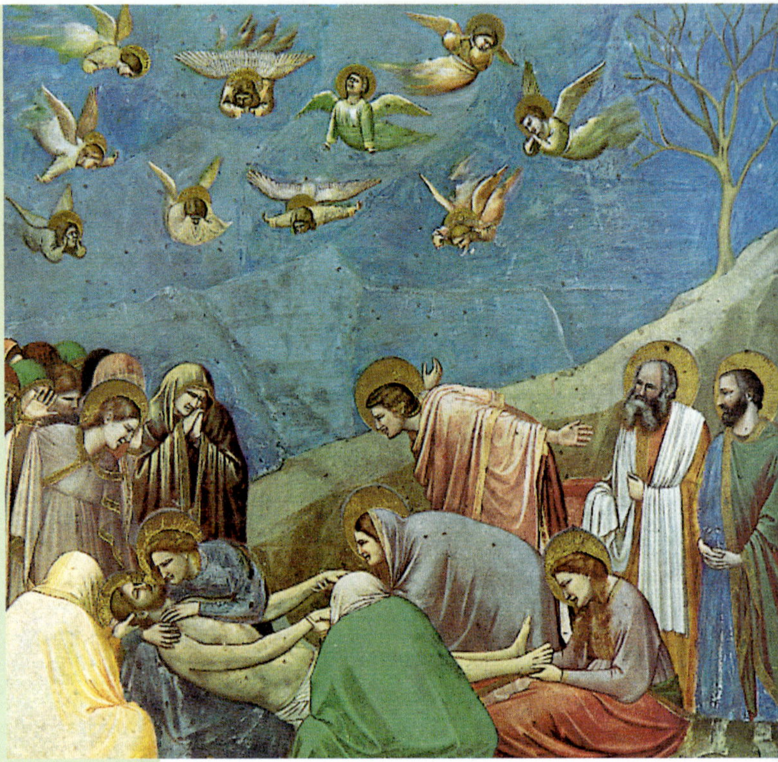

The Lamentation

Giotto (Giotto di Bondone)
(Colle di Vespignano, Florence, 1266/67–Florence, 1337)

- 1303–5
- fresco
- 185 x 200 cm
- Arena Chapel, Padua

Despite his training in the Byzantine style, which prevailed in Trecento Italy, Giotto is regarded as one of the first modern painters insofar as he broke with the medieval canon, adopting a style that introduced new ideals of naturalism and created a convincing sense of pictorial space. He placed particular emphasis on different aspects of volumetry, on the superimposition of planes in the distance and on integrating figures into the background to form a cohesive whole. In this work the dead body is depicted with remarkable naturalism, utterly unlike the rigid figures of his predecessors. The arms are heavy and manifest the inertness of his wrists on being held. The head is tilted back slightly and supported by a woman with a glory and a mourner whose back is turned toward the spectator. One extraordinary feature of this work is the treatment of the flesh tones, which include blue, brown and green hues that model the volumes and subtle shadows.

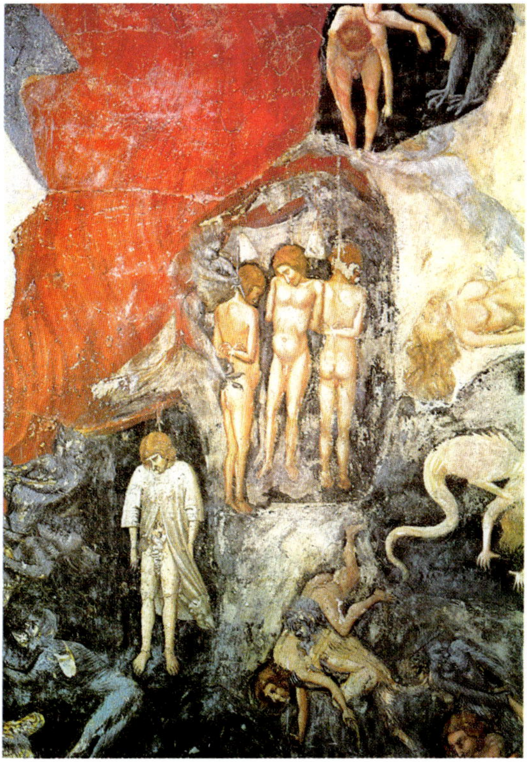

Giotto is sometimes regarded as the first modern painter in the history of art. The monumentalism which he brought to the treatment of his subjects no less than the realism he accorded his figures broke with all preceding trends. The minute one compares the nudes in this work, for instance, with those of earlier artists, or even of his contemporaries, the developments that Giotto introduced in his conception of anatomy can no longer be overlooked: his figures are well modeled, they show realistic three-dimensionality and individual perceptions are more naturalistic. The three figures at the center of this canvas reveal the painter's mastery of draftsmanship and human anatomy, especially in respect of the foreshortening that is present here to an almost kaleidoscopic degree. The foreshortening of the figure at the top of the fresco, for example, is remarkable for its complexity in conveying a bent posture: executed with realistic naturalism, the trunk appears to advance towards the spectator, while the legs seem to recede into the cave.

Hell (Scene from The Last Judgment)

Giotto (Giotto di Bondone)
(Colle di Vespignano, Florence, 1266/67–Florence, 1337)

- ca. 1303/10
- fresco
- Cappella degli Scrovegni all'Arena, Padua

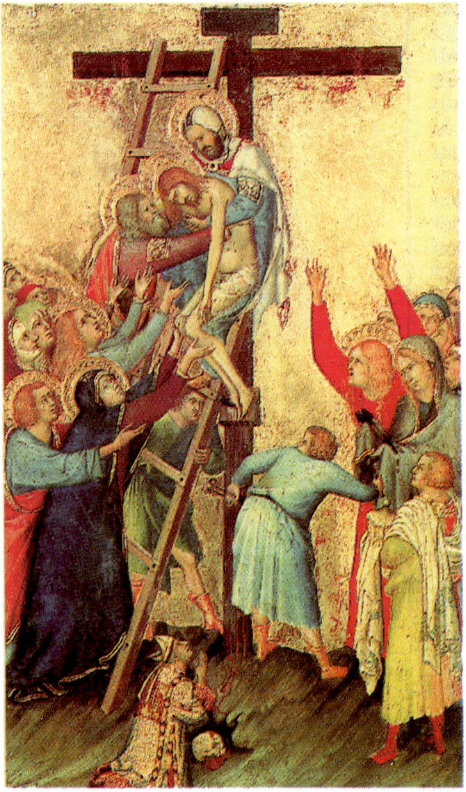

The Deposition

Simone Martini
(Siena, 1280/85–Avignon, 1344)

- ca. 1315
- tempera on panel
- 29.7 x 20.5 cm
- Koninklijk Museum voor Schone Kunsten, Antwerp

The composition of this small panel painting is filled with figures, without appearing crowded. The spaciousness is achieved by means of perspective, whereby the characters have been arranged in order of importance, with the donor, Cardinal Orsini, kneeling in the foreground. The man standing at the foot of the Cross may represent Simone Martini himself. The body of Christ is executed with striking naturalism, his inert arms being supported by the figures around him. Although still rather crude, the individual elements of the painting have been depicted with the utmost care.

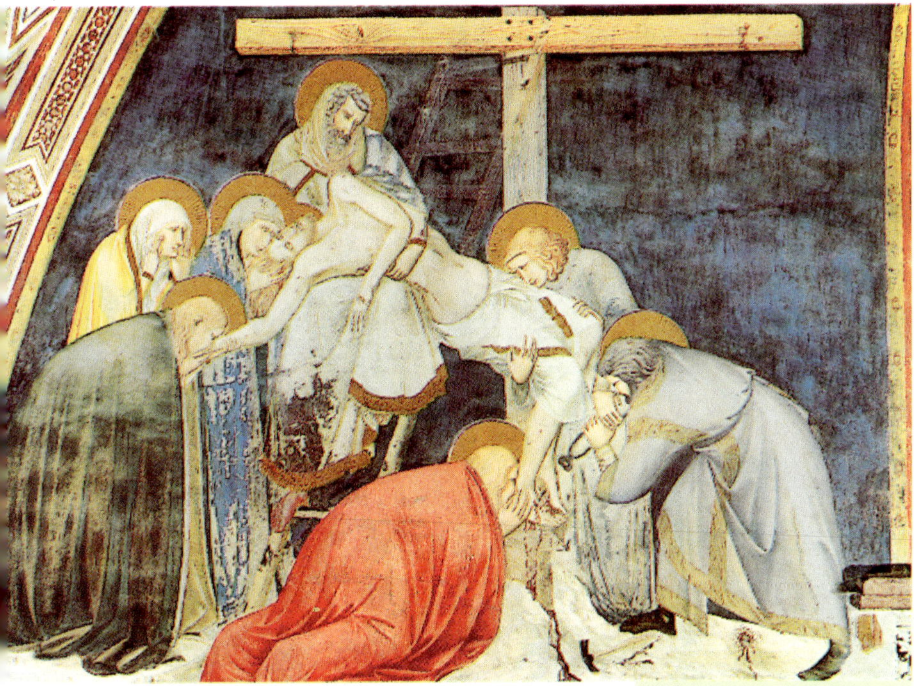

The representation of Christ's death on the Cross and the martyrdom of saints provided artists with the ideal opportunity to circumvent the stringent moral codes of orthodox doctrine and to include nude figures in the scene. It is no wonder, then, that these subjects were taken up with alacrity. In this work, Lorenzetti presents a scene in the Gothic style, with a highly stylized figure of Christ, whose slender body is not a symbol of weakness, but, rather, of svelteness and elegance. The attenuated arms and legs form a harmonious compositional parallel to the vertical lines of the ladder in the background. Unlike the ascetic representations of Christ's body in other works dealing with the same subject, this one contains blood, which is particularly notable on the feet. This was to become widespread in the Netherlandish and other northern painting traditions, in which blood is shown gushing from Christ's naked body.

The Deposition

Pietro Lorenzetti
(Siena, 1280/90–ca. 1348)

- 1320–30
- fresco
- 232 x 337 cm
- Lower Chapel of the Church of St. Francis, Assisi

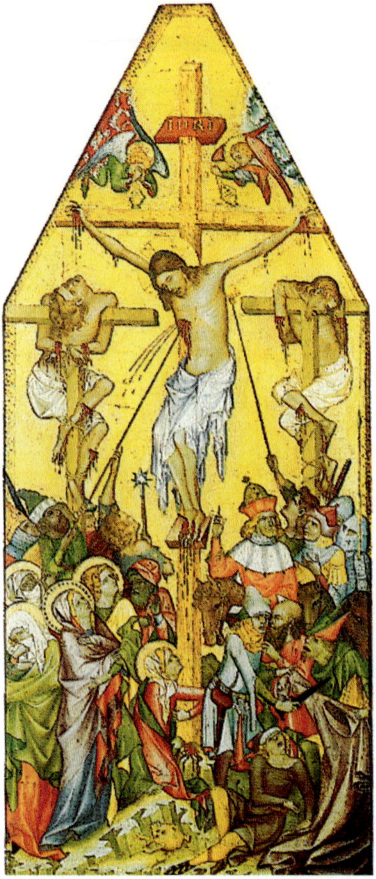

The Crucifixion

Master of the Kaufmann Crucifixion

- ca. 1340
- tempera on panel
- 67.7 x 30.3 cm
- Staatliche Museen Preussischer Kulturbesitz, Gemäldegalerie, Berlin

Despite his penchant for angular, convoluted forms, the Bohemian master who painted this panel was clearly inspired by Italian models. The anatomical studies are remarkably naturalistic: the agony suffered by the three crucified figures finds dramatic expression in their writhing bodies. The good thief, to the right of Jesus, stares repentantly up to heaven; the bad thief, who is depicted with wounds, looks down at the ground. The symmetry of these figures is disrupted by a soldier piercing Jesus' right side with a lance, from which blood issues, in the shape of an arc.

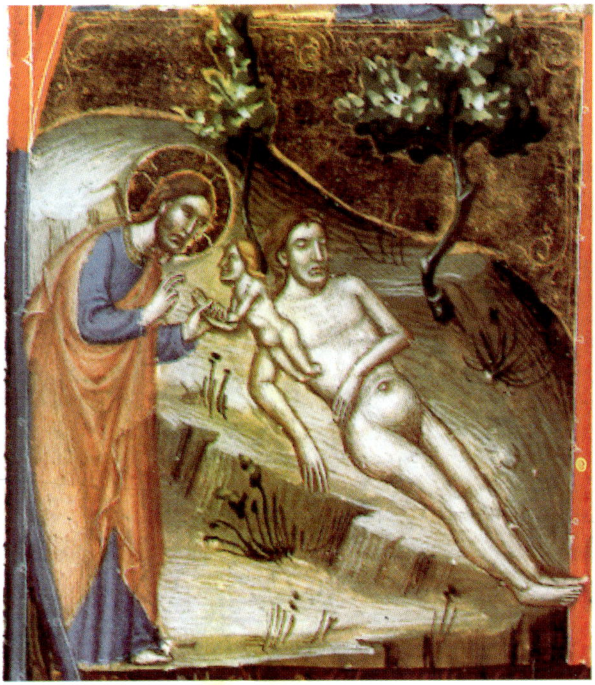

God is depicted here in the form traditionally reserved for Jesus. Adam is portrayed nude and in deep sleep. His body is well modeled and all its features have been correctly drawn. Its three-dimensionality has been achieved through a magnificent interplay of highlights and shadows that evince the artist's true skill. Notable are the figure's bulging abdomen (a typical feature of Gothic iconography), enormous eye-shaped navel, and outstandingly-drawn facial expression and features. The figure appears to levitate rather than to be recumbent, and Eve is shown emerging from Adam's flank, to which her legs are still attached. Despite the diminutive size of the figure, the artist has managed to bring out the figure's svelte, feminine forms. Once again, as is characteristic of such works, the artist has concerned himself solely with didactic aspects.

The Creation of Eve

Ferrer Bassa
(ca. 1285/90, Tortosa –Barcelona, 1348)

- ca. 1340/48
- illumination
- Anglo-Catalan Psalter, Bibliothèque Nationale, Paris

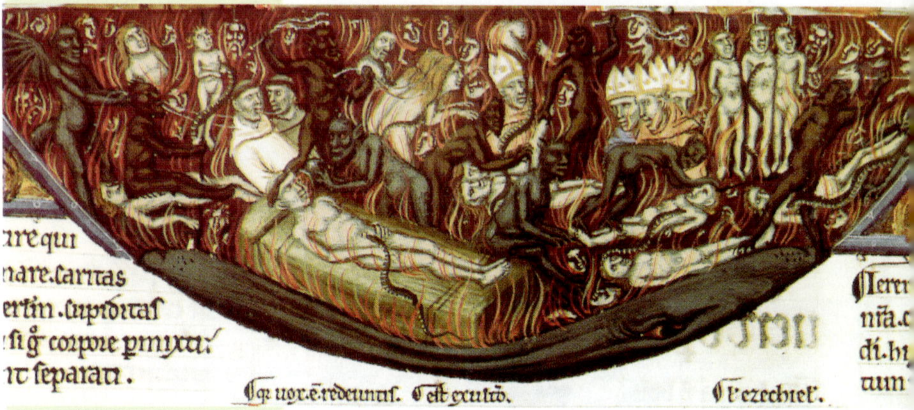

Vision of Hell

Ferrer Bassa

(ca. 1285/90, Tortosa –Barcelona, 1348)

- ca. 1340/48
- illumination
- Anglo-Catalan Psalter, Bibliothèque Nationale, Paris

This work depicts a vision of Hell, in which different ecclesiastical characters play a leading role. A serpent is shown attacking a recumbent figure in the foreground, naked, recently deceased, while his bed begins to burn. Others are being dragged along by black-skinned demons whose appearance is terrifying. Far right, a group of three are hanging by their necks. Archbishops and other clergymen, amidst demons and women, are enveloped in flames. The scene is a reference to the difficult, convulsed times in which significant sections of the clergy often led scandalous lifestyles. The work depicts the future in store for such individuals. Despite the relative simplicity of the work's techniques and its treatment of figures, its visual impact is stunning. There is no doubt this artist was a remarkable communicator who perfectly understood the psychology of his public.

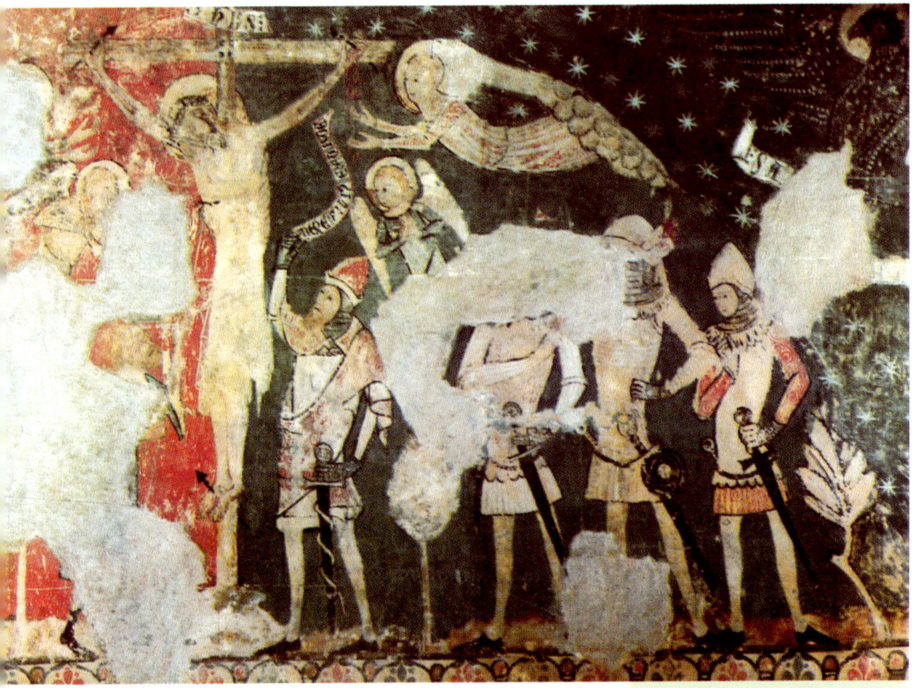

Crucifixion

Anonymous

- ca. 1350
- fresco
- Sant Miguel de Cardona, Museu Diocesà i Comarcal de Solsona, Lérida

This detail from a huge mural decoration depicts the Crucifixion. Time has obliterated many of the figures, so that apart from Christ, only a group of Roman soldiers is visible. Christ himself here is a poignant image of death and downcast humanity. The artist has highlighted whatever most fittingly reflects the horror of martyrdom: the body emaciated and stretched, the ribs plainly visible, an overall heaviness. The dark-blue starry sky, which forms the background to a large part of the composition, lends the scene an air of solemnity and heightens the tragedy of the moment. The whole has great dramatic power and breathes splendor. Everything in the work is designed to move the viewer and to foster prayer and devotion.

The Deposition

Pietro da Rimini
(Rimini, first half of the 14th century)

- first half of the 14th century
- panel
- 44 x 31 cm
- Musée du Louvre, Paris

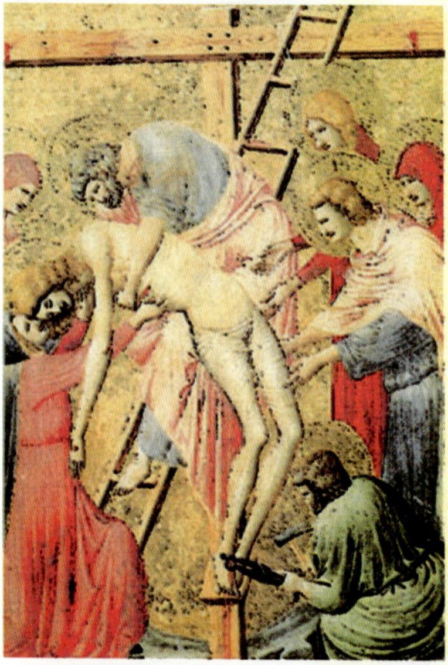

Pietro da Rimini, one of the most skilled and influential of second-generation artists of the Rimini School, presents a scene laden with drama and emotion, whose function is to arouse pious devotion in the viewer. Against a light golden background appear the stylized, attenuated figures, emphasizing their spirituality. Christ is depicted in an unnatural pose and wears a transparent loincloth.

The Damned (Detail from The Last Judgement)

Orcagna (Andrea di Cione Arcangelo)
(Florence?, ca. 1308–1368)

- ca. 1360
- fresco (detail)
- overall size: 700 x 334 cm
- Museo dell'Opera di Santa Croce, Florence

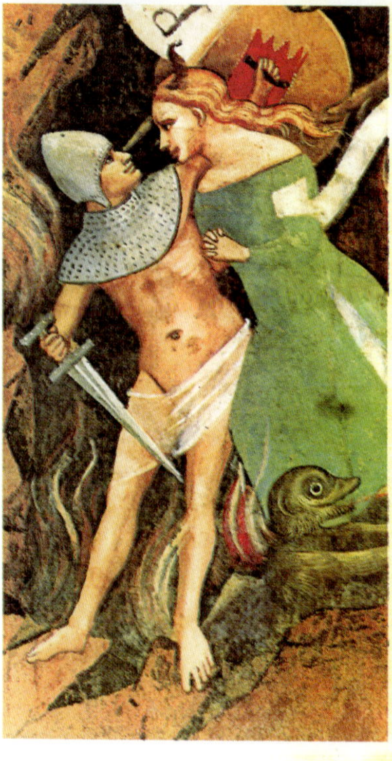

Orcagna's pictorial work influenced Florentine painting towards the end of the 14th century with its great expressive power and its technique. In the present detail, we see two extremely naturalistic figures: a nude soldier protecting one of the damned. The soldier's nude body is fundamentally realistic and rather sensually portrayed, a characteristic that is accentuated by the transparent veil covering his loins.

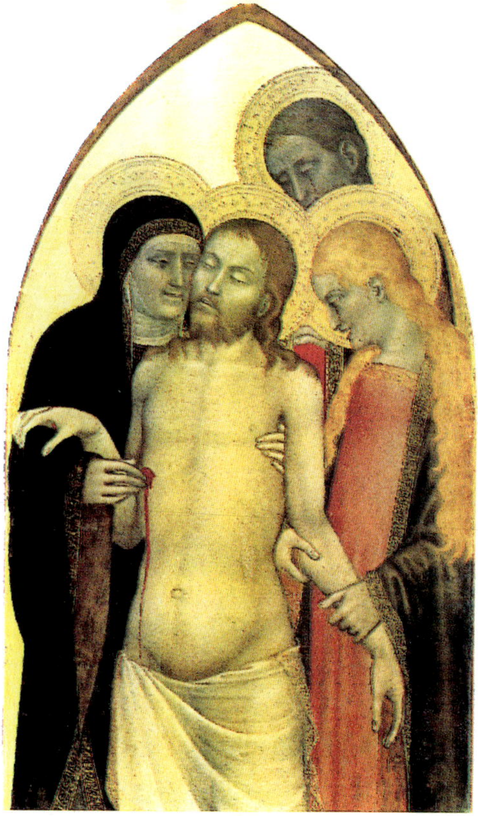

Pietà

Giovanni da Milano

(Caversaccio, near Como; active 1346–69)

- 1365
- tempera on panel
- 122 x 58 cm
- Galleria dell'Academia, Florence

Originally in the church of San Girolamo della Costa in Florence.

lere, we see the Virgin, Jesus, St. John and Mary Magda-ene. The feeling of anguish shared by Christ and his mother nds symbolic expression in the way their faces touch, and her gesture of pointing to the wound at Jesus' side. The aces are composed of simple features, whose expressions re somewhat crude. The figure of Christ is not that of a orpse, but rather of a beautiful nude sleeping serenely. The oft modeling of the forms reveal a painstaking anatomical tudy in which light and shadow blend together in seamless radations. The painting depicts a remarkably harmonious ude, certainly ahead of its time, and contains clear refer-nces to Byzantine iconography. The painting has an extra-rdinary narrative quality. The figures are fluid, not hieratic, nding a subliminal dynamism to the scene, which was later be taken up and further developed in the Renaissance nd which recurs in Netherlandish painting, with its crisply elineated, almost aggressive compositional lines.

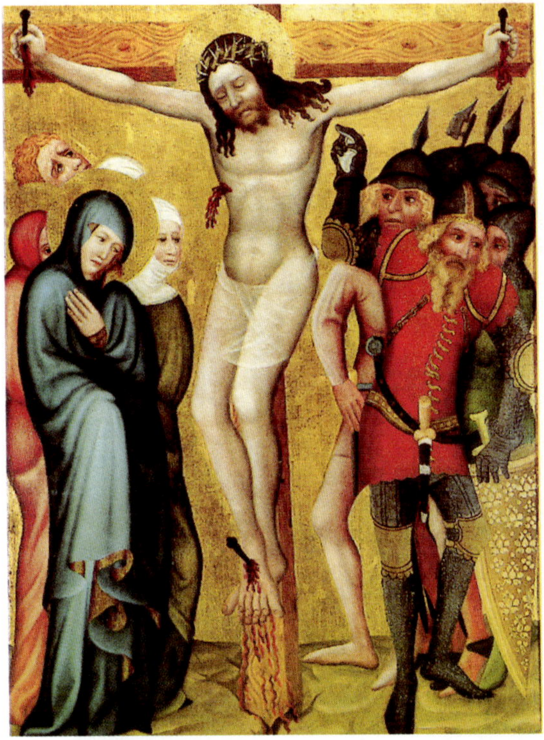

The Crucifixion

Master Theoderic
(Bohemia, active 1359–81)

- ca. 1370
- tempera on panel
- 132 x 98 cm
- Národni Galeri, Prague

Master Theoderic was undoubtedly one of the most brilliant and original Bohemian artists of his age, serving as court painter to Charles IV in Prague. This panel is conceived as a sculptural group, in which the figures' three-dimensionality is one of the artist's principal concerns. The symbolism is revealed in the arrangement of the various groups of figures: on Jesus' right we see his followers; on the left his executioners, dressed in red. Christ's body exhibits a high degree of plasticity, as if it were modeled in clay; the precision with which it has been rendered attests to the artist's sound anatomical knowledge. This does not mean, however, that certain details, such the area where the legs overlap, were not inspired from models. Master Theoderic has filled the picture plane with so many figures that it looks as though they can scarcely be contained within the painting's frame. By using various color gradations and half-tones, the artist imbues each individual figure with an almost mystical quality.

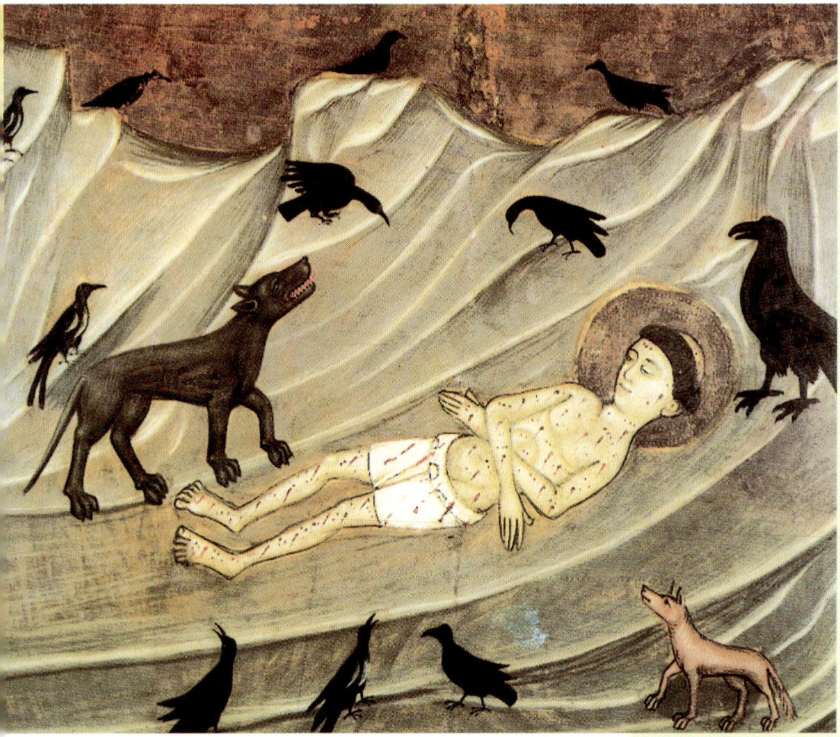

The body of the saint is portrayed abandoned in the mountains and at the mercy of wolves and carrion crows. Such depictions were eminently didactic, aiming to bring fundamental religious tenets home to the faithful with a minimum of elements. Despite his martyrdom, the saint's expression is serene, demonstrating that suffering cannot touch one who has faith in God.

Martyrdom of St. Vincent

Anonymous

- 1370–80
- paint on panel
- Museu Nacional d'Art de Catalunya, Barcelona

This altarpiece was in the parish church of Sant Vicenç d'Estimariu.

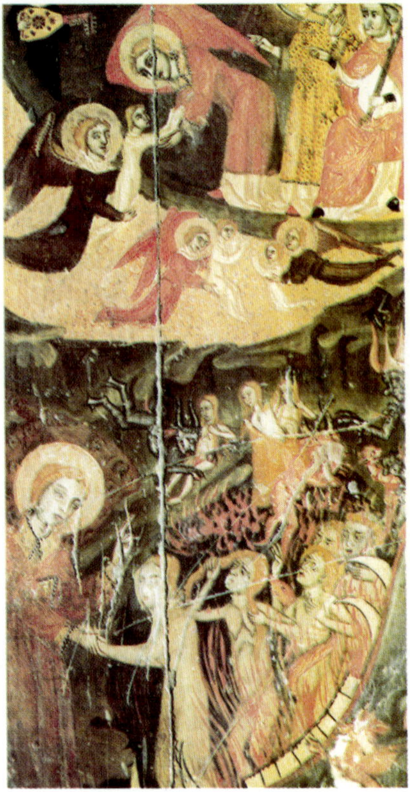

Scene from the Life of St. Michael

Master of Elna
(14th/15th century)

- ca. 1375/1400
- tempera on panel
- Cathedral of Santa Eulàlia d'Elna, Rosellón

This two-tiered painting depicts St. Michael in Purgatory freeing the souls of the righteous and sending them to heaven, where they are received by angels in the presence of God, who is dressed as a bishop and assisted by a deacon. The souls are portrayed as nude figures, their forms somewhat schematic and indistinct. The bodies in Purgatory are partially covered by the purificatory flames. The artist has concentrated his attention on the facial expressions of the subjects, who gaze upwards in hope. The souls in heaven are portrayed in naked innocence, their features childlike, which also explains the delicate way in which the angels are holding them.

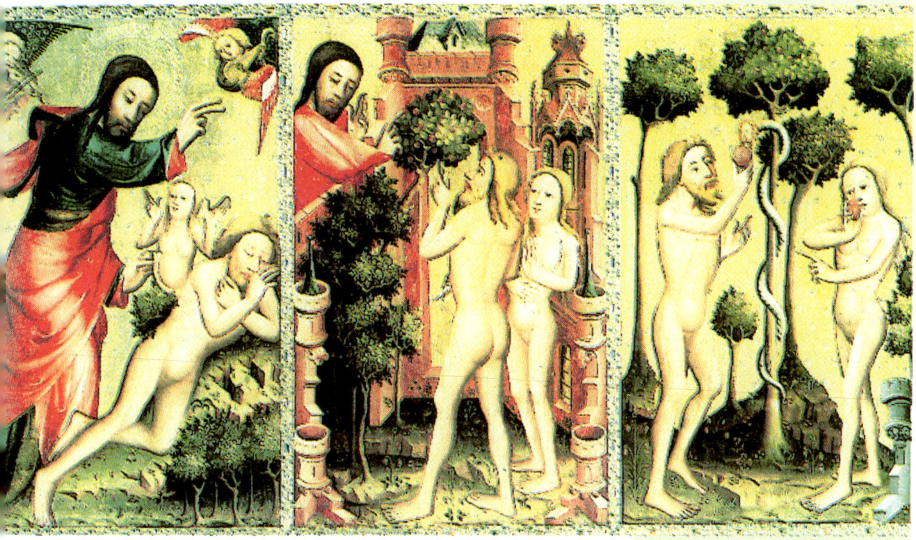

Scenes from the Book of Genesis

Master Bertram
(Minden, Westphalia, 1340/45–ca. 1415)

- 1383
- paint on panel
- 86 x 172 cm
- Kunsthalle, Hamburg

These three scenes illustrate the story of Adam and Eve as described in the Book of Genesis: God creates Eve from Adam's rib; God tells Adam and Eve not to eat of the forbidden fruit; the Fall. In keeping with the style of the times, these paintings are simple in conception, although the artist has seen to it that the most important details are manifest, enabling the viewer to understand the moral of the story readily. Adam and Eve are represented as nudes, who exhibit disproportionately large heads and feet, slender legs and bulging abdomens, in the Gothic tradition. These are exceedingly beautiful, almost lyrical paintings, whose perfectly outlined figures stand out against a golden background, together with the vegetation, representing the Garden of Eden.

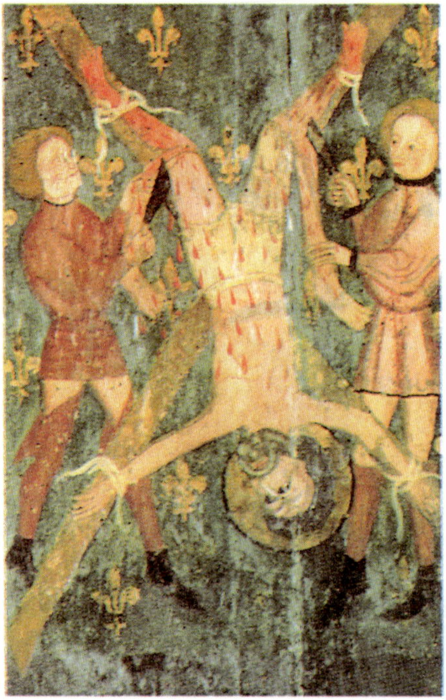

The Martyrdom of St. Bartholomew

Anonymous

- ca. 1400
- paint on panel
- Museu Nacional d'Art de Catalunya, Barcelona

Of unknown origin, the panel originally belonged to the Maricel Collection, Sitges, and was acquired by the Museum in 1986.

Bartholomew, one of the twelve disciples, was martyred at king Astyages' behest. His brother Polimius had been converted and his sister had been exorcised of evil spirits by Bartholomew. Bartholomew is said to have suffered martyrdom by being flayed alive. As a result he was proclaimed patron of all guilds that worked with hide, which is why many panels were painted of him. This one is the lower left-hand panel of an altarpiece dedicated to the saint. Against a blue background decorated with fleurs-de-lis, the seminude saint is depicted tied to a cross, upside down and flanked by his executioners. Using knives, they are removing his skin. Blood is flowing and has already bespattered the body of the saint, who yet shows no sign of pain. Bartholomew's naked body is rendered along early Gothic lines. The work of course had a fundamentally catechetical purpose.

The iconography of this panel is not uncommon in depictions of this episode in the life of Christ. Jesus is shown submerged in water up to the lower waist. The water, however, is not opaque: like a translucent veil, it scarcely conceals his naked limbs. While stylized, the figure does show more naturalistic elements, its brightness enhanced by the relative dark of its surroundings.

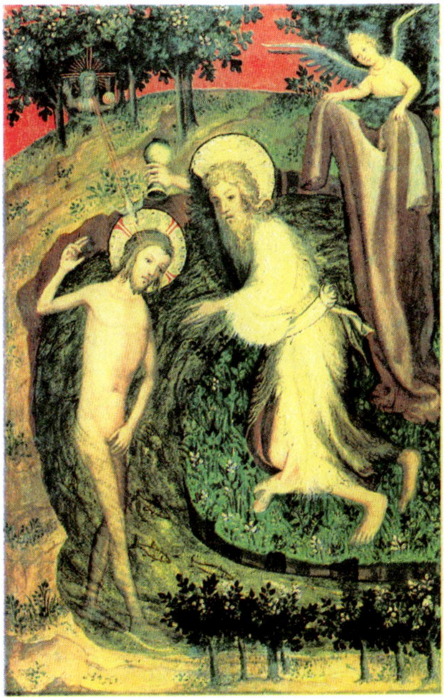

The Baptism of Jesus

Anonymous (Gelderland?)

- ca. 1400
- panel painting
- The Walters Art Gallery, Baltimore

Museum Mayer van der Bergh, Antwerp

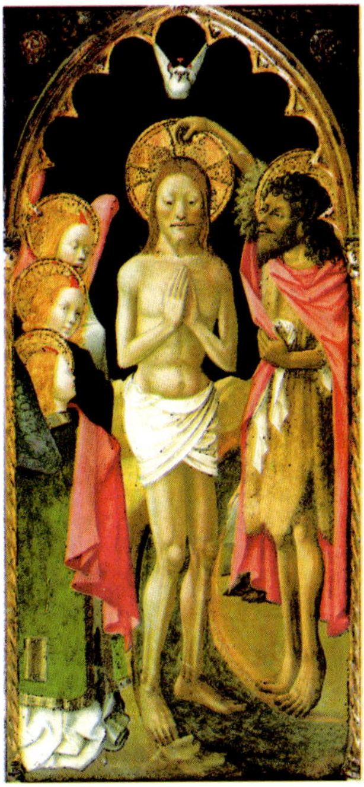

Baptism of Christ

Jacopo Duranti
(active in France between 1454 and 1469)

- tempera on panel
- Museo Massena

Duranti's style manifests typically Renaissance approaches to painting that are of a Provençal origin. The artist strove to achieve a certain naturalism in his work, as in this panel, which radiates tremendous spirituality. Christ's rather skinny legs are skilfully modeled, and are remarkable as well for the way the skin colors, including direct applications of green and blue, have been deployed.

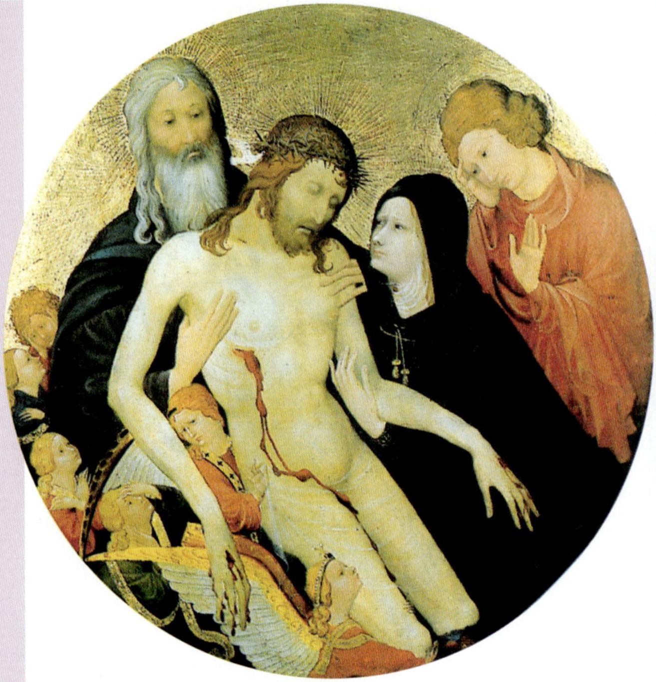

Pietà

Jean Malouel
(or **Maelwael**)
(Nijmegen, before 1370–Dijon, 1415)

- 1400
- tempera on panel
- diameter: 64.5 cm
- Musée du Louvre, Paris

The circular shape of this work was no doubt inspired by Italian tondi, a format that was highly popular at the European courts. This pietà resembles a Deposition, which the artist did not depict in order to ensure that enough space was left for the figures in the foreground. It shows Christ, after the descent from the Cross, of great physical beauty, with well-proportioned and stylized limbs and modeling achieved by the presence of a flood of golden light. The consummately executed study of the hands is particularly noteworthy, as is the delicate, transparent veil with which the angels are shown covering the lower part of Christ's body, which heightens the sensuality of the figure. The work is attributed to the Netherlandish artist Jean Malouel, who maintained close ties with the Limburg brothers, and was perhaps even their uncle. Executed in the so-called International Gothic style, it combines aspects of Netherlandish painting, Sienese painting, which had made its way to Paris toward the end of the 14th century, and Parisian stylization.

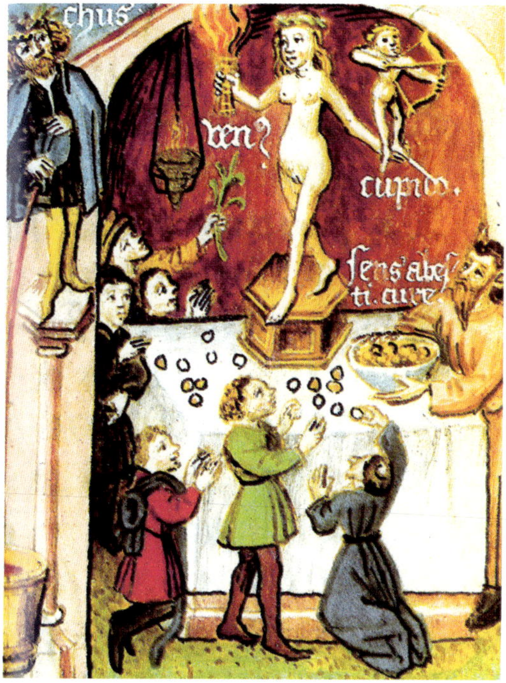

The Chapel of Venus

Anonymous

- 15th century
- tempera on parchment

'arious figures from the clergy and the bourgeoisie are
epicted around a table that is laid with a variety of fruit and
ther delicacies, in a cheerful, festive atmosphere. To the left,
erched atop a column, Bacchus is shown pouring wine; on
dais at the center of the table, Venus is walking in dynamic
tride and bears a torch in her right hand. To her left is her
on, Cupid, who has drawn back his arrow, ready to shoot.
'enus is portrayed entirely nude, exhibiting physical attributes
hat are unusual for paintings of the time. She is the epitome
f sensuality, candidness and provocation. The artist was
learly more concerned with a naturalistic treatment of light
han the figure's volumes, whose shadows are suggested
ith only slightly darker colors than the rest of the skin. The
lethora of colors aptly conveys the atmosphere sought by
ne artist, who, with this work, aimed to denounce the
nchecked libertine lifestyles of certain members of the bour-
eoisie and the clergy.

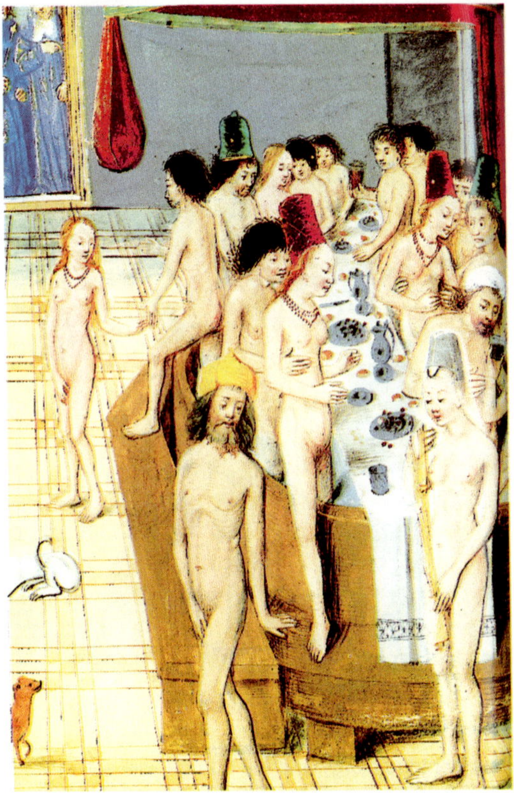

Orgiastic Scene

Anonymous

- 15th century
- tempera on parchment

In this miniature the artist makes interesting use of central perspective, enabling the beholder to view the scene from an elevated vantage point, ensuring that no details are over-looked. The figures represent male and female guests at a party who are completely naked save the occasional toga or hat. They are shown merrymaking in a bath across which a table containing cherries has been placed. Observed by a fully clothed couple in the top left-hand corner, the guests mingle freely in the warm atmosphere of the room, showing neither embarrassment nor inhibition. The figures reflect the ideal of beauty of the day, a canon that other artists explored on canvas or panel. The women, with stylized bodies, small breasts and bulging abdomens, resemble pubescent girls. The man in the foreground has such a slim build that his bones can be seen protruding through his skin.

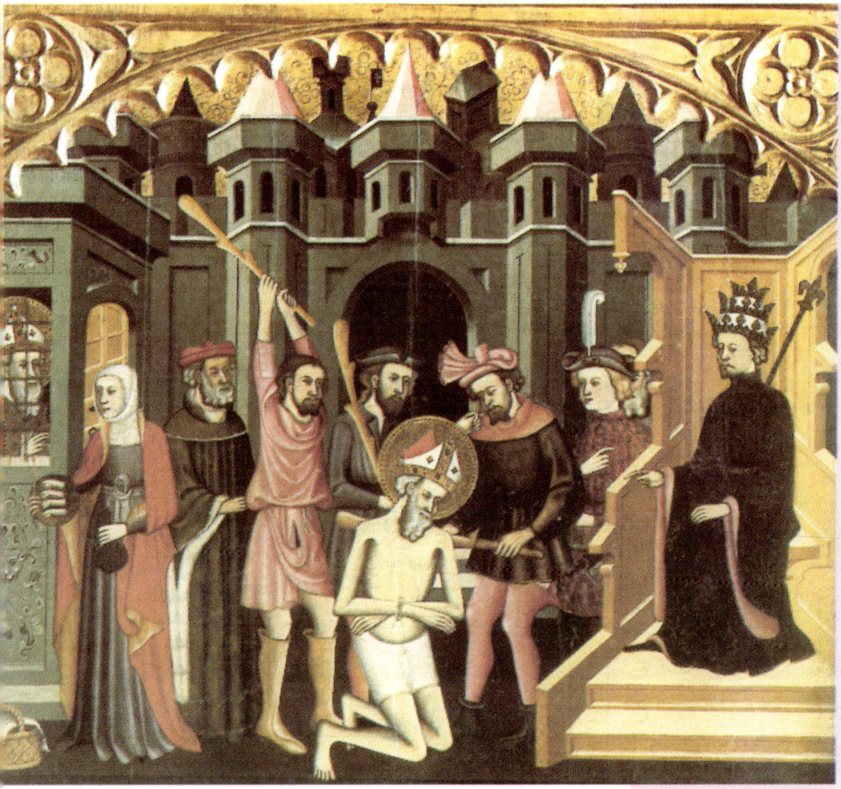

This painting, part of an altarpiece, depicts the saint's martyrdom. Kneeling, miter on head, dressed in underwear, his hands bound, St. Blas receives the blows of his executioners with resignation. His body has all the qualities of a good drawing, the pale color of his skin highlighting the figure against the dark background. The saint's body is old and thin, doubtless the result of an ascetic lifestyle. Pose and facial expression indicate an ordinary, well-meaning person, whose faith in God reduces the agony of the martyrdom he is being subjected to. Some of the complementary figures here are mandatory for the theme (Agricola, for instance, depicted on a throne with the attributes of a king); others appear to have been included at random.

Martyrdom of St. Blas

Pere Vall
(documented Barcelona ca. 1405–1411)

- 1408
- tempera on panel
- Sant Vicenç de Cardona, private collection

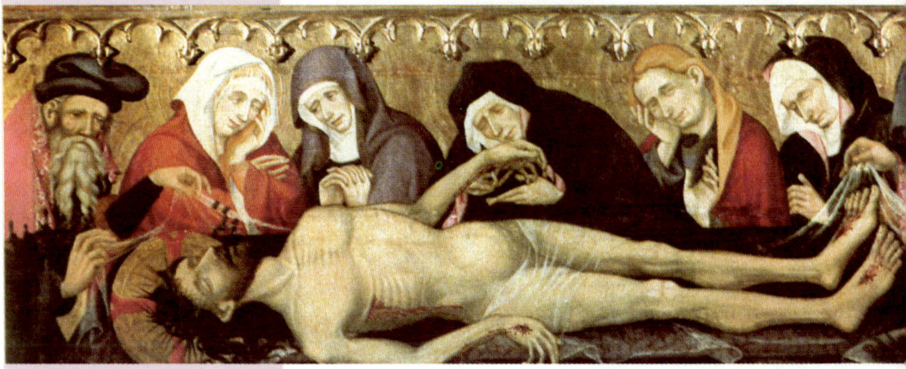

Lamentation

Luis Borrassà
(documented Gerona, ca. 1380 –Barcelona, ca. 1424-26

- 1410
- tempera on panel
- 99 x 235 cm
- Santa Maria de Manresa, Barcelona

The panel depicts the moment immediately following Christ's descent from the Cross. Standing on one side of Christ laid out on a slab is Mary, his mother, who is shown kissing her son's hand. Behind her are the three Marys, and on the far left Joseph of Arimathea. The body of Christ, rigidly depicted, brings home the bare reality of death. Veins, muscles and bone structure illustrate how the artist has utilized his firm grounding in human anatomy to achieve this aim. The bulging abdomen is in keeping with other nude representations of the time. A transparent veil covers Christ's intimate parts. The panel is one of the finest works of Catalan painting of the period.

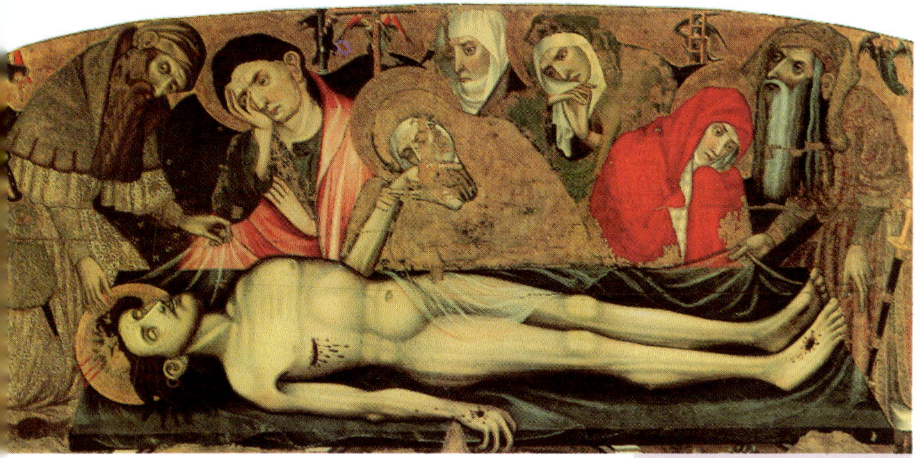

This work, unusually, was a single, independent panel forming an entire altarpiece. Christ is depicted lying on a slab of black marble on a large, transparent veil held by Joseph of Arimathea and Nicodemus. Mary devoutly kisses her son's hand before the disconcerted and forlorn gazes of St. John the Evangelist and the three Marys. The expressivity in the faces of the bystanders no less than Christ's body itself deserve attention, the latter being a forceful, definitive image of his human condition. The figure is presented in a conventional manner because the artist was not interested in naturalistic depiction but rather wished to elicit feelings of compassion and spirituality in the viewer.

Pietà

Jaume Cabrera
(d. 1432)

- ca. 1410/20
- egg tempera on panel
- 122 x 250 cm
- Museu d'Art, Gerona

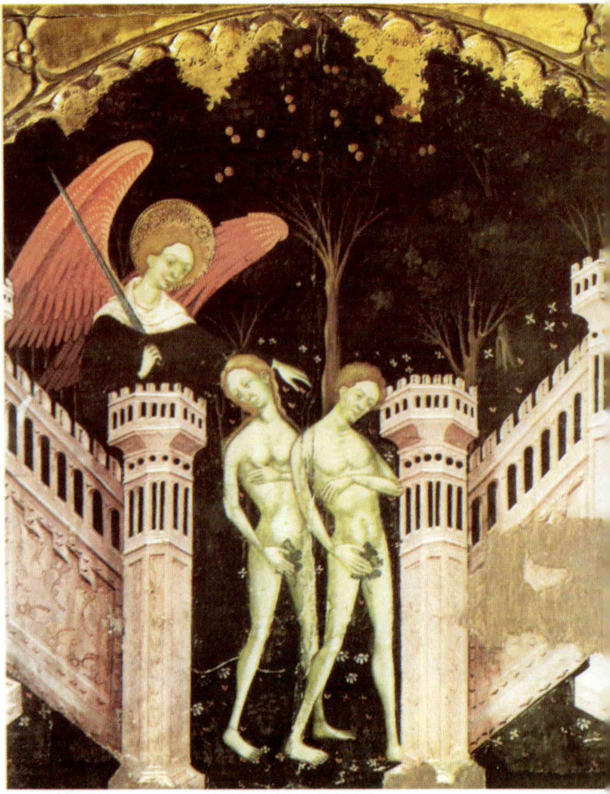

The Expulsion of Adam and Eve from Paradise

Ramon de Mur
(died ca. 1435)

- 1412
- tempera on panel
- 120 x 101 cm
- San Sebastián de Guimerà, Museu Episcopal de Vic, Barcelona

The panel depicts architectural constructions that are both background and frame for the human subjects. Adam and Eve are two magnificent figures here, as much for their poses as for their position at the center of the work. In addition to conveying the reality of what they are experiencing, their stylized and schematic bodies, slender legs and mannered forms, compose a harmonious and dynamic whole of notable aesthetic merit. The painting is an exquisite example of Mur's style: lissom, delicate anatomies, skilled distribution of elements, rich chromatism and balance of forms, compositional simplicity and overall elegance.

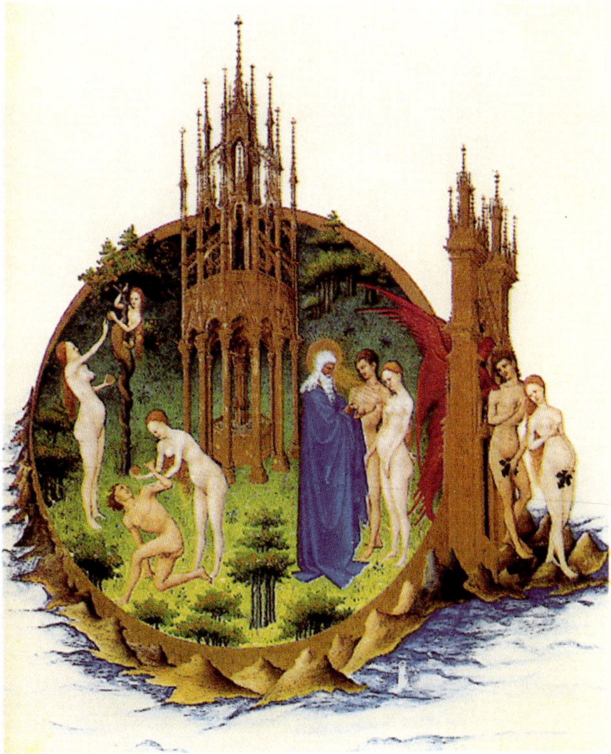

This miniature is an illustration in a book of hours—a prayer book used by laymen for private devotion, containing prayers or meditations appropriate to certain times of the day, week, month or season. It illustrates the Fall of man: the serpent is shown offering the apple to Eve, who, in turn, tempts Adam with it, causing them to lose their primal innocence. God punishes the couple for the sin they have committed by having an angel expel them from Paradise. The nudes reflect the erotic ideal of the early 15th century, especially the figure of Eve, who has sloping shoulders, small round breasts and a large abdomen. The flesh tones of the two figures differ, the woman's being much whiter than that of the man, a characteristic that was intended to heighten the sensuality of the figure, for, at the time, white skin was considered a sign of beauty. Particularly notable features of this miniature include its painstaking execution and its remarkable composition, which is seen from a slightly elevated point of view.

Les Très Riches Heures: Expulsion from Paradise

Limburg (or **Limbourg**) **Brothers: Herman, Jean (Jannequin) and Paul (Pol)**
(active 1385–1416)

- 1414–16
- illuminated manuscript
- 29 x 21 cm
- Musée Condé, Chantilly

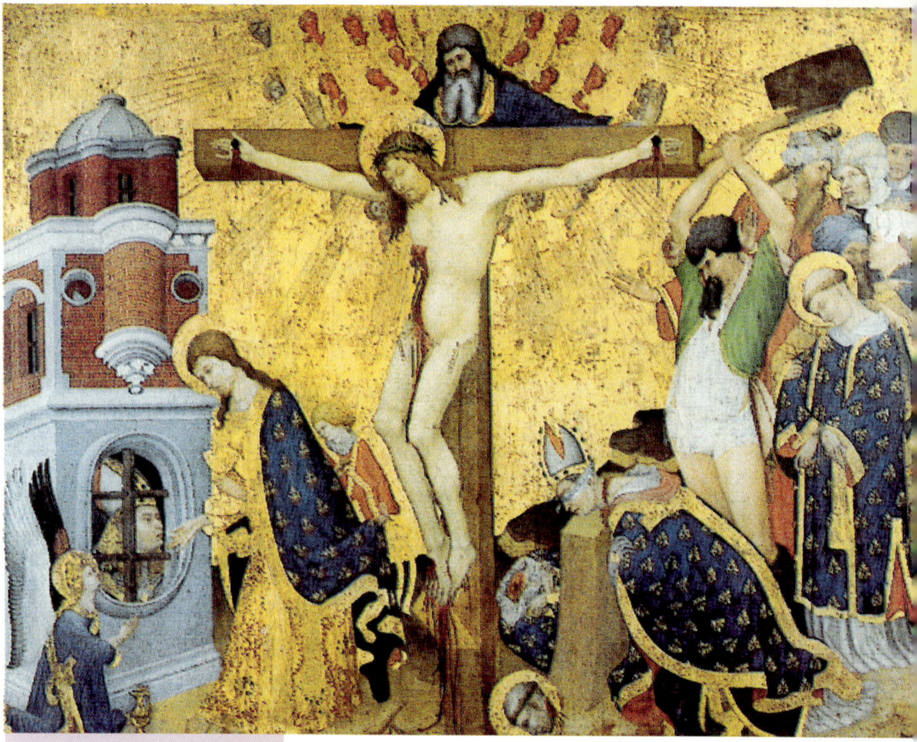

The Martyrdom of St. Denys

Henri Bellechose
(Brabant?, ca. 1380 –Dijon, 1440/44)

- 1416
- tempera on panel, transferred to canvas
- 162 x 211 cm
- Musée du Louvre, Paris

At the center of this painting appears Christ crucified, above whom a rather human figure of God the Father can be seen. Two scenes flank Christ: on the left Denys, also known as Dionysius, the first bishop of Paris and an avid promoter of Christianity in Gaul, is shown receiving his last communion in prison; on the right, we see his martyrdom on Montmartre, where he was beheaded along with two companions, Rusticus, a priest, and Eleutherius, a deacon. The blue and golden pattern on the liturgical vestments evoke the traditional royal colors of the fleurs-de-lys. The naturalism and crudeness with which the naked figure of Christ is portrayed is moving. His arms are outstretched above the saint, signifying that both the patron saint of France, and of the French royal family, is suffering martyrdom under the shelter of Divine protection. Christ is completely nude and the blood dripping down his torso serves as a discreet loincloth. This nude is notable for its anatomically perfect limbs, the smoothness of its contours and its delicate modeling, which is scarcely perceptible. The luminous figure blends subtly with the golden background.

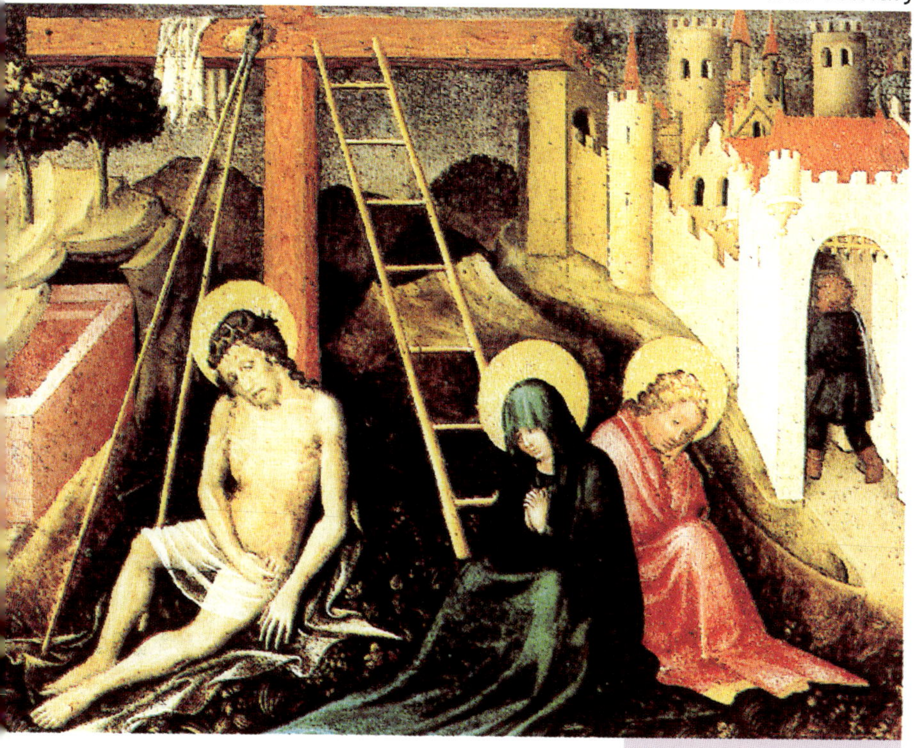

'he size of this panel suggests that it was a private devotional nage intended for an oratory or small room. The painting has een associated with Fra Angelico, but several details indicate quite distinctive, personal style. The figures contrast strongly ith the dramatic style characteristic of much Bohemian painting. The body of Christ appears at the foot of the Cross, sepa-ated from the Virgin and St. John, who are shown praying in esigned poses in the other half of the panel. The naked body f Christ is rendered with a naturalism far removed from the gorous schematization of other contemporary depictions. espite the imperfect state of preservation, the artist's mas-ry of anatomy is clear, particularly in the figure of Christ. This especially evident in the arm and leg joints and in the fore-ortening of the figure as it leans against the Cross.

Christ at the Foot of the Cross with the Virgin and St. John

Master of the Presentation in the Temple

(Austrian, active ca. 1420–40)

- ca. 1420
- mixed media on panel
- 25 x 34 cm
- Staatliche Museen Preussischer Kulturbesitz, Gemäldegalerie, Berlin

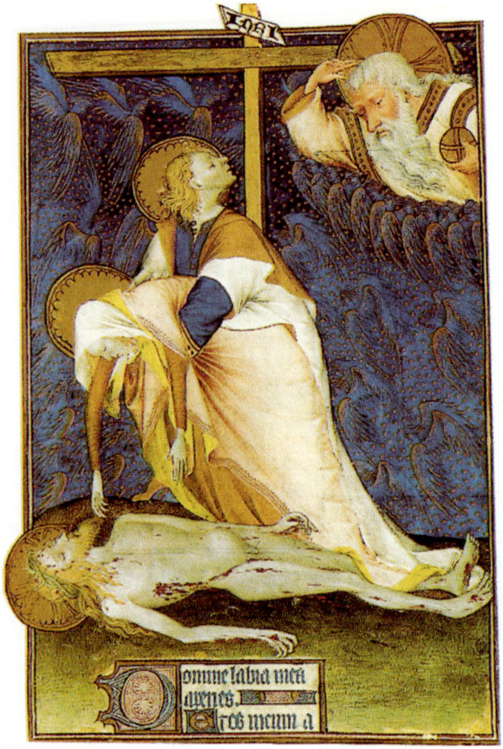

The Lamentation

Master of the Rohan Hours
(French, active 1420–30)

- 1420–27
- illuminated manuscript
- 29 x 21 cm
- Bibliothèque Nationale, Paris

The miniatures painted by the Limburg brothers in their books of hours paved the way for two artistic styles: one of them led to the Jan van Eyck style; the other was more expressionistic, and can be observed in this work. In this miniature, the figures are stylized and exaggeratedly dramatic. The saturated tonal values provide sharp color contrasts. The nude body of Christ, which has already been taken down from the Cross, is shown lying on the ground. Its proportions and features are more in keeping with expressionism than naturalism. Although Christ's face shows no signs of pain, pathos is evoked, both in the Virgin's moving reaction to the scene and in the blood issuing from Jesus' side, staining his cadaverous skin. The sober, naturalistic depiction of the deceased's skin, which covers his angular yet well-defined limbs with gray tones, is remarkable indeed.

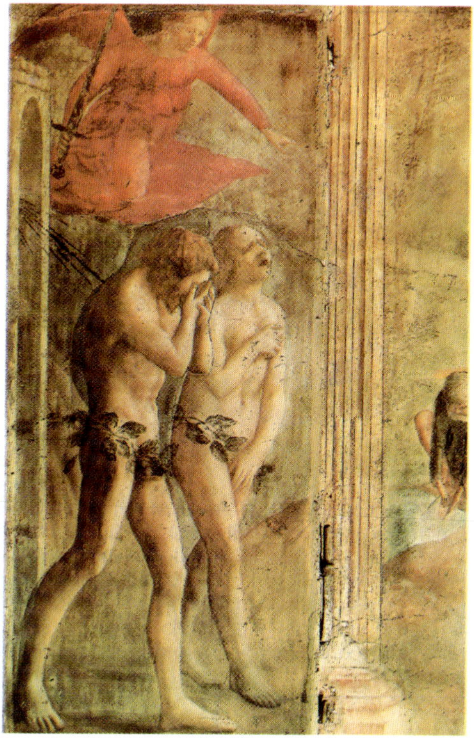

The Expulsion from Paradise

Masaccio (Tommaso di Ser Giovanni di Mone)
(Castel San Giovanni [San Giovanni Valdarno], Tuscany, 1401–Rome, 1428)

- 1424–25
- fresco
- 208 x 88 cm
- Santa Maria del Carmine, Florence

search of a new artistic idiom, Masaccio broke with the edieval Gothic tradition, from 1417 onward, favoring stead a style that was to change the face of Western art. nis scene, which is part of a fresco cycle in the Brancacci napel of Santa Maria del Carmine, Florence, shows two uman forms reduced to schematic bodies that verge on xpressionism. The artist's primary aim was to convey Adam nd Eve's shame and dejection after being expelled from aradise. The nudes are extraordinary in the way they lend e composition a sense of rhythm—a quality that was utterly ew in painting at the time. Masaccio did not seek to stylize e figures in this work; on the contrary, they consist of natu-listic anatomical volumes, whose modeling provides dark eas against which the limbs stand out.

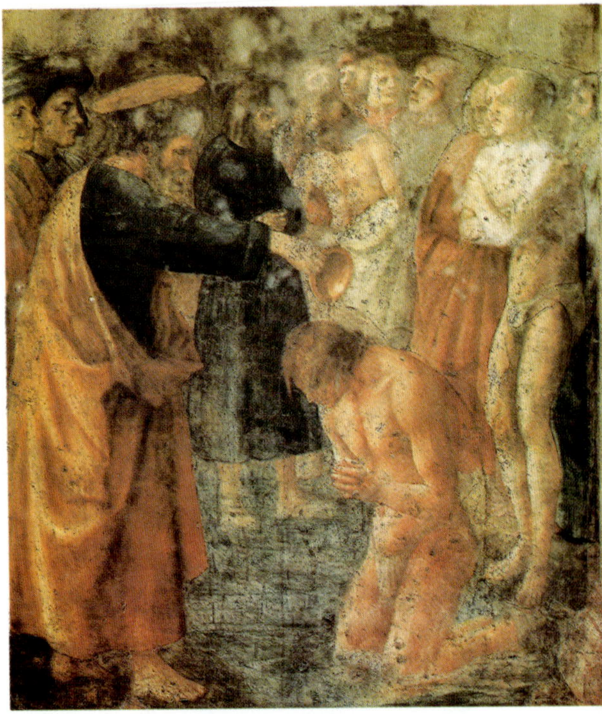

St. Peter Baptizing the Neophytes

Masaccio (Tommaso di Ser Giovanni di Mone)
(Castel San Giovanni [San Giovanni Valdarno], Tuscany, 1401–Rome, 1428)

- 1424–25
- fresco
- 225 x 162 cm
- Santa Maria del Carmine, Florence

This fresco, together with others recounting scenes from the life of St. Peter, is arguably the church's most famous. It shows the saint baptizing newly converted Christians. Unlike the nudes in The Expulsion from Paradise, these handsome figures are idealized, although this was not intended by the artist. Masaccio's mastery of human anatomy in demonstrated in this fresco, in which the figures' muscles are skillfully modeled with light and shade. This work reveals Masaccio's grasp of and profound interest in perspective. The colors in the foreground are quite bright, providing contrasts, whereas those in the background are fainter. The chapel in which the fresco is located has undergone of a number of alterations over the years; the frescoes we see today are the results of the restoration work carried out in 1990. In addition to removing certain elements that had been applied to cover the intimate parts of the nudes, the fresco's original freshness and intensity has been restored.

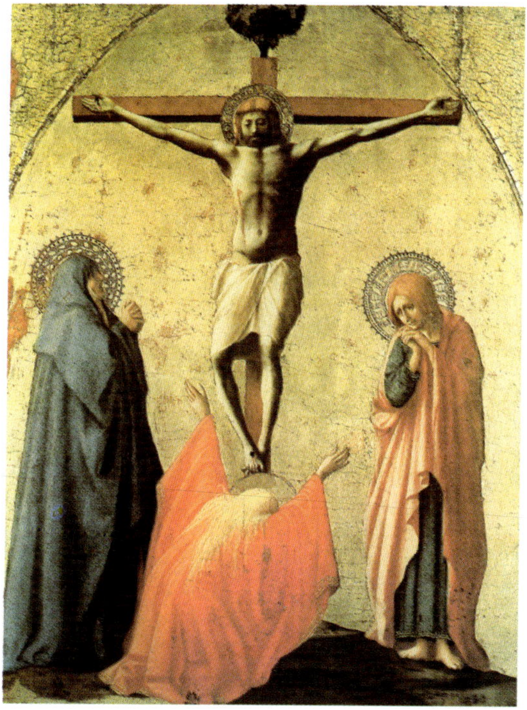

The Crucifixion

Masaccio (Tommaso di Ser Giovanni di Mone)
(Castel San Giovanni [San Giovanni Valdarno], Tuscany, 1401–Rome, 1428)

- 1426
- tempera on panel
- 83 x 63 cm
- Museo di Capodimonte, Naples

his work contains typical Gothic elements, such as the gold ackground, as well as some modern features, such as the rrangement of the figures. The expressive gestures of the rotagonists lend drama to the scene, especially those of ary Magdalene, whose arms are outstretched in despera- on. The naturalistic figure of Christ stands out against the ackground owing to the treatment of the shadows, which roduce harsh modeling, with a limited range of tonal values. ne highlighted areas of the flesh are subtly blended with e shadow. Several errors were made in the foreshortening the figure, notably in the head, although this may have een deliberate attempt to create an optical illusion, whereby e artist would have taken into account the height at which e panel was originally to be viewed.

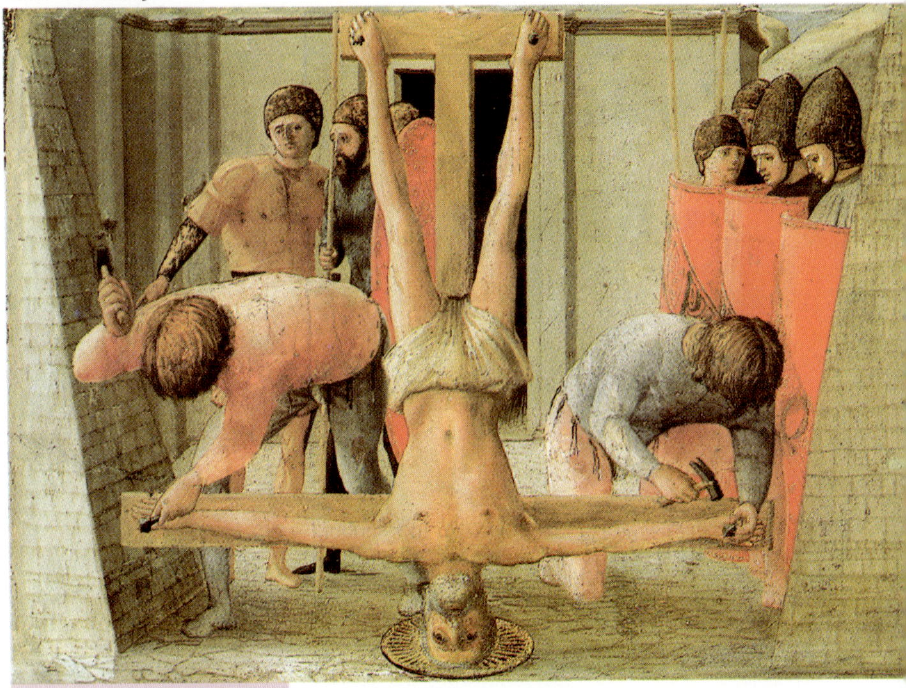

The Crucifixion of St. Peter

Masaccio (Tommaso di Ser Giovanni di Mone)
(Castel San Giovanni [San Giovanni Valdarno], Tuscany, 1401–Rome, 1428)

- 1426
- tempera on panel
- 21 x 30.5 cm
- Staatliche Museen Preussischer Kulturbesitz, Berlin

In the few paintings in which Masaccio uses architecture to obtain a sense of depth, he does so to fine effect. The walls framing this scene are an example. The subject decreed that St. Peter be depicted as a stiff figure. As in most Crucifixion scenes, he is shown frontally. At first sight, the nude may appear to be a step back in the history of the representation of the human figure, especially when one compares it with the dynamism of figures in other works by this painter. Concentrating on the nude to the exclusion of the rigorously centralized, symmetrical composition, however, one notes how detailed and aptly proportioned the anatomy is, the volumes clearly defined. The shading does not emphasize individual muscles, but articulates the bone structure, the joints and the chief muscles. Highlights in the shaded areas grant the figure a remarkable realism.

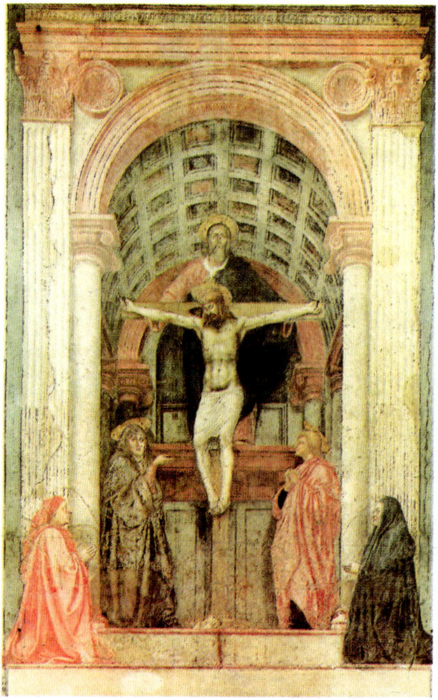

The Trinity

Masaccio (Tommaso di Ser Giovanni di Mone)
(Castel San Giovanni [San Giovanni Valdarno], Tuscany, 1401–Rome, 1428)

- 1426–28
- fresco
- 667 x 317 cm
- Santa Maria Novella, Florence

his work may have been painted with the help of Filippo runelleschi, be it in an advisory capacity or as a fellow ainter. The new science of perspective is evident in this esco, in which particular attention is given to the technically npeccable composition of the crucifixion scene. The rangement of the figures is the result of careful study, for e artist has taken into account the vantage point of the ewer. The artist places special emphasis on sculpting the ucified figure of Christ with light. Details of the anatomy e readily discernible: the tensed muscles in the arms and e rib cage, stretched such that the spaces between the os are revealed. The modeling of the abdomen down to the ubis is executed with remarkable anatomical exactitude.

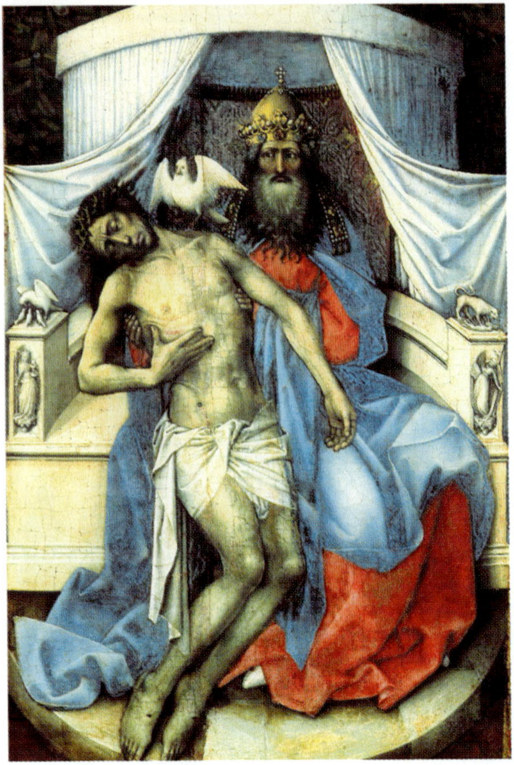

Holy Trinity

Master of Flémalle (Robert Campin)
(Tournai, 1378/79–Tournai, 1444)

- 1433–35
- oil on canvas
- 34.3 x 24.5 cm
- Hermitage, St. Petersburg

In this painting the Master of Flémalle depicts the Holy Trinity under a solemn baldachin, with God the Father, sitting on a majestic throne, as a venerable old man. Christ is supported by God the Father, and the Holy Ghost appears between them in the form of a dove. The triangular composition underscores the symbolism of the scene, the triangle representing the mystical number three, alluding to the Trinity. Clearly influenced by Gothic sculpture, this group of figures is exceptionally beautiful, particularly that of Christ, who, despite having been taken down from the Cross and showing signs of his martyrdom, is alive, touching his side with his right hand. The ashen skin covers lean yet well-defined muscles, which are meticulously modeled. The well-proportioned bone structure is that of a tall, slender youth.

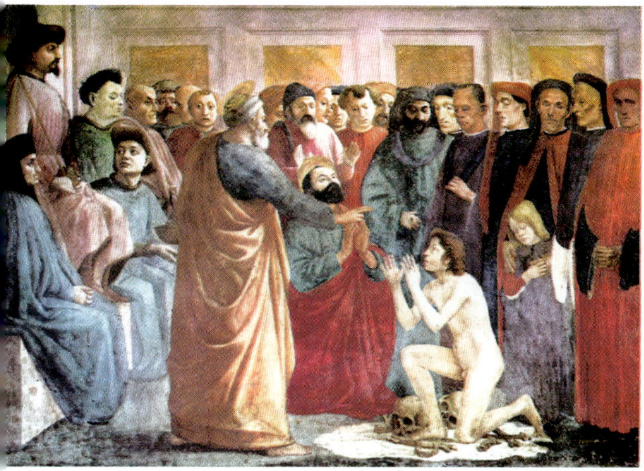

St. Peter Raising Theophilus' Son

Masaccio (Tommaso di Ser Giovanni di Mone)
(Castel San Giovanni [San Giovanni Valdarno], Tuscany, 1401–Rome, 1428)

- 1428
- fresco
- overall size: 230 x 598 cm
- Santa Maria del Carmine, Florence

This fresco depicts the Apostle bringing back to life the Prefect of Antioch's son, an act that moved its inhabitants to convert to Christianity. The work is remarkable for the way human subjects and architecture have been integrated. In the figure of the adolescent nude we see just how much realism has flowed into the work, while it is the extraordinarily subtle treatment of light that gives rise to the subtler modeling of forms and the sense of the man's three-dimensionality.

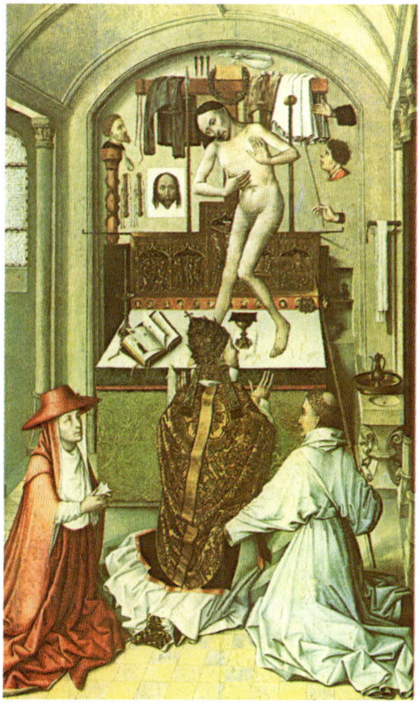

Mass of St. Gregory

Master of Flémalle (Robert Campin)
(Tournai, 1378/79–Tournai, 1444)

- painting on panel
- Musées Royaux des Beaux-Arts, Brussels

This work is an original interpretation of the mass Pope St. Gregory is said to have held in St. Peter's, during which Jesus appeared with all the instruments of the Passion, displaying his wounds. The nude figure here is essentially synthetic, lacking sexual characteristics, which emphasizes the supernatural quality of the occurrence. The modeling of the body is near-perfect, despite its paleness.

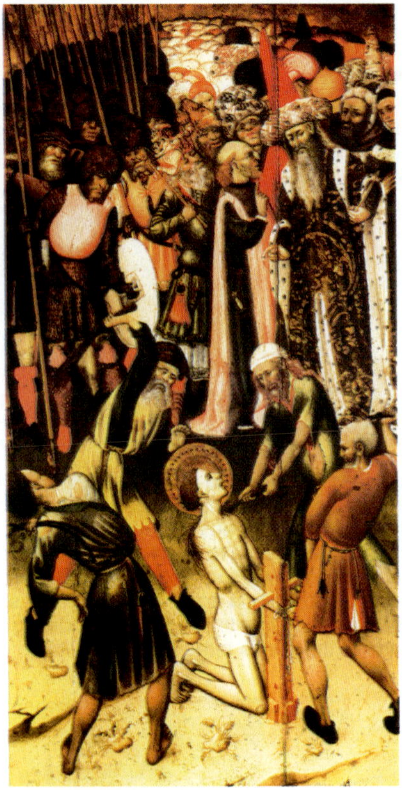

The Flagellation of St. George

Bernardo Martorell
(Sant Celoni, Vallès Oriental; active in Barcelona 1427–52)

- ca. 1430
- panel
- 107 x 53 cm
- Musée du Louvre, Paris

This painting was executed in the International Gothic style, which was widespread in Europe by the first quarter of the 15th century and is marked by a striking mannerism that sought to capture pure forms by eschewing naturalistic elements, thereby causing the actual drama to recede into the background. This altarpiece wing is one of four from a polyptych bearing scenes from the life of St. George. The nude is rendered motionless; the other figures also appear stiff and attenuated, recalling the austere art of the Romanesque period. We cannot, however, date the painting to this time, for more modern elements are in evidence: the modeling of the muscles of the saint's naked body and the illuminated skin th stands out against the background, which has been darkene to achieve this contrast. A feature of the Gothic nude is the clear delineation of contours, a technique that does not serve to idealize the body, but rather to achieve an overarching aes thetic, whereby all the elements serve to embroider the them

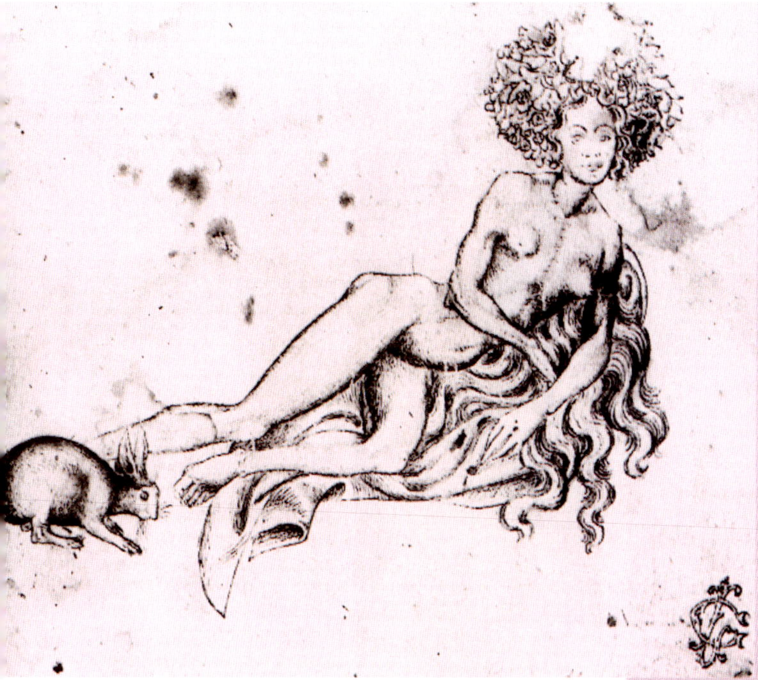

'his allegory is executed in a technique closer to that of con-
ɜmporary art than of Pisanello's own era. The woman's body
; well-proportioned, exhibiting a lithe and delicate slender-
ess. The sinuous curve of the back and hips forms a rhyth-
ıic S-shape, heightening the sensuality of the nude. The
roticism of the figure is evident in many details: one feature,
vhich recurs throughout the history of art, is the provocative
ensuality of her pose and the way in which she challenges
ıe viewer. The volumes are modeled naturalistically, with a
ght source above, accentuating the chest and abdomen.
)ther erotic features include the woman's long locks of hair,
ıe flower garland and the hare, a symbol of fecundity.

Allegory of Lust

Pisanello (Antonio Pisano)
(Pisa?, ca. 1395 –Mantua?/Rome?, 1450/55)

- ca. 1430
- pen and ink
- 19.2 x 15.2 cm
- Graphische Sammlung Albertina, Vienna

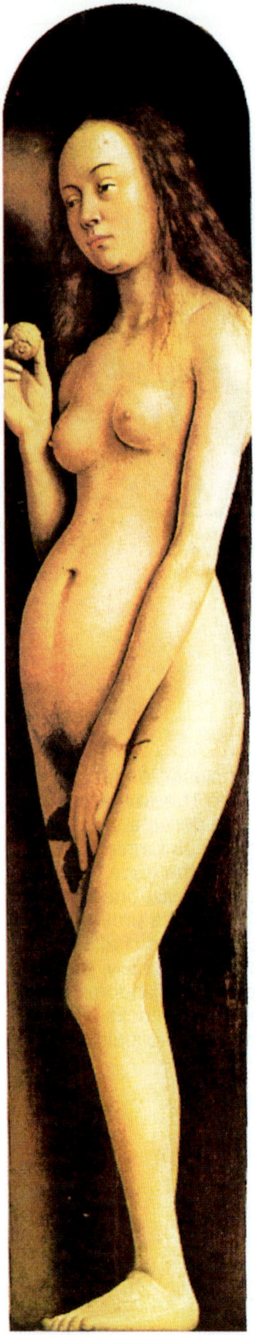

Eve

Jan van Eyck

(Maaseyck, Limburg, ca. 1390 –Bruges, 1441)

- 1432
- painting on panel
- wing of the Ghent altar
- overall size: 350 x 45 0 cm
- Saint-Bavon, Ghent

This canvas depicts a woman painted from life according to the standards of beauty fashionable at the time: a stylized figure with narrow, sloping shoulders, firm but small breasts, a thin waist, large, protruberant abdomen and long, thin legs lacking volume. Eve is holding a small apple in her right hand while covering her intimate parts with a leaf. The figure combines two clearly distinct interests: the naturalism of the model and the exquisite artistic treatment. This artist's work represents the culmination of medieval art and the threshold to the Renaissance.

'he artist has learly sought to ender Christ's ody naturalistical-', while yet pre-erving an interest features of the nedieval tradition. he muscles of hrist's left shoul-er display a narked torsion, eightening the ramatic interest. lis hips are dis-roportionately 'ide in comparison his waist. mongst other nings, they display his painting's ves-gial allegiance Gothic.

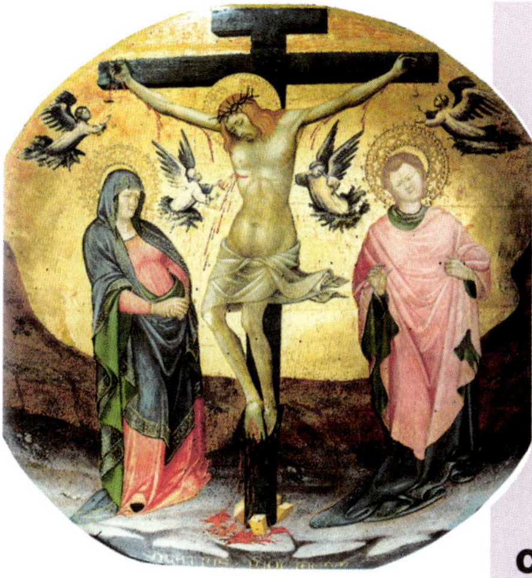

Crucifixion

Orazio di Jacopo

- 1435
- tempera on panel
- Chiesa dell'Osservanza, Bologna

his work still hows the influ-nce of the pre-eding, Gothic eriod. The dra-natic facial xpressions of e participants this deposition fluence how e perceive the ead figure of hrist. His body hows Gothic ements, such the way the ear definition features marks ut each corpo-al part.

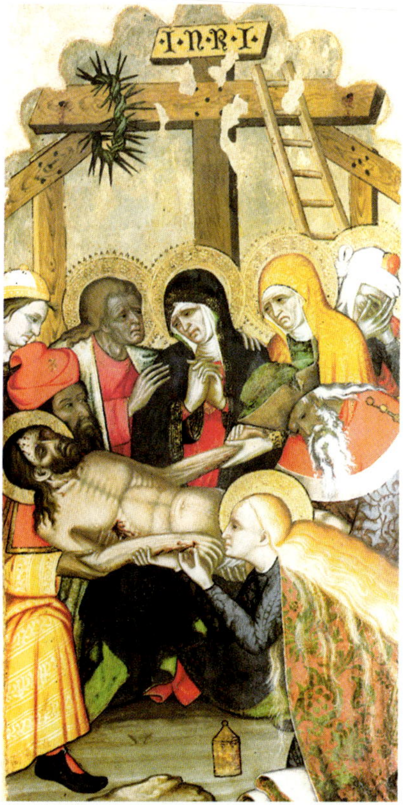

Lament for Christ

Guglielmo da Chieri

- tempera on panel
- Galleria Sabauda, Turin

Trinity

Master of the Trinity of Turin

- oil on panel
- Museo Civico d'Arte Antica, Turin

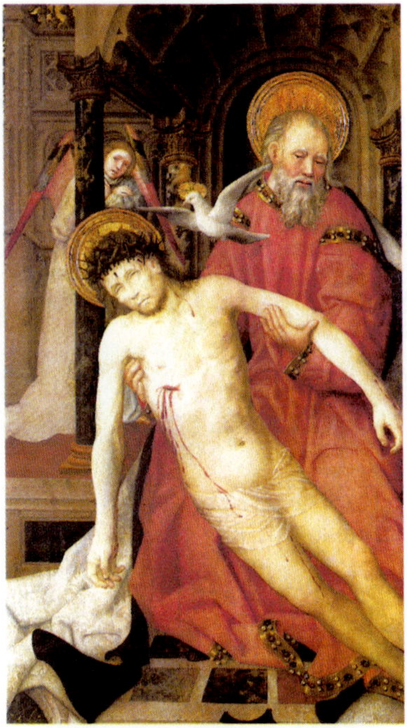

Due to a certain idealizing penchant perhaps, the depiction of pain in Italian painting was seldom allowed to prevail over the mystical nature of a theme. Here we see God holding the body of his son. The naturalistically-depicted features indicate a thorough grounding in anatomy, where all influence of Flemish painting has disappeared. The body's corporeality is subtly modeled by means of delicate tonal variations.

Temptations of St. Benedict

Michele Giambono (?)

(Venice?, 1420–1462)

- paint on panel
- Museo Poldi Pezzoli, Milan

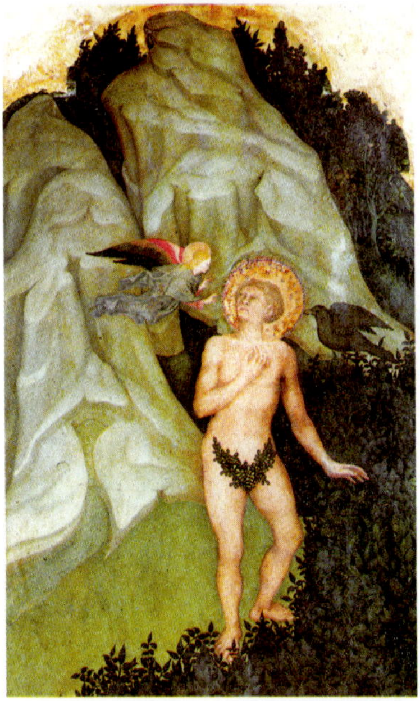

Giambono, a late Gothic painter, had ideas concerning the depiction of the human body that tended more to the naturalistic, and his approach is regarded as decidedly modern. The figure here has dynamism and it lacks the rigidness typical of most Gothic art. Harsh contrasts and the employment of a strong line have yielded to plasticity and subtle tonal gradations.

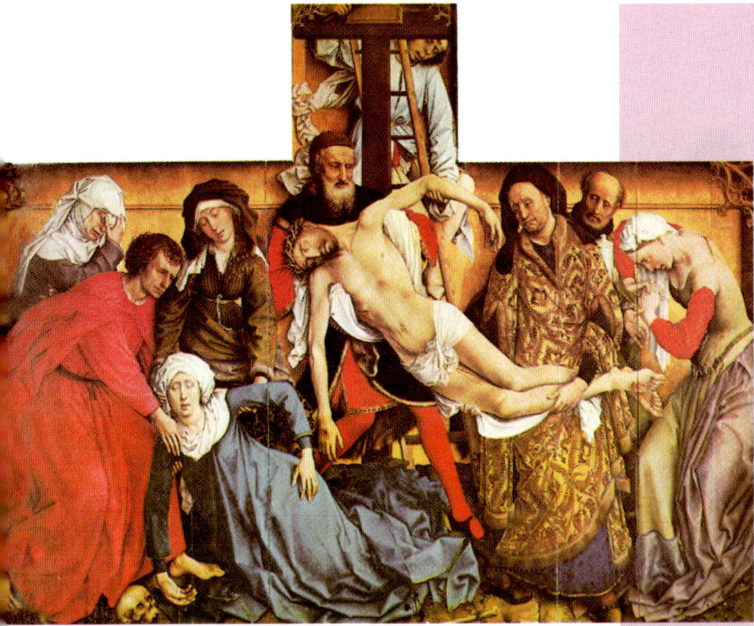

ne work of this artist, an exponent of early Netherlandish aturalism, reaches the height of its expressive powers this altarpiece. The drama of the painting is conveyed in ach individual element. The flat background offsets the sumuous colors of the garments, breathing life into the figures nd lending them a near sculptural plasticity that creates an npression of real rather than painted images. Christ appears nguid, with sinuous curves. The way in which his arm danes and the points on which his body rests heighten the realm of the scene. The shroud in which he is being wrapped ings out the consummate painterly handling of the flesh, allid and painstakingly modeled by means of a masterly play light. The figure of Jesus exudes a certain sensuality that ombines with the pathos of the scene. The nude figure ppears delicate and helpless, revealing the fragility of the ody, in contrast to the soul. Seen in formal terms, this work es somewhere between Gothic and Renaissance art.

The Deposition

Rogier van der Weyden (Rogier de la Pasture)

(Tournai, ca. 1400 –Brussels, 1464)

- 1436
- panel
- 220 x 262 cm
- Museo del Prado, Madrid

This painting at one time belonged to Mary of Hungary. It was inherited by Philip II of Spain, who deposited it in El Escorial, where it remained until the Spanish Civil War of 1936–39, after which time it entered the Museum.

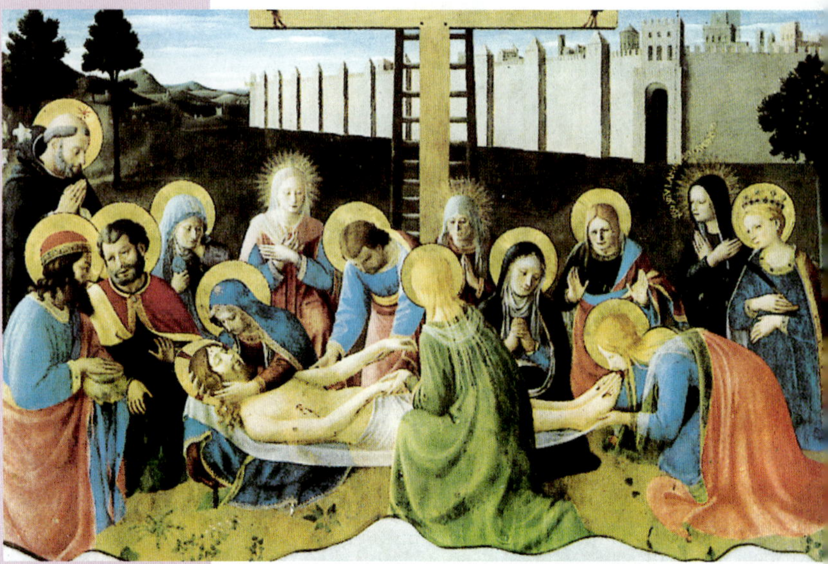

The Lamentation

Fra Angelico
(or **Guido** or **Guidolino di Pietro, Brother Giovanni da Fiesole**)
(Vicchio di Mugello, Tuscany, 1395/1400–Rome, 1455)

- 1436
- tempera on panel
- 108 x 165 cm
- Museo di San Marco Florence

In his paintings, Fra Angelico sought to go beyond merely depicting the scene at hand; instead, the devout artist attempted to incite religious contemplation in the viewer, which he achieves through his balanced, compelling compositions. This scene shows the body of Christ, which has just been taken down from the Cross, being placed on a shroud in which he is to be transferred to the tomb. Unlike in other works by the artist, the anatomical details of Christ's body are not painstakingly recorded; instead, the naturalism of the scene lies in the depiction of Jesus' naked body. Various skin tones are not employed to suggest muscles; some modeling is, however, achieved by the use of shadows. Notable are Christ's remarkably expressive hands, whose slight flexion at the joints attests to their lifelessness.

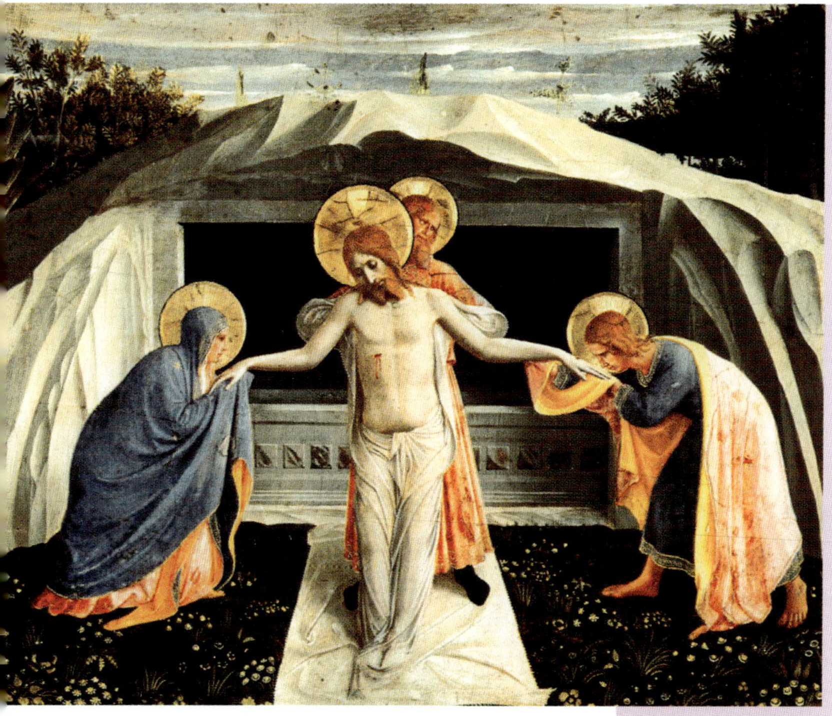

ıis work was the central panel of five that once formed the edella gracing the high altar of the church of San Marco, orence, which is dedicated to SS. Cosmas and Damian, e patron saints of the Medici family, who donated the altar-ece. One cannot help but take note of the great transpar-ıcy of forms in this painting, which may be indebted to the ork of Domenico Veneziano. This painting bears witness to ı important development in painting that took place at the ne with regard to the treatment of figures and breaks with e traditional manner of handling this subject in two ways: reshortening is employed and the figures are rendered nat-alistically. The varied palette, which includes richly contrast-g skin tones, as well as light and shadow subtly articulate ırist's musculature, which is somewhat idealized. Although sthetic considerations were not foremost in the artist's nd, his tendency toward euphuism cannot be denied. This -pervading elegance allows Fra Angelico to achieve his al: to inspire contemplation and prayer.

The Entombment

Fra Angelico
(or **Guido** or
Guidolino di Pietro, Brother Giovanni da Fiesole)
(Vicchio di Mugello, Tuscany, 1395/1400–Rome, 1455)

- 1438–43
- tempera on panel
- 37.9 x 46.4 cm
- Alte Pinakothek, Munich

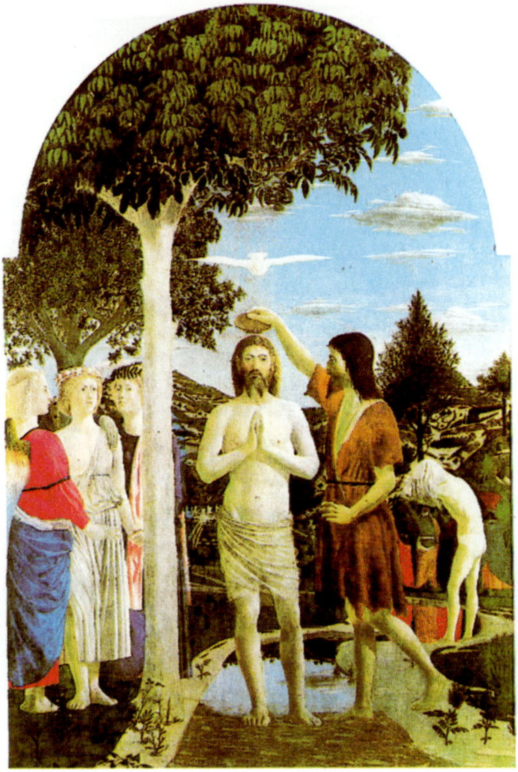

The Baptism of Christ

Piero della Francesca (or **Piero di Benedetto** or **Piero dal Borgo**)
(Borgo de San Sepolcro, Arezzo, 1416/17–1492)

- 1440–45
- tempera on panel
- 168 x 116 cm
- National Gallery, London

This is one of the first works in which the human figure is firmly embedded in its spatial surroundings, an approach initiated by Masaccio. In its naturalism and perspective construction the landscape is typical of Quattrocento art. The light figure of Christ dominates the center of the composition, baptized by his cousin John beneath the dove symbolizing the Holy Ghost. The three winged figures are angels, an allusion to the Decree of Union between the Eastern and Western churches issued in 1439 by the Council of Florence. The modeling of the nudes is exceptionally fine, although the white light in which they are bathed diminishes their three-dimensionality and lifelike quality. Christ's serenity contrasts with the animated movement of the figure undressing in the background in order to receive baptism.

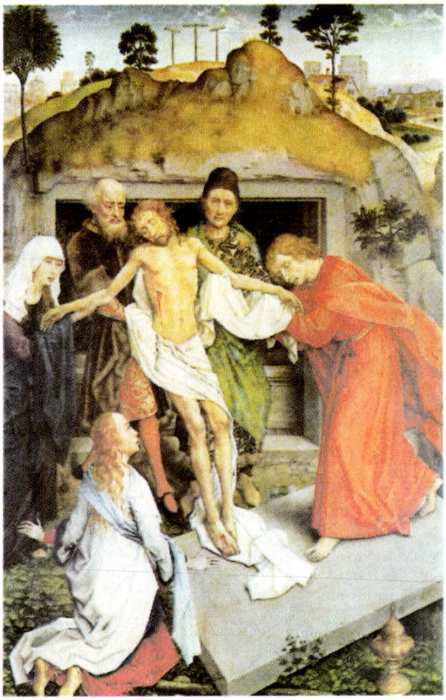

;ommissioned by
ıe Medici, this
ıainting is a copy
ıf a work by Fra
ıngelico. It is a
ıeautiful rendering
ıf Christ being laid
ı the tomb and
ıas all the theatri-
ality typical of its
ge as well as fea-
ıring a thoroughly
ıaturalistic treat-
ıent of the body.
;hrist's well-pro-
ıortioned bodily
ame is brought
ıut by the thinness
ıf his limbs, pre-
enting us all in all
ıith a fragile and
ignified figure.

The Deposition of Christ

Rogier van der Weyden (Rogier de la Pasture)

(Tournai, ca. 1400 - Brussels, 1464)

- ca. 1449
- oil on panel
- 110 x 96 cm
- Galleria degli Uffizi, Florence

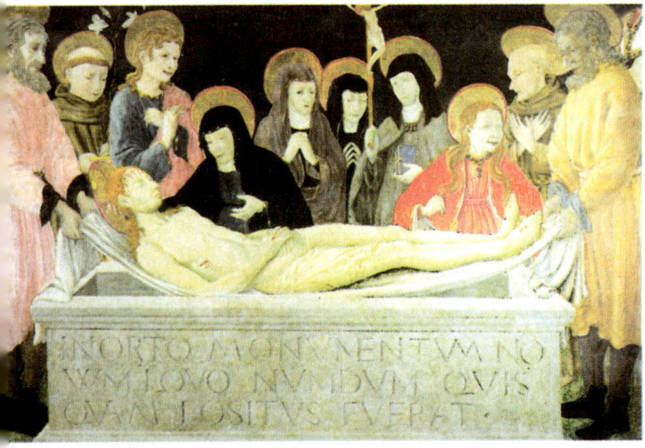

ompared to the other figures in this panel, that of Christ is ıll, and if its anatomical details are stylized, its proportions re nevertheless perfect. The grayish-green skin tones con-asting with lighter areas give the whole its radiance. The ody's deathly aspect, reinforced by the grays that model it, ıake it seem almost ghostly, an effect that is accentuated y its red hair.

The Deposition of Christ

School of Ferrara

- 1450–55
- oil on panel
- Pinacoteca Nazionale, Ferrara

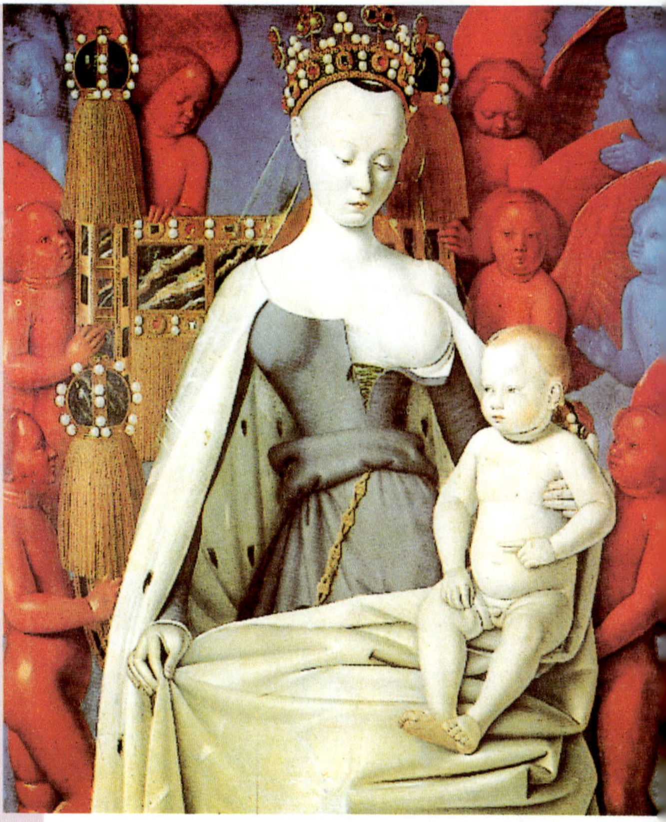

The Virgin and Child

Jean Fouquet
(or **Foucquet**)
(Tours, ca. 1420–ca. 1481)

- ca. 1450
- tempera on panel
- 91 x 81 cm
- Koninklijk Museum voor Schone Kunsten, Antwerp

The skillfully rendered depiction of the Virgin's face here reveals that it is a portrait (traditionally it is thought to be of Agnes Sorel, mistress of Charles VII, though Catalina Budé, the wife of the donor, has also been suggested). In the other panel of this diptych, in which Etienne Chevalier is shown kneeling, the flesh tones are warm and varied, establishing a notable difference between the earthly and the divine. The Virgin's white skin in this painting forms a striking contrast to the red angels, making her bare, round breast appear almost mystical. Contrary to the ideal of beauty of the day, her breasts are full and round, indicating that the artist did not intend her to be erotic.

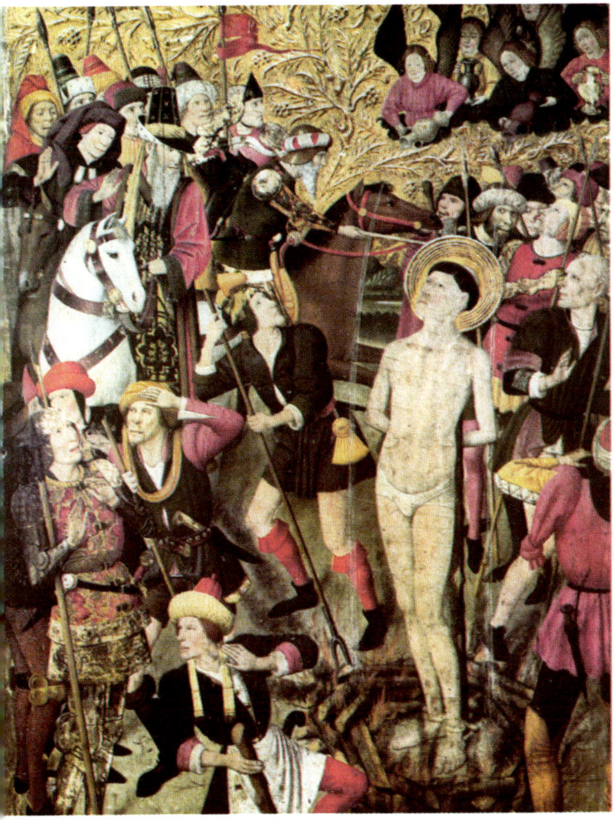

The work shows the saint bound to a stake piled around with logs that have just been ignited. The saint's gaze is serene and trusting, his eyes staring up toward heaven. The paleness of his skin contrasts strongly with the rest of the panel and makes him the focus of a composition otherwise brimming with figures. The golden background is decorated with plant motifs that lend the scene a hint of sumptuousness. The saint's body shows no suggestion of sensuality as the artist has concerned himself solely with religious objectives.

Martyrdom of St. Vincent

Jaime Huguet
(Valls, Tarragona, ca. 1415 –Barcelona, 1492)

- 1450–56
- tempera on panel
- 166 x 98 cm
- Sant Vicenç de Sarrià, Museu Nacional d'Art de Catalunya, Barcelona

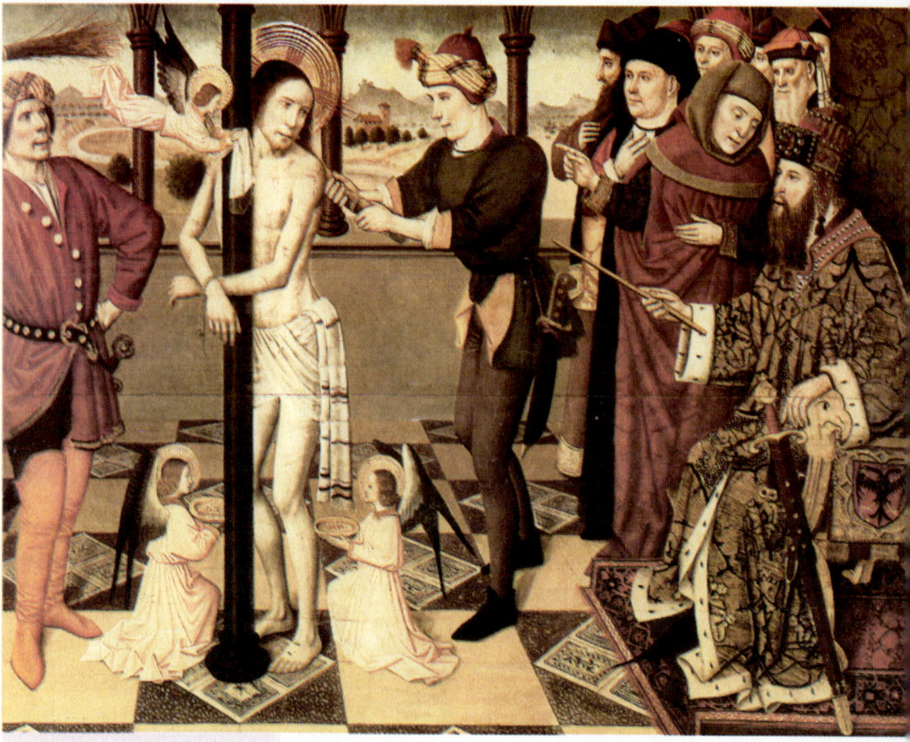

Flagellation of Christ

Jaime Huguet
(Valls, Tarragona, ca. 1415 –Barcelona, 1492)

- ca. 1450/56
- tempera on panel
- 90 x 195 cm
- Musée du Louvre, Paris

In a room with beautiful floor tiles and windows, Caiaphas and representatives of the Sanhedrin look on as two henchmen flagellate Jesus, who is bound to a column and aided by three black-winged angels. The artist has sought to convey Christ's hopelessness in the face of his enemies. Despite the rigidity and sharp angles of the drawing, the work is rated amongst the artist's finest, recalling here Flemish painting, especially van Eyck.

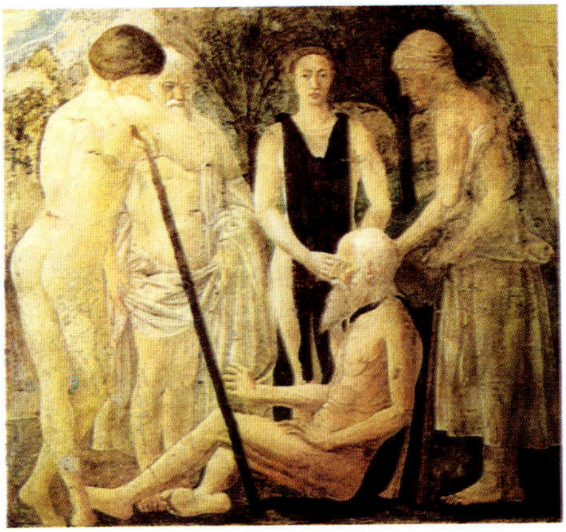

The Death of Adam

Piero della Francesca (or **Piero di Benedetto** or **Piero dal Borgo**)
(Borgo de San Sepolcro, Arezzo, 1416/17–1492)

- 1452–66
- fresco
- overall size: 390 x 747 cm
- San Francesco, Arezzo

According to legend, Adam died at the age of 930. He is depicted here seated on the ground, directing his son Seth to go in search of the seed of forgiveness. Behind him, attentive but resigned, Eve is supporting her husband's head. The nude figures are portrayed with great realism, which is brought out yet more clearly by the shaft of light they are bathed in, so that the scene acquires a sculptural air. In this work, Piero abandoned for good his Gothic aesthetic.

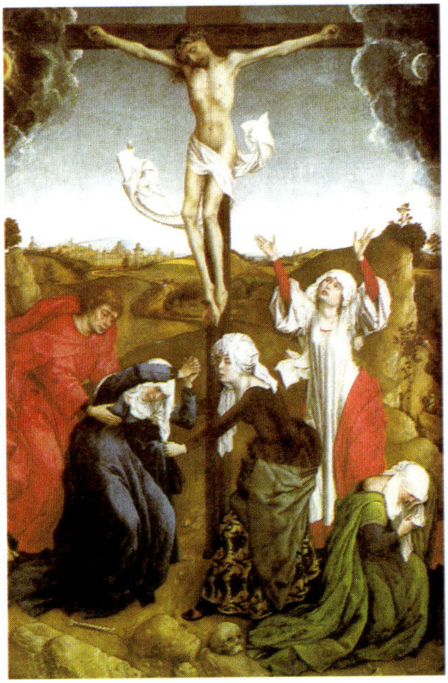

Crucifixion

Rogier van der Weyden (**Rogier de la Pasture**)
(Tournai, ca. 1400 - Brussels, 1464)

- oil on canvas
- Abegg Stiftung, Berne

During the Quattrocento, van der Weyden was instrumental in breaking with preexisting styles. Especially in the development of modern, more naturalistic conceptions of painting, his influence was profound. The figure of Christ is so executed here as to express the weakness of the human condition with great sensitivity. Despite its extremely fragile appearance, the proportions of Christ's body are both balanced and physical.

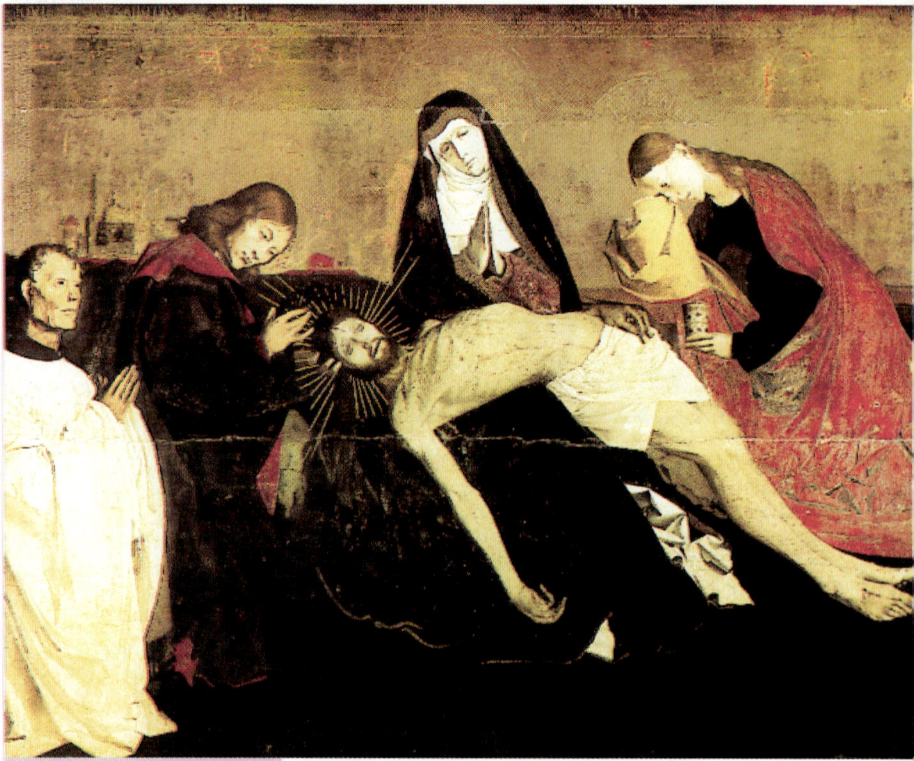

Avignon Pietà

Enguerrand Quarton
(or **Charreton, Carton, Charton, Charonton**)
(Laon, ca. 1410–Avignon, ca. 1466)

- 1454–56
- tempera on panel
- 162 x 271 cm
- Musée du Louvre, Paris

This work, attributed to Enguerrand Quarton, is an exceptionally elegant, delicate painting of the dead Christ, who is shown here laid out on his mother's lap, in the company of Mary Magdalene and the Apostle Paul, who is seen removing the Savior's crown of thorns. On the far left appears the donor, who is lost in prayer. This panel belongs to the final period of French Gothic. The figure of Christ is extremely naturalistic, in both complexion and anatomy. The bright light, which is cast on the body from the right, accentuates his luminous skin, which stands out against the dark background. The shadows on Christ's torso bring out his bone structure, heightening the drama of the scene. The realism of the painting recalls Flemish art, whereas the spontaneous stylization of the figures is more akin to the art of Italy.

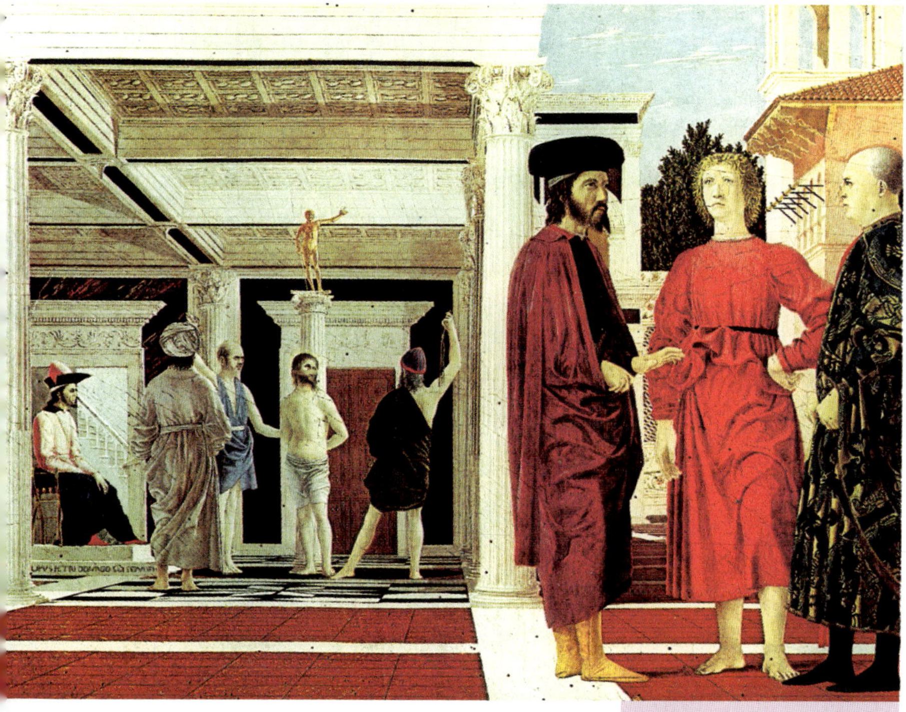

his work combines the attention to detail of early Nether-
ındish painters with the central perspective developed in
ıe artist's native Italy. Piero employs perspective to un-
sual iconographic effect, as he directs the viewer's gaze
› a bound Christ who is placed not in the center fore-
round but in the far background on the left. Though this
ude is finely proportioned, its height in relation to the fig-
res of Christ's tormenters produces a strange effect. The
ıodeling is especially fine, the shaded areas on the side
pposite the light source granting the whole figure a lumi-
ous quality. The painting depicts two events: the flagella-
ɔn of Christ and the conspiracy of 1444 to kill the brother
f Duke Federico of Urbino, Oddantonio da Montefeltro,
ho is seen on the right between two advisors who, with
eir evil counsel, flagellate the young nobleman morally
s the Romans had flagellated Jesus physically.

The Flagellation

Piero della Francesca (or **Piero di Benedetto** or **Piero dal Borgo**)
(Borgo de San Sepolcro, Arezzo, 1416/17–1492)

- 1455
- tempera on panel
- 59 x 81.5 cm
- Galleria Nazionale delle Marche, Urbino

Madonna of the Milk

Marco Zoppo (Marco di Antonio di Ruggero)

(Cento, 1433–Venice, 1478)

- oil on canvas
- Musée du Louvre, Paris

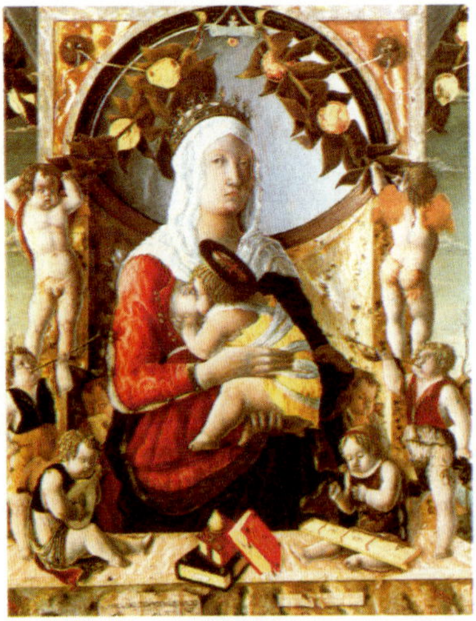

This exquisite work is remarkable for the figures of cherubs adorning it, since, with the exception of crucifixions and martyrdoms, few nudes were painted during the period. Artists therefore would sometimes resort to this device. The diminutive forms are well modeled, although they are represented as having adults' rather than children's bodies.

Pietà

Cosimo (or **Cosmè**) **Tura**

(Ferrara, ca. 1430–1495)

- ca. 1460
- tempera on panel
- 48 x 33 cm
- Museo Correr, Venice

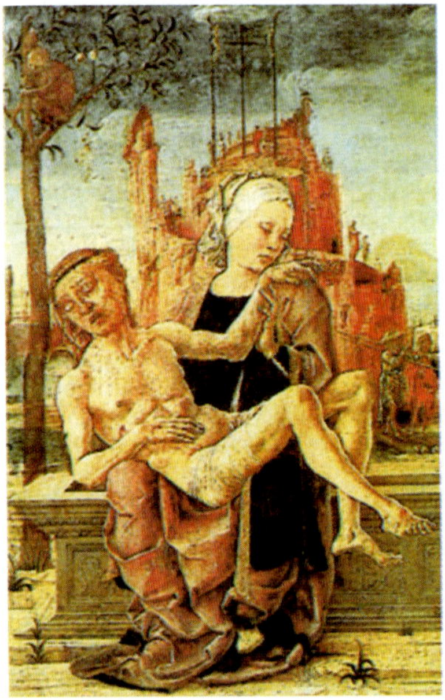

Held in high esteem by the Romantics, Cosimo Tura was th first major exponent of the School of Ferrara, where he was appointed court painter to the Este family in 1452. His work was highly infl enced by a wide range of painters, and is notable for its crisp lines and the dramatic tension in the figures' facial expressions. In this mystical painting, he drew on German art, meticulously executing formal aspects with the so intention of impress ing the viewer.

This woodcut alludes to a miracle said to have taken place in a mass celebrated by Pope Gregory in St. Peter's, Rome. The figure of Christ is expressionistic for the rigor of its naturalism, which breaks with medieval aesthetic norms and ideals. The draftsmanship is clean, and via numerous carefully described details, the well-defined outlines delineate an emaciated man.

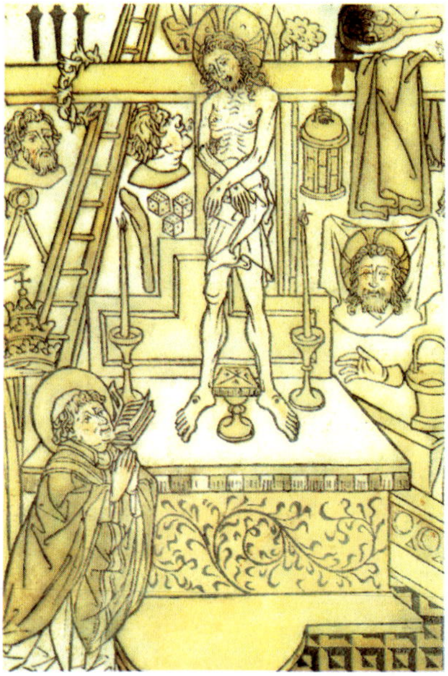

Mass of St. Gregory

Anonymous

- 1460
- woodcut
- 25.2 x 18.1 cm
- Germanisches Nationalmuseum, Nuremberg

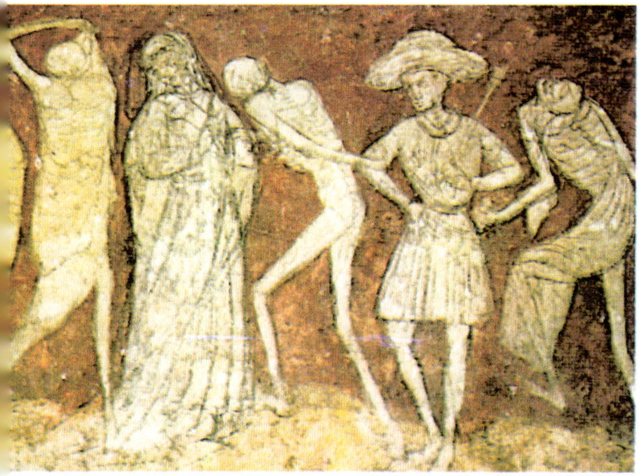

Dance of Death

- ca. 1460/70
- fresco
- Chaise-Dieu Abbey, Haute-Loire, France

This moralizing motif was very popular in the Middle Ages. In this fresco, Death, personified by gaunt corpses, is shown walking among figures of different social standing, both rich and poor. The whole presentation is dynamic, an unusual enough trait for the period. The nude figures are highly stylized and their grotesque movements are combined with anecdotal details, such as the one corpse divesting itself of its shroud in order to dance more freely.

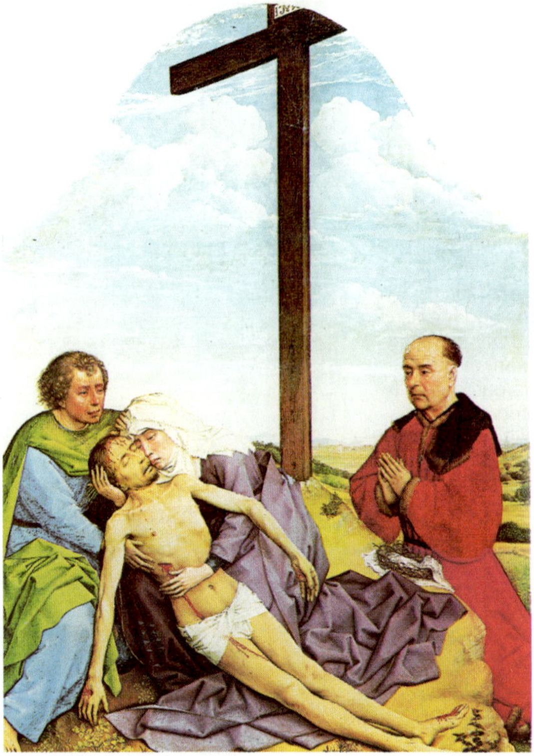

Pietà

Rogier van der Weyden (Rogier de la Pasture)

(Tournai, ca. 1400 –Brussels, 1464)

- panel
- 47 x 35 cm
- Museo del Prado, Madrid

This panel was acquired by the Museum in 1924 from the Dukes of Mandas.

This painting betrays a pathos seldom observed in works executed in this style. The intensity with which Christ's pain is conveyed here is only increased by the compelling expressiveness of this figure, who has just been taken down from the Cross. His mouth is slightly ajar and the eyelids are somewhat swollen—this is a corpse, displaying clear signs of death. The body, exhibiting symptoms of rigor mortis, does not demonstrate the lively aspect common in iconography of this type. The torso bends only at the waist; the limbs are stiff and rigid. The extended legs are slightly knock-kneed, and the stiff arms evince the pain they have suffered. The painstaking details lend a dramatic beauty to the scene, such as the blood running down the body's side and beyond the loincloth. The figure on the right is one of the donors, possibly a member of the Broers family of Malinas, of whom similar portraits exist. A nearly identical work can be found in the Gemäldegalerie in Berlin.

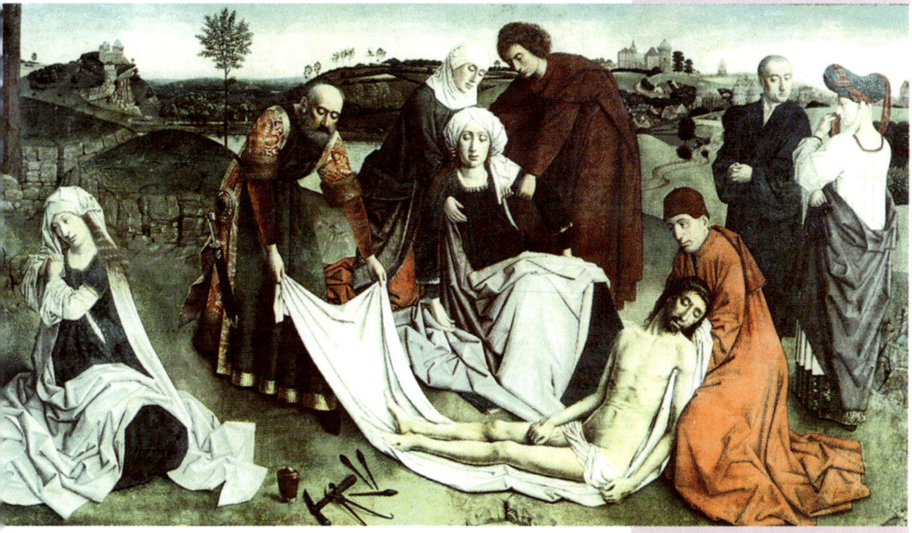

Lamentation

Petrus Christus
(Baerle, Gante, ca. 1420–Bruges, ca. 1473)

- oil on panel
- 101 x 192 cm
- Musées Royaux des Beaux-Arts, Brussels

An air of tragedy pervades this scene, whose figures are arranged in the shape of an arch under which the figure of Christ appears slightly off-centered. He has been rendered with great realism and his emaciated body bears all the marks of death. This well-proportioned nude displays a high degree of plasticity, given that the sense of death is not as explicit as in other works that take this subject as their theme. On the contrary, although naturalistically rendered, the dead Christ is almost beautiful here, lending the scene a mystical quality that encourages prayer and devotion, the primary function of such works from this period.

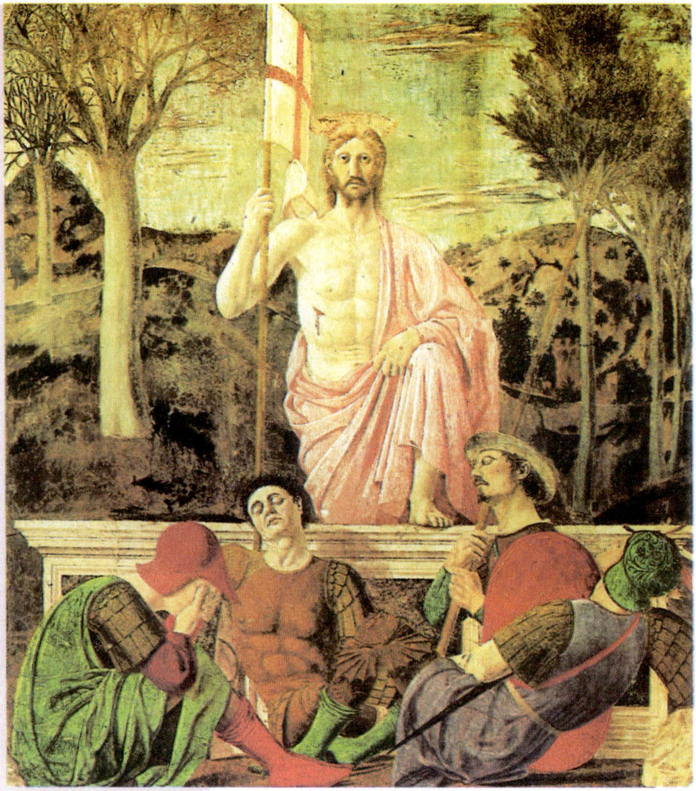

The Resurrection

Piero della Francesca (or **Piero di Benedetto** or **Piero dal Borgo**)
(Borgo de San Sepolcro, Arezzo, 1416/17–1492)

- 1463–65
- fresco
- 225 x 200 cm
- Pinacoteca Communale, Sansepolcro

This religious subject, painted after the artist's frescos of the Legend of the True Cross in Arezzo, is given a profoundly human dimension. The two landscapes flanking Christ are symbolic: one depicts the dead, barren nature of winter, the other evokes a return to life symbolized by summer. Having conquered death, Jesus rises from his grave as a figure of heroic proportions, his majestic serenity exuding a reassuring air. The broad bone structure and the athletic build of this nude bring to mind depictions of Classical gods. The body is subtly modeled in luminous tones, making it stand out against the far darker background as though the figure emanated its own light.

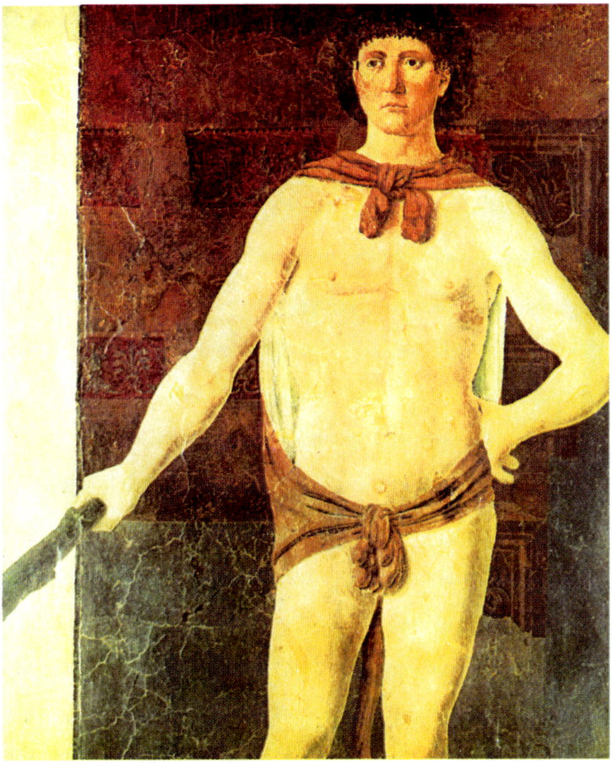

Hercules

Piero della Francesca (or **Piero di Benedetto** or **Piero dal Borgo**)
(Borgo de San Sepolcro, Arezzo, 1416/17–1492)

- 1465
- fresco
- 151 x 126 cm
- Isabel Stewart Gardner Museum, Boston, MA

In this work the artist betrays his solid knowledge of human anatomy, using light to model forms with an almost sculptural precision against a dark background that focuses attention on the figure. The effect of volume is achieved by subtle shading in the lightest areas and by bordering the darkest parts with a luminous outline. This nude is not simply an in-depth anatomical study, for it possesses a marked erotic charge. The lion skin emphasizes Hercules' nakedness: tied in a knot with the lion's paws exactly over the genitals, it serves to flaunt the hero's sexuality while ostensibly preserving decorum.

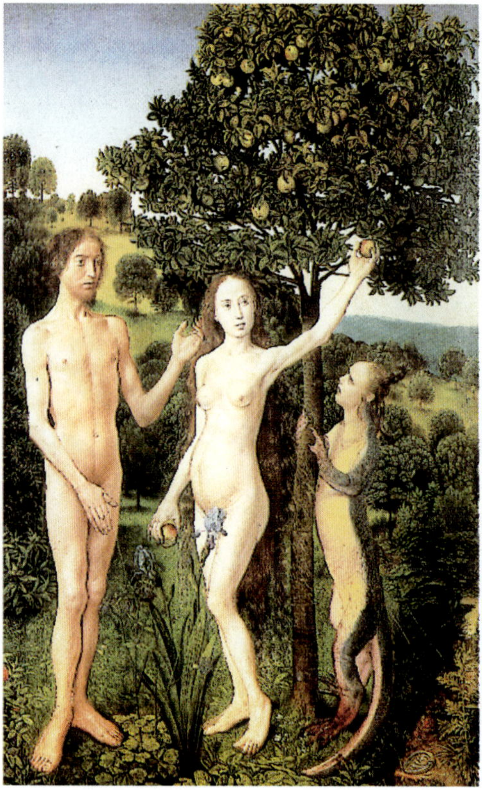

The Fall

Hugo van der Goes

(Goes, Zeeland?, 1435/45–Roode Kloster, near Brussels, 1482)

- 1470
- oil on panel (left panel of diptych)
- 34 x 23 cm
- Kunsthistorisches Museum, Vienna

This small panel, which forms part of a diptych, is one of Hugo van der Goes' most curious and disturbing works. His luxuriant Paradise is replete with numerous details, all of which have been meticulously studied and skillfully rendered. The accuracy with which he paints can be observed in the figures' hair, the leaves, the blades of grass and the numerous details in the background, all of which consist of individual brushstrokes. So many details make the painting look somewhat crowded. The facial expressions of the figures are somewhat contorted around the edges. The naturalistic nudes are skillfully executed, their faces recalling portraits. Adam is natural if somewhat rigid; Eve's sensual, curvaceous body reflects the ideal of beauty of the day.

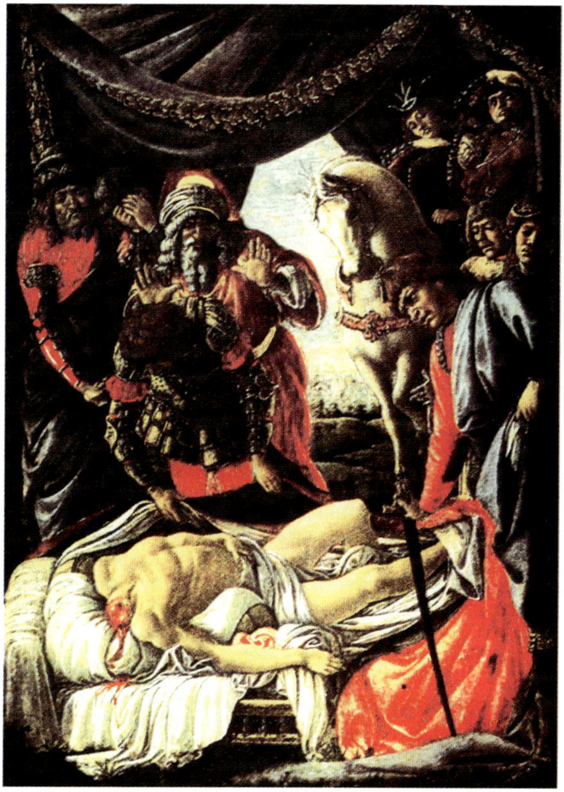

The painting captures the moment after the Assyrian general Holofernes was beheaded by Judith, the widowed Jewish woman, who used her beauty, bravery and cruelty to save her people from being besieged. The position of Holofernes' body breaks with the hieraticism with which Botticelli usually executed his figures. At once static and dynamic, the painting is remarkable for its boldly foreshortened figure of the warrior in the foreground and for its striking composition. The pictorial treatment of the light and volume lends the figure a sculptural quality. Holofernes' athletic build is enhanced by a balanced distribution of light and shadow, which offsets the intense contrasts between the reds and whites. The figures' undulating garments are a typical feature of Botticelli's works.

The Discovery of the Murder of Holofernes

Sandro Botticelli (Alessandro di Mariano Filipepi)
(Florence, 1445–1510)

- ca. 1470
- oil on panel
- 31 x 25 cm
- Galleria degli Uffizi, Florence

The Suffering of Christ

Geertgen tot Sint Jans
(active Haarlem, second half of the 15th century)

- oil on panel
- 26.2 x 25.2 cm
- Rijksmuseum Het Catharijneconvent, Utrecht

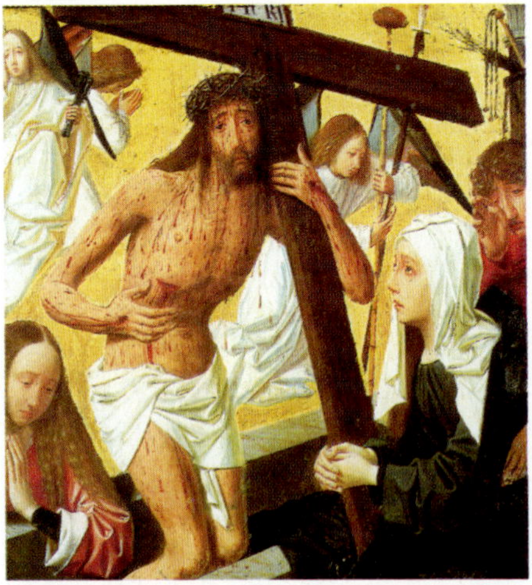

The pathos of this panel is self-evident and requires no comment. Gesture and color combine in a unique rendering of the figure of Christ, his gaze fixed on the observer. Treated in the manner of certain figures by Brueghel or Hieronymus Bosch, this one is rich in contrasts, its large dimensions giving it, if anything, a slightly grotesque air.

Pietà

Giovanni Bellini (Giambellino)
(Venice, ca. 1430–1516)

- ca. 1470
- oil on panel
- 107 x 86 cm
- Pinacoteca di Brera, Milan

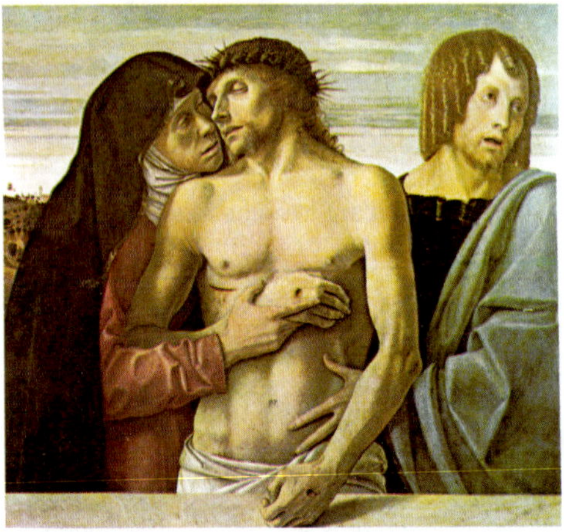

Bellini painted this subject several times, employing Quattrocento iconography, and each time he tried out a different treatment of the central figure. In this work he relies on light, and on the distance between the body and the left arm extended slightly to the front, to give Christ's figure a great deal of plasticity. While the figure does have its sculptural qualities, a strong interest in naturalism is also evident.

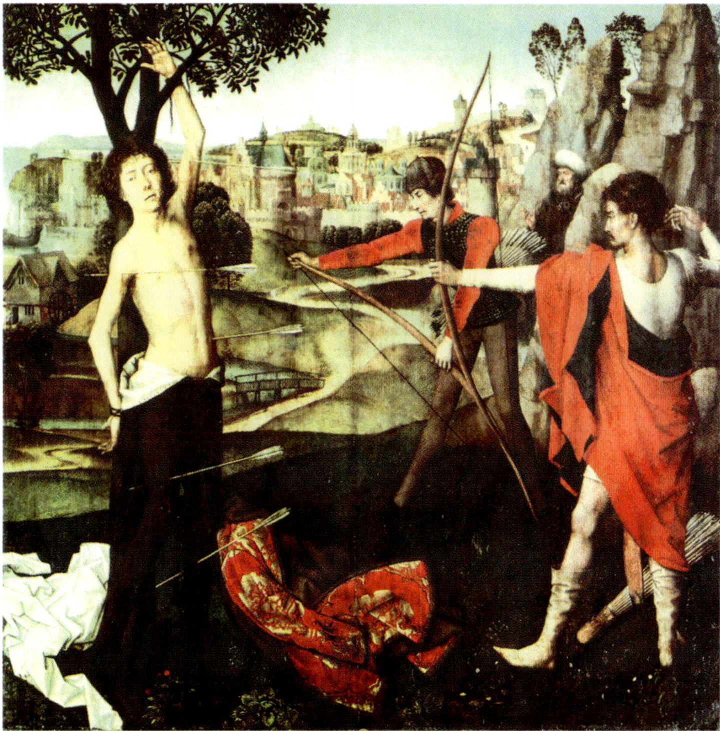

Jnlike more conventional depictions of St. Sebastian, this figure is not the least bit sensual, and is rendered in an artistic style that is clearly indebted to Gothic art. His thin, androgynous body has been modeled with extraordinary skill. The figure refrains from showing any signs of pain, which is left o the viewer's imagination, and gazes out of the picture with what appears to be an expression of resignation. The work contains elements that heighten the drama of the scene and end the saint a human aspect, making it easier for the viewer o identify with him. This type of painting, which combines dealism and emotion with a simple composition and bright colors, lyricism and narrative force, is designed solely to instruct, using a visual language that is readily intelligible to all.

The Martyrdom of St. Sebastian

Hans Memling
(Seligenstadt, near Aschaffenburg, Hessen, ca. 1435–Bruges, 1494)

- ca. 1470
- oil on panel
- 67 x 68 cm
- Musées Royaux des Beaux-Arts, Brussels

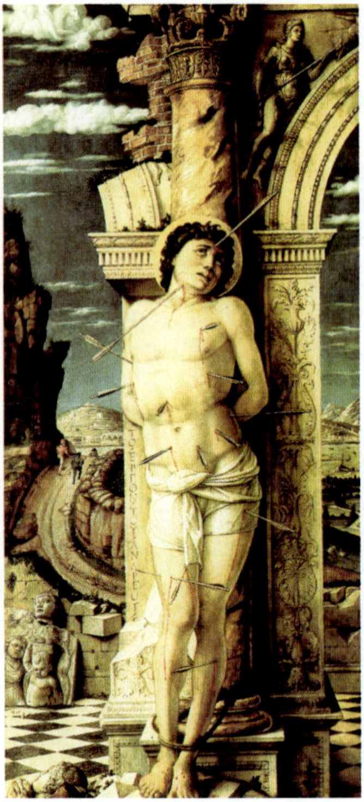

St. Sebastian

Andrea Mantegna
(Isola di Carturo, near Padua, ca. 1431–Mantua, 1506)

- ca. 1470
- tempera on panel
- 68 x 30 cm
- Kunsthistorisches Museum, Vienna

SS. George and Sebastian have traditionally served as leading exemplars of ideal male beauty. At the time when Mantegna flourished, Adam and the martyred St. Sebastian were about the only subjects of male nudity that were permissible, which is one reason why there are so many of these renderings. Despite the large number of arrows that have pierced St. Sebastian's body, Mantegna has included only a few drops of blood, which may not enhance, yet they certainly point up, the beauty of this well-proportioned figure. The artist in this work established a close link between architecture and the human figure. The Renaissance generally sought to draw human concerns closer to all fields of art and the sciences. The work, which has been painstakingly elaborated in every detail, reveals the artist's preoccupation with space and perspective; the checkered floor recalls some of the works of Piero della Francesca.

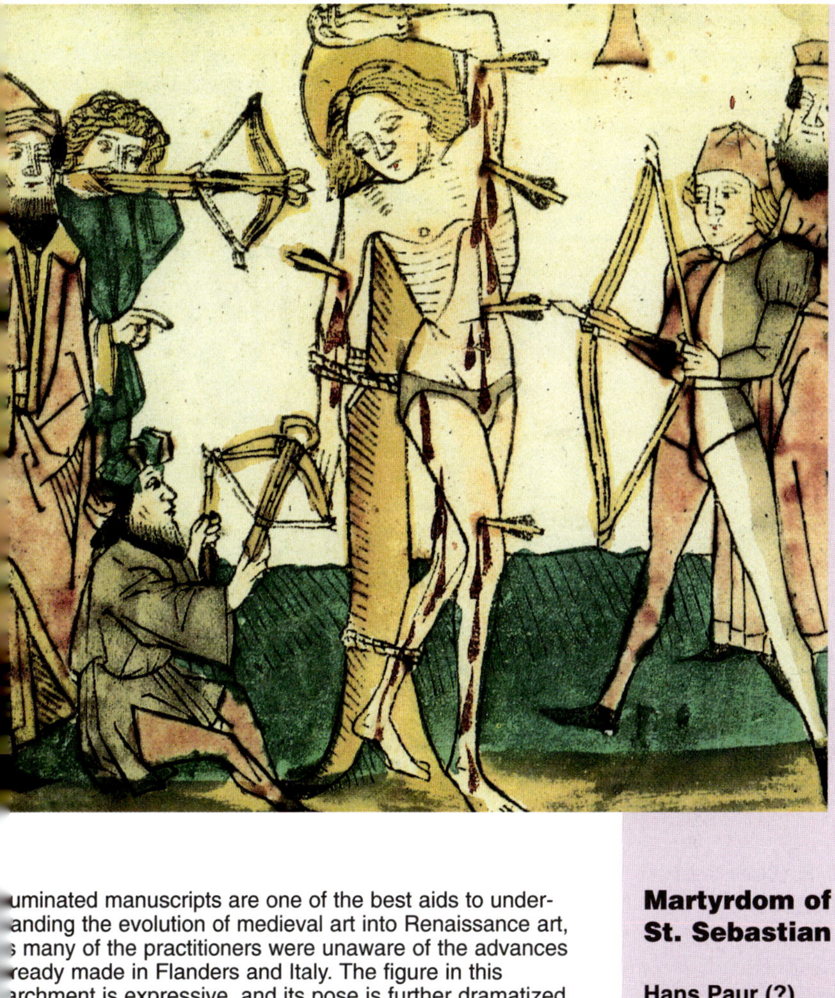

uminated manuscripts are one of the best aids to underanding the evolution of medieval art into Renaissance art, s many of the practitioners were unaware of the advances ready made in Flanders and Italy. The figure in this archment is expressive, and its pose is further dramatized y the arrows and blood. The absence of modeling and the rong line serve to lend the figure great power.

Martyrdom of St. Sebastian

Hans Paur (?)
(active Nuremberg, 1455–1472)

- ca. 1472
- miniature on parchment
- 25.5 x 18.5 cm
- Staatliche Graphische Sammlung, Munich

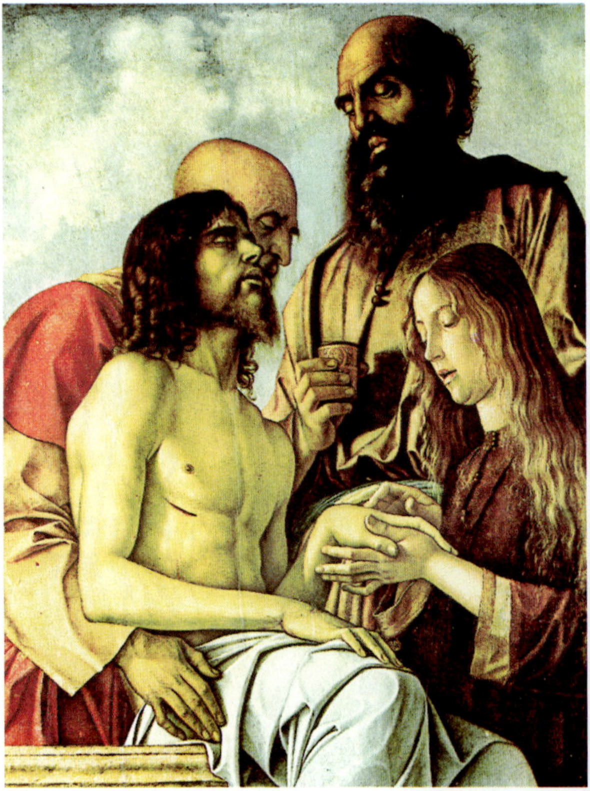

The Entombment of Christ

Giovanni Bellini (Giambellino)
(Venice, ca. 1430–1516)

- 1470–75
- oil on canvas
- 107 x 84 cm
- Pinacoteca, Vatican

The dramatic interest here, while foregrounded to a certain extent, does not prevail over the essential message. Christ's nude figure is that of a young man, its complexion golden, in contrast to the more natural skin coloration of those around him. To this extent one can say there is an attempt at idealization, as the painter does not content himself with the usual ashen colors. Such treatment differs from other works by the same artist. Thus, for example, in 1508 Bellini painted a Pietà using a far more realistic skin coloration than is found here. This naked Christ evidences the great capacity of this key Venetian Quattrocento artist to understand and express the human figure. The work is pervaded by a certain intimacy, doubtless attributable to the tastes of his patron, who came from a wealthy Venetian family.

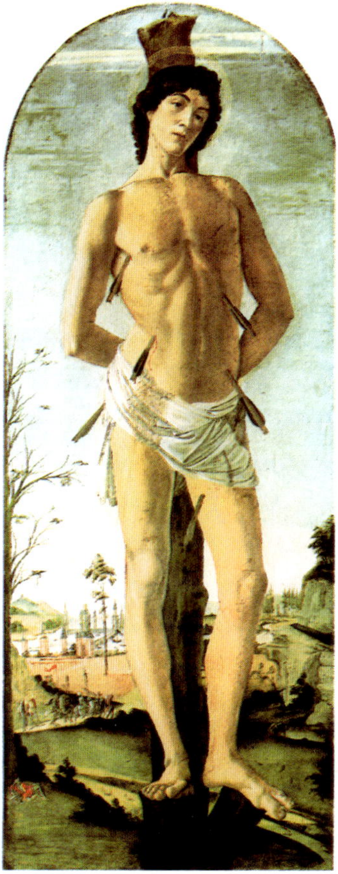

lthough influenced by his mentor, Filippo Lippi, Botticelli mploys more delicate and subtle lines and his figures are ıore skillfully modeled. Yet they still betray a somewhat gid treatment, far removed from the painterly lyricism of is later work, which might explain why he is more interest-d here in the saint's anatomy than his human aspect. The gure's contrapposto pose recalls that of a sculpture. otticelli's figures would henceforth possess such compell-ıg three-dimensionality. The chiaroscuro modeling of the ell-proportioned body is extraordinary indeed. The artist's uest for beauty leads him to stylize the figure, a feature ıat was to become ever more prevalent in his work.

St. Sebastian

Sandro Botticelli (Alessandro di Mariano Filipepi)
(Florence, 1445–1510)

- 1473
- tempera on panel
- 195 x 75 cm
- Staatliche Museen Preussischer Kulturbesitz, Berlin

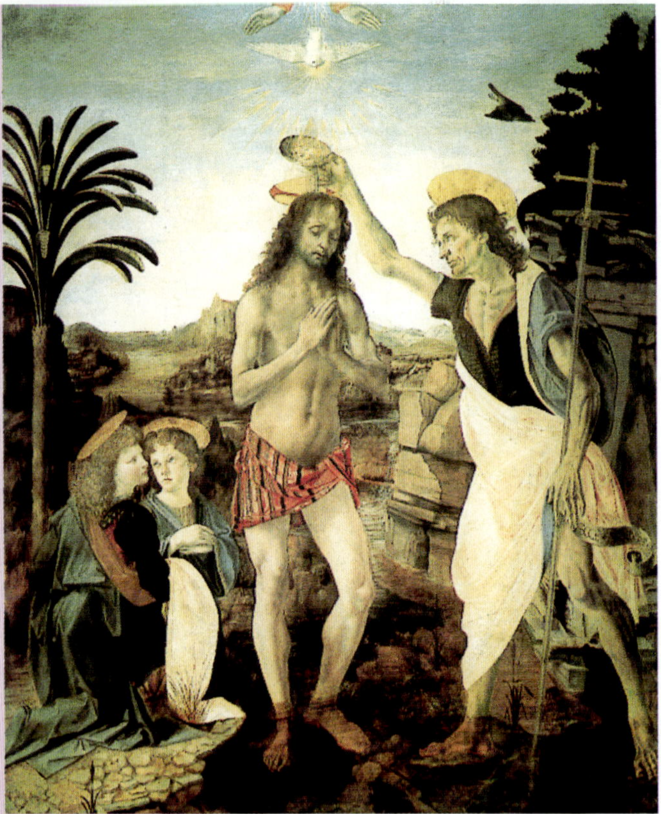

Baptism of Christ

Andrea del Verrocchio (Andrea di Cioni)
(Florence, ca. 1435 –Venice, 1488)

- ca. 1470
- tempera on panel
- 177 x 151 cm
- Galleria degli Uffizi, Florence

Andrea di Verrocchio was a multifaceted artist, who devoted most of his time to sculpture, a discipline that exerted a decisive influence on his painting. The works that are attributed t the artist were not painted exclusively by him. In this work, fc example, the hand of Leonardo da Vinci, who was a pupil of Verrocchio, can be discerned in the landscape and in the tw angels on the left, which are executed in a completely differe style from that of the painting's protagonists. Another, less ce ebrated pupil painted the dove and the hands that appear above Christ, who possesses a distinguished presence owin to his sculptural volumes, a characteristic that lends his body hard and angular appearance. However, the figure recalls a stone sculpture, failing to display the naturalism that was so sought after in the Renaissance. The figures are well integra ed into the landscape, whose depth is achieved by using cer tral perspective, another preoccupation of Renaissance artis

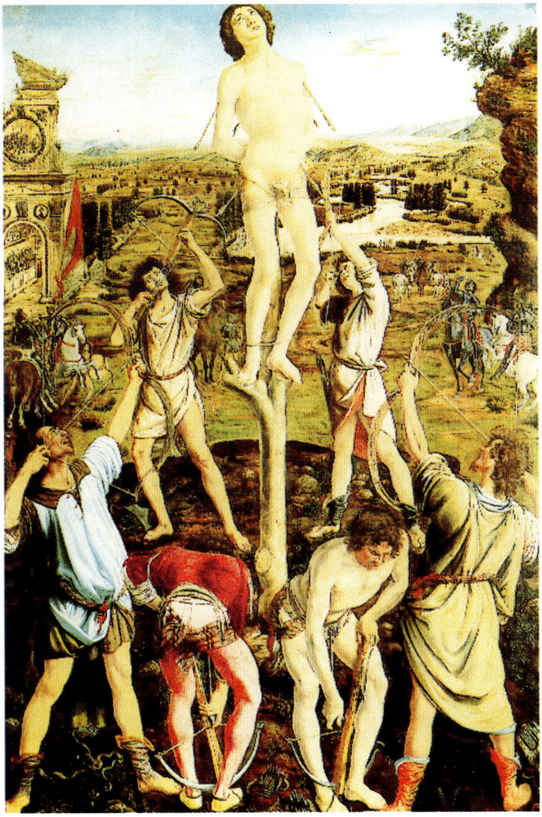

ntonio del Pollaiuolo shared a painting, sculpture and gold-mith's studio with his brother Piero. Comparisons of works igned by Piero with others from the studio suggest that ntonio was the greater painter of the two. This work, influnced by Andrea del Castagno and Donatello, clearly reveals close study of anatomy, especially of flexed muscles. For xample, the muscles of the figure bending over his cross-ow in the right foreground are perfectly defined, and his ace betrays the effort involved. The anatomy of Pollaiuolo's gures is so realistic, the flesh and muscles attached so cor-ectly to the bone structure, that one is tempted to believe hat he anticipated Leonardo da Vinci in dissecting corpses.

The Martyrdom of St. Sebastian

Antonio Pollaiuolo (Antonio Benci)
(Florence, ca. 1432–Rome, 1498)

- 1475
- tempera on panel
- 292 x 203 cm
- National Gallery, London

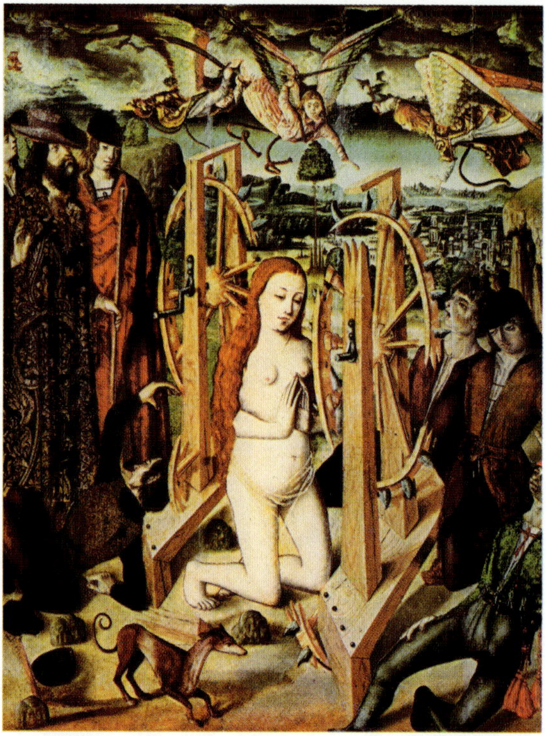

The Martyrdom of St. Catherine

Fernando Gallego
(active 1466/67–1507)

- panel
- 125 x 109 cm
- Museo del Prado, Madrid

According to a legend from the 11th century, Catherine of Alexandria was a highly educated young Christian woman from an aristocratic family who, after defending her Christian principles and protesting the persecution of Christians by the Roman Emperor Marcus Aurelius Valerius Maxentius, was tortured to death. She was tied to a wheel to be dismembered, but it miraculously broke, so she was beheaded instead. The painting is attributed to Fernando Gallego, although it is not signed. This is a work of great plasticity, though its quality is inferior to the Pietà, or The Fifth Sorrow of the Virgin. The saint's delicate beauty forms a sharp contrast to the crude figures of the executioners surrounding her. The artist clearly intended to depict the nude in a naturalistic manner, which he certainly achieved in the curve of Catherine's hips and thighs in the positioning of her feet, in the palms of her hands and the inclination of her head. The treatment of the breasts, on the other hand, is unrealistic, unlike other works by the artist.

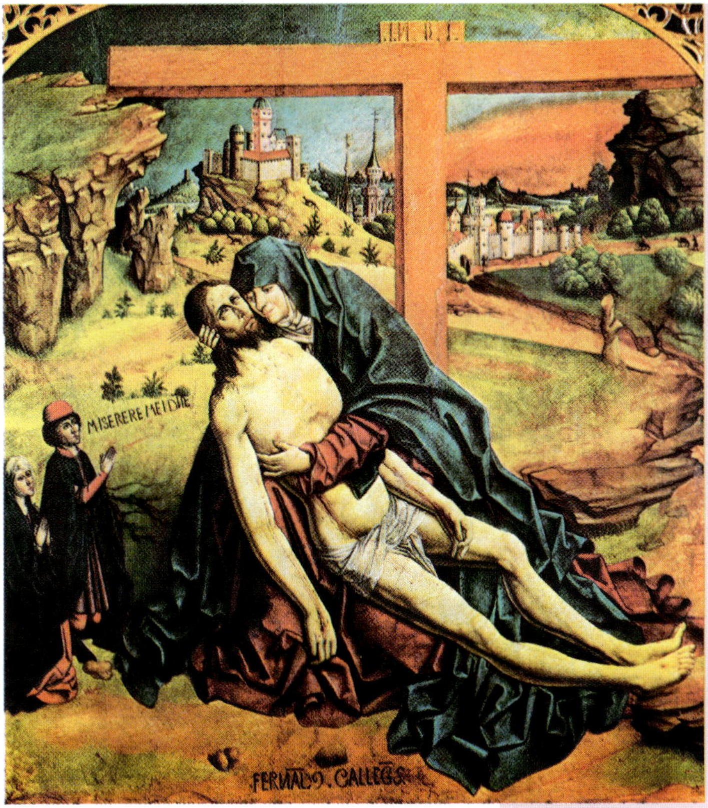

Pietà, or **The Fifth Sorrow of the Virgin**

Fernando Gallego
(active 1466/67–1507)

- panel
- 118 x 102 cm
- Museo del Prado, Madrid

'he artist of this work employs an undiluted Flemish style, ,hich is evident in the overall impression of the picture as ,ell as in such details as his treatment of folds in the drap- ry. The figure of Christ clearly expresses suffering. This rude expressionism does not seek to idealize or portray eauty; on the contrary, the artist seems deliberately to ave avoided this. Nonetheless, the work demonstrates im- eccable painterly technique and the diffusion of the light is emarkable. The bright illumination of the body contrasts ,ith the shaded areas, producing a nearly perfect treatment f light. The body, in turn, is modeled in shadow. The nude oignantly conveys the tragedy of the scene. The image of strong yet lifeless body having suffered such ruthless tor- ıre calls for reflection and prayer.

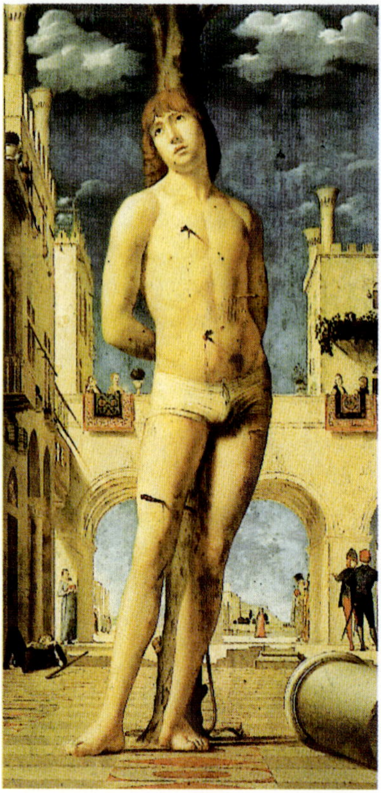

St. Sebastian

Antonello da Messina
(Messina, ca. 1430–Venice, 1479)

- 1475
- tempera on panel transferred to canvas
- 171 x 86 cm
- Gemäldegalerie Alte Meister, Dresden

This is regarded as one of the artist's masterpieces. Created in Venice, it had a considerable impact on late 15th-century painting in that city. The beholder sees the saint from a very low vantage point. This extreme viewpoint recalls the work of Mantegna, an artist also brought to mind by the strict use of central perspective to generate a sense of depth. Removed from the scene of his martyrdom, St. Sebastian is shown standing in Venice, bound to a tree and with several arrow wounds from which blood flows—a feature reminiscent of the more drastic imagery of Netherlandish painting. The body is perfectly modeled and the entire image flooded with light in a way that eradicates contours. This atmospheric type of lighting was later to be taken up by Titian.

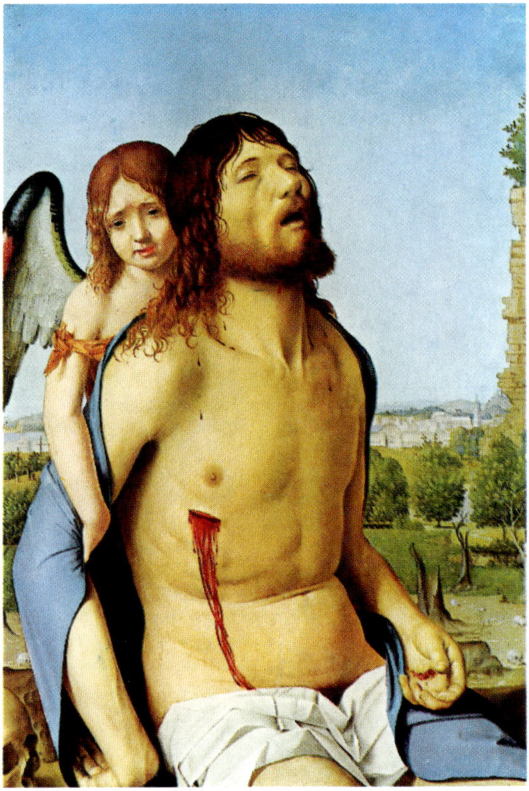

he work of Antonello da Messina was fundamental to the evelopment of Italian painting. During his training in Sicily nd Naples, he produced works that were influenced by oth Italian and Flemish schools. The present picture, one f many small panel paintings by the artist, is sublime in its etailed treatment of the figure and the exquisite sensuality ith which the subject is portrayed. The expression of hrist is profoundly serene. The well-proportioned nude is ositively sculptural in its modeling: the gradations of light eveal every anatomical feature of the figure. The muscles re not pronounced, enabling the artist to render the dead ody not as if sleeping, but instead as if in a trance-like ate. The angel's expression is dramatic but not overly so. is supporting Christ's body, as if he might bring the Savior ack to life. However, a number of details, such as the ositioning of the hands, confirm that the figure is dead.

The Dead Christ Supported by an Angel

Antonello da Messina
(Messina, ca. 1430–Venice, 1479)

- 1475–78
- panel
- 74 x 51 cm
- Museo del Prado, Madrid

St. Sebastian with Archers

Master of Amsterdam
(active Upper Rhine, 1470–1500)

- 1475–80
- drypoint
- 12.9 x 19.2 cm
- Rijksmuseum, Amsterdam

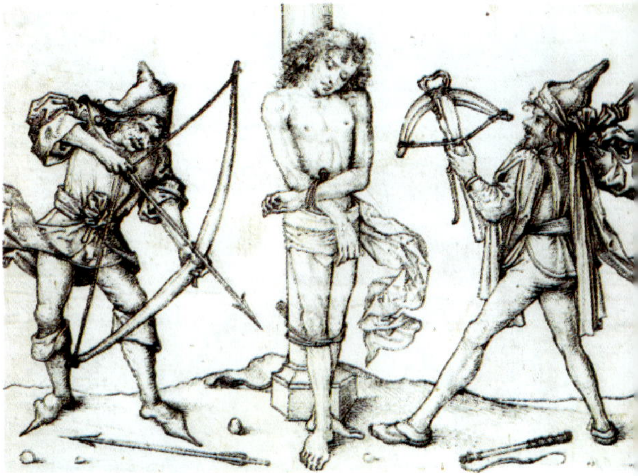

Dürer advocated a more naturalistic treatment of the human figure, and although he came from Nuremberg, his influence was felt throughout German-speaking Europe. St. Sebastian in this work is expressive in a traditionally German manner, and Dürer's attention to anatomical detail was rigorous. Musculature is rendered by subtle shading in the form of cross-hatching where denser grays were desirable.

Lament for the Crucified

Domenico da Tolmezzo
(Friuli, 1448–1507)

- paint on panel
- part of an altarpiece in Santa Lucia
- Museo Cívico, Udine

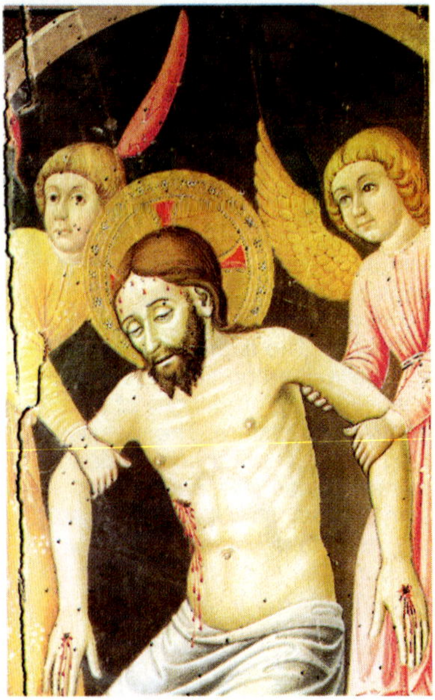

This painter's preservation of various aspects of early Renaissance painting is more apparent than real, given that the nude figure reveals a firm grounding in anatomy. Against the dark background, the delicate skin tones become yet more ethereal. Bodily proportions are dignified and accurate, and the bone structure, displaying areas of occasional tension, is scrupulously observed.

Pietà

Ercole de Roberti

- paint on panel
- Walker Art Gallery, Liverpool

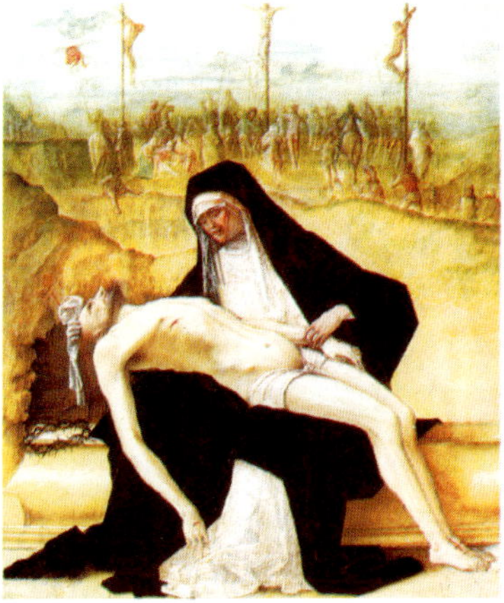

'he modeling of the central figure can make this seem a ather aloof work, yet the humanity and mystery inherent in its ubject matter were common features in the works of 15th-entury artists at the Court of the Este in Ferrara. The work is nusual for the trompe l'oeil effects it employs. Christ's torso s realistically depicted and has great physicality.

Resurrection and Descent into Limbo

Master of Vignola

- fresco
- Castle chapel, Modena

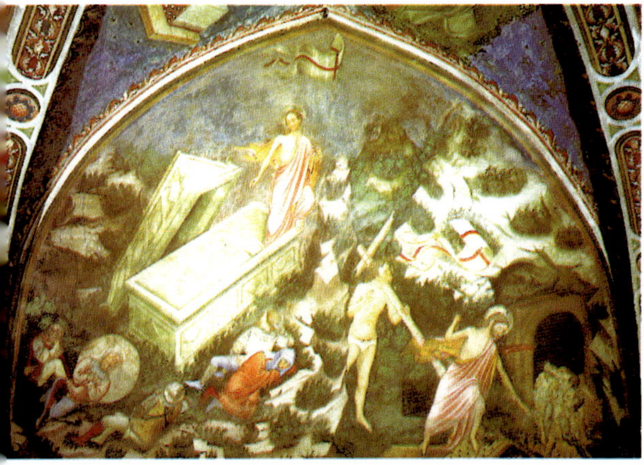

Jp until the 19th century the Master of Vignola had a sig-ificant following and his work was an obligatory subject of tudy in many art schools. His relatively late-Gothic figures eralded certain of the advances to modernity, including a narked interest in naturalistic treatment. The central figure f this fresco displays definite developments, in style and conography, as in its dramatic action.

Crucifixion

Antonello da Messina
(Messina, ca. 1430–Venice, 1479)

- ca. 1470
- oil on canvas
- 52.5 x 42.5 cm
- Koninklijk Museum voor Schone Kunsten, Antwerp

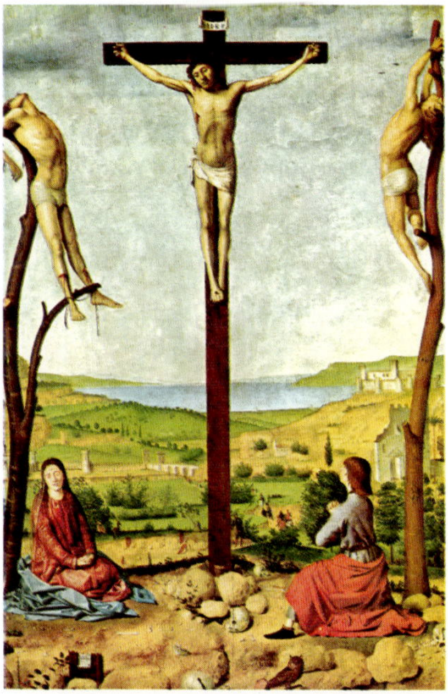

True to a stylistic tradition of the Flemish school, this painter establishes a set of dramatic contrasts in this scene. The tortured contortions of the two thieves, attached to their tree trunks set off against the serene figure of Jesus, his two companions and the peaceful landscape, go towards creating a most impressive effect.

Madonna and Child with SS. Job, Francis, John the Baptist, Dominic, Louis of Toulouse, and Sebastian

Giovanni Bellini (Giambellino)
(Venice?, ca. 1430–Venice, 1516)

- oil on panel
- part of the altarpiece of San Giobbe
- 471 x 258 cm
- Galleria dell'Accademia, Venice

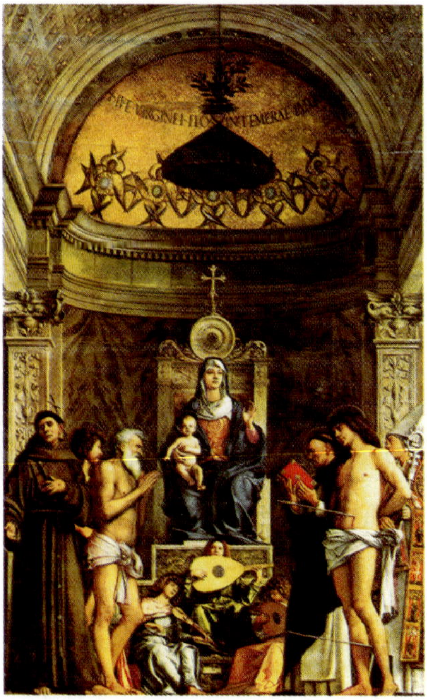

The nude figures in this panel are of an exquisite beauty, the foreshortening well-executed, and anatomical details naturalistically depicted. Independent of subject matter, one notes the sensual treatment of the human body, which is of interest given that it was to become a primary concern from the 16th century onwards.

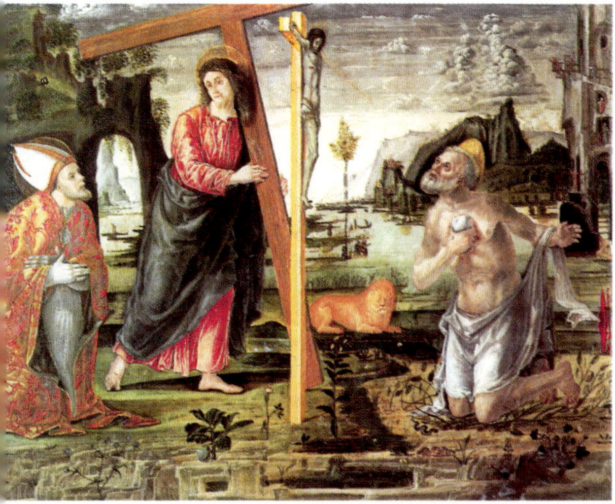

Christ Carrying the Cross between SS. Augustine and Jerome

Bernardino Parenzano
(Parenzo, 1450–Padua?, 1500)

- oil on panel
- Galleria Estense, Modena

t. Jerome, here, with the lion he is often depicted as sit-
ng beside, is magnificently sculptural in conception, the
raftsmanship attending minutely to anatomical details.
;ontrasting light and dark areas create a sense of depth
nd help generate the impressive foreshortening.

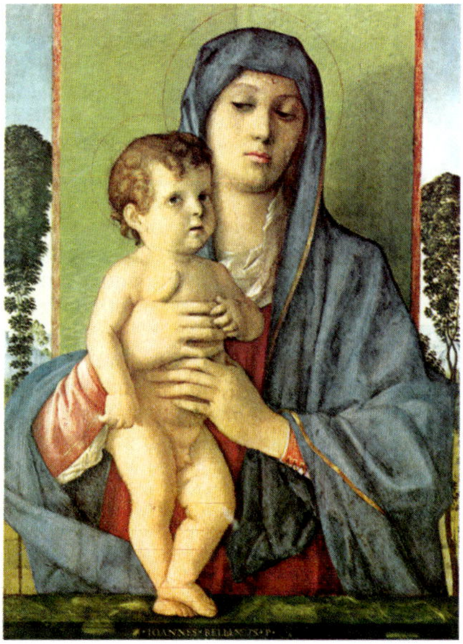

Madonna of the Little Trees

Giovanni Bellini (Giambellino)
(Venice, ca. 1430–Venice, 1516)

- ca. 1480
- oil on canvas
- 74 x 56 cm
- Galleria dell'Accademia, Venice

leld in front of
ie Virgin, with
er brightly col-
red garments
s a background,
ie appearance
f this Christ child
wholly natural.
t a slight angle
the viewer,
ie boy's facial
xpression is,
deed, notable,
s is Mary's.

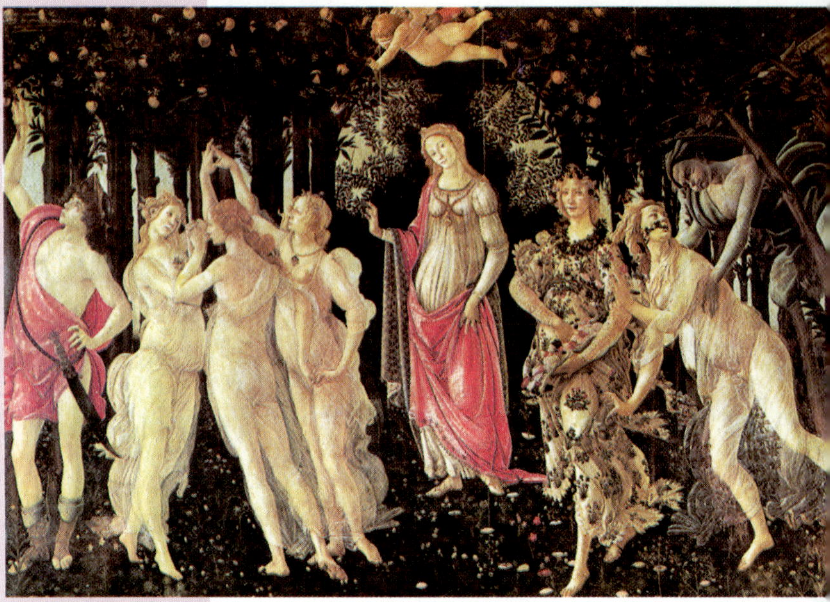

Primavera

Sandro Botticelli (Alessandro di Mariano Filipepi)
(Florence, 1445–1510)

- ca. 1478
- tempera on panel
- 203 x 314 cm
- Galleria degli Uffizi, Florence

The theme, taken from several tercets in Politian's Stanze per la giostra del Magnifico Giuliano de' Medici, is highly complex, combining many mythological figures, as if in a puzzle, but without reference to a known mythological event. On the right, Aeolus embraces Briseis. The goddess Flora, pregnant and wearing a floral dress, heralds spring. In the center is Venus, the goddess of beauty and love, wearing a white dress and a red shawl. Her son, Cupid, is shown flying overhead while aiming his arrow at the Three Graces. On the far left Mercury stands alone, looking away from the scene. Some of the figures in this work are covered with only thin veils, contributing to their eroticism. Far from reproducing the classical Renaissance view, which imagined a new humanity in a world of harmonic order and architecture, Botticelli seems to depart here from a style that he had been cultivating for over 50 years, allowing himself to be guided by a sense of nostalgia instead.

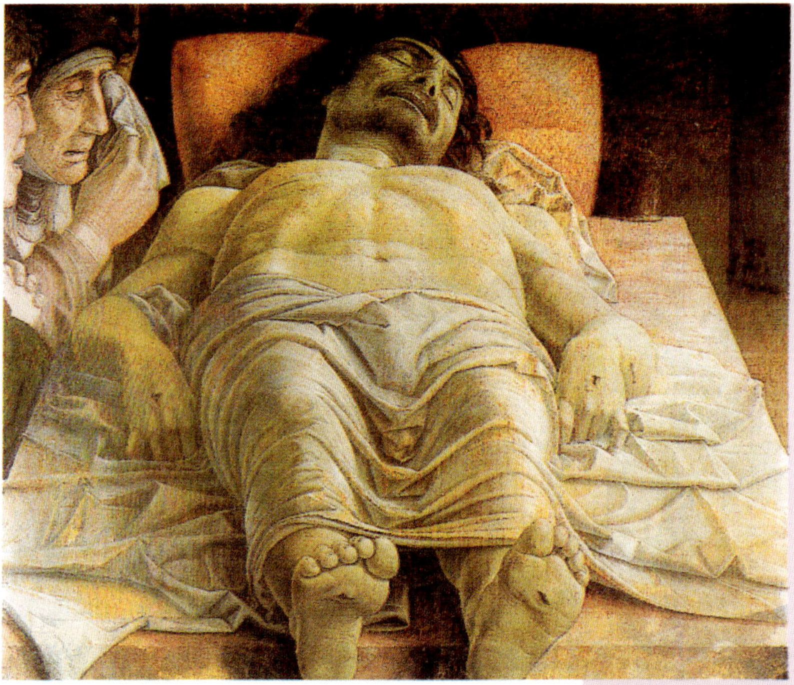

ts most unusual point of view makes this one of the most riginal images of Italian Renaissance art. The portrayal of he dead body of Christ scandalized the artist's contempo- aries, who were nonetheless astounded by his mastery of erspective and geometry. Mantegna applied mathematical aws to a series of given measurements in order to arrive at his strongly foreshortened figure seen in central perspective. rom this angle, the spectator perceives the dead Christ, nd indeed death itself, in a completely new manner, the em- hasis placed on the wounds in the feet and the hands, the unken stomach, the half-open lips and the pallid flesh. In ome ways, this extraordinary study of human anatomy, car- ed out in a characteristically hard, almost sculptural style, epresents the culmination of Mantegna's oeuvre.

The Lamentation over the Dead Christ

Andrea Mantegna
(Isola di Carturo, near Padua, ca. 1431–Mantua, 1506)

- 1480
- tempera on panel
- 66 x 81 cm
- Pinoteca di Brera, Milan

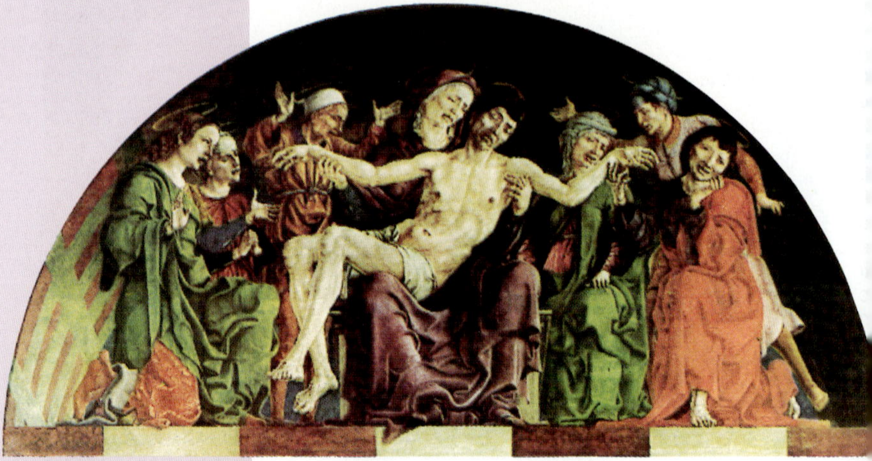

Pietà

Cosimo
(or **Cosmè**) **Tura**
(Ferrara, ca. 1430–1495)

- 1480
- oil on panel
- 132 x 267 cm
- Musée du Louvre, Paris

This work is part of a polyptych that Cosimo Tura painted for a family from his native city. The dramatic scene betrays almost expressionistic qualities. Dominated by a plastic figure of Christ at the center, the composition assumes the shape of a lunette. The brightest light falls on Christ's naturalistically rendered body, evoking the figures of Andrea Mantegna. His pale skin is crisscrossed with a frenetically rhythmic network of lines. The foreshortening is accentuated by the torsion of the figure's limbs. Christ appears ethereal, indeed weightless which is confirmed by the points on which the figure rests. Athletic and perfectly proportioned, Christ's body is lent an idealized form in this anatomical study, in keeping with Renaissance notions of beauty. The artist uses the nudity of the figure to convey Christ's humanity by emphasizing the humiliation he suffered through death.

The pathos in Christ's facial expression reinforces the physical aspects of his grotesque figure, with its elongated thorax and sunken abdomen; Christ's ribs are visible, and his arms seem about to snap under the weight of his body. That this harrowing image is turned towards the observer only adds extra expressive force to it, causing the other elements to retreat into the background.

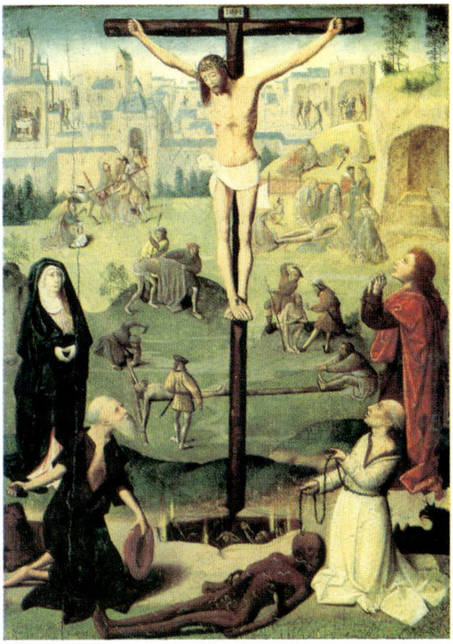

Christ on the Cross

Geertgen tot Sint Jans

(active Haarlem, second half of the 15th century)

- 1480
- egg-based tempera on panel
- 26.8 x 20.5 cm
- National Gallery of Scotland, Edinburgh

This painter's style, which is possibly of German derivation, played an important role in 14th- and 15th-century Mannerism in and around Seville. The rendering of the nude figure appears to betray Flemish influences with a tendency to distort facial features and the figure as a whole. The figure of Christ shows fine attention to detail, however, and the carefully modelled limbs and trunk endow it with great physicality.

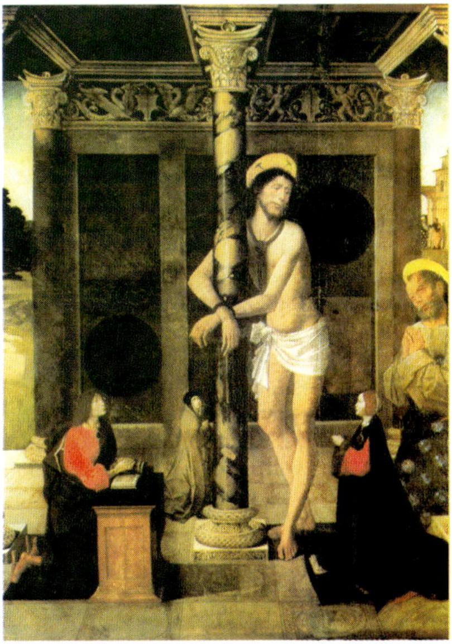

Christ Bound to a Pillar

Alejo Fernandez

(Córdoba, 1470–Seville, 1546)

- Oil on panel
- Museo Provincial de Bellas Artes, Córdoba

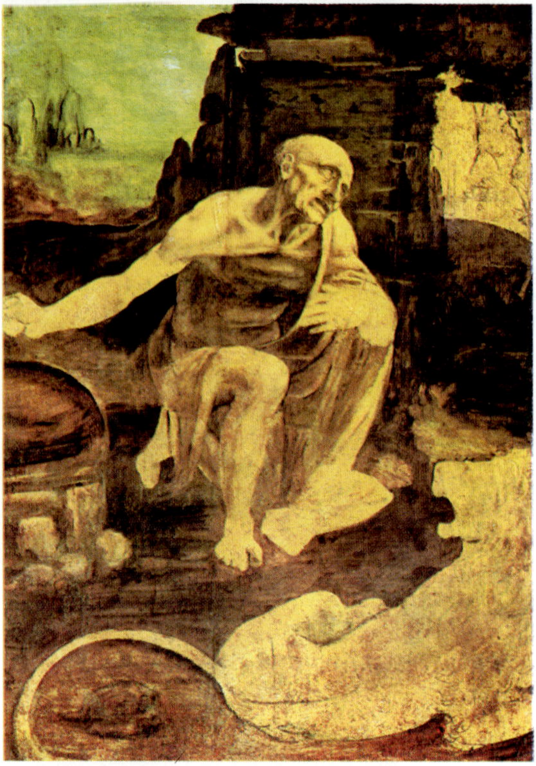

St. Jerome

Leonardo da Vinci
(Vinci, Tuscany, 1452
–Cloux, France, 1519)

- 1482
- oil on panel
- 103 x 75 cm
- Pinacoteca, Vatican

In this painting the penitent, old saint is portrayed as an emaciated figure, recalling Leonardo's anatomical studies The most detailed treatment can be observed in the figure's face, although the body exhibits skillfully rendered features as well, such as the articulation of the muscles, the interplay of light and the foreshortening. The bright highlights of the body against shaded areas give rise to highly naturalistic volumes and textures, just as the dark background makes the figure as a whole stand out. The nude appears ascetic and austere, its pose suggesting great piety, especially in the torsion of the arm extended as in intense prayer. It is clear that, in this painting, the artist was more concerned with evoking a dramatic scene than he was with aesthetic considerations.

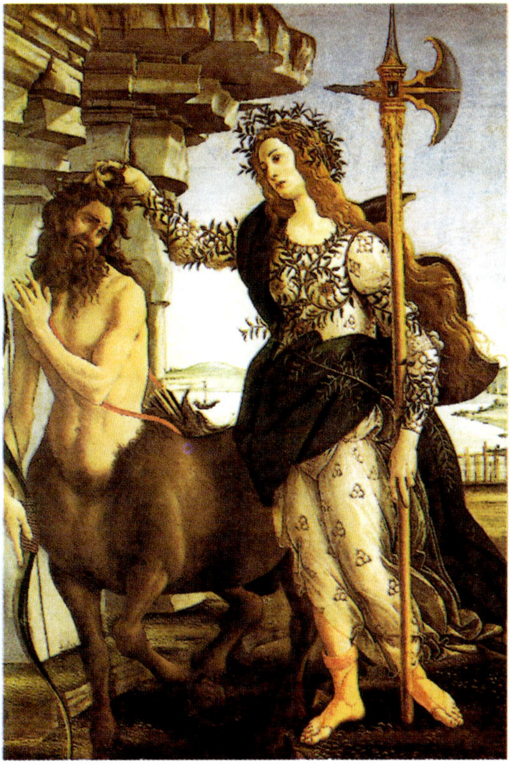

n Classical mythology, Pallas Athena was the goddess of var, and hence of victory and peace. The daughter of Zeus ınd Metis, she was born fully armed, springing from the nouth of Zeus after he had devoured his pregnant wife. 'he centaurs were children of Ixion and Nephele. Half man, alf horse, these wild creatures inhabited the mountains of 'hessaly. The figure of Pallas Athena (called Minerva by the Romans) is represented here in a transparent dress decorat- d with the symbol of the Medici family, three intertwined ngs. The goddess is grasping the centaur's hair, who looks t her with an expression of pained submission. The painting ymbolizes the triumph of chastity over vice. Both figures are erfectly formed, the play of light and shade granting them a ertain grandeur without depriving them of a sense of move- nent.

Pallas Athena and the Centaur

Sandro Botticelli (Alessandro di Mariano Filipepi)
(Florence, 1445–1510)

- 1482-85
- tempera on canvas
- 207 x 148 cm
- Galleria degli Uffizi, Florence

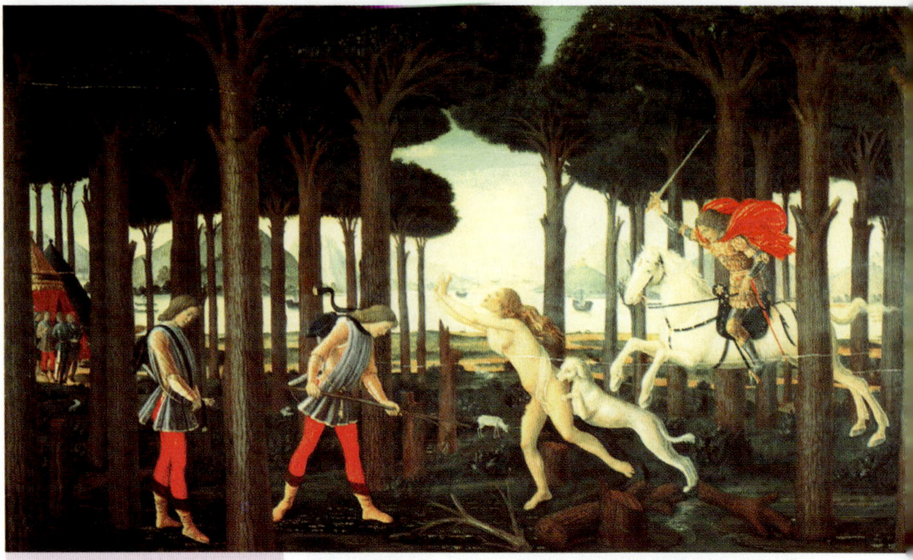

The Story of Nastagio degli Onesti, First Episode

Sandro Botticelli (Alessandro di Mariano Filipepi)
(Florence, 1445–1510)

- 1483
- tempera on panel
- 83 x 138 cm
- Museo del Prado, Madrid

This painting is part of a series of four, three of which were part of the Cambó Collection in Barcelona from 1929 to 1941, before being transferred to the Prado. The fourth is in a private collection in London.

The theme of this work has been taken from Bocaccio's Decameron, in which Nastagio's amorous advances are rejected by Paola Traversari. While wandering through the woods, sad and dejected, he has a vision: a nude woman flees in terror, chased by a rider and his hounds. Botticelli narrates the episodes in detail, as if creating a sort of storyboard. The boughs of the trees, sturdy and rendered in saturated colors, dominate the top third of the picture plane. In the distance a bright marine background can be seen. The woman's naked body is draped in a small veil whose shape and position—in addition to suggesting movement—are carefully conceived so that neither her breasts nor her pubis are visible. This nude, which defies the traditional hieraticism of the pose, is dynamic, an aspect that implies a great advance in painting, since figures in motion had not hitherto been executed in sketches. The woman is shown in profile, with the exception of her left leg.

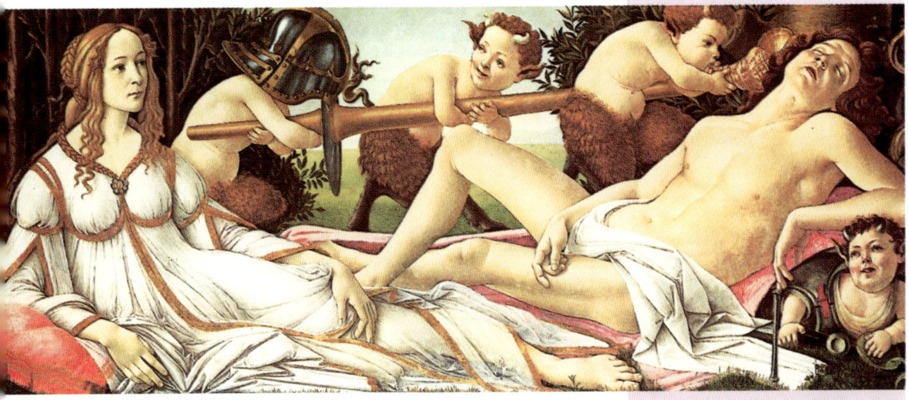

The figures in this painting represent Simonetta Vespucci and Giuliano de Medici. The nude Mars, the god of war, is in a deep sleep, despite the busy fauns around him who, with their half-human, half-goat bodies and horns on their heads, lend the painting a picaresque air. Mars' delicate body is exquisitely rendered, with smooth skin and fine brown lines, while his torso is skillfully foreshortened. The nude is extremely sensual and much more dynamic than the dressed figure of Venus on the left, who exhibits a refined beauty in her facial expression. Despite the painting's consummate composition, the superb treatment of light, which imbues the entire scene, and the evocative palette, in which light colors predominate, the scene is somewhat hieratic and affected.

Venus and Mars

Sandro Botticelli (Alessandro di Mariano Filipepi)
(Florence, 1445–1510)

- ca. 1485
- tempera and oil on panel
- 69.2 x 173.4 cm
- National Gallery, London

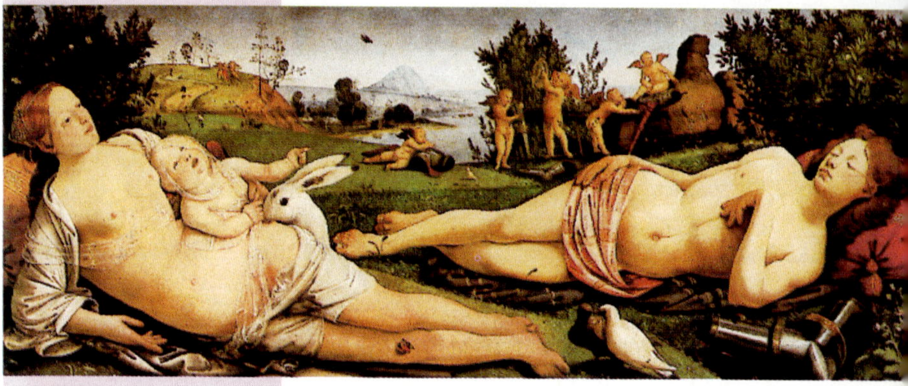

Venus, Mars and Cupid

Piero di Cosimo (Piero di Lorenzo di Chimenti)
(Florence, 1461/62–after 1515)

- 1488
- oil on panel
- 72 x 182 cm
- National Gallery, London

In this tranquil scene Mars sleeps soundly beside his wife, Venus. As in Botticelli's painting, the goddess is shown to be awake, serenely contemplating her husband while holding her son, Cupid, who, snuggling up to her, plays with a rabbit, a symbol of fertility. Both nudes are magnificent, positively exuding sensuality and eroticism. Indeed, Mars' curvaceous forms recall the body of a woman. Venus' recumbent pose lends her a more erotic aspect than Mars, whereby the curious torsion of the hip evokes Gothic iconography, which was losing ground by the time this picture was painted. Mars' body exhibits finer proportions and the arrangement of his limbs engenders a remarkable compositional rhythm. This work attests to Piero's consummate skill in depicting light and naturalistic figures, be they religious or mythological.

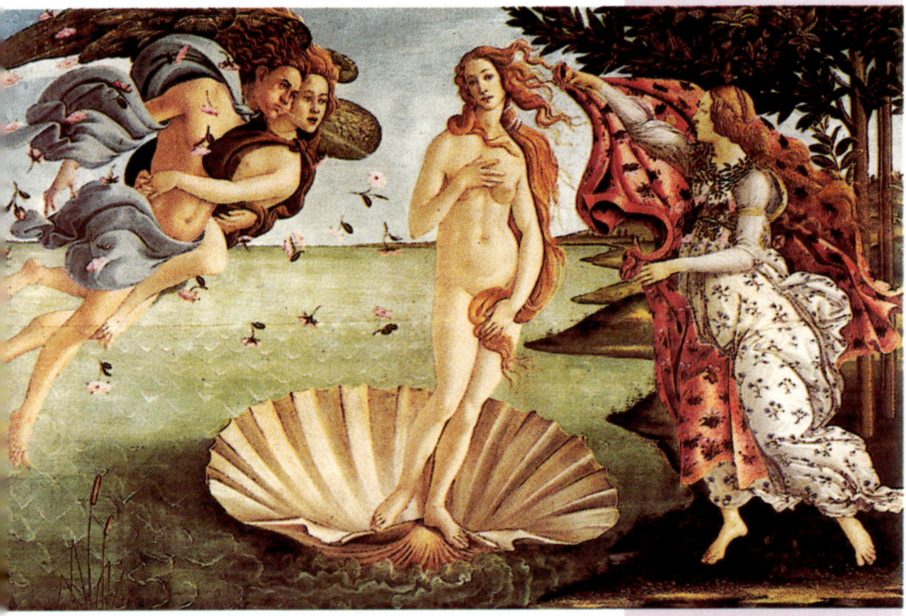

'enus is shown reaching the island of Cyprus in a sea shell fter emerging from the foam. The goddess, Classical in ppearance and pose, is shown being propelled to land by ne breath of Zephyr and Chloe, mild winds. On the right tands the goddess Flora, who is attempting to cover the aked Venus with her shawl. The suggestion of a land-cape in the right background is limited to a rugged coast-ne with sparse vegetation. This does not mean that the ainter rejected the technical advances of perspective that vere so central to Renaissance painting; they were simply ot his primary concern. Venus' slim, elegant figure has a ather mystical, sensual air, which is heightened by the inuous, flowing lines of her body. Her tranquil attitude con-rasts with the dynamism of her long, undulating hair, which iscreetly covers her intimate parts. Simonetta Vespucci robably sat as model for the artist.

The Birth of Venus

Sandro Botticelli (Alessandro di Mariano Filipepi)
(Florence, 1445–1510)

- ca. 1489
- tempera on canvas
- 175 x 278 cm
- Galleria degli Uffizi, Florence

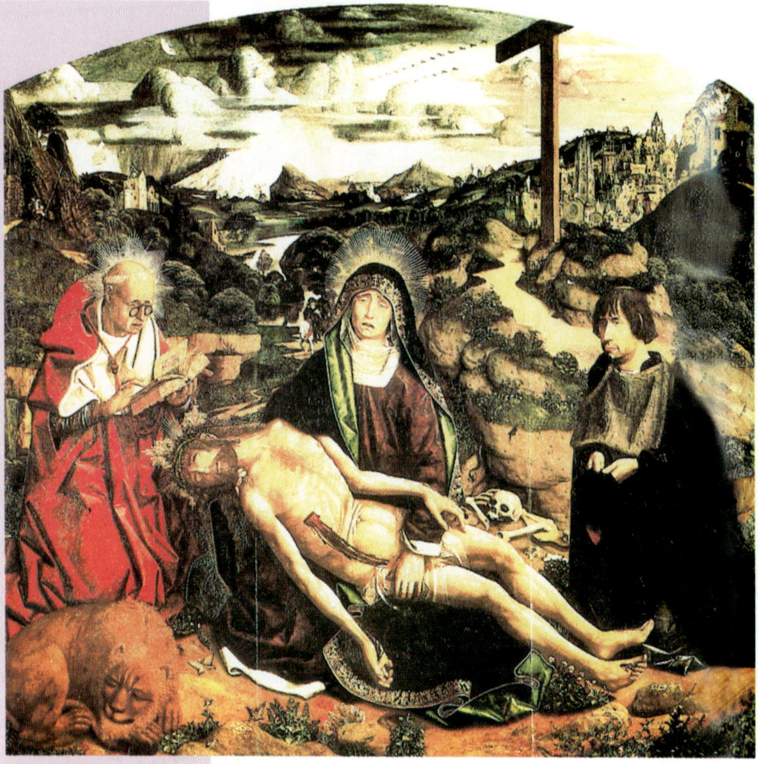

Pietà

Bartolomé Bermejo
(Córdoba?,–Barcelona, 1498; active 1474–95)

- 1490
- panel
- 175 x 189 cm
- Museo de la Catedral, Barcelona Cathedral

The influence of Netherlandish realism is evident in many aspects of this work, such as the painstakingly rendered background, an illuminated landscape that lends the scene a sense of depth. Although the artist was not unduly concerned with aesthetic considerations, he conceived a forceful composition. In his inimitable style, the painter makes consummate use of light and shadow. And with the palette he adopts, he lends the image an impressive poignancy, which is reinforced by the harrowing facial expressions of the two protagonists. The drama culminates in the nude figure of Christ, whose limp body, attenuated arms and subtle modeling contribute to the pathos of the scene.

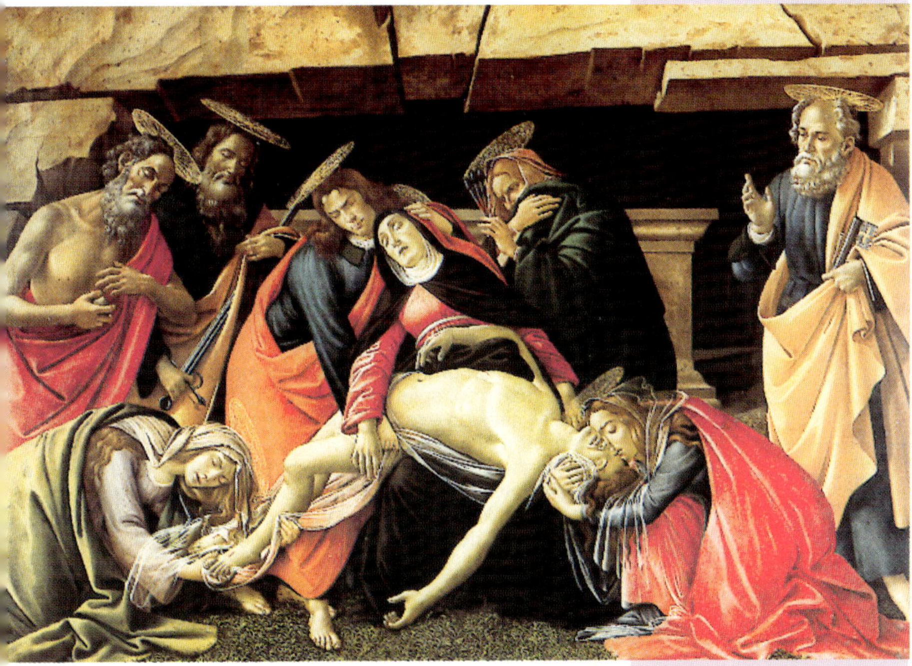

This dramatic scene, set at the entrance to Christ's tomb, shows the figure of the Savior lying arched in his mother's lap in a way designed to appeal to the viewer's emotions. The magnificent, strongly illuminated figure of Christ is less serene than most of Botticelli's figures. Modeled with an almost sculptural boldness, it accurately represents the well-proportioned body of an athletic young man. This picture, which Botticelli probably executed with the help of assistants, is one of a series of religious subjects painted towards the end of the artist's life that give expression to his profound mysticism. In its bright colors it reverts to an earlier style of painting.

Pietà

Sandro Botticelli (Alessandro di Mariano Filipepi)
(Florence, 1445–1510)

- after 1490
- tempera on panel
- 110 x 207 cm
- Alte Pinakothek, Munich

Pietà

Giovanni Bellini (Giambellino)

(Venice?, ca. 1430–Venice, 1516)

- 1475
- oil on panel
- 91 x 131 cm
- Pinacoteca Comunale, Rimini

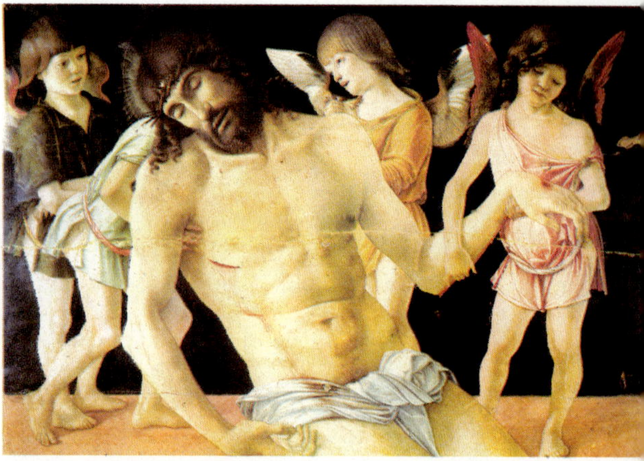

The execution of this panel is fluid and expressive. Bellini was a master of spiritual scenes, which he painted frequently, seeking ever new points of view. Christ here, attended by child-angels, is depicted with a well-built torso on which death seems to have had remarkably little effect. However, the limp body is scarcely that of a sleeping person, either. It seems instead to reflect the mystery surrounding death and the resurrection.

Allegory of Inconstant Fortune

Giovanni Bellini (Giambellino)

(Venice, ca. 1430–1516)

- ca. 1490
- panel
- 34 x 22 cm
- Galleria dell'Accademia, Venice

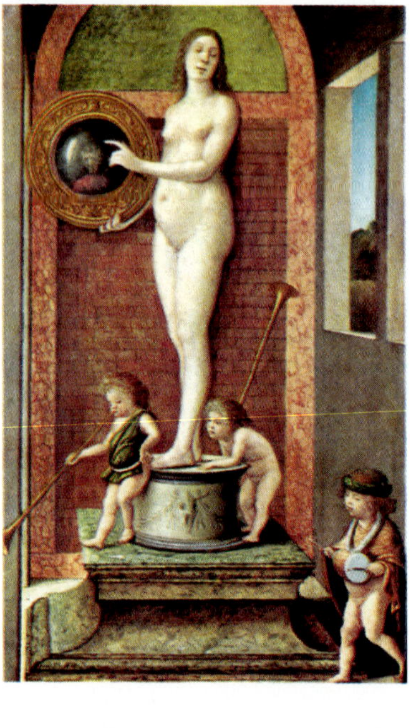

The painter here celebrates the female figure by placing it among architectural elements. Turned at a slight angle, it features rather diminutive breasts that contrast curiously with the figure's more abundant abdomen and buttocks.

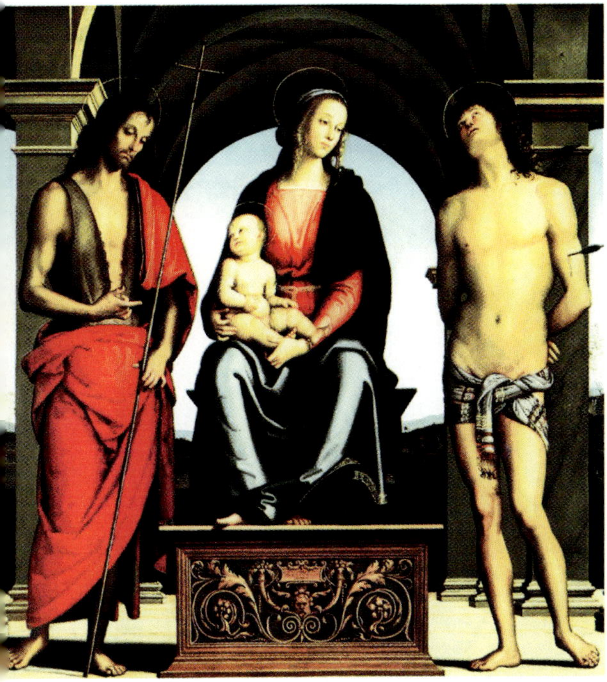

This work portrays the Virgin holding the Christ child on her lap, flanked by St. John the Baptist on the left and St. Sebastian in his martyrdom on the right. The magnificent nude has a fine finish that puts it on a par with Raphael's art. The entire body has a black outline that blends subtly into the background and emphasizes the body, a technique that was used for many years. The body of St. Sebastian is brightly illuminated and static, eschewing harsh shadows and revealing a modeling that defines the muscles with exquisite subtlety. His torso is elongated and his genitals covered with a small loincloth, lending the figure a certain sensuality—one of the most notable features of Perugino's nudes.

The Madonna between St. John the Baptist and St. Sebastian

Pietro Perugino (Pietro Vannucci)
(Città della Pieve, near Perugia, Romagna, ca. 1448–Fontignano, near Perugia, 1523)

- 1493
- oil on canvas
- 178 x 164 cm
- Galleria degli Uffizi, Florence

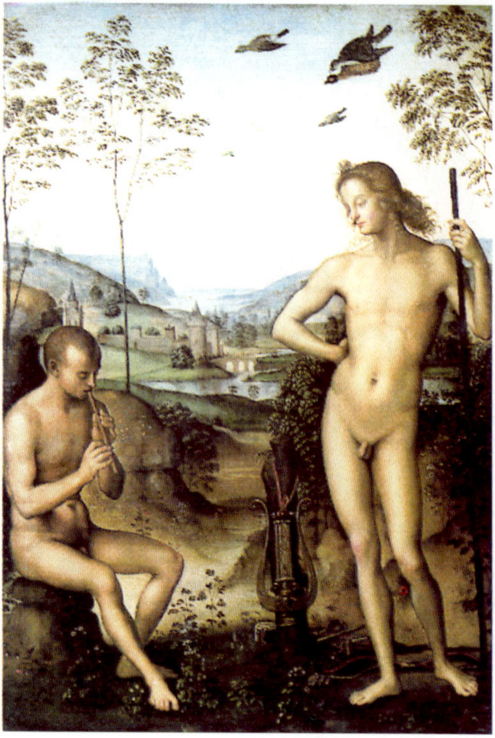

Apollo and Marsyas

Pietro Perugino (Pietro Vannucci)
(Città della Pieve, near Perugia, Romagna, ca. 1448–Fontignano, near Perugia, 1523)

- ca. 1459
- tempera on panel
- 39 x 29 cm
- Musée du Louvre, Paris

Marsyas was a Phrygian satyr who challenged Apollo to a music competition using a flute that had once belonged to Athena and had been discarded by her. Apollo won, flayed Marsyas alive and hung his skin in a cave. The scene depicted here is set in a peaceful landscape rendered in central perspective. This creates a background of great depth, with stylized trees with slender trunks and several large birds. Marsyas concentrates on playing his flute while Apollo looks on, listening attentively and observing his opponent with contempt. Both subjects have svelte, delicate bodies and stylized figures, which are magnificently modeled. Their flawless anatomical volumes have been painstakingly studied, a characteristic of the painter's work, and positively radiate sensuality, calling attention to the stark contrast between their fine physical beauty and the depth of their feelings and intentions. It should come as no surprise to learn that the work of Pietro Perugino exerted a considerable influence on Raphael, his pupil.

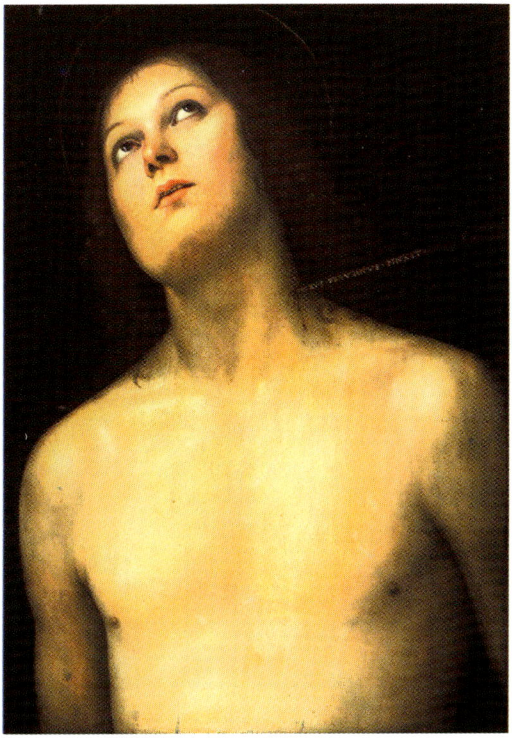

St. Sebastian

Pietro Perugino (Pietro Vannucci)
(Città della Pieve, near Perugia, Romagna, ca. 1448–Fontignano, near Perugia, 1523)

- 1459
- tempera on panel
- 53.8 x 39.5 cm
- Hermitage, St. Petersburg

;ebastian was one of the most widely painted saints during ne Renaissance, as it was believed that it would provide rotection against the Black Death, which was ravaging Europe at the time. Here, the artist has made use of a wide ange of technical means to evoke this extraordinary figure, ome recalling the work of Raphael, who visited Pietro Perugino's studio about a year after this work was completed. 'he figure of Sebastian is remarkable for its modeling, btained by the use of sfumato, and for the reflection of the olden atmosphere on the skin. In order to heighten the motional intensity of the scene, the artist has used virtually ne entire picture plane, leaving a small area behind the aint for a dark background that highlights the figure further till. In this work Perugino lends the martyr a svelte, handome anatomy; the skin is treated with remarkable sensitivity nd the rather effeminate face is idealized, displaying a cerain degree of sensuality. This religious subject provided rtists of the day with an excuse to paint a nude, whose feaures could be rendered with painstaking detail.

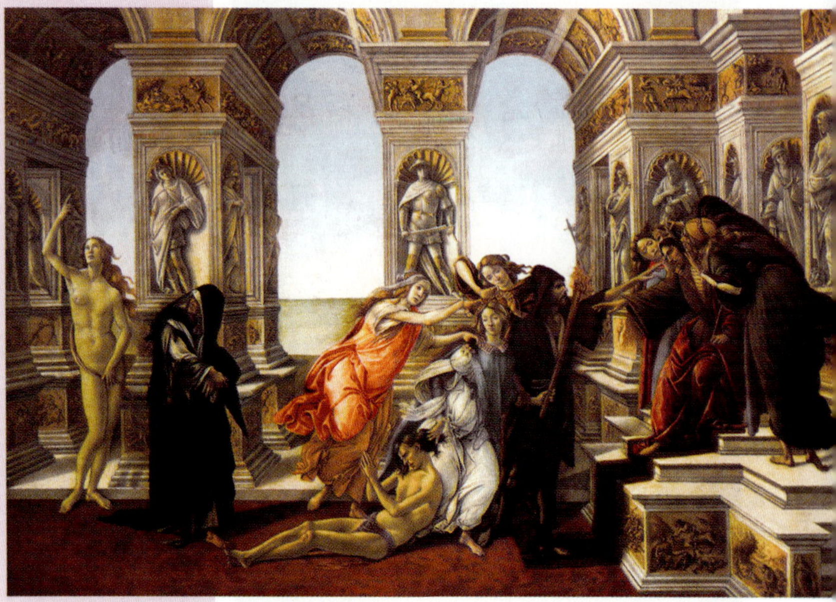

The Calumny of Apelles

Sandro Botticelli (Alessandro di Mariano Filipepi)
(Florence, 1445-1510)

- 1495
- tempera on panel
- 62 x 91 cm
- Galleria degli Uffizi, Florence

The canvas depicts the Greek painter Antiphilos accusing Apelles of incitement to rebellion against Ptolemy IV, for which he was unjustly imprisoned. The woman at the left, shown concealing her pubis with her flowing hair, represents Truth. She recalls the figure in The Birth of Venus. Corruption, dressed in black, stands nearby. We see Apelles being dragged to his judgement by Calumny, while two seductive female figures, Treachery and Imposture, comb her hair. The man holding Calumny's hand is Hatred. The king, with the ears of an ass, attends to what Ignorance and Suspicion have to say. Certain critics claim that the work concerns the allegation against Raphael that he had maintained homosexual relations with his students. Despite the dramatic splendor and masterful composition of the scene, the work falls short of the perfection of The Birth of Venus, which is generally considered to be Botticelli's masterpiece.

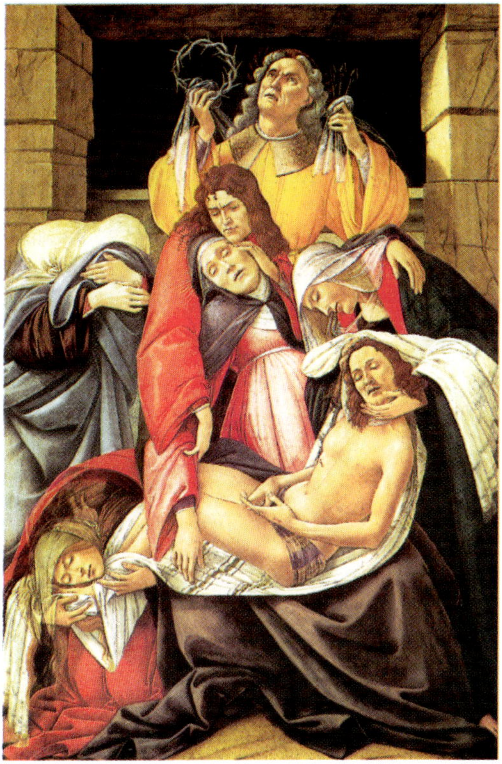

'he pyramidal composition of this painting lends the whole reat cohesion, whereas the lines provide dynamism and armony. The nude body of Christ, about to be wrapped in typical Jewish shroud, is S-shaped, disrupting the traight lines with which the scene is replete. The white hroud frames Christ's body like an aura, making it stand ut against the dark tones of the tunics around him. The ody possesses neither the slenderness nor the rhythm of ther nudes by the artist, and the muscles, although pre-ent, are scarcely perceptible. Christ's limp arms, hands nd head, which seems practically detached from his ody, reveal that he is dead. The skin tones are rich and nore brilliant than in earlier works by the artist.

The Lamentation

Sandro Botticelli (Alessandro di Mariano Filipepi)
(Florence, 1445–1510)

- 1495
- tempera on panel
- 107 x 71 cm
- Museo Poldi Pezzoli, Milan

The Virgin between Saints

Girolamo da Treviso

(Treviso?, 1480–Boulogne, 1544/48?)

- oil on panel
- Cathedral, Treviso

This scene is part of an altarpiece.

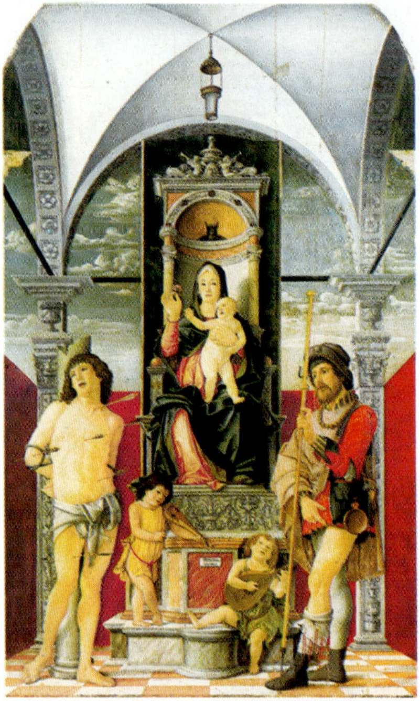

Advances effected in technique and style, as well as a yearning for a return to more classical themes and interest in the human body, were all instrumental in the development of nude painting. St. Sebastian's role in conveying physicality, even sensuality, became an almost mandatory feature. Here his well-built body, if slightly mannered in its presentation, has been executed according to an ideal of beauty found in early sculpture.

Crucifixion

Pietro Perugino (Pietro Vannucci)

(Città della Pieve, near Perugia, Romagna, ca. 1448–Fontignano, near Perugia, 1523)

- ca. 1495
- fresco
- Convent of Santa Maria Magdalena dei Pazzi, Florence

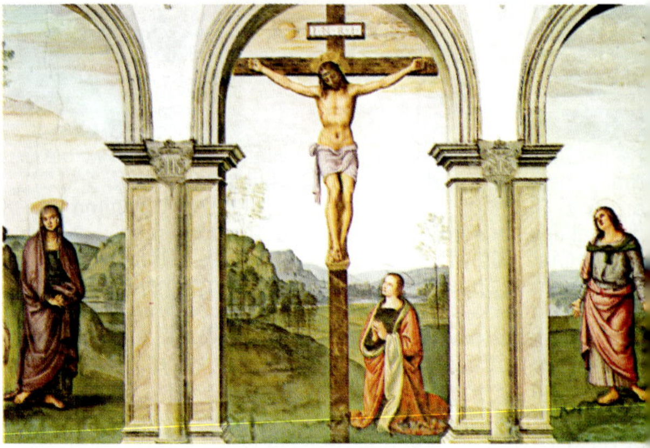

This fresco depiction of the crucifixion features a remarkably naturalistic figure, a characteristic Michelangelo exploited in the ceiling of the Sistine Chapel. The body's three-dimensionality comes out superbly despite the very bright background, a system of tonal blending being used for the purpose, which had a considerable influence on Renaissance artists.

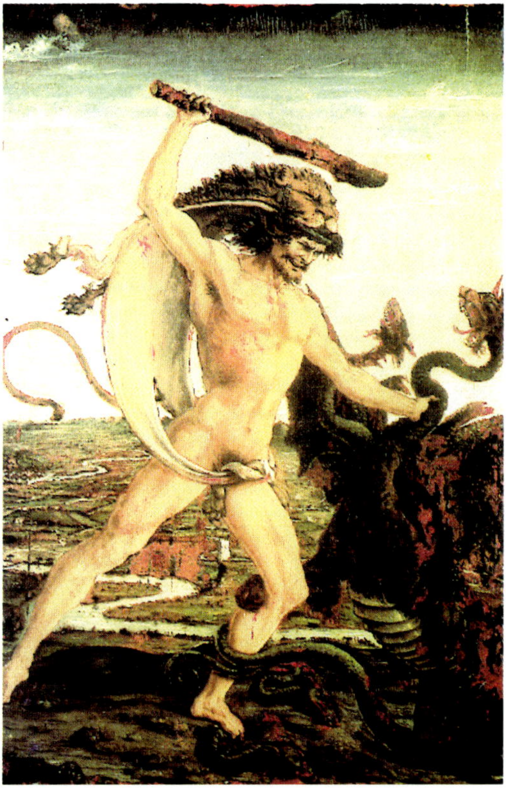

Hercules and Hydra

Antonio Pollaiuolo (Antonio Benci)
(Florence, ca. 1432–Rome, 1498)

- ca. 1460
- tempera on panel
- 17 x 12 cm
- Galleria degli Uffizi, Florence

ne Hydra was a water-serpent with a hound's body that ed in the swamps of Lerna, near Argos. The monster had ven heads and, when one was cut off, another would mediately grow to replace it. Hercules was able to slay e Hydra by cauterizing the neck with a firebrand after cutg off all nine heads with a single strike. Antonio Pollaiuolo ptures the moment when Hercules delivers the mortal ow. Although the creature resembles a terrifying dragon, it es not frighten the hero, who here boasts a muscular and werful body. The painter has executed a naturalistic and instakingly detailed anatomical study and made wise use light, which describes, models and lends volume to the markable figure of Hercules. The artist reserved the dark lors to convey the repugnant beast and avoided stark ntrasts, which may have detracted from the hero.

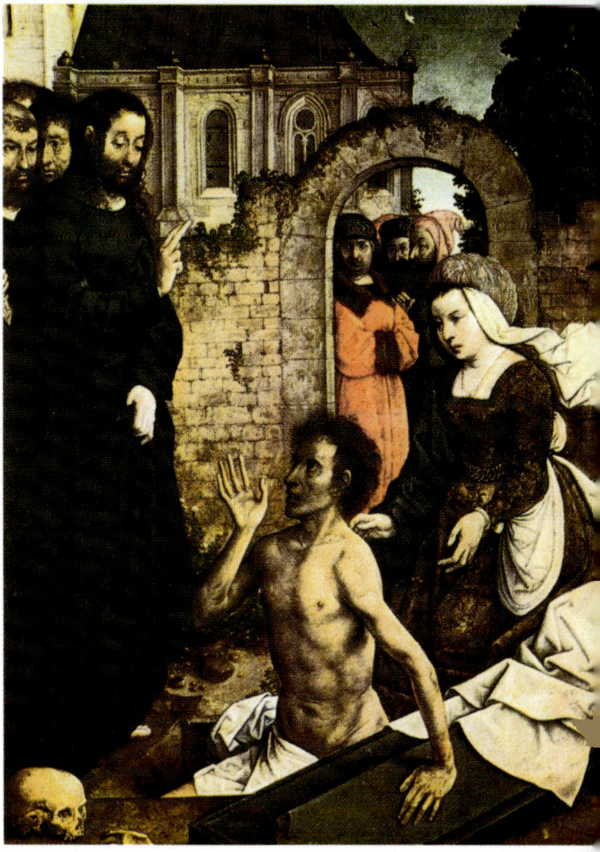

The Raising of Lazarus

Juan de Flandes
(ca. 1465–Palencia, 1516)

- panel
- 110 x 84 cm
- Museo del Prado, Madrid

The work of this painter must have been highly regarded in his day, for in 1496 he received the title "Painter of the Catholic Queen," whom some believe is represented in the female figure on the right. Juan de Flandes approached the theme of the painting, The Raising of Lazarus, one that many other painters have depicted, in a novel manner. In traditional renditions the figure of Jesus is the focus of attention. Here, however, Lazarus occupies the center of the picture, where the composition's principal lines of perspective converge. This cadaverous figure is portrayed in a naturalistic fashion. The shadows in the painting are one of its most unnerving aspects, evoking the work of Leonardo da Vinci in their painterly handling, particularly in the contrast between the foreground and background.

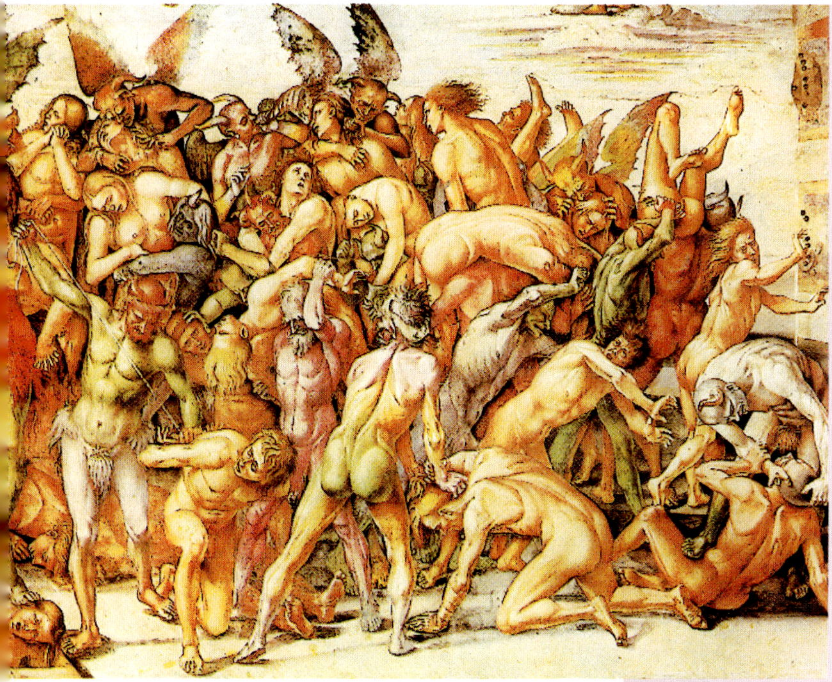

The End of the World

Luca Signorelli
(Cortona, ca. 1445/50–1523)

- 1499–1504
- fresco
- approx. 670 cm long
- San Brizio Chapel, Orvieto Cathedral

his painting is part of a fresco series representing some f Signorelli's finest work. The artist was commissioned to ontinue the work that Fra Angelico, to whom the iconog- aphy is attributed, had commenced in 1477. In this grand ainting Signorelli displays his mastery of the nude, with ighly sophisticated and realistic foreshortening. One otable feature of his figures is the muscular tension of eir bodies, which suggests that the artist drew them from ature. The group of figures is highly dramatic, making the arsome demons more credible. Despite the fact that the gures exhibit various defects (a general heaviness in rm, a somewhat stylized anatomy, a slightly imbalanced omposition), this bold, monumental work is a fine exam- e of Quattrocento painting.

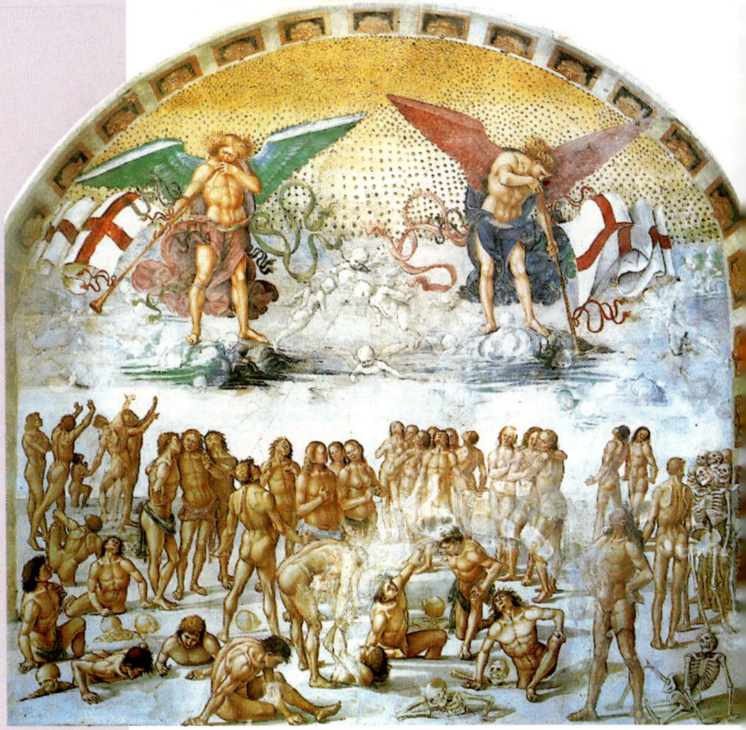

The Resurrection of the Dead

Luca Signorelli
(Cortona, 1445/50–1523)

- 1499–1504
- fresco
- San Brizio Chapel, Orvieto Cathedral

This scene is part of a magnificent series of six frescos that are considered to be Luca Signorelli's finest works. It shows the moment before the Last Judgment, with the bodies of the risen responding to the sound of the trumpets played by the two angels in the sky, surrounded by little cherubs. The artist has filled the painting with nudes, most of which are male, in a variety of poses and typologies. The bodies are stylized with sophisticated modeling, well-defined musculature, fair skin and sensual lines. These figures have been painted with a warm tone that emerges from a bluish-gray background, and look both admiringly and expectantly at the apparition in the sky. The drama is played out in solemn theatricality. The bold foreshortening and colorism of the nudes prefigure the virtuoso work of Michelangelo and Giulio Romano.

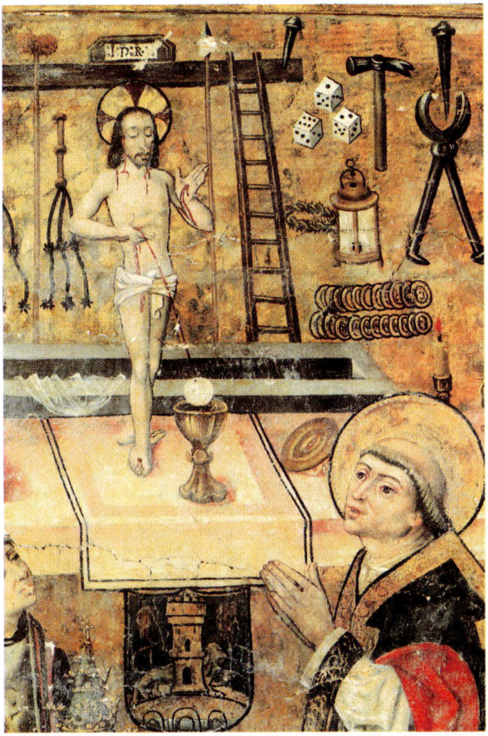

Mass of St. Gregory

School of Castille

- ca. 1500
- tempera on panel
- 81 x 73 cm
- Museu Diocesà, Lérida

ıis panel depicts that legend in the life of the saint accord-
g to which, upon doubting the Transubstantiation at one of
s masses, Christ resurrected, accompanied by the attrib-
es of the Passion, appeared to Gregory. Despite the
tist's evident efforts to present the scene as realistically
possible, the work remains naïve and traditional.
evertheless, this was not particularly important, since this
pe of work did not aim at fulfilling academic norms, rather
was designed to be an instructional aid for the faithful.
ırist is shown with a head that is huge in relation to the
st of the body, and there are other idiosyncratic details.

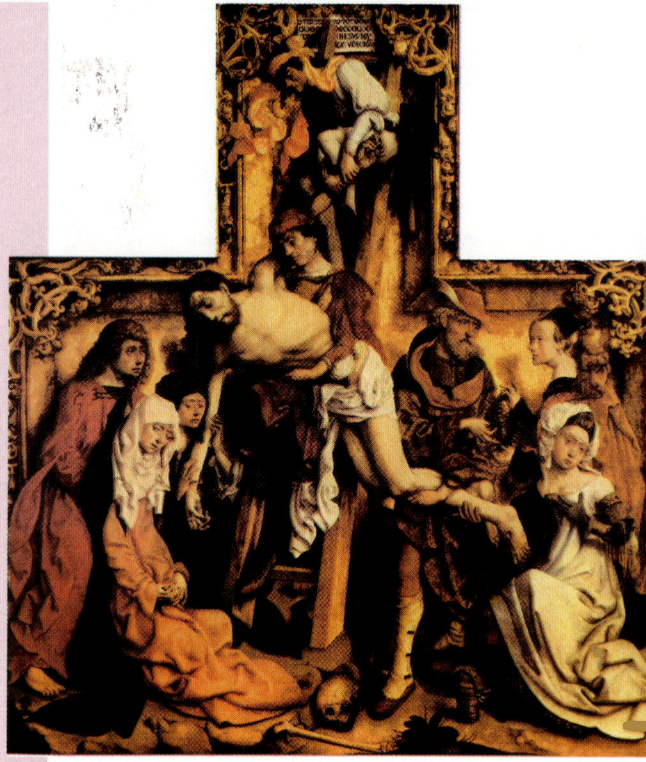

The Deposition

Master of St. Bartholomew
(end of the 15th century –beginning of the 16th century)

- ca. 1500
- panel
- 220 x 214 cm
- Musée du Louvre, Paris

In this painting Christ is clearly depicted as a human being, languid and heavy; there is no sign of the floating weightlessness of other interpretations. The failure of the Divine in the face of human malice is seldom portrayed in Gothic art, in which Christ is not one who has died a torturous death, but one who triumphs over it. Here Christ's hands, stiff with rigor mortis, contrast with the serene expression of his face, which is haggard and drawn. The realistic study of the muscles and bone structure, enhanced by the treatment of the skin, attests to the artist's sound anatomical knowledge. Sof tonal modeling renders the volumes realistic. The composition, painted on gold leaf, appears to be worked in bas-relie The painting's depth, which is suggested by the shadows, serves only to increase the realism of the scene. This impression is heightened by superimposing the figure of Christ onto the frame.

ermejo, who as trained in landers, nbraced the emish style, een here in the aturalism that npregnates this eautifully com- osed work. The cial expressions the figures are so notably elo- uent. The nudes e represented ith bulging odomens, in the othic style. The e veil covering e intimate parts some helps nvey the purity the expectant ouls.

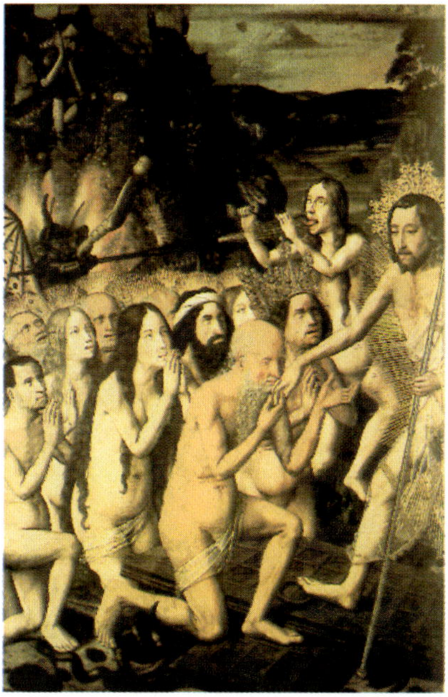

Descent into Limbo

Bartolomé Bermejo
(Córdoba, before 1450 –Catalonia, after 1498)

- ca. 1500
- oil on canvas
- 88.5 x 68 cm
- Museu Nacional d'Art de Catalunya, Barcelona

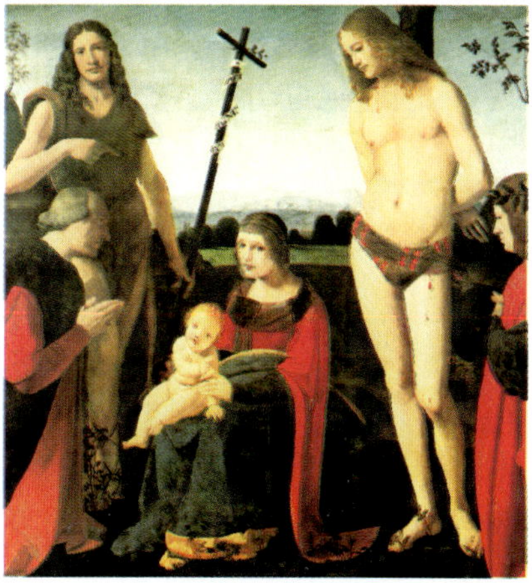

Madonna Casio

Giovanni Antonio Boltraffio
(Milan, 1467–1515)

- 1500
- oil on panel
- Musée du Louvre, Paris

s quite likely that this artist, who was a pupil of Leonardo da nci, actually painted some of the works now attributed to the aster. The treatment of anatomical details and composition re are flawless. There is a touch more hardness to the style an we find in works by Leonardo himself. Both the figure and e pose of St. Sebastian's convey a self-evident sexual ambi- ity. Lacking any overt dramatic interest, the graceful curva- e of the saint's slender body radiates serenity.

Simonetta Vespucci

Piero di Cosimo (Piero di Lorenzo di Chimenti)
(Florence, 1462–1521)

- oil on panel
- 57 x 42 cm
- Musée Condé, Chantilly

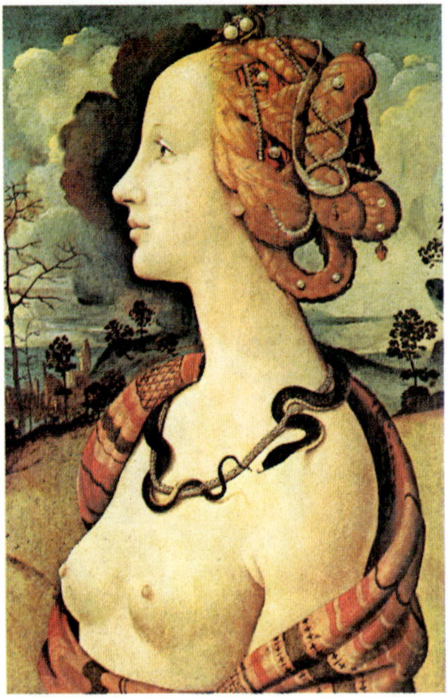

The garment draped around thi young woman causes her nude torso to stand out all the more prom nently, in particula her breasts and the necklace with entwined snake. The sinuous profi of the woman's face and the skilf use of contrasts with respect to th background help bring out yet mor strongly the work' manifest eroticism

Pietà

Giovanni Bellini (Giambellino)
(Venice?, ca. 1430–Venice, 1516)

- ca. 1500
- oil on panel
- 65 x 87 cm
- Galleria dell'Accademia, Venice

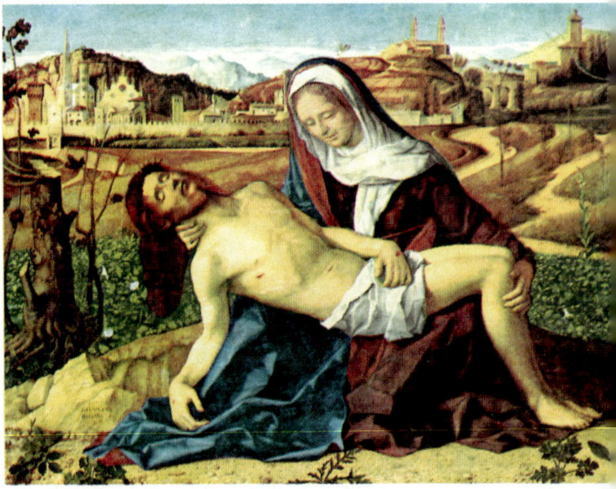

The variegated landscape with buildings in the background, some of which are rather imposing, points up by means of contrast the dramatic tragedy enacted in the foreground. The body of this dead Christ is classically handsome. Except for the stigmata, all sign of suffering having been eliminated from the portrayal, while the Virgin wears an expression of deep pain on her face.

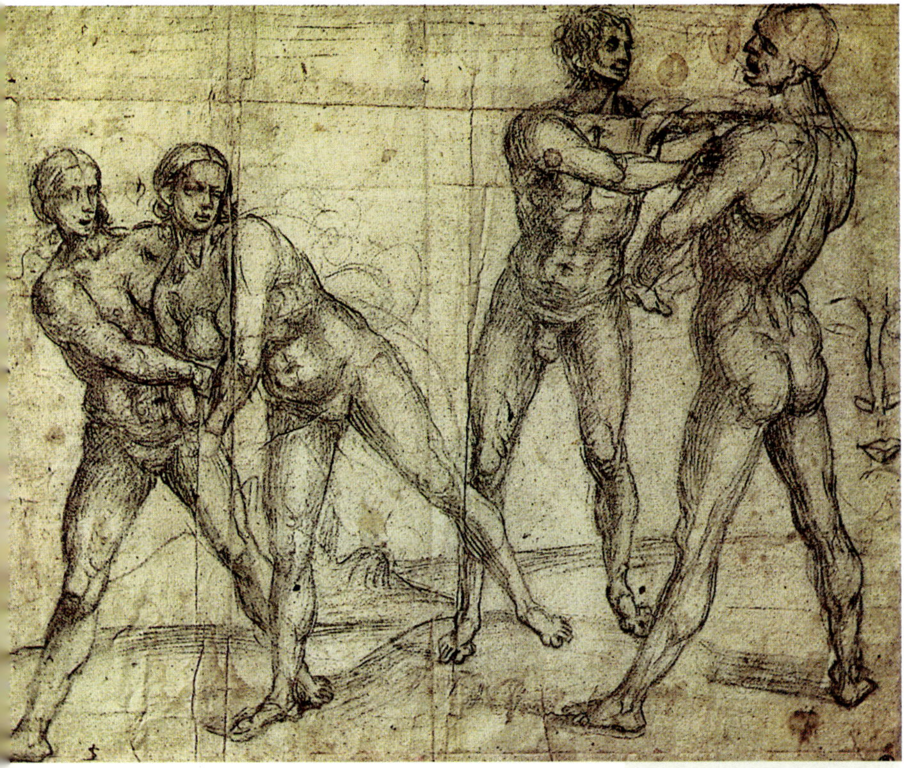

ather than draw a group of interrelated figures, the artist as executed four independent figure studies here, with an nderlying theme. The four figures appear as in movement, rawn with multiple lines that, in addition to modeling the ody, describe body masses, shapes and details, as well as rovide highlights and shading. The artist's humanist inten- ons are clear here in his attempt to present the human natomy as being something of sublime value that must be culpted until perfection is finally achieved. Seen in this light, nd in view of his humanist concerns, it is not surprising that ichelangelo was moved profoundly by Signorelli's works.

Four Nude Figures Preparing to Wrestle

Luca Signorelli
(Cortona, ca. 1445/50-1523)

- pen and ink drawing
- 29.5 x 36.8 cm
- Musée du Louvre, Cabinet de Dessins, Paris

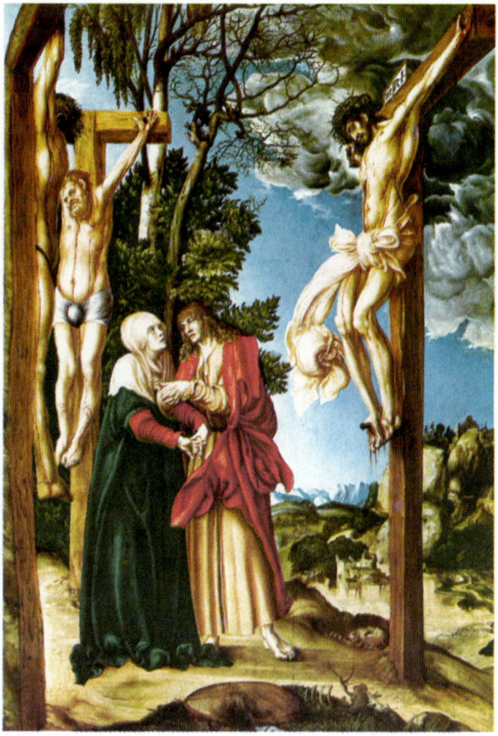

The Crucifixion

Lucas Cranach the Elder
(Kronach, Franconia, 1472–Weimar, 1553)

- 1503
- oil on canvas
- 136 x 99 cm
- Alte Pinakothek, Munich

By lending the human body three-dimensionality, Cranach the Elder was able to convey human torture in all its graphic brutality. This highly original composition shows the human body from different vantage points. All three nudes are depicted with their muscles stretched and their rib cages protruding, yet each has been lent its own peculiar attributes. Christ, for example, is the only figure to have his feet nailed to the Cross and his arms are spread wider apart than those of the others. Although they all exhibit similar flesh tones, Christ's are the most luminous as he is set against a background of dark clouds. Another noteworthy feature is the loincloth covering his genitals with an enormous knot, which gives it an unreal elegance. The painter achieves a scene resembling a stage set by arranging the crosses so that they blend into the landscape, underscoring the tragedy of the moment.

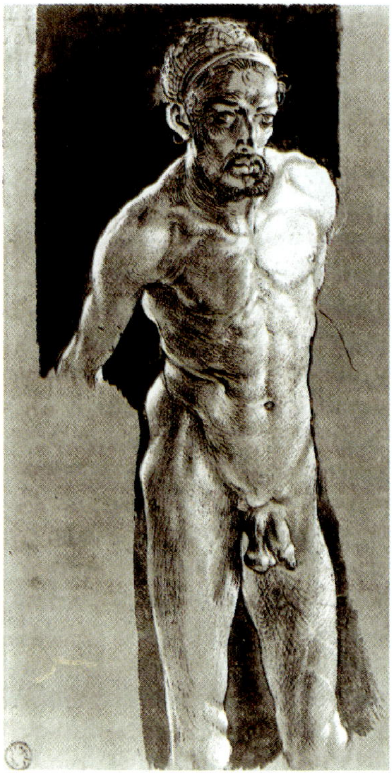

All of Dürer's works have one point in common: in their conception and composition they belong unreservedly to the Renaissance tradition, yet, in their detailed treatment, they are certainly indebted to Gothic art, as is evident in this work. This meticulously studied nude has been given an unusual pose and a highly expressive face. The light, which emanates from two different sources, models the figure's muscles and the folds of his skin, lending the portrait an air of levity, despite its predominant dark tones. To this end, the artist uses a wide range of grays to articulate the volumes, avoiding black so that even the darkest areas contribute to the extraordinary modeling. This work eloquently attests to the high degree of technical perfection reached by the artist in his lifetime.

Self-Portrait

Albrecht Dürer
(Nuremberg, 1471–1528)

- ca. 1506
- pen and India ink on gray paper
- Graphische Sammlung, Weimar

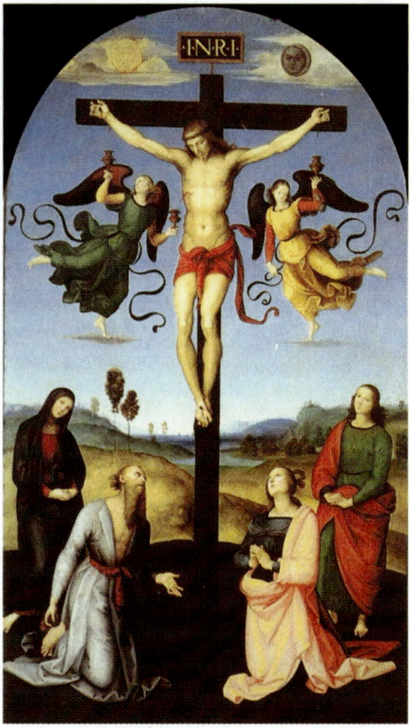

The Crucifixion

Raphael (Raffaello Santi or **Sanzio)**
(Urbino, 1483–Rome, 1520)

- 1503
- oil on panel
- 280.7 x 165.1 cm
- National Gallery, London

This work is part of a group of three altarpieces which the artist was commissioned to paint in his early period for the church of Città di Castello. Numerous elements in the panel call to mind Perugino, and certain compositional aspects are shared with works by Piero della Francesca. No pictorial element necessary to fascinate a viewer is lacking: great balance and harmony of composition, and a brilliant palette, so that compositional and chromatic rhythms interact. Christ's figure stands out at the center, contrasted against the blue sky. Such powerful contrasts enabled the artist to dispense with halos as means of enhancing his figures, as Christ's very skin glows, filling the painting with vitality, while his body's sinuous forms both capture attention and invite contemplation. Christ's body is carefully proportioned, stylized, yet without ever becoming deformed. This serene image of Christ is a far remove from the pathos of Flemish art, being more an icon of exceptional purity instead.

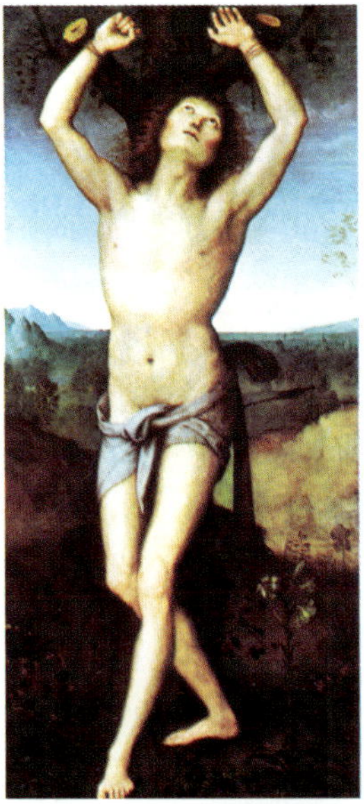

St. Sebastian

Pietro Perugino (Pietro Vannucci)
(Città della Pieve, near Perugia, Romagna, ca. 1448–Fontignano, near Perugia, 1523)

- oil on panel
- 174 x 88 cm
- Nationalmuseum, Stockholm

Pietro Perugino painted many renditions of this saint: in a variety of poses, alone and in company. In this work, he sought an innovative composition. The saint's arms, raised as he looks up to heaven, provide the air of mysticism that the artist strove to create. The legs are boldly foreshortened and the painterly handling of the figure recalls the work of Raphael, particularly the contours and the modeling of the volumes. This delicately treated semi-nude, depicted without the customary arrows piercing his sides, is highly erotic.

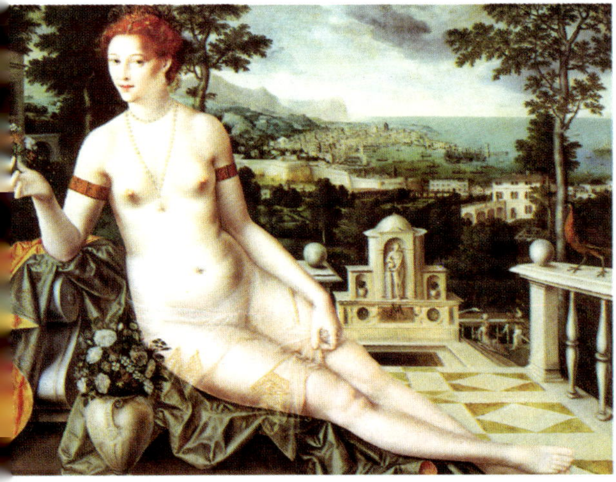

Venus

Quentin Massys (Matsys or Metsys)
(Louvain, 1466–Antwerp, 1530)

- oil on canvas
- 130 x 156 cm
- Nationalmuseum, Stockholm

Despite the cool emotionalism with which this nude has been treated, the figure radiates an ardent eroticism, both in her forms and her attitude. Her pubescent breasts seem to form part of the jewelry adorning her naked body, and her exposed genitals are covered with a delicate, gold-embroidered, transparent veil. Rather than a classical treatment of the flesh, the skin has a metallic appearance, an aesthetic feature that took root in this style of Mannerism, which betrays a certain degree of classicism as well as Italian influences.

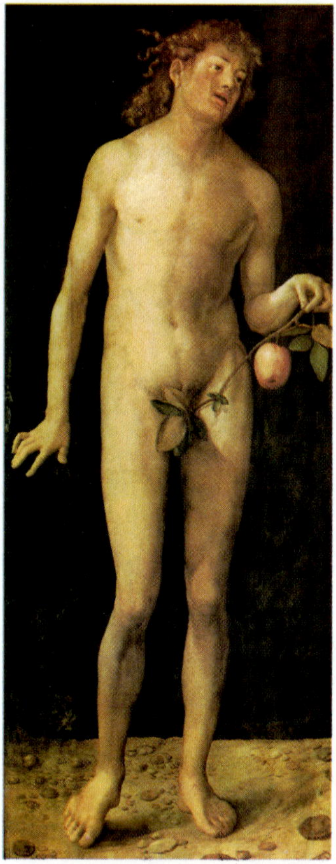

Adam

Albrecht Dürer
(Nuremberg, 1471–1528)

- 1507
- oil on panel
- 209 x 81 cm
- Museo del Prado, Madrid

This figure of Adam, along with an exquisite Eve, form a diptych in which Albrecht Dürer's handling of each figure varies subtly. With this figure the painter achieves a realistic, non-allegorical nude of beautiful proportions, despite the fact that they are not idealized. The figure's volumes resemble those of Michelangelo's sculpture of David. Indeed, its volumes and modeling exhibit affinities with Italian art. Adam's body is Apollonian, Mediterranean and Classical. The figure's tranquility is in keeping with the formal rhythm of the body, which is shown in a slight contrapposto. The naturalism of the nude recalls the serenity of sculptures from Classical Antiquity, although viewed through an intellectual filter that lends the figure utterly human qualities.

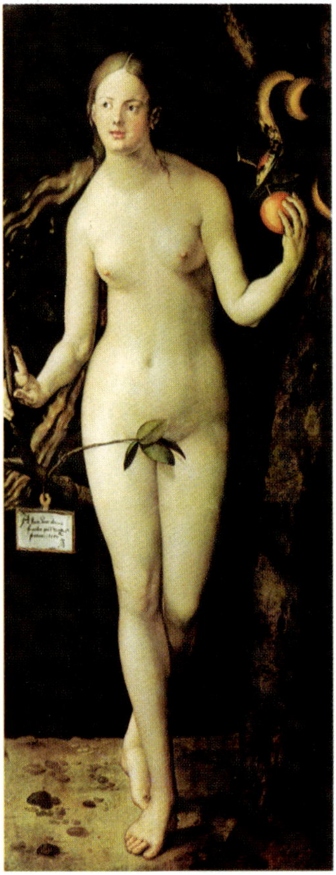

'wo panels, this one of Eve and one of Adam, form a diptych. 'he beauty of this figure is evoked by combining the Italian umanist spirit with certain Gothic elements, such as the pro- ounced slope of the shoulders and the bulging abdomen. Ionetheless, the anatomy does not represent an archetype, ut rather contemporary notions of beauty, which have influ- nced ideas of the ideal female body to this day. Dürer devoted nuch of his time to studying the mathematical laws of ideal uman proportions, beginning with the teachings of Euclid and 'itruvius. In the two panels of this diptych, the painter records is ideal notion of beauty. One extraordinary aspect is the sug- estion of movement in the figure of Eve, who, like Adam, vokes the sculptures of Classical Antiquity. The figure of Eve is elicately and precariously balanced owing to its slightly off- entered placement in the painting. The pale, luminous tones of er skin, which contrast with the tanned hues of her compan- on, also bear testimony to the aesthetic tastes of the period.

Albrecht Dürer
(Nuremberg, 1471–1528)

- 1507
- oil on panel
- 209 x 80 cm
- Museo del Prado, Madrid

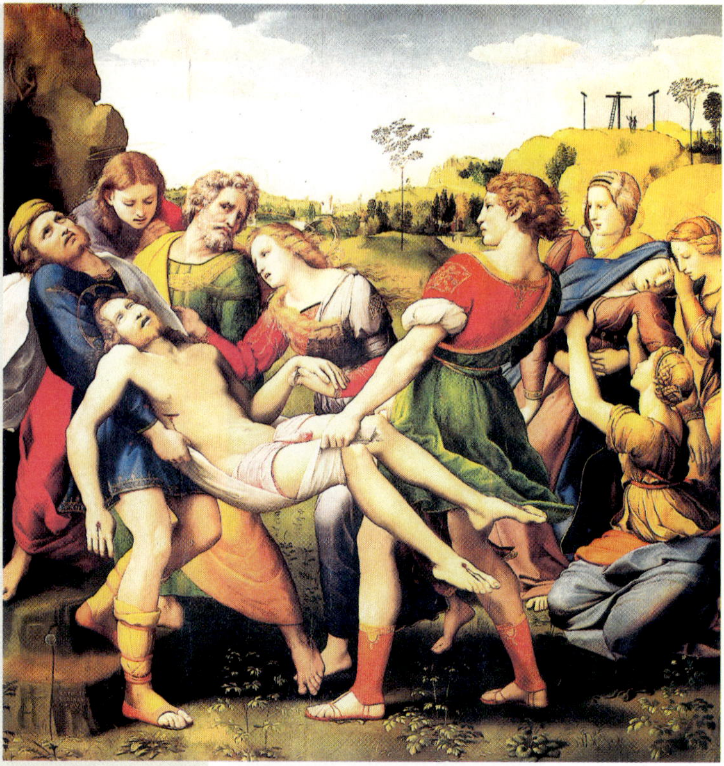

The Holy Burial

Raphael (**Raffaelo Santi** or **Sanzio**)
(Urbino, 1483–Rome, 1520)

- 1507
- oil on panel
- 184 x 176 cm
- Galleria Borghese, Rome

Christ's body presents a series of significant features. To begin with, the drafting is more concerned with the outlines of forms than the anatomy of the body. Since the flesh colors are so brilliantly illuminated, the modeling of the bodies is minimal, although there are tonal values so subtle that all the anatomical details can be inferred. The necessary shadows are accentuated through sfumato, used only along those outlines that are least illuminated. The treatment of the nude lends it a particularly mysterious and mystic air. Christ approaches spiritual purity, and is surrounded by vivid colors that significantly accentuate this characteristic. Jesus' human state is also evident in his weight, which is so great that those carrying him are making a great effort, reflected in their gestures and facial expressions. Although the scene presents a tragic moment, expressed in the protagonist's face, the painter has avoided emphasizing the physical evidence—such as the blood and the wounds—of his horrible martyrdom.

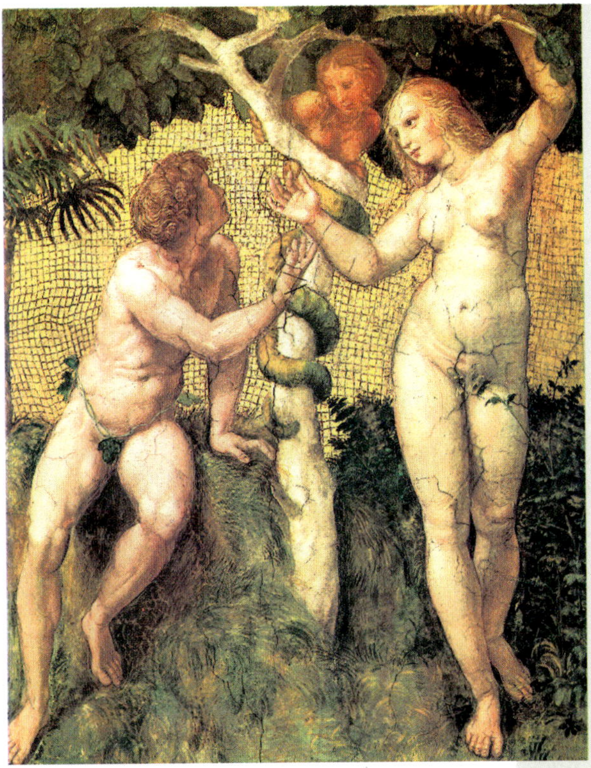

The figure of Adam, portrayed with a muscular, handsome and well-proportioned build, is the result of technically complex foreshortening, whereby the extreme torsion of the upper body is combined with frontally rendered legs, which are bent because he is seated. Eve, voluptuous and sensual, is depicted in a harmonious contrapposto that enhances her beauty. The play of her hips and powerful thighs accentuate the curves of her figure. Her torso is also twisted, and her left leg foreshortened, as if her movement had been frozen in time. Eve's body combines a slender, well-proportioned torso with a swollen abdomen and long legs. The treatment of light lends volume to both nudes, whose extreme realism is striking.

Adam and Eve

Raphael (Raffaello Santi or **Sanzio)**
(Urbino, 1483–Rome, 1520)

- 1508
- fresco
- 120 x 105 cm
- cupola in the Stanza della Segnatura, Vatican City

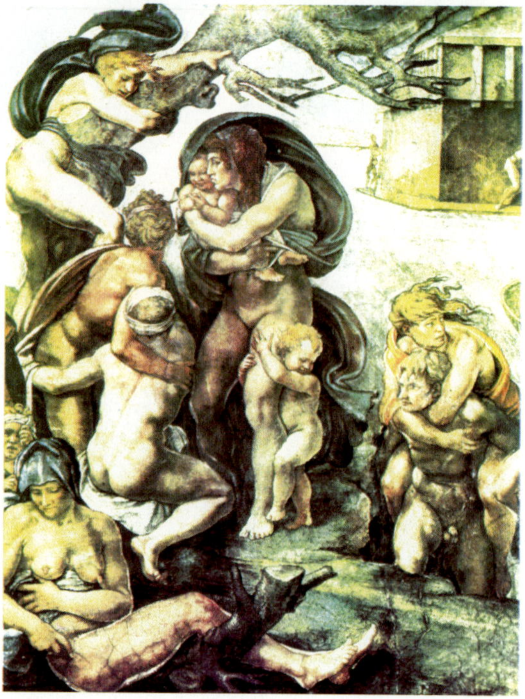

The Deluge (detail of ceiling)
Michelangelo (Michelangelo Buonarroti)
(Caprese, Tuscany, 1475 –Rome, 1564)

- 1508–9
- fresco
- 280 x 570 cm (entire fresco)
- Sistine Chapel, Vatican

This painting depicts the Deluge as recounted in the Bible. The present detail shows a group of figures fleeing from the catastrophe, all of which are naked and have muscular, well-proportioned bodies in heroic poses. In this monumental, tragic scene, the figures perfectly convey the terror and helplessness of humanity in the face of the tragedy. Their full bodies bear witness to the artist's mastery of draftsmanship. Yet he considered himself to be first and foremost a sculptor, hence his penchant for rendering volumes by means of careful modeling. The artist's interest in showing the degeneration of the body is also evident here, for example, in the female figure on the left, who shows clear signs of aging.

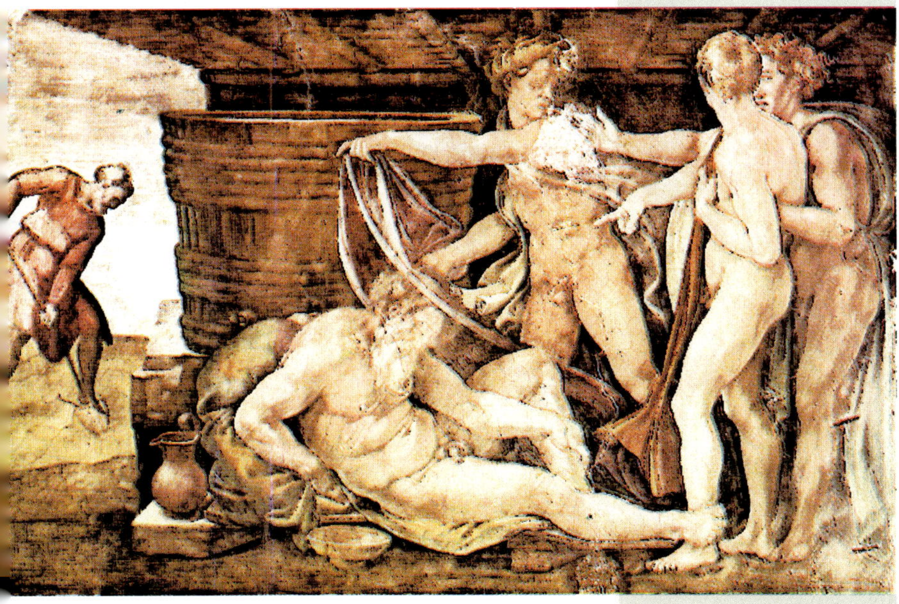

The Drunkenness of Noah (detail of ceiling)
Michelangelo (Michelangelo Buonarroti)
(Caprese, Tuscany, 1475 –Rome, 1564)

- 1509
- fresco
- 170 x 260 cm
- Sistine Chapel, Vatican

this biblical scene, Noah is shown lying next to a jug, eeping off his drunkenness after imbibing generous nounts of wine. His daughters rush to cover his naked ody, for they wish to conceal their father's drunken state order to save their own honor. The classical beauty of e nudes, some of which have rather androgynous pects, is one of their most notable features, although, rough his peculiar style, Michelangelo sought to establh a human standard that goes beyond anatomy taken om real life. In biblical scenes by the artist such as this, e bodies of the figures are treated like sculptures, exhibng a powerful build and daring foreshortening, positively iallenging the viewer to discern the two-dimensional ane on which the plastic volumes are rendered.

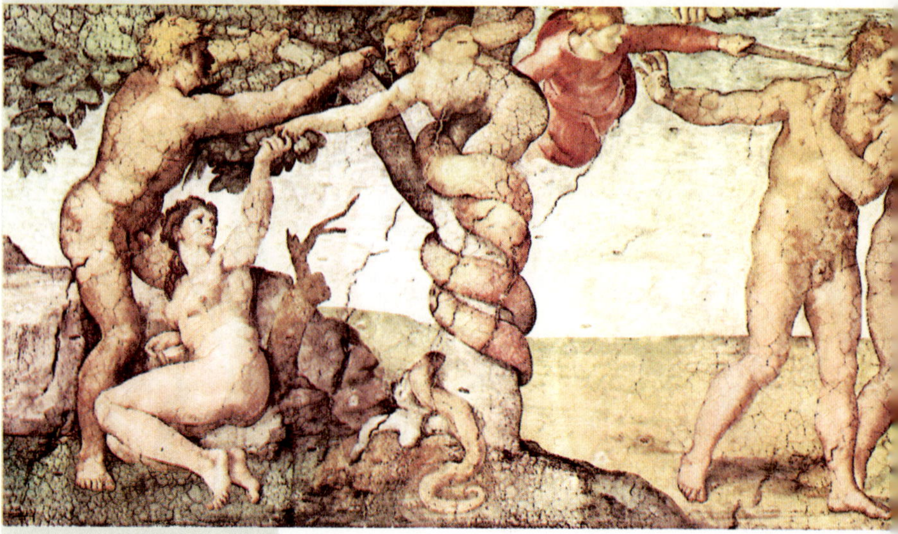

Original Sin (detail of ceiling)

Michelangelo (Michelangelo Buonarroti)
(Caprese, Tuscany, 1475 –Rome, 1564)

- 1509–10
- fresco
- 280 x 570 cm (entire fresco)
- Sistine Chapel, Vatican

Two scenes from the biblical story of the Fall of humanity are depicted in this magnificent fresco. In the center appears a large tree around which a serpent is coiled. Instead of having a serpent's head, the body of the creature ends in that of a woman, who is shown offering the forbidden fruit to Adam and Eve on the left, who take it. To the right of the tree Adam and Eve are punished for the sin they have committed: both figures are shown being expelled from Paradise by an angel. The nudes in this scene represent a veritable lesson in anatomy, demonstrating the artist's profound knowledge of the human body. The modeling and volumes are rendered naturalistically with a monumental style bearing a closer resemblance to that of a sculptor than that of a painter. The figures on the left convey tranquility and peace, in their gentle gestures and in Eve's beautiful face, whereas on the right their faces reveal dramatic expressions, betraying their fear of God's punishment, and are deliberately made ugly. The nude bodies of the figures are powerful, exhibiting a painstakingly executed musculature. The lines heighten the sensuality of the figures, attesting to Michelangelo's keen interest in human anatomy.

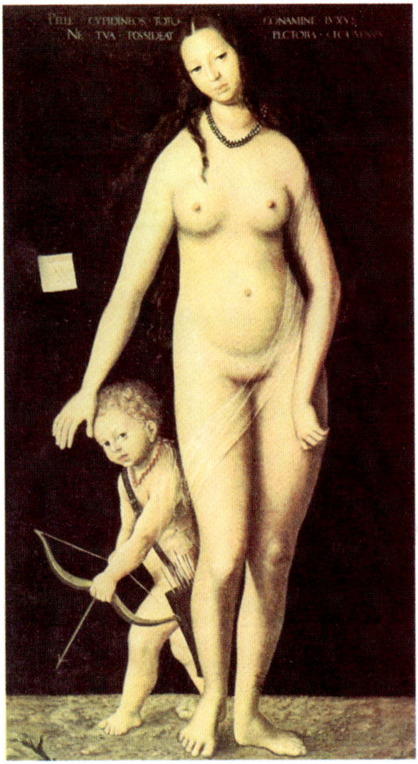

Venus and Cupid

Lucas Cranach the Elder
(Kronach, Franconia, 1472–Weimar, 1553)

- 1509
- oil on canvas
- 213 x 102 cm
- Hermitage, St. Petersburg

Before being acquired by the Museum in 1769, this painting belonged to the Brühl Collection, Dresden.

This painting is the first known nude with a mythological theme in German art. It is far removed from typical Italian Renaissance representations of the goddess, and is unlike any later works by the artist. Its message is conveyed in the Latin couplet inscribed across the top of the painting, attributed to Scheurl or Sibutus: "Flee from Cupid and all of his pleasures, lest Venus take your heart prisoner." Therefore, the painting warns the viewer of the dangers of Venus, the Roman goddess of love, and Cupid, her son, who shoots his arrows to light the flame of desire in the hearts of mortals. The goddess, who stands before a dark background devoid of distracting elements, has a slender, sensual body draped in a delicate transparent veil. She appears at once unapproachable, impassive and self-assured, the living image of an invincible woman. Cupid is shown drawing his arrow, preparing to shoot it at his next victim when Venus commands it.

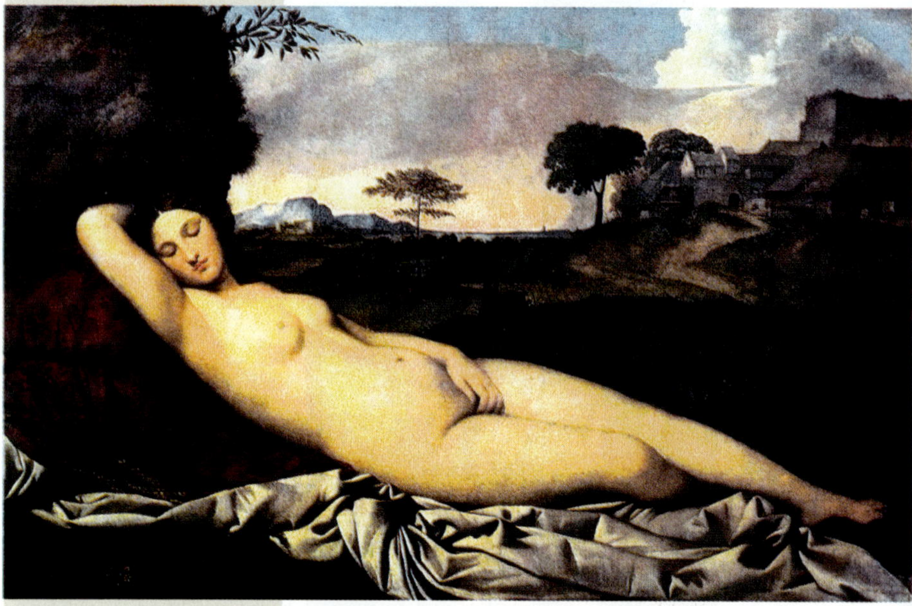

Venus Sleeping

Giorgione (Giorgio da Castelfranco or **Giorgio Barbarelli)**
(Castelfranco, ca. 1477 –Venice, 1510)

- ca. 1509
- oil on canvas
- 108 x 175 cm
- Gemäldegalerie, Dresden

The exquisitely elongated proportions of this nude figure give a clear example of the Renaissance ideal of female beauty. In addition to poeticism, it combines great sensuality and charm. The woman's sinuous forms invite the viewer's gaze to linger, while a series of details render her pose openly erotic: her right fore-arm, placed behind her head, causes her breast to rise and stand firm; her head is slightly inclined, face relaxed in sleep; and her left hand seems to toy with her pubis, while her crossed legs draw her thighs together. The artist clearly marshaled these elements with the aim of suggestiveness in mind. He succeeded in integrating the figure into the landscape with great intelligence. By placing Venus against a darker area, Giorgione brings out the luminosity of her body.

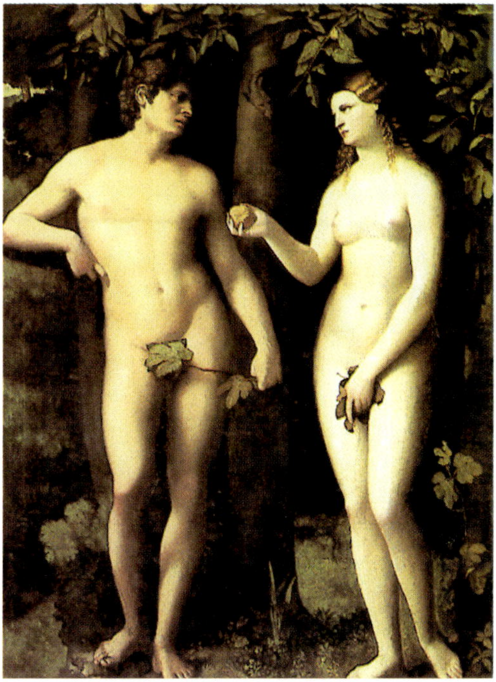

Adam and Eve

Palma Vecchio (Jacomo Palma)
(Serina, Bergamo, ca. 1480–Venice, 1528)

- ca. 1510
- oil on canvas
- 292 x 152 cm
- Herzog Anton Ulrich Museum, Braunschweig

Although Palma Vecchio grew up in the Quattrocento, he adopted the new ideas of the Cinquecento in his paintings, particularly those of figures set in a landscape, such as this one. Here the artist has used the tree and vegetation to create a dark, dense background, against which the figures' pale flesh tones stand out clearly. Stylized along Renaissance lines, the elongated figures and compact forms, modeled subtly with shade, breathe great sensuality. Both the heroic body of Adam and the stylized body of Eve have been idealized, in keeping with Renaissance notions, when the study and celebration of human anatomy had become an obsession. The figures display notable expressive force and the canvas pays homage to the human body in its most humanist manifestation. These figures are extremely academic in both conception and execution.

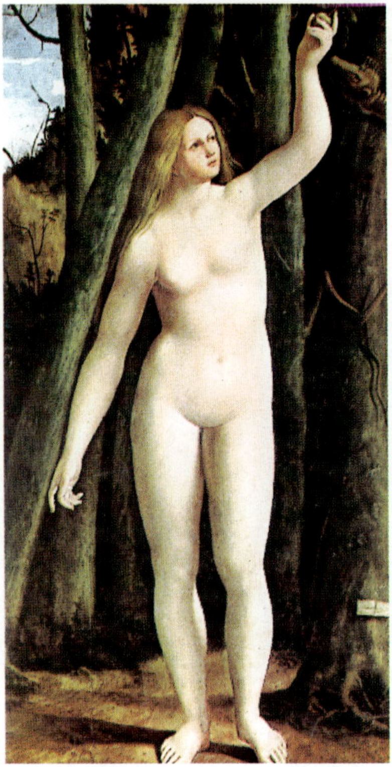

Eve

Marco Basatti
(Venice, 1460?–1525)

- oil on panel
- 150 x 82 cm
- Galleria Borghese, Rome

In this painting, Marco Basatti portrays the figure of Eve in much the way his contemporaries north of the Alps would have depicted a Venus: her head is disproportionately small in size, and Basatti's Eve recalls Classical sculptures of allegorical or mythological figures in the roundness of her forms, the smooth, marble-like quality of her skin, the dramatic position of her arms and her pose. She lacks the sensuality that one expects of nudes. Indeed, her sexual organs, although not concealed, appear unfinished: her breasts are executed with minimal modeling and her genitals are practically nonexistent. Moreover, the figure's contrapposto pose fails to lend even the subtlest erotic aura to the figure.

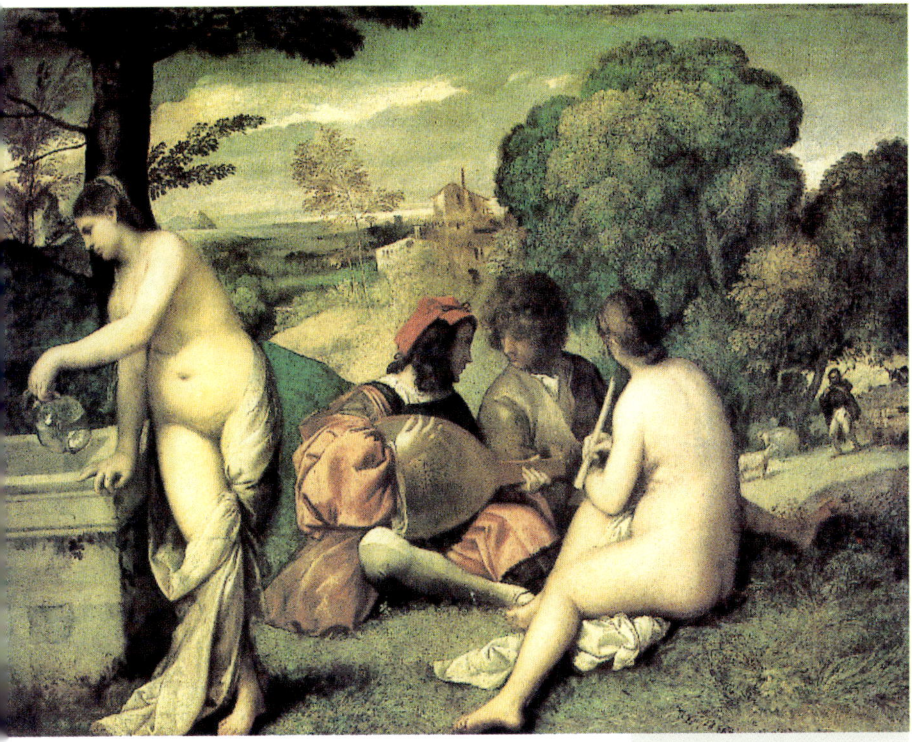

This is a highly sensual work, in which two naked women, utterly unconcerned with their nudity, are depicted in the company of two musicians, who are discussing the piece they are about to play. The woman sitting on the grass parts part in the conversation, while the woman standing up, languid and distracted, pours water from a glass pitcher into a well. The nudes are extremely elegant, as much in form as in execution. Their skin reflects the golden light that pervades the landscape. The dark background makes the women's bodies appear luminous, imbuing the scene with an atmosphere of tranquility and desire. This is an outstanding example of the work of Giorgione, exhibiting a sophisticated Venetian palette while forging a link between figure and landscape.

Le Concert Champêtre

Giorgione (Giorgio da Castelfranco or Giorgio Barbarelli)
(Castelfranco, ca. 1477 –Venice, 1510)

- ca. 1510
- oil on canvas
- 110 x 138 cm
- Musée du Louvre, Paris

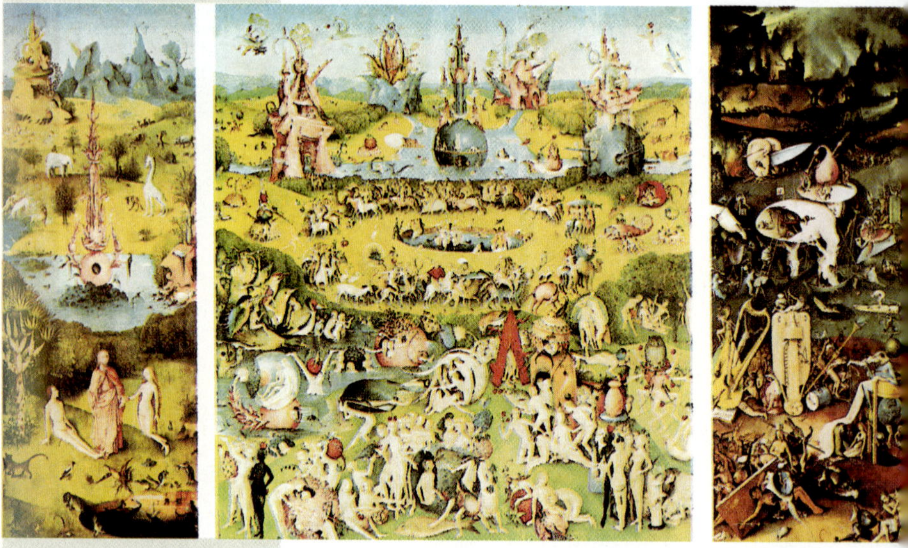

The Garden of Earthly Delights

Hieronymus Bosch (Jerome van Aeken)
('s-Hertogenbosch, Brabant, ca. 1450–1516)

- ca. 1510
- oil on canvas
- 220 x 389 cm
- Museo del Prado, Madrid

This triptych portrays the genesis and end of the world. When closed, it shows a scene from Genesis. When open, the right wing depicts the creation of hell, the left wing the creation of the world and the middle panel earthly life. The landscapes are populated with imaginary creatures, beasts, plants with human forms and a multitude of human nudes that recall worms burrowing their way through a large piece of fruit that i the world. In hell naked sinners are subjected to various forms of torture by demons or with contraptions. Bosch's work, whic is at a unique historical crossroads of art history, conveys the conflict of ideas of its day, and is open to all manner of interpretation: some consider it to be moralistic, others as an attack on heretics and some even contend that the work itself is heretical. In any case, it is the dreamscape of a visionary.

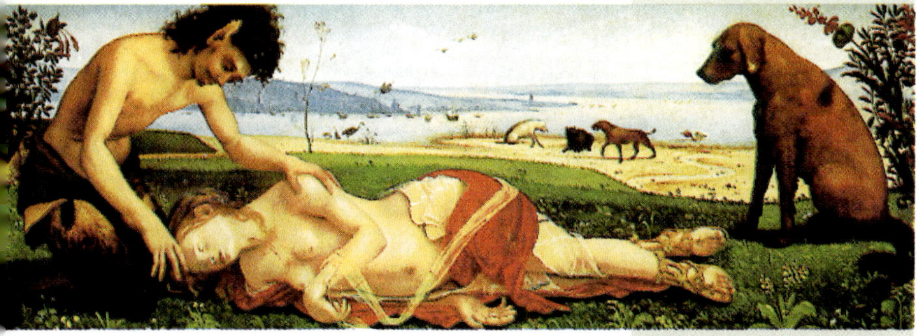

Death of Procris

Piero di Cosimo (Piero di Lorenzo di Chimenti)
(Florence, 1461/62–1521)

- ca. 1495
- oil on panel
- 65.4 x 184.2 cm
- National Gallery, London

ephalus was married to Procris. Doubting his wife's fidelity, e decided to test her faithfulness. Humiliated, she retreated the forest, where Diana gave her a spear and a hunting og. Cephalus, feeling remorse for what he had done, went find her. Later, Procris, resentful of her husband, followed m on a hunt, concealing herself in some bushes; Cephalus istook the movement of the branches for a hidden boar, and lled her by mistake. This painting shows Procris being ourned by a satyr. Her naked body lies peacefully on the ass, where it stands out against the luminous background. ne treatment of the volumes is realistic, unlike the modeling the shadows. The study of the forms and the forlorn pose the satyr lend great pathos to the scene. This, and other orks by Piero, combines fantasy, elegy, emotion and poetry.

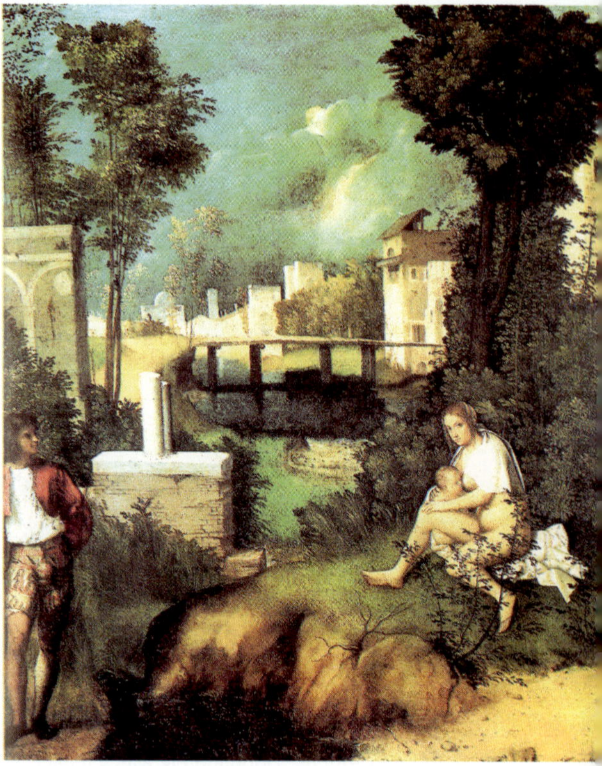

The Tempest

Giorgione (Giorgio Barbarelli)
(Castelfranco, Veneto, 1477/78–Venice, 1510)

- ca. 1510
- oil on canvas
- 78 x 72 cm
- Galleria dell'Accademia, Venice

The group of elements in this painting would appear to represent a strange and encrypted code. Some say they can be linked to the cabalism and mysticism so common in Venice at the time. On the right, a young mother is seated on a blanket, which partly covers the baby she is suckling, while staring out at the viewer with disarming candidness, as if in another reality. The naturalism of the nude is enhanced by elements in the foreground, which help to establish a sense of pictorial depth. One unusual feature is the podium with two truncated columns. On the left appears a nobleman staring longingly at the woman. With this work the artist takes Venetian painting one step further by making the landscape itself an important aspect of the painting, whose atmospheric treatment deserves special attention.

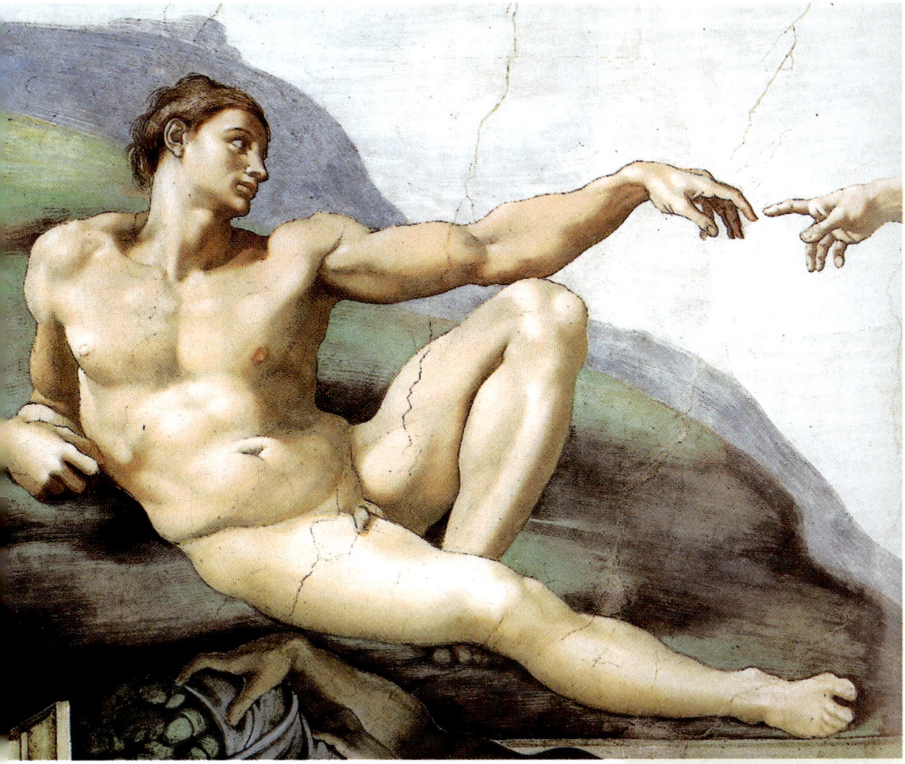

The Creation of Adam

Michelangelo (Michelangelo Buonarroti)
(Caprese, Tuscany, 1475 –Rome, 1564)

- ca. 1510
- fresco
- 280 x 570 cm
- Sistine Chapel, Vatican City, Rome

fter creating the world and all its creatures, God created ıan in his own image, fashioned from dust. In this work dam's hand is shown touching that of God, who thus reathes life into him. This fresco features one of the finest udes ever to have been painted. The heroic figure of Adam achieved by a virtuoso, sculptural modeling, with subtle ghlights and few, yet perfectly placed, shadows. The propor- ons of his body are based on an ideal of male beauty that urvives to this day. It is foreshortened with remarkable real- m, as can be observed in the arm supporting the weight of ıe body or in the elegant bending of the upright torso. This a monumental work and the artist, who regarded himself remost as a sculptor, reveals his mastery of draftsmanship this figure, which recalls a work of sculpture in its striking ıree-dimensionality.

Avarice

Albrecht Dürer
(Nuremberg, 1471–1528)

- 1507
- oil on canvas
- 35 x 29 cm
- Kunsthistorisches Museum, Vienna

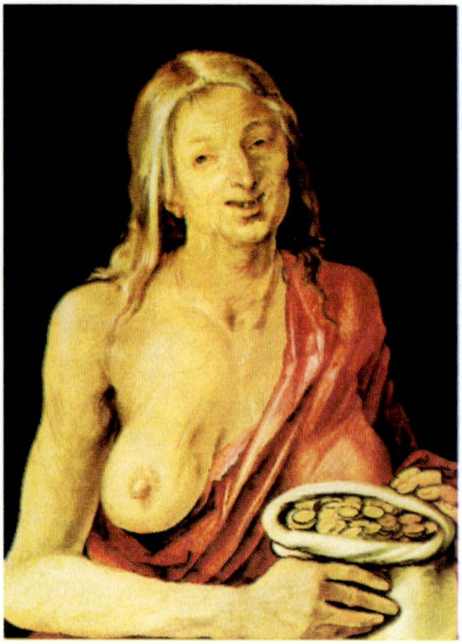

In this allegorical painting, Avarice is represented as a naked crone, whose grotesque physique and painterly handling bring out all the meanness of this mortal sin. Seldom in the history of painting, with the exception of Brueghel, Cranach and Bosch has an artist rendered so unsightly a figure, which, here is achieved with hideous features, skin that is as wrinkled as paper and a breast that, at one time large, is now shriveled like an empty wineskin.

The Baptism of Jesus

Giovanni Battista da Conegliano (Cima da Conegliano)
(Conegliano, Venetia, ca. 1459–ca. 1517)

- ca. 1510
- oil on panel
- 350 x 210 cm
- San Giovanni in Bragora, Venice

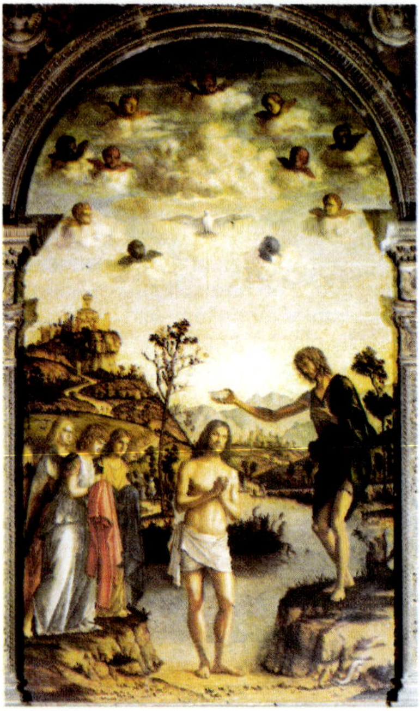

The nude figure in this panel seems to alternate between staid Realism and something more physically involving. Its soft tonalities permit skilful modeling that creates the illusion of depth no less effectively than the foreshortening of the limbs. To avoid affectedness, the artist eschewed the usual contrapposto, depicting Jesus in an almost vertical stance instead, with only a slight inclination and twist of his trunk.

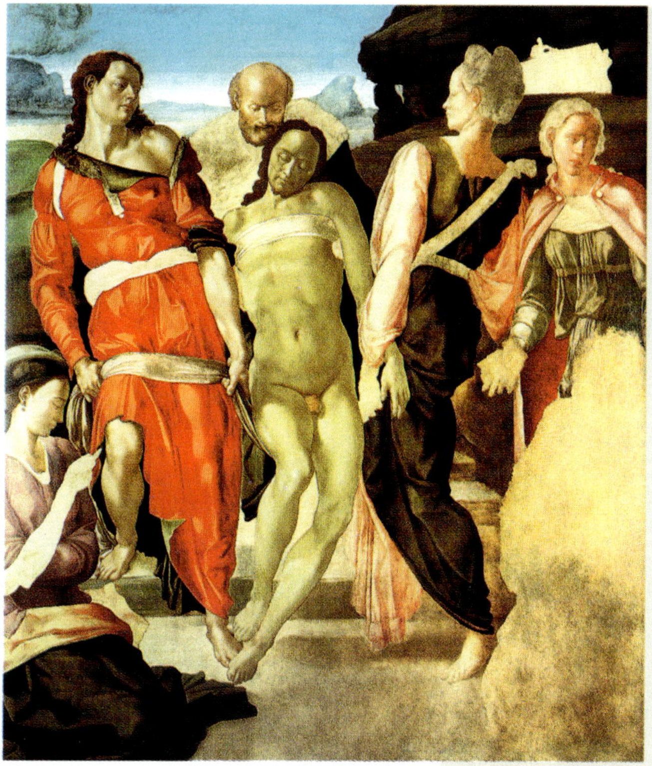

The Entombment

Michelangelo (Michelangelo Buonarroti)
(Caprese, Tuscany, 1475 –Rome, 1564)

- 1500–1501
- oil on panel
- 161.7 x 149.9 cm
- National Gallery, London

his panel may not be a real Michelangelo, for it contains umerous corrections. It could be the work of one of his upils, corrected afterward by the master. The figures embody e very monumentality that marks this artist's extraordinary euvre, and the harmonious composition offsets the dramatic nsion engendered by the scene's intense light and profusion colors. The delicate, naked figure of Christ is finely outlined nd his legs foreshortened. The proportions are idealized and e volumes, treated with diffuse, light hues to avoid a hard- ning of the forms, is reminiscent of marble sculptures in hich the transition from light to shadow is smooth (we must ot forget that Michelangelo considered himself to be first and remost a sculptor). This same pictorial treatment would later e taken up by Salvador Dalí in many of his nudes.

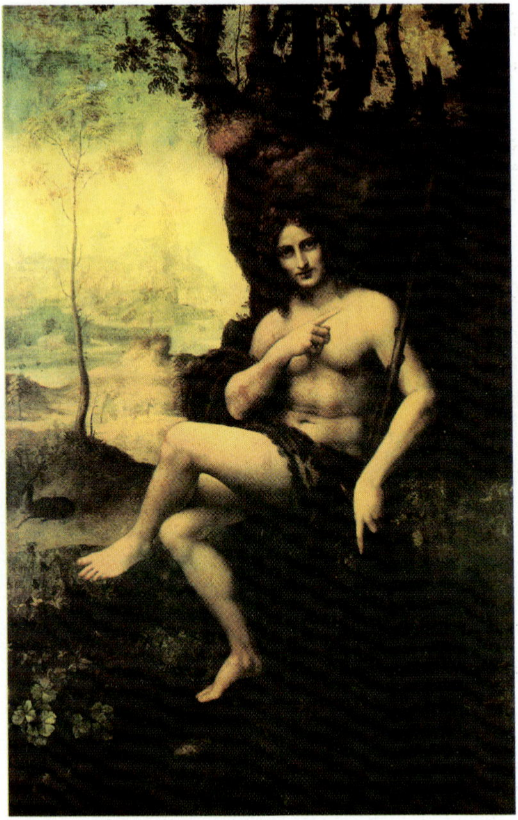

Bacchus

Leonardo da Vinci
(Vinci, Tuscany, 1452–Le Clos-Lucé, Amboise, 1519)

- ca. 1515
- oil on panel
- 177 x 115 cm
- Musée du Louvre, Paris

The nude in this painting exudes a sensual beauty. Curiously enough, the model is the same as the one used for his St. John the Baptist, a man with ambiguous features, which allowed him to play with the aesthetic duality of masculinity and femininity. Yet it was not sexual duality that Leonardo sought in his work, but, rather, as he affirms in his Treatise on Painting, he had "... two principal objectives: the person and the intention within his soul." The face of this sitter resembles that of the Mona Lisa, painted about 1505. The figure's modeling and well-defined volumes make it appear to emerge from the shadows, while the highlighted areas transform the skin into a source of golden light. The sfumato technique with which the forms are rendered creates diffuse shadows.

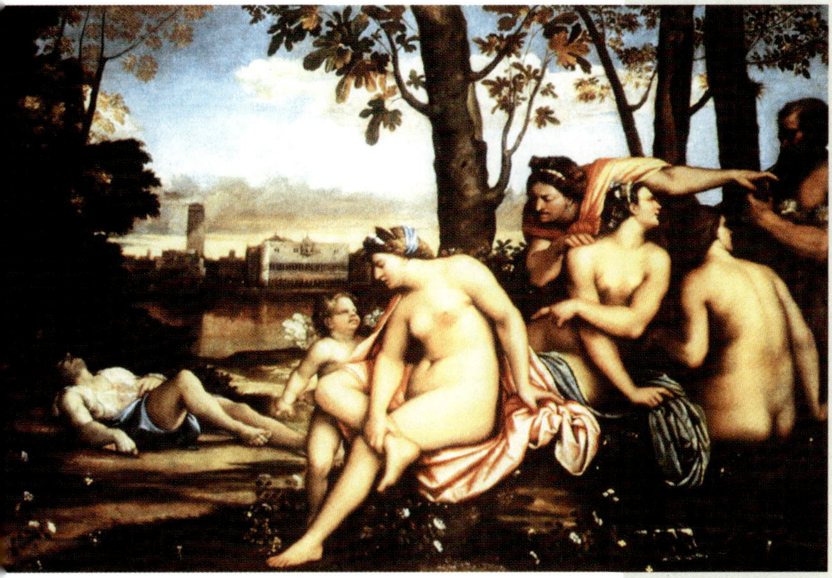

The Death of Adonis

Sebastiano del Piombo (Sebastiano Luciani)
(Venice, ca. 1485–Rome, 1547)

- ca. 1512
- oil on canvas
- 189 x 295 cm
- Galleria degli Uffizi, Florence

'he death of Adonis—murdered by Mars, who had turned imself into a wild boar out of jealousy—is a mythological ıeme that has been taken up by artists time and again. Yet ıis scene substitutes the drama inherent in the episode for paradisiacal vision, in which lewdness and eroticism pre-ominate. Thus the main subject (the death of Adonis) is llocated to the background and, curiously enough, is por-ayed dressed while Venus, his lover, and her nymphs ppear naked in the foreground. This contrast between the ressed and nude bodies accentuates the eroticism of the cene. The nudes have been executed with the utmost care nd introduce a sense of rhythmic movement to the compo-ition. The sensuality of the three women is heightenede y their attitudes, blurred contours and the way they present ıemselves to the viewer, especially the central nymph, /hose arms are crossed under her breasts and whose torso twisted, revealing her splendid anatomy.

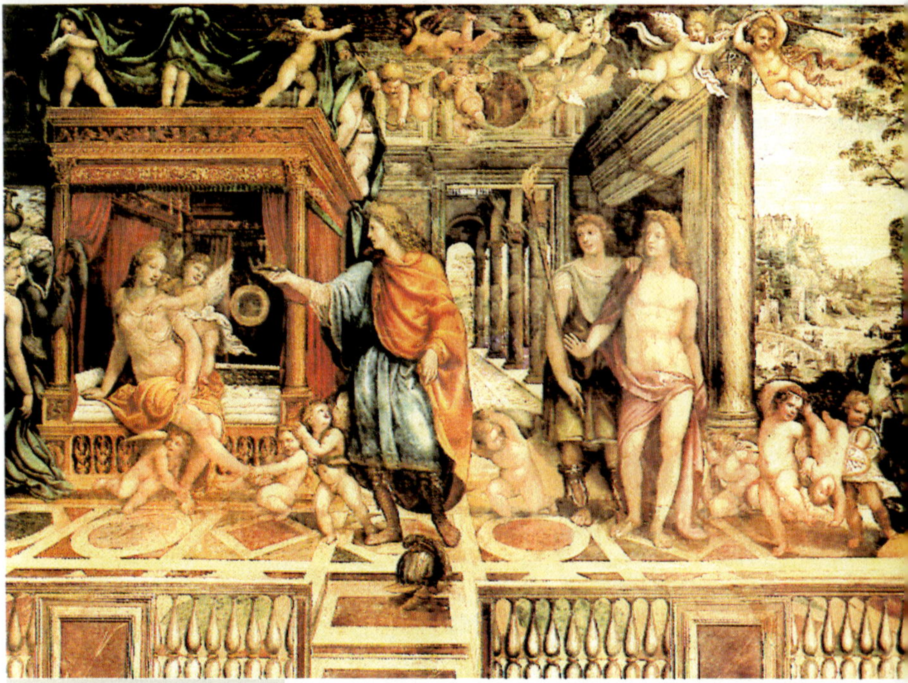

The Marriage of Alexander and Roxane

Il Sodoma (Giovanni Antonio Bazzi)
(Vercelli, 1477–Siena, 1549)

- 1516–17
- fresco
- 460 x 670 cm
- Villa Farnesina, Rome

The protagonists in this work are Alexander the Great, King of Macedonia, and his newly wed wife, Roxane, daughter of a Bactrian nobleman. They are presented with all the solemnity that befits the event and the legend surrounding the historical personage of Alexander. Curiously, the painter has presented the two figures as if they were Venus and Mars, together with various large cherubs, no doubt to recall the love between them, in a composition that illustrates how painters of the time blended mythology, history and a large measure of imagination and fantasy in their work. Roxane is seated on a bed covered by a baldachin, awaiting her husband, who appears to the right in a heroic pose. In keeping with an established practice of the Renaissance, the figures, with their well-proportioned bodies, are juxtaposed with a number of architectural elements, the aim of which was to draw a parallel between the meticulous study of the human body and the precise proportions of the architecture.

Pietà

Andrea del Sarto (Andrea d'Agnolo di Francesco)
(Florence, 1486–1530)

- 1320?
- fresco
- 182 x 113 cm
- Galleria dell'Accademia, Venice

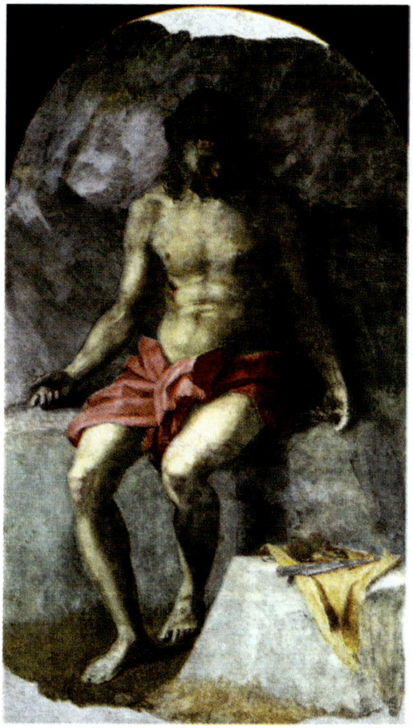

Del Sarto's style, insofar as it concerns his treatment of color, has characteristics typical of Venetian art. The presentation of Jesus solo in a pietà is highly unusual in traditional iconography. The seated figure is depicted in frontal foreshortening, the draftsmanship perfect, although no attempt is made to define the forms perfectly. The shadows and light are very much in the style of Leonardo da Vinci, with sfumato darker and lighter tones merging atmospherically. Del Sarto combines techniques from a preceding generation to create an eclectic personal style in the service of a moderate yet dramatic expressionism.

Anatomical Studies

Leonardo da Vinci
(Vinci, Tuscany, 1452–Le Clos-Lucé, Amboise, 1519)

- ca. 1513
- drawing in black ink
- anatomical sketchbooks (Vol. V, p. 22 r.)
- Royal Collection, Windsor Castle

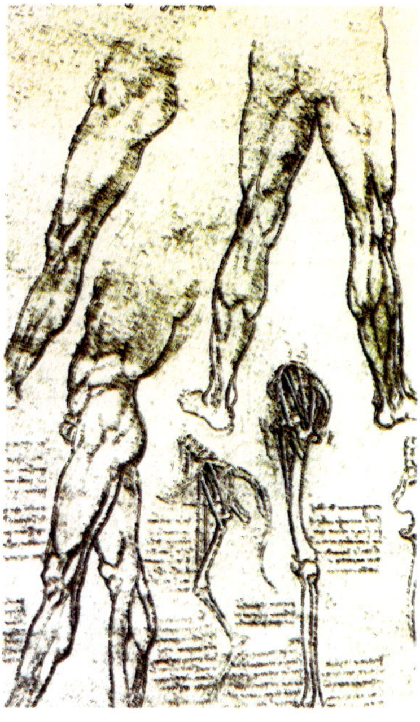

At a time when the Inquisition was persecuting those who dissected corpses, Leonardo carried out an in-depth study of the structure of the human body, using either living models or cadavers. His investigations remain valid to this day. His resolute and scientifically just draftsmanship here reveals the depth of his interest in human anatomy, which, in this work, is treated comparatively alongside the hind leg of a horse.

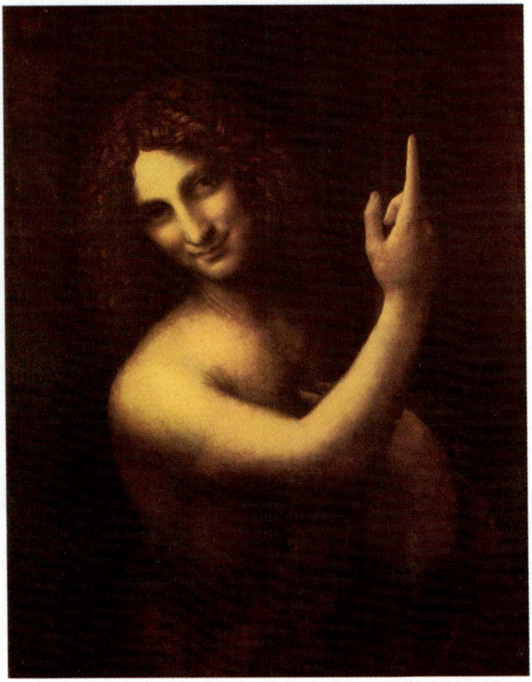

St. John the Baptist

Leonardo da Vinci
(Vinci, Tuscany, 1452–
Le Clos-Lucé, Amboise, 1519)

- 1513–16
- oil on panel
- 69 x 57 cm
- Musée du Louvre, Paris

This work belongs among the most beautiful nudes painted by Leonardo da Vinci. In fact, owing to its ambiguous nature, the face could perfectly well be the same as that in the Mona Lisa, although it was painted many years earlier. The flesh tones, modeled with extreme sensitivity, lend the figure tender and sensual qualities. It appears as if Leonardo's interest in anatomy were relegated to the background here, for the focus of this work would seem to lie in the spiritual realm. The body emerges from the darkness, scarcely revealing the saint's soft skin. Despite the darkness that envelops the figure, the skin is exhibits rich, warm hues. The saint's relaxed gesture and serene facial expression are perhaps the most compelling features of this work, which would seem to prefigure Caravaggio's use of chiaroscuro. The torso's volumes are defined largely by the artist's treatment of the shadows. With impasto he creates highlights, displaying an unprecedented painterly technique. The outlines of the figure are blurred on account of Leonardo's characteristic use of sfumato.

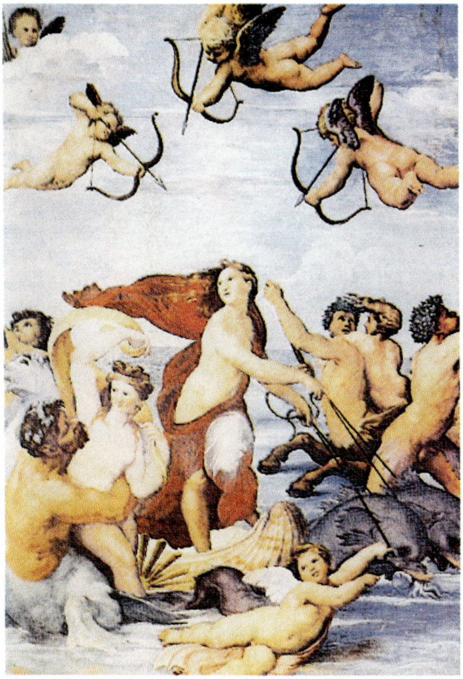

Classical mythology Galatea was a sea nymph with whom e Cyclops Polyphemus became infatuated. According to vid, however, she preferred a young shepherd called Acis. hen the latter two were discovered together by olyphemus, Galatea jumped into the sea. Acis, crushed by rock hurled at him by Polyphemus, was then turned into a ream and followed Galatea. Among cherubs and anthropo- orphic creatures Galatea is embraced by Acis, who has ready been partly transformed into a river. With this paint- g Raphael has created a freely conceived composition full color and movement, with a blue background against nich the warm complexions of the figures shine splendidly. though these are gods, their human aspect is in keeping ith the Renaissance notion that human beings are the cen- r of the universe. The body must therefore be perfect and, hen depicted, should be the purest expression of ideal auty. The painting embraces typical classical forms and e naked figures, with their dynamic gestures and bold col- s, move in a heavenly atmosphere of sensuality.

Galatea

Raphael (Raffaello Santi or **Sanzio)**
(Urbino, 1483–Rome, 1520)

- 1511–12
- fresco
- 300 x 220 cm
- Villa Farnesina, Rome

Flora

Titian (Tiziano Vecellio di Gregorio)
(Pieve di Cadore, Veneto, 1488/89–Venice, 1576)

- 1514
- oil on canvas
- 80 x 63.5 cm
- Galleria degli Uffizi, Florence

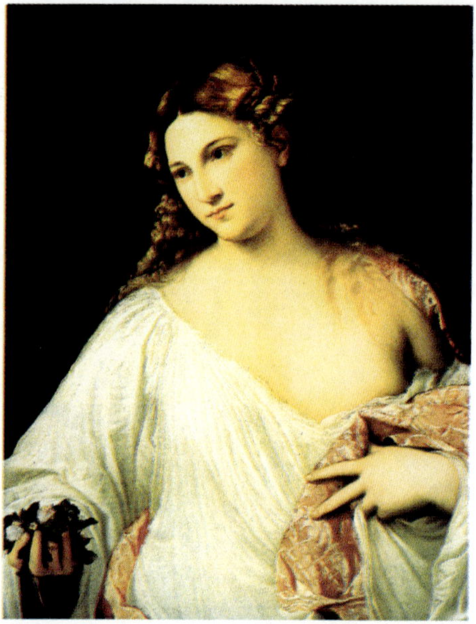

Although this Flora is highly sensual, the treatment of the figure ultimately evokes a saint, not a goddess. The serene facial expression and the submissive inclination of the head contrast with the libertine pose of the torso. Although this is a seminude, the study of light falling on the figure's clothed areas as well as certain details serve to heighten her sensuality.

Sacred and Profane Love

Titian (Tiziano Vecellio di Gregorio)
(Pieve di Cadore, Veneto, 1488/89–Venice, 1576)

- ca. 1515
- oil on canvas
- 118 x 279 cm
- Galleria Borghese, Rome

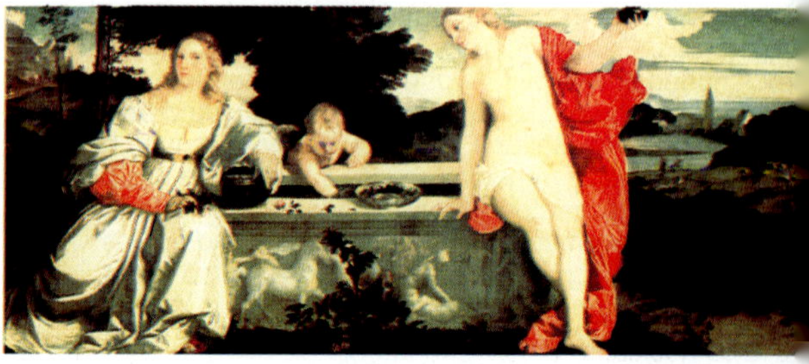

A balanced composition, with skillfully executed figures and an intelligent application of light and color, this enigmatic allegory personifies two types of love: while both are sensual, sacred love is shown here to embody abundance, plenitude and nobility, symbolized by a woman wearing sumptuous clothing, while profane love represents beauty, sexual attraction and provocation. Yet, for all her bare skin, the second figure seems indeed to be lacking something.

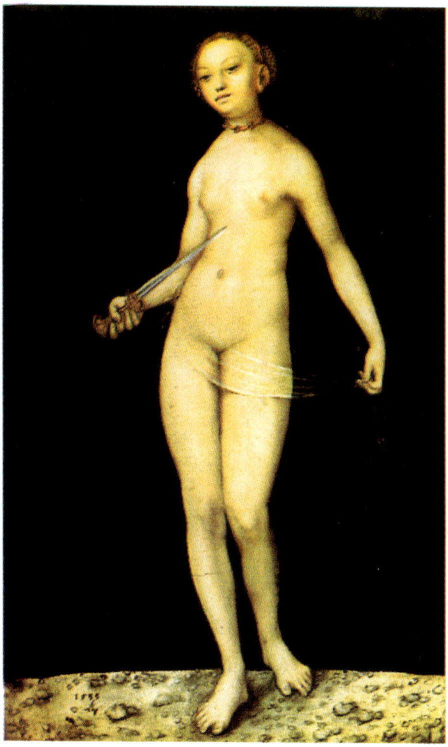

Lucretia

Lucas Cranach the Elder
(Kronach, Franconia, 1472–Weimar, 1553)

- 1515
- tempera on panel
- 35.5 x 21.5 cm
- Gemäldegalerie Dahlem, Berlin

fter being raped by her brother-in-law Sextus, the son of ome's last emperor, Tarquinius Superbus "the Proud," ucretia took her life in order to save her family's name. This ude, the very embodiment of cool elegance and ardent sen-uality, is one of Cranach the Elder's most impressive. The gure is set against a black background for no other reason an to draw the viewer's undivided attention to the woman's udity and her gesture of suicide. She is depicted in a static, ontrapposto pose, and has large thighs, the breasts of an dolescent, sloping shoulders, a long neck and a languid verall appearance. The erotic features of the portrait are as ıbtle as they are effective, beginning with her coiffure and recious necklace, which lend the nude a certain opulence. he transparent gauze accentuates the refined elegance and ensuality of the figure.

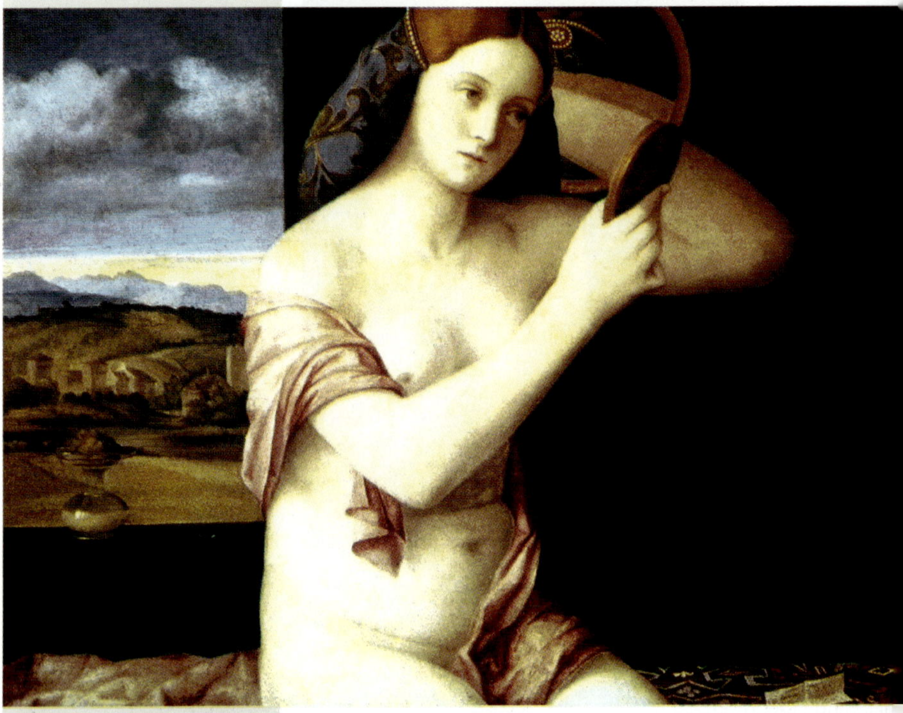

Woman with a Mirror

Giovanni Bellini (Giambellino)
(Venice, ca. 1430-1516)

- 1515
- poplar panel
- 62 x 79 cm
- Kunsthistorisches Museum, Vienna

The idealized anatomy of this sensual, elegant nude is studied and monumental, drawing on Classical representations of mythological figures. The treatment of the skin lends the figure a bright, almost milky, aspect, something that was eventually to be taken up again and developed by Ingres. Although the figure is anatomically correct, the dictates of naturalistic imagery yield to an interest in sinuous forms. The mirror the woman is holding implicates the viewer in an act of intimacy, which is underlined by the mirror behind reflecting her beautiful coiffure. In his late works, Bellini adopted many of the techniques of his younger contemporaries, but without their more severe Classicism.

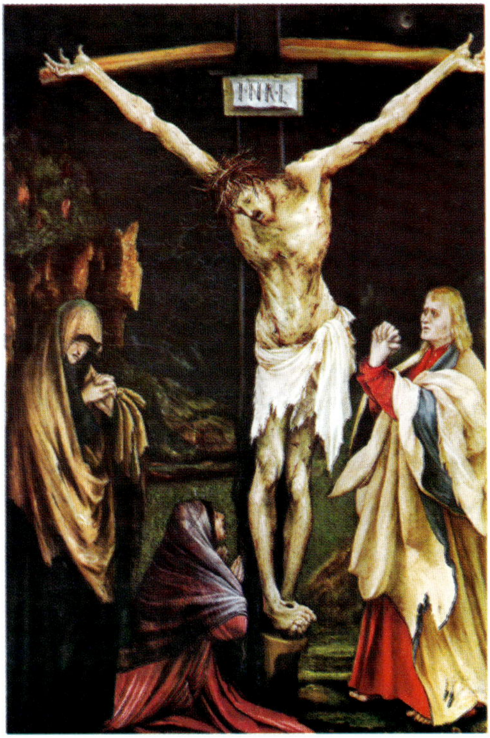

Small Crucifixion

Matthias Grünewald (Mathis Gothardt or **Neithardt)**
(Würzburg, 1475/80–Halle, 1528)

- 1511–20
- oil on panel
- 61.3 x 46 cm
- National Gallery of Art, Samuel H. Kress Collection, Washington, D.C.

nlike the work of his contemporary Albrecht Dürer, Matthias rünewald's art was not imbued with Renaissance ideas. His xtremely dramatic style surpasses in individuality and emo- nal intensity even that of the Netherlandish painters of his ay. Grünewald concentrated exclusively on religious emes, and in particular on the Crucifixion, a subject that he as to make his own. This painting, likened by some to the enheim Altarpiece, which is thought to be the artist's mas- rpiece, presents the Crucifixion as it is described in the ble, with a black sky and dark brown earth. The figure of hrist dominates the scene; his hands and, in particular, his et are shown contorted with agony. His arms stretch under e weight of his own body, making the thorax look as if it ere about to separate from the torso. The head shows all e signs of death, with a gaping mouth and a vacant expres- on. Curiously, the painter has included in this scene the fig- e of St. John the Baptist, who died before Jesus.

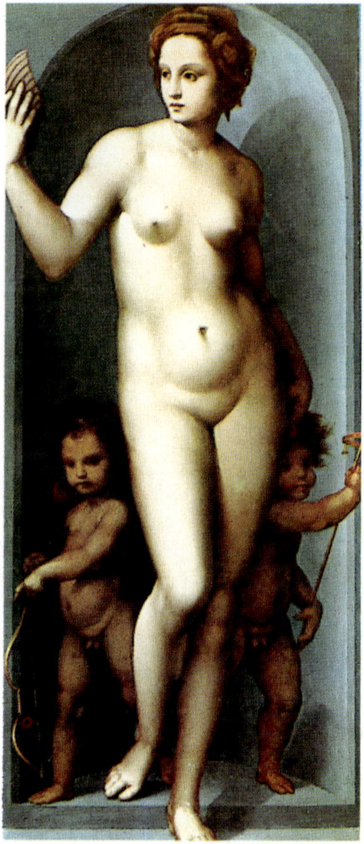

Venus and Two Cherubs

Andrea di Giovanni del Brescianino
(active 1502–25)

- oil on canvas
- 168 x 67 cm
- Galleria Borghese, Rome

This painting of Venus, who appears to be stepping out of th niche, recalls the legend of Pygmalion and Galatea. Accordin to the legend, Galatea is sculpted by Pygmalion, the King of Cyprus, who prays earnestly to Aphrodite to bring his artwork to life—a wish that the goddess grants him. The figure is exe cuted according to Classical criteria, and its Mannerist featur clearly betray the influence of Bronzino, both in the modeling of forms and in the arrangement of the principal figure and th two cherubs. The latter are executed with much darker colors in order to emphasize the luminous complexion of the goddess, who is well proportioned, with the forms of a beautiful, noble young woman. She has a smooth, well-modeled body, small but firm breasts and a fine face and head, which is crowned with an elaborate coiffure. Her hemispheric breasts and abdomen are remarkable features of her anatomy.

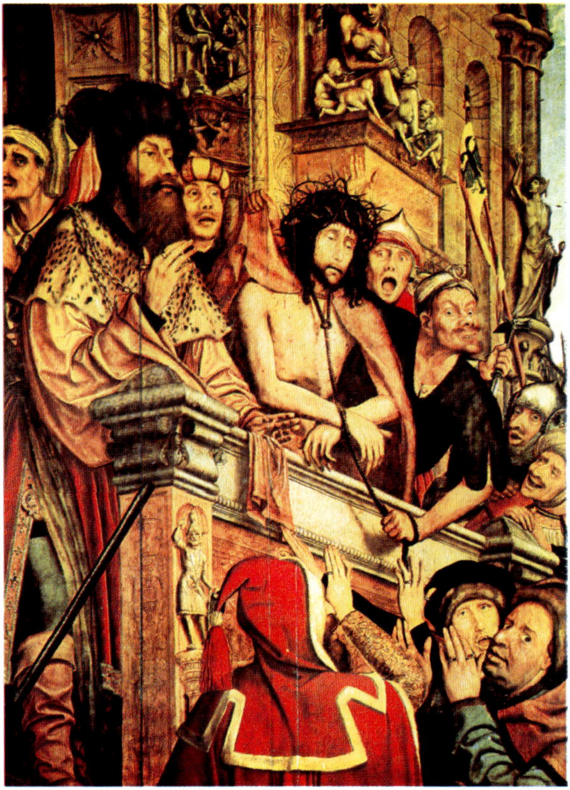

his painting is depicted from a curious point of view. As pectators, we feel that we are amid the throng, yet be-ause the protagonists are not looking in our direction we re made to feel like anonymous witnesses of the scene. he crude facial expressions of the figures evoke Leonardo a Vinci's caricatures, pointing to an influence of the Italian enaissance, which is also evident in the scene's architec-ire. The accurate manner in which the sumptuous clothing rendered, on the other hand, betrays a Netherlandish tyle. Christ's bare torso is emaciated, with numerous marks nd wounds on his skin, and his face wears an expression utter exhaustion. The group of figures on the landing is ndered by means of an unusual perspective, which ex-nds to include Christ's body and face. It would seem that e artist, in an attempt to foreshorten the figure, applied the ame rules of perspective to Christ's body as he did to the rchitectural surroundings.

Ecce Homo

Quentin Massys (Metsys, or **Matsys)**
(Louvain, 1466–Antwerp, 1530)

- ca. 1515
- panel
- 160 x 120 cm
- Museo del Prado, Madrid

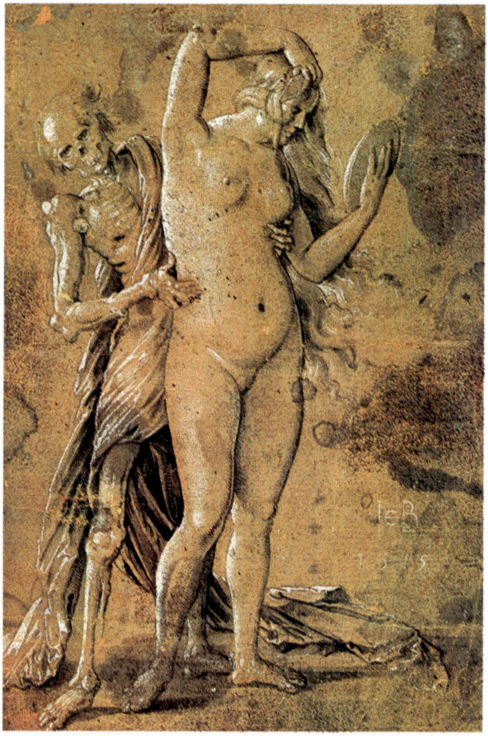

Death and the Maiden

Hans Baldung
(called **Grien**)
(Schwäbisch Gmünd, Swabia, 1484/85–Strasbourg, 1545)

- 1515
- pen and black ink with chalk
- 30.6 x 20.4 cm
- Staatliche Museen Preussischer Kulturbesitz, Kupferstichkabinet, Berlin

A nude woman is looking in a mirror and arranging her hair while Death appears at her back and clasps her. The work is clearly to be understood in the nature of a memento mori: everything in life, beauty included, is transient, death is omnipresent and omnipotent. The influence of Dürer is clearly felt in this work, in whose atelier in Nuremberg Baldung had worked from 1503–1507. In general treatment and composition, the drawing puts one in mind of a painting. However, the nude figure itself gives the impression that Baldung was content to sketch out a seductively elegant figure without bringing it to technical perfection. Noteworthy is the chalk heightening and the proximity of the two figures, which intensifies the dramatic effect of the drawing.

'hile the machin-
'y of martyrdom
certainly in evi-
ence, the delicate
eatment of the
ıde figure does
erve, if only for a
oment, to relegate
e horror to the
ackground. The
ıysique is excep-
onally athletic and
ıe in an idealizing
ay. The skin has
een given an
most satiny finish
ıd harsh shadows
ave been avoided.

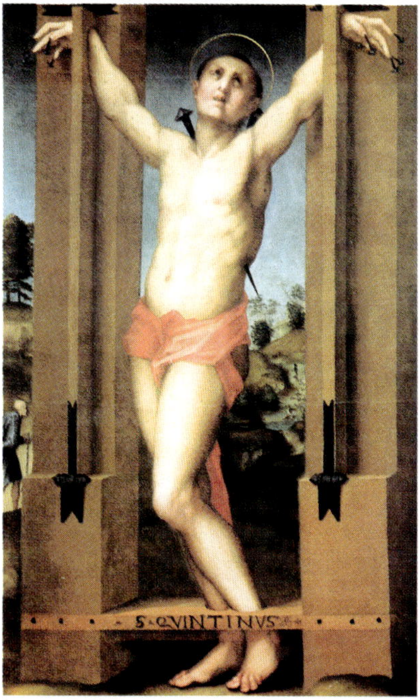

St. Quentin

Pontormo (Jacopo Carucci)
(Pontormo, Tuscany, 1494–Florence, 1557)

- 1515
- oil on panel
- 65 x 103 cm
- Museo Civico, Borgo San Sepolcro

'pical characteris-
:s of Flemish
ainting here are
e details of cloth-
g, and the
oman's facial
xpressivity, which
onveys pain and
so something
strionic. The
xposed parts of
er body, her dress
athered together
w down at the
aist, revealing a
ft of pubic hair,
eate a powerful
ıysicality, while
er open bodice,
less than the
agger with which
e is about to take
er own life, draw
e viewer's gaze
eluctably to her
easts.

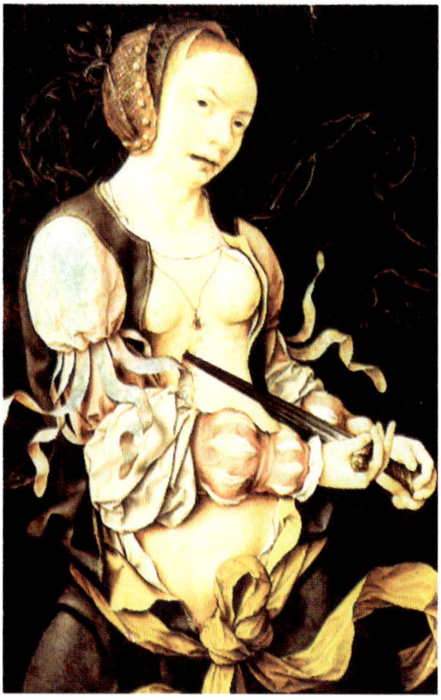

Lucrece

Joos van Cleve
(Cleves, North Rhine-Westphalia, ca. 1485–Antwerp, ca. 1540)

- 1515–18
- oil on canvas
- Kunsthaus, Zurich

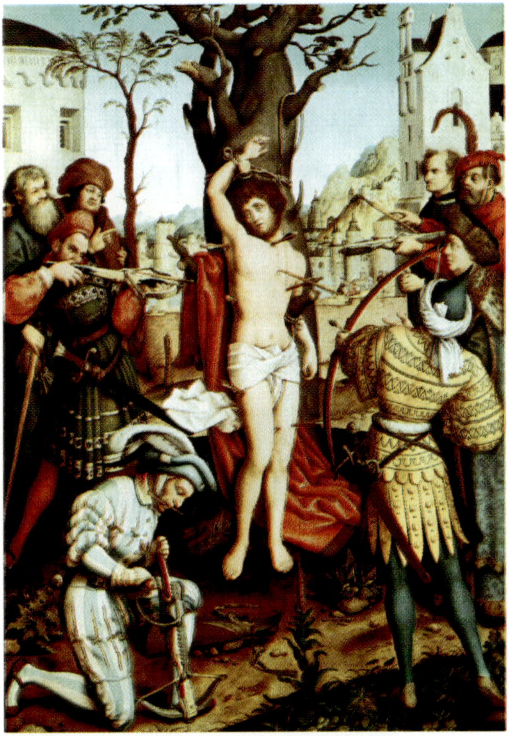

The Martyrdom of St. Sebastian

Hans Holbein the Elder
(Augsburg, 1465–Isneheim, 1524)

- 1516
- paint on panel
- 153 x 107 cm
- Alte Pinakothek, Munich

St. Sebastian is clearly the main protagonist of this work—remarkable for its superb composition and painterly handling—for he is situated in the center of the panel, flanked by the soldiers who only moments before were under his orders and have now become his executioners. The saint is shown being tortured, bound to a tree in the customary fashion, that is, by tying one of his arms over his head and the other to his side. The martyr's pose harmonizes with the composition and is highly erotic. His face betrays no hint of pain, despite the fact that he has been pierced by numerous arrows, but instead seems to be overcome with ecstasy. The body has been rendered in accordance with the German painting tradition, with hieratic volumes and a painstaking articulation of the muscles.

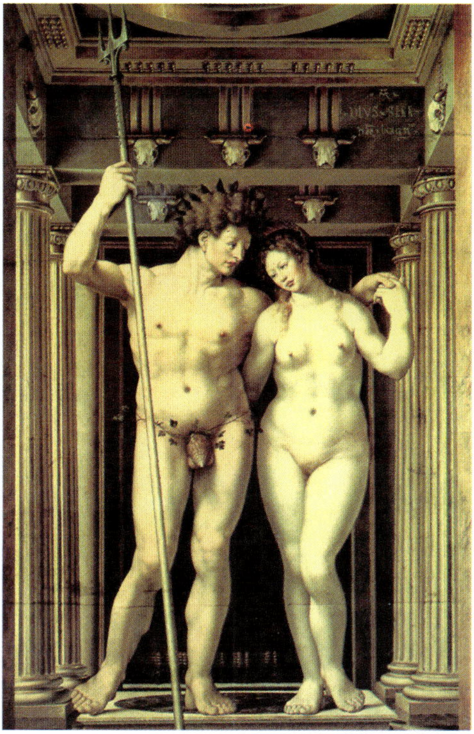

dam and Eve were obligatory motifs in times of religious rvor. However, when it was not necessary to resort to reli- ous motifs in order to justify painting a nude, mythological nd profane themes became the subject of most painting. e development from the Renaissance, via an exacerbat- d period of Mannerism, to the Baroque paved the way for w aesthetic styles, whereby the intellectualization of assical forms transformed the nude into an almost sculp- ral element, far removed from earlier realism. This work Jan Gossaert, who introduced Italian Renaissance inting to the Netherlands—the nude in particular—shows eptune with his wife, Amphitrite, one of the Nereids. The ell-defined musculature and generously proportioned bod- s resemble living sculptures, which the painter placed in architectural setting in an effort to idealize them and vest them with an air of monumentality. The graceful con- apposto of both figures lends a harmonic rhythm to the mposition. The most interesting aspect of the painting, wever, is the modeling and foreshortening of the limbs.

Neptune and Amphitrite

Jan Gossaert
(or **Gossart**; also called **Mabuse**)
(Maubeuge, 1478 –Antwerp, 1532)

- 1516
- oil on canvas
- 188 x 124 cm
- Staatliche Museen Preussischer Kulturbesitz, Berlin

Acquired from the Solly Collection in 1821.

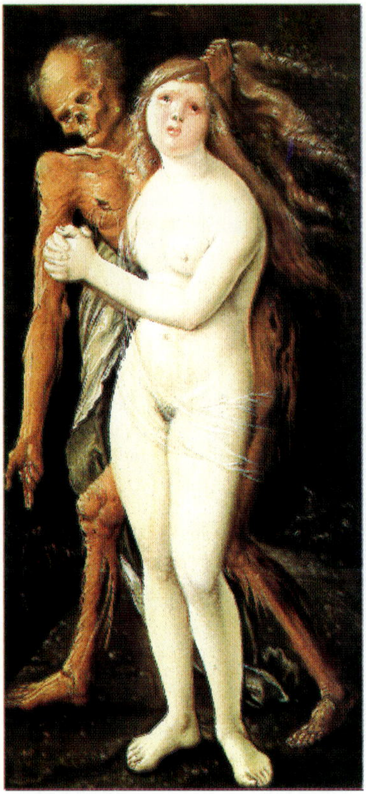

Death and the Maiden

Hans Baldung
(called **Grien**)
(Schwäbisch-Gmünd, 1484-Strasbourg 1545)

- 1517
- tempera on wood
- 30 x 15 cm
- Öffentliche Kunstsammlung, Kunstmuseum, Basel

Baldung's painting is a monument to human fragility in the face of death. Here we see Death, personified as a semi-decomposed corpse, clutching by the hair a naked woman in her prime. Her imploring attitude calls to mind contemporaneous Italian renderings of Venus, her shape and form in accordance with prevailing ideals of beauty of the period, although her shoulders are shown rounded almost to the point of deformity. This savage, symbolic image of death accosting youth in its prime, the erotic associations nicely brought out by a transparent veil at the girl's waist, was of course intended to have moral force.

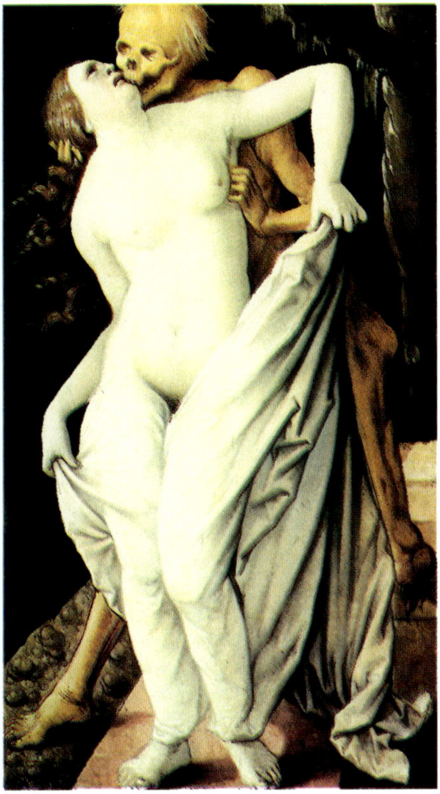

Repulsion and morbidity converge in this work to form allegories of Life and Death, which appear in other works by Hans Baldung, in moralistic contexts. Neither the young nor the beautiful escape the terrible embrace of Death. In a scene of great anguish and drama, Death kisses Life with relentless persistence. Life could scarcely wear a more horrified expression on her face, which is reflected in her averted eyes and twisted mouth. An incongruent aspect of the scene is the maiden's demeanor, a gesture of submission that would verge on eroticism were it not for the presence of the work's real protagonist behind her. Both nudes testify to the artist's profound knowledge of anatomy: on the one hand, the corpse, whose execution recalls that of Hieronymus Bosch; on the other hand, the maiden, whose body is rendered in typical Italian Renaissance fashion and is positively expressionistic in its painterly handling.

Death and the Maiden

Hans Baldung Grien
(Schwäbisch Gmünd, Swabia, 1484/85–Strasbourg, 1545)

- 1517
- tempera on panel
- 30 x 14.5 cm
- Öffentliche Kunstsammlung, Kunstmuseum, Basel

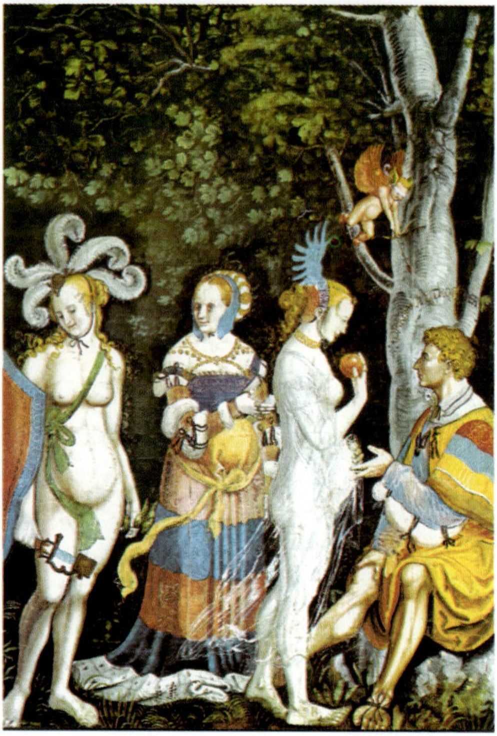

The Judgment of Paris

Niklaus Manuel Deutsch
(Bern, 1484–1530)

- 1517–18
- tempera on canvas
- 223 x 160 cm
- Öffentliche Kunstsammlung, Basel

Attending the wedding of Peleus and Thetis uninvited, the goddess Eris flung down a golden apple inscribed "for the fairest." At the behest of Zeus, the three goddesses who claimed this title requested that Paris, son of the king of Troy, decide which of them was the most beautiful. He chose Aphrodite, who had bribed him by promising him the most beautiful woman in the world. This was Helen, wife of the king of Sparta, whose elopement with Paris unleashed the Trojan War. The clothed figures in this painting—Juno and Paris—are dressed not in the classical manner, but in the fashion current in the early 16th century in Germany. Both in their poses and anatomical detail, the elegantly sensual nudes—Athena (on the left) and Aphrodite—recall the female figures of Albrecht Dürer.

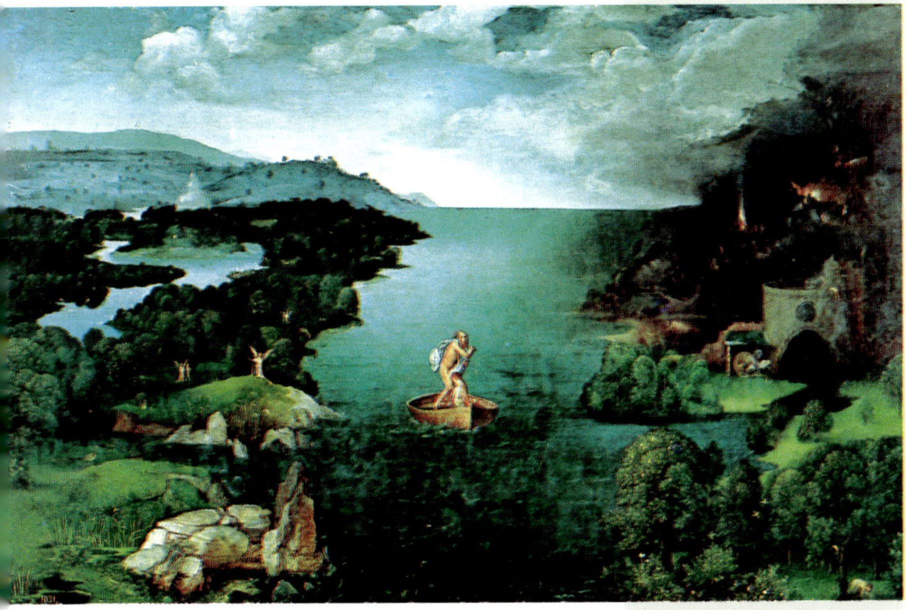

oachim Patinir was the first early Netherlandish artist to
nake a landscape the subject of a painting, for, unlike
oday, landscapes in his day were employed merely as
cenery. Here, he uses the landscape to relate a narrative
cene in which small figures have been depicted. The tiny
ude at the center recalls Bosch's iconography. It is Charon,
ne boatman who ferries the souls of the dead from the
orld of the living across the River Styx to Acheron, the
nderworld. On the left, Paradise is evoked with glass struc-
ures and, on the right, Avernus is enveloped in fire, smoke
nd darkness. The imagined landscape, with its high hori-
on, covers a vast area, which is painted with a threefold
olor scheme, containing contrasts of light and shadow and
elicately rendered details. Charon is depicted as an old
nan with tanned skin and is well proportioned. The study of
novement is executed with perfection: the figure's legs are
ent at the knees and his back leans slightly forward, evok-
g the exertion required to push the boat forward.

Charon Crossing the Styx

Joachim Patinir
(Patinier or **Patenier)**
(Bouvignes, 1475/86
–Antwerp, 1524)

- panel
- 64 x 103 cm
- Museo del Prado, Madrid

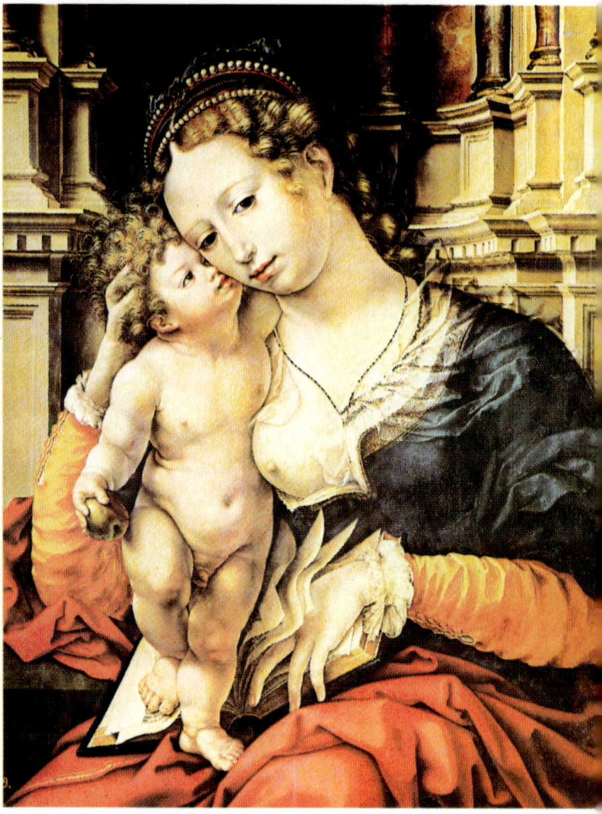

The Virgin and Child

Jan Gossaert (or **Gossart**; also called **Mabuse**)
(Maubeuge, 1478 –Antwerp, 1532)

- panel
- 63 x 50 cm
- Museo del Prado, Madrid

This artist, who introduced the Italian Renaissance nude to the Netherlands, demonstrates the artist's clear intention to leave behind the traditional style of that region in favor of Italian impulses. Here, the Virgin evokes the sweetness of Netherlandish figures, whereas the muscular child recalls the anatomical studies of Italian Renaissance artists. The white flesh tones of the Virgin's bare breast set against the dramatic folds of her dress adds a note of sensuality to the scene. The volumes of the nude Christ child are modeled with great skill, exhibiting a powerful and pronounced musculature. The study of the child's flesh tones is extraordinary, in particular the bold red and yellow hues that reflect those of his mother's dress. The artist's eye for detail, evident here in the articulation of forms and the detailed rendition of the hair, betray his Netherlandish training.

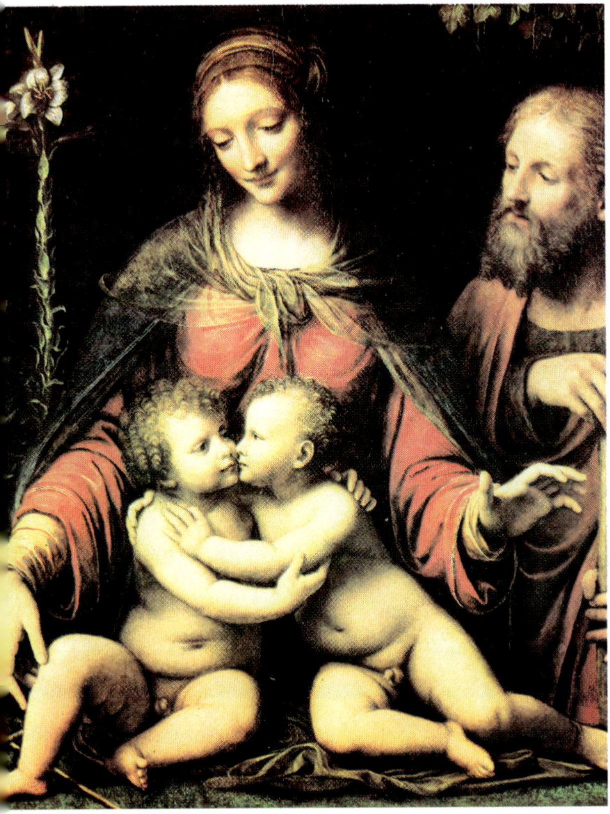

This composition is based on a drawing by Leonardo da Vinci. In contrast to the delicate handling of the other figures, St. Joseph is notably rigid and archaic in treatment. Both children—Jesus and his cousin John the Baptist—are exquisitely executed. The sfumato technique employed by the artist lend the figures an astonishing degree of plasticity and vitality; at the same time, however, a sense of mystery is conveyed. This work reveals a certain sensuality, despite the fact that its main subjects are two boys. Indeed, it is precisely their innocence that brings this erotic quality to the fore. The image of two boys kissing, not an infrequent motif in art, was typical of Leonardo's work and an attempt to project adult sentiments onto children.

The Holy Family

Bernardino Luini
(Luino, Lake Maggiore, 1480/90–Milan, 1532)

- panel
- 100 x 84 cm
- Museo del Prado, Madrid

When he was in Florence, this painting was presented to Philip II of Spain, who was given to believe that it was the work of Leonardo da Vinci. It was kept at El Escorial from 1574 to 1839.

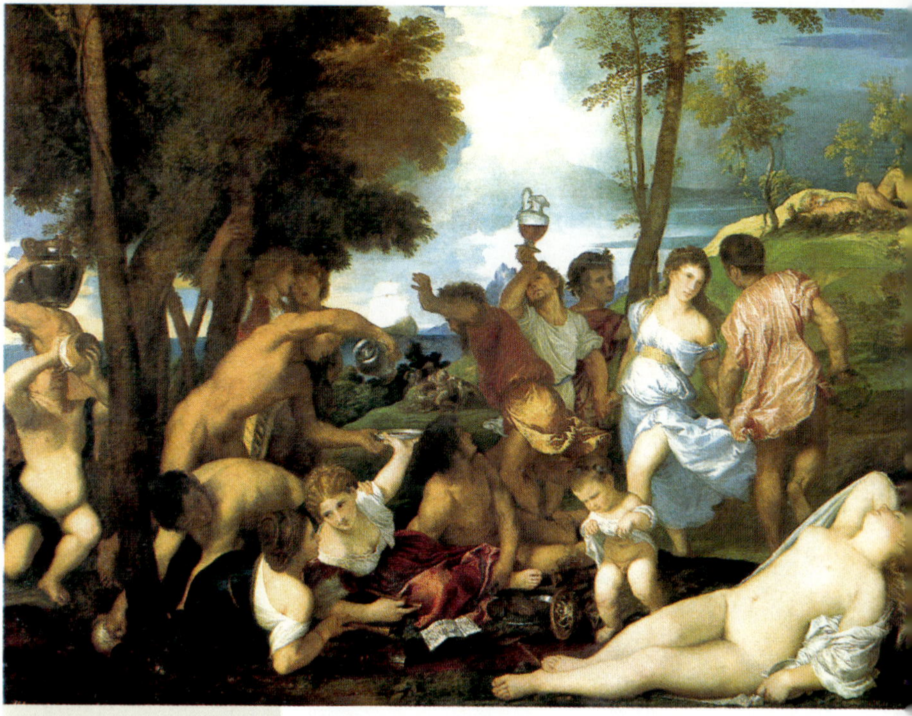

Bacchanal

Titian (Tiziano Vecellio di Gregorio)
(Pieve di Cadore, 1488/89 –Venice, 1576)

- ca. 1518
- oil on canvas
- 175 x 193 cm
- Museo del Prado, Madrid.

This painting represents one of the stories of Philostratus, which has come down to us through the poems of Catullus. The scene is a veritable celebration of life and the joys it brings—and entails a large dose of eroticism! Violante, Titian's mistress at the time he painted this work, appears at the center in a white blouse and red dress. The most notable nude, who appears in the right foreground, is a reclining female figure of great sensuality. She is voluptuous and well proportioned, and her skin is so bright that the details of her anatomy could scarcely be distinguished were it not for the soft modeling of her forms. The rest of the picture radiates varying intensities of light that combine with the sinuous lines of the bodies to form a composition that is at once dynamic and harmonious. The removal of this work from Rome, when it was given to Philip IV, caused a great stir for it is an exquisite example of Neo-Venetian Baroque art.

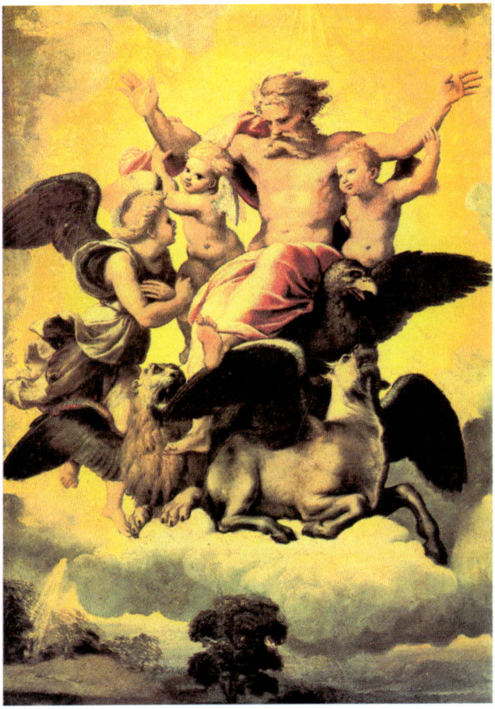

Ezekiel's Vision

Raphael (Raffaello Santi or **Sanzio)**
(Urbino, 1483–Rome, 1520)

- 1518
- oil on panel
- 40 x 30 cm
- Galleria Palatina, Florence

ı this painting Raphael depicts God the Father accompanied ·y the attributes of the four Evangelists: an eagle (John), a ›on (Mark), an angel (Matthew) and an ox (Luke). The sacred ›ature of the scene is heightened by the golden atmosphere ›nveloping the figures and pervading the entire composition. 'he circular arrangement of the figures is remarkable, ıcreasing the sense of solemnity and transcendence of the ›cene. In the lower left edge of the painting, in the back-round, a miniature image of the Prophet can be seen, illumi-›ated by a ray of light. The figure of God, muscular and beau-fully executed, is colossal and recalls Olympic gods in its ›eroic aspect, grave facial expression and majestic bearing.

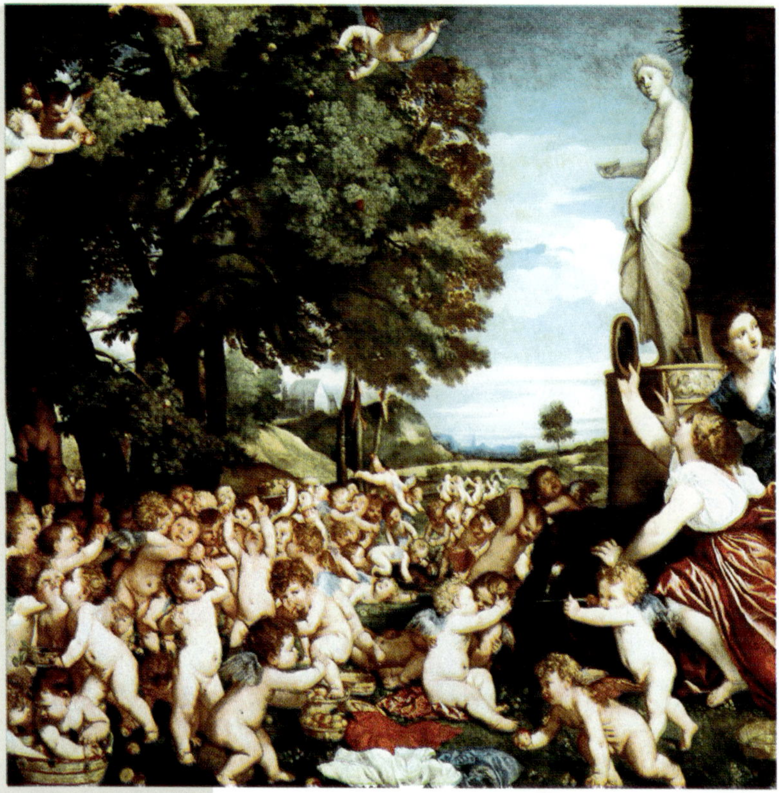

Worship of Venus

Titian (Tiziano Vecellio di Gregorio)
(Pieve di Cadore, 1488/89 –Venice, 1576)

- 1518–19
- oil on canvas
- 172 x 175 cm
- Museo del Prado, Madrid

A nude statue of Venus, standing on a pedestal, is shown modestly holding her fallen dress by the corner to cover her genitals. At the base of the pedestal numerous cherubs take delight in a wide variety of activities: eating fruit, playing, climbing trees, sleeping and even flying, for these mythical creatures, heirs of Cupid, have wings. The artist rendered every child with great realism, granting each figure its own individual physiognomy and personality, which prevents the composition from becoming a mass of faceless figures. The study of light on the small bodies makes them appear highly sculptural, albeit mobile as well. This work, which reinvents mythological iconography, is highly naturalistic, with a bold composition and a rich color scheme. It is a marvelous example of the painter's inventive skill.

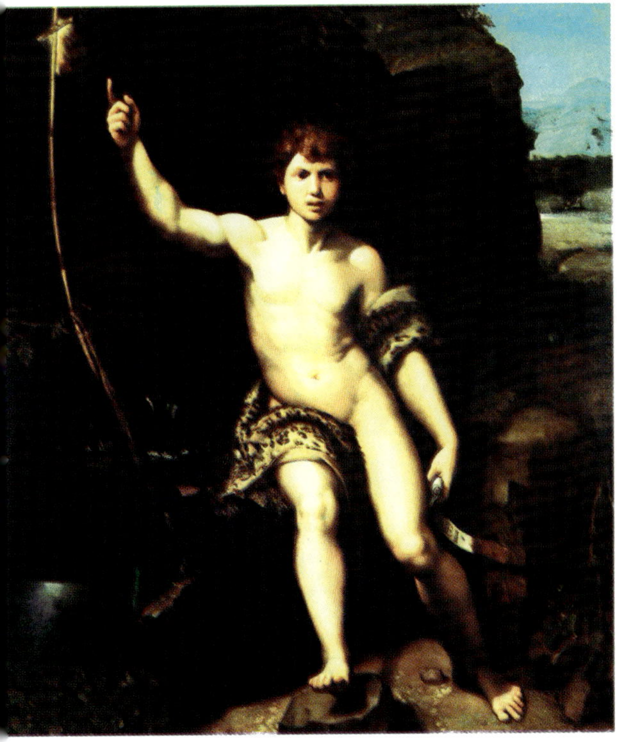

Raphael placed this figure of St. John in front of dark rocks to create the strong contrast we see here. The complexion is sculptural, with a marble-like modeling that recalls the steely bodies of Netherlandish painting, although the pictorial treatment here is more sophisticated and impressive. The shadows surrounding him are subtly blended with the modeled volumes, rendering the outlines of his body somewhat blurred. This beautiful nude has the body of a youth rather than that of a boy, judging from the shoulder width and proportions. The masterly foreshortening is so well executed that it is scarcely noticeable. It was not by chance that, until the later 19th century, Raphael was regarded almost universally as the greatest painter ever to have lived.

St. John the Baptist in the Desert

Raphael (**Raffaello Santi** or **Sanzio**)
(Urbino, 1483–Rome, 1520)

- 1518–20
- oil on panel
- 165 x 147 cm
- Galleria degli Uffizi, Florence

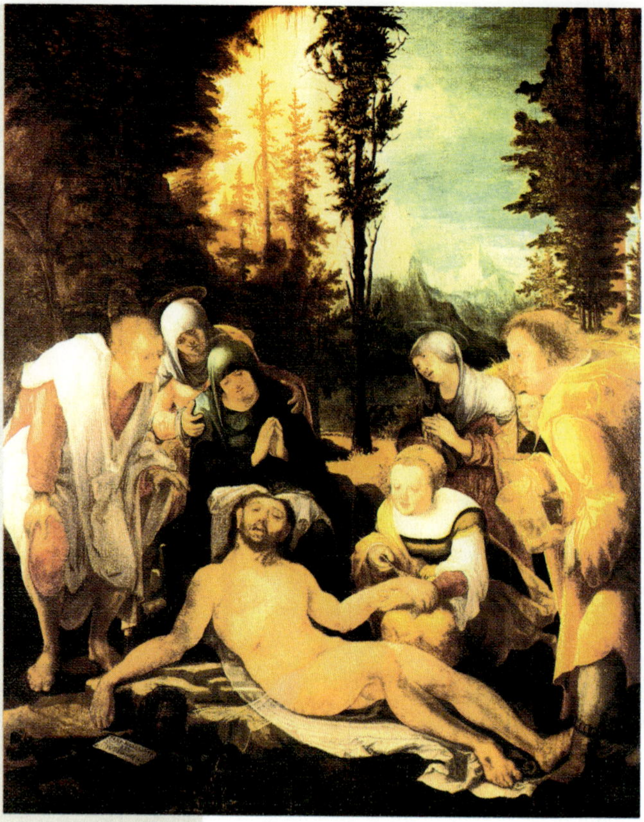

The Lamentation

Wolf (or **Wolfgang**) **Huber**
(Feldkirch, Vorarlberg, 1485–Passau, 1553)

- ca. 1519
- panel
- 105 x 86 cm
- Musée du Louvre, Paris

Wolf Huber used this painting—one of the few surviving works by the Austrian artist, a leading exponent of the so-called Danube School—to portray its donors and his family, who are actively part of the drama. They can be identified by their contrasting and colorful attire compared to that of the other figures. In this scene the reclining Christ looks as though he were sleeping. Even his leg, slightly bent, suggests a certain trance-like state. One could argue that the figure of Christ is not perfect owing to its somewhat inexact anatomy, particularly the foreshortened leg and the right forearm. The effect, however, may have been a deliberate attempt to enhance the dynamism of the scene. Assuming this is so, it is not a defect, but rather an aesthetic device.

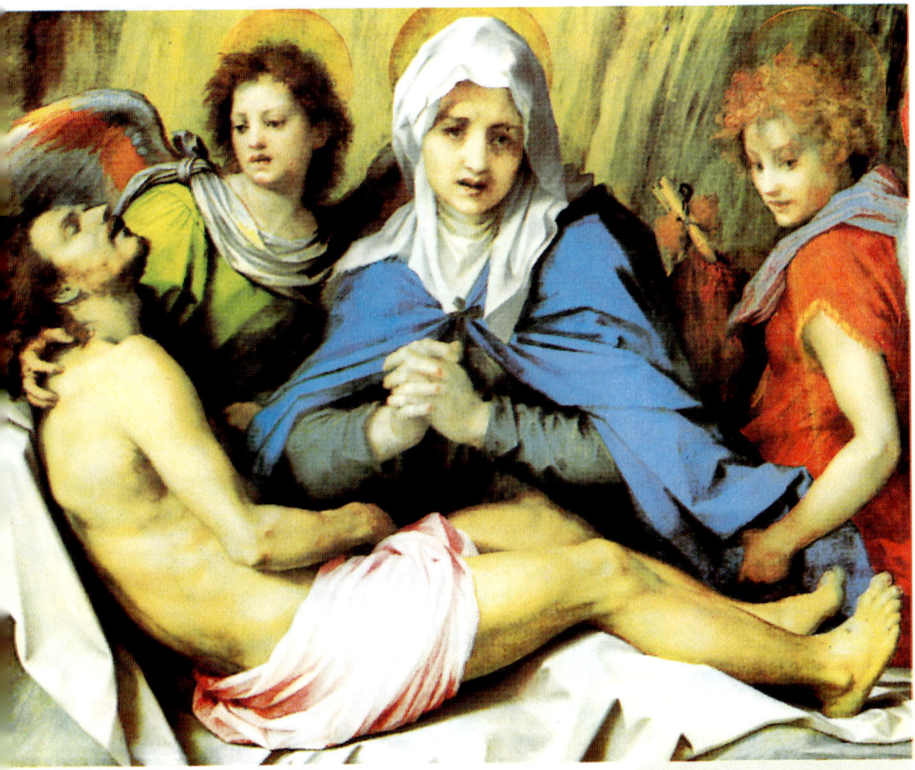

Andrea del Sarto's type of Pietà differed from that of his Florentine predecessors. The relationship between mother and son is not portrayed as close; indeed, it is one of the angels who supports the body of Christ descended from the Cross. The artist employs a classical composition, which is achieved by a vivid color scheme of pure, luminous tones so characteristic of the Florentine school. The figure of Christ exhibits human characteristics and is not idealized. The curvature of the figure's back skillfully conveys the weight of the dead body. The modeling of the body is classical in execution, in contrast to such areas as the background. Instead of a traditional background, the artist opted for an abstract one against which his subjects are placed. It is a simple in design, executed with merely a few brushstrokes, and serving no other purpose than to fill the void behind the protagonists.

Pietà

Andrea del Sarto (Andrea d'Agnolo di Francesco)
(Florence, 1486–1530)

- 1519–20
- oil on panel
- 99 x 120 cm
- Kunsthistorisches Museum, Vienna

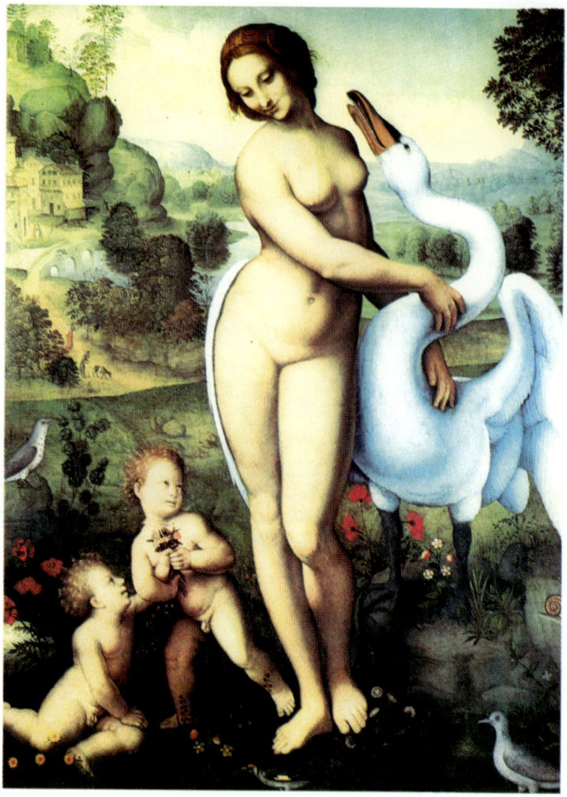

Leda and the Swan

Anonymous

- oil on panel
- 112 x 86 cm
- Galleria Borghese, Rome

Jupiter, according to legend, fell in love with Leda, queen of Sparta and wife of Tyndareus, and turned himself into a swan in order to seduce her. The theme enjoyed immense popularity and has been immortalized by numerous painters, including Leonardo da Vinci, whose version of it was destroyed in the burnings carried out by Savonarola and his followers. The author of this work is not known, although it appears to be derived from Leonardo's. The painting, of course, is exceptionally sensual, both for the way Leda's pose and gestures complement her rotund, suggestive forms and for the almost aggressive voluptuousness of the swan. The eroticism, however, is rather blatant, and lacks the subtlety and mysteriousness we find in Leonardo's works. Nevertheless, the artist has achieved a faithful reproduction of a face the master painted many times. He almost certainly copied it directly from one of Leonardo's drawings.

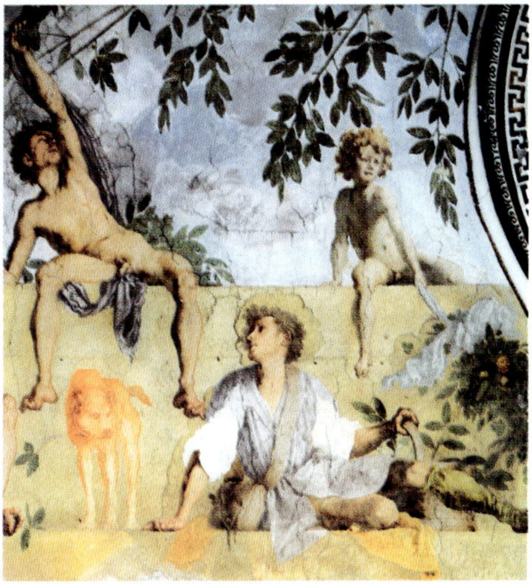

Vertumnus and Pomona

Pontormo (Jacopo Carucci)
(Pontormo, Tuscany, 1494–Florence, 1557)

- 1519–21
- fresco
- Villa Medicea, Poggio a Caiano

Pomona was the Italo-Roman goddess of crops and orchards. The treatment of Vertumnus, who was in love with the goddess, is boldly realistic, not only for its total nudity, which ncludes a clearly-displayed male member, but for its deployment of effective trompe-l'oeil. The artist will no doubt have felt freer because the work was privately commissioned. Modeling and execution of this figure are exceptionally modern.

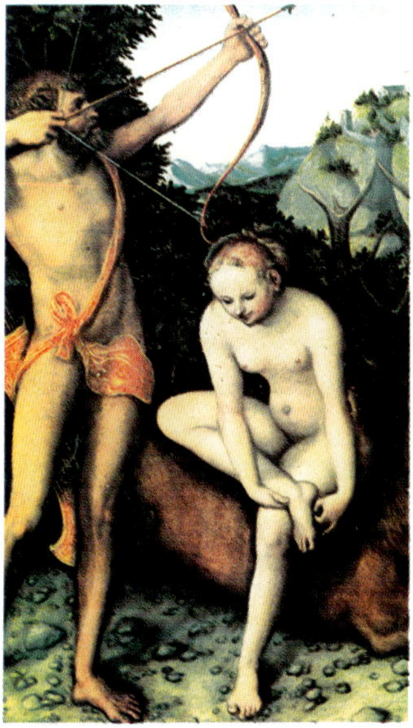

Apollo and Diana

Lucas Cranach, the Elder
(Kronach, Franconia, 1472–Weimar, 1553)

- 1530
- painting on panel
- 45 x 31 cm
- Musée Royal des Beaux-Arts, Antwerp

n this work, two naked, beautiful and sensually attractive bodies are portrayed. Apollo, god of arts and music, is depicted more in the fashion of Hercules than as the prototype of the kind of beauty he stood for. Diana, goddess of hunting, is depicted seated on a deer, removing a thorn rom her foot. The curves of her body are accentuated by foreshortening. Apollo, erect, bow drawn, creates an elegant curve that sets up an interplay with the forms and shape of his sister.

Charity

Lucas Cranach the Elder

(Kronach, Franconia, 1472–Weimar, 1553)

- oil on panel
- 119 x 81 cm
- Musée Royal des Beaux-Arts, Antwerp

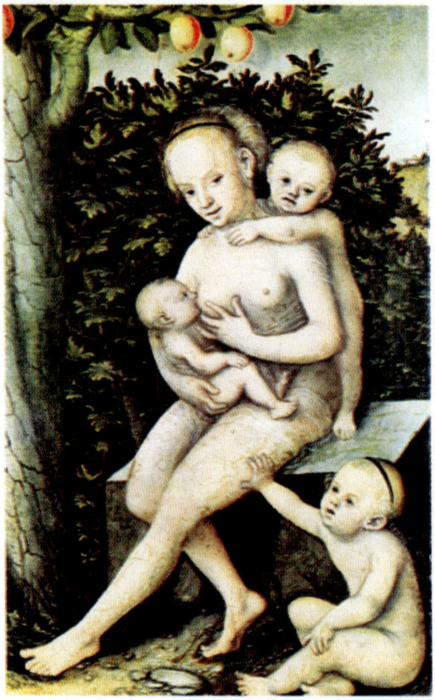

Cranach developed a unique style combining psychological vision and eroticism. Here, both aspects are in evidence, enhanced by intelligent iconography. Not only the woman's attitude and pose make her sexually explicit, but also her provocative gaze, which draws the viewer in. One can say, without exaggeration, that the figure has clear erotic designs on the viewer, where the childishly small breasts and mischievous facial expression play a definite role.

Diana Bathing

Palma Vecchio (Jacomo Palma)

(Serina, Bergamo, ca. 1480–Venice, 1528)

- 1525
- oil on canvas
- 77.5 x 124 cm
- Kunsthistorisches Museum, Vienna

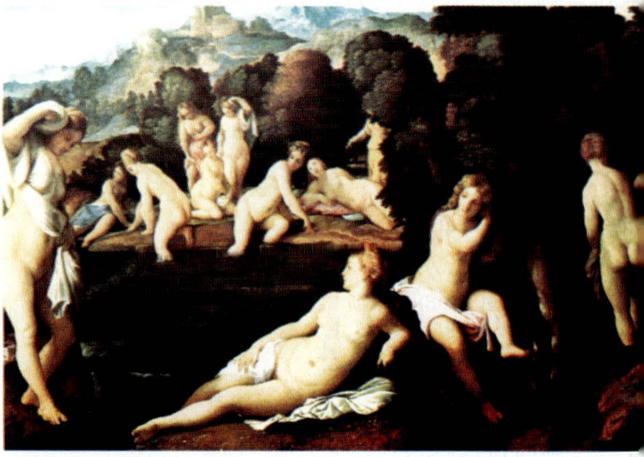

In this work, which betrays the influence of Bellini and Giorgione, the figures are rendered in a Mannerist style, recalling the work of Titian. Here, Diana is depicted in a natural setting, surrounded with luxuriant vegetation, together with her nymphs, who are resting at the water's edge after a day of hunting. The nudes are strong and robust, but their gestures are graceful, their poses erotic and the atmosphere sensual.

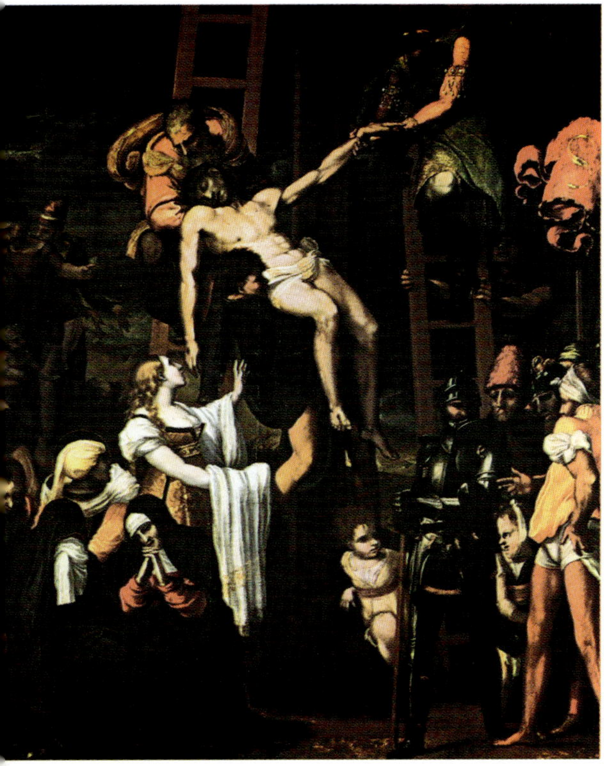

The Deposition

Pedro Machuca
(Toledo, ca. 1490
–Granada, 1550)

- panel
- 141 x 128 cm
- Museo del Prado, Madrid

'his artist was clearly inspired by the work of Michelangelo, f whom he was presumably a pupil, and by that of Raphael, lthough Pedro Machuca's handling of light is entirely his wn. The intense chiaroscuro in this painting is juxtaposed vith patches of intense color, which contribute to the dynaıism of the scene. The crucified Christ has a heroic aspect, ıuscular but inanimate. The limbs, in a show of almost xaggerated realism, hang under their own weight. The forehortening of the outstretched arms, which were dislocated y the weight of Christ's body on the Cross, is executed with onsummate skill. The head hangs lifelessly from a flaccid eck. The almost tangible suffering of the scene is accentuted by the artist's virtuoso handling of light. The scene ecalls a stage set, with spotlights ingeniously positioned to ighlight individual volumes and exaggerate the shadows to mphasize the muscular anatomy.

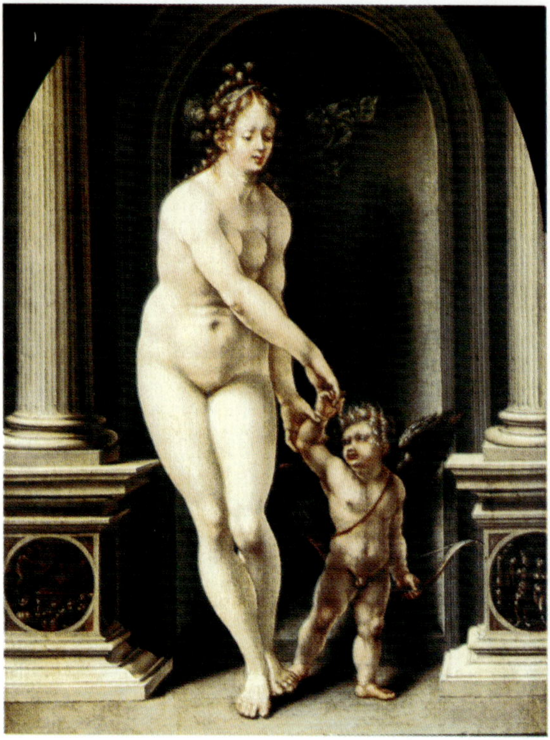

Venus and Cupid

Jan Gossaert
(or **Gossart**; also called **Mabuse**)
(Maubeuge, 1478 –Antwerp, 1532)

- 1521
- oil on panel
- 36 x 23.5 cm
- Musées Royaux des Beaux-Arts, Brussels

Despite Mabuse's Netherlandish training, he employed, as can be observed in this work, a number of artistic means to give his figures a sculptural appearance, in the style of the Italian Renaissance. Nonetheless, his meticulous treatment of the skin betrays his Netherlandish background, giving rise to a figure of remarkable beauty that is rendered with the steely flesh tones of northern art. The striking effect is intensified by the contrasts that arise from the dark background against which the figures have been set. The sense of movement evoked by the goddess, which Dürer had already employed in his Eve, marks a turning point in the work of Jan Gossaert. Venus' curvaceous body is imbued with a harmonious sensuality and her rotund, feminine forms are beautiful to behold.

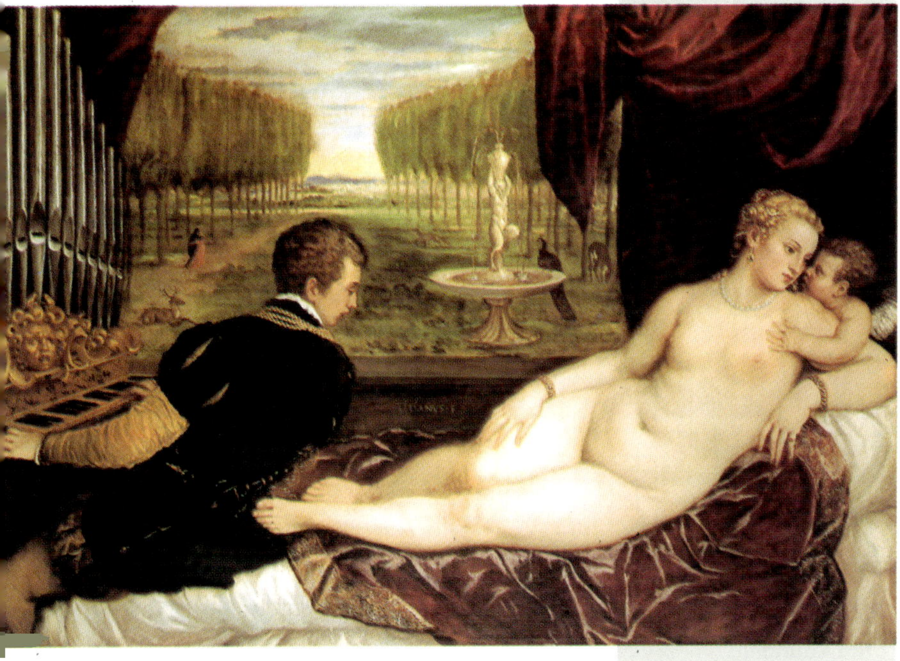

Venus with Cupid and an Organist

Titian (Tiziano Vecellio di Gregorio)
(Pieve di Cadore, 1488/89 –Venice, 1576)

- ca. 1518
- oil on canvas
- 148 x 217 cm
- Museo del Prado, Madrid

ery few works depicting nudes in a landscape have come own to us from before Titian's time. This painting is one of e most beautiful allegories of eroticism. The scene shows voluptuous Venus reclining on a bed, attentive to the hispers of her child, Cupid, the symbol of love, while listening to the music of a young organ player whose glance fixed on her pubis. Venus is elegant, suggestive and rovocative. The curve of her torso harmonizes with the potioning of her arms and legs, resembling one of Rubens' irens. Unlike other goddesses, this is a real woman, who mbodies the northern ideal of beauty. Her head is somehat small, her shoulders narrow and her breasts small. he influence of Rubens is evident in the treatment of the esh tones and the broad shape of the hips. The artist ainted other versions of this theme as well.

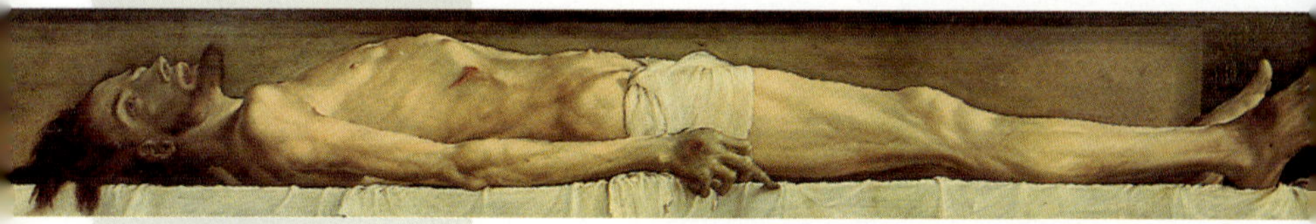

Christ in the Tomb

Hans Holbein the Younger

(Augsburg, 1497–London, 1543)

- 1521
- tempera on panel
- 30.5 x 200 cm
- Öffentliche Kunstsammlung, Kunstmuseum, Basel

This corpse displays all the signs of the traumatic death it suffered: purple hands and feet; rigor mortis, which can be observed in the mouth; and the contraction of the fingers. This is realism taken to the extreme. The body is that of a very tall man of harmonious proportions, whose extreme slenderness further accentuates the brutality of his death. The flesh tones would seem to be fading and the skin becoming progressively more opaque and ashen. To increase the dramatic effect, the corpse is not presented in an open space, but portrayed in the confined space of a tomb to emphasize the extreme humiliation to which he was subjected. This work is an eloquent example of German expressionism, which lasted from late Gothic period to the work of Grünewald, whose influence here is indisputable.

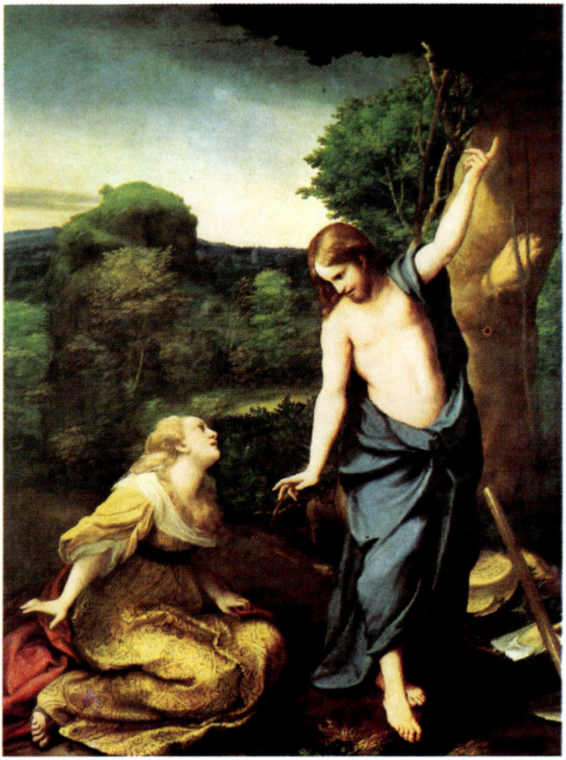

orreggio attains a nearly feminine sensuality in his nudes at would seem to herald the dynamic movement, intense olors and fervent emotions that characterize Baroque art, l of which are in evidence in this painting. A trembling and istraught Mary Magdalene kneels before Jesus, whose hysique, bearing and gestures are rendered in a stylized anner. His bare chest is the focal point of the scene, which ere is interpreted as eliciting sentiments in Mary Magdalene at may go beyond purely religious fervor. The figure of hrist is even more dramatic in expression. His unnatural, xaggerated pose, in which his arms form a diagonal, indiates his intention to flee. Against the velvety, dark green ndscape his resplendent white skin is brought to the fore, pparently without regard for the lighting in the rest of the cene.

Noli me tangere

Correggio (Antonio Allegri)

(Correggio, near Parma, Emilia, ca. 1489–1534)

- ca. 1522–23
- panel transferred to canvas
- 130 x 103 cm
- Museo del Prado, Madrid

This painting originally belonged to Charles I of England. After it was acquired by the Duke of Medina de las Torres, he gave it to Philip IV of Spain. It remained in El Escorial until 1839.

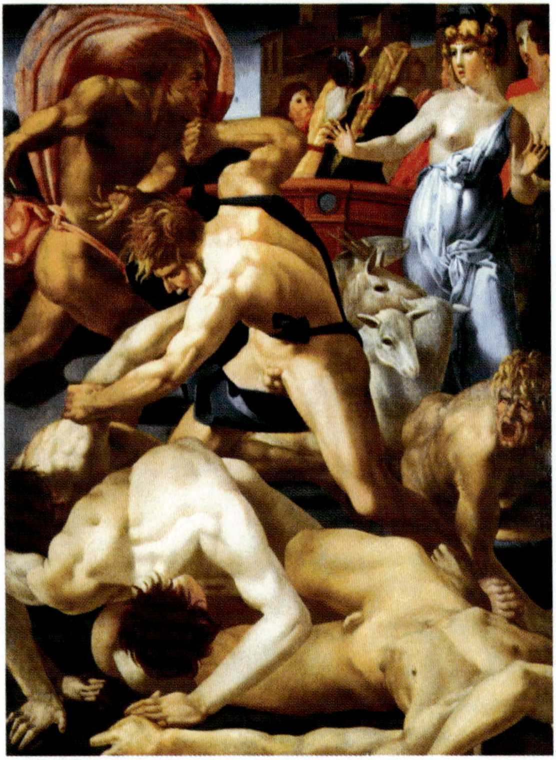

Moses and the Daughters of Jethro

Giovanni Battista Rosso (called **Rosso Fiorentino**)
(Florence, 1495–Paris, 1540)

- ca. 1523
- oil on canvas
- 160 x 117 cm
- Galleria degli Uffizi, Florence

This painting takes an episode from the Book of Exodus as its theme: the daughters of Jethro, priest of Madian, were accosted by some shepherds while taking water from a well to give to their cattle. Moses, who was resting nearby, got up and fought them, freeing the women from their captors. In gratitude, Jethro offered Moses his daughter Sebora's hand in marriage. This scene shows Moses' combat with the shepherds. His appearance is heroic, with a sculptural quality approaching that of Michelangelo's figures in the Sistine Chapel. The foreshortening of the figures is technically complex, evoking a violent dynamism. The compositional rhythm is carefully studied and each nude is a singular anatomical study, such that each one is visually distinct from the others. Despite its crowded composition, the painting has been rendered in central perspective.

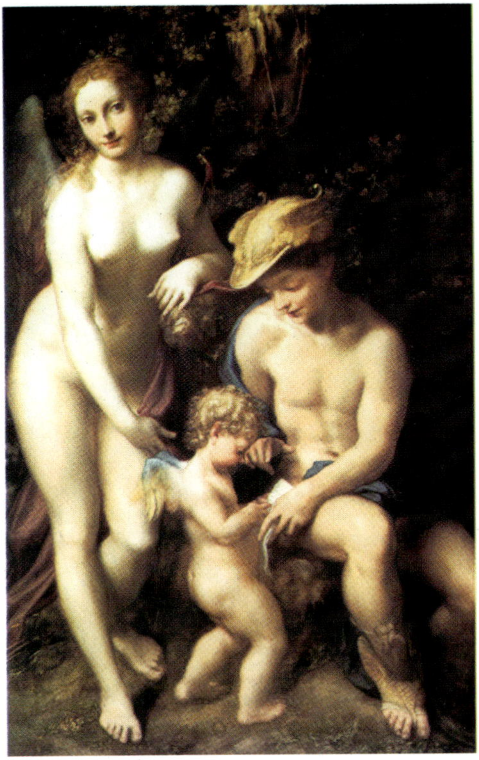

School of Love

Correggio (Antonio Allegri)
(Correggio, near Parma, Emilia, ca. 1489–1534)

- 1524–26
- oil on canvas
- 155 x 91.5 cm
- National Gallery, London

ederico II Gonzaga commissioned Correggio to paint two ythological works with nude figures, which the painter car- ed out in depictions of Venus, Cupid and Mercury. This work epicts Mercury teaching Cupid to read. Venus, portrayed as n exceedingly beautiful woman with a powerful body, uses er son's bow in the manner of a staff, while she glances at e spectator out of the corner of her eye. Correggio em- oyed various stylistic techniques for these figures, which evitably recall the hand of Leonardo da Vinci: the velvety nish, chiaroscuro and sfumato tones; even the conception f Venus herself. Winged (unusual for depictions of Venus), pronounced contrapposto, she recalls Leonardo's sensual eda as we know her from the copy. These nude figures' ensuality and tenderness are accentuated by their entirely atural foreshortening and by their outstanding execution. his style of treatment heralds the advent of Baroque as it as developed later by Rubens.

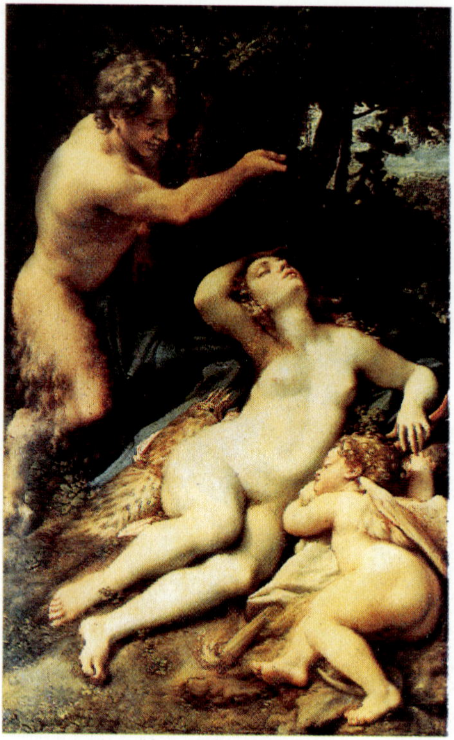

Venus and Cupid with a Satyr

Correggio (Antonio Allegri)
(Correggio, near Parma, Emilia, ca. 1489–1534)

- 1525
- oil on canvas
- 190 x 124 cm
- Musée du Louvre, Paris

The style and subject of this painting are clearly influenced by the work of Leonardo da Vinci, whereas the painterly tech nique recalls that of the Venetian School. The sensuality of the feminine forms is heightened by the painting's soft illumi nation, which envelops Venus' body, lending it a provocative expression. The scene is dominated by the innocent contem- plation of beauty by Cupid, who is also nude and rather cor- pulent, and by the more libertine instincts of the nude Satyr, who is at once naïve, as is suggested by his child-like body, and mischievous, as revealed by the direction in which his gaze is fixed. There is a clear complicity between the two on- lookers. Venus, self-absorbed, is portrayed abandoning her- self to her dream, apparently not preoccupied by the nudity of her body, but aware of the fact that it is the object of desir of her two companions. Venus' eroticism in this painting is achieved by means of rotund, feminine shapes, accentuated curves and smooth, well-defined volumes.

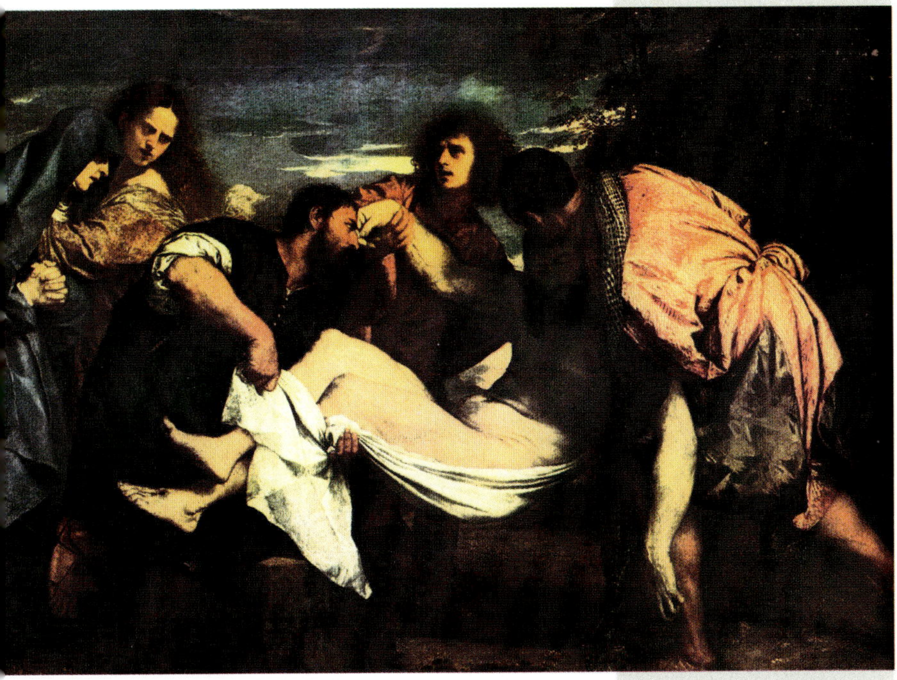

The Entombment

Titian (Tiziano Vecellio di Gregorio)
(Pieve di Cadore, 1488/89 –Venice, 1576)

- 1525
- oil on canvas
- 148 x 205 cm
- Musée du Louvre, Paris

ılike in other Renaissance compositions, the figure of Christ this work is not glorified, nor is the sensuality characteristic so many paintings of the period in evidence here. Instead, e artist has depicted a strong, inanimate body that is so ıavy that Joseph of Arimathea, John the Apostle and Nicoımus must take great pains to lift it. The lower half of hrist's body is bathed in bright light, whereas the torso is ıst in shadow, heightening the drama of the scene. The pale ;in, tinged with blue and green, suggests death, although ere are no signs of rigor mortis. Instead, the figure appears have fallen into a deep sleep. This nude displays a high ıgree of naturalism, unlike the eroticism inherent in many ıintings with religious subjects. Although Titian portrayed his ıdes with great realism, eschewing any attempt to idealize s subjects, it is evident that he set great store by the selecon of his models.

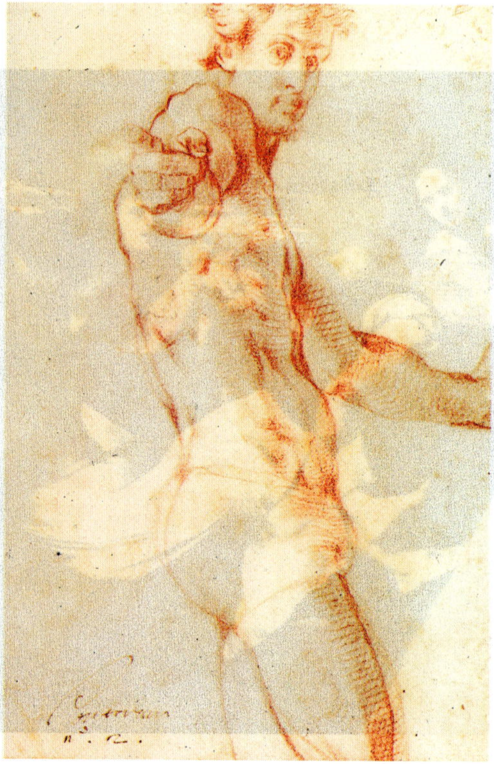

Study of a Male Nude (Self-Portrait)

Pontormo (Jacopo Carucci)
(Pontormo, Tuscany, 1494–Florence, 1557)

- 1525
- red chalk
- 24.4 x 20.2 cm
- British Museum, London

The principal interest of this work lies in the dramatic foreshortening of the figure. The artist used a mirror to draw himself, a task requiring him repeatedly to take up the pose and then correct the errors, which can be observed in the back, the buttock and the right leg. Many corrections were probably carried out, but in this drawing they cannot be seen clearly since they have been erased and covered with new lines. Th drawing is not a masterpiece, for it displays certain errors of draftsmanship that are caused by the visual problem posed b observing the model at such close range. The top part of the back, for example, would have been observed from a completely different point of view than the throat. The foreshortening of the arm and the treatment of light are two aspects that merit closer examination; the shadows model the entire front area, yet they are executed with lines, rather than by means of stumping, recalling methods employed in engraving.

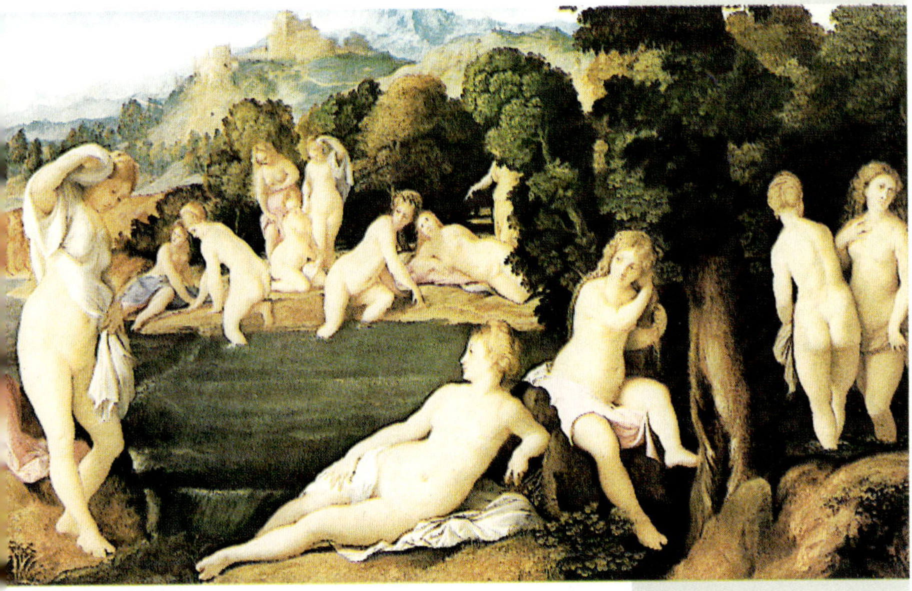

Diana Discovers Callisto's Pregnancy

Palma Vecchio (Jacomo Palma)
(Seria, near Bergamo, ca. 1480–Venice, 1528)

- ca. 1528
- oil on canvas
- 77.5 x 124 cm
- Kunsthistorisches Museum, Vienna

Callisto, a nymph who vowed to remain a virgin and became one of Artemis' (Diana's) maidens, is visited by Zeus, who falls hopelessly in love with her. In the guise of Artemis, Zeus lures her into his embrace, leaving her pregnant. Once her pregnancy is apparent, Artemis turns her into a bear. Other versions of the story recount that it was Hera, who, out of jealousy, ordered Callisto's transformation, or even that Zeus, in order to prevent his wife from learning of his lover, turns her into the constellation of Ursa Major, the Great Bear. The dynamism of the nudes lend this painting a sense of movement. Of all the figures only the goddess appears relaxed, contemplating her condition. The combination of figure and landscape is a typical attribute of Cinquecento painting. As in other works by this artist, the feminine bodies are rotund and voluptuous, whose sensuality is underscored by the remarkable chromatic harmony of the painting.

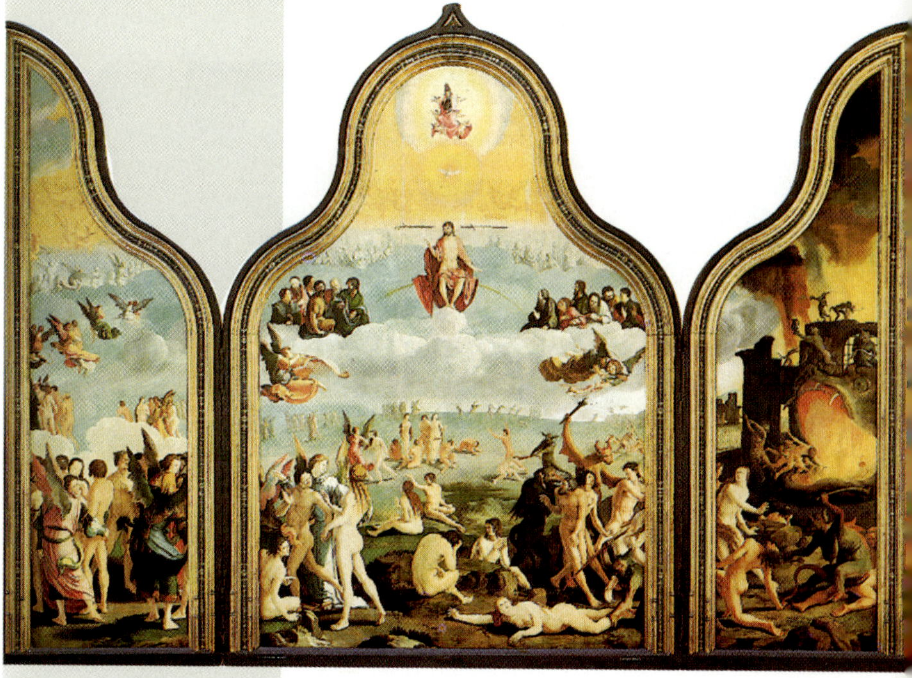

The Last Judgment

Lucas van Leyden (Lucas Huyghensz)
(Leiden, 1494–1533)

- 1526–27
- tempera on panel
- 271 x 185 cm (central panel); 266 x 176 cm (wings)
- Stedelijk Museum de Lakenhal, Leiden

The three scenes in this triptych recount scenes from the Gospel. The top part of the central panel shows God on high. Below him, flanked by his apostles and angels, is the risen Christ, who has returned to earth for the Last Judgment. The left wing shows the righteous entering light-filled heaven; the right panel shows the damned entering hell and being punished by devils. The painter has carried out an intricate study of light in these paintings, in which the brilliant colors and completely white areas stand out. The relatively few figures in the three scenes are rendered with painstaking precision. The beautiful, sensual nudes are arranged in groups and take up a variety of naturalistic poses, some of which suggest movement. The artist has perfectly combined the luminosity of the flesh tones with the dark colors of the background in order to highlight the figures.

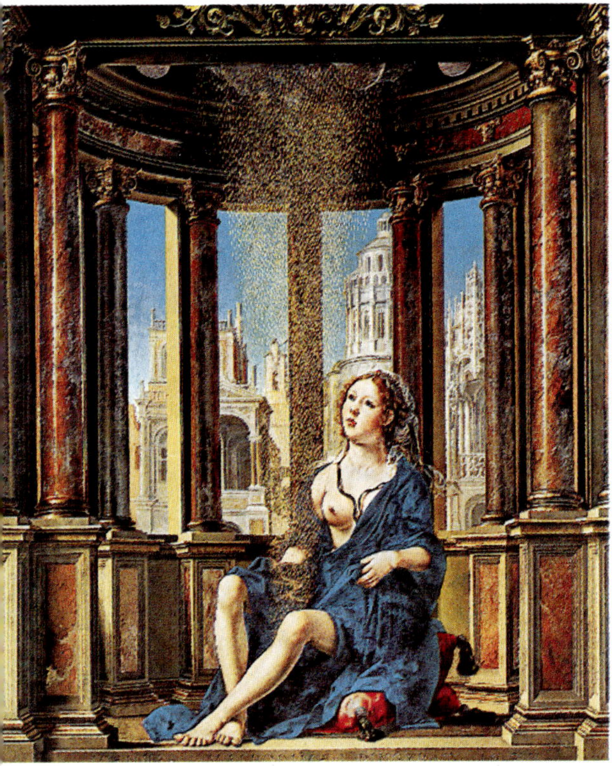

This picture depicts Danaë showered with the golden rain into which Zeus had transformed himself. The artist has absorbed elements of 16th-century Italian painting without grasping the spirit behind the letter of Renaissance imagery. He has exchanged Gothic forms for Roman-style architecture, for example, but paints it and everything else in the Netherlandish style. The partly naked figure of Danaë is meticulously modeled in a rather sculptural manner, the slightly cold, steely flesh not impeding the creation of an intensely erotic aura. This treatment tends to diminish the importance of color, light and, to a certain degree, the psychology of the protagonist. That is not to say that Danaë's pose, her legs partly bared and slightly apart, does not indicate her complicity, as she removes her garment to allow Zeus' golden rain to soak her body.

Danaë

Jan Gossaert
(or **Gossart**; also called **Mabuse**)
(Maubeuge, 1478
–Antwerp, 1532)

- 1527
- tempera and oil on canvas
- 113.5 x 95 cm
- Alte Pinakothek, Munich

St. John Evangelist

Pontormo (Jacopo Carucci)
(Pontormo, Tuscany, 1494 –Florence, 1557)

- 1525-26
- oil on panel
- 70 cm diameter
- Cappella Capponi, Santa Felicità, Florence

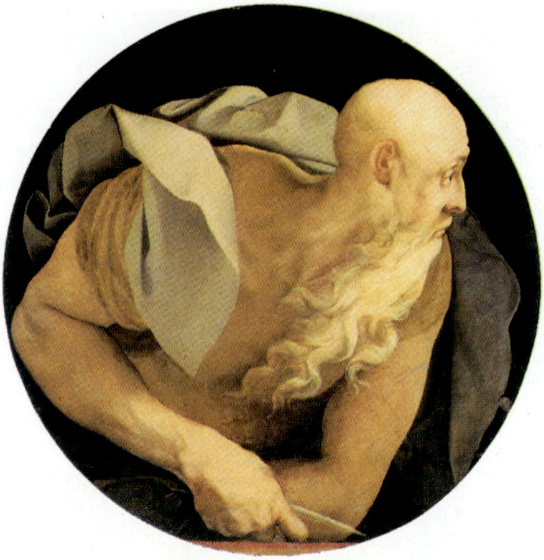

The conception underlying Pontormo's panel, in which the influence of Raphael and Michelangelo is manifest, seeks a certain ideal beauty by using powerful, sculptural forms. The Evangelist is depicted with an extremely well-built body, whose proportions are at once substantial and stylized. The foreshortening and the treatment of light in this painting are remarkable.

St. Jerome

Pontormo (Jacopo Carucci)
(Pontormo, Tuscany, 1494 –Florence, 1557)

- 1527-28
- oil on panel
- 105 x 80 cm
- Niedersächsisches Landesmuseum, Hanover

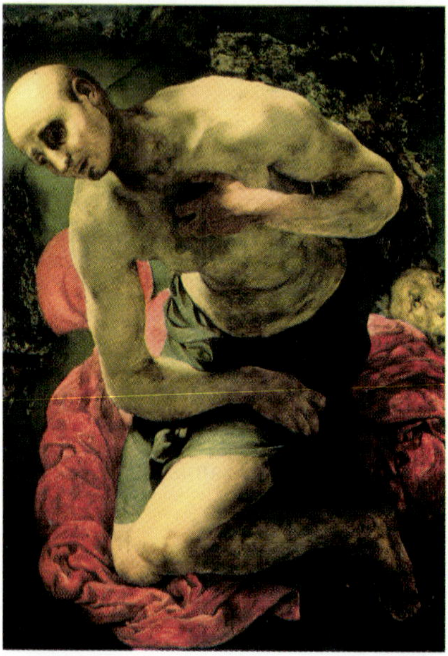

This painting is innovative both in conception and execution. The figure of St. Jerome is bathed in warm light falling from above to produce realistic chiaroscuro effects on trunk and limbs. The figure's forms are stylized, yet full of beauty. The skin coloration employs extremely unusual tones, greenish-grays, for instance, of a kind that Rubens was later to adopt.

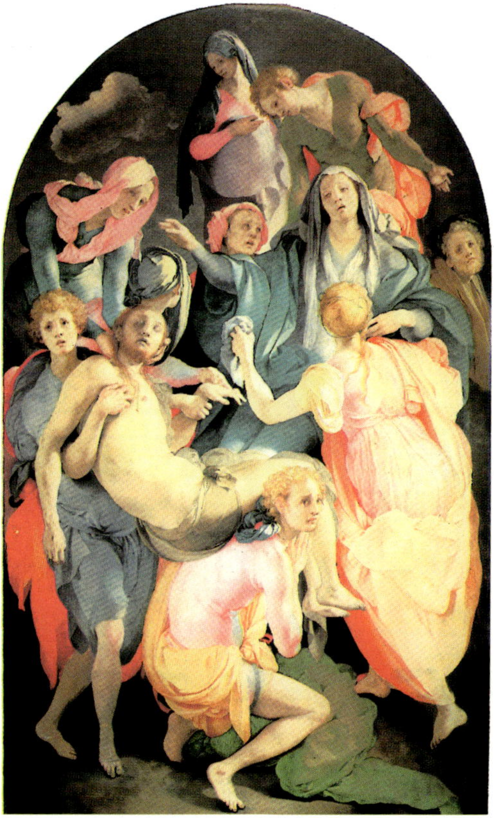

The Deposition

Pontormo
(Jacopo Carucci)
(Pontormo, Tuscany, 1494–Florence, 1557)

- 1526
- panel
- 313 x 192 cm
- Church of Santa Felicità, Capponi Chapel, Florence

ontormo, influenced by Albrecht Dürer, was concerned with voking elegance in his art, with almost immaterial subjects, f sinuous lines and flawless contours, and Mannerist, albeit istinctly Florentine, compositions. This work is a fine example of the artist's style, showing the lengths to which he went o break with the style of his early work. The painting is emarkable for its balanced composition, which is populated y figures in a variety of poses, making various gestures and lonning flowing drapery. It is also notable for its singular olor scheme: in the foreground the figures are luminous; as ney recede into the background, the colors become darker nd more intense. All this lends drama to the scene, whose rotagonist, with his dynamic pose and diagonal positioning, reaks the verticality of the other figures.

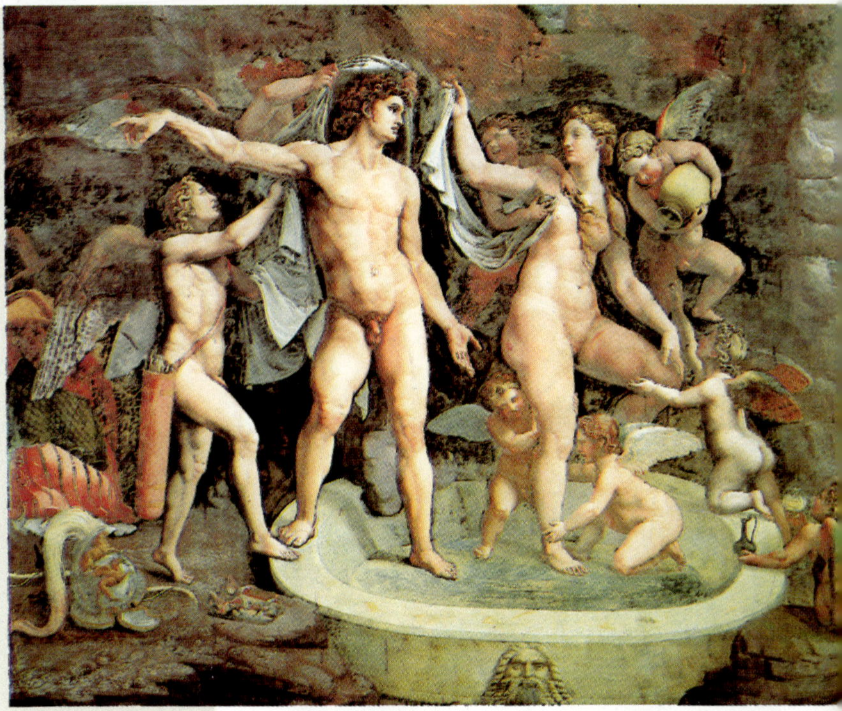

Cupid and Psyche's Bath

Giulio Romano (Giulio Pippi)
(Rome, prob. 1499 –Mantua, 1546)

- 1527–31
- fresco
- Palazzo del Tè, Hall of Psyche, Mantua

This Mannerist painting, with its majestic, grandiloquent pictorial treatment, is reminiscent of the work of Michelangelo. The scene abounds with nudes, each of which represents a unique anatomical study. Psyche, who symbolizes the soul and its feelings, will and intelligence, has powerful thighs and well-modeled, copious muscles. Attended by a group of cherubs, she stands with her legs slightly apart, in a stance that enhances the composition and increases the erotic quality of the painting. The male figure accompanying Psyche has an elegant body with carefully modeled muscles. He is also attended by cherubs, and by Cupid, an adolescent who appears on the left with his arrows. The three-dimensional figures in this elegant, theatrical scene are highly expressive and reflect the ideal of beauty that prevailed in the Renaissance.

Adam

Lucas Cranach the Elder
(Kronach, Franconia, 1472–Weimar, 1553)

- 1528
- oil on canvas
- 172 x 63 cm
- Galleria degli Uffizi, Florence

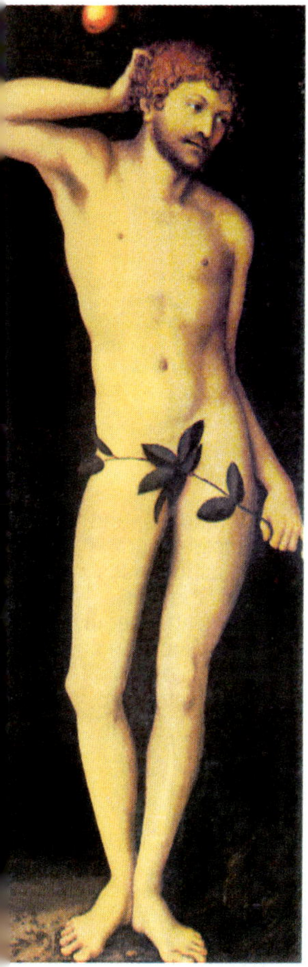

'his work is one of many
n religious or mythological
iemes by this important
epresentative of German
ainting. The dark back-
round and markedly ner-
ous profile are reminiscent
f Dürer, although in concep-
on the nude is closer to
enaissance traditions.

Eve

Lucas Cranach the Elder
(Kronach, Franconia, 1472–Weimar, 1553)

- 1528
- oil on canvas
- 167 x 61 cm
- Galleria degli Uffizi, Florence

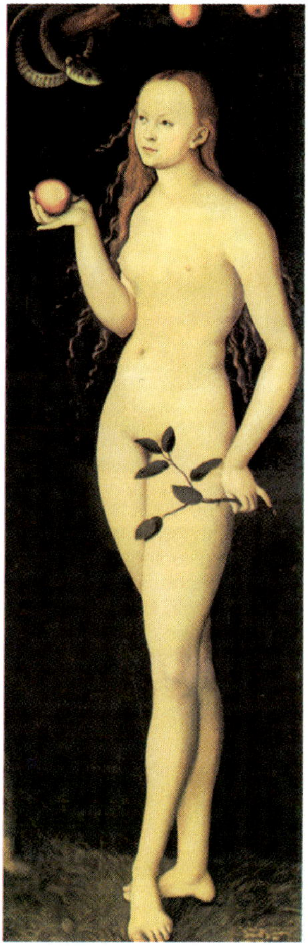

The painting hints at this artist's complex role as a Protestant who painted numerous works on religious or mythological themes, while maintaining a fine erotic sensibility very much in the Renaissance tradition. Works such as this one were so much in demand that Cranach had to paint a great number of them.

Martyrdom of St. Maurice

Pontormo (Jacopo Carucci)
(Pontormo, Tuscany, 1494–Florence, 1557)

- 1529–30
- oil on panel
- 65 x 73 cm
- Palazzo Pitti, Florence

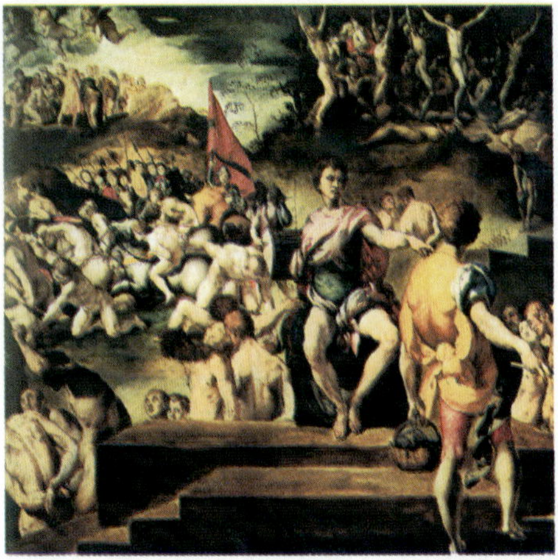

This scene depicts the martyrdom of St. Maurice, and the punishments inflicted on him by his soldiers at the Emperor Diocletian's behest, for his refusal to persecute the Christians. Monumental in conception, the work employs bold foreshortening in its figures, enhanced by an equally bold interpretation of light. The execution of the nude soldiers is distinctly naturalistic, while the dramatic lighting on their skin anticipates chiaroscuro.

Bacchus and Ariadne

Titian (Tiziano Vecellio di Gregorio)
(Pieve di Cadore, 1488/89 –Venice, 1576)

- 1520–23
- oil on canvas
- National Gallery, London

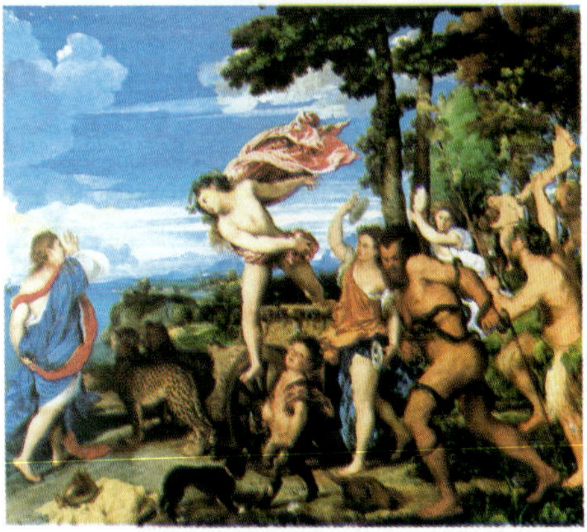

Ariadne, daughter of Minos, king of Crete, fell in love with Theseus, whom she supplied with the thread that ultimately enabled him to escape from the labyrinth. This composition presents the first encounter of hero and heroine in a setting where many other nude or half-nude figures create a warm and ravishing atmosphere.

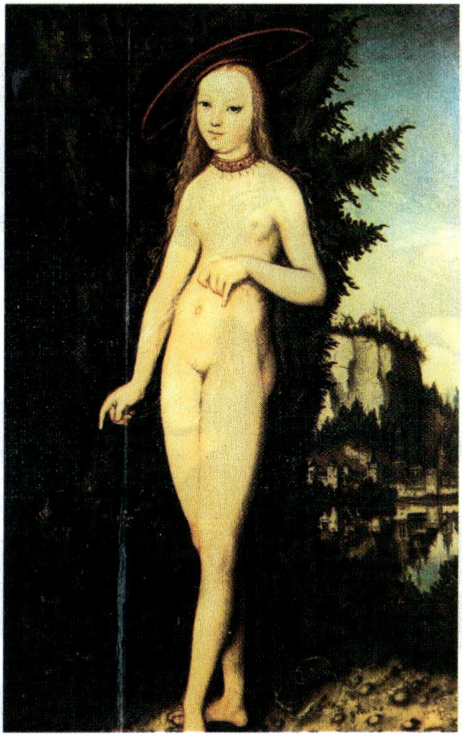

ılbrecht Dürer's Adam and Eve was probably what inspired ;ranach and other artists to take Venus as their subject for ıany years to follow. Cranach was an advocate of the Refor-ıation, a fact that contradicted his interest in the Renais-ance; for this reason, the painter preferred to align himself ,ith the teachings of Erasmus of Rotterdam, despite the diffi-ulties this entailed. Even though executing such nudes was ıe artist's way of taking up the Renaissance spirit, leaving .side all religious considerations, this Venus is radically dif-erent from the kind that was being painted in Italy at the me. Cranach's nude is not inspired by an aesthetic ideal, ut rather conceived from a critical standpoint. His Venus ,as painted as though it were destined for an altarpiece, ven though the painterly handling is clearly appropriate to a ortrait. The figure's body is made more sensual by the use f a transparent veil, which does not even cover the goddess' ıtimate parts. Cranach's ideal of beauty is revealed in the gure's slender body, with a slightly bulging stomach and nar-ɔw hips and shoulders.

Venus

Lucas Cranach the Elder
(Kronach, Franconia, 1472–Weimar, 1553)

- 1529
- panel
- 33 x 26 cm
- Musée du Louvre, Paris

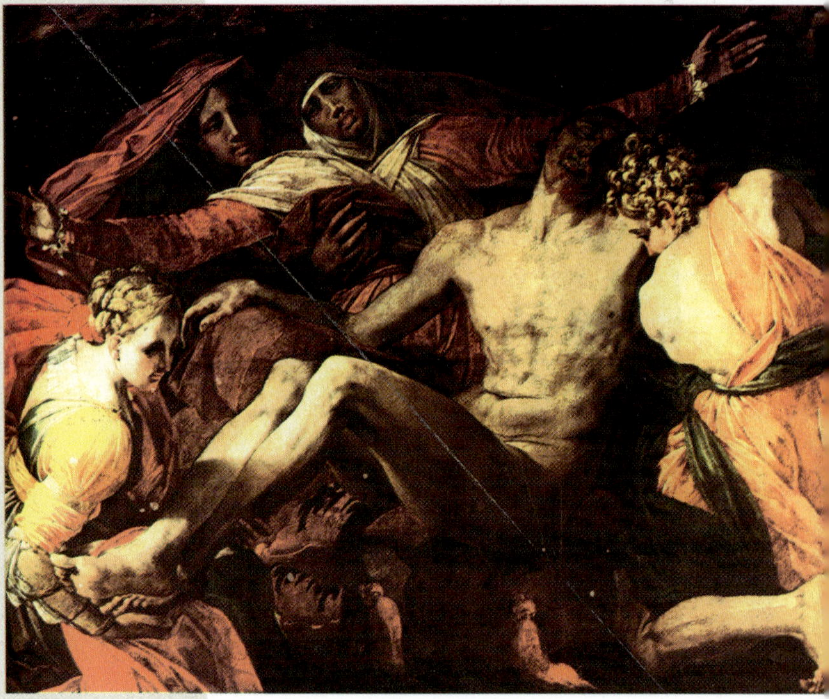

The Lamentation

Rosso Fiorentino
(Florence, 1494–Paris, 1540)

- original painting on panel, later transferred to canvas
- 125 x 159 cm
- Musée du Louvre, Paris

Rosso Fiorentino was a tormented artist. Summoned to France by Francis I, who undertook to emulate the Italian courts, the artist founded the Fontainebleau School. This is his last, and probably his finest, work. Commissioned by Anne de Montmorency for the chapel at Ecouen Palace, the anguish and high drama of the scene is achieved by the composition; at the same time the work is both harmonious and compelling in expression. Dürer's influence is apparent in Fiorentino's work, which is also informed by the compositions of Michelangelo. Evidence of this can be found in the plastic modeling of the figure of Christ, who is an element of calm in the midst of so much despair. He is portrayed as having an elongated body, which is drawn with a clean line and modeled in the Classical manner. Particular emphasis is placed on the study of light. The shadows that envelop the figure lend it volume and thus a sculptural quality.

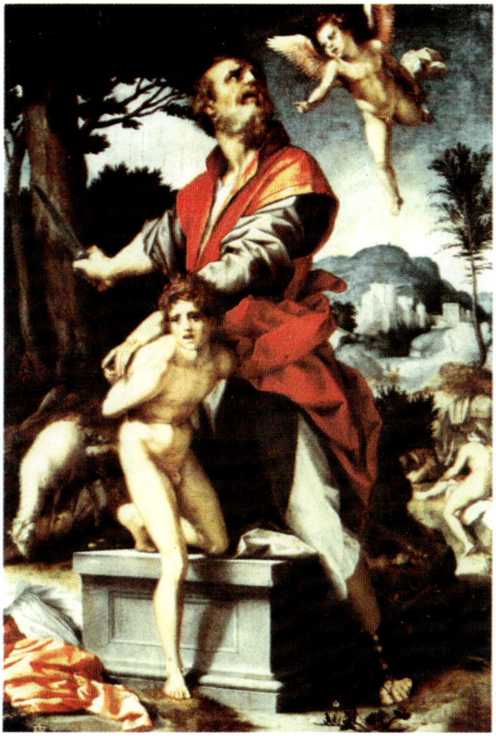

Sacrifice of Isaac

Andrea del Sarto (Andrea d'Agnolo di Francesco)
(Florence, 1486–1530)

- ca. 1529
- oil on canvas
- 98 x 69 cm
- Museo del Prado, Madrid

ıe consummate draftsmanship, the idealized forms and the ;e of starkly contrasting grays, reds and blues make this an :quisite composition, in which the drama being played out is legated to a secondary status, giving preference to aesthet- ;. The sensual, nude figure of Isaac kneels on an altar with ıe knee while terrified, looking toward the spectator and eading for mercy. His body is foreshortened and his back ınt forward. Although this is a perfectly executed body, as in ıer classical works, the boy's proportions are not those of a ıild but of an adult, albeit on a smaller scale. This manner of presenting figures was employed for aesthetic reasons and in keeping with similar criteria of the ancient Egyptians: the ;e of the subject indicates both age and social status.

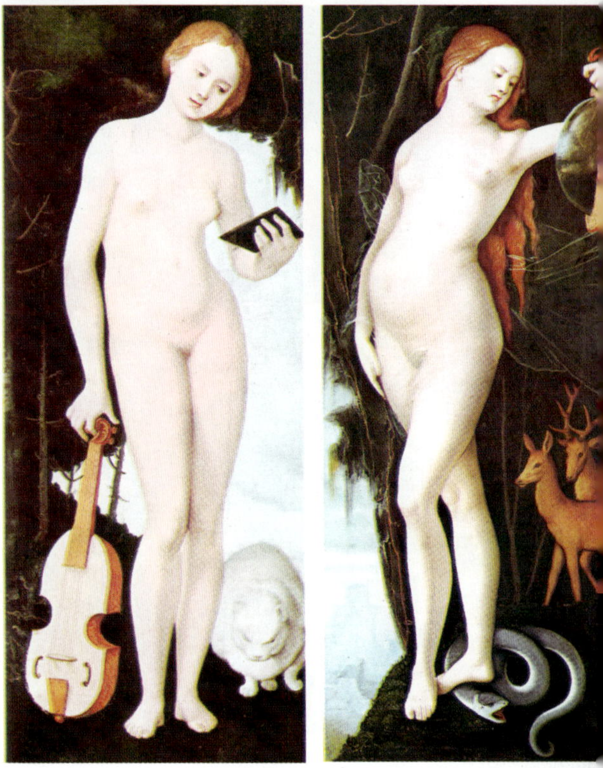

Music and Vanity

Hans Baldung
(called **Grien**)
(Schwäbish Gmünd, Swabia, 1484/85–Strasbourg, 1545)

- 1529
- panel
- 83 x 35 cm (each panel)
- Alte Pinakothek, Munich

These two allegorical figures reflect the ideal of beauty that prevailed in the 16th century. Baldung strove to introduce Italian Renaissance art to Germany during the Reformation, albeit by employing a traditional German iconography. The figure of Vanity exhibits certain Gothic traits, while the nude on the left, Music, possesses forms that are closer to the Renaissance style. Whereas Music has very soft forms, Vanity's are angular. Music's shoulders are straight, while those of Vanity are sloping, a characteristic of Gothic art. Another Gothic feature is the bulging abdomen, while that of the figure on the left is more harmonious. These two figures convey an intense eroticism that seeks to marry the Renaissance ideal of beauty with German symbolism, a fact that makes this artist one of the leading exponents of German Mannerism.

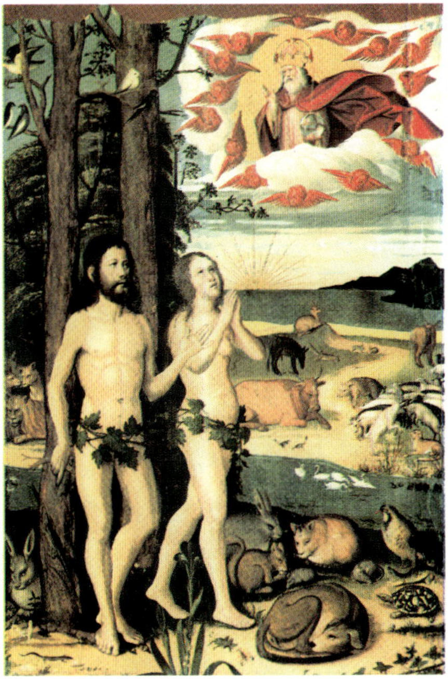

God has just finished creating the world. Sun, moon, nature, animals, Adam and Eve are peacefully admiring the Creator, portrayed on high, amidst clouds and surrounded by angels. Adam and Eve's loins are covered, which of course deviates from the biblical tradition, for there they are completely naked until they have sinned. Adam and Eve's painstakingly-executed faces and bodies, slender, delicate and sensual in line and form, contrast markedly with the naïve representations of the animals. The whole is pleasant and well-balanced and it achieves an orderly, considered and didactic narration. The panel, which displays numerous not always compatible influences, holds a balance between Renaissance innovation and Catalan High Gothic.

The Creation

Pere Mates

(Sant Feliu de Guíxols, Gerona, ca. 1490–Gerona, 1558)

- ca. 1530
- tempera on panel
- 109 x 61 cm
- Museu d'Art, Gerona

This panel was taken from the church of Santa María de Segueró, Garrotxa, Gerona.

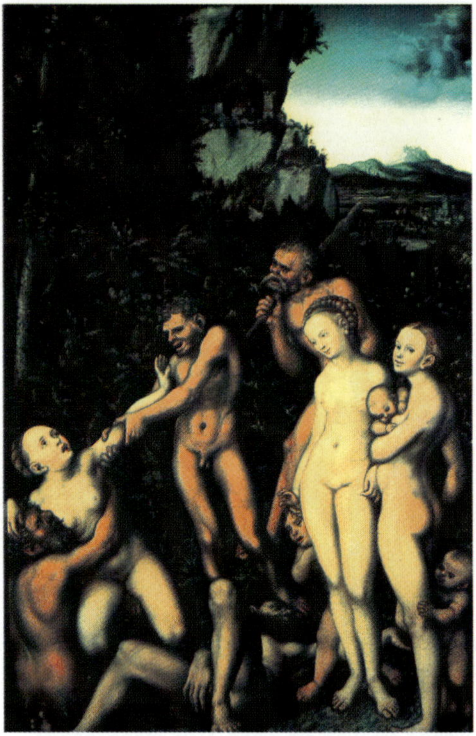

The Age of Silver

Lucas Cranach the Elder
(Kronach, Franconia, 1472–Weimar, 1553)

- 1530
- oil on panel
- Pushkin Museum, Moscow

This work is an allegory of jealousy, one of man's greatest weaknesses. The nudes in this work represent excellent anatomical studies, in which the ideal of beauty betrays male, almost grotesque attributes. The reason for the artist applying different flesh tone is plain to see: it not only served to distinguish between male and female beauty, but also to underscore it. Unlike other works by Cranach, the ideal of beauty depicted here bears a closer resemblance to that of the Italian Renaissance than of Gothic art, upon which he had based his subjects until then. Here, the female forms are softer and more graceful; certain aspects, such as the bulging abdomen, are given less importance, and, although the shapes of the breasts have remained the same, their volumes are merely suggested. Prior to executing this work, the artist had painted primarily themes of a religious nature. Henceforth, he was to receive numerous commissions for paintings of female nudes.

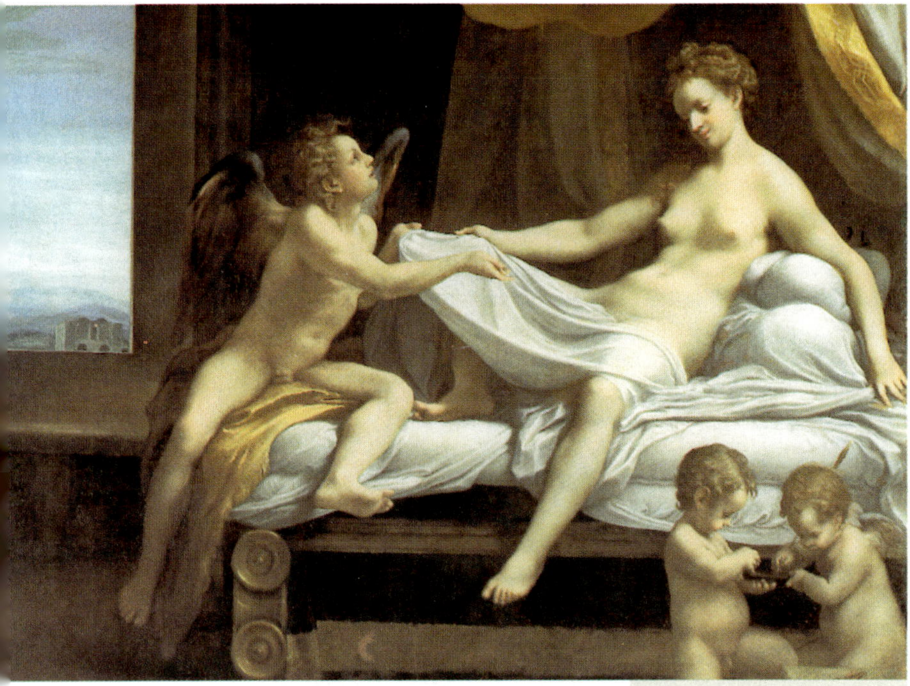

anaë was the daughter of Acrisius, King of Argos. As it as prophesied that her son would cause the death of the ing, he had her imprisoned in a bronze tower. Here Zeus escended upon her in the form of a shower of golden ain; and the son she bore him was Perseus. The image is ighly erotic. Young Danaë, with her legs spread slightly part, shows her complicity and willingness to receive her ver. Cupid gazes at Zeus, lifting the sheet that covers anaë's naked body, which is exquisite indeed. The light mphasizes her pubescent breasts, while she looks at her enitals, waiting for her lover to possess her. Cupid is rep- esented as a well-proportioned young man. The pictorial eatment betrays Leonardo's influence and makes use of n intense play of light and shade on the nudes.

Danaë

Correggio (Antonio Allegri)

(Correggio, near Parma, Emilia, ca. 1489–1534)

- 1530–32
- oil on canvas
- 161 x 193 cm
- Galleria Borghese, Rome

This painting belonged to the collection given to Charles V by the Duke of Mantua at his coronation in Bologna. It was part of Christina of Sweden's collections. Through acquisition by Prince Camilo Borghese in 1823, it became part of the present collection.

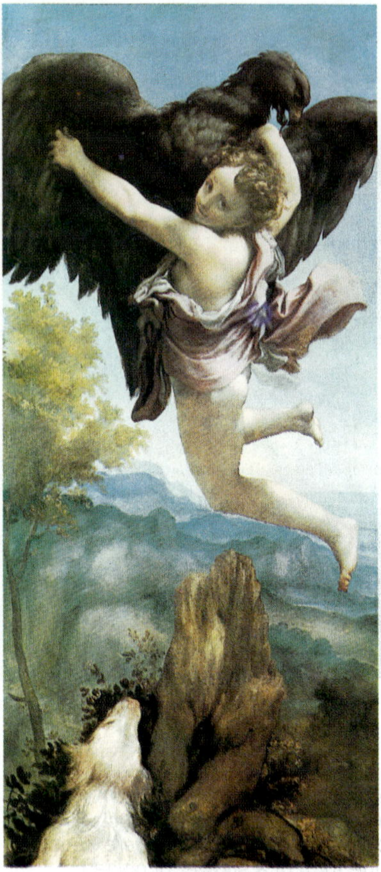

The Abduction of Ganymede

Correggio (Antonio Allegri)
(Correggio, near Parma, Emilia, ca. 1489–1534)

- 1530–32
- oil on canvas
- 163.5 x 70.5 cm
- Kunsthistorisches Museum, Vienna

As Ganymede, a handsome Trojan prince, became the object of Zeus' desire, the god turned himself into an eagle and carried Ganymede off to Olympus. In the eagle's grip, the youth looks resignedly towards the spectator, who views him from a lower vantage point. With this daring foreshortening Correggio achieves a sensual and elegant nude that is well proportioned. The treatment of light on the figure engenders magnificent flesh tones that reflect the luminosity of the scene, thus subtly integrating the nude into the landscape. The format contributes to the vertical compositional line, which is echoed in the hanging figure of Ganymede, the tree on the left and the rock at the center.

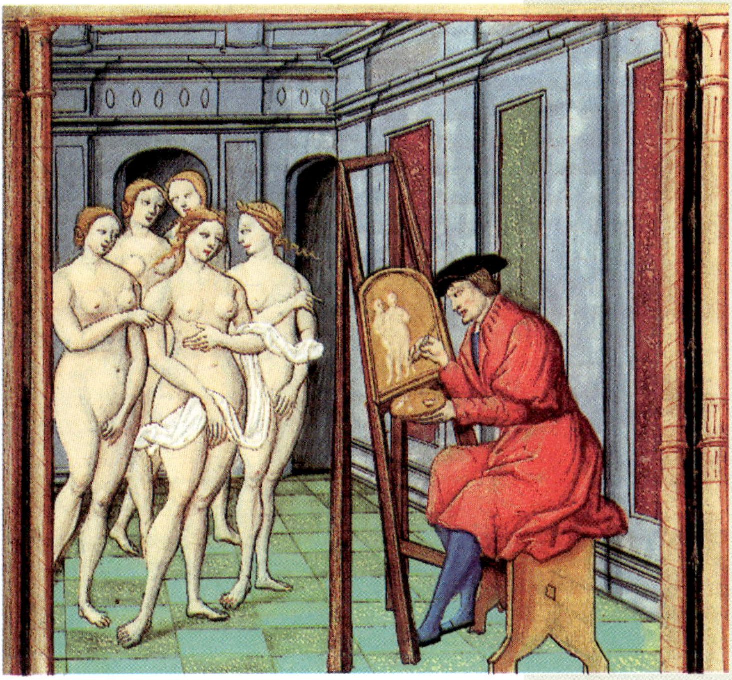

Zeuxis Painting the Daughters of Croton

Anonymous

- 1530–40
- miniature
- Pierpont Morgan Library, New York

'he subject of this painting derives from an account of Pliny ıe Elder: Zeuxis was invited to Croton to paint a picture of lelen of Troy, in the Temple of Juno. The artist ordered that search be carried out to find the most beautiful maiden of ;roton, who was to sit for him and provide inspiration. Since ıe ideal girl was not found, he chose the five most beautiful ı order to combine the most perfect parts of each one to reate a figure of ideal beauty. The female figures in this /ork are carefully rendered, showing the artist's interest in uman anatomy. Although the painting is marked by humanst refinement, a characteristic of the Renaissance, the figres betray Gothic influences in their clearly delineated outnes and schematic anatomy. Moreover, the maidens' poses nd facial features are nearly identical, attesting to a some-hat outdated treatment of the figures.

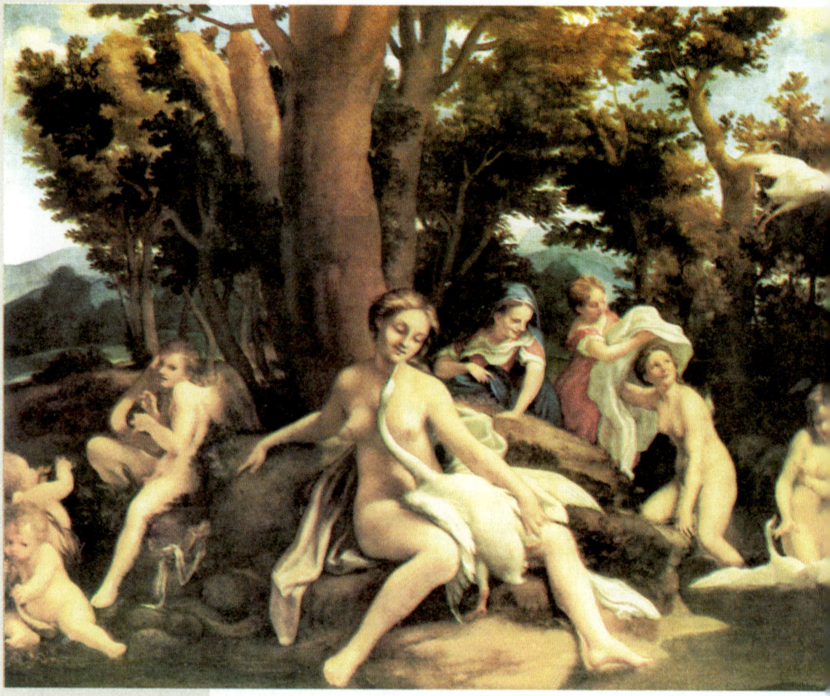

Leda and the Swan

Correggio (Antonio Allegri)
(Correggio, near Parma, Emilia, ca. 1489–1534)

- 1531–32
- oil on canvas
- 152 x 191 cm
- Staatliche Museen Preussischer Kulturbesitz, Gemäldegalerie, Berlin

In this painting, Correggio depicts Jupiter, in the guise of a swan, seducing Leda. Positioned between her legs, he stretches his shapely neck over her body, between her breasts until his beak touches her chin. Her head is slightly inclined in a gesture of mystical submission. The scene is set in a forest, which serves as a backdrop against which the golden luminosity of the nudes is further accentuated. An air of eroticism pervades the scene, finding its most perfect expression in the figure of Leda, who is shown coquetting with the swan. The masterly handling of light lends the foreshortening of the figures and the subtle chiaroscuro remarkable realism. It is precisely this treatment that gives the figures their soft and dreamy appearance.

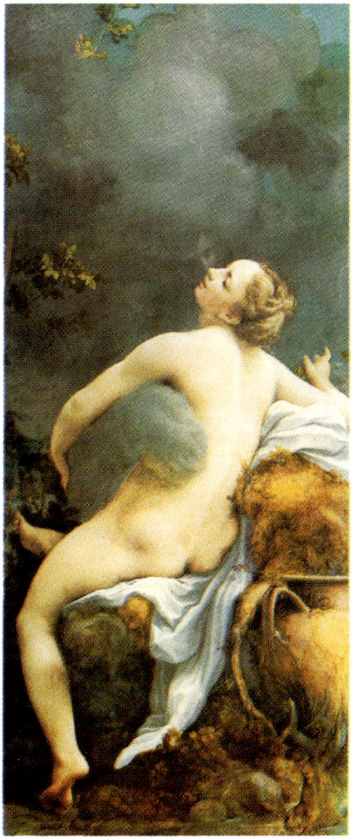

ɘus, enamoured of Io, spreads a cloud of darkness over e woods in which he makes love to her. Zeus' wife, Hera, ıspecting what has happened, decides to investigate. ɘfore the goddess is able to catch them in the act, Zeus rns Io into a heifer. This is one of Correggio's most ravish- g nudes, no doubt influenced by Leonardo da Vinci. The oportions of this extremely sensual female nude are bal- ıced and harmonious. The foreshortening of her limbs lend e amorous scene a sense of slow, rhythmic movement. ith this work Correggio heralds the arrival of Mannerism, wing the seed that was to become Baroque art.

Zeus and Io

Correggio (Antonio Allegri)
(Correggio, near Parma, Emilia, ca. 1489–1534)

- 1531–32
- oil on canvas
- 163.5 x 74 cm
- Kunsthistorisches Museum, Vienna

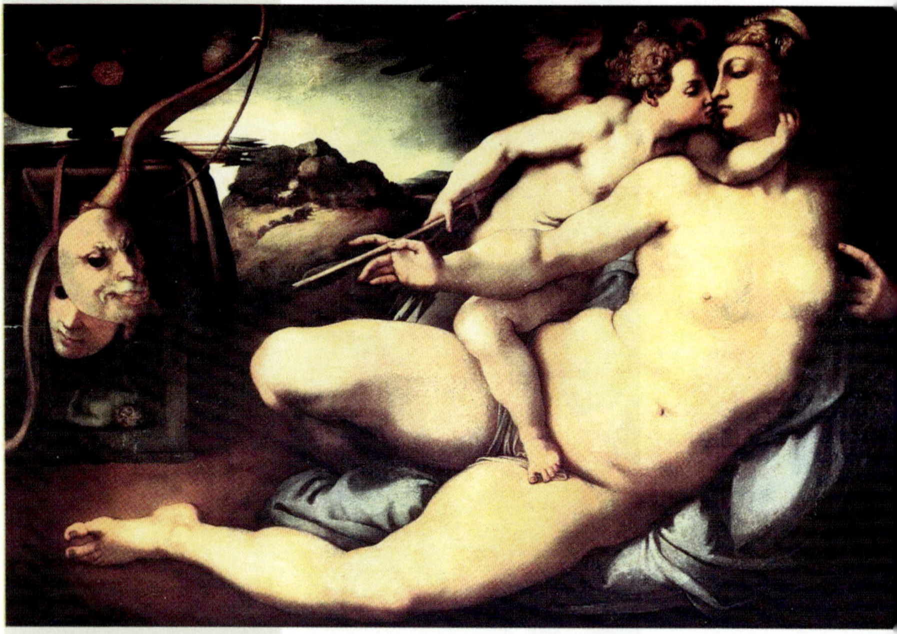

Venus and Cupid

Pontormo (Jacopo Carucci)
(Pontormo, Tuscany, 1494–Florence, 1557)

- 1533
- oil on canvas
- 128 x 197 cm
- Galleria dell'Accademia, Venice

With this painting, Pontormo created a unique pattern for the depiction of the goddess, in which she appears almost as a giantess, her bodily proportions approaching the point of deformation if aesthetics or composition so require. Here, Venus' nude body is provocatively exhibited, offering itself to the viewer with parted legs and trunk twisted towards the left. Her head, relatively small in size, emphasizes the goddess' bodily strength. The skin tints are executed in an extremely rich palette full of tonal variations, so that Venus' body contrasts brightly with the surrounding dark, while the interaction between the two protagonists is deliberately ambiguous: innocence and sensuality, provocation and eroticism, love and pleasure, all have a place here. This painter's art is elegant and typical of Florentine Mannerism with its sinuous, almost immaterial forms, well-defined profiles and an abundance of cool tones.

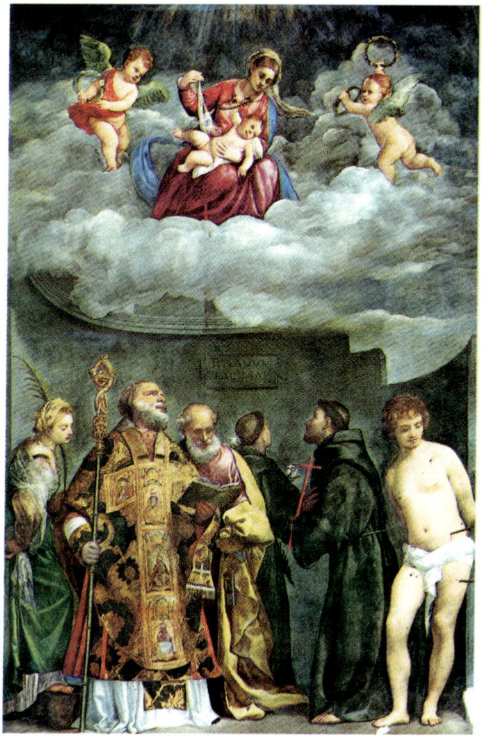

The Madonna of San Nicolas dei Frari

Titian (Tiziano Vecellio di Gregorio)
(Pieve di Cadore, 1488/89 –Venice, 1576)

- 1533–35
- oil on canvas
- 388 x 270 cm
- Pinacoteca, Vatican

this work, various structural divisions give rise to a lay-
d composition. The iconographic program is, although
entirely original, uncommon, at once complicating and
iching the narrative. The lower register contains the fig-
s of various saints, with St. Sebastian standing out on
right, forming a compositional diagonal that harmonizes
n that of the Virgin. Unlike in more conventional depic-
ns the martyr is not looking up to heaven here, but,
ner, at the ground. This nude, although rendered in a
king contrapposto pose, is not as sensual as other rep-
entations of the Saint, perhaps on account of the fact
t here he is not the protagonist of the scene. Titian has
trayed the figure of Sebastian naturalistically and with
ninine features, eschewing any attempt at idealization.

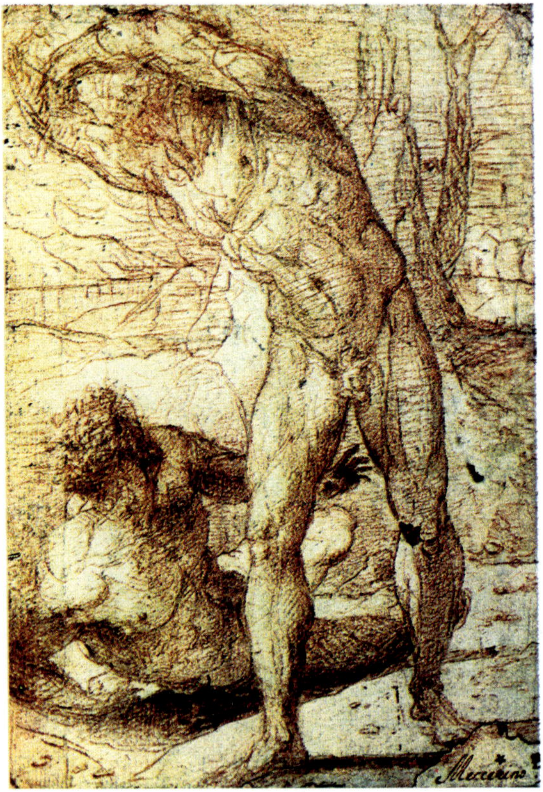

Two Naked Men in a Landscape

Domenico Beccafumi (Domenico di Giacomo de Pace)
(Valdibiena, Siena, 1486- Siena, 1551)

- sanguine
- 22.4 x 15.8 cm
- Devonshire Collections, Chatsworth

This artist was acquainted with the works of the Renaissance painters, all of whom had a decisive influence on his paintings. Later, his style came closer to the Mannerist style of Rosso and Pontormo, with an interest in subtlety and symbolism, rather than in compositional structure. The painter's preoccupation with the problems of light and shadows in his works presages the chiaroscuro technique. This drawing is a study of forms and light. The line is fluid and the shadows display a delicateness and luminosity that evoke the drawings of Leonardo da Vinci. The pose, the structure and the general conception of these two figures seem to be inspired by the spectacular sculptural models by Michelangelo, with their well-studied dramatic poses. Despite the apparent bulkiness of these bodies, they appear to move with unhindered grace. More than a unitary scene, it seems as if the artist had combined two independent studies in this work, given that there is no relationship between the two.

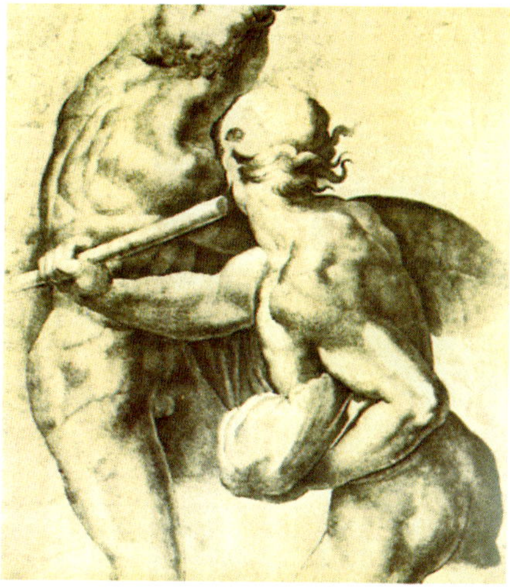

Two Nude Torsos from Behind

Michelangelo (Michelango Buonarroti)
(Caprese, Tuscany, 1475 –Rome, 1564)

- drawing
- Galleria dell'Accademia, Venice

l are familiar with Michelangelo's surpassing interest the human body and in finding new ways of repre-nting it. For this reason he even dissected corpses to ırsue his anatomical studies, for which he was put on al. The exaggeratedly clear forms and gestures here e a part of Michelangelo's search for an ideal beauty.

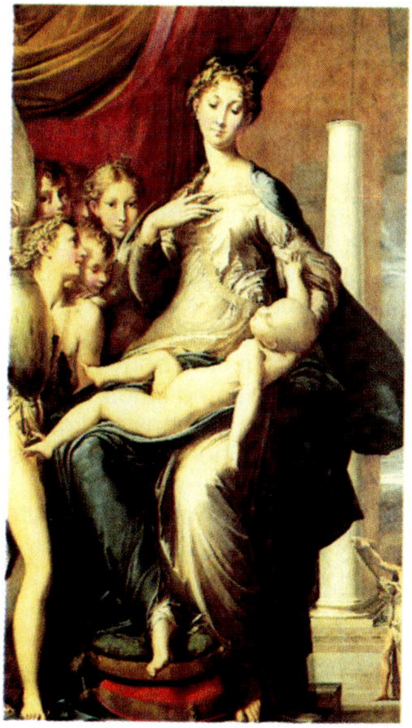

Madonna of the Long Neck

Parmigianino (Girolamo Francesco Mazzola)
(Parma, 1503–Casalmaggiore, Cremona, 1540)

- ca. 1535
- oil on canvas
- 214 x 133 cm
- Galleria degli Uffizi, Florence

is canvas, the work of a inter who studied under rreggio, exhibits formal gance and delicate nsuality. Its spiritual ture is heightened by attenuated figures in ected, static poses, the phuism of forms and the icate treatment of the es, lending the painting eat refinement. The fig- of Christ can be seen eep on his mother's lap, ibiting his penis, which scrutinized by one of the ıres on the left.

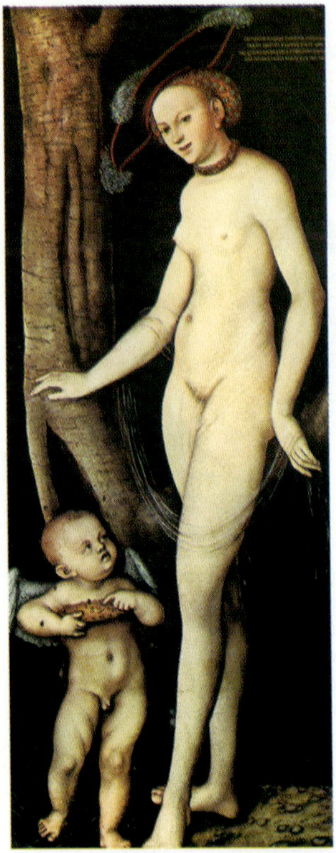

Venus and Cupid with a Honeycomb

Lucas Cranach the Elder
(Kronach, Franconia, 1472–Weimar, 1553)

- 1531
- tempera on panel
- 170 x 73 cm
- Galleria Borghese, Rome

This Venus is remarkable for her disarmingly candid gaze a the viewer, her mischievous facial expression and her sensu al body. In his nudes, Cranach did not seek realism, but, rather, a sophisticated blending of the religious with the profane, the transcendental with the commonplace. Here, Venu cold sensuality is enhanced by the elegant hat she is wearin (which appears in other works by the artist), the jewelry adorning her body and the transparent veil that brushes against her naked body. This adolescent-looking figure has fragile, attenuated limbs with small, firm breasts and a grac ful neck. The emphasized curves along her left side, from h breast, along her abdomen, down to the front leg, is in keep ing with the figure's sensuality. The incipient pubic hair, a highly unusual detail, is executed here with great delicacy.

oses and forms in
ontormo's drawings
re often somewhat
xaggerated, a prev-
lent verticality and
light unnaturalness
f appearance being
allmarks of the first
eneration of Flor-
ntine Mannerism.
Ve see these char-
cteristics in this
emale nude depict-
ig an allegorical
ersonage, the artist
aving distorted the
ose with a view to
iving the figure a
iore idealistic and
ream-like feel.
lowever, outlines
nd areas of light
nd shade are clean
nd sharp; the resul-
nt three-dimen-
onality creates an
ttractive figure of
reat vitality.

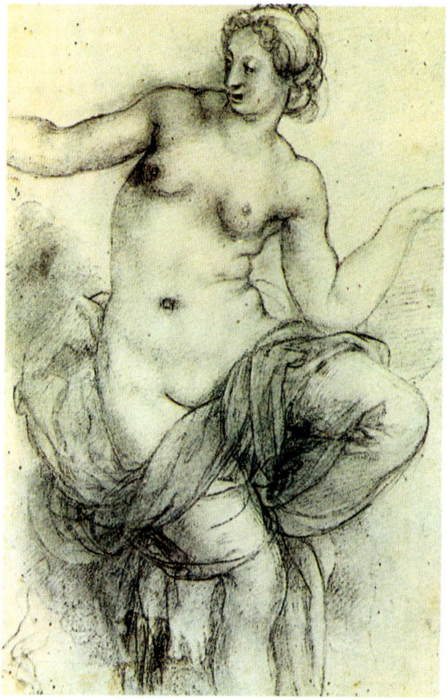

Female Allegory

Pontormo (Jacopo Carucci)
(Pontormo, Tuscany, 1494–Florence, 1557)

- pencil and wax
- 35.3 x 26.2 cm
- Kunsthalle, Hamburg

nis artist's richly
culptural style of
ainting has had a
ofound and endur-
g influence on all
ibsequent art.
though he never
oked on himself
a painter, his rep-
sentations of the
iman body are
me of the best
at have ever been
oduced. Their
iatomical precision,
well as the
asterful use of
reshortening, lend
chelangelo's fig-
es uniquely monu-
ental qualities.

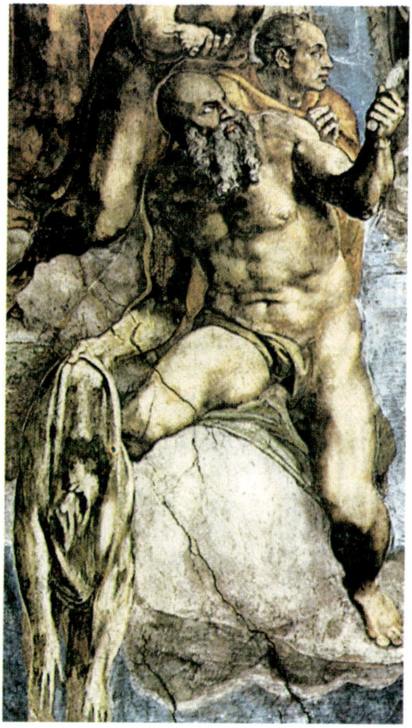

Detail of the Last Judgement

Michelangelo (Michelango Buonarroti)
(Caprese, Tuscany, 1475 –Rome, 1564)

- ca. 1536–41
- fresco
- 1483 x 1330 cm (overall size)
- Sistine Chapel, Vatican City

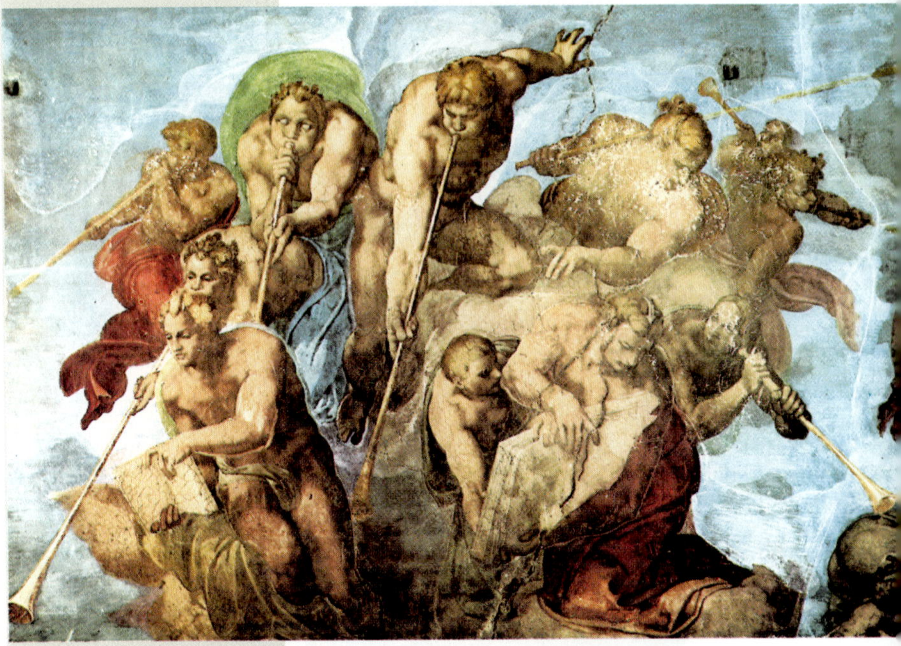

Angels with Trumpets and Books (detail of The Final Judgment)

Michelangelo (Michelango Buonarroti)
(Caprese, Tuscany, 1475 –Rome, 1564)

- 1537–41
- fresco
- 1370 x 1220 cm
- Sistine Chapel, Vatican

This group of figures, which seems to emerge from a brilliant blue background, has great visual impact and serves to emphasize the divine glory and justice of the scene. The bodies of the figures are heroic in aspect and exhibit a high degree of plasticity owing to the detailed study of tonal values, the vi tuoso draftsmanship and the subtle use of half-light in the modeling. The light colors highlighting the figures lend them astounding realism. This combined with a strong compositior rhythm produces a dynamic visual effect. Considering that these frescos are monumental in size, are located far above the viewer and that the entire Sistine Chapel is full of nudes, the overall visual effect is extraordinary indeed.

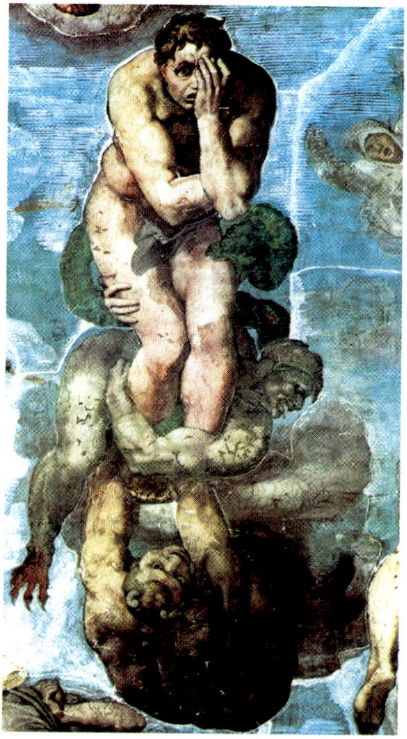

The Damned (detail of The Final Judgment)

Michelangelo (Michelango Buonarroti)

(Caprese, Tuscany, 1475 –Rome, 1564)

- 1537–41
- fresco
- 1370 x 1220 cm
- Sistine Chapel, Vatican

his is one of the most celebrated nudes in the Sistine hapel owing to its dramatic expression and gesture of hor- r. Facing the viewer, the figure is boldly foreshortened and artly covering his face with his left hand. He conveys a ense of foreboding, particularly in the twisted shape of his outh. Several devils are tugging at his legs, dragging him own to hell. The body of this damned soul, rotund despite s muscles, is the very embodiment of human helplessness the face of destiny. The anatomy is complex, which is par- cularly evident in the figure's contorted limbs. The figure's xtreme plasticity is achieved through a skillful application of ght and shadow, as well as through the use of various flesh nes: in the upper body, sienna tones predominate, where- s in the lower body, warm flesh tones prevail.

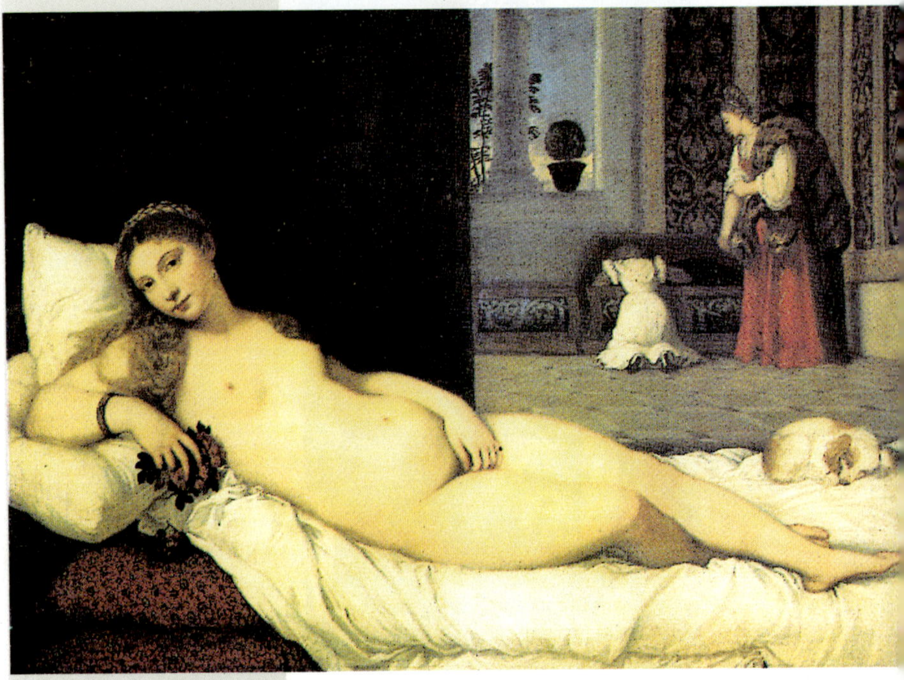

Venus of Urbino

Titian (Tiziano Vecellio di Gregorio)
(Pieve di Cadore, 1488/89 –Venice, 1576)

- ca. 1538
- oil on canvas
- 119 x 165 cm
- Galleria degli Uffizi, Florence

This was the first figure of Venus painted by Titian and, of all his works, it was to have the greatest impact on future generations of artists. The splendid young woman is shown reclining on a bed whose white sheets reflect the brightness of the room. She looks out of the scene, inviting the viewer to enjoy her company. The provocative character of the painting is underscored by the nonchalance with which she suggestively rests her left hand on her pubis. Another erotic feature of the nude is her hair, which falls demonstratively around her shoulders, a detail that in Titian's time was considered to be highly erotic as it was customary for women to put their hair up, letting it down only in intimate settings. The nude is extremely naturalistic in style, which only serves to enhance her beauty. The two figures in the background wonderfully offset the nude in the foreground.

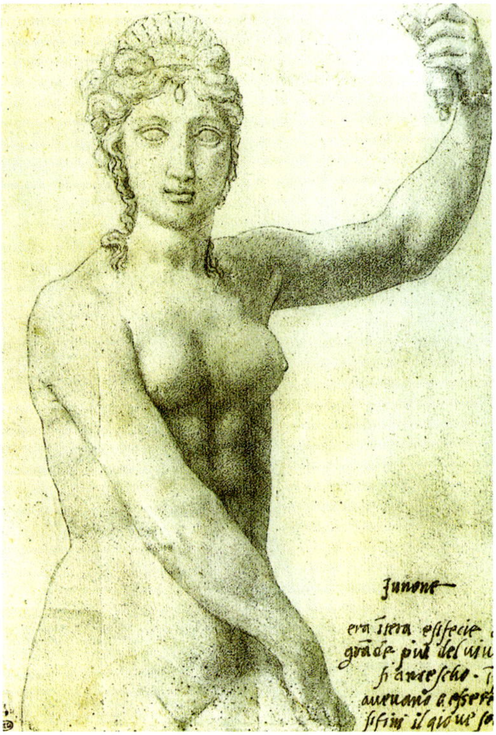

though fewer than a dozen drawings in all have been tributed to this artist, they are so exceptional that Cellini ill ranks among the finest draftsmen of the Tuscan Cinque- ento. The subject of this drawing is Juno, the ancient oman queen of heaven. Arguably the artist's finest drawing, e sketch was originally made for a set of bronze cande- bras (never actually made) to be decorated with goddesses id commissioned by king Francis I in 1540. This no doubt plains why the drawing employs a decidedly sculptural eatment, suggesting a work in marble or bronze. It is exe- ited along purest Classical lines: pose static, figure ideal- ed, meticulously modeled and rich in tonal gradations, with ely-wrought, expressive musculature. Highlights and shad- vs blend perfectly through an abundance of complex gray nes that also give the motif great subtlety.

Female Study (The Goddess Juno)

Benvenuto Cellini
(Florence, 1500–1571)

- 1540
- black pencil
- 24.7 x 18.6 cm
- Musée du Louvre, Cabinet des Dessins , Paris

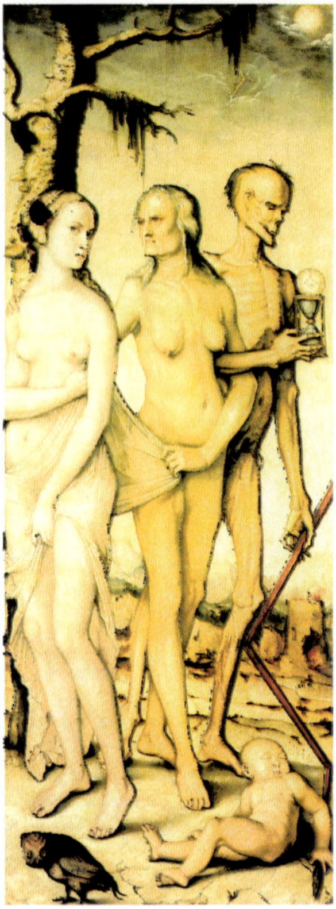

The Three Ages of Man

Hans Baldung
(called Grien)
(Schwäbisch Gmünd, Swabia, 1484/85–Strasbourg, 1545)

- ca.1540
- oil on panel
- 151 x 61 cm
- Museo del Prado, Madrid

This painting has belonged to the Spanish royal collection since the reign of Philip II.

This work, which formed part of a diptych, shows three stages of life, as well as Death, the keeper of time and the fate of every human being. The tense facial expressions and the relationship between the figures evoke pathos and displeasure at once. The artist has, however, made a concerted effort to portray them in an aesthetically appealing and idealistic manner. The young woman, with her round shoulders, bulging abdomen and small, distinct breasts, represents the Gothic ideal of beauty. Her facial expression betrays a matur form of expressionism with certain naturalist influences. This style is accentuated further still in the old woman, whose humanist naturalism is most apparent. The figure of Death is surreal to the point of being grotesque. It is based on Romanesque and Gothic reliefs, in which he is represented as a dancer who is both a caricature and terrifying.

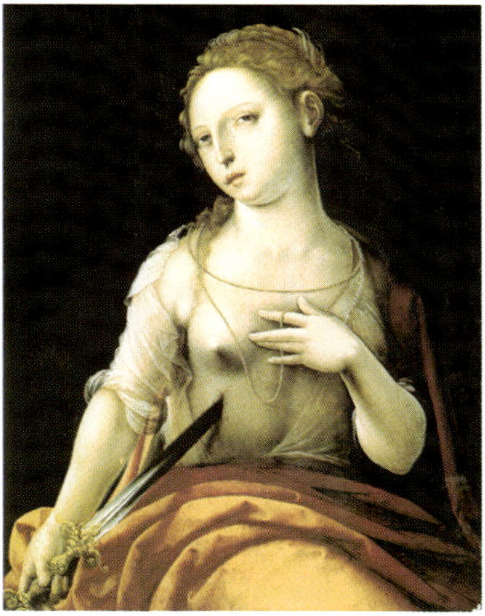

Lucrece's Suicide

Master of the Parrot

- first half of the 16th century
- oil on panel
- 48 x 38 cm
- Museo del Prado, Madrid

'he work has been attributed to several artists. Its elabo-ate execution recalls Flemish art in contact with the Italian enaissance. Lucrece is presented here as a woman of mall, almost child-like build, whose somewhat pallid com-lexion goes to heightening her physical appeal.

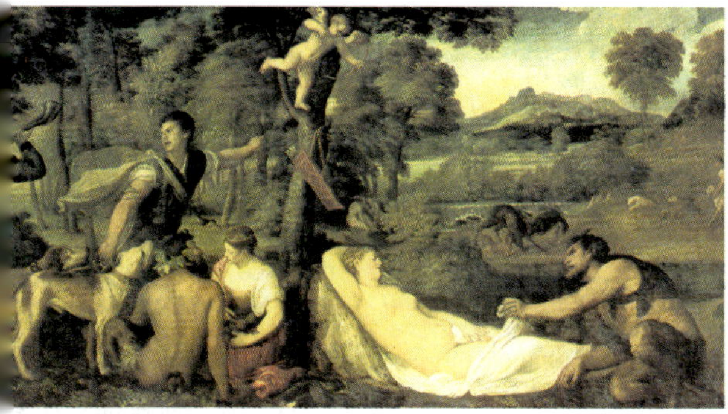

Jupiter and Antiope (Pardo Venus)

Titian (Tiziano Vecellio di Gregorio)

(Pieve di Cadore, 1488/89 –Venice, 1576)

- 1540–42
- oil on canvas
- 196 x 385 cm
- Musée du Louvre, Paris

a natural setting and with a slightly hazy atmosphere that iaracterizes his works, Titian composed this bucolic scene, hich includes a remarkably luminous figure of Venus. The oddess appears asleep, shrouded in an air of mystery. Her aked body is sensual and rotund, with comely shapes, and set in a pose that bears the hallmark of Titian's work, a ombination of innocence and self-assurance and a synthe-s of uninhibited boldness, beauty and sensuality.

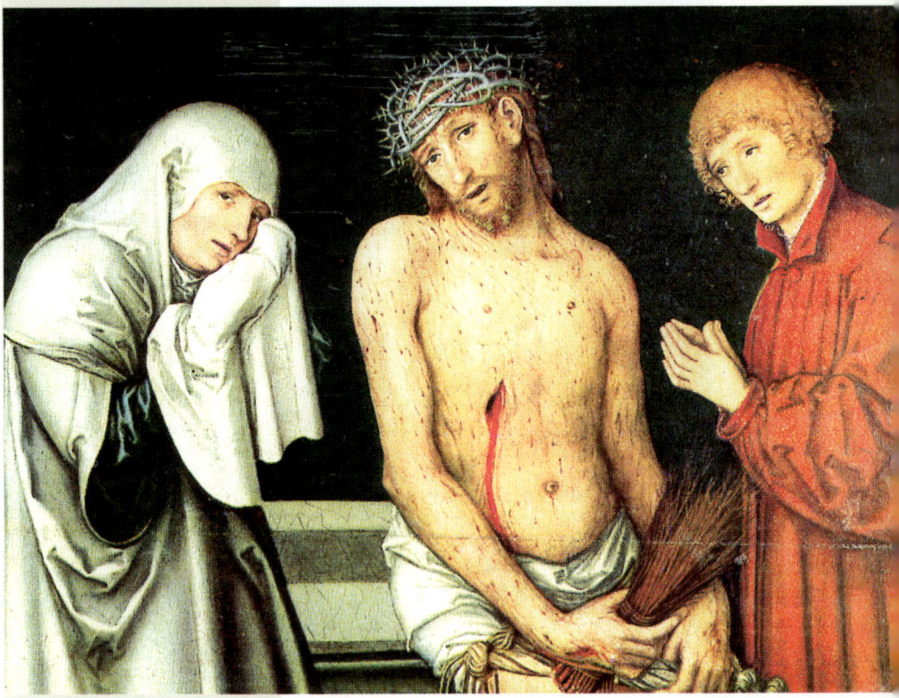

Pietà

Lucas Cranach the Elder
(Kronach, Franconia, 1472–Weimar, 1553)

- 1540
- oil on panel
- 54 x 74 cm
- Pinacoteca, Vatican

The work of Cranach the Elder epitomizes the transition between German Gothic and Renaissance art. His friendship with Martin Luther led him to become one of the artists who best served the Protestant cause. This figure of Christ, though exhibiting signs of a Renaissance conception of the human body, bears a closer resemblance to Gothic images. Although the modeling of the volumes gives rise to a certain naturalism, the figure's bone structure, pose and attitude betray its alignment with German Gothic. The anatomical forms have been conceived as a set of masses such that the muscles are scarcely perceptible. Cranach's skillful draftsmanship is brought to the fore by the outlines of his figures, which form a striking contrast to the background, a technique that was to persist in German art for many years to come. The figure of Christ is imbued with remarkable expressive force, as is typical of early German Renaissance painting.

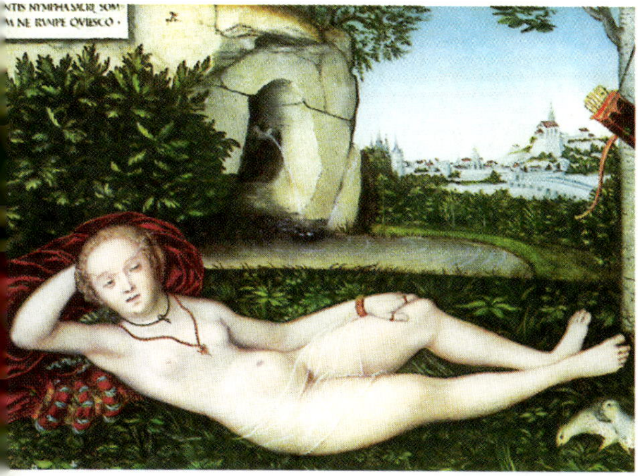

The Nymph of the Spring

Lucas Cranach the Elder

(Kronach, Franconia, 1472–Weimar, 1553)

- after 1537
- oil on panel
- 48.5 x 72.8 cm
- National Gallery of Art, Gift of Clarence Y. Palitz, 1957, Washington, D.C.

ı this allegorical work, Cranach presents a nymph sleeping ı a natural setting, next to a spring. Some of the elements ıcluded in this work, such as the quiver and the arrows in ·ont of the tree trunk, recall the goddess Diana. The nude ·reathes sensuality, which is accentuated by the tiny transpar- ·nt veil covering her genitals, yet which does little to conceal ·er nude body from the spectator's view.

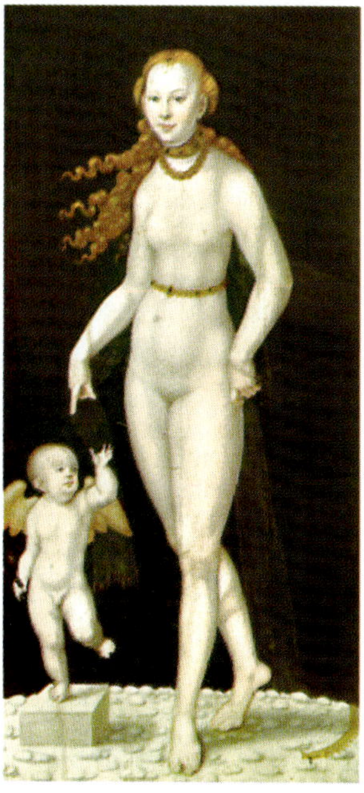

Venus and Cupid

Lucas Cranach the Younger

(Wittenberg, 1515 –Weimar, 1586)

- oil on panel
- 196 x 89 cm
- Alte Pinakothek, Munich

·his Venus, of Gothic concep- ·on, reflects the German ideal ·f beauty of Cranach's day. ·he figure's round shoulders ·omplement the long neck. ·er small, almost puerile, ·reasts, appear above a ·ollow torso that accentuates ·er bulging abdomen, and an ·xquisite belt is wrapped ·round her waist. The figure set against a dark back- ·round, making the flesh ·ppear extremely pale, in- ·eed almost marmoreal. The ·olumes, modeled with gray- ·h tones, serve to heighten ·e subtle sensuality of the ·oddess of love.

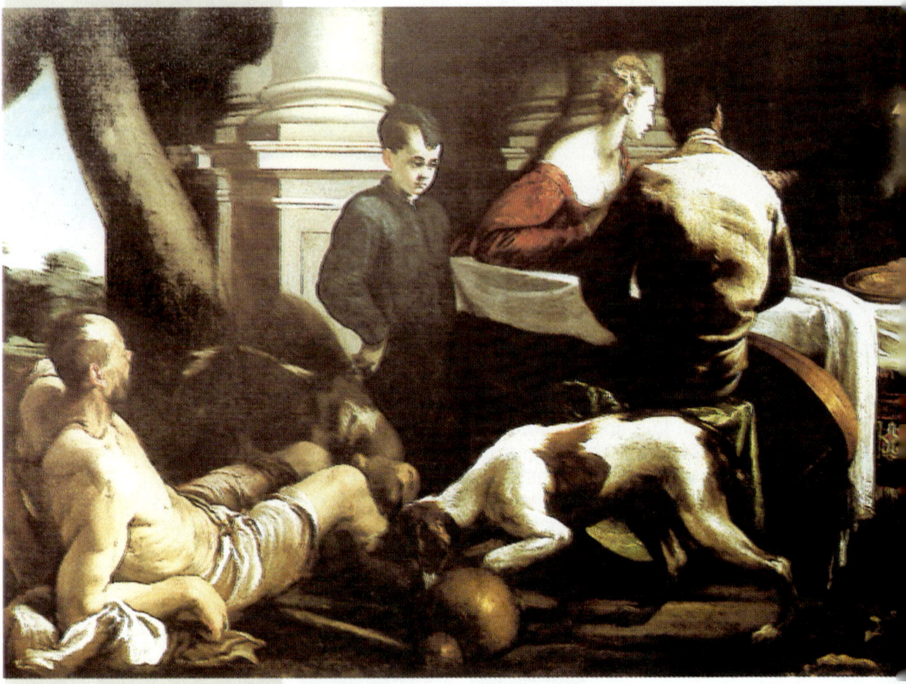

Lazarus and the Rich Man

Jacopo Bassano (Jacopo da Ponte)

(Bassano, ca. 1518–1593)

- 1540
- oil on canvas
- 146 x 221 cm
- Cleveland Museum of Art, Cleveland, OH

This painting illustrates a parable from the Gospel according to St. Mark. Lazarus was a beggar who went in vain to the gate of a rich man's house in search of food. When both men die, Lazarus goes to heaven, whereas the rich man is banished to hell. Jacopo Bassano has lent the figure of Lazarus great dignity, eschewing any sense of pathos, while faithfully rendering the scene described in the Gospels, including the table that has been laid and even the dog licking Lazarus' wounds. With chiaroscuro the artist evokes a highly atmospheric and compelling scene. Against the dark, saturated colors of much of the painting, many of the details and illuminated areas are brought to the fore, giving rise to a highly dramatic work. Moreover, the painter took great pains to depict the quotidian objects in the scene.

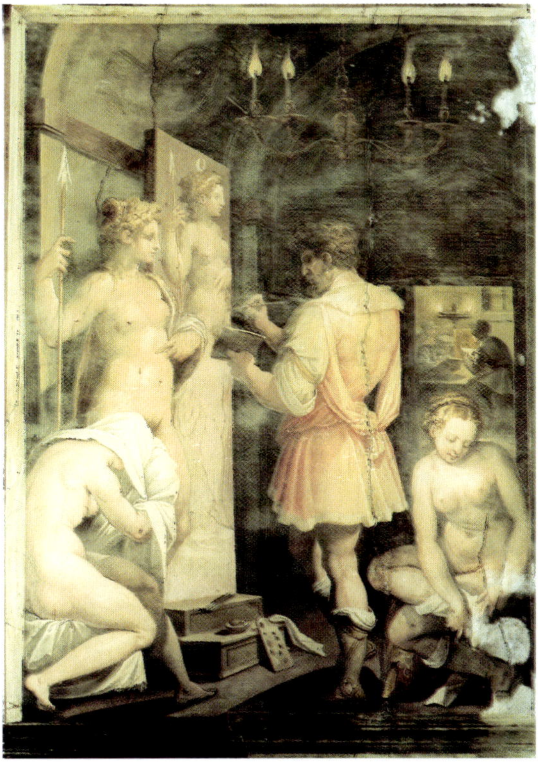

The Studio of Apelles at Ephesus

Giorgio Vasari
(Arezzo, 1511–Florence 1574)

- 1542
- fresco
- Casa Vasari, Arezzo

he influence of Michelangelo is evident in the robust, muscu-
ır bodies in this painting, although they do not display the
uid forms so characteristic of the figures of the great master.
ı this fresco the artist demonstrates a clear interest in the
lay of light and shadow on the human body. Each of the
ıree female nudes has been afforded a different treatment.
he flesh colors most reminiscent of those of Michelangelo's
gures belong to the nude in the left foreground, who resem-
les one of master's sibyls. The body's build, on the other
and, recalls Mannerist depictions of Venus from the Baroque
eriod. The more academic figure posing with a lance is dis-
nguished by the bright areas that punctuate the earth tones
 his body. The most sensual of the three figures is the one
n the right, whose candid and unconcerned pose recalls the
udes in Bathsheba at Her Toilet and Susanna and the Elders.

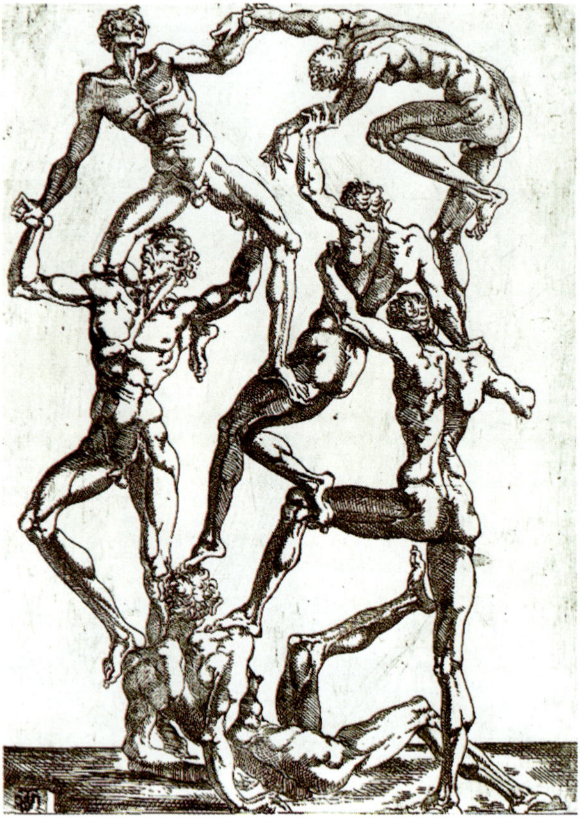

Pyramid of Men

Juste de Juste
(Tours, 1505–1559)

- etching
- 26.6 x 20 cm
- Paul Prouté Collection, Paris

The most interesting feature of this etching of a group of stylized, muscular male nudes is its composition, which determines both the proportions and forms of the figures, breaking, uncharacteristically, with the academic conventions of the day. Unlike later etchings, in which large shaded areas were evoked by means of hatching, in early etchings the pure line predominated. The present figures are treated in an entirely linear manner, whereas the shadows are evoked by means of fine hatchwork in which the underlying white of the paper remains in evidence. Despite the distorted proportions and the unusual arrangement of the figures, this work is a study of musculature and poses, a fitting concern of a Renaissance artist.

his painter, a pupil f Andrea del Sarto nd Pierino del 'aga, was one of ie artists who intro- uced the Florentine nd Roman tradi- ons of Mannerism) Venice. Strongly ıfluenced by Michel- ngelo, the artist resents a magnifi- ent allegory in this 'ork: an elegantly ressed woman enerously offers er breasts to sever- ' chubby children 'ho avidly seek ıem. The scene is ıonumental and the gures sensual.

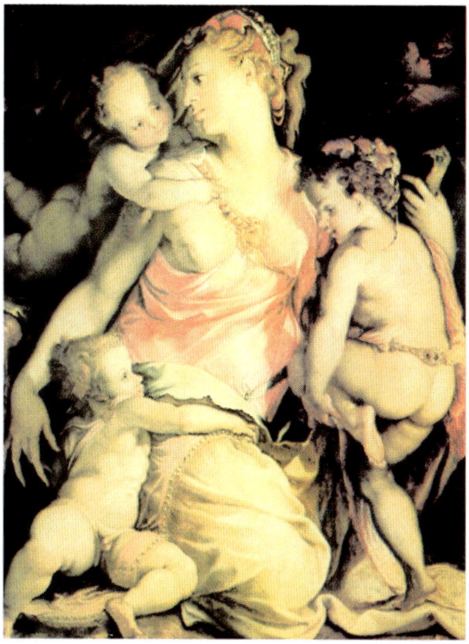

Charity

Francesco Salviati (Francesco de' Rossi)

(Florence, 1510–Rome, 1563)

- 1543–45
- tempera on panel
- 156 x 122 cm
- Galleria degli Uffizi, Florence

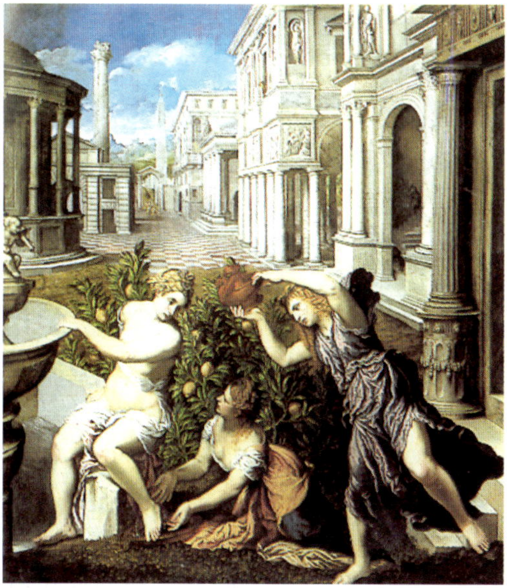

his painting was executed during a period in which the artist as in the employ of the Fugger family in Augsburg. Inspired y Sebastiano Serlio's architecture, the buildings in the back- round are remarkable for their painstaking detail, and the ghly sculptural figures for their subtle colorism. Bathsheba splays all the sensuality characteristic of the figures of Titian nd Giorgione, to whom Bordone's art is indebted.

Bathsheba Bathing

Paris Bordone

(Treviso, Veneto, 1500 –Venice, 1571)

- 1543–46
- oil on canvas
- 234 x 217 cm
- Wallraf-Richartz Museum, Cologne

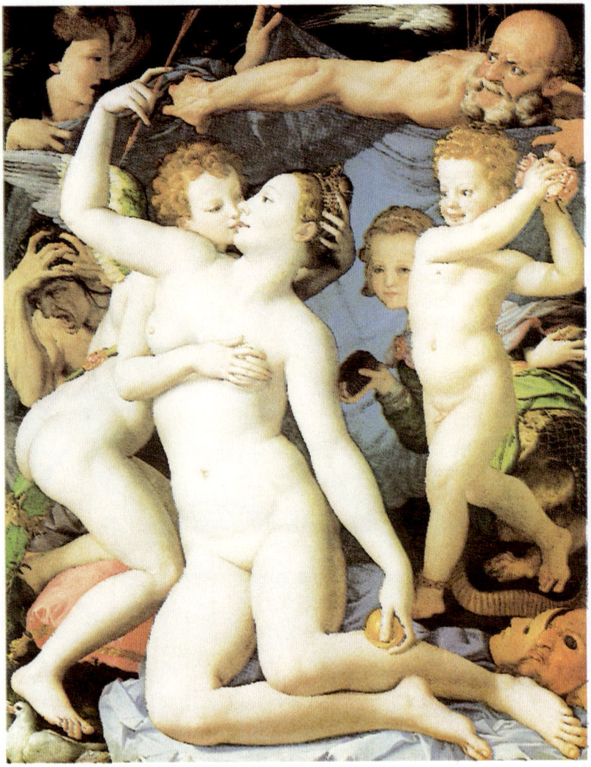

An Allegory with Venus and Cupid

Agnolo Bronzino (Agniolo di Cosimo di Mariano)
(Monticelli, near Florence, 1503 –Florence, 1572)

- 1540–50
- oil on panel
- 146.1 x 116.2 cm
- National Gallery, London

This painting is a complex allegory combining numerous elements, both mythological and symbolic. The nude figures and the colors carry connotations that mysteriously mix the earthly with the divine. The almost sculptural nudes are the very embodiment of carnal love. Here, Bronzino demonstrates his mastery of draftsmanship and human anatomy, arranging the figures in elegant, amorous attitudes. Both Venus and Cupid display a certain androgynous quality, heightening the tension of the scene. Whereas the goddess is given an imposing build, her son has an extremely effeminate figure. Indeed the delicacy with which he touches his mother's breast recalls a lesbian relationship charged with passion. In this work, the artist gives free rein to his capricious and extreme formal demands, demonstrating his virtuosity as a painter.

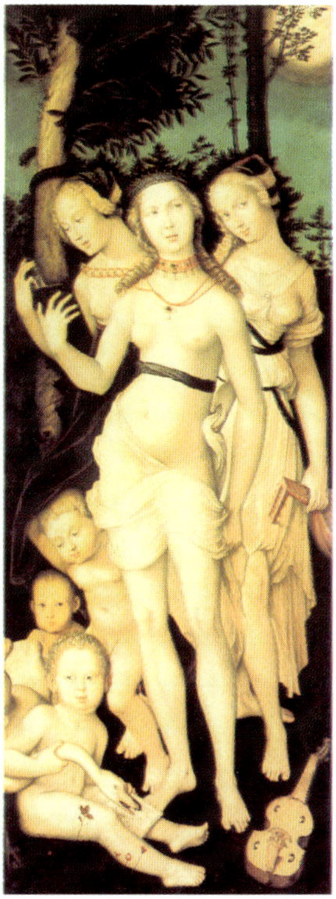

Harmony, or **The Three Graces**

Hans Baldung
(called Grien)
(Schwäbisch Gmünd, Swabia, 1484/85–Strasbourg, 1545)

- ca. 1545
- oil on canvas
- 151 x 61 cm
- Museo del Prado, Madrid

This work, together with The Three Ages of Man, forms a diptych. The three graces, daughters of Zeus and Eurynome, went by the names of Euphrosyne, Thalia and Aglaia. In this work, they exhibit attributes of the senses and knowledge, and two of them are semi-nude. The splendid central figure is the focal point of the painting, bearing a closer resemblance to Italian Renaissance figures than to those of the German Renaissance tradition, which was more closely related to the Central European Gothic. The woman's striking contrapposto pose and the manner in which the cloth rests on one hip and falls away from the other heightens the eroticism of the figure, whose genitals are barely covered by the fabric. Another element that enhances the beauty and sensuality of this figure is the dark ribbon wrapped around her torso, just beneath her small breasts, for it emphasizes her nudity and white complexion. Hans Baldung, a major exponent of the German Renaissance, does not idealize his subjects in this work, but presents skillful studies of the female body.

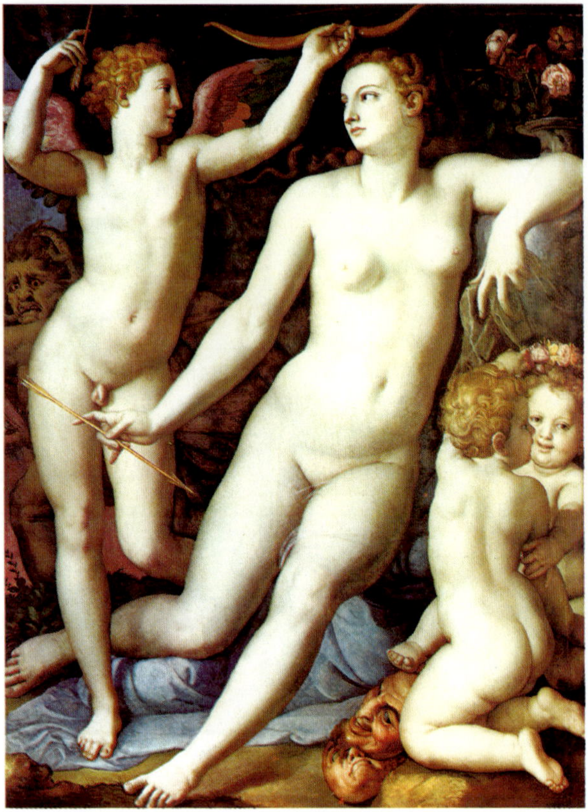

Venus, Love and Jealousy

Agnolo Bronzino (Agniolo di Cosimo di Mariano)
(Monticelli, near Florence, 1503 –Florence, 1572)

- ca. 1545
- oil on canvas
- 192 x 142 cm
- Szépmüvészeti Múzeum, Budapest

The highly sensual, elegant figures in this work are reminiscent of those in Bronzino's Allegory (Venus, Cupid, Folly, and Time), although here, their sensuality is less explicit and they are used as subtle compositional devices. The artist, not content with merely depicting a scene, transforms the curves of his nudes into highly harmonious visual rhythms. While Venus forms a diagonal, Cupid is portrayed in a marked contrapposto pose, which, in turn, is offset by the cherubs on the right. Both protagonists display a cold, marmoreal beauty and bear a remarkable resemblance to the foreshortened figures of Michelangelo, particularly in the way their forms are outlined.

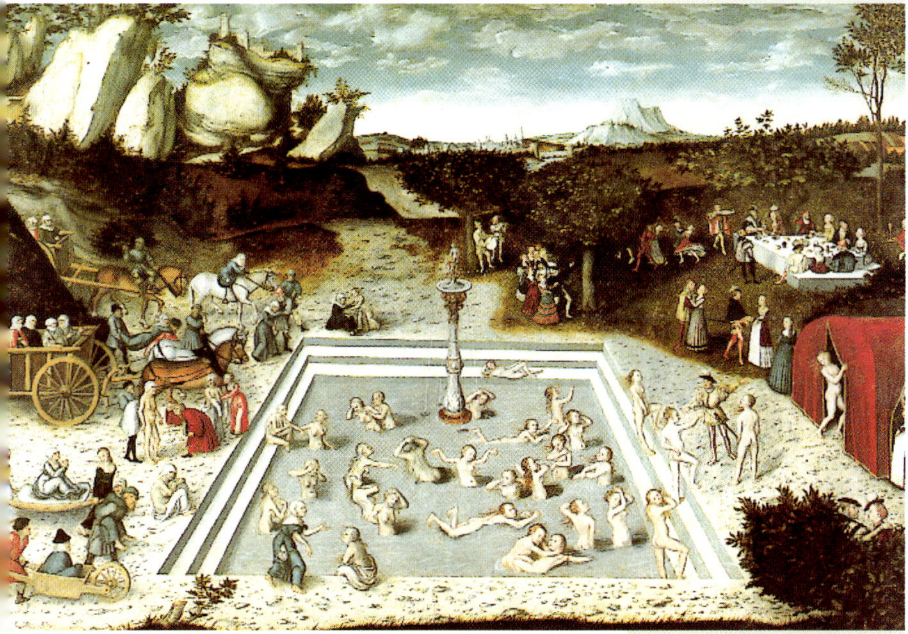

'his complex work has been attributed by some to Lucas ;ranach the Younger, yet many of its characteristics can be ɔund in the work of both painters. Although the composition etrays certain medieval features, the figures correspond to ıe ideal of beauty that was prevalent north of the Alps during ıe Renaissance, with their slender legs, narrow, sloping houlders and round abdomens. The special properties of the ɔuntain of youth are obvious: those leaving its waters are ejuvenated. Coming from the barren, mountainous landscape n the left, old, decrepit women approach or are transported y relatives. On the right, the women leave the bath refreshed. ewly attired and adorned they abandon themselves to the ɔys of life: feasting, music, dancing and love. In this work, hich was no doubt intended to have a moralizing function, ıe painter was inspired by scenes from courtly life of the day.

The Fountain of Youth

Lucas Cranach the Elder

(Kronach, Franconia,1472 –Weimar, 1553)

- 1546
- oil on panel
- 121 x 184 cm
- Staatliche Museen Preussischer Kulturbesitz, Gemäldegalerie, Berlin

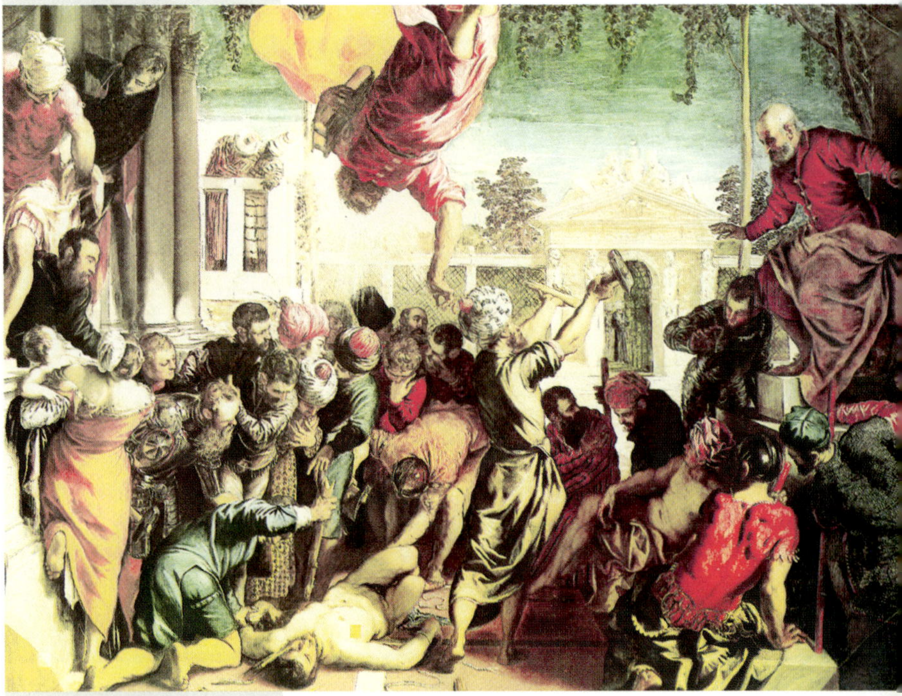

Miracle of the Slave

Tintoretto (Jacopo Robusti)
(Venice, 1518–1594)

- 1548
- oil on canvas
- 415 x 541 cm
- Galleria dell'Accademia, Venice

This dynamic scene, executed with harmonious colors characteristic of the Venetian School, was commissioned by the Scuola Grande di San Marco, a well-endowed brotherhood associated with Venice's patron saint. After Mark the Evangelist, companion of the Apostle Peter, founded a Christian community in Alexandria, he was captured by pagans, who dragged him through the streets of the city, eventually throwing him into the sea. A slave who wished to pray at Mark's grave was condemned to be brutally tortured for having abandoned his master. Yet the instruments of torture miraculously broke, sparing the slave. Surrounded by a large crowd, the figure of the slave, which is boldly foreshortened, and above which the merciful St. Mark hovers, forms the focal point of the scene. A bright shaft of light illuminates his torso, making it stand out amid the throng and against the ground. Careful observation reveals that not all the figures are looking at Mark, which serves to heighten the dramatic tension of the scene.

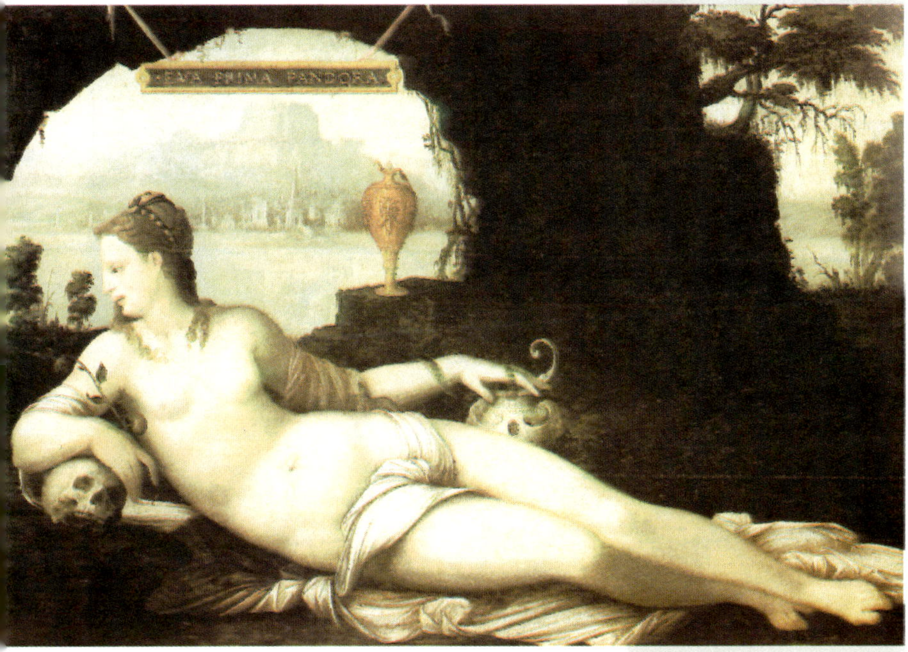

ean Cousin the Elder, a painter, engraver, designer and ook illustrator, is one of the foremost exponents of French enaissance art. His work betrays a strong Italian influence, earing remarkably little resemblance to the prevailing style f the Fontainebleau School. This painting, one of the few hat are firmly attributed to the artist, must be considered in nis light. In it, the painter presents a classical, idealized emale figure with a slender, subtly modeled body of great lasticity. She is portrayed in a studied pose, occupying the ntire length of the panel, and stands out against the dark ackground, which makes her the focal point of the painting. he trees in the upper right-hand corner, the landscape and uildings in the upper left-hand corner and the garden in the niddle contribute to the sensual atmosphere of the scene.

Eva Prima Pandora

Jean Cousin the Elder

(Sens, Yonne, 1490 –Paris, ca. 1560)

- ca. 1550
- panel
- 97.5 x 150 cm
- Musée du Louvre, Paris

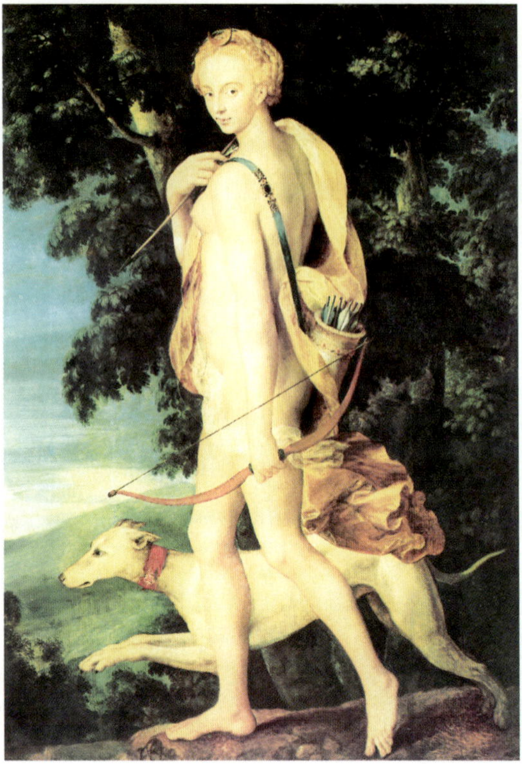

Diana

Anonymous Fontainebleau School

- ca. 1550
- oil on panel
- 192 x 133 cm
- Musée du Louvre, Paris

Diana was the Roman goddess of the woodlands and hunting, who was identified with the Greek goddess Artemis. The figure in this work could be Diane de Poitiers, mistress of Henry II of France. She is portrayed as a well-proportioned woman, although the artist did not intend to accentuate her femininity in doing so. She stands tall, with an athletic build, and displays a small, taut breast. The face does not appear to belong to the body, a common characteristic of works of this nature. The semi-transparent veils covering the goddess' intimate parts, for example, serve only to heighten the visual ambiguity of the rather masculine body. Unlike other works that feature veils or semi-naked figures, this painting was not intended to carry erotic connotations.

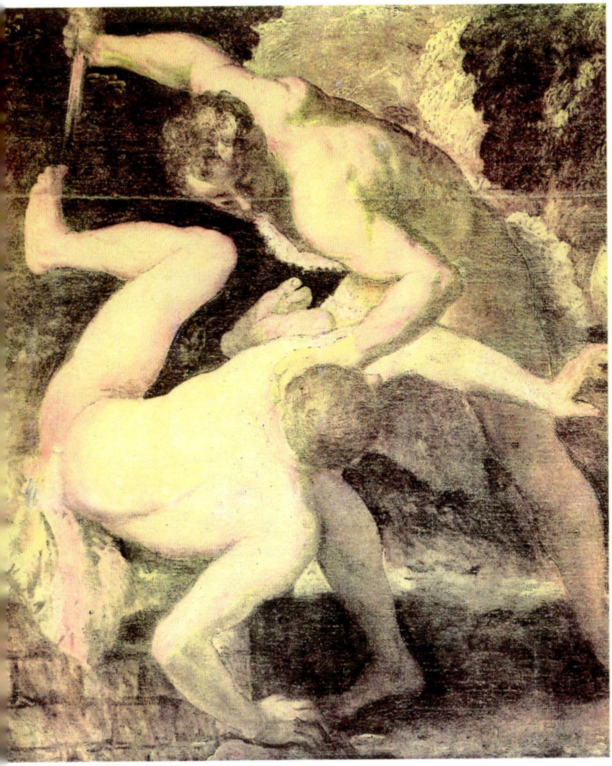

Cain and Abel

Tintoretto (Jacopo Robusti)
(Venice, 1518–1594)

- 1550–53
- oil on canvas
- 140 x 196 cm
- Galleria dell'Accademia, Venice

In this painting, executed for the Scuola della Trinità in Venice, Tintoretto illustrates the biblical scene in which Cain, consumed by envy, kills his own brother—after which he becomes a wanderer until he finally settles in the land of Noh, where he founds the city of Enoch. Here, the two brothers are shown locked in mortal combat. The dramatic composition is treated with fresh and spontaneous artistic verve. Both contenders exhibit corpulent bodies, especially Cain, who is stronger and looks more like a warrior. They are portrayed with technically complex foreshortening and modeled with chiaroscuro, creating a remarkable sense of depth. Their skin is bathed in a warm light, which is particularly bright on Abel's back, producing various intermediate tonal values and shadows on the figure of Cain.

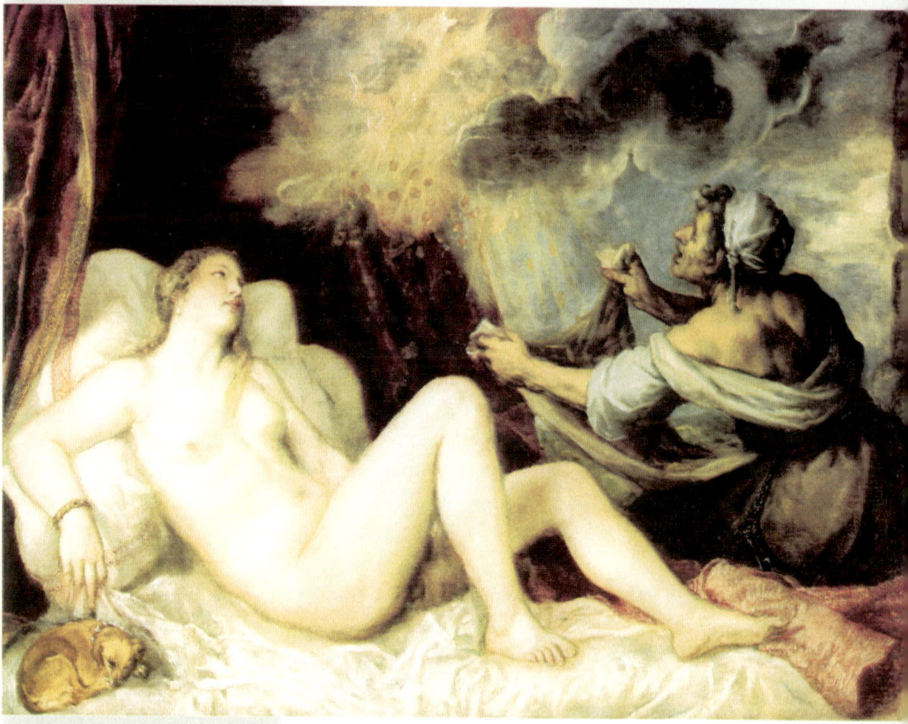

Danaë and the Golden Rain

Titian (Tiziano Vecellio di Gregorio)
(Pieve di Cadore, Veneto, 1488/89–Venice, 1576)

- 1553
- oil on panel
- 129 x 180 cm
- Museo del Prado, Madrid

This sensual scene, which depicts a mythological theme, was painted for Phillip II of Spain. In Classical mythology Danaë was the daughter of Acrisius, King of Argos. When he learned that one of Danaë's sons would put him to death, he resolved to imprison her so that the prophecy would not be fulfilled. Zeus foiled the king, however. In the guise of golden rain, he gained access to her room, in which their son Perseus was conceived. When Michelangelo saw an early drawing of the painting, he severely criticized the figures for their lack of plasticity. Titian, however, conveyed movement by means of cursory, vigorously articulated lines. This sensual figure of Danaë was executed with extraordinary sensitivity. Her classical beauty is accentuated by the soft, rotund volumes of her body. Her rapt expression and expectant pose draw the beholder into the scene, making him a voyeur.

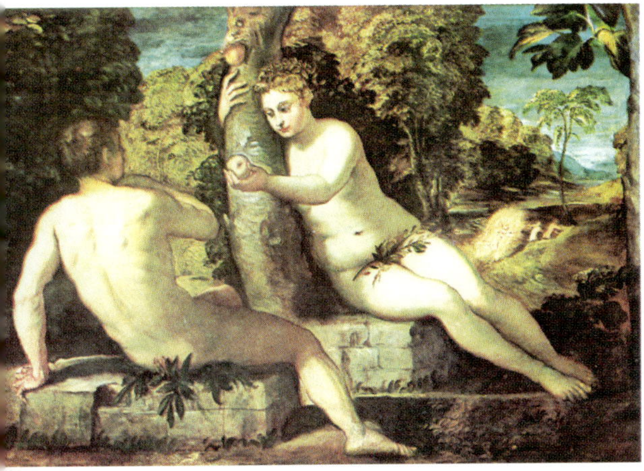

Adam and Eve

Tintoretto (Jacopo Robusti)
(Venice, 1518–1594)

- ca. 1550
- oil on canvas
- 150 x 220 cm
- Galleria dell'Accademia, Venice

In this work, we see Eve offering the apple to Adam. Abundant foreshortening, deep perspective, a beautiful landscape of an almost Titianesque quality, and bright, intense colors, were all characteristic of this painter's works around this time. The nude rendering of Adam is in the tradition of the Renaissance, while Eve, whose face alone is of portrait quality, is plump and voluptuous.

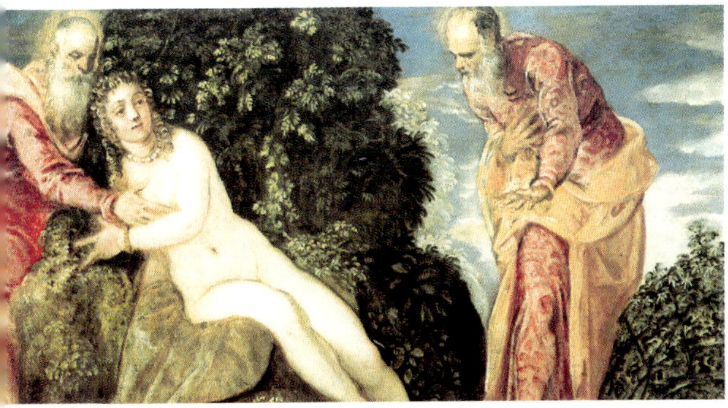

Susanna and the Elders

Tintoretto (Jacopo Robusti)
(Venice, 1518–1594)

- 1553–55
- oil on canvas
- 58 x 116 cm
- Museo del Prado, Madrid

When Susanna rejected the advances of the two elders, they accused her of adultery. In the sequel, however, when the truth came out, they, and not she, were sentenced to death. Susanna's body is young and physically attractive, her skin almost luminous. Contrapposto and foreshortening combine to make the figure extremely realistic. Susanne's reaction is interesting: in order to avoid one of the men, she leans to one side, unwittingly nearing the other, who seizes the opportunity to touch her breast.

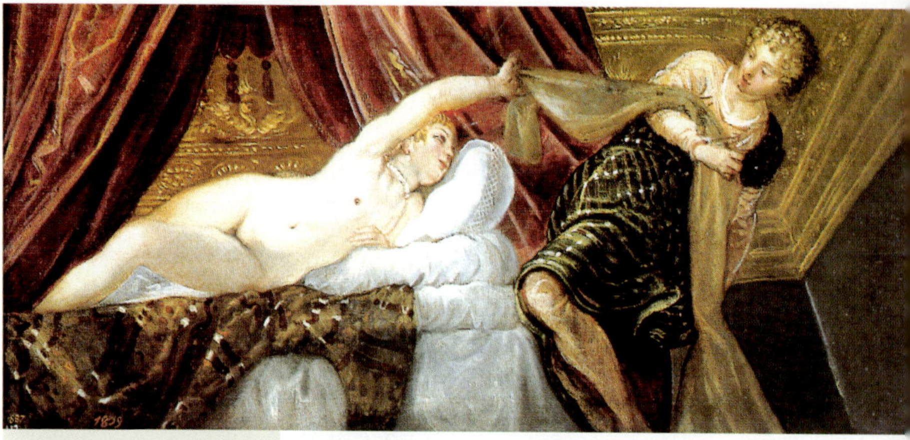

Joseph and Potiphar's Wife

Tintoretto (Jacopo Robusti)
(Venice, 1518–1594)

- 1553–55
- oil on canvas
- 54 x 117 cm
- Museo del Prado, Madrid

Affronted by Joseph's spurning her advances, Potiphar's wife informed her husband he had tried to rape her. This nude figure is seductive, not only in pose and attitude, but through the artist's treatment of color as well: the cool palette accentuates the foreshortening of areas in shadow, while the feminine qualities of Potiphar's wife are further emphasized by local variations of tone.

Purification of the Captured Virgins of Midian

Tintoretto (Jacopo Robusti)
(Venice, 1518-1594)

- 1553 - 55
- oil on canvas
- 295 x 181 cm
- Museo del Prado, Madrid

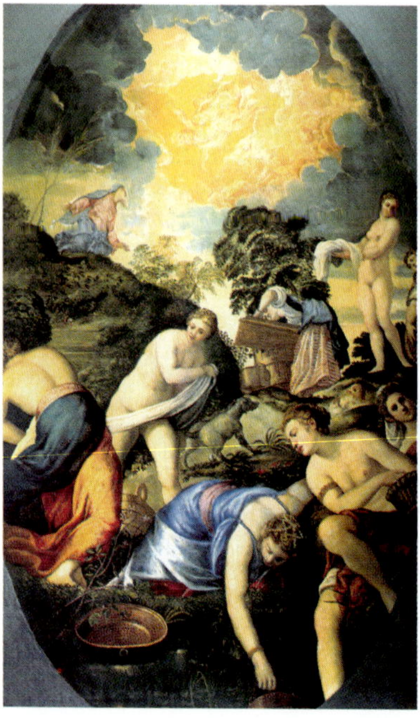

Following the war against the Midianites, Moses was ordered by God to cleanse the spoils of war, in this case prisoners taken, by fire and water. All the men, male children and the women no longer virgins were to be killed, while virgin women were to be allocated to the troops. Here, we see the women prisoners cleansing themselves with water. Not only the pictorial treatment but also the skilful use of foreshortening lend the nude figures great vitality, creating a dynamic and aesthetically pleasing interplay of human forms.

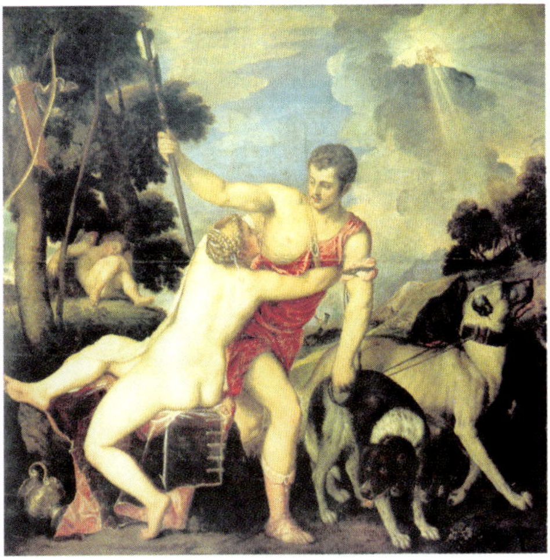

Venus and Adonis

Titian (Tiziano Vecellio di Grigorio)
(Pieve di Cadore, 1488/89 -Venice, 1576)

- 1554
- oil on canvas
- Museo del Prado, Madrid

Adonis and his hunting dogs come across Venus in a bucolic scene, and, filled with passion, the goddess embraces him, hoping he will reciprocate. In the background, Cupid is sleeping peacefully, bow and arrows hanging from a tree. The goddess is intoxicated with desire, while her pose clearly demonstrates her intentions and sentiments. The warm colors reflect the passion of the moment.

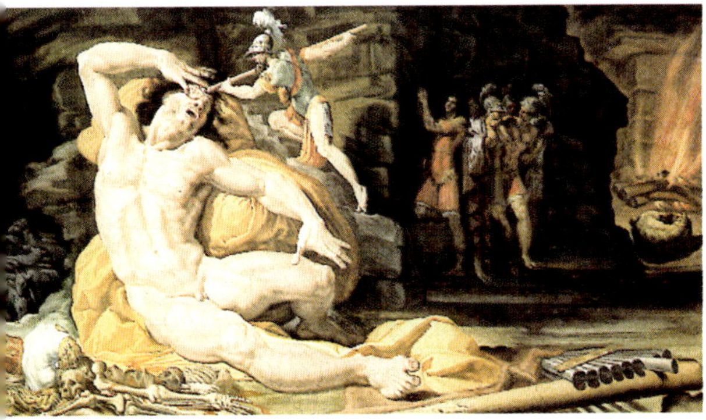

Ulysses Blinding Polyphemus

Pellegrino Tebaldi
(Puria di Valsolda, 1527 –Milan, 1591)

- 1554/56
- oil on canvas
- Palazzo Poggi, Bologna

The motif is derived from the Odyssey. We see Ulysses, having intoxicated his enemy Polyphemus with drink, driving a lance through his one eye and blinding him. While the awe-inspiring, naked giant, in an exaggerated and complex pose, displays his terrifying strength, the treatment of Ulysses is heroically idealized—a spectacular painting that considerably influenced Spanish painters of the period.

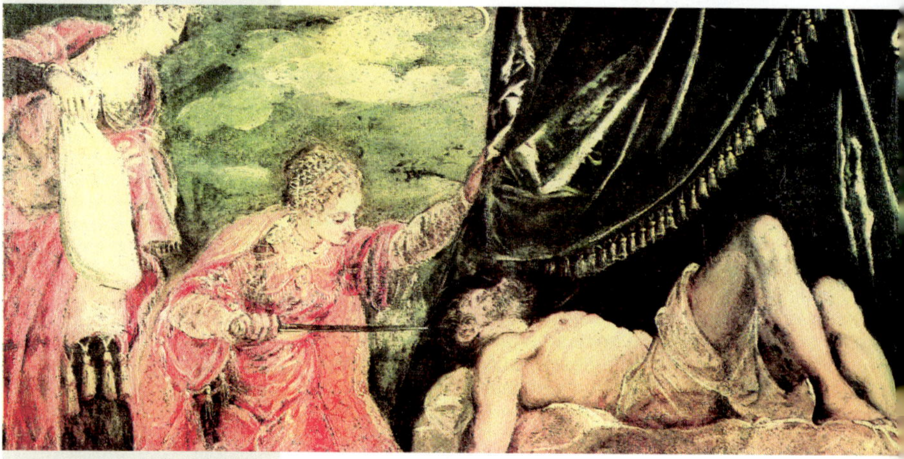

Judith and Holofernes

Tintoretto (Jacopo Robusti)
(Venice, 1518–1594)

- ca. 1555
- oil on canvas
- 56 x 119 cm
- Museo del Prado, Madrid

In the Bible, Judith beheads the Assyrian general Holofernes to save her people from being besieged. The artist captures the moment before she commits the murder. Judith draws the curtain to reveal the naked man sleeping, while, behind her, a maid holds the bag in which Holofernes' head is to be placed. In this well-studied composition, Tintoretto, despite his youth, achieves great elegance, with the three figures forming a diagonal that increases the dramatic tension of the moment. The foreshortened body of Holofernes lends depth to the composition, causing the viewer to forget that the painting is executed on a flat surface. The figure of the general is rendered naturalistically by a varied treatment of light. The body is painstakingly articulated, with a well-studied muscle and bone structure. The flesh tones are influenced by the atmospheric light, enhanced by reflections from the women's sumptuous clothing.

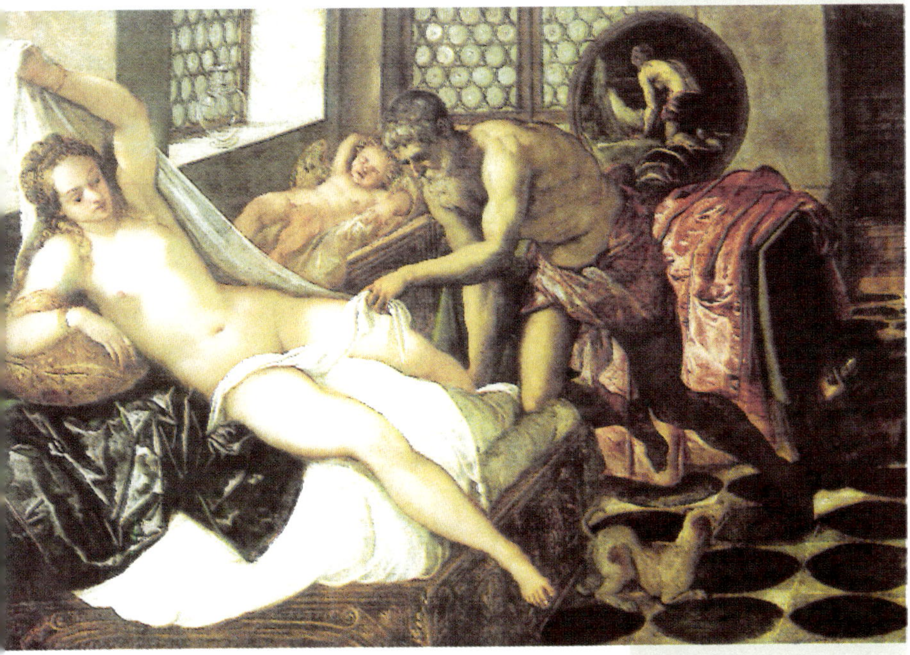

Mars and Venus, Surprised by Vulcan

Tintoretto (Jacopo Robusti)
(Venice, 1518–1594)

- ca. 1555
- oil on canvas
- 134 x 198 cm
- Alte Pinakothek, Munich

Vulcan, apprised of the love affair between Venus and Mars, fashions a sturdy net with which to catch the lovers. When he discovers them, Mars attempts to hide under the sheets. The work presents the moment in which Vulcan enters the bedroom and searches among the sheets. Venus is surprised, although she attempts to conceal her feelings. In reality, she is still sexually united with Mars, for he cannot free himself. Venus' body is young and beautiful, the light highlighting her breasts and one of her perfect, long legs. The naked goddess is extremely sensual and her pose provocative. Her pubis, shown at the moment when Vulcan removes the sheet covering it, is just about to be exposed, heightening the eroticism of the scene. Foreshortening is employed throughout the scene, in which the artist demonstrates his mastery of central perspective, which lends the scene great dynamism. The colors are saturated and the light is modeled in chiaroscuro.

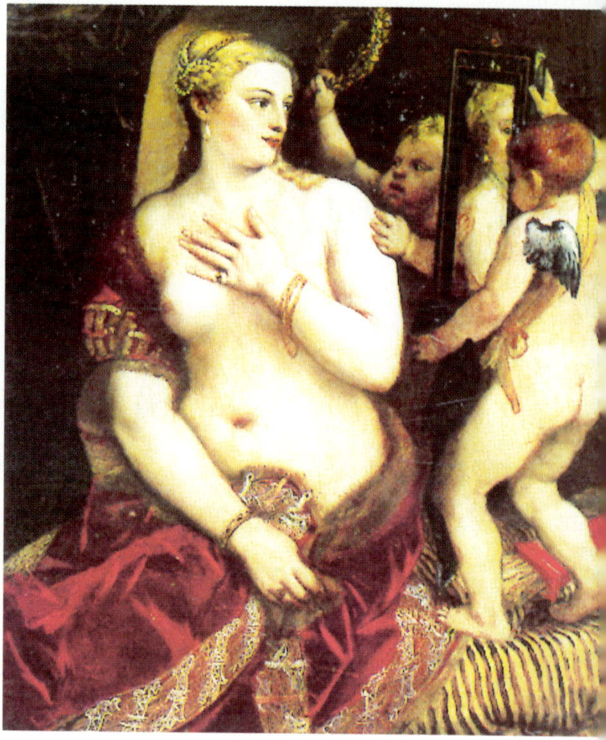

Venus with a Mirror

Titian (Tiziano Vecellio di Gregorio)
(Pieve di Cadore, 1488/89–Venice, 1576)

- ca. 1555
- oil on canvas
- 124.5 x 105.5 cm
- National Gallery of Art, Andrew W. Mellon Collection, Washington, D.C.

Titian was the first artist to portray Venus at her toilet. Regrettably, this is the only surviving example thereof by the artist. The artist himself likened this imaginary mythological, erotic scene with "poesy." The woman, seemingly unaware of the viewer's presence, covers her right breast with her left hand, while in her right hand she holds a sumptuous red cloak with gold embroidery in front of her genitals. Her beauty is heightened by her pale, white skin, which is illuminated by a bright, warm light that creates an atmosphere of intimacy. The artist's color scheme is rich and his brushwork vigorous and cursory, producing blurred contours. The brushstrokes can be discerned close up, but are imperceptible when viewed from a distance. This highly dramatic and expressive work, painted in the Venetian style, is a remarkable display of atmosphere and light.

e Kempeneer,
ho lived in
eville, exerted a
onsiderable influ-
nce on Spanish
aroque by his
ntroduction of
lannerism and an
riginal approach
the nude figure.
this latter
espect, his paint-
ngs display cer-
ain affinities with
l Greco. The fig-
re of this Christ,
vith its elongated
roportions, is full
f grace and phys-
cal presence. The
ontal display
llows the artist to
emonstrate his
nasterful grasp
oth of foreshort-
ning and of ana-
omical detail.

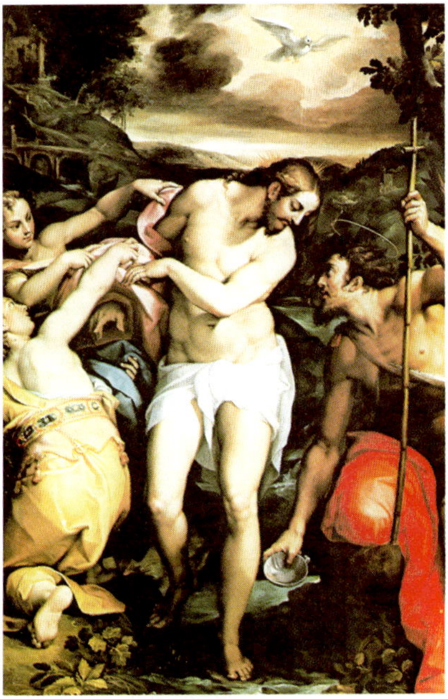

Baptism of Christ

Pieter de Kempeneer (Pedro de Campaña)
(Brussels, 1503–1580)

- ca. 1555
- oil on canvas
- Museum Lazaro Galdiano, Madrid

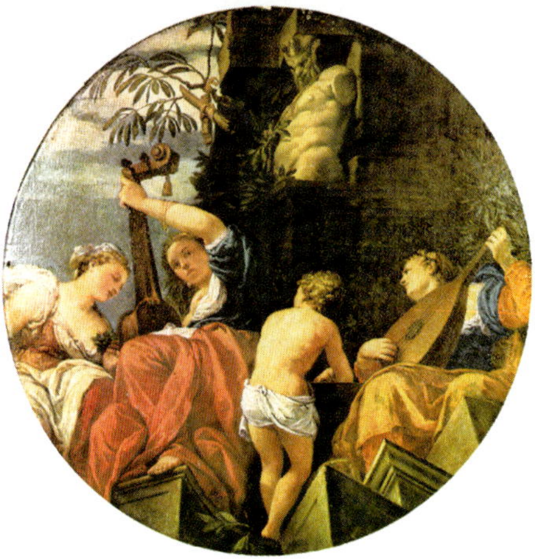

his allegorical painting is described by Vasari. It depicts,
mong other things, Cupid, his back turned, and wingless, in
n unusual but, under the circumstances, necessary rendering.
he painter exhibits how music is born of love, which, without
ings, cannot fly. The figure of Cupid is delicate and, if it lacks
ne sensuality customarily accompanying it, nevertheless
vinces the artist's great skill in handling anatomical detail.

Music

Paolo Veronese (Paolo Caliari)
(Verona, 1528–Venice, 1588)

- 1556
- oil on canvas
- 230 cm diameter
- Biblioteca Marciana, Venice

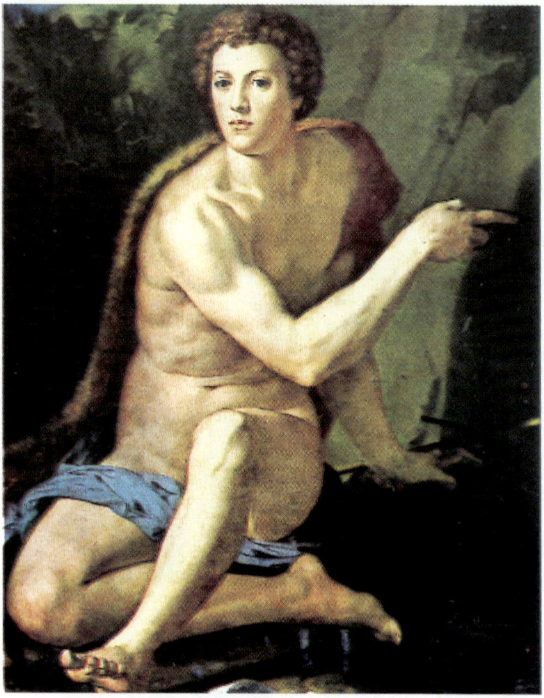

St. John the Baptist

Agnolo Bronzino (Agniolo di Cosimo di Mariano)
(Monticelli, near Florence, 1503 –Florence, 1572)

- oil on canvas
- 120 x 92 cm
- Galleria Borghese, Rome

In this painting, Bronzino demonstrates his skill as a keen observer of human anatomy and as a master draftsman, as seen in the bold foreshortening of the figure. This work was executed early in the artist's career and contains some of the features associated with his early artistic period, such as rough forms and acrid colors. This young man of stylized proportions is extremely sensual, his forms inviting the viewer to enjoy what they see. A harmonic sense of movement gives rise to the painting's dynamism. In the foreground, an arm and leg form a diagonal that breaks with the symmetry and verticality of the torso. The greenish shadows in the background serve to isolate the figure and enhance its complexion. The luminous blue cloth lends the figure a highly distinguished, dignified air.

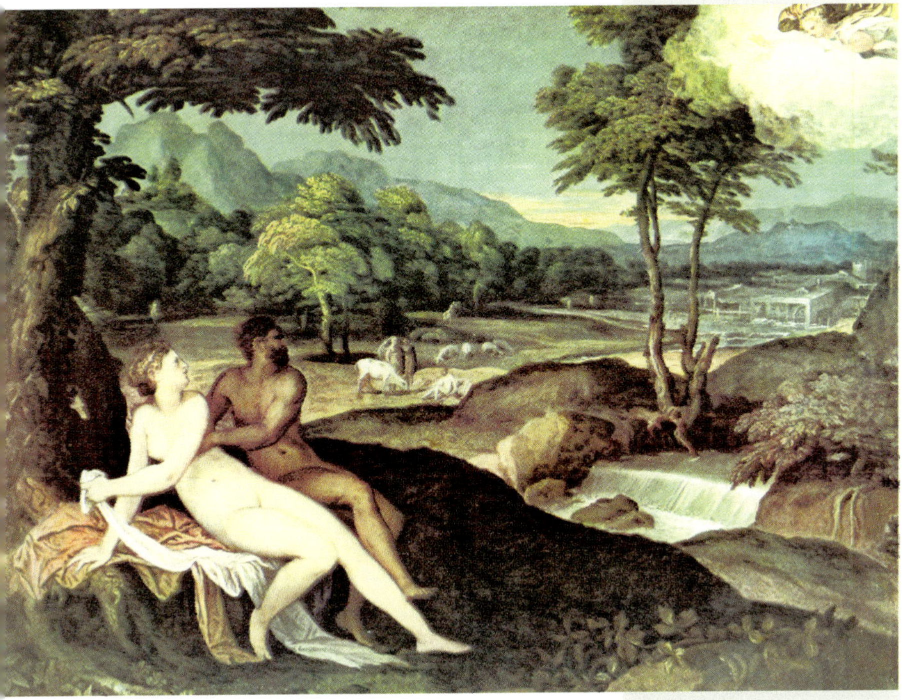

Landscape with Jupiter and Io

Andrea Schiavone (Andrea Meldolla)
(Zara, Croatia, ca. 1510 –Venice, 1563)

- oil on canvas
- 205.5 x 275. 5 cm
- Hermitage, St. Petersburg

uno, the jealous wife of Jupiter, surprises him while he is ying with Io the nymph. In order to protect her from his wife's nevitable revenge, Jupiter turns Io into a heifer, which Argos s entrusted to protect. The landscape is the dominating aspect of this painting, in which the figures would seem to play a subsidiary role. Its consummate composition reveals hree distinct chromatic planes, which serve to complement he painting's protagonists. The middle ground, for example, vith its dominating brown tones, forms an ideal background against which the two figures can be shown to best effect, providing, at the same time, a frame for the pastoral landscape, which exhibits great vitality and chromatic harmony. It appears to herald the ideas that were later to preoccupy the painters of the Bolognese School. Andrea Schiavone portrays the two nude figures with great dignity, accentuating heir human side in the way they are surprised at being discovered. Io, depicted with elegant and delicate lines and esplendent white skin, attempts to cover herself; Jupiter, vith a tanned muscular body, makes as if to protect his lover.

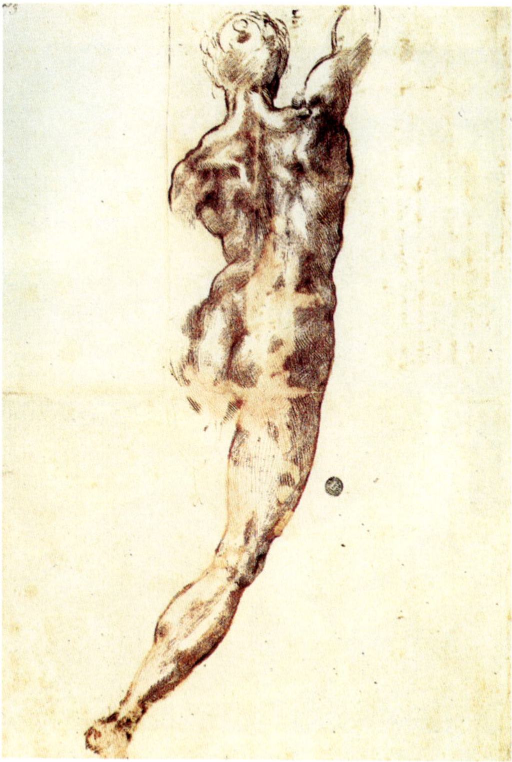

Male Nude from behind (study for the Battle of Cascina)

Michelangelo (Michelango Buonarroti)
(Caprese, Tuscany, 1475 –Rome, 1564)

- pen and pencil
- 40.8 x 28.4 cm
- Casa Buonarroti, Florence

Michelangelo left us over 500 drawings, most of them figure studies for use in murals or canvases. This nude eloquently exemplifies his style, drawn by one whose mastery of male anatomy was complete and who was particularly drawn to male figure work, in part possibly as a consequence of homosexual inclinations. The present figure is stylized and heroically idealized in pose. It would doubtless have been hard to find so graceful a body in real life, yet Michelangelo saw to it that everything harmonized in this representation, thus laying down norms for new ideals. The technique is worthy of attention, cross-hatched areas modeling the figure in the manner of a drypoint etching.

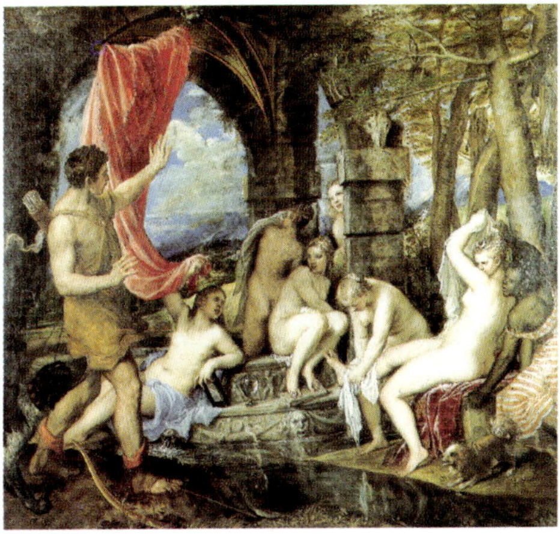

Diana and Actaeon

Titian (Tiziano Vecellio di Gregorio)
(Pieve di Cadore, 1488/89 –Venice, 1576)

- 1556–59
- oil on canvas
- 191 x 207 cm
- National Gallery of Scotland, Edinburgh

n this scene amongst ruins, Titian revises the classical opos of Actaeon discovering the goddess and contemplat-ng her beauty. The monumental nudes are executed with he chromatic plasticity typical of Venetian painting. The light ends the figures depth, focusing on the goddess, who is overing her body, while the highlights serve to accentuate er role as protagonist.

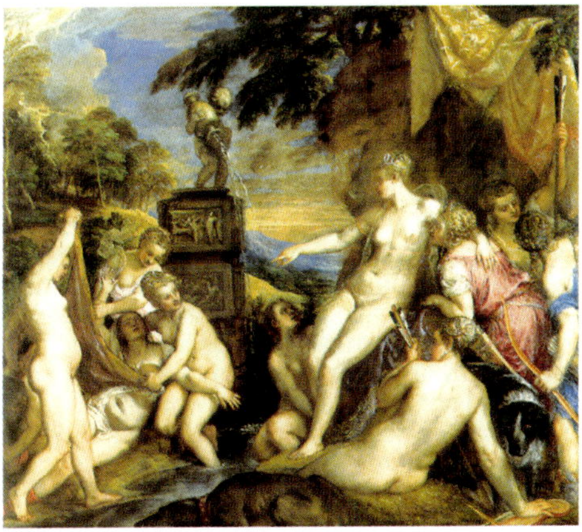

Diana and Callisto

Titian (Tiziano Vecellio di Gregorio)
(Pieve di Cadore, 1488/89 –Venice, 1576)

- 1556–59
- oil on canvas
- 187 x 205 cm
- National Gallery of Scotland, Edinburgh

ragedy stalks Callisto, who was seduced by Jupiter having aken on the form of Diana. Here, her fellow nymphs are lisplaying her pregnancy to the real Diana, who reproaches er despite her innocence. These powerful, sculptural udes are well integrated in a dense, sensual atmosphere hat saturates the light, especially on the principal volumes.

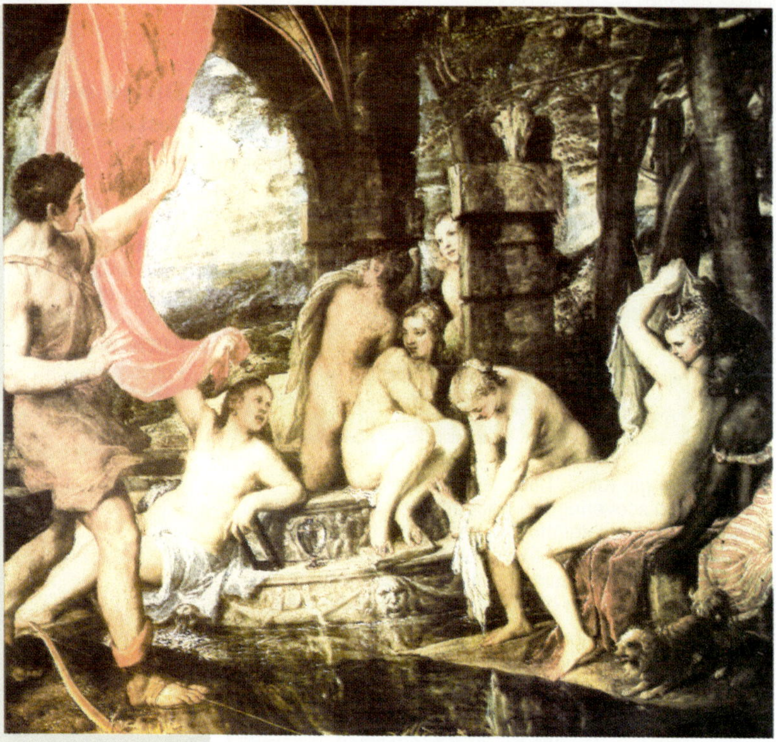

Diana and Actaeon

Titian (Tiziano Vecellio di Gregorio)
(Pieve di Cadore, 1488/89 –Venice, 1576)

- 1556–59
- oil on canvas
- 191 x 207 cm
- National Gallery of Scotland, Edinburgh

This scene, illuminated as if it were indoors, portrays a group of nymphs of the goddess Diana, bathing after a day of hunting. Diana, on the right, is attended by a servant while, on the left, the hunter Actaeon appears on the scene and beholds the nude goddess. The figures are rendered in Classical academic poses, skillfully arranged to create a harmonious, balanced composition. The female bodies are executed with loose, vigorous brushwork and a subtle treatment of light, recalling certain works of Tintoretto. The sensuality of the scene is heightened by the candid poses of the female figures, their freshness and spontaneity, and the slightly morbid flesh tones of their pallid skin, which was so fashionable at the time. The dark scene accentuates the paleness of the figures' skin and the elegant contours of their feminine forms.

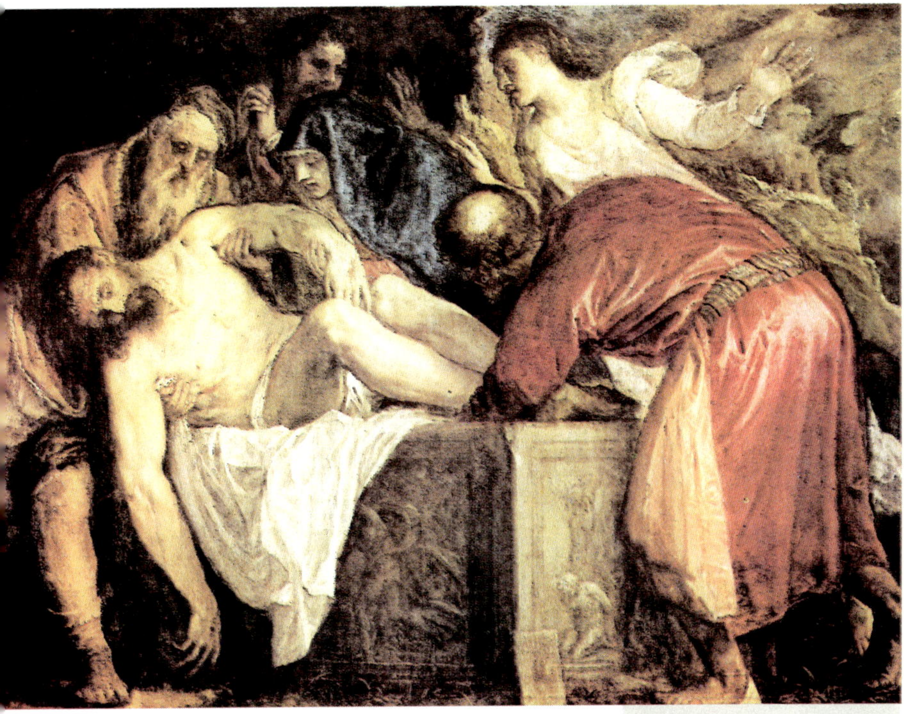

The Entombment

Titian (Tiziano Vecellio di Gregorio)
(Pieve di Cadore, 1488/89 –Venice, 1576)

- 1559
- oil on canvas
- 137 x 175 cm
- Museo del Prado, Madrid

'his work is a copy of an earlier painting that has been lost. ı a letter to Philip II of Spain, who commissioned the work, itian mentioned his intention of improving on the now un-'aced painting. This work exhibits an extraordinarily diverse ictorial idiom. The brushwork, which is free and lively, would ppear to presage Impressionism, although the painterly andling belongs to different styles. Whereas Christ's face is ainted with thick, expressive brushstrokes, the body is far ıore Classical in form, with almost sculptural modeling, ecalling Michelangelo's rotund figures. The various flesh olors lend volume to the figure in a tonal modeling that sur-asses realism. The nude, which is large and well built, ppears weighed down by the gravity of death—an impres-ion that is confirmed in the figure's lifeless arms and legs, 'hich are supported by the group around him. The drama of ıe scene is heightened by the desperate gesture of Mary 'Iagdalene's raised arms, which is reminiscent of represen-ıtions on some early sarcophagi.

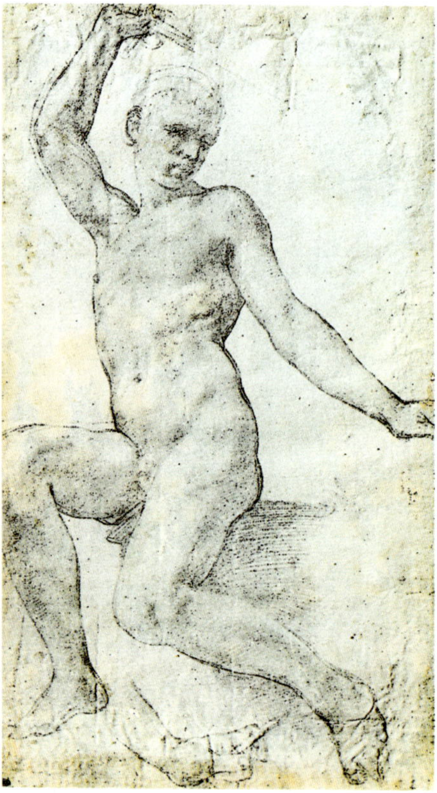

Naked Man Wielding a Weapon

Agnolo Bronzino (Agniolo di Cosimo di Mariano)
(Monticelli, near Florence, 1503 –Florence, 1572)

- black pencil on cerulean paper
- 30.5 x 25.5 cm
- Musée du Louvre, Cabinet des Dessins, Paris

The few drawings we have by this artist all lead one to believe he must have been a refined, aristocratic individual who knew how to get down on paper the dark, introverted representations of the first Mannerists with meticulous and decorative elegance. As such, he is ranked among the second generation of Florentine Mannerists. The present work is academic, yet dominated by a general sense of refinement, seen in the intensity of its tones, which oscillate between white and full gray; very dark tones are avoided, and black is reserved for outlines, as in the subtly delineated muscles, which are never overpowering or forced. The superb handling of light helps bring out the figure's three-dimensionality without coarsening it—despite its masculinity, it is not aggressive. Such handling of light also helps tone down exaggeratedly dramatic elements, a technique we find deliberately utilized in the work of Michelangelo and Pontormo.

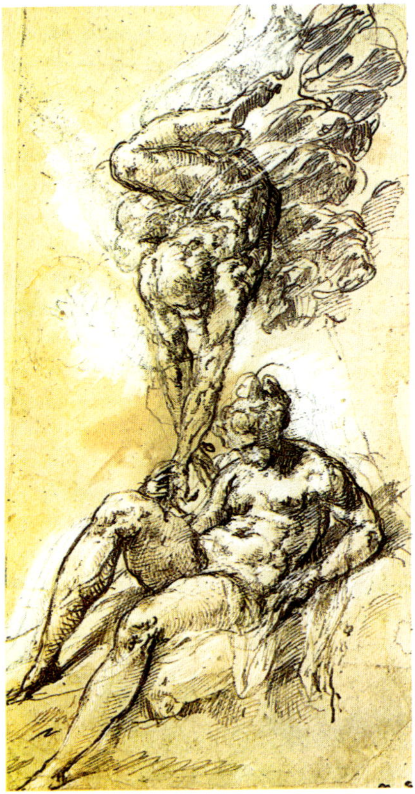

Zephyr and Psyche

Niccolò dell'Abate (or **Abbate**)
(Modena, ca. 1509 –Fontainebleau, 1571)

- pen, brown ink, white and red chalk on paper
- 35 x 18.3 cm
- Ashmolean Museum, Oxford

:ephyr, god of the air, and Psyche, goddess of the soul, ›ave been brought together here in a scene from the artist's magination, in which Zephyr, as a soft, western breeze, is lepicted caressing Psyche. This artist's drawings are in general highly imaginative and strive for exaggerated effects, in vhich respect they show their derivation from Dosso, while he attractiveness of their forms recalls Correggio and their lelicacy of line Parmigianino. The two figures here are balinced so as to bring out each figure's actions, while their ›oses never appear forced. Through his weightlessness and he swirl of his clothes, Zephyr expresses agility and ethereility, while Psyche's nude, partially recumbent body radiates feeling of melancholy. Preoccupied by her lover's absence, he is yet willing to receive Zephyr's caresses to assuage ier loneliness.

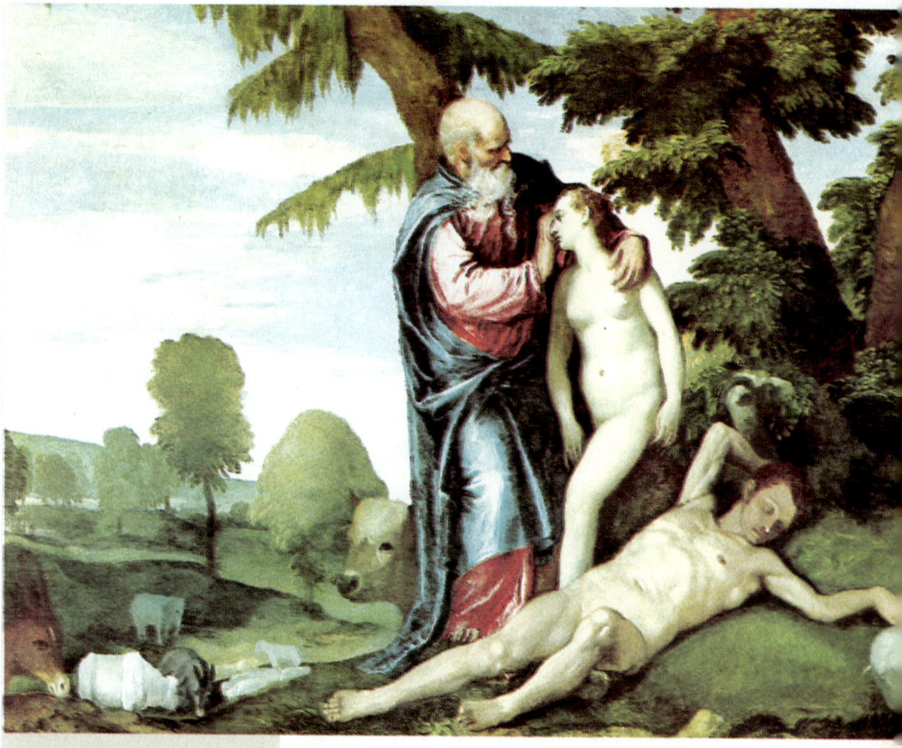

The Creation of Eve

Paolo Veronese (Paolo Caliari)
(Verona, 1528–Venice, 1588)

- oil on canvas
- 81 x 102.2 cm
- The Art Institute of Chicago, Chicago, IL

According to the Book of Genesis, God created Eve, from one of Adam's ribs, so that he would not feel lonely. The Eve depicted in this painting has not yet been brought to life, her muscles flaccid and her gaze vacant. Her body is like that of a mannequin and her complexion is extremely pallid. Adam, who is also very pale, is shown sound asleep. His beautiful, slender figure has perfectly defined muscles, contrasting with Eve's unfinished body. The sensuality of this painting culminates in the figure of Adam, whose foreshortened leg conceals his genitals. Much in the spirit of Venetian painting, the artist achieves a consummate composition by employing a harmonious combination of light and color as well as formal dynamism. His mastery of perspective and foreshortening is remarkable.

'he central figure in this ıassive depiction of St. ;ebastian is one of this rtist's most successful ıale nude figures gener- lly. His handling of light, vhich causes the upper art of the saint's body ɔ appear darker, while ıe lower portions are ɘlatively bright, is un- sual. His body is heroic- lly proportioned, its hysicality almost palpa- le, while its torsion, as e strains to glimpse the 'irgin throned in splendor bove him, accentuates is athletic musculature.

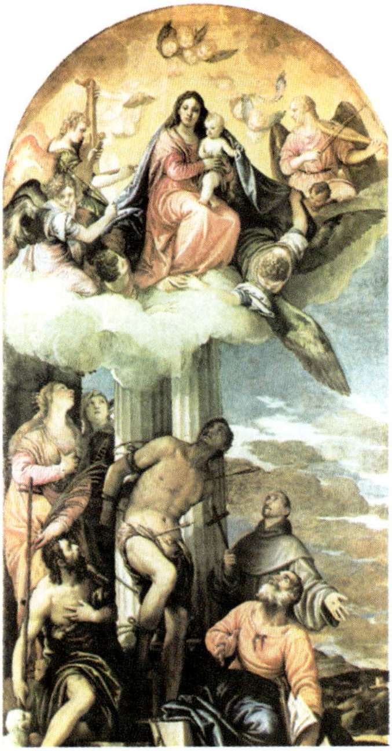

Madonna and Child in Glory with St. Sebastian and Other SS.

Paolo Veronese (Paolo Caliari)
(Verona, 1528–Venice, 1588)

- 1559–61
- oil on canvas
- 420 x 230 cm
- San Sebastiano, Venice

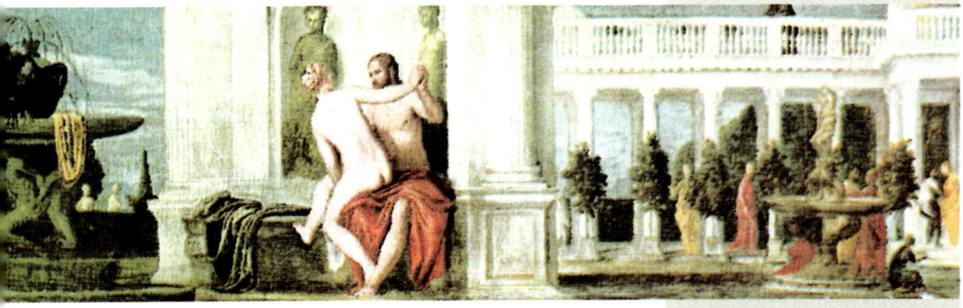

upiter is portrayed here seated and dallying with 'enus on his lap. The monumental surroundings re notable, no less than their successful integra- on into an atmosphere of luxurious sensuality.

Venus and Jupiter

Paolo Veronese (Paolo Caliari)
(Verona, 1528–Venice, 1588)

- 1560
- oil on canvas
- 108 x 25 cm
- Museum of Fine Arts, Boston

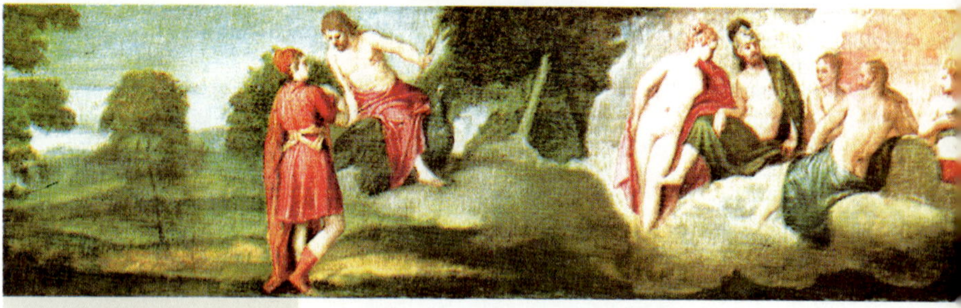

Olympus

Paolo Veronese (Paolo Caliari)
(Verona, 1528-Venice, 1588)

- 1560
- oil on canvas
- 108 x 25 cm
- Museum of Fine Arts, Boston

Jupiter briefs Mercury while a group of gods on the right confabulate. Mars, Diana and Venus are of their number, the last of the three mentioned facing the viewer so as to display her seductively unclothed body. The artist has made her the painting's real focus of attention. Through its brilliance as well as its inclined position, her figure serves as a counterpoint to Jupiter's.

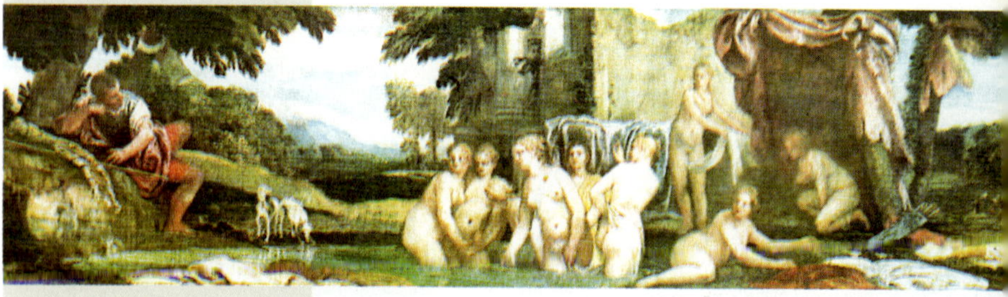

Actaeon Watching Diana Bathing

Paolo Veronese (Paolo Caliari)
(Verona, 1528-Venice, 1588)

- 1560
- oil on canvas
- 108 x 25 cm
- Museum of Fine Arts, Boston

Actaeon is watching Diana and her nymphs who, alerted to his presence, are clustering together. The result is a group of beautiful, harmoniously-disposed bodies, whereby each individual figure maintains its own identity due to the skilful handling of light and shade. On the one hand forceful, the figures are also extremely light and dynamic. As a group, they were destined to provide a point of reference and contact for many future artists.

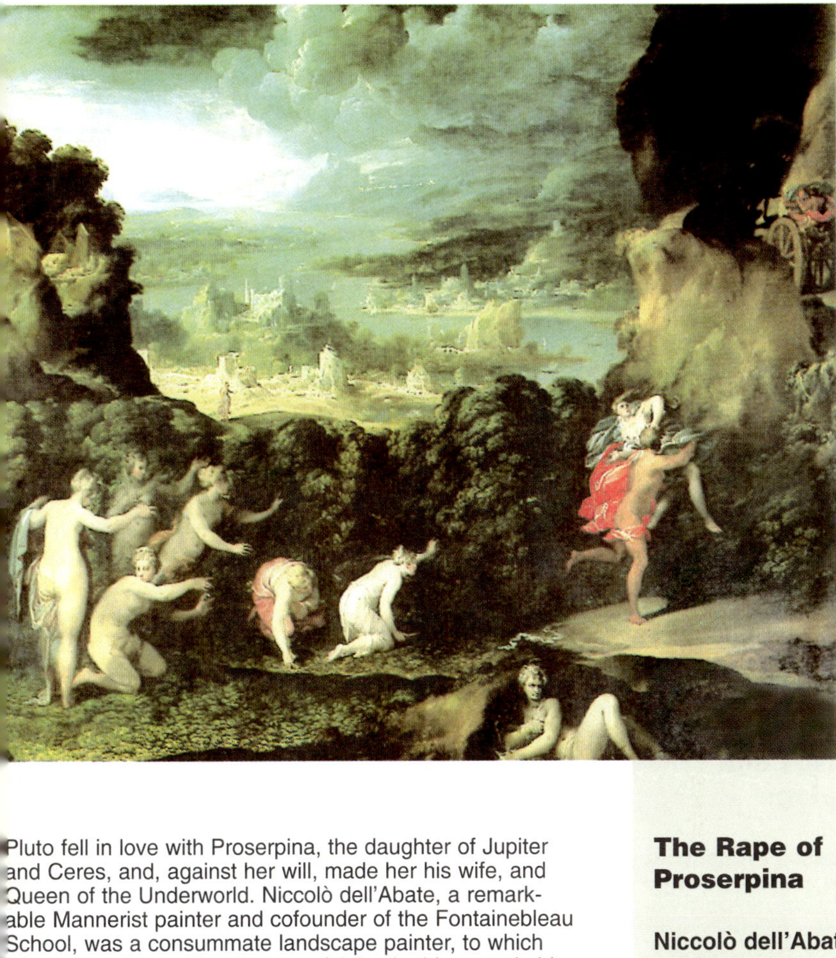

Pluto fell in love with Proserpina, the daughter of Jupiter and Ceres, and, against her will, made her his wife, and Queen of the Underworld. Niccolò dell'Abate, a remarkable Mannerist painter and cofounder of the Fontainebleau School, was a consummate landscape painter, to which this scene attests. The drama unfolding in this remarkable landscape, which is populated by nymphs, captures the moment at which Pluto abducts Proserpina, who is draped over his shoulder. The nymphs are represented as nudes and semi-nudes, covered only by transparent veils, concealing very little of their delicate, sensual bodies, which are depicted in static, unnatural poses. The figures would seem to be mere staffage, animating the scene, which is remarkable as much for its various planes as for its high drama and the intense white light in which it is bathed.

The Rape of Proserpina

Niccolò dell'Abate
(or **Abbate**)
(Modena, ca. 1509
–Fontainebleau, 1571)

- ca. 1560
- oil on canvas
- 196 x 215 cm
- Musée du Louvre, Paris

Venus and Cupid

Titian (Tiziano Vecellio di Gregorio)
(Pieve di Cadore, 1488/89 –Venice, 1576)

- ca. 1560
- oil on canvas
- 139 x 195 cm
- Galleria degli Uffizi, Florence

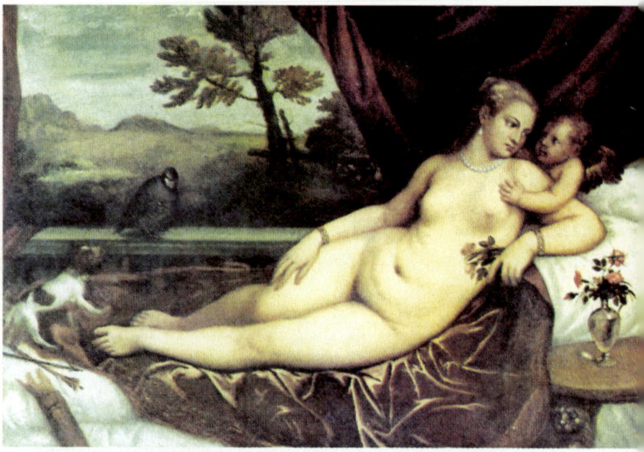

Theme and conception here are much the same as in the Venus of Urbino. If not with quite the same elegance, they still enable Titian to portray here a female nude, an unknown contemporary, with all the characteristic attributes and features considered to be beautiful at the time.

Ulysses and Penelope

Francesco Primaticcio
(Bologna, ca. 1504–Paris, 1570)

- ca. 1560
- oil on canvas
- 115 x 123 cm
- Museum of Art, Toledo, Ohio

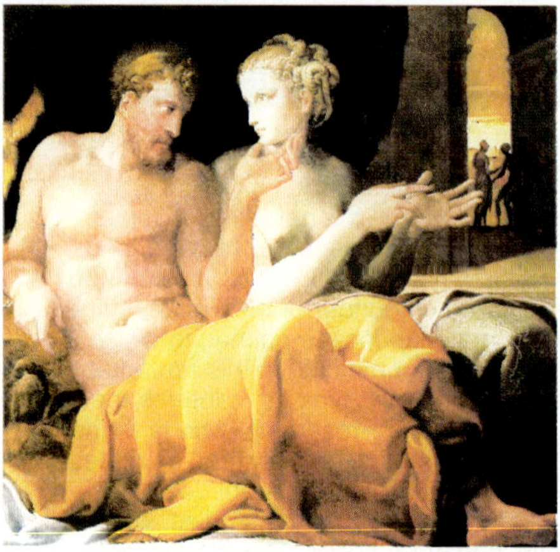

Penelope was the paradigm of the faithful wife, although some have questioned this—according to one myth, she is reputed to have conceived Pan with Hermes. In this canvas, we see her in the foreground, next to her husband Ulysses after he has returned from the Trojan War and ten years of wandering. The body of Ulysses has received a decidedly sculptural treatment that reveals strong Mannerist influences, and foreshortening as found in Michelangelo.

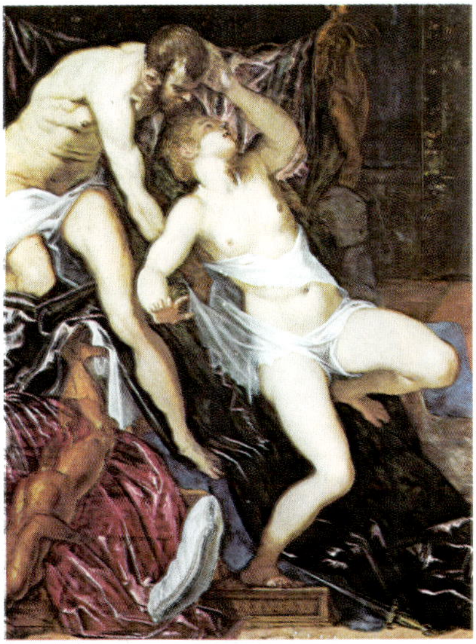

The violence done by Tarquin to his sister-in-law finds brilliant expression in this painting. The dagger, with which Lucrece will later commit suicide, is lying on the floor near her foot. The bodies of the two figures are extremely expressively executed, while, as not infrequently in depictions of this sort, violence is played off against overt eroticism, in this case, as we experience it in Lucrece's position and in her torn, diaphanous clothing.

Tarquin and Lucrece

Tintoretto (Jacopo Robusti)
(Venice, 1518–1594)

- ca. 1560
- oil on canvas
- 175.2 x 152.4 cm
- Art Institute, Chicago

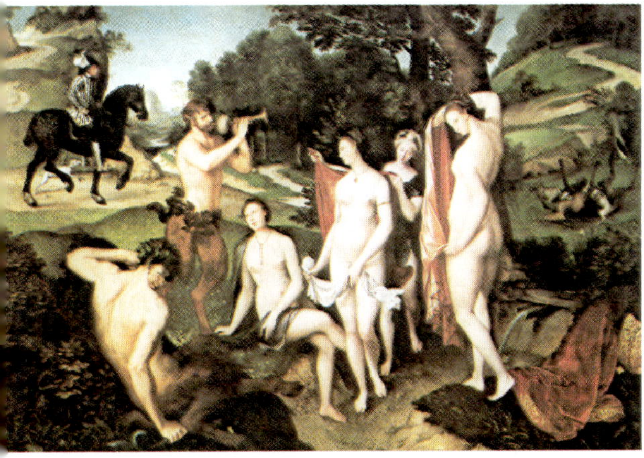

Cool sensuality is one of the surprising and attractive features of the First School of Fontainebleau. In Clouet's treatment of the present theme, Actaeon is portrayed as a rider dressed in clothing of the artist's own period. The well-delineated nude figures represent the culmination of a somewhat affected style, which gives rise to a certain formality and inertness in its effects.

Diana Bathing

François Clouet (or **Janet Clouet**)
(Tours, ca. 1510–Paris, 1572)

- ca. 1560
- oil on canvas
- Musée des Beaux-Arts, Rouen

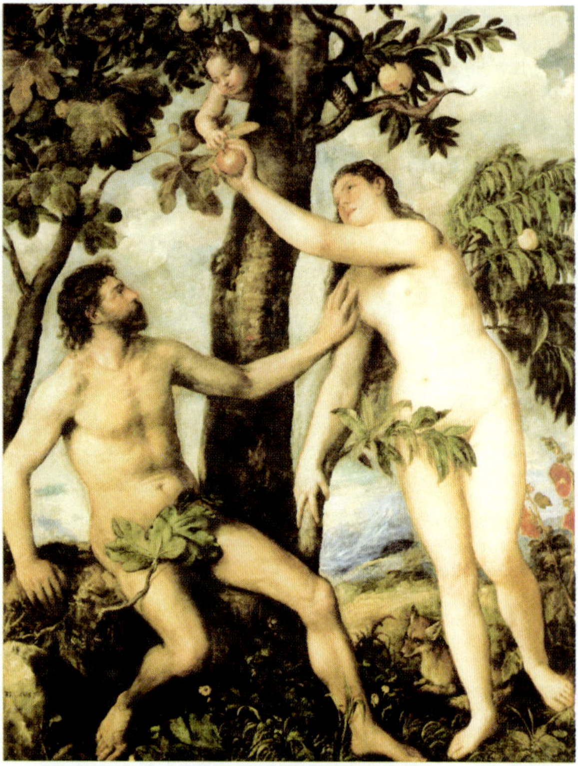

Adam and Eve

Titian (Tiziano Vecellio di Gregorio)
(Pieve di Cadore, 1488/89 –Venice, 1576)

- 1560
- oil on canvas
- 240 x 186 cm
- Museo del Prado, Madrid

The influence of the work of Michelangelo is apparent in the great plasticity and athletic build of these two figures, although Titian surpasses him in both respects. His vigorous brushwork lends the volumes diffuse flesh tones. This painterly handling had a large impact on Peter Paul Rubens, for whom Titian was a spiritual mentor. The two figures portrayed here are suffused with eroticism. Adam, who is shown trying to stop Eve with his arm, brushes her breast with his hand, increasing the sensuality of the scene. The figures' poses have been painstakingly studied, enhancing the composition as a whole. Eve's body is executed in a manner that is entirely characteristic of the painter. The modeling of the figures' skin contributes to the erotic quality of the painting, in which Eve's luminous body comes to the fore.

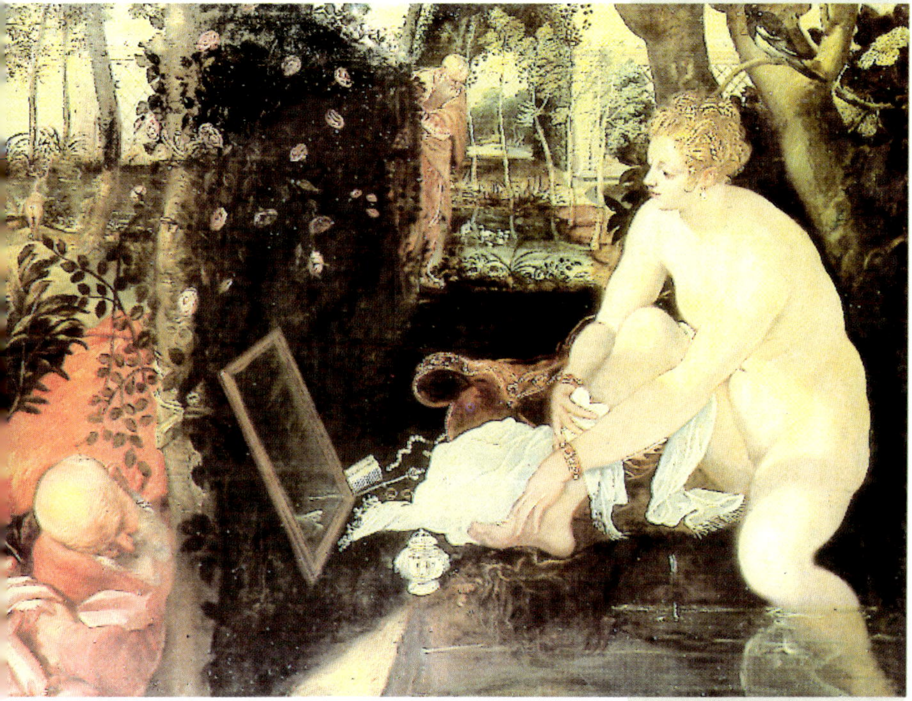

Susanna and the Elders

Tintoretto (Jacopo Robusti)
(Venice, 1518–1594)

- 1560–65
- oil on canvas
- 146.6 x 193.6 cm
- Kunsthistorisches Museum, Vienna

t was difficult for artists to find a socially acceptable pretext or painting nudes, unless they were set in mythological or eligious scenes. The theme of chaste Susanna allowed intoretto to paint a female nude in a religious context. Two lderly judges are shown spying on the woman as she athes. When she declines their propositions, they accuse er of adultery and condemn her to death. Daniel, however, ntercedes in favor of the young woman, denouncing the alumny of her accusers, who are summarily executed in er stead. Susanna is clearly the protagonist of the compo-ition. She bathes in an intense beam of golden sunlight, hich highlights her smooth, white, sensual skin. The work etrays a Venetian influence, evoking the work of Titian. A ew notion of landscape is apparent in the painting, whose ccentuated brightness of certain colors is notable.

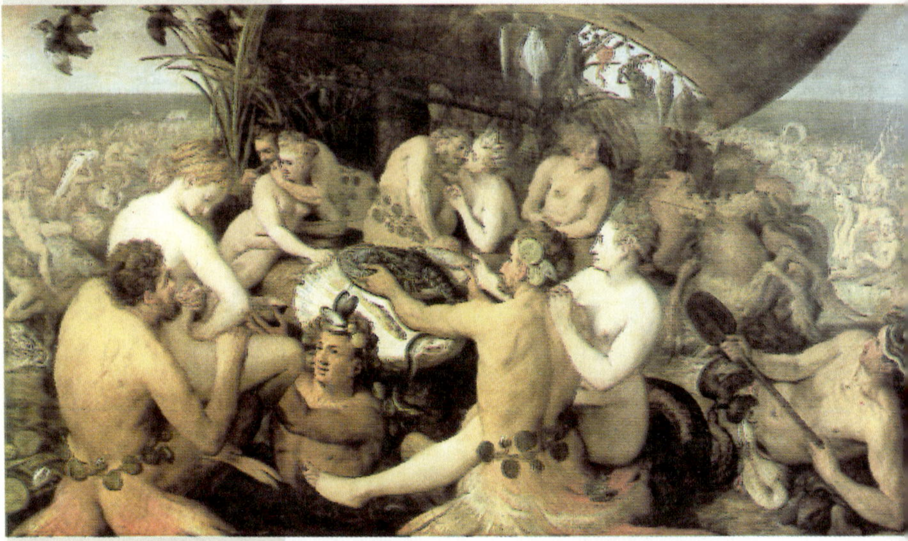

The Banquet of the Sea Gods

Frans Floris (Frans de Vriendt)
(Antwerp, 1519/20–1570

- 1561
- oil on canvas
- National Museum, Stockholm

The nudes in this work have formal elegance and each displays its individual personality. The canvas is literally packed with figures: an oval-shaped group in the foreground, while in the atmospheric background, a dense throng can be seen. Sinuous outlines lend the foreground nudes immense sensuality, and their aroused gestures are animated. The handling of coloration, from figure to figure, as well as between foreground and background figures, is also noteworthy.

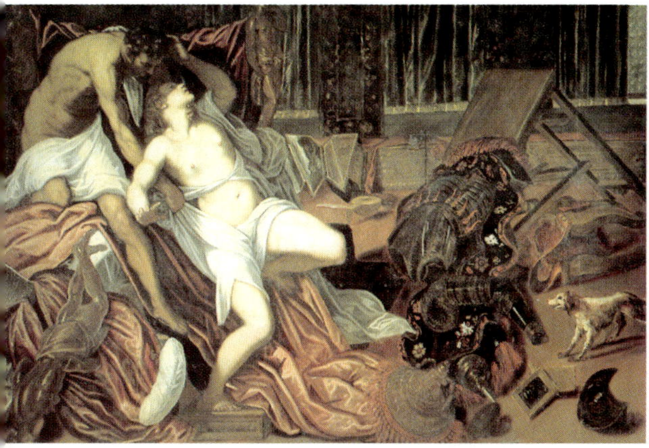

Tarquin and Lucrece

Tintoretto (Jacopo Robusti)
(Venice, 1518–1594)

- oil on canvas
- 181 x 271 cm
- Museo del Prado, Madrid

Tintoretto repeatedly painted this disturbing scene, with slight variations. We see Tarquin attacking Lucrece violently from behind, so that her naked body is fully revealed, the equivocal eroticism of the moment heightened by the drape about to be torn from her lower body.

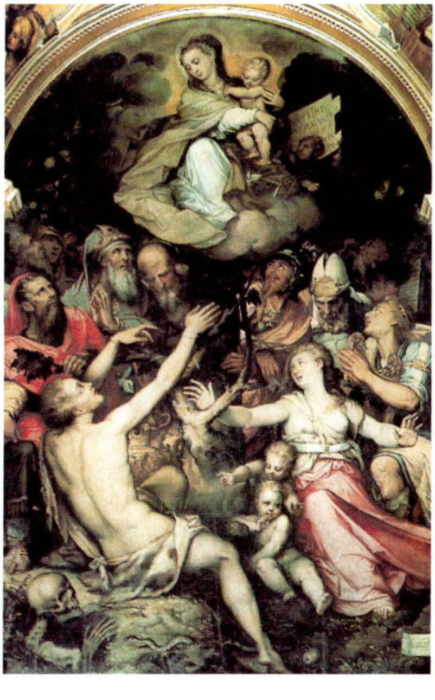

Vision of Christ

Luis de Vargas
(Seville, 1505–1567)

- 1561
- paint on panel
- Seville Cathedral

This altarpiece was, and is still, sometimes, referred to as 'la gamba', a Spanish word for leg, in deference to the masterful foreshortening used in the depiction of Adam's right leg. His delicate yet masculine figure attracts attention: the anatomical details are worked out in Baroque terms, with Manneristic elements that recall the monumental figures of Michelangelo.

The Rape of Europe

Titian (Tiziano Vecellio di Gregorio)
(Pieve di Cadore, 1488/89 –Venice, 1576)

- 1562
- oil on canvas
- 178 x 205 cm
- Isabella Stewart Gardner Museum, Boston

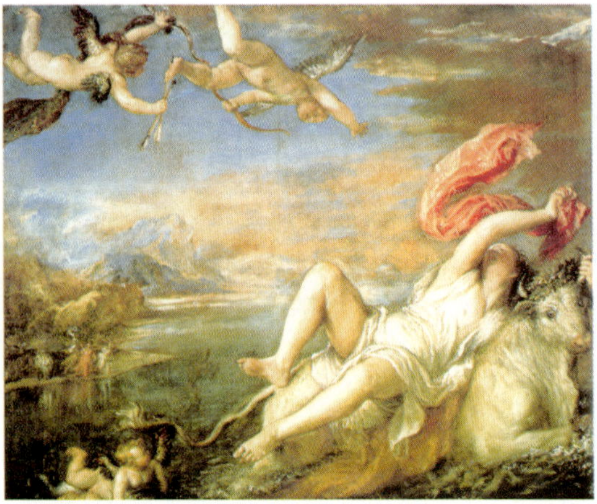

In a seascape, surrounded by cherubs, the enamored Jupiter has transformed himself into a bull in order to bear Europe away and possess her. Her pose indicates the violence of the god's actions and captures the moment with almost snapshot-like precision. Intense colors, vehement brushwork and accentuated dynamism make the work exceedingly expressive.

Danae

Gaspar Becerra
(Baeza, Jaén, 1520 –Madrid, 1570)

- 1562–68
- mural painting
- Palacio del Pardo, Madrid

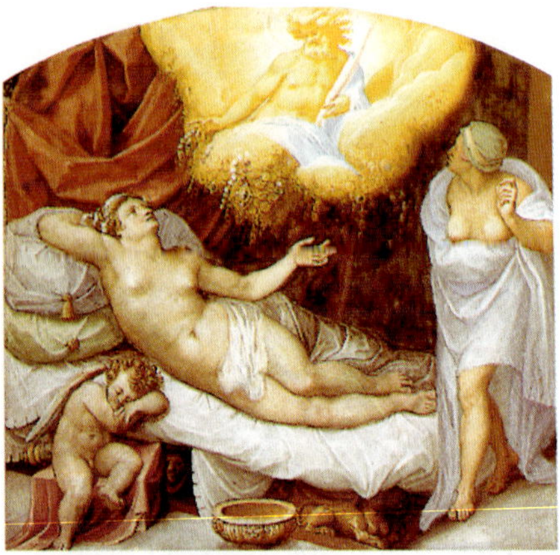

Jupiter, appearing in a golden aureole, scatters gold, pearls and jewels, while Danae, reclining on her bed, relaxed and seductive, reaches out her hand. Rather generously, she is displaying her nudity under the attentive gaze of a servant who, despite her veil, also shows her considerable charms. Cupid is sleeping next to the bed.

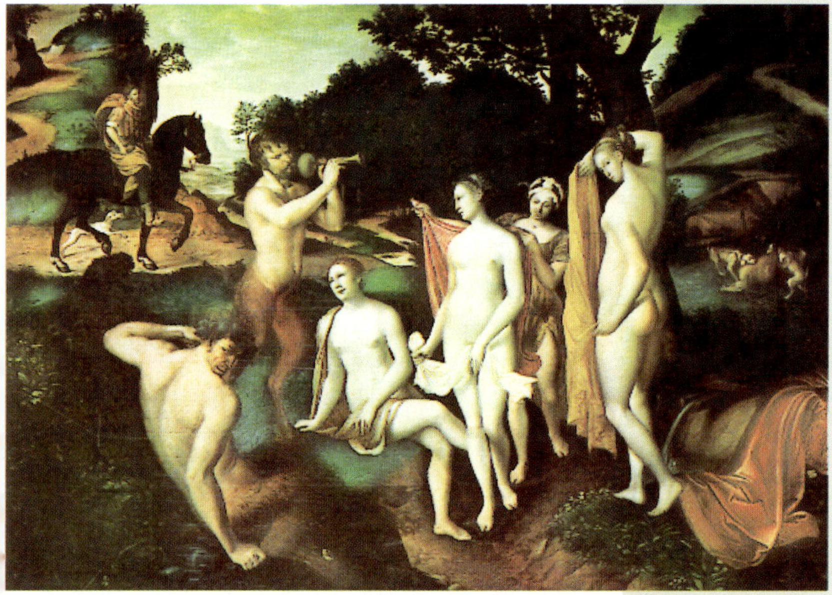

This work is typical of the Fontainebleau School. Taking as its subject the mythological episode in which Actaeon observes Diana while she bathes, the scene is set in a luxuriant landscape. When discovered, Actaeon is punished by being turned into a deer and torn apart by his own hounds. The figures portrayed here are members of the French court, whose real features and personalities are rendered in only a somewhat modified form to suit the narrative. The nudes are stylized according to the artist's own ideal of beauty, which differs only slightly from that of the time. Although they suggest a certain degree of movement, the figures are hieratic and rather cold, recalling sculptures. The female figures are more erotic than the one depicted in Lady in Her Bath by the same artist. The bodies are beautifully modeled and the forms are firm, suggesting smooth complexions. In his modeling of the figures, François Clouet has focused primarily on creating idealized nudes, whereby aesthetic considerations far outweigh naturalistic ones.

Diana at Her Bath

François Clouet
(or **Janet Clouet**)
(Tours, ca. 1510–Paris, 1572)

- ca. 1562
- oil on panel
- 78 x 110 cm
- Museu de Arte, São Paulo

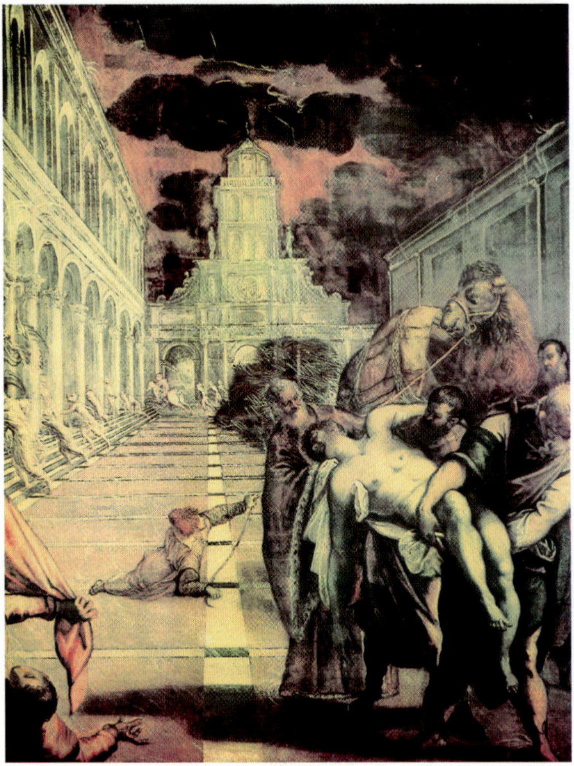

The Stealing of the Dead Body of St. Mark

Tintoretto (Jacopo Robusti)
(Venice, 1518–1594)

- 1562–66
- oil on canvas
- 398 x 315 cm
- Galleria dell'Accademia, Venice

According to legend, the Apostle Peter, head of the early Christian Church, appointed Mark Bishop of Alexandria. When Mark went to the city, where he founded a Christian community, he was abducted and flogged, whereupon he was thrown into a dungeon, where the same torture awaited him the next day. Unable to recover, the martyr died in the dungeon. During the night, his followers stole his body, as shown in this scene. The nude body is boldly foreshortened, similar in form, if not in conception, to the Dead Christ by Mantegna. The brushwork is loose and vigorous, blending the atmosphere with the figures in a fascinating play of light and shadow. These light effects lend Mark's body great drama, with his limbs surrounded by dense shadows and his torso shining brilliantly. Indeed, his body is so full and heavy that it recalls a sculpture.

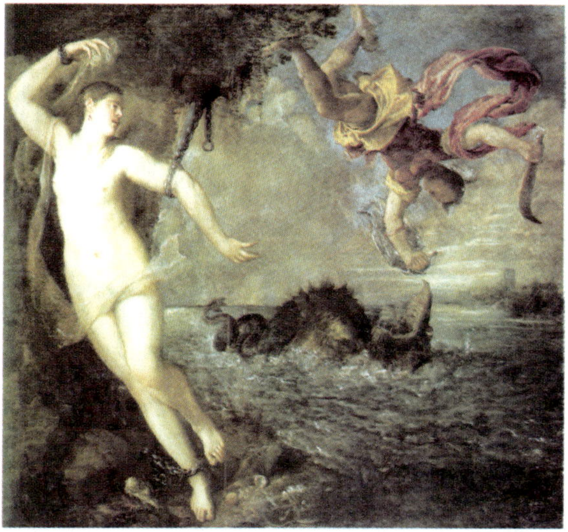

Perseus and Andromeda

Titian (Tiziano Vecellio di Gregorio)
(Pieve di Cadore, 1488/89 –Venice, 1576)

- ca. 1565
- oil on canvas
- Wallace Collection, London

'erseus rescued Andromeda from being killed by a sea mon-ter. Here, we see him leaping into the sea to do battle with ıe creature, while Andromeda struggles to escape her chains. 'he brilliance of her naked body, due to incident light falling 'om the left, attracts the spectator's eye. In her sensual forms re combined force and generosity, weakness and fear.

'he climax of .ucrece's tragedy .nd the start of the ownfall of the Roman kings is epicted here. arquin threatens his ister-in-law in order ɔ rape her, which vill lead to her even-ual suicide. Her ody, diffusely ren-ered, reflects the bruptness of the ttack. Her relatively vell-defined face and ands heighten the rama. The figure is lastic and delicate ı tonal range, while ıe sheet discreetly ɔvering her pubis ıcreases the 'oman's sensuality.

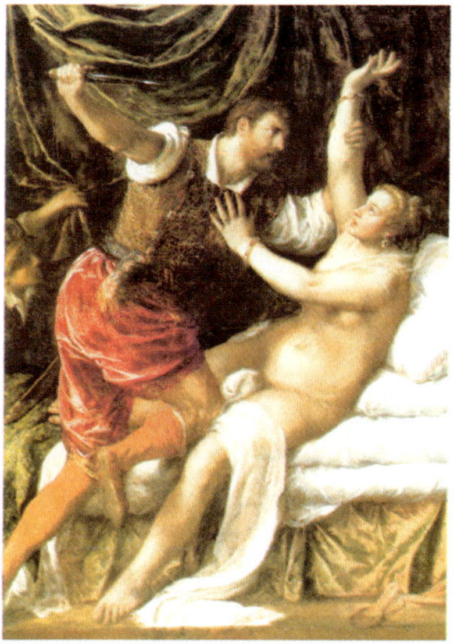

Tarquin and Lucrece

Titian (Tiziano Vecellio di Gregorio)
(Pieve di Cadore, 1488/89 –Venice, 1576)

- ca. 1565
- oil on canvas
- Fitzwilliam Museum, Cambridge

The Martyrdom of St. Sebastian

Paolo Veronese (Paolo Caliari)

(Verona, 1528–Venice, 1588)

- 1565
- oil on canvas
- 355 x 540 cm
- San Sebastiano, Venice

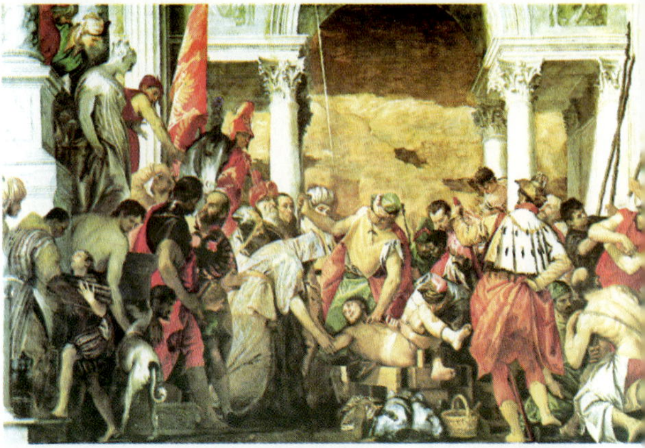

The artist demonstrates skilful draftsmanship and employs extremely bold foreshortening in this painting. Having refused to abjure his faith, St. Sebastian is about to be attacked by the mob. His nude figure is magnificently portrayed, its modeled forms recalling antique heroes, while the foreshortening gives it depth and a sense of realism.

Allegory of Love: Respect

Paolo Veronese (Paolo Caliari)

(Verona, 1528–Venice, 1588)

- 1565
- oil on canvas
- 184 x 193 cm
- National Gallery, London

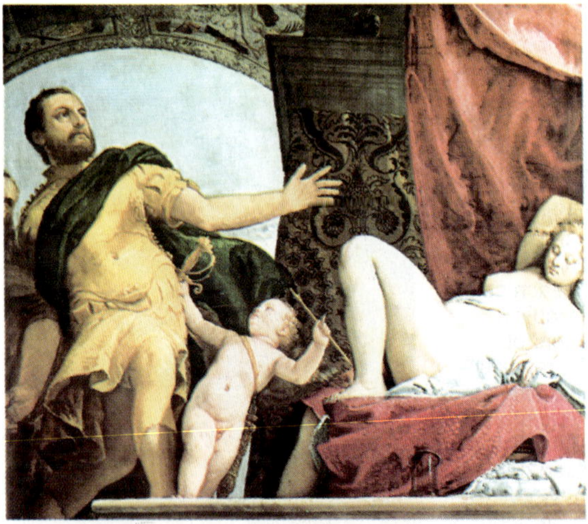

The sleeping female form is imbued with overt erotic appeal. The bright colouring of the skin, together with the red drapes combine to create a warm, voluptuous atmosphere. The figure's form is entirely in keeping with the taste of the period.

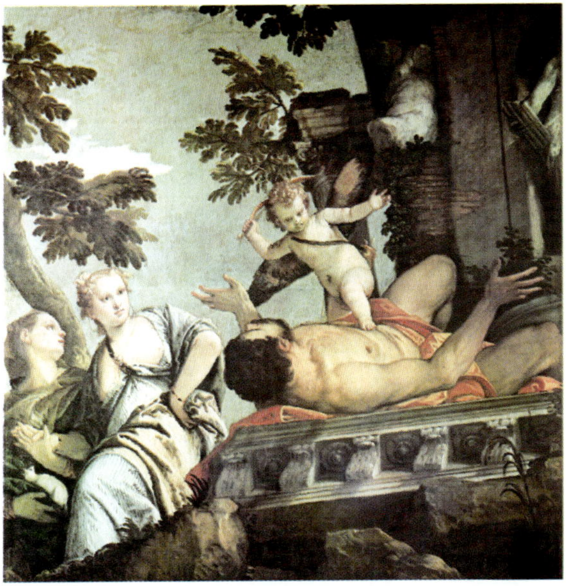

Allegory of Love: Disillusionment

Paolo Veronese (Paolo Caliari)

(Verona, 1528–Venice, 1588)

- 1565
- oil on canvas
- 185 x 193 cm
- National Gallery, London

Cupid attacks the man responsible for disappointing his mistress, who is being consoled. The foreshortening of the man's trunk and limbs is wonderfully deceptive, while the masterful deployment of light over his reclined body creates planes that appear to be at different distances from the spectator.

In this complex depiction of a nude figure, the dark background, Lucrece's somber look and the luminous complexion of her skin are set off against each other. After Tarquin's ravishment of her, her face reflects grief and shame, which are reinforced by the lethargy expressed by her sagging body. Yet we see her as beautiful rather than the reverse, her dignified moral integrity reinforced by the physical attractiveness of her body.

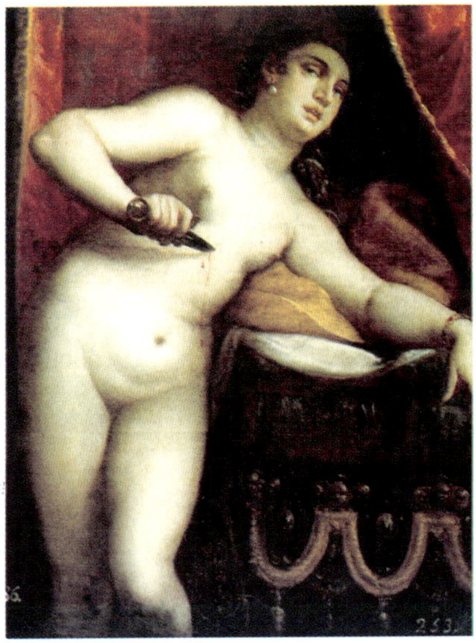

The Death of Lucrece

Luca Cambiaso

(Moneglia, Liguria, 1527 –El Escorial, 1588)

- oil on canvas
- 123 x 120 cm
- Museo del Prado, Madrid

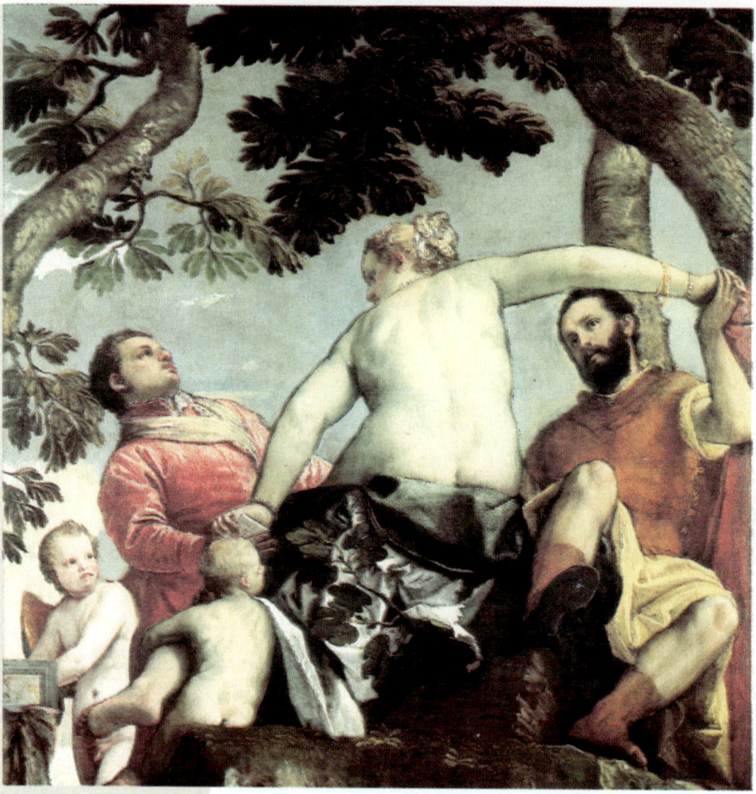

Allegory of Love, I ("Unfaithfulness")

Paolo Veronese (Paolo Caliari)
(Verona, 1528–Venice, 1588)

- 1565
- oil on canvas
- 190 x 190 cm
- National Gallery, London

The subject represented here is unfaithfulness, a popular topic during the Baroque period. The artist's genius does not lie solely in the painting's consummate execution, but also in the way it seeks to involve the viewer in the scene. The manner in which this is achieved is complex, for, when conceiving the work, the artist must have taken into account the height at which it was to be viewed. Consequently, Veronese has executed the painting in perspective, distorting the figures such that the scene appears to be viewed from a lower level than that on which it takes place. Although the scene abounds with somber tones, the colors are superbly luminous, offering striking contrasts between cool and warm hues; this is also true of the flesh tones, which even include shades of blue, green and carmine. The outline of the nude woman is executed with a dark line, highlighting its forms against the leaden tones of the sky.

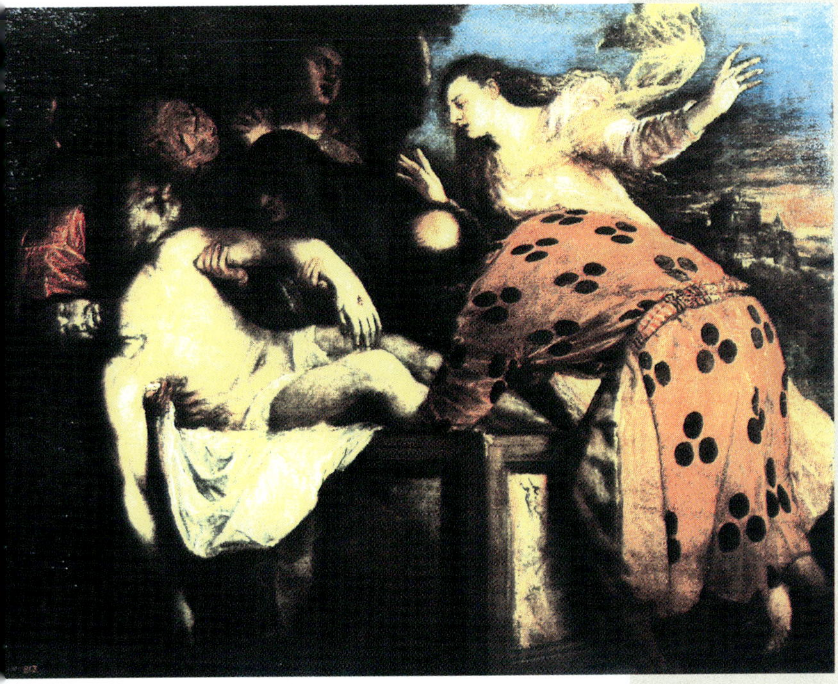

This nude, whose legs and one arm are boldly foreshortened, occupies a large part of the painting. Not content with a simple dark background, Titian sought to make the figure stand out further by rendering only the area of the background against which Christ appears black, whereas in the right half we see a colorful sky. The body of Christ is skillfully modeled with light and shadow, and a terrifying sense of death pervades the scene. The nude displays all the signs of recent death, such as the gaping mouth, the tightly closed eyes and the golden-yellow flesh tones, as well as the way in which the lifeless body's own weight causes it to sag. The signs of man's failure before God could not be any clearer. The solemnity and high drama of the scene are intended to bolster the beholder's devotion.

The Deposition

Titian (Tiziano Vecellio di Gregorio)
(Pieve di Cadore, 1488/89 –Venice, 1576)

- 1566
- oil on canvas
- 130 x 168 cm
- Museo del Prado, Madrid

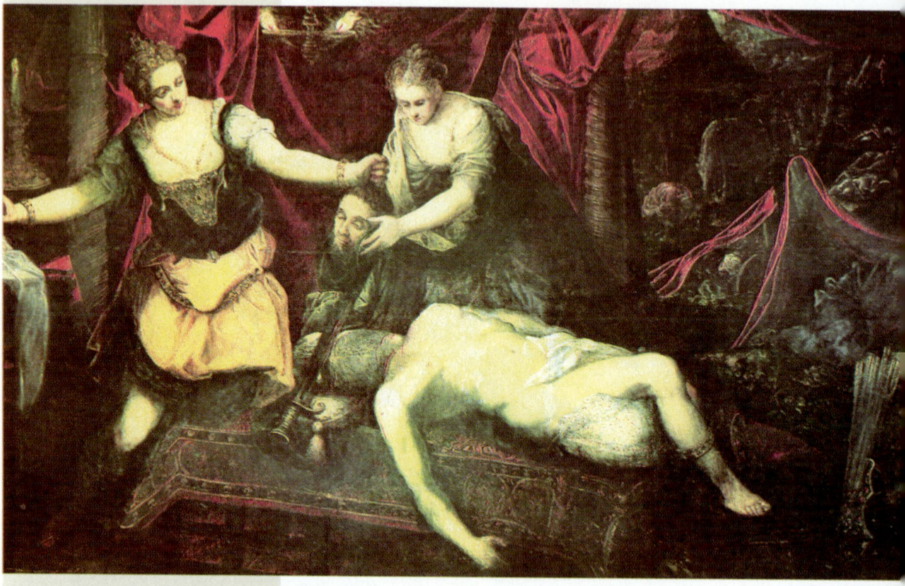

The Death of Holofernes

Tintoretto (Jacopo Robusti)
(Venice, 1518–1594)

- ca. 1570
- oil on canvas
- 98 x 325 cm
- Museo del Prado, Madrid

Despite its horrific subject, the painting scarcely conveys a sense of horror. Both Judith and her assistant are calm and collected, the former with her skirts slightly lifted, and allowing her breasts to be seen through a transparent brassiere—a sure sign of the amorous encounter she has just had with the unfortunate general, whose naked, headless body is strikingly beautiful and luminous. The figure's slight foreshortening lend depth to the scene, although he appears somewhat smaller than his murderess, a rather unusual feature. Holofernes' well proportioned body is brightly illuminated, with subtly modeled flesh tones, and exhibits skillfully articulated muscles. Through the remarkable light and the drama inherent in the theme, reir forced here by the emotional aloofness of the women, the artist demonstrates his skill at achieving astonishing effects, a fact that was to influence Mannerist as well as Baroque artists

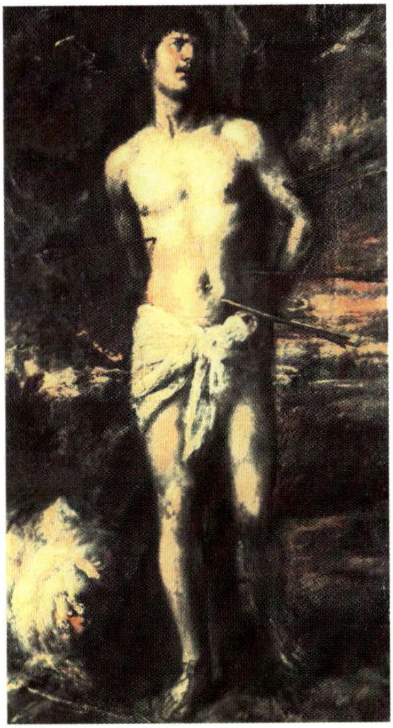

his is one of the last works painted by Titian, who lived to e almost ninety years old. The Venetian colors so charac- ristic of the artist's early work were never completely aban- oned by him, although in this work they are combined with ch grays and browns. Titian painted this canvas with xceptional speed, employing virtuoso, vigorous brushwork, hose chief function is to lend the figure plasticity. The saint shown resigned to his fate, illuminated by a halo that nderlines his masculinity. The modeling of the flesh tones veals the direction from which the light is emanating, ren- ering the shadows more intense and bringing to the fore ne of the aspects of Titian's work that was to make a deep npression on Rubens: the inclusion of greens and blues in e skin. The apparent informality of the work and the spec- cular lighting effects—the result of a study similar to intoretto's—mark Titian's late work, in which he distanced mself from the line and volume to concentrate on synthe- s, in which everything is represented in cursory brushwork nd impastoed patches of color.

St. Sebastian

Titian (Tiziano Vecellio di Gregorio)
(Pieve di Cadore, 1488/89 –Venice, 1576)

- 1570
- oil on canvas
- 212 x 116 cm
- Hermitage, St. Petersburg

Leda

Tintoretto (Jacopo Robusti)
(Venice, 1518–1594)

- ca. 1570
- oil on canvas
- 162 x 218 cm
- Galleria degli Uffizi, Florence

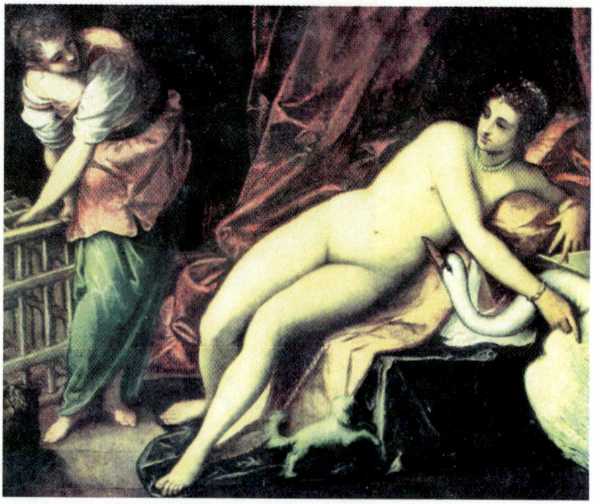

In this rendering of the myth of Leda being seduced by Jupiter in the form of a swan, Tintoretto presents us with a slender figure, more sinuous than curvaceous, with budding breasts. The result is a delicate and extremely sensual image. Appurtenances such as the curtains and dog are frequently found in similar works by other artists.

Pietà

Luís de Morales
(Badajoz, ca. 1510–ca. 1586)

- ca. 1570
- paint on panel
- 124 x 94 cm
- Real Academia de Bellas Artes de San Fernando, Madrid

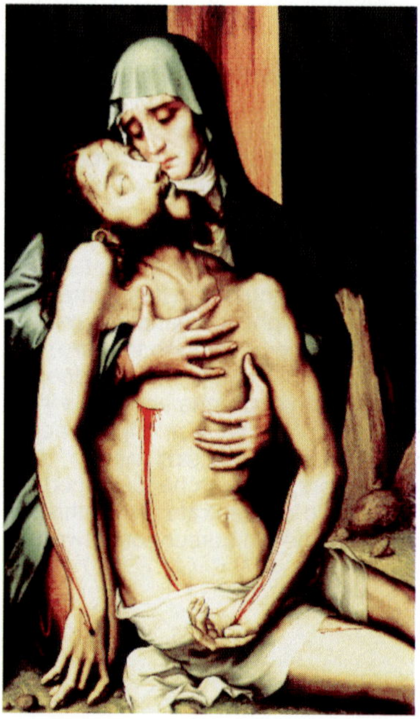

The paintings of Luís de Morales incorporate characteristics of various artistic trends. This work betrays a certain affinity with Flemish art in Portugal, with engravings but also with Italian Mannerist works. His style is dry, but meticulous and euphuistic in its execution and in the details, with peculiar colors and a certain elongation of the figures, which lends them spontaneity and, in the case of Christ, sensuality.

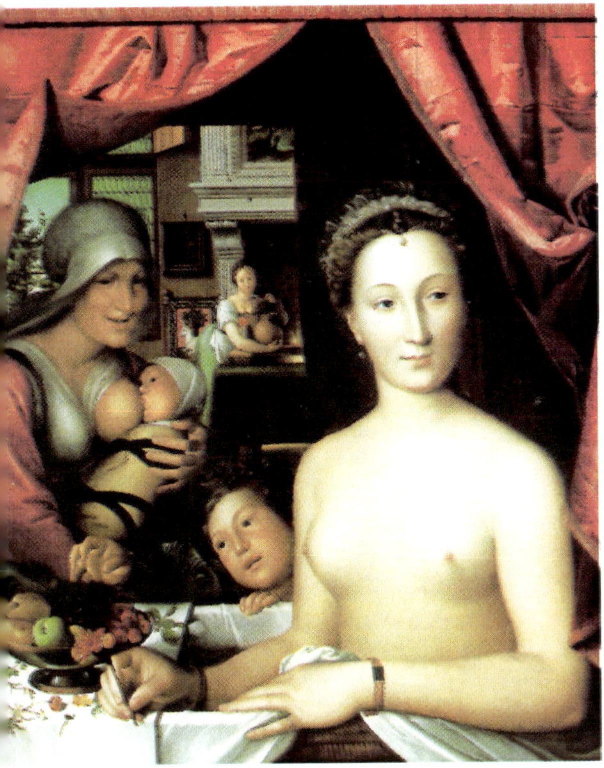

his artist painted in a Mannerist style like that practiced by
rtists of the Fontainebleau School, the combination of real-
sm and decorativeness betraying the influence of Italian
rt. The figure in the foreground, traditionally identified as a
ortrait of Diane de Poitiers, is given wider significance by
er surroundings. The nude torso, with its fine skin, small,
rm breasts and taut skin, is both sensual and coldly dis-
ant. Its particular brand of sensuality derives from the con-
rast between the almost hard beauty of the face and the
oft, blurred forms of the body. This is a characteristic fea-
ure of the Fontainebleau style and can be seen in another,
losely related work probably by the same artist, Gabrielle
'Estrées and One of Her Sisters.

Lady in Her Bath

François Clouet
(or **Janet Clouet**)
(Tours, ca. 1510–Paris, 1572)

- 1570
- oil on panel
- 92 x 81 cm
- National Gallery of Art, Washington, D.C.

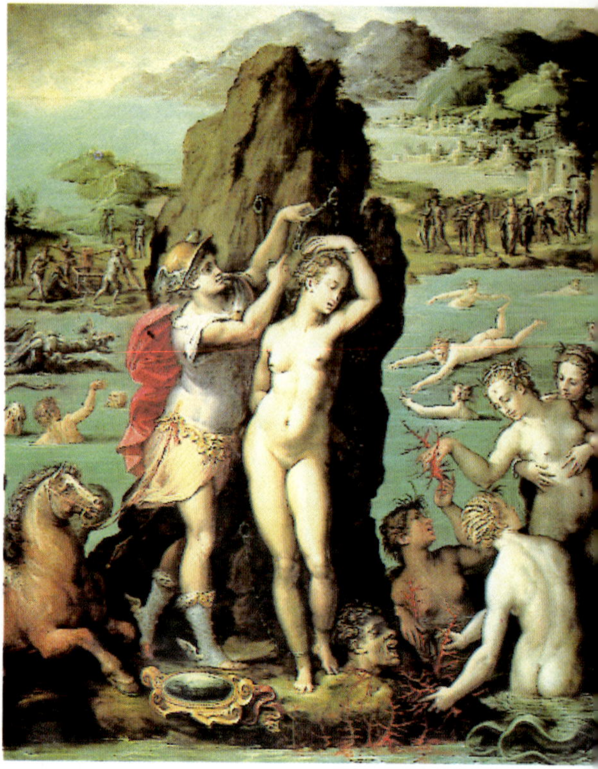

Perseus and Andromeda

Giorgio Vasari
(Arezzo, 1511–Florence, 1574)

- 1573
- fresco
- 117 x 100 cm
- Palazzo Vecchio, Florence

Andromeda was the daughter of Cepheus, King of Joppa in Palestine (called "Ethiopia" in most sources), and Cassiopeia, herself a daughter of Hermes' son Arabus. Her mother once boasted that Andromeda was the fairest of the Nereids, which infuriated Poseidon, who sent a sea-monster to devastate the country. Andromeda was bound to a rock near the sea and left for the monster to devour her. Perseus intervened, however, rescuing her from her horrible fate and then marrying her. In this fresco, Giorgio Vasari skillfully combines figure and landscape, lending both great dynamism by using a color scheme of intense and contrasting hues. The spectacular landscape has great depth, with a sea that reaches the foreground, filled with the sensual bodies of the Nereids in various poses. Andromeda, who strikes a classical pose, is depicted as a ravishing young woman with a body that is modeled with light and shade.

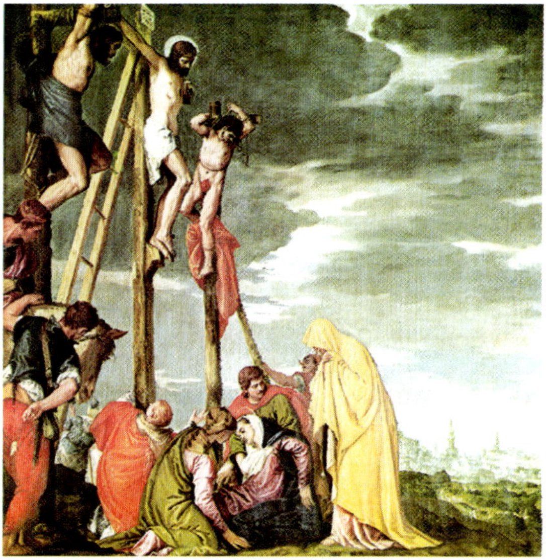

The Crucifixion

Paolo Veronese (Paolo Caliari)
(Verona, 1528–Venice, 1588)

- 1570–80
- oil on canvas
- 102 x 102 cm
- Musée du Louvre, Paris

ne pictorial conception lying behind this painting of the rucifixion is highly original. The dynamic regression of the cene, breaking as it does with the traditional frontal view, accentuated by the dramatic sky. The nude figures are oldly executed, in particular the thief on the right, the moding of whose trunk, limbs and muscles is exceptional.

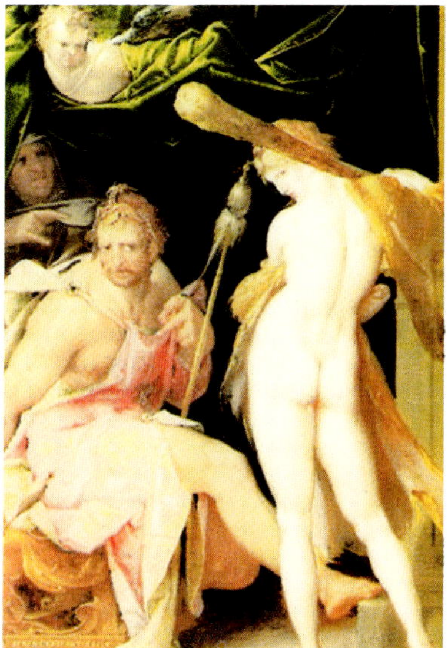

Hercules and Omphale

Bartholomäus Spranger
(Antwerp, 1546–Prague, 1611)

- 1575–80
- oil on leather
- 24 x 19 cm
- Kunsthistorisches Museum, Vienna

artholomäus pranger's penchant r small formats can obably be traced ack to his Netherndish background. ney enabled him to oncentrate on etails, as if working enamel. The atmosnere of the painting skillfully evoked, as e the figures, creatg a perfect stage for e drama of mphale and ercules to unfold on.

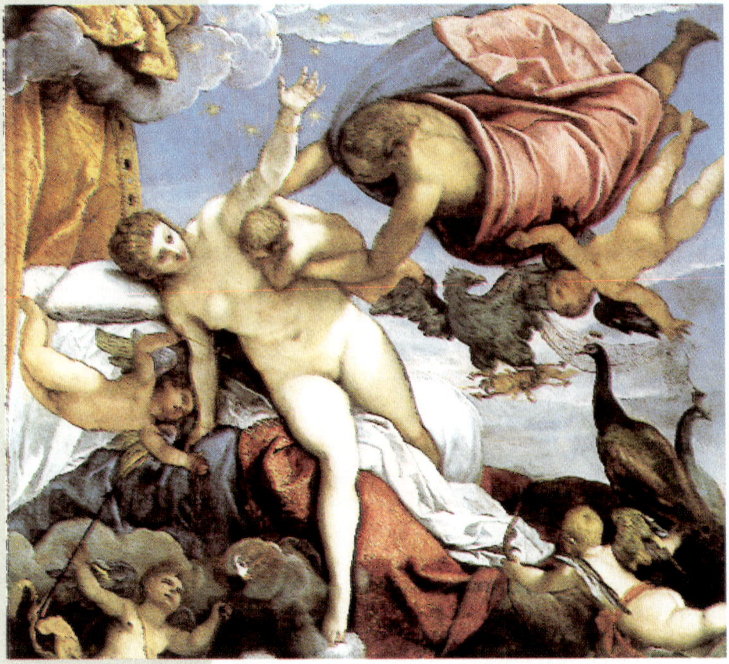

The Origin of the Milky Way

Tintoretto (Jacopo Robusti)
(Venice, 1518–1594)

- 1575–80
- oil on canvas
- 148 x 165.1 cm
- National Gallery, London

The female figure in the center of the scene, the goddess Juno, is shown in an affected pose. Instead Tintoretto would seem to have been more concerned with the overall composition of the painting and the arrangement of the figures around her. Her idealized, monumental body reflects the ideal of beauty of the day. The painting's extraordinary sensuality, color and light betray its Venetian origins. A black profile outlines the figures, and, although the light comes from the right, the figure of Juno is not cast in shadow. The painter has used a combination of intense, vivid and crisp colors, engendering a lively image with a distinctive palette. This and the elegant swathes of cloth lend the painting grandeur and drama.

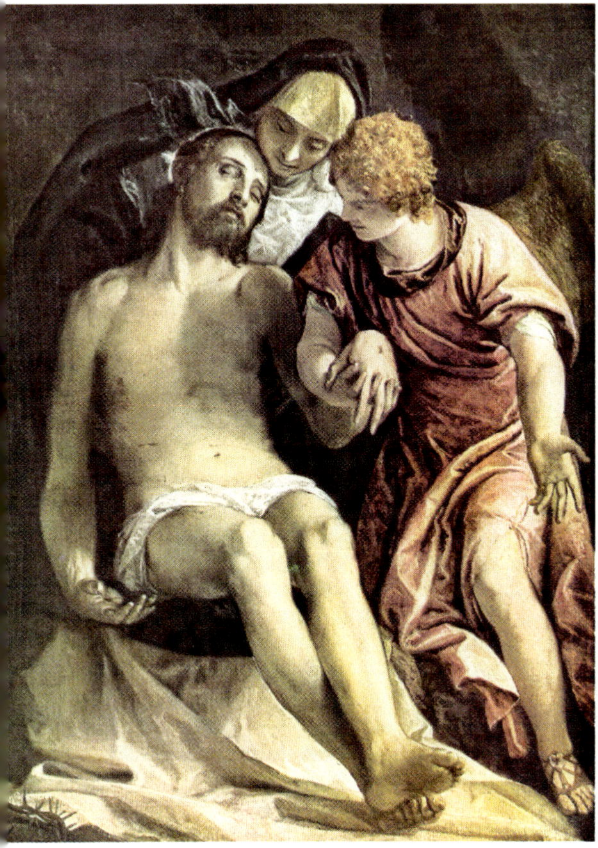

ıis scene, which is not of a real biblical event, shows the ərt body of Christ, together with the Virgin and an angel, ter having been taken down from the Cross. The artist əems to have had difficulties finding a suitable means of proaching the subject, for the painting has undergone ountless alterations. The austerity of the work perfectly nveys the gravity and solemnity of the moment. The dark ıckground causes the spectator's attention to be drawn to e three figurers. The painter has used an extensive ılette of restrained tones, which enhance the impact of the ht and the resulting contrasts that heighten the drama of e scene. The figures, whose well-balanced color scheme eates the impression of being a cohesive whole, are high- sculptural in character.

Pietà

Paolo Veronese (Paolo Caliari)

(Verona, 1528–Venice, 1588)

- 1576–82
- oil on canvas
- 147 x 111.5 cm
- Hermitage, St. Petersburg

In the first half of the 17th century this painting was purchased by Charles I of England. Following the sale of the English royal collection, it went to France, where it passed through several hands—including those of the Duke of Longueville, Count d'Armagnac and Crozat, whose collection was acquired by the Museum in 1772.

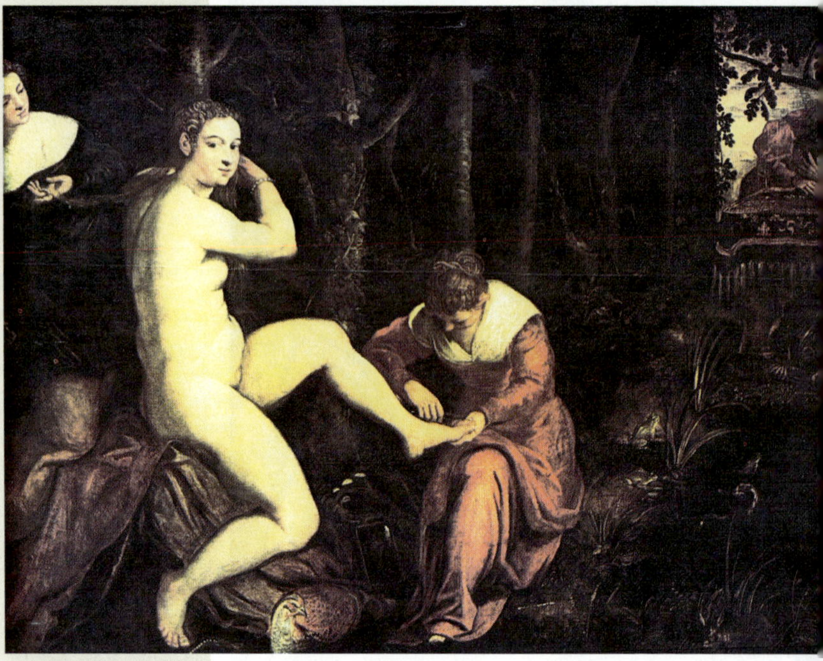

Susanna and the Elders

Tintoretto (Jacopo Robusti)
(Venice, 1518–1594)

- 1550
- oil on canvas
- 167 x 238 cm
- Musée du Louvre, Paris

Susanna, naked after bathing, is shown being attended to by her maid. The scene recalls a stage flat; the landscape, like a theater curtain, projects into the background diagonally to the right. On the left, an old woman takes delight in the sight of Susanna's naked body. The subject, in turn, whose marble-white skin is illuminated by a soft light, is shown looking out of the scene with such disarming candidness that she appears to invite the beholder into the intimate setting. Her seductive expression is accompanied by a provocative pose in which her lower abdomen and one of her breasts are exposed to view. The work is an incitement to voyeurism and draws the viewer into an uneasy exchange of glances with its subject.

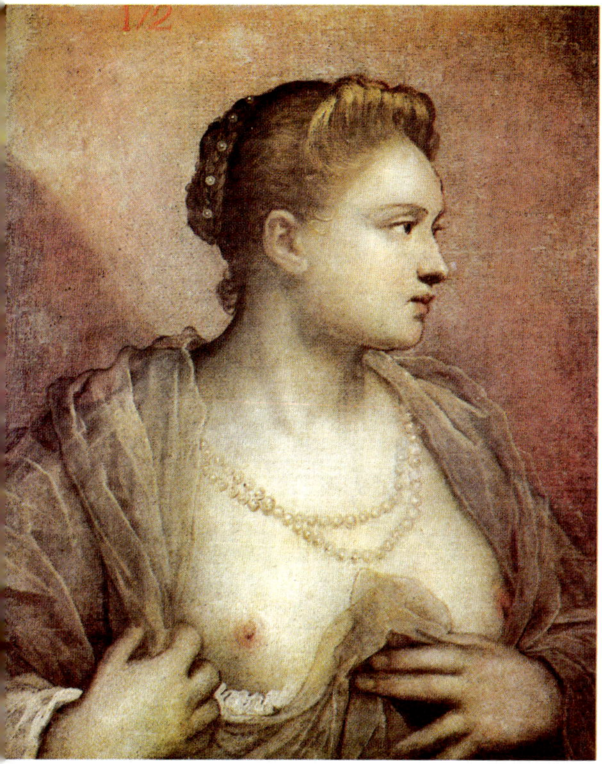

is not clear who the subject of this painting is: some say is the daughter of the artist, Marieta, who was also a ainter; others believe it is Veronica Franco, an exceed- gly beautiful Venetian courtesan, who was known for er refinement. The eroticism of this portrait is heightened the predominating mauve in which it was painted. The verall composition evokes an air of grandeur and phistication; the figure's expression fluctuates between opriety and restraint. The subject is graced with mar- elously luminous skin, and the loose-fitting dress accen- ates her beauty. The way in which she holds the dress gainst her body underlines her well-executed, soft yet m breasts. A precious string of pearls adorns her neck.

Woman Revealing Her Breasts

Tintoretto (Jacopo Robusti)
(Venice, 1518–1594)

- oil on canvas
- 61 x 55 cm
- Museo del Prado, Madrid

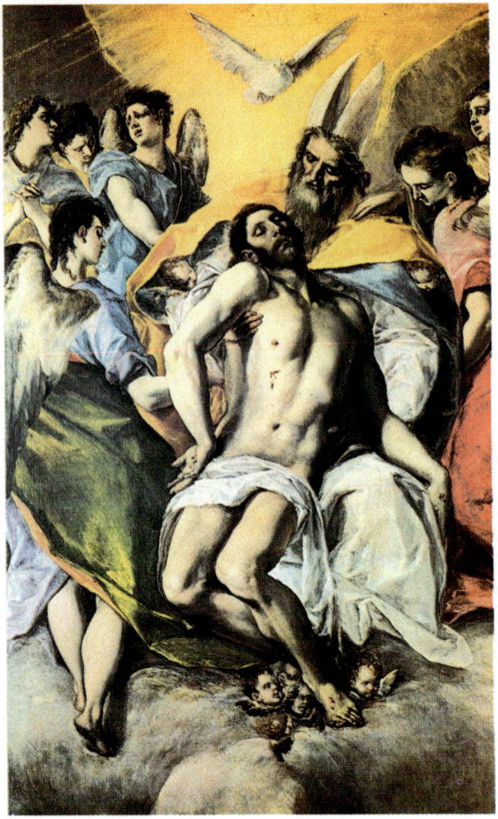

The Trinity

El Greco (Domenikos Theotokopoulos)
(Crete, 1541–Toledo, 1614)

- 1577
- oil on canvas
- 300 x 179 cm
- Museo del Prado, Madrid

This large work, conceived for the altarpiece of the monastery of Santo Domingo el Antiguo in Toledo, was the first commission undertaken by El Greco after moving to that city. Its wide range of cool colors reveals an Italian influence, notably the work of Tintoretto. The naturalistically rendered, athletic figure of Christ also recalls the figures of Michelangelo. With the exception of the wound in Christ's side, the painter has eschewed signs of pain and suffering in favor of beautiful imagery. The body's volumes and contours are brought out through the play of light and shadow, lending the work its remarkable dynamism. The bold S-shaped figure of Christ gives the painting a mannered air.

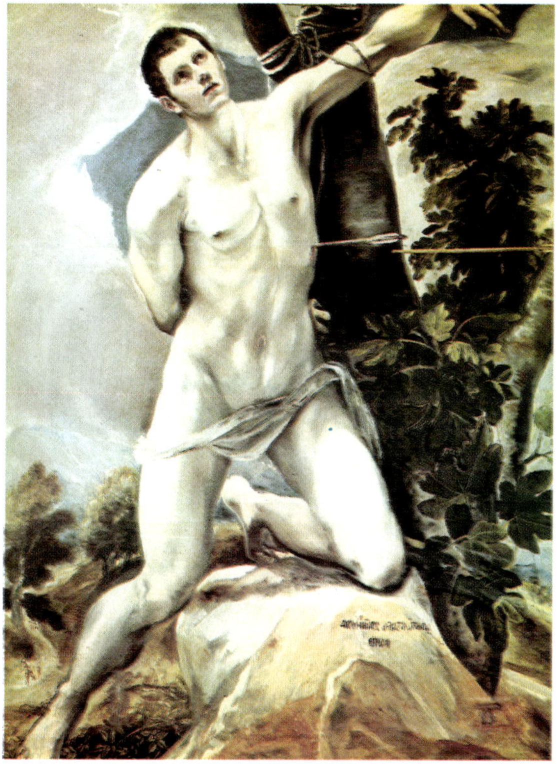

lthough Sebastian is being martyred, rather than reveal any ign of suffering, his face displays serenity as he stares pward, as if conversing with God. Unusual in this work from n art-historical point of view is the mother-of-pearl skin color, hich vies with the lead-white of the clouds, thus forcing the rtist to accentuate the blues over the figure. The young man's road proportions dominate the entire composition, which is in e form of an X, one bar of which is composed by the left arm nd right leg and the other by the tilted head and left leg.

St. Sebastian

El Greco (Domenikos Theotokopoulos)
(Crete, 1541–Toledo, 1614)

- 1577–78
- oil on canvas
- 191 x 145 cm
- Cathedral of Palencia

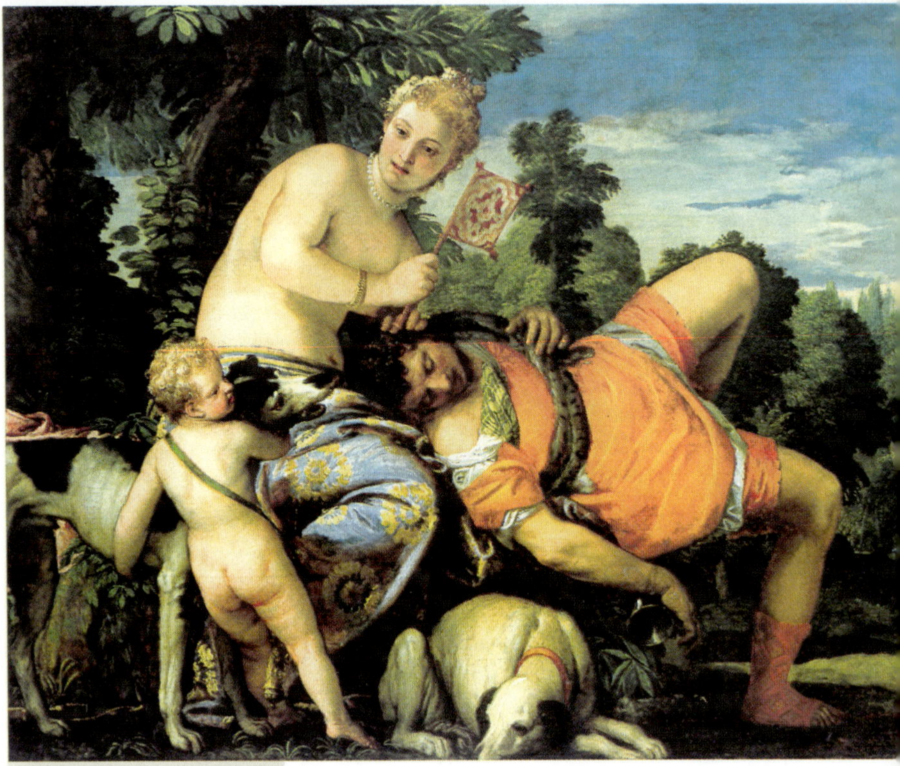

Venus and Adonis

Paolo Veronese (Paolo Caliari)
(Verona, 1528–Venice, 1588)

- ca. 1582
- oil on canvas
- 212 x 191 cm
- Museo del Prado, Madrid

On his second trip to Italy, Diego Velázquez acquired this painting for Philip IV of Spain.

Venus betrayed her husband, Vulcan, with numerous amour Adonis was one of her many conquests, a youth of great beauty, who was killed by a wild boar and from whose blood anemones were born. This painting exhibits stylistic affinities with the mythological works of Titian, in which gods are also made to look utterly human. Here, the goddess, who is partly covered in sumptuous fabric, caresses her sleeping lover, whose head rests on her lap, while the light that filters throug the trees plays about her skin. The figure of Cupid symbolize the couple's illicit love. The nude goddess unashamedly covers one of her breasts with her right arm while her other breast is just visible behind it. In this candid gesture lies the eroticism of this image, which is heightened by the goddess' voluptuous, round forms. The vibrant colors by which she is surrounded bring out her rosy skin.

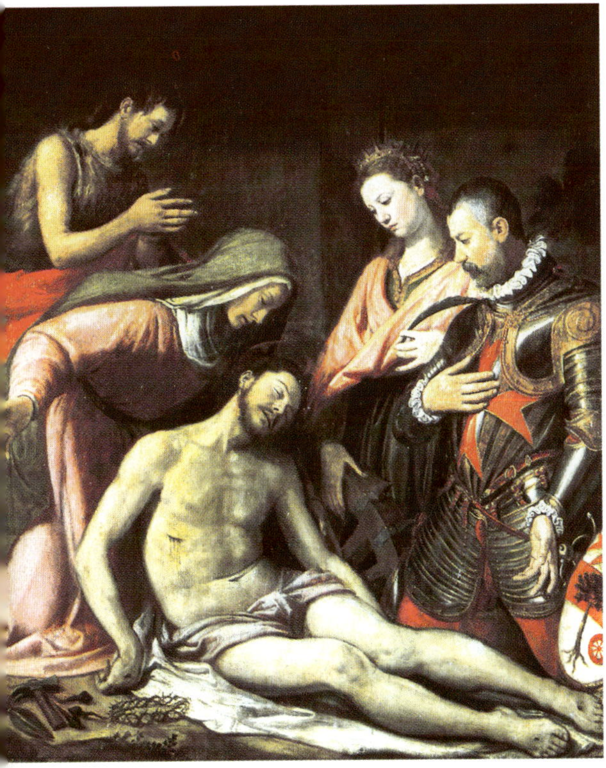

This painting depicts human despair in the person and figure of Christ, who has just suffered martyrdom. Yet melodrama is absent, whether in Christ or in those around him, who are grave, meditative and devout. Jesus' body, its complexion ashen, is a cadaver after rigor mortis has set in: complete langor, and a realistic facial expression. The realism does not extend to the signs of his martyrdom, the blood and wounds, because the artist is more interested in instilling devotion than in depicting tragedy. The foreshortening of the legs is extremely simply yet effectively resolved, since their depth is achieved through draftsmanship and not by means of contrast. The treatment of light is remarkable, picking out as it does the central figure's body and the faces of the by-standers, and lending their expressions sublimity.

Deposition with the Virgin, Saints and Patron

Santi di Tito
(Borgo San Sepolcro, 1536 –Florence, 1603)

- oil on canvas
- Galleria dell'Accademia, Venice

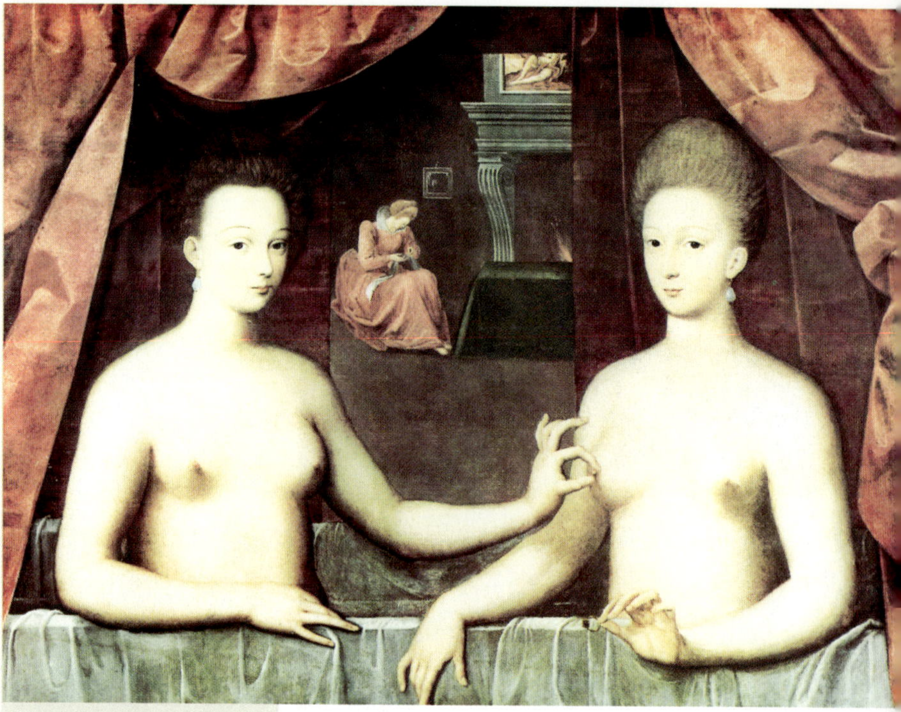

Gabrielle d'Estrées and One of Her Sisters

Anonymous Fontainebleau School

- oil on canvas
- 96 x 125 cm
- Musée du Louvre, Paris

At the behest of Francis I of France, a cultural center was founded in Fontainebleau, which initially consisted exclusively of major Italian, and later included French, artists. Its influence extended into the 17th century, leaving its mark even on Parisian artists. The work of the Fontainebleau artists is marked by an elegant yet emotionally cool style; it embraces the tradition of Italian Mannerism, but with local and Flemish influences. The setting of this work corresponded to the tastes of the day, when paintings on easels were frequently incorporated into pictures. The identity of the sitters remains obscure but it has been suggested that the two women in the foreground are Gabrielle d'Estrées, the king's mistress, and her sister, the Duchess of Villars. The scene is undeniably erotic. The subjects' smooth, white skin, which contrasts with the dark background, is extremely sensual, as are the figures' soft, well-formed contours. This is underlined by the gesture of the woman on the left, who is shown pinching the other woman's nipple. Far from the Baroque ideal of beauty, these courtesans are not graced with voluptuous bodies, but rather androgynous ones.

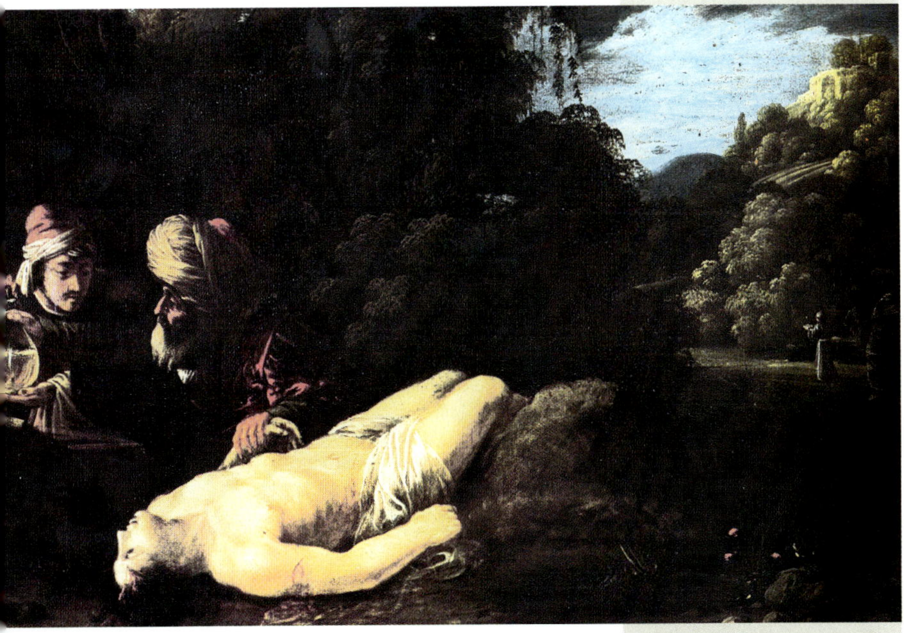

fter moving to Italy, this painter became fascinated by the
ork of Caravaggio, in particular his use of chiaroscuro.
espite the Flemish influences that can be observed in Adam
lsheimer's work, it has a very personal style. In this paint-
ng, the brightest light falls on the wounded figure in the fore-
round, the product of bold and masterly foreshortening. The
nanner in which the figure is placed in the scene and the
ght falls on it make the landscape seem unreal and mysteri-
us. The picture takes up the theme of human mortality,
eminding the viewer that anyone can have a fateful moment,
egardless of his or her social status or age. Every detail is
endered with the utmost care, such as the wounds from
vhich blood is flowing in small, scarcely perceptible rivulets,
r the thin, transparent cloth covering the figure's loins.

The Good Samaritan

Adam Elsheimer
(or **Ehlsheimer**)
(Frankfurt am Main, 1578
–Rome, 1610)

- oil on copper
- 21 x 26 cm
- Musée du Louvre, Paris

Diane de Poitiers

Anonymous Fontainebleau School

- oil on canvas
- 111.5 x 98.5 cm
- Öffentliche Kunstsammlung, Basel

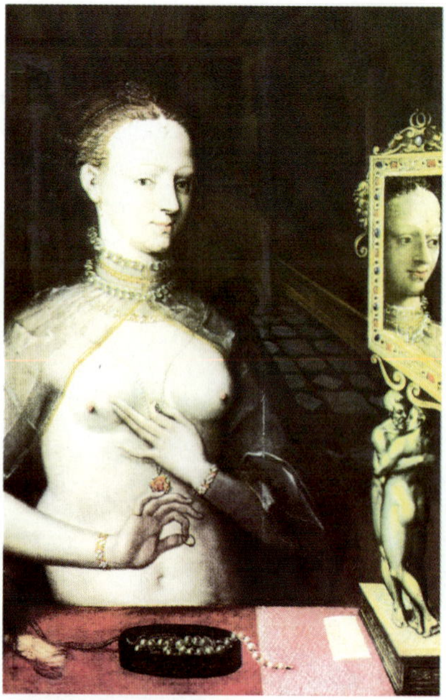

Diane de Poitiers, an ambitious courtesan of undeniabl beauty and seductive charms, was the mistress of Henry II of France. Portrayed here as both commanding and sensual, her naked body acquires an air of mystery and the flesh tones stand out against the dark background. Depicted as if she were looking into a mirror, she shows the viewer her jewelry, framing her breasts with a string of pearls anc a transparent veil.

The Choice of Hercules

Annibale Carracci
(Bologna, 1560–Rome, 1609)

- oil on canvas
- 168 x 238 cm
- Museo e Gallerie Nazionali, Campodimonte

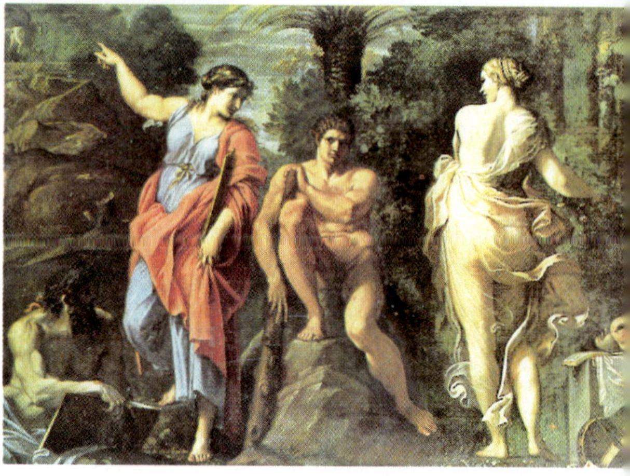

Hercules is attempting here to choose between the two women, Virtue (struggle) and Vice (passivity). The figure of the hero is executed along the lines of Greek sculptural models, if with a somewhat less mature physique. Young and full of vitality, he seems to have stepped out of one of Michelangelo's frescos. The nude figure radiates great strength, the lighting lending it, with its impressive foreshortening, a monumental aspect.

enebrist realism
ave rise to an
nportant school
iat still exists
oday. Influenced
i its foreshorten-
ig by Ribera, this
ainting depicts a
culptural nude ac-
entuated by light
alling from the left,
/hich creates
tmosphere and
ilds the figure
/ith warm tones.

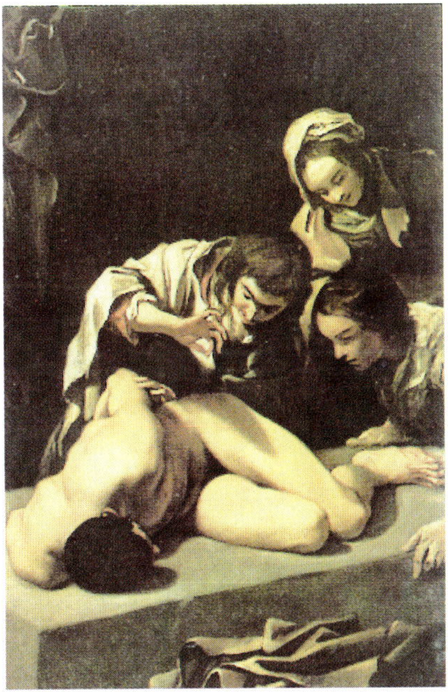

St. Sebastian Attended by Pious Women

Bartolomeo Schedoni
(Formegine, 1570–Parma, 1615)

- oil on canvas
- 188 x 126 cm
- Museo e Gallerie Nazionali, Campodimonte

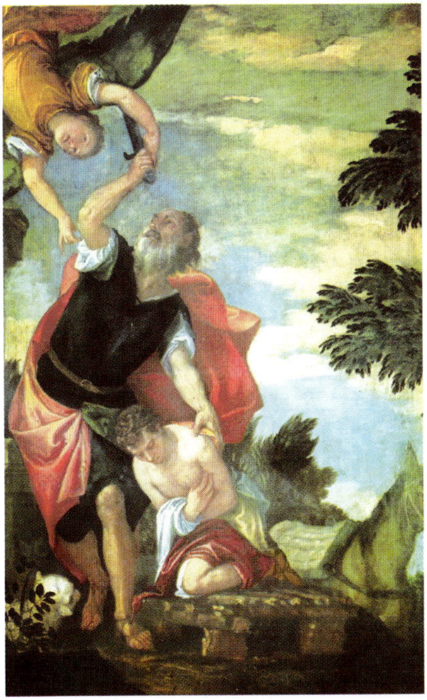

Abraham's Sacrifice

Paolo Veronese (Paolo Caliari)
(Verona, 1528–Venice, 1588)

- ca. 1580
- oil on canvas
- 95 x 129 cm
- Museo del Prado, Madrid

saac is inclining
orward in expecta-
on of death.
.lthough not fully
aked, the fore-
hortening
dmirably reveals
is youthful and
eautifully-propor-
oned trunk with its
gorous modeling.

The Last Judgment

Maerten de Vos
(Antwerp, ca. 1532–1603)

- ca. 1580
- oil on canvas
- Museo Provincial de Bellas Artes, Seville

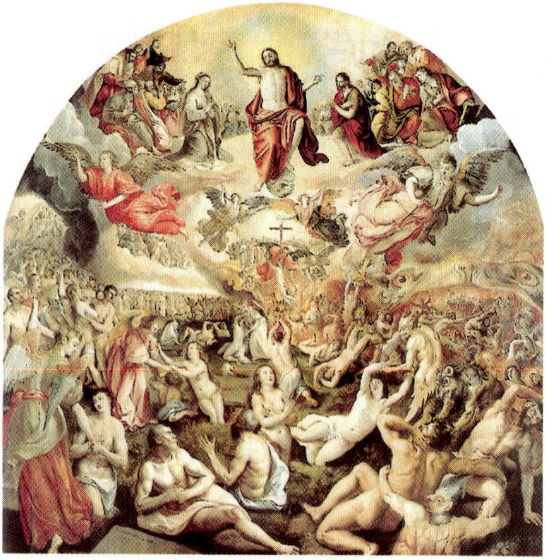

This monumental and sensational scene comprises a large aggregate of nude figures of both sexes in various dynamic poses exhibiting a wide range of foreshortening and gestures. The figures offer themselves to display without inhibition, the male bodies being muscular and strong, the female delicate and sensual.

Portrait of a Sculptor

Paolo Veronese (Paolo Caliari)
(Verona, 1528–Venice, 1588)

- ca. 1580
- oil on canvas
- 126 x 95 cm
- Metropolitan Museum of Art, New York

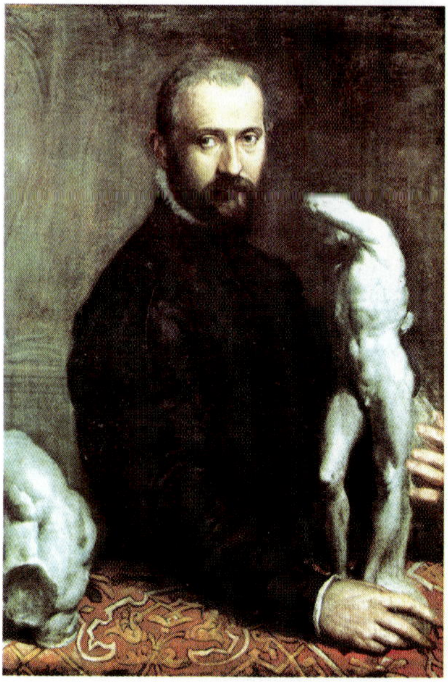

A middle-aged man—possibly the sculptor Alessandro Vittoria—is holding a nude statue of Hercules. The statue itself is remarkable for its forceful, plastic treatment, where highlights and tonal contrasts create a figure that appears to be literally sculpted on the canvas. Typical of this artist's male nudes, its proportions are also of great beauty.

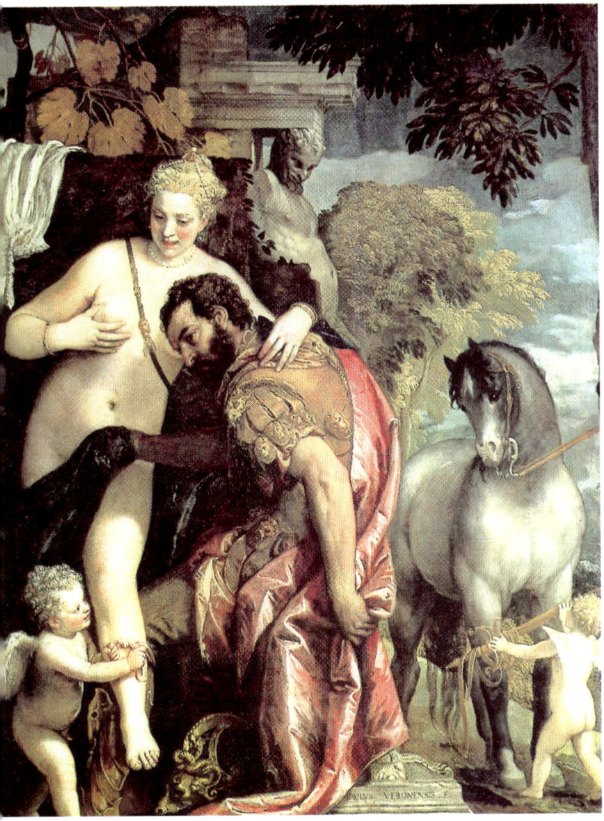

The figures in this composition are concentrated in the left half of the painting in order to accentuate the idea of union and intimacy. Veronese uses the landscape and the architecture as complementary background elements against which the figures stand out, particularly Venus, whose body is pale and well lit. She exhibits a robust anatomy, although her forms are soft, with all the sensuality appropriate of the goddess. Mars is depicted as a Roman centurion. The faces of the two figures are probably of well-known people of the day. Cupid, who brings Venus and Mars together by means of a thin rope tied around their legs, is not portrayed as cunning, as in other works, but as an innocent child, with which the artist accentuates tenderness, the work's main theme.

Mars and Venus United by Cupid

Paolo Veronese (Paolo Caliari)
(Verona, 1528–Venice, 1588)

- ca. 1580
- oil on canvas
- 206 x 161 cm
- Metropolitan Museum of Art, New York

Flagellation of Christ

Ludovico Carracci
(Bologna, 1555–1619)

- ca. 1580
- oil on canvas
- 189 x 265 cm
- Musée de la Chartreuse, Douai

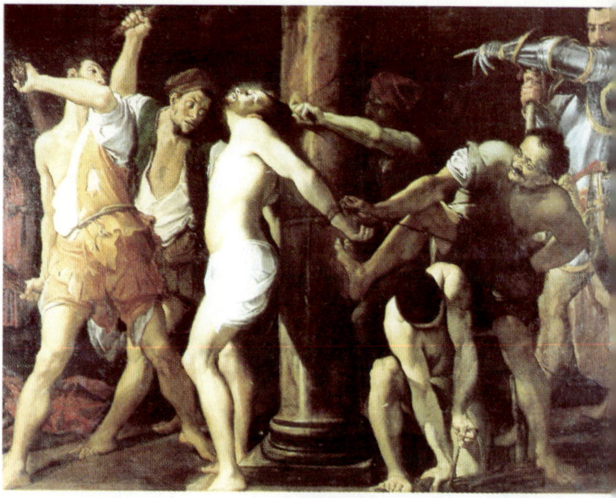

Tenebrist painting completely revolutionized approaches to light and dramatic action. The dynamism of Carracci's works facilitated a style of realism hitherto unattained in art, in which the freezing of action serves to heighten the drama enacted. Christ here has the body of an ordinary man with no great capacity for suffering.

Christ on the Cross, with Two Donors

El Greco (Domenikos Theotokopoulos)
(Crete, 1541–Toledo, 1614)

- ca. 1580
- oil on canvas
- 250 x 180 cm
- Musée du Louvre, Paris

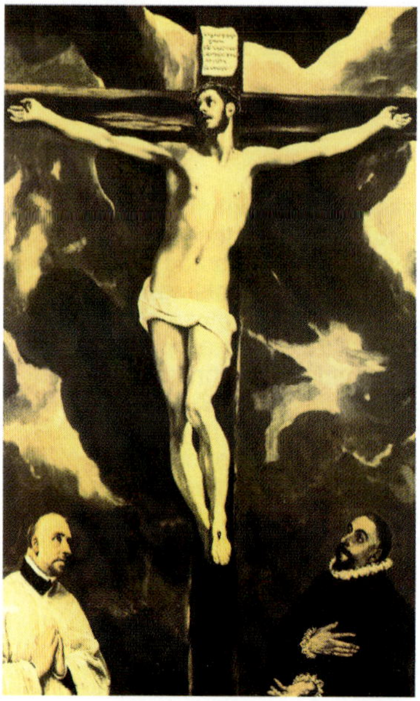

The proportions of the figure do not represent deformations, but an idealization, through which a consummate composition is achieved. The outline of Christ's perfectly proportioned body is sinuous, eliminating all traces of rigidity and making the nude appear light and ethereal. The image of the crucified Christ is idealized here; his humiliation and suffering thus recede into the background.

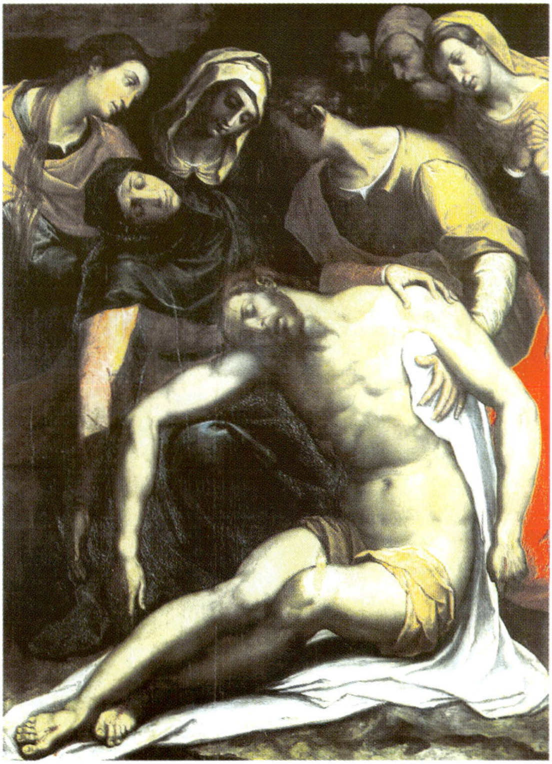

ieri has succeeded in creating a full, well-balanced composi-
on, with rhythm and dramatic interest. The painter has
epicted the nude and inert body of the crucified Jesus, with-
ut blood or the wounds of martyrdom, so that mysticism is
verlaid on tragedy and suffering. Chiaroscuro effects domi-
ate the scene. The figures around Christ, as complementary
lements, retreat in shadow, while the figure of Jesus is high-
ghted by strong side illumination that brings out the perfect,
uscular body of a man of near-heroic proportions. The con-
asting light and shade give the body a sculptural aspect. The
ody describes an arc at the center of the painting, arresting
e viewer's gaze at the same time as serving the painter's
ligious intention, while the impassive, meditative faces of
e onlookers contribute powerfully to the overall atmosphere.

Descent from the Cross

Stefano Pieri
(1542–1629)

- ca. 1585
- oil on canvas
- Galleria dell'Accademia, Venice

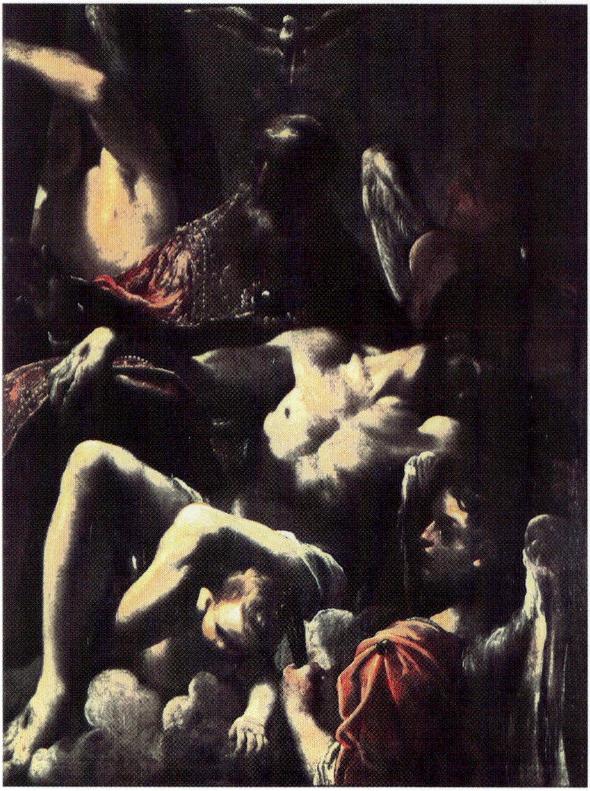

Trinity with Dead Christ

Ludovico Carracci
(Bologna, 1555–1619)

- ca. 1590
- oil on canvas
- Pinacoteca, Vatican

This work is typical of the style of composition pursued by the painter throughout his career. None of the standing figures is entire, the draftsmanship is supreme, the foreshortening bold, and no space is left unfilled. The foreshortening used for the depiction of Christ is extreme; with legs and torso prominent, while the abdomen remains in shadow, it is as if the figure were literally bathing in light. The effect is highly dramatic and thoroughly suited to fostering a mixture of religious passion, devotion and mystery. The work replaces Caravaggio's naturalism with a kind of Classicism, and Mannerist symbolism with an allegorical style that lay well within the public reach. As a result, religious iconography, until then rather grandiose and pompous, is simplified.

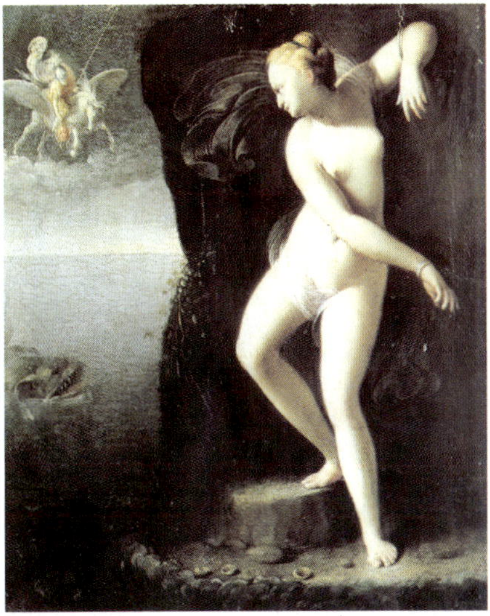

ɴndromeda
:hained to a rock
ɪnd about to be
ɪevoured by a
nonster, while
ᴾerseus
ɪpproaches in
ɪrder to rescue
ɪer, is the subject
ɪf this panel.
ɴndromeda's pale
gure has a
vraith-like quality,
ɪnd, unlike many
ɪther depictions
ɪf the same
cene, she lacks
ɪeauty.

Andromeda Chained

Carlo Saraceni
(Venice, ca. 1579–1620)

- 1592–93
- oil on panel
- 26 x 22 cm
- Musée des Beaux-Arts, Dijon

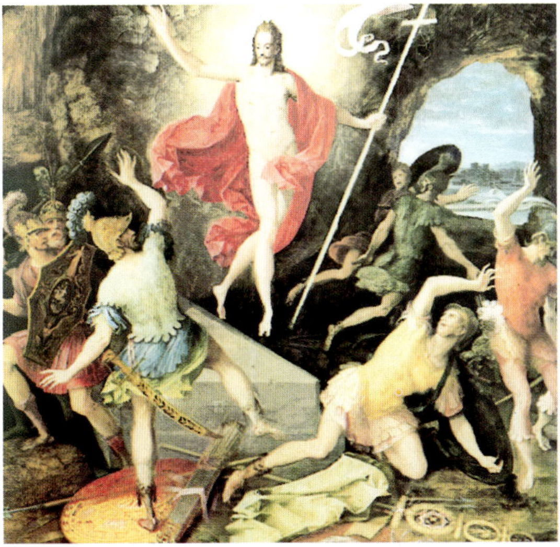

Resurrection of Christ

Antoine Caron (?)
(Beauvais, Île-de-France, 1521 –Paris, 1599)

- ca. 1594
- oil on canvas
- Musée du Département d'Oise, Beauvais, France

;aron's art, with its clear debt to Manneristic trends, is eopled with figures that display their creator's profound cquaintance with the details of human anatomy. The setng they appear in is often theatrical to an extreme. Christ, iumphant and in splendor, seems oblivious to the panic e is creating amongst the Roman soldiers. His nude figre is depicted here radiating brightness, which, however, oes not end up obscuring the physical details, as often ccurs in representations of a similar kind.

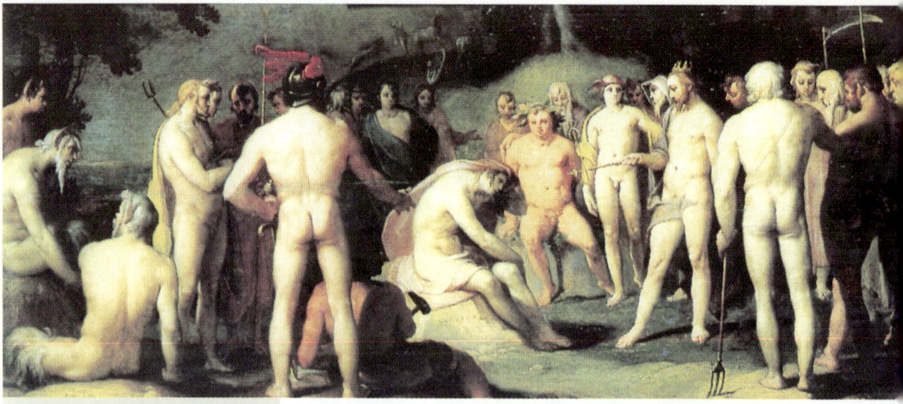

Apollo Before the Tribunal of the Gods

Cornelis van Haarlem (Cornelis Cornelisz)
(Haarlem, 1562–1638)

- 1594
- oil on panel
- 44 x 98 cm
- Museo del Prado, Madrid

The scene may have some reference to Apollo and Venus' illicit union. Caught in flagrante in a trap set by Venus' consort, Vulcan, he displays their adultery to the rest of the gods. It might, however, refer to Jupiter's judgement of Apollo for the killing of the Cyclops. These naturalistically-rendered, powerfully-modeled nudes have great plasticity and beauty.

Diana and her Nymphs Surprised by Actaeon

Dirck van der Lisse (?)
(b. Breda; d. The Hague, bur. 31 Jan 1669)

- ca. 1600
- painted on copper
- 29 x 41 cm
- Museo de Bellas Artes, Cordoba

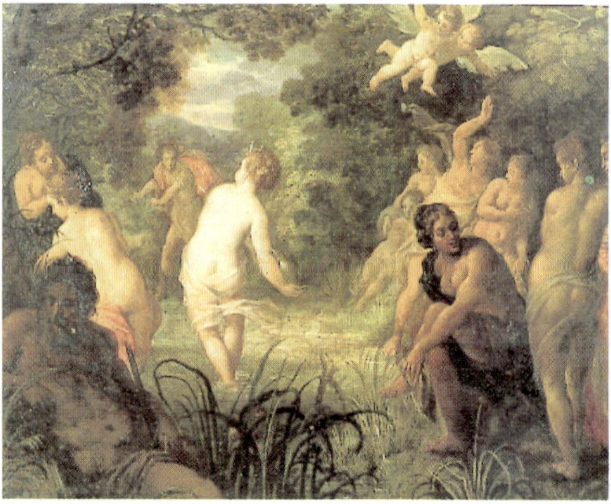

This exquisite oil painting on copper, with its dark tones and gradations of colour, varies the usual depiction of the theme. Here, alarmed by the discovery of the intruder, the nymphs scatter in all directions, while Diana, to the right, seems undaunted.

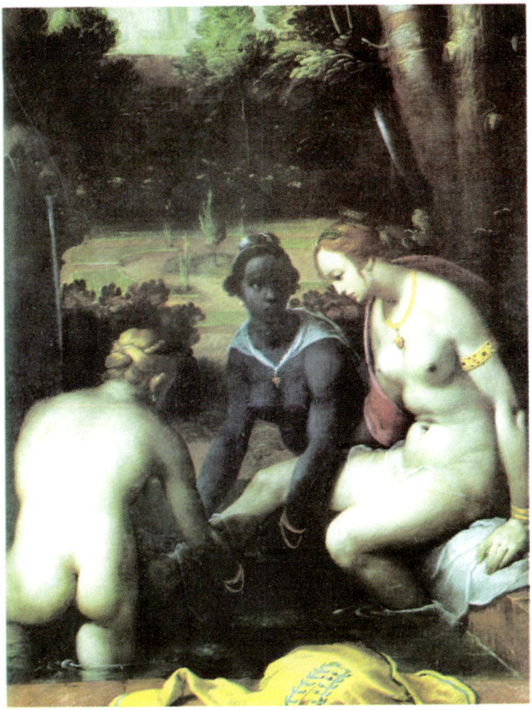

Bathsheba, attended by two maids, does not realize that King David is watching her from afar. He falls in love with her, although she is married to Uriah, an officer in his army. After consummating their love, Bathsheba is with child. In order to marry his lover, the king cunningly sends Uriah to his death on the front. The painting's landscape in the background combines with the figures in the foreground to evoke a mysterious mood, which pervades the entire scene. The women's white bodies are bathed in a studied light, bringing out their forms and enhancing the voluptuousness of their volumes. The shadows modeling the figures blend into the magical atmosphere, making the lighter areas stand out against the dark landscape. The women's natural and uninhibited poses add to their sensuality, as do their corpulent bodies and marmoreal complexions. The exotic, colored servant is visually striking, although the bluish tones of her skin are difficult to distinguish from the black of the shadows on her body.

Bathsheba at Her Bath

Cornelis van Haarlem (Cornelis Cornelisz)
(Haarlem, 1562–1638)

- 1594
- oil on canvas
- 77.5 x 64 cm
- Rijksmuseum, Amsterdam

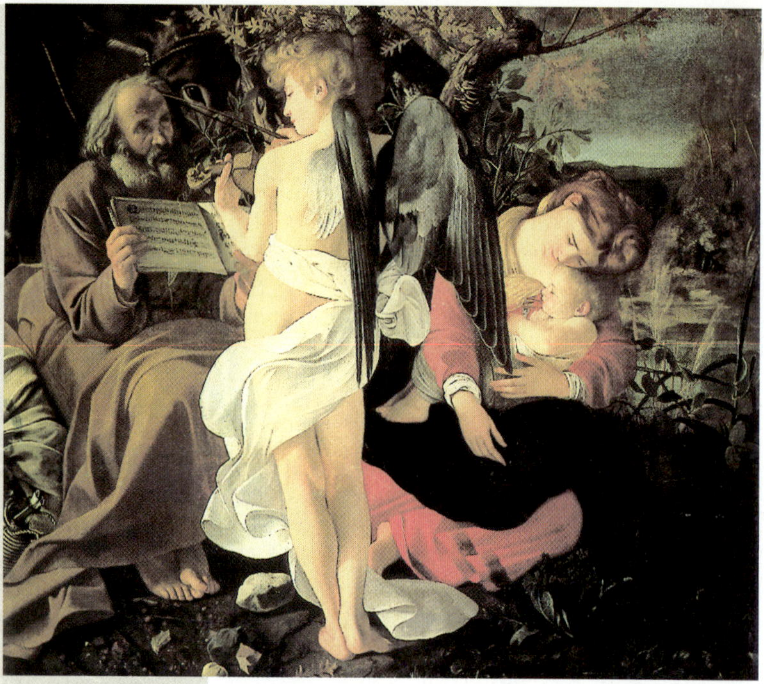

Rest on the Flight to Egypt

Caravaggio (Michelangelo Merisi or **Amerighi da Caravaggio)**
(Caravaggio, Lombardy, 1573 –Port'Ercole, Tuscany, 1610)

- 1594–96
- oil on canvas
- 130 x 160 cm
- Galleria Doria Pamphili, Rome

Caravaggio fought hard to earn his living as a painter, virtually leading the life of a vagrant at one point because he was unable to sell many works. Eventually, in the 1590s Cardinal del Monte became interested in his work and took it upon himself to protect the painter. Caravaggio now began to receive commissions, including this work, which displays his extraordinary mastery of painting and drawing. Although the subject is religious—an imaginary biblical scene, as it were —it appears here in an almost profane guise. Sexual ambiguity characterizes many of the artist's figures: in this painting, for example, the appearance and artistic treatment of the angel playing the violin, an early instance of Caravaggio's dramatic use of light, resemble those of a woman. The position of the feet gives the angel a light, feminine grace, while the contrapposto is that of a Venus rather than a male figure. Such figures occur time and again in this artist's work, along with boldly masculine ones.

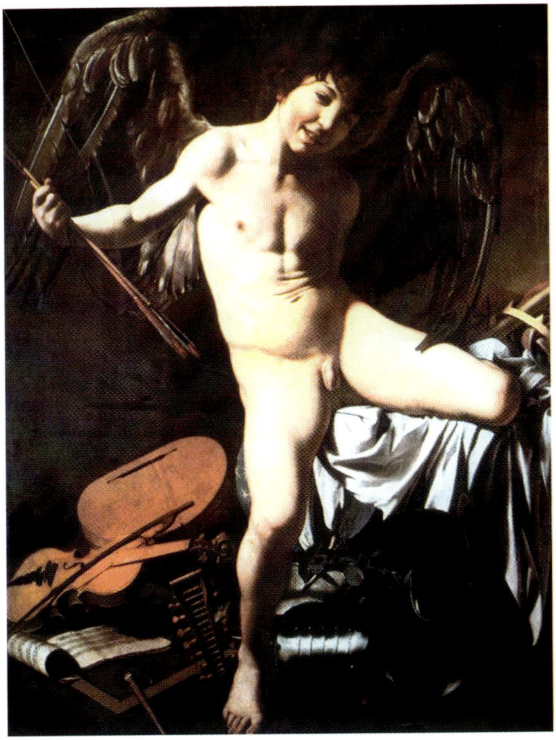

Caravaggio's model, a street urchin, displays his sensual body without reserve and with a mischievous, teasing smile. Amor triumphant innocently tramples the worldly glories of science, riches, art, even war, as he descends from his bed of love in a delightfully cheeky pose, his wings a sparrow's, a common enough bird. The work parodies Michelangelo's work of the same name. The anatomical draftsmanship is perfect and exhibits a body full of vigour. The lighting is harsh and facilitates very powerful modeling, which, however, does not reach some of this artist's extremes of chiaroscuro. As well as concluding 16th-century Italy's series of artistic transformations, Caravaggio's tenebrism and chiaroscuro formed the gateway to Baroque realism.

Cupid

Caravaggio (Michelangelo Merisi or **Amerighi da Caravaggio**)
(Caravaggio, Lombardy, 1573 –Port'Ercole, Tuscany, 1610)

- ca. 1595
- oil on canvas
- 154 x 110 cm
- Gemäldegalerie Dahlem, Berlin

The work was acquired by the gallery in 1815.

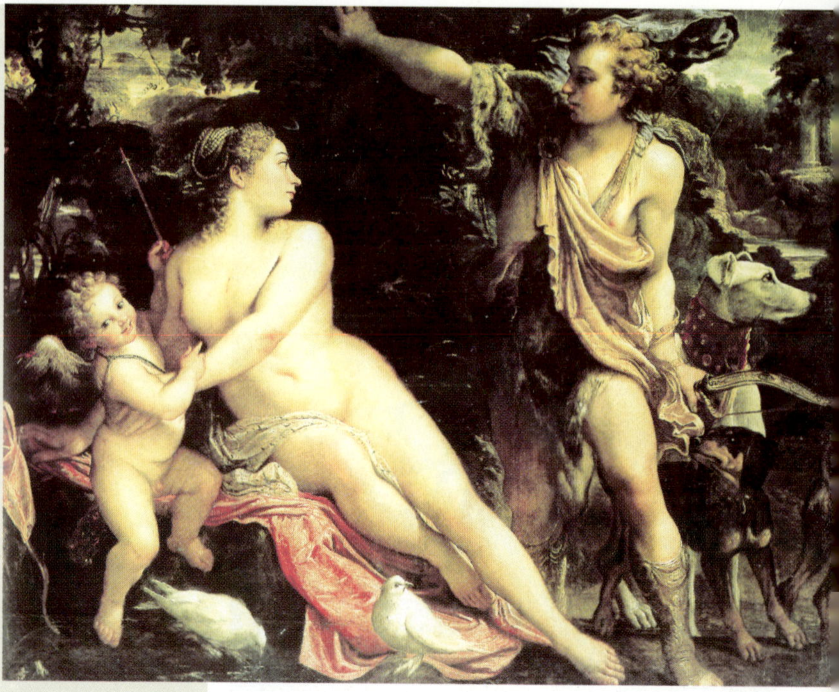

Venus and Adonis

Annibale Carracci

(Bologna, 1560–Rome, 1609)

- ca. 1595
- oil on canvas
- 212 x 268 cm
- Museo del Prado, Madrid

This painting, executed after the artist's return from a trip to Venice, pays tribute to the work of Titian and Paolo Veronese. Its round and sensual forms evoke the compositions and colors of the Venetian School. It depicts the amorous encounter of Venus and Adonis. Carracci's style evokes the compositions of Raphael; the plasticity of the figures is characteristic of the artist's work. Carracci's ideal of the human body is reflected above all in the balance and harmony of the figures. He does not exaggerate their proportions to achieve aesthetic effects. Rather, he endeavors to attain a real, almost tangible beauty in his nudes. Particularly notable details of the painting include the treatment of the flesh tones, the palette used for the skin, which is different for each nude, and the subtly rendered illuminated areas, which do not appear artificial.

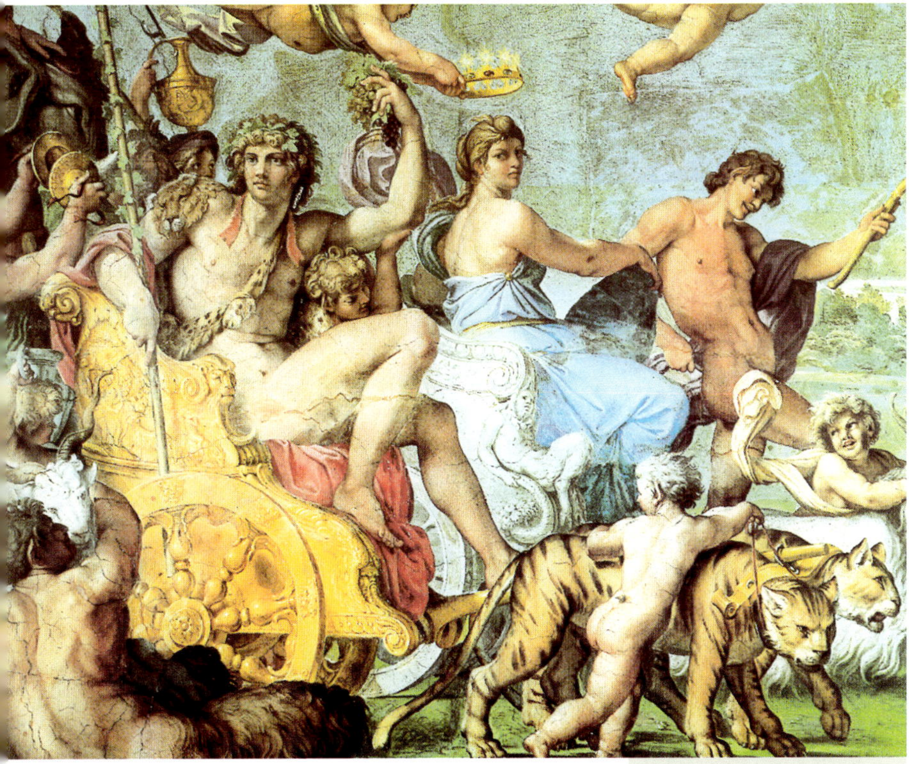

ˉhis painting represents the love between Bacchus and ٨riadne, daughter of Minos, King of Crete. Abandoned on the sland of Naxos by Theseus, the princess was rescued by ßacchus, who took her to Olympus as his wife. The theme is aken from Ovid's The Loves of the Gods. This classical work nakes reference to the triumphal marches of the Roman em-›erors upon their return from military campaigns. The painter ׀as clearly influenced by the frescos of Michelangelo, as is ւpparent in the monumentality of the figures, whose volumes ւre nearly sculptural. The sensuality of the figures is accentu-ւted by the corpulence of their androgynous bodies. Possibly or this reason, Carracci makes the facial features of Ariadne nore extreme. Bacchus, bearing a certain resemblance to ›ne of Michelangelo's Herculean sibyls, is foreshortened like ℟aphael's figures. The nudes are striking, not only in their ophisticated foreshortening, but also in their arrangement vithin the painting.

The Triumph of Bacchus and Ariadne (detail)

Annibale Carracci
(Bologna, 1560–Rome, 1609)

- 1595–1605
- fresco
- Palazzo Farnese, Rome

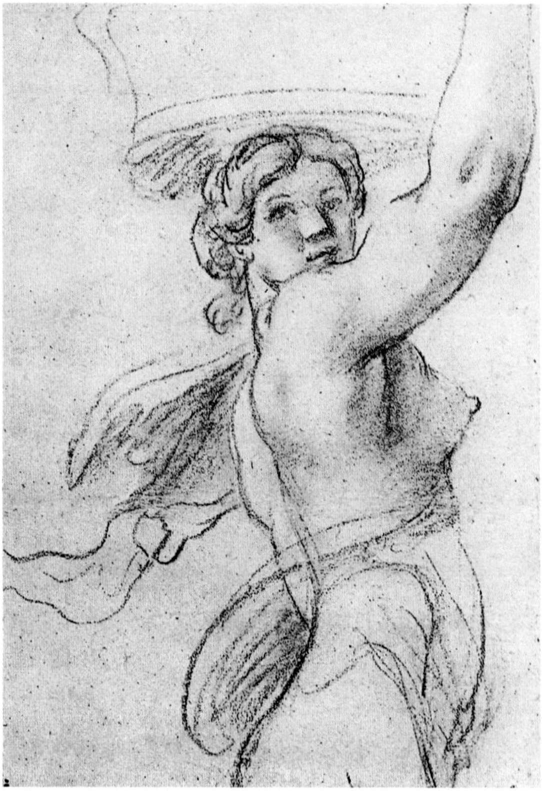

Woman Carrying a Basket on her Head

Annibale Carracci
(Bologna, 1560-Rome, 1609)

- ca. 1597
- black chalk heightened with white
- 42.8 x 28.7 cm
- Musée du Louvre, Cabinet des Dessins, Paris

The artist's treatment of his theme in this drawing is thoroughly Classical—a woman in profile, of powerful build and full bosom, enhances her features by reaching her arms up above her head to hold a basket. Her strong physique contrasts with and is moderated by, the transparent veil flowing around her. As a result, the figure is idealized and attains to the status of symbol or allegory. The pose is academic, yet the facture is modern, the woman's outline boldly confident, despite some loose lines. Noteworthy is the slow, solemn rotational movement of her entire body that brings her to face the viewer. The artist has ensured that the tones remain soft and delicate.

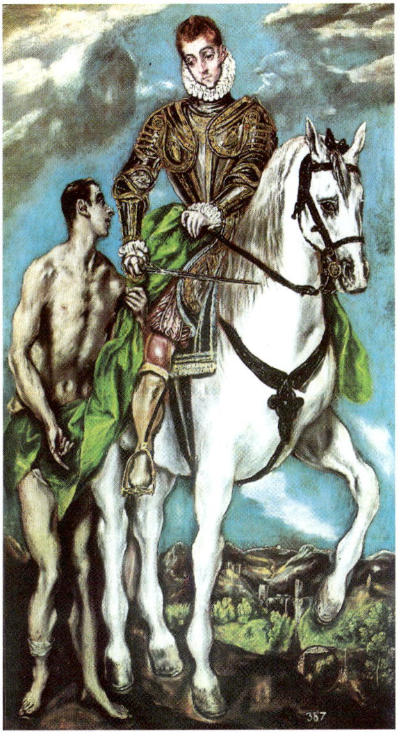

The saint in this painting is a well-proportioned figure, while the beggar and the horse are of much thinner, elongated proportions. The beggar's body is further remarkable for the treatment of light evinced on his skin: the illumination bathing the figure appears to be reflected off its surface. Each curve in the beggar's body is lent rhythm, emphasizing his dynamic musculature in a highly expressive way—a set of painterly solutions that astounded his contemporaries no less than they still astound us today. As in other works by this painter, verticals are accentuated to a maximum. It is not true, as some believe, that the artist distorted his images because of bad eyesight. He did this in order to surprise the spectator and to foster feelings of admiration and devotion.

St. Martin and the Beggar

El Greco (Domenikos Theotokopoulos)
(Crete, 1541–Toledo, 1614)

- 1599
- oil on canvas
- 193 x 103 cm
- National Gallery of Art, Washington D.C.

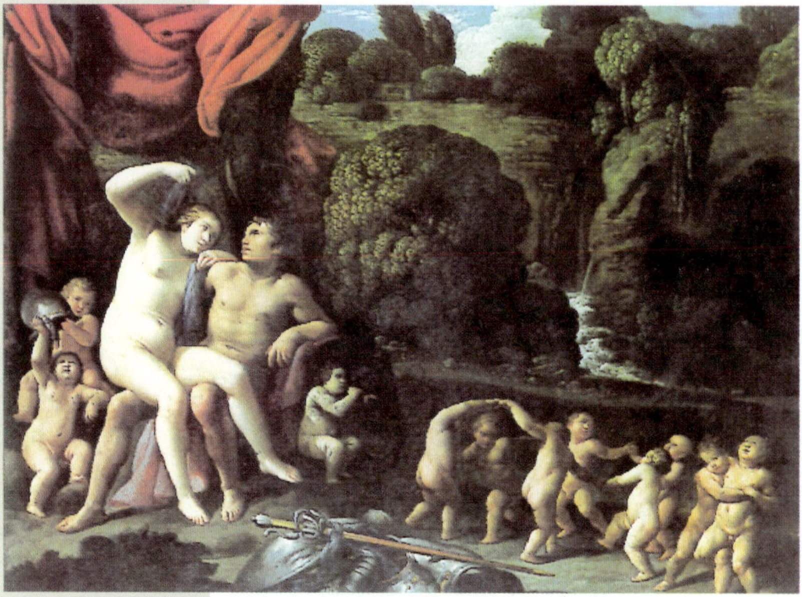

Venus and Mars

Carlo Saraceni
(Venice, ca. 1579–1620)

- oil on canvas
- 39 x 52 cm
- Museu de Arte, São Paulo

Scarcely anything is known about this Mannerist painter. His art was clearly influenced by the Venetian School and Caravaggio's naturalism. In this painting, Venus and her husband, Mars, appear in a setting that combines an indoor scene with a landscape to produce a highly decorative work. The well-modeled nude bodies of the protagonists, as well as those of the dancing cherubs, have somewhat rotund bodies. The figure of Venus is brightly illuminated, accentuating her feminine curves. The goddess is seated on Mars' Apollonian lap, in keeping with the tastes of the French Academy. Although the nudes are not profound figures, on account of the work's decorative nature, the cherubs playing and dancing in celebration of the gods' love are veritable miniature masterpieces. The luxuriant vegetation, consisting primarily of trees rendered in saturated colors, serve to complement the figures, particularly those in the foreground.

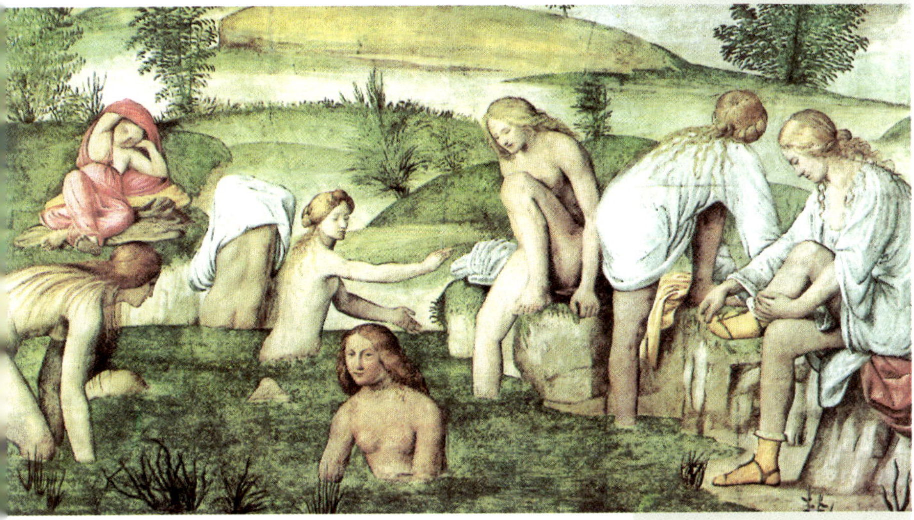

Bernardino Luini was one of the artists who best understood the works of Leonardo da Vinci, from whom he learned the technique of sfumato, taking up his style and adapting it to simpler themes. Based on the master's techniques, he concentrated on representing mythological as well as religious themes, lending a certain bucolic air to his scenes. This stylistic treatment brought Leonardo's complicated ideas to a wider audience. This scene, showing naturalistically-rendered female nudes in various foreshortened poses while bathing, makes a voyeur of the viewer. Although the female forms are rather androgynous, certain aspects, such as their postures and long, loose hair, evoke feminine sensuality. The painter demonstrates his narrative abilities in this scene, which is imbued with rhythmic plasticity and freshness.

Women Bathing

Bernardino Luini

(Luino, Lake Maggiore, 1480/90–Milan, 1532)

- ca. 1518
- fresco
- 35 x 250 cm
- Pinacoteca di Brera, Milan

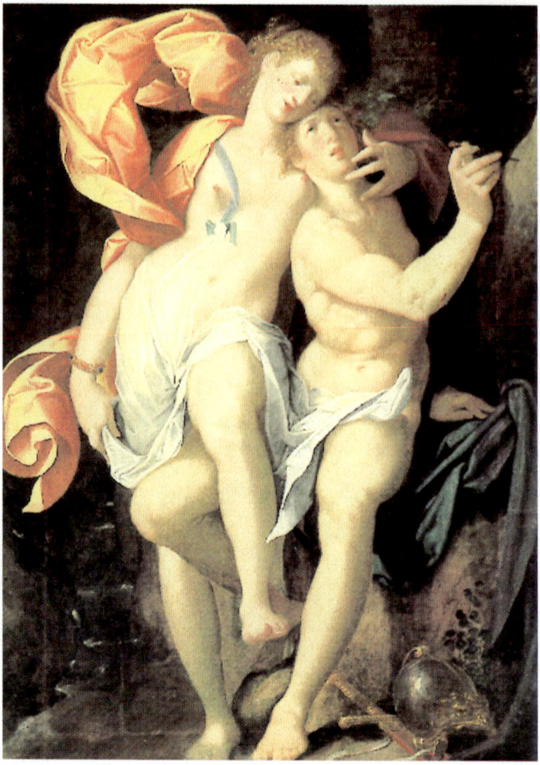

Angelica and Medoro

Bartholomäus Spranger
(Antwerp, 1546–Prague, 1611)

- oil on canvas
- 107.5 x 79.5 cm
- Alte Pinakothek, Munich

Bartholomäus Spranger's exposure to Italian art is evident in this painting, which is one of many the artist executed of this type. His works are conceived with the most impeccable compositions and display a remarkable facture. This canvas shows Angelica, who has been unfaithful to Orlando, with a new lover, Medoro. The figures recall deities with their majestic poses, idealized anatomies and divine appearance. Another notable feature is the drapery that swirls around the figure of the princess. Medoro, depicted with an athletic body, is spellbound by his lover's sensuality. The euphuistic painting, which exhibits several typical features of the Fontainebleau School, is a fine work of Mannerism, which was much in vogue among the nobility of the day. The painting should be understood as an allegory, as an ode to love and liberty—a bold message for the time.

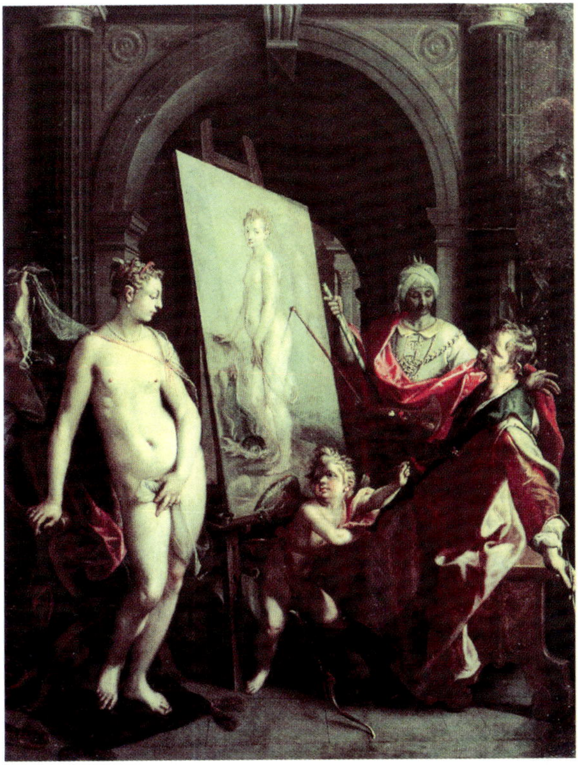

Campaspe, the wife of Alexander the Great, was painted and seduced by Apelles, the emperor's personal painter. The scene conveys the artist's ardent passion for her before the distracted gaze of the king. Jodocus van Winghe places two exquisite nudes of Campaspe in a lavish atmosphere: one as the model, who is slender, realistic and sensual; the other on Apelles' canvas, idealized by his virtuoso hand. In both, the figure embodies the Baroque ideal of beauty in its voluptuous curves and graceful slenderness, whereby the hips are wide and the breasts just beginning to form, suggesting her youthfulness. The pose is a typical one for female, mythological and historical nudes. In an effort to emphasize her body, van Winghe has painted the room in a half-light, creating an ideal background, against which Campaspe's brightly lit body can become the focus of the painting and of the viewer's attention. The contrapposto, the transparent veil and the woman's discreet gesture of covering her intimate parts with her hand are details that increase the nude's suggestiveness and lend it a refined sensuality.

Apelles Painting Campaspe

Jodocus (or **Josse**) **van Winghe**
(Brussels, 1542/44
–Frankfurt, 1603)

- ca. 1600
- oil on canvas
- 210 x 175 cm
- Kunsthistorisches Museum, Vienna

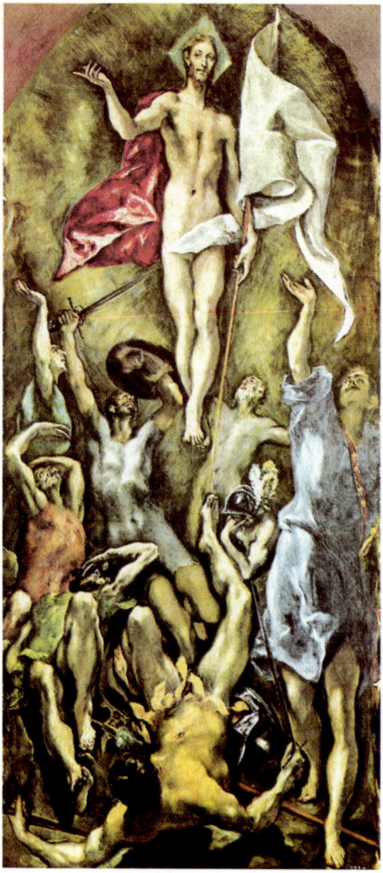

The Resurrection

El Greco (Domenikos Theotokopoulos)
(Crete, 1541–Toledo, 1614)

- ca. 1600
- oil on canvas
- 275 x 127 cm
- Museo del Prado, Madrid

The format of the painting creates a composition of elongated forms, showing the great plasticity and spiritual forcefulness of El Greco's work. The theme is charged with violence and anguish, contrasting with the serene aspect of the resurrected Christ. The figures form a circle around Jesus, who triumphantly rises above the living, holding a great white banner. The mysterious light emanating from the figure models each nude in a different way. The boldly foreshortened figure in the foreground reveals strong contrasts of light and shadow, whereas the bodies in the background appear to emerge from the darkness. In the middle, the weightless figure of Christ is slender and sensual, both in gesture and in movement. Sensuality is, however, not the subject of this work, but, rather, the triumph of beauty, as a platonic concept, over sin and human imperfection.

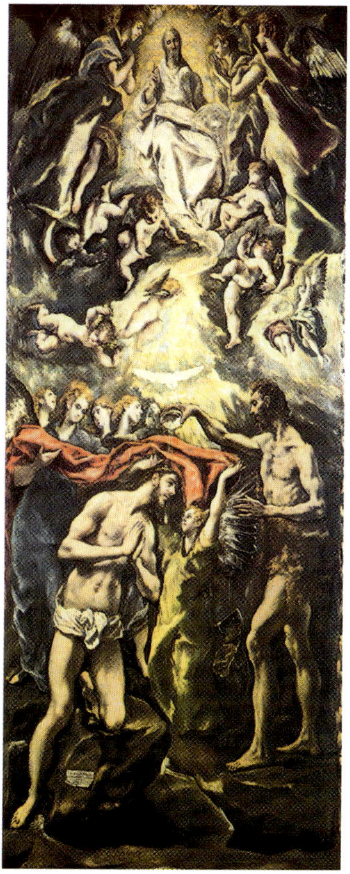

Comparing this painting with earlier works by El Greco reveals a development in the artist's palette as well as in his interpretation of the theme. He increasingly shuns a naturalistic style, allowing himself be guided by his emotions. The bodies are elongated, becoming weightless and ever more idealized. Here the colors appear to be "dirtier" and weaker owing to a diminished chromatic vibrancy. Yet a certain tension is achieved in the composition and in the interpretation of the figures. The nudes are stylized, their limbs attenuated: in this way the artist endeavored to develop a more spiritual idiom, in which formal beauty was of little consequence. The two protagonists are utterly different in character. Christ is depicted as a young man with predominantly soft, but also angular, forms, whereas John the Baptist has a mature and bony build, with much more clearly defined muscles.

The Baptism of Christ

El Greco (Domenikos Theotokopoulos)
(Crete, 1541–Toledo, 1614)

- ca. 1600
- oil on canvas
- 350 x 144 cm
- Museo del Prado, Madrid

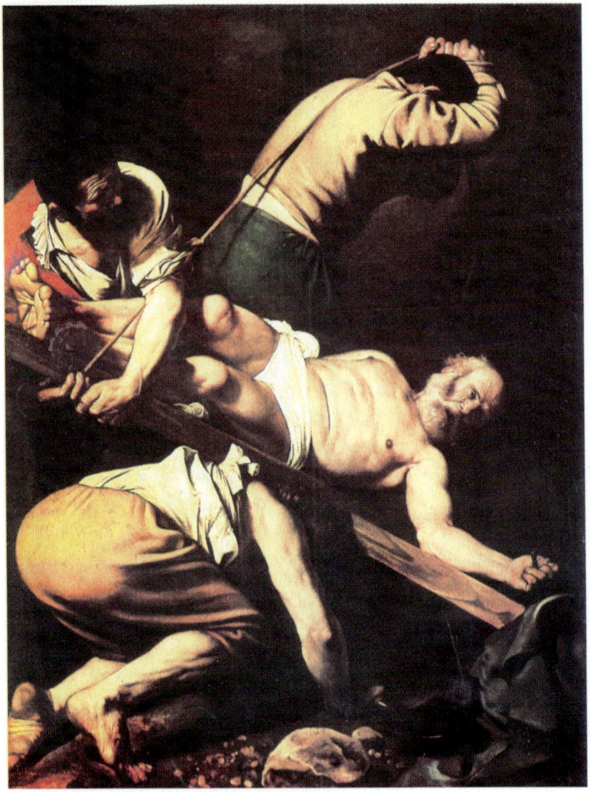

The Crucifixion of St. Peter

Caravaggio (Michelangelo Merisi or **Amerighi da Caravaggio)**
(Caravaggio, Lombardy, 1573 –Port'Ercole, Tuscany, 1610)

- 1600–1601
- oil on canvas
- 230 x 175 cm
- Sta Maria del Popolo, Rome

Unlike the peaceful attitude of his contemporaries, Caravaggio led a very turbulent life, in which he was involved in gambling and fights. He would paint for a time, then spend two or three months drinking and brawling. This canvas is one of Caravaggio's finest. Everything about it is extraordinary, from its composition to the chiaroscuro treatment of the figures. The interplay of light and shade recreate the moment with great drama and draw the beholder's attention to the subject, with the help of the main shaft of light. The image of the nude St. Peter is extremely naturalistic; the movement of the executioners and that of the saint himself appears to have been perfectly frozen in time. The martyr's muscular physique suggests that the artist used a peasant as a model. Caravaggio frequently used the same model for more than one work.

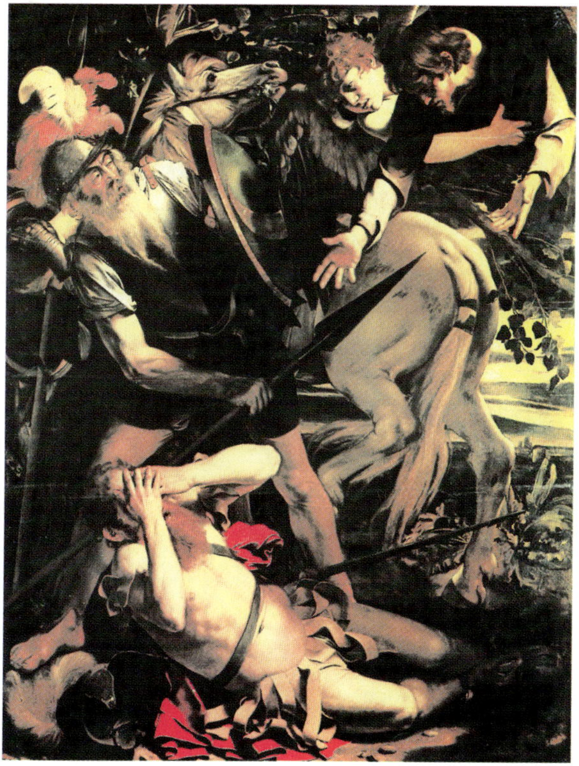

rior to receiving a commission to execute paintings for the ontarelli Chapel in S. Luigi dei Francesi in Rome, Caraaggio had painted for a severely limited number of patrons. enceforth he was to concentrate on dramatic, intensely ealistic depictions of religious subjects in which the action ppears frozen on the canvas. In this work, painted, together ith the Crucifixion of St. Peter, for the Cerasi Chapel in anta Maria del Popolo in Rome, the shaft of light entering e image from the top right creates a strong diagonal, focusg attention on the fallen St. Paul, who covers his face with s hands. The chiaroscuro is of unparalleled drama, the usculature possessing an almost sculptural quality intensied by the complex foreshortening of the arms.

The Conversion of St. Paul

Caravaggio (Michelangelo Merisi or **Amerighi da Caravaggio)**

(Caravaggio, Lombardy, 1573 –Port'Ercole, Tuscany, 1610)

- 1601
- oil on canvas
- 237 x 189 cm
- Odescalchi Balbi Collection, Rome

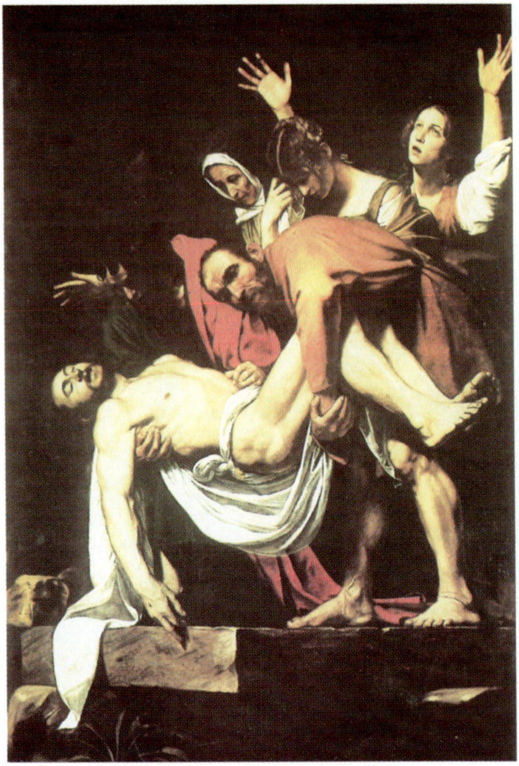

The Entombment

Caravaggio (Michelangelo Merisi or **Amerighi da Caravaggio)**
(Caravaggio, Lombardy, 1573 –Port'Ercole, Tuscany, 1610)

- 1602–4
- oil on canvas
- 300 x 203 cm
- Pinacoteca, Vatican

Caravaggio's method of painting his figures from life gives his scenes a theatrical quality, which he enhances by employing chiaroscuro. The artist frequently depicted his saints with rustic faces and the hands of peasants. The athletic body of Christ shown in this work is both beautiful and sensual. The light cast on the left-hand side of the painting accentuates the figure's luminous flesh tones, while shadows form an almost perfect profile around his body. Caravaggio employs a tenebrist chiaroscuro (the utilization of light and dark to create a sense of form and space) in order to underscore the work's religious theme and to invite the viewer to contemplate the scene. The work is executed with a sober palette and is devoid of unnecessary details.

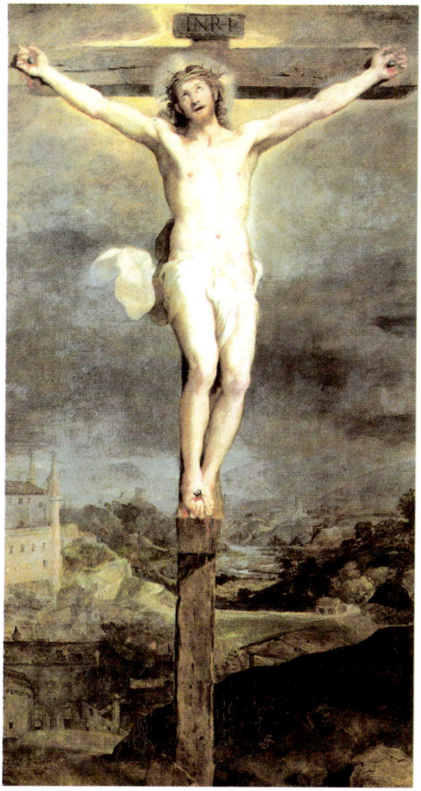

Christ on the Cross

Federico Barocci (Federico Fiori)
(Urbino, 1528–1612)

- 1604
- oil on canvas
- 374 x 246 cm
- Museo del Prado, Madrid

ederico Barocci—a harbinger of the Baroque—cultivated a yle of Mannerism recalling that of Correggio and Taddeo ıccari. The Counter-Reformation is reflected in the pathos this nude, whose dramatic expression borders on ecstasy. ıe painterly handling of the body, which is rendered in soft rms, is reminiscent of that of Rubens and Murillo. The symetry of the body lends the theme a note of serenity, diminning the dramatic force of the image. This is continued in e treatment of forms and the luminosity of the volumes, obably deriving from Correggio. At the same time, the artist ıs taken this opportunity to depict the beautiful setting of bino. The fascinating landscape in the background, bathed a mysterious half-light, accentuates the light radiating from e figure of Christ.

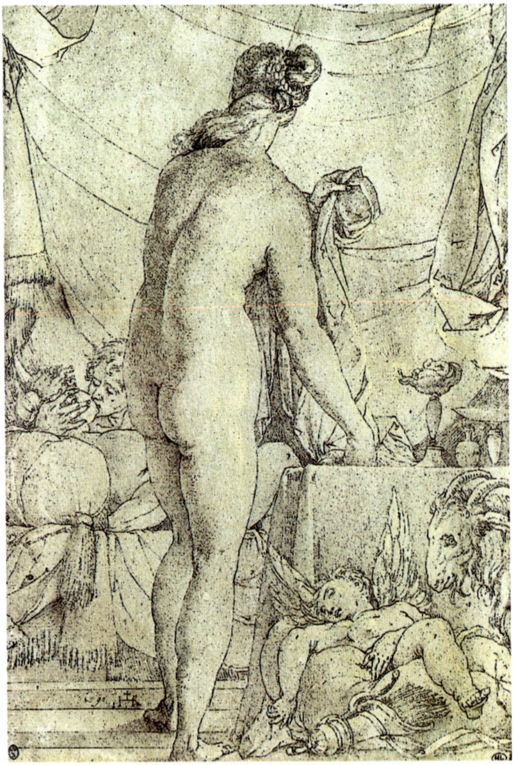

Venus and Sleeping Cupid

Jacopo Ligorzi
(Verona, 1547–Florence, 1627)

- pen, ink and watercolor, heightened with gold
- 30 x 19.7 cm
- Musée du Louvre, Cabinet des Dessins, Paris

This drawing of the interior of a room in Venus' sanctuary shows the goddess, back to the spectator, contemplating a couple making love. In the foreground, Cupid is sleeping soundly with his arrows at his side, while Malice, depicted as a male goat, is entering at the right. The artist has placed each element in his picture precisely, and defined its role and function clearly, so as to convey an atmosphere of lasciviousness and passion. The figure of Venus is presented in an academic pose: a somewhat full-bodied woman yet finely built, of considerable height and beautifully modeled. The treatment of tones is consistently delicate. Black has been avoided, which enhances the overall sensuality of the sketch.

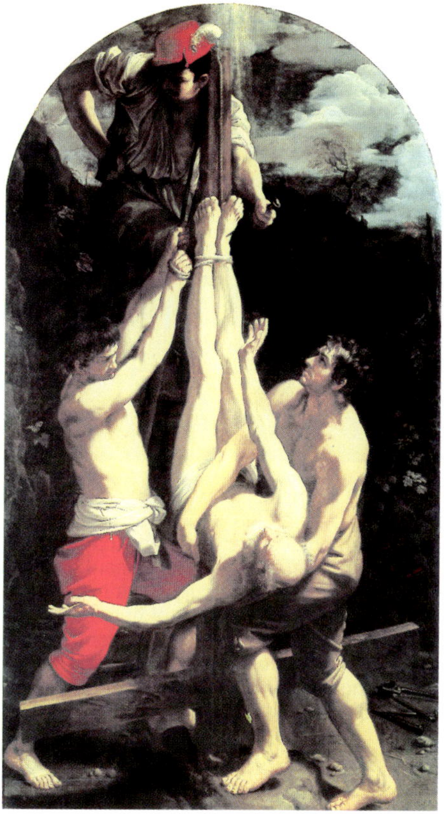

The Crucifixion of St. Peter

Guido Reni
(Bologna, 1575–1642)

- 1604–5
- oil on canvas
- 305 x 175 cm
- Vatican Museum, Rome

this scene, a distinct undercurrent of violence is felt, but ɔt shown. Guido Reni seems to have been intent on com- ning the beauty of Classical sculpture with the painterly andling of Correggio and Carracci, of whom he was a pupil. e apparently took great pains to create a suitably dramatic, mospheric background for the scene. Although somewhat ude in expression, the two men hoisting Peter's body are ɔble and monumental in stature. The principal figure, St. eter, does not draw the viewer's attention away from the hers, as in Correggio's depictions of the martyr—here, he merely another element of the composition. The figure of eter is impeccably rendered and resolved with great verisi- ilitude, despite being the subject of technically difficult fore- ıortening. Executed for the church of St. Paul of the Three ɔuntains in Rome, this painting presages the artist's tenden- toward a naturalism that eschewed ugliness and vulgarity.

Mercury and Argus

Peter Paul Rubens
(Siegen, Westphalia, 1577–Antwerp, 1640)

- oil on canvas
- 63 x 87.5 cm
- Staatliche Kunstsammlungen, Dresden

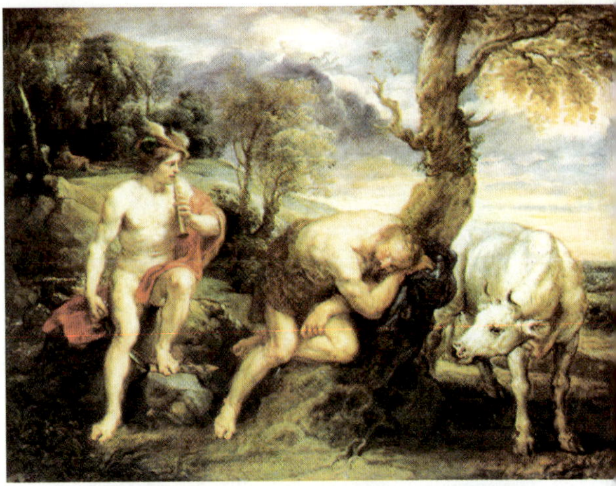

Rubens executed his paintings with restless, vigorous brushwork, engendering blurred contours that cause his figures to blend harmoniously into the landscape. Mercury, the messenger of the gods, plays his instrument to send Argus to sleep. When this occurs Mercury slays him with his sword. The painter, whose mastery of human anatomy is apparent in this scene, presents two different types of body: Mercury's is sensual, covered merely by a red cloak that highlights his smooth, pallid skin, whereas Argus' volumes are somewhat cruder and his skin darker in color.

Trinity with Christ Crucified, SS. Peter and Bernard

Ventura Salimbeni
(Siena, 1568–1613)

- ca. 1600
- oil on canvas
- 164 x 118 cm
- Musée Fesch, Ajaccio

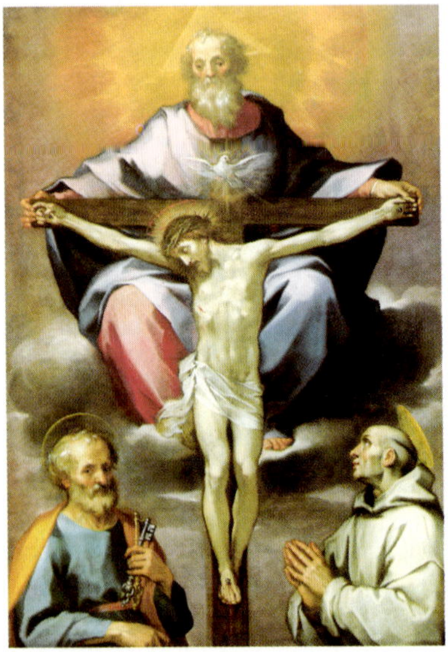

This work creates depth of field witho any referential elements, such as surrounding objects that might help set up a perspectival frame. In comparison to his son, God the Father is gigantic. The figure of Christ, true to the traditions of Spanis Baroque, is portrayed as being extremely beautiful and evinces no dramatic interest at all. The light comin from above helps t define the corporea elements.

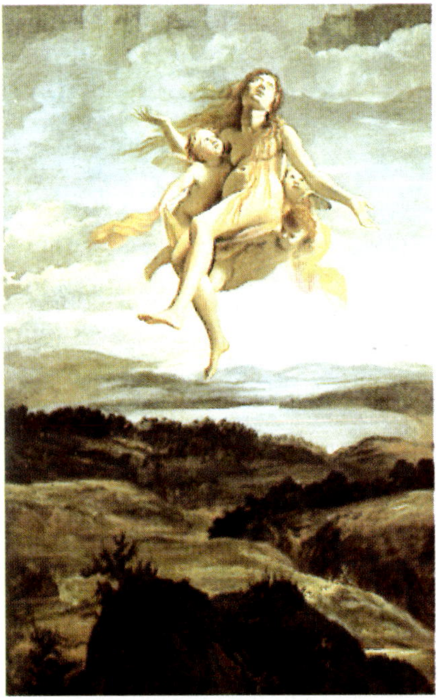

St. Magdalene Carried by an Angel

Giovanni Lanfranco
(Terenzo, near Parma, 1582–Rome, 1647)

- 1605
- oil on canvas
- 110 x 72 cm
- Galleria Nazionale di Capodimonte, Naples

Giovanni Lanfranco was a pupil of Annibale Carracci, whose precision he took up in his own work. In this highly expressive painting, the artist plays with the contrast between light and shadow to create a realistic landscape and an excellent study of central perspective. Floating above the countryside are two nude figures, which are boldly foreshortened, have smooth skin and sensual shapes and dominate the scene as if they were transcendental beings.

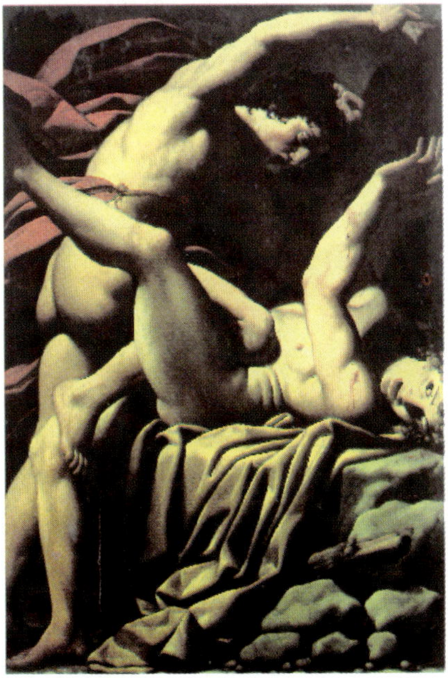

The Death of Abel

Lionello Spada
(Bologna, 1576–Parma, 1622)

- oil on canvas
- 54 x 46 cm
- Museo e Gallerie Nazionali, Campodimonte

The influence Caravaggio exerted on many painters of the 15th century and after is not hard to understand given his tenebrist realism. The drama of this scene is accentuated by a use of light that almost violently expresses the muscular tension of the two young bodies. A certain over-dramatization typical of tenebrism is apparent, an effect of action frozen by light used in order to startle the viewer.

The Fall of Icarus

Carlo Saraceni
(Venice, ca. 1585–Rome, 1620)

- oil on canvas
- 41 x 53 cm
- Museo e Gallerie Nazionali, Campodimonte

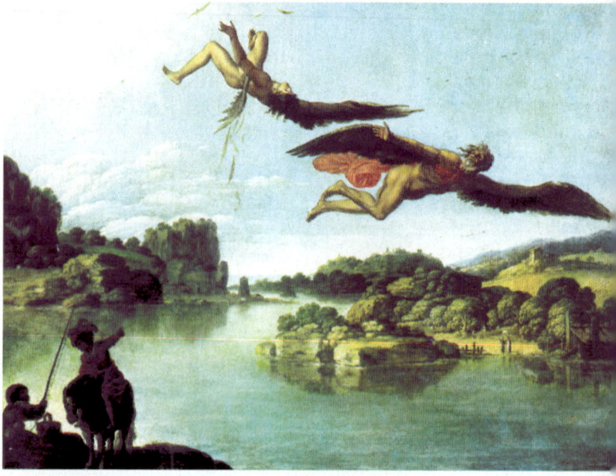

Daedalus and his son, Icarus, imprisoned in Minos' labyrinth on the island of Crete, made their escape using wings constructed of feathers and wax. Icarus flew too close to the sun despite his father's warnings, so that the wax melted and he fell to his death in the ocean.The nude figures are of an extremely beautiful execution, heroically distinguished by the light accentuating their forms.

Salmacis and Hermaphroditus

Carlo Saraceni
(Venice, ca. 1585–Rome, 1620)

- oil on canvas
- 41 x 53 cm
- Museo e Gallerie Nazionali, Campodimonte

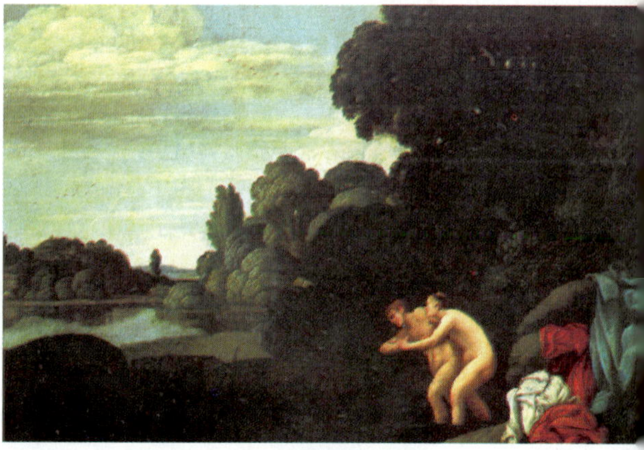

Hermaphroditus was the son of Hermes and Aphrodite. Whe[n] the nymph Salmacis fell in love with him, and he refused her, she begged the gods to be allowed to embrace him, and so powerfully that nothing could ever separate them. Her wish was granted, and as she embraced him their bodies fused physically. Hence the word "hermaphrodite" for a person com bining both sexes in one body.

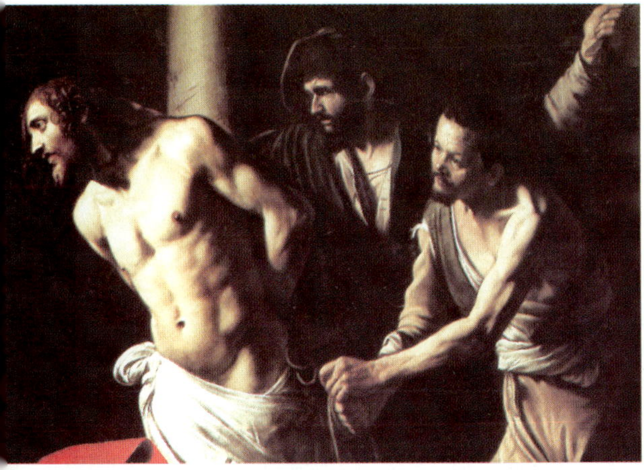

Flagellation of Christ

Caravaggio (Michelangelo Merisi or **Amerighi da Caravaggio)**
(Caravaggio, Lombardy, 1573 –Port'Ercole, Tuscany, 1610)

- 1606–07
- oil on canvas
- 134.5 x 174.5 cm
- Musée des Beaux-Arts, Rouen

Caravaggio has adapted his figures here to the format of the canvas, meticulously defining the details by means of chiaroscuro. The figure of Jesus is superbly modeled, Apollonian and possesses enormous physicality. The loin-cloth, which the painter has allowed to fall away slightly, reveals a corner of Jesus' intimate parts, albeit through its being in shadow, with infinite discretion.

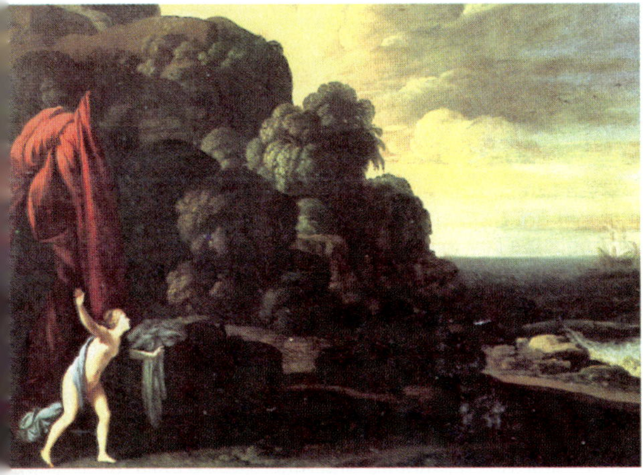

Ariadne Abandoned

Carlo Saraceni
(Venice, ca. 1585–Rome, 1620)

- oil on canvas
- 41 x 53 cm
- Museo e Gallerie Nazionali, Campodimonte

Theseus abducted Ariadne and then abandoned her on the island of Naxos, whence Bacchus rescued and then wedded her. As early as Bosch or Brueghel, we find works that integrate figures and landscape admirably. The splendidly luminous and ample woman's figure here is close to Giorgione in its hieratical pose, while its well-defined outlines serve to create the impression of movement.

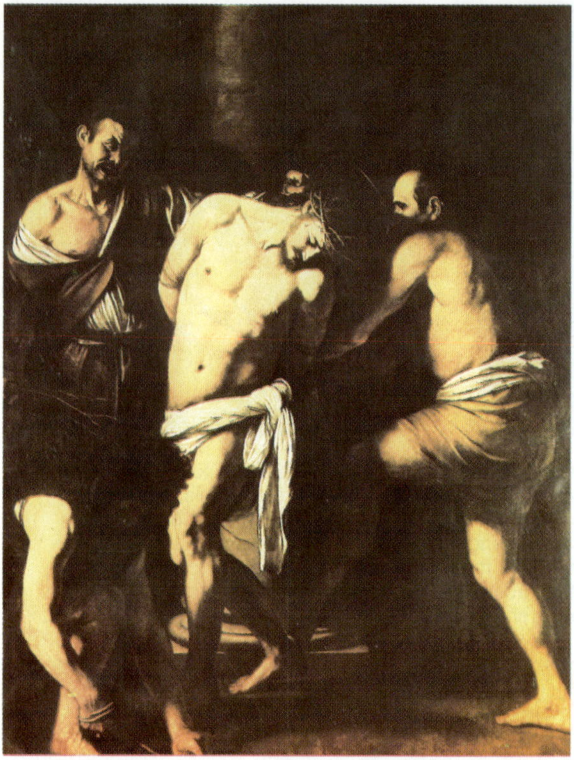

The Flagellation

Caravaggio
(**Michelangelo Merisi** or **Amerighi da Caravaggio**)
(Caravaggio, Lombardy, 1573 –Port'Ercole, Tuscany, 1610)

- ca. 1607
- oil on canvas
- 286 x 213 cm
- Museo di Capodimonte, Naples

No one was able to furnish a work with the drama of the moment like Caravaggio. The expertise of capturing the instant is the key to tenebrism. The solution may appear overly dramatic and the palette somewhat limited, but it is precisely what the painter wished to achieve. This Flagellation shows Christ immediately before he is to be scourged. The accentuated anatomical volumes reveal the artist's treatment of the nude to be more sculptural than painterly. The source of light is never shown in Caravaggio's works, increasing the dramatic impact of the protagonist. Instead, the light would seem to emanate from a supernatural presence. In this work, the painter employs a dramatic and monumental style, while combining Classical and Mannerist elements. Marked by a bold use of light and shade, Caravaggio's paintings extol the most primitive aspects of the human condition.

Toilet of Venus

Johann Liss (or **Lys**)
(Oldenburg, ca. 1597–Venice, 1631)

- oil on canvas
- 88 x 69 cm
- Galleria degli Uffizi, Florence

This painting illustrates a characteristic feature of Baroque art: the combination of various conceptual elements in a single work, in this instance an oneiric vision, heightened sensuality, naturalistic and comely figures and a high degree of plasticity and theatricality. The erotic force of these figures is increased by the light, which illuminates a vivid red, the diaphanous nature of the clouds, the movement of the drapery and the cherubs in the top left-hand corner of the painting.

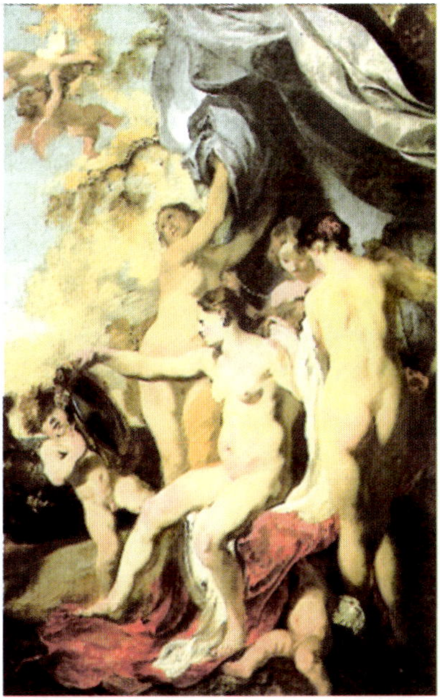

The Judgement of Paris

Peter Paul Rubens
(Siegen, Westphalia, 1577–Antwerp, 1640)

- ca. 1607–9
- oil on panel
- 91 x 114 cm
- Museo del Prado, Madrid

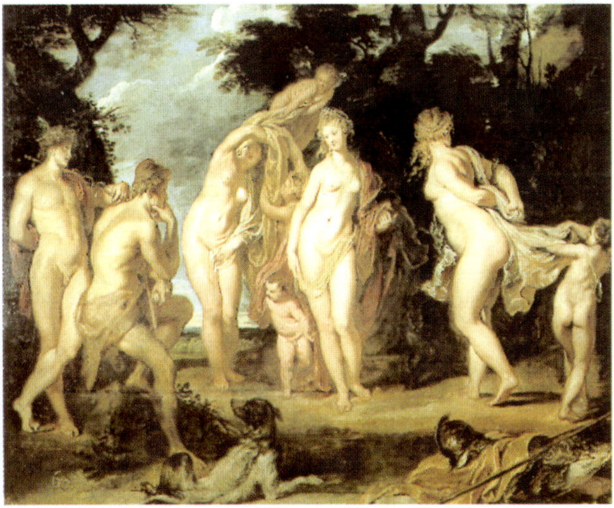

The serious treatment of colour in this painting, and the elongated, sculptural figures in rather affected poses, are certain of the means by which this work, rather than honoring its title, consitutes a homage to Venus, whose brightly–lit figure forms the resplendent center of the composition.

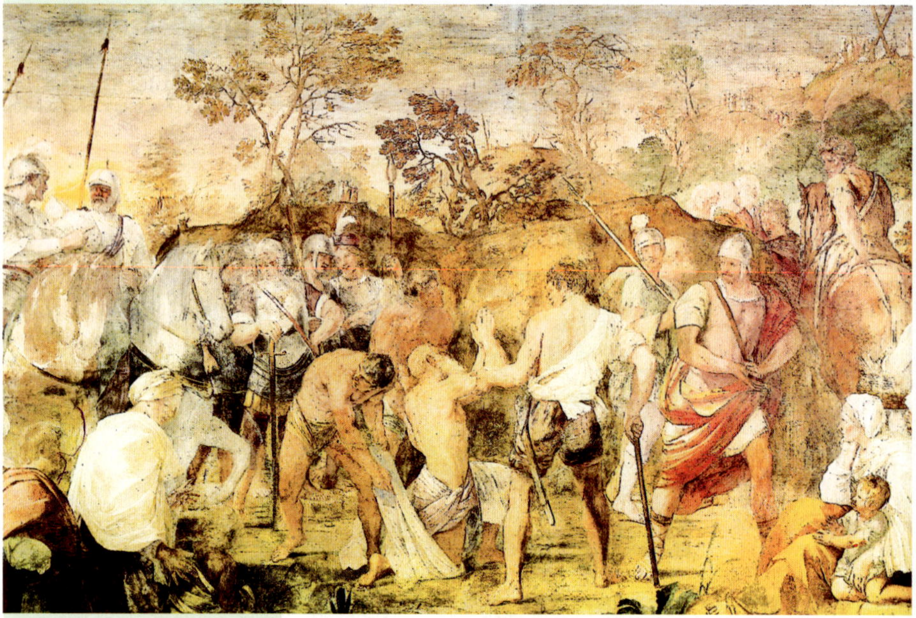

St. Andrew before His Martyrdom

Guido Reni
(Bologna, 1575–1642)

- 1608
- fresco
- 410 x 640 cm
- San Gregorio al Celio, St. Andrew's Oratory, Rome

Guido Reni was, above all, a brilliant draftsman, as demonstrated in this monumental fresco. In his anatomical studies he was concerned with achieving technically complex foreshortening. This work was executed during one of the artist's most productive periods, combining certain Raphaelesque elements with a modern atmospheric landscape. A close examination of the individual figures reveals skillfully modeled bodies, whose muscles are well positioned and whose rhythmic tension fills the scene. The palette lacks the intensity of other oil paintings by the artist.

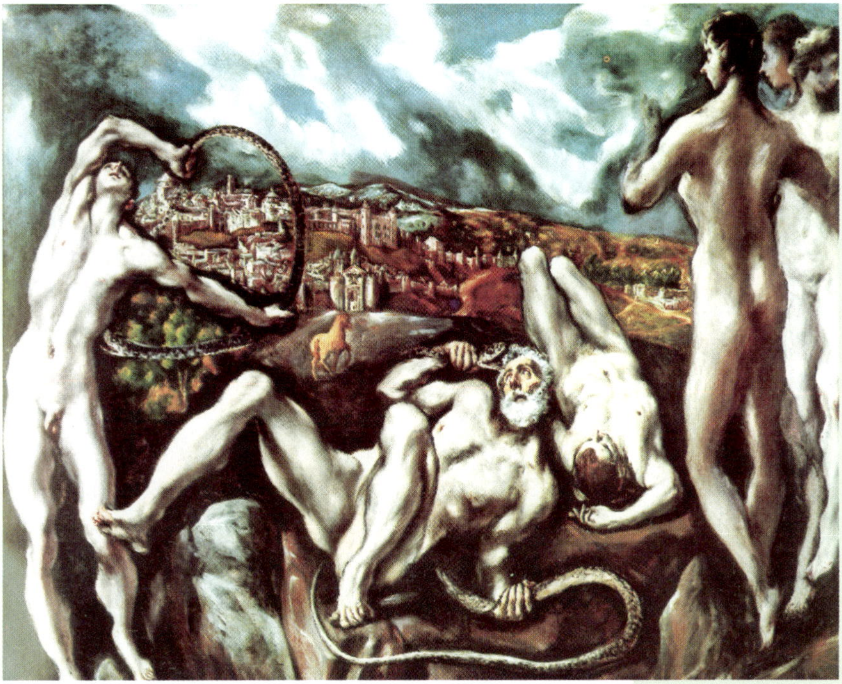

Laocoön was a priest of Apollo, who, during the Trojan War, warned the Trojans against bringing into the city the Wooden Horse that the Greeks had left on the beach. Just as he is about to take a pickax to it, two enormous sea serpents emerge from the waters and strangle Laocoön and his two sons as punishment for having married Antiope, who bore him the sons. All the nudes are situated in the foreground and are illuminated by an uncanny light that lends them an almost phantasmagoric appearance, with pale skin modeled in numerous gray tones. The limbs are highly stylized, acquiring tubular forms. Despite the fact that this is an unfinished work, the painter has rendered it with his typical expressiveness. The subjects are depicted with contorted and attenuated bodies. This, coupled with the artist's singular style, heightens the drama of the scene. Interestingly, the city in the background representing Troy is in fact Toledo, where the painter resided.

Laocoön

El Greco (Domenikos Theotokopoulos)
(Crete, 1541–Toledo, 1614)

- 1610–14
- oil on canvas
- 137.5 x 172.5 cm
- National Gallery of Art, Washington, D.C.

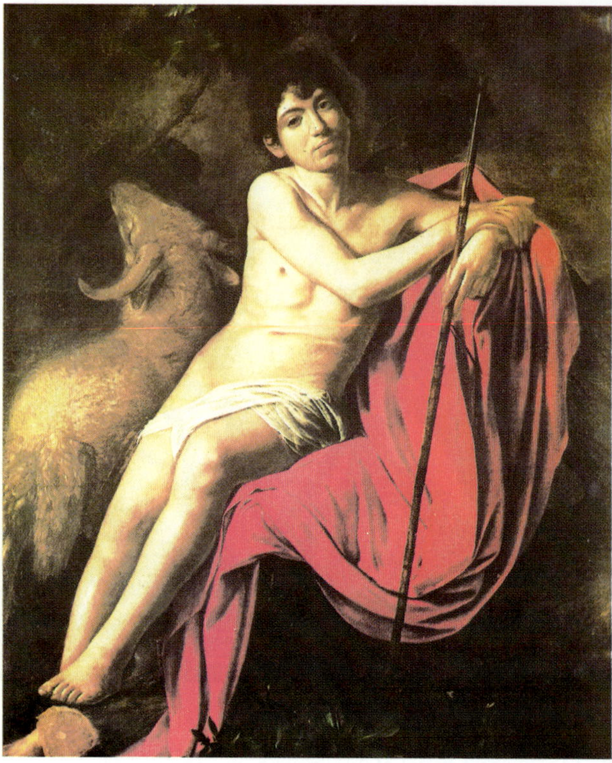

St. John the Baptist

Caravaggio (Michelangelo Merisi or **Amerighi da Caravaggio)**
(Caravaggio, Lombardy, 1573 –Port'Ercole, Tuscany, 1610)

- 1609–10
- oil on canvas
- 159 x 124 cm
- Galleria Borghese, Rome

Like the painter himself, Caravaggio's figures are often shrouded in an aura of sexual ambiguity. Both in the models he used and in the iconography of his religious imagery, the artist departed from traditional norms. Though severely rebuked for this, his great technical skill guaranteed him the support of several powerful families. This painting shows St. John the Baptist on the verge of manhood, a highly sensual, enticing figure depicted in a stylized, almost feminine manner. His face is not especially handsome, the wrinkles perhaps those of an adult not wishing to betray his age. Pose and face evince a deep sadness, while the hands appear to be bound—perhaps the artist here had a premonition of the illness that would eventually kill him. Ending his life an outlaw, Caravaggio had remained faithful to his artistic principles, painting saints with almost a low-life air about them in everyday settings and, precisely through this sober, realistic treatment, granting them nobility and a profoundly spiritual dimension.

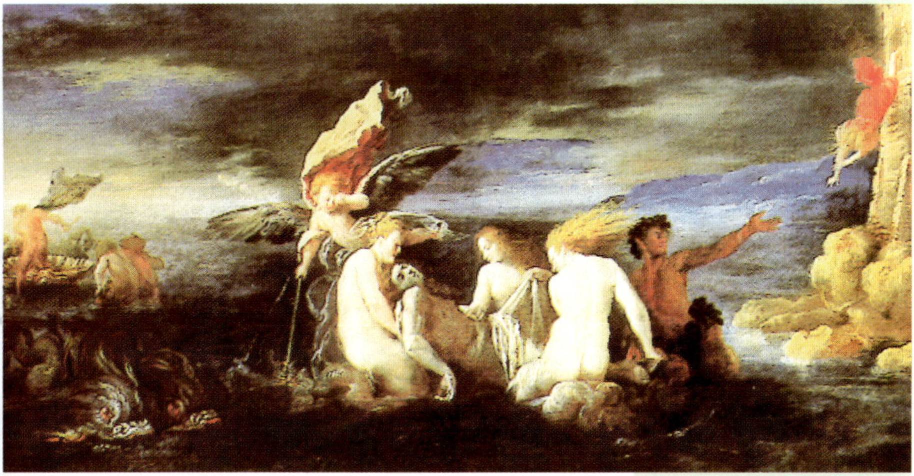

Hero, a priestess of Aphrodite, was in love with Leander, a young man from Abidos, who swam across the Hellespont every night to see her, guided by the torch that Hero lit in her castle. One night, when the wind blew out the torch, Leander lost his way and drowned. When she learned of the incident, Hero threw herself from the tower in despair. The painting represents the priestess' assistants recovering Leander's body while, on the right, Hero throws herself to her death. The bold composition coupled with the surging, dark sea and vibrant colors of the brightly lit figures lend dynamism to the scene, whereas the dark clouds and intense colors of the stormy sky make it extremely atmospheric. The sensual, voluptuous nudes contrast with the tragic subject of the painting. This exquisite work prefigures a composition that was to be taken up with alacrity in Venetian painting, as well as in Italian Baroque art generally.

Hero and Leander

Domenico Fetti
(or **Feti**)
(Rome, ca. 1589–Venice, 1623)

- panel
- 41 x 97 cm
- Kunsthistorisches Museum, Vienna

Samson and Delilah

Peter Paul Rubens
(Siegen, Westphalia, 1577 –Antwerp, 1640)

- ca. 1609
- oil on panel
- 185 x 205 cm
- The National Gallery, London

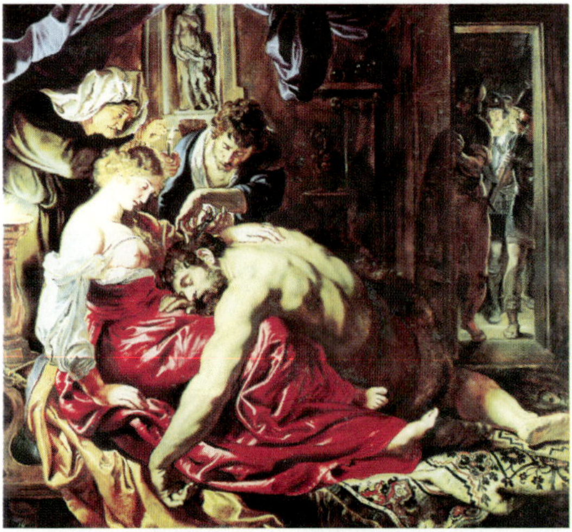

Rubens has depicted Samson asleep on his wife Delilah's lap, while an accomplice is cutting his hair in order to rob him of his strength. His nude figure is prodigiously robust. The light falling obliquely across it throws every detail into relief and creates a powerfully expressive atmosphere.

Landscape with Psyche and Jupiter

Paul Brill
(Antwerp, 1554–Rome, 1626)

- 1610
- oil on canvas
- 93 x 128 cm
- Museo del Prado, Madrid

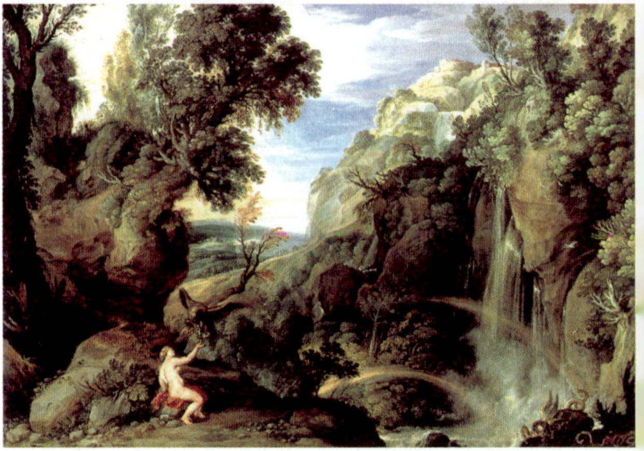

Cupid's consort, Psyche, is aided by Jupiter, in the form of an eagle, to fill a cup with water from the River Styx, which runs through the Underworld. Brill has placed Psyche's ample, nude form in the immense theatricality of the landscape, as a counterbalance and human reference point amongst so much non-human grandeur.

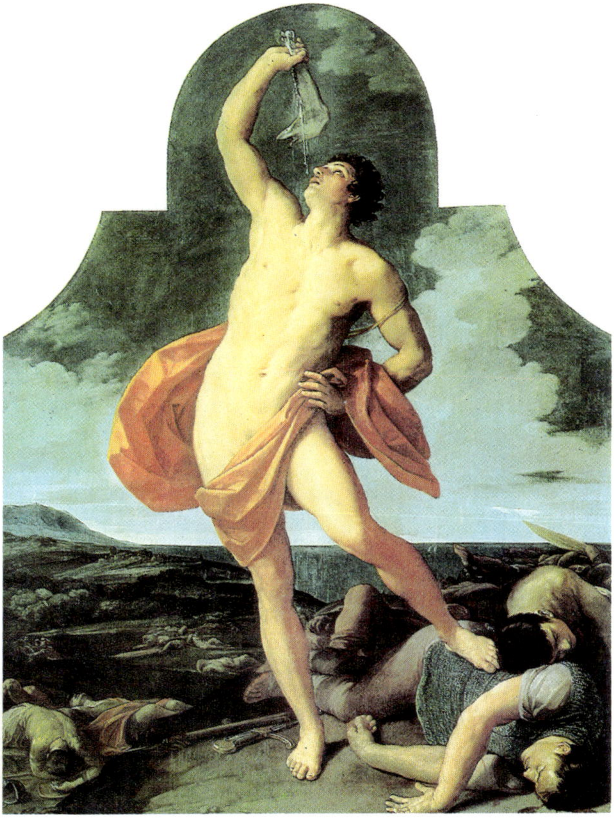

Far removed from the biblical version of Samson, this highly erotic, graceful figure strikes a pose encountered frequently in sculpture from Classical Antiquity. Against the muted background the body appears to radiate a golden light. Inspired by the frescos of Raphael in the Vatican, in its color scheme and the rhythm of the figure, this work is a fine example of European classicism in the 17th century. In keeping with his preoccupation with beauty and harmony, the artist renders Samson in a contrapposto pose. Despite the elegant torsion of his body and the smoothness of his skin, he is not effeminate in appearance. This is probably owing to the three-dimensional quality of the forms.

Samson Victorious

Guido Reni

(Bologna, 1575–1642)

- 1611–12
- oil on canvas
- 260 x 233 cm
- Pinacoteca Nazionale, Bologna

Ceres and Pomona

Peter Paul Rubens
(Siegen, Westphalia, 1577 –Antwerp, 1640)

- 1611/28
- oil on canvas
- 223 x 162 cm
- Museo del Prado, Madrid

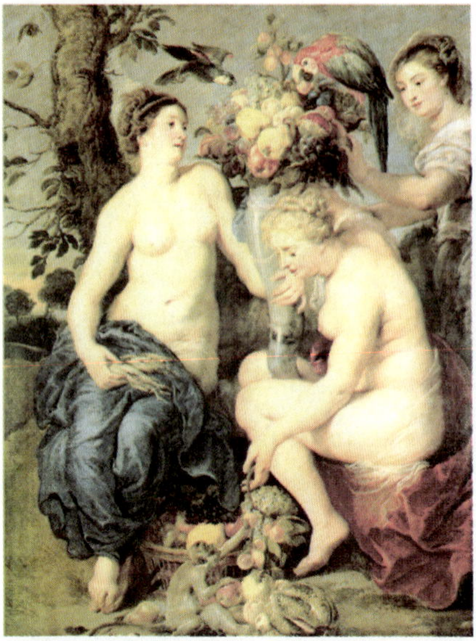

The two chief figures in this painting may be Ceres and Pomona, although they could also be two nymphs charged with filling a cornucopia. The painting came from Rubens' workshop, which had a high turnover, with Rubens painting the bodies and Snyders the birds and fruit. The nude bodies are very naturally handled, and display Rubens' skill in draftsmanship and in the coloring of skin.

Male Nude Knoeling

Peter Paul Rubens
(Siegen, Westphalia, 1577–Antwerp, 1640)

- drawing
- Boymans van Beuningen Museum, Rotterdam

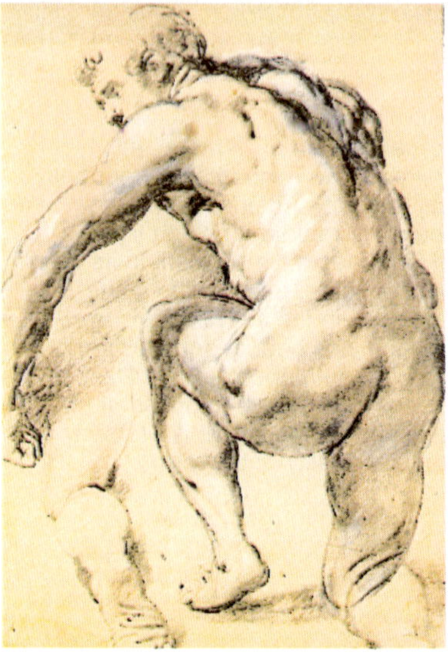

Few artists have been able to render the human figure as Rubens did. Given his paintings, it is perhaps not entirely surprising that he left behind hundreds of anatomical studies with the power and magnificence of this one. The anthropocentric, value-oriented Renaissance is much in evidence. The sketch evinces Rubens' search for ideal beauty, with the stamp of Baroque magnificence.

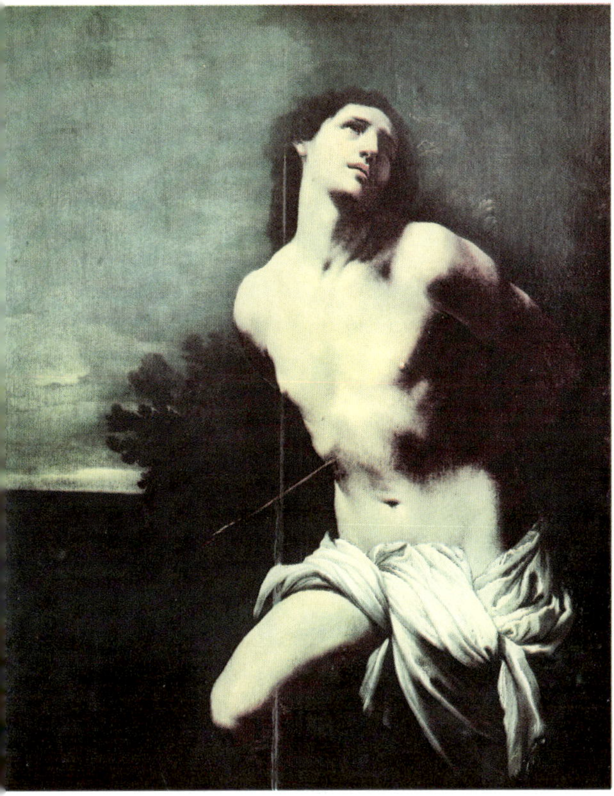

St. Sebastian is frequently portrayed as the very embodiment of sensuality, of which this work is an excellent example. The treatment of the figure seems to eclipse the subject itself, causing the viewer not to empathize with the martyr, but, rather, to become caught up in the mysticism of the moment. The eroticism of the figure is striking indeed. The drama of the scene is heightened by the tension that is established between its horror and beauty, which lends the whole a sultry air. Guido Reni employs chiaroscuro in which shadow predominates, bringing to the fore the figure of the saint. The subtle modeling of the effeminate body refrains from defining the muscles. For the artist an ideal of beauty is conveyed through ideas, which is how one forms a union with God.

St. Sebastian

Guido Reni
(Bologna, 1575–1642)

- oil on canvas
- 170 x 133 cm
- Museo del Prado, Madrid

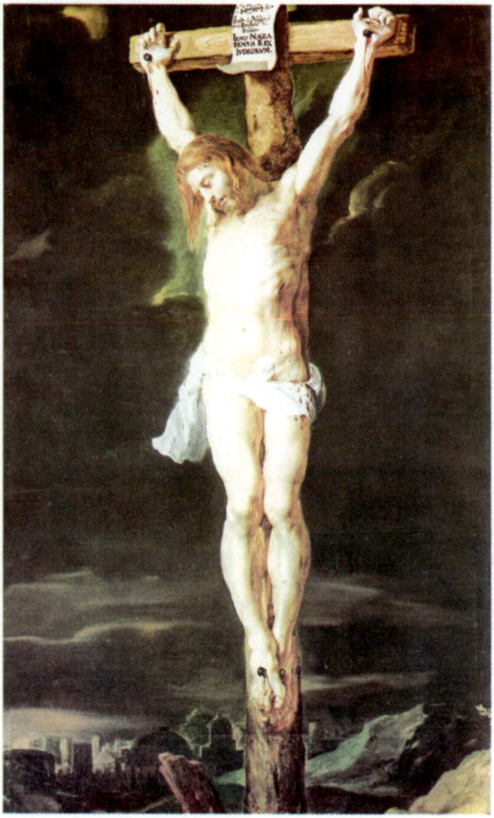

Christ on the Cross

Peter Paul Rubens
(Siegen, Westphalia, 1577–Antwerp, 1640)

- 1612–15
- oil on panel
- 145.3 x 91.8 cm
- Alte Pinakothek, Munich

Although this nude occupies the center of the painting, the work departs from a symmetrical composition in that the figure's face is not seen frontally, but at an angle, such that the upper torso and head are slightly foreshortened, lending the scene more dynamism. The intensely luminous figure is highlighted with pearly skin tones that positively shine against the dense, dark colors of the background. In other parts of the body, such as the legs, the tones are more smoothly integrated into the background. This superbly executed nude is a well-built, exceedingly handsome man. The artist's sagacious treatment of the shadows enhances further still the brightest areas, although there is no attempt to evoke the drama of tenebrism. In addition to achieving a highly harmonious work by means of a subtle palette, with this work Rubens presents a plastically daring painting.

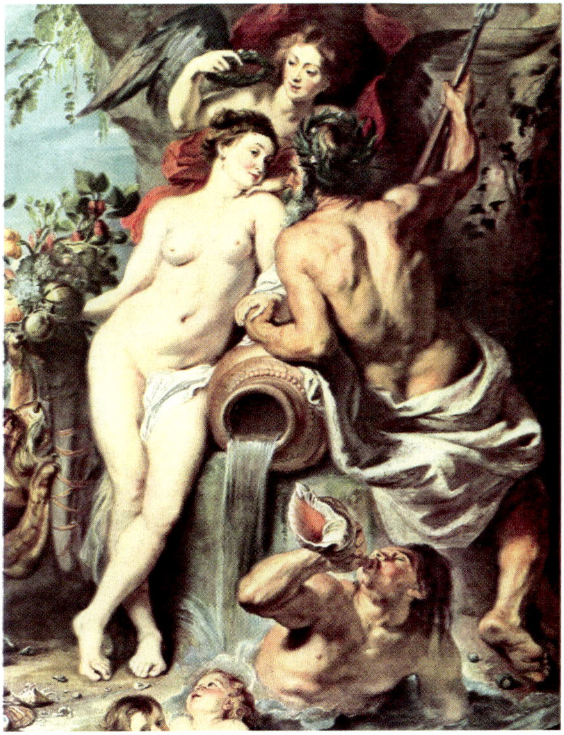

This painting, with Cybele and what must be Poseidon, judging from his trident, depicts an allegory of the union of Antwerp and the Schelde River, a waterway that was important at the time for industry and commerce, and which is represented by the bodies emerging from the water. The composition recalls a pyramid, within which all the figures are arranged. It is based on classical Renaissance models, and the painter may have been inspired by a fresco by Francesco Primaticcio at Fontainebleau. The charming figure of Cybele, voluptuous and elegant, with soft, well-modeled curves and milky skin, is shown allowing herself to be courted by Poseidon. The latter is represented with the muscular body of a warrior and dark, leathery skin. Two aspects of this work are particularly notable: the treatment of color, whose clarity and brilliance lend the image great forcefulness and vitality, and the modeling of the figures, which is executed with the utmost care.

The Union of Earth and Water

Peter Paul Rubens
(Siegen, Westphalia, 1577–Antwerp, 1640)

- ca. 1615
- oil on canvas
- 224 x 184 cm
- Hermitage, St. Petersburg

This painting was at one time part of the Chigi Collection in Rome, and was acquired by the Hermitage between 1789 and 1800.

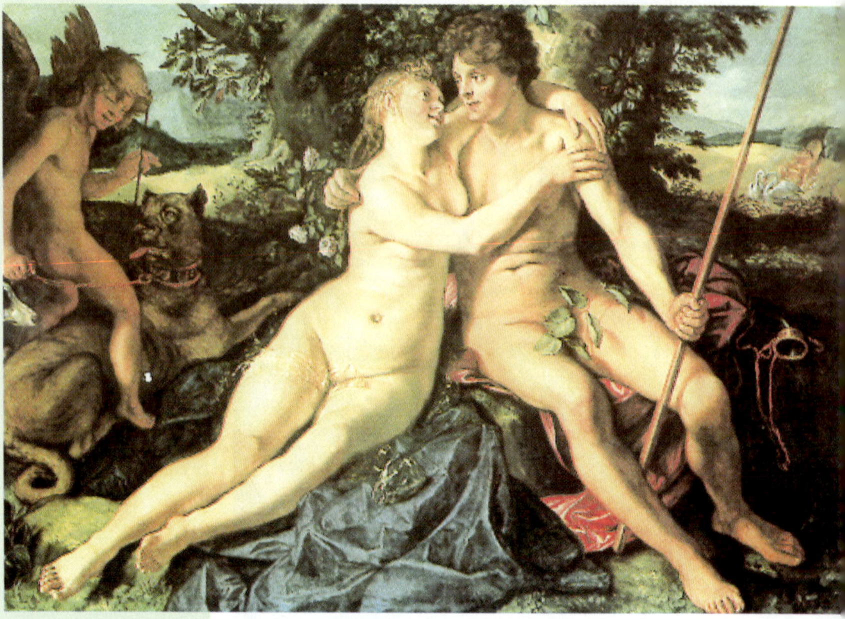

Venus and Adonis

Hendrick Goltzius
(Mulebrecht, 1558
–Haarlem, 1617)

- 1614
- oil on canvas
- 114 x 191 cm
- Alte Pinakothek, Munich

Here Hendrick Goltzius presents two nudes. The figure of Adonis corresponds to an Apollonian youth of delicate lines, smooth skin and effeminate facial features. A small branch discreetly covers his loins. The body of Venus is much more complex in conception, for it is foreshortened, inclined and slightly twisted in order to embrace her lover. Her lower abdomen is round and voluptuous, in keeping with the tastes of the period, while she discreetly covers her breasts with her arm. The scene is romantic and sensual. Certain aspects of the painting evoke the work of Peter Paul Rubens, such as the vivid colors, the texture of the bodies, the luxuriant setting and the smilingly, triumphant Cupid, who is cast in shadow and shown straddling a dog on the far left of the painting.

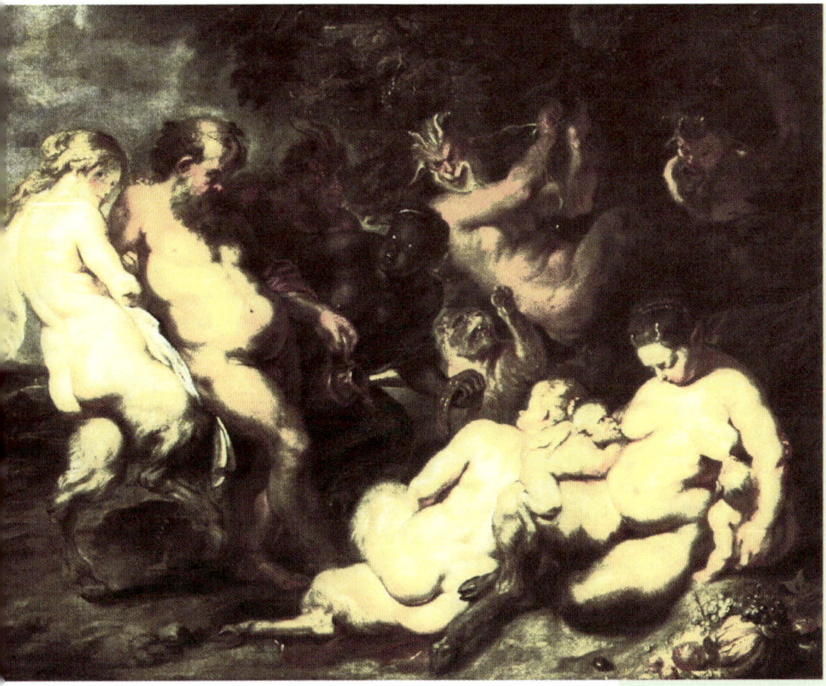

this work, Rubens presents a group of naked, inebriated atyrs given over to the pleasures of wine, while Bacchus, so overcome with drunkenness, is being supported by a oluptuous female nude, whose cunning and mischievous aze is directed at the spectator. In the bottom right-hand orner, two women complete the orgiastic scene, one of em offering her breasts to some cherubs. This group is arked by Rubens' customary iconography, brimming with e and brilliantly illuminated. Sensual features have been ade grotesque, and the nude figures are neither impres-ve nor heroic, as Rubens' figures normally are, owing to eir naturalistic proportions. The artist's aim in this work is represent figures overcome by, rather than triumphing ver, delirium and lechery. Here, Rubens shows himself to ave an extremely fertile imagination and to be a master realizing mythological figures.

Bacchanal

Peter Paul Rubens
(Siegen, Westphalia, 1577–Antwerp, 1640)

- 1615
- oil on canvas
- Pushkin Museum, Moscow

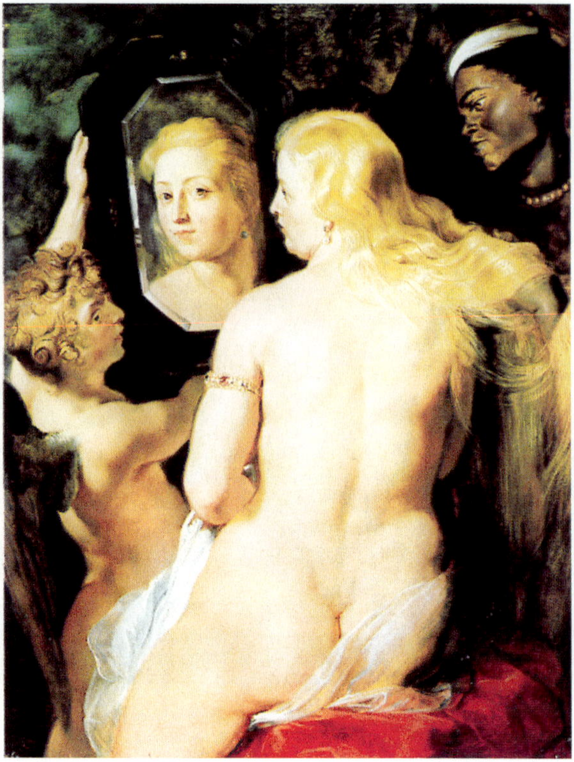

Venus and the Mirror

Peter Paul Rubens
(Siegen, Westphalia, 1577–Antwerp, 1640)

- 1615
- oil on panel
- 124 x 98 cm
- Collection of the Prince of Liechtenstein, Vaduz

This is one of the most commonly depicted themes in the history of art. Here, it contains no mythological references other than the name of the goddess, a mere pretext to paint a nude woman, who is given the title and name of the goddess of beauty so as not to offend the viewer's sense of propriety. The voluptuousness of the woman's body eclipses all other aspects of the scene, which is imbued with her grace and beauty. The modeling of Venus' idealized volumes is achieved by means of a palette rich in golden flesh tones. Not only is her body delightful; her pose—her upright body, her back to the viewer, the reflection of her provocative, mischievous face in the mirror—is also a striking aspect of the painting. The figure of Cupid holding up the mirror and the face of the black servant contribute to its sensual atmosphere.

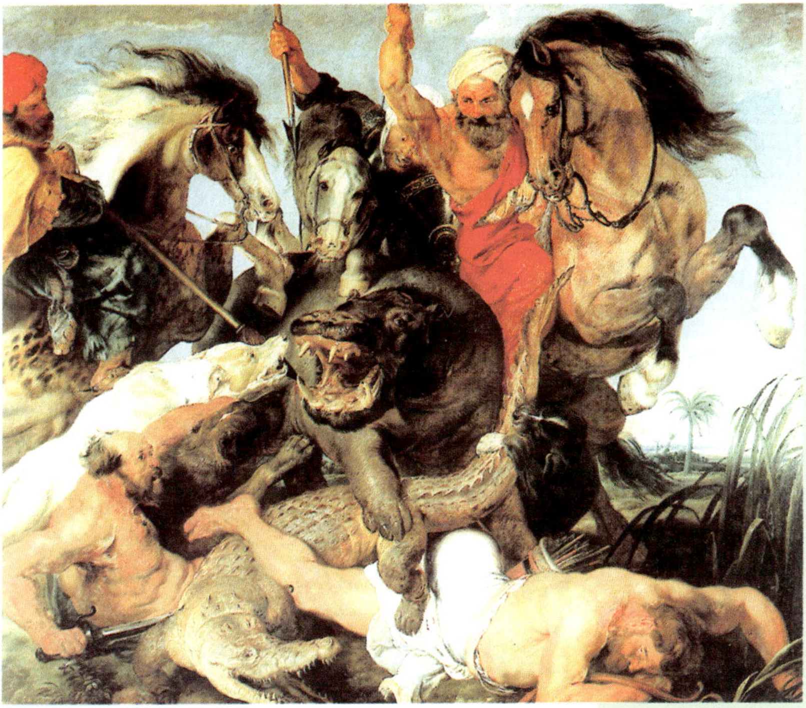

ʼor this painting, Rubens carried out preliminary studies of ıe two wild animals to achieve greater realism. Intertwined ʋith the fierce animals below the mounted hunters, the two ude figures on the ground are impressive in their dyna-ıism. Again, Rubens exhibits his profound knowledge of uman anatomy, presenting the figures in daring foreshorten-ıg, full of vitality and movement. The flesh tones, applied to owerful, sculptural bodies, are achieved by means of curso-y brushstrokes and a palette rich in blues, greens and reds. 'he composition enhances the magnificence and theatricality f the figures, which are skillfully arranged in the painting, lling the entire canvas. Rubens, whose oeuvre represents ıe culmination of a style of painting begun by Titian, is one f the finest exponents of Baroque art.

The Hunt of the Hippopotamus and the Crocodile

Peter Paul Rubens
(Siegen, Westphalia, 1577–Antwerp, 1640)

- 1615–16
- oil on canvas
- 248 x 231 cm
- Alte Pinakothek, Munich

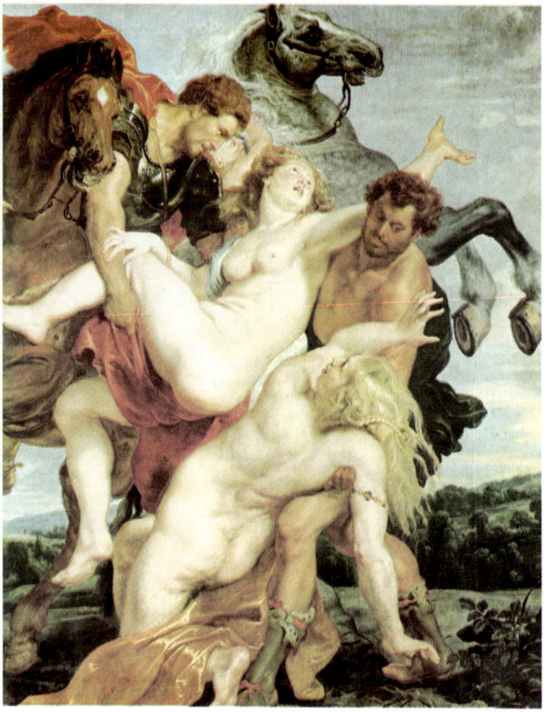

Castor and Pollux Abducting the Daughters of Leucippus (The Rape of the Sabine Women)

Peter Paul Rubens
(Siegen, Westphalia, 1577–Antwerp, 1640)

- 1616–18
- oil on canvas
- 222 x 209 cm
- Alte Pinakothek, Munich

In this scene, Castor and Pollux, conferred with great vitality, are shown abducting two daughters of Leucippus. The drama is heightened by the choreographic-like rhythm with which Rubens depicts the action. The two women are dynamic and forceful in execution. Despite the fullness of their bodies, they appear light in the arms of their abductors. The technically superb foreshortening combines with an elaborate composition to contribute to the scene's sense of movement. One model was used for both female nudes, in two different poses. Their sensuality is revealed when their sumptuous clothing suddenly falls to the ground, exposing splendid, strong and supple bodies, typical characteristics of Rubens' female nudes. In this work, the artist shows one of his principal strengths to best effect: compositional perfection achieved by means of interrelated forms, colors and light. Corpulent bodies lent a certain weightlessness are characteristic of Baroque art.

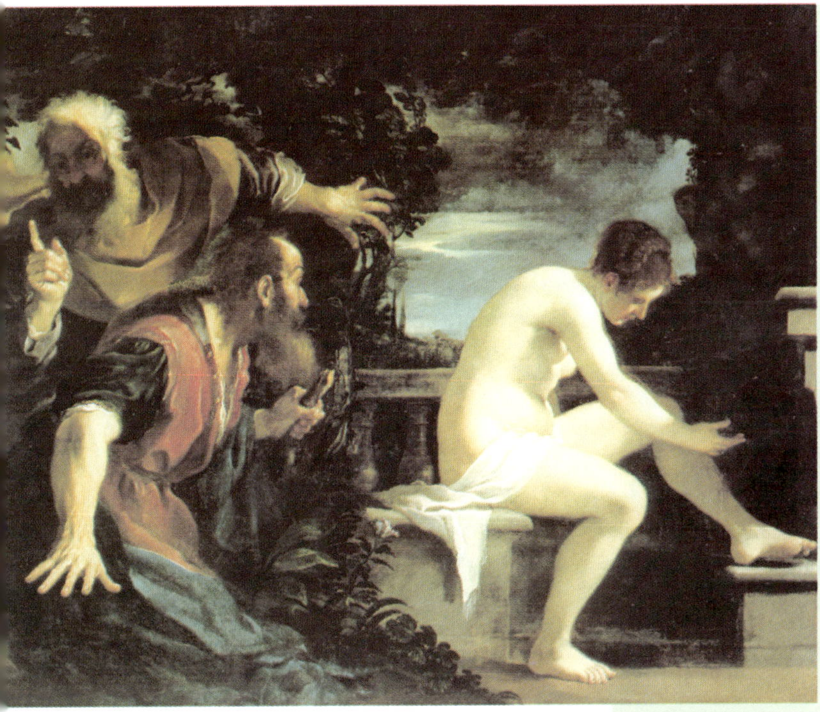

Susanna and the Elders

Il Guercino (Giovanni Francesco Barbieri)
(Cento, near Ferrara, 1591–Bologna, 1666)

- 1617
- oil on canvas
- 175 x 207 cm
- Museo del Prado, Madrid

This painting, along with others by the same artist and some by Titian, were given to Philip IV of Spain by Cardinal Ludovisi and kept at El Escorial for many years.

Venetian influence is evident here in the vibrant colors ıd the resolution of the light, a style far removed from Cara-ıggio's. This theme has been painted often: while bathing, sensual Susanna reveals, unawares, her naked charms to ʋo lecherous old men. The subtle handling of the woman's ɔdy, which is brightly illuminated, contrasts with the saturat-ɪ colors of the figures on the left. The areas of the skin that ˈe cast in shadow are rosy in color, creating an impression freshness that underscores the beauty and youthfulness the figure. Il Guercino's sensitive rendering of the subject as to influence the work of later artists, up to the Pre-aphaelites. The round, clearly delineated forms and the ɔnsummate, strictly classical treatment of the scene are ɔme of the painting's most notable attributes. The overall ıpression is one of serenity, owing to the harmonious figure Susanna, while, at the same time, a certain dynamism is ɛt in motion through the excited figures on the left.

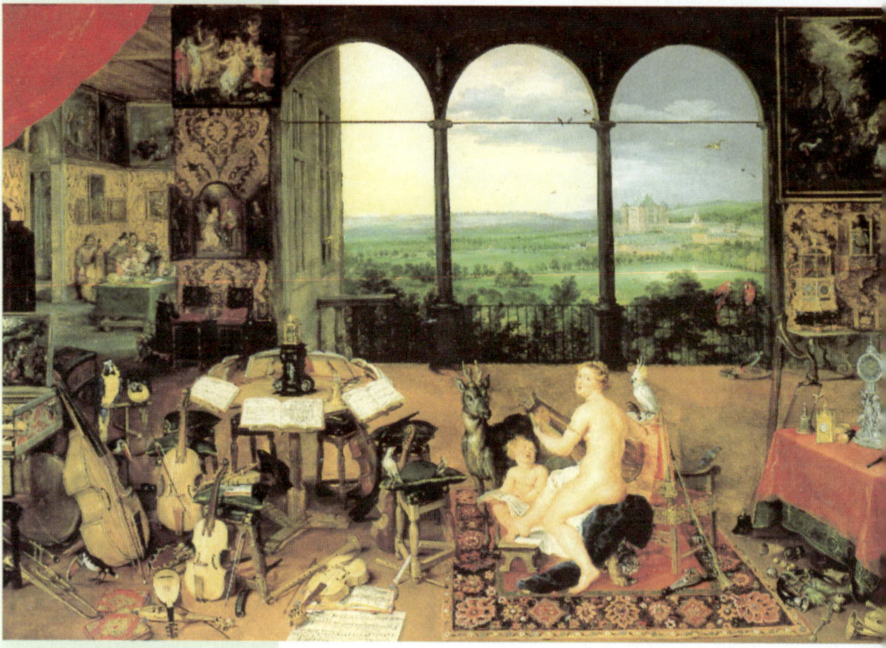

Allegory of Hearing

Jan Brueghel "de Velours"
(Brussels, 1568–Antwerp, 1625)

- 1617–18
- panel
- 65 x 107 cm
- Museo del Prado, Madrid

"De Velours" (Velvet Brueghel) was the sobriquet given to Ja son of Pieter Brueghel the Elder, on account of the velvetee finish of his paintings and the luxurious atmospheres evoke in them. This is one of a series of five panels entitled "The Senses," each of which is devoted to one of the sense orga The generous proportions, the virtuoso, luminous modeling and, above all, the lifelike expression of the female nude at the center reveals the influence of Rubens, with whom the artist collaborated, most closely from 1615 to 1618. Nonetheless, the overall composition is somewhat rigid. The artis rendition of the figure is remarkable. The light appears to be emanating from her skin, making her the brightest point in th painting. Another extraordinary feature is the line of vision th leads from the child via the female figure to the viewer. Whil the child looks up at her, enthralled by her music, she turns her gaze toward the viewer, inviting him to listen, too.

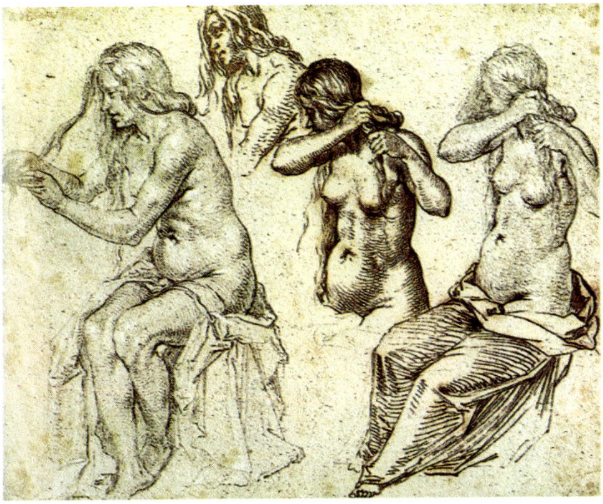

Four Studies of a Female Nude

Jacopo II de Gheyn
(Antwerp, 1565
–The Hague, 1629)

- charcoal, pen, brush and sepia
- 26.2 x 33.5 cm
- Musées Royaux des Beaux-Arts, Brussels

is painter is associated with the broad movement of ıropean Mannerism. In this sheet, we see several studies that idence his skill at exceptionally detailed naturalistic work, hough the poses are academic and static, despite the fact ıt the woman has been depicted in mid-action. The sculptural ree-dimensionality of the well-built body, with its full forms and aceful lines, displays rare sophistication of technique.

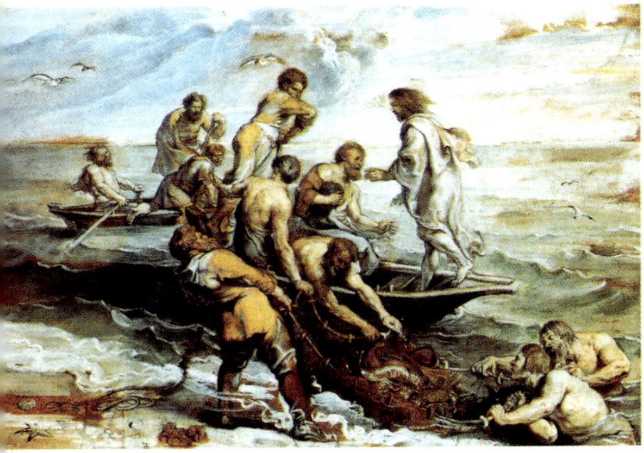

The Miracle of the Fish

Peter Paul Rubens
(Siegen, Westphalia,
1577–Antwerp, 1640)

- 1618
- pencil, ink and oil on paper mounted on canvas
- 54.5 x 84.5 cm
- The National Gallery, London

ıen Jesus was preaching at the sea of Galilee, he com-ınded Peter and Andrew to cast their nets. The catch was abundant that they needed the help of another boat. The eshortened torsos of the fishermen are compact and pow-ul, while the handling of light displays their muscles. The erall draftsmanship is extremely accomplished, and puts e in mind of Michelangelo's figures in the Sistine Chapel.

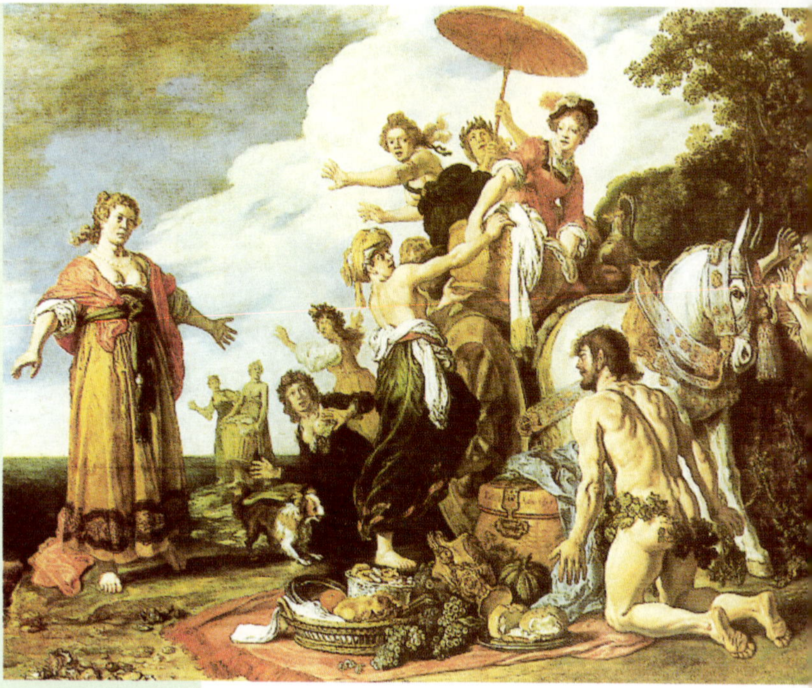

Odysseus and Nausicaa

Pieter Lastman
(Amsterdam, 1583–1633)

- 1619
- oil on panel
- 91.5 x 117.2 cm
- Alte Pinakothek, Munich

This scene, from Homer's epic poem The Odyssey, represer the episode in which Odysseus finds himself shipwrecked or an island and he meets Nausicaa, daughter of Arete and Alcinous, king of the Phaeacians, who takes him in at her father's palace. The modeling of the hero's body clearly defines his muscles, which exhibit a high degree of plasticity The painting contains many contrasts, and the illumination of the nude creates a moment of tension and drama in whicl theatricality is given top priority, to the detriment of the painte ly handling. This is also evident in the affected gestures of the figures, the excessively pleated garments and the strikin juxtaposition of incongruous colors. Despite these flaws, the painting possesses great expressive force.

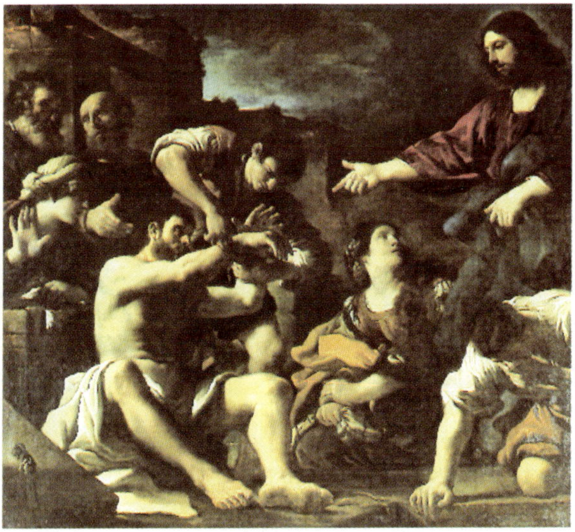

The Resurrection of Lazarus

Il Guercino (Giovanni Francesco Barbieri)
(Cento, near Ferrara, 1591–Bologna, 1666)

- ca. 1619
- oil on canvas
- 201 x 233 cm
- Musée du Louvre, Paris

ɩuercino, a pupil of Ludovico Carracci and influenced by
› Venetian School, despite undergoing a period of certain
nity with Guido Reni, was always conditioned by academic
:eria. This is evident in the present canvas, both in the
mposition and in the manner in which the figures are repre-
ıted, particularly the classical, nude figure of Lazarus.

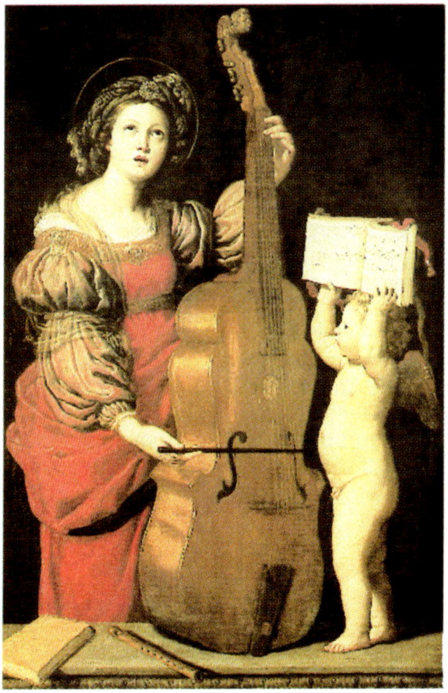

St. Cecilia

Domenichino (Domenico Zampieri)
(Bologna, 1581–Naples, 1641)

- 1620
- oil on canvas
- 60 x 120 cm
- Musée du Louvre, Paris

e present paint-
ı shows St.
cilia, the patron
musicians, as
licated by the
strument she
ıolding. The
ures in the pre-
nt painting,
th refined and
phuistic, pos-
ss highly ex-
essive, if some-
at affected,
es. The naked
gel, probably
inted from a
odel, is the very
ıbodiment of
ldlike innocence
d candor.

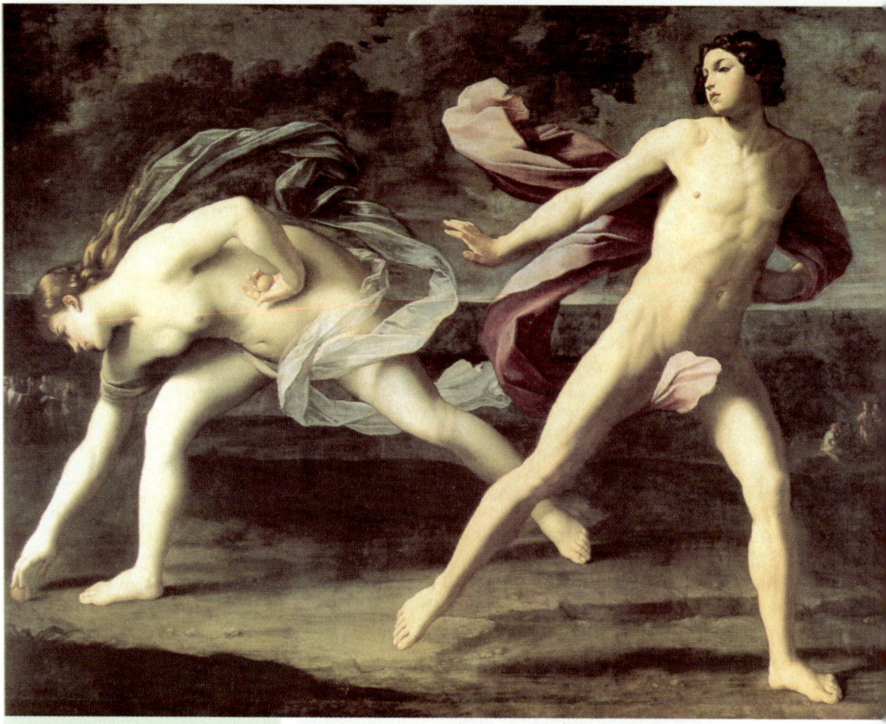

Hippomenes and Atalanta

Guido Reni
(Bologna, 1575–1642)

- 1620
- oil on canvas
- 206 x 279 cm
- Museo del Prado, Madrid

This painting was added to the Spanish royal collection in the 17th century. Deposited at the University of Granada in 1882, it entered the Prado in the 1960s.

Atalanta became Hippomenes' wife after outrunning her in a race that she had proposed. The painting shows Atalanta's distraction as she stops to pick up an apple, causing her to lose the race and marry the victor. The figures are executed in an accentuated Manneristic style. The classical figures are at once beautiful and harmonious. The composition, a symphony of colors, is skillfully constructed around two diagonals, achieving a perfect equilibrium. The two figures, portrayed in carefully composed, dynamic postures, exhibit a high degree of plasticity. They are fine anatomical studies whose naturalistic articulation is in keeping with the lyricism of the theme. The rhythm of the nudes attains its kinetic force through the frozen movement of the veils covering the loins of the two figures. Another version of the painting is in the Capodimonte National Gallery in Naples.

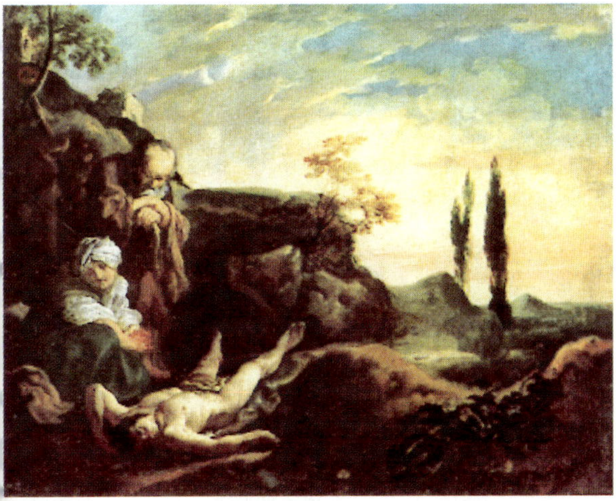

Abel Mourned by his Parents

Johann Liss (or **Lys**)
(Oldenburg, 1595–Venice, 1630)

- ca. 1620
- oil on canvas
- 67 x 84 cm
- Galleria dell'Accademia, Venice

e way Abel is lying in the picture is both sensational and ocking. The dramatic background, with its studied effects llumination, further enhance these aspects.

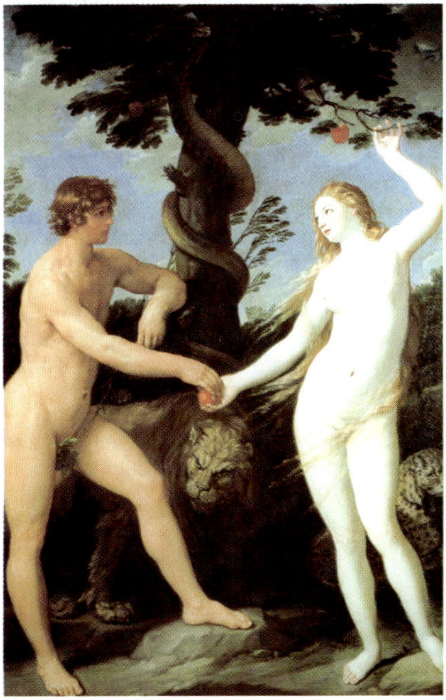

Adam and Eve

Guido Reni
(Bologna, 1575–1642)

- 1620
- oil on canvas
- 277 x 196 cm
- Musée des Beaux-Arts, Dijon

deled as if y were marble tues, the ooth outlines d composition hese two fig-s conform to early 17th ntury classical al of beauty. eir elegant ms combine h their com-xions and ir hair—am's meticu-s curls, Eve's g flowing ks—to en-nce their physi- attractiveness.

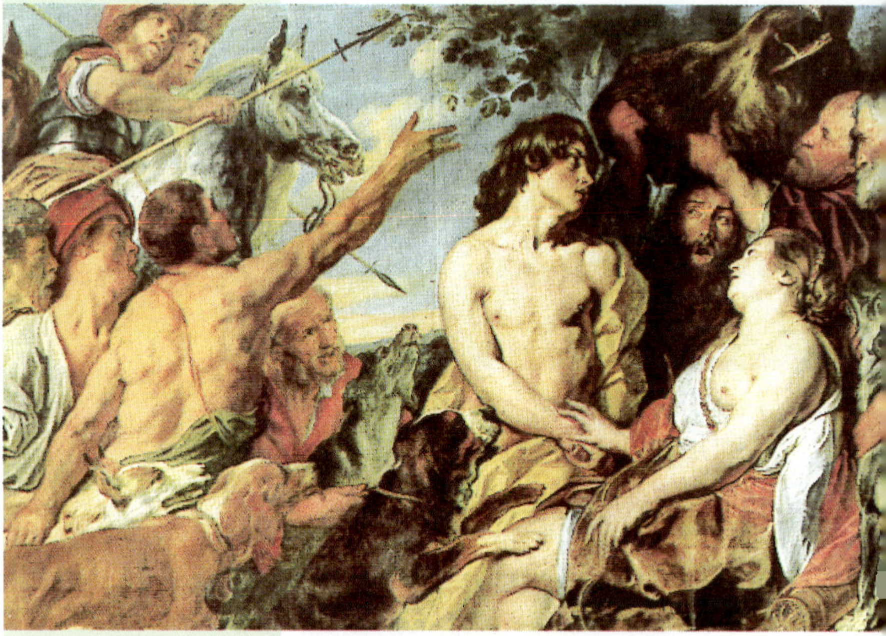

Meleager and Atalanta

Jacob Jordaens
(Antwerp, 1593–1678)

- 1620
- oil on canvas
- 151 x 241 cm
- Museo del Prado, Madrid

Together, Atalanta and Meleager slew the Calydonian boar. As a token of his gallantry, Meleager gave Atalanta the animal's head and its hide. The rest of the hunters resented him for this, which explains why the two figures on the right background can be seen attempting to steel the trophy, whil Meleager makes as if to unsheathe his sword, a gesture that is thwarted by Atalanta. The semi-naked subjects are foreshortened. Meleager has a torso of an Apollonian youth, with an effeminate face, whereas Atalanta is portrayed with a corpulent build. The contrast between the serene facial expressions of the protagonists and the unsettling compositional rhythm of the whole conveys an air of violence. The nudes, of great vitality and sculptural roundness, recall the figures of Rubens, Jordaens' teacher, with their powerful an idealized bodies, executed with a wide-ranging palette of luminous flesh tones.

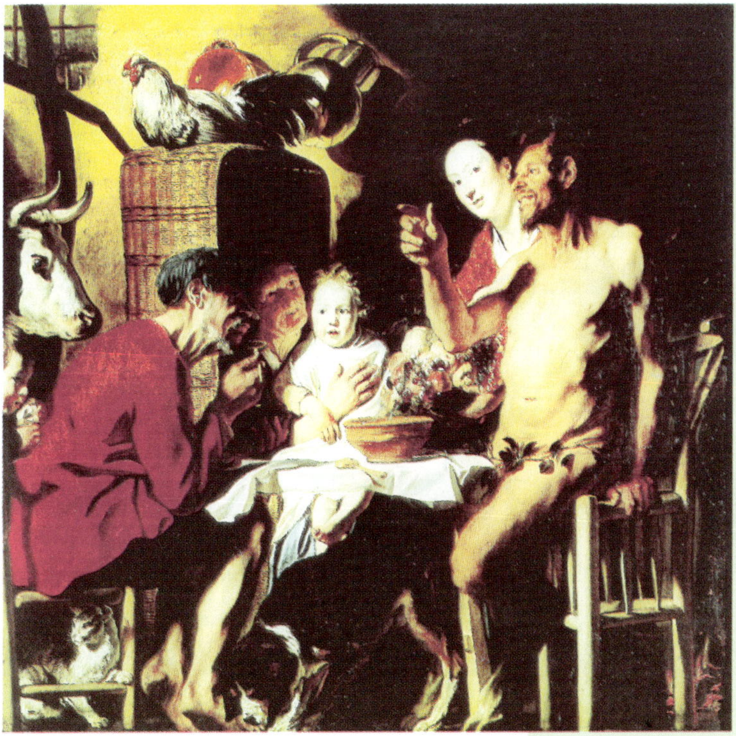

Satyr with Peasants

Jacob Jordaens
(Antwerp, 1593–1678)

- after 1620
- oil on canvas and panel
- 174 x 205 cm
- Alte Pinakothek, Munich

ıis painting, a depiction of one of Aesop's fables, shows a ·asant farmer, who has invited a satyr to supper with him ıd his family. Seeing how the farmer blows on his hands to ırm them, and then blows on his soup to cool it down, the .tyr—at first bewildered—assumes the man is out to make ı of him. The everyday realism of Jordaens' figures are ways impressive, whether in portraits or, as here, in sacred ıd mythological themes. In this work, he contrives to hieve enormous vitality by means of strong illumination and rich range of colours. Numerous people from the real world ure in the painting: the baby is the artist's daughter and the oman behind the satyr his wife. The satyr, his body human ıd his legs those of a goat, is perfectly integrated into the nre scene, and is outstanding for the realism of his portray- —his wrinkled skin, muscles and mature male torso that uld easily be that of a model. The satyr is shown pointing, if he has suddenly realized what is happening, while his t arm, its hand clasping his chair, expresses great tension.

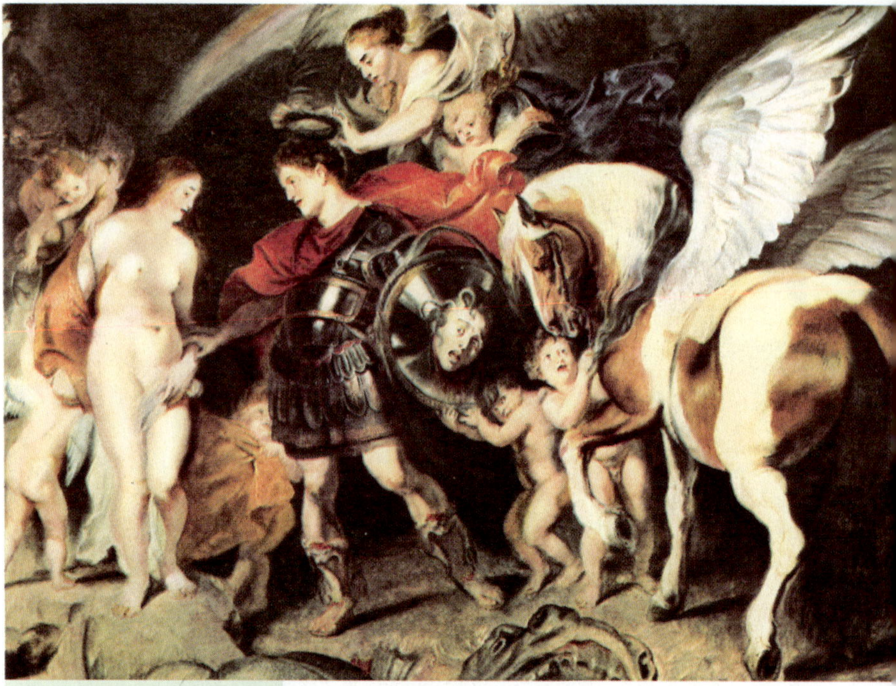

Perseus and Andromeda

Peter Paul Rubens
(Siegen, 1577–Antwerp, 1640)

- 1620/21
- oil on canvas
- 99.5 x 139 cm
- Hermitage, St. Petersburg

Originally part of the Schönborn Collection, this painting was sold at auction in 1738 to the Brühl Collection, Dresden, from which the Museum acquired it in 1769.

In order to pacify the Nereids, a sea monster was sent by Poseidon to devour Andromeda, daughter of Cassiopeia, the Queen of Ethiopia, because her mother boasted that she wa[s] more beautiful than the Nereids. Perseus, son of Zeus and Danaë, kills the Gorgon, from whose bleeding neck the winged horse Pegasus emerges. It is upon this horse that he rides to Andromeda's rescue. The painting depicts the moment of rescue: several angels free the maiden, untying the ropes that had bound her to the rock; others attempt to cover her naked body while she herself conceals her intimate parts; still others hold up Perseus' shield with an image of Medusa's head on it; and another keeps hold of Pegasus. At the same time, a celestial figure holds a crown over Perseus head in reward for his heroism. The well-executed painting is highly expressive, exhibiting a variety of notable details: Andromeda with the appearance of a young Flemish woman the angels with innocent children's faces; the highlights on Perseus' armor; the virtuoso treatment of colors, to name only a few. The movement of the painting is suggested by th[e] horse's wings and the clothing billowing in the wind. The composition is arranged such that the beholder's gaze is automatically drawn to Andromeda, who is brightly lit.

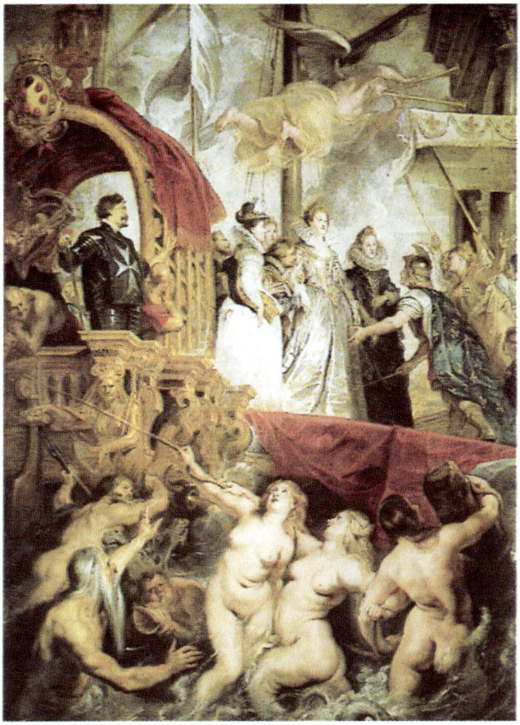

The Landing of Marie de Medici at Marseilles

Peter Paul Rubens
(Siegen, Westphalia, 1577–Antwerp, 1640)

- 1621
- oil on canvas
- 394 x 295 cm
- Musée du Louvre, Paris

ı this allegorical painting, historical personages are juxtaosed with mythological figures. The lower section is occuied by a group of Tritons and three Naiads, whose robust odies are articulated with loosely drawn, dynamic lines. hese figures are highly erotic, although this is not the ainting's principal objective, and become luminous against ıe play of contrasts in the background. The generous proortions of the Herculean Tritons evoke the figures of ichelangelo. The femininity of the Naiads is underscored y their voluptuous, sensual curves. However, these erotic udes are not the protagonists of the painting; instead they rm the divine audience receiving Marie de Medici and her tinue in Marseilles. Every one of Rubens' nudes is a asterpiece owing to their round, harmonious forms and markable vitality. They are marked by a majestic dignity precedented in the history of art. Although they give the npression of being rather heavy, the powerful, heroic bods display an agility that renders them weightless.

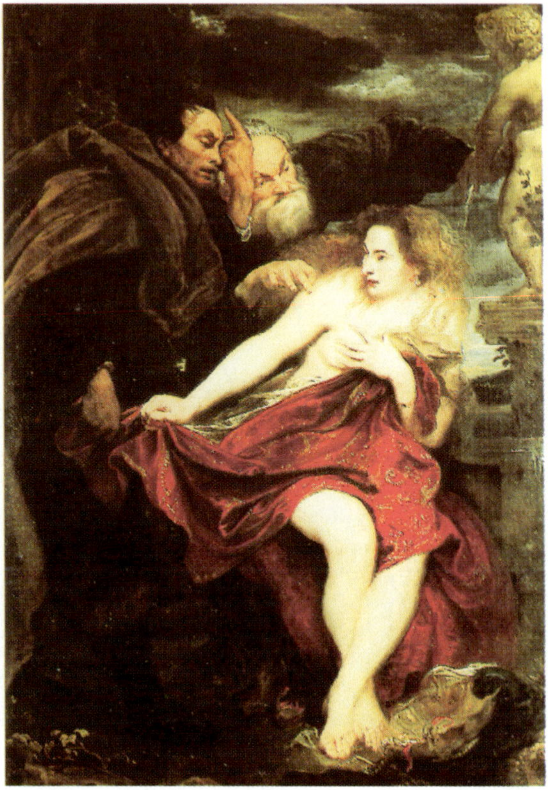

Susanna and the Elders

Anthony van Dyck
(Antwerp, 1599–London, 1641)

- 1621–22
- oil on canvas
- 194 x 144 cm
- Alte Pinakothek, Munich

In this painting, the artist portrays Susanna as a common woman, who is being harassed by two old men, one of whom puts his hand on her shoulder, the other threatening her with his raised hand while pulling at the cloth with which she is covering herself. Susanna, who looks both humiliated and frightened, is surprised and defenseless. In accordance with contemporary tastes, the artist represents her with a plump figure, brightly illuminated, making her the focal point of the scene. In this work, Anthony van Dyck demonstrates his compositional skills and his mastery of draftsmanship. His treatment of light enhances the painting's palette and attests to the artist's skill at rendering volumes. Moreover, the painterly handing of the folds in the drapery is clearly influenced by Venetian and Bolognese art.

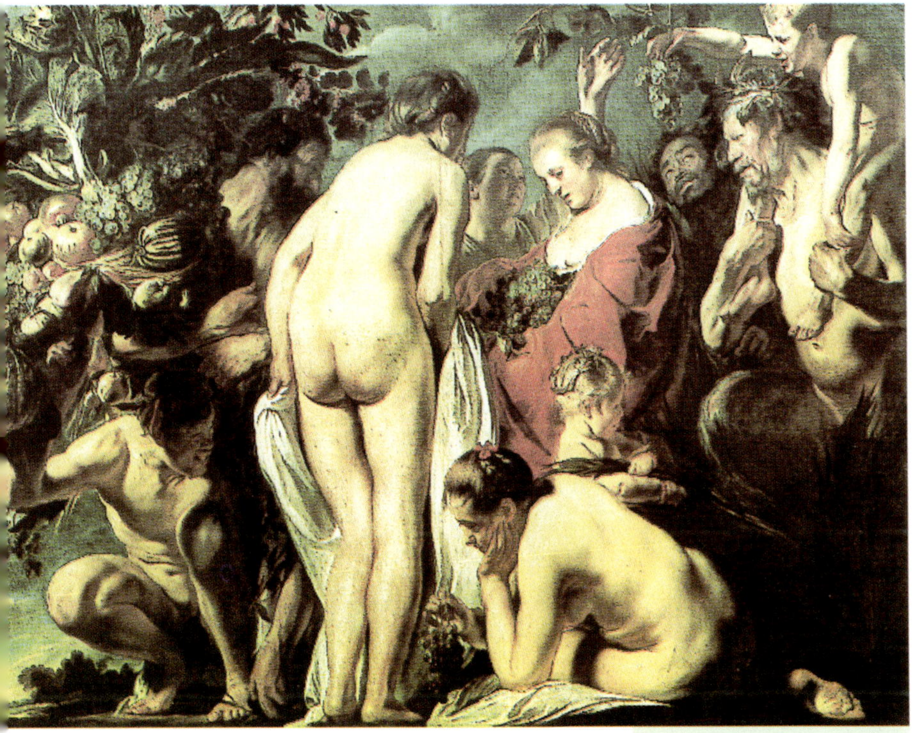

In this allegory, Fertility is depicted with a rotund figure; dressed in red appears Pomona, the goddess of fruit and its cultivation. Several nude figures crowd around her: satyrs, nymphs, children, all of them symbols of human carnality and procreation. The satyr is the symbol of lust, women the source of life and children the fruits of human desire. These exquisite nudes exhibit a sophisticated foreshortening and different male and female attributes. The figures' modeling is executed with chiaroscuro, accentuating her female forms. Their impeccable execution attest to Jordaens' sound knowledge of human anatomy. As in other works by the artist, the painting's most remarkable attributes include its palette, comprising light tones of great chromatic force, and the movement and arrangement of the figures, which is typical of Baroque art.

Homage to Pomona: Allegory of Fertility

Jacob Jordaens
(Antwerp, 1593–1678)

- ca. 1622
- oil on canvas
- 180 x 241 cm
- Musées Royaux des Beaux-Arts, Brussels

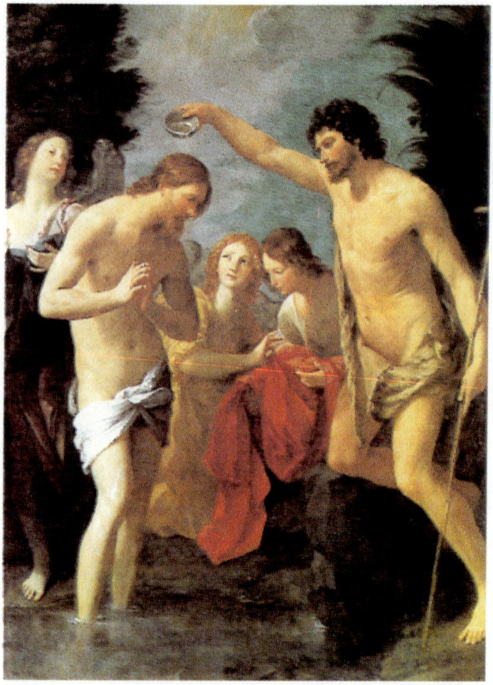

The Baptism of Christ

Guido Reni
(Bologna, 1575–1642)

- ca. 1623
- oil on canvas
- 263.5 x 186.5 cm
- Kunsthistorisches Museum, Vienna

The spirituality of this painting, simple in composition, is in part achieved by the atmosphere evoked in its fore-, middle and background. The focal point of the composition is the baptism of Christ by John, whose body forms an arc that ends above Jesus' head. Behind these figures, in the middle ground, the angel on the left holds Jesus' garments. The background comprises the landscape and sky, from which the Holy Ghost descends in the form of a dove. Each of the three grounds was executed with a different color scheme in order to establish perfect harmony among the painting's various elements and principal nudes. A strong whitish light falls on the figure of Christ, emphasizing the fact that he is the protagonist of the painting; the light falling on John, on the other hand, is golden. Both have different builds, Jesus' being more languid, while the figure of John is more corpulent, with more clearly defined and larger muscles. Without abandoning classicism, Reni is primarily concerned with the beauty and harmony of his figures.

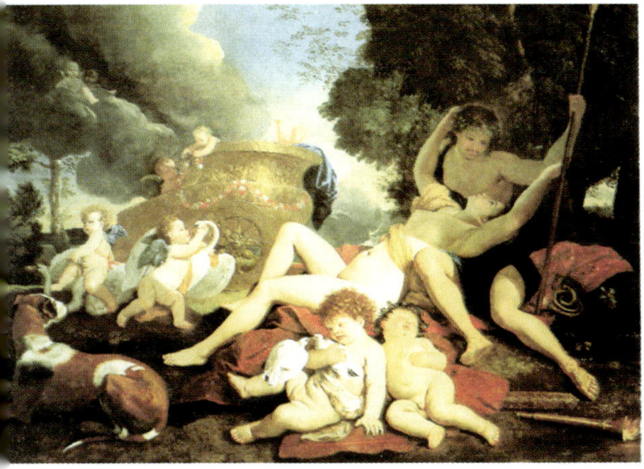

Venus and Adonis

Nicolas Poussin
(Les Andelys, 1594–Rome, 1665)

- 1624–25
- oil on canvas
- 98.5 x 134.6 cm
- Kimball Art Museum, Fort Worth, Texas

In a landscape populated with cherubs, Venus abandons herself to her lover's gaze in a pose of total surrender. Her position shows off her attractive body to advantage: slender, sensual and sheathed in light.

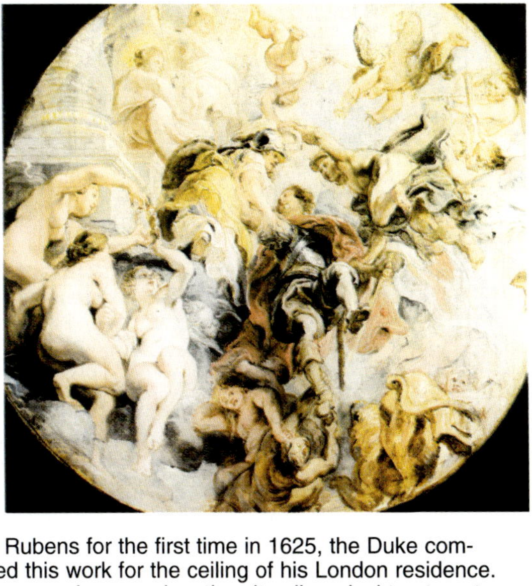

Minerva and Mercury Bearing the Duke of Buckingham to the Temple of Virtue

Peter Paul Rubens
(Siegen, Westphalia, 1577 –Antwerp, 1640)

- 1625
- oil on panel
- tondo, 62 cm diameter
- The National Gallery, London

Meeting Rubens for the first time in 1625, the Duke commissioned this work for the ceiling of his London residence. The theme needs no explanation. Its allegorical treatment is sensual and rich in erotic undertones. The nude figures of the three graces show great beauty. The foreshortening used in depicting them is extremely bold.

St. Sebastian Attended by the Holy Women

Hendrick Terbrugghen
(Deventer, ca. 1588–Utrecht, 1629)

- 1625
- panel
- 149.5 x 120 cm
- Allen Memorial Art Museum, Oberlin, OH

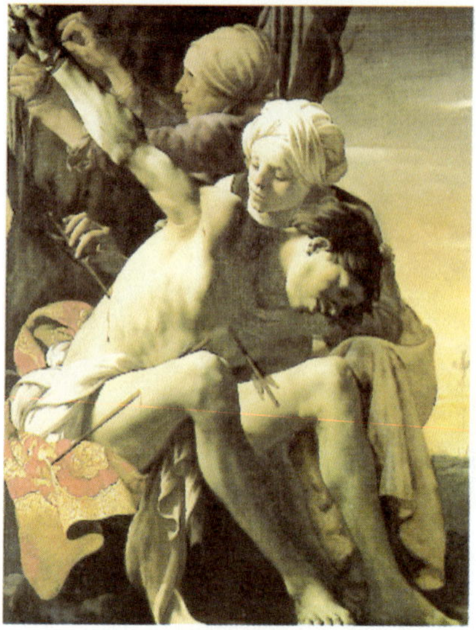

Considered one of the finest exponents of Caravaggism in northern Europe, Hendrick Terbrugghen was chiefly a painter of religious scenes, but he also produced some remarkable genre works. His paintings recall those of Orazio Gentileschi and are notable for their subtle tonality and psychological intensity. This is one of his most emotive works, with a singular composition. It is a scene full of sensuality, candor and tenderness, enhanced by a studied lighting and a balanced color scheme.

Cleopatra

Rembrandt (Rembrandt Harmensz van Rijn)
(Leiden, 1606–Amsterdam, 1669)

- red chalk on cream-colored paper
- Het Rembrandthuis, Amsterdam

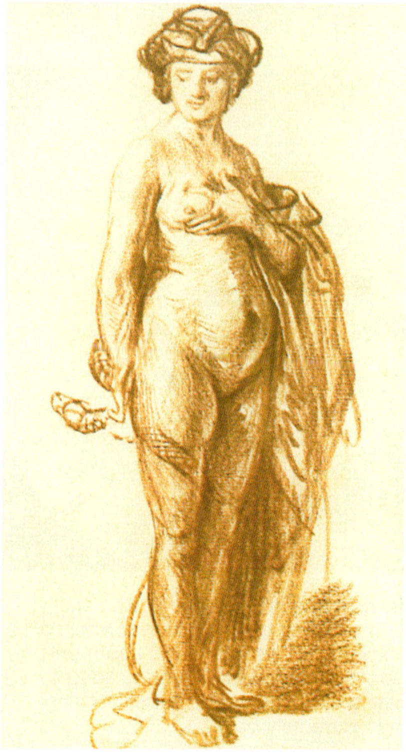

Rembrandt was arguably the best and most prolific draftsman the history of art has ever known. In the present work he has depicted an historical figure, who happened to become a legend, in the most demystifying manner conceivable. Cleopatra is portrayed as a plump, rather short and unattractive female figure.

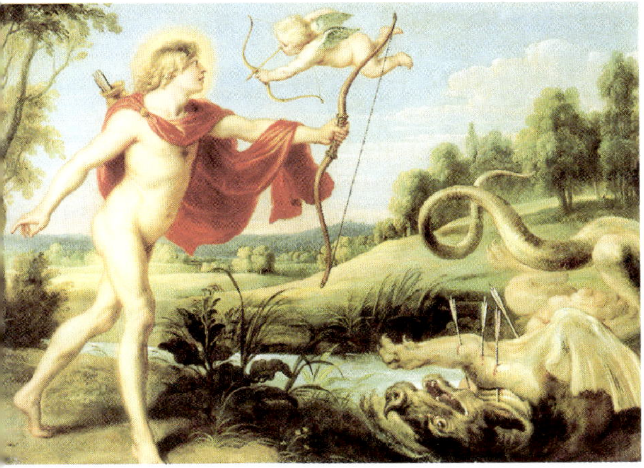

Apollo and the Python

Cornelis de Vos

(Hulst, 1584–Antwerp, 1651)

- oil on canvas
- Museo del Prado, Madrid

Despite a certain exaggerated mannerism in this painting, certain formal innovations are discernible in respect of how the body of Apollo is portrayed, at once theatrically and naturalistically, with a somewhat rarefied idealization. The result is a decidedly non-heroic youth, whose beauty is more evident in his face than in his body. The way Apollo's movement appears as if frozen is also noteworthy.

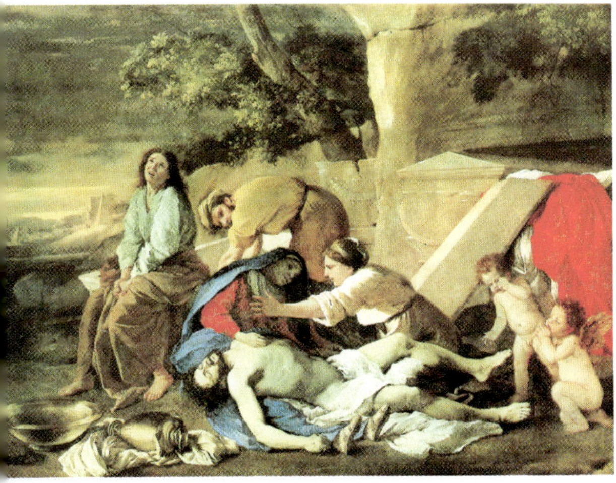

Lamentation for the Dead Christ

Nicolas Poussin

(Les Andelys, 1594 –Rome 1665)

- 1625
- oil on canvas
- 102.7 x 146 cm
- Alte Pinakothek, Munich

Portrayed with various figures and two cherubs, the dead body of Christ is shown in his mother's lap. Despite the martyrdom he has undergone, the body displays no marks. The anatomy is svelte, with a modeling that has been achieved with a filtered light that brings out the forms. The work conveys all the expressiveness and drama of the moment.

Penitent St. Jerome

Georges de La Tour

(Vic-sur-Seille, Lorraine, 1593–Lunéville, 1652)

- 1620–30
- oil on canvas
- 153 x 106 cm
- Nationalmuseum, Stockholm

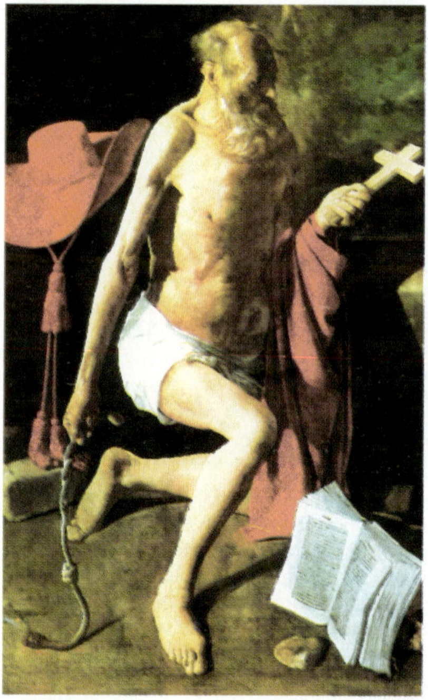

The contrasts of light give way to an almost photographic image of the saint as an old man, whose stylized and well-proportioned body represents a fine example of French Baroque realism. The lateral lighting foreshortens the left half of the figure, while the part in shadow appears to recede into the loincloth he is wearing. The work is remarkable in the away the red of the cloak draped over his left arm is reflected on the saint's skin, modifying the intensity of the shadows.

Bacchanal

Nicolas Poussin

(Les Andelys, 1594–Rome, 1665)

- ca. 1625–26
- oil on canvas
- 122 x 169 cm
- Museo del Prado, Madrid

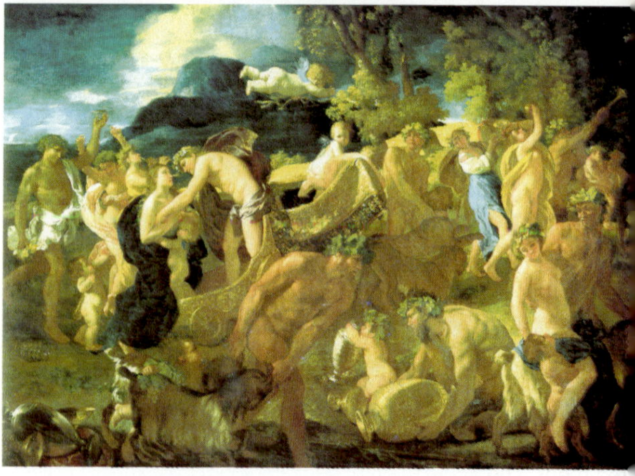

The nude figures here, excited by wine, are dancing and revelling. Ariadne and Bacchus stand out from the rest, the latter in particular being a meticulously executed figure. The composition is complex, and its overall effect is more one of confusion than of celebration, as not infrequently occurs also in Titian's work.

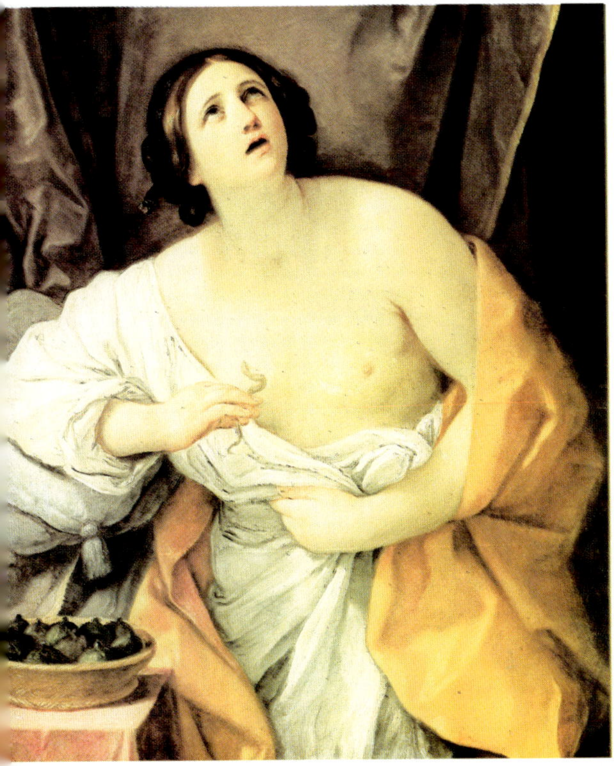

Cleopatra

Guido Reni
(Bologna, 1575–1642)

- 1635–40
- oil on canvas
- 122 x 96 cm
- Galleria Palatina, Palazzo Pitti, Florence

The subject of this painting is taken from Plutarch's Lives. Cleopatra, upon hearing of her lover, Mark Antony's, defeat, takes her life by succumbing to the fatal bite of an asp, which can be seen being taken from a basket of figs here. This was a common theme in 17th-century painting and literature. Guido Reni, embracing the fashion of the day, executed a total of five paintings on the subject between 1625 and his death, in 1642. During this period, women were the artist's favorite subjects, combining elegance, spirituality, theatricality and great expressiveness. These works were highly valued and brought the artist great acclaim. The treatment of Cleopatra could well be that of the Virgin or another saint. The modeling of this classical nude is almost sculptural in treatment. The figure's torso is somewhat androgynous in its generous volumes and diminished forms.

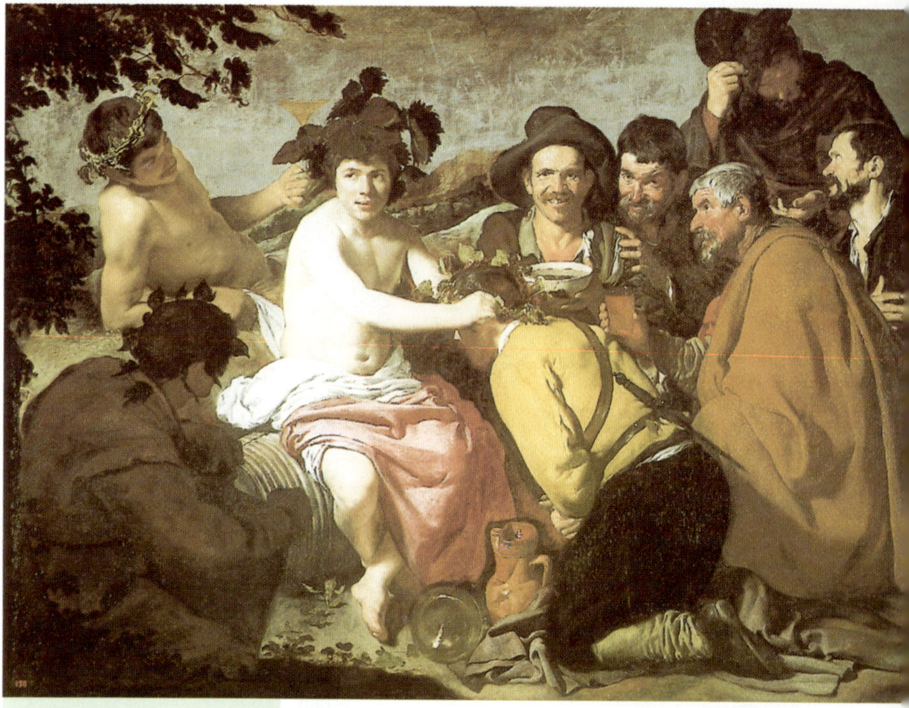

The Drunkards, or The Triumph of Bacchus

Diego Rodríguez de Silva y Velázquez
(Seville, 1599–Madrid, 1660)

- 1626
- oil on canvas
- 165 x 188 cm
- Museo del Prado, Madrid

This is one of the most famous paintings by Diego Velázquez, and is perhaps his best composition. The left half of the painting is influenced by Italian art: the beautiful, sensual and somewhat ambiguous figure of Bacchus resembles some of Caravaggio's models, while the nude figure appearing behind him holding a goblet evokes Titian's style. As an element of contrast, a dressed figure has been placed in the dark lower left-hand corner of the painting. On the right several drunkards with expressive faces crowd about a soldier who is being crowned by the god. The gestures and poses of this group recalls a biblical scene, the Adoration of the Magi. It is curious that, despite its mythological character, the representation is not idealized. Perhaps this is due to the artist's Christian convictions, which may have led him unconsciously to discredit the validity of pagan beliefs.

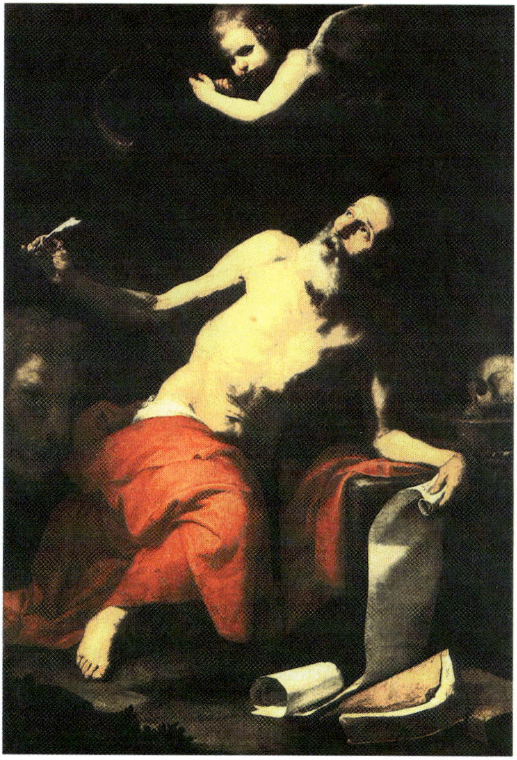

St. Jerome and the Angel (St. Jerome Listening to the Trumpets that Announce the Final Judgment)

José (Jusepe) de Ribera (called **Lo Spagnoletto**)
(Jàtiva, Spain, 1591 –Naples, 1652)

- 1626
- oil on canvas
- 185 x 133 cm
- Hermitage, St. Petersburg

masterly handling of light, the element of surprise, an air f mystery and, frequently, affable or picaresque episodes re characteristic of Ribera's oeuvre. He was criticized on ore than one occasion for his depictions of saints, which either possessed the appearance nor the intelligence of ore conventional images of the day. Ribera does little to ealize his models, determining only the pose and the ghting in order to heighten the drama of the scene and emonstrate what he believed was the divine hand that as able to render such magnificence. In this painting, the rtist does not make the old man's body appear ugly, but, ther, lends it dignity, evincing a thin but well-proportioned ude of noble dimensions. The tenebrist chiaroscuro brings ut the sharp angles of the subject's bone structure, thereby achieving an interesting transition between the highghts and the shadows. Like other works by Ribera, this anvas breathes the refinement of drama and solemnity.

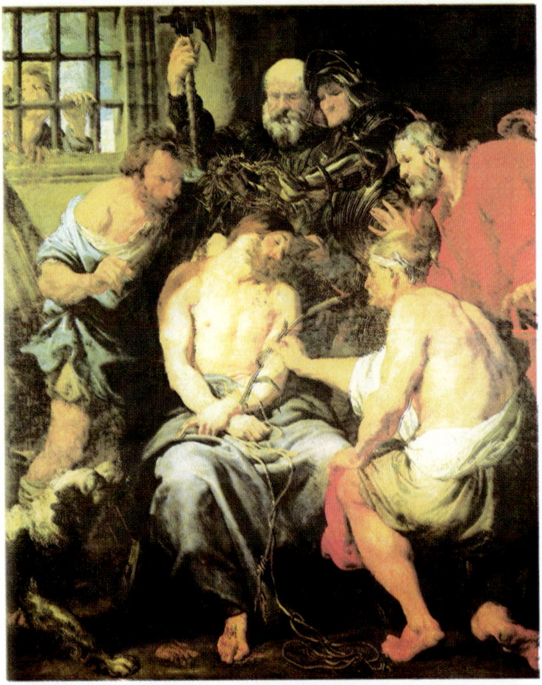

The Crowning with Thorns

Anthony van Dyck
(Antwerp, 1599–London 1641)

- 1618
- oil on canvas
- 223 x 196 cm
- Museo del Prado, Madrid

Given by the artist to Rubens, whose collection passed to Philip IV.

This youthful work by Van Dyck, inspired by Titian's famous treatment of the subject, exhibits a compositional scheme to which the artist was to return in later years. Here, he is interested in the play of light on the naked human figure. The semi-nude body of Christ, treated with majestic dignity despite his physical and psychological state, is given an almost Herculean appearance, somewhat akin to a triton by Rubens. This heroic dimension is complemented by such intensely human elements as the weary look on Christ's face and the slackness with which his powerful arms rest in his lap. Attention focuses on the luminous flesh of Christ's body, emphasized by the dark surroundings and heightening his divine aura. The modeling, which recalls the work of Caravaggio, carefully renders the chiaroscuro of light and shade, the half-lights accentuated by surrounding colors. The Gemäldegalerie in Berlin possesses a similar painting by Van Dyck.

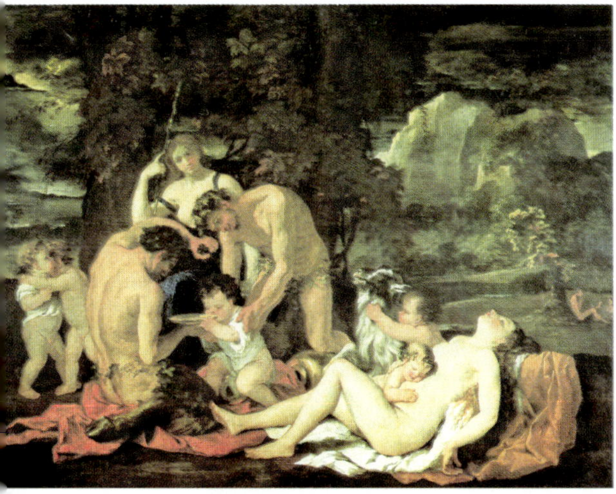

Nurture of Bacchus

Nicolas Poussin
(Les Andelys, 1594–Rome, 1665)

- 1626–27
- oil on canvas
- 97 x 136 cm
- Musée du Louvre, Paris

Zeus is portrayed here holding a plate from which the child Bacchus is eating, while his mother, Semele, sleeps on drapery laid on the ground. The scene has all the ingredients of an allusive vision: an abundance of nude figures and a treatment of light that contributes to the mysterious, dream-like air of the painting.

Disguising himself as a bunch of grapes, Bacchus seduced Erigone, daughter of Icarus, a humble Athenian peasant, by intoxicating her. In this painting, the god of wine has covered his genitalia with several vine leaves, and a cherub holds the grapes that Bacchus will give to Erigone. He has been given a youthful, strong and athletic body, unlike more conventional depictions of the god. This work betrays the influence of Italian painting, particularly in the treatment of the shadows.

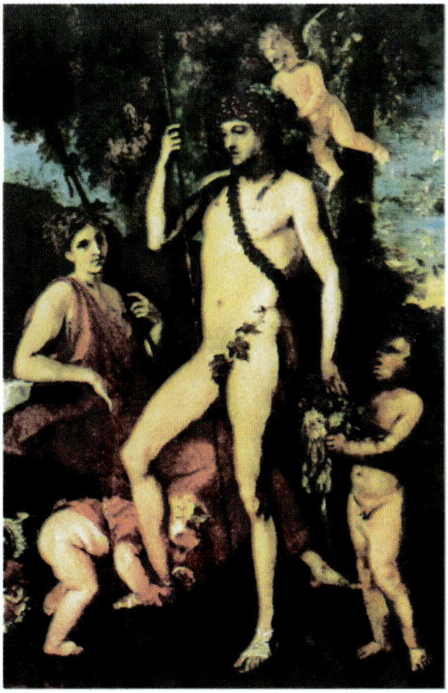

Bacchus and Erigone

Nicolas Poussin
(Les Andelys, 1594 –Rome, 1665)

- 1626–27
- oil on canvas
- 98 x 74 cm
- Nationalmuseum, Stockholm

St. Sebastian Tended by St. Irene

Georges de La Tour

(Vic-sur-Seille, Lorraine, 1593–Lunéville, 1652)

- oil on canvas
- 167 x 131 cm
- Musée du Louvre, Paris

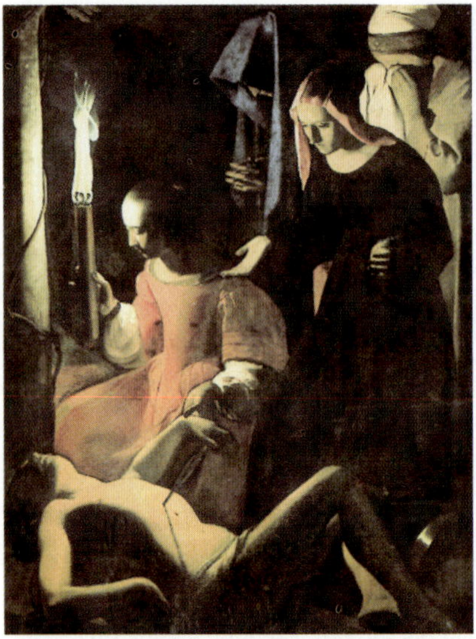

Georges de La Tou was interested in studying and expe imenting with light in dark settings. In this nocturnal scene, the artist creates a mysterious, artificial atmosphere through l ight and color, and radically simplifies the figures, reducing volumes to sim ple planes. The artist has sought to minimize the fea tures of his sensua Sebastian in favor of a static theatricality, which marks the entire work.

Scene with Bacchus

Nicolas Poussin

(Les Andelys, 1594–Rome, 1665)

- 1626–28
- oil on canvas
- 74 x 60 cm
- Museo del Prado, Madrid

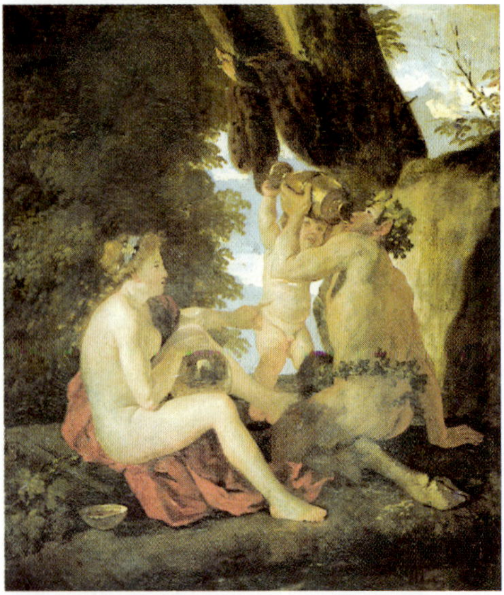

Renderings of Bacchus often provided painters with an opportunity to depict nude figures in a landscape. The scene here, far from being orgiastic, rather resembles in its tranquillity a family outing. The female figure, not overly sensual in appearance, its lateral position reminiscent of certain archaic works, nevertheless evinces a perfect handling of anatomical detail, and its outlines are very finely drawn.

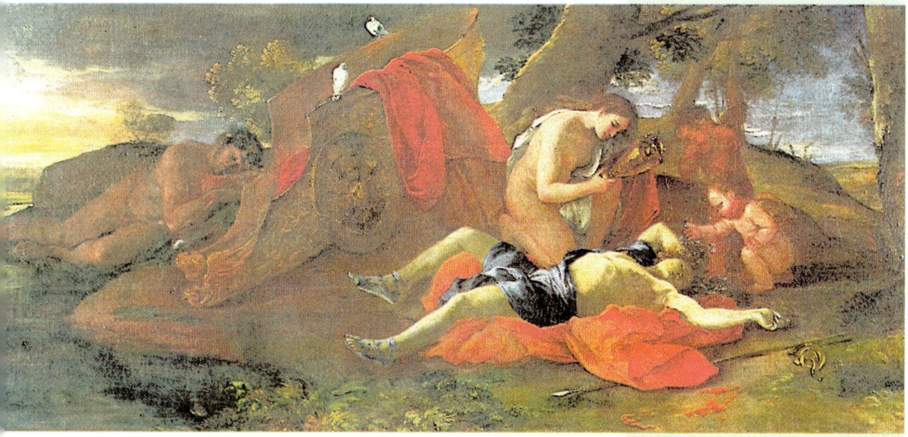

Calliope determined that Persephone and Venus should share Adonis in the course of the year. Venus then persuaded him to avoid Persephone, whereupon Persephone, jealous, told Mars, who turned into a boar and killed Adonis. Here we see Venus pouring nectar over Adonis from whom anemones bloom. Adonis' pose is similar to the dead Christ Poussin painted, an indication of the relationships he established in his paintings between the Catholic Church and pagan culture. The chiaroscuro illumination of Adonis recalls Caravaggio and the foreshortening employed in the figure is complex. The nude figure of Venus by way of contrast is simple, sensual and rather faint, most of her body being dark, but with highlighted arm and face. Poussin, of course, subscribed to a distinctly Classical aesthetic, as can be seen from the historical and mythological themes he was so fond of painting. Caravaggio's naturalism and Guido Reni's lightness of style are diametrically opposed to his, which is closer to Raphael and Titian.

Venus with the Dead Adonis

Nicolas Poussin
(Les Andelys, 1594–Rome, 1665)

- ca. 1627
- oil on canvas
- 57 x 128 cm
- Musée des Beax Arts, Caen

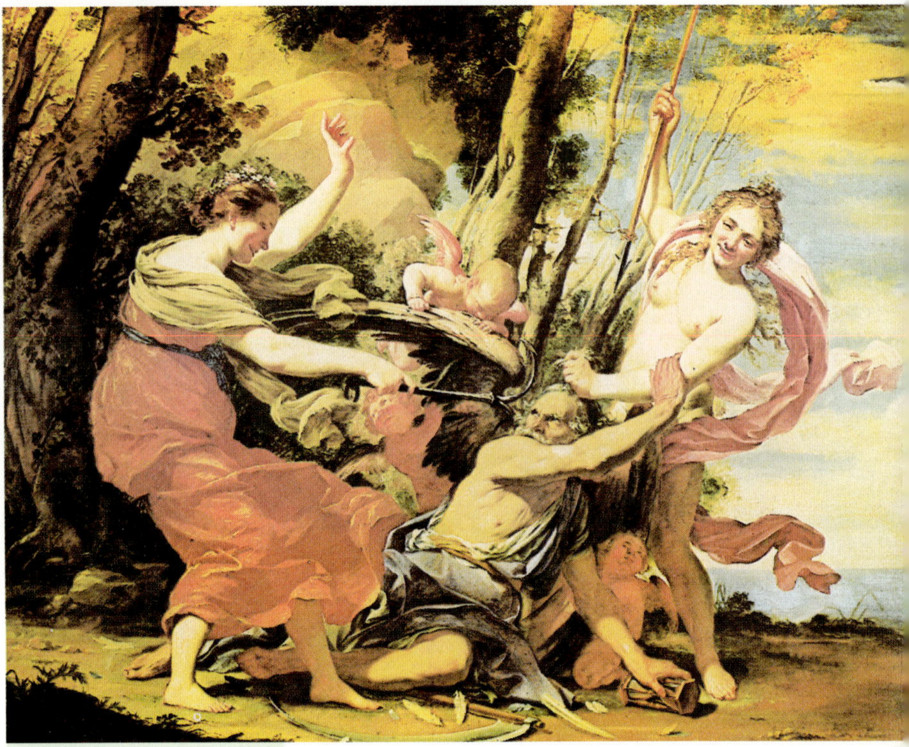

Time Defeated by Youth and Beauty

Simon Vouet
(Paris, 1590–1649)

- 1627
- oil on canvas
- 107 x 142 cm
- Museo del Prado, Madrid

Simon Vouet was one of the principal promoters of the French Academy, founded in 1648, a year before his death. His style was to exert a formative influence on official art during the reign of Louis XIV. The present work shows a treatment of light typical of Caravaggio, an intensely naturalistic depiction of anatomy reminiscent of Gentileschi and brilliant, light colors indebted to those of the Venetian School. These influences combine to form a highly individual style, notable for firmly rounded volumes and striking contrasts. The anatomy of the nude figure of Youth, with its smooth skin, for example, contrasts with that of Time, represented as an old man with leathery skin. The brilliance of the flesh tones and the bold modeling of the slightly androgynous female bodies contribute to the powerful sensuality of the painting.

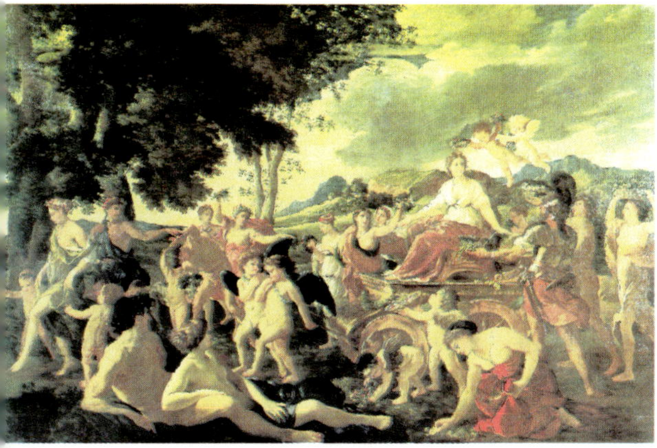

The Triumph of Flora

Nicolas Poussin

(Les Andelys, 1594–Rome, 1665)

- 1627
- oil on canvas
- 165 x 241 cm
- Musée du Louvre, Paris

Possibly painted for Cardinal Saccheti, the work was in the possession of Cardinal Omodei when acquired by Louis XIV in 1684.

In this canvas, Poussin has depicted a feast in honor of Flora, the goddess of flowers, in which poetry and something like Romanticism are delightfully combined. As befitted the feasts as they were held annually in honor of this goddess in ancient times, the present painting is a celebration of liberty, life and optimism.

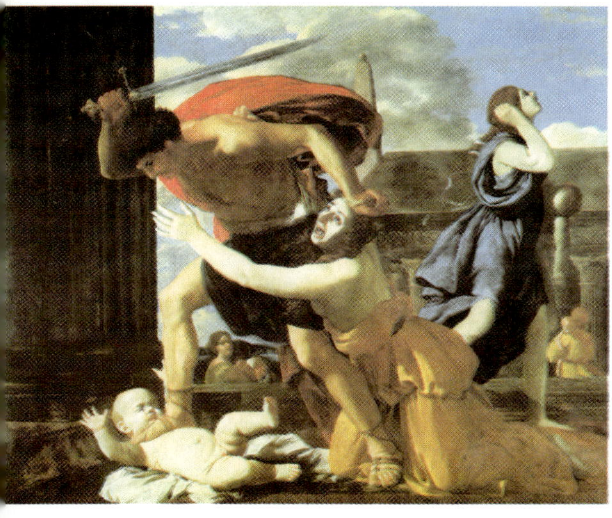

The Massacre of the Innocents

Nicolas Poussin

(Les Andelys, 1594–Rome, 1665)

- 1628–30
- oil on canvas
- 147 x 171 cm
- Musée Condé, Chantilly

The work belonged to various British collections as well as to the collections of the Marquis Vincenzo Giustiniani and of Lucien de Bonapart. It was acquired by the Duke of Aumale in London in 1854.

Bathed in clear, bright light, the figures are presented as a sculptural group against a darker architectural background. The soldier's cruelty, the mother's terror as she attempts to stop him, the distraction of another mother already bereft of her child, as of other fleeing mothers, come together here to compose a scene full of drama and horror.

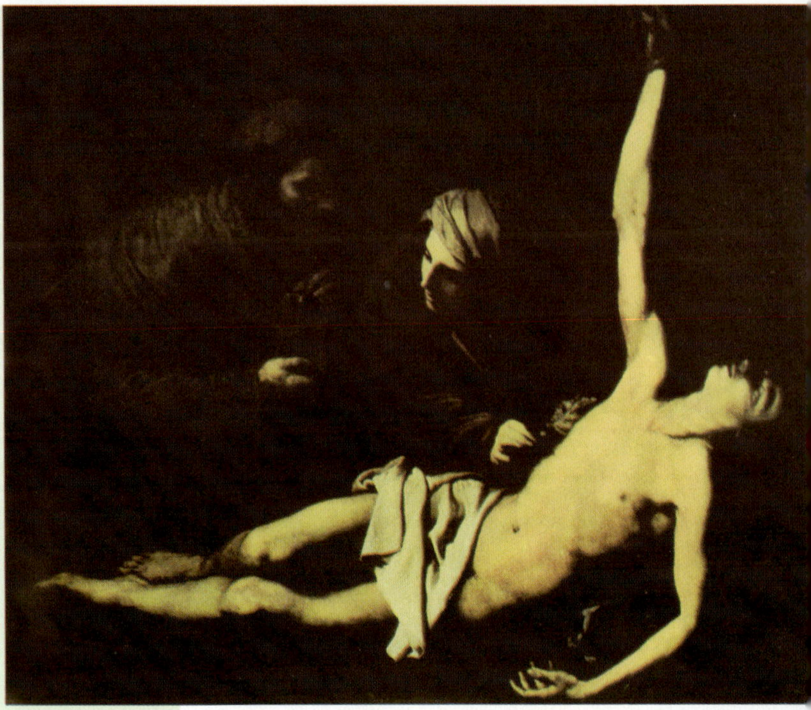

SS. Sebastian and Irene

José (Jusepe) de Ribera (called **Lo Spagnoletto**)
(Jàtiva, Spain, 1591 –Naples, 1652)

- 1628
- oil on canvas
- 156 x 188 cm
- Hermitage, St. Petersburg

This painting was acquired by the Museum in 1829 from the Duchess of Saint Lieu.

Sebastian, a Roman soldier who was converted to Christianity, was to suffer an agonizing death under Diocletian. As patron saint against the Plague, he was a very popular saint and was made the subject of many paintings, particularly in the 15th century, in which he appears as an attractive young man who is tied to a tree and pierced with numerous arrows. In the 17th century, his martyrdom was embellished by the legend of Irene, a wealthy widow who attempted to heal the martyr's wounds with the help of her assistant and who stood by him in his plight. The drama and solemnity of this moment are evoked in the striking contrast between the intense, dark colors of the painting, which almost completely engulf the figures of the two women, and the brightly lit body of St. Sebastian. The soft skin and effeminate forms of the young and slender martyr serve to underscore the his sensuality. The painting is a masterly combination of delicacy, lyricism and tragedy, with the body of the saint as its centerpiece.

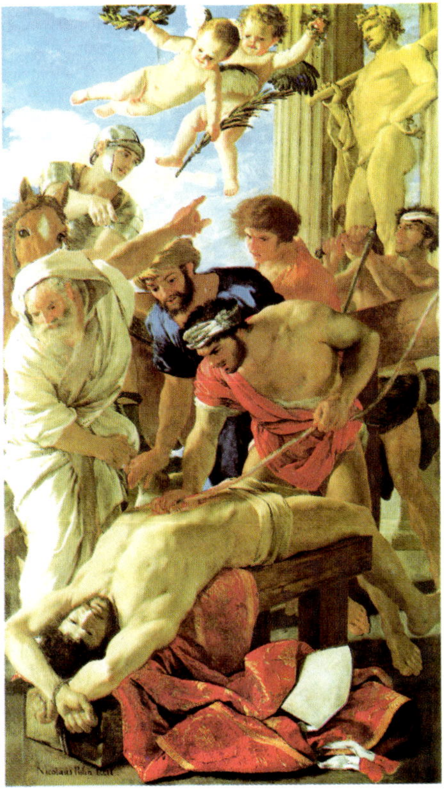

n Rome, Poussin achieved such renown as a painter of large-ormat religious themes that he was commissioned to execute aintings for nearly all the churches in the city. This work was ctually supposed to be carried out by Pietro da Cortona but, hanks to Casiano dal Pozzo and Cardinal Barberini, it was iven to Poussin instead. Perhaps it was for this reason that he work was received with indifference. Erasmus, bishop of ormiae in the Campagna, was arrested at the behest of iocletian and subjected to various types of torture, including isembowelment, as shown here. The nude evokes the work f Caravaggio in the treatment of light and in the way the ction has been conceived. The saint's body is boldly fore-hortened, which was the source of much criticism at the time. Although the painting can be ascribed to Baroque canons, it lso attests to the artist's interest in classicism, both in the reatment of the figure and of the picture as a whole.

The Martyrdom of St. Erasmus

Nicolas Poussin
(Les Andelys, 1594–Rome, 1665)

- 1628–29
- oil on canvas
- 320 x 186 cm
- Pinacoteca, Vatican

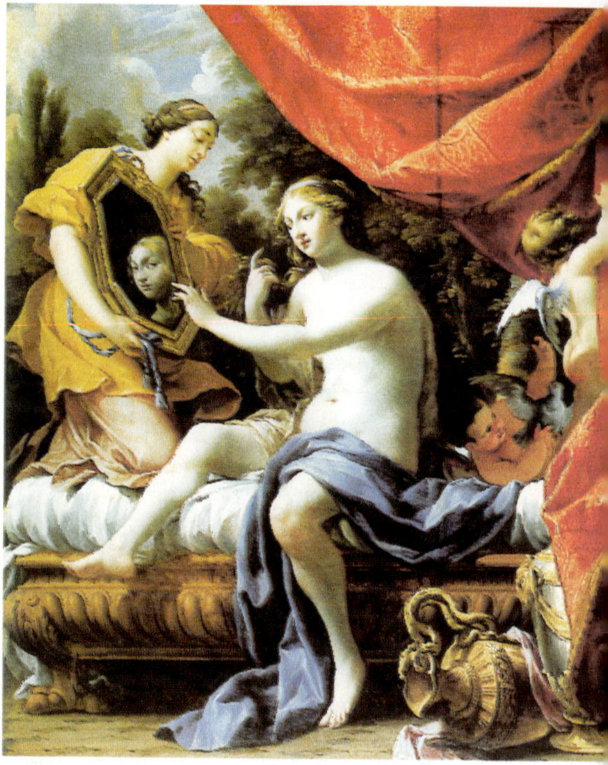

The Toilet of Venus

Simon Vouet
(Paris, 1590–1649)

- 1628–39
- oil on canvas
- 183.8 x 153 cm
- Cincinnati Art Museum, Cincinnati, OH

French Baroque art is marked by an academic style, of which Simon Vouet is a fine exponent. The artist's works, in keeping with court tastes and so-called official art, are a far cry from the vigorous painterly handling of the Baroque art of other countries. In this painting, Venus is not like the goddess at her toilet painted by contemporary artists—here, her beauty is cold, both in the treatment of the figure and in the palette. The pallid, marble-like flesh tones contrast with the crimson curtain, a preoccupation of the French Neoclassicists. A highly creative painter, who worked with great speed, Vouet's works were well received by the French court.

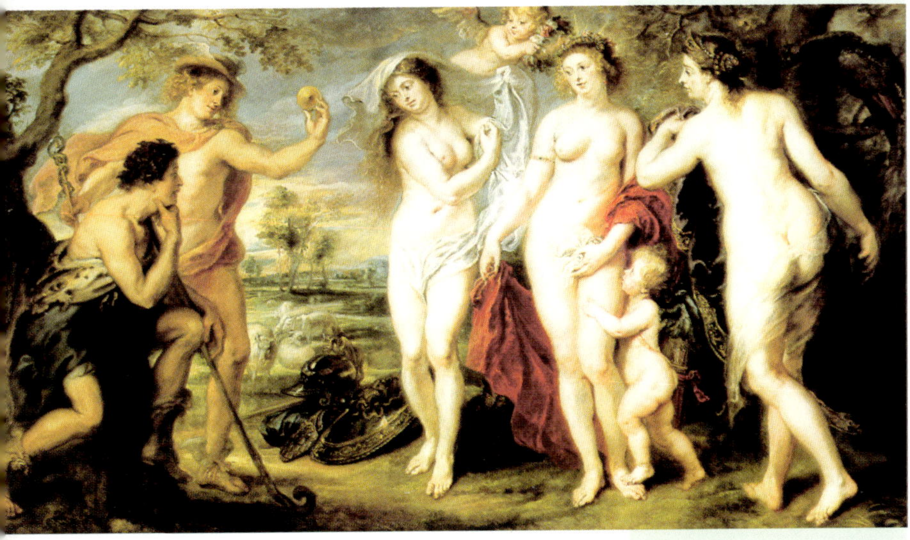

Zeus entrusted Paris with deciding who was the most beautiful goddess. Hera, Athena and Aphrodite attempted to bribe the unsuspecting mortal. Aphrodite, the goddess holding an apple, was victorious after promising Paris the love of the most beautiful woman, Helen, wife of the King of Sparta. This painting, inspired by an engraving by Marcantonio Raimondi, represents the goddesses with extraordinary beauty, their opulent rounded forms illuminated by a golden light. Only Rubens was capable of imbuing depictions of human flesh with this succulent quality. His image conveys the serenity of the Olympic deities with all the vibrancy of the Baroque style, the agitated brushwork of the modeling combining with the clearly articulated rhythm of the three nudes. According to the Infante Cardinal, brother of Philip IV of Spain and commissioner of the work, Aphrodite is a portrait of Rubens' wife and favorite sitter, Helena Fourment, who inspired many of his paintings.

The Judgment of Paris

Peter Paul Rubens
(Siegen, Westphalia, 1577–Antwerp, 1640)

- 1628–30
- oil on canvas
- 199 x 379 cm
- Museo del Prado, Madrid

War and Peace

Peter Paul Rubens
(Siegen, Westphalia, 1577–Antwerp, 1640)

- 1629
- oil on canvas
- 203.5 x 298 cm
- The National Gallery, London

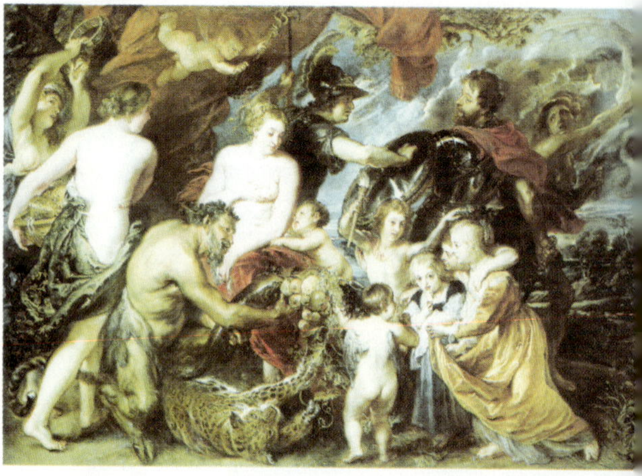

While on a diplomatic mission to negotiate peace between Spain and England, Rubens painted several works for the English king. War and Peace is one of the best. Minerva is portrayed here together with Mars, the god of war, and Horror, while Peace and Prosperity, pale-skinned and beautiful, fill the middle ground. Peace has a hand raised to her breast in readiness for suckling the nearby infant.

The Judgment of Paris

Francesco Albani
(Bologna, 1578–1660)

- oil on canvas
- 113 x 171 cm
- Museo de la Real Academia de Bellas Artes de San Fernando, Madrid

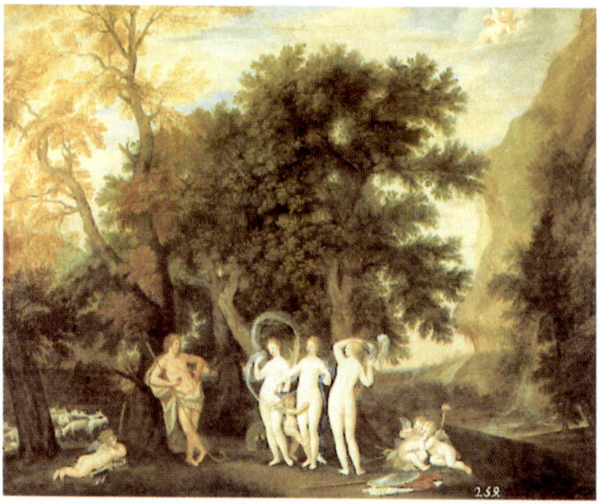

The painter of this work was held in high esteem during the 17th and 18th centuries. Once again, we see here a mythological theme providing the occasion for a painter to explore the nude human figure in a landscape setting. The present treatment is fresh, clean and poetic, and the figures are powerfully expressive.

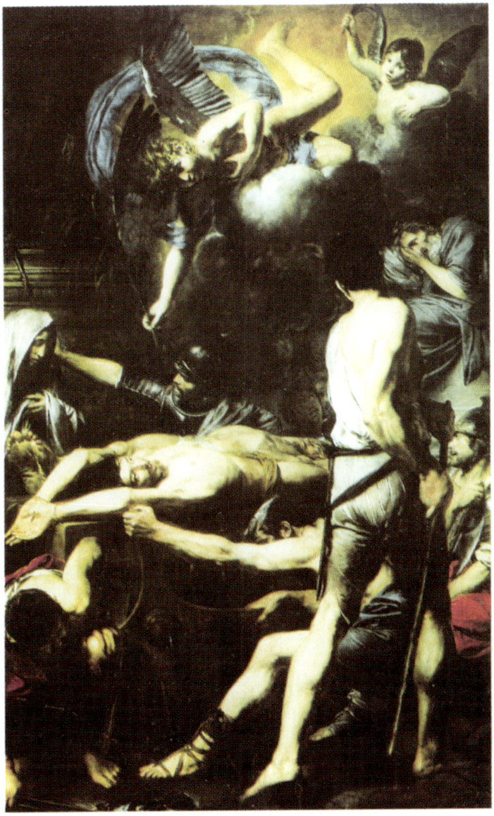

An interesting feature of this magnificent work, painted for St. Peter's in Rome as a pendant to Nicolas Poussin's Martyrdom of St. Erasmus, is the way the figures have been cut off to lend the painting greater realism. In his treatment of the figures, Le Valentin, a French Caravaggesque painter active in Rome, demonstrates that he is master draftsman and adept at employing central perspective by means of foreshortening. Yet the most extraordinary aspect of this painting is the artist's painterly handling of light, which, in addition to making the scene more dramatic, emphasizes painstakingly rendered muscles, recalling anatomical studies. The light also contributes to the modeling of the figures, which are rendered in a highly naturalistic manner.

Martyrdom of SS. Processus and Martinian

Moïse Valentin (Valentin de Boulogne, also called **Le Valentin)**
(Coulommiers en Brie, 1591–Rome, 1632)

- 1629–30
- oil on canvas
- 302 x 192 cm
- Pinacoteca, Vatican

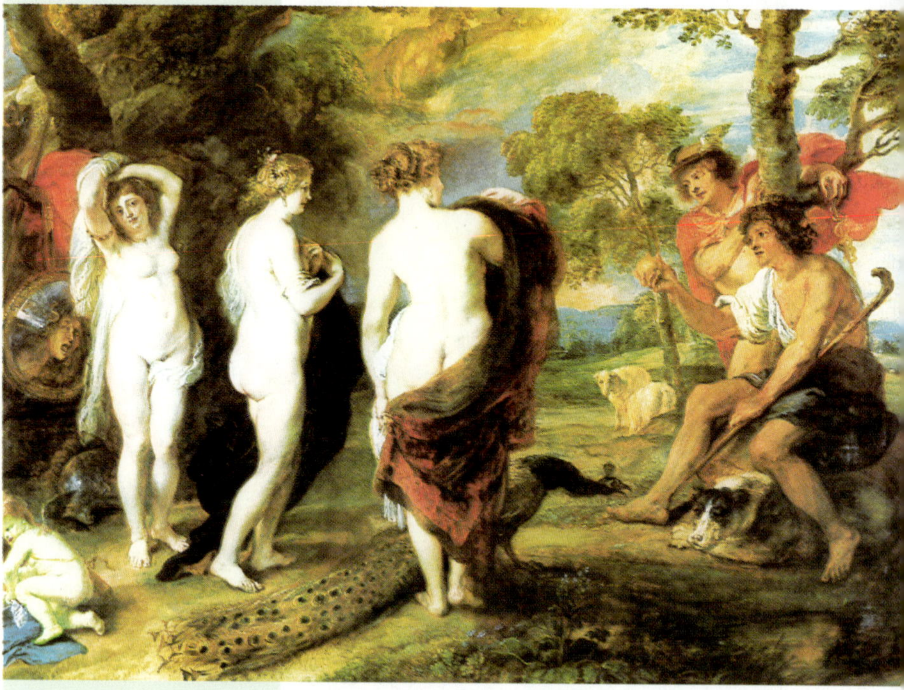

The Judgment of Paris

Peter Paul Rubens
(Siegen, Westphalia, 1577–Antwerp, 1640)

- 1632–35
- oil on panel
- 144.8 x 193.7 cm
- National Gallery, London

Jupiter asks Paris, a prince of Troy, to decide which of the three goddesses—Juno, Minerva or Venus—is the most beautiful and to award a golden apple "to the fairest." Paris is shown seated on the right, offering the apple to Venus, who has promised him the most beautiful woman in the world as his wife. The nudes appear in a sequence of movements in which the female body is shown from the front, side and back. All three figures were based on the same model. They are graceful and sculptural, with subtle modeling and blue and green flesh tones, which accentuate their pale complexions. The almost mother-of-pearl color of the three bodies contrasts with the background and they are brightly illuminated, making them the focal point of the scene. Behind Paris appears Mercury, Jupiter's messenger, who observes the action, while Cupid plays in the left foreground, secure in the knowledge that his mother, Venus, will be chosen.

Allegory of Rome

Valentin de Boulogne
(Coulommiers, 1594
–Rome, 1632)

- ca. 1630
- oil on canvas
- Institutum Romanum, Finland

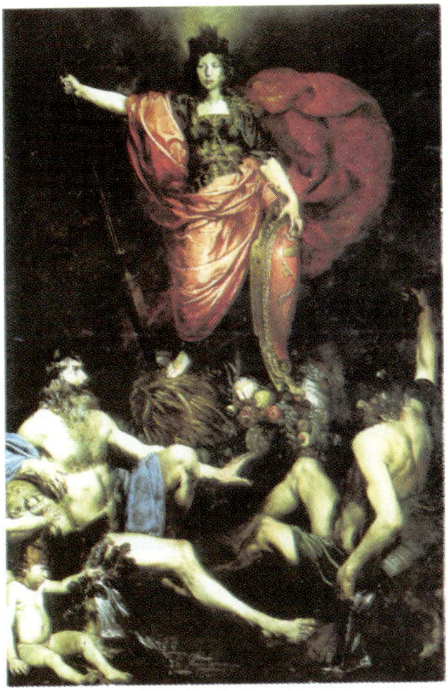

The nude personification of the River Tiber in this tenebrist canvas is remarkable. Unlike many traditional representations, this one shows a mature man, with hirsute chest and bodily features appropriate to his age. The great dignity and physical strength he nevertheless retains are due in large part to the dark background his figure has been placed against.

The Exposing of Moses

Nicolas Poussin
(Les Andelys, 1594–Rome, 1665)

- ca. 1630
- oil on canvas
- 146 x 196 cm
- Gemäldegalerie, Dresden

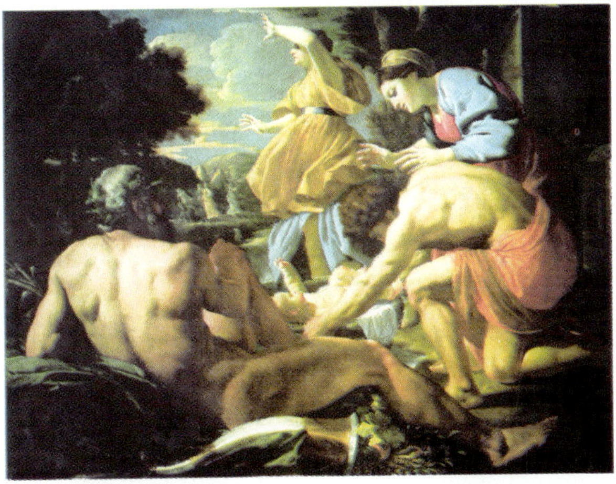

When Pharaoh ordered the killing of all the Hebrew, male, new-born children, the wife of a man of the house of Levi, having just given birth to a boy, took her son and laid him in an ark of bulrushes and placed him in the reeds beside the River Nile. The nude male figure in the foreground is a personification of the river. Near his right thigh lies a large cornucopia. His powerful body has been treated in the manner of a Classical sculpture.

Abel's Sacrifice

Charles Mellin
(1600–1649)

- ca. 1630
- oil on canvas
- Musée Historique Lorrain, Nancy

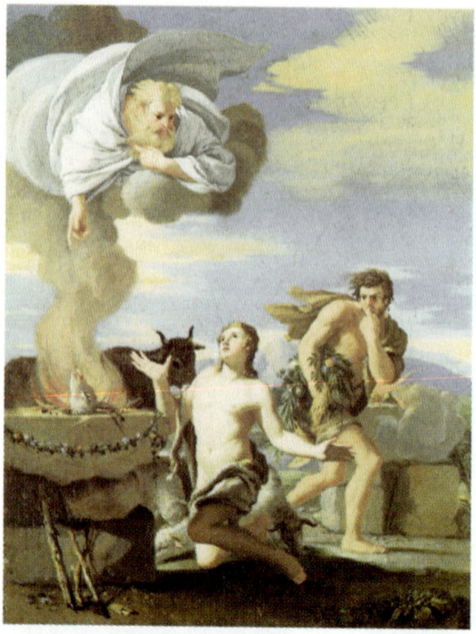

When Cain offered up his best crops to God, and Abel sacrificed his best lamb, God accepted the latter's and rejected Cain's offering. Abel's beautiful nude figure as depicted here, in contrast to that of Cain, is feminine in facial features, gestures and complexion, its sensual aspects heightened yet further by the sheepskin that is about to fall away from his loins.

The Birth of Venus

Peter Paul Rubens
(Siegen, Westphalia, 1577 –Antwerp, 1640)

- ca. 1630
- ink and grisaille on panel
- 61 x 78 cm
- The National Gallery, London

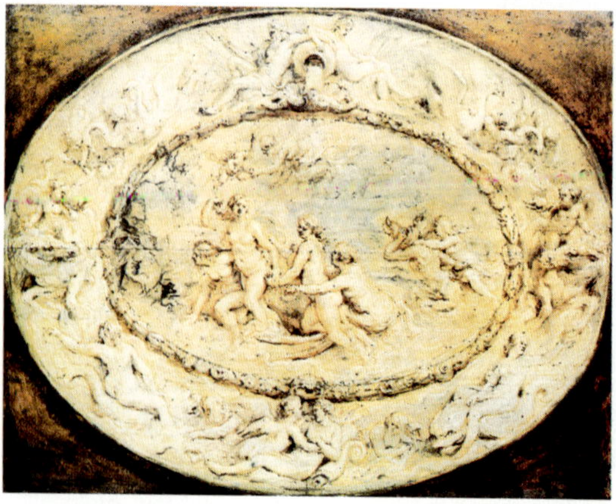

Rubens, here, depicts Venus' arrival at the island of Cythera shortly after being born from the sea. She is accompanied by Aeolus, her son, Cupid, and various Nereids. The work attests to Rubens' extraordinary skill in drawing the human body.

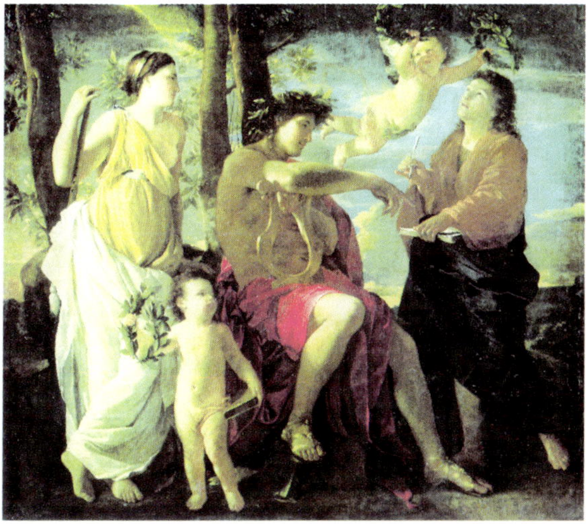

The Inspiration of the Epic Poet

Nicolas Poussin
(Les Andelys, 1594–Rome, 1665)

- ca. 1630
- oil on canvas
- 182 x 213 cm
- Musée du Louvre, Paris

'he inspiration for this work came ultimately from Classical terature, something that Poussin was very skilled in transnitting to canvas. A muse accompanies Apollo who, semiıude, guides the poet's hand. Hardly any points of light ctually reach his body, the surfaces of which are treated ıs flat color masses, although a certain amount of modeling till manages to suggest corporeality.

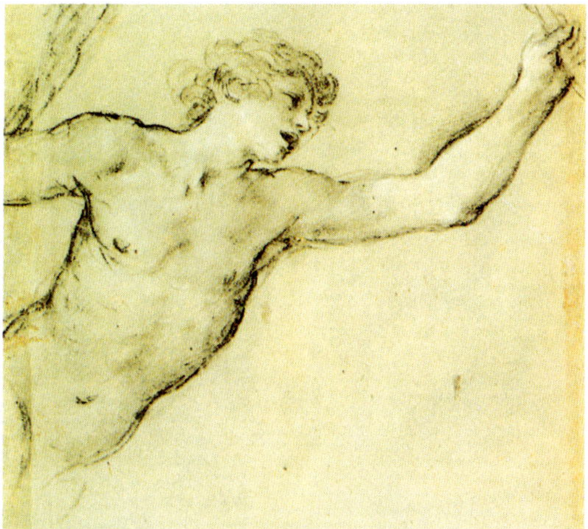

Study of a Young Man

Pietro da Cortona (Pietro Berrettini)
(Cortona, 1596–Rome, 1669)

- ca. 1630
- sepia on paper
- drawing collection, Galleria degli Uffizi, Florence

ıterest in naturalistic representations of the human body rew throughout the 17th century. This nude torso of a handome youth strives, if not without moral undertones, to delinate the perfections as well as the defects of the human form.

Pietà

Anthony van Dyck
(Antwerp, 1599–London, 1641)

- ca. 1630
- oil on canvas
- 135 x 208 cm
- Koninklijk Museum voor Schone Kunsten, Antwerp

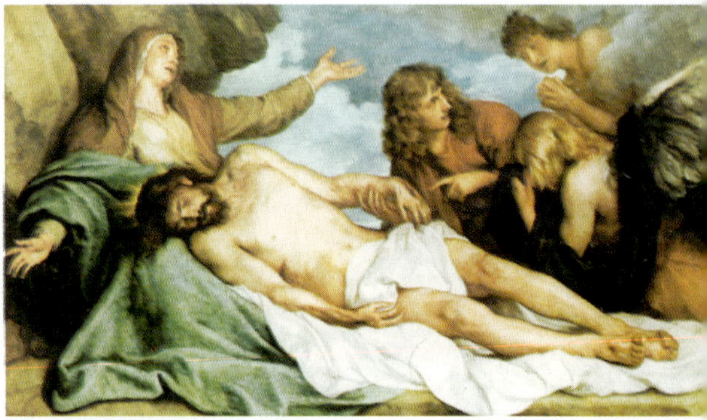

The painting belongs to a period in the artist's career when he was receiving many commissions from the various churches. Dignity, grace and pathos are expressed in this body of Christ.

Pietà

Anthony van Dyck
(Antwerp, 1599–London, 1641)

- ca. 1630
- oil on canvas
- 303 x 225 cm
- Koninklijk Museum voor Schone Kunsten, Antwerp

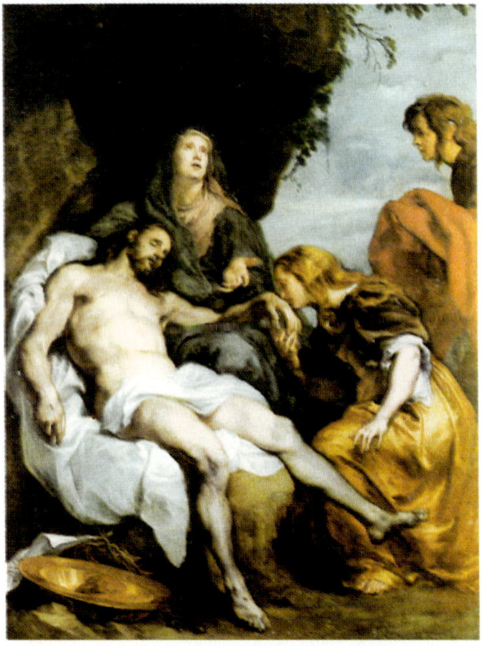

Although a disciple of Rubens, van Dyck's style is far less elaborate, and is more delicate and discreet in its treatment of sensuality. The nude body of Christ lacks all but the faintest traces of physical suffering and has been portrayed with consummate care. Dignity and devotion pervade the scene.

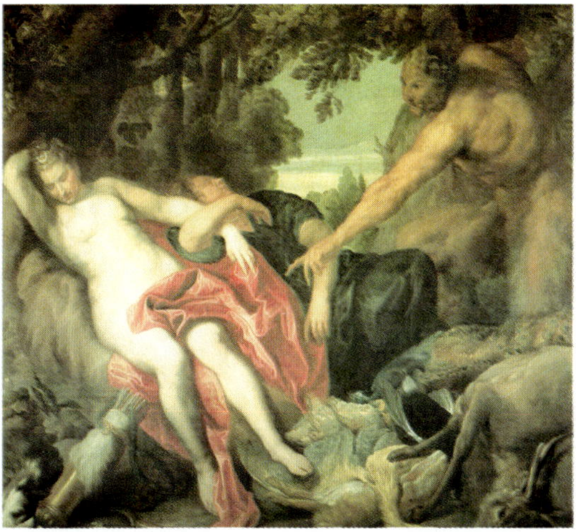

Diana and Endymion

Anthony van Dyck
(Antwerp, 1599–London, 1641)

- ca. 1630
- oil on canvas
- 144 x 163 cm
- Museo del Prado, Madrid

his work identifies Diana with Selene, whose relationship ith the handsome youth Endymion issued in fifty daughters. ndymion asked Zeus to be allowed to sleep forever in order remain eternally young. Selene displays her charms, oblivius to the satyr's attentions, accentuating the eroticism of the cene. This nude's abundant and powerful flesh, while inclinng towards plumpness, nevertheless defines a shapely, not to ay heroic, body.

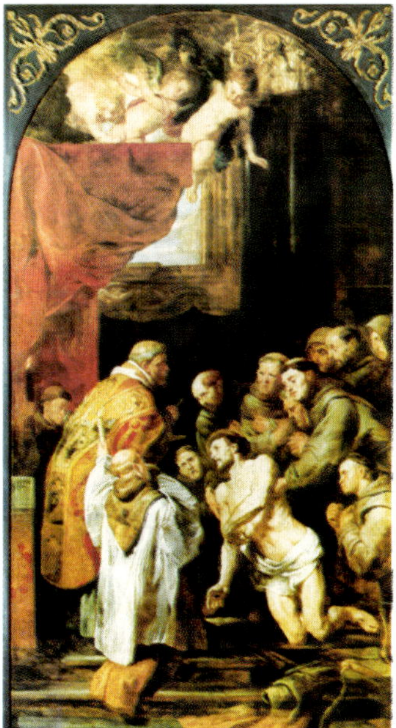

The Last Holy Communion of St. Francis

Peter Paul Rubens
(Seigen, Westphalia, 1577–Antwerp, 1640)

- oil on canvas
- 422 x 226 cm
- Koninklijk Museum voor Schone Kunsten, Antwerp

eep sadness and pirituality pervade this ork, despite the Baroque umptuousness, which is resent in all its splendor.

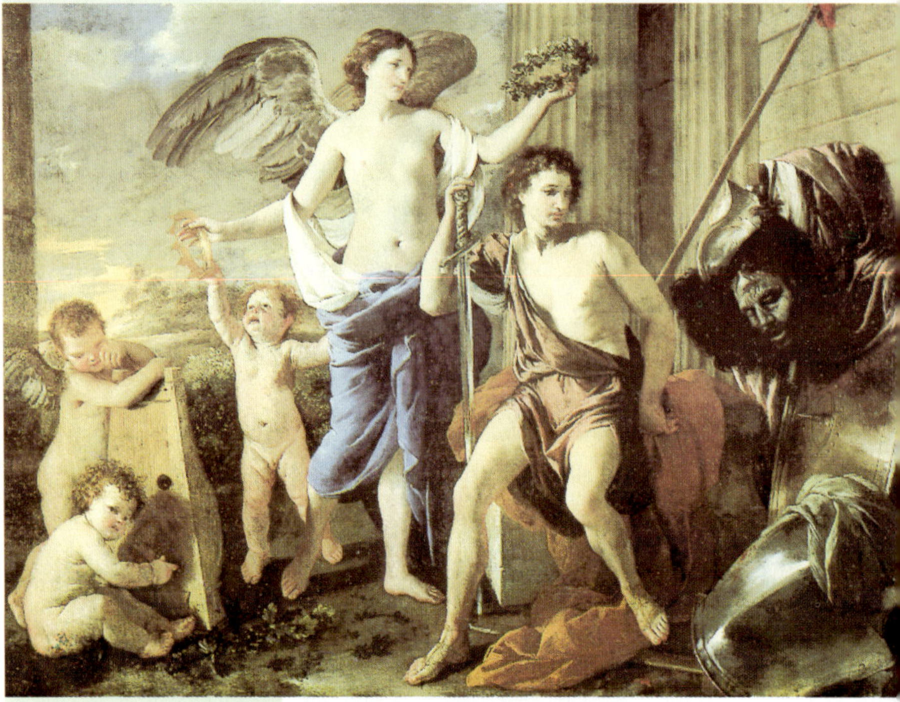

The Triumph of David

Nicolas Poussin
(Les Andelys, 1594 –Rome, 1665)

- ca. 1630
- oil on canvas
- 100 x 130 cm
- Museo del Prado, Madrid

The biblical theme depicted here is combined with mythological elements, such as the putti, which evoke certain reliefs by François Duquesnoy, or the Classical figure of Victory. The painting shows a young David who, after having vanquished Goliath, contemplates the giant's head, which he has just severed, while being crowned by the allegorical figure, who is rendered in the most undiluted Classical style. Victory, who is sexually ambiguous, evokes Roman friezes, although feminine forms predominate, especially in the hips. The figure of David is that of a hero, albeit in a somewhat rigid pose, compared with the expressive plasticity of the children, exhibiting a dynamic naturalism. In this work, the artist's treatment of light is indebted to that of Caravaggio, although without the dramatization typical of the Italian painter's work and in a more restrained style.

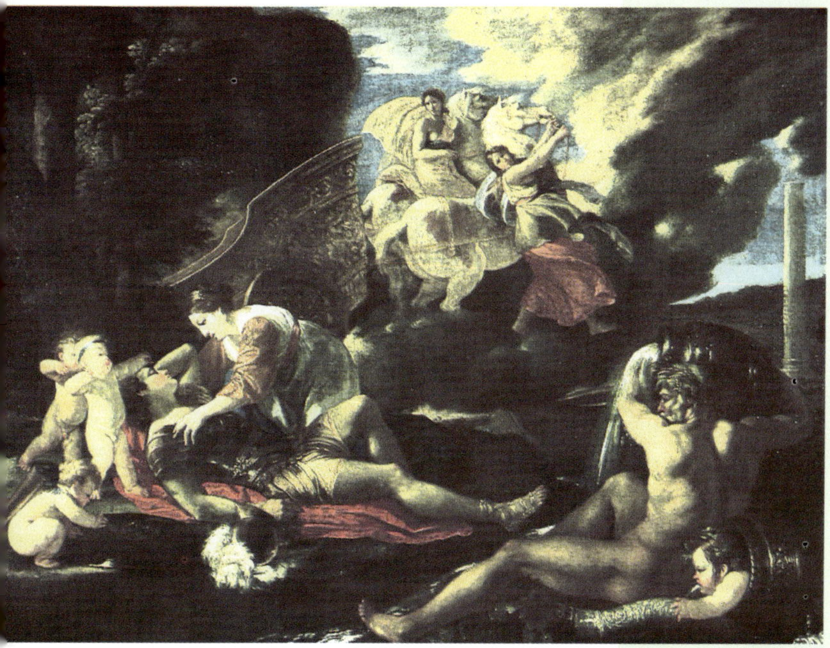

Rinaldo and Armida

Nicolas Poussin

(Les Andelys, 1594–Rome, 1665)

- 1630
- oil on canvas
- 95 x 113 cm
- Pushkin Museum, Moscow

ɔllowing a fierce struggle between the powers of the under-ɔrld, the sorcerer Hidraot asks Armida, an exceedingly ɘautiful woman possessing the cunning of a witch, to go the military camp of the soldiers besieging Jerusalem and put one of them, Rinaldo, under a spell. As can be seen this work, he succumbs to her irresistible charms. Poussin ainted this scene during a period in which he embraced ɘrtain conventions of the day. The nude on the left is an egory of Water, while the figure of an old man on the right, own pouring water from a bottomless vessel, personifies a ver. This extraordinary anatomical study recalls the figures Michelangelo in the Sistine Chapel, although Poussin ɔdeled his figures with dark hues, which contrast with the d drapery, lending his figures a highly sculptural quality. though the work has a mid-sized format, it conveys the ɔnumentality of the artist's larger compositions.

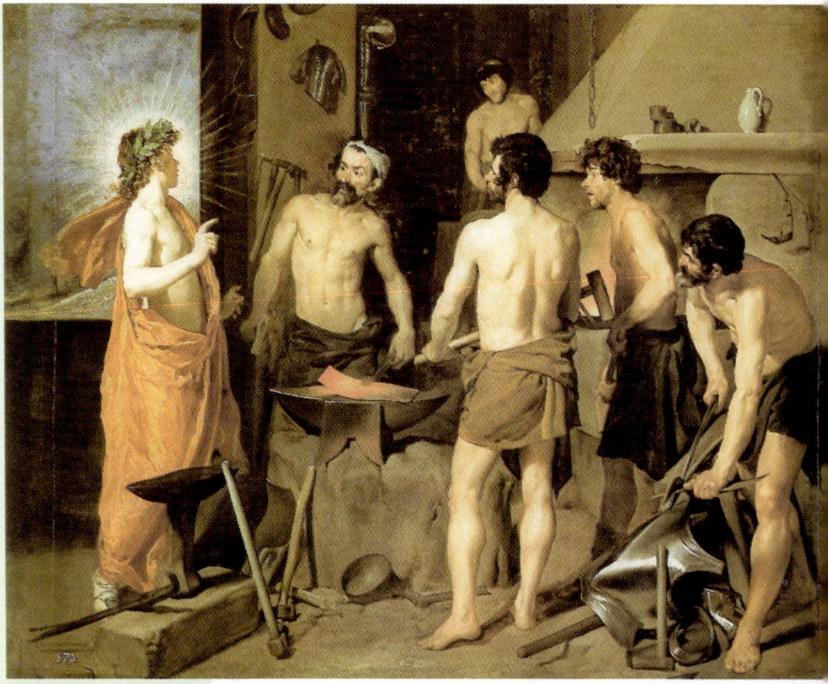

The Forge of Vulcan

Diego Rodríguez de Silva y Velázquez
(Seville, 1599–Madrid, 1660)

- 1630
- oil on canvas
- 223 x 290 cm
- Museo del Prado, Madrid

Apollo, depicted here as a somewhat androgynous youth, is smooth-skinned and of delicate build, his head crowned with laurel leaves and a radiant halo. Vulcan, consort of Venus, is holding an incandescent strip of iron on an anvil and listening as Apollo informs him of his wife's adultery with Mars, for whom the smiths are making a suit of armor. The painting deviates from existing versions of the legend, but provides Velázquez with subject matter of great flexibility and compositional beauty. Each of the smiths is interesting in his own right: the smith with his back to the viewer recalls ancient Classical statuary; the smith on the right is prodigiously dynamic and mobile; the smith whose profile we see is unkempt and wears an expression of surprise. Velázquez gave the painting two chief points of light and animated the whole with numerous details, such as the luminous halo of the god against the blue sky, the incandescent iron, the fire in the chimney and the small ceramic vase.

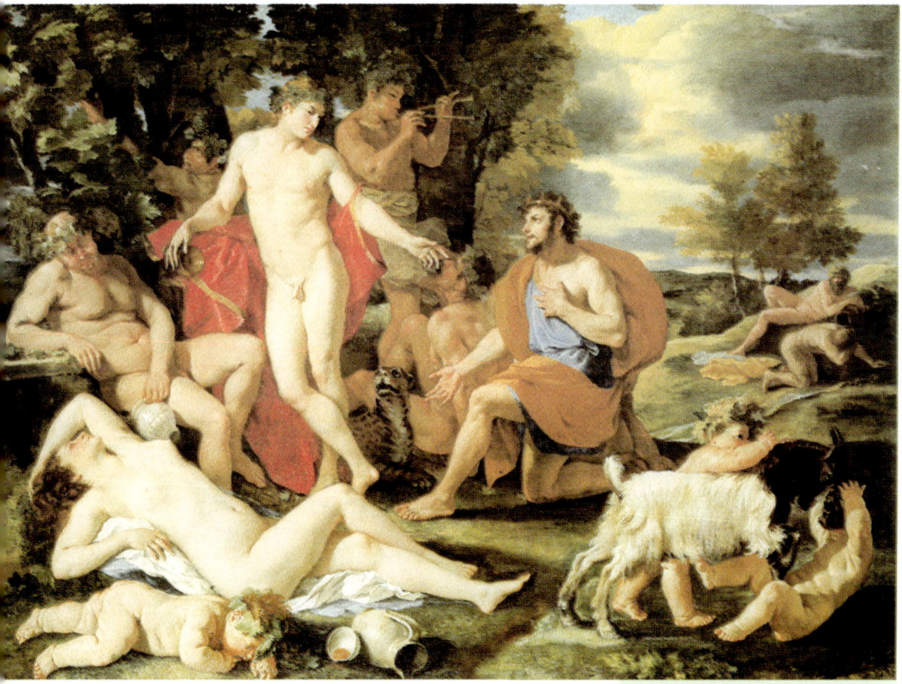

Midas and Bacchus

Nicolas Poussin
(Les Andelys, 1594 –Rome, 1665)

- ca. 1630
- oil on canvas
- 98 x 153 cm
- Alte Pinakothek, Munich

ɿis work illustrates a story from Ovid's Metamorphoses. It lls how Bacchus granted Midas the power to turn all that ɘ touched into gold. When he realized that even his food ' drink were being transformed into the precious metal, ɘ begged the god to be returned to his previous state, as ɘ was hungry and thirsty. Bacchus did so by telling him to ash in the Pactolus River, which henceforth was rich in ɔld dust and nuggets. In this scene, Poussin shows the oment when Midas is thanking the god for saving him. ıe style of the figures is indebted to the sculpture of lassical Antiquity. The great naturalism and sensuality of s nudes is achieved through their anatomy, poses and ›sh tones. The body of Bacchus and that of the woman clining in the foreground are remarkably beautiful.

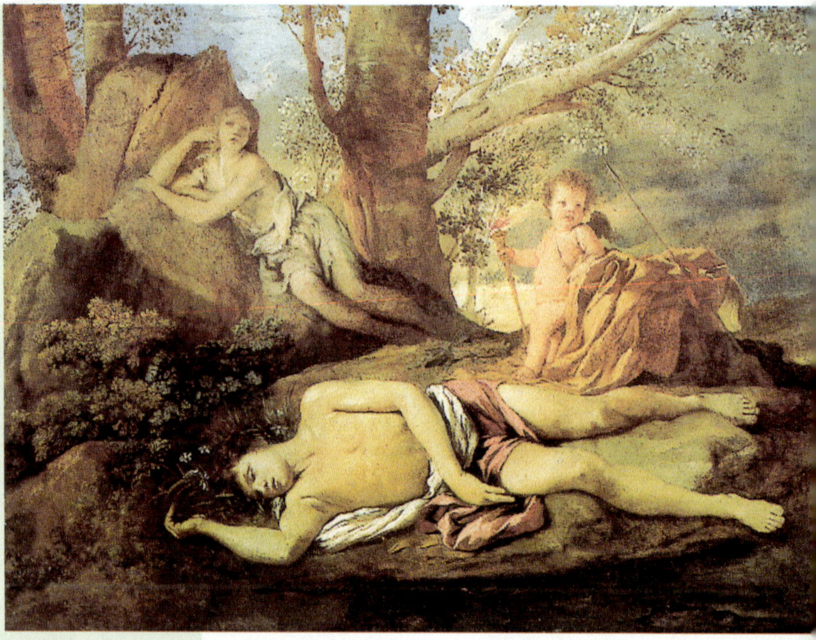

Echo and Narcissus (The Death of Narcissus)

Nicolas Poussin
(Les Andelys, 1594 –Rome, 1665)

- 1627–28
- oil on canvas
- 74 x 100 cm
- Musée du Louvre, Paris

Echo was enamoured of the beautiful Narcissus, who rejecte the love of all women. When she realized that she could not win his heart, Echo retired to a solitary place in the woods ar was turned to stone. Only her echoing voice remained. The goddess Nemesis, who personified retribution, became angr and decided to punish Narcissus by making him look at his own reflection in a river. He found himself to be so beautiful that he fell in love with himself and died lost in the contempla tion of his own image. In the place where he died, the flower named after him was born. In this work, Narcissus is portrayed dead, with Cupid behind him and petrified Echo in the background. Narcissus, whose body is slightly foreshortened reclines near the water's edge. Although the well-proportione youth is not athletic in build, he is not as sexually ambiguous as the figures of many other artists. Poussin has presented a scene that resembles a stage set. The figures' poses eschev any suggestion of movement and the love of the two protago nists finds expression in the warm colors of the scene.

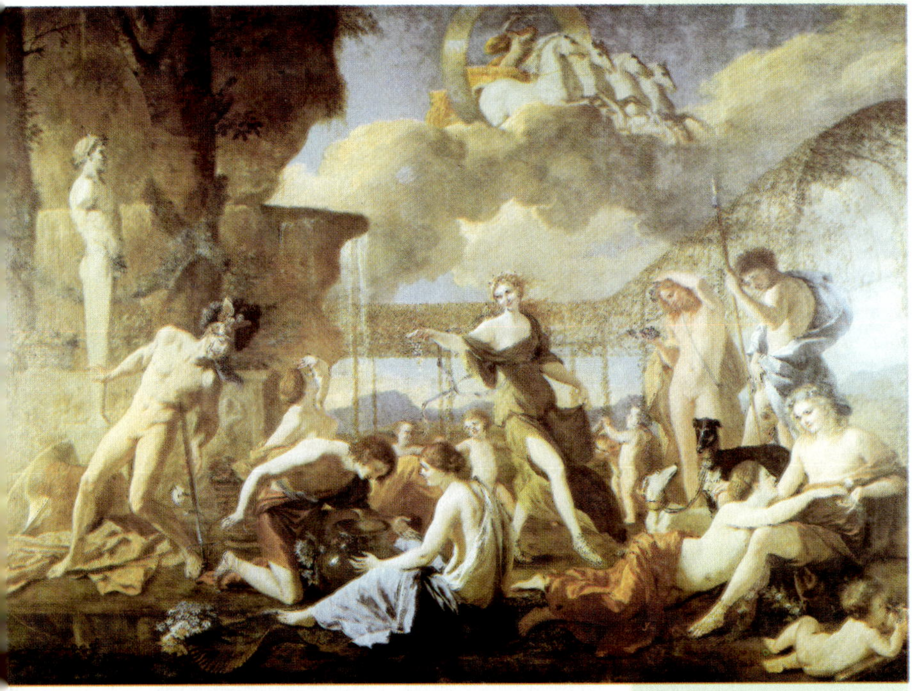

This work pays homage to the Roman goddess Flora, in whose honor the Ludi Florales (Floral Games), or Floralia, were held every year in Rome in April–May. The artist composed the painting such that the figures are more or less symmetrically arranged, and the background includes various architectural and natural elements, even apparitions. This creates a fitting atmosphere, which is animated by the figures' dynamic poses and the vitality and joy conveyed by the young bodies, emphasizing the happy side of life, just as the Roman festival did. In representations of this nature, Poussin achieves, like few others, extraordinary results indeed. In any case, not all the works of this artist convey such optimism.

Flora's Empire

Nicolas Poussin
(Les Andelys, 1594
–Rome, 1665)

- ca. 1630
- oil on canvas
- 131 x 181 cm
- Gemäldegalerie, Dresden

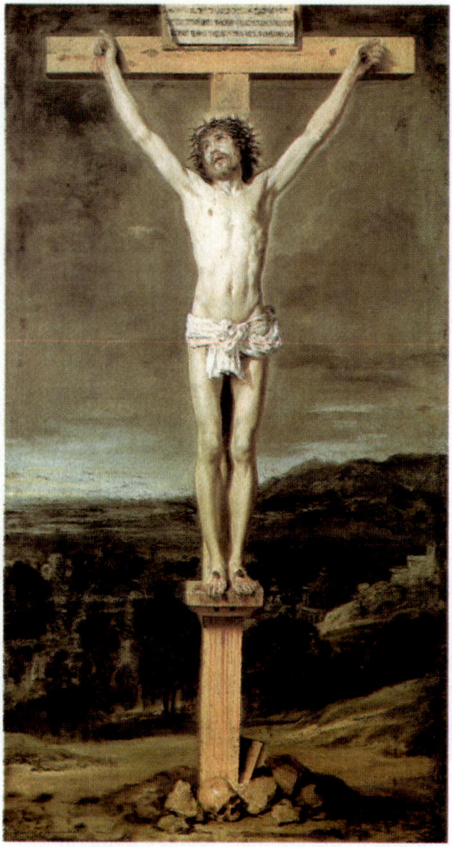

Christ on the Cross

Diego Rodríguez de Silva y Velázquez
(Seville, 1599–Madrid, 1660)

- 1631
- oil on canvas
- 100 x 57 cm
- Museo del Prado, Madrid

This is one of the few works that the artist ever signed and dated, and while it is highly sophisticated, it is not obviously in Velázquez's established style, especially when one bears in mind the dramatic facial expression, at once pathetic and desperate. The position of the arms, rather close to one another, gives the figure an imploring aspect and increases the tension of the picture. The background is dark to bring out the body: a sky of gray clouds, as documented by scripture, and a dark landscape with profuse vegetation and some buildings; by way of contrast, the horizon is defined by a clear sky. Planted in the ground, the Cross is held tight by a small wedge and a mound of stones. The skull in the foreground symbolizes the Redemption through Christ's death of the sin of Adam, which brought death into the world.

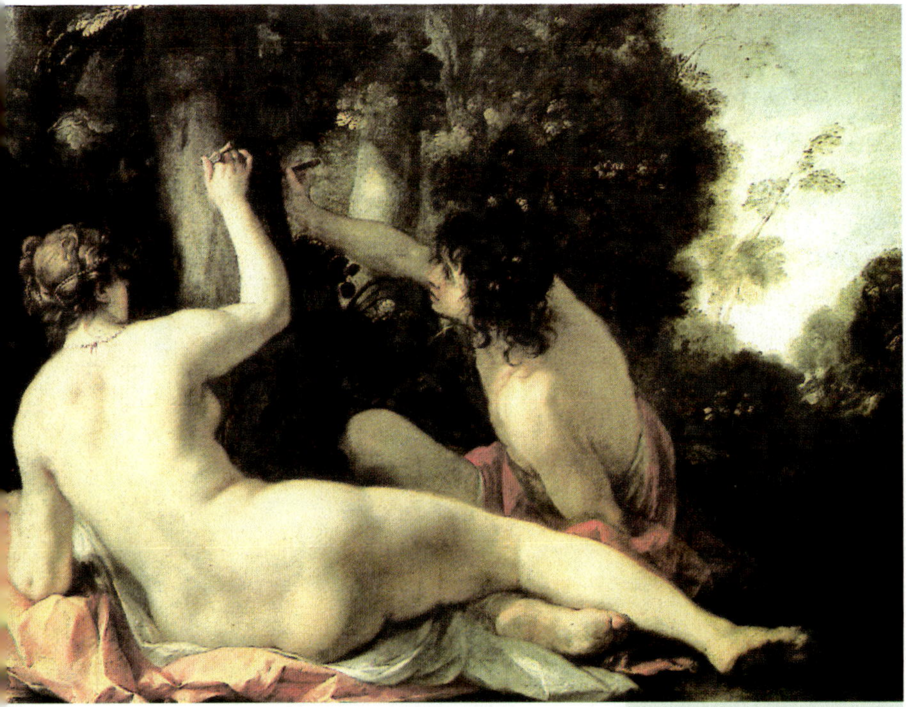

The beautiful, seductive and fickle Angelica, Queen of Cathay, was brought to Europe by her lover, Orlando. After having fallen in love with Medoro, a young Saracen soldier, she returns with him to his country, where he is crowned king, to Orlando's ire. The pose of the two lovers is singular indeed, and Angelica is portrayed as a normal woman, with a voluptuous body and her back to the spectator. Medoro, younger than Orlando, is portrayed with a youthful face and a sensual torso. The subjects are shown carving their names into the trunk of a tree with a knife. The artist has placed the lovers in a forest, giving the scene an intimate, bucolic setting. The artist's style reflects Baroque developments in Rome and the sensuous richness of Venetian painting in the clarity of the colors, the dramatic contrasts obtained with shadows and the iridescent light.

Angelica and Medoro

Jacques Blanchard
(Paris, 1600–1638)

- 1631–33
- oil on canvas
- 121.5 x 176 cm
- Metropolitan Museum of Art, New York

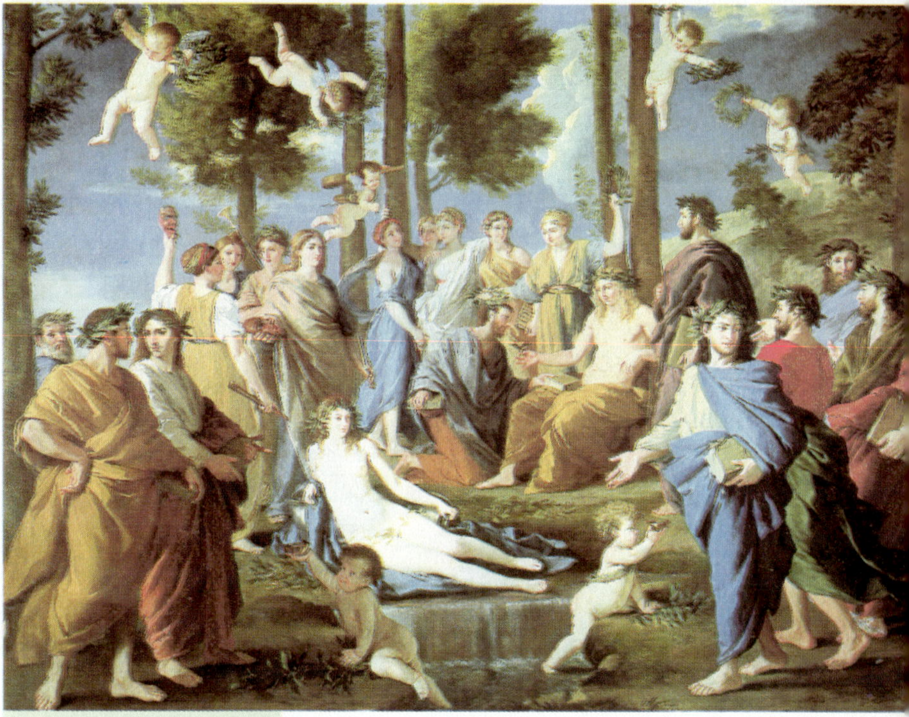

Mount Parnassus

Nicolas Poussin
(Les Andelys, 1594–Rome, 1665)

- 1631–33
- oil on canvas
- 145 x 197 cm
- Museo del Prado, Madrid

From the Spanish royal collection, probably acquired by Philip V.

This profoundly Classical work contains two nudes. An artist notable for his intellectual stringency, Poussin banished any hint of sensuality from these figures. Their bodies, Classical in pose and anatomy, are rendered in dispassionately descriptive terms, flawless in their draftsmanship. The artist is interested not in eroticism but in the literary background to his depiction of Parnassus, the home of the Muses in Classical mythology. His style here recalls Raphael's paintings in the Vatican Stanze's apartments, while the cherubs and spring in the foreground pays homage to Titian's Bacchanal. Poussin deprives the naked figures of their sensuality by giving them a hieratic appearance and by playing down their curves.

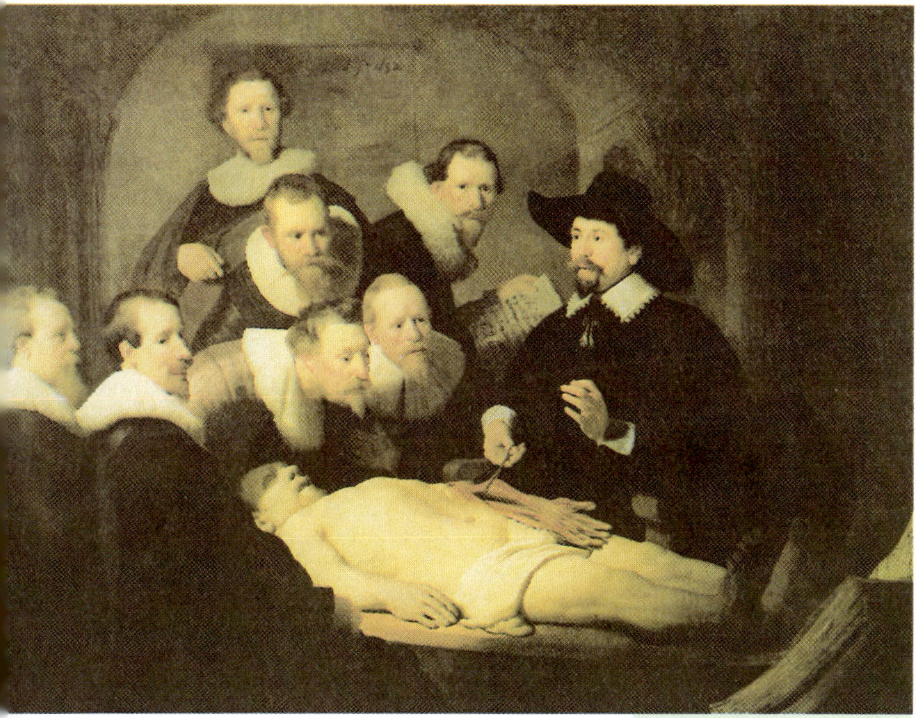

Anatomy Lesson of Dr. Tulp

Rembrandt (Rembrandt Harmensz van Rijn)
(Leiden, 1606–Amsterdam, 1669)

- 1632
- oil on canvas
- 169.5 x 216.6 cm
- Mauritshuis, The Hague

When the dissection of corpses ceased to be a criminal offence in the Netherlands, Dr. Tulp gave a public anatomy lesson, using the dead body of a criminal. The city's guild of surgeons commissioned the painting to record the event. The style of the painting is characteristic of the artist's early work, and represents one of the best depictions of a corpse ever to be painted. The rigor mortis of the figure leaves no room for doubt: the artist must have witnessed the scene first-hand. He presents the corpse by means of bold foreshortening so as not to detract from the group of surgeons; however, it is so bright that it invariably becomes the focus of the painting. The skin of the cadaver is an opaque yellow, devoid of warmer colors. The dead body provides a considerable amount of information: how long the person had been dead, the state of the body's preservation at the morgue and, to a certain extent, the kinds of experiment that were then carried out on corpses.

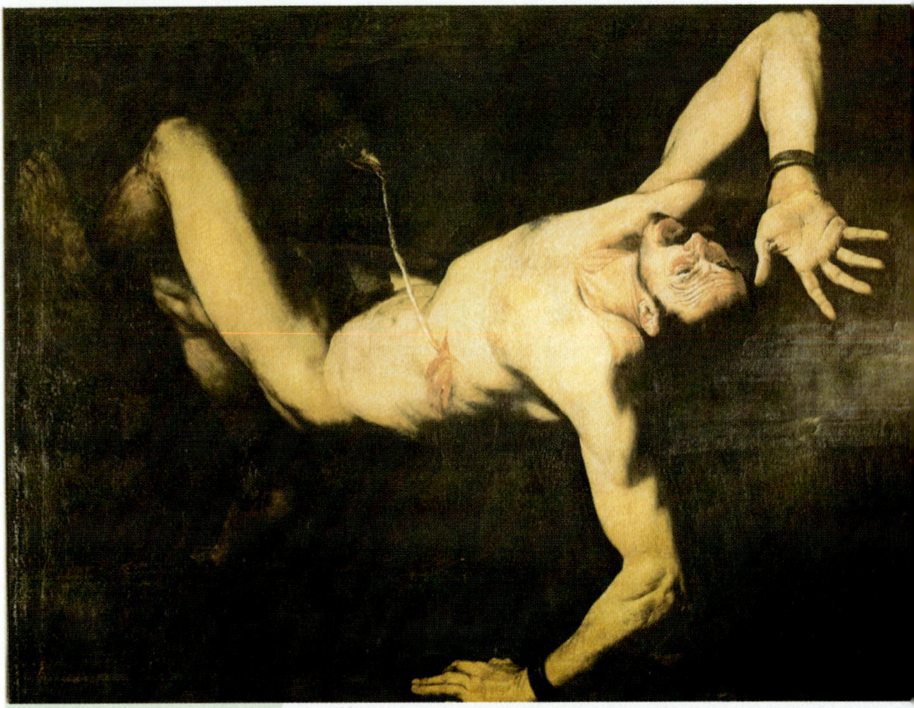

Tityus

José (Jusepe) de Ribera (called **Lo Spagnoletto**)
(Jàtiva, Spain, 1591 –Naples, 1652)

- 1632
- oil on canvas
- 227 x 301 cm
- Museo del Prado, Madrid

Tityus, the giant, was the product of Zeus' seduction of Elare behind his wife Hera's back. As punishment for having attempted to rape Leto, mother of Apollo and Artemis, Tityus was bound to the ground in Tartarus, where a pair of vultures, or two serpents, according to another version of the story, eternally pecked at his liver. Ulysees, upon seeing him, was surprised at how large he was, for he occupied nine acres of land. This painting by Ribera is highly dramatic, revealing a certain liberty the artist has taken in his interpretation of the story. Here, a large cow is included instead of the animals mentioned in the legend. The body, articulated in a brilliant display of chiaroscuro, shows a muscular man in an exaggeratedly dramatic pose, a result of the torture to which he is being subjected. The realism of Ribera's nudes is remarkable in the way they reveal such details as age and physical condition, making them perfect anatomical studies. The modeling of the shadows evokes tense muscles as well as wrinkles and folds.

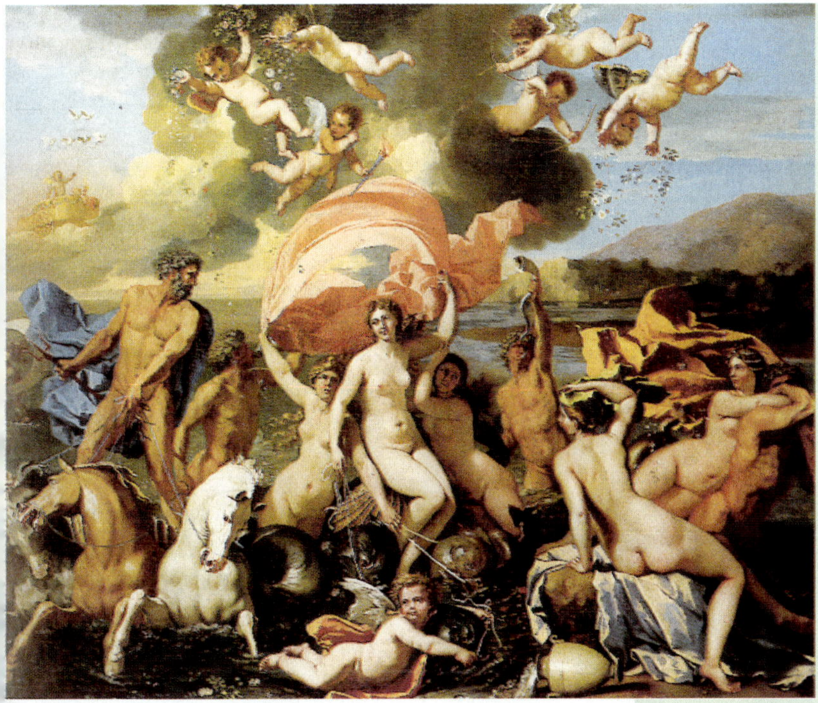

The influence of Titian and Raphael (The Triumph of Galatea) is evident in this painting, which was executed in a classicist aesthetic appropriate to a mythological theme. The scene is set in an idealized landscape presided over by Amphitrite, goddess of the sea, surrounded by an entourage of nymphs, tritons and cherubs, and by Neptune, god of the sea, mounted on his marine steeds. All the figures are nude and are shown in a variety of contorted poses suggesting movement. The billowing cloth, the vibrant colors and dramatic setting give rise to a painting of great dynamism. The artist was clearly influenced by Italian art (he lived in Rome for several years), which can be observed in the nudes, who recall some of the greatest figures in Renaissance art. They are vigorous and sensual, strike daring and elegant poses, and exude a heroic, monumental air.

The Triumph of Neptune and Amphitrite

Nicolas Poussin

(Les Andelys, 1594 –Rome, 1665)

- 1634
- oil on canvas
- 114.5 x 146.6 cm
- Philadelphia Museum of Art, Philadelphia, PA

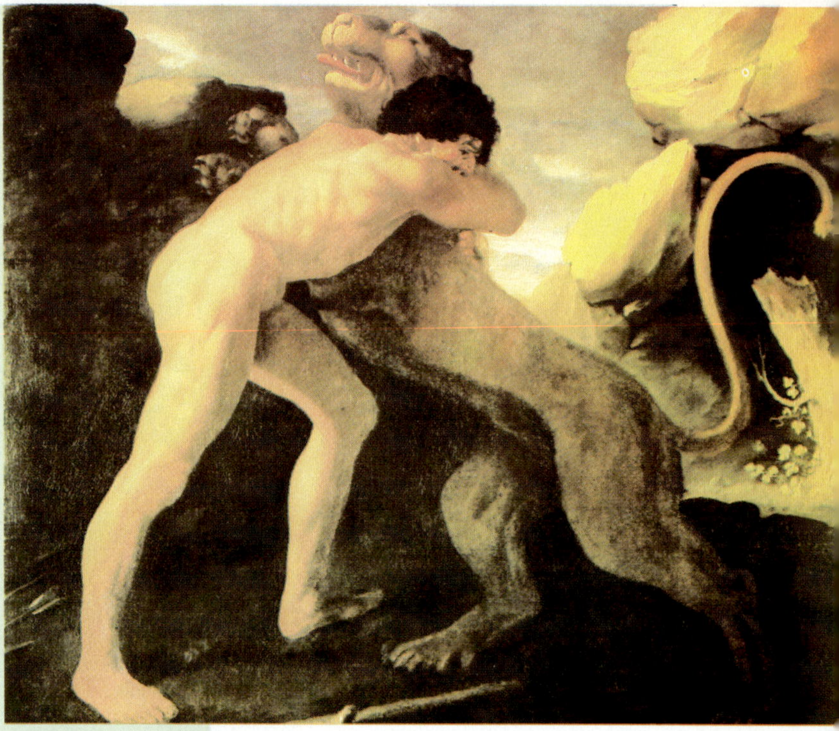

Hercules Fights the Lion of Nemea

Francisco de Zurbarán
(Fuente de Cantos, Andalusia, 1598–Madrid, 1664)

- 1634
- oil on canvas
- 151 x 166 cm
- Museo del Prado, Madrid

The first of the Twelve Labors of Hercules was to slay and skin the lion that kept the people of the valley of Nemea in a constant state of alarm. When Hercules saw that the arrows simply bounced off the lion, he grabbed it by the neck, squeezed it to death and skinned it. Here, the hero is shown in mortal combat with the beast. The nude, one of the few by the artist, who painted primarily saints and religious figures, is a splendid academic study of a muscular man. Whereas the figure of Hercules is perfectly studied and modeled, exhibiting certain influences of tenebrist realism, as was popular in Seville at the beginning of the 17th century, the lion is a product of the painter's imagination. Despite the requirements of the scene, movement is not suggested in the static poses of the figures.

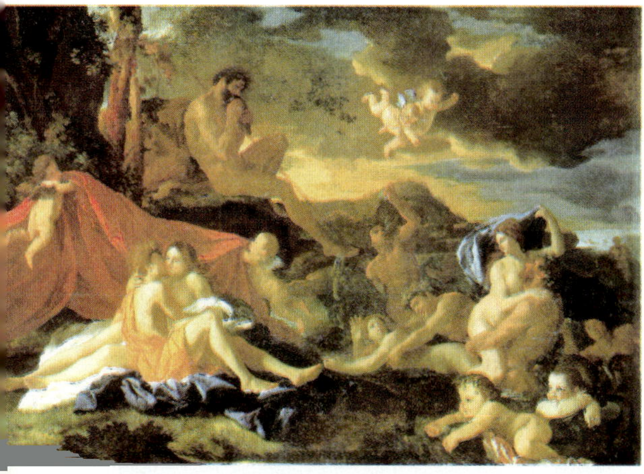

Acis and Galatea

Nicolas Poussin
(Les Andelys, 1594
–Rome, 1665)

- 1634
- oil on canvas
- 98 x 137 cm
- National Gallery of Ireland, Dublin

n a wilderness region, amongst fawns and cherubs, various couples are abandoning themselves to love-making. The atmosphere and lighting of the painting are warm and intimate. The protagonists of the piece are depicted on the left, illuminated in a shaft of brighter light. In the other couples, Poussin makes play of the juxtaposition of darker-skinned male bodies and paler-skinned female bodies.

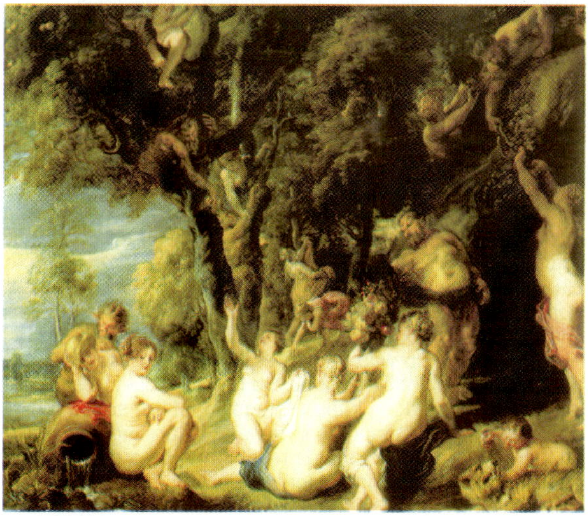

Nymphs and Satyrs

Peter Paul Rubens
(Siegen, Westphalia,
1577–Antwerp, 1640)

- ca. 1635
- oil on canvas
- 133 x 165 cm
- Museo del Prado, Madrid

Titian enjoyed combining landscape and figures, as in this work. The female body is rendered nude here in a variety of poses that are all very expressive and vivid. The painting radiates a sense of vitality and optimism that is accentuated by the sensuality of the bodies.

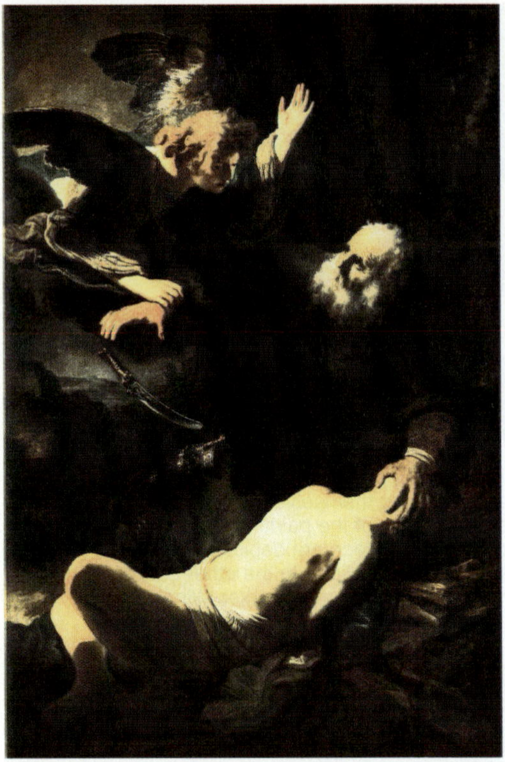

The Sacrifice of Isaac

Rembrandt (Rembrandt Harmensz van Rijn)
(Leiden, Westphalia, 1606–Amsterdam, 1669)

- 1635
- oil on canvas
- 193 x 133 cm
- Hermitage, St. Petersburg

Testing his faith, God commanded Abraham to sacrifice his own son, Isaac, with which he and his wife had been blessed in old age. Just as he was about carry out God's command, a voice from heaven ordered him to sacrifice a lamb in Isaac's place. Here, an angel stops Abraham (most likely a model from the Amsterdam ghetto), just as he is about to slit his son's throat. The knife is shown falling to the ground while Abraham looks up with an expression of astonishment. A bright shaft of light illuminates the boy's boldly-foreshortened, sensual body, making it the protagonist of the scene. This early work of Rembrandt is indebted to Caravaggio, exhibiting an incipient naturalism that is heightened by a chiaroscuro tha enhances the three-dimensional quality of the composition.

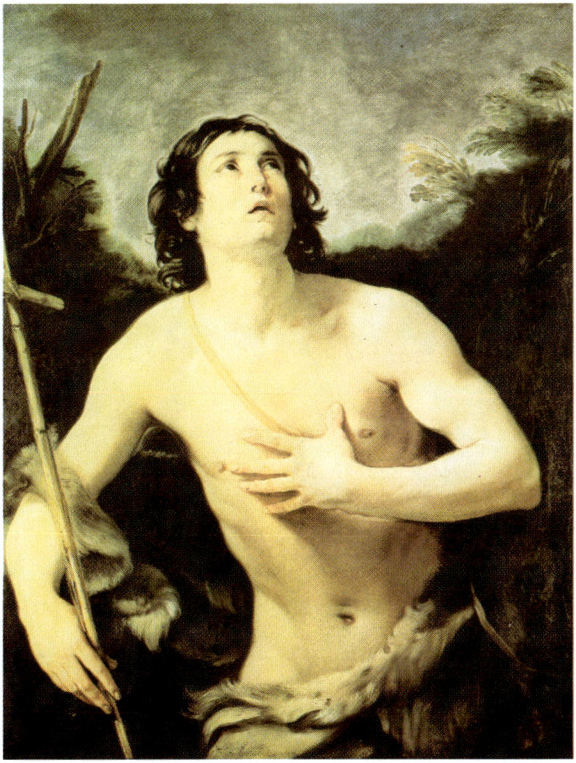

John the Baptist, represented here with his characteristic attributes, has a mystical air in this painting. The framing, which includes only half the body, allows the artist to indulge in a painstaking study of the torso of a muscular young man with fine features. Set against a dark background, the figure is luminous. The gradated skin tones are blended smoothly together without dense shadows. The figure is given just enough muscles to conform to the ideal of beauty of the day. In other paintings executed by the artist toward the end of his life, Reni evokes highly spiritual figures, distancing himself from Raphaelesque compositions and the classical canon in favor of a remarkable lyricism that makes him one of the greatest painters of his time.

St. John the Baptist

Guido Reni
(Bologna, 1575–1642)

- 1635–40
- oil on canvas
- 112 x 92 cm
- Galleria Sabauda, Turin

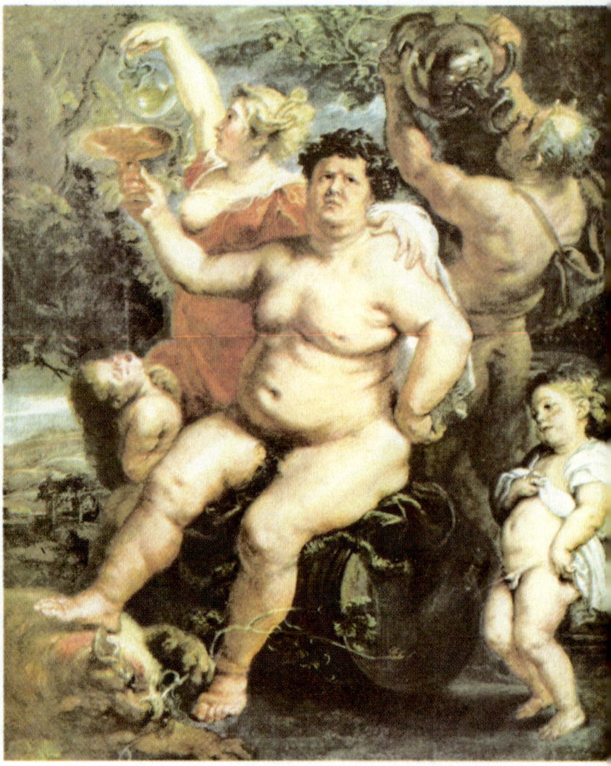

Bacchus

Peter Paul Rubens
(Siegen, Westphalia, 1577–Antwerp, 1640)

- 1635–40
- oil on canvas
- 191 x 160 cm
- Hermitage, St. Petersburg

This work represents one of Bacchus' orgiastic feasts, in which wine is the real protagonist. The half-drunken, corpulent god, whose foot is shown resting on a tiger sleeping off his drunkenness, extends his goblet for one of his priestesses to fill, while a child tilts his head to catch the runoff. On the right, a faun indulges in a swig of wine, straight from the jug. In the foreground, a child, also inebriated, gathers up his shirt while he unabashedly urinates into the foreground. The light concentrates on the upper part of the maenad's body, which is set against the dark colors of the background, accentuating her voluptuous body. Grotesque in appearance and attitude, the figures are interested only in the wine and their faces reveal that they are overcome by its effects.

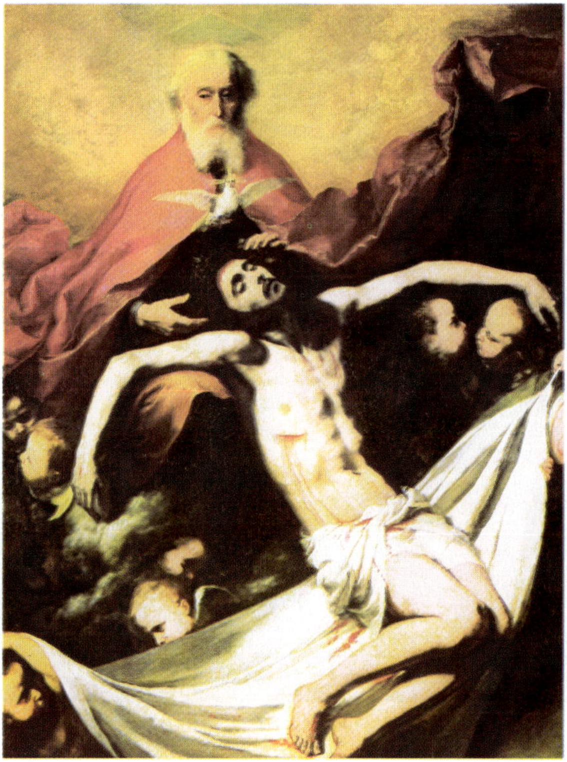

This work combines the tenebrism of Caravaggio and certain classical aspects of Carracci, the two most important trends in Italian Baroque art. It contains a complex set of stylistic references, ranging from classical realism (the figure of God the Father) to an exaggerated chiaroscuro (the naturalism of Christ). The figure of God exhibits human qualities, recalling a portrait. The extraordinary figure of Christ is illuminated from above, casting well-defined shadows onto his body. The strong diagonal line made by his outstretched arms above the vertically aligned body is picked up by the dove above, which symbolizes the Holy Ghost. The eye is taken further upwards to the head of God the Father, drawing the elements into a strong pyramidal form. The apparent weightlessness of Jesus' body contrasts with the sunken state of his thorax.

The Holy Trinity

José (**Jusepe**)
de Ribera (called
Lo Spagnoletto)
(Jàtiva, Spain, 1591
–Naples, 1652)

- ca. 1636
- oil on canvas
- 226 x 181 cm
- Museo del Prado, Madrid

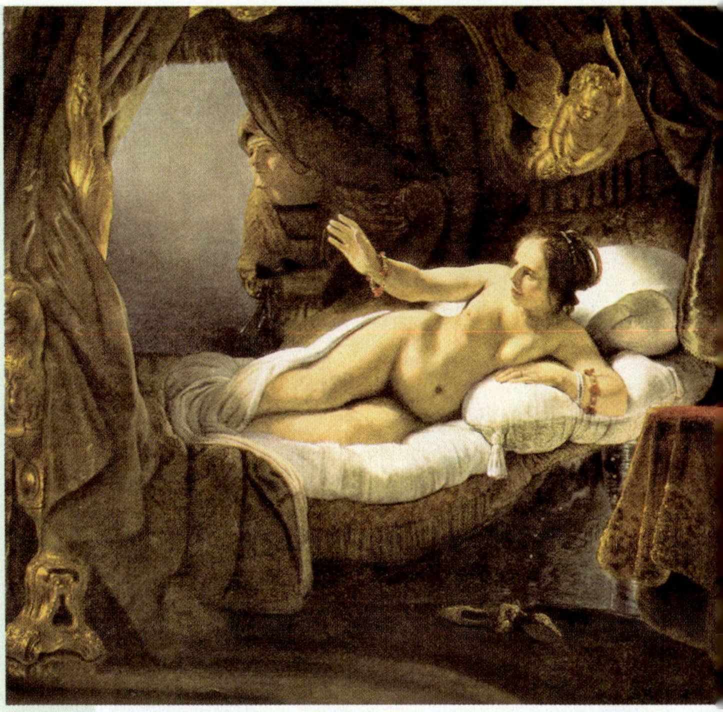

Danaë

Rembrandt (Rembrandt Harmensz van Rijn)
(Leiden, 1606–Amsterdam, 1669)

- ca. 1636
- oil on canvas
- 185 x 202 cm
- Hermitage, St. Petersburg

Danaë was the daughter of Acrisius, King of Argos, and Euridice. Imprisoned in a tower, she is visited one night by Zeus, who is disguised as golden rain, and they conceive a child, Perseus. In this work, Rembrandt substitutes the golden rain with an intense light, which pervades the room and is cast across Danaë's body, while a servant draws the heavy drapery. Rembrandt captured like no one else the anxious expression on Danaë's face as she awaits the arrival of Zeus. The painting's details are executed with the utmost care. The drapery, the gold-colored Cupid, Danaë's bracelets, the brocade slippers, the sheets: all are enveloped in a baroque rhythm. Many experts consider this to be one of the most intricate works painted by Rembrandt during the period around 1630. Some have identified the subject as Venus, others as Mesalina; it is even possible that it is a biblical character.

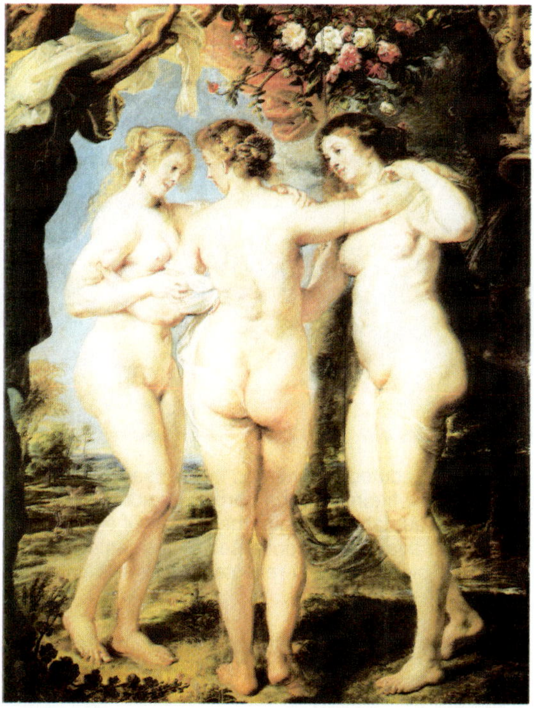

n this work, Rubens distances himself from the classical nude and strikes a new note, giving us more corpulent women, who no doubt reflect the prevailing ideal of his day. The three Graces Aglaia, Thalia and Euphrosyne, daughters of Eurynome and Zeus, were seen as brightening nature and man's works with beauty and charm, of which they are themselves the embodiments. Here, they are about to dance n a ring on a raised foreground overlooking a bucolic scene that radiates peace and serenity. The perfection of the composition is primarily a result of the interplay of forms, colors and highlights. The figure on the right has been identified as Rubens' first wife, Isabella Brandt, while that on the left is his second wife, Helena Fourment. The painter has taken visible pleasure in depicting these voluptuously-modeled women's bodies. The scene is bathed in a golden and silvery light, which symbolizes joy in life. Such exuberant sensuality was very bold for its time, and it is not inconceivable that there is some truth in the legend that Helena Fourment was anxious o destroy the painting after her husband's death.

The Three Graces

Peter Paul Rubens
(Siegen, Westphalia, 1577–Antwerp, 1640)

- ca. 1636/38
- oil on canvas
- 221 x 181 cm
- Museo del Prado, Madrid

The Sense of Smell

Jan Brueghel (also called **"Velvet" Brueghel**)
(Brussels, 1568–Antwerp, 1625)

Peter Paul Rubens
(Siegen, Westphalia, 1577–Antwerp, 1640)

- ca. 1636
- oil on canvas
- 65 x 109 cm
- Museo del Prado, Madrid

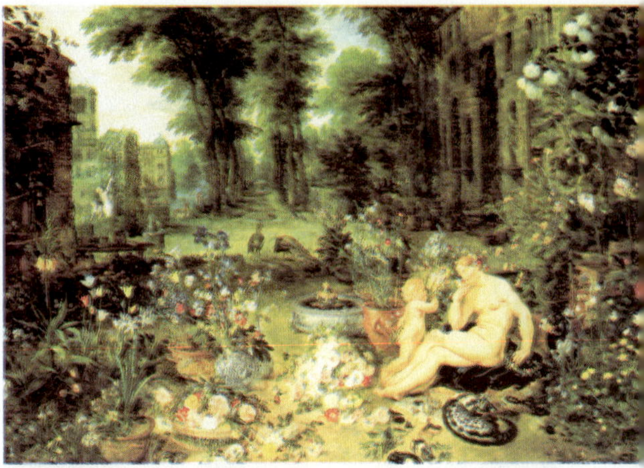

Brueghel executed a series on the senses, with Rubens providing the figures. In the garden depicted here, we see Venus, presumably indulging her sense of smell. Her figure stands out against the cool tones of the setting, certain of which are picked up and reflected in her skin tints.

The Birth of Venus

Cornelis de Vos
(Hulst, 1584–Antwerp, 1651)

- ca. 1636
- oil on canvas
- 187 x 208 cm
- Museo del Prado, Madrid, Torre de la Parada Collection

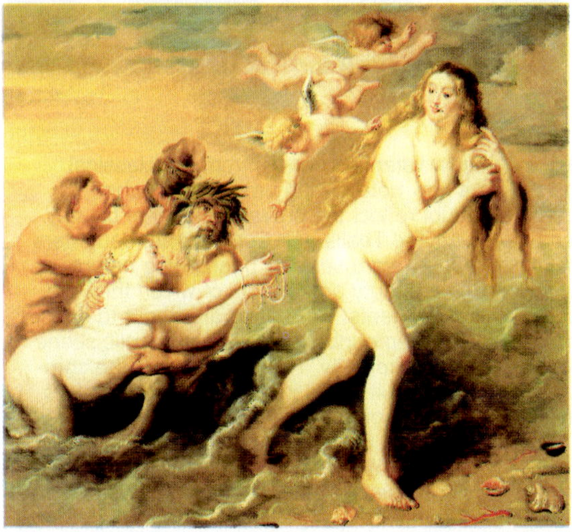

Although Venus' body is Rubenesque in conception and execution (the painting was actually based on one of his sketches), its forms are softer and its outlines more clear-cut, and generally the style of this painting is less "modern" than that of Rubens.

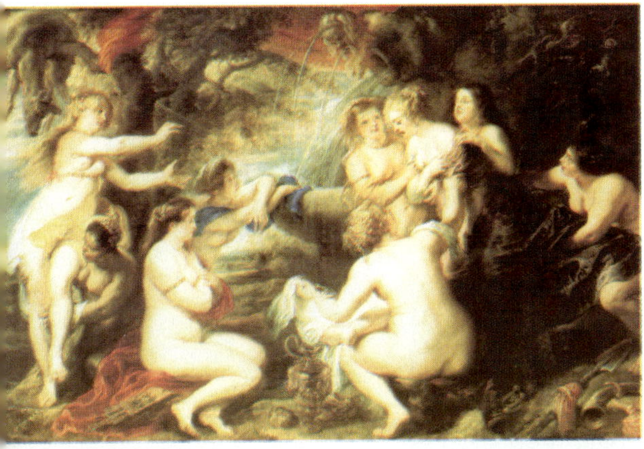

Diana and Callisto

Peter Paul Rubens
(Siegen, Westphalia, 1577–Antwerp, 1640)

- ca. 1636
- oil on canvas
- 202 x 323 cm
- Museo del Prado, Madrid

Callisto vowed chastity to Diana, but was seduced by Jupiter having taken on the form of Diana for the purpose. When she refused to undress to bathe, the other nymphs removed her clothes and so revealed her pregnant state. Rubens' wife herself stood model for Callisto. These joyful and uninhibited nude figures have great strength of presence, while the bold skin hues accentuate the powerful physicality of their bodies.

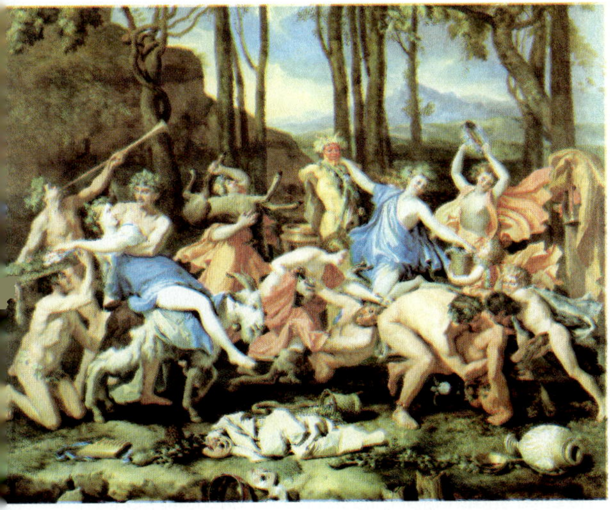

The Triumph of Pan

Nicolas Poussin
(Les Andelys, 1594 –Rome, 1665)

- 1636
- oil on canvas
- 138 x 157 cm
- National Gallery, London

The painting is extraordinarily dynamic, involving a large number of nude figures in a festival of flowers, music and pleasurable activities. The god Pan, depicted at the center, with the legs of a goat, is practically hidden in the mêlée. Pleasure, sensuality and joie de vivre are the predominant themes here, in accordance with the licentious spirit of the god.

Landscape with St. Jerome

Nicolas Poussin
(Les Andelys, 1594–Rome, 1665)

- 1636–37
- oil on canvas
- 155 x 234 cm
- Museo del Prado, Madrid

This work was commissioned by Phillip IV to decorate his Buen Retiro Palace, Madrid.

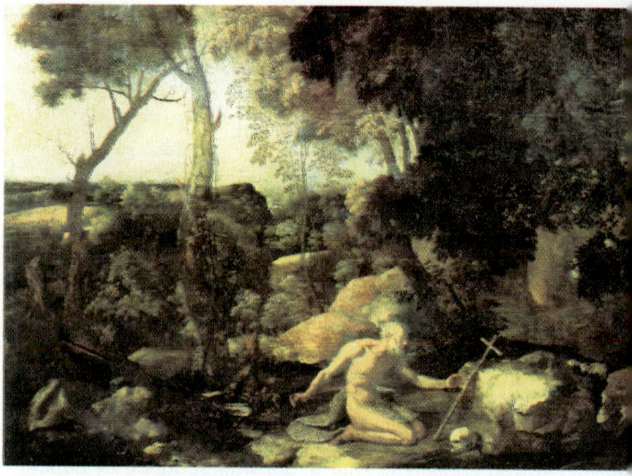

The saint is depicted here as an old man with an expressive face. His body meticulously modeled, he personifies abstinence and penitence. Lost almost amidst the dark, luxuriant vegetation, the setting elaborates on a different plane his emotional and spiritual state.

The Origin of the Milky Way

Peter Paul Rubens
(Siegen, Westphalia, 1577–Antwerp, 1640)

- 1636–38
- oil on canvas
- 181 x 244 cm
- Museo del Prado, Madrid

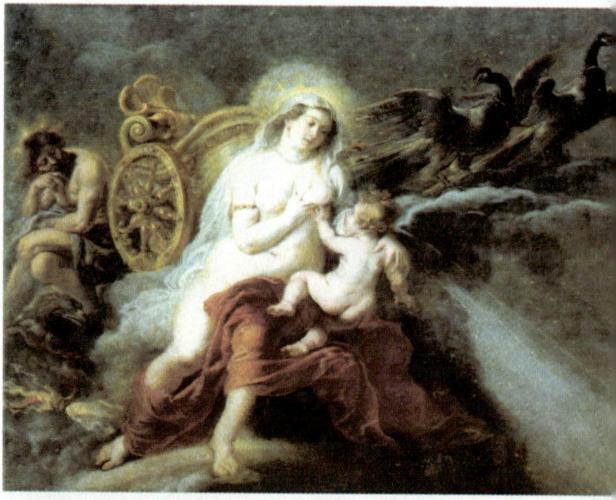

The child shown taking sustenance from Juno's breast here is Hercules, whom Jupiter had placed next to his wife while she slept. When the goddess awoke and caught sight of her adulterous husband's son, the milk from her breast spilt, creating the Milky Way. The goddess' body is remarkable both for its matronly dimensions and for the way it successfully dominates the action within the depicted scene.

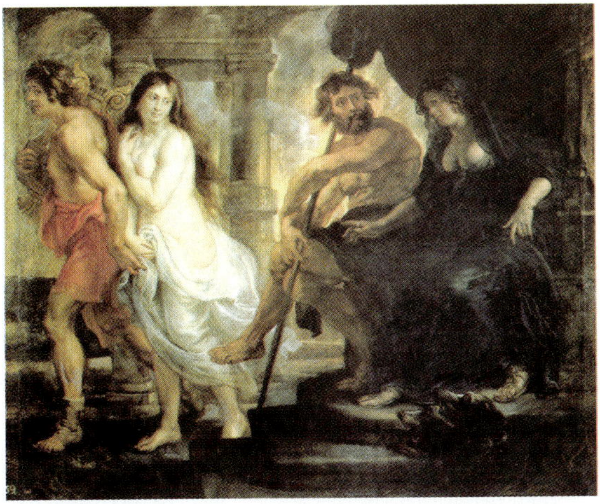

Orpheus and Eurydice

Peter Paul Rubens
(Siegen, Westphalia, 1577–Antwerp, 1640)

- 1636–38
- oil on canvas
- 194 x 245 cm
- Museo del Prado, Madrid

Orpheus descends into the underworld and rescues Eurydice in the presence of Pluto and Proserpine, who are enchanted by his song. The scene foreshadows the sequel, for the condition of Orpheus' receiving back his wife is that he not look back, which he is evidently on the point of doing. Both nude figures are most expressive. In Orpheus' case we see his strength, in Eurydice's her tender delicacy, rich in charm and sensual appeal.

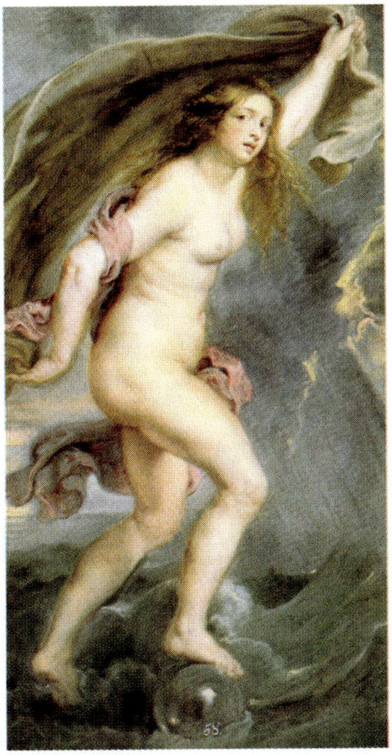

Fortune

Peter Paul Rubens
(Siegen, Westphalia, 1577 –Antwerp, 1640)

- 1636–38
- oil on canvas
- 179 x 95 cm
- Museo del Prado, Madrid

Rubens' models, like this one, represented the northern ideal of beauty: an ample and curvaceous, large-proportioned body of voluptuous appearance. This highly dynamic painting is also extremely unusual, as the goddess is gazing directly at the viewer, inviting the eye to enter the picture and to take part in the action.

The Nurture of Jupiter

Nicolas Poussin
(Les Andelys, 1594
–Rome, 1665)

- 1637
- oil on canvas
- 95 x 118 cm
- Dulwich Picture Gallery, London

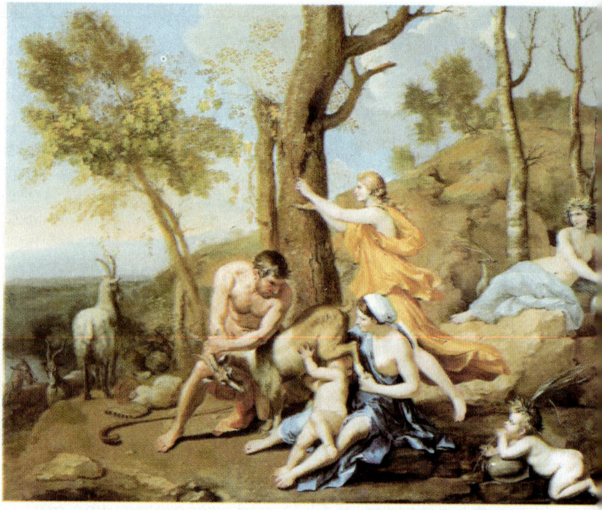

Both theme and figures here are notable. The child Jupiter is depicted suckling a goat held by a muscular and somewhat weather-beaten Chronos aided by one of the three slender, milky-skinned nymphs in the picture. The colors further heighten the physicality of this work.

Pan

Nicolas Poussin
(Les Andelys, 1594
–Rome, 1665)

- 1637
- oil on canvas
- 106.5 x 82 cm
- Staatliche Kunstsammlungen, Dresden

The work was painted for Nicolas Guillaume de la Fleur. Acquired by Auguste III of Saxony in Paris in 1742.

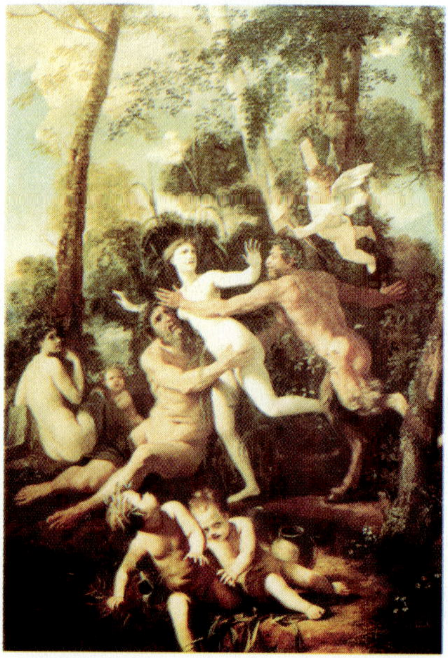

Pan, god of flocks and shepherds, had the legs and horns of a goat and was in the habit of chasing nymphs and frightening those who had strayed into the countryside. He is shown here up to his usual pranks. While the landscape is tranquil, and the figures in it all in various states of activity, over the whole there lingers an atmosphere of sexuality and appetite.

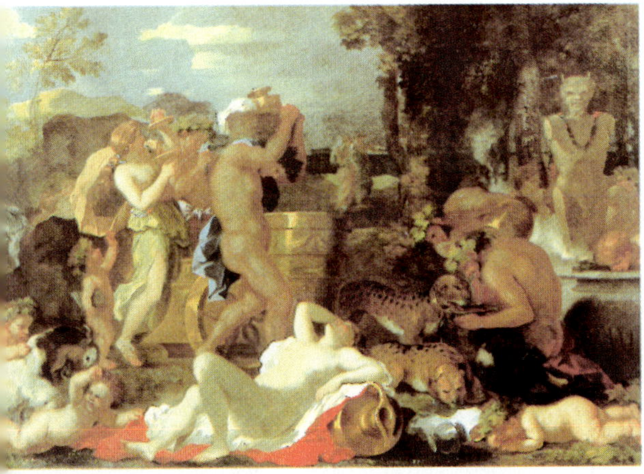

Bacchanal

Sébastien Bourdon
(Montpellier, 1616–Paris, 1671)

- ca. 1637
- oil on canvas
- 79 x 101 cm
- private collection, France

his work, depicting, amongst others, Pan and Bacchus, ·as for a time attributed to Poussin. The beauty and sen-uality of the nude figure in the foreground are brought ut by the almost harsh lighting; contrasting strongly with ıe dark background, it helps to delineate the forms of the gure as well as to accentuate the foreshortening.

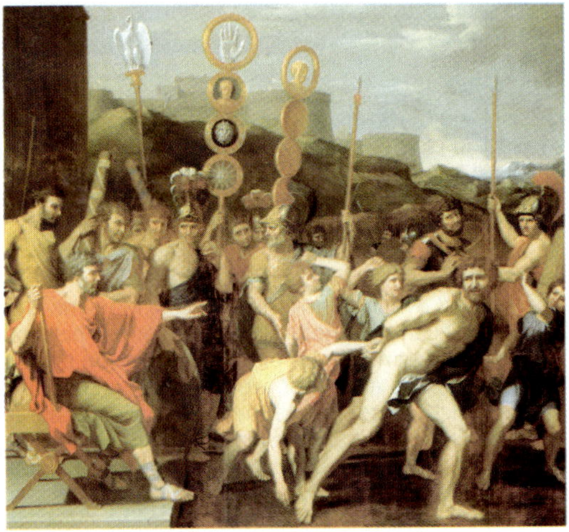

Camillus and the Schoolmaster of Falerii

Nicolas Poussin
(Les Andelys, 1594–Rome, 1665)

- 1654
- oil on canvas
- 252 x 265 cm
- Musée du Louvre, Paris

ıaked, hands bound at his back, a schoolmaster who as inflicted cruel punishments on his pupils is delivered ver to them and left to their mercy. Poussin's profound cquaintance with human anatomy is in evidence here, o less than his ability to generate eroticism, even in a tuation overflowing with violence.

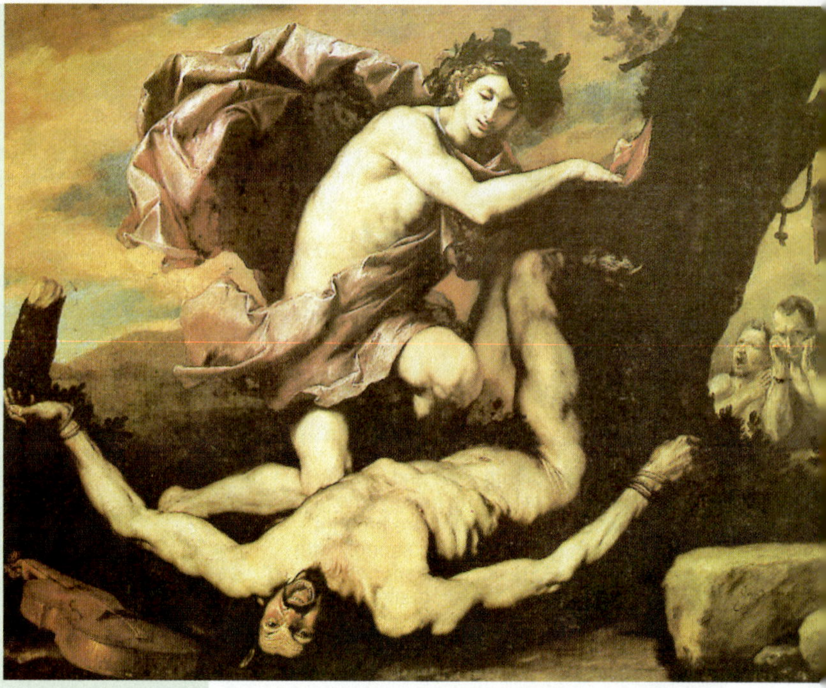

Apollo and Marsyas

José (Jusepe) de Ribera (called **Lo Spagnoletto**)
(Jàtiva, Spain, 1591 –Naples, 1652)

- 1637
- oil on canvas
- 185 x 226 cm
- Museo di San Martino, Naples

Apollo and Marsyas held a competition to see which of the two could play their musical instruments better. Apollo won, skinned his opponent alive and hung the skin in a cave. This painting shows Marsyas lying bound to the ground, just moments before being flayed. The scene belongs among the best mythological motifs of the artist, as much for its scenery and lighting effects as for the painterly handling of the figures' evenly-illuminated bodies. Marsyas is depicted as a well-built man, not so much to convey his strength as to create an atmosphere of extreme tension and desperation. Apollo has a slender, well-proportioned body with smooth skin. Marsyas has the tanned face of an adult, whereas the winner's is refined and effeminate, accentuating his cruelty. The painter has endeavored to idealize the scene, as attested to by Apollo's gesture, the victory laurel on his head and his windblown cloak. The sensuality of the figures is underscored by the warm and intense colors.

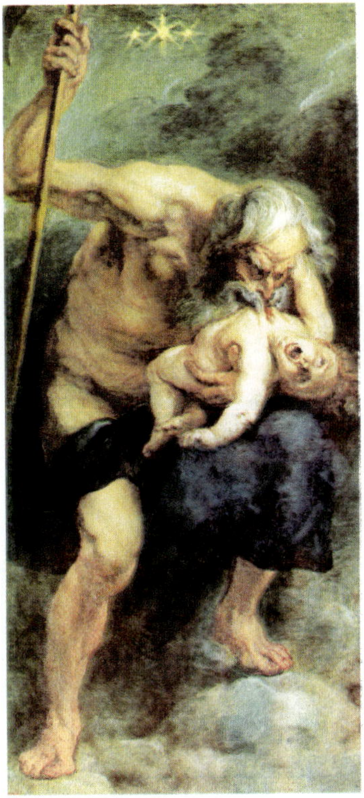

Saturn Devouring One of His Sons

Peter Paul Rubens
(Siegen, Westphalia, 1577–Antwerp, 1640)

- 1637–38
- oil on canvas
- 180 x 87 cm
- Museo del Prado, Madrid

'his scene was inspired by the episode in Ovid's Meta-
ıorphoses in which Saturn, the god of the Titans, devours
ıis sons to prevent them from overthrowing him. Rhea, their
ıother, is able to save only Zeus. The characterization
ınd dramatic nature of the nude god evokes the figures of
/ichelangelo. Here, Saturn is represented as an elderly man
vith a skillfully-rendered, Herculean body. The magnificent
ıead is bent forward to heighten the drama of the action.
.eaning on his scythe, the symbol of agriculture and its pow-
ır over life, Saturn avidly tears at the chest of one of his
hildren, who writhes in pained agony. The figure of Jupiter is
everely foreshortened, with one leg placed before the other.
ɪis torso is cast in a half-light, rendering the details indiscern-
ɔle, a pictorial technique that enhances the luminosity of the
hild, whose body constitutes the painting's focal point.

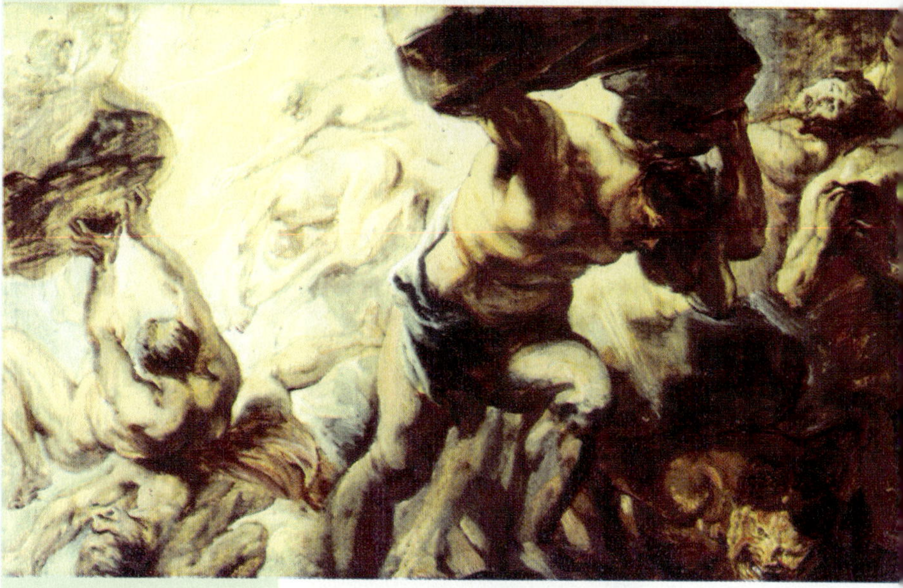

The Fall of the Titans

Peter Paul Rubens
(Siegen, Westphalia, 1577 Antwerp, 1040)

- 1637–38
- oil on canvas
- Musées Royaux des Beaux-Arts, Brussels

This painting depicts a story taken from Ovid's Metamorphose in which the giants of the underworld attempt to overthrow the gods of Olympus by piling up rocks to form a mountain tall enough to reach it. Zeus, whose discovery of them sends him into a rage, destroys the mountain and defeats the Titans. These Herculean nudes, clearly influenced by the work of Michelangelo, demonstrate the artist's remarkable mastery of his art. They are foreshortened in a manner akin to trompe l'o determining the vantage point from which they are intended to be viewed. When observed from the correct height, an optical illusion is produced and the monumentality of the scene is heightened, thanks to a careful study of volume and light.

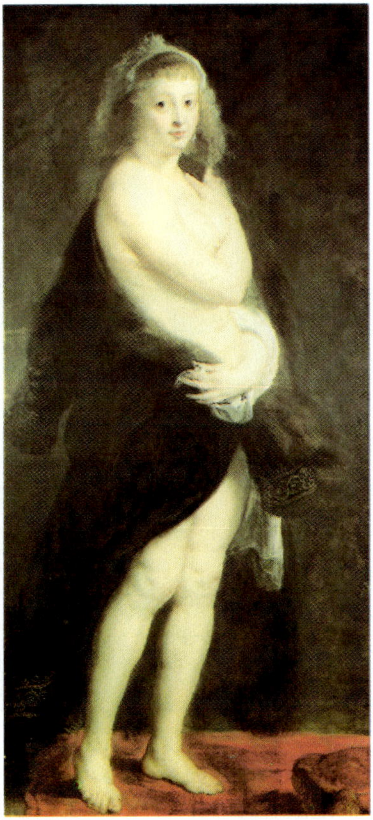

The Fur Coat

Peter Paul Rubens
(Siegen, Westphalia, 1577–Antwerp, 1640)

- 1638
- oil on canvas
- 176 x 83 cm
- Kunsthistorisches Museum, Vienna

elena Fourment, who had been Rembrandt's muse and wife om the age of sixteen, is portrayed here with a corpulent ody. She sat as model for most of the artist's nudes that ere painted from 1630 onward. A close emotional tie etween the model and the artist is so strong that it is almost ngible in this painting. It is said that when Rubens executed is work, he was suffering from arthritis, which caused him reat pain in his hands. This, however, did not stop him from apturing the remarkable eroticism of his sitter with the same acrity as when he was a young man. The model does not ppear to be indifferent to the spectator, but seems to pro- oke the viewer with her disarmingly candid gaze. Her seduc- ve qualities go beyond this, and include her falsely modest esture of attempting to cover her breast, which rests on one rm, while the other arm keeps her fur coat in place.

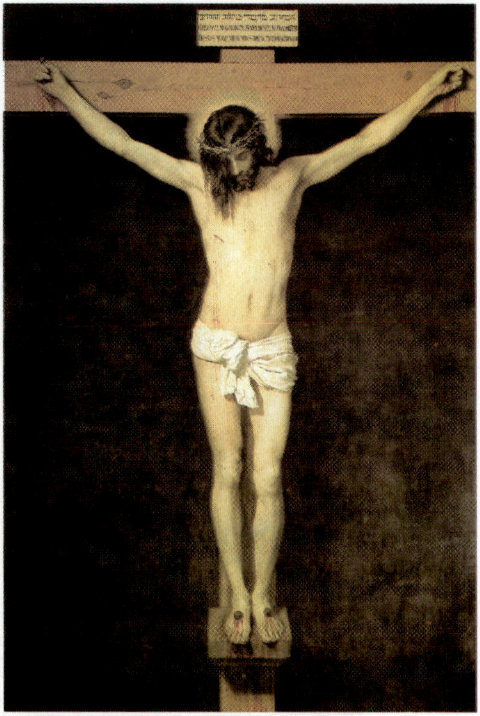

Christ on the Cross

Diego Rodríguez de Silva Velázquez
(Seville, 1599–Madrid, 1660)

- 1632
- oil on canvas
- 248 x 169 cm
- Museo del Prado, Madrid

This may be the most important religious painting executed by Velázquez, not only for its superb technique, aesthetic appeal and emotive force, but also for the stories to which it has given rise over the years. According to the most famous one, the work was commissioned by Philip IV in atonement for his illicit amorous affair with a young nun. The figure of Christ on the Cross, positively luminous against the dark background, is serene and heroic. Despite his nudity, he displays a remarkable dignity. He wears a crown of thorns and his loose hair conceals part of his face. The light enters the scene from the left, producing a subtle modeling with tenuous shadows, so that a sense of spirituality and devotion eclipses that of high drama and dynamism. Christ's majestic head is remarkable for its highly expressive, sculptural quality.

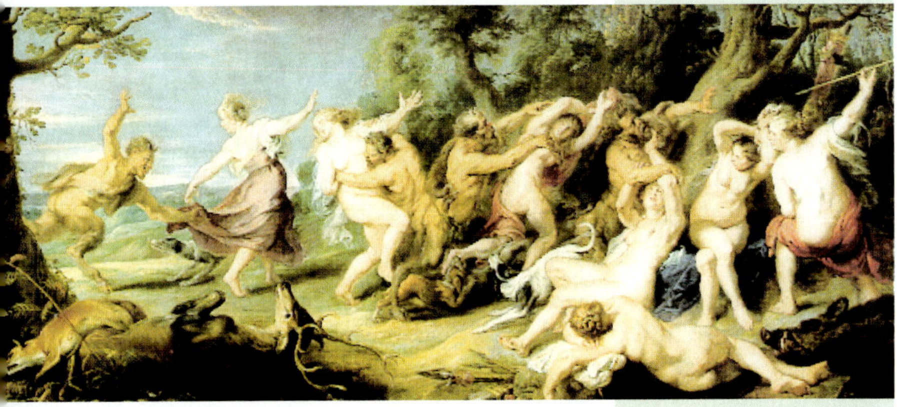

reek mythology has long provided painters with a source
' erotic imagery, granting respectability to many a work that
ould otherwise have been branded as immoral. Baroque
tists, and Rubens in particular, relished such subjects. This
mplex composition is considered one of the artist's finest.
ne frantic movements of the female nudes seem to have
fected the idyllic landscape surroundings. The naked fig-
es exude a powerful sensuality, most notable in the sleep-
g nymph in the lower right-hand corner. Each body evinces
different kind of eroticism. All the female forms, from the
htly clad semi-nudes to the completely naked figures, are
eated with exquisite taste, suppressing the violence of the
ıbject in favor of a beautifully "choreographed" whole.

Diana and Her Nymphs Surprised by Fauns

Peter Paul Rubens
(Siegen, Westphalia, 1577–Antwerp, 1640)

- ca. 1539
- oil on canvas
- 128 x 314 cm
- Museo del Prado, Madrid

A Dance to the Music of Time

Nicolas Poussin
(Les Andelys, 1594–Rome, 1665)

- 1638–40
- oil on canvas
- 83 x 105 cm
- Wallace Collection, London

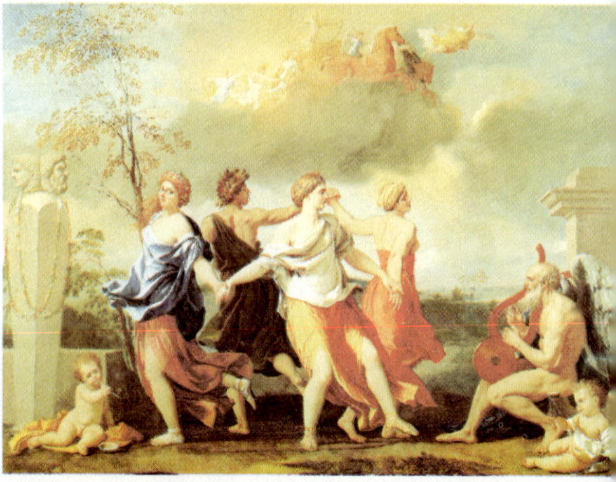

The canvas is an allegorical poem on life and the passage of time. Time, elderly but equipped with a magnificent body, is seated playing the lyre, while in the center, four figures, representing the four seasons, are dancing in a circle. On the left, a cherub is blowing soap bubbles. Apollo, in his chariot, presides in the sky. Lightness and evanescence pervade the scene.

Venus Bringing Arms to Aeneas

Nicolas Poussin
(Les Andelys, 1594–Rome, 1665)

- 1639
- oil on canvas
- 105 x 142 cm
- Musée des Beaux-Arts, Rouen

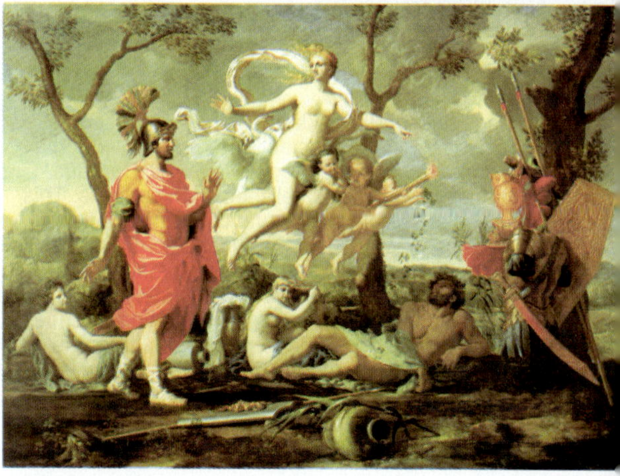

An episode from Virgil's Aeneid is depicted here. Venus is shown presenting her son with the weapons she has asked Vulcan to fashion for him so that he can do battle against the Rutulians and settle the Trojans in the region of Latium, and ultimately found the city of Rome. The painting is allegorical and its figures are equipped with heroic attributes.

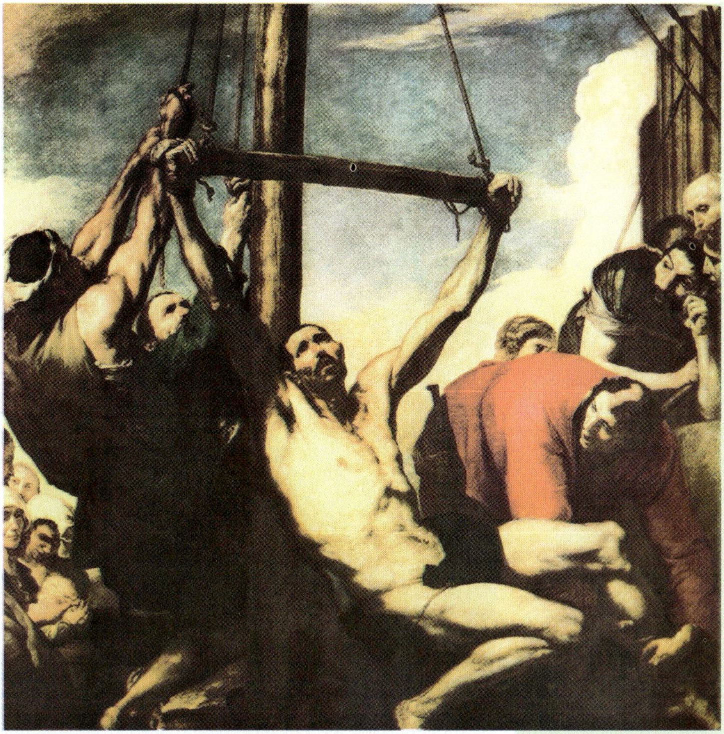

ccording to legend Bartholomew, one of the twelve Apostles,
as flayed alive by Roman soldiers. Despite the title of the
ork, the painting does not show the martyrdom itself, but
ther the moment prior to it, leaving the horrifying event to
e viewer's imagination. The naked figure of the Apostle is
tremely moving; he has a desperate but resigned expres-
on on his face, which gazes up at heaven while the execu-
oners—captured with photographic precision—prepare to
oist the victim's body. The detail of Bartholomew's anatomy
executed with the utmost skill: both the foreshortening and
e modeling of the forms break with the Classical ideal of
auty, favoring instead a strong, natural body that is none-
eless old enough to have wrinkles (in the abdomen). One
her noteworthy aspect of the work is the virtuoso illumination
the martyr's body: the torso is brightly lit, whereas the face,
ms, legs and feet are bronze in color.

The Martyrdom of St. Bartholomew

José (Jusepe) de Ribera (called **Lo Spagnoletto**)
(Jàtiva, Spain, 1591 –Naples, 1652)

- 1639
- oil on canvas
- 234 x 234 cm
- Museo del Prado, Madrid

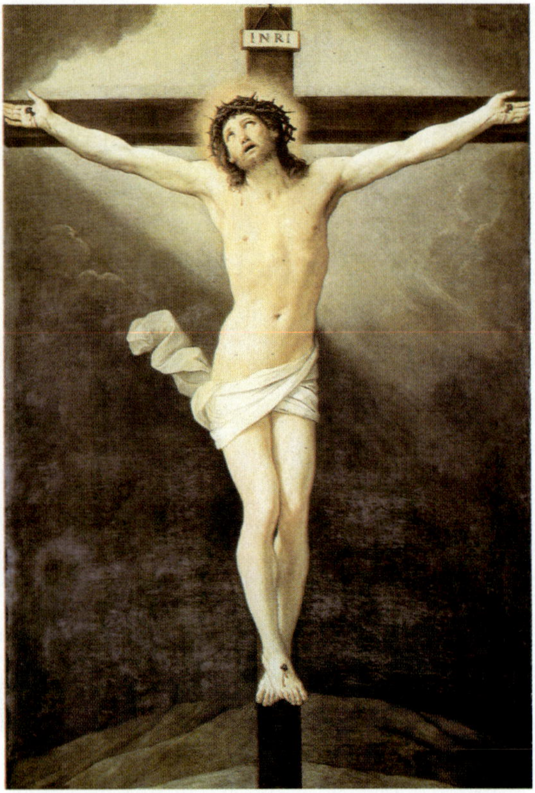

The Crucifixion

Guido Reni
(Bologna, 1575–1642)

- 1639
- oil on canvas
- 261 x 174 cm
- Galleria e Museo Estense, Modena

During the last five years of his life Guido Reni employed a palette dominated by gray, mother-of-pearl and pinkish tones. These colors gave rise to a progressively more spiritual art, evoked by means of impasto, which produced an unfinished effect. Although, particularly by today's standards, the conception and execution of this work is of a high quality, the real reason for this change in the artist's style was that he was forced to work quickly in order to pay off his gambling debts. The somber palette engenders an almost monochromatic work, in which the skin of the carefully rendered figure stands out against the dark, ominous background. The message of the painting is clear: Christ's spiritual ecstasy far outweighs the pain he suffers on the cross.

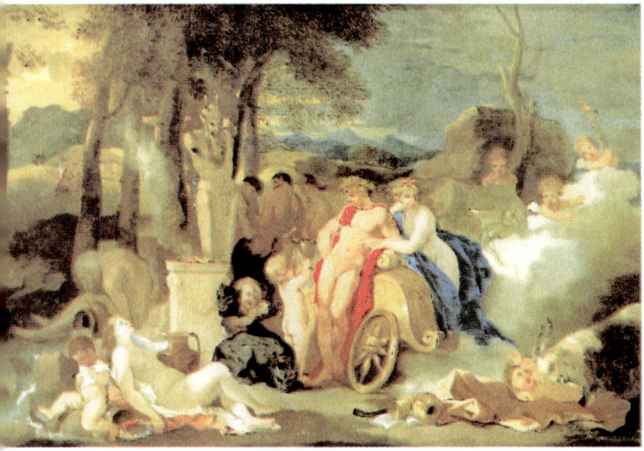

Bacchus and Ceres

Sébastien Bourdon
(Montpellier, 1616–Paris, 1671)

- ca. 1640
- oil on canvas
- 51 x 77.5 cm
- Szépmüvészeti Múzeum, Budapest

ı the foreground, left, a young woman is sleeping off the ffects of wine. The red cloak draped around Bacchus' body ot only frames but also dignifies it, while Ceres, also de-icted as a draped nude figure, contemplates the the scene om behind. As goddess of crops and agriculture, she is ssociated with Bacchus, the god of wine, who, in his turn, ; associated with Pan, the god of procreation, but also an ager drinker of the juice of the grape.

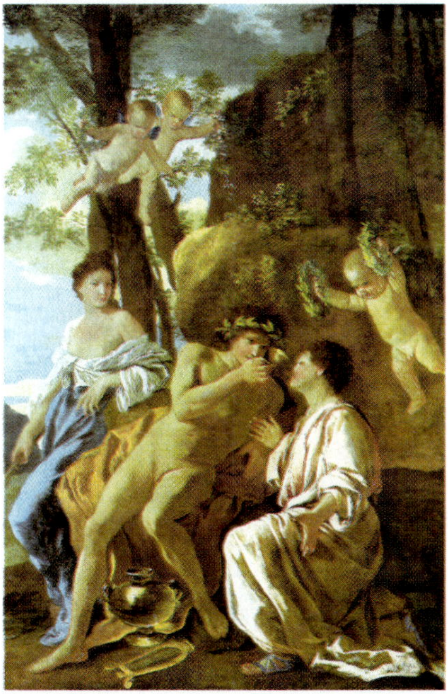

'enus and Apollo ıre portrayed ıere as sources ıf poetic inspira-ion, as Apollo ıives a sandaled oung poet omething to 'rink. The nude gure of Apollo ıas been lovingly 'rawn, and the ›reshortenings it omprises evince ıumerous tech-ıiques. Shadows ıre precisely elineated gainst lighter ıreas, and the ody's torsion is emarkable for its ıaturalistic feel.

The Inspiration of the Lyric Poet

Nicolas Poussin
(Les Andelys, 1594 –Rome, 1665)

- ca. 1640
- oil on canvas
- Niedersächsische Landesgalerie, Hanover

The Holy Family and St. John Baptist

Jacob Jordaens
(Antwerp, 1593–1678)

- ca. 1640
- oil on panel
- 123 x 93.9 cm
- The National Gallery, London

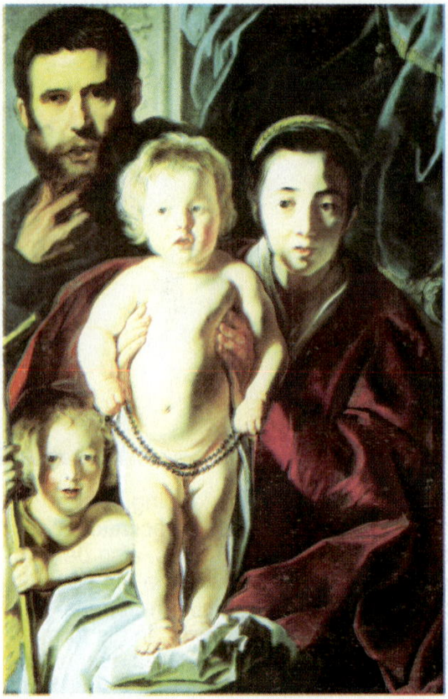

Jordaens' Protestantism did not prevent him from painting this eminently Catholic panel. Caravaggio's influence is evident in the treatment of light and shadows, while the naturalistic handling of all the figures is exceptional. The Christ child is not only beautiful to look at, but the modelling of his figure, both in conception and execution, is supreme.

The Golden Age

Pietro da Cortona (Pietro Berrettini)
(Cortona, Tuscany, 1596–Rome, 1669)

- ca. 1640
- fresco
- Palazzo Pitti, Florence

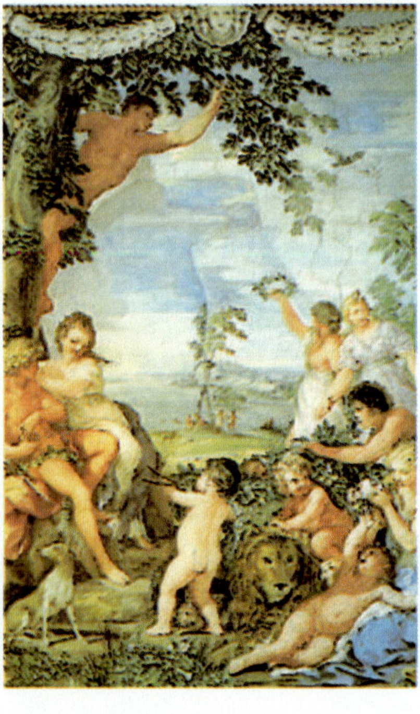

This is an exuberant and monumental scene filled with voluptuous nudes, and is a typical example of the Baroque style with which the artist decorated the Sala della Stufa in the Palazzo Pitti with his pupil Ciro Ferro. In accordance with the title, the work is a veritable celebration of life, as is reflected in the landscape, the plants, the animals and the figures, which convey a sense of prosperity, in a festive atmosphere of sensuality.

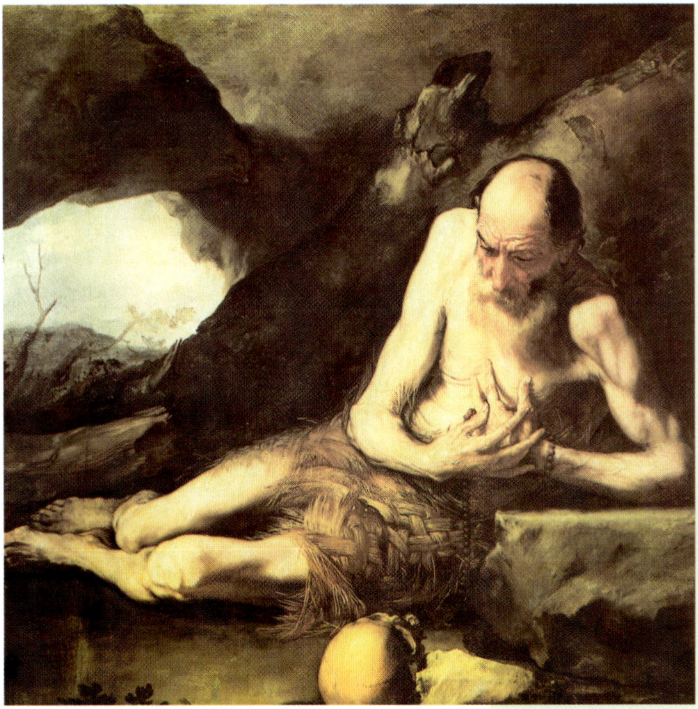

Lo Spagnoletto was a master of tenebrist realism, a style he adopted in Italy—although Italian tenebrism probably owes more to Ribera's art than to that of Caravaggio. This work presents a naturalistic figure of St. Paul, albeit with a typical tenebrist dramatization that verges on theatricality. The build of the nude alone evokes a sense of profound meditation. The saint's body is long and gaunt, yet nonetheless muscular. This is not a decrepit or ill old man, but one in good physical condition, captured in a moment of reflection. His introspection is given expression in his wrinkled brow and in the tension created by holding his hands against his chest. The study of light on the skin reveals bright flesh tones and a texture that has rarely been achieved in the history of art. Another remarkable aspect is the foreshortening of the figure, which draws the viewer's attention to the most important parts of the body.

St. Paul the Hermit

José (Jusepe) de Ribera (called **Lo Spagnoletto**)
(Xàtiva, Spain, 1591 –Naples, 1652)

- 1640
- oil on canvas
- 143 x 143 cm
- Museo del Prado, Madrid

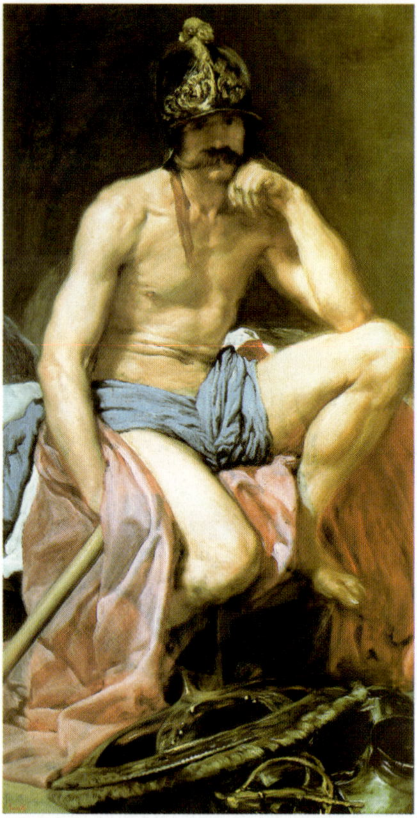

Mars

Diego Rodríguez de Silva Velázquez
(Seville, 1599–Madrid, 1660)

- 1640
- oil on canvas
- 179 x 96 cm
- Museo del Prado, Madrid

In keeping with his penchant for ridiculing mythological figures, Velázquez, here, presents a human-looking Mars, defeated, melancholic and wearing a vacant expression on his face. He is dressed in a simple blue cloth, has a mustache typical of infantry soldiers and is shown seated, with his head resting on his left hand in a pose recalling the figures of Michelangelo. The flesh colors and the texture of the skin and muscles lend the figure realism, emphasizing the human qualities that the artist wishes to ascribe to the god. The long handle on his right, the helmet, the jousting shield, the hilt of the sword and the armor are the attributes of a fallen warrior, the ridiculed god, so diametrically opposed to Italian representations. The painter is confident in his painterly handling and his treatment of color, based on juxtaposing cool tones with vivid, warm hues, reveal that his work is more indebted to the French painting tradition than to the Venetian School.

Andromeda, tied to her rock and about to be devoured by the sea monster, is being freed by Perseus. The cherubs above his head indicate his love for her, and the heroine's pose, necessitated on the one hand by her bonds, serves the double purpose of allowing Rubens freely to display her provocative bodily charms.

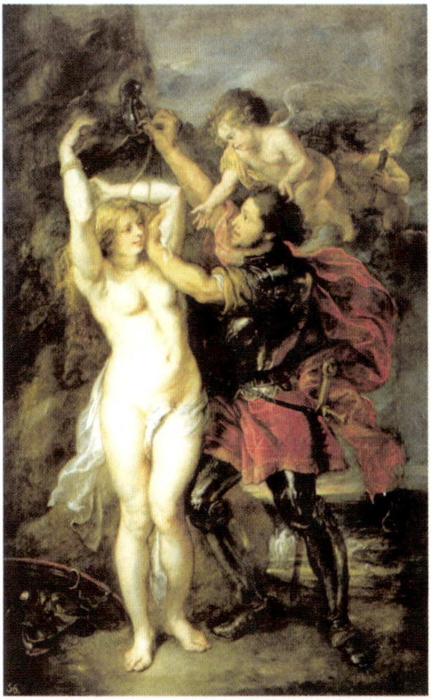

The Rescue of Andromeda

Peter Paul Rubens
(Siegen, Westphalia, 1577–Antwerp, 1640)

- ca. 1640
- oil on canvas
- 265 x 160 cm
- Museo del Prado, Madrid

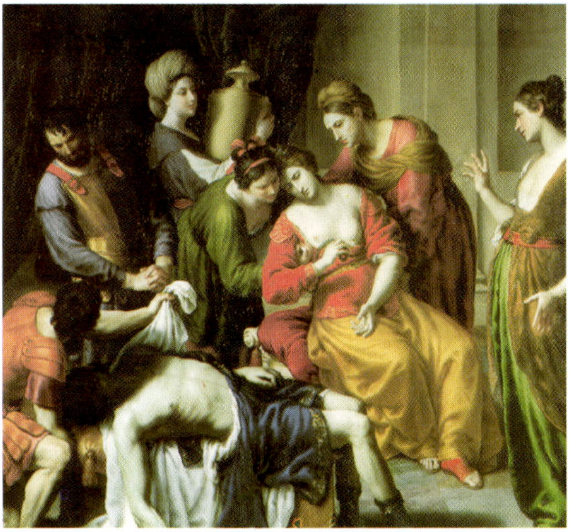

Commissioned by the French collector Phélypeaux de la Vrillière, this painting is classical in conception and evidences great formal purity. Its somewhat moderated tenebrism goes hand in hand with a Baroque style modified to suit French taste.

The Death of Cleopatra

Alessandro Turchi (L'Orbetta)
(Verona, 1578–Rome, 1649)

- 1640
- oil on canvas
- 255 x 267 cm
- Musée du Louvre, Paris

Cupid

Copy after Parmigianino

- oil on canvas
- 135 x 65,3 cm
- Museo del Prado, Madrid

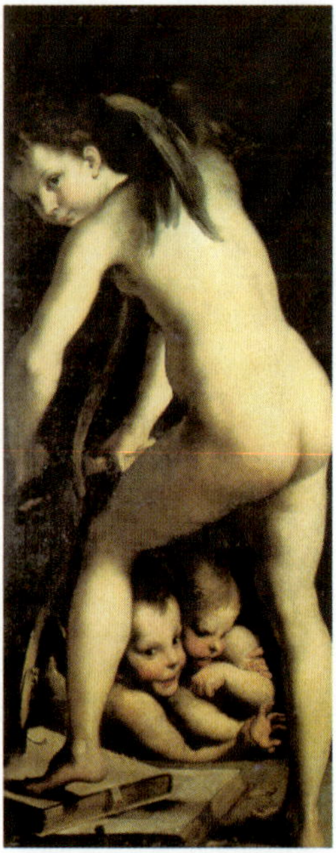

This copy of a painting by Parmigianino depicts a curious figure of somewhat uncertain sex, having the shapeliness and gentleness of a woman and the head of an ostensibly innocent boy. This equivocal candidness would seem to be alluded to by theburlesque smiles of the two cherubs between his legs.

Eolus

Erasmus Quellin (Quellinus)

(Antwerp, 1607–1678)

- oil on canvas
- 140 x 126 cm
- Museo del Prado, Madrid

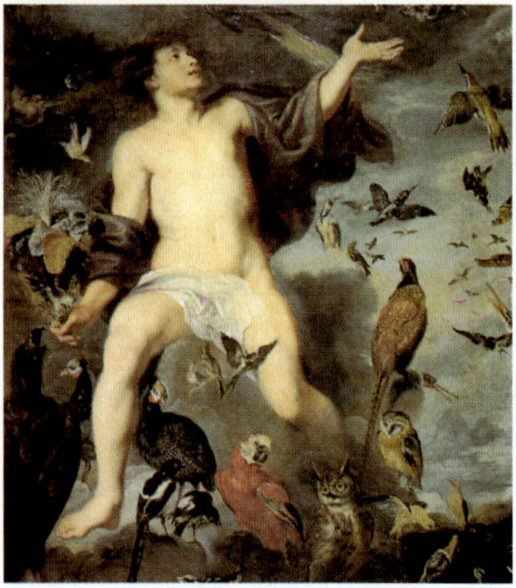

Eolus' body, in shape and form, is definitely Rubenesque. While Rubens' flamboyant brushstroke is not in evidence, the work could easily have been executed by an apprentice, perhaps Quellinus. Eolus is depicted as a self-assured, full-bodied and muscular young man, who, in accordance with Baroque ideals, is also treated fairly naturalistically.

Nude drawing became part of the standard repertory of artistic practices for all academic artists. Forms were idealized, and a set of criteria established that often ruled out certain anatomical features, even though they were thoroughly realistic. The present drawing, for example, while outstanding as a drawing, nevertheless sets anatomical realism aside in order to concentrate on other things, such as dramatic interest and the heroic.

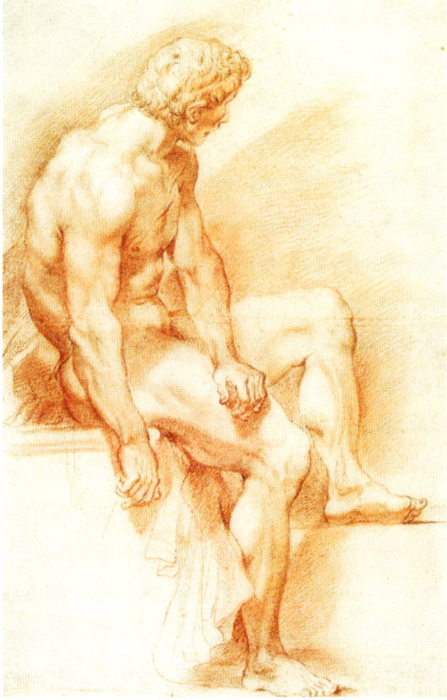

Study of a Seated Man

Sébastien Bourdon
(Montpellier, 1616–Paris, 1671)

- red chalk on paper
- 43 x 55 cm
- Musée du Louvre, Paris

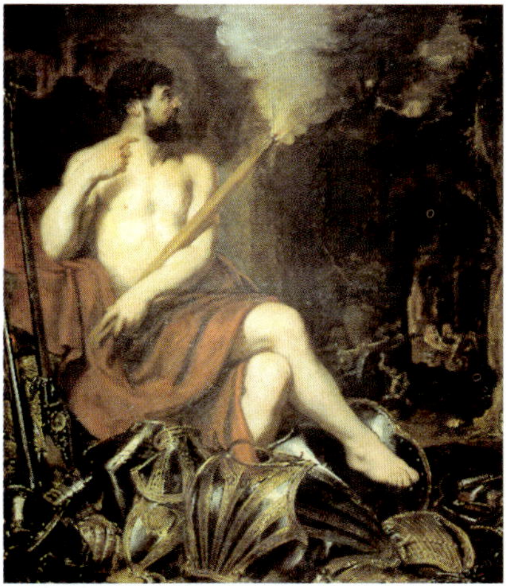

Vulcan

Erasmus Quellin (Quellinus)
(Antwerp, 1607–1678)

- oil on canvas
- 140 x 126 cm
- Museo del Prado, Madrid

Unusual, if not daring, at a time when buyers of paintings were for the most part men, this nude study of Vulcan with identifying attributes is elegant, severe and refined. The god's body is muscular and heroic, characteristics that were typically found in works of the French Academy. The style reveals skilled draftsmanship as well as detailed knowledge of the human anatomy.

Christ between the Two Thieves

Peter Paul Rubens
(Siegen, Westphalia, 1577 –Antwerp, 1649)

- 1620
- oil on canvas
- 429 x 311 cm
- Koninklijk Museum voor Schone Kunsten, Antwerp

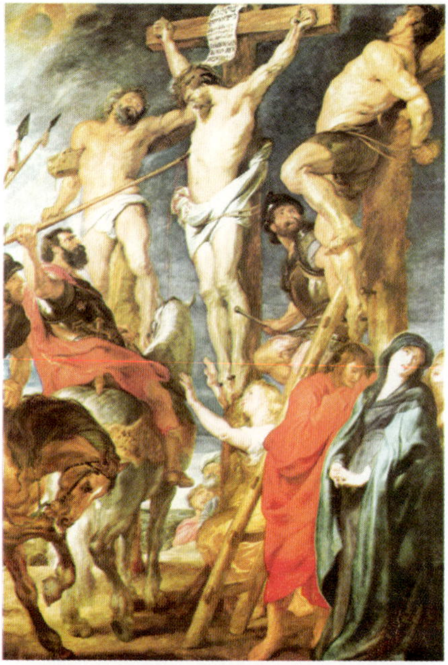

Rubens impresses and moves the spectator through his use of color, naturalistic detail and a spectacular painterly language, all of which create a powerfully expressive vision. The tense nude bodies in this painting, foreshortened and contorted, are exceptionally compelling.

Lot and His Daughters

Guercino (Giovanni Francesco Barbieri)
(Cento, Bologna, 1591 –Bologna, 1666)

- oil on canvas
- Monasterio del Escorial, Province of Madrid

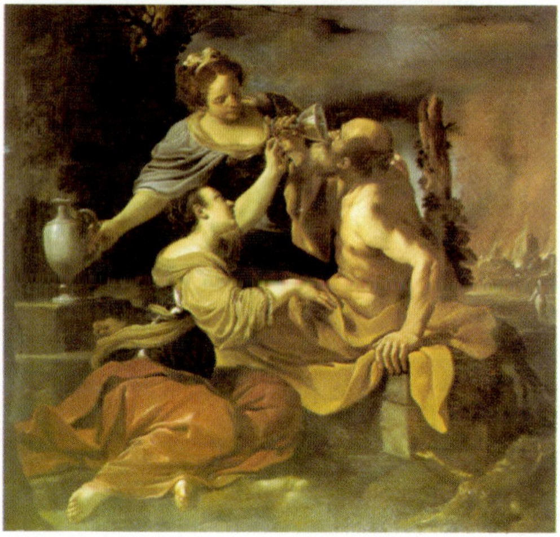

Lot's daughters made him drunk in order to sleep with him and so become pregnant with child by him. In this work, the elderly man's undraped trunk is especially prominent, its powerful muscles accentuated by strong lighting producing highlights and shadows.

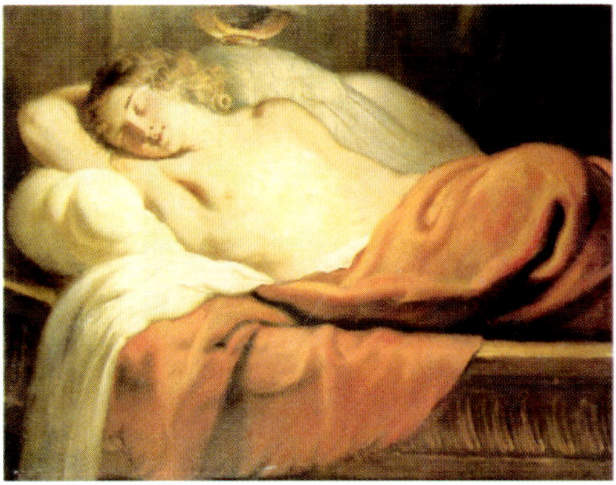

Cupid Asleep

Erasmus Quellin (or **Quellinus**)
(Antwerp, 1607–1678)

- oil on canvas
- Museo del Prado, Madrid

This Cupid's sensuality seems to have been taken over directly from images by Rubens. The body is well defined, which however does not mar the tonal softness or the depicted corporeal amplitude. Athletic and muscular, Cupid here is far from the young, often ambiguous body forms he is portrayed as having in other paintings, while the shadows framing his form imbue him with eroticism.

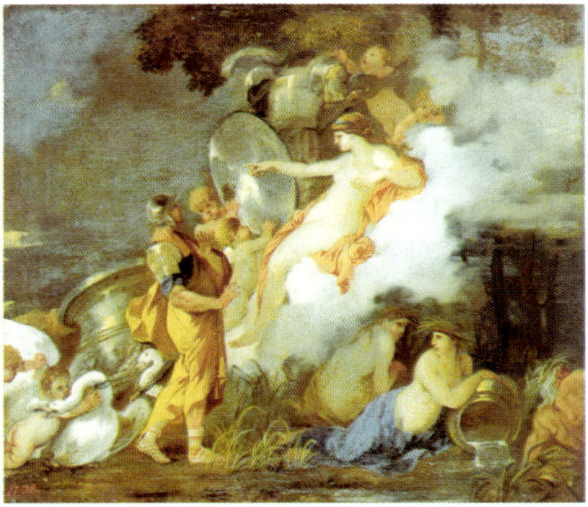

Venus Showing Aeneas his Arms

Sébastien Bourdon
(Montpellier, 1616–Paris, 1671)

- first half of the 17th century
- oil on canvas
- 43.5 x 54.5 cm
- Hermitage, St. Petersburg

Having induced Vulcan to forge arms of war for her son, Venus is shown here presenting him with them so that he will be invincible in battle. The goddess is depicted in an orange cloak, leaning on a cloud. Bourdon would often tone down the erotic overtones of his figures in order to bring them out more effectively within the composition as a whole. The slightness of Venus' breasts here contrast pleasingly with the heaviness of her abdomen and legs.

Christ's Descent into Limbo

Alonso Cano
(Granada, 1601–1667)

- 1640–50
- oil on canvas
- 168 x 199 cm
- County Museum, Los Angeles

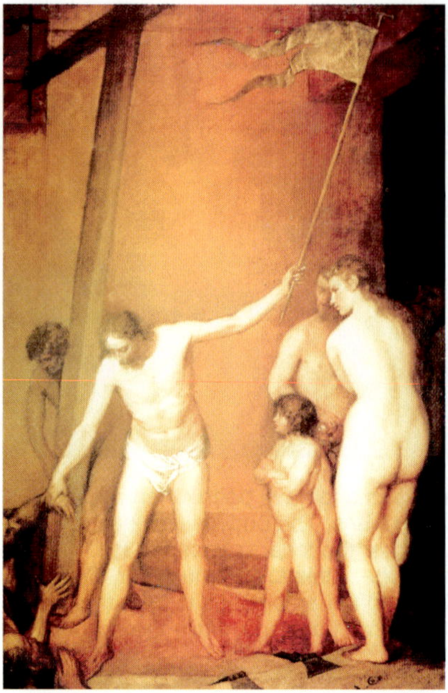

Cano's well-designed scheme avoids sharply-defined forms in favour of a more rounded sort, in the manner of Titian or Rubens. This canvas depicts a group of nude figures who, having been rescued from Limbo, are waiting to be taken to Heaven. The luminosity of the bodies is offset by tones that merge imperceptibly with the atmosphere, by which means Cano masterfully integrates background and figures.

Female Nude

Alonso Cano
(Granada, 1601–1667)

- ink on paper
- Museo del Prado, Madrid

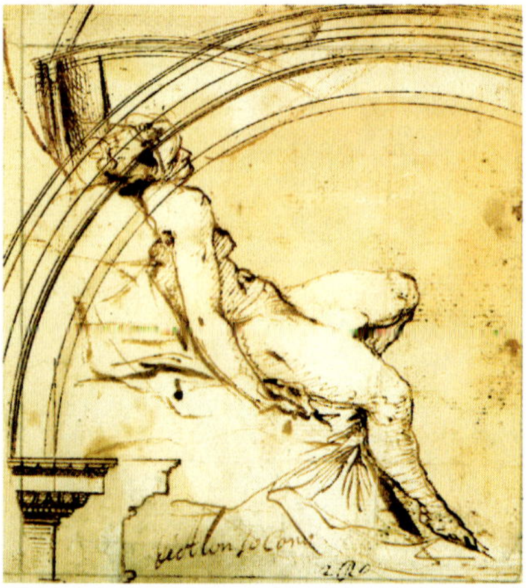

The strong lines composing this foreshortened, sleeping figure lend it conviction and freshness, while the remarkable roundness of the limbs and torso give it a sculptural feel. The lines of breast and abdomen are naturalistic. The problem of depth is solved by shading in the form of parallel lines that cause those parts of the body that are foreshortened to recede.

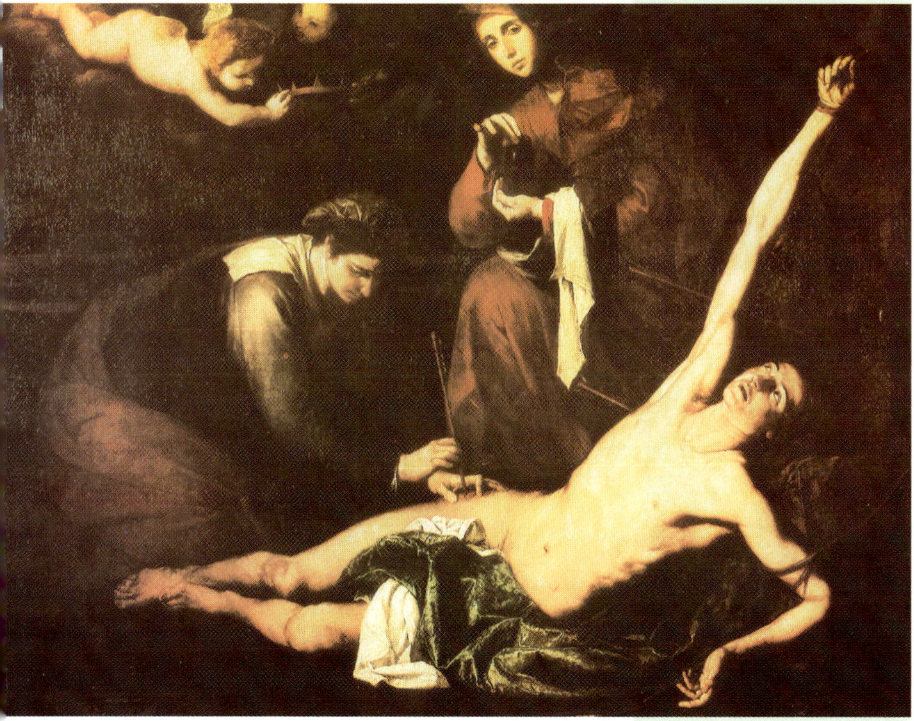

St. Sebastian is frequently portrayed as a paragon of sensuality, with effeminate features or in a provocative pose, failing to convey the pain and tragedy of his martyrdom. Indeed, the pain of the wounds and the immobility of the pious, resigned saint are elements that elicit multilayered, contradictory sentiments in the viewer. The brightly illuminated nude contrasts with the darkness of the rest of the painting, forming a nearly perfect diagonal that divides the work in two. Here, the body of the young saint does not exhibit signs of having been tortured. His elegant but muscular build and attenuated limbs combine to form an extremely handsome body. The scene is charged with eroticism through the gesture of the completely dressed female figure on the left, who is tending to Christ's the martyr's with great tenderness.

St. Sebastian Attended by Irene

José (**Jusepe**) **de Ribera** (called **Lo Spagnoletto**)
(Jàtiva, Spain, 1591 –Naples, 1652)

- oil on canvas
- 206 x 152 cm
- Museo Provincial de Bellas Artes, Valencia

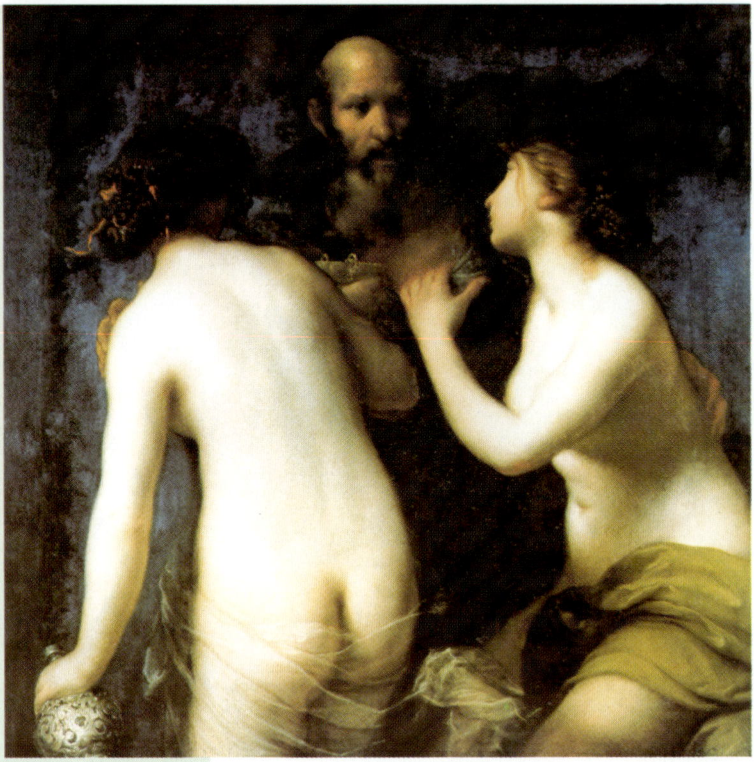

Lot and His Daughters

Francisco Furini
(Florence, 1603–1646)

- ca. 1634
- oil on canvas
- 123 x 120 cm
- Museo del Prado, Madrid

The Duke of Tuscany presented this painting to Philip IV of Spain and Mariana of Austria as a wedding present in 1649.

The work shows a scene from the Book of Genesis: Lot, advanced in age, lives with his two daughters in a cave. Because there are no men there to marry, the daughters conspire to ply their father with wine in order to seduce him. As a result, they each bear him a son, Moab and Ammon. An air of lustful intent and subliminal eroticism is subtly evoked in this work. The painterly treatment of the scene is inextricably and symbolically linked with this atmosphere. The figure of Lot, which is only vaguely outlined, blends in to the mysterious background haze, creating an atmosphere of restlessness. The brightly illuminated bodies of the daughters are the very embodiment of purity and are modeled with very little shade, causing certain areas to be merely suggested. The transparent veil in which the left-hand figure is enveloped increases the sensuality of the scene.

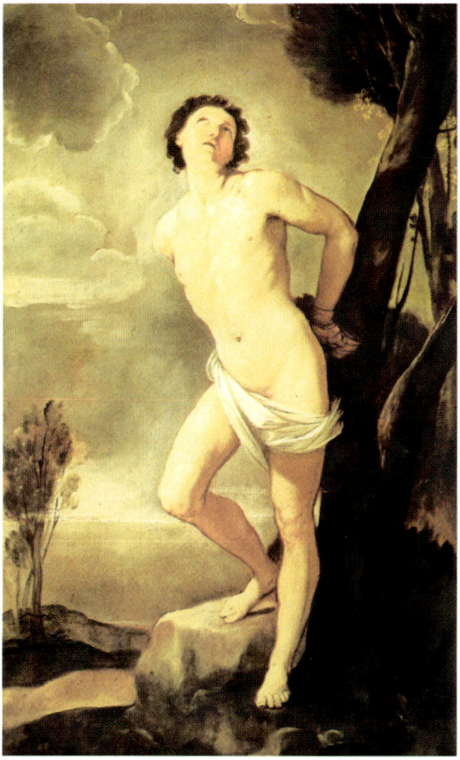

This painting abounds with pink tones, made slightly gray by a transparent layer of brown, which offsets the figure from the background. The sculptural treatment of the nude is heightened by the sense of depth created by the painting's various grounds. In the works painted by the artist during the final years of his life, Reni combines the classicism that he had always sought with mysticism arising from his Catholic faith. In any case, eroticism is inherent in this figure of St. Sebastian, who exhibits no signs of his martyrdom. The pose, the line of the body and the smooth surface of the skin all grant him sensuality, as does the loincloth that hangs provocatively across his loins, revealing a small area of pubic hair. This remarkably handsome nude represents a harmonious balance between pose, proportions and composition.

St. Sebastian

Guido Reni
(Bologna, 1575–1642)

- 1640–42
- oil on canvas
- 232 x 135 cm
- Pinacoteca Nazionale, Bologna

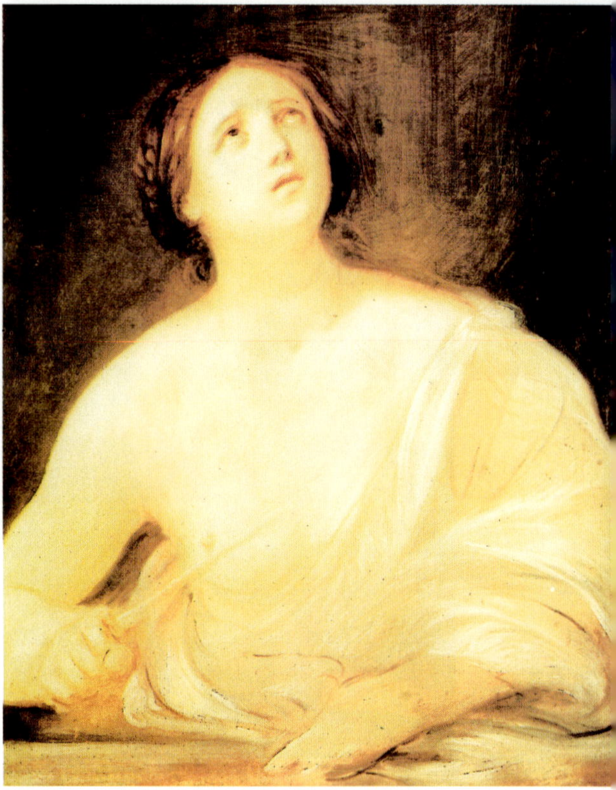

Lucretia's Suicide

Guido Reni
(Bologna, 1575–1642)

- 1640–42
- oil on canvas
- 91 x 73 cm
- Pinoteca Capitolina, Rome

Lucretia, the sister-in-law of Tarquinius Superbus, the seventh and last king of Rome (534–510 BC), was raped by the king's son, Sextus. In order to spare her husband and family humiliation, she committed suicide by stabbing herself. Although the torso is brightly illuminated, forming a stark contrast to the dark background, white highlights are reserved exclusively for areas of the drapery. This full nude, which exhibits very few tonal values, is the very embodiment of morality, and therefore is not intended to be the least bit erotic. Nonetheless, the figure of Lucretia possesses sensual features, enhanced by the treatment of color and light, which renders the volumes of her breasts scarcely discernible. The woman's facial expression conveys the profound sadness and despair that drives her to suicide.

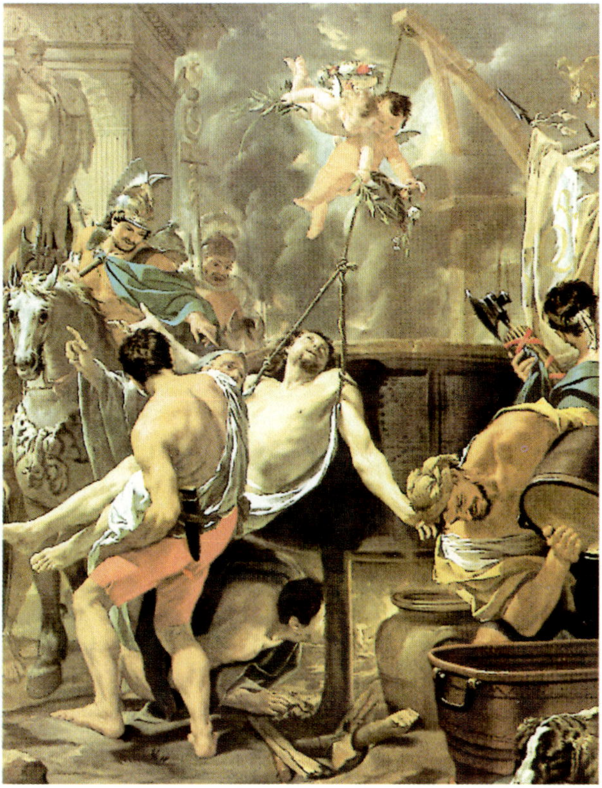

In this painting, aside from the evident influence of Poussin, the treatment of the figure and light approaches that of Caravaggio. The artist, named first painter to the king under Louis XIV and an exponent of French Neoclassicism, was under the protection of Cardinal de Richelieu and later Jean-Baptiste Colbert. This scene shows the martyrdom of St. John, who was arrested in Rome at the Latin Gate at the behest of Emperor Domitian and condemned to be burned in a cauldron of boiling oil. The fortunate saint not only survived the martyrdom, but was rejuvenated by it. Here, the apostle offers no resistance to his persecutors. The seminude bodies are extremely elegant, such as that of the athletic man holding the saint's legs as he is being hoisted. The effect produced by the light falling on the two figures is extraordinary, John's body shining brightly, thus heightening the drama and spiritual nature of the scene.

The Martyrdom of St. John the Evangelist before the Latin Gate

Charles Lebrun
(Paris, 1619–1690)

- 1641–42
- oil on canvas
- 282 x 224 cm
- Saint-Nicolas du Chardonnet, Paris

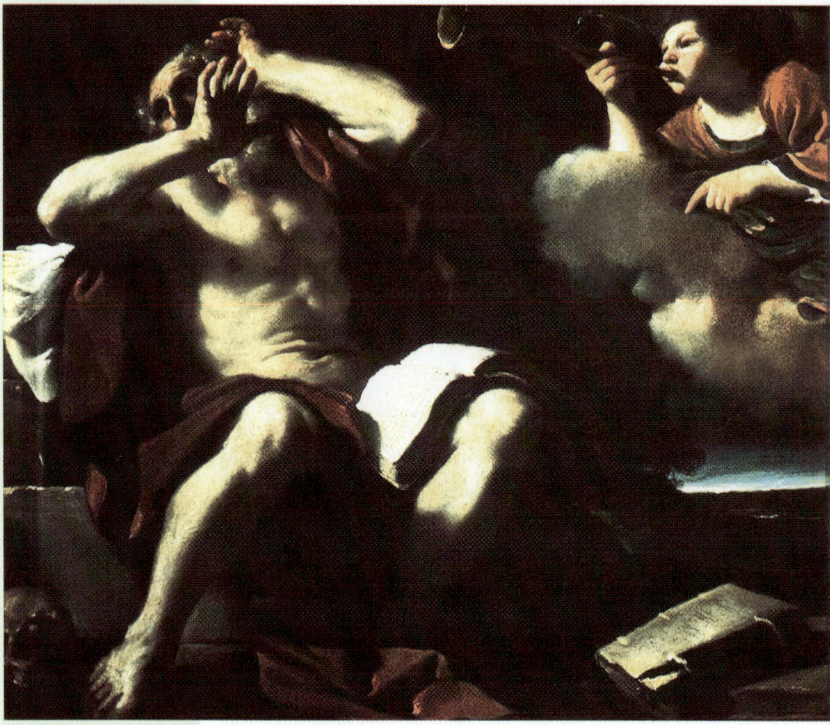

The Vision of St. Jerome

Il Guercino (Giovanni Francesco Barbieri)
(Cento, near Ferrara, 1591–Bologna, 1666)

- ca. 1642
- oil on canvas
- Pushkin Museum, Moscow

In this painting, St. Jerome appears terrified by the trumpets heralding the Last Judgment. The painting, which takes up the same theme as Ribera's St. Jerome, is here recreated in a composition that reveals certain affinities with tenebrism. The saint has a heroic body, which is appropriate neither to the figure's age nor to his condition. Nevertheless, it is remarkable for the treatment of flesh tones, which recall the work of Peter Paul Rubens and Titian, and for the green and blue hues, which are combined with intense light. Another interesting aspect is the way in which the highlights are used to create a sense of three-dimensionality of alarming realism. In keeping with works of this nature, this intensely dramatic scene fulfills the artistic criteria of the Baroque, albeit with a touch of classicism.

The dramatic dynamism of this work breaks with almost all the preceding treatments of the same theme, in a manner which is yet akin to Ribera's realism. The naked figure of St. Peter has been painted impasto, with thick layers of paint, the effects of which, however, have been softened by the skilful deployment of tonal gradations. As a result, the draftsmanship of the central figure is remarkably fluid, especially in the highlights.

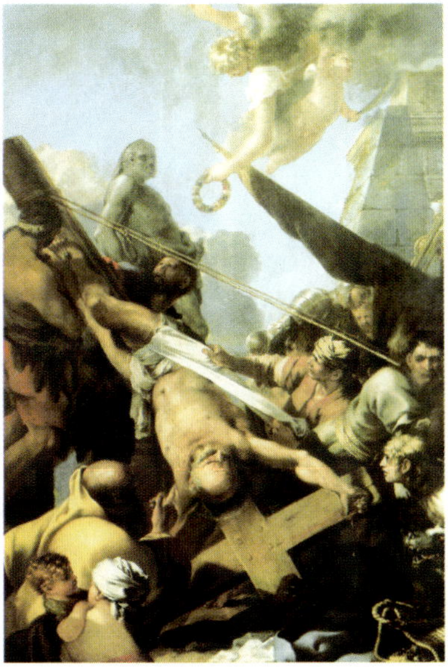

Crucifixion of St. Peter

Sébastien Bourdon
(Montpellier, 1616–Paris, 1671)

- ca. 1643
- oil on canvas
- 360 x 260 cm
- Notre-Dame, Paris

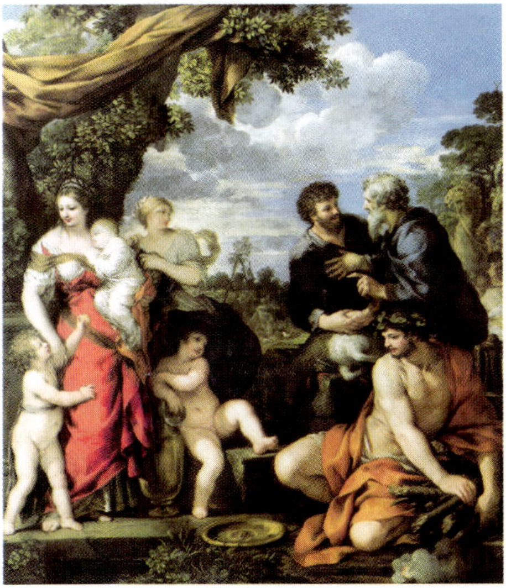

Jacob Meets Laban Again

Pietro da Cortona (properly **Pietro Berrettini**)
(Cortona, 1596–Rome, 1669)

- oil on canvas
- Musée du Louvre, Paris

After working for Laban for many years, Jacob returned to his father's land with all he had acquired. Laban followed, wishing to reproach him for departing so abruptly. The semi-nude figure in the foreground draped with an orange robe is one of Laban's sons. The physicality of the modeling is Classical, and Pietro evinces superb mastery of scaling and foreshortening.

Martyrdom of St. Bartholomew

Sébastien Bourdon
(Montpellier, 1616–Paris, 1671)

- oil on canvas
- 44.5 x 36 cm
- Musée des Jacobins, Morlaix

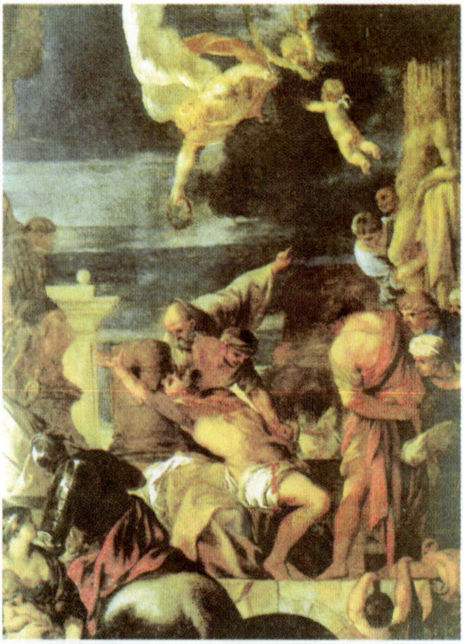

This canvas depicts the flaying of St. Bartholomew. The painterly treatment of his figure, from an anatomical point of view, is exceptionally thorough. The exemplary foreshortening of the body introduces movement into the scene, indeed provides it with its chief dramatic element, while the prevailing warm reddish light softens the bloodiness of the deed and endows unity.

Descent from the Cross

Sébastien Bourdon
(Montpellier, 1616–Paris, 1671)

- oil on canvas
- 303 x 157 cm
- Musée du Louvre, Paris

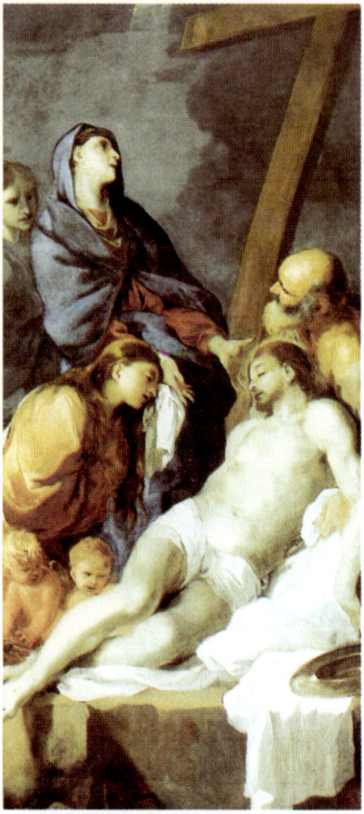

For its subtle attention to anatomical detail and forms, as well as its gravity, this is an exceptionally fine nude. Certain stylistic features are reminiscent of El Greco and Rubens. Dignified proportions and sculptural moulding combine to convey spirituality and grace. The pale greenish hue of the skin, while not entirely original, has been given close attention, both in respect of highlights and physical detail.

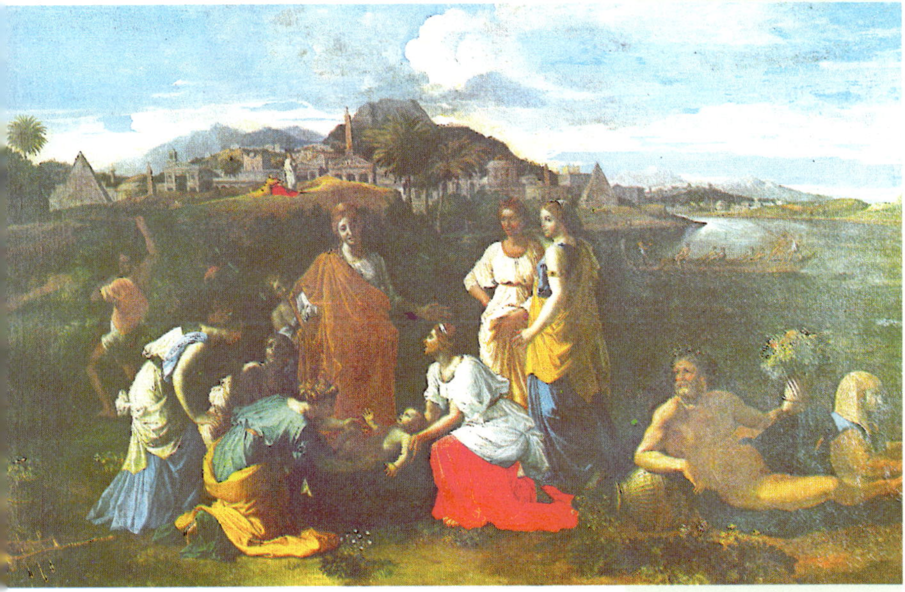

The Finding of Moses

Nicolas Poussin
(Les Andelys, 1594
–Rome, 1665)

- 1647
- oil on canvas
- 121 x 195 cm
- Musée du Louvre, Paris

This biblical scene captures the moment in which Moses, having just been rescued from the waters, is handed to the Pharaoh's daughter. The focal point of the work is the Egyptian princess, surrounded by her servants. On the right, a muscular male nude, resembling depictions of Neptune, is shown lying next to a sphinx, symbolizing the Nile River. This figure features in many paintings in which the Nile is alluded to. Despite its secondary role, the anatomical volumes are well studied; the wide range of hues in the shadows accentuate the figure's extraordinary beauty. The torso is cast in shadow, while the face and right arm are illuminated by a bright light. This work is remarkable for the way in which the artist has placed such well-executed figures in a landscape of equal artistic quality. This lends the painting a natural and fresh quality, freeing the work from solemnity and idealization.

St. Benedict Carried to Heaven by the Theological Virtues

Sebastiano Mazzoni
(Florence, ca. 1611 –Venice, 1678)

- 1648
- oil on paper on panel
- 41 x 29 cm
- Musée des Beaux-Arts, Nantes

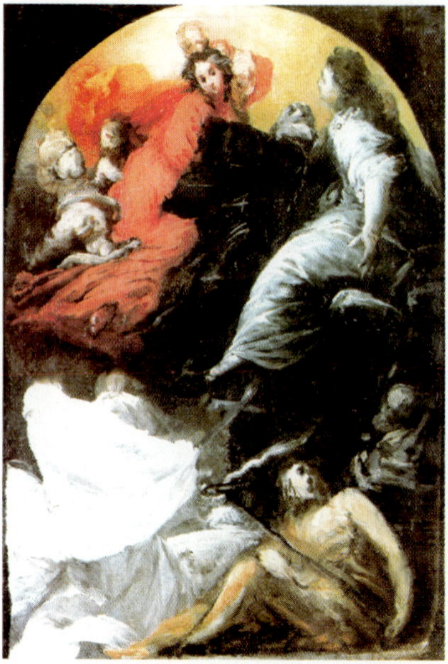

This painting in oils is a study for a larger work. The iconographic program and the compositional scheme are already well established, as also are the symbolic colors of the virtues: white for Faith, greenish-blue for Hope and red for Charity. St. Benedict is wearing a black habit. At the foot of the study, naked and disconsolate, Death is seated.

Bacchanal

Peter Paul Rubens
(Siegen, Westphalia, 1577 –Antwerp, 1641)

- ca. 1648
- oil on canvas
- Nationalmuseum, Stockholm

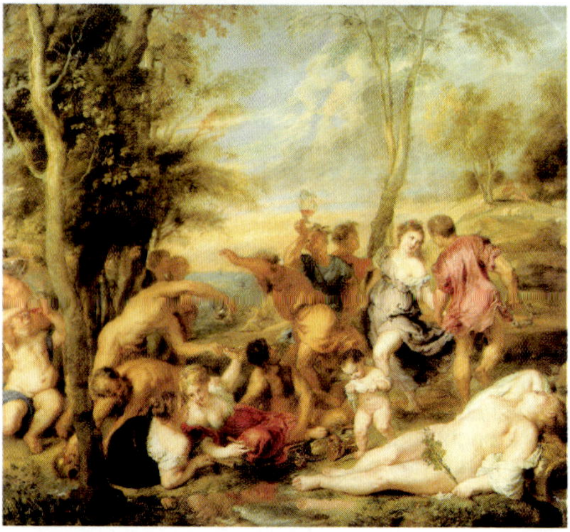

This painting is a copy of the one Titian had executed years earlier. With its dynamic, Baroque figures and its rather bombastic pictorial language, the scene is placed in a diaphanous, oneiric atmosphere dominated by voluptuousness and pleasure. The sleeping woman in the lower right corner embodies the quintessence of such qualities.

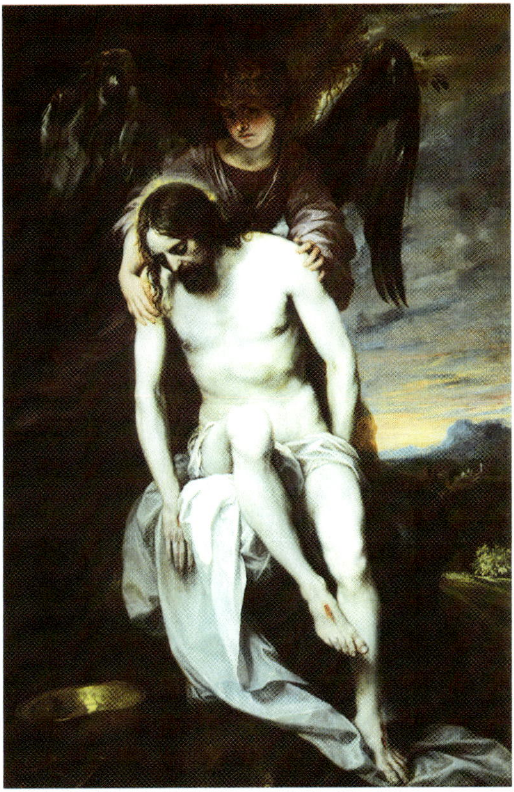

'his composition has a remarkable color scheme and
3aroque aspect, recalling Venetian Mannerism. The sub-
me anatomical study of the figure of Christ is illuminated
y a bright light, engendering a dramatic image reminiscent
f the work of Caravaggio. Set against a dark background
levoid of excessive spatial references, the marmoreal fig-
re of Jesus is clearly the focal point of the scene. His skin
s modeled in white, gray and pinkish hues, which are
eflected on the shroud. Next to him appear several ele-
nents that are presented in the manner of a still life, such
s the Crown of Thorns, almost hidden in the half-light. The
ainter appears to have been most interested in capturing
deal beauty and in utilizing the light to best effect, render-
ng it in many subtle gradations, in the Venetian manner.

Pietà

Alonso Cano
(Granada, 1601–1667)

- 1448–52
- oil on canvas
- 178 x 122 cm
- Museo del Prado, Madrid

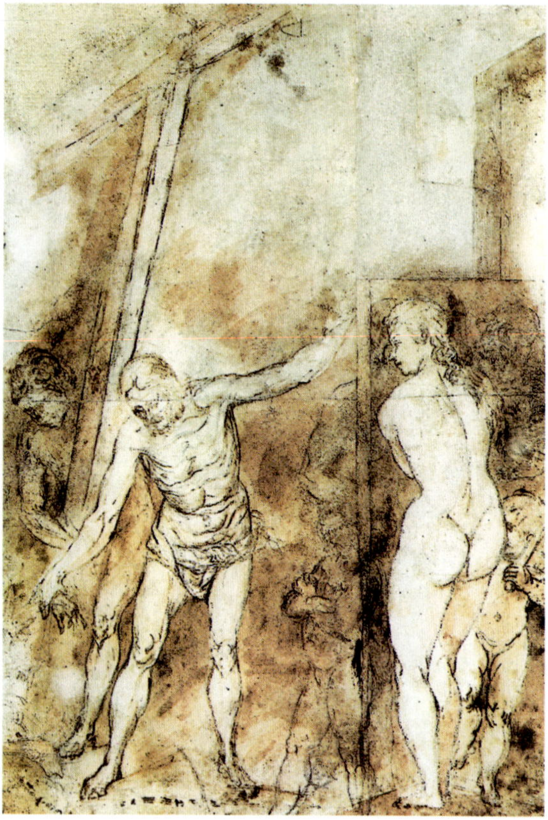

Christ's Descent into Limbo

Alonso Cano
(Granada, 1601–1667)

- pencil, ink, sepia and watercolor
- 27.2 x 19.2 cm
- Real Academia de Bellas Artes de San Fernando, Madrid

Cano was one of the very few Spanish artists of the 17th century to execute drawings on a very wide range of themes. His style is rather eclectic. In this drawing, Christ is depicted after the Crucifixion, on his descent into limbo to redeem the righteous on the Day of Judgment. The soul of one of the elect in the form of a naked woman, back turned to the viewer, is shown on the right. The artist traces the female figure in sensual, tenuous lines that are quite unique in Spanish Baroque, evoking delicacy and softness of skin. The figure of Christ is rendered in confident, dark lines that lend him more pronounced modeling.

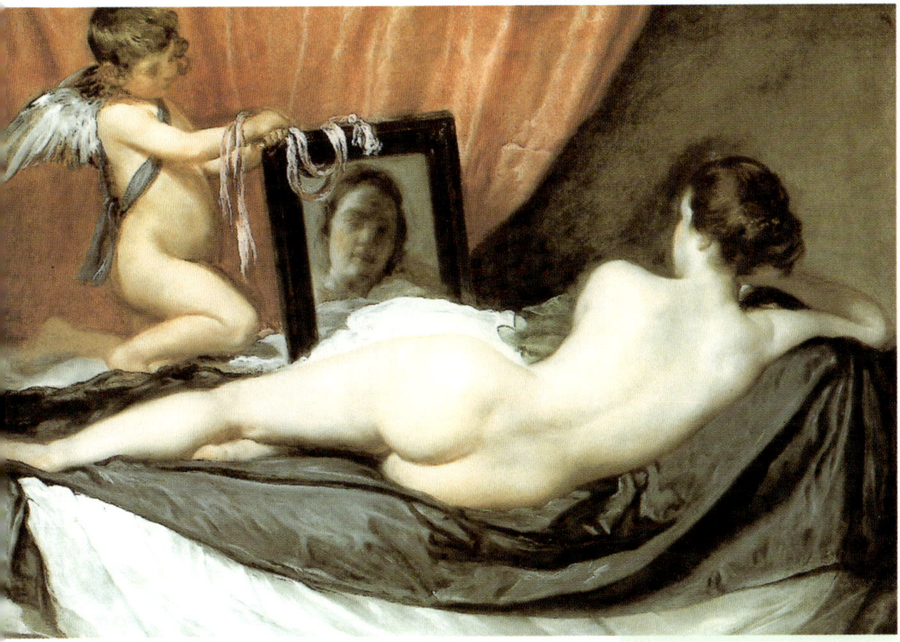

The Toilet of Venus

Diego Rodríguez de Silva Velázquez
(Seville, 1599–Madrid, 1660)

- 1647–51
- oil on canvas
- 122.5 x 177 cm
- National Gallery, London

he only surviving painting of a female nude by Velázquez, ıis attractive, sensual figure of Venus, with her back to the ıewer, reclining on a bed and resting her head on her right and, contemplates her own beauty in a small mirror held by winged Cupid. In his customary manner, the painter demy-ıologizes Venus, although the silk sheets, curtains and tmosphere give rise to a certain majestic air, to which the killfully modeled, smooth body contributes. Indeed, the pose f the goddess may have been inspired by Classical statuary. he woman is emotionally cool and distant, as is her child, for hom she shows not the slightest interest. Cupid nonetheless erves his mother attentively. The painting has a subliminal ıessage: Love is always a slave to Beauty. In May of 1914, woman stabbed the painting seven times. Thanks to excel-ent restoration work, the marks are scarcely noticeable today.

Baptism of Christ

Sébastien Bourdon
(Montpellier, 1616–Paris, 1671)

- oil on canvas
- oval, 150 x 116.2 cm
- The Metropolitan Museum of Art, New York

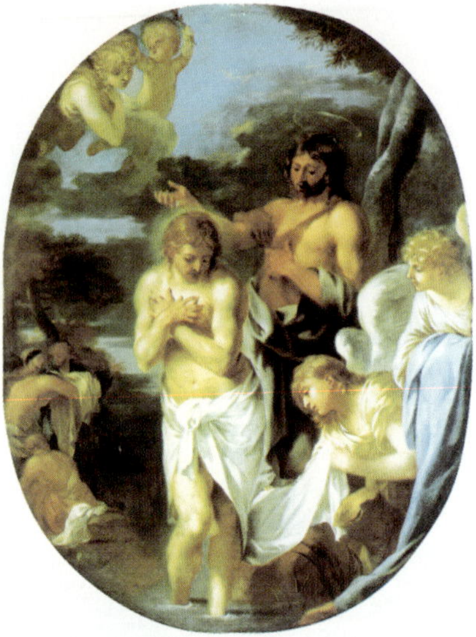

The pictorial treatment and dynamics of the figures in this work recall a mythological scene. The figures are delicate, rather sensual, and even exuberantly depicted. John the Baptist's purposefulness contrasts starkly with Christ's meekness, his seminude body appearing almost to emit its own light, in an attitude as humble as he is religiously devout.

Martyrdom of St. Andrew

Sébastien Bourdon
(Montpellier, 1616–Paris, 1671)

- after 1649
- oil on canvas
- 305 x 260 cm
- Musée des Augustins, Toulouse

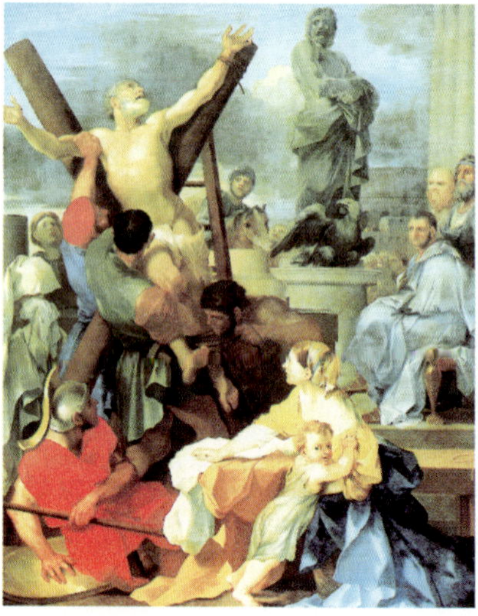

The artistic execution of the saint's body is both fastidious and beautiful, despite the tortures being visited upon it. The subtle tonal modulations of the skin enabled the artist to elaborate quite intricate forms, without having to resort to abrupt transitions in the level of light. The young, athletic body does not really fit the elderly face, a practice acceptable to the Academy, which was often more interested in idealization than in realism.

The Rape of Europe

Peter Paul Rubens
(Siegen, Westphalia, 1577 –Antwerp, 1640)

- oil on canvas
- Museo del Prado, Madrid

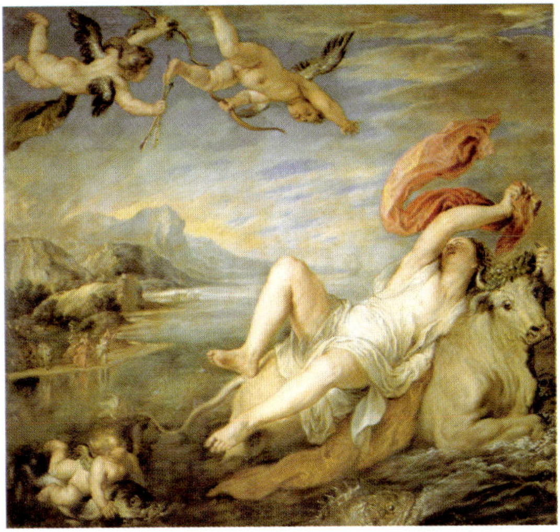

ı this work, Rubens creates a copy of a Titian painting more ır less down to the last detail, albeit in his own style: essential haracteristics remain the same, yet technique and formal spects change. In contrast to Titian's original, Rubens' work ; softer and less vehement, although hardly less erotic.

The Holy Family with Six Putti

Nicolas Poussin
(Les Andelys, 1594–Rome, 1665)

- 1651
- oil on canvas
- 96.5 x 133 cm
- The J. Paul Getty Museum, Malibu, and The Norton Simon Foundation, Pasadena

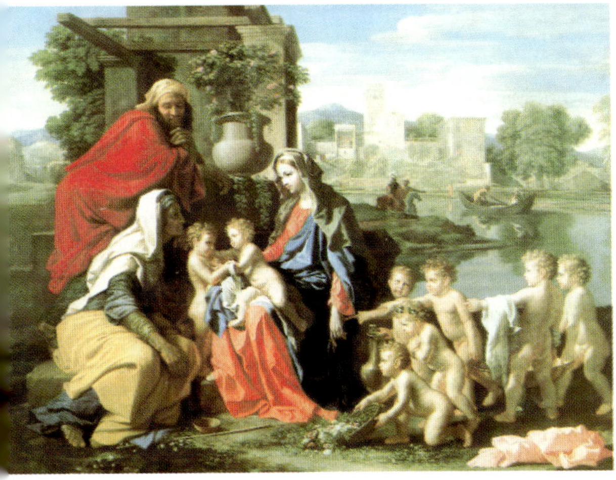

'oussin has grasped the opportunity in this depiction of ıe Holy Family to paint a fascinating series of nude child gures. Their varied poses, expressive faces and the andor they transmit make them personifications of innoence. Despite their tender age, their bodies are slender, vith harmonious, well-modeled forms.

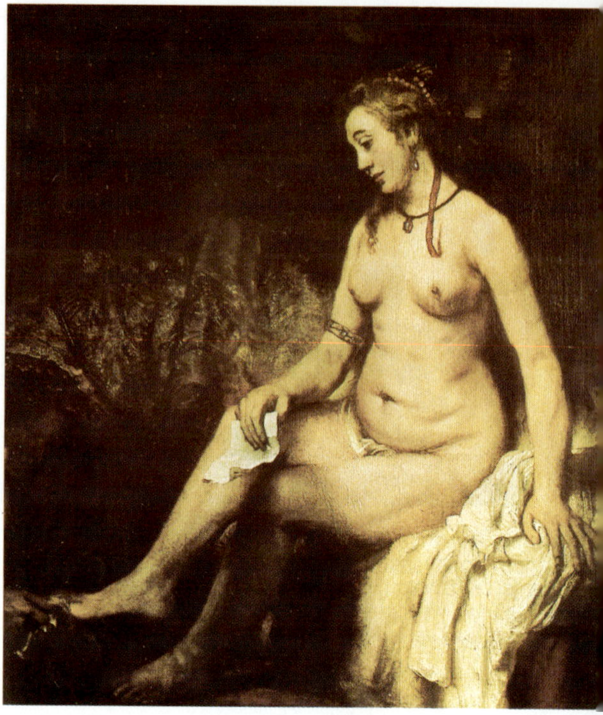

Bathsheba at Her Toilet

Rembrandt Harmensz van Rijn
(Leiden, 1606–Amsterdam, 1669)

- 1654
- oil on canvas
- 142 x 142 cm
- Musée du Louvre, Paris

Toward the end of a period in which he concentrated on biblical themes, Rembrandt painted this picture of his mistress of nearly six years, Hendrickje Stoffels, as Bathsheba. She had come to work as a maid in the Rembrandt household in 1646 Until 1662, one year before her death, she was the painter's preferred model. Here Rembrandt foregoes any attempt at an idealistic representation, producing instead a highly naturalistic one that reveals both virtues and imperfections. The limited chromatic range is predominated by numerous earth tones. The artist's use of chiaroscuro enables him to highlight the figure against a dark background without delineating clear contours, subtly blending the shadows with the illuminated areas. For Rembrandt, the nude was, above all else, an ideal genre in which to experiment with the play of light on the human body. The voluptuousness of his subjects is due more to this fact rather than any interest in eroticism.

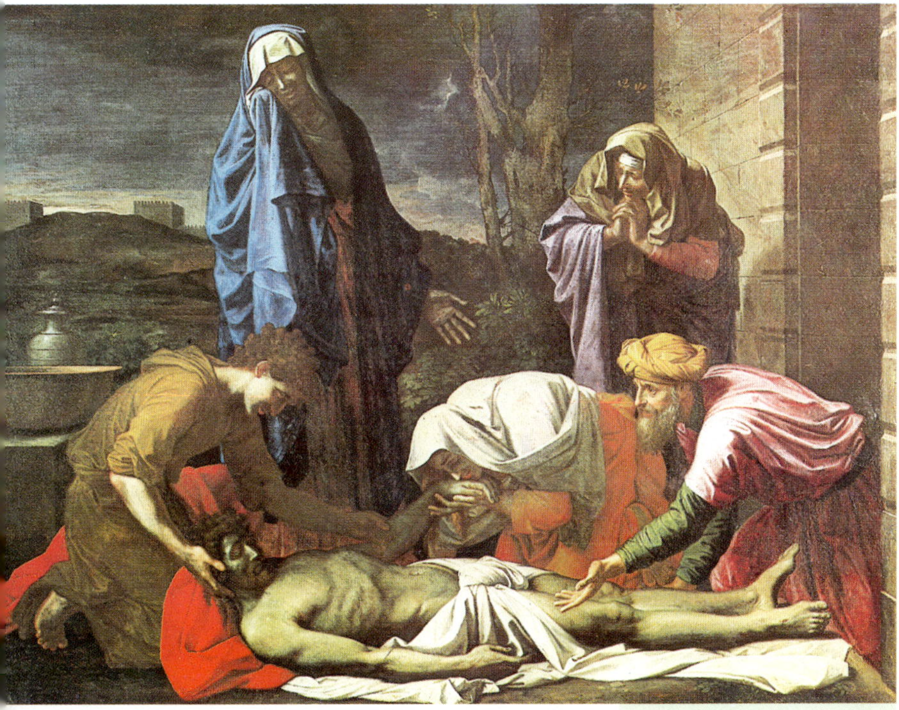

The Lamentation

Nicolas Poussin
(Les Andelys, 1594
–Rome, 1665)

- ca.1654–57
- oil on canvas
- 94 x 130 cm
- National Gallery of Ireland, Dublin

this work, an interesting chiaroscuro technique is used in e modeling of the figures, of which Christ is given the most iorough treatment. The consummately rendered body of the ecumbent figure is attenuated, conveying a muscular, athtic man, whose greenish gray skin reveals that he is dead. ne sober realism of this image is extraordinary indeed. The reshortened figure conveys all the tragedy of the moment, nding the scene a meditative quality. The treatment of the nadows, which almost enshroud the schematic face, confer n air of mystery to Christ, whose only visible facial features e the high cheekbones, the temples and the nose. The nadows cast across the body are dense, modeling the adaver with sculptural clarity. The solemn drama played out y the various figures in the scene creates a sense of emoonal cohesion among the protagonists.

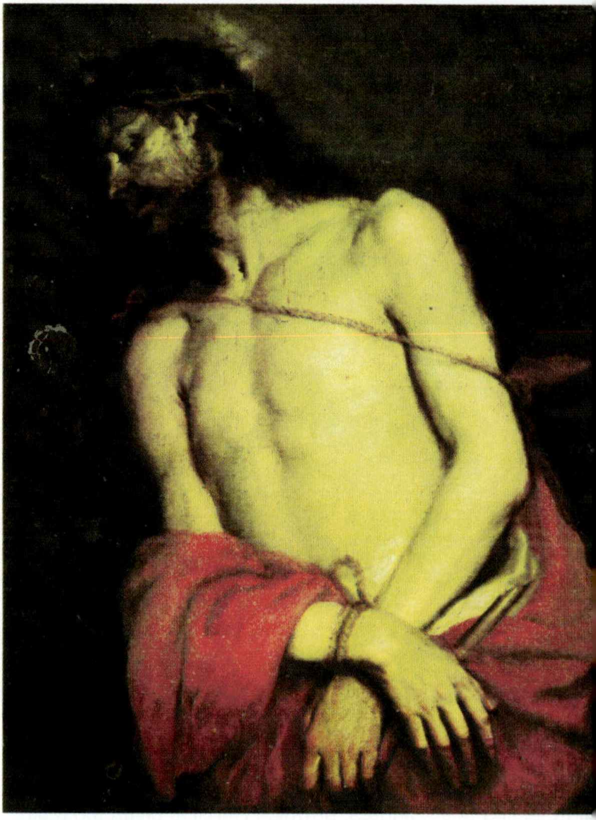

Ecce Homo

Mateo Cerezo the Younger
(Burgos, 1626–Madrid, 1666)

- oil on canvas
- 98 x 75 cm
- Szépmüvészeti Múzeum, Budapest

This sensitively rendered portrayal of Christ is exceedingly beautiful, a characteristic of most of the artist's figures. Not only does it reveal Cerezo's artistic mastery, but also his skill at conceiving striking compositions. Christ's pose, in which h leans slightly to the left, leaves the face immersed in a half-light, making the torso the focal point of the painting, which is bathed in an intense light emanating from the right. This com position lends the motif an air of gravity and mystery. The cloak that covers part of the figure is secured by a cord that runs across the top half of Christ's chest and over his left arm a detail that heightens the sensuality of his naked body, whic is wrapped in a crimson, half-fallen tunic. With this work, the painter achieves an image of unparalleled realism, revealing himself to be a fine exponent of the Spanish Baroque.

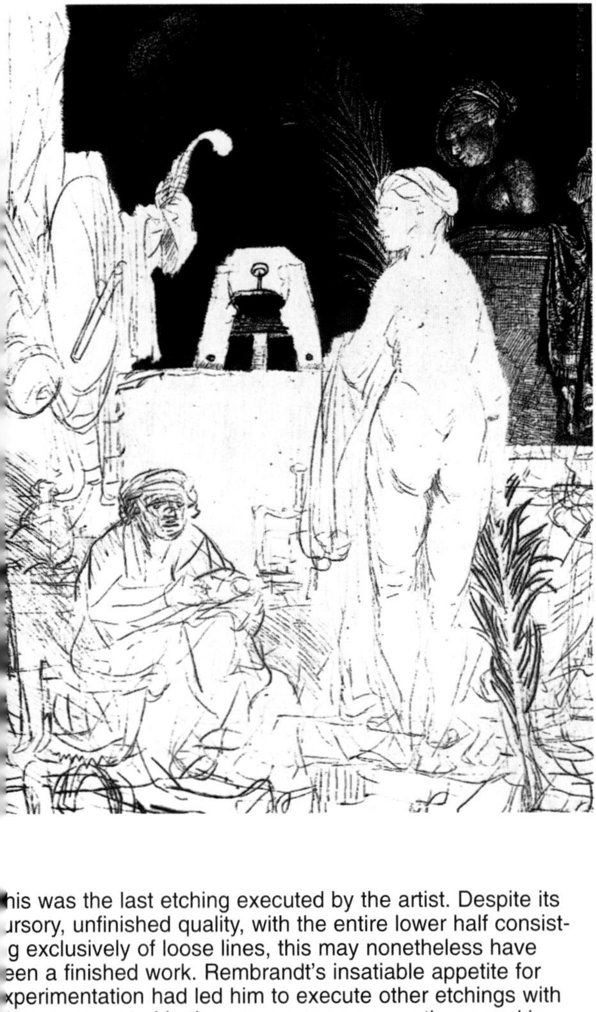

ɦis was the last etching executed by the artist. Despite its ɹrsory, unfinished quality, with the entire lower half consist- g exclusively of loose lines, this may nonetheless have een a finished work. Rembrandt's insatiable appetite for xperimentation had led him to execute other etchings with gures presented in the same manner, sometimes working n a single plate for over ten years. Throughout the course f his life the painter depicted many nudes, evoking the roticism of the female body in particular in his own inimi- ıble style. In this instance, the model, with her back to the pectator, is rendered naturalistically.

An Artist Drawing a Model

Rembrandt (Rembrandt Harmensz van Rijn)
(Leiden, 1606–Amsterdam, 1669)

- ca. 1639
- etching
- 23.1 x 18.4 cm
- Graphische Sammlung Albertina, Vienna

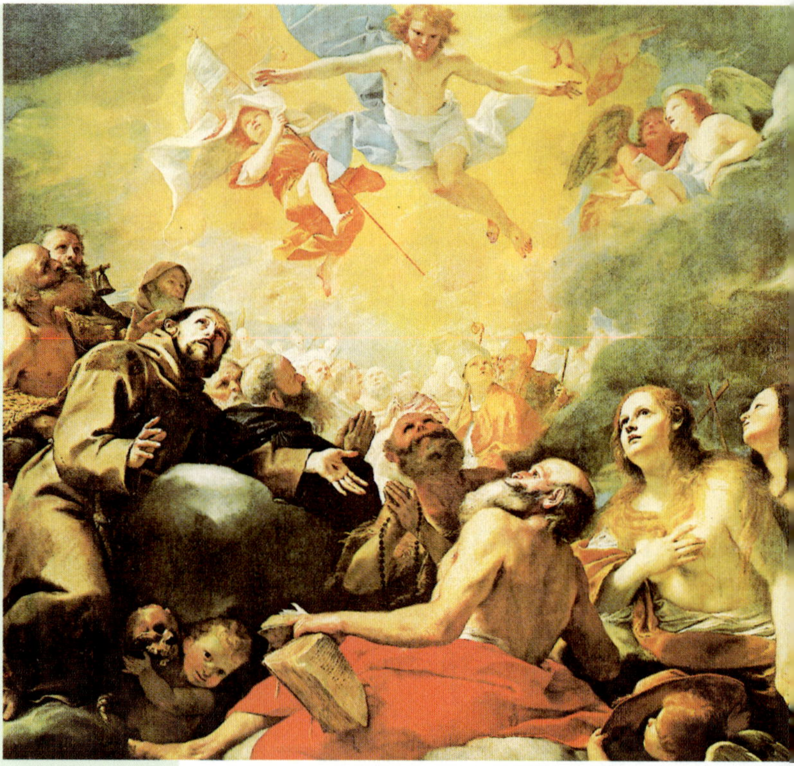

Christ in Glory with Saints

Mattia Preti (also called **Il Cavaliere Calabrese**)
(Taverna, Calabria, 1613 –La Valletta, Malta, 1699)

- ca. 1656
- oil on canvas
- 220 x 253 cm
- Museo del Prado, Madrid

This intricate work is a highlight of the so-called decorative Baroque, and draws together elements as diverse as Caravaggio's treatment of light, Veronese's palette and Correggio's handling of the human body. It was designed to be hung from the ceiling, where it achieves its most astonishing optical effect. The half-nude figures are portrayed in an extremely realistic fashion, with subtle modeling that takes into account the light radiating from the glorified Christ. Although the painting is not exactly depicted in an exaggeratedly puritanical manner, the foreshortening of the figures causes them to appear almost entirely clothed. The aesthetic function of the figures is to convey the elation of the saints anxiously anticipating Christ's appearance. Their expressions range from a feverish ecstasy to mysticism, which is accomplished without the scene eclipsing the theme it depicts.

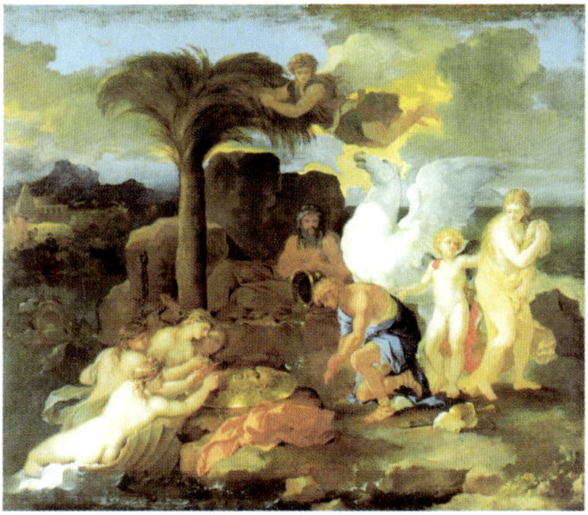

Perseus and Andromeda

Sébastien Bourdon
(Montpellier, 1616–Paris, 1671)

- oil on canvas
- 113 x 140.8 cm
- Alte Pinakothek, Munich

erseus cut off the head of the Medusa, and her face became mblazoned upon his shield. Pursuing his flight, he saved ndromeda from being devoured by a sea monster. This cene depicts the sea nymphs presenting him with the coral to which the Medusa's blood had been turned. The attractive ensuality of the nymphs is enhanced by their poses and right skin coloration, which contrasts starkly against the dark- r elements both of the foreground and the background.

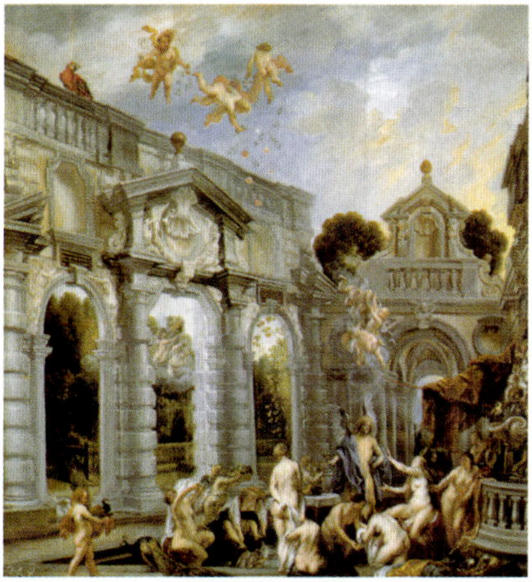

Goddesses and Nymphs After the Bath

Jacob Jordaens
(Antwerp, 1593–1678)

- oil on canvas
- 131 x 127 cm
- Museo del Prado, Madrid

ne scene would seem to have some reference to the gend of Cupid and Psyche. The opulent nude figures e wonderfully carnal, that of Cupid in particular stand- g out from the rest. The work is conceivably a osthumous) homage to Rubens, since, amongst other ings, the scene is set in the gardens of his house.

Lamentation

Sébastien Bourdon
(Montpellier, 1616–Paris, 1671)

- oil on canvas
- 46 x 55 cm
- Musée Fabre, Montpellier

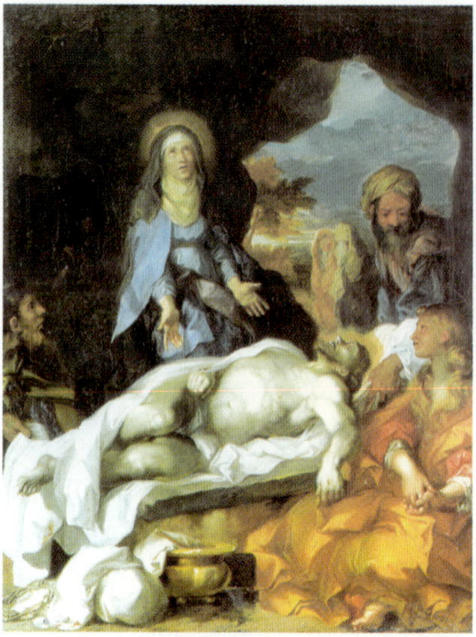

The figure of Chri laid out on the tomb is one of Bourdon's finest achievements. Here, there is nor of the tenderness that often characterizes his brushwork. Instead, he has focused on corporeal bulk, foreshortening an on conveying the beauty a powerfu masculine body can display. Ther is no overlooking death here, yet oddly enough it does not diminish the beauty of wha is presented.

Time Destroying Beauty

Giovanni Domenico Cerrini
(1609–1681)

- oil on canvas
- 258 x 229 cm
- Museo del Prado, Madrid

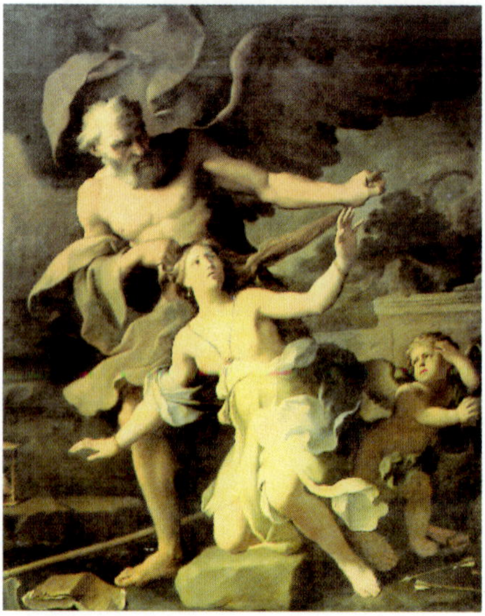

This Baroque painting is an allegory of Time. An elderly man about to kill a young woman (representing beauty and love) i the presence of Cupid, on the right, who is sighing. The youn woman's body is physically attractive, her garment providing frame for her young breasts. The coolness of her expression attenuates the melodrama of the scene, a formal quality that grew steadily more popular with Neoclassicist painters.

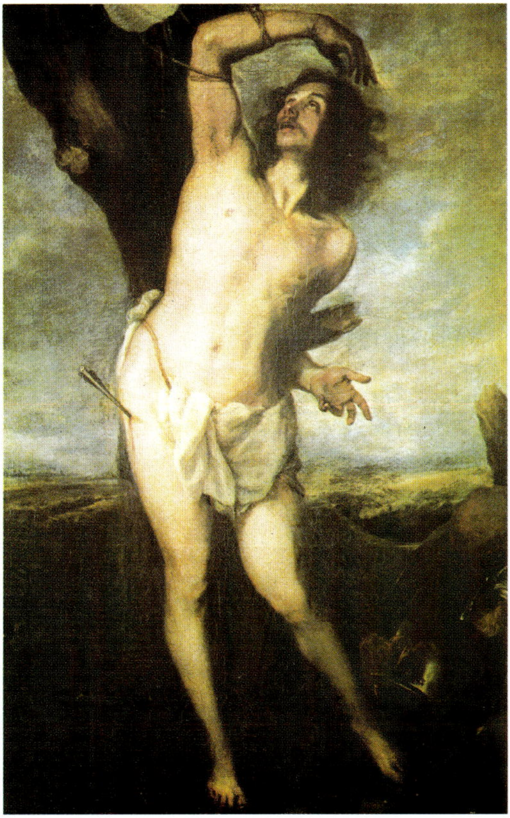

St. Sebastian

Juan Carreño de Miranda
(Avilés, 1614–Madrid, 1685)

- 1656
- oil on canvas
- 171 x 113 cm
- Museo del Prado, Madrid

his work shows a highly erotic nude. Indeed, in the Baroque eriod, St. Sebastian was frequently portrayed with great sen-uality. This may have been a way of distracting the viewer om the horrible torture scene. With curved hips and delicately odeled legs, the contrapposto figure appears almost femi-ne. The rhythm of the torso is achieved by means of sinuous nd straight lines that form an extension of those beginning in e legs. The raised arm, together with the right leg, form a e that divides the painting in two, whereas the hip marks the oint of flexion of the torso with which a highly refined plasticity achieved. Sensuality, elegance and a Mannerist aesthetic ontrast sharply with the painting's tragic theme, which is omewhat softened by the beauty of the scene.

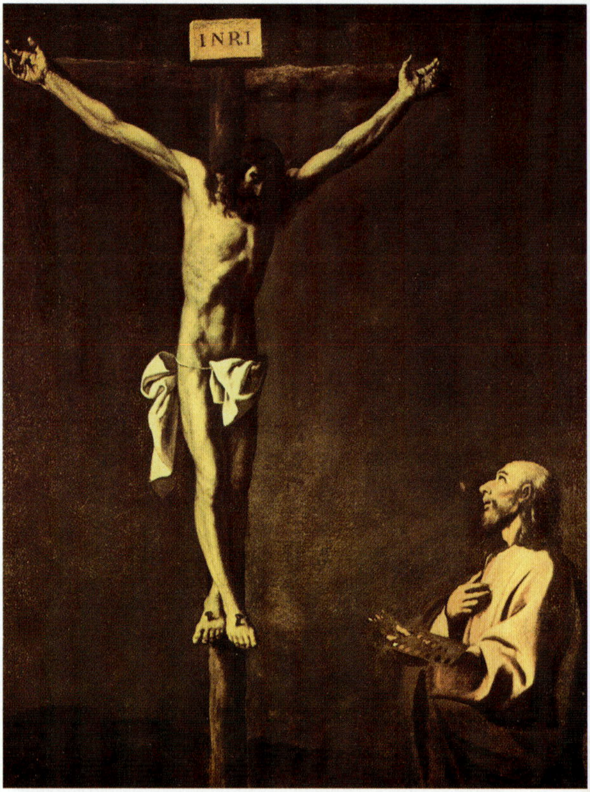

St. Lucas Contemplating Christ on the Cross

Francisco de Zurbarán
(Fuentedecantos, Andalusia, 1598–Madrid, 1664)

- 1635–40
- oil on canvas
- 105 x 84 cm
- Museo del Prado, Madrid

A notable characteristic of this Crucifixion scene is the extraordinary tension conveyed in the figure of Christ. The sober colors and the way in which only one side of Christ's bare body is illuminated heighten the drama of the scene, inviting contemplation and introspection. The arms reveal that death has triumphed, for, under the weight of Christ's body, they have stretched and the chest has been raised, resulting in death by suffocation. Because this work was intended as a devotional image, no blood is to be seen, which is perhaps the most striking difference between it and more traditional depictions of the Crucifixion. The originality of this painting can, however, be observed in other elements as well, notably the way in which the body of Christ has been modeled with light and shade, giving rise to a dramatic image indeed.

Lucrece

Guido Cagnacci (Canlassi)
(Santarcangelo di Romagna, 1601–Vienna, 1663)

- 1657
- oil on canvas
- 87 x 66 cm
- Musée des Beaux-Arts, Lyon

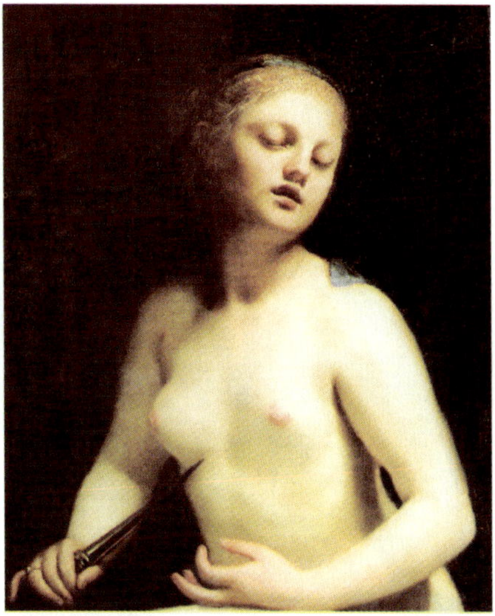

Young, smooth-skinned and firm-breasted, although only her torso and part of a thigh are visible, this Lucrece is depicted completely naked, which serves to underline her helplessness. The drama of the moment is perfectly described, and while the black background makes her pale, bright figure stand out, it also emphasizes the sense of her desolation and loneliness.

The Birth of Bacchus

Nicolas Poussin
(Les Andelys, 1594 –Rome, 1665)

- 1657
- oil on canvas
- 122 x 179 cm
- Fogg Art Museum, Cambridge, MA

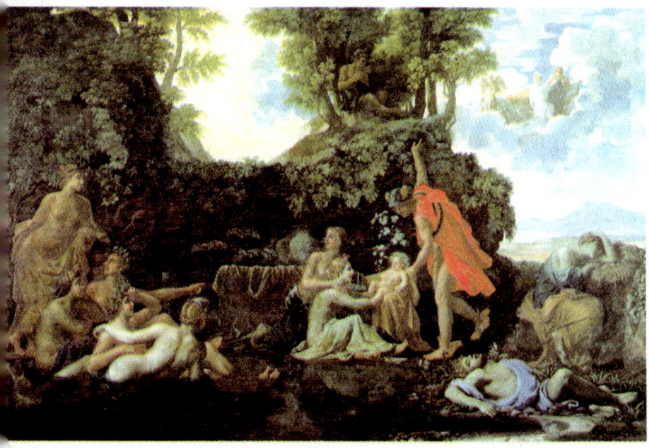

Mercury is depicted entrusting Bacchus to the nymphs who will suckle him. He has just been removed from the thigh of Jupiter, who can be seen in the sky, lying on a bed and being tended by Hera. Left, we see the god Pan in the company of several lovely nymphs. Right, Echo mourns over the dead body of Narcissus.

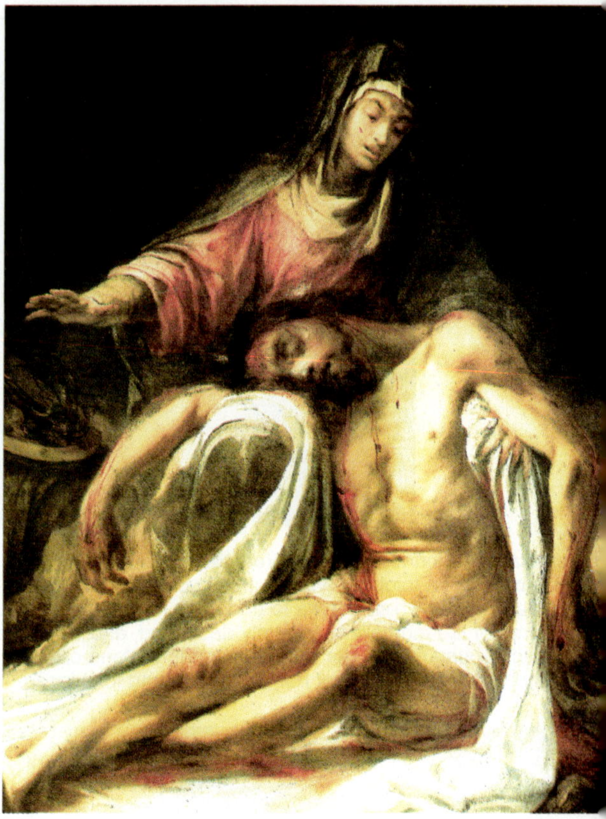

Pietà

Juan de Valdés Leal
(Seville, 1622–1690)

- 1657–59
- oil on canvas
- 144 x 160 cm
- Metropolitan Museum of Art, New York

This composition forms a triangle, which begins along Christ's legs and moves up to the Virgin's head and down her right arm. The figure of Christ is remarkable for its striking verisimilitude and pathos. Sitting on the ground and resting his head on the Virgin's lap, he exhibits an elaborate treatment of light that increases the drama of the scene. The muscles are executed in the sfumato technique, such that the profiles of the figures are somewhat blurred. The foreshortening of the bent leg is executed in a highly naturalistic manner, and all the joints are depicted with wounds covered in blood. The figure stands out against the surrounding darkness, as does the white shroud that the Virgin wraps around her son, giving rise to a moving scene, conceived to impress and arouse fervent devotion in the viewer.

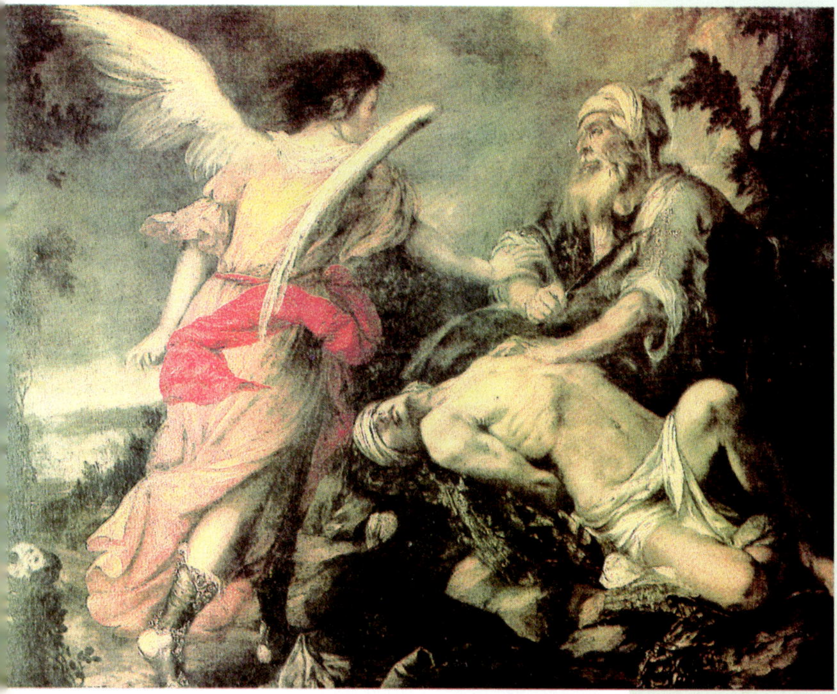

To put Abraham's faith to the test, God commands the elderly man to sacrifice his son. The scene shows the moment in which an angel, sent by God, stops the patriarch from carrying out God's will. Despite his youth, Isaac, blindfolded and bound, has been given the sensual body of an adult. The execution of this nude is masterly, the foreshortening daring. The artist fully involved himself both in its conception and execution. The rather unnatural pose of this figure heightens the dramatic tension of the scene. The light subtly models the figure, whose contorted pose creates a torsion in the back. The thorax is stretched, revealing the pectoral and dorsal muscles, while the abdomen is taut and smooth.

The Sacrifice of Isaac

Juan de Valdés Leal
(Seville, 1622–1690)

- 1657–59
- oil on canvas
- 189 x 249 cm
- private collection, Palma de Mallorca

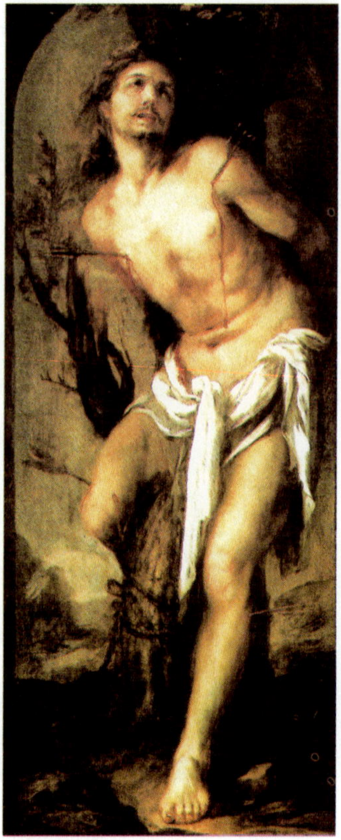

St. Sebastian

Juan de Valdés Leal
(Seville, 1622–1690)

- ca. 1659
- oil on canvas
- 141 x 53 cm
- Mary Magdalene, Chapel of the Fifth Sorrow, Seville

In this painting, St. Sebastian exhibits a powerful, tall and slender body and, in accordance with the ideal of beauty of the time, lacks well-defined muscles, creating an androgynous impression and increasing the sensuality of the scene. Compared to other works in which the martyr is depicted in a static pose, this nude exhibits an extraordinary dynamism, which is heightened by the warm light in which he bathes. His twisted pose, a result of the pain he is suffering, is enhanced by the naturalistically rendered loincloth covering his genitals. The saint's weight rests on one leg, his luminous body is set against a dark background and his facial expression has an almost mystical quality.

he execution of
ese two figures
technically bril-
ant and, due to
e almost metallic
ghlights of the
kin coloration,
ensually speaking
ther cool. The
anvas calls to
ind certain
lemish works
fluenced by the
alian Renais-
ance, although, in
ct, it is Baroque,
nd approaches
rench Neo-
assicism in cer-
in respects. The
gures display
old foreshorten-
g, in particular
at by means of
hich Adam's con-
entional decency
ensured.

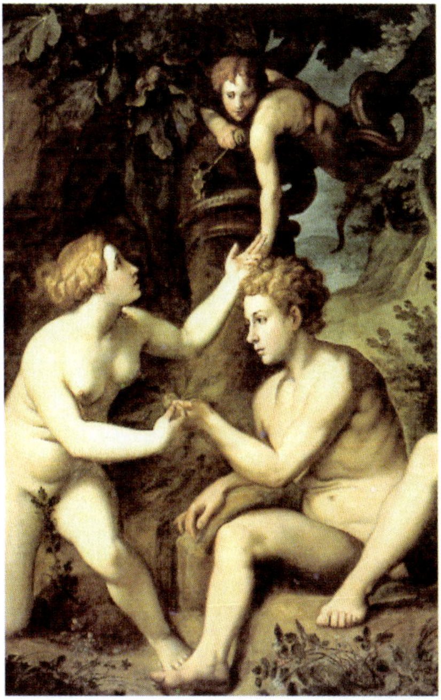

Adam Receiving the Forbidden Fruit from Eve

Pietro Fachetti or Fracchetti

- oil on canvas
- Museo del Prado, Madrid

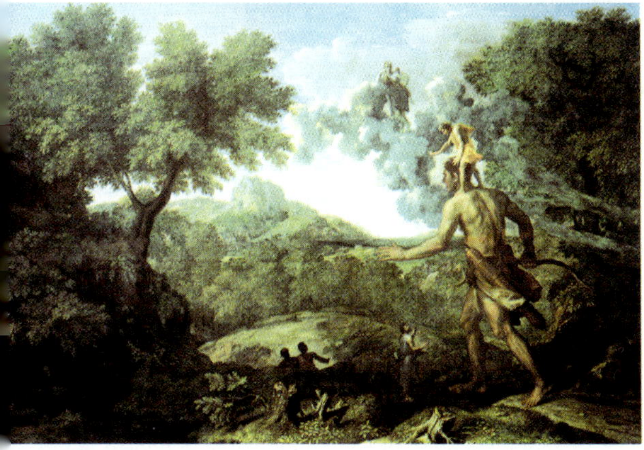

Landscape with Orion

Nicolas Poussin
(Les Andelys, 1594 –Rome, 1665)

- 1658
- oil on canvas
- 119 x 83 cm
- Metropolitan Museum of Art, New York

linded by Enopion, king of Chios, for having attempted to ape his daughter, and accompanied now by his guide, edalion, who is standing on his shoulders, the giant Orion alks east in search of a cure for his blindness. While his ngainly figure does have presence, its skin coloration tends merge with that of the landscape, thus involving the view- r far less than it otherwise might.

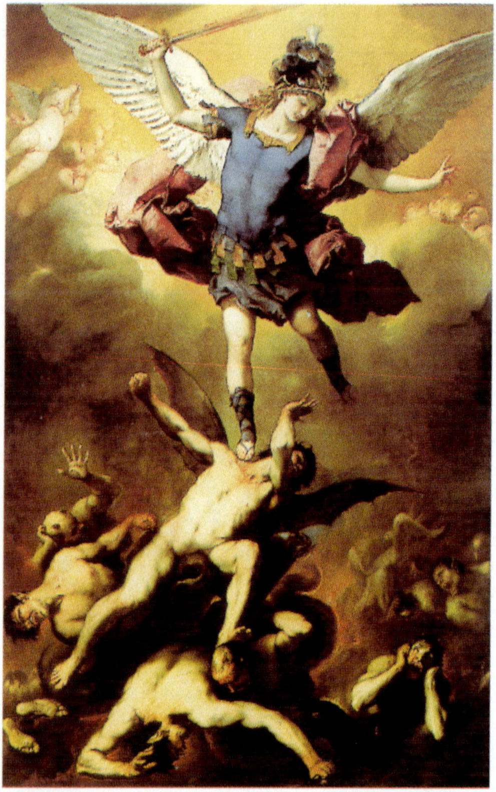

The Fall of the Rebel Angels

Luca Giordano
(Naples, 1634–1705)

- 1666
- oil on canvas
- 419 x 283 cm
- Kunsthistorisches Museum, Vienna

Luca Giordano was sometimes called "Luca fa presto" because of the speed with which he executed his works. The fall of the rebel angels was a controversial point during the Counter-Reformation. This work symbolizes the triumph of light over darkness, and the artist uses it as an opportunity to conceive a dramatic image of the struggle between heaven and hell by employing chiaroscuro. The nudes constituting the group of fallen angels display a high degree of dynamism. Giordano's virtuoso treatment of light and bold foreshortening heighten the tension of the scene. The armed angel, Michael, treads on the writhing bodies of the vanquished in a grand gesture of victory. Illuminated from above, the bodies are muscular and the shadows they cast create a mysterious atmosphere typical in tenebrism.

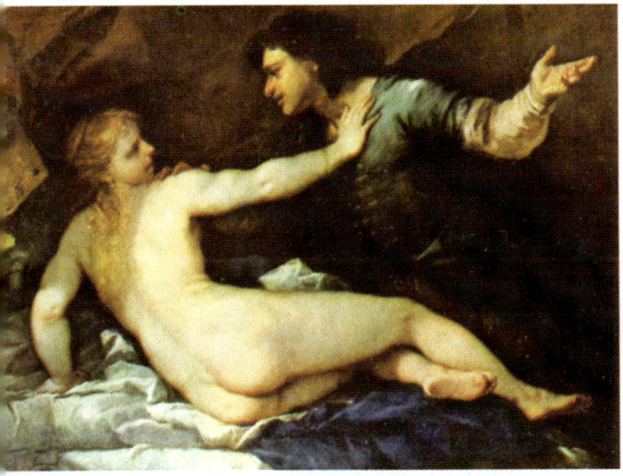

Lucrece and Tarquin

Luca Giordano
(Naples, 1634–1705)

- oil on canvas
- 138 x 188 cm
- Museo e Gallerie Nazionali, Capodimonte

ucrece took her life after being raped by Tarquin, the son f her brother-in-law Tarquinius Superbus, king of Rome. he painting depicts a somewhat amiable Lucrece, the arm tones of her naked body heightening her attractive-ess, so that she seems almost to be inviting rather than ejecting. This nude figure is elegant and pleasantly mod-led, with stylistic details that recall Titian's art.

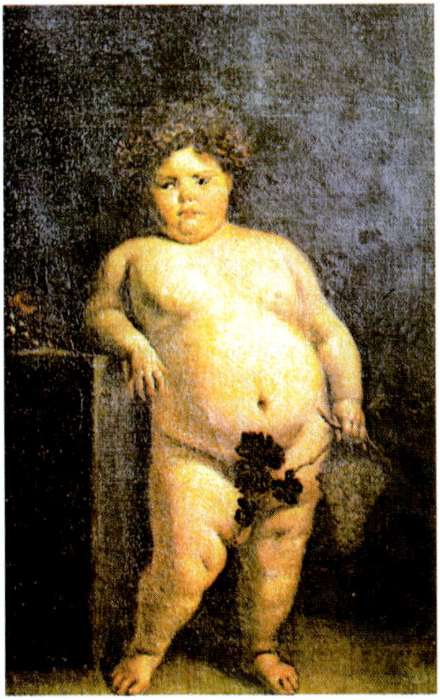

The Nude Monster

Juan Carreño de Miranda
(Avila, 1614–Madrid, 1685)

- ca. 1670
- oil on canvas
- 200 x 101 cm
- Museo del Prado, Madrid

nfluenced by Titian nd Rubens, this ainting shows the rtist's clear affilia-ons with the Real-sm of the Madrid School. The treat-nent of light is ex-eptionally accom-lished, describing erfectly the forms nd outlines of this verweight dwarf gure with its xpressive face, robably one of the nany dwarfs kept at ourt as jesters and ntertainers.

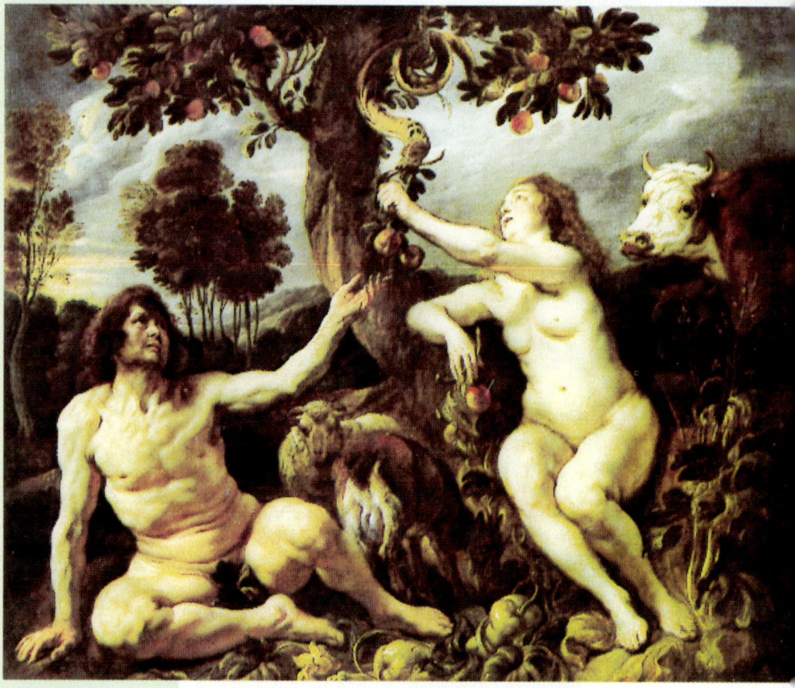

Original Sin

Jacob Jordaens
(Antwerp, 1593–1678)

- 184.5 x 221 cm
- Szépmüvészeti Múzeum, Budapest

The painterly handling of this work betrays the influence of Rubens. The nudes' intense highlights combine with the warmer flesh tones to create a distinctive body type, recalling the figures of Caravaggio. Although these two nudes are remarkable for their exceptional quality, it is the figure of Adam that is most interesting, for it is boldly foreshortened and displays a remarkable treatment of the flesh, which brings out all the subtleties of the skin and musculature. Both bodies are consummately executed and modeled with the utmost care. Adam, muscular and well built, is depicted with his legs spread. Eve is extremely voluptuous, with smooth, white skin. The lines of her body form a contrast and a counterpoint to those of her companion, while both display great vitality and sensuality.

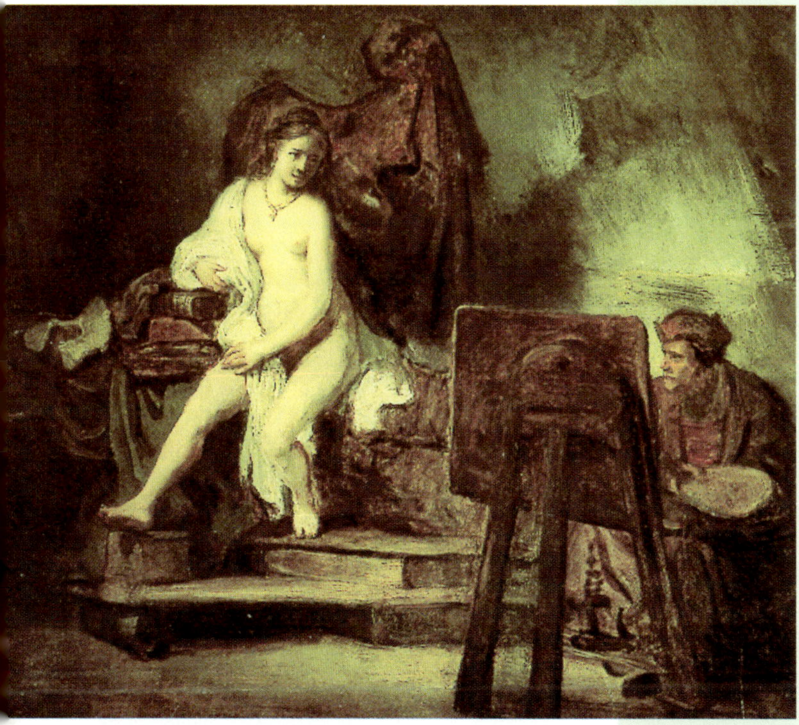

Rembrandt Painting Hendrickje Stoffels

School of Rembrandt

- oil on panel
- 53 x 60.6 cm
- Museum and Art Gallery, Glasgow

his work, painted by an anonymous artist, is an obvious tempt to emulate Rembrandt's style. Although loose ushwork is employed, there is a learned Mannerism about that makes the painting a harmless simulacrum. The nude odel, Rembrandt's mistress, is explicitly resolved, while e extended leg and the arm in full view appear somewhat iff. Through a studied illumination, the artist has created e proper atmosphere, with the darkness instilling a certain r of intensity and mystery, in which the brightly illuminated gure becomes the focal point of the picture. The flesh cols are accurate in their luminosity, yet the modeling falters the extended leg. Certain details rendered with excessive are, such as the face, reveal this work to be of an epigone the Dutch master.

The Sacrifice of Iphigenia

Jean Baptiste Jouvenet
(Rouen, 1644–Paris, 1717)

- 1685
- oil on canvas
- 190 x 133 cm
- Musée des Beaux-Arts et d'Archéologie, Troyes

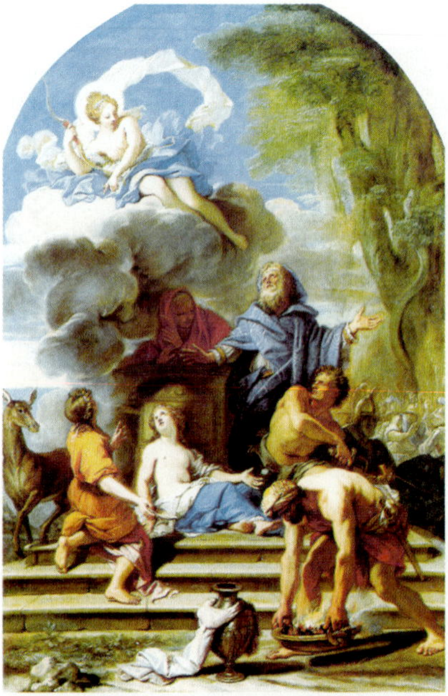

After becalming Agamemnon's fleet, Artemis demanded that he sacrifice his daughter, Iphigenia, before she would allow the ships to set sail again. At the last minute, the gods intervened, transporting Iphigenia to the land of the Tauri. The femininity and sensuality of the female nudes in this canvas is heightened by the contrast they establish with the men's heroically powerful, muscular bodies.

Lamentation

Sébastien Bourdon
(Montpellier, 1616–Paris, 1671)

- 1690s
- oil on canvas
- 92 x 103 cm
- Musée Fabre, Montpellier

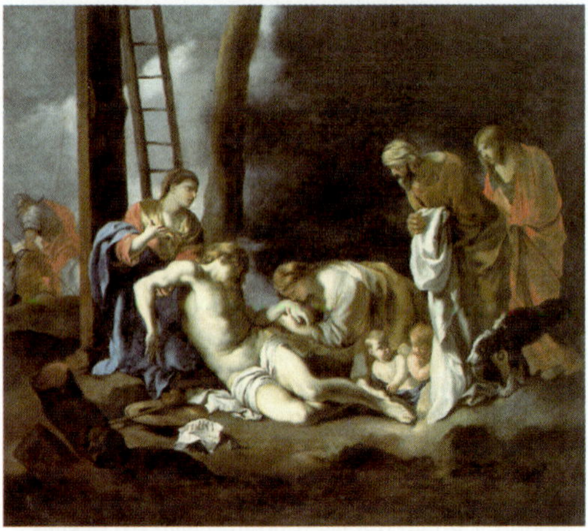

The study of anatomy for artistic purposes became obligatory in the French Academy of Painting, and the nude, which until then had been, so to say, a sideline became a central theme. Christ's body is depicted here with much volume and depth, proportions majestic. Its beauty and size distinguish it from the other figures. Light and shade here show the influence of tenebrism, one half of the body and face being plunged in shadow, which lends the figure as a whole its sculptural appearance.

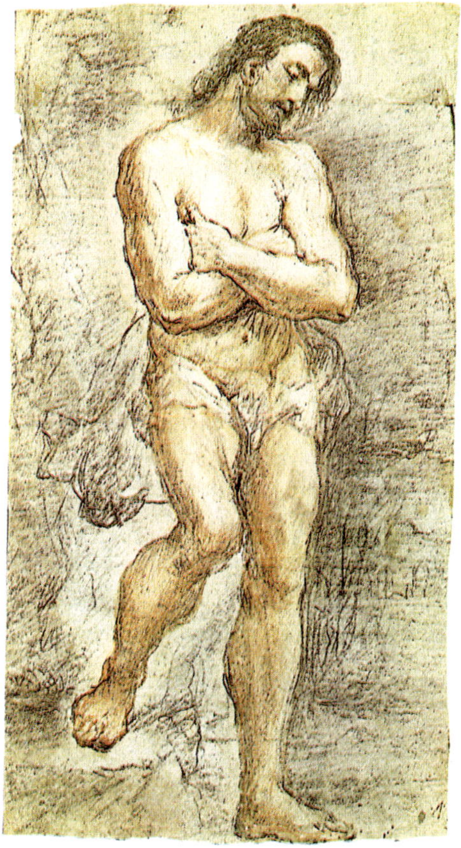

'his artist's paintings and drawings show the influence of letherlandish art, notably that of van Dyck and Rubens, s well as of the Venetian School. In this work, Christ is epicted waiting to be baptized by John. The background as been lightly shaded in with black pencil, creating an bstract surface of lines from which the figure of Jesus eems to emerge. Christ's skin is rendered largely in red halk, which the artist has applied with great virtuosity. lodeling and shadows are rendered by means of short, ense, black lines, generating a well-defined, meticulously tudied drawing of great vigor and dynamism.

Christ about to be Baptized

Juan Carreño de Miranda
(Avilés, 1614–Madrid, 1685)

- pencil and red chalk
- 41 x 23 cm
- Museu del Prado, Madrid

Clytië Transformed into a Heliotrope

Charles de la Fosse
(Paris, 1636–1716)

- 1688
- oil on canvas
- 131 x 159 cm
- Musée National des Châteaux de Versailles et de Trianon

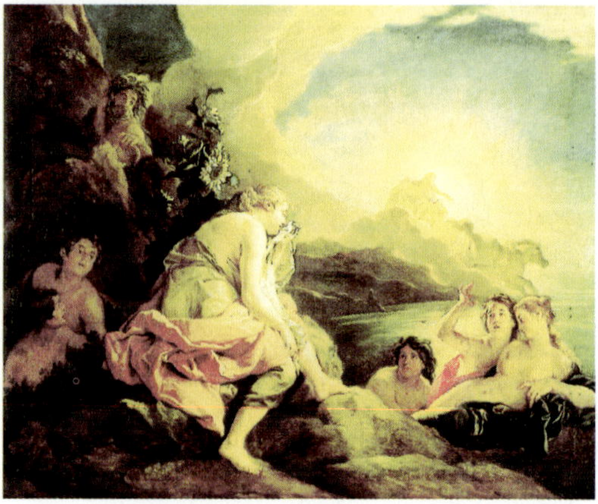

Clytië, a nymph or water naiad who fell in love with the sun god, Apollo, used to follow him with her gaze every morning when he stepped out of his chariot. To put an end to her suffering, she was converted into a sunflower, despite which she never stopped looking at the sun. The nude nymph on the right in this painting is remarkable, bathed as she is in the golden light of dawn. The lighting generally lends the bodies great physicality.

Pan and Selene

Pierre Mignard
(Troyes, 1612–Paris, 1695)

- ca. 1688–90
- oil on canvas
- 71 x 96 cm
- Sarah Campbell Blaffer Foundation, Houston

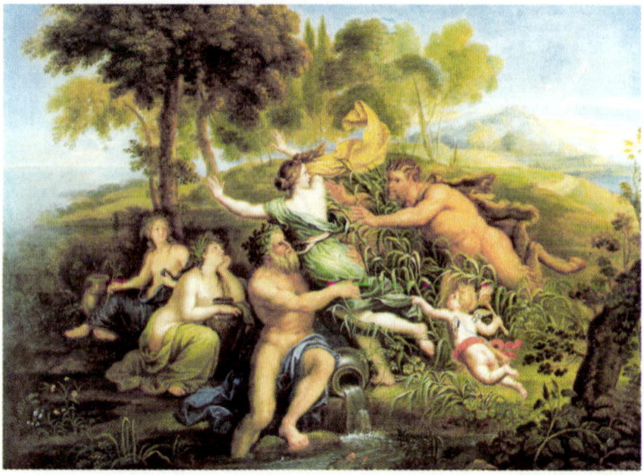

Pan, protector of shepherds and flocks, could never resist a pretty nymph, and many were those he enjoyed, including Selene, whom he deceived disguised as a lamb. The present canvas depicts the moment when, aided by the river god and in the presence of the nymphs of the springs, he attempts to ravish her. The execution of the river god is particularly complex and recalls Michelangelo in the details of its foreshortening.

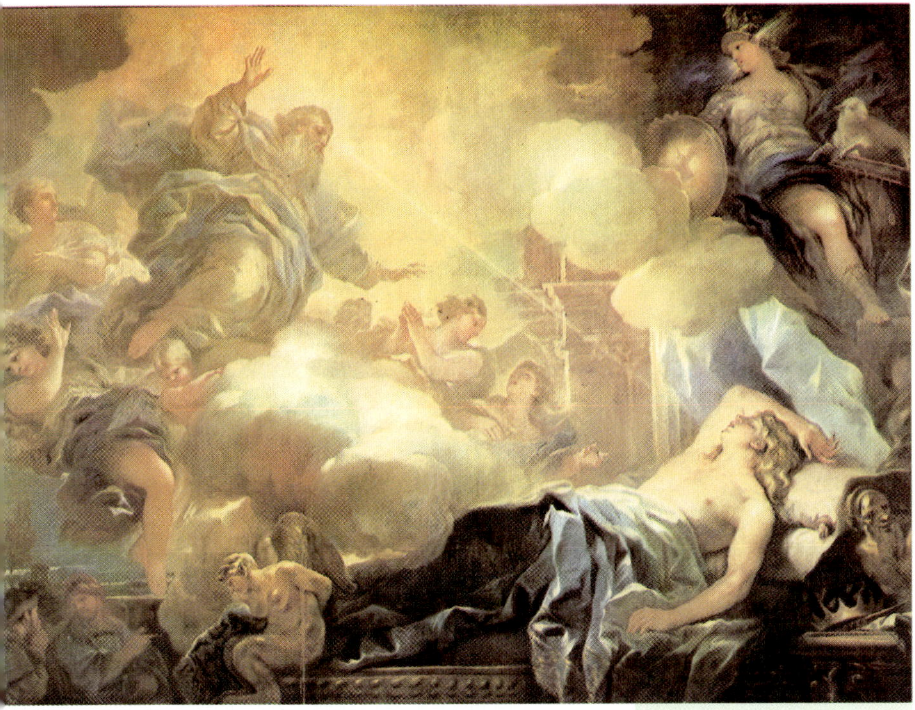

Solomon's Dream

Luca Giordano
(Naples, 1634–1705)

- 1693–94
- oil on canvas
- 245 x 361 cm
- Museo del Prado, Madrid

Luca Giordano was an ambitious pupil of José de Ribera in Naples. This painting is from a series illustrating the story of David and Solomon. This painting is a reworking of the frescos executed by the artist in the vaulting of the monastery at El Escorial at the behest of Charles II of Spain. The work shows God instilling in Solomon wisdom, represented here by the mythological figure of Minerva, in a dream. The young man, who is depicted here with an athletic build, has clearly fallen into a restless sleep. The artist skillfully integrates two separate realities into the scene: the dream, in which figures are enveloped in a haze, and reality, with the sleeping king, in which the contrasts are accentuated and the figure's individual volumes are clearly modeled by the light.

The Good Samaritan

Luca Giordano
(Naples, 1634–1705)

- 1650
- oil on canvas
- 135 x 165 cm
- Musée des Beaux-Arts, Rouen

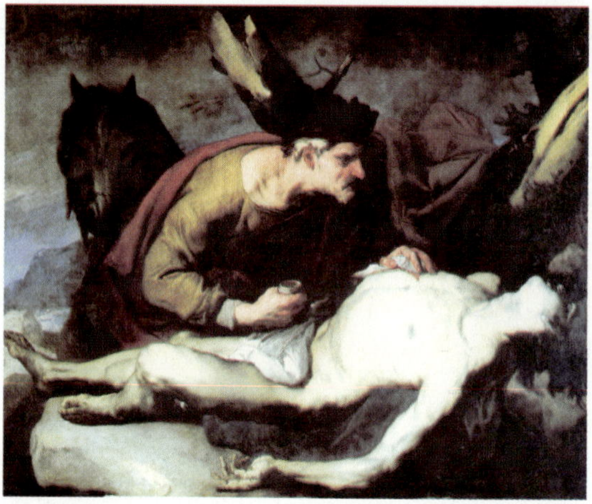

This work was influenced by Ribera's tenebrism. The highly realistic and expressive chiaroscuro effect lends the painting a modern feel. The naked body of the wounded man seen from the side, its rigid, tense muscles and pale skin, give clear expression to his helplessness.

Bathsheba at her Toilet

Luca Giordano
(Naples, 1634–1705)

- ca. 1699
- oil on canvas
- 219 x 212 cm
- Museo del Prado, Madrid

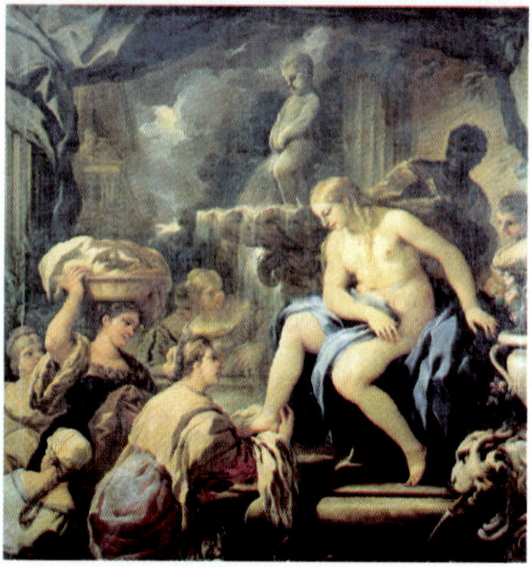

Seeing Bathsheba at her toilette, and captivated by her beauty, David took her to wife. We see her elegant charm here, while the brilliant rendering of her skin captures the viewer's inner eye. Bathsheba is less sensual in appearance here than in many other representations of her, perhaps in deference to her legendary fidelity to her husband.

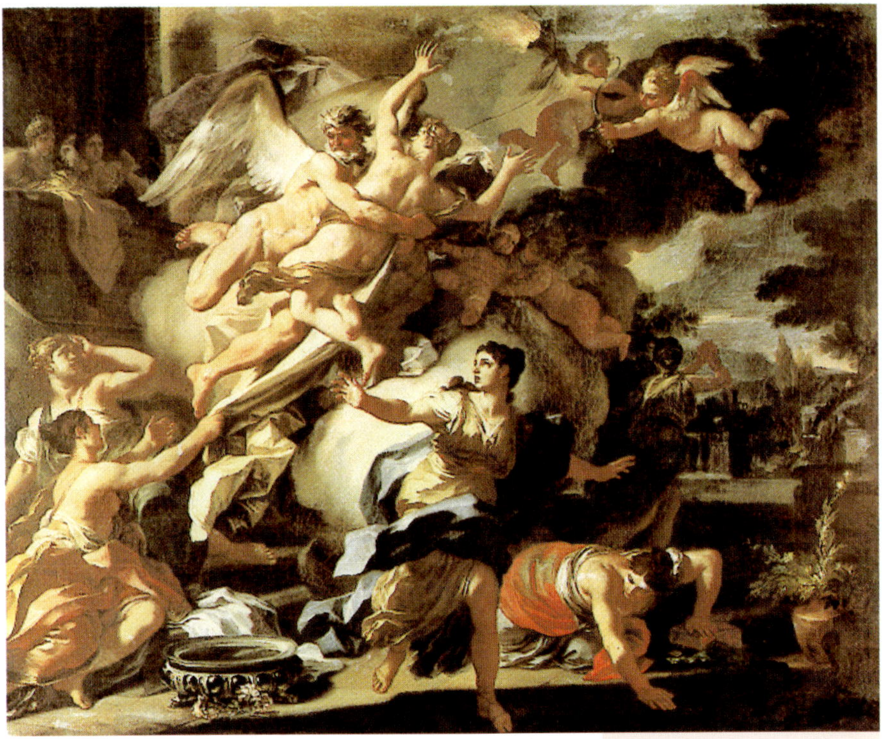

In Classical mythology, Boreas, the god of the North Wind, courted Oreithyia, daughter of Erechtheus, an Athenian king. When she resisted his advances, he wrapped her in a cloud and carried her off to Thrace, where he made her his queen. In this work, the painter used all the means available to him to depict this highly dramatic scene, which is as remarkable for its various figures as it is for its studied effects of light. Boreas is shown as a naked old man with large wings and a muscular body hardened by battle. Oreithyia, too, has a powerful body, which is likewise shown unclothed. Her raised arms not only serve to evoke the rapture of the moment and a sense of movement, but also call attention to the stylization of her body. The various figures, with their expressive gestures, reinforce the action and heighten the drama being played out. Francesco Solimena, concerned with rendering the minutest details, was a much sought-after painter of monumental Baroque works, to which the many commissions he received to decorate the rooms of Italian and Spanish palaces and churches attest.

The Rape of Oreithyia

Francesco Solimena
(Canale di Serino, 1657 –Barra, 1747)

- 1700
- oil on canvas
- 101 x 138 cm
- Galleria Spada, Rome

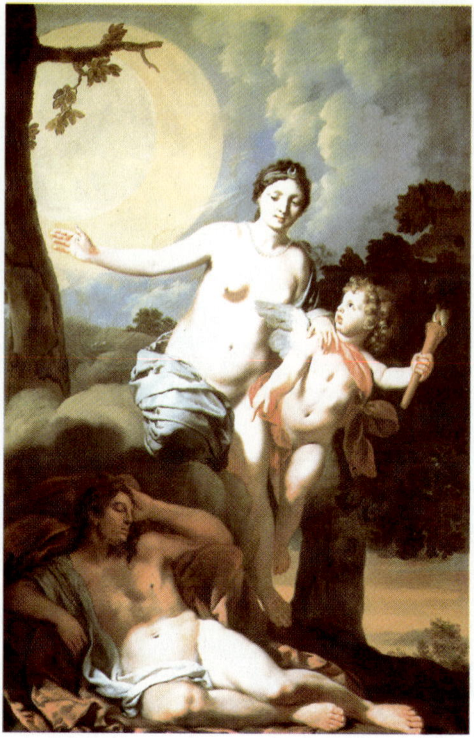

Selene and Endymion

Gerard de Lairesse
(Liège, 1641–Amsterdam, 1711)

- oil on canvas
- 177 x 188.5 cm
- Rijksmuseum, Amsterdam

Endymion was an exceedingly beautiful youth, beloved of Selene, the Moon goddess, who came to him every night in the cave where he slept, on Mount Latmus. The youth has an exquisite body, whose lower half is luminous and whose upper half is cast in a half-light, no doubt to best convey the oneiric and mysterious nature of the scene. The comely figure of Selene is portrayed with smooth, pallid skin; her gesture is one of calm, innocence and sensuality. A cherub lights the way with a torch. The nighttime landscape is treated with cool, dark tones. The two subjects are naked in readiness for their rendezvous, with their genitals skillfully covered by drapery. This dramatic work portrays a static, classical scene. Gerard de Lairesse has also rendered the figures' volumes in a classical fashion, blending them with both the cool and warm tones of the painting in a style all his own.

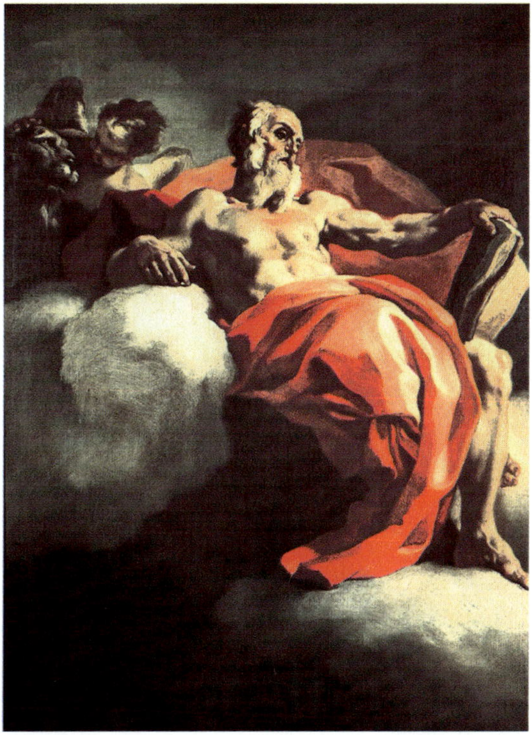

ʒt. Jerome is portrayed here as distinguished and solemn, ›eated on a throne of clouds and contemplating the world ·rom on high. Luminous red drapery covers the saint's body, vhich has been treated with utmost care. It is the body of a ›ero, recalling a figure of Moses by Michelangelo. The ›culptural treatment of the torso gives rise to an extremely nuscular build. This iconography became widespread in eligious painting in the 17th and 18th centuries, when different types of Renaissance and Baroque perspective were ›sed to assimilate certain dramatic aspects of tenebrism, ›lbeit with an evident classicist style.

St. Jerome

Francesco Solimena
(Canale di Serino, 1657 –Barra, 1747)

- oil on canvas
- Pushkin Museum, Moscow

Susanna Bathing

Jean-Baptiste Santerre

(Magny-en-Vexin, Val d'Oise, 1651–Paris1717)

- 1704
- oil on canvas
- Musée du Louvre, Paris

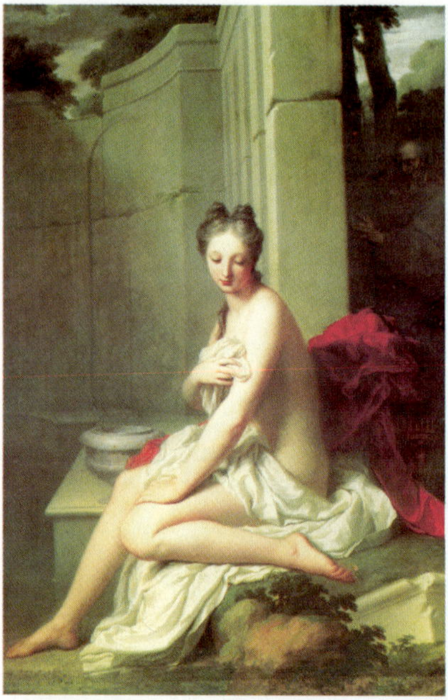

Susanna is depicted here by means of soft tonal modeling as an elegant and rather long-boned woman, who is self-absorbedly enjoying the private intimacy of the moment. Her obliviousness to the lecherous Elders spying on her sets up a dramatic tension more subtle than we find in certain other depictions.

Perseus Displaying Medusa's Head

Jean-Marc Nattier

(Paris, 1685–1766)

- 1705–10
- oil on canvas
- 113.5 x 176.6 cm
- Musée des Beaux-Arts, Tours

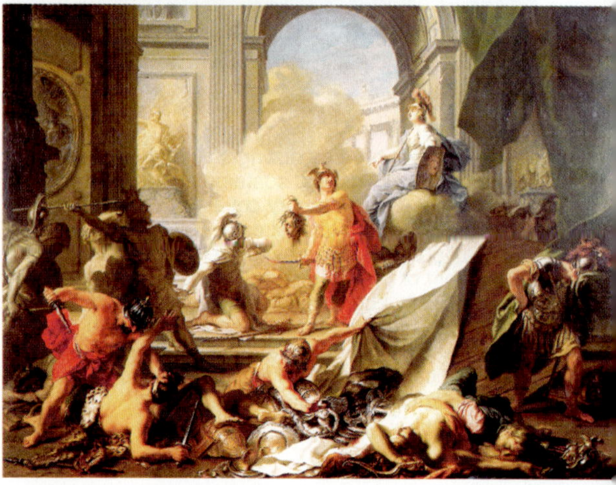

After he had slain Medusa and saved Andromeda from the sea monster, Perseus turned Polydectes and his followers to stone by showing them Medusa's head. The nude figures here are depicted with a good deal of foreshortening.

Vatteau's amiable style eventually developed nto a taste for something closer o sultry eroticism bordering on the pornographic. The depiction of his nude figure, or instance, has all the ingredients necessary o induce a viewer's gaze to inger on the young woman's ntimate parts; her very pose, and the way she s depicted establishing direct eye-contact, amounts to ittle less than an open invitation.

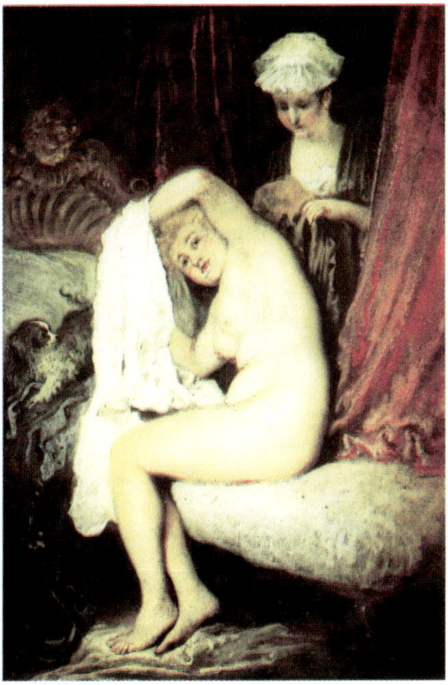

A Lady at her Toilet

Jean-Antoine Watteau
(Valenciennes, 1684–Nogent-sur-Marne, 1721)

- ca. 1705
- oil on canvas
- 45.2 x 37.8 cm
- Wallace Collection, London

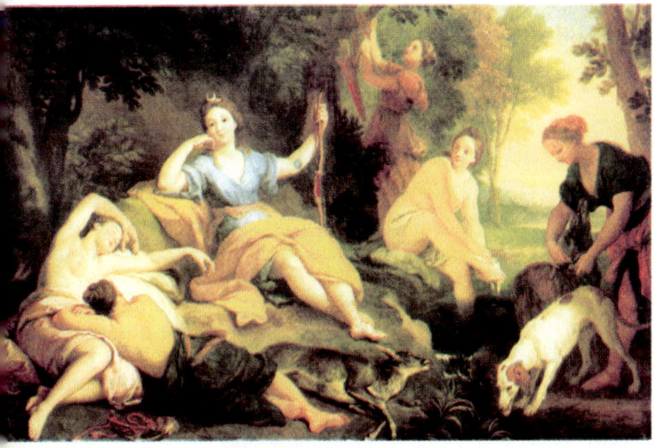

Diana at Rest

Louis de Boullongne
(Paris, 1654–1733)

- 1707
- oil on canvas
- 105 x 163 cm
- Musée des Beaux-Arts, Tours

Diana gazes triumphantly at the viewer, while two of her nymphs lie asleep at the left, torsos bared. The difference in skin coloration of the two stimulates the interest the viewer takes in their bodies, which are treated here in greater detail than the rest of the scene. Yet another nymph, completely nude, is bathing while she looks towards the goddess. Her body displays qualities that are more Baroque, and while she is generally larger and heavier than her sisters, her pose s nonetheless agile and sensual.

Christ About to be Crucified

Claude Gillot
(Langres, 1637–Paris, 1722)

- ca. 1710
- oil on canvas
- 180 x 212 cm
- parish church, Noailles

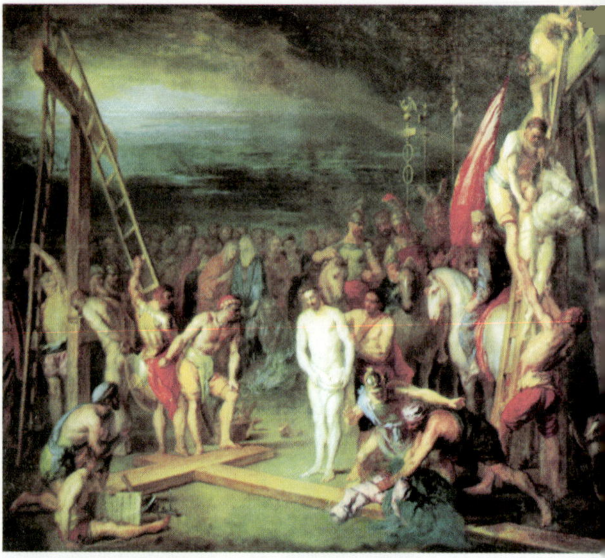

The treatment of religious themes in this period had acquired a good deal of freedom. What makes this work original are developments that have their roots in Caravaggio and Ribera, and which have to do with the way the imminence and realism of the dramatic events are brought out. The naked figures of the condemned men are visually powerful because their depiction rests on a careful utilization of anatomical detail.

Bathing

François Lemoyne
(Paris, 1688–1737)

- ca. 1710
- oil on canvas
- Musée Boucher de Perthes, Abbeville

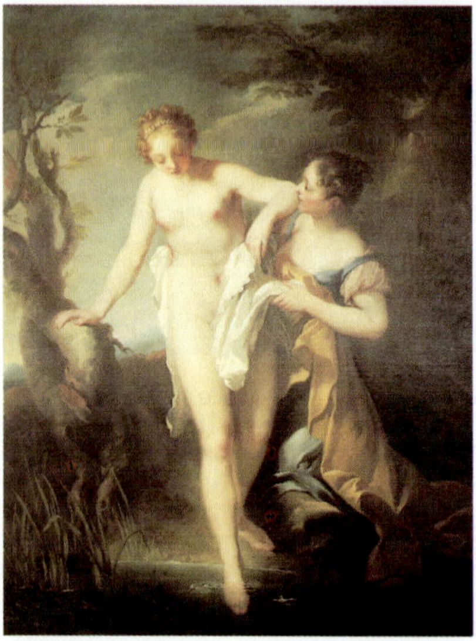

In depictions of Diana bathing, artists often dispensed with mythology in order to concentrate on producing a study of female beauty. The present figure is both physically attractive and elegant, the woman's skin seeming to glow with light, which however does not obscure the delightful forms of her body. Relatively weakly defined outlines produce a warm and pleasing atmosphere.

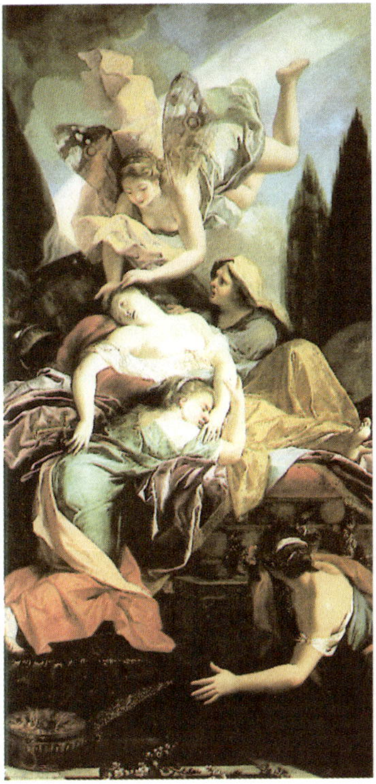

The Death of Dido

Antoine Coypel
(Paris, 1661–1722)

- 1714–17
- oil on canvas
- 387 x 190 cm
- Musée Fabre, Montpellier

According to Virgil's Aeneid, Dido was the legendary founder queen of Carthage, after the murder of her husband, Sichaeus, by her brother, Pygmalion. To escape Pygmalion's tyranny, she fled to Crete with her husband's treasures, where she had 50 maidens abducted and married them to the men accompanying her. She then proceeded to found Carthage. Jarbas, the king of the country, asked for her hand in marriage. Dido, still in love with her deceased husband, accepted his proposal only to protect the lives of her entourage. Three months later, she committed suicide by stabbing herself. The painting shows her just after her suicide. With it, the artist captures the spectacular, magnificent quality of mythological works, with a palette recalling that of Peter Paul Rubens and a grace and dynamism typical of the work of Correggio. To heighten the drama and underline the message of the scene, the queen's firm, bare breasts are revealed, symbolizing her generosity and commitment to her people.

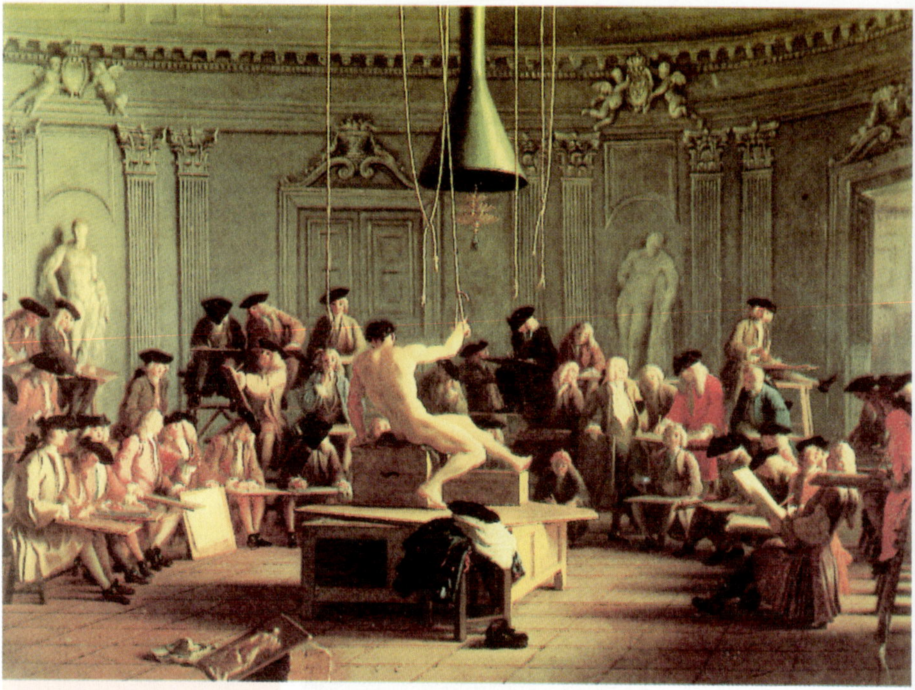

The Art Academy

Michel-Ange Houasse
(Paris, 1680–Arpajon, Île de France, 1730)

- ca.1715
- oil on canvas
- 61 x 73 cm
- Palacio Real, Madrid

The Académie des Beaux-Arts was one of the most rigid and immutable institutions of artistic control to exist in France. It not only prescribed the style of painting and the type of figures that were deemed acceptable, but also the subject matter. Only those who met its criteria were considered "true" artists. The tests to which candidates were subjected were extremely rigorous. In this painting, Michel-Ange Houasse takes one of the Académie's drawing classes as his theme. A naked male model is posing at the center and the class is well attended, exclusively by male pupils. The model adopts a dramatic, heroic pose, an indispensable element of an academic painting. The modeling of the skin, one of the most important features of a nude, exhibits a wide variety of tonal values, particularly in the shadows.

Susanna's distress is a mirror of her chastity. Her nude figure is vigorous in both color and lighting. An intricate interplay of purity and sensuality is thereby established.

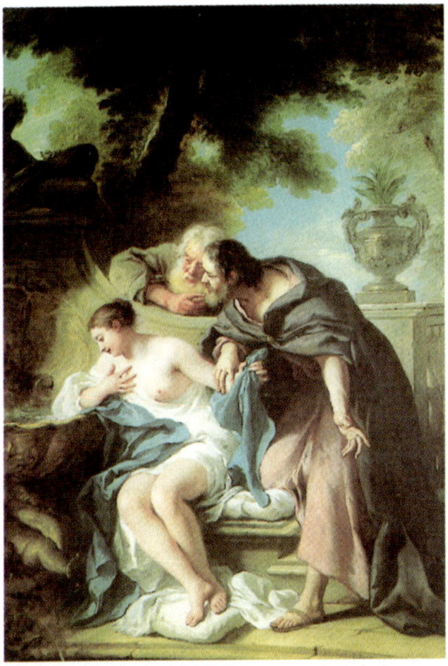

Susanna Bathing

Jean-François de Troy
(Paris, 1679–Rome, 1752)

- oil on canvas
- Musée des Beaux-Arts, Rouen

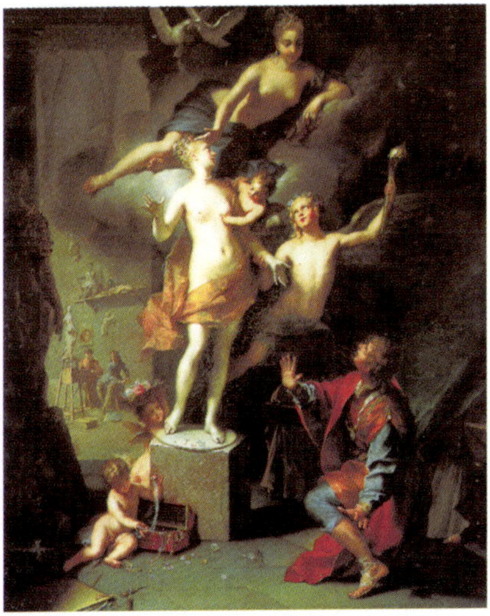

Pygmalion

Jean Raoux
(Montpellier, 1677–Paris, 1734)

- ca. 1715
- oil on canvas
- 134 x 100 cm
- Musée Fabre, Montpellier

Raoux's canvas depicts Venus, in response to Pygmalion's prayer, bringing his sculpture to life, and is reminiscent of Venetian art, its tenebrism lending it an air of mystery. The nude figures have been very finely executed, that of Galatea, in particular, standing out for its brilliance.

Diana at her Bath

Jean-Antoine Watteau
(Valenciennes, 1684–Nogent-sur-Marne, 1721)

- 1715–16
- oil on canvas
- 81 x 101 cm
- Musée du Louvre, Paris

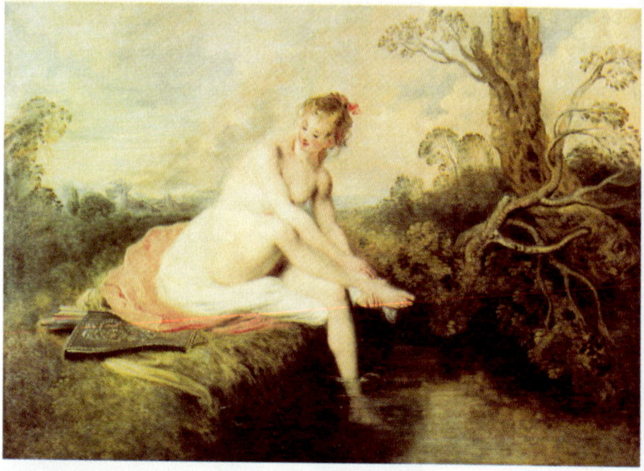

Watteau was a master of gallant and erotic painting. Here, we see Diana, her figure combining forceful robustness and a nearly ethereal weightlessness that is largely a result of the light it gives off. The latter technique, so often used by this artist, caused the nude to virtually blend into the surrounding atmosphere. The vibrancy of the brushwork in certain areas creates a rather indefinite profile.

Nymph and Satyr, or Jupiter and Antiope

Jean-Antoine Watteau
(Valenciennes, 1684 –Nogent-sur-Marne, 1721)

- 1715–16
- oil on canvas
- 73.5 x 107.5 cm
- Musée du Louvre, Paris

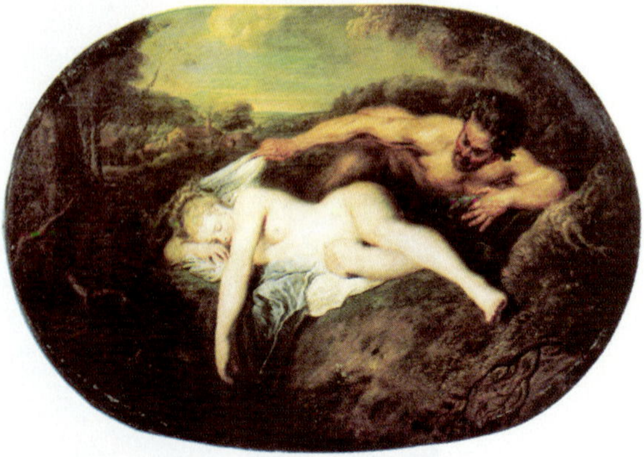

Attracted by Antiope's great beauty, Zeus possessed her in the form of a satyr. This painting depicts the moment when the god discovers the young woman, her resplendent body set off by the dark tones surrounding it. Highlights placed skilfully on her skin enhance the three-dimensionality of her body. The satyr observes her lustfully, thereby sullying her innocence, which lends an oppressive note to the otherwise erotic scene.

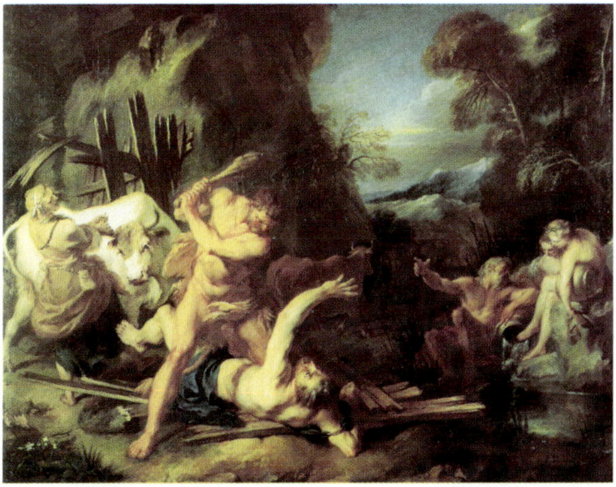

Hercules Striking Cacus

François Lemoyne
(Paris, 1688–1737)

- ca. 1716
- oil on canvas
- 131 x 170 cm
- École Nationale Supérieure des Beaux-Arts, Paris

Hercules pursues and slays Cacus, who had stolen some of his cattle. The painting is full of dynamism, with Hercules' figure in particular standing out for its muscularity, bulk and—from the artistic point of view—its foreshortening. On the right, we see the river nymphs casually discussing the event with the river god.

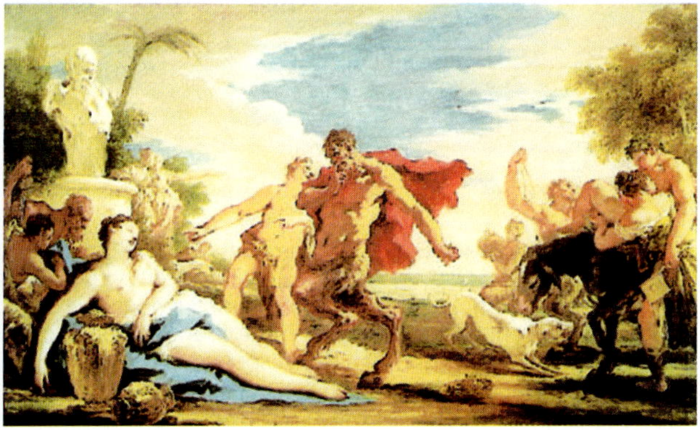

Bacchanal

Giovanni Antonio Pellegrini
(Venice, 1675–1741)

- oil on canvas
- Staatsgalerie, Stuttgart

This artist—who, along with Sebastiano Ricci and Jacopo Amigoni, was responsible for reviving Venetian art—presents a monumental work here, in the style of grand mythological painting. The figures are idealized and each represents a concept, namely sensuality, strength, vice and evil. The work is more like an allegorical scene than a bacchanal. The muscular male figures evoke sheer physical strength, whereas the voluptuous female figures are the very embodiment of sensuality. Together, they create a harmonious symphony of form and color.

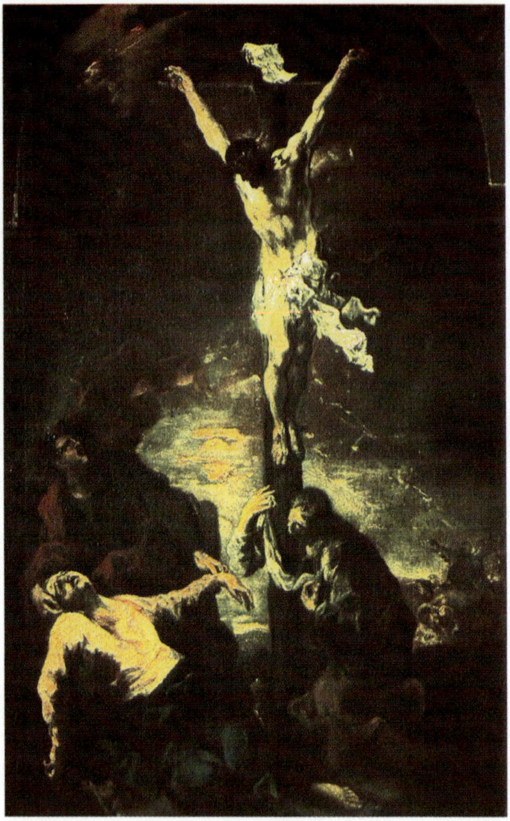

The Crucifixion

Alessandro Magnasco
(called **Il Lissandrino**)
(Genoa, 1667–1749)

- oil on canvas
- Pushkin Museum, Moscow

With the skill and deftness of Rubens, Alessandro Magnasco evokes a muscular body of Christ, suspended on the Cross. The painter has employed a number of artistic means to intensify the scene's drama: a dark background of dense colors and a mysterious light, nature's response to the tragedy of the event. Christ crucified, contorted on the Cross, appears to be in the throes of death. His loincloth flaps in the wind while the figures at the foot of the Cross are shown in dramatic poses that convey their shock and profound sorrow. In addition to lending the scene mystery, the treatment of the light heightens the drama and brings to the fore the powerful musculature of Christ, who is given heroic proportions. This nude is extremely sensual, as much for its anatomical study as for the elegant lines of its undulating loincloth.

After slaying the Minotaur, Theseus carried Ariadne away with him, only to abandon her on the island of Naxos at the behest of the gods. There, she was found by Bacchus, who wedded her and took her to Olympus. Bertin's formal influences are numerous. Ariadne's bosom, for instance, recalls Rubens in its treatment of light and skin tints. Both nudes have been executed with extreme subtlety, their proportions idealized. Bacchus' body in particular is not only athletic and sensual, but effeminate as well.

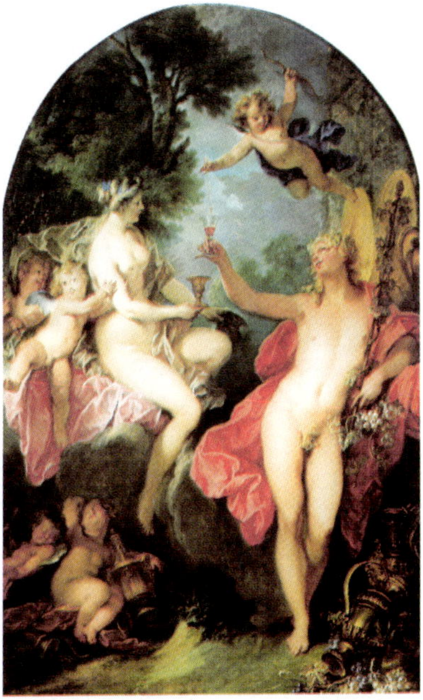

Bacchus and Ariadne

Nicolas Bertin
(Paris, 1668–1736)

- ca. 1715/19
- oil on canvas
- 75 x 50 cm
- Musée d'Art et d'Industrie, Saint-Etienne

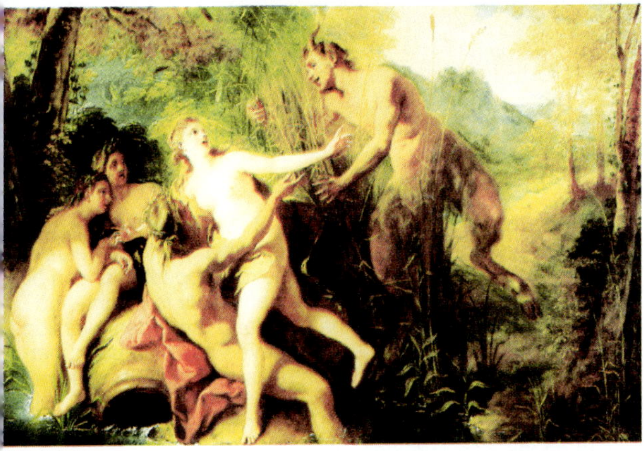

Pan and Selene

Jean-François de Troy
(Paris, 1679–Rome, 1752)

- ca. 1722–24
- oil on canvas
- 74.3 x 92 cm
- The J. Paul Getty Museum, Malibu

The nymph Selene is being held fast by the river god so that Pan can possess her. The nudes display great beauty, their surprise making Pan's intentions all the more dramatic. Selene's nude body is the brightest of all and, thus, the focus of attention, while the others are bathed in a warmer, less glaring light. The nymphs are anxiously awaiting the outcome; the one furthest left is well-built, her shapeliness accentuated by the light falling across her side.

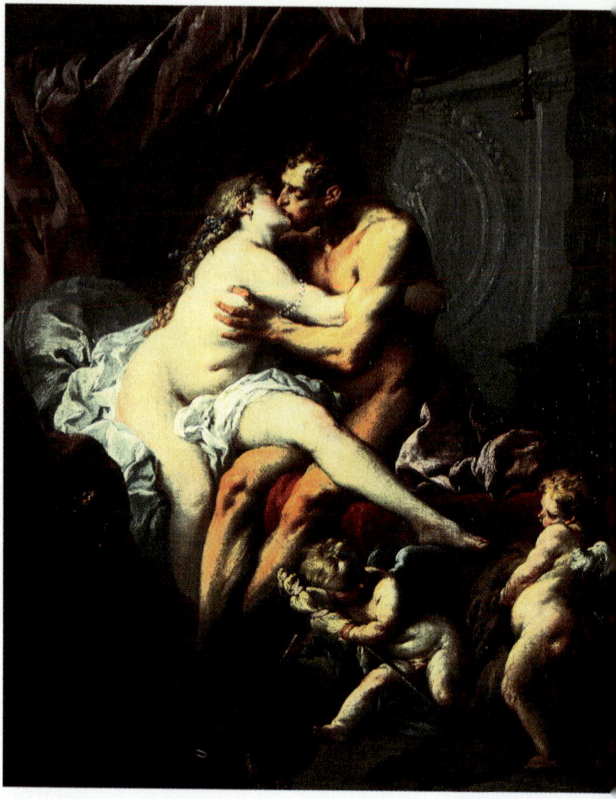

Hercules and Omphale

François Boucher
(Paris, 1703–1770)

- 1731–344
- oil on canvas
- 90 x 74 cm
- Pushkin Museum, Moscow

To avenge the death of Iphitus, son of Eurytus, Hercules was bound a slave to Omphale, queen of Lydia, for three years. She had him satisfy her insatiable sexual appetite, as can be seen in this scene. Omphale's soft sensuality is heightened by Hercules' tanned, masculine body and the ardent passion of the figures' embrace. She is portrayed as voluptuous, her legs spread slightly, one of which rests on those of her lover. Hercules is depicted as a powerful but submissive brute, willing to fulfill the queen's every desire. The figure of Omphale, based on the Baroque ideal of beauty, exhibits a magnificent body, whose torsion requires the artist to foreshorten the legs, lending the figure great dynamism.

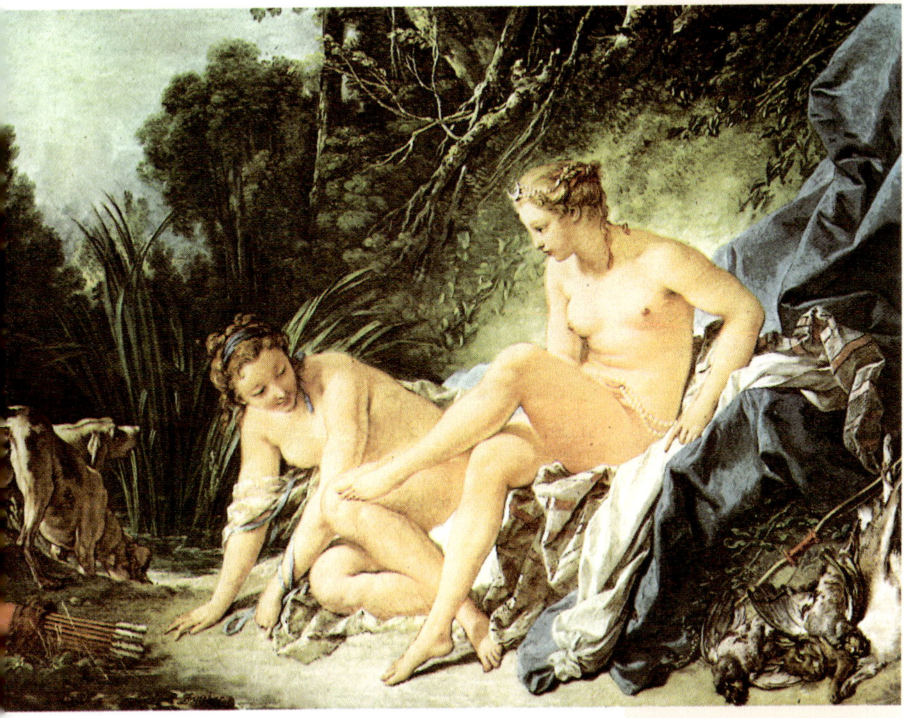

ı Classical mythology, the young hunter Actaeon spied on)iana, the goddess of hunting, while she was bathing. To revent his boasting of this exploit, she turned him into a tag, whereupon he was devoured by his own hounds. In this ainting, François Boucher's nude figures display both lyrical nd frivolous qualities. After Jean-Antoine Watteau's death, in 721, painting became more decorative and affected, schewing profound subject matter in favor of an erotic harge. Although the elegance of the present figures cannot e denied, their histrionic quality is certainly their most otable attribute. The background recalls a backdrop in a tage set. The two women appear complacent in their sensu- l and intimate gestures. The string of pearls and the sumptu- us cloth serve to heighten the sensuality of their elegant, oluptuous bodies.

Diana Resting after Her Bath

François Boucher
(Paris, 1703–1770)

- 1742
- oil on canvas
- 57 x 73 cm
- Musée du Louvre, Paris

Diana at her Bath with Nymphs

Jean-François de Troy
(Paris, 1679–Rome, 1752)

- ca. 1722–24
- oil on canvas
- 74.3 x 92 cm
- The J. Paul Getty Museum, Malibu

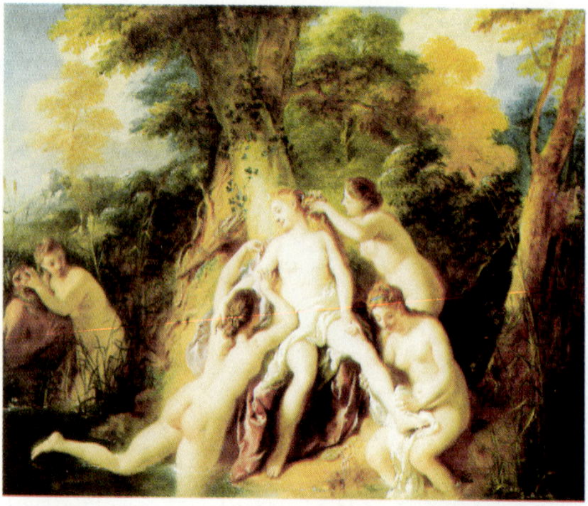

In depictions of this theme, Actaeon is usually shown hidden somewhere in the distance, whereas here, one of Diana's nymphs is covering his eyes so that he can no longer see. Diana and the nymphs attending to her have still not noticed his presence. The delicately-modeled bodies of this central group are firm and strong, their outlines often rather tenuous, although their solidity is almost palpable.

Diana and Actaeon

Louis Galloche
(Paris, 1670–1761)

- ca. 1725
- oil on canvas
- 81 x 121 cm
- Hermitage, St. Petersburg

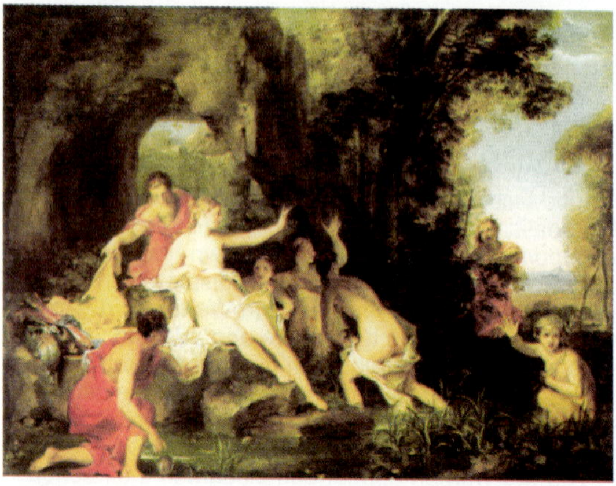

When, during a break from the hunt, Diana and her nymphs happened to be bathing, Actaeon took advantage of their nudity and spied on them in secret, a deed that eventually led to his death. This dynamic and sensuously elaborated scene depicts the moment of Actaeon's discovery. The play of light and shade brings out the three-dimensionality of the nude bodies very pleasantly.

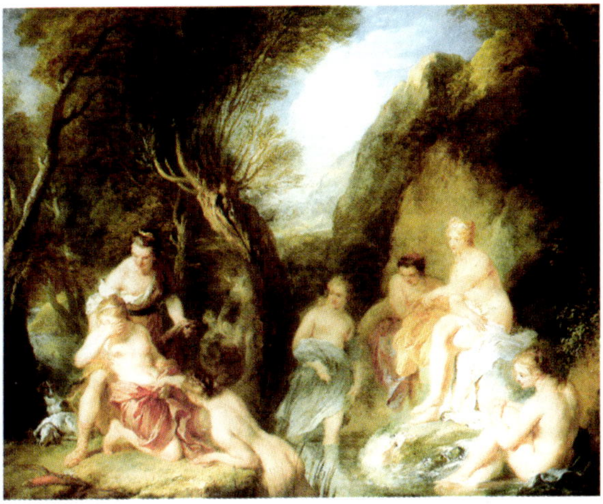

Diana and Callisto

François Lemoyne
(Paris, 1688–1737)

- 1725–28
- oil on canvas
- 76 x 95 cm
- Alex Wengraf Collection, London

Callisto, a hunter of Diana, had vowed chastity to her mistress, which did not daunt Zeus, who.seduced her in the guise of Diana herself. Her pregnancy becoming evident, she was expelled from the huntress' entourage and turned into a bear. In this painting, one of her sister nymphs pulls down Callisto's garment to expose her pregnant condition. The resplendent nude figures combine with the ethereal atmosphere to imbue the scene with great charm and sensuality.

The three "Graces", Euphrosyne (Joy), Aglaea (Radiance) and Thalia (Flowering), personified charm, grace and beauty. This work is an allegory of life's pleasures, in which the virtues and beauty are personified, the latter, here, in the shape of Venus, and Bacchus symbolizing joie de vivre and ebullience. Rubens' influence is evident in the fullness of the Graces' bodies, while Venus is more delicate and rarefied.

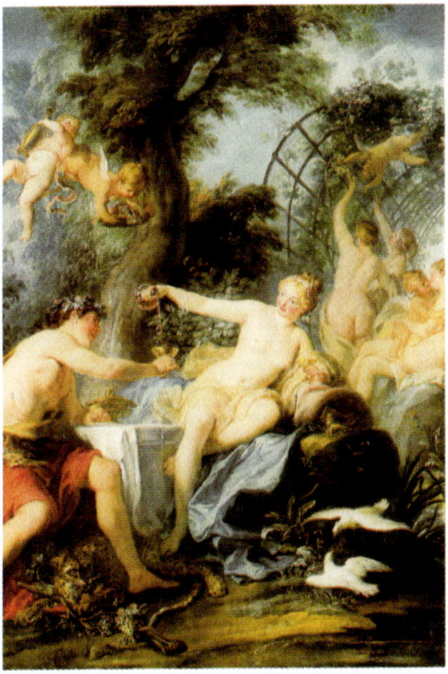

Venus, Bacchus and the Three Graces

Noël-Nicolas Coypel
(Paris, 1690–1734)

- 1726
- oil on canvas
- 101 x 82 cm
- Musée d'Art et d'Histoire, Geneva

The Rescue of Andromeda

Charles-Antoine Coypel
(Paris, 1694–1752)

- 1726–27
- oil on canvas
- 131 x 196 cm
- Musée du Louvre, Paris

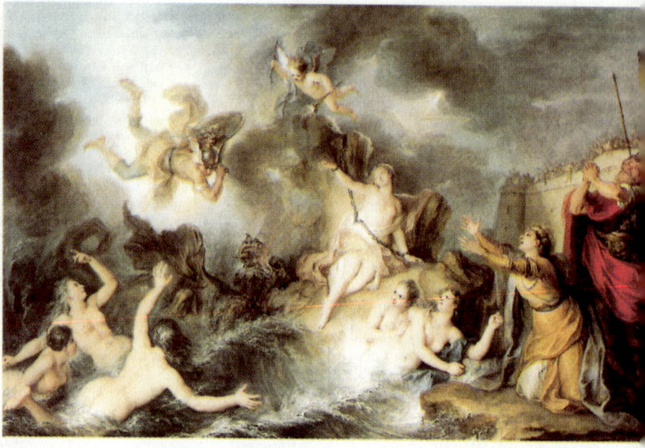

While the composition of this scene resembles certain seascapes by Rubens, the solution of numerous of its aesthetic problems are far removed from his. The figures have been executed according to a rather rigid scheme. The handling of skin tints, while it allows ample enough body volumes to arise, is somewhat oversubtle, especially in the case of certain of the Nereids in water.

Hercules and Omphale

Jacques Dumont
(Paris, 1701–1781)

- 1728
- oil on canvas
- 133.5 x 167 cm
- Musée des Beaux-Arts, Tours

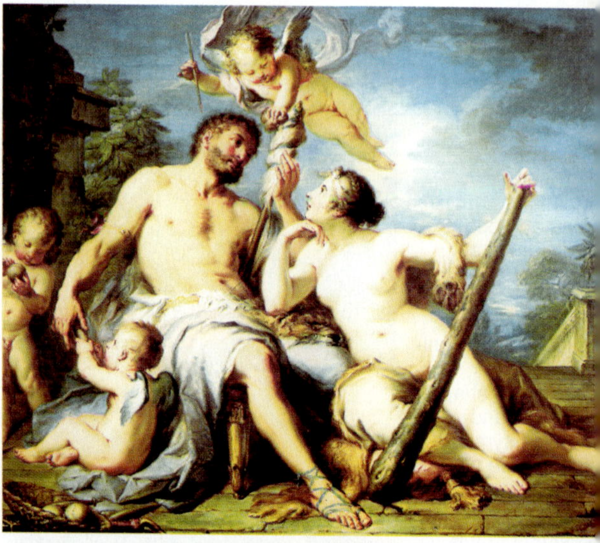

The capricious Omphale is holding Hercules' cudgel, a fairly obvious phallic symbol, her nudity tastefully offset by the garment draped over her leg.

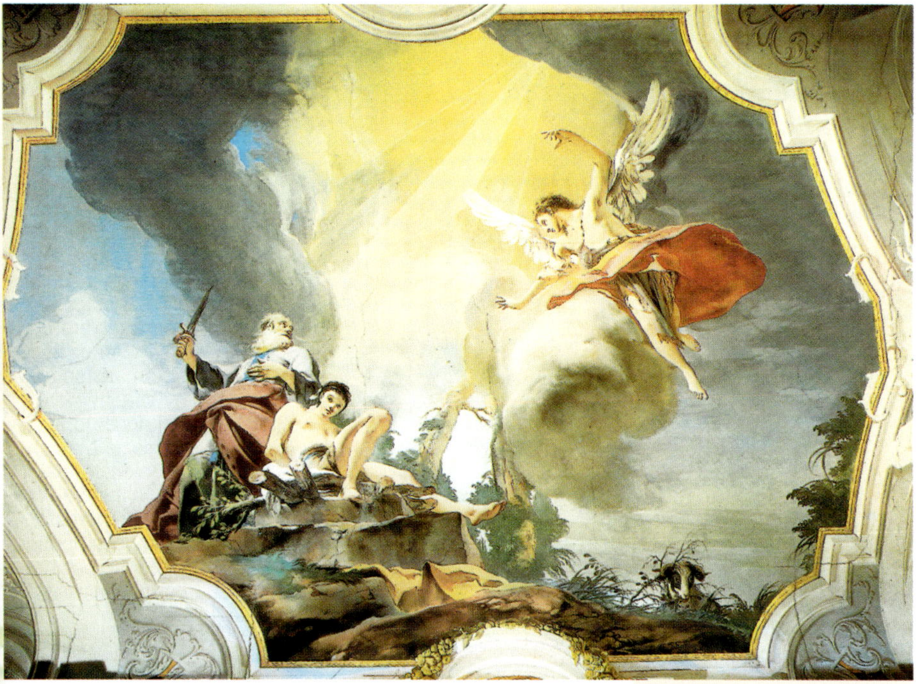

The Sacrifice of Isaac

Giovanni Battista (Giambattista) Tiepolo

(Venice, 1696–Madrid, 1770)

- 1726–28
- fresco
- 400 x 500 cm
- Archbishop's Palace, Udine

This fresco captures the moment in which the angel stops Abraham from slaying his son, Isaac. Notable is the artist's handling of color and his skill at employing central perspective. Since the composition had to be adapted to a ceiling, it creates an optical illusion. Isaac is shown bound and naked, looking toward the viewer resignedly. The handsome nude exhibits generous proportions and technically complex foreshortening. The body is illuminated by a ray of sunlight, which lends the flesh tones great luminosity. The shadows modeling the figure are naturalistically articulated and the trompe l'œil achieves the desired optical effect. The works painted by Tiepolo in Ubine at this time marked a significant turning point in his style.

The Judgment of Paris

Noël-Nicolas Coypel
(Paris, 1690–1734)

- 1728
- oil on canvas
- 101 x 82 cm
- Nationalmuseum, Stockholm

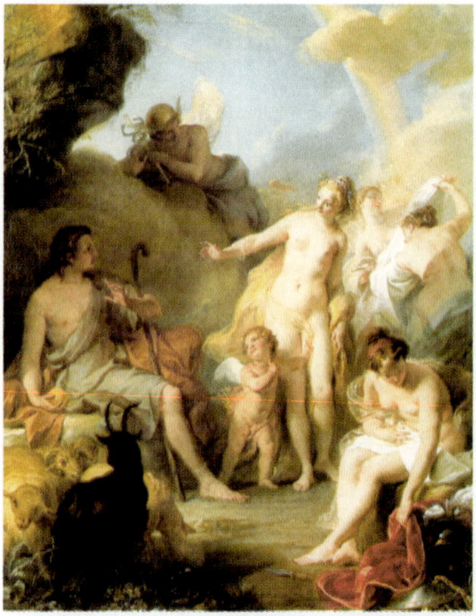

Paris was forced to choose which of the three goddesses, Venus, Athena or Hera, was the most beautiful. Bribed by Venus, he specified her. Athena and Hera undressing as he decides, the work employs a subliminal language of remarkable eroticism. Venus' nude figure, accentuated by shadows that enhance her forms, is a splendid piece of painting. A thin veil covers her intimate parts, contributing to her somewhat crafty, knowing aspect.

Venus and Adonis

François Lemoyne
(Paris, 1688–1737)

- 1729
- oil on canvas
- 92 x 73 cm
- Nationalmuseum, Stockholm

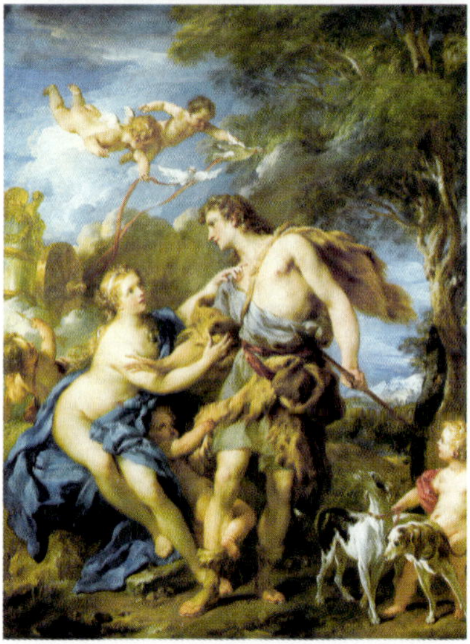

In this scene, Venus is attempting to seduce the youth, who seems to offer resistance. The goddess is depicted as a voluptuous young woman, the foreshortening used accentuating her feminine forms. The fabric in which she is draped contrasts with and heightens the radiant tones of her skin.

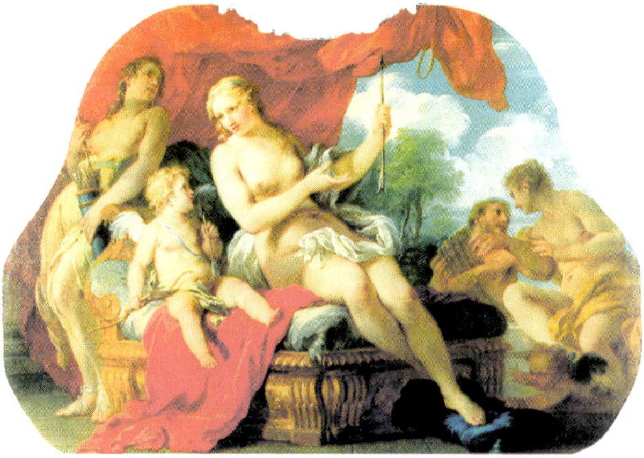

Venus Showing Cupid the Power of his Arrows

François Lemoyne
(Paris, 1688–1737)

- 1729–30
- oil on canvas
- 109 x 164 cm
- Musée Rodin, Paris

Amongst flowing fabrics in bright red shades, Venus teaches her son what his arrows can do, how they can incite love or incline a person towards poetry or music. Her nude figure is far more shapely than was general in baroque art, which tended to prefer ample bodies and small breasts. Although well-proportioned, the goddess, as she is presented here with rounded breasts, has something more human about her.

Deceived and accused of robbery, Hercules killed Iphitus and was sold into slavery to seductive Omphale. She had him dress as a woman and set him to woman's work. The queen is seen here draped in the skin of the Nemean lion, holding a phallic scepter. Hercules, half draped in some gorgeous fabric, and touched by Cupid, gazes spellbound at her.

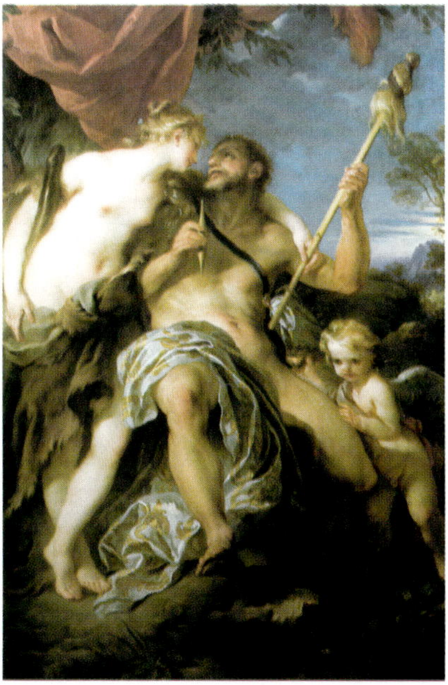

Hercules and Omphalë

François Lemoyne
(Paris, 1688–1737)

- ca. 1730/35
- oil on canvas
- 136 x 95 cm
- private collection

Jupiter Abducts Ganymede

Charles-Joseph Natoire
(Nîmes, 1700–Castel Gandolfo, 1777)

- ca. 1731
- oil on canvas
- 123 x 108 cm
- Musée des Beaux-Arts et d'Archéologie, Troyes

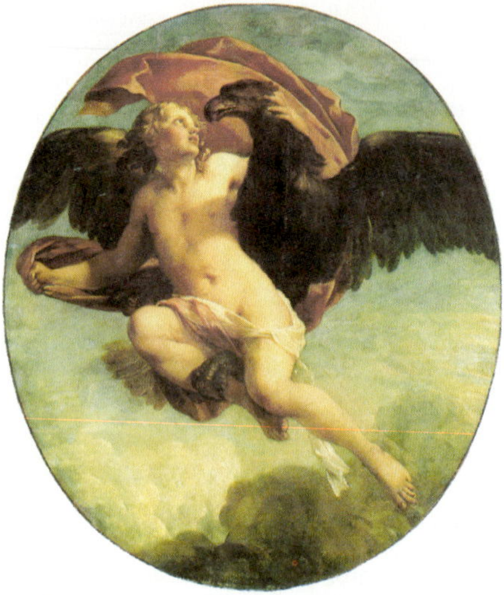

Ganymede's beauty induces Jupiter to fall in love with him. In order to possess him, he metamorphoses into an eagle. The work is powerfully dynamic, both in its treatment of figure and for the action it depicts. The figure of Ganymede is reminiscent of Tiepolo. Light, modeling and skin tones are all highly allusive.

Venus Asking Vulcan for Arms for Aeneas

François Boucher
(Paris, 1703–1770)

- 1732
- oil on canvas
- 252 x 175 cm
- Musée du Louvre, Paris

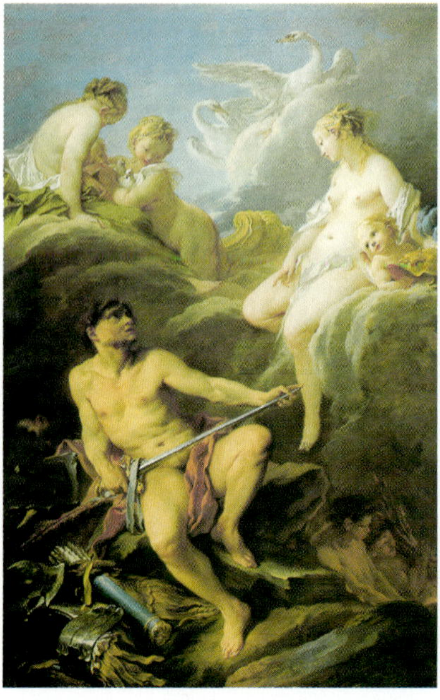

Venus is using her physical and emotional allures to win over her consort. Belly exposed, she parts her legs slightly as part of her argument. The treatment of Vulcan here is in accord with mythological texts: his body is indeed that of a strong young man, yet his largeness of limb and his facial appearance make him a relatively unrefined god, and closer to a simple smith.

In order to show Cephalus that his beautiful and cunning wife, Procris, could be bought, the dawn goddess, Aurora (Greek Eos), transformed him into the semblance of another man. Seeing that Procris accepted his advances in exchange for money, he spurned her and fell in love with Aurora instead, depicted here as a small-breasted young woman with a pale complexion. Her intelligent, aloof beauty is finely counterbalanced by Cephalus' physical robustness.

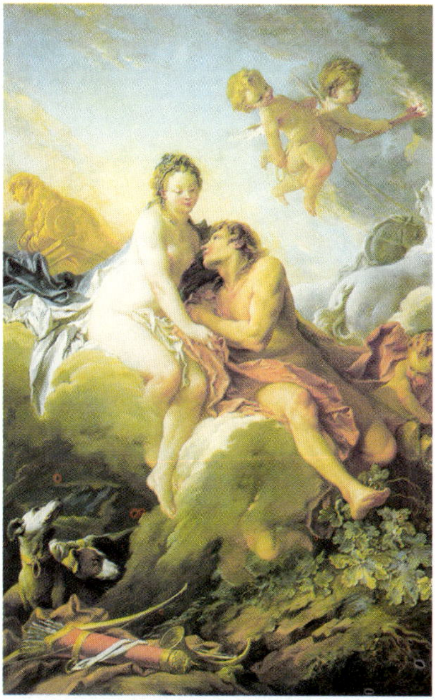

Aurora and Cephalus

François Boucher
(Paris, 1703–1770)

- 1733
- oil on canvas
- 250 x 175 cm
- Musée des Beaux-Arts, Nancy

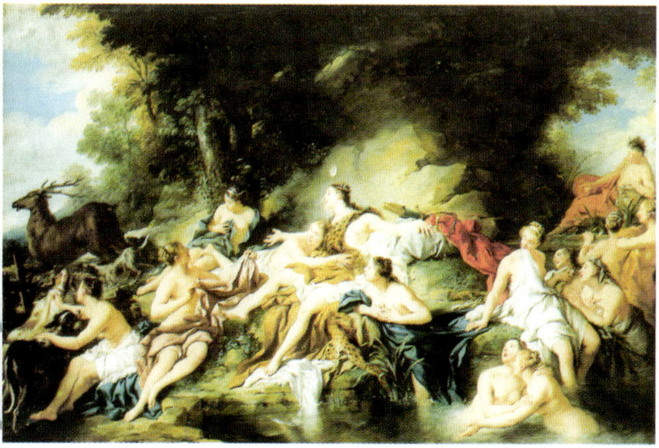

Diana Surprised by Actaeon

Jean-François de Troy
(Paris, 1679–Rome, 1752)

- 1734
- oil on canvas
- 129 x 193 cm
- Öffentliche Kunstsammlung, Kunstmuseum, Basel

In this depiction of the well-worn theme, de Troy concentrates his and the viewer's attention on the nymphs surrounding the goddess. The women are greatly agitated, their nude bodies enriched by the vivid colors and the movement of their robes as they attempt to cover themselves. The two nymphs embracing in the water stand out in particular for their sensuality and for the expressions of surprise on their faces.

Venus Asking Vulcan for Arms for Aeneas

Charles-Joseph Natoire

(Nîmes, 1700–Castel Gandolfo, 1777)

- 1734
- oil on canvas
- 192 x 138 cm
- Musée Fabre, Montpellier

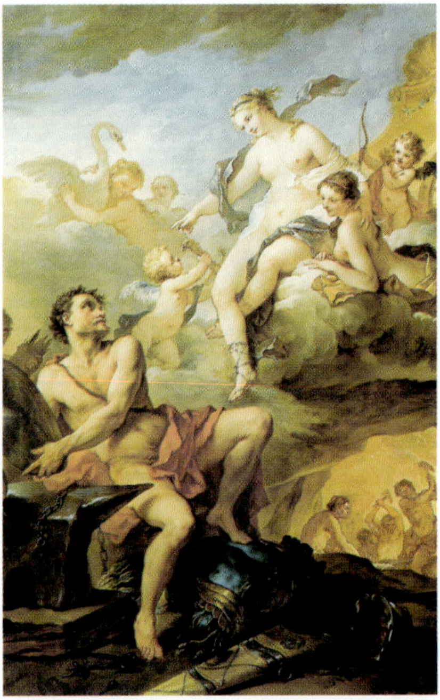

Aeneas was the son of Venus and Anchises, a human whom the goddess seduced by transforming herself into Otreo, the King of Phrygia's daughter. Here, Venus is asking Vulcan for weapons to equip her son in the war against Turnus. Vulcan, naked himself and in a somewhat mannered pose, easily stands his own against the goddess' delicate sensuality.

Venus and Adonis

Jacopo Amigoni

(Naples, 1675–Madrid, 1752)

- oil on canvas
- 45 x 75 cm
- Galleria dell'Accademia, Venice

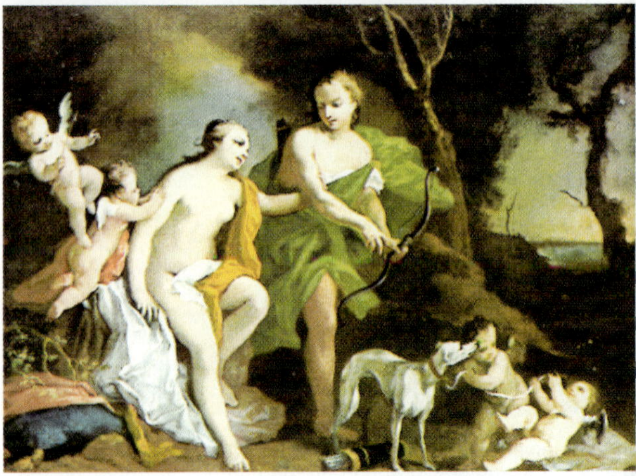

In a style more casual than the rich composition would seem to demand, the painter presents the two lovers accompanied by winged cherubs. Adonis is portrayed, if anything, as having a somewhat feminine air about him. The figures lack the symbolic and allegorical gravity so typical of similar Renaissance figures.

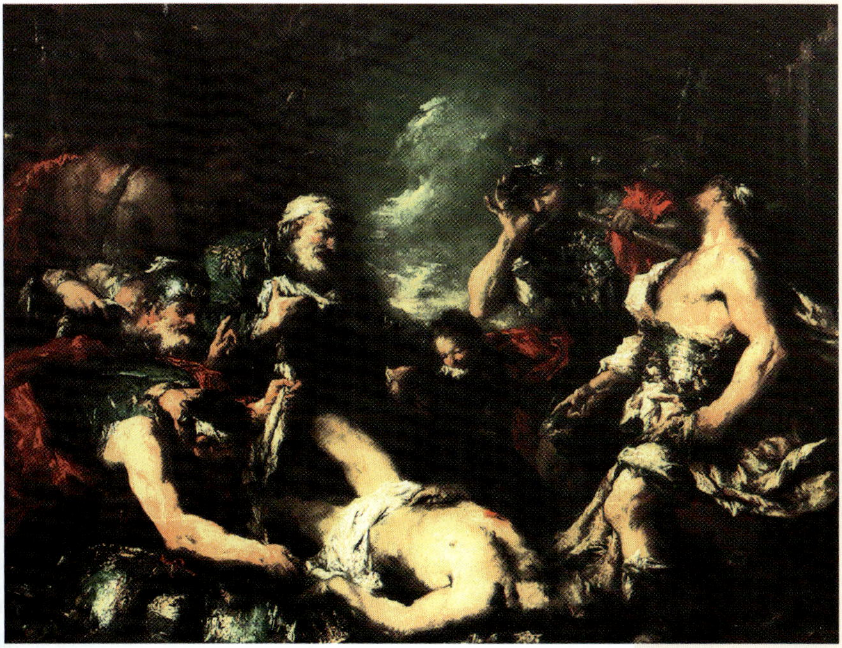

Alexander before the Body of Darius

Francesco Guardi
(Venice, 1712–1793)

- 1740
- oil on canvas
- Pushkin Museum, Moscow

After being defeated at the battle of Issus by Alexander the Great, Darius III, king of Persia, fled the country, while his family was captured. Since Alexander refused the 10,000 talents of gold and the territories west of the Euphrates as ransom, Darius assembled a large army to attack him, but he was once again defeated, and killed by his own soldiers. This canvas shows Alexander the Great before the dead body of Darius, which lies majestically on the ground. The foreshortened body, wearing nothing save a loincloth, is strong and heroic. The scene is obscured by a dense penumbra, whereas Darius' torso is brightly illuminated, making it the focal point of the painting. Francesco Guardi has used the sfumato technique to render the almost misty quality of the atmosphere, in which intense red highlights can be seen. This ambience serves to blend the figures into the landscape and to evoke movement.

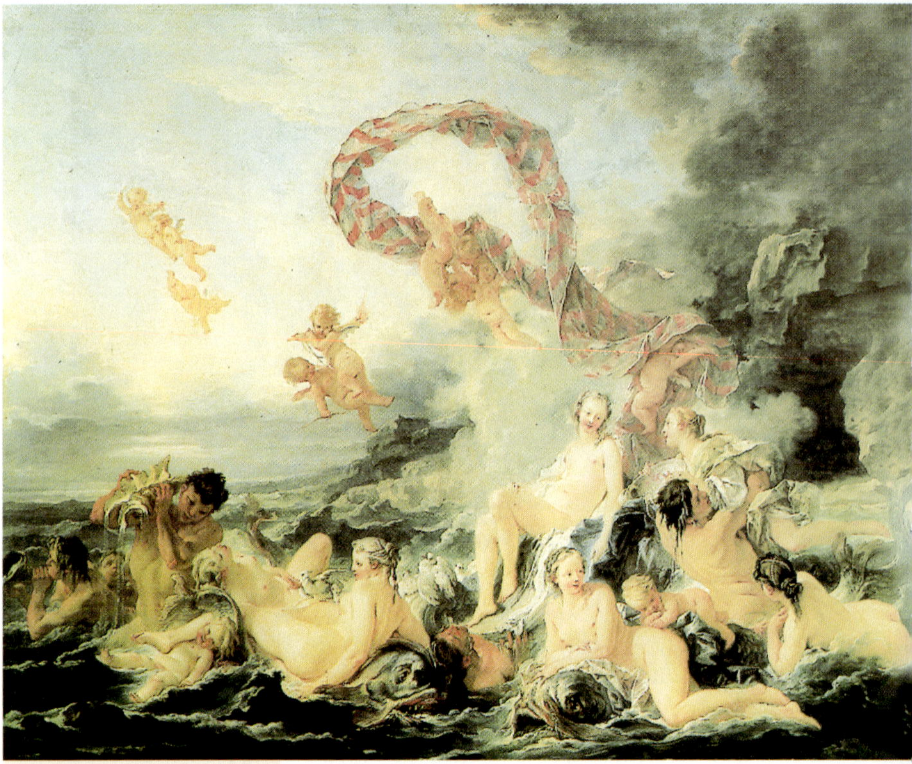

The Triumph of Venus

François Boucher
(Paris, 1703–1770)

- 1740
- oil on canvas
- 130 x 162 cm
- Nationalmuseum, Stockholm

The elegant and dynamic poses, the resourceful combination of curves and the highly erotic quality of these female nudes by François Boucher earned the artist high acclaim in his day, by the public and critics alike, who waxed positively lyrical about his Rococo mythological scenes. Intent on evoking the grandeur of Venus, the artist conceived this magnificent painting, generously exhibiting the naked bodies of the nymphs by depicting them in a variety of poses, giving rise to a writhing, sensual scene. With these remarkable figures, the artist demonstrates his profound knowledge of human anatomy.

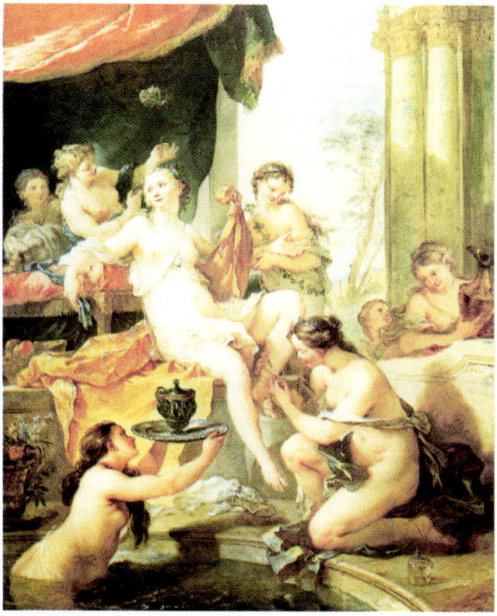

Psyche at her Toilet

Charles-Joseph Natoire
(Nîmes, 1700–Castel Gandolfo, 1777)

- ca. 1735
- oil on canvas
- 198 x 169 cm
- Museum of Art, New Orleans

Youngest of three daughters of an Asian king, Psyche was beautiful but superficial. The scene shows the princess being attended at her toilette by her servants. Her nude figure radiates great sensuality, while conveying her nature as well. The especially lustrous treatment of her skin tones makes her stand out in contrast to those around her.

Diomedes, barbarous king of the Thracian Cicones, was eventually devoured by his own team of man-eating mares. Here, we see Hercules pushing him towards them. The bold foreshortening employed in the depiction of the hero's figure brings out the power of his frame. The golden lighting suffusing many parts of the picture helps to set the representation in a mythological, legendary framework.

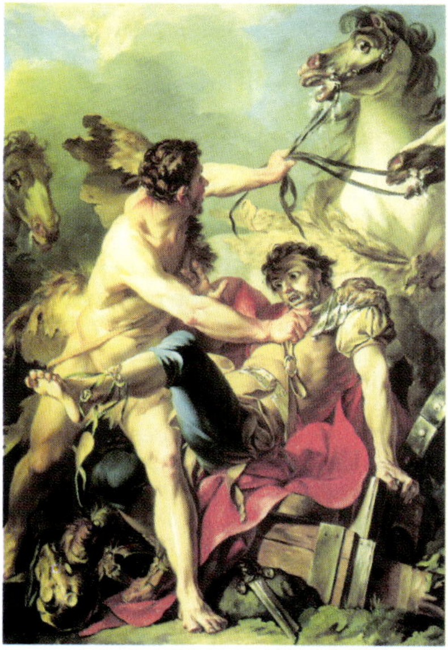

Diomedes and Hercules

Jean-Baptiste-Marie Pierre
(Paris, 1713–1789)

- 1741
- oil on canvas
- 191 x 138 cm
- Musée Fabre, Montpellier

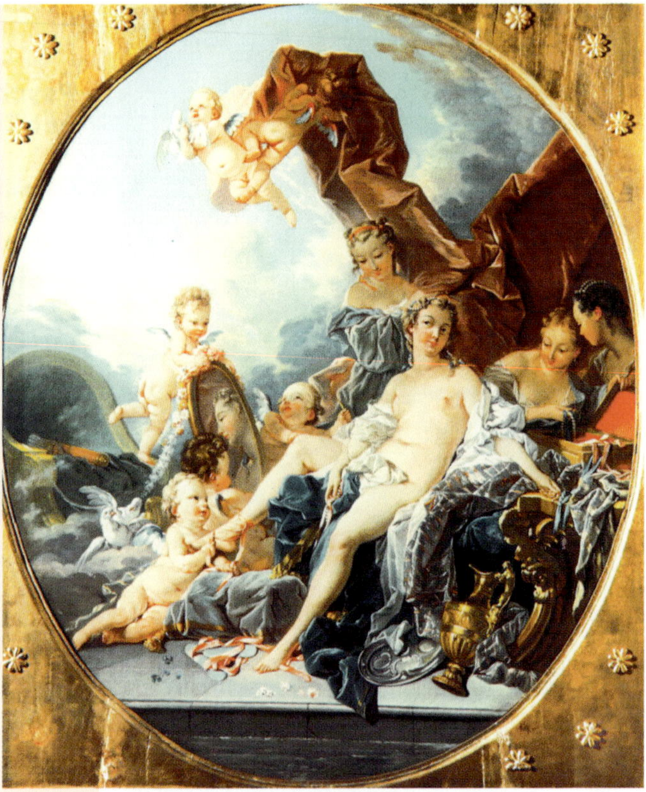

Venus at Her Toilet

François Boucher
(Paris, 1703–1770)

- 1742
- oil on canvas
- 101 x 86.7 cm
- Hermitage, St. Petersburg

This painting shows a frivolous, candid scene replete with erotic details. Together with The Triumph of Venus, it constitutes a diptych that combines a series of highly interesting visual elements. The nude of Venus, placed in a mysteriously sensual setting, is far removed from the staid mythological representations of more conventional works on the subject. Here, the goddess, who is portrayed with flushed cheeks, gazes haughtily down at the viewer, with her legs spread apart in a provocative pose. The subtle modeling of her skin is executed with painstaking meticulousness. The Baroque ideal of beauty, with its penchant for grand, voluptuous figures, no longer obtains here, although certain aspects, such as the small breasts, were retained and continued to be considered beautiful until the 20th century. With this type of painting, Boucher shows himself to be one of the primary exponents of the Rococo.

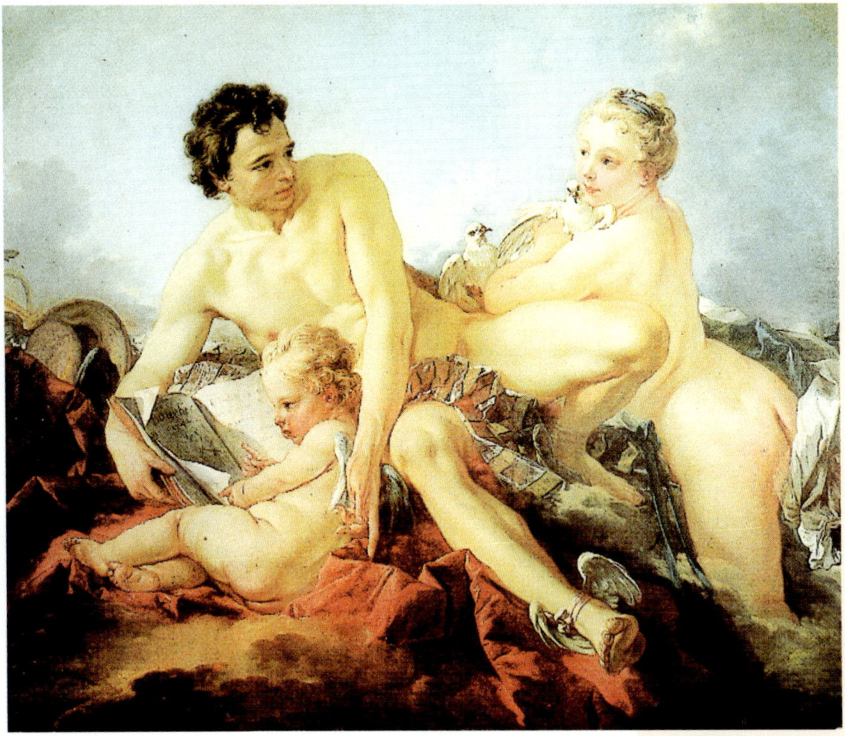

Venus and Mercury Instructing Cupid

François Boucher
(Paris, 1703–1770)

- 1742
- oil on canvas
- 118 x 136 cm
- Staatliche Museen, Berlin

Venus is depicted, here, watching as Mercury instructs their child, Cupid. Cupid's presence softens Mercury's otherwise somewhat sluggish nature so he is captivated by the goddess' alluring gaze and pose, the latter very similar to the pose used by Boucher in his Blond Odalisque (1752). The two nude figures are imbued with eroticism, not only through their intimate positions and their painterly handling, but also on account of the disturbing relationship between them: complicitous looks and gestures seem to signal the inevitable amorous dénouement. Boucher's technical mastery is impeccable, the subtle atmosphere created being enhanced by even the very skin tones of the figures. If the figure of Mercury is more naturalistic than that of Venus, relatively speaking an idealization having certain Rubenesque characteristics, Boucher's approach to human anatomy is never anything but precise and purposeful.

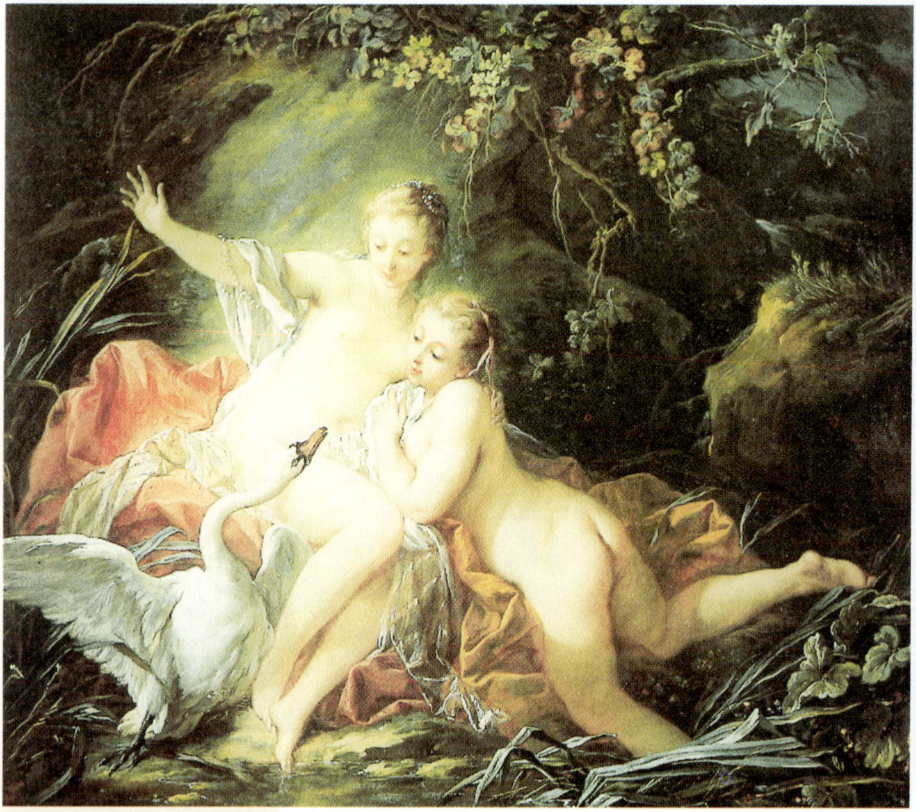

Leda and the Swan

François Boucher
(Paris, 1703–1770)

- 1742
- oil on canvas
- 60 x 74 cm
- Collection of Mr. and Mrs. Stewart Resnick

The work is an excellent specimen of Boucher's refined style at its most exquisite. The young women are graceful and cultivated, yet uninhibited. The treatment of the nymph is more carnal than that of Leda. In certain areas the light is so bright that outlines are concealed, while at the same time related areas are endowed with tones that allow the clear depiction of every anatomical feature.

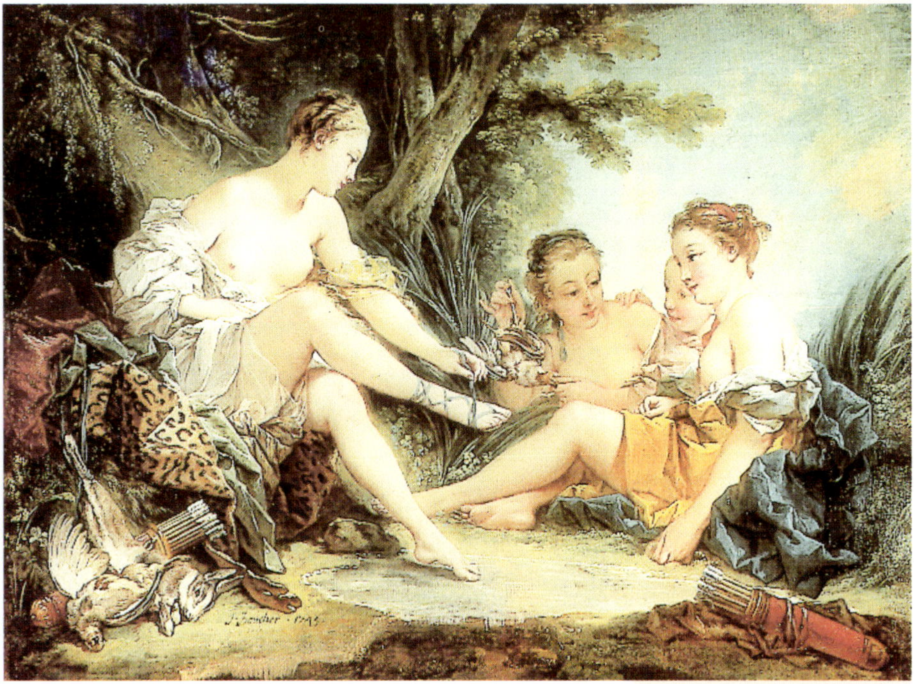

This work is a sensual, nude study of the goddess Diana relaxing after hunting and just before being observed by Actaeon, who will duly be punished. Boucher captures a moment of intimacy that is full of beauty and sensuality. The goddess exhibits a dazzling body in a hazy, warm atmosphere. Her skin tones are subtle and contribute effectively to an unusually graceful style of modeling, which helps entice the viewer into the scene. Erotic minutiae are abundant, from Diana's complete lack of selfconsciousness, to the seductive manner in which she crosses her legs, while the transparency of the veils above her thigh enhances her delicate nature.

The Return of Diana from the Chase

François Boucher
(Paris, 1703–1770)

- 1745
- oil on canvas
- 94 x 132 cm
- Musée Cognacq-Jay, Paris

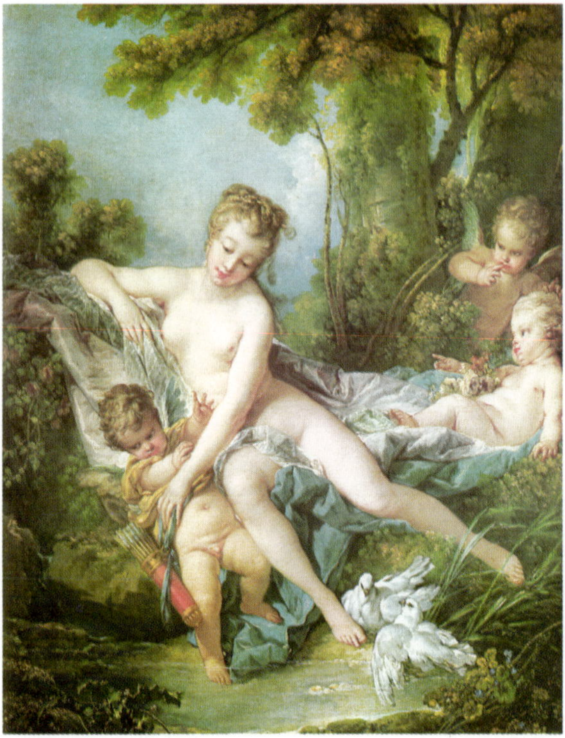

Venus Consoling Cupid

François Boucher
(Paris, 1703–1770)

- oil on canvas
- 107 x 85 cm
- National Gallery of Art, Washington, D.C.

Venus, represented as a sensual young woman, is shown patiently disarming Cupid of the arrows he uses to inflict desire on his victims. The goddess' frontal pose reveals her breasts and her legs, which are spread slightly in a carefree attitude, with the end of the drapery carefully placed over her genitals. Although far from being those of a heroic woman, the forms of her body are balanced, fragile and sophisticated, with pink flesh tones and alluring features. The figures are situated in a luxuriant setting, whose beauty is enhanced by the drapery and the precious diadem that crowns Venus' head. The artist, in accordance with a style that was much in vogue at the time, has used the mythological theme to capture the splendid body of the nude. Executed with great skill and subtlety, the eroticism of the scene is heightened by the facture of the composition and the elegance of the figures.

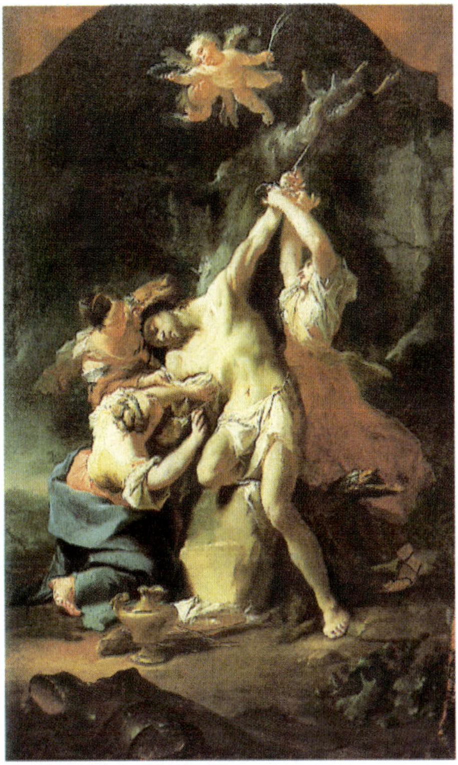

Troger depicts the saint, commander of the Praetorian guard, after suffering martyrdom for his refusal to renounce the Christian faith. St. Irene and two other women attend. The saint's head has no halo, symbol of divine election. Instead, we see a doomed human being, shattered and at his end, with no succor but that offered by the three women. The theme of St. Sebastian was traditionally the locus par excellence where the male nude could be explored, as artists felt freer and more at ease with the human body here than in, say, the Crucifixion. Here, while there is no overt eroticism, there are nevertheless strong emotional and dramatic elements, emphasized by powerful chiaroscuro, with the figure of the saint as the central focus. Anatomical realism and pose stand out and transmit an effect of sagging weight. Contrasting colors, vibrant brushwork and sinuous forms go to produce a work of great power.

St. Sebastian, St. Irene and Two Women

Paul Troger
(Welsberg, Pustertal, 1698 –Vienna, 1762)

- ca. 1746
- oil on canvas
- 60 x 37 cm
- Österreichische Galerie, Belvedere, Vienna

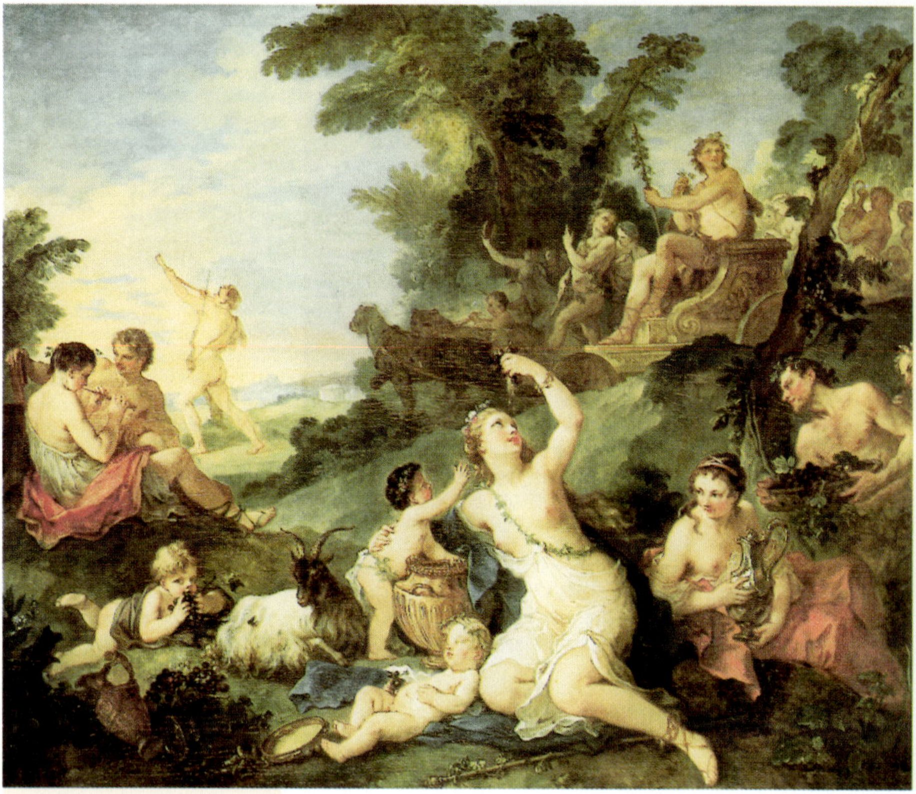

The Triumph of Bacchus

Charles-Joseph Natoire
(Nîmes, 1700–Castel Gandolfo, 1777)

- 1747
- oil on canvas
- 199 x 225 cm
- Musée du Louvre, Paris

Bacchus is depicted parading triumphantly in his chariot. The beautiful young nude, with eloquent facial expression in the foreground, is Erigone, in whose honor the celebrations are being held. Erigone's body is of monumental dimensions, yet perfectly proportioned. Her pose reveals her attractive allures, the sensuality heightened by her diaphanous clothing.

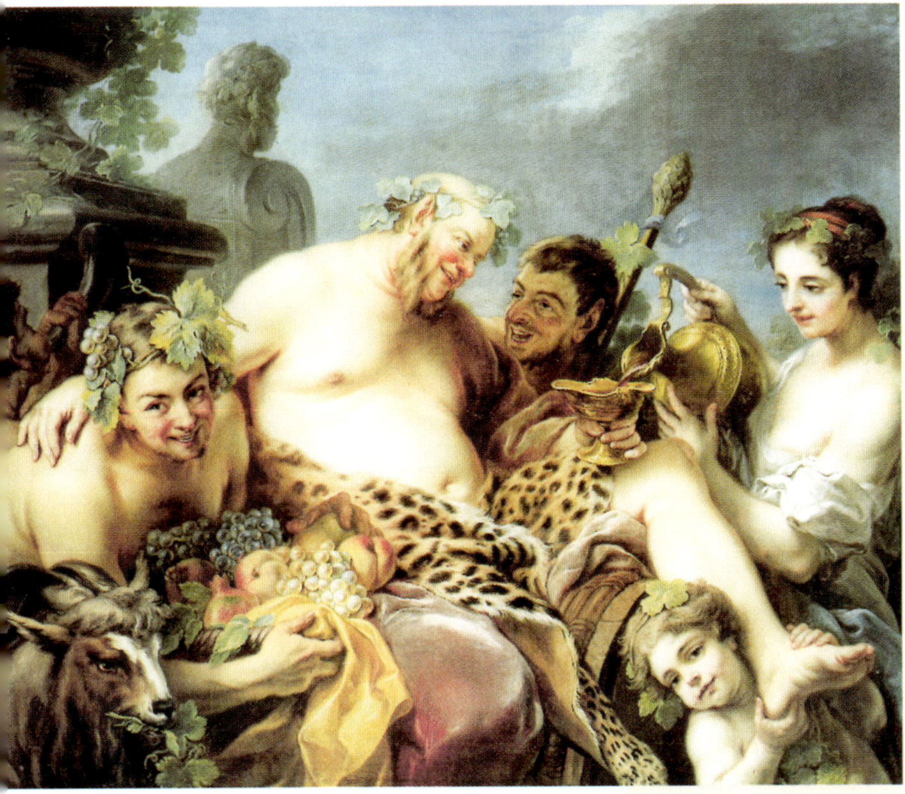

ilenus, sometimes described as the son of Pan, is depicted
ere with satyrs, who were part of Bacchus' entourage. There
little beauty in the figures, who, nevertheless, are invariably
njoying life's pleasures to the full. The satyrs here are repre-
ented as short, chubby human beings, while Silenus is more
orpulent still, as well as tipsy. His somewhat grotesque torso
erfectly reflects his personality. His flabbiness and large
elly give him a jovial, good-natured appearance.

Silenus

Charles André van Loo

(Nice, 1705–Paris, 1765)

- 1747
- oil on canvas
- 164 x 195 cm
- Musée des Beaux-Arts, Nancy

Bacchanal

Charles-Joseph Natoire
(Nîmes, 1700–Castel Gandolfo, 1777)

- 1749
- oil on canvas
- 79.3 x 100 cm
- Museum of Fine Arts, Houston

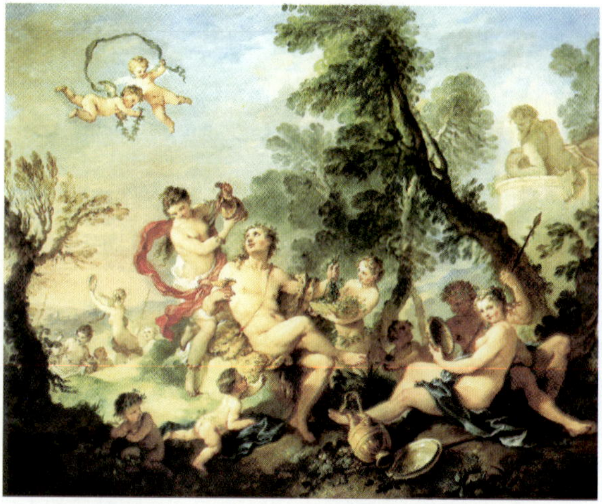

The women are young and rather heavyset, yet the composition is balanced. There is an echo of the joviality we find in the works of Rubens. The figure of Bacchus also manifests a change in attitude towards the male nude. The pronounced foreshortening of his body contributes to an execution that is highly sensual, a far cry from the heroic ideal of the Baroque.

The Education of Cupid

Louis Michel van Loo
(Toulon, 1707–Paris, 1771)

- ca. 1750
- oil on canvas
- Real Academia de Bellas Artes de San Fernando, Madrid

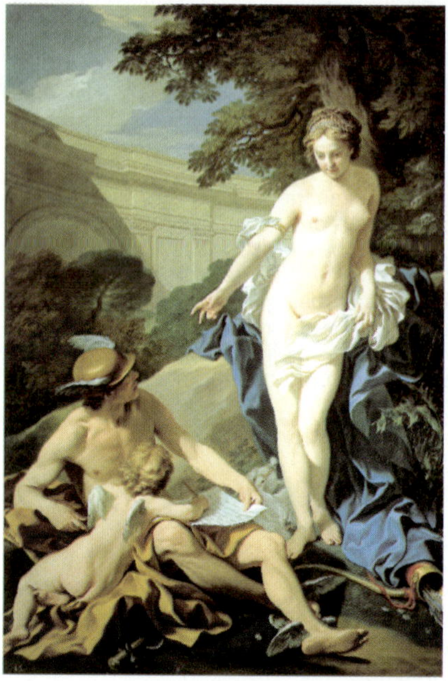

Despite its overt Classicism, the painting breathes a certain romantic intention as well, with its splendidly erotic depiction of Venus. The forms of the female figure are moderate compared to the often overwhelming exuberance of Baroque art. The contrapposto is sculptural, approaching the style of Classical statuary—breasts and hips small and well-modeled—and the figure has a resplendent complexion.

'he complex foreshortening of the udes, the different figures in arious poses, ɔgether with the azzling palette, emonstrate the ɹrtist's mastery ·f draftsmanship ɹnd painterly echnique. Tiepolo ombines myth ·ith reality to reate a transcendental quality that ·clipses the allegorical nature of he scene.

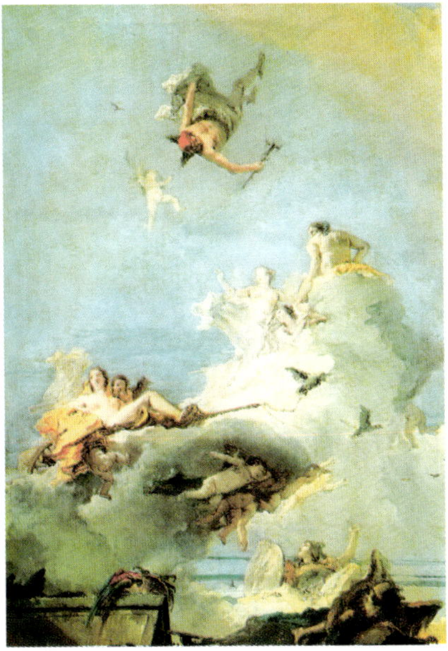

Mount Olympus

Giovanni Battista (Giambattista) Tiepolo
(Venice, 1696–Madrid, 1770)

- oil on canvas
- 86 x 62 cm
- Museo del Prado, Madrid

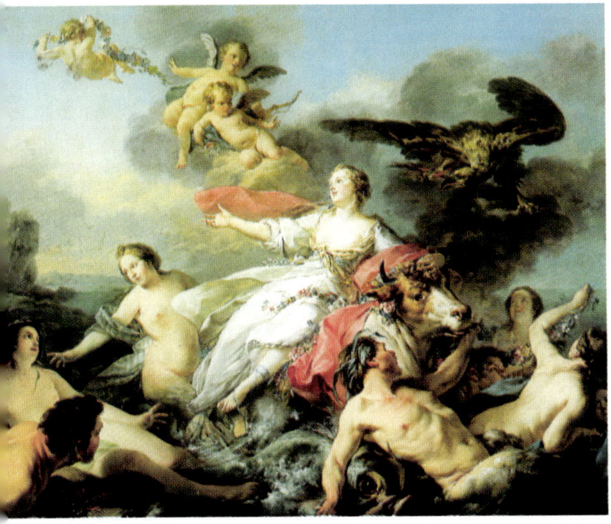

The Rape of Europa

Jean-Baptiste-Marie Pierre
Paris, 1714–1789)

- 1750
- oil on canvas
- 240 x 274.4 cm
- Dallas Museum of Art, Foundation of the Arts Collection, Mrs John B. O'Hara Fonds

The work draws for its charm and strength on the contrasts ɔetween Europa's beauty and gentleness, the force of the ·ea and the movement of the naked bodies floating around he bull, as if they were performing a magical dance. These ·econdary figures have been elaborated to a high degree. The masterful forshortening in the male figures is thoroughly ɿatural and dynamic.

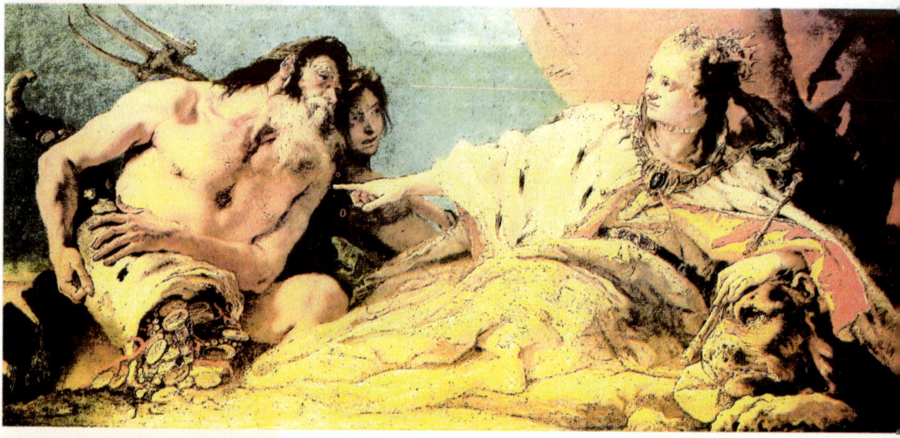

Neptune Offering Gifts to Venice

Giovanni Battista (Giambattista) Tiepolo
(Venice, 1696–Madrid, 1770)

- 1750
- oil on canvas
- 135 x 275 cm
- Doge's Palace, Venice

This is an allegory of the gifts received by the city of Venice, here represented as a queen in regal attire, with her arm resting on a lion's head, which symbolizes St. Mark, the city's patron saint. Neptune, who pours out the riches from a horn, is depicted as a battle-hardened, muscular old man with a white beard. The artist employs a color scheme of harmonious warm hues. The light emanates from the left, modeling Neptune's naked torso as well as Venice's sumptuous robes, leaving the background in a half-light, thus arresting the viewer's attention as the figures seem to emerge from it. Tiepolo has granted the allegorical scene just the amount of formalism and grandiloquence that it calls for.

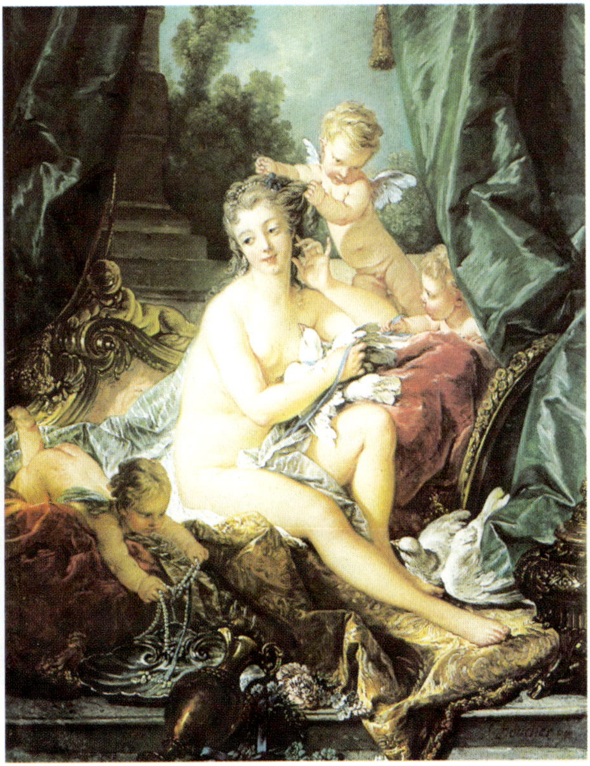

The Toilet of Venus

François Boucher
(Paris, 1703–1770)

- 1751
- oil on canvas
- 108 x 85 cm
- The Metropolitan Museum of Art, New York

lad we to characterize Boucher by one particular trait, then would have to be the sensuality of his female nudes. The ssence of this painter's work lies in the Baroque sentinents that it expresses in respect of eroticism and of the ariegated world of colors and shapes. Venus, here, is hown sitting in extravagant and carefree splendor while herubs sport around her. The room, serving as a backdrop, luxuriously decorated and the goddess is flanked by goreous fabrics, jewelry and a sumptuous golden divan. They erve to frame this young, nude woman, who is mischieous enough to show herself seductively rather than exhibionistically. The exuberant skin coloration of Venus is in the tyle of Rubens, with bluish and greenish hues among iaphanous pinkish tones. The goddess is shown glancing oquettishly to one side, while the fabric between her legs lays its role in heightening the eroticism of the moment.

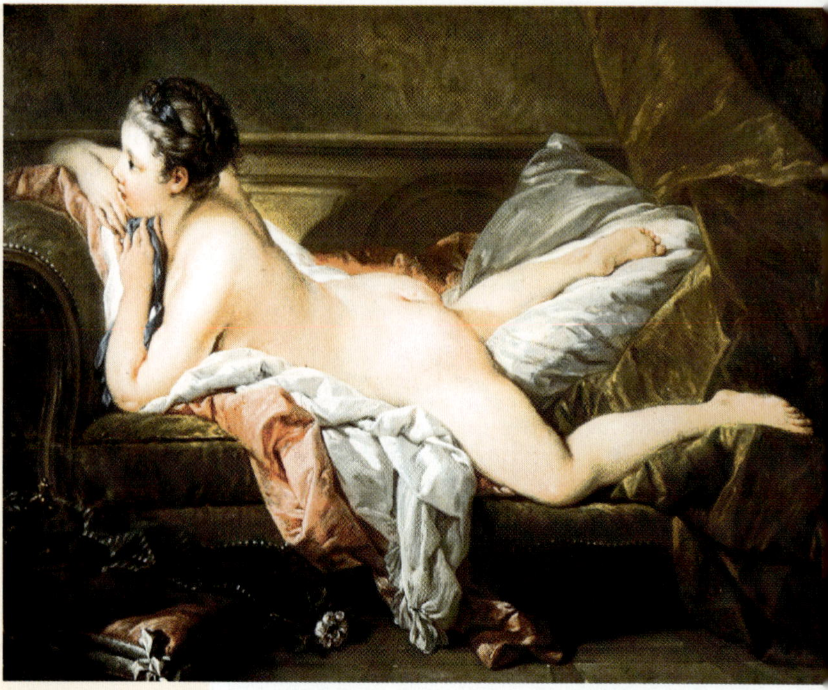

The Blond Odalisque

François Boucher
(Paris, 1703–1770)

- 1752
- oil on canvas
- 59 x 73 cm
- Alte Pinakothek, Munich

In this painting, Boucher is considered by some to have portrayed Louise O'Murphy, a young Irish woman who modeled for him and who became Louis XV's mistress in 1753. Her pose is unequivocally lascivious, legs parted and belly pressed against the bedclothes below, and while the young woman's pose suggests innocent relaxation, everything is, in fact, highly studied. The nude body, modeled with the aid of subtle shadows, reflects much light and her skin in some areas seems to have the quality of mother-of-pearl. The model's position describes a slight diagonal as she directs her gaze, as if expecting somebody to enter at that very moment. In such paintings, Boucher laid aside the tenderness and delicacy typical of so many treatments of the female nude in order to use a more direct approach, seeking high-intensity eroticism combined with subtle and piquant undertones. Although Boucher himself was looked on as a libertine, his art had a considerable following in Parisian high society in his day.

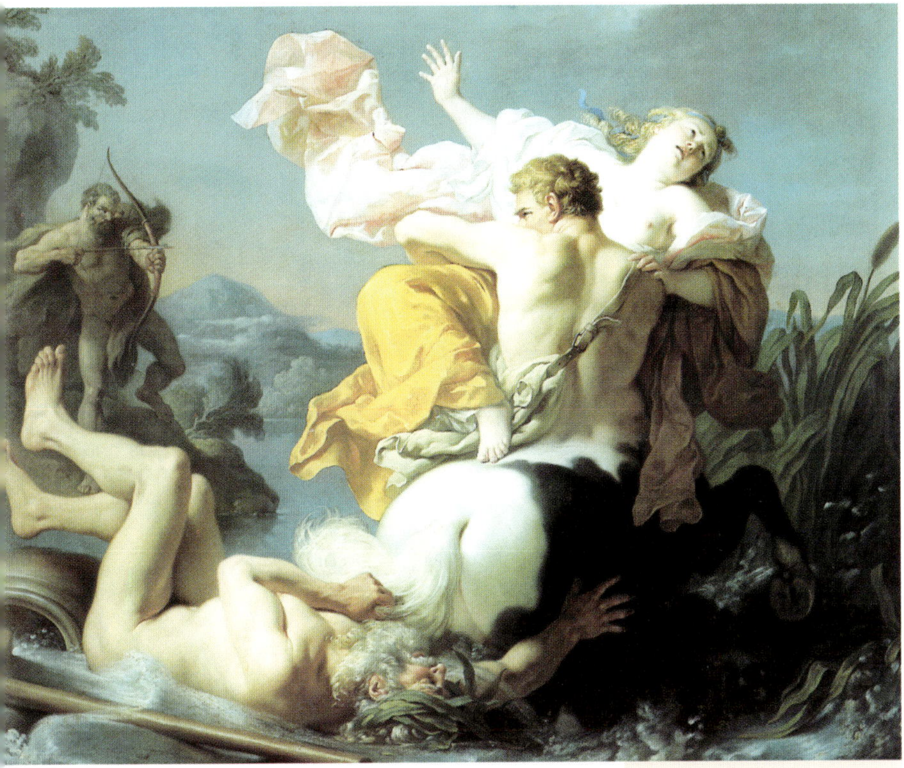

The Centaur Nessus fell in love with and abducted Deianira, Hercules' last wife, and upon Hercules' pursuing and shooting him with an arrow, the dying Centaur, in revenge, instructed Deianira to impregnate a garment for Hercules with his blood, claiming that this would function as a potent love-charm and render him faithful to her forever. Deianira followed his instructions. However, when Hercules later donned the garment, it burnt him because it was poisoned, and, unable to remove it, such was the manner of his death. The centaur's torso and Deianira are splendidly executed here, the handling of both their figures rather delicate and smooth despite the fact that they are muscular and strong.

Nessus Abducting Deianira

Louis-Jean-François Lagrenée (the Elder)
(Paris, 1725–1805)

- 1754
- oil on canvas
- 157 x 185 cm
- Musée du Louvre, Paris

Venus Disarming Cupid

François Boucher
(Paris, 1703–1770)

- 1751
- oil on canvas
- 142 x 114 cm
- Collection of Mr. and Mrs. Stewart Resnick

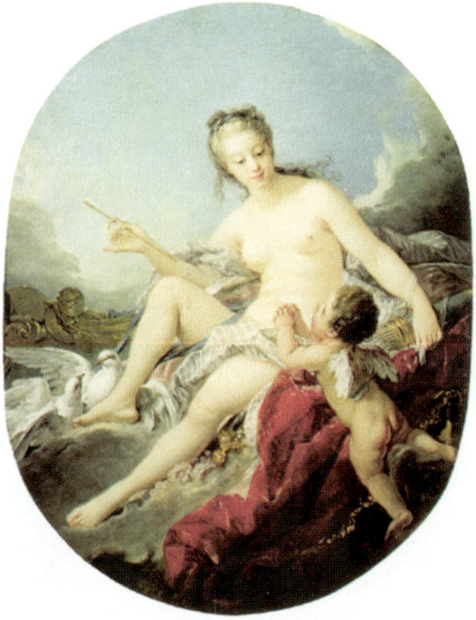

Boucher celebrates the female nude in representations of goddesses, such as this one of Venus exercising her manifest superiority over her son, Cupid, from whom she has just confiscated one of his dangerous arrows. The figure is gracefully elegant, the positioning of her fingers and hands refined, while her gaze combines tenderness and majesty. Her relatively slender body is not without an idealized touch of realism.

Emperor Severus Reproaching Caracalla

Jean-Baptiste Greuze
(Tournus in Ardèche, 1725 –Paris, 1805)

- 1755
- oil on canvas
- 124 x 160 cm
- Musée du Louvre, Paris

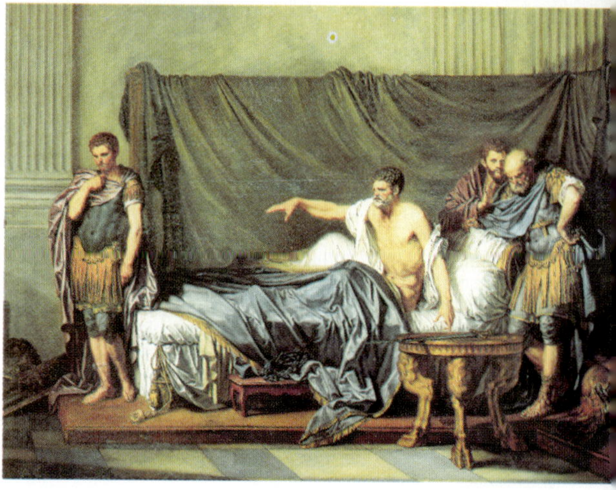

Historical themes were frequent in French academic painting, where naked figures were often employed to inject dramatic interest into a scene. Here, we see the emperor Severus sitting up and reproaching Caracalla, his eldest son, whom he accuses of having attempted to assassinate him. The depiction of his body is natural enough, although clearly it has been executed in a somewhat academic style.

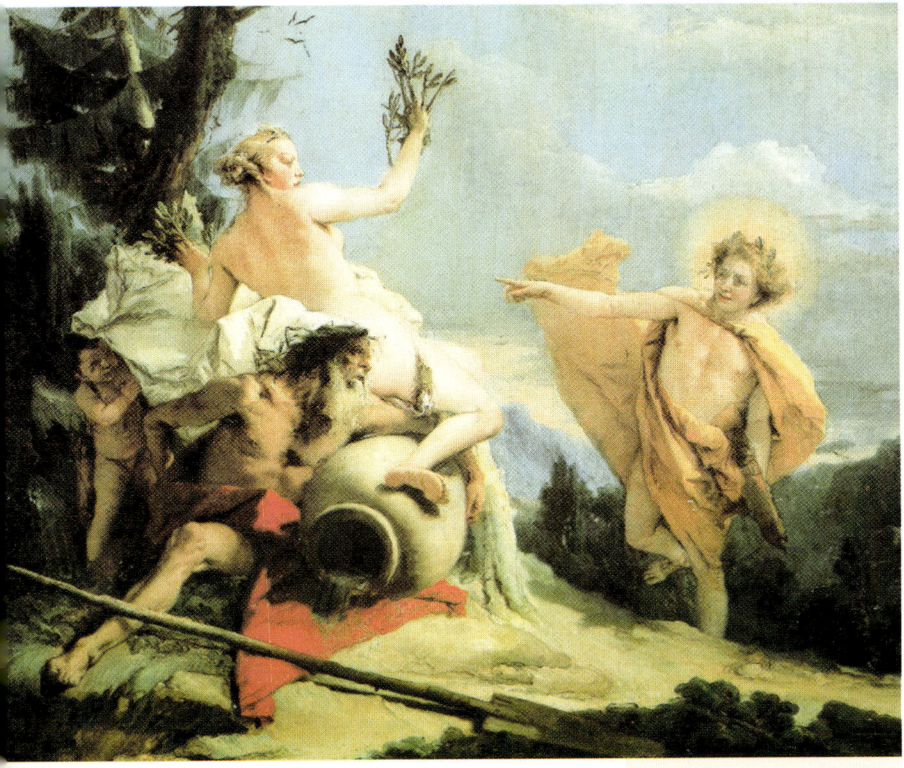

When Apollo slew the python, he ridiculed Cupid, mocking his diminutive stature and the fact that he carried bow and arrows. Cupid took his revenge by shooting Apollo with one of these arrows, which made Apollo fall in love with the nymph Daphne. Cupid shot a second arrow to make Daphne spurn Apollo's love. The work shows Apollo flying to Daphne, who is seated by her father, Peneus, the river god. Cupid, far left, is all but hidden from view. Daphne asked her father for help, which he gave by turning her into a laurel tree. Tiepolo is a master of the nude figure, which he executes here with sensuality and romantic realism. Noteworthy here is how varied the treatment of the three figures is.

Apollo Pursuing Daphne

Giovanni Battista (Giambattista) Tiepolo
(Venice, 1696–Madrid, 1770)

- 1755–60
- oil on canvas
- 68.8 x 87.2 cm
- National Gallery of Art, Washington

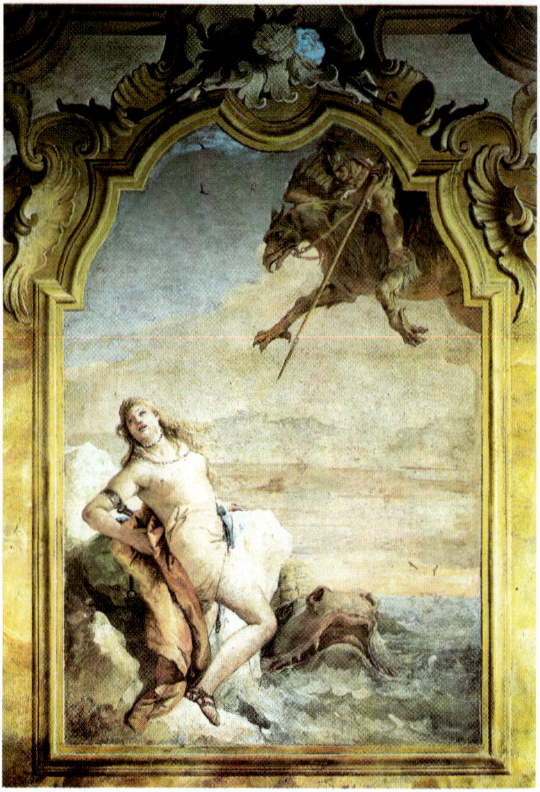

Ruggero Saves Angelica from the Sea Monster

Giovanni Battista (Giambattista) Tiepolo
(Venice, 1696–Madrid, 1770)

- 1757
- fresco
- 250 x 175 cm
- Villa Valmarana, Vicenza

Although the draftsmanship of this nude does not compare with that of other works by the artist, it is interesting for the modern manner in which it has been rendered and for its imaginative execution. The bold foreshortening and the volumes of Angelica's torso have been articulated with the deftness of a master draftsman. Since the subject of this work was taken from Classical mythology, and in keeping with his singular style, Tiepolo has conceived a magnificent work evoking the epic tales of antiquity, for which he was so renowned. This painting is also remarkable for its treatment of light, which creates a bright background from which the subject appears to emerge, producing contrasts in the manner of a relief.

ector slew atroclus, friend Achilles, who turn slew ector, dragging s corpse behind s chariot round e walls of Troy nd finally leaving unburied. The ude figure of enus is delicate, hile Hector's anly frame eflects the coldess of death.

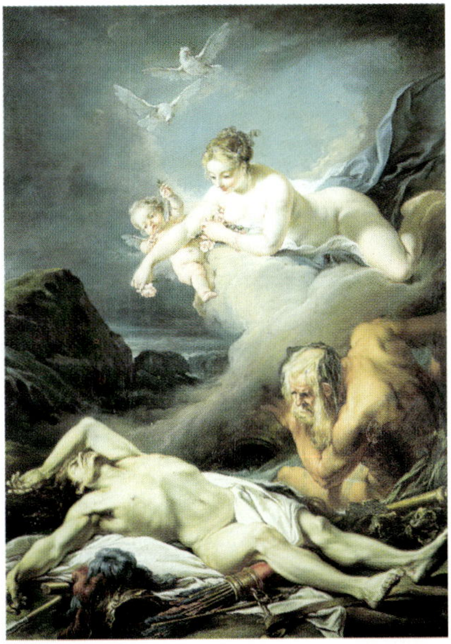

Hector Abandoned on the Banks of the Scamander

Jean-Baptiste Deshays
(Colleville, near Rouen, 1729–Paris, 1765)

- 1758
- oil on canvas
- 244 x 180 cm
- Musée Fabre, Montpellier

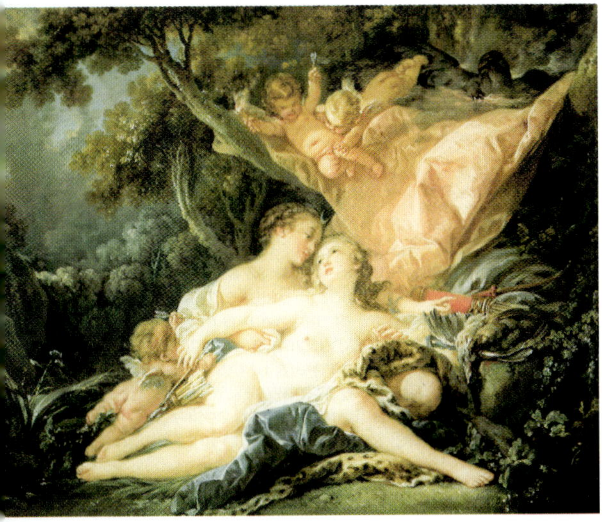

Jupiter Seducing Callisto

François Boucher
(Paris, 1703–1770)

- 1759
- oil on canvas
- 56 x 74 cm
- The Nelson-Atkins Museum of Art, Kansas City, Missouri

oucher's art frequently has an extremely high erotic charge: outhful bodies exposed without inhibition, budding breasts, aresses and looks. Here, a most sensual moment is portrayed. upiter has transformed himself into Diana and is seducing allisto, who surrenders to his charms. Callisto is shown as an nocent girl enraptured by her cunning seductress. Her body adiates both innocence and lasciviousness.

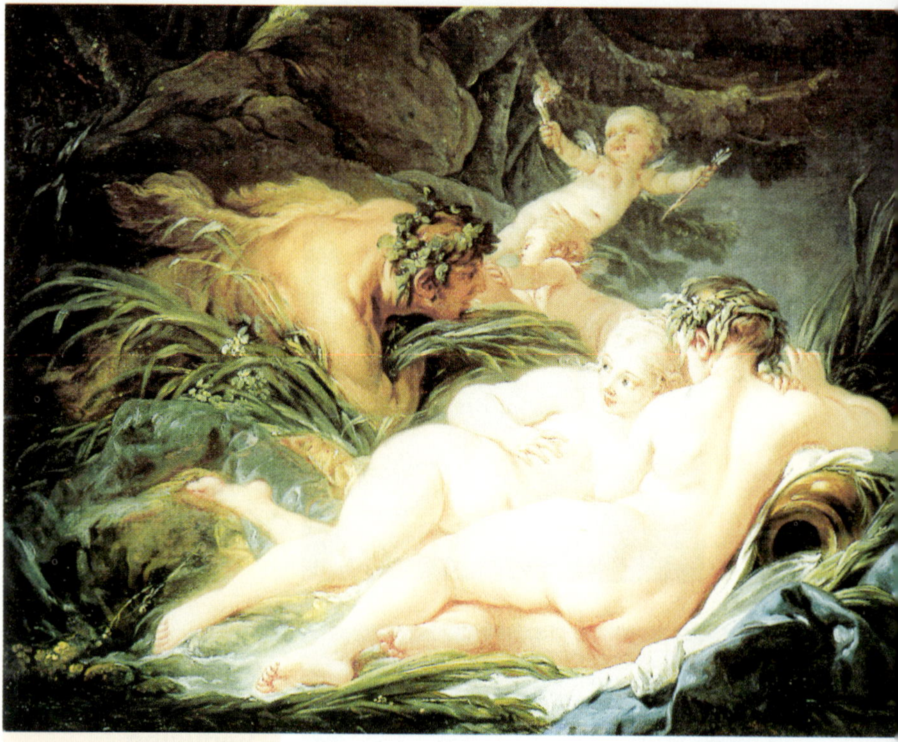

Pan and Selene

François Boucher
(Paris, 1703–1770)

- 1759
- oil on canvas
- 32.5 x 41.5 cm
- The Trustees of the National Gallery, London

Pan, disguised as a lamb, charmed Selene and persuaded her to take a ride with him around a meadow, requesting that she fulfil one wish of his in return. Selene does not appear in the least startled by Pan's sudden appearance. Boucher depicts a resplendent Selene, her radiance illuminating her surroundings, at play with a river nymph, while a corpulent Pan is shown emerging from undergrowth. Both nymphs recall Rubens' treatment of the human anatomy, although these figures are somewhat more restrained than in Rubens, and more authentic. Their bodily positions, as well as the wonderful treatment of skin tints heightened with red tones, convey great sensuality.

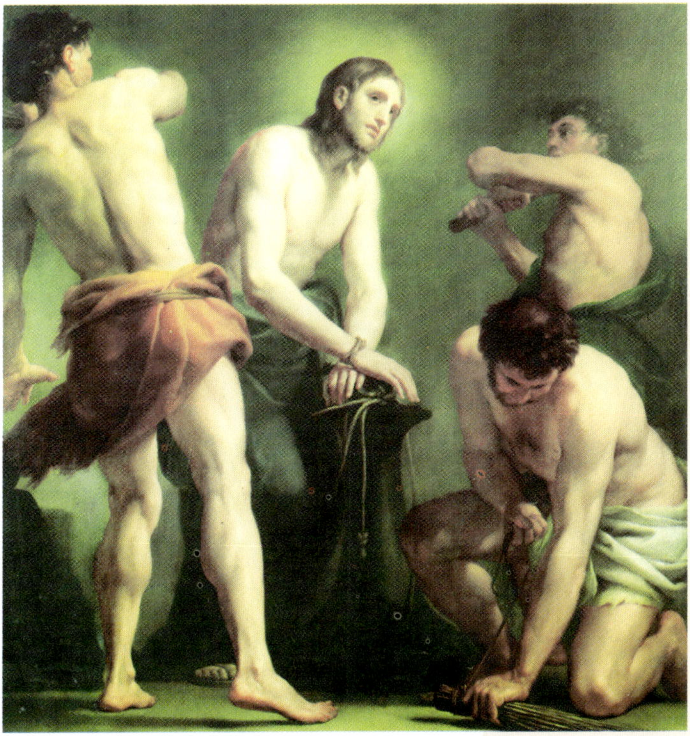

engs' future was marked out for him from his earliest infan-
/. His father, obsessed with the idea that his son would
ecome a great artist, subjected him to a strict upbringing.
/hilst still in his cot, paper and pencil were his only toys. The
tist lived a tormented life, obsessed with attaining perfection
his works, to which the present painting attests. The
natomical studies of the various figures are of an exception-
ly high quality, with special emphasis placed on the muscu-
ture, which in Mengs' treatment always acquires a dull,
zzy appearance. Although these foreshortened figures illus-
ate the artist's remarkable skill at rendering the human
ody, his figures appear somewhat overly dramatic and pos-
ess a certain listlessness, even those that require a more
gorous treatment. Despite the fact that the figures are well
xecuted, as a whole, the work is somewhat static and cold.

The Flagellation

Anton Raffael Mengs
(Aussig, Bohemia, 1728 –Rome, 1779)

- 1791–69
- oil on canvas
- 185 x 185 cm
- Palacio Real, Madrid

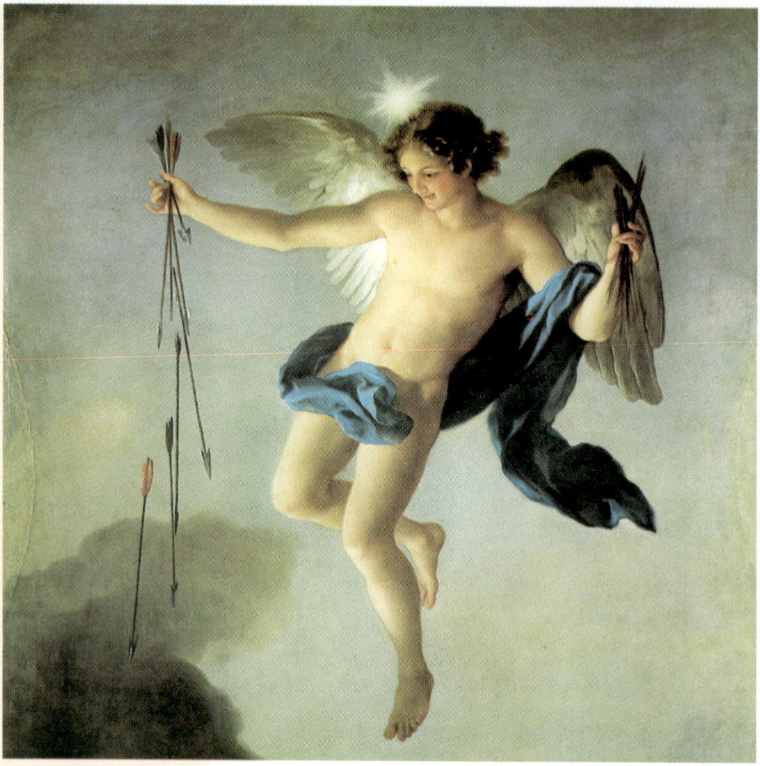

Afternoon

Anton Raffael Mengs
(Aussig, Bohemia, 1728 –Rome, 1779)

- ca. 1765
- oil on canvas
- 210 x 200 cm
- Palacio de la Moncloa, Madrid

This elegant, winged nude resembles an ordinary boy with somewhat androgynous features and an athletic body that eschews a clearly defined musculature. Virtually none of the figures rendered by Mengs has the heroic bearing that other artists have given their nudes. The influence of Raphael is apparent in this work in the treatment of the flesh tones and in the palette. The modeling of the skin is of the highest quality, a hallmark of the painter's work, even if the painterly treatment is somewhat bland. The sensitivity with which the artist has resolved the lighting is masterly, as much in the background, which is smooth and luminous, as in the resplendent body, which is modeled with subtle shadows and exhibits a color scheme that underscores its beauty. This striking work is academic in both conception and execution.

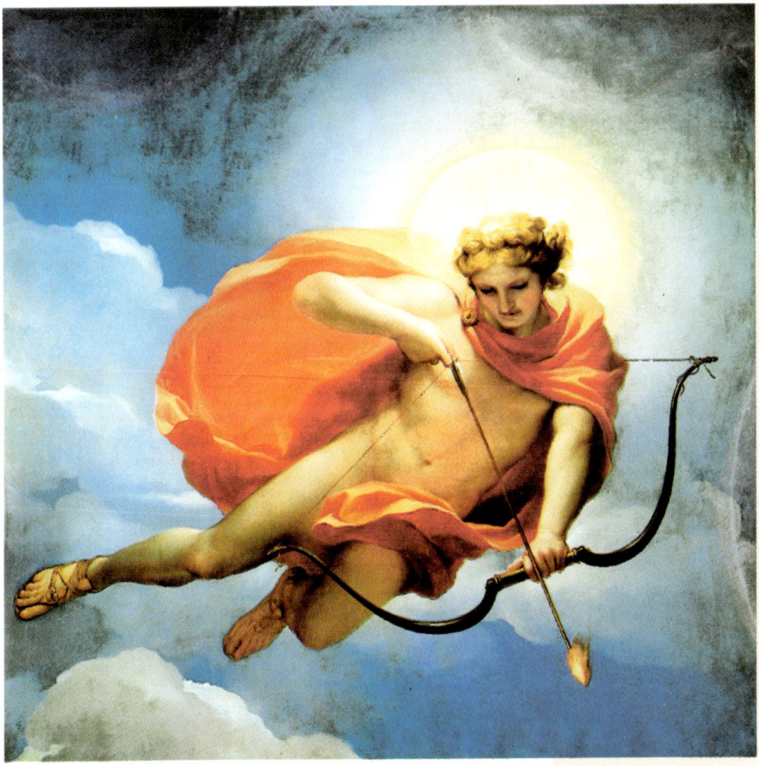

ıidday is represented here as a youthful archer about to ıoot a flaming arrow. The body of the nude has been ealized and behind his head appears a brilliant sun, sembling an aureole. The figure's shoulders are so bright- illuminated that they are almost as blinding as the sun. ne rest of the body, on the other hand, consists of dense nal values, the result of back lighting, although they never ɔpear hard, for one of the most characteristic features of engs' nudes is their soft modeling, recalling the figures Correggio and Raphael. The work is remarkable for its terplay of the luminous, intense colors of the figure and e cool tones of the background.

Midday

Anton Raffael Mengs

(Aussig, Bohemia, 1728 –Rome, 1779)

- ca.1765
- oil on canvas
- 210 x 200 cm
- Palacio de la Moncloa, Madrid

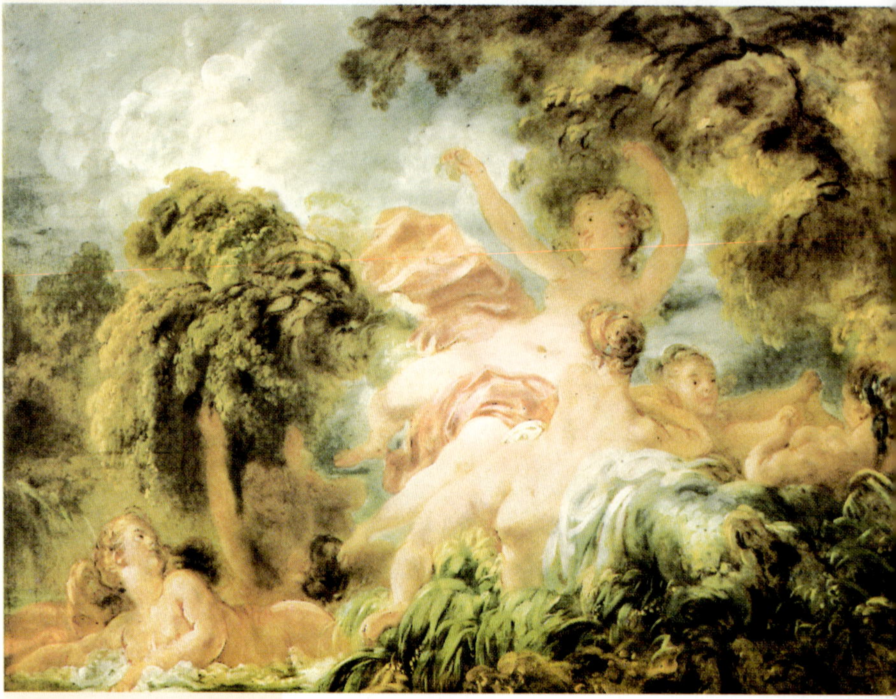

The Bathers

Jean-Honoré Fragonard
(Grasse, 1732–Paris, 1806)

- 1765
- oil on canvas
- 64 x 81 cm
- Musée du Louvre, Paris

This sensual painting depicts both a festive and an erotic scene with a warm atmosphere in soft focus. What appear to be nymphs at play are young, voluptuous women, recalling the figures of Peter Paul Rubens in the fullness of their bodies, their rhythmic movement and the harmony established between the pastel colors and the scene they depict—something that was later to be taken up again by the Impressionists. The hazy atmosphere blends almost imperceptibly with the gradations of the women's skin, accentuating their nudity. The volumes are well articulated, indeed, nearly sculptural, particularly in the half-light, where the play of light and shade model their bodies. In the lighter areas, however, the skin appears nearly flat.

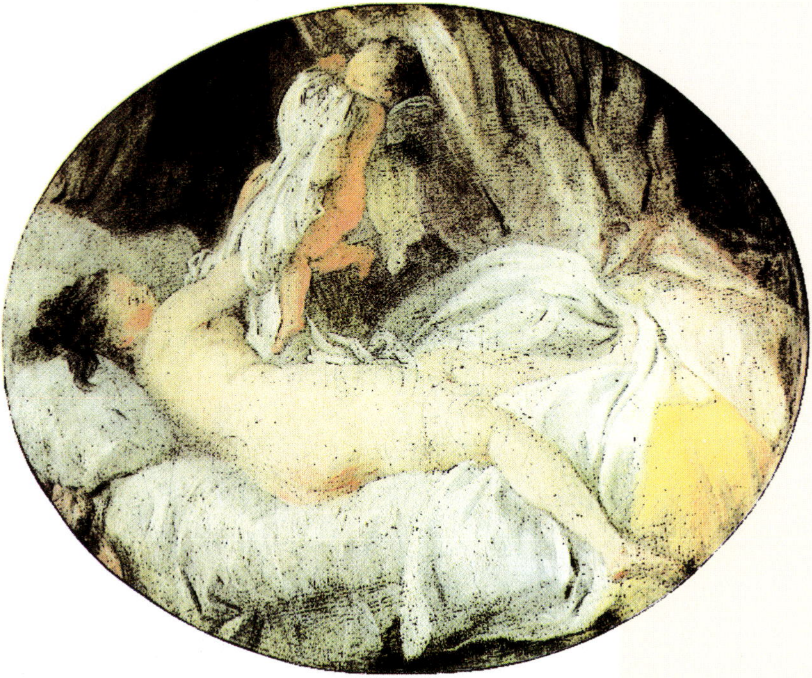

This depiction of a beautiful woman being unclothed has been described as a scene between Venus and Cupid. However, some hold that it is only a cherub, mischievously removing a young woman's nightgown, since Venus, it is pointed out, is rarely portrayed as being dressed. The loose brushwork is very bold, so that outlines disappear almost completely, creating a hazy atmosphere that stirs the spectator to become a voyeur. The figure's brightness virtually precludes modeling. Light reddish tints on cheeks and buttocks tend toward the kind of treatment of sensuality that the artist's predecessors brought to the nude. Decorative aspects prevail, yet Fragonard's treatment of anatomy is exceptionally subtle, and the figure very nearly blends with the sheets underneath. From 1767 on, Fragonard had begun to paint scenes such as this one, gallantly frivolous, yet full of charm and sensuality. This was generally in line with prevailing taste. His loose, vibrant brushwork is a prelude to Impressionism.

La Chemise enlevée

Jean-Honoré Fragonard
(Grasse, 1732–Paris, 1806)

- 1767/72
- oil on canvas
- 36.5 x 43 cm
- Musée du Louvre, Paris

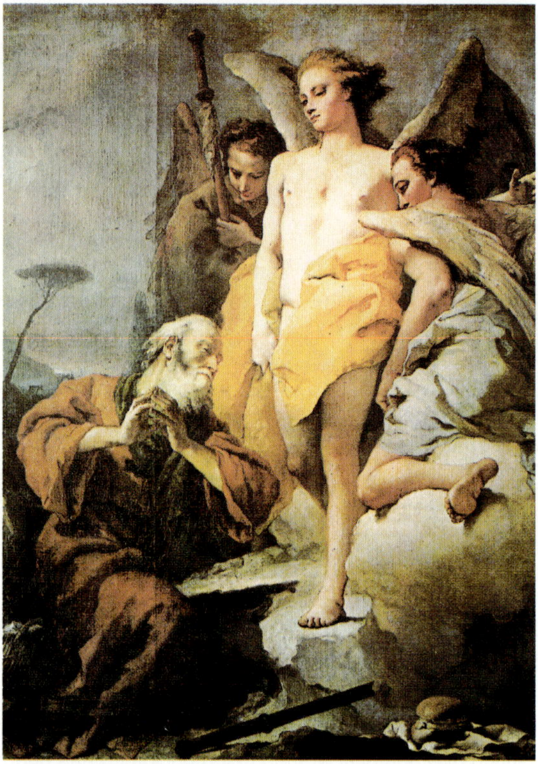

Abraham and the Three Angels

Giovanni Battista (Giambattista) Tiepolo
(Venice, 1696–Madrid, 1770)

- ca. 1768
- oil on canvas
- 197 x 151 cm
- Museo del Prado, Madrid

The theme of this work is taken from the Book of Genesis: Abraham, advanced in years and despondent because his wife, Sarah, is unable to bear a child, is resting. One day, three men appear before him, whom he invites in. One of them promises to return the following year, claiming that by then Sarah will have had a child, despite her age. The skillfully rendered androgynous angels are not shown flying through the air, but treading on thick clouds. The central figure, a youth of slight build and partly covered by a cloth, has the face of a woman, which is not an uncommon feature of Tiepolo's male nudes. Although well-proportioned, the figure represents an ideal of beauty that is far removed from that of Classical Antiquity. The treatment of the skin, with its soft modeling of volumes by means of bright light and tenuous shade, is striking indeed. The figure's slight contrapposto and the position of the hand, similar to that of David, evoke the grace of Michelangelo's nudes.

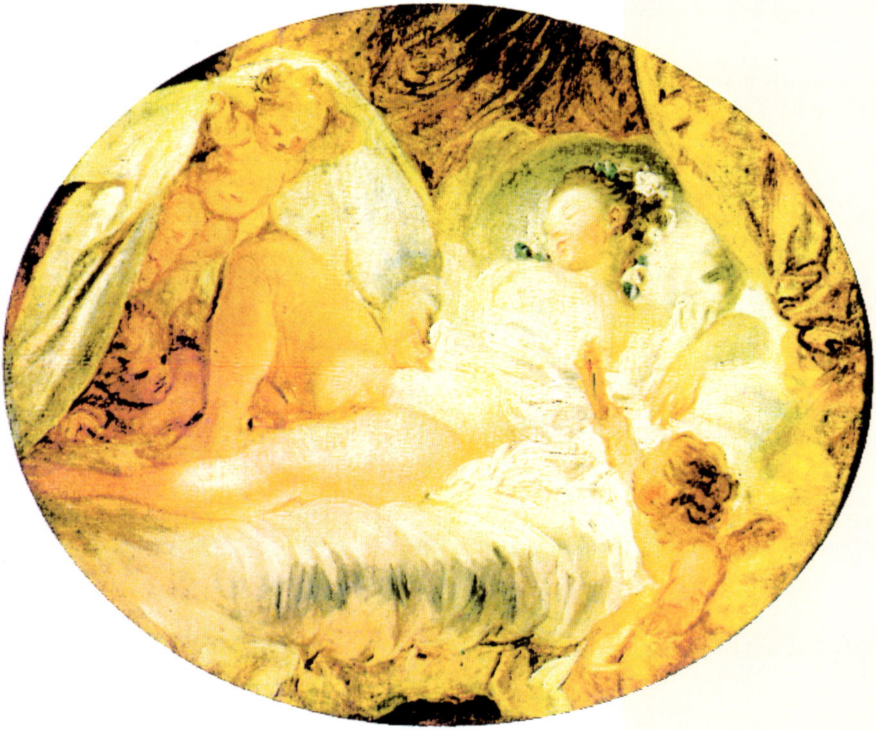

This painting shows several nude cherubs next to a beautiful, young woman who is sound asleep with her legs open, revealing her genitals. The cherubs are holding phallic objects in their hands. One of them uses his to caress the young woman between her legs. The female nude is boldly foreshortened and the luminous, vigorous brushwork almost blends the figure into the warm colors of the background. The utterly relaxed yet provocative pose of the naked woman, the various expressions of the cherubs, ranging from innocence to mischief, the dream-like atmosphere, the diffuse light and ardent red tones combine to heighten the sensuality of the scene, which would have conformed precisely to the tastes of certain sections of French society at the time.

Dream of Love

Jean-Honoré Fragonard
(Grasse, 1732–Paris, 1806)

- 1786
- oil on canvas
- Musée du Louvre, Paris

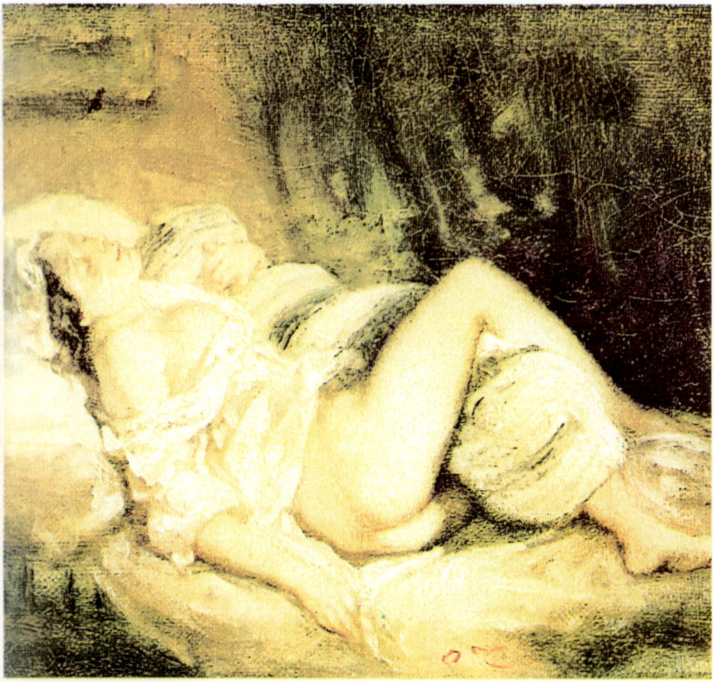

Dream of Love

Jean-Honoré Fragonard
(Grasse, 1732–Paris, 1806)

- 1768
- oil on canvas
- Musée du Louvre, Paris

This woman, unaware that she is being observed, lies sound asleep on a bed, absorbed in her dream. She is portrayed venting her passion, as if with her lover, by embracing a pillow, part of which is positioned between her legs. Fragonard makes the spectator a hidden and silent observer. Vigorous brushwork, which blurs the forms, and a euphuistic technique, which brings out each and every detail, mark the painter's style. The brightly illuminated figure stands out against a dark background. Nonetheless, in an effort to underscore the oneiric nature of the scene, the artist renders the contours fuzzy, making the nude blend harmoniously into the golden atmosphere.

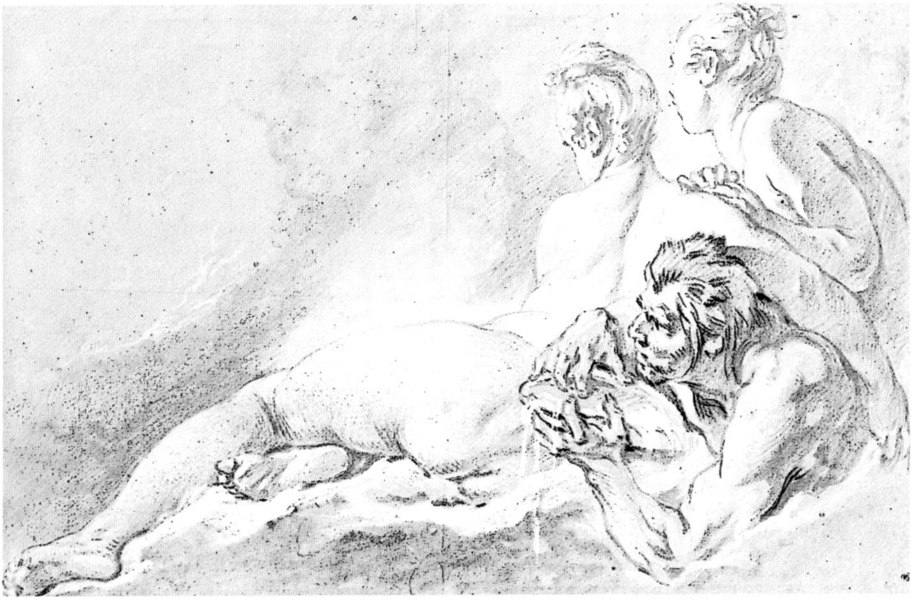

Triton and Naiads

François Boucher
(Paris, 1703–1770)

- pencil and red chalk
- 29.1 x 46.9 cm
- Musée du Louvre, Cabinet des Dessins, Paris

With over ten thousand drawings to his name, Boucher was one of the most prolific Rococo artists of his day. He had a penchant for depicting female nudes, particularly ones that exhibited a refined eroticism. The Naiads, daughters of Zeus, were water nymphs. Triton, a minor sea god, and the son of Poseidon and Amphitrite, aided the Argonauts in their quest for the Golden Fleece. His presence in this drawing is probably due to the artist's desire to juxtapose him with the nymphs, who epitomize sensual beauty. Their voluptuous bodies have been meticulously modeled with a subtle treatment of light.

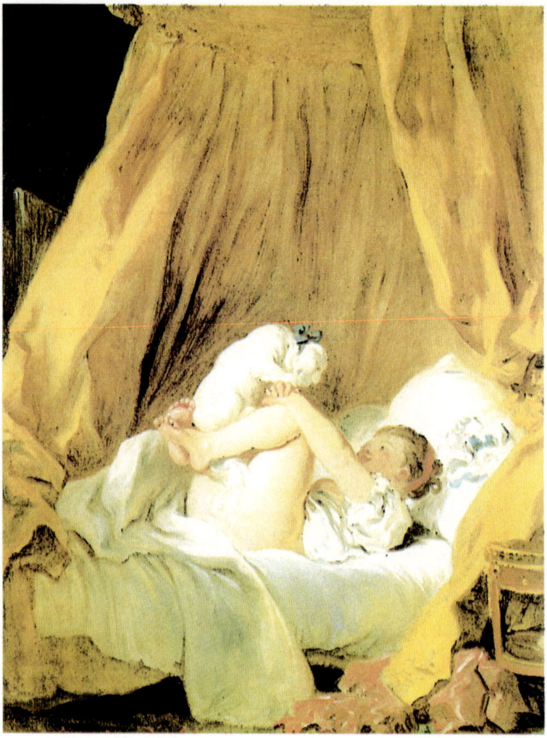

Gimblette

Jean-Honoré Fragonard
(Grasse, 1732–Paris, 1806)

- 1770
- oil on canvas
- Musée du Louvre, Paris

Erotic scenes often include elements that are intended to heighten the sensuality of the scene. In this work, an innocent girl is depicted in an utterly uninhibited pose, without undergarments and with a blouse that accentuates her nudity and provocatively reveals her firm breasts. Undistracted, she raises her legs into the air, revealing her genitals and a delicate body. Her luminous skin reveals striking highlights that suggest smooth and taut skin. Her open legs, crossed only at the feet, provide a seat for her inoffensive and loving pet dog, whose wagging tail accidentally caresses the girl's genitals in an explicit sexual game. The girl, rather than showing displeasure, appears to be enjoying it. This gives rise to further sexual innuendo with which the eroticism of the work is increased.

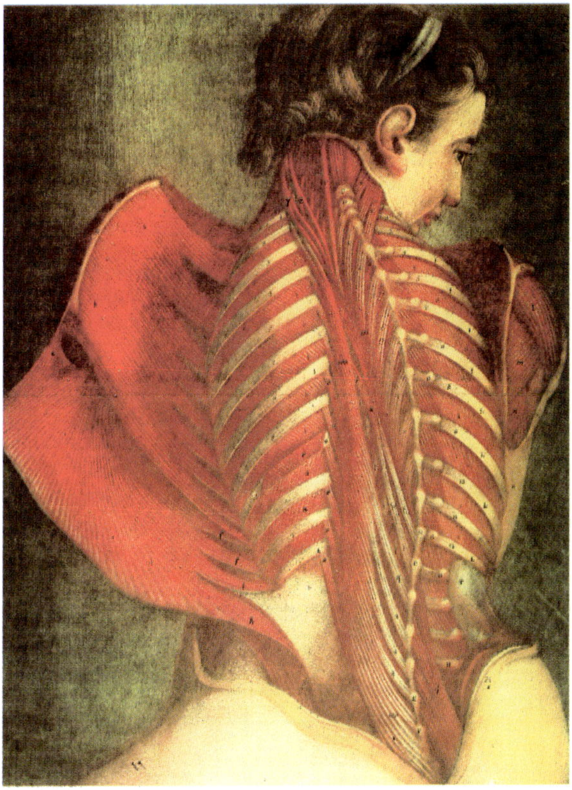

The Anatomical Angel

Jacques Gautier d'Agoty
(1710–1781)

- color etching
- 60.5 x 46 cm
- Public and University Library, Geneva

Several seemingly scatological subjects occupy an outstanding place within the genre of the nude. One such example is this anatomical study. Prior to the advent of photography color, etchings had been nearly perfected. It had become fashionable among doctors as well as the general public to use etchings for educational and cultural purposes. The figures depicted in these works were known as "anatomical angels" because of the way the skin was peeled back, much like wings, to reveal the internal anatomy. Such figures were not depicted dead, but very much alive, sometimes even in provocative poses. The perfectly executed anatomy in this work, which is indebted to Neoclassical aesthetics, includes numbers in it, which refer to captions that originally accompanied the pictures.

Boreas Abducting Oreithyia

François-André Vincent
(Paris, 1746–1816)

- 1770
- oil on canvas
- 260 x 195 cm
- Musée du Louvre, Paris

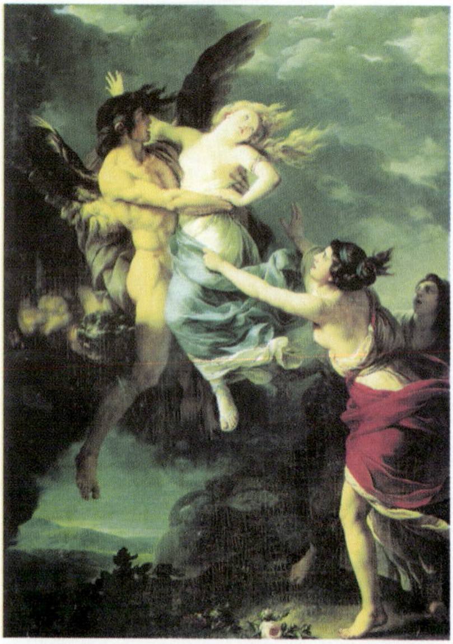

Oreithyia, daughter of a legendary king of Athens named Erechtheus, was dancing near a river when Boreas abducted her and bore her to Thrace. God of the north wind, and of the lineage of the Titans, Boreas is often depicted winged, as here, his physique that of an athlete of sturdy and harmonious proportions.

Narcissus

Nicolas-Bernard Lépicié
(Paris, 1735–1784)

- 1771
- oil on canvas
- 113 x 143 cm
- Musée Antoine Lécuyer, Saint-Quentin

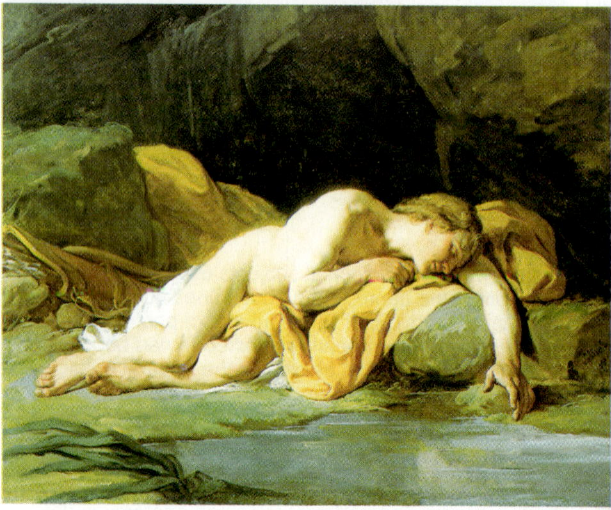

The handsome youth Narcissus was doomed to fall in love with himself alone. According to Tiresias' oracle delivered to Narcissus' mother, Tyriope, he would live just as long as he did not look at himself. However, seeing his reflection in a pool, he fell madly in love with it and drowned attempting to kiss it. The well-molded, ample forms of this figure, its muscles well-defined and perfectly proportioned, never quite reach a fully mannerist treatment.

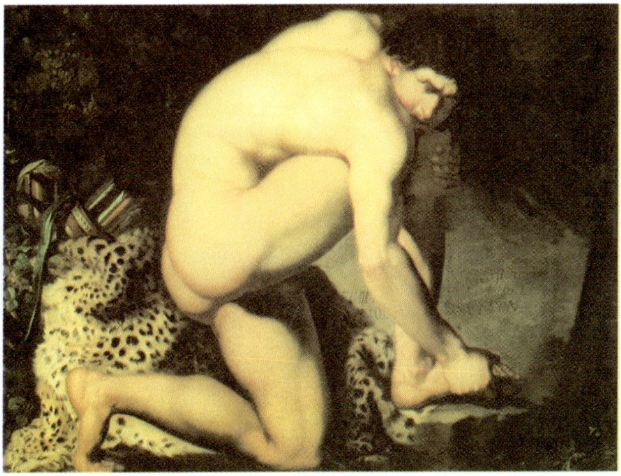

Philoctetes Wounded

Nikolai Abraham Abilgaard
(Copenhagen, 1743 –Frederiksdal, 1809)

- 1774–75
- oil on canvas
- 123 x 173.5 cm
- Statens Museum for Kunst, Copenhagen

The model's posture here is designed to give expression to the pain a foot wound can produce. Containing a wealth of warm, golden colors, the body almost glows out against its dark background, and the contrasts over it highlight its main anatomical details.

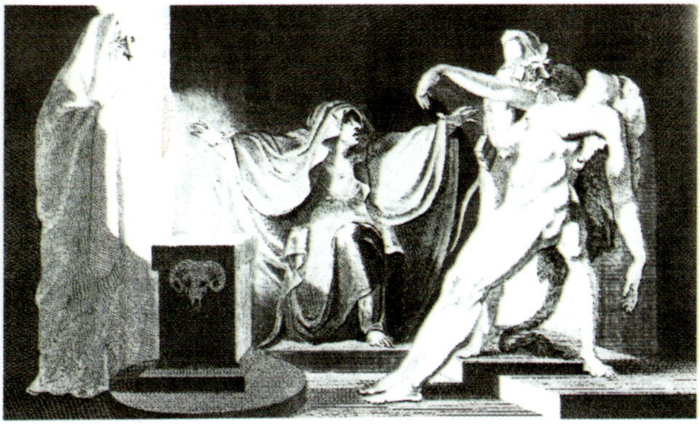

Witch of Endor

Henry Fuseli (Johann Heinrich Fuessli or **Füssli)**
(Zurich, 1741–London, 1825)

- 1777
- preliminary study for an engraving
- Columbia University, New York

While this sketch is certainly schematic in effect, its expressive secondary figures, the pose of the nude figure, and the modeling nevertheless convey the drama of the situation most effectively.

Learning Attempting to Detain Time

François-Guillaume Ménageot
(London, 1744–Paris, 1816)

- 1777
- oil on canvas
- 225 x 184 cm
- École Nationale Supérieure des Beaux-Arts, Paris

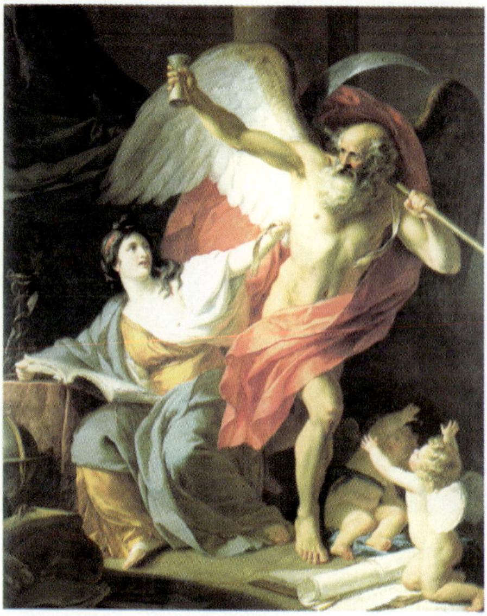

Time's semi-nude figure here has been executed with a good deal of attention to naturalistic detail, although it is more an ideal, youthful body than that of an old man. Harsh contrasts, amongst other things, go towards lending it a somewhat severe air.

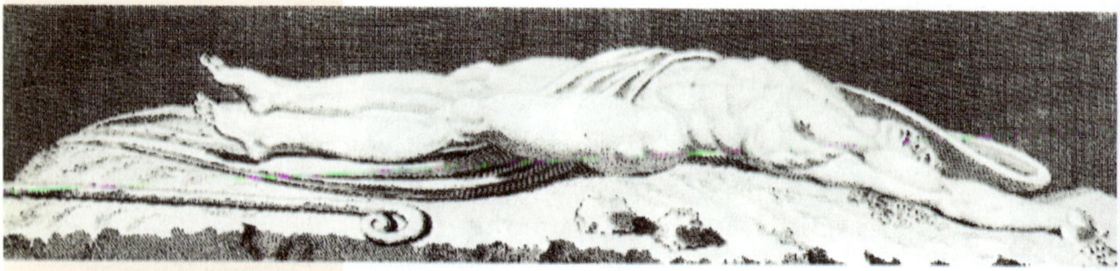

Death of Abel

Henry Fuseli (Johann Heinrich Füssli)
(Zurich, 1741–London, 1825)

- ca. 1779
- preliminary study for an engraving
- Columbia University, New York

The artist's excellent treatment of shadows here is largely responsible for the way this figure's shape and muscularity, despite its prostration, manage to assert themselves. The handling of the figure shows the application of Classical ideas to a biblical theme.

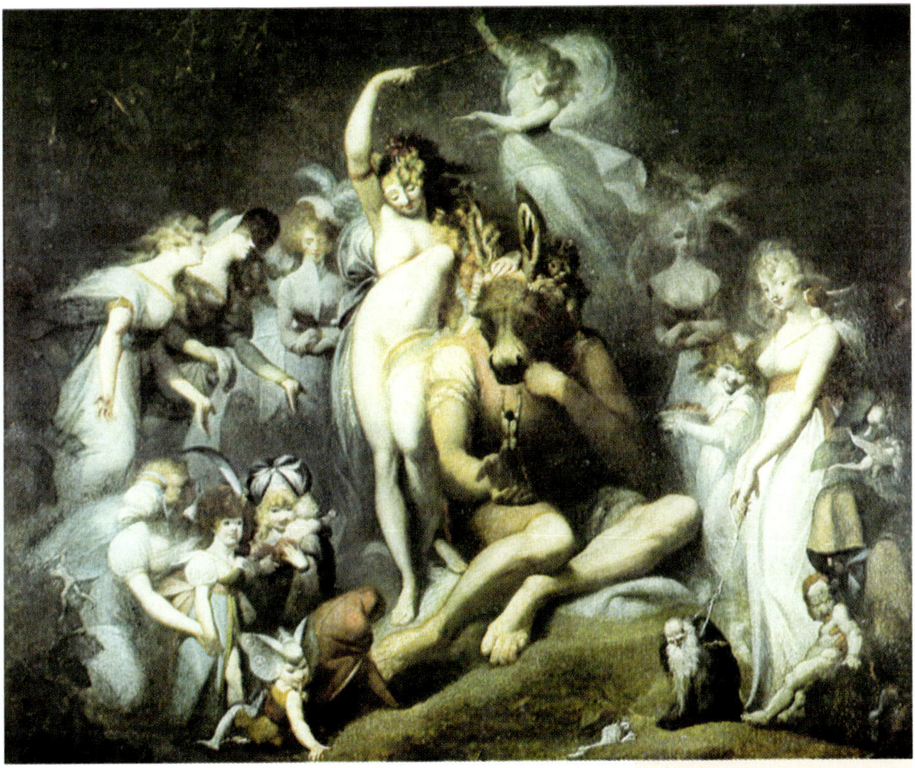

A great admirer of Shakespeare's works, Fuseli here presents a scene based on A Midsummer Night's Dream, portraying Titania as Venus in triumph surrounded by characters from the play. The painter investigates the world of dreams and the subconscious, creating an air of fantasy and mystery against a dark and diaphanous background. The scene has subsequently fed the imaginations of many illustrators, writers and filmmakers, often giving rise to exceptional results. The nude Titania, sensual and graceful, embodies both coquetry and shyness. Despite the complex distribution of light, and thanks to her forceful figure, young Titania is the focus of attention. The treatment of colour makes her body almost gleam with a rosy white hue. Her figure is sculptural, with firm and well-defined, slender forms, exemplifying a romantic ideal of beauty.

Titania and Bottom

Henry Fuseli (Johann Heinrich Fuessli or **Füssli)**
(Zurich, 1741–London, 1825)

- ca. 1780/90
- oil on canvas
- 216 x 274 cm
- Tate Gallery, London

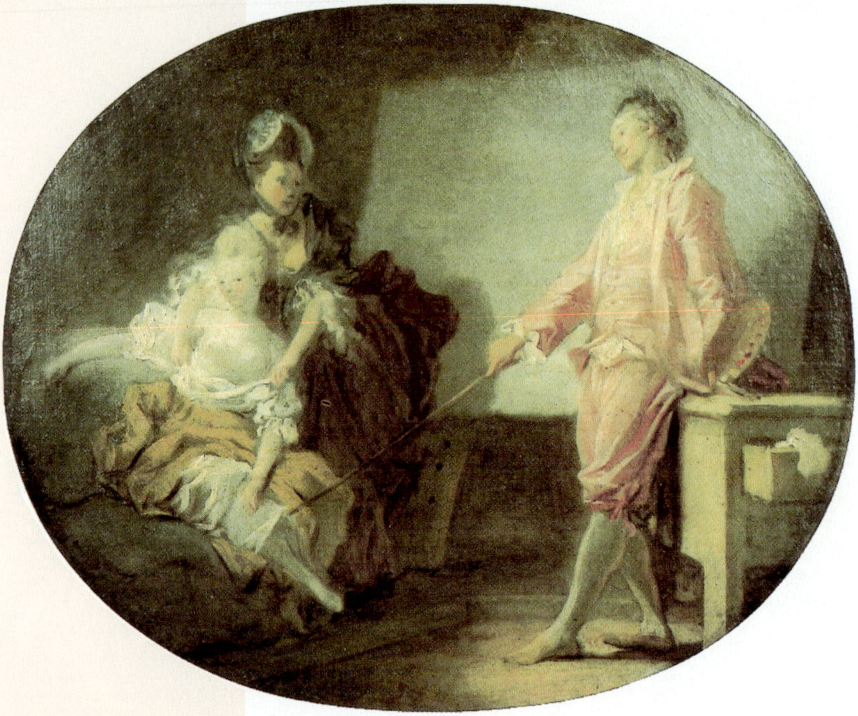

The Model's Debut

Jean-Honoré Fragonard
(Grasse,1732–Paris, 1806)

- oil on canvas
- 50 x 63 cm
- Institut de France, Musée Jacquemart-André, Paris

This painting captures the moment at which a model reveals her naked body to an artist for the first time. Her expression of demure modesty make her more erotic than most nudes. Scenes such as this were very much in vogue in Fragonard's day and were used to decorate the homes of the upper middle classes, their sole purpose being decorative. The young woman's skin is pallid and her cheeks pink with rouge. Her bare breasts, firm and round, form a diagonal that meets the extended line of the artist's arm, in the middle of the painting.

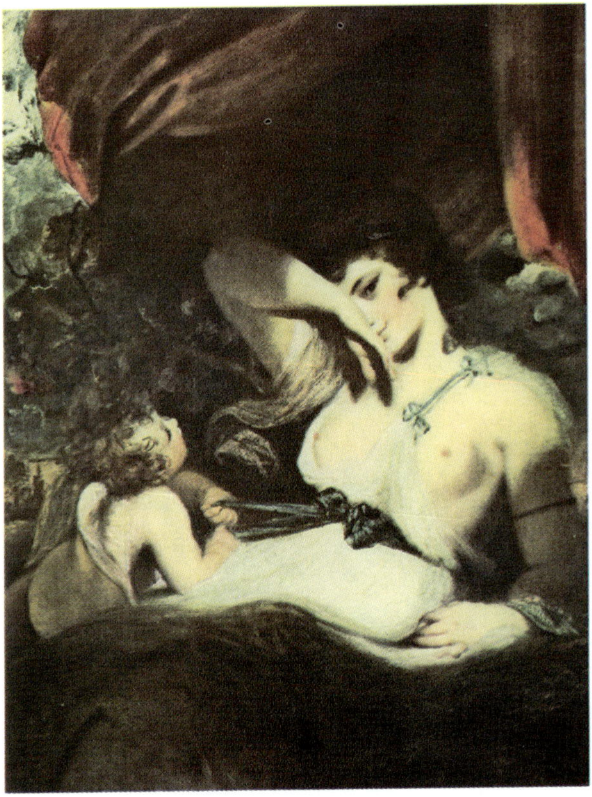

Venus and Cupid

Joshua Reynolds
(Plympton, Devon, 1723 –London, 1792)

- 1784–88
- oil on canvas
- 127.5 x 101 cm
- Hermitage, St. Petersburg

This painting was acquired from the artist by Prince G. A. Potemkin in 1788, via Lord Carysfort, for £105. In 1791, it entered the Museum as part of the prince's collection.

This work is one of the few mythological themes painted by Joshua Reynolds. The scene and Venus' demure pose, with her hand partly covering her face, are typically English, far removed from Italian art of the time. The scene does not illustrate any particular mythological episode but, rather, an imaginary, intimate moment. The erotic figure of Venus is presented as a mother, in the company of her son, Cupid, whose wings are merely ornamental. Cupid represents innocence, whereas Venus exhibits a tender sensuality. The identity of the model used for the goddess' face has been a matter of great conjecture. It was probably Emma Lyon, a celebrated beauty of the time, who began as a servant, posed as a model for the artist and then became Lady Hamilton through her marriage with William Hamilton, the ambassador to Naples.

Pygmalion and Galatea

Louis-Jean-François Lagrenée

(Paris, 1734–1805)

- 1781
- oil on canvas
- 58.42 x 48.26 cm
- The Detroit Institute of Arts, Detroit

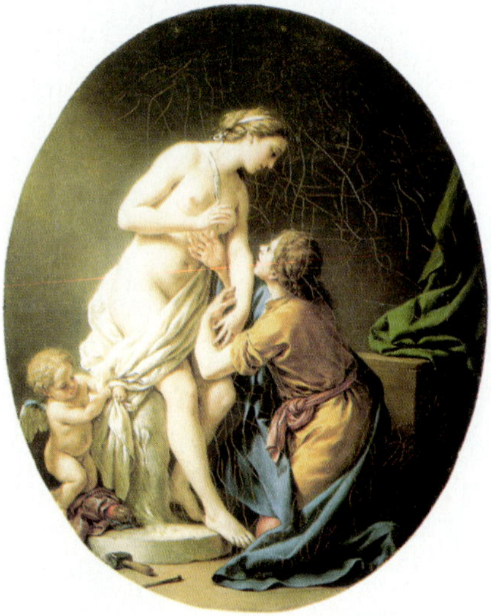

Pygmalion sculpted a statue of Venus that was so realistic and beautiful that he fell in love with it. He then begged the goddess to help him find the statue's flesh-and-blood counterpart. Venus answered his wish by bringing the sculpture to life and naming the woman Galatea, and the artist then took her gratefully in wedlock. Galatea is portrayed here as being thoroughly beautiful, her forms both Classical in conception as in their proportions.

Venus Tending Aeneas' Wounds

Jean-Charles-Nicaise Perrin

(Paris, 1754–1831)

- 1786
- oil on canvas
- 197 x 163 cm
- École Nationale Supérieure des Beaux-Arts, Paris

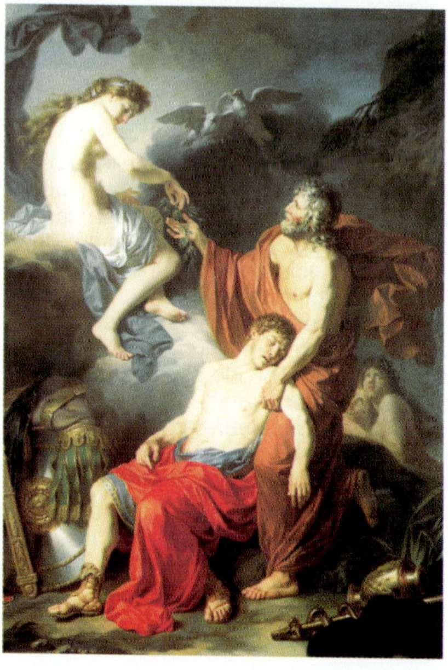

After Aeneas has been wounded in combat against Turnus, king of Ardea and of the Rutulians, Venus comes to the aid of her son, bringing a medicinal herb from Mount Ida. The figures here are attractive, not least for their highly-individuated characters.

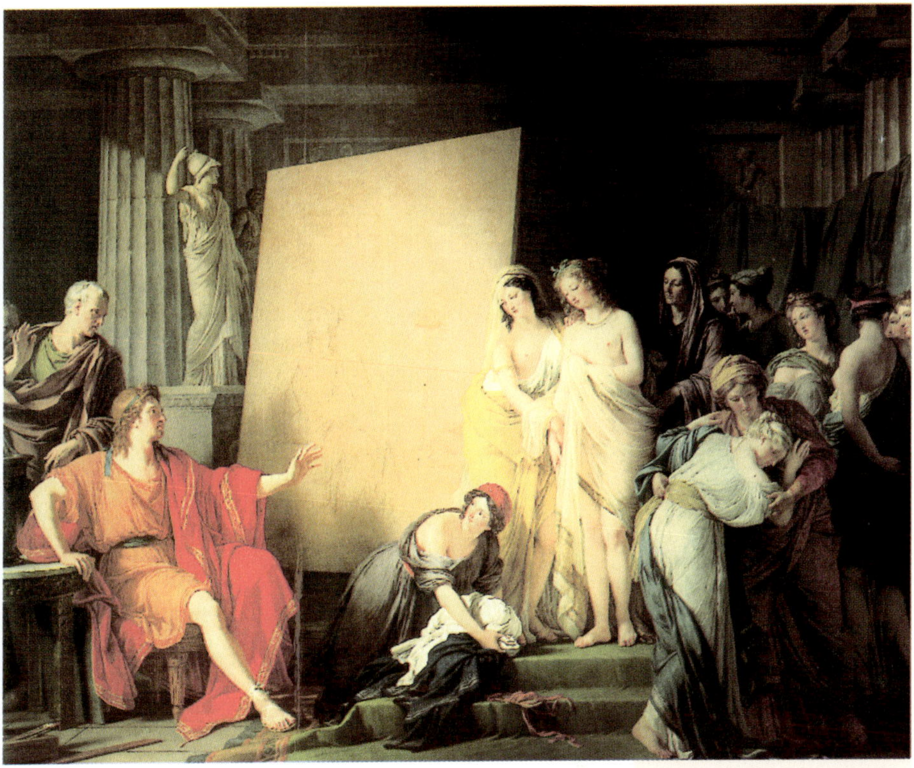

Zeuxis Painting the Daughters of Croton

François-André Vincent
(Paris, 1746–1816)

- 1789
- oil on canvas
- 323 x 415 cm
- Musée du Louvre, Paris

The subject of this painting derives from an account of Pliny the Elder: Zeuxis was invited to Croton to paint a picture of Helen of Troy, in the Temple of Juno. The artist ordered that a search be carried out to find the most beautiful maiden of Croton, who was to sit for him and provide inspiration. Since the ideal girl was not found, he chose the five most beautiful in order to combine the most perfect parts of each one to create a figure of ideal beauty. The female figures in this work are carefully rendered, showing the artist's interest in human anatomy. Although the painting is marked by humanist refinement, a characteristic of the Renaissance, the figures betray Gothic influences in their clearly delineated outlines and schematic anatomy. Moreover, the maidens' poses and facial features are nearly identical, attesting to a somewhat outdated treatment of the figures.

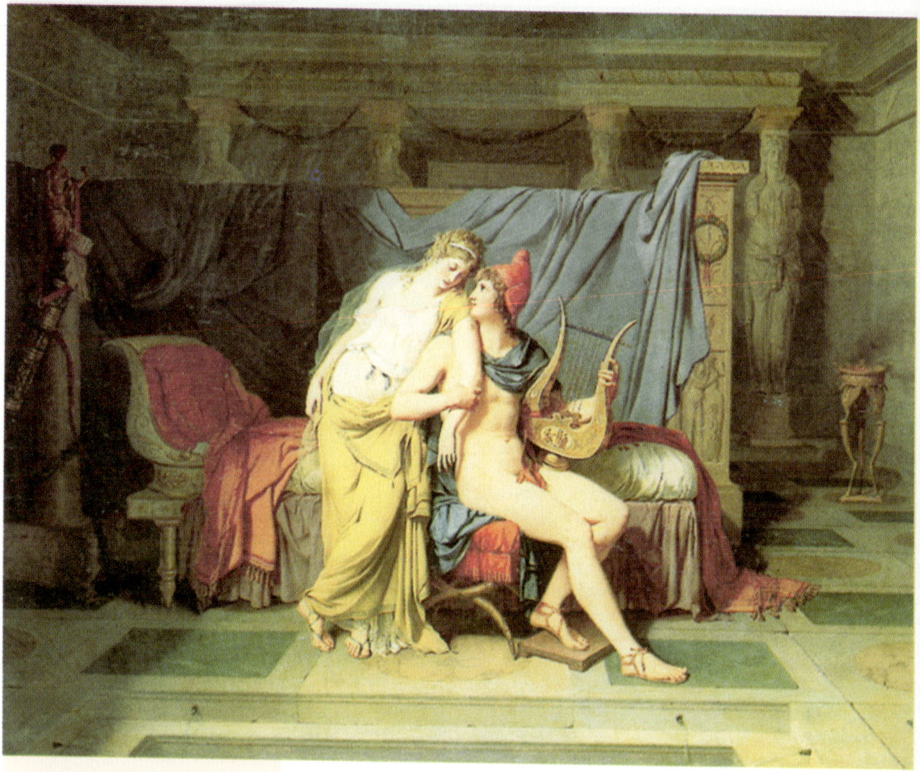

Paris and Helen

Jacques-Louis David
(Paris, 1748–Brussels, 1825)

- 1789
- oil on canvas
- 144 x 174 cm
- Musée des Arts Décoratifs, Paris

In return for his judging her the most beautiful goddess and awarding her the apple of discord, Venus promised Paris Helen. Upon his abducting her, Helen's consort Menelaus declared war on the city of Troy, which was then ruled by Paris' father, Priam. David was the Neoclassical painter par excellence. The proportions of his nudes exhibit definite stylizations and their proportions correspond to an ideal rather than being realistic. Paris is depicted here as being of a young and attractive physique, albeit without the attributes of a hero or a god. He is wearing a Phrygian hat.

A fine example of the ‹ind of study carried ɔut at the end of the 18th century and which ;ombined two basic ɜlements: practice in :echnique and drawing 'rom nature.

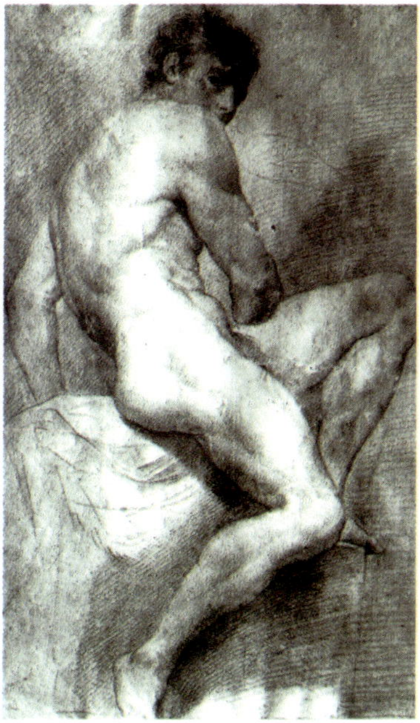

Male Nude

Pere Pau Montaña
(Barcelona, 1773–Madrid, 1803)

- ca. 1790
- pencil
- Museu Nacional d'Art de Catalunya, Barcelona

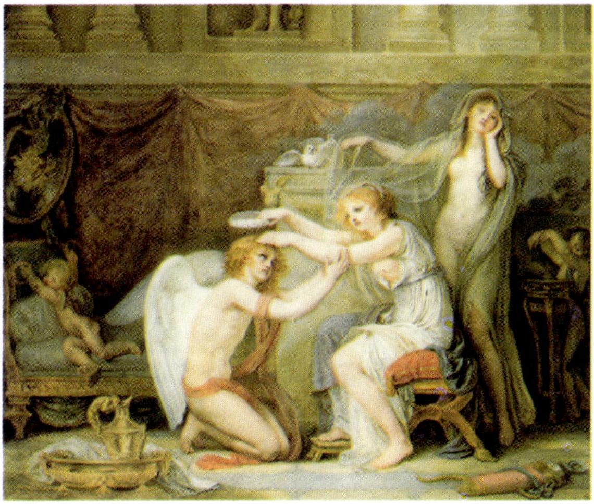

Psyche Crowns Cupid

Jean-Baptiste Greuze
(Tournus, 1725–Paris, 1805)

- 1790
- oil on canvas
- 147 x 180 cm
- Musée des Beaux-Arts, Lille

ᵓsyche's beauty was such that Cupid fell in love with her, and nade her his wife. In this canvas, a nude Cupid is portrayed ıs he surrenders to her. His delicate, sensual physique is in :ccord with and, at the same time, underlines his divine ;tatus. The outlines of his body are relatively weakly-defined :reating the effect of a certain aura surrounding his figure.

The Bather, or **Diana at her Bath**

Antoine-Jean Gros
(Paris, 1771–1835)

- 1791
- oil on canvas
- 99 x 81 cm
- Musée des Beaux-Arts et d'Archéologie, Besançon

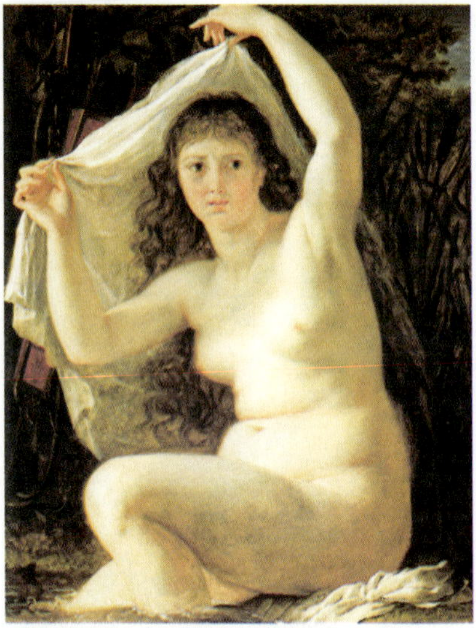

The nude figure of Diana in this painting has been executed with great subtlety and feeling. Her body is shapely and its outlines, while definite, are not absolutely clear-cut. One is put in mind of Rubens' dynamic brushstrokes as well as of Renoir's later pictorial conception. Diana's body seems to emit more light than it can have received the treatment of every area is remarkable, both for its definition and for the way it focuses attention on the whole.

Los and Orc

William Blake
(London, 1757–1827)

- ca. 1792
- pen and watercolor
- 21.7 x 29.5 cm
- Tate Gallery, London

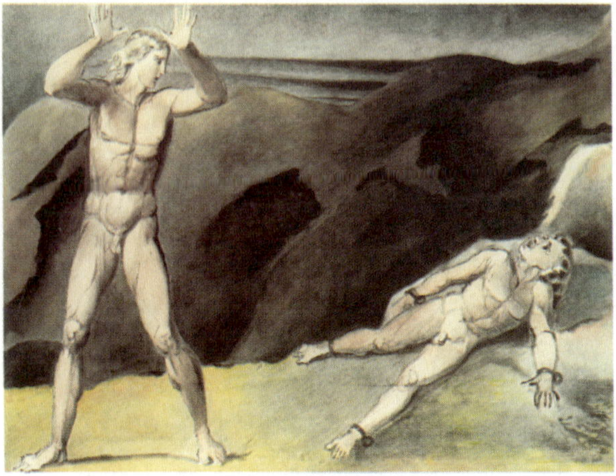

Blake, here, as so often, depicts mythological figures in a composition of great simplicity. The bodies combine idealism and a high degree of expressivity.

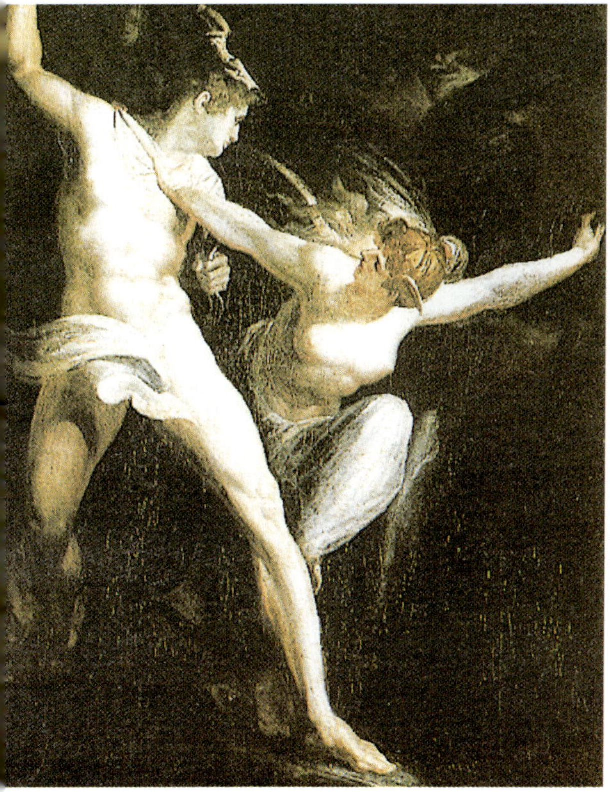

ʼuseli executed this painting during the time that he taught
ɩt the Royal Academy of Arts in London. Many of his works
ɩre based on themes taken from mythology, Italian literature
ɩnd German or British theater. In this Romantic painting,
ɩeautiful, subtly-modeled figures with light, blended shadows
ɩnd well-defined volumes emerge from a dark background in
tudied poses that are both dynamic and sensual. The fig-
ɩres are highly naturalistic, demonstrating the artist's pro-
ɔund knowledge of human anatomy and mastery of
raftsmanship. Although the figures are executed with great
are, their expressiveness takes on more importance than
ɩlastic or aesthetic aspects, achieved by placing the bodies
ı the poses and gestures that best serve this objective.

Satan and Death Separated by Destiny

Henry Fuseli (Johann Heinrich Fuessli or **Füssli)**
(Zurich, 1741–London, 1825)

- 1792–1802
- oil on canvas
- 91.3 x 71.1 cm
- Neue Pinakothek, Munich

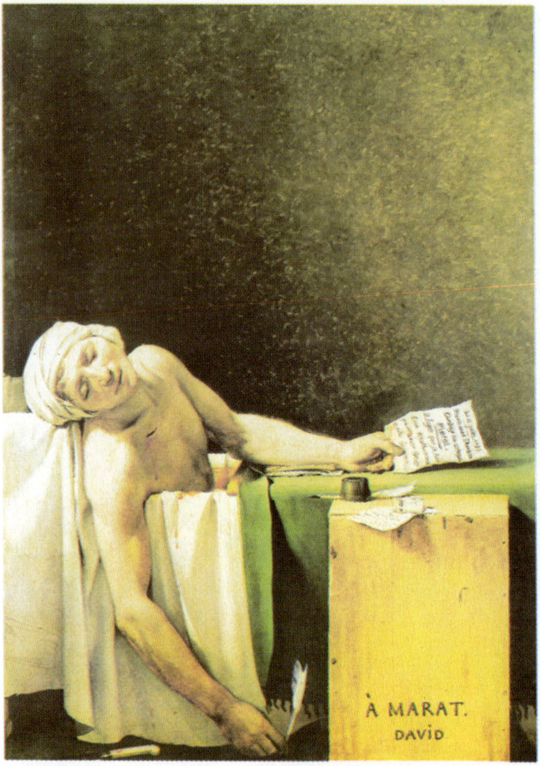

The Death of Marat

Jacques-Louis David
(Paris, 1748–Brussels, 1825)

- 1793
- oil on canvas
- 165 x 128 cm
- Musées Royaux des Beaux-Arts, Brussels

Ties of friendship connected Marat and Jacques-Louis David. Great patriot that Marat was, he played an important role in the founding of the French Republic, and was forced by a skin disease to spend long hours in therapeutic baths, where he even worked and received visitors. In 1793, Marie Charlotte Corday stabbed him while visiting him at his bath. The politician's arm is seen having fallen heavily while still gripping the quill with which he was writing. In the other hand, he holds the paper the assassin used to procure entry. The modeling of this nude figure is stringent and highly dramatic. The light-source is to the left and behind the figure. The emptiness of the entire upper half of the painting creates a dense, silent atmosphere appropriate to the solemnity of the theme. It is a tragi-heroic work of great force and depth of feeling, its simplicity measured and its asceticism evocative.

;uperhumanly owerful, the god 'hor emerges 'om the dark ackground of nis canvas to do attle with the erpent. \natomical letails such as ne sinewy, knot- ed muscles of is body empha- ized by the lat- ral light-source elp to endow ne god with his eroic aspect.

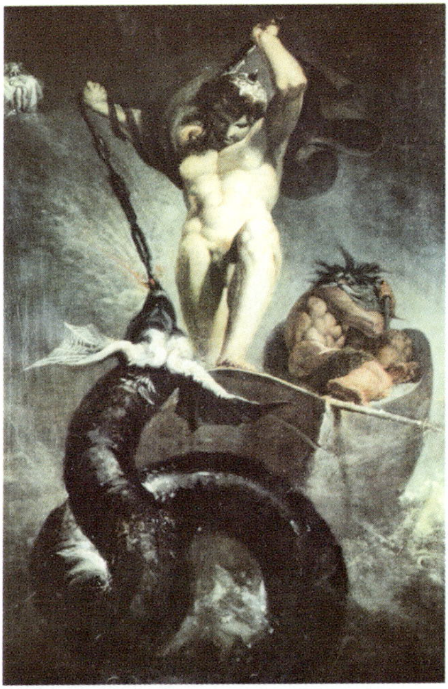

Thor, in the Boat of Hymir, Battering the Midgard Serpent

Henry Fuseli (Johann Heinrich Fuessli or **Füssli)**
(Zurich, 1741–London, 1825)

- 1790
- oil on canvas
- 131 x 92 cm
- Kunsthaus, Zurich

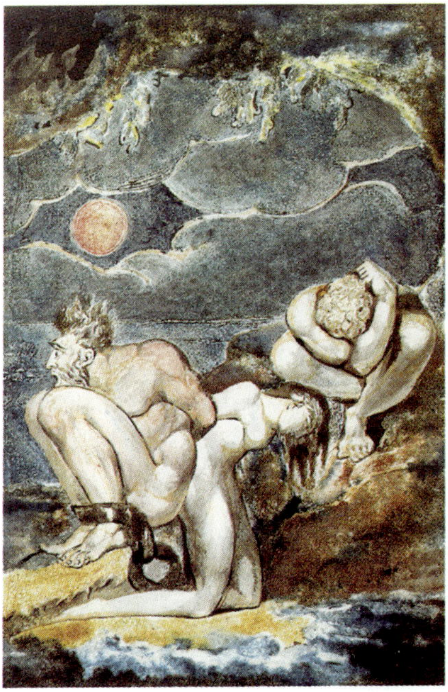

Frontispiece to the Visions of the Daughters of Albion

William Blake
(London, 1757–1827)

- 1793–95
- color print finished in pen and watercolor
- 17 x 12 cm
- Tate Gallery, London

Ve see here nree nude fig- res in a terrify- ng landscape. 'heir bodies, at east two of them hained, are epicted in highly nnatural posi- ons. Despite neir simplicity ney are wonder- ılly expressive.

Pity

William Blake
(London, 1757–1827)

- ca. 1795
- engraving
- 42.5 x 43.9 cm
- Tate Gallery, London

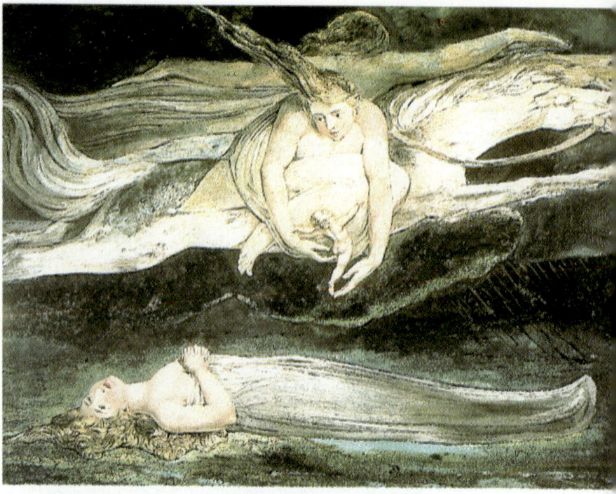

William Blake, one of the most remarkable artists of the Romantic period, possessed visionary powers from a young age and used a highly personal symbolism to express his mystical philosophy. This work, which depicts a recumbent, sleeping figure of a woman and her oneiric vision above,is a paragon of candor, prefiguring Fauvism, particularly in the treatment of the hair and the figures' clothing.

Pietà

Pere Pau Montaña
(Barcelona, 1773–Madrid, 1803)

- end of 18th century
- oil on canvas
- Iglesia de la Merced, Barcelona

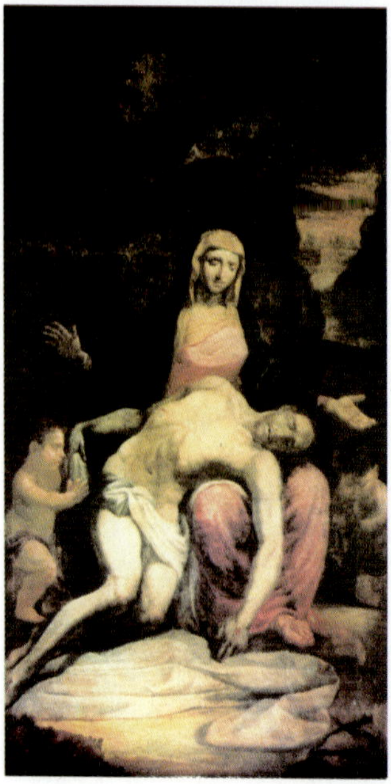

This artist, whose work bears similarities to that of Anton Raffael Mengs, paints in a Neoclassical academic style that breaks with the Baroque spirit of religious representations current at that time. Christ's body is executed in a meticulously studied pose and skilfully modeled through a fine handling of light.

'or this painting, ıe artist has aken a perfectly ırdinary male ıodel, whose ody is neither vell-propor-oned nor espe-ially beautiful. 'he work is a tudy in the ıodeling of the uman form, ınd its excellent 'eatment of light as enabled the ırtist to describe ıany of the ıan's muscles ı great detail.

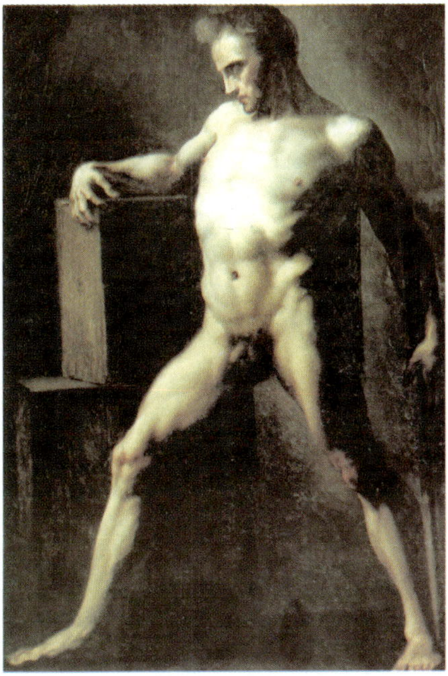

Academic Study of the Nude

Théodore Géricault
(Rouen, 1791–Paris, 1824)

- ca. 1816
- oil on canvas
- 81 x 65 cm
- Musée des Beaux-Arts, Rouen

ıgainst a dense, redominantly ark back-round, 'éricault has epicted this owerfully-built ude man, 'uminated by ttenuated light ıat brings out ıe surface etails of his ody with great larity. An xcellent display f this painter's ıasterful rasp of human natomy.

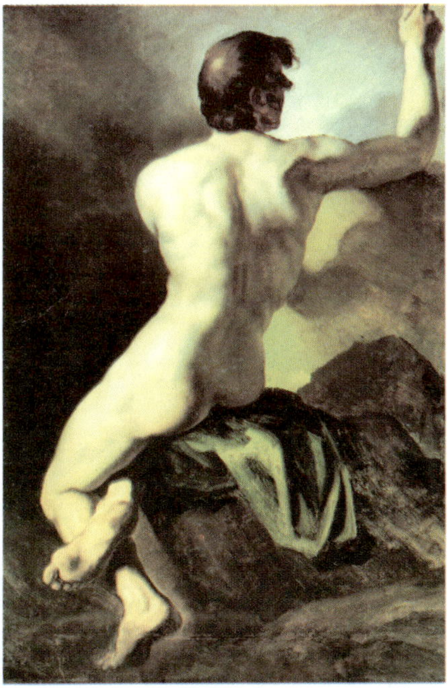

Academic Study of the Nude

Théodore Géricault
(Rouen, 1791–Paris, 1824)

- ca. 1816
- oil on canvas
- 89.5 x 64 cm
- Musées Royaux des Beaux-Arts, Brussels

Leda and the Swan

Théodore Géricault
(Rouen, 1791–Paris, 1824)

- pencil, wash and watercolor on paper
- 21.7 x 28.4 cm
- Musée du Louvre, Département des Arts Graphiques, Paris

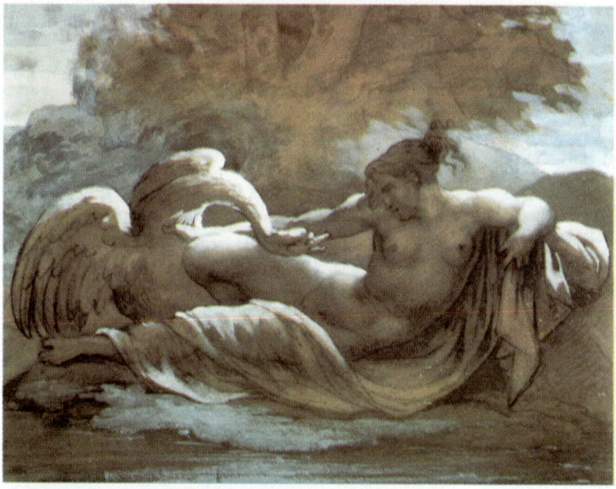

The theme of Jupiter turning himself into a swan in order to seduce Leda is represented with great expressiveness. The protagonist's receptive attitude, evident through her pose and the gesture she is making with her arm, combines with the mystery created by a theatrical backlighting that leaves the figures in a warm and intimate darkness, which gives rise to a highly erotic setting.

Four Youths Holding a Running Horse

Théodore Géricault
(Rouen, 1791–Paris, 1824)

- 1817
- oil on canvas
- 48.5 x 60.5 cm
- Musée des Beaux-Arts, Rouen

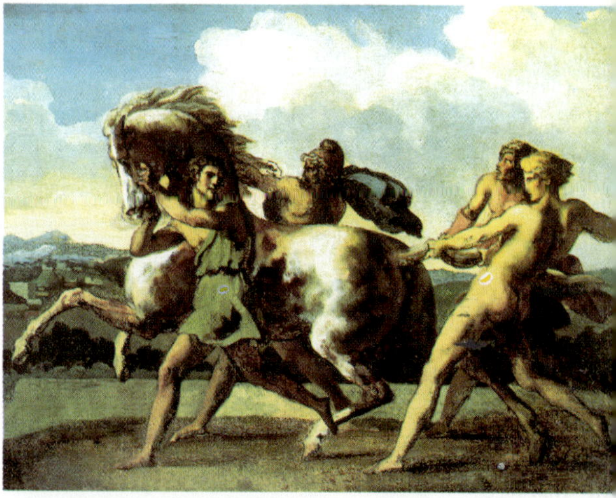

The work is one in a series on horses done by the artist. The scene has great dynamic potential and is, at the same time, a fine study in color and light. The nude slave is beautifully and expressively modeled.

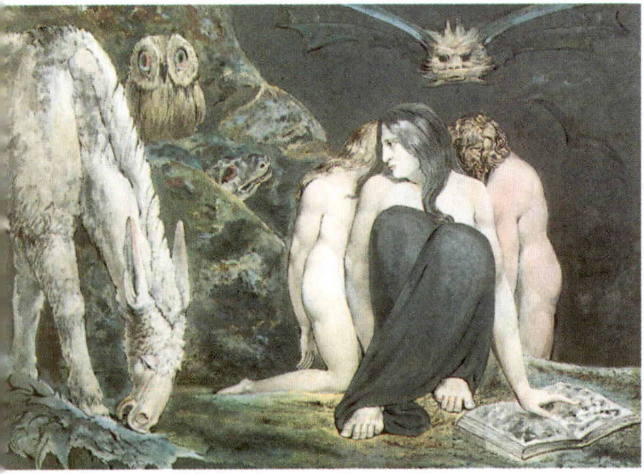

Hecate

William Blake
(London, 1757–1827)

- ca. 1795
- color print finished in pen and watercolor
- 43.9 x 58.1 cm
- Tate Gallery, London

'he artist here combines pale and somber colors that ırow their reflection on the skin-colour of the figures, ıdding to their air of mystery.

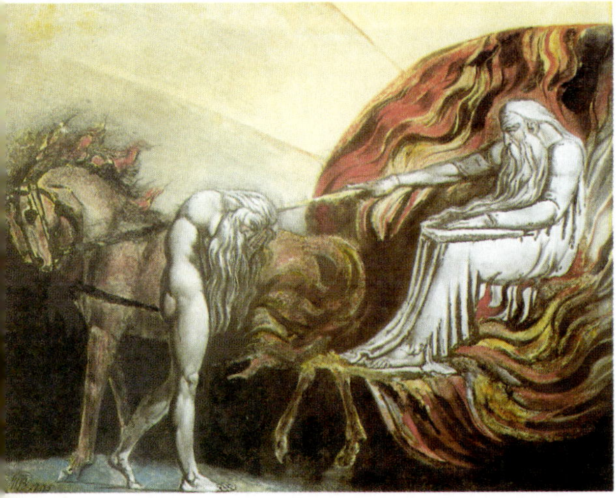

God Judging Adam

William Blake
(London, 1757–1827)

- 1795
- color print finished in pen and watercolor
- 43.2 x 53.5 cm
- Tate Gallery, London

'he Creator of the Universe is riding a chariot of fire pulled ›y a fiery-maned steed. Before him, his hair long and white ınd his body muscular, Adam humbles himself.

The House of Death

William Blake
(London, 1757–1827)

- 1795
- color print finished in pen and watercolor
- 48.5 x 61 cm
- Tate Gallery, London

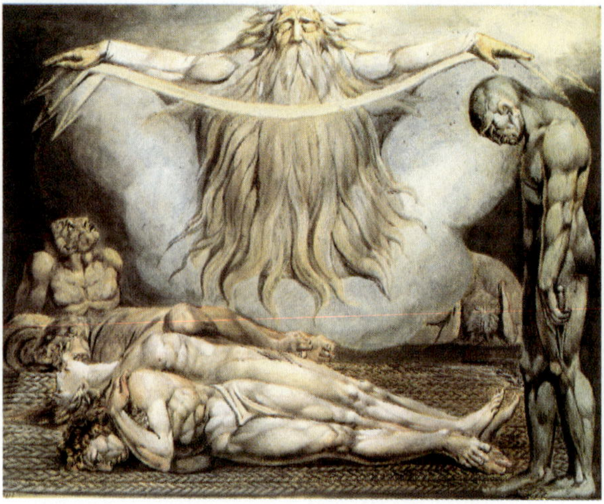

The muscular figures in this spectacular setting result in a remarkable composition, which is both somber and awe-inspiring.

Allegory of the Peace of Basel

Pere Pau Montaña
(Barcelona, 1773–Madrid, 1803)

- 1799
- oil on canvas
- Real Academia de San Fernando, Madrid

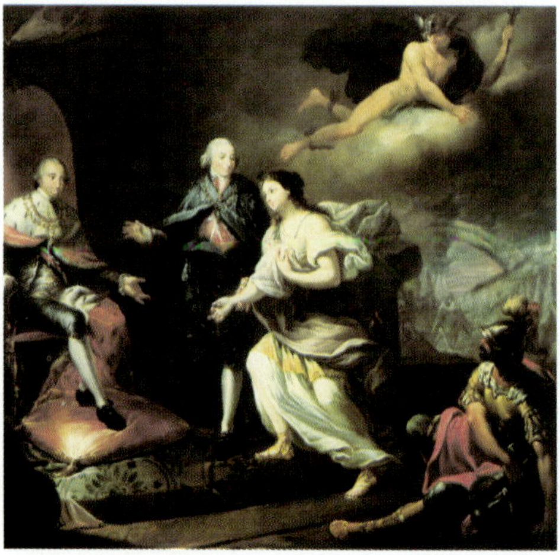

The painting has for its subject the peace treaty signed in 1795 whereby Spain ceded to France the eastern half of the island of Santo Domingo (now Haiti) and France returned the Spanish territory it had occupied. Charles IV is receiving a female figure, representing Peace, while a soldier is relegated to the bottom-most right-hand corner of the painting. Mercury is depicted above.

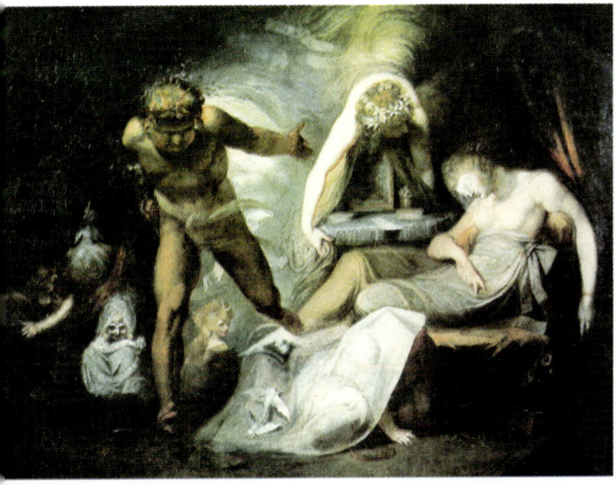

The Cave of Spleen

Henry Fuseli (Johann Heinrich Fuessli or **Füssli)**
(Zurich, 1741–London, 1825)

- 1799
- oil on canvas
- 103 x 123 cm
- The Vancouver Art Gallery

'he painter's studied treatment of light and color here rings out the delicacy of the reclining woman's body, /hile the male figure, tanned and muscular, with fore-hortening that creates the illusion of vigorous motion, ets up tension through contrast.

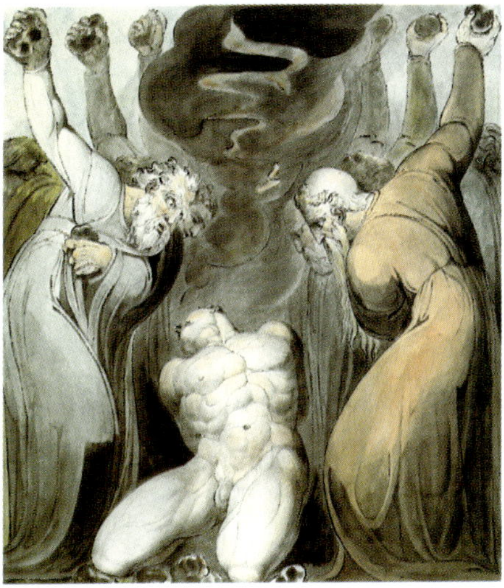

The Stoning of Achan

William Blake
(London, 1757–1827)

- ca. 1800
- pen and watercolor
- 38.1 x 34.1 cm
- Tate Gallery, London

'he work illustrates a passage from Leviticus, where ne punishment Yahweh ordains for blasphemy is toning to death outside the city walls. One of Blake's haracteristically powerfully-modeled bodies is the ocus of this particular depiction.

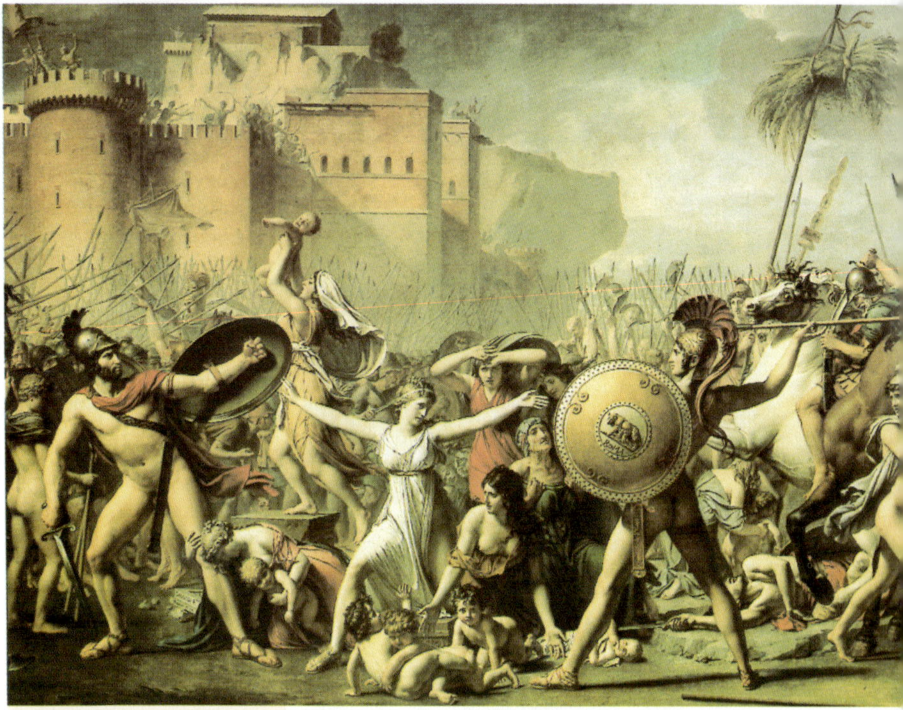

The Intervention of the Sabine Women

Jacques-Louis David
(Paris, 1748–Brussels, 1825)

- 1794–99
- oil on canvas
- 385 x 522 cm
- Musée du Louvre, Paris

After founding Rome, Romulus sent messengers to the Sabine territory, requesting that their daughters marry his subjects. When his proposal was rejected, Romulus had Roman youths raid the Sabine territory and carry off all the women they could find, while the Roman menfolk were at a festival. This led to war. Tassius, king of Ceres, entered the city, laying siege to the Romans, only to be stopped by the Sabine women themselves, who were now the wives and mothers of the Romans, and peace was made. The painting captures the heat of the battle between the two factions, with the Sabine women separating the warriors and showing them their children. This work is highly dramatic, with gesticulating figures in exaggerated poses. The extremely sensual nude figures enhance the stylistically perfect scene, which recalls a bas-relief from Classical Antiquity.

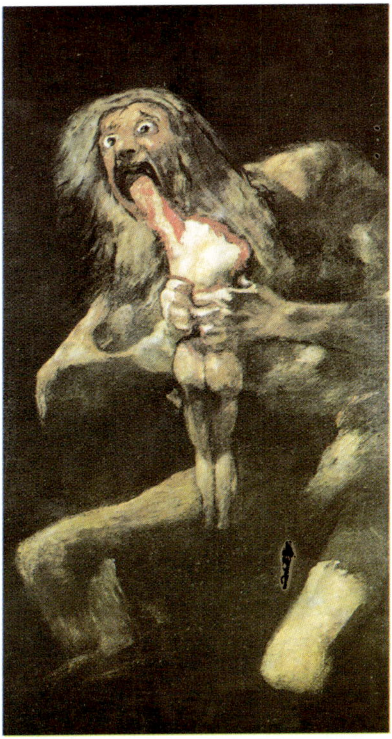

Saturn Devouring One of His Sons

Francisco de Goya y Lucientes

(Fuendetodos, Aragon, 1746–Bordeaux, 1828)

- fresco transferred to canvas
- 146 x 83 cm
- Museo del Prado, Madrid

When he moved to France, in 1823, Goya bequeathed his home, located on the outskirts of Madrid and in which he had painted this and other murals, to his grandson. In 1873 the house was purchased by the Belgian Baron Emile d'Erlanger, who had the paintings transferred to canvas, whereupon he donated them to the Museum.

Goya's so-called Black Paintings were executed on the walls of his house known as the Quinta del Sordo (House of the Deaf Man), which he had bought in 1819. By then, the painter had grown old and embittered, and was becoming deaf, as the name of the house would suggest. The paintings of this period were executed with a palette dominated by grays, blacks and browns, reflecting the artist's profound pessimism and the critical view he took of life toward the end of his own. This is one of the most horrific of the Black Paintings. It depicts Saturn, the ancient Roman deity identified with the Greek god Cronos, devouring one of his sons. The nudes were executed with an almost ferocious intensity and freedom of handling, prefiguring Expressionism, one of the principal artistic movements in Europe following World War II. Saturn's deformed body is resolved with strong contrasts, on which points of light are all that give form to his body.

Portrait of a Black Woman

Marie-Guillaume Benoist
(Paris, 1768–1826)

- ca. 1800
- oil on canvas
- 81 x 65 cm
- Musée du Louvre, Paris

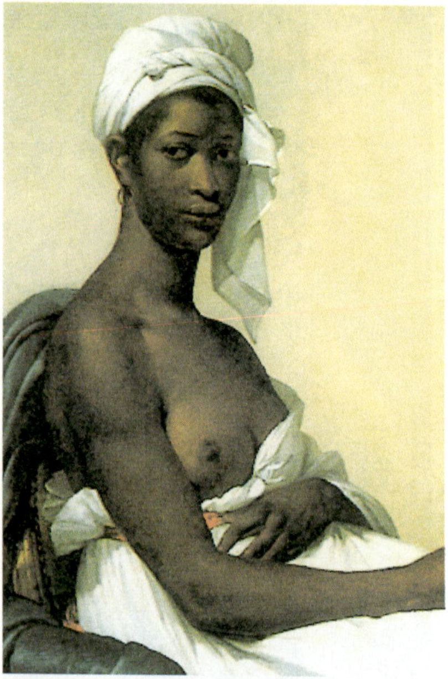

The intensity conveyed by this painting, which combines Neoclassicism and Romanticism, is a result of the meticulousness of its execution, the outstanding treatment of light and shade and the exoticism of the figure.

Fortune and Sleeping Boy

Pierre Bouillon
(Thiviers, 1776–Paris, 1831)

- 1801
- oil on canvas
- 139 x 171 cm
- Musée des Beaux-Arts, Rouen

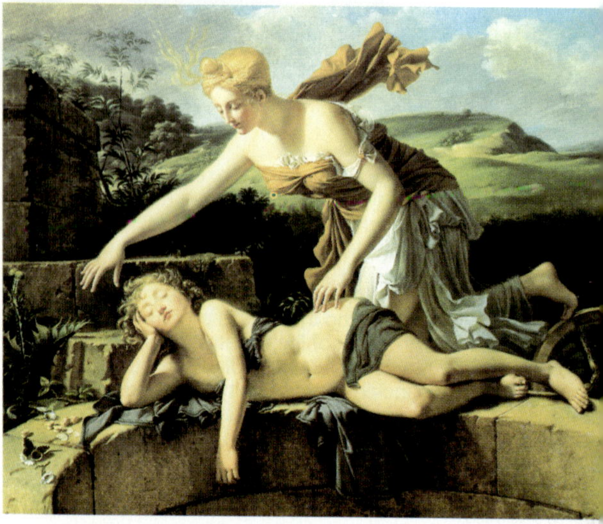

Although the reclining figure is a boy, the painter has depicted him with deliberate ambiguity: skin color, bodily shape, even clothing, could be those of a girl. The overall atmosphere of the work is finely sensual and poetic.

3athed in light, :he goddess strews flowers along her path as she walks, :he warm aura of her golden brilliance enhancing her attractiveness. Particularly notable is her mystical expression and the way her arms, crossed over her chest, emphasize her firm breasts and occupy the visual center of the canvas—a composition of deliberately heightened eroticism.

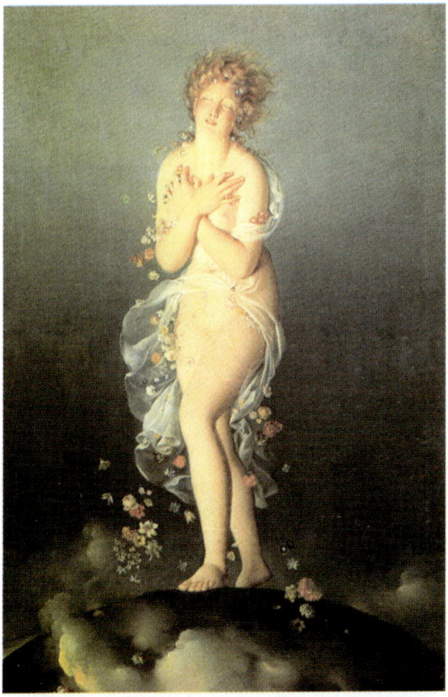

Flora

François Gérard
(Rome, 1770–Paris, 1837)

* ca. 1802
* oil on canvas
* 168 x 105 cm
* Musée des Beaux-Arts, Grenoble

'his rendering of Eve as a long-haired woman of modernity rather than of any biblical age is enhanced by the large, dark tree at her back. The devil is depicted as a vast serpent with a winged head and human features.

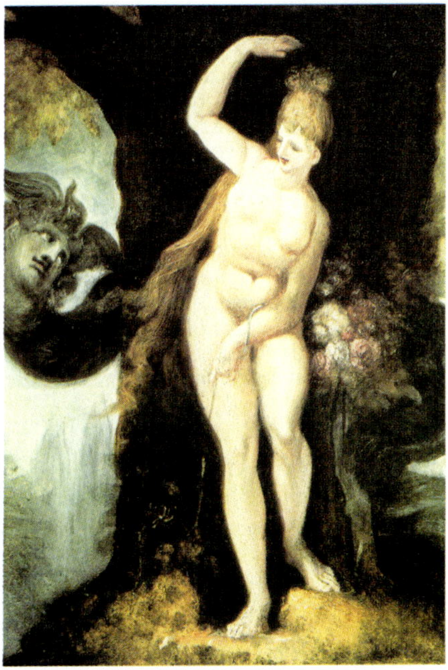

Satan's First Address to Eve

Henry Fuseli (Johann Heinrich Fuessli or **Füssli)**
(Zurich, 1741–London, 1825)

- 1802
- oil on canvas
- 30.2 x 23.8 cm
- Art Gallery, Auckland

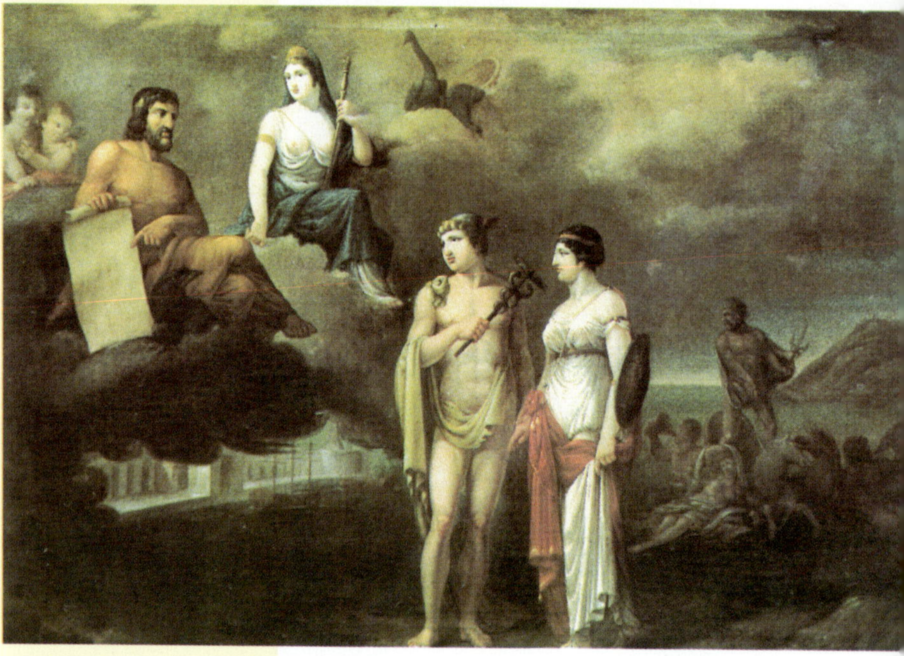

Allegorie des Handels

Bonaventura Planella i Couxello
(Barcelona 1772–1844)

- 1803
- oil on canvas
- Escuela de Artes y Oficios, Barcelona

The canvas won a prize in 1803. It is an outstanding example of the French-influenced Neoclassical style that prevailed at the time and which was adopted by many of the most important artists of the period for allegories and mythological themes. The work is remarkable for its iconography, depicting Trade personified as a woman right of center. She is shown being introduced to Zeus, seated on a cloud, by Mercury, the god of commerce. In the background, on the right, Neptune calms the waters, represented here by Nereids and sea gods. The nudes are classically drawn. Mercury's pose and attire have been copied from a Roman sculpture. The milky-white bust of the goddess seated beside Zeus provides an element of contrast amidst the mass of dark color.

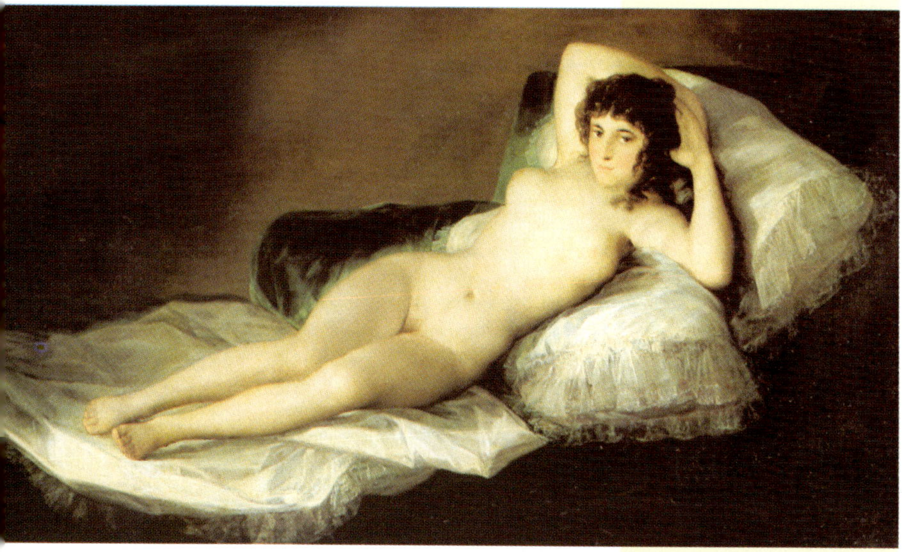

Naked Maya

Francisco de Goya y Lucientes
(Fuendetodos, Aragon, 1746–Bordeaux, 1828)

- 1803–6
- oil on canvas
- 98 x 191 cm
- Museo del Prado, Madrid

his work was painted by Goya during his second creative eriod, between 1793 and 1808. As legend has it, both laja paintings by the artist, the Clothed Maja and the laked Maja, were fitted with a secret mechanism in the uchess of Alba's La Moncloa Palace in Madrid, which llowed one of the paintings to be lowered in front of the ther. The naked maja is shown reclining on a divan, with er hands behind her head in a provocative and defiant ose, intended to accentuate her beauty. The painter does ot portray a goddess but a real woman who is fully aware f her seductive powers. Her smooth skin is illuminated by cool, impersonal light. The painting is devoid of the ccessories present in so many other paintings of nudes, uch as silk and flowers. The maja's gaze is challenging, er smile provocative and proud. With this work, Goya not nly initiated a new approach in depicting nudes; he also edefined the relationship between man and woman.

Standing Nude

Pierre-Paul Prud'hon

(Cluny, 1758–Paris, 1823)

- black pencil and crayon on light blue paper
- 58 x 33.9 cm
- Musée du Louvre, Cabinet des Dessins, Paris

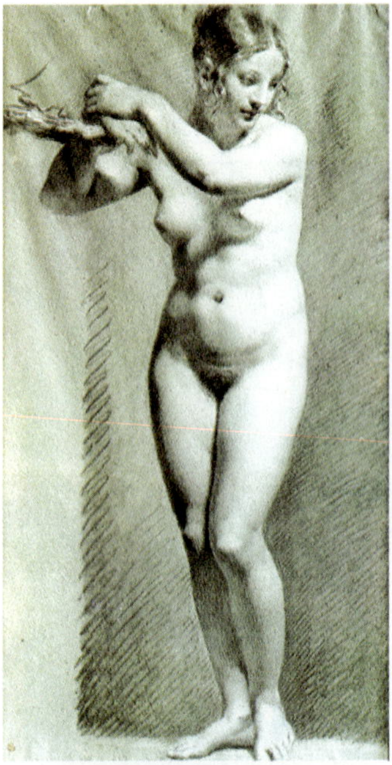

Prud'hon spent several years in Italy, where he developed a style based on sfumato techniques following the example of such painters as Leonardo and Correggio. The execution of this nude is unequivocally Classical in style and technique and shows that Prud'hon was a master of the human figure. The young woman's body is relatively slender, attractive and well-modeled, and bears a closer resemblance to sculpture or bas-relief than drawing. The treatment of light gives rise to a balanced composition recalling the chiaroscuro of Delacroix or Géricault.

Napoleon Visting the Victims of the Plague at Jaffa

Antoine-Jean Gros

(Paris, 1771–1835)

- 1804
- oil on canvas
- 532 x 720 cm
- Musée du Louvre, Paris

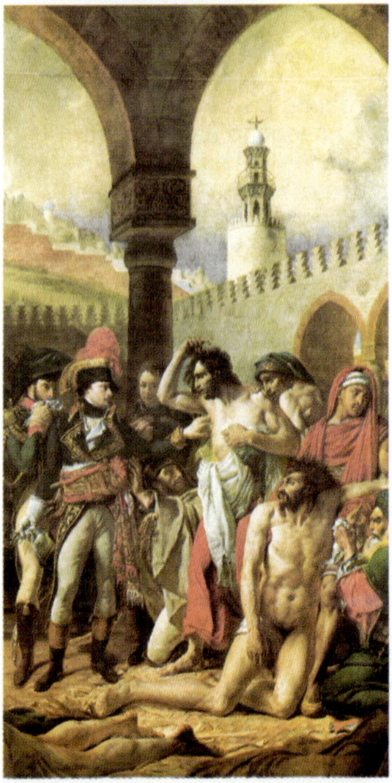

Despite its Neoclassical character, this work approaches Romanticism of which Eugène Delacroi was later to become an exponent. Far from the th atricality of Neoclassical art, it depicts Napoleon a his troops on a military campaign in Syria. Suffering from the Plague the nudes exhibit clear signs of pain, both in thei poses as well as in their facial expressions. The nude shown on his knees in the foreground is a com pelling image of an ill, exhausted man. The brigh flesh tones are brought o by the modeling of the shadows, which lend defi tion to the figures' muscle

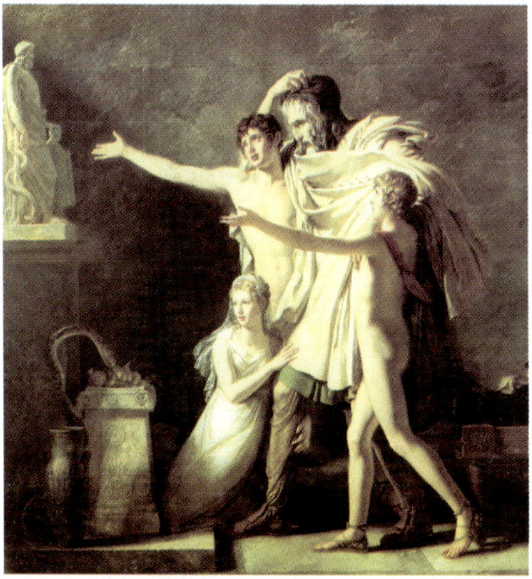

Offering to Aesculapius, or **Filial Devotion**

Pierre-Narcisse Guérin
(Paris, 1774–Rome, 1833)

- 1803
- oil on canvas
- 291.5 x 259.5 cm
- Musée des Beaux-Arts, Rouen

n elderly man, accompanied by his children, is rendering n offering to a statue of Aesculapius, son of Apollo and the od of medicine. The brightly illuminated figures of the two oys stand out against the dark background. Their soft skin nd delicate modeling, together with their rather slender orms, go to create fine, if somewhat effeminate, bodies.

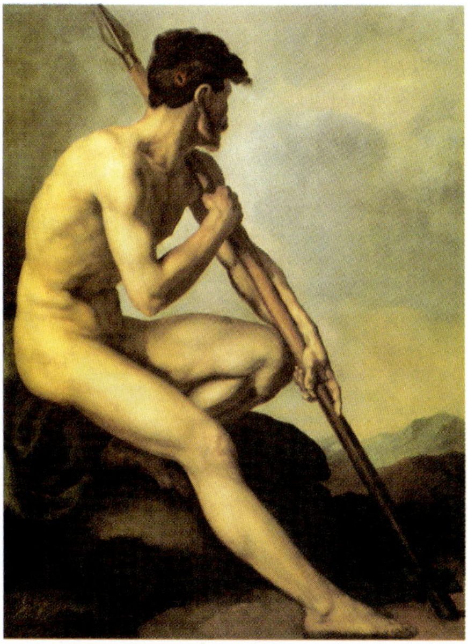

Naked Warrior with a Lance

Théodore Géricault
(Rouen, 1791–Paris, 1824)

- 1808–12
- oil on canvas
- 92 x 73 cm
- National Gallery of Art, Chester Dale Collection, Washington D.C.

'he draftsmanship of this ude figure is npeccable. 'he handling of ght and shade s seen in the orporeal suraces is also emarkable, nd brings out nusculature nd underlying one structure.

Oedipus and the Sphinx

Jean-Auguste-Dominique Ingres
(Montauban, 1780–Paris, 1867)

- 1808
- oil on canvas
- 189 x 144 cm
- Musée du Louvre, Paris

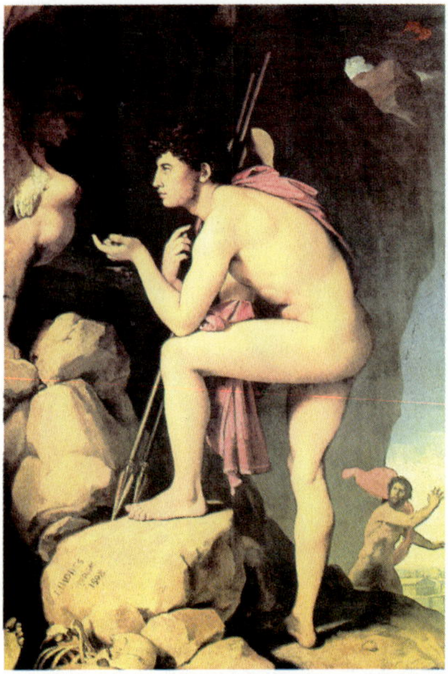

The nude figure of Oedipus recalls a Classical sculpture the ideal of beauty employed in its cre ation giving rise to a perfectly-propor- tioned body. The careful treatment of anatomy here is academic in the strictest sense, and is executed in a Classical manne

Exequies of Julius Caesar

Blai Amatller i Rotllan
(Barcelona, 1768–Madrid, 1841)

- 1008 22
- copper engraving
- 70.5 x 54 cm
- Biblioteca Nacional, Madrid

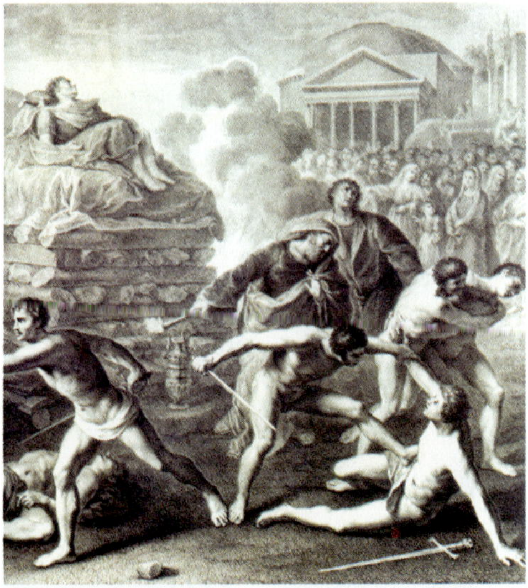

This work is a copy. The series of male nudes in different poses show a great deal of dynamism and the technique of their execution is exceptionally polished.

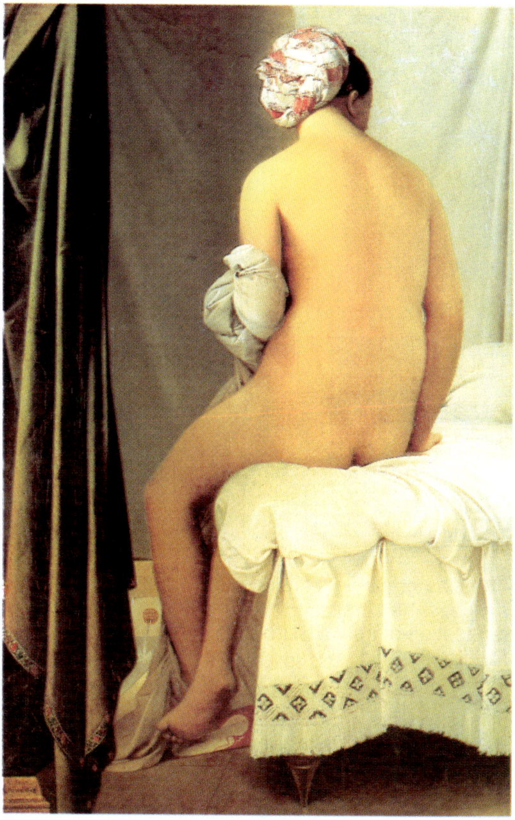

Valpinçon Bather

Jean-Auguste-Dominique Ingres
(Montauban, 1780–Paris, 1867)

- 1808
- oil on canvas
- 146 x 97.5 cm
- Musée du Louvre, Paris

This elegant painting is a fine example of Ingres' most undiluted style, as can be observed in the clean, fluid lines, the uncompromising subordination of color to drawing and the delicate feminine forms that lend the figure harmony and apparent dexterity. The sinuous curves of the nude's body are extremely sensual. The subtle neckline breaks with formalism in favor of aesthetics. Virtually no muscles can be discerned on the woman's body, which serves only to heighten her sensuality. Despite its pronounced academic character, Ingres' painterly handling of the nude exerted a decisive influence many artists, such as Edgar Degas.

Gothic Bathroom

Jean-Baptiste Mallet
(Grasse, 1759–Paris 1835)

- 1810
- oil on canvas
- Musée de Dieppe

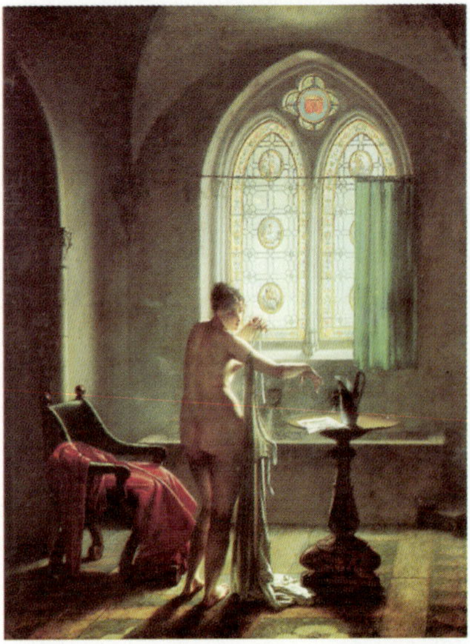

The play of the light filtering through the window here exposes the details of this nude figure. It is not so much a question of chiaroscuro inherited from the Baroque. Rather, the buttocks and thighs are saturated in red tones that modulate at points to something approaching complete darkness.

Three Women, an Amorino and a Prostrate Man

Henry Fuseli (Johann Heinrich Fuessli or **Füssli)**
(Zurich, 1741–London, 1825)

- 1811
- pencil on paper
- 20 x 27.1 cm
- Art Gallery, Auckland

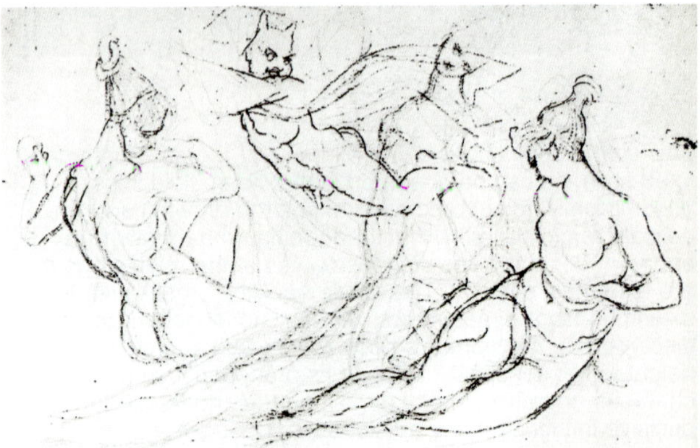

In this drawing, the artist's style as well as his highly individual vision are apparent. The women are muscular, with powerfully-developed bodies, while the man is very faintly drawn, lying, as if vanquished. The "cherub," here, complete with masculine attributes and the devil's face and horns, would appear to represent love.

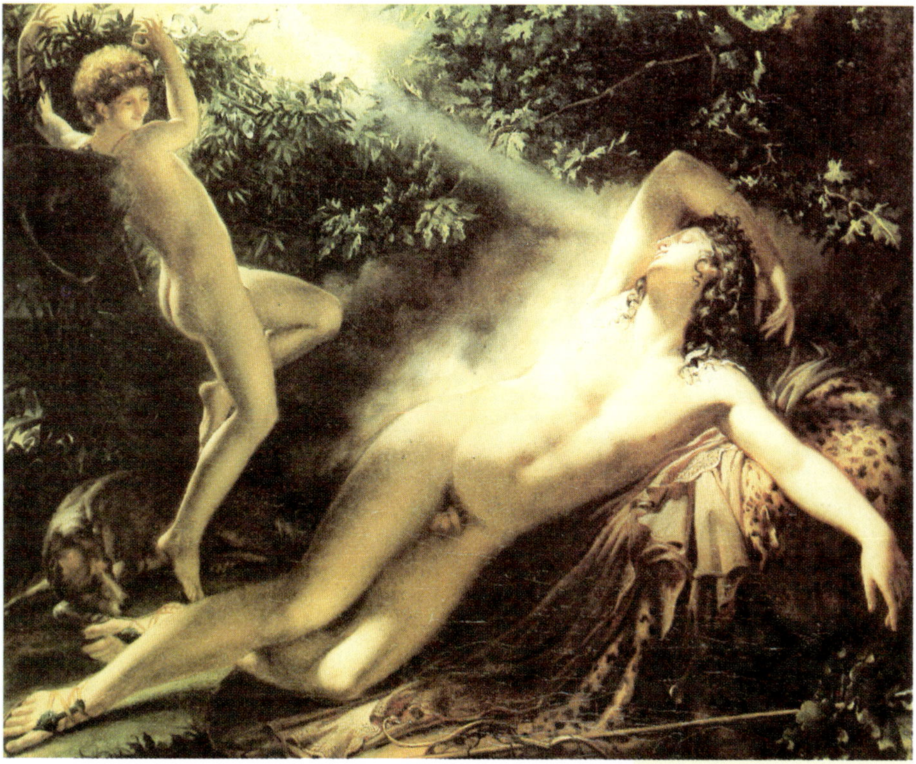

Endymion's Dream

Anne-Louis Girodet de Roucy Trioson
(Montargis, Loiret 1767–Paris, 1824)

- oil on canvas
- 197 x 260 cm
- Richard L. Feigen & Co., New York

This canvas, which seems to foreshadow certain characteristics of pre-Raphaelite aesthetics, depicts Endymion in the process of having his wish for eternal sleep fulfilled. However, some have doubted this interpretation, for Cupid is pulling back the foliage in order to allow Selene, or Diana, whose hunting equipment is strewn around him, to reach the young man in the guise of a moonbeam. Endymion's sensual appeal needs no comment. His adolescent body is long-limbed and attractively shaped. The strong shaft of light striking and bathing his body in golden vapor is reminiscent of Danaë receiving the golden rain.

Jupiter and Thetis

Jean-Auguste-Dominique Ingres
(Montauban, 1780–Paris, 1867)

- 1811
- oil on canvas
- 327 x 260 cm
- Musée Granet, Aix-en-Provence

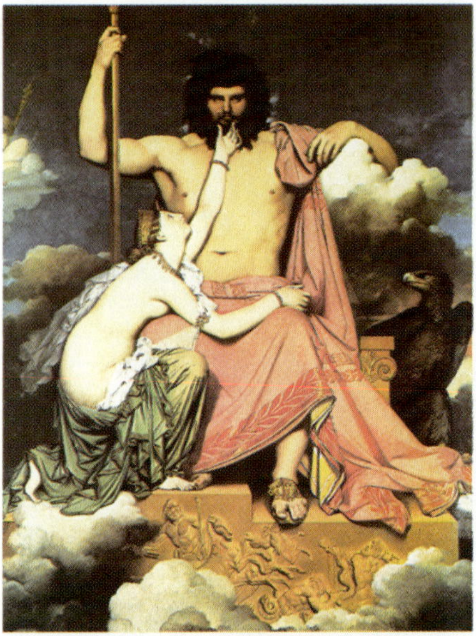

It is one of Ingres' best-known works, and was severely criticized in its day owing to its mannered treatment of feminine proportions in favour of aesthetic ends. Nevertheless, Ingres has lent the figure notable sensuality. Thetis' body is smooth, sinuous and insinuating. Jupiter, motionless and statuesque, appears to be scrutinizing the infinite.

Venus and Adonis

Pierre-Paul Prud'hon
(Cluny, 1758–Paris, 1823)

- 1812
- oil on canvas
- 244 x 172 cm
- Wallace Collection, London

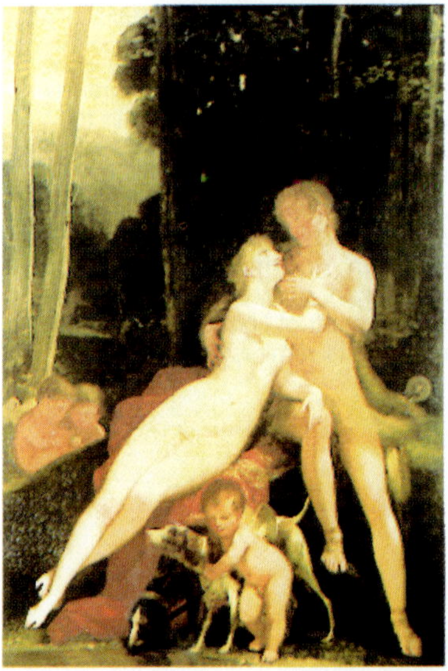

This work, commissioned by Marie-Louise for the Tuileries Palace, is chromatically elegant, romantically refined and full of freshness and originality, characteristics of 18th-century art. The light illuminates the slender, smooth-skinned, well-modeled bodies, which are shown entwined in an amorous embrace laden with eroticism. Although both figures are totally nude, their poses discreetly conceal their loins.

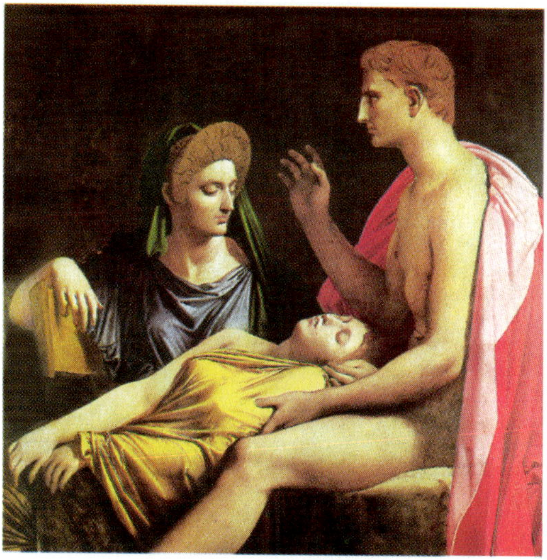

Virgil Reading the Aeneid before Augustus

Jean-Auguste-Dominique Ingres
(Montauban, 1780–Paris, 1867)

- 1812 or 1819
- oil on canvas
- 138 x 142 cm
- Musées Royaux des Beaux-Arts, Brussels

The classicizing style with which this nude has been treated recalls Roman sculptures of the Emperor, although here, Ingres has included a dramatic hand gesture, as if Augustus sought to ward off the death of Octavia's son.

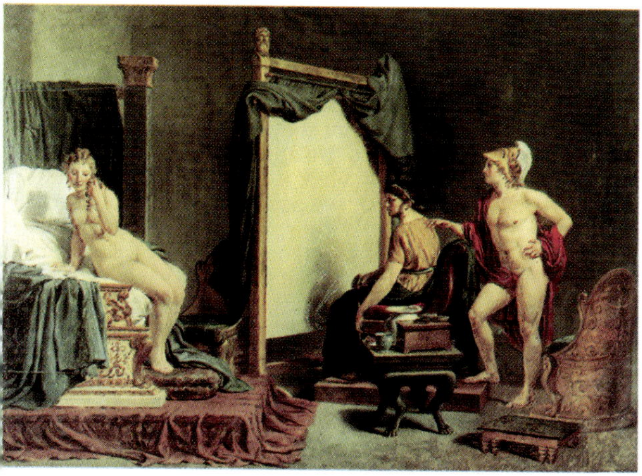

Apelles Painting Campaspe in the Presence of Alexander

Jacques-Louis David
(Paris, 1748–Brussels, 1825)

- 1812–13
- oil on canvas
- 96 x 136 cm
- Musée des Beaux-Arts, Lille

This motif enabled David to depict a glorious nude and to create an emotionally rife, sensual scene. The sentiments of each figure find expression here, as well as the curious relationships between them. Campaspe, aware that her charms and power of seduction have affected the artist, is shown posing coyly and blushing.

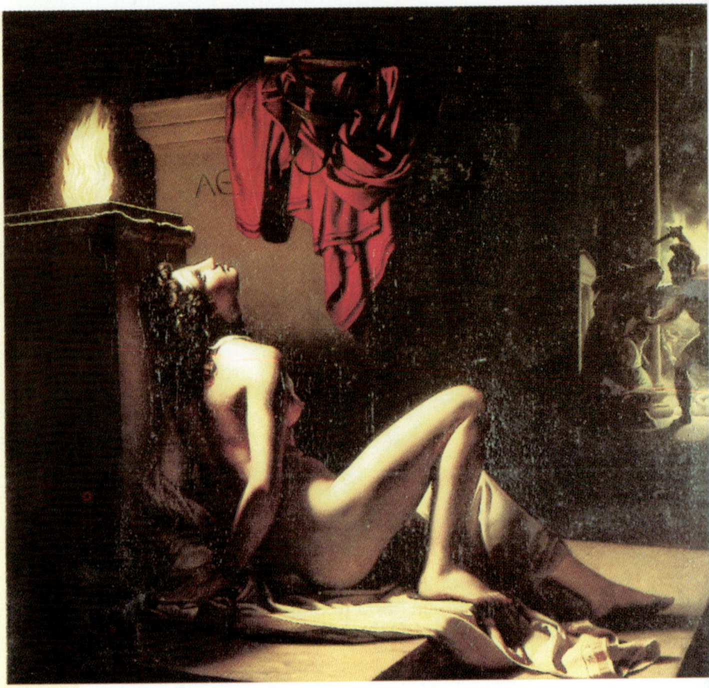

Cassandra

Jérôme Langlois
(Paris, 1779–1838)

- ca. 1815
- oil on canvas
- 180 x 193 cm
- Musée des Beaux-Arts, Chambéry

After the Greeks had taken Troy, Cassandra, daughter of king Priam and sister of Paris, hid behind the altar of Athena, in an attempt to save herself. But she was discovered and taken prisoner by Ajax. Here, we see her naked and helpless, hands bound, pleading with Athena for revenge. Her highly sensual body is illuminated by a powerful shaft of light, while the candle on top of the altar illuminates the sanctuary. Right, in the background, we see the burning city that backlights a soldier cutting someone down. The painting's flawless draftsmanship and composition also counterbalance Cassandra's sensuality. The work is unusually mannered compared to the dominant movements of the day.

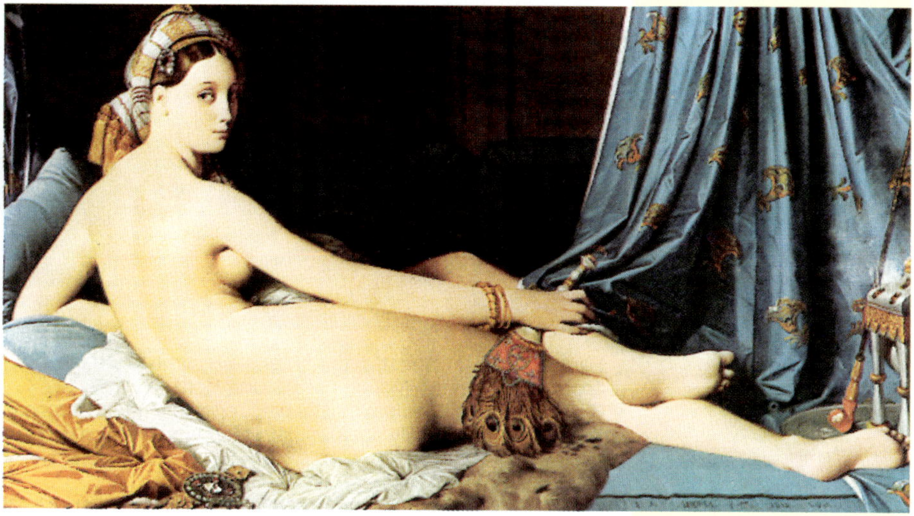

La Grande Odalisque

Jean-Auguste-Dominique Ingres

(Montauban, 1780–Paris, 1867)

- 1814
- oil on canvas
- 91 x 162 cm
- Musée du Louvre, Paris

Ingres frequently turned to Oriental themes for inspiration, for they provided an ideal pretext to paint idealized female nudes charged with eroticism. This odalisque, whose back has been made disproportionately long owing to aesthetic considerations, represents a fine example of harmony prevailing over realism. The figure of the odalisque recurs in Ingres' oeuvre, such as in the Turkish Bath. The scene, evoking the sensuality of the Orient, is rendered in rich colors and is brightly illuminated. The pose of this majestic nude is candid if somewhat static. While reclining, she looks back and gazes at the viewer with disarming candidness and aloofness.

The Dying Paris Rejected by Œnone

Jean-Baptiste Antoine Thomas
(1791–1834)

- 1816
- oil on canvas
- 114 x 146 cm
- École Nationale Supérieure des Beaux-Arts, Paris

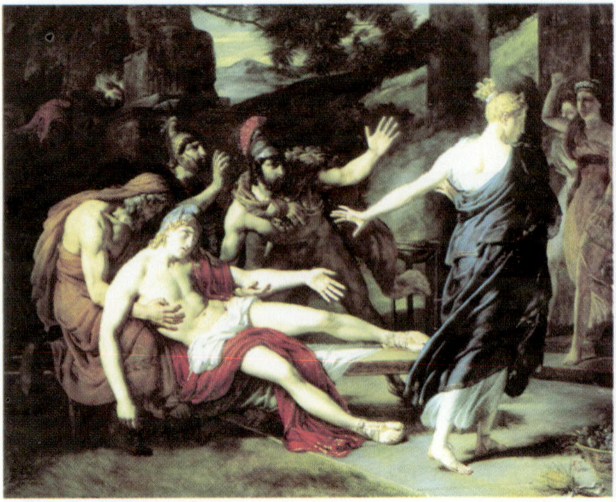

Paris' union with Helen, wife of Menelaus, unleashed the Trojan War. Here, although her consort Paris is dying, Œnone refuses to help him. His pale, effeminate body stands out almost ridiculously against that of the warriors aiding him.

The Raft of the Medusa

Théodore Géricault
(Rouen 1791 — Paris 1824)

- 1818/19
- oil on canvas
- 65 x 83 cm
- Musée du Louvre, Paris

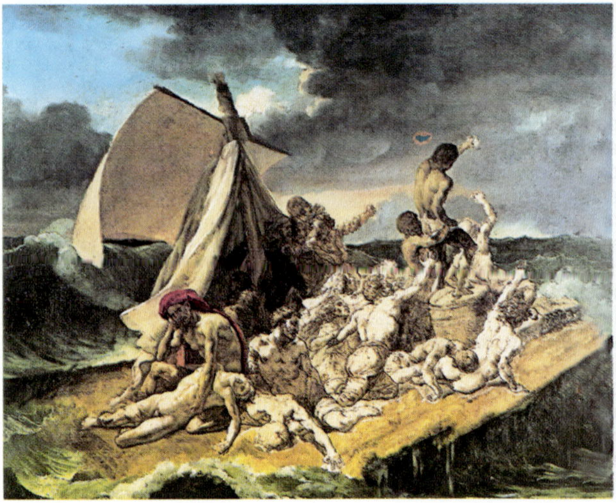

This is one of the preliminary paintings Géricault produced for his definitive work of the same title (1819). He pursued in-depth research, sketching people in psychiatric wards and hospitals, as well as corpses in morgues. The various nudes in different stages and states give us an idea of his working process.

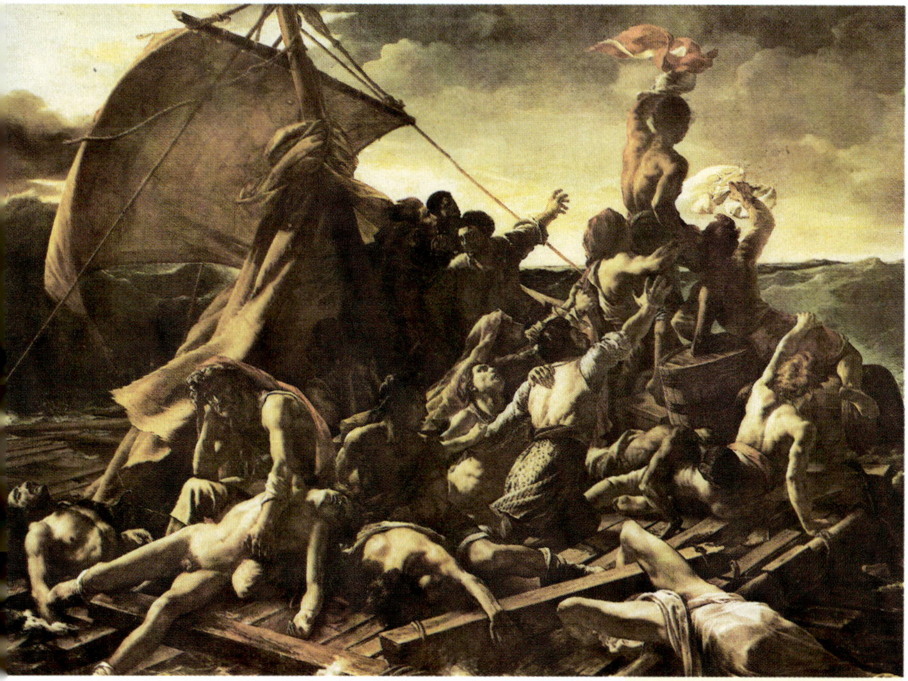

The Raft of the Medusa

Théodore Géricault
(Rouen, 1791–Paris, 1824)

- 1819
- oil on canvas
- 491 x 716 cm
- Musée du Louvre, Paris

'his is one of Géricault's most important works. The new ıpproaches that it inaugurated in respect to the academic radition gave rise to practices that broke with rigid historicist ıorms. The sculptural nudes in this work testify to Géricault's eing influenced by Michelangelo, although the overall npression made by the painting is nearer to ancient bas-eliefs. The Baroque dynamism of the composition mingles vith the rich treatment of light on the bodies, heightening ıe dramatic interest. The scene is based on events that took lace upon the shipwreck of the frigate Medusa in 1816, ıvolving 149 victims, many of whom perished after undergoıg pitiful ordeals on the rescue raft. Géricault studied human orpses, dying people and the mentally ill in preparation for ıis work. The bodies depicted show various states of rictus nd other extreme conditions that can only be understood as esulting from severe physical and mental ordeal.

Angelica

Jean-Auguste-Dominique Ingres
(Montauban, 1780–Paris, 1867)

- 1819
- oil on canvas
- 84 x 42.5 cm
- Musée du Louvre, Paris

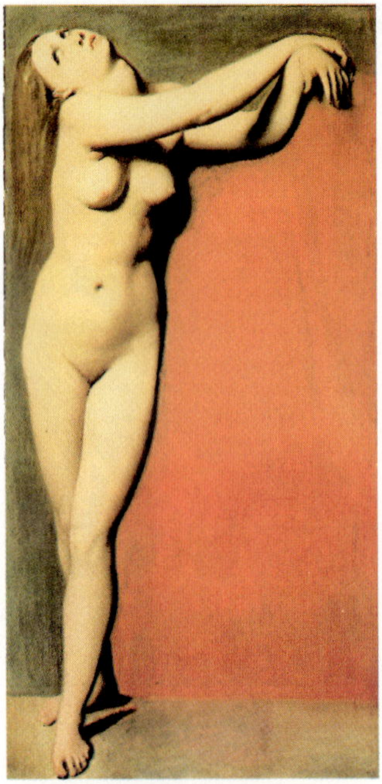

Although Ingres was evidently intent on eliminating excessive curvature of the hips, the forms are not those of a girl, but of a mature woman whose sensuality is heightened by the careful treatment of the figure's intimate parts: shaven genitals that leaves the sexual organ in plain view, something that is uncommon in representations of women of the time; and full, perfectly formed breasts. These elements are offset by the woman's languid facial expression and her dramatic, swan-like neck.

Standing Female Nude

Théodore Géricault
(Rouen, 1791–Paris, 1824)

- gouache, indigo and pencil
- 19.8 x 13 cm
- Musée des Beaux-Arts, Rouen

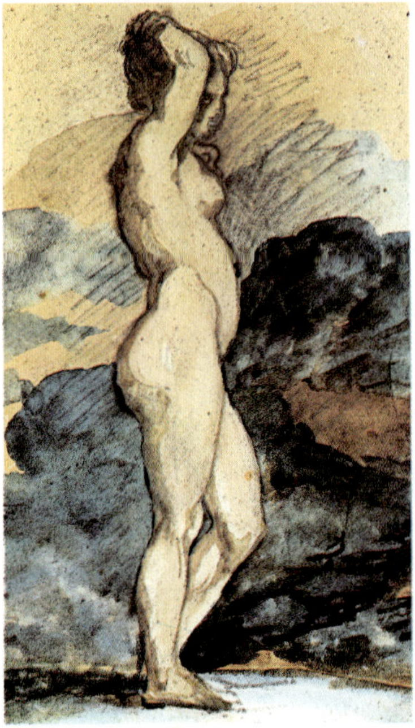

This work bears witness, among other things, to the energetic handling of paint that we can observe in many of his works. The figure is intriguing. The painting's color scheme consists of a harmonious combination of subdued tones. Against a background of darker hues, the artist has applied rough, thick, even violent brushwork, lending the scene dramatic tension.

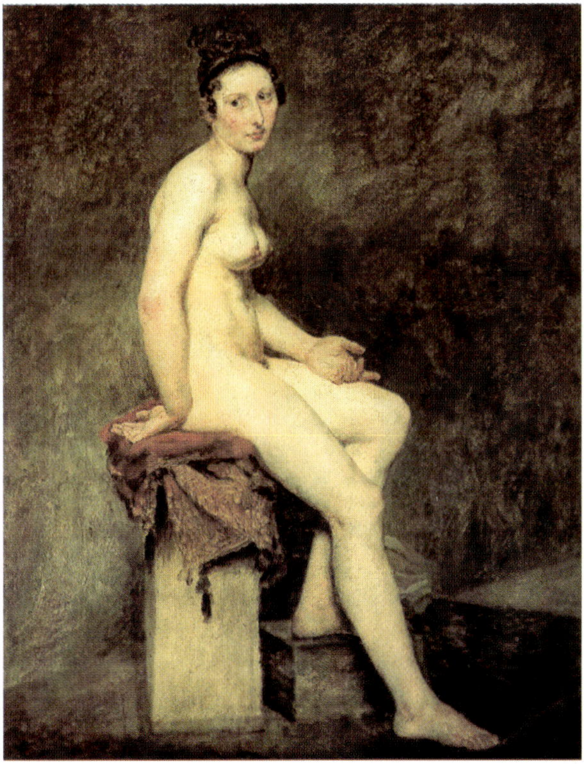

Delacroix's subtle palette, particularly the flesh tones, are indebted to the work of Rubens and Titian, which he deeply admired. In this nude, treated with a surprising naturalism, the artist shows a keen interest in realism. The artist took great pains to perfect this figure, yet he conceived it in a manner that was far removed from the academic style of such artists as David or Ingres. Nonetheless, Delacroix does not neglect his interest in composition, which is manifest here: from head to foot the figure forms an S, boldly dividing the painting in two with a brightly lit body that stands out against the dark brown background. The figure is painted in the manner of a portrait, with relaxed shoulders and arms, and gazes at the artist, not the viewer.

Seated Nude (Mademoiselle Rose)

Eugène Delacroix
(Charenton-Saint-Maurice, near Paris, 1798–Paris, 1863)

- ca. 1821
- oil on canvas
- 81 x 65 cm
- Musée du Louvre, Paris

Samson and Delilah

Joseph-Désiré Court
(Rouen, 1797–1865)

- 1821
- oil on canvas
- 25 x 33 cm
- École Nationale Supérieur des Beaux-Arts, Paris

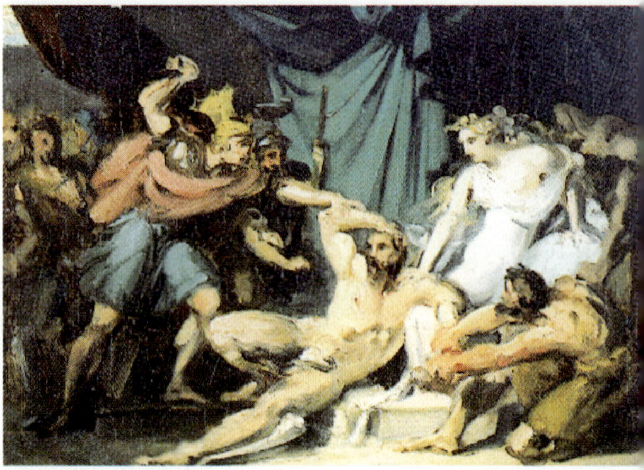

The work captures a great deal of violence and movement in a small space. Samson, at Delilah's feet, is depicted in a complicated yet expressive pose, his body extremely powerful, as befits this hero.

The Serpent Attacking Buoso Donati

William Blake
(London, 1757–1827)

- ca. 1824
- pen and watercolor
- 37.2 x 52.7 cm
- Tate Gallery, London

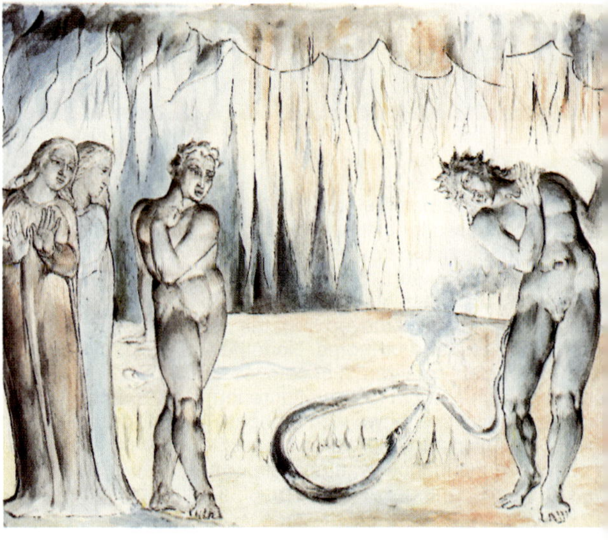

Another illustration for the Inferno in Dante's Divine Comedy. The nudes show sculptural modeling and depth, with well-defined muscles and powerful, flowing bodies. The work also displays a superb handling of light and color.

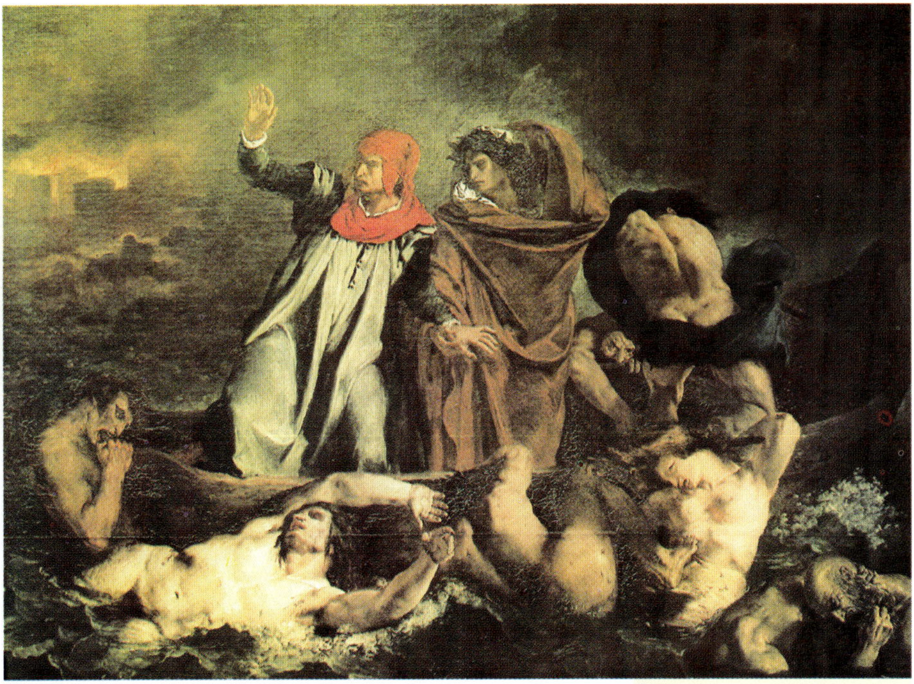

Dante and Virgil are shown traveling to Hell on Charon's boat. In the background appears the infernal city of Dis. The nude bodies attempting to clamber into the boat are those of the damned. They are illuminated, while the poets are cast in shadow. The considerable foreshortening of the damned betray the influence of Michelangelo and Rubens. Their bodies are monumental, exhibiting heroic proportions and powerful muscles. Their contorted poses lend drama to the scene. Of the writhing, expressive figures, the one on the left, who has the tip of the boat between his teeth, is the most striking. The struggle in the water evokes a vivid image of humanity triumphing in the face of adversity.

Dante and Virgil in Hell

Eugène Delacroix
(Charenton-Saint-Maurice, near Paris, 1798–Paris, 1863)

- 1822
- oil on canvas
- 189 x 246 cm
- Musée du Louvre, Paris

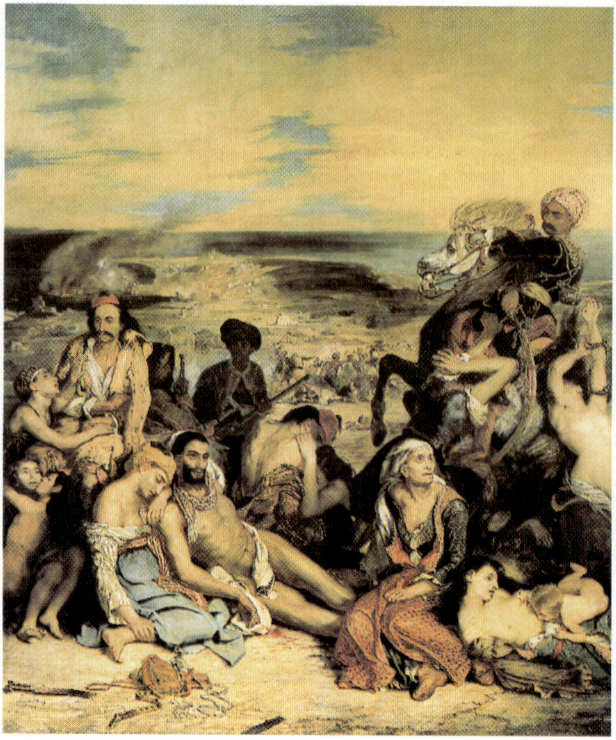

Scenes from the Chios Massacres

Eugène Delacroix
(Charenton-Saint-Maurice, near Paris, 1798–Paris, 1863)

- 1824
- oil on canvas
- 417 x 354 cm
- Musée du Louvre, Paris

In 1822, the Greek inhabitants of the island of Chios rose up against their Turkish overlords, incurring 20,000 casualties. This painting, based on that tragedy, shows Delacroix championing a new style in opposition to the Classicism of Ingres. While the figures are grouped as in a Classical relief, the modeling and rich, dense colors evoke Rubens' Baroque style. The figures in this scene, their skin coloring extraordinarily rich and facial expressions extremely varied, are the victims of war. Individual nudes are naturalistically rendered and skilfully foreshortened. The artist has set his painstakingly-executed figure-studies in a landscape with a brightly-lit sky that underscores the dramatic tension of the events taking place.

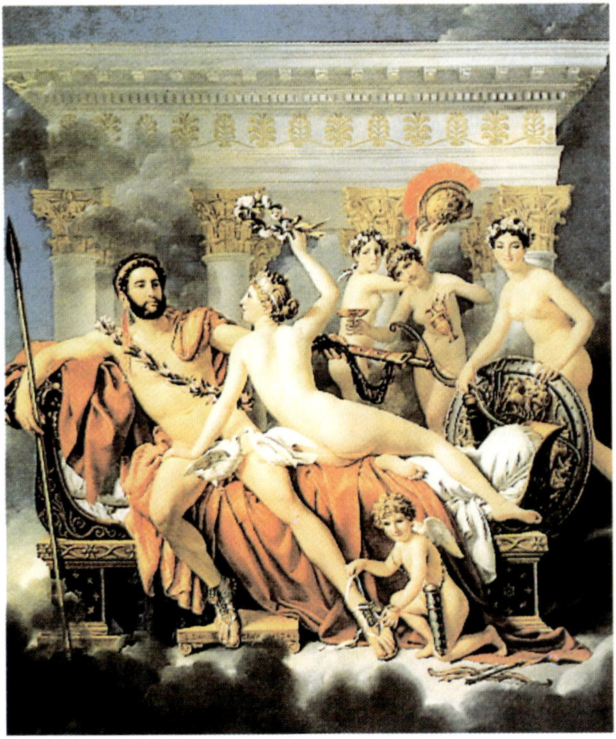

This painting was executed after David had decided to go into exile in Belgium. There, he set up a studio with his former pupils and began to execute monumental paintings inspired by ancient mythology and literature, of which this work is an example. Venus and her husband, whose ankle is being tied by Cupid, are partly reclining in the company of the Three Graces. The painting, combining architecture with the purest form of the human figure, the nude, is an attempt to approximate Classical art, on which the artist bases the general aesthetic, rhythm and color scheme of the painting. In addition to the sensuality achieved through the colors, the atmosphere, with its clouds and ethereal nature, and the physical beauty of the nudes, the painter sought a meaning, an ideological objective, whether it be a spiritual conviction or an affirmation of certain artistic criteria. The nudes are treated with great euphuism, and are remarkable for their elegant lines and proportions.

Venus Disarming Mars

Jacques-Louis David
(Paris, 1748–Brussels, 1825)

- 1824
- oil on canvas
- 308 x 265 cm
- Musées Royaux des Beaux-Arts, Brussels

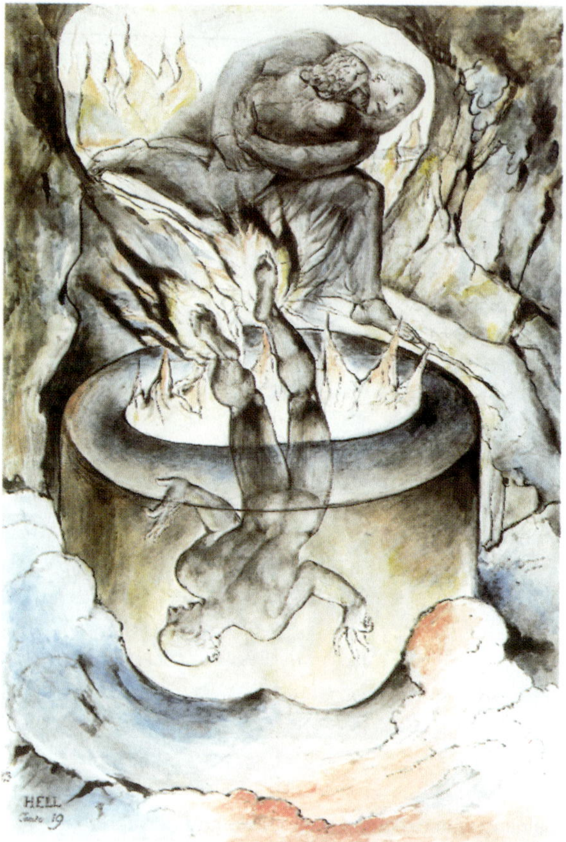

The Simoniac Pope

William Blake
(London, 1757–1827)

- 1824
- pen and watercolor
- 52.7 x 36.8 cm
- Tate Gallery, London

The watercolor illustrates a passage from the Inferno in Dante's Divine Comedy concerning the punishment of Pope Nicholas III for nepotism and simony. The cavern and abyss of hell, full of fire and smoke, the pit of fire for the damned, and the figure who dispatches them to their punishment, have all been represented with great schematic simplicity. Well-defined lines, juxtaposition of cool and warm tones and the figures themselves go to create a scene of great visual impact.

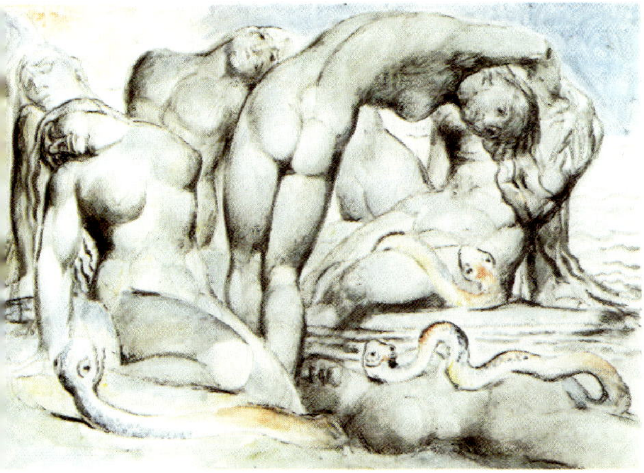

The Punishment of Thieves

William Blake
(London, 1757–1827)

- 1824
- black chalk, pen and watercolor
- 37.2 x 52.7 cm
- Tate Gallery, London

The inspiration for this pencil and watercolor piece is, once again, an episode from the Divine Comedy. The artist presents a group of male and female nude figures, in both varied and expressive poses. The work is a marvellously sensual study in figures.

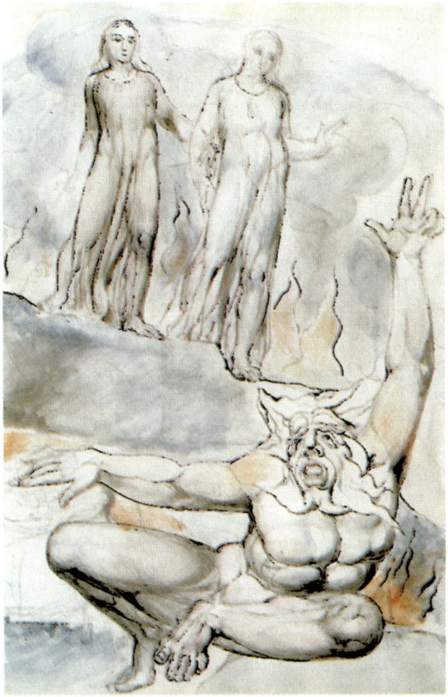

Plutus

William Blake
(London, 1757–1827)

- 1824
- pen and watercolor
- 52.7 x 37.1 cm
- Tate Gallery, London

Plutus, the god of wealth, is shown seated at the edge of the Circle of the Avaricious clutching his money-sack.

The Mulatta Aline

Eugène Delacroix
(Charenton-Saint-Maurice, near Paris, 1798–Paris, 1863)

- 1824–26
- oil on canvas
- 80 x 65 cm
- Musée Fabre, Montpellier

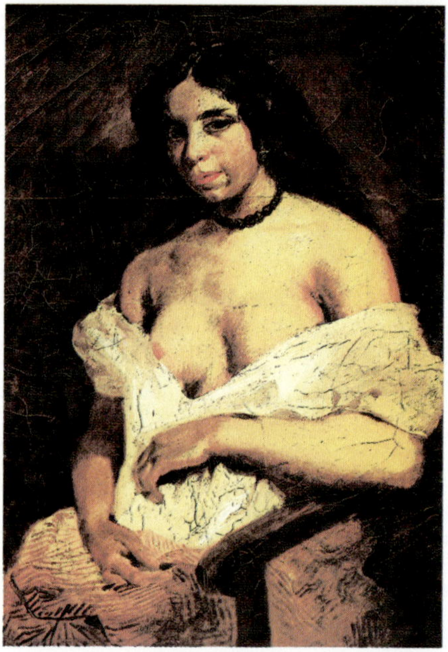

The woman has a timid aspect and a captivating gaze. Her strong generous body skillfully modeled with light and shadow. The brushwork and the synthetic manner of resolving forms recall the work of Velázquez. The woman allows one of her breasts to be seen, although she seems to want to cover her torso, demonstrating a certain modesty, which adds to her sensual appeal.

The Prisoner

François-Joseph Heim
(Belfort, 1787–Paris, 1865)

- ca. 1825
- oil on canvas
- 105 x 140 cm
- Musée Municipal, Semur-en-Auxois

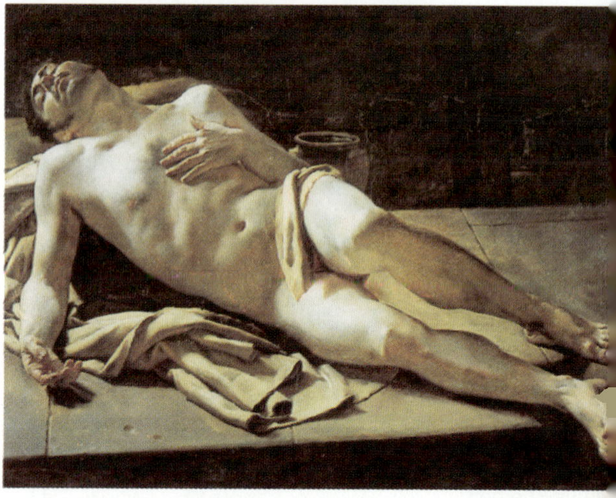

The subject depicted here might almost be a saint, and, in fact, the artist did receive numerous church commissions. The work is a superb academic figure study, incisively and masterfully executed. The diagonal of the composition, the contrasts of light and dark, and the color range, lend both an erotic as well as a violent air to this naked figure.

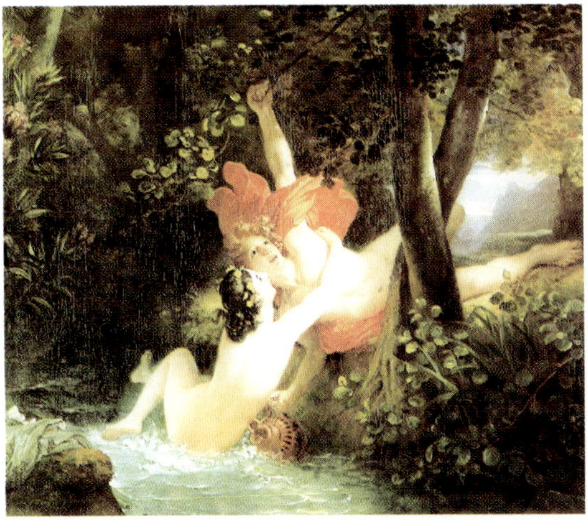

Hylas and the Nymph

François Gérard
(Rome, 1770–Paris, 1837)

- 1825–26
- oil on canvas
- 173 x 203 cm
- Musée Baron-Gérard, Bayeux

Hylas, son of the king of the Dryopes, took part in the expedition of the Argonauts. One day he came across a spring and, being thirsty, knelt down to drink. A beautiful nymph suddenly emerged from the water and dragged Hylas under, drowning him. The execution of the two nude and semi-nude figures here is meticulous.

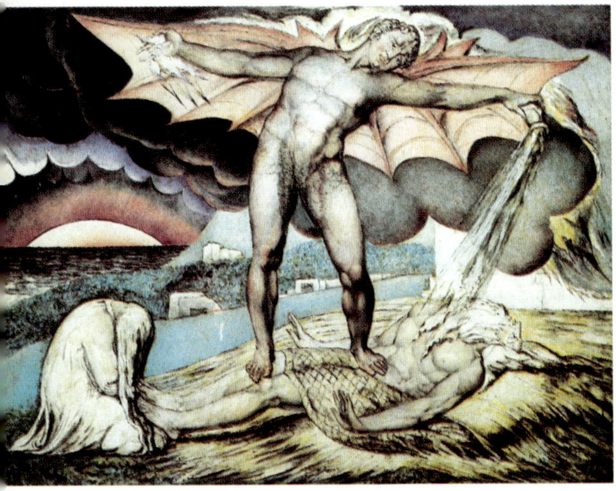

Satan Smiting Job with Sore Boils

William Blake
(London, 1757–1827)

- ca. 1826
- pen and tempera on mahogany
- 32.6 x 43.2 cm
- Tate Gallery, London

A work freely illustrating the Book of Job. Prostrate and impotent despite his strong body, Job is shown here being tortured by Satan who, standing on his body, pours a potion down on him. Satan is depicted as a powerful, well-built figure, his spread wings casting darkness across the Earth.

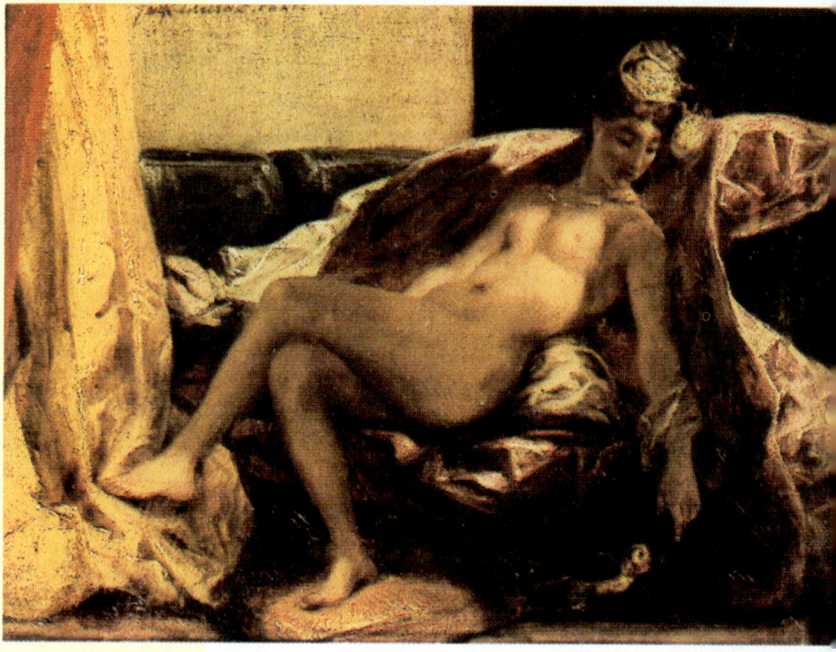

Woman with Parrot

Eugène Delacroix
(Charenton-Saint-Maurice, near Paris, 1798–Paris, 1863)

- 1827
- oil on canvas
- 24 x 32 cm
- Musée des Beaux-Arts, Lyon

Delacroix was undoubtedly the greatest French painter of the Romantic movement, with a predilection for exotic and emotionally-charged subject matter. He refused to use models for his works, which led him to make some errors of draftsmanship. This painting was executed early in the artist's career, when he delighted in meeting contemporary artists and intellectuals. It betrays a penchant for the Baroque and for theatricality, with a color scheme based on complementary colors, and taking advantage of all the intensities of a single range, tempered by the effects of light. It was precisely these characteristics, along with the emotional force of his works, that captivated the Impressionists, who considered him to be a harbinger of their movement. His influence on Manet's work from the 1860s is indisputable.

The artist here manifests his mastery of draftsmanship, and even though it is only a sketch, Delacroix has managed to bring together in it rhythm and elegance of figure, graceful, sensual lines, an expressive pose, movement and dramatic interest, as well as numerous incidental details, such as the footwear, hair and white veil.

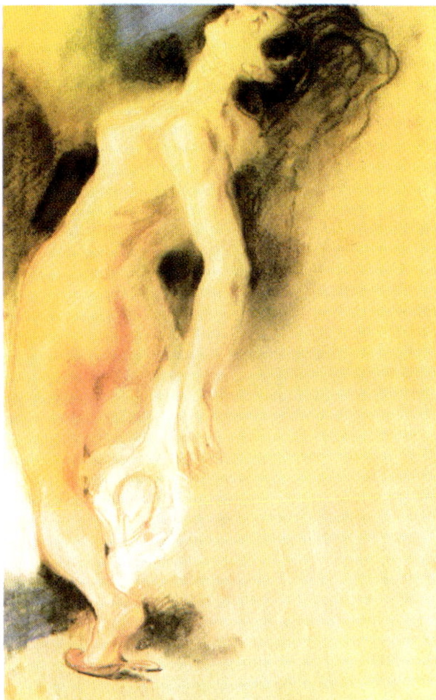

Study for The Death of Sardanapalus

Eugène Delacroix
(Charenton-Saint-Maurice, near Paris, 1798–Paris, 1863)

- 1826
- pastel on paper
- Musée du Louvre, Cabinet des dessins, Paris

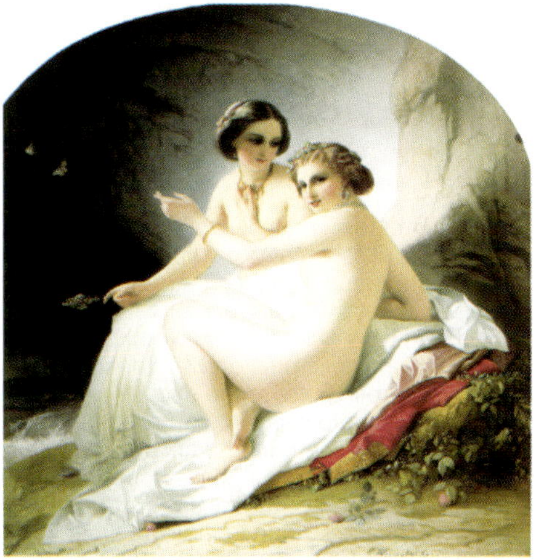

Bathers

Louis Hersent
(Paris, 1777–1860)

- 1830
- oil on canvas
- 130 x 137 cm
- Roy Miles Gallery, London

The delicacy of his present treatment of these bathers is such that even the unconcealed lesbianism that the picture reveals is not offensive, since the work's aesthetic qualities relegate it to second place.

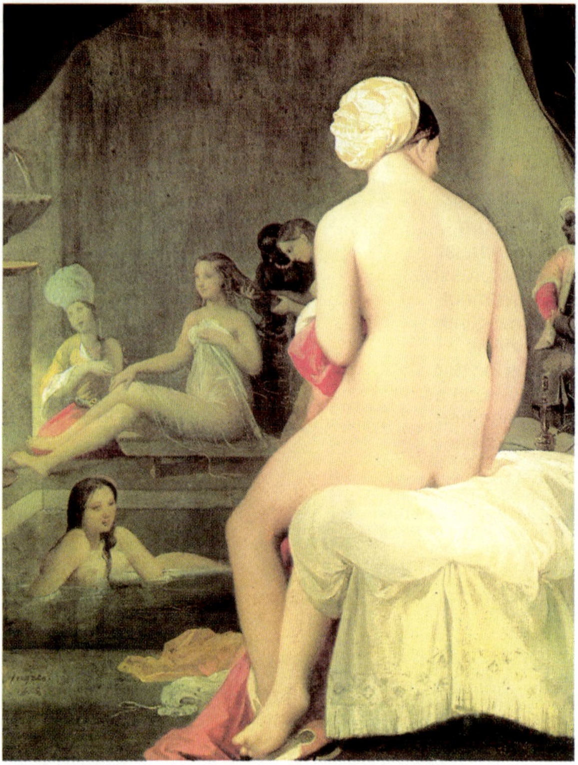

The Petite Baigneuse

Jean-Auguste-Dominique Ingres
(Montauban, 1780–Paris, 1867)

- 1828
- oil on canvas
- 35 x 27 cm
- Musée du Louvre, Paris

In addition to this small canvas, two other versions of the theme exist (The Bather of Valpinçon and The Turkish Bath) in which the same figure appears, with slight variations. The main subject of the work, of course, is the bather, who is shown with her back to the viewer. Her body appears to radiate light. Her skin is pale and soft, lending the representation a distinctly erotic note. In the middle ground, barely sketched, a young, natural-looking woman is bathing, her pose charmingly seductive. The darker background is peopled with bathers and attendants in static poses and with rather expressionless faces. Ingres seems to have stinted somewhat on such background details in order to devote his attention all the more effectively to the female nude in a traditional academic pose.

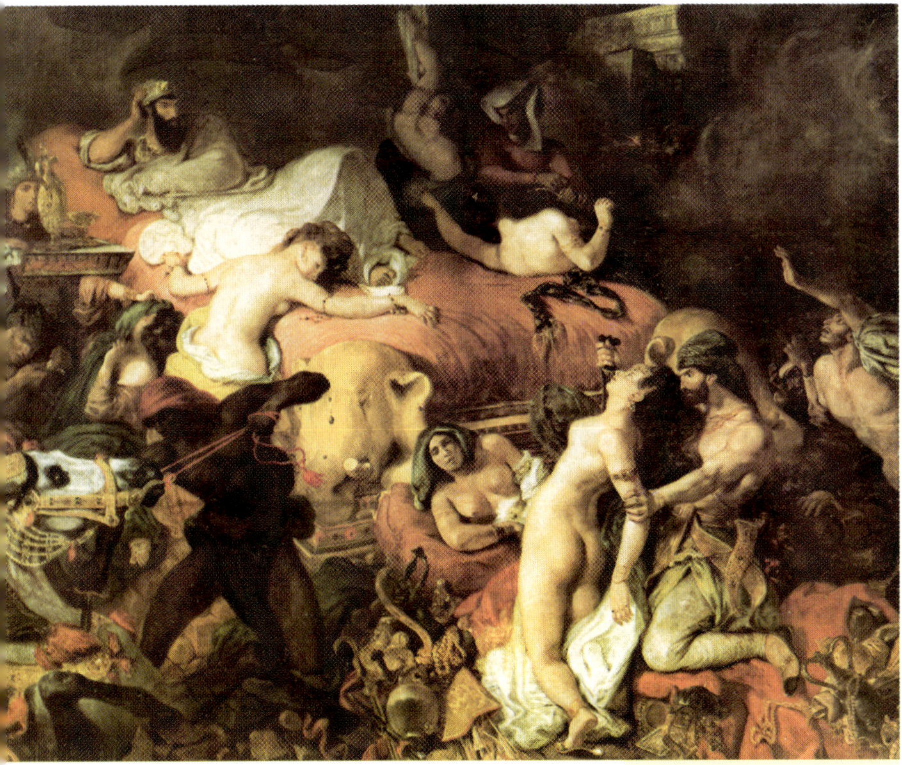

The Death of Sardanapalus

Eugène Delacroix
(Charenton-Saint-Maurice, near Paris, 1798–Paris, 1863)

- 1827–28
- oil on canvas
- 395 x 496 cm
- Musée du Louvre, Paris

his monumental painting represents an outright attack on the lassical style of academic painting as practiced by the pupils f Jacques-Louis David. The scene depicts the moment when ie last Assyrian king, Sardanapalus, seeing that his capital is bout to capitulate during a siege, orders his concubines, laves and horses to be killed before burning himself. Rubens' ifluence is felt in this distinctly Baroque work, particularly in s writhing figures and composition. The naturalistic propor-ons of his sensual female nudes are rendered with a striking, enetic line painted over a study of a model, unlike the sub-ective interpretations of the artist's rival Ingres. Rembrandt's ifluence can be discerned in the subtle blending of the hadows and in the impasto, as well as in such details as the orse's head in the lower left-hand corner of the scene.

Gros' Advanced Studio Session

Auguste Massé
(1795–ca. 1836)

- 1830
- oil on canvas
- 80 x 100 cm
- Musée Marmottan, Paris

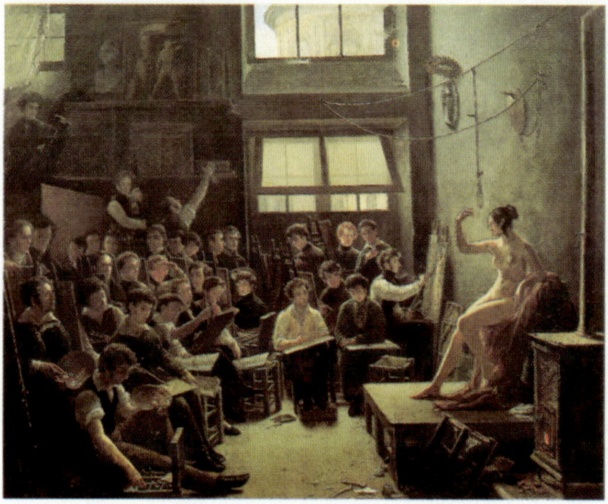

The nude adopts a classical pose, which suggests that the class is practicing foreshortening. The vantage point from which the scene is viewed makes the beholder feel as though he or she were one of the pupils.

King Candaules

William Etty
(York, 1787–1849)

- 1830
- oil on canvas
- 50 x 61 cm
- Tate Gallery, London

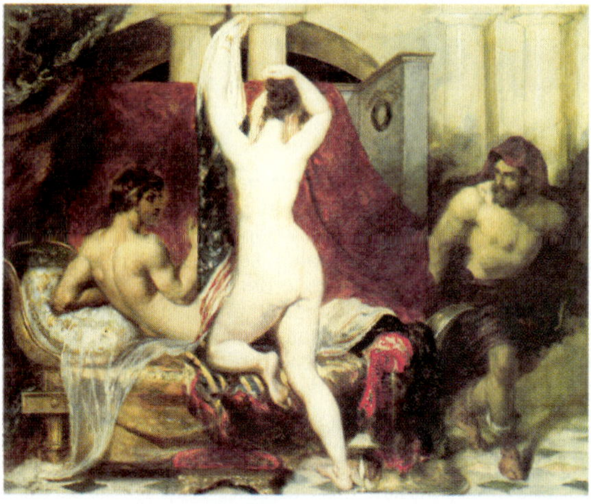

In order to convince his favorite, Gyges, of his wife's beauty King Candaules allows him to enter his chamber and see her naked. Gyges is smitten with love for her, and the king later pays for his rashness with his life. The nude figure here, displaying ample curves and a provocative positioning of her legs, is expressive of sensuality to a high degree.

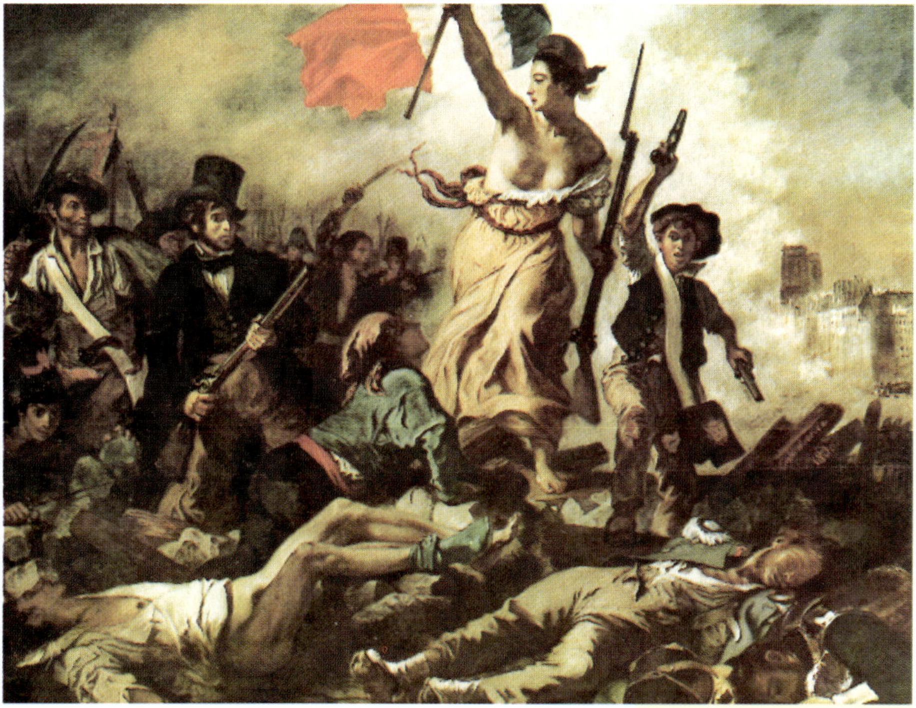

Liberty Leading the People

Eugène Delacroix
(Charenton-Saint-Maurice, near Paris, 1798–Paris, 1863)

- 1831
- oil on canvas
- 260 x 325 cm
- Musée du Louvre, Paris

After meeting Théodore Géricault, Delacroix attended the Ecole des Beaux-Arts, where he copied paintings with historical and mythological subjects in order to study their harmonious palettes, compositions as well as the creative force underlying them. This Romantic spirit led him to conceive this painting, an allegory of the uprising of July 28, 1830. The figure of Liberty exhibits the qualities of a leader who is able to mobilize and guide the masses. Shown in combat, her robust, naked torso recalls sculptures of Michelangelo. Although the fallen dress reveals her breasts, she is not intended to be provocative, but, instead, to reinforce the allegorical nature of the work. The light and shadow modeling the torso are harsh, the breasts firm and round, revealing the artist's intention to idealize the figure. The fact that Delacroix portrays himself in the painting (the figure with the top hat) indicates his support of the uprising.

Bathsheba at her Bath

Francesco Hayez
(Venice, 1791–Milan, 1882)

- 1834
- oil on canvas
- 77 x 107 cm
- Pinacoteca di Brera, Milan

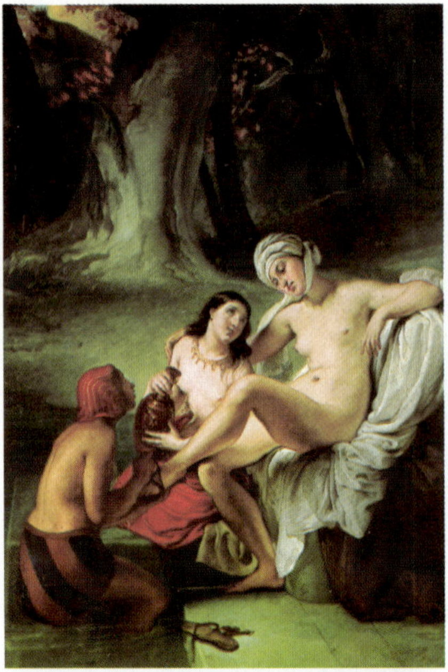

The lines of her body are harmonious and sinuous, illustrating an important change in the ideal of beauty following the Baroque period. The body is smoother and younger, the breasts are just beginning to form, and an attempt is made to emphasize their firmness. The limbs are attenuated, lending the figure a graceful aspect.

Woman before a Mirror

Christoffer Wilhelm Eckersberg
(Blaakrog, southern Jutland, 1783–Copenhagen, 1853)

- ca. 1837
- oil on canvas
- 32 x 25 cm
- Den Hirschsprungske Samling, Copenhagen

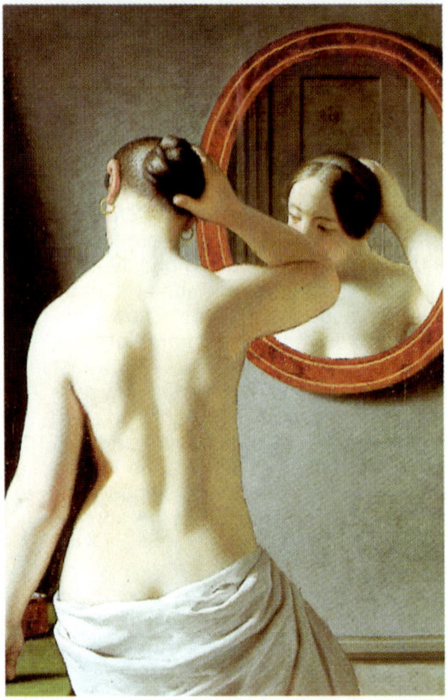

This elegantly classical nude possesses marble-like flesh, which is modeled with considerable subtlety. The only shadows present are those that define the major muscle groups, which are treated with great smoothness and finesse. The figure's full female forms appear graceful and weightless.

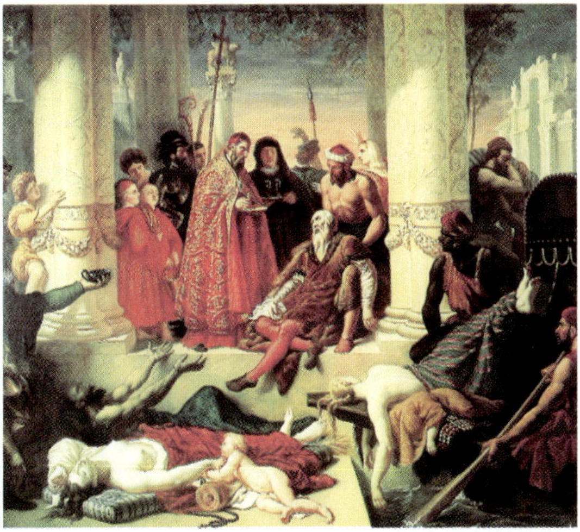

The Death of Titian

Pierre-Nolasque Bergeret
(Bordeaux, 1782–Paris, 1863)

- 1833
- oil on canvas
- 167 x 200 cm
- Musée Girodet, Montargis

This painting depicts the death of the great Venetian painter, Titian, who died a wealthy and highly-respected man aged 89 as a result of the plague. The foreground includes a number of figures recognizable from several famous Titian paintings.

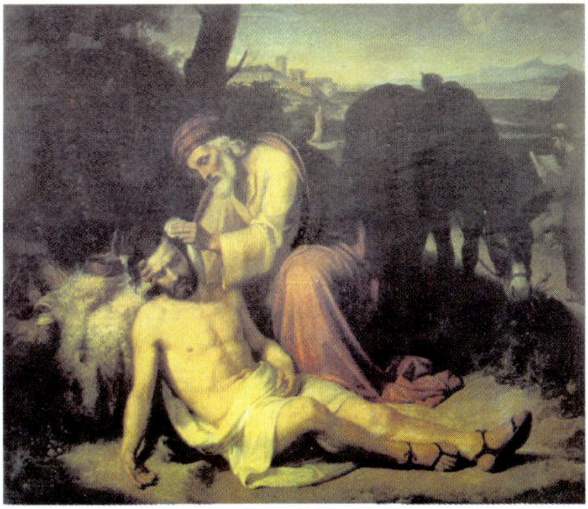

The Good Samaritan

Pelegrí Clavé i Roqué
(Barcelona, 1811–1880)

- 1839
- oil on canvas
- 241 x 187 cm
- Real Academia de Bellas Artes de Sant Jordi, Barcelona

This work is by one of the leading exponents of Catalan romanticism. Composition, the depiction of anatomical details, the use of chiaroscuro, as well as the coloration of the work are all impressive.

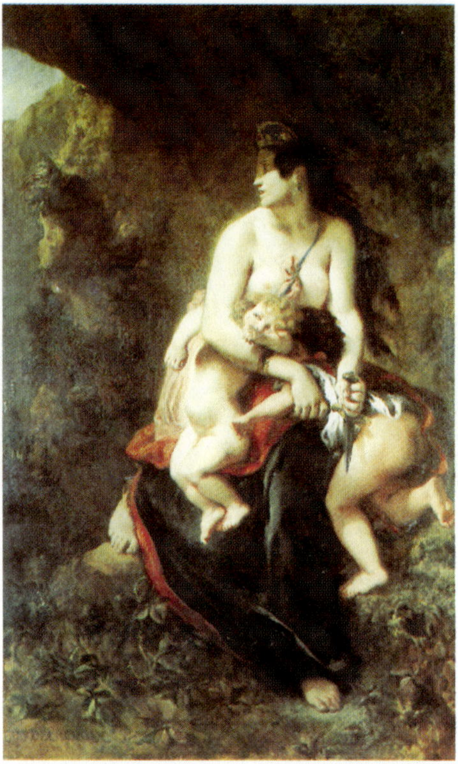

Medea

Eugène Delacroix
(Charenton-Saint-Maurice, near Paris, 1798–Paris, 1863)

- 1838
- oil on canvas
- 260 x 165 cm
- Musée des Beaux-Arts, Lille

The work was exhibited at the 1838 Salon. Medea, daughter of Aeëtes, king of Colchis, and lover of Jason of the Argonauts, eventually became his wife. But Jason did not hesitate to reject her later, in order to marry Creusa, daughter of the king of Corinth. Distressed, Medea planned revenge. She not only gave her rival a small case, a dress and a crown, all of which were poisoned, but she also murdered her two children by Jason, Mermesus and Feres. Here, she is portrayed as a large-breasted woman grasping her sons unlovingly, against a dark background whose chromatism highlights her pale skin coloration.

n this biblical scene, the patriarch expels the slave and the son she bore him, in order to put an end to his wife Sarah's jealousy. The work displays great naturalism. Noteworthy is he backlighting, which brings out he colour of smael's body by darkening it.

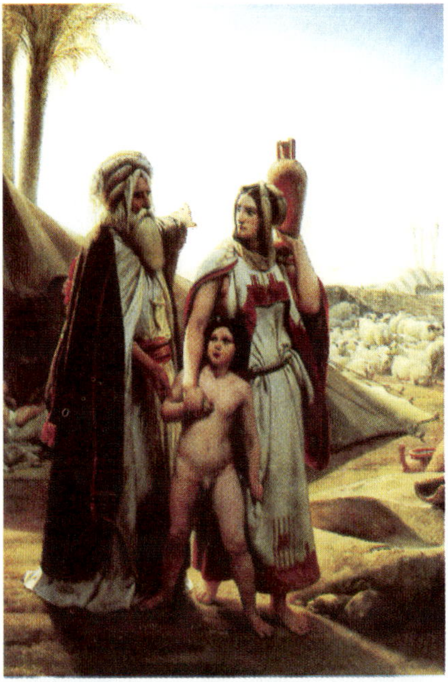

Abraham Expelling Hagar

Émile-Jean-Horace Vernet
(Paris, 1789–1863)

- 1839
- oil on canvas
- 81 x 61 cm
- Musée des Beaux-Arts, Nantes

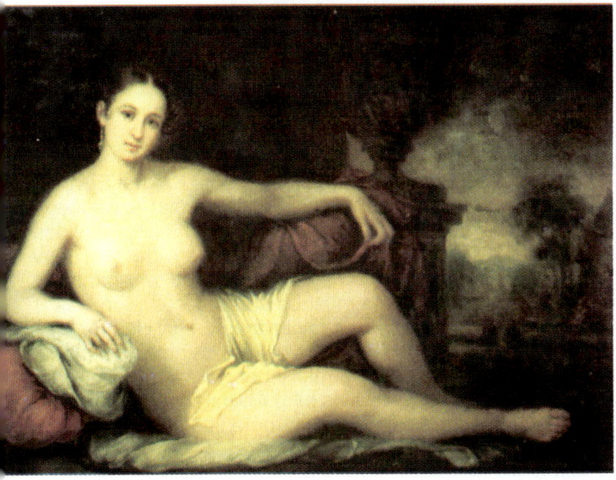

The Nude Maja

José Gutiérrez de la Vega
(Seville, 1791–Madrid, 1865)

- 1840
- oil on canvas
- 105 x 45 cm
- Museo del Prado, Madrid

José Gutiérrez is an important exponent of Spanish Romanticism. The confident pose of this nude figure, if somewhat academic in handling, is nevertheless surprisingly naturalistic. Eroticism here is unconcealed. The figure calls to mind certain renderings of Venus in similar poses. The artist was concerned in this painting to give a dignified portrayal of the female type as found in Seville.

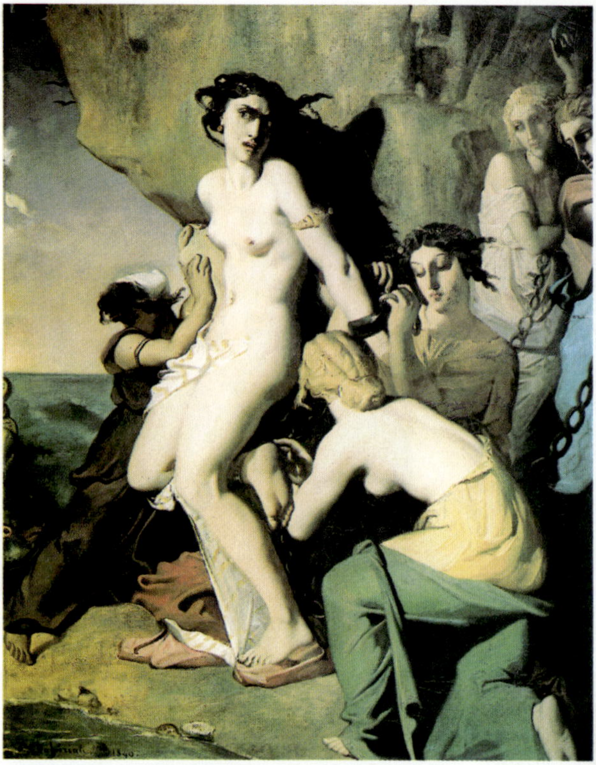

Andromeda Bound to the Rocks by the Nereids

Théodore Chassériau
(Samaná, Dominican Republic, 1819–Paris, 1856)

- 1840
- oil on canvas
- 92 x 74 cm
- Musée du Louvre, Paris

Andromeda was the daughter of Cepheus, King of Egypt, and Cassiopeia. Her mother once boasted that Andromeda's beauty surpassed that of the Nereids, which sent Poseidon into a rage—so much so that he sent a sea monster to devastate the country, to which the oracle of Jupiter Ammon declared that Andromeda must be surrendered. She was accordingly chained to a rock near the sea and left for the monster to devour her. She was delivered, however, by Perseus, who proceeded to marry her. This work shows the moment at which the Nereids bind Andromeda to the rock. The elegant, sinuous lines of Andromeda's body, which is duly modeled, her penetrating expression of horror, her pose, which befits her sensuality, and an air of mystery are just some of the painting's striking features. Chassériau frequently used models to whom he felt particularly close—such as his sister Adéle, Alice Ozy and Princess Cantacuzène—which explains the unique attraction of his nudes.

Harem scenes gave painters the opportunity to explore the mystery and sensuality of the Orient, where a woman was sometimes considered an unattainable jewel. Here, we see the biblical figure of Esther, attended by servants. Her sinuous profile, the left flank burnt in with dark shadow, is both pleasing and provocative.

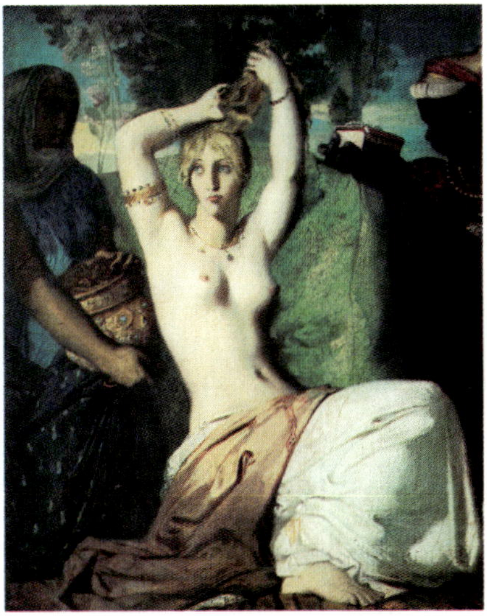

Esther's Toilet

Théodore Chassériau

(Samaná, Dominican Republic, 1819–Paris, 1865)

- 1841
- oil on canvas
- 49.5 x 33.5 cm
- Musée du Louvre, Paris

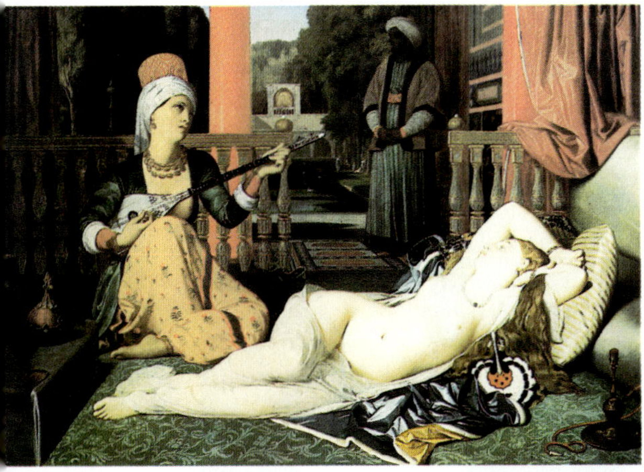

Odalisque with Slave

Jean-Auguste-Dominique Ingres

(Montauban, 1780–Paris, 1867)

- 1842
- oil on canvas
- 76 x 105.4 cm
- Walters Art Gallery, Baltimore

Ingres depicts a nude here in a somewhat studied pose: hips showing to advantage, foreshortening of thighs, together with an air of enforced relaxation. It was the Classicism of Ingres' settings, more than anything else, that enabled his work to find acceptance in an otherwise repressed and repressive society.

The Origins of the Harp

Daniel Maclise
(Cork, 1806–London, 1870)

- 1842
- oil on canvas
- 110.4 x 85 cm
- City of Manchester Art Galleries

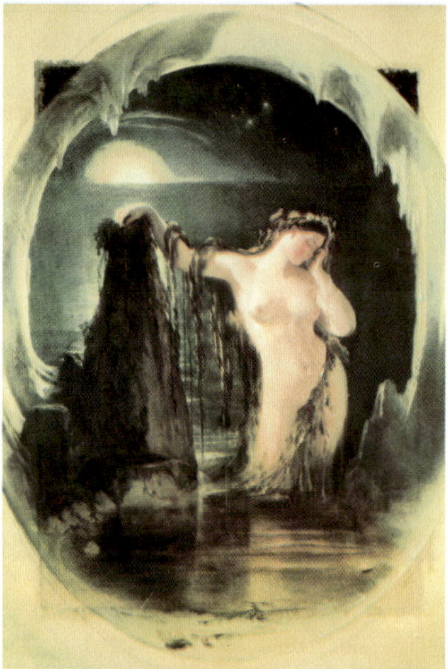

A sensual and, at the same time romantic nude study. Modeling, full breasts, narrow waist and broad hips do not fail in their accustomed effects.

Beautiful Rosina

Antoine Wiertz
(Dinant, 1806–Brussels, 1865)

- 1843
- oil on canvas
- 140 x 100 cm
- Musées Royaux des Beaux-Arts, Brussels

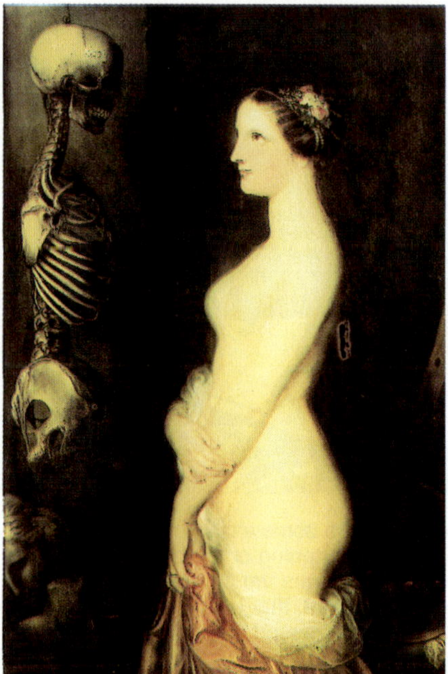

This figure's highly erotic body is impeccably rendered in the Neoclassical style, which is particularly evident in the individual features and in the skillful modeling of the volumes. The flesh tones are rendered with a staggering realism, particularly in the hands, and the nude's sensuality is heightened by its juxtaposition with the skeleton.

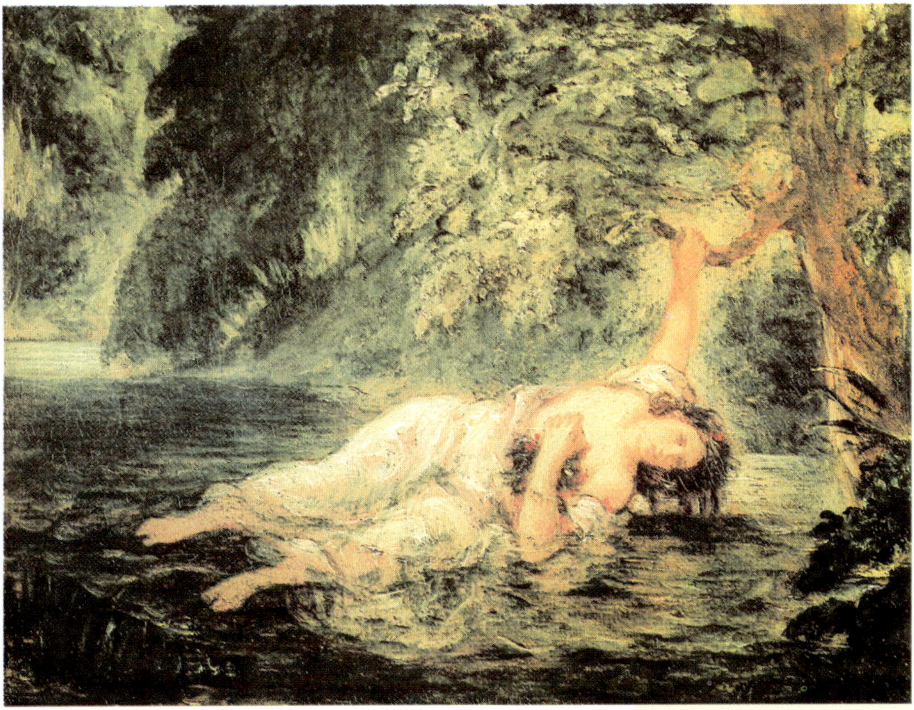

With this figure, the artist presaged one painted by the Pre-Raphaelite John Millais in 1851. The technique is Impressionistic both in its cursory brushwork and rough impasto, evoking shapes by juxtaposing color fields. Although the theme of this work is romantic, Delacroix clearly attempts to paint for painting's sake, independently of the subject matter. Ophelia's foreshortened torso is bare, though her breasts remain completely covered. The outline of her body is blurred, blending into the background. The light lends the body, which is enveloped in a vigorous red line, contrasting tonalities and solidity. The shadows give way to chromatic tones that differ from those employed in the light areas.

The Death of Ophelia

Eugène Delacroix
(Charenton-Saint-Maurice, near Paris, 1798–Paris, 1863)

- 1844
- oil on canvas
- 23 x 30.5 cm
- Musée du Louvre, Paris

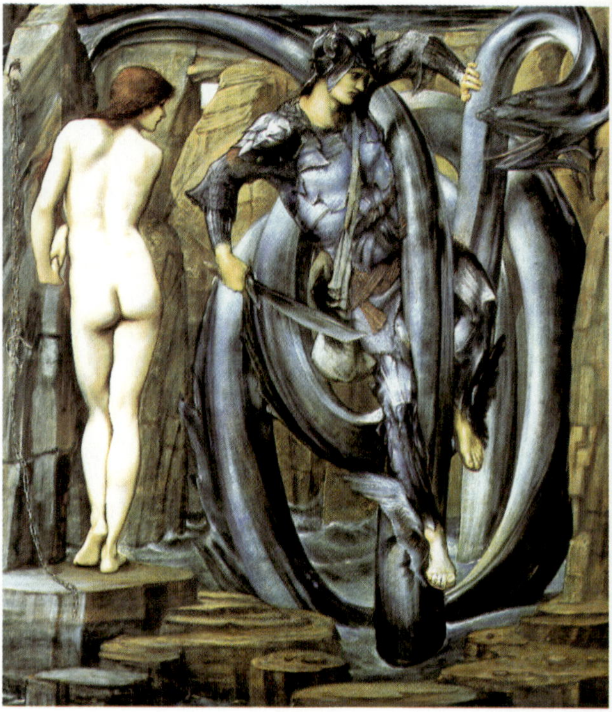

From the Perseus Series

Edward Burne-Jones
(Birmingham 1833
—London 1898)

- 1884/85
- gouache
- 155.8 x 158.4 cm
- Southampthon City Art Gallery

This painting is taken from the Perseus Series. After his victory over Medusa, Perseus set out to free Andromeda, who had been chained to a rock and was being threatened by a sea monster. He attacked the huge serpent, which is depicted here in a somewhat futurist fashion and structure, its metallic coloring being akin to that of a knight's armor. The iconographic concept of the scene draws on the legend of Saint George and the Dragon, whereby the sensual and strongly scuptural nude figure of Andromeda belongs to Burne-Jones' most admired works. Here, posture lends the painting a seductive note. The painting's contrasting palette and the calligraphical means used to incorporate the figure into the composition as a whole by means of curved lines, as well as the fight between Perseus and the sea monster, form a harmonious picture imbued with both erotic and violent elements.

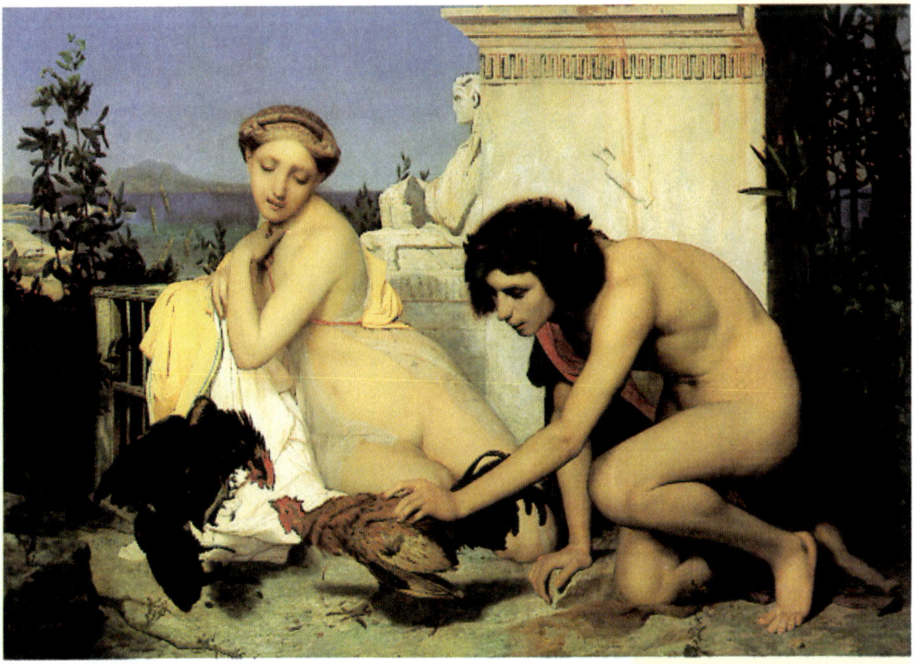

Cockfight

Jean-Léon Gérôme
(Vesoul, 1824–Paris, 1904)

- 1846
- oil on canvas
- 143 x 204 cm
- Musée d'Orsay, Paris

Jean-Léon Gérôme's interest in Classical Antiquity is apparent in some of the themes of his works, with their finished academic style. This canvas was exhibited at the Paris Salon of 1847, which earned the artist high acclaim. Here, he presents a young Greek couple with comely bodies. The figure of the young man has an Apollonian aspect—slender, delicate and sensual—with smooth skin and subtle modeling. The female nude, whose body is foreshortened and twisted to one side, is placed at a slight distance from him. She is shown covering her breasts with her arms while a light, transparent veil reveals her nudity. Like her companion, she has a sensual body, with broad hips and a large abdomen. The landscape in the background, the architectural fragments near the figures and the crisp, vibrant colors of the dress that the young woman has taken off and is reclining on engenders a warm, intimate atmosphere.

Christ on the Cross

Eugène Delacroix
(Charenton-Saint-Maurice, near Paris, 1798–Paris, 1863)

- 1845
- oil on panel
- 37 x 25 cm
- Museum Boymans van Beuningen, Rotterdam

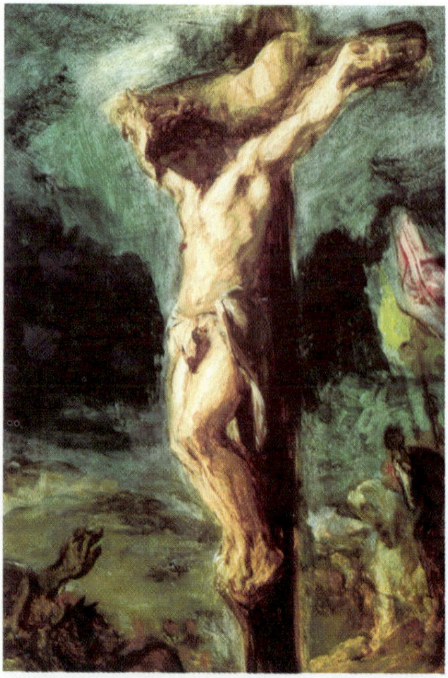

The artist used this sketch as a study for a more conventional crucifixion. The vigorous brush-strokes with which the muscles of this Christ's anatomy are alluded to are reminiscent of Rembrandt, and certain deformations of the body recall German masters. Dramatic interest at a painterly level is high in this panel.

Christ on the Cross

Eugène Delacroix
(Charenton-Saint-Maurice, near Paris, 1798–Paris, 1863)

- 1846
- oil on panel
- 80 x 64.2 cm
- The Walters Art Gallery, Baltimore

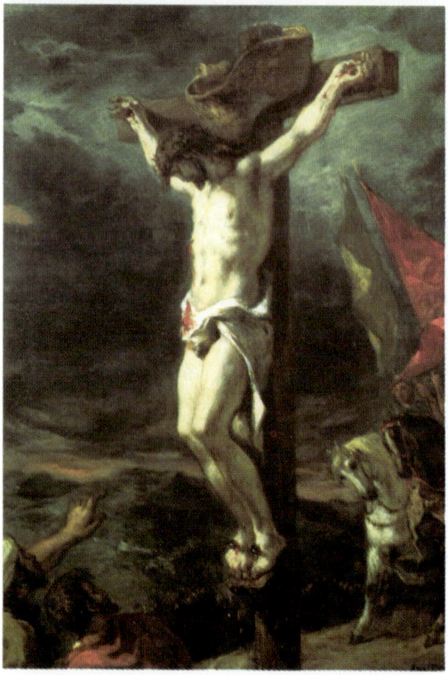

This painting is more finished than the sketch made of the same subject a year earlier. The treatment of Christ's body through strongly contrasting light against dark is reminiscent of some tenebrist works. Moreover, certain innovations, such as the near-photographic framing of the people in the lower left corner, have been introduced.

The painter has depicted a group around the young, attractive figure of Venus. Her pose is rather uninhibited, and she seems to be fully aware of her superior beauty. Cupid's figure has a certain seductiveness about it, too.

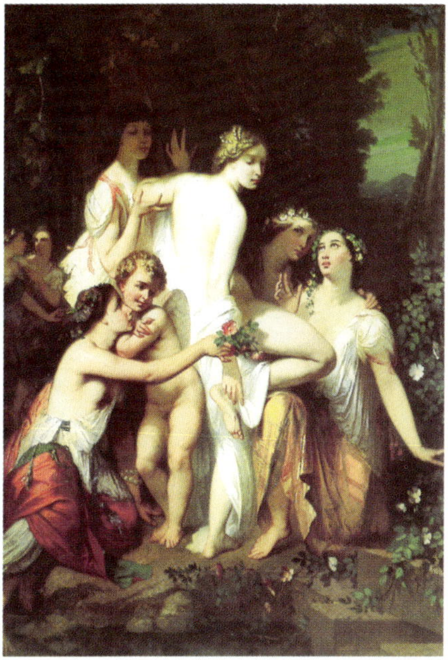

The Blood of Venus

Auguste-Barthélemy Glaize

(Montpellier, 1807–Paris, 1893)

- 1846
- oil on canvas
- 276 x 213 cm
- Musée Fabre, Montpellier.

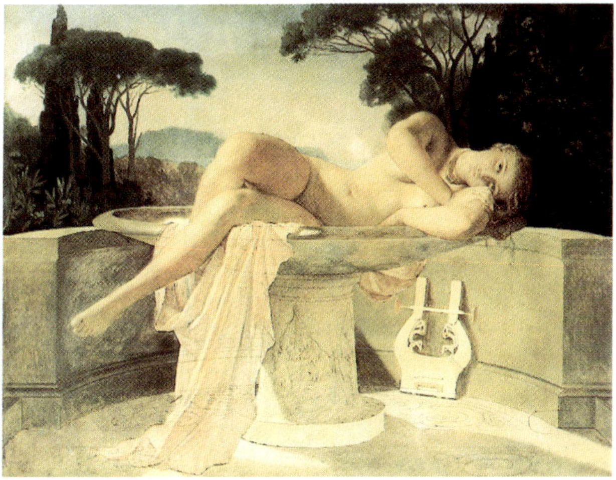

In this curiously enigmatic scene, a young woman, wearing only a necklace, is portrayed lying on a marble fountain, from which a drape hangs. The background landscape is Mediterranean. Pose and sensuality, as well as the lyre, suggest there may be some connection to the Greek lyric poet Sappho.

Young Woman on a Fountain

Paul Delaroche (Hippolyte Delaroche)

(Paris, 1797–1856)

- 1846
- oil on canvas
- 154 x 192 cm
- Musée des Beaux-Arts, Besançon

Anacreon, Bacchus and Cupid

Jean-Léon Gérôme
(Vesoul, 1824–Paris, 1904)

- 1848
- oil on canvas
- 134 x 203 cm
- Musée des Augustins, Toulouse

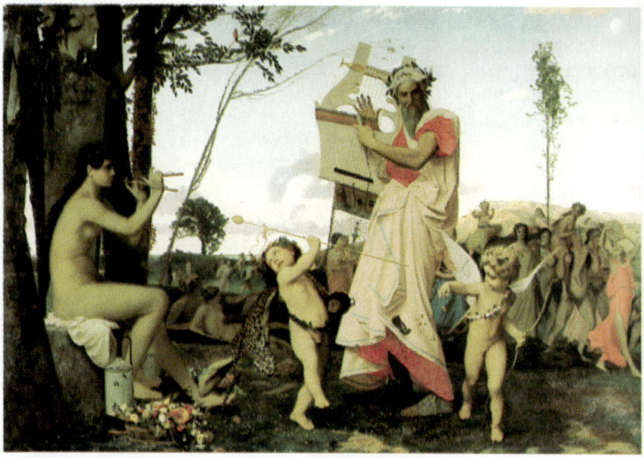

Exhibited at the 1848 Salon, this Neoclassical work is a homage to the poet Anacreon. The painter chose to concentrate his attention on classical and conventional details of pictorial content, while his handling of the problems of colour lends the nude figures a mythical and mysterious air.

Perseus and Andromeda

Eugène Delacroix
(Charenton-Saint-Maurice, near Paris, 1798–Paris, 1863)

- 1849–53
- oil on marouflé cardboard on panel
- 43.2 x 33.6 cm
- The Baltimore Museum of Art, Baltimore

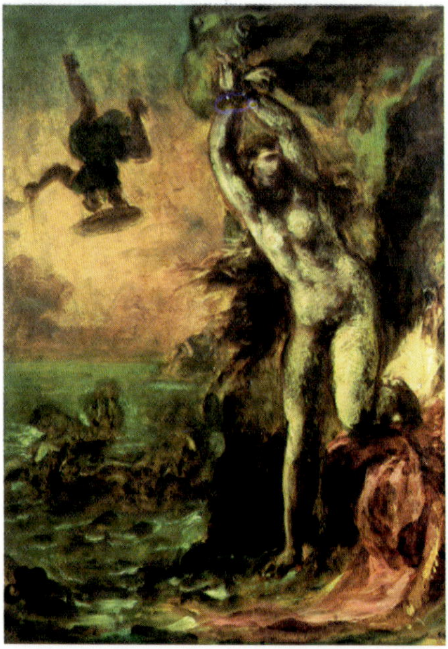

Advanced for his time, the artist understands the nude in this panel as a mass of paint, providing a minimum of detail and carrying expressionism to its limit. There is no search for sensuality, with two possible options arising: one towards painting for painting's sake; another towards the interpretation of anatomical forms.

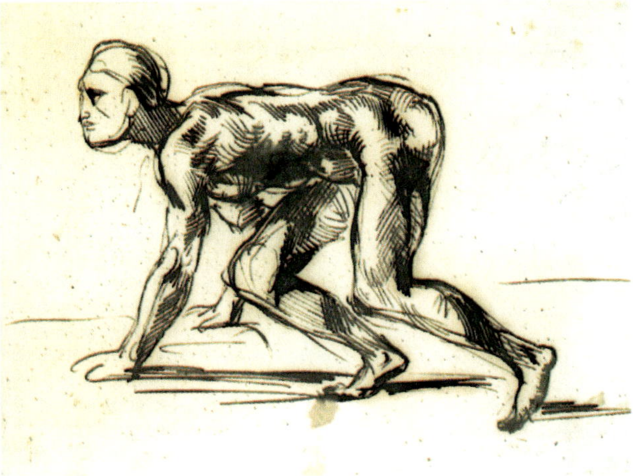

Male Nude Squatting

Eugène Delacroix
(Charenton-Saint-Maurice, near Paris, 1798–Paris, 1863)

- ca. 1850
- pen and brown ink
- 15.8 x 20.3 cm
- Musée du Louvre, Département des arts graphiques, Paris

The forms of the body are analyzed without seeking idealization. The reworking of the outline—something wholly unthinkable in Ingres—refines the overall study. The artist isolates areas of light with categorical blacks, thus determining the principal muscular areas and volumes of the body.

The theme of Susanna and the Elders is interpreted here along lines laid down by academic painting in Seville at the time. The woman's shapeliness is dignified through her pose, while the naturalism of the treatment tones down the lasciviousness of the scene. Susanna's disapproving gesture directed towards the elders displays one side of her body openly, so that its modelling is brought out yet more clearly.

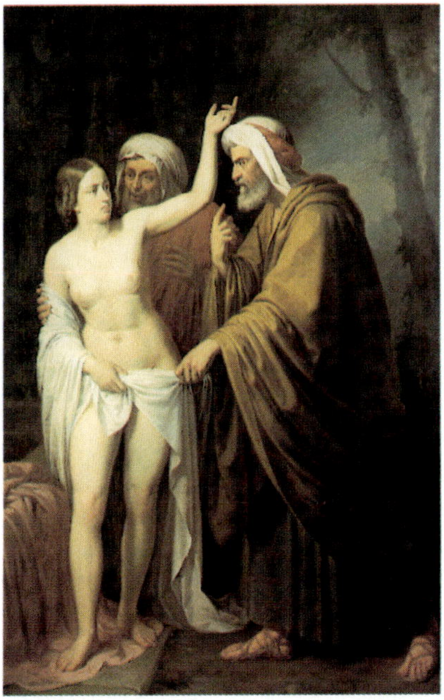

The Chaste Susanna

Antonio María Esquivel
(Seville, 1806–Madrid, 1857)

- ca. 1850
- oil on canvas
- Museo de Bellas Artes, Sevilla

Susanna and the Elders

Eugène Delacroix
(Charenton-Saint-Maurice, near Paris, 1798–Paris, 1863)

- 1850?
- oil on cardboard
- 31 x 24.8 cm
- Musée des Beaux-Arts, Reims

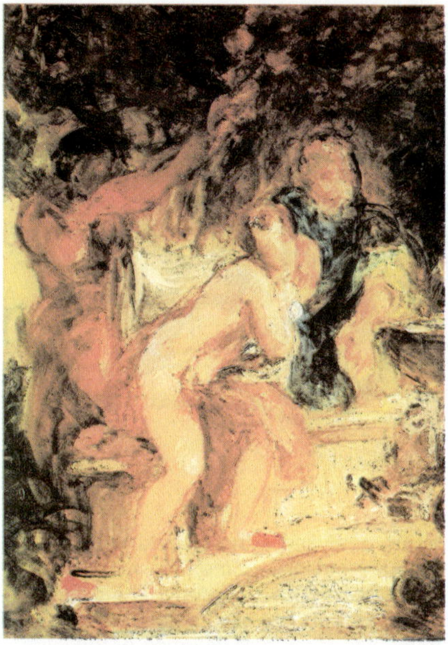

The treatment of the nude is extremely modern for the time. The body is composed of fields of paint with bold, cursory brushwork. The figure is far removed from those in traditional figure painting, for it is the object of an experiment instead of the reason for the painting. The work is a careful study of the effects of light on color, rendered with expressiveness and drama.

Marfisa and Pinabello's Lady

Eugène Delacroix
(Charenton-Saint-Maurice, near Paris, 1798–Paris, 1863)

- 1850–52
- oil on canvas
- 82 x 101 cm
- The Walters Art Gallery, Baltimore

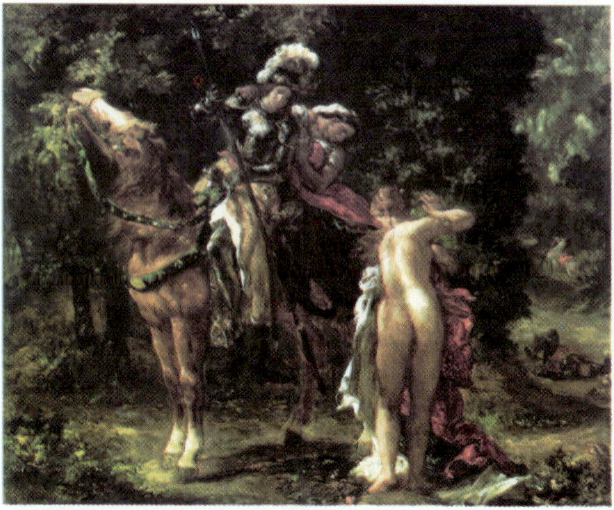

The work has reference to Ariosto's romantic epic poem Orlando Furioso. The nude female figure is powerful and strongly drawn, with strong highlights that lend it depth. The torsion of the trunk, as well as the shape of hips and thighs, bring especially feminine qualities to expression.

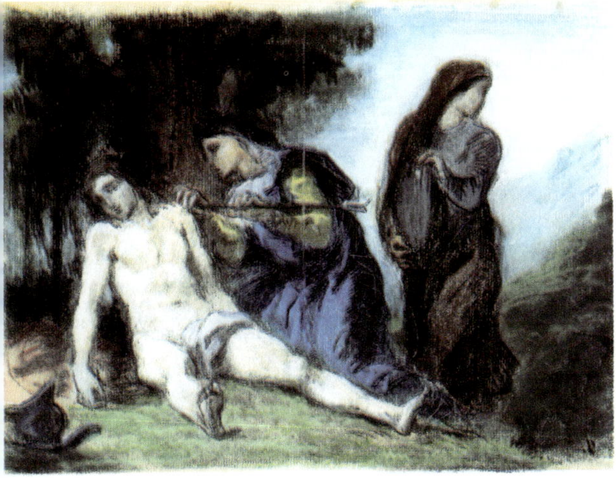

St. Sebastian Tended by the Holy Women

Eugène Delacroix
(Charenton-Saint-Maurice, near Paris, 1798–Paris, 1863)

- 1850–54
- pastel
- 18.2 x 26.5 cm
- private collection

The work depicts a male figure in strong foreshortening akin to that found in Renaissance and Baroque art. Against a dark background, illuminated body areas combine with grayer parts to define a deeply-imagined figure.

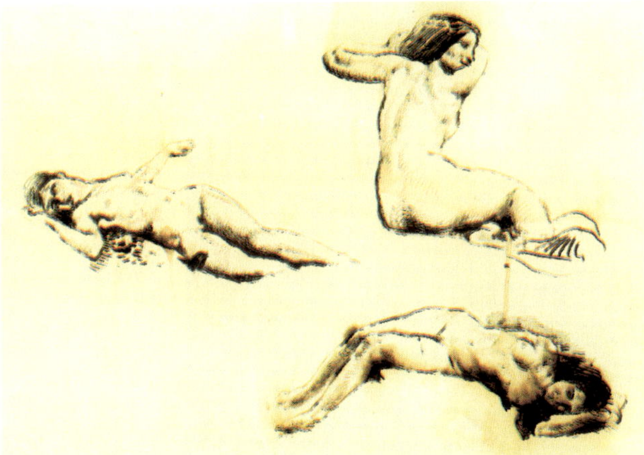

Three Studies of a Female Nude

Eugène Delacroix
(Charenton-Saint-Maurice, near Paris, 1798–Paris, 1863)

- 1850–55
- pen, brown ink and lead pencil
- 26.5 x 42.3 cm
- Musée du Louvre, Département des arts graphiques, Paris

Delacroix was greatly interested in the analysis of reality, these studies being evidence thereof and showing his skill as a draftsman. The forms are sensual, accentuated by the lines defining them, and the foreshortenings show an interest in eroticism, evident in the abandoned poses of the reclining women.

Harem Scene

Eugène Guérard
Nancy, 1821–1866

- 1851
- oil on canvas
- 32.5 x 41 cm
- Eyre and Hobhouse Ltd., London

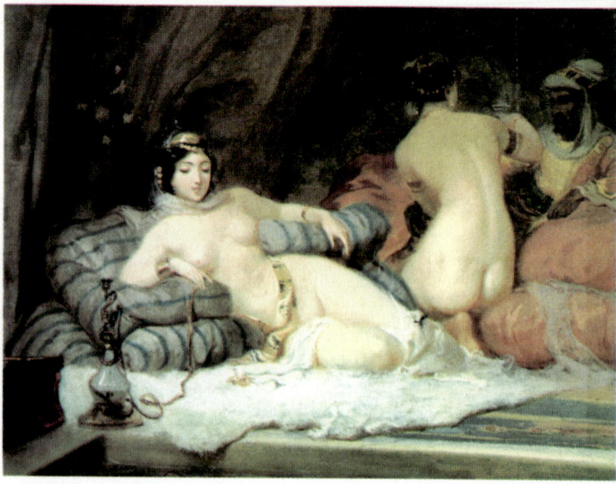

The painter has skilfully captured the mysterious intimacy of this scene, where details such as the pipe, unusual head-wear, cushions, drapes, and the presence of a bearded man function as a rich setting for the somewhat diffusely-rendered nude figures.

Sketch for Apollo Defeating the Python

Eugène Delacroix
(Charenton-Saint-Maurice, near Paris, 1798–Paris, 1863)

- 1852
- oil on canvas
- 137.5 x 102 cm
- Musées Royaux des Beaux-Arts, Brussels

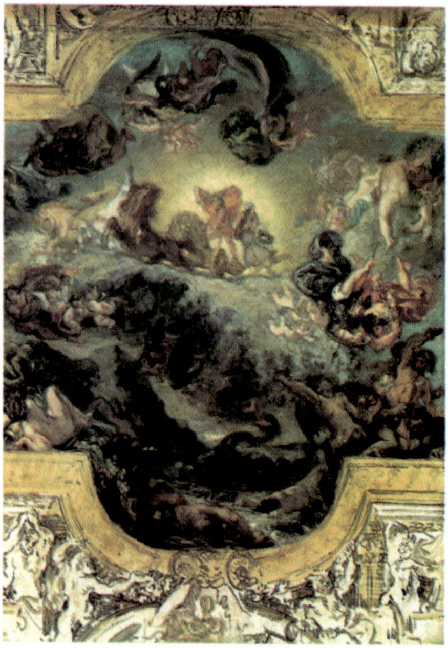

Apollo defeated the python and then mocked Eros, who, in revenge, made him fall in love with Daphne and her reject him. The rounded nudes in this work are executed quickly, with a vibrant brush and great skill in the underlying drawing and the foreshortening of the figures.

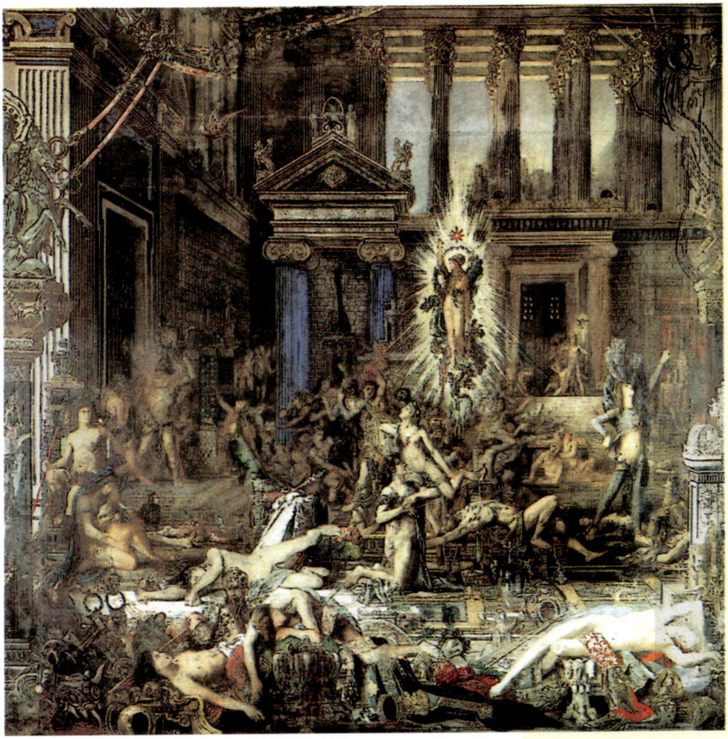

The Pretenders

Gustave Moreau
(Paris, 1826–1898)

- after 1852
- oil on canvas
- 385 x 343 cm
- Musée Gustave Moreau, Paris

Gustave Moreau developed a style that was highly distinctive in both subject and technique. His preferred subject matter included mystically intense images evoking long-dead civilizations and mythologies, which he treated with extraordinary sensuousness. His paintings are ornate, frequently including Neoclassical architecture and lively figures. These characteristics can be seen in this work, marked by symbolism and an enormous array of details, the result of his limitless visions and fertile imagination. This led the artist to execute countless preliminary studies in watercolors. He would start a work and leave it, then return to it and retouch it numerous times. Many of the nudes in this painting are brilliantly conceived. The artist took great care to cover their genitalia and many of their poses, in addition to being highly unusual, create a remarkable sense of uninhibited movement and great expressiveness. The bodies, modeled with shade, have a delicate appearance and carefully-drawn forms, which enhance the sensual atmosphere of the scene.

Female Nude

William Mulready
(Ennis, 1786–Bayswater, London, 1863)

- 1853
- pencil on paper
- 18.5 x 13 cm
- private collection

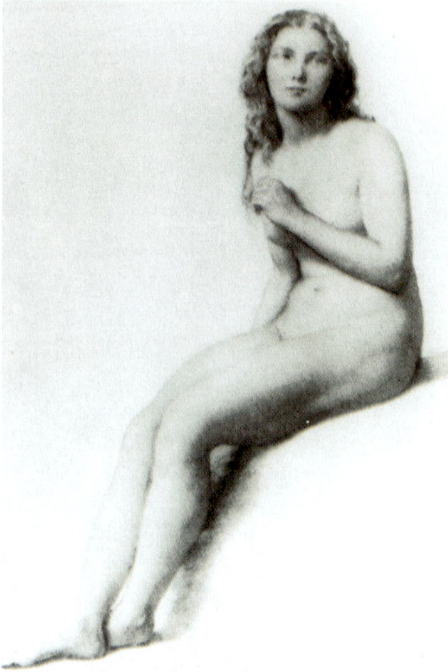

Mulready, who was a member of the Royal Academy, presents here a skilfully-executed female study of an almost sculptural quality. The subtle shading succeeds in lending the figure great plasticity.

The Apotheosis of Napoleon

Jean-Auguste-Dominique Ingres
(Montauban, 1780–Paris, 1867)

- 1853
- oil on canvas
- 48 x 48 cm
- Musée Carnavalet, Paris

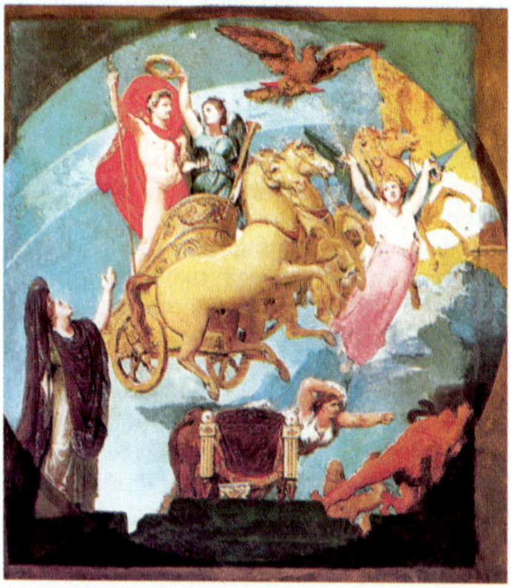

Napoleon is depicted nude and idealized as a hero; his face is that of a Roman emperor, while his body is a Greek hero's, and yet there is a certain, at least facial, resemblance between the real person and the representation. Ingres evidently intended to produce an image that would give rise to ridicule, as Napoleon's stature was completely unlike the Olympian proportions given him here.

In this abstract study, the figures and objects are depicted in a conventional manner. The finish is precise and the female forms are distinguished by an interest in traditional iconography, while the light enhances the volumes.

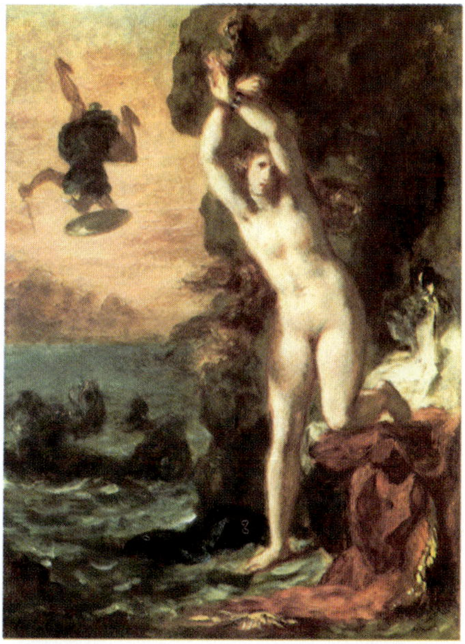

Perseus and Andromeda

Eugène Delacroix
(Charenton-Saint-Maurice, near Paris, 1798–Paris, 1863)

- 1853
- oil on marouflé paper on canvas
- 43.8 x 32.2 cm
- Staatsgalerie, Stuttgart

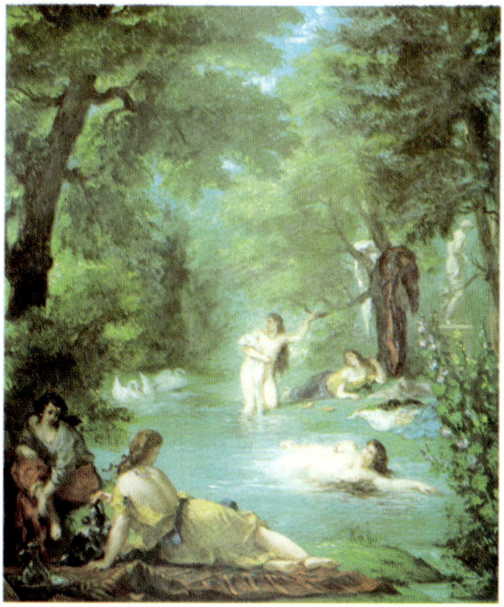

Women at Turkish Bath

Eugène Delacroix
(Charenton-Saint-Maurice, near Paris, 1798–Paris, 1863)

- 1854
- oil on canvas
- 92 x 78 cm
- Wadsworth Atheneum, Harford

In an exotically diffuse setting, the painter has placed his very precisely imagined scene of tranquil enjoyment, where cool colors hold aloof from and, at the same time, merge with the soft complexions of the bathers' bodies. It is the painterly record of a spontaneous moment, at once poetic and sensual, yet handled with delicate meticulousness.

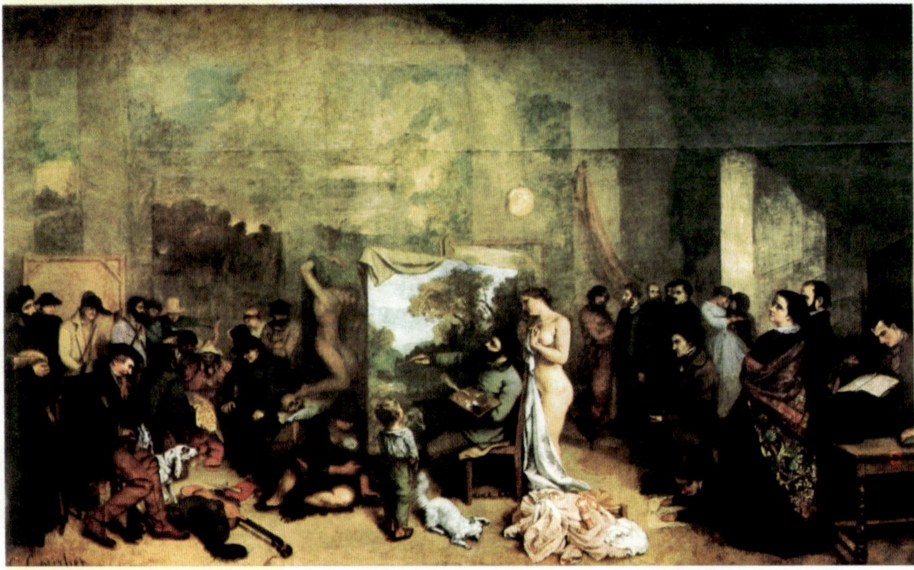

The Painter's Studio

Gustave Courbet
(Ornans, 1819–La Tour-de-Peilz, Switzerland, 1877)

- 1854–55
- oil on canvas
- 360 x 598 cm
- Musée d'Orsay, Paris

This painting is an allegory that sums up Courbet's artistic life. In it he portrays both his studio and himself, as the artist-hero. The composition contains portraits of some of the painter's contemporaries and friends, as well as various references to social topics of the day. The figures are arranged in three groups: on the right we see the painter's friends; in the middle, the artist himself, and on the left, both wealthy and impoverished members of society. The naked woman next to Courbet is the muse who inspires his art. Although she has a comely body, she is far from idealized. The shadows modeling her smooth, glowing skin lend it a marble-like quality. As its brightest element, she forms the focal point of the painting. Her naked body is executed with particular care, for she represents the painter's devotion to his art and to the viewer.

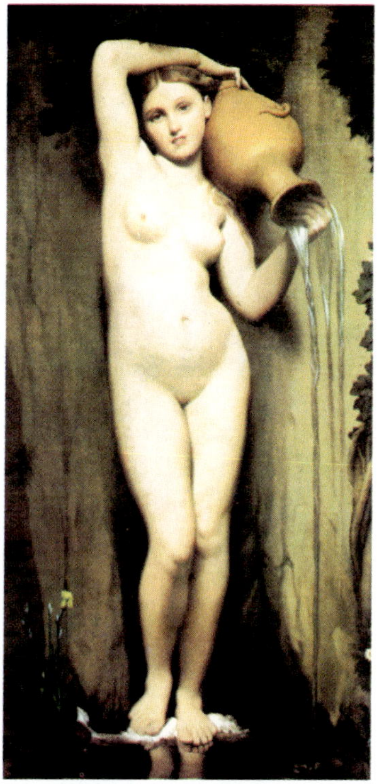

The Spring

Jean-Auguste-Dominique Ingres

(Montauban, 1780–Paris, 1867)

- 1856
- oil on canvas
- 164 x 82 cm
- Musée du Louvre, Paris

In this work, Ingres makes the female figure symbolize the source of a river, with a direct influence of his own work Venus Anadyomene, from 1808. The artist painted two similar works on the subject, the last one a year before his death. The highly sensual nude recalls an adolescent, and the genre of painting derives from Renaissance art, in which nymphs, children and elderly men frequently symbolize rivers and springs. The woman's forms are naturalistically rendered, not deformed for the sake of aesthetics, as in other works by this artist. The proportions, modeling and volumes are so exquisite that the complexion appears almost tactile to the eyes. The gesture of the woman's right arm, raised above her head, is remarkably coquettish. Her candid gaze at the viewer is nearly hypnotic and her forms recall the gentle flow of water.

The Triumph of Genius

Eugène Delacroix
(Charenton-Saint-Maurice, near Paris, 1798–Paris, 1863)

- pen and sepia ink with lead on paper
- 26.3 x 35.1 cm
- The Metropolitan Museum of Art, New York

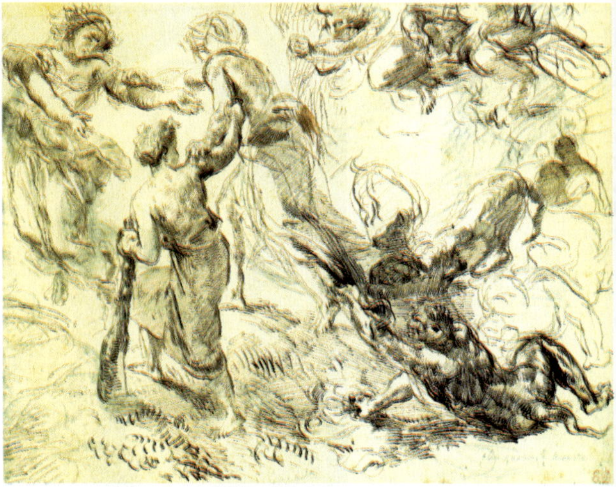

These nudes, executed with great spontaneity, are not far removed from the artist's paintings. He still abides by academic rules here, although there is a certain preoccupation to break with the most traditional artistic forms.

The Flutist

Marià Fortuny i Marsal (Mariano José Bernardo Fortuny y Marsal)
(Reus, Catalonia, 1838–Rome, 1847)

- 1859
- lithograph
- 61 x 46.5 cm
- Real Academia de Bellas Artes de Sant Jordi, Barcelona

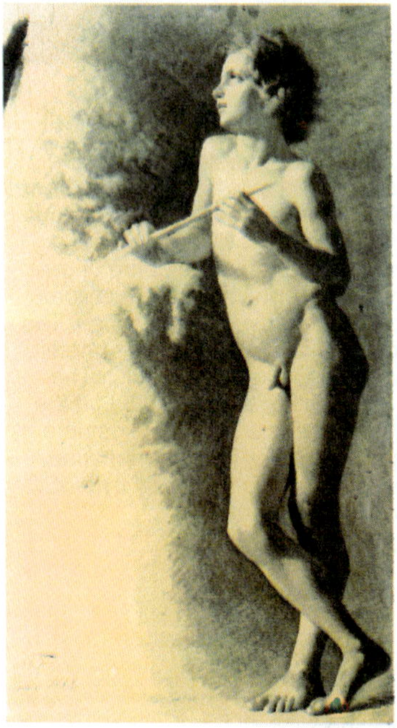

Fortuny was one of the best draftsmen of his age. His acquaintance with human anatomy was profound, and he was a skilled and meticulous observer. His nudes are highly romantic, yet extremely precise, and they display enormous virtuosity. This boy, with the brilliantly-lit area to the left, is an outstanding example of how draftsmanship can transcend realism while remaining in contact with truth.

The drawing is a striking illustration of the countless possibilities the human body has to offer and how the competent artist discovers and reflects his subject matter, without the need to resort to concepts or complementary images.

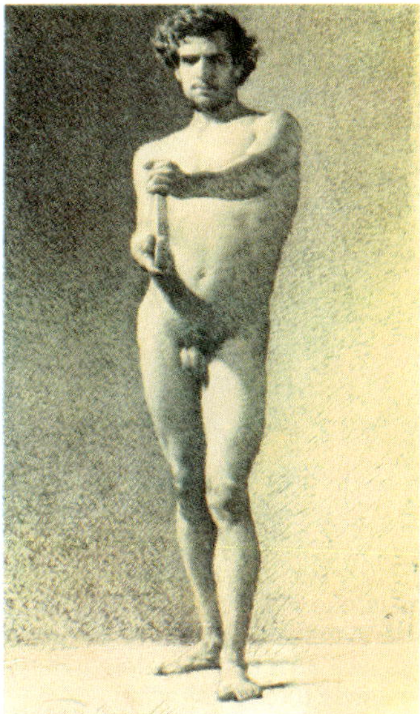

Discus Thrower from the Front

Marià Fortuny i Marsal (Mariano José Bernardo Fortuny y Marsal)
(Reus, Catalonia, 1838–Rome, 1847)

- ink on pink paper
- Real Academia de Bellas Artes de Sant Jordi, Barcelona

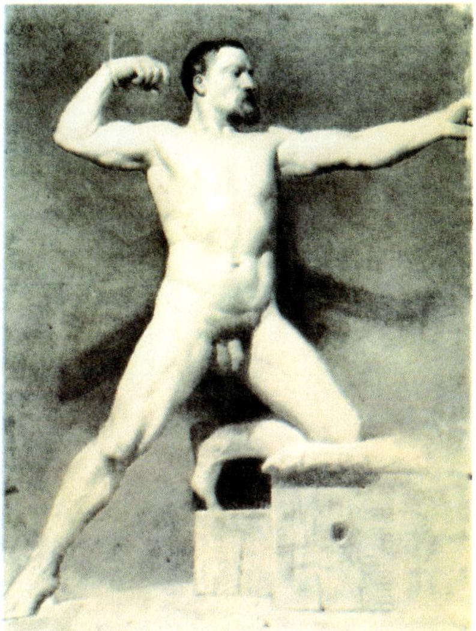

Archer

Marià Fortuny i Marsal (Mariano José Bernardo Fortuny y Marsal)
(Reus, Catalonia, 1838–Rome, 1847)

- 1859
- charcoal on paper
- Real Academia de Bellas Artes de Sant Jordi, Barcelona

This drawing is a compendium of everything an artist aspires to. Without resorting to any particular technique or system of idealization, the artist manages to convey all the strength, expressiveness and sensuality encapsulated in this masculine body; a homage to humanity, an ode to each of the values with which he is endowed. It is not surprising that these works made the impression they did throughout Western Europe.

Semi-nude Male and Reclining Lion

Eugène Delacroix
(Charenton-Saint-Maurice, near Paris, 1798–Paris, 1863)

- 1856
- pen, brown ink and brown wash
- 23.3 x 35.8 cm
- Musée du Louvre, Département des arts graphiques, Paris

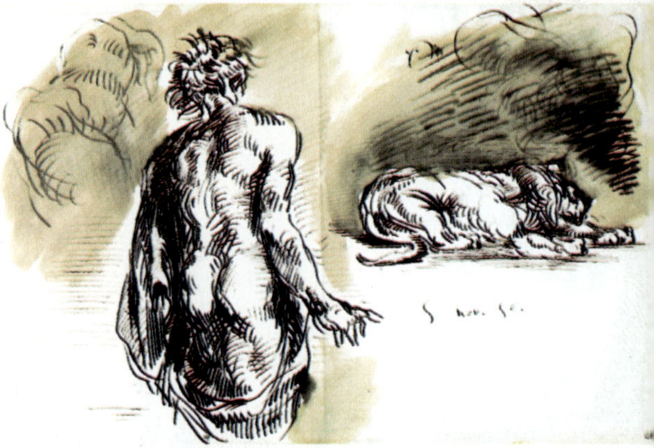

This male nude seen from behind is interesting for the distance of the figure's conception from academic formality. Nonetheless, there is an unusual foreshortening of the arm as well as a distinct interest in defining the principal muscle masses through shading.

Diana and Actaeon

Eugène Delacroix
(Charenton-Saint-Maurice, near Paris, 1798–Paris, 1863)

- 1856–63
- oil on canvas
- 198 x 165.7 cm
- Museu de Arte, São Paulo

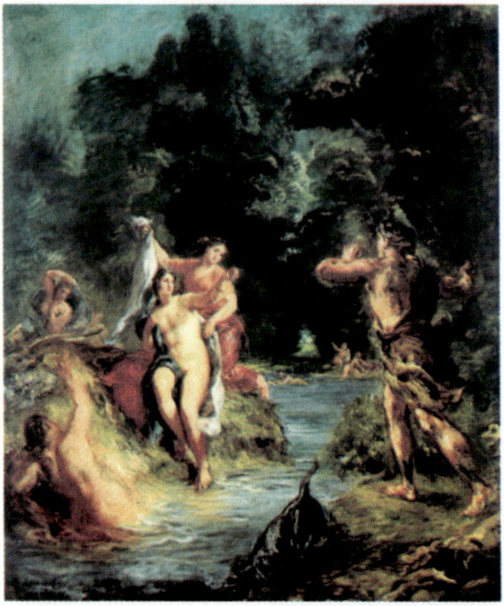

Diana's nude figure is clearly defined, in accordance with Neoclassical ideals. She is of near-heroic proportions and somewhat androgynous.

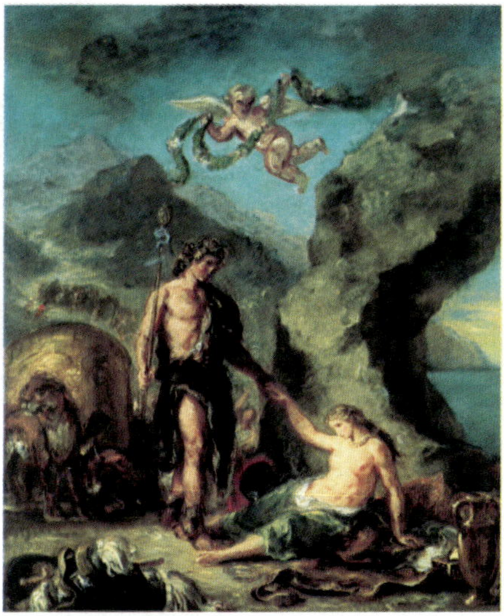

Bacchus and Ariadne

Eugène Delacroix
(Charenton-Saint-Maurice, near Paris, 1798–Paris, 1863)

- 1856–63
- oil on canvas
- 198 x 165.7 cm
- Museu de Arte, São Paulo

Bacchus discovers Ariadne on the island of Naxos after she has been abandoned by Theseus. Her naked body is robust and recalls certain rapid sketches done by Rubens, her shape almost sculpturesque and the handling of narrative pictorial elements spontaneous and fresh.

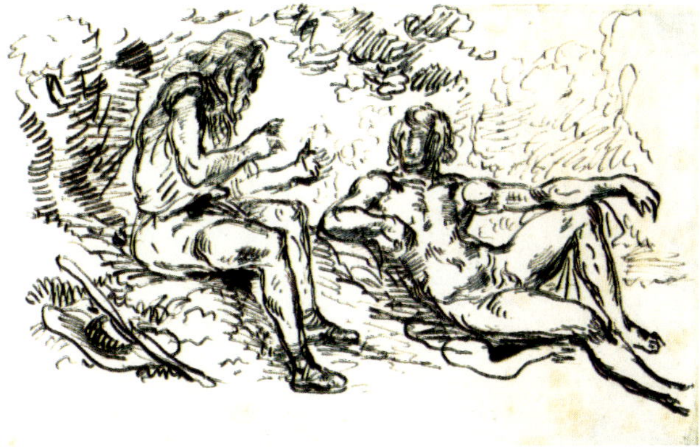

Aged Traveler Conversing with a Youth in a Landscape

Eugène Delacroix
(Charenton-Saint-Maurice, near Paris, 1798–Paris, 1863)

- 1858–62
- pen and brown ink
- 20.1 x 30.6 cm
- Musée du Louvre, Département des arts graphiques, Paris

The nude of the reclining man is an academic drawing with a habitual pose. The frontal foreshortenings of the leg and arm on the other figure are executed fluently, with a resolute, rapid line. Nevertheless, the details are dispensed with once again in this work, and only the most essential embellishments are included.

Young Spartans Exercising

Edgar Degas
(Paris, 1834–1917)

- ca. 1860
- oil on canvas
- 109.2 x 154.3 cm
- National Gallery, London

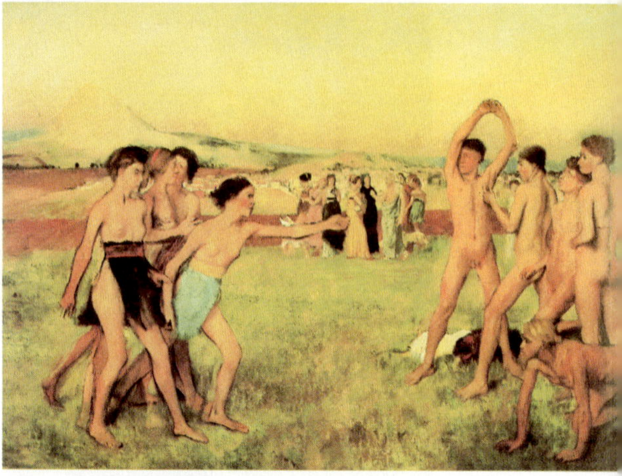

The boys in the right foreground seem to be showing off in front of the girls, who are responding to them. The three groups of figures are arranged in a semicircle and the canvas is imbued with a golden light that models the bodies. Degas shows his interest in combining different body types in a variety of poses within a single scene. The artist once confessed to having used Parisian street urchins as models for this work.

Two Studies of a Male Nude Seated on a Stone

Eugène Delacroix
(Charenton-Saint-Maurice, near Paris, 1798–Paris, 1863)

- 1860
- pen and brown ink
- 23.5 x 35.7 cm
- Musée des Beaux-Arts et d'Archéologie, Besançon

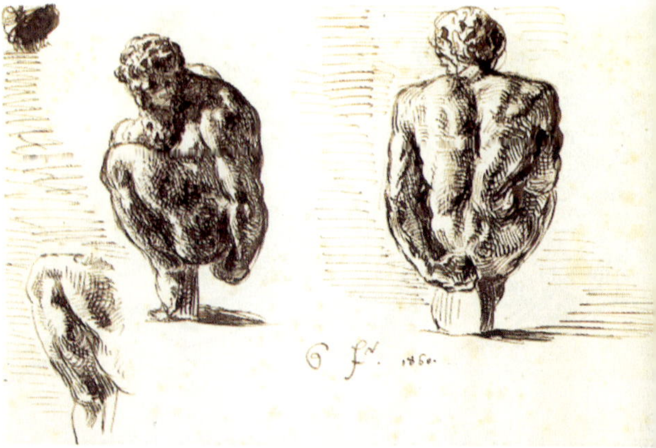

In this nude of sculptural volumes, the man consists of a compact mass, the illumination of which allows his muscular and anatomical details to be distinguished. The shadows are dense, such that the bright areas acquire presence and greater luminosity as a result of the contrast.

This study verges on near-photographic realism, which seems to issue from the hand of a sculptor more than that of a painter.

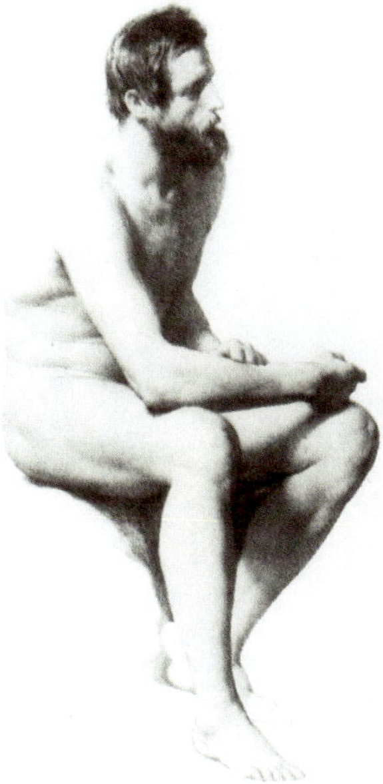

Male Nude Study

William Mulready
(Ennis, 1786–Bayswater, London, 1863)

- 1860
- pencil on paper
- 53 x 32 cm
- National Gallery of Ireland, Dublin

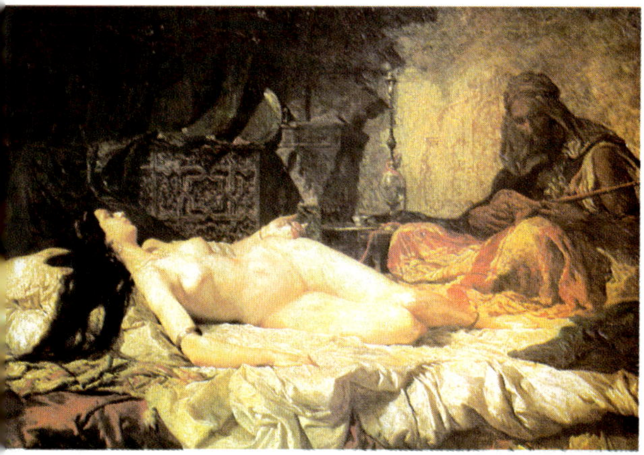

Oriental themes were much in vogue among 19th-century artists, such as Ingres or Delacroix. Fortuny also created works of great beauty in the style, as we may see here. The naked figure of the woman is plunged in powerful light, which contrasts strongly with the dark background, whereby depth and plasticity are conferred on her. Fortuny worked this figure up from a simple sketch.

Odalisque

Marià Fortuny i Marsal (Mariano José Bernardo Fortuny y Marsal)
(Reus, Catalonia, 1838–Rome, 1847)

- 1861
- oil on cardboard
- 54 x 79 cm
- Museo de Arte Moderno, Barcelona

The Chaste Susanna Bathing

Jean-Jacques Henner
(Bernwiller, Alsace, 1829 –Paris, 1905)

- 1864
- oil on canvas
- Musée Henner, Paris

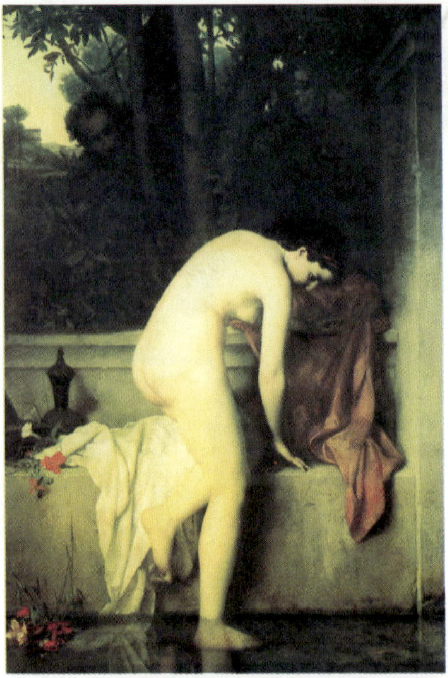

Suggestiveness and mystery have often pushed aside the biblical theme and focused attention on Susanna, as is the case here. As viewers we thus become accomplices of the Elders, depicted here spying on her from the dark background. For us, however, Susanna stands out almost luminously, the curves of her body accentuated by her pose.

The Bathers, or Bathers in the Seine

Edouard Manet
(Paris, 1832–1883)

- 1862–65
- oil on canvas
- 132 x 98 cm
- Museu de Arte, São Paulo

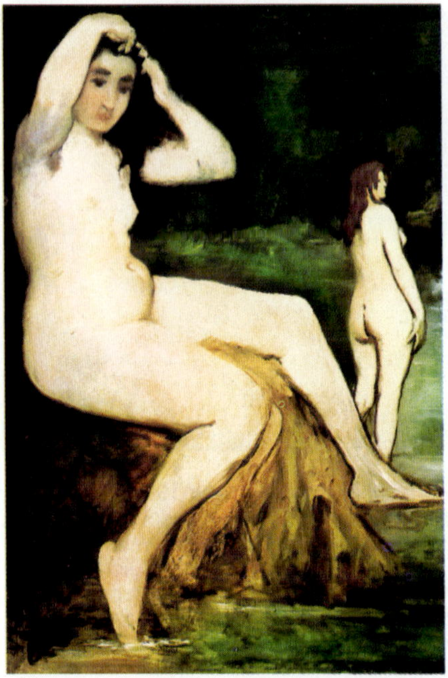

The nudes are rendered with loose brushwork, engendering two large fields of bright paint, in which only the most basic forms can be discerned, that is, the outlines of the figures' bodies and some form-lending shadows, such as those used to articulate the buttocks of the nude in the background. The nude in the foreground is so brightly lit that her breasts seem scarcely three-dimensional.

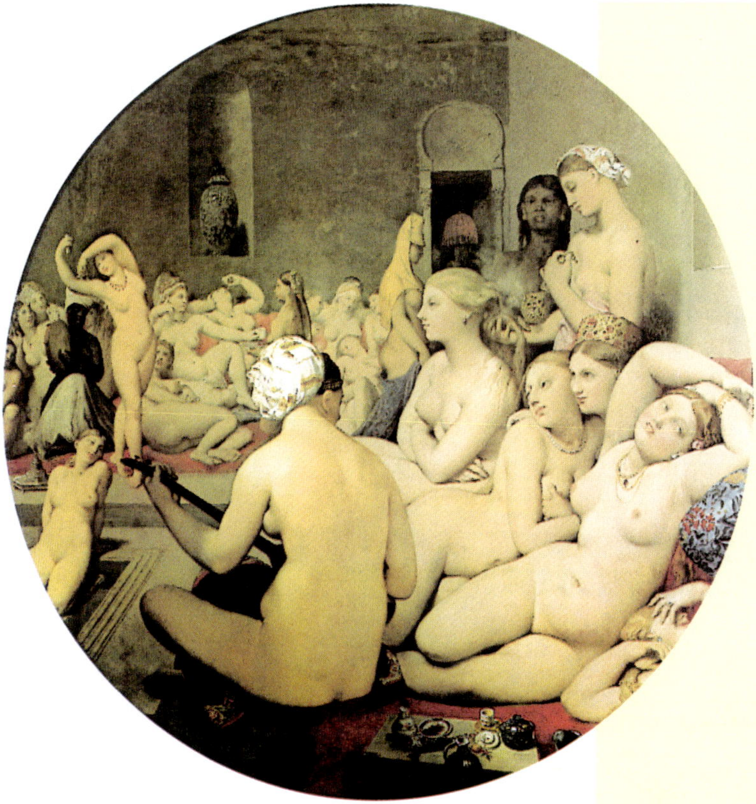

he sensuous, not to say sensual, nude figures in this scene onstitute a veritable ode to female beauty. Their outlines ave been softened, lines have been altered and blurred in he interest of aesthetic qualities. The room's palpable tmosphere causes the figures beyond the guitar-playing voman to become progressively less well-defined, until they irtually merge into the background. The painting is a fine xample of the work of this classicist and academic artist, vho strongly influenced many moderate European romantics, hampioning balanced composition and the superiority of raftsmanship over color. The work demonstrates the ease nd mastery with which he painted the human figure. Ingres, owever, did not lack his detractors, owing to his intolerant ttitude towards the newer artistic developments of his time.

The Turkish Bath

Jean-Auguste-Dominique Ingres
(Montauban, 1780–Paris, 1867)

- 1862
- oil on canvas
- 108 cm diameter
- Musée du Louvre, Paris

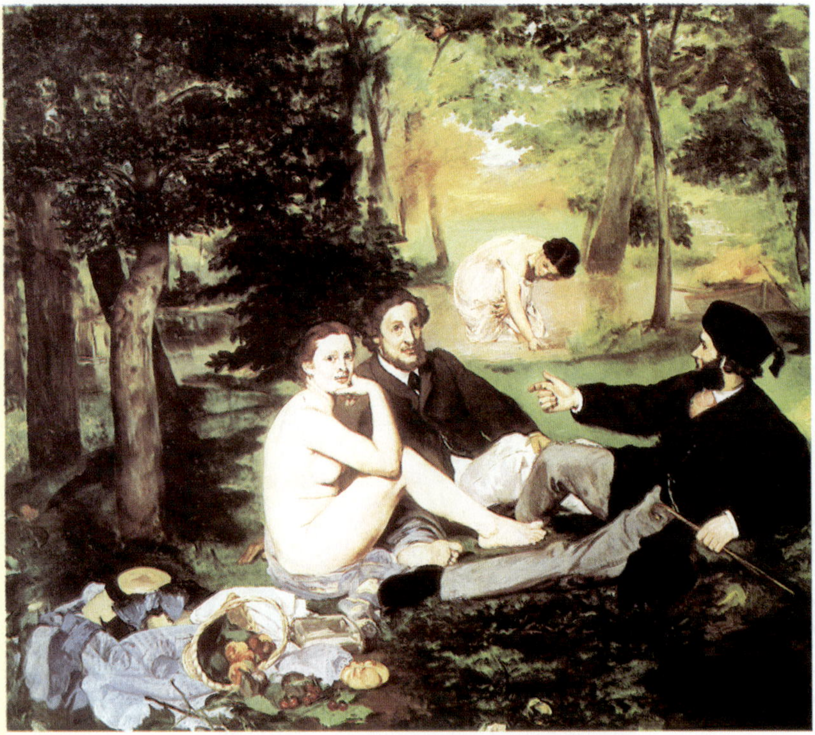

Déjeuner sur l'Herbe

Edouard Manet
(Paris, 1832–1883)

- 1863
- oil on canvas
- 214 x 270 cm
- Musée d'Orsay, Paris

Edouard Manet is considered to be a harbinger of Impressionism. This canvas, owing to the candid, self-assured gaze of the naked woman in it, received harsh criticism from no lesser a figure than Napoleon III. Other contemporaries of the artist dismissed it as "anti-academic." The scene shows two gentlemen, Eugène Manet, the painter's brother, and Ferdinand Leenhoff, the painter's brother-in-law, seated on the floor of a forest, conversing with a woman, Victorine Meurend, Manet's favorite model. The other woman, in the background, wearing a white garment, is washing her feet in a brook. In the left foreground is a basket of fruit with the leftovers of the luncheon. The painting is executed with flat, starkly contrasting colors, its most original aspect being the unusual manner in which the light is reflected on the men's dark frock coats as well as on the pinkish white skin of the nude. The landscape contains several areas of bluish green tones, where the foliage is reflected in the water's surface.

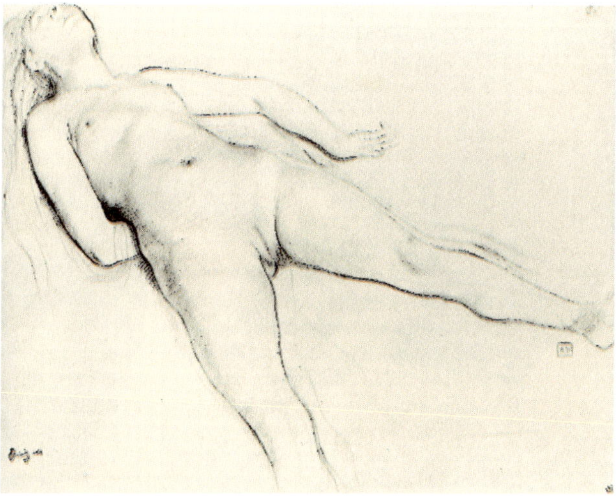

Nude

Edgar Degas
(Paris, 1843–1917)

- ca. 1863
- charcoal
- 26.5 x 35.1 cm
- Musée du Louvre, Cabinet des Dessins, Paris

The figure is the sole element of the drawing, with one or two shadows that define the outlines of her body. Even though the pose is modern and somewhat risqué, the drawing is executed in accordance with academic criteria, as much in the line as in the volume. The perfectly rendered figure conveys all the artist wishes to convey: a sensual body in an attractive, striking pose. This work bears witness to Degas' fascination with the female nude.

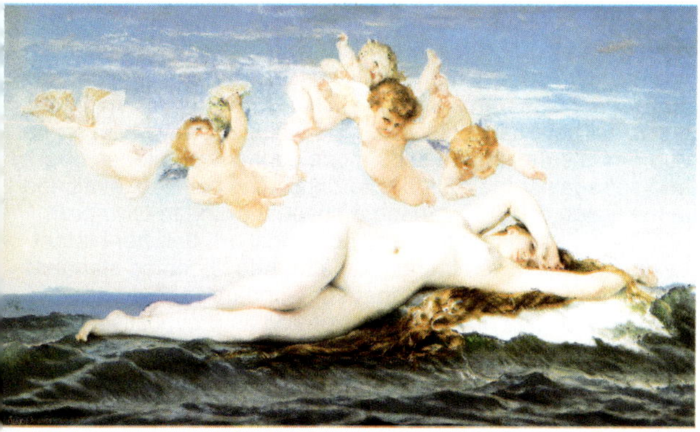

The Birth of Venus

Alexandre Cabanel
(Paris, 1823–1889)

- 1863
- oil on canvas
- 130 x 225 cm
- Musée d'Orsay, Paris

The surface innocence of the scene contrasts sharply with the erotic connotations with which the subject is imbued: the goddess not only displays her beauty, but entices the viewer. With its meticulous draftsmanship and modeling, the painting is a fine example of Second Empire work, against which the Impressionists were later to rebel.

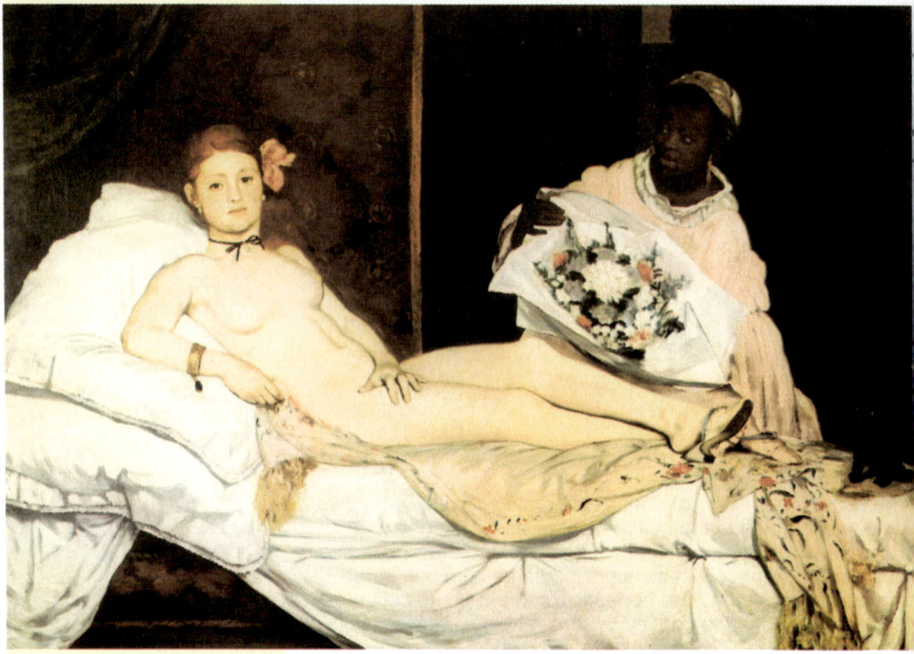

Olympia

Edouard Manet
(Paris, 1832–1883)

- 1863
- oil on canvas
- 130 x 190 cm
- Musée d'Orsay, Paris

In 1890 this painting was donated to the Musée du Luxembourg. In 1908 it was transferred to the Musée du Louvre, in Paris.

Here, Manet strips the subject of all idealization and concerns himself solely with painting a young nude courtesan, lying on a bed, her arrogant face gazing defiantly at the viewer, and paying no attention to the servant who offers her a bunch of flowers. The painter has skillfully captured her strong character, her delicate forms and pink flesh, with a well-illuminated body that contrasts subtly with the white sheets, which reveal numerous creases and folds modeled in various tones of gray and set against the dark background. The painting, exhibited in the Salon of 1865, caused a scandal owing to Olympia's pose, which appears to parody classical art, and her blatant sexuality, which was thought an affront to accepted standards of decorum. Even the fact that she appears to cover her genitals with one hand was interpreted as provocative—and certain sections of Parisian society found her insolent, insouciant expression to be offensive.

The artist's interest in light and color is evident, although the influence of Spanish and French academic painting is clearly far greater. Indeed, adopting such a style was necessary in order to take part in art competitions of the day

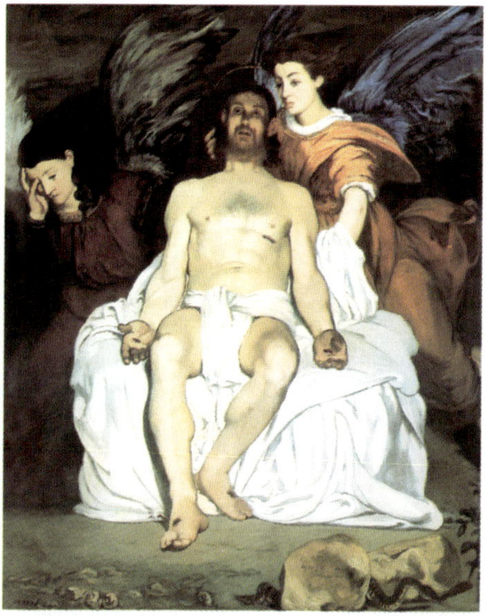

The Dead Christ and the Angels

Edouard Manet
(Paris, 1832–1833)

- 1864
- oil on canvas
- 179.4 x 149.9 cm
- Metropolitan Museum of Art, New York. Bequest of Mrs. H. O. Havemeyer, 1929, from the H.O. Havemeyer Collection

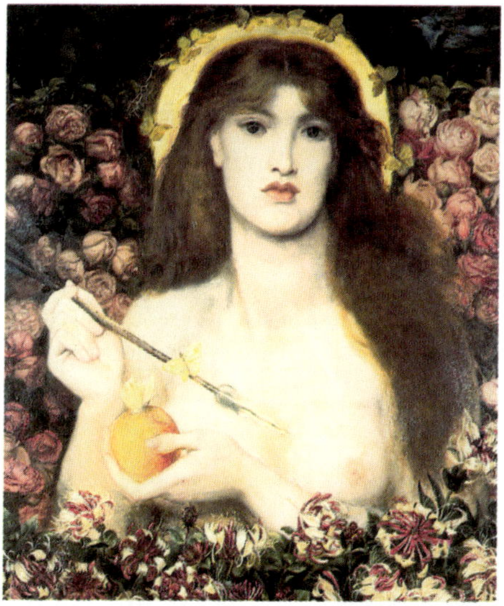

Venus Verticordia

Dante Gabriel Rossetti
(London, 1828–Birchington-on-Sea, 1882)

- 1864–68
- oil on canvas
- 38 x 27.5 cm
- Cotes Art Gallery and Museum, Bournemouth

This Venus' markedly androgynous features are nonetheless sensual. Her angularity and fullness of body, which we see here particularly in the jaw and neck, are reminiscent of certain figures by Raphael. A soft atmospheric veil seems to hang over parts of the picture.

Torso

Théodore Géricault
(Rouen, 1791–Paris, 1824)

- ca. 1865
- black pencil and watercolor
- 55.7 x 45.1 cm
- Musée Ingres, Montauban

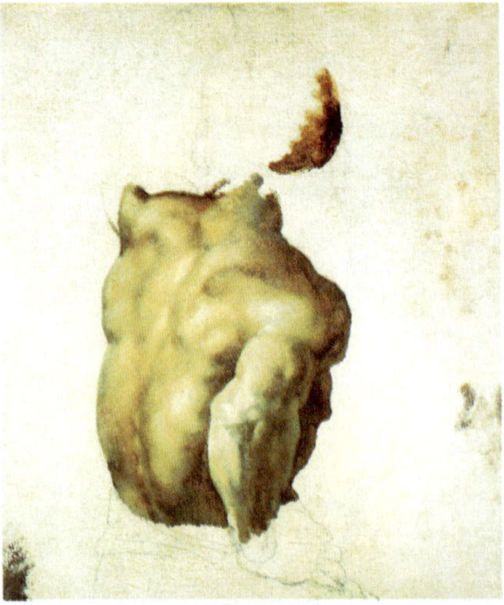

Here the artist has created a powerfully expressive torso in mixed media. Chromatically very well balanced, the muscles and spinal column have been brought out beautifully through the use of light and shade. Anatomical detail here has received scrupulous attention.

Jason and Medea

Gustave Moreau
(Paris 1826–1898)

- 1865
- oil on canvas
- 204 x 115 cm
- Musée d'Orsay, Paris

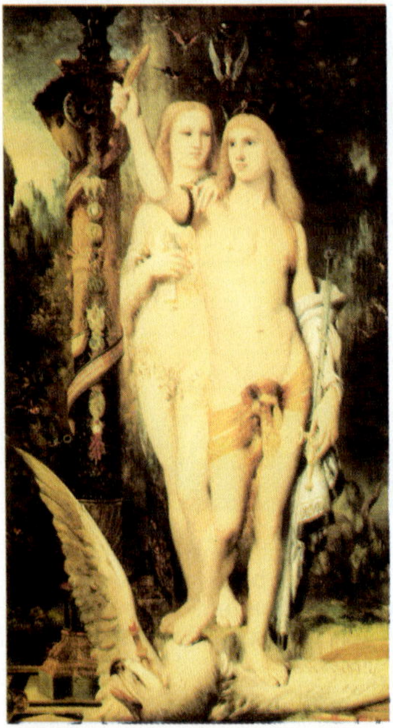

The nude of Jason is as ambiguous as that of Medea. Moreau's vision of the nude was different to that of the Academy. The forms of his nudes were androgynous, thus establishing an original canon diverging from that of neoclassicism and providing a vision approaching symbolism.

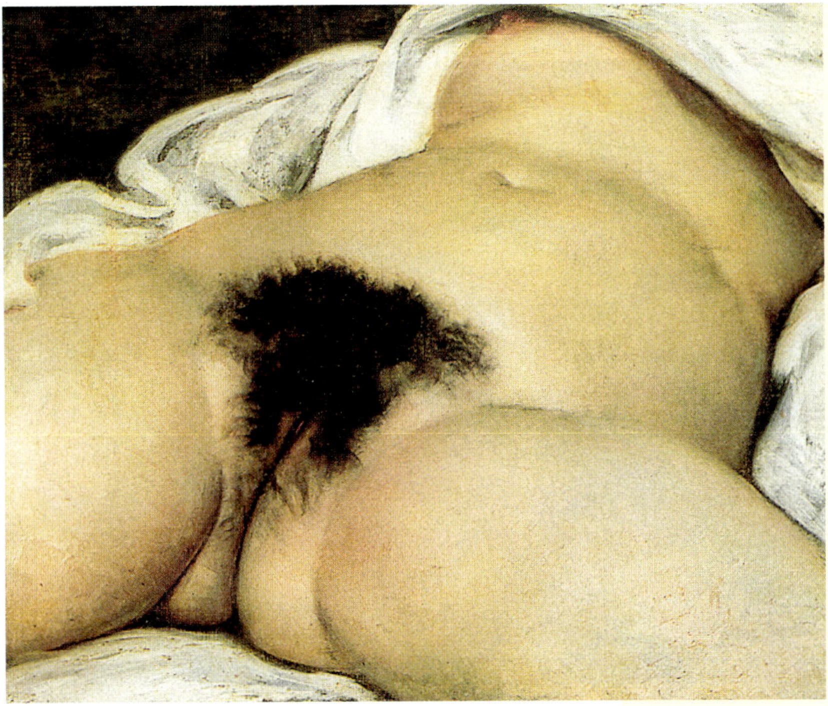

The Origin of the World

Gustave Courbet
(Ornans, 1819–La Tour-de-Peilz, Switzerland, 1877)

- 1865–66
- oil on canvas
- 55 x 46 cm
- Musée du Louvre, Paris

Between the painting of this canvas and its arrival in the Louvre, a considerable time elapsed. In an era of double standards, which outwardly shunned sex and the representation of it, this work both attracted and repelled. Courbet, however, was open-minded and psychologist enough to know that sex lies not in any representation of it but in the mind, and he often dealt with the topic in a candid and explicit manner, heedless of conventional sensibility. This won him admirers as well as critics. Flawless composition and technical execution give rise here to a work of powerful realism. The theme's ambiguity, woman's intimate parts as nest of pleasure and as cradle of life, makes it a work that it is difficult to be indifferent to. Courbet's mistress Joanna Hiffierman was his model.

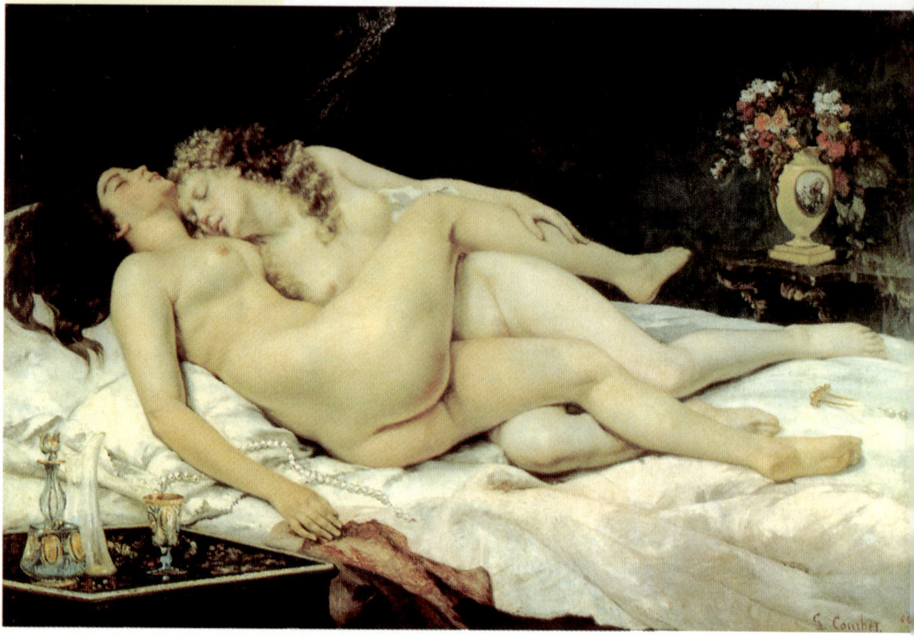

Sleep

Gustave Courbet
(Ornans, 1819–La Tour-de-Peilz, Switzerland, 1877)

- 1866
- oil on canvas
- 135 x 200 cm
- Musée du Petit Palais, Paris

Gustave Courbet depicted highly realistic scenes of remarkable formal beauty. Owing to his unconventional subject matter, and to the controversy surrounding it, his works were frequently deemed scandals, even among his friends. In this painting, two women are shown making love. Lesbian love was also depicted by other artists, who, for very little money, hired prostitutes to pose as models. Courbet demonstrates here his mastery of the female nude. The poses, the expressive faces and the decoration are all painstakingly executed. Combined, the various pictorial elements lend grace and sculptural beauty to the scene. The figures are sensitively rendered, their bodies delicate and their soft, voluptuous forms highly sensual. Such technical perfection and restraint underscore the painter's provocative intention.

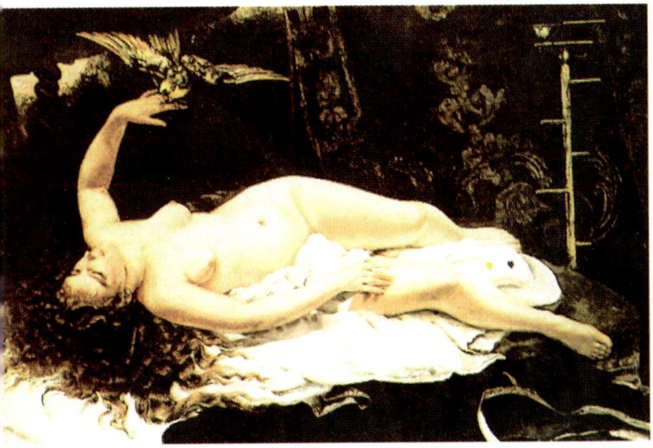

Woman with a Parrot

Gustave Courbet
(Ornans, 1819–La Tour-de-Peilz, Switzerland, 1877)

- 1866
- oil on canvas
- The Museum of Modern Art, New York

This canvas is an elegant example of the artist's work. His lines are steady yet spontaneous, evoking a singular beauty, lyricism and emotion. It is precisely these values that heighten the erotic and expressive force of the painting, which the artist conveys in the woman's daring pose, her luminous naked body set against a dark background, her lack of modesty and her disconcertingly provocative gaze.

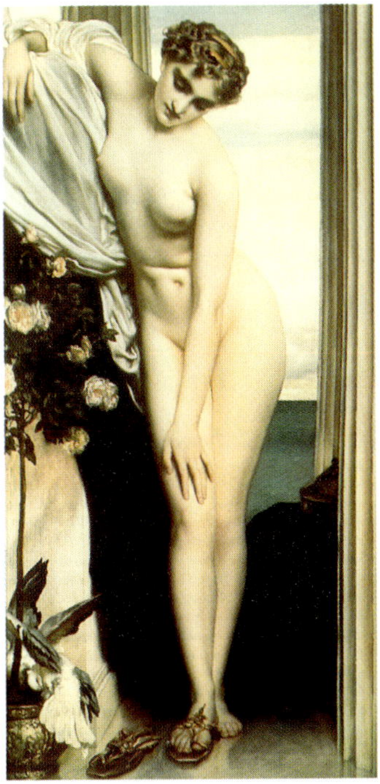

Venus Disrobing for the Bath

Frederic Leighton
(Yorkshire, 1849–1917)

- 1866–67
- oil on canvas
- 200.8 x 90.2 cm
- Royal Academy, London

Venus, depicted here with somewhat androgynous facial features, is shown undressing to bathe. The soft shadows bring out her bodily shapes, while her upraised arm causes her right breast to appear in profile. The contrapposto of her position accentuates the curve of her hip.

Diana

Pierre-Auguste Renoir

(Limoges, 1841–Cagnes-sur-Mer, 1919)

- 1867
- oil on canvas
- 199.5 x 129.5 cm
- National Gallery of Art, Chester Dale Collection, Washington, D.C.

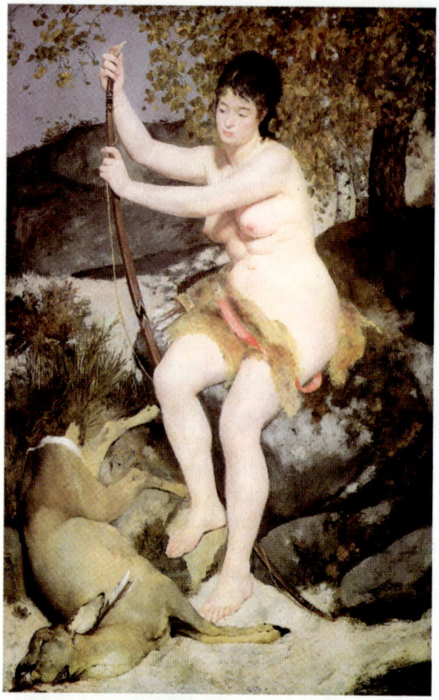

Although the protagonist portrayed here exhibits the attributes of a goddess, she is clearly an ordinary woman disguised as Diana. Our detection of this fact can be ascribed to Courbet's uncanny brand of realism, which is far removed from that of the academic tradition

The Abduction

Paul Cézanne

(Aix-en-Provence, 1839–1906)

- 1867
- oil on canvas
- 89.5 x 116.2 cm
- The Provost and Fellows of King's College, Cambridge, Keynes Collection. On loan to the Fitzwilliam Museum

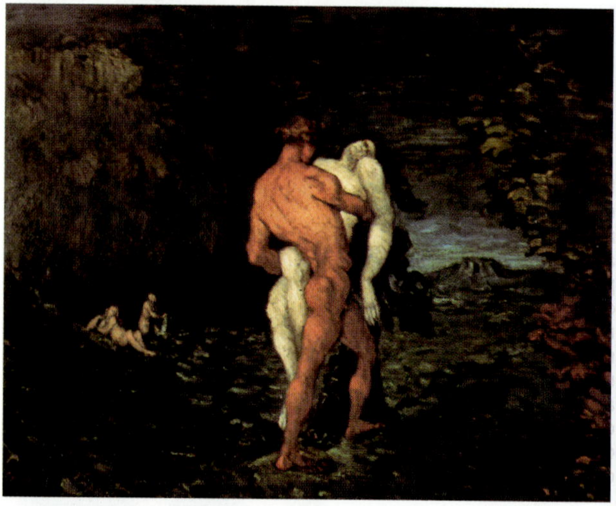

Despite the schematic nature of the figures, the artist skillfully conveys the action of the two protagonists, an image of great emotional intensity, in which man's physical power over woman is lent visual expression.

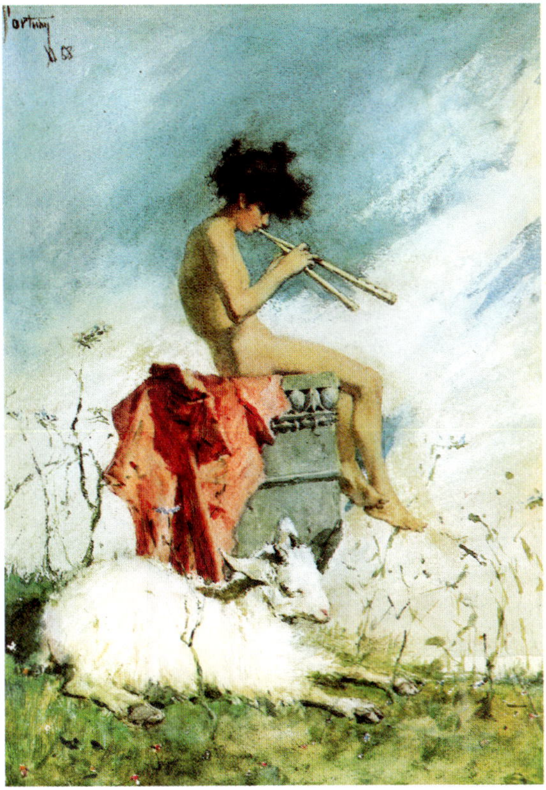

Fortuny painted this well-built, adolescent, nude boy playing music in a sensuous bucolic scene. His luminous flesh tones make him the focal point of the painting. The figure's contours are blurred, blending seamlessly into the atmosphere. The pilaster on which the boy sits provides the motif with a classical element that evokes the greatness of antiquity, giving rise to all manner of interpretation: innocence, musical idyll, melancholy. The painting is remarkable for its euphuistic, luminous landscape and the artist's brilliant painterly technique and singular style, recalling that of the Impressionists. These qualities, which mark the artist's work dating from this period of his career, led Marià Fortuny i Marsal to be regarded in his day as one of the greatest painters ever to have lived.

Idyll

Marià Fortuny i Marsal (Mariano José Bernardo Fortuny y Marsal)
(Reus, Catalonia, 1838–Rome, 1847)

- 1863
- watercolor on paper
- 31 x 22 cm
- Museo del Prado, Madrid

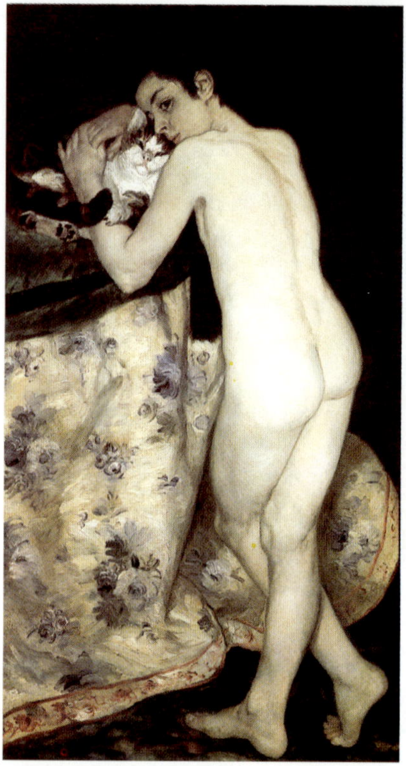

Boy with Cat

Pierre-Auguste Renoir
(Limoges, 1841–Cagnes-sur-Mer, 1919)

- 1868
- oil on canvas
- 124 x 67 cm
- Musée d'Orsay, Paris

Although the pose of this puerile, rather androgynous figure is indebted to academic painting, the ambience and composition are less conventional. The marmoreal skin is the true protagonist of this work, which is highlighted against a black background. The position of the legs, with the right one supporting the weight of the body and the left one crossing the latter, lends a delicate rhythm to the candid scene. The face of the figure and that of the cat are remarkable for their exquisite details, expressive force and innocent tenderness. The boy's face is rendered with a large nose, a sensual mouth with pale red lips—the color that predominates in the flesh tones—and penetrating eyes. It is conceivable that Renoir used one of the many Italian boys who worked as models in the ateliers and art schools of Montmartre and the Latin Quarter of Paris.

The sculptor Pygmalion's prayers to Venus resulted in one of his sculptures being brought to life: Galatea, the goddess' spitting image, became Venus' supposed human incarnation. Again, this figure's facial features in particular are markedly androgynous.

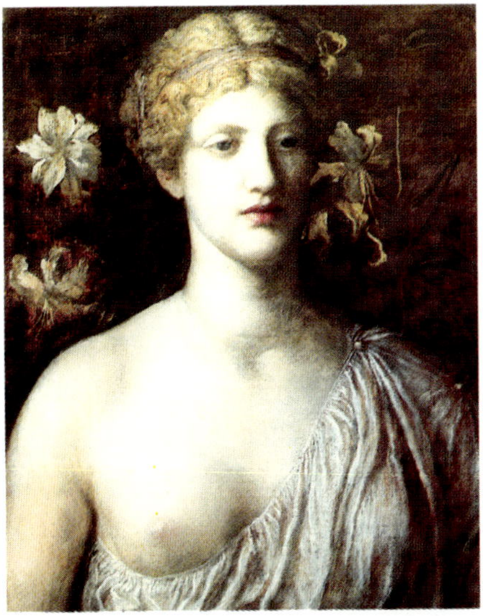

Pygmalion's Wife

George Frederick Watts

(London, 1817–Compton, Surrey, 1901)

- 1868
- oil on canvas
- 26.5 x 21 cm
- Faringdon Collection Trust, Buscot Park, Oxfordshire

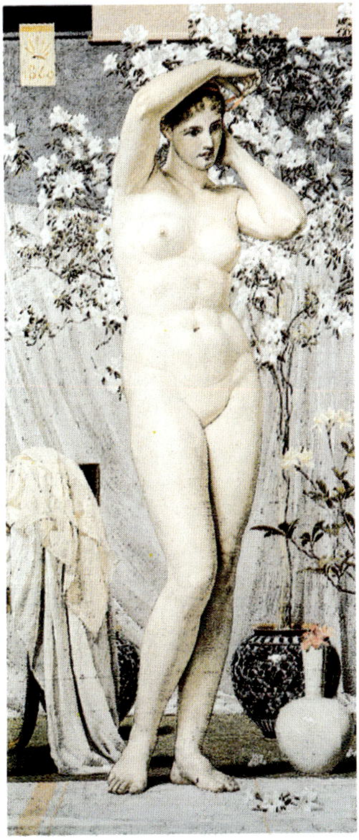

Venus

Albert Joseph Moore

(York, 1841–1893)

- 1869
- oil on canvas
- 63 x 30 cm
- York City Art Gallery

Given the muscular attributes and complexion of this figure, one might be forgiven for thinking, however briefly, of a statue of a Greek hero. In other respects, the goddess' feminine charms are fully in evidence.

Pygmalion and his Statue: I. Heart's Desire

Edward Burne-Jones
(Birmingham 1833
—London 1898)

- 1868/69
- oil on canvas
- 66 x 51 cm
- private collection

The artist received the commission for this series of paintings in 1868 from Euphrosyne Cassavetti, the mother of his muse at that time, Maria Zambaco.

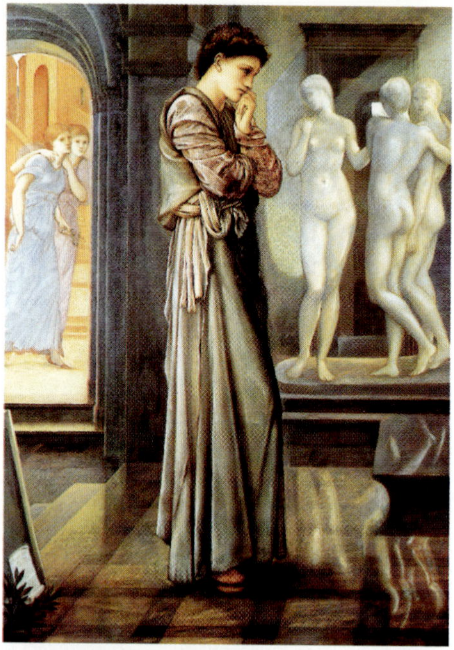

This is the first of the paintings of the Pygmalion Series. Pygmalion is depicted as an androgynous figure, lost in contemplation of his work, the Three Graces executed with precision and with a degree of eroticism. The artist is struck by the idea of creating the perfect sculpture.

Pygmalion and his Statue: II. The Hand Pauses

Edward Burne-Jones
(Birmingham 1833
—London 1898)

- 1868/69
- oil on canvas
- 66 x 51 cm
- private collection

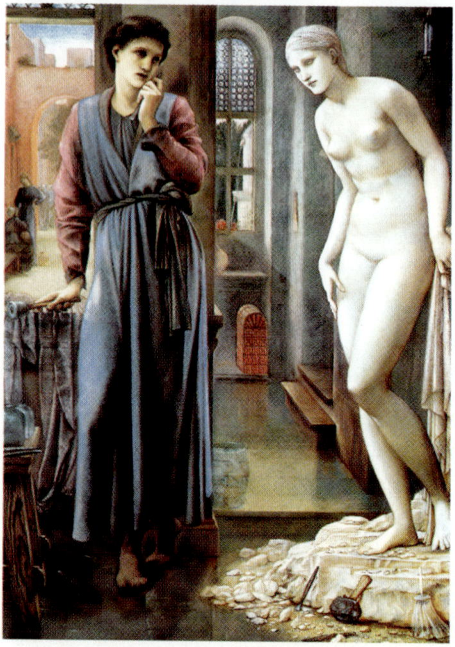

Pygmalion is looking at the sculpture he has just completed. Its perfection disturbs him so much that he is plunged into an abyss of uncertainty. Feelings stir within him as well as the painful acceptance that such beauty is void of life.

/enus
ıppears in
ınswers to
Pygmalion's
ɔleas, and
ɔreathes life
nto the sculp-
ure. It
ıssumes the
igure and
ıppearance
ɔf the god-
łess, so
nuch so that
t is trans-
ormed into
he very
mage of the
ɔoddess. The
ɔerfectly pro-
ɔortioned
ɔodies exude
ı disturbingly
ɜnigmatic
ɔeauty of
heir own.

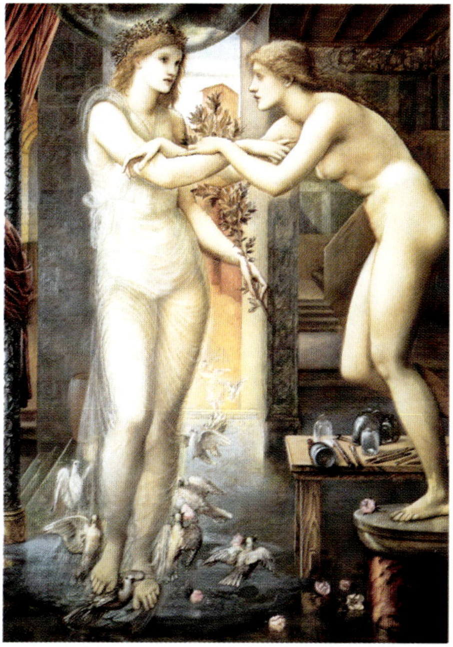

Pygmalion and his Statue: III. The Embrace of the Goddess

Edward Burne-Jone
(Birmingham 1853
—London 1898)

- 1868/69
- oil on canvas
- 66 x 51 cm
- private collection

The transfor-
nation of the
culpture into
ı mortal be-
ng is the ulti-
nate answer
ɔ the artist's
rayers. Cap-
ured by the
irl's beauty,
e kneels
own before
er. This se-
ies of paint-
ngs remained
ontroversial
ınd was the
ource of
nuch criti-
ism. W.A.I.
Benson and
Maria
Zambaco
cted as
nodels.

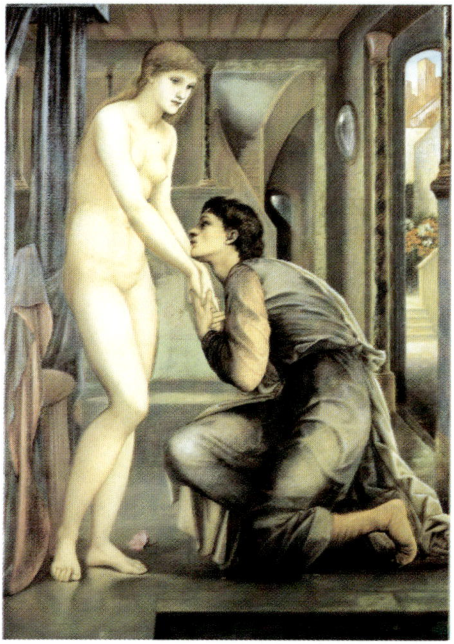

Pygmalion and his Statue: IV. The Waiting Soul

Edward Burne-Jones
(Birmingham 1833
—London 1898)

- 1868/69
- oil on canvas
- 66 x 51 cm
- private collection

Daedalus and Icarus

Frederic Leighton
(Scarborough, 1830 –London, 1896)

- 1869
- oil on canvas
- 138 x 104.5 cm
- Faringdon Collection Trust, Buscot Park, Oxfordshire

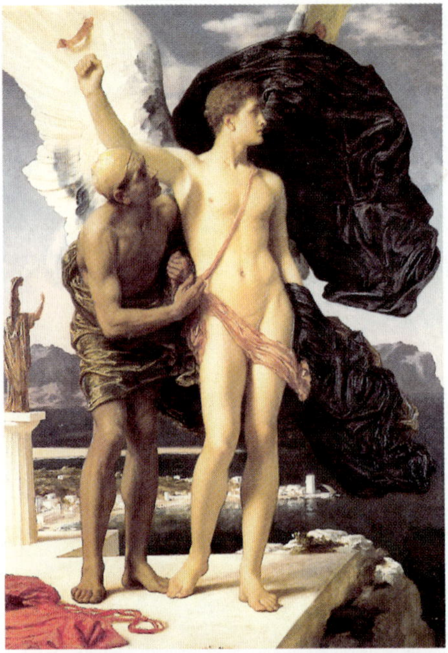

Daedalus is affixing wings to his son, Icarus, and warning him not to fly too close to the sun. Portrayed in slight contrapposto, the figure of Icarus is classical in its proportions, while his uplifted arm lends the whole an heroic air.

Happiness, Chance and Madness

Francesc Sans i Cabot
(Gerona, 1834–Madrid, 1881)

- 1871
- oil on canvas
- 225 x 180 cm
- Museu d'Art, Gerona

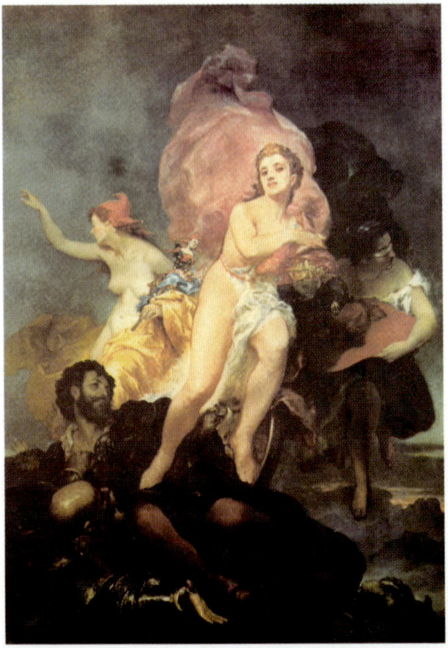

This work is more that of a professional artisan than of an artist, an example of art that was still romantic during the realist period.

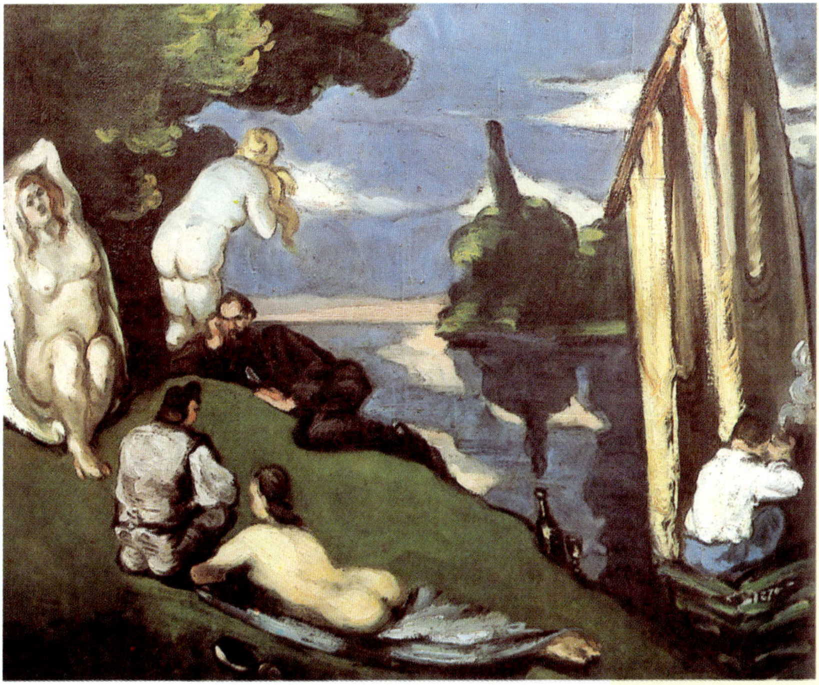

The scandal caused by Edouard Manet's Déjeuner sur l'Herbe had still not died down when Cézanne took the theme one stage further: the artist painted himself lying on the ground in a bucolic landscape, surrounded by voluptuous, naked women in provocative poses, set in an idyllic scene of vibrancy and passion. Cézanne appears to have just arrived on the boat moored at the right, enticed there by the seductive sensuality of the women. The surroundings also appear to induce lust and the artist has painted an unmistakable phallic form amid the vegetation in the background, which is reflected in the water. The boatman, smoking a pipe with his back to the viewer, is the only note of sexual neutrality in the midst of such lasciviousness. The landscape, executed with intense, flat colors, brings out the figures' forms, which are evoked with only a few loose and descriptive lines, demonstrating the artist's mastery of the female nude and a technique suited to the volume of the bodies. The work is an affirmation of artistic freedom in a society obsessed with established norms.

Pastoral (Idyll)

Paul Cézanne
(Aix-en-Provence, 1839–1906)

- 1870
- oil on canvas
- 65 x 81 cm
- Musée d'Orsay, Paris

After the Bath

Frédéric Bazille
(Montpellier, 1841–Beaune-la-Rolande, Loiret, 1870)

- 1870
- oil on canvas
- 41 x 30 cm
- private collection

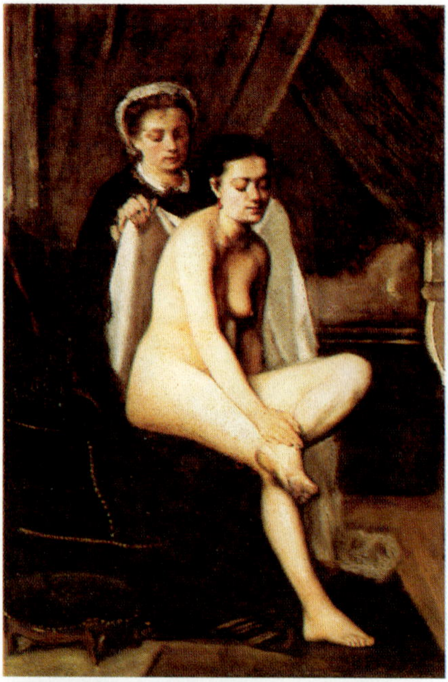

The nude's sophisticated modeling, illuminated throughout, manifests the work of a master draftsman capable of lending his figures great physical presence. Dressed in black so as not to detract from the protagonist, the servant's face alone is illuminated, and is highly expressive.

Bather

Pierre-Auguste Renoir
(Limoges, 1841–Cagnes-sur-Mer, 1919)

- 1870
- oil on canvas
- 184 x 115 cm
- Museu de Arte, São Paulo

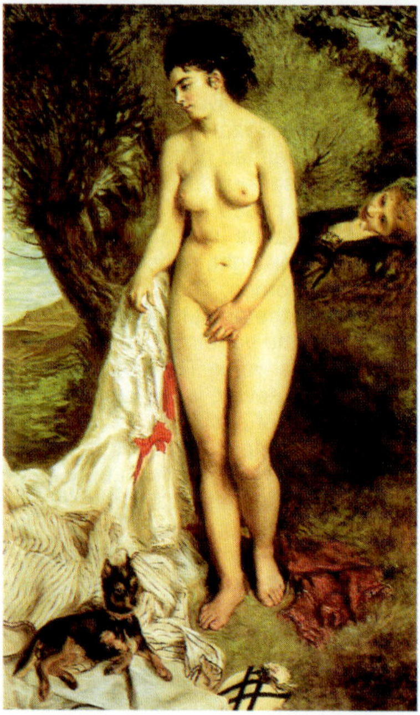

This work is the first in a series of nudes painted by Renoir throughout his lifetime. The artist was renowned for his reactionary and chauvinistic attitude toward women, whose only attraction, for him, lay in the fact that they possessed sufficient qualities to paint. Consequently, he invariably painted plain-looking women, who lacked sophistication and idealism, such as the subject of this work.

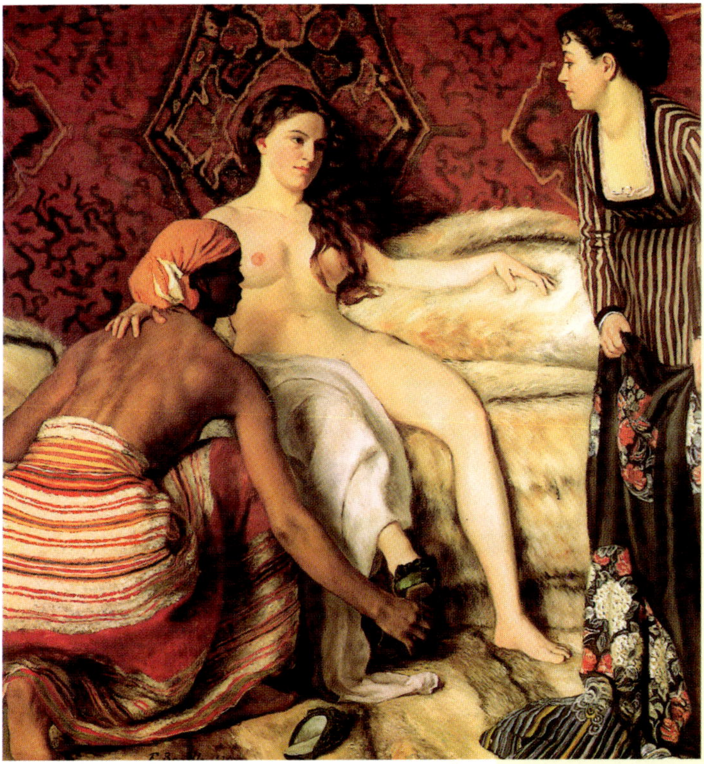

This scene shows a woman at her toilet, a favorite subject among many 19th-century painters, from Degas' scenes of erotic voyeurism, to the cruelest realism of Toulouse-Lautrec, to the narcissism of Berthe Morisot or Mary Cassatt. This painting, reminiscent of The Bather painted by Renoir in the same year, shows a young, aristocratic woman after her bath, reclining on a bed and being dressed by two servants, one white and the other black. The girl has soft skin, full breasts and a well-proportioned body. The erotic nature of the scene is heightened by the black servant's nude torso, which, although more muscular, is equally sensual. The decoration and the colors lend the scene the sumptuousness so prevalent in many of Delacroix's works. Presented in the 1870 Salon, the work was rejected because it was deemed to be provocative.

La Toilette

Frédéric Bazille
(Montpellier, 1841–Beaune-la-Rolande, 1870)

- 1870
- oil on canvas
- 211 x 201 cm
- Musée Fabre, Montpellier

Phyllis and Demophon

Edward Burne-Jones
(Birmingham 1833 —London 1898)

- 1870
- oil on canvas
- 36 x 18 cm
- Birmingham City Art Gallery

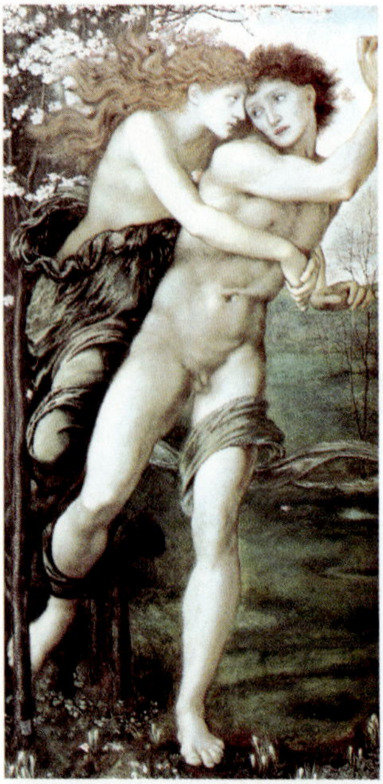

Demophon's nude figure here is not unrelated in the working out of its anatomical forms to Michelangelo's figures. These forms tend towards simplicity, although the handling of lighting creates a clear sense of depth and volume. They are also somewhat effeminate, just as the pose is rather affected.

Pan und Psyche

Edward Burne-Jones
(Birmingham 1833 —London 1898)

- ca. 1872/74
- oil on canvas
- 61 x 54,6 cm
- private collection

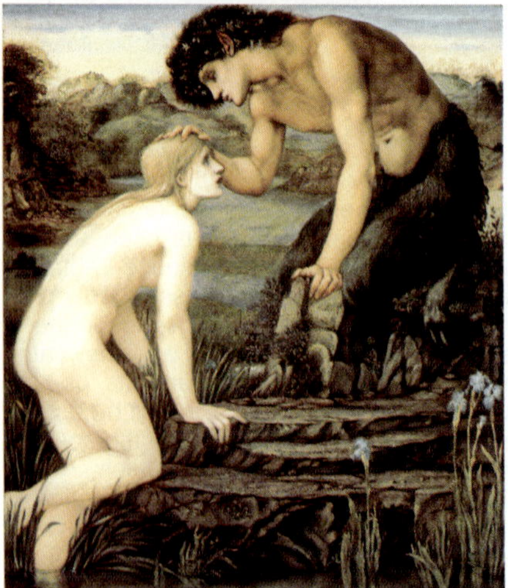

Pan's athletic torso, in striking contrasts to the rest of his body, is used to full effect to win over the beautiful nymph Psyche. Her innocence is in absolute opposition to the intention of the god of shepherds and flocks with his goat's legs, and her situation seems to be beyond hope.

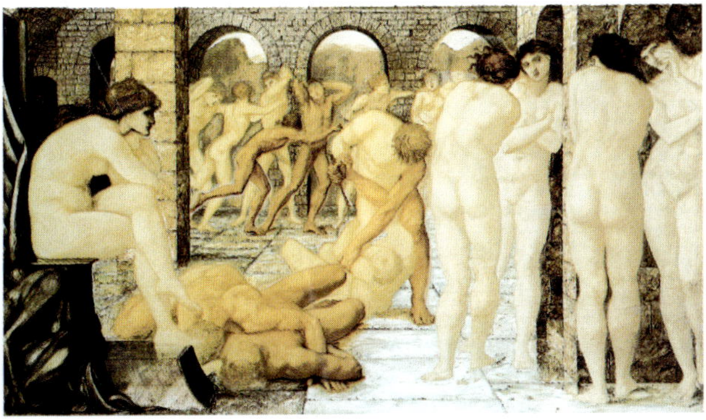

Venus Discordia

Edward Burne-Jones

(Birmingham 1833
—London 1898)

- 1872/75
- oil on canvas
- 128,2 x 209,8 cm
- National Museum and Gallery, Cardiff, Wales

Incited by the Venus Discordia, a number of male figures are engaged in the violent consequences of baser human passions, namely in a fight, reminiscent of scences from the Renaissance. On the right are the four female figures representing the four Vices (Anger, Envy, Suspicion and Strife).

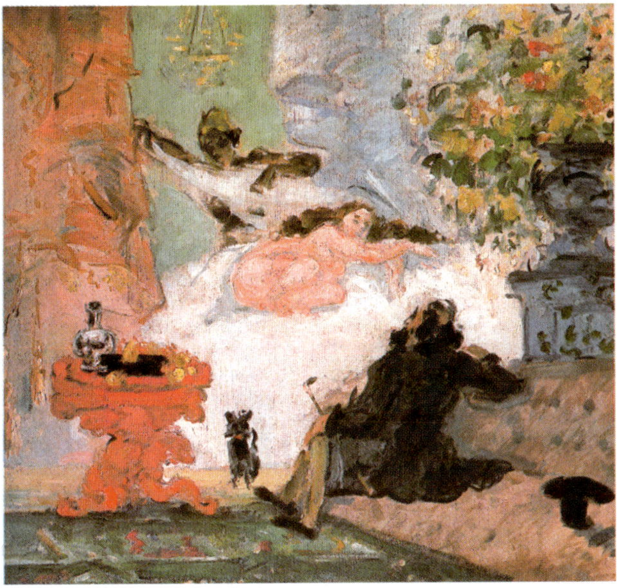

A Modern Olympia

Paul Cézanne

(Aix-en-Provence, 1839–1906)

- 1873
- oil on canvas
- 46 x 55 cm
- Musée d'Orsay, Paris

Olympia's pose and forms are a deliberate provocation, causing the viewer to doubt what he sees and what he yearns for. Cézanne, the greatest exponent of Post-Impressionism, juxtaposes various intense colors so as to enhance them, the result of which underscores the sensuality of the work.

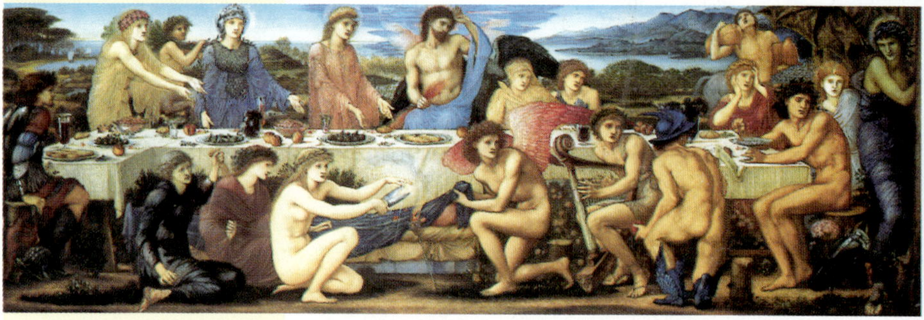

The Feast of Peleus

Edward Burne-Jones
(Birmingham 1833
—London 1898)

- ca. 1872/81
- oil on canvas
- 37.5 x 100.2 cm
- Birmingham Museum and Art Gallery

This painting depicts the feast following the marriage of one of the Nereids, Thetis, with Peleus, a king of the Myrmidons. Various gods are present, being served by centaurs. On the far left are the gods Mars and Vulcan and, on the right, Bacchus with Proserpina, with Ceres in the background. Apollo clutches the harp, Amor—in the foreground and in the center of the painting, prepares the matrimonial bed while the Three Fates are spinning the threads of fortune. On the far right, attracting the attention of all the figures present, is Eris, the goddess of discord, depicted with an ominous expression, the wings of a bat and the skin of a serpent. She has not been invited to the celebration and is shown in subdued colors, lurking in the shadows. Murcury is portrayed from behind, clad in a helmet and winged footware of a brilliant blue; in his left hand he holds the apple which Eris has just rolled into the scene and, in his right hand, he has a sheet of parchment on which the words 'Detur Pulcherrimae' (the most beautiful) can be seen. This ultimately releases the quarrel between Aphrodite/Venus, Athena/Minerva and Hera/Juno, recognisable on the left of the painting next to Zeus. In this work, the assembly of beautiful, gracefully slim bodies, delicately painted and softly outlined, form a striking contrast to the grim figure of Eris.

The forms utilized by this artist were strongly influenced by Raphael and Michelangelo's frescos. His search for beauty led him to distort anatomical detail and so to create images having a mysteriously dream-like air.

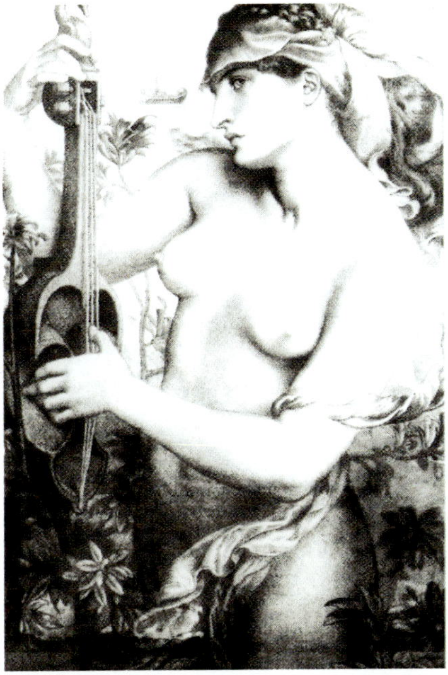

The Siren Ligeia

Dante Gabriel Rossetti
(London, 1828–Birchington -Sea, 1882)

- 1873
- pencil on papel
- 31.5 x 21 cm
- private collection

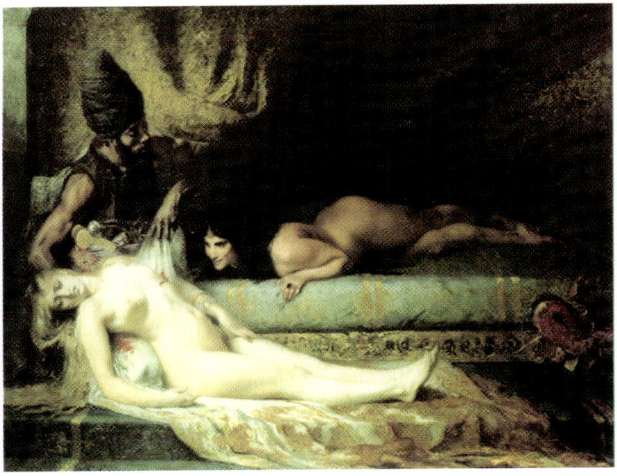

Jealousy in the Harem

Fernand Cormon (Fernand-Anne Piestre)
(Paris, 1845–1924)

- 1874
- oil on canvas
- 160 x 220 cm
- Musée des Beaux-Arts et d'Archéologie, Besançon

A drama not uncommon in harems is depicted in a claustrophobic and mysterious atmosphere. Abetted by a eunuch, a woman has just murdered a fellow concubine and rival. The powerful sensuality of the two nude bodies contrasts with the crime that has just been committed and the evident satisfaction of the murderess.

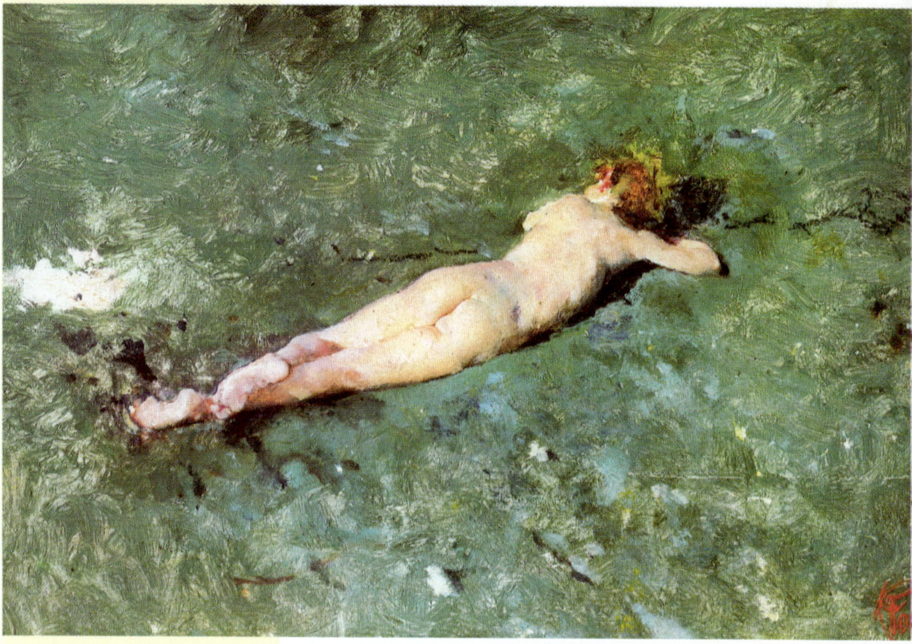

Nude on the Beach of Portici

Marià Fortuny i Marsal (Mariano José Bernardo Fortuny y Marsal)
(Reus, Catalonia, 1838–Rome, 1847)

- 1874
- watercolor on paper
- 13 x 19 cm
- Casón del Buen Retiro, Madrid

The most remarkable aspect of this work is its simple composition: a luminous nude that is highlighted against a solid background. Despite its stationary position, the figure is dynamic and vibrant, as Fortuny allows the light to breathe through the green ground enveloping the figure, causing the light to be perceived as an atmospheric value. The artist has depicted his subject as a young, rather androgynous figure, placing special emphasis on certain elements that are traditionally female, such as the curvature of the back, the slight torsion of the hips or the coquettish pose with the foreshortened leg crossed over the other. Owing to the technique used to resolve the intense green background—by means of loose brushwork with a wide range of hues—and the virtuoso treatment of the light, this work ranks among some of the finest Impressionist paintings.

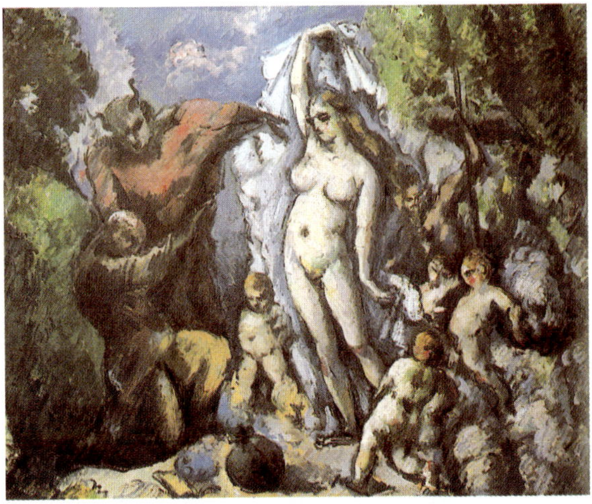

The Temptation of St. Anthony

Paul Cézanne
(Aix-en-Provence, 1839–1906)

- ca. 1875–77
- oil on canvas
- 47 x 56 cm
- Musée d'Orsay, Paris

Here, the painter has clearly rejected Mannerist modes in favor of Impressionist ones. Cézanne uses intense colors and vigorous brushwork to achieve the sole aim of this work: to present a woman of disarming beauty in all her naked splendor.

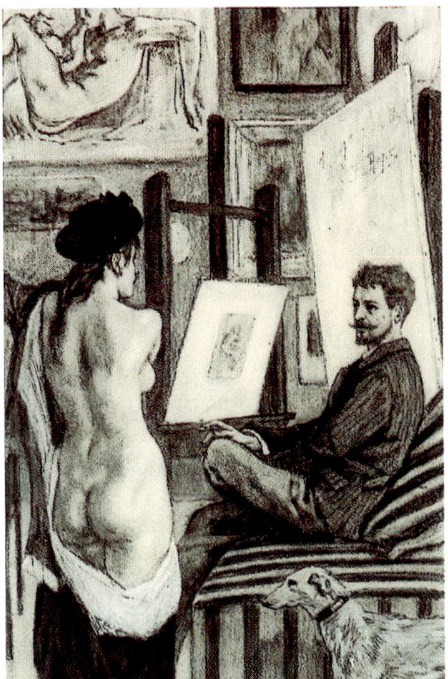

Self-Portrait with Model in the Studio

Félicien Rops
(Namur, 1833–Essonnes, 1898)

- 1875
- pencil on paper
- 22 x 15 cm
- Musée Provincial Félicien Rops, Namur

Revering the nude, the artist here no longer stands before her as an observer, but becomes an active participant in the scene. The model has voluptuous forms and a marked femininity, whose modeling is executed along classical lines. The dark contrasts in the background highlight her luminous body, whose volumes are naturalistically articulated.

Harem Assistant

Paul-Désiré Trouillebert
(Paris, 1831–1900)

- 1874
- oil on canvas
- 130 x 97 cm
- Musée des Beaux-Arts Jules Chéret, Paris

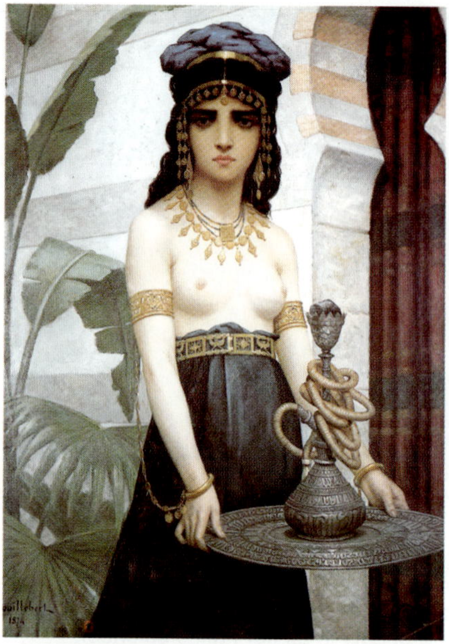

The exposed breasts, the highly unusual headgear and clothing, the directness of her stare and the lowering black eyebrows of this harem assistant make a powerful impression on the viewer.

The Garden of Pan

Edward Burne-Jones
(Birmingham, 1833 –London, 1898)

- 1876–77
- oil on canvas
- 152.5 x 186.7 cm
- National Gallery of Victoria, Melbourne

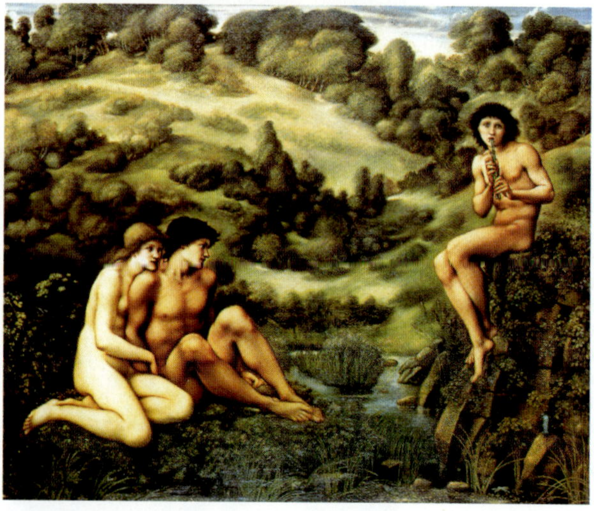

The subject of Pan in his garden brings to mind certain Renaissance works. Two young nude figures are set in a bucolic landscape here.

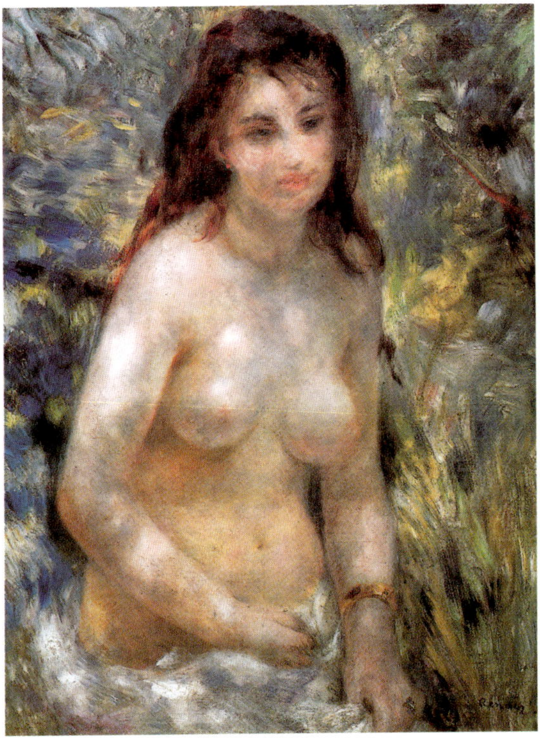

The figure in this work is shown seated, in a pose slightly turned to one side and set against a dense background of trees. The effects of light and color on the nude are executed in the Impressionist manner. The figure's body bears all the hallmarks of the painter's technique: vaporous colors, soft skin and voluptuous, and sensual forms dappled with small white patches of sunlight. The vegetation, rendered with dense brushstrokes, applied in different directions, is deliberately made abstract, causing the young woman to stand out. The artist has depicted her with carefully-rendered details, such as the innocent expression on her face, the realism of her hair, the torso's slight inclination and the way in which she modestly holds her dress across her lower abdomen.

Torso in the Sun

Pierre-Auguste Renoir
(Limoges, 1841–Cagnes-sur-Mer, 1919)

- 1875
- oil on canvas
- 81 x 65 cm
- Musée d'Orsay, Paris

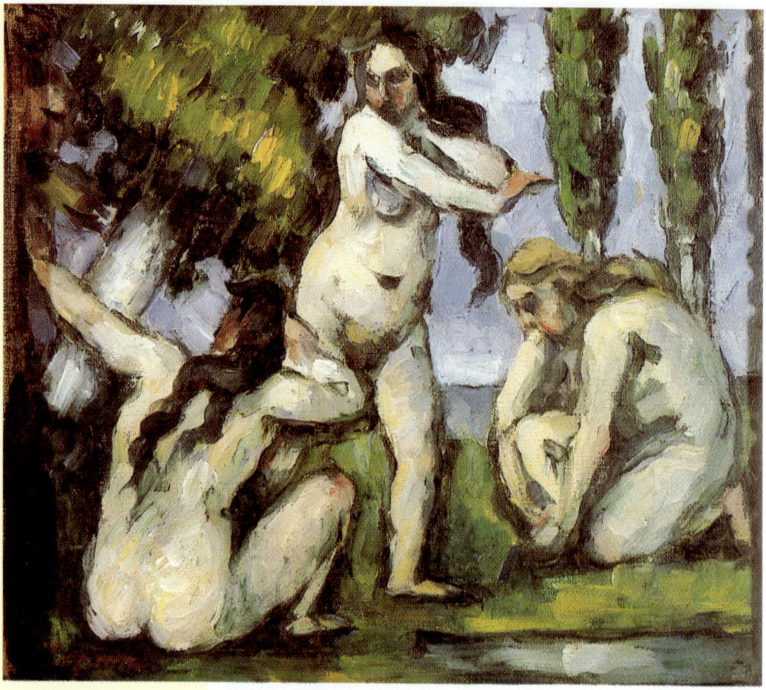

Three Bathers

Paul Cézanne
(Aix-en-Provence, 1839–1906)

- 1875–77
- oil on canvas
- 22 x 19 cm
- Musée d'Orsay, Paris

Three naked women are shown bathing in a landscape when, suddenly, a man on the far left surprises them. Each woman reacts in a different way: the one on the left attempts to keep him at bay; the woman in the center turns her back to him in order to conceal her nudity; and the one on the right remains kneeling, covering her body as best she can. The influence of Impressionist painting techniques are evident in this striking pyramidal composition. The vegetation is represented with numerous intense greens and yellows, which harmonize with the light blue sky. The women's bodies, executed with broad brushwork, stand out against the background. So many saturated colors in such a confined space could have produced a crowded, chaotic composition, but the artist has skillfully avoided this by including the vertical and diagonal forms of the trees, which lend the figures a sense of movement and levity, attesting to the painter's mastery of his art.

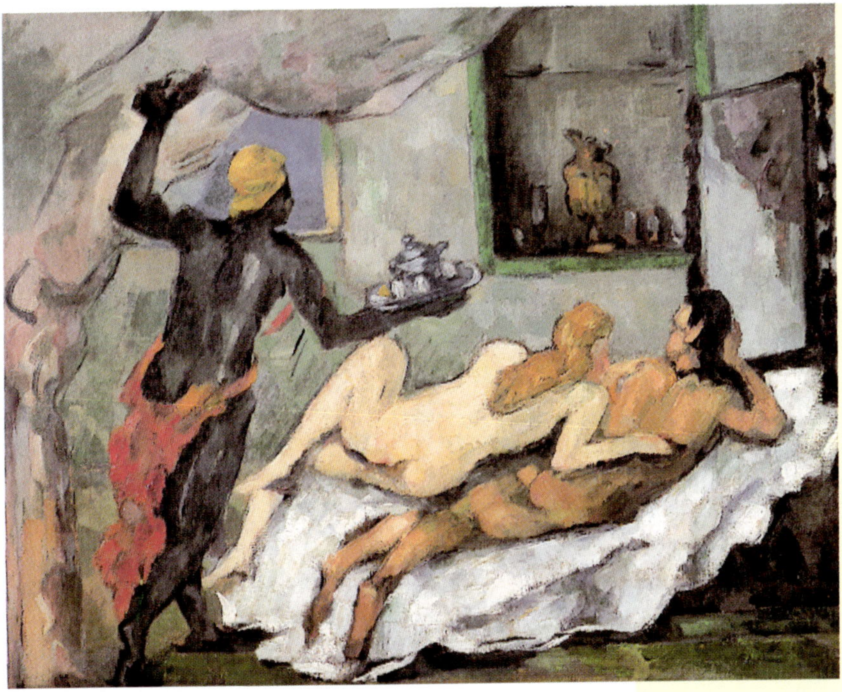

Afternoon in Naples

Paul Cézanne
(Aix-en-Provence, 1839–1906)

- ca. 1875–77
- oil on canvas
- 37 x 45 cm
- National Gallery of Australia, Canberra

This canvas was painted when Cézanne appeared to be emerging from a period of great emotional distress, dominated by his sexual frustration, which was to plague him throughout his lifetime. His relationship with Hortense Fiquet seemed to alleviate his condition somewhat, evidence of which is shown in his erotic works of colorful, romantic scenes, which omit the violence and atmosphere of tension of The Abduction. In this scene, the bodies of the two lovers form the main subject, although the black servant also represents an important chromatic and compositional element. The servant's gesture, her body leaning forward, holding a bowl in one hand while drawing back the curtain with the other, is a fine example of the painter's ability to arrange the various pictorial elements such that the scene is lent a sense of movement and drama.

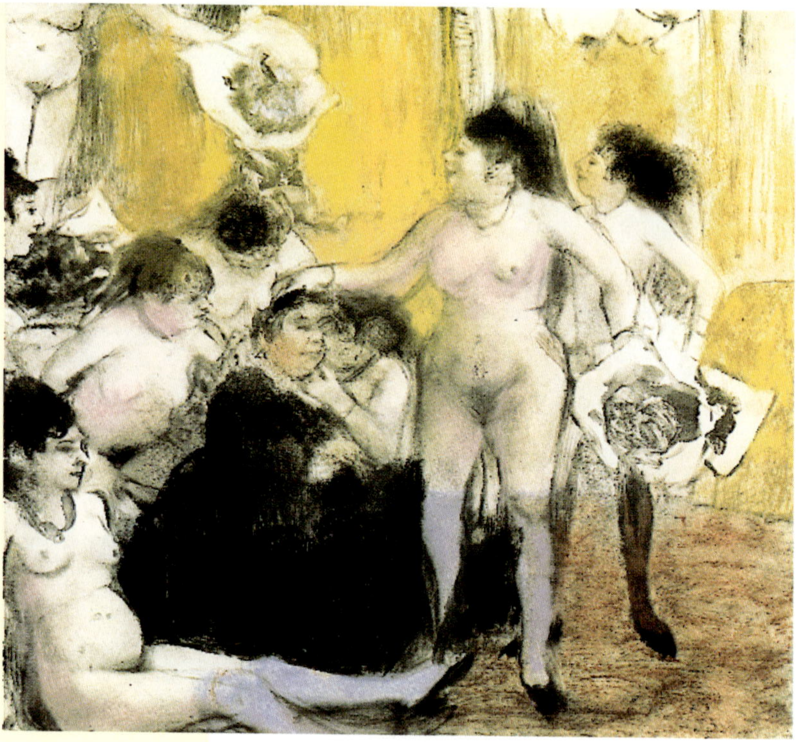

The Name Day of the Madam

Edgar Degas
(Paris, 1834–1917)

- 1876–77
- pastel over monotype on paper
- 26.6 x 29.6 cm
- Musée Picasso, Paris

Degas enjoyed portraying women in moments of their everyday intimacy, especially those in which they could be portrayed nude. Here, the painter presents a sort of snapshot, in which the spontaneity of the moment, the sordid milieu and the, arguably, comeliness of the prostitute's bodies are brilliantly conveyed. The work's composition is striking, as is the singular arrangement of the figures, the fresh, ethereal and almost mysterious quality of the pastels and the candidness of the figures' poses. The fact that it is a cursory sketch (it may have been a preliminary study for another work) gives it an agility and virtuosity appropriate to the figures and the atmosphere. Life inside a brothel was no mystery to Degas. As the work reveals, he possessed sound knowledge of female anatomy and mastered the technique of drawing as few others. The result is a skillfully executed work of captivating charm.

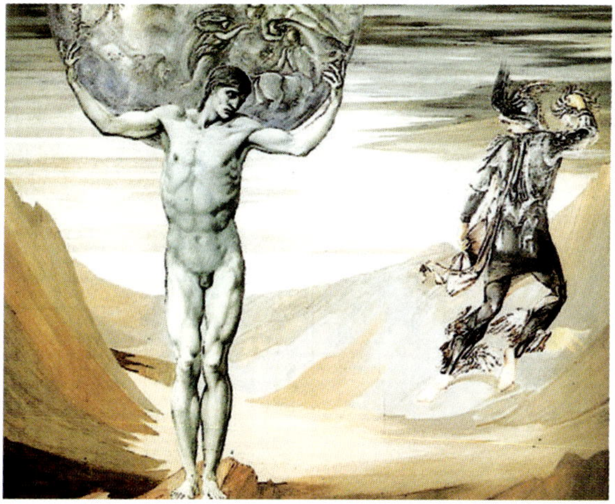

Atlas Lifting the Earth

Edward Burne-Jones

(Birmingham, 1833 –London, 1898)

- 1876–88
- oil on canvas
- 152.5 x 190 cm
- City Art Gallery, Southampton

Standing in an imaginary landscape, Atlas, despite his muscular build and sensual anatomy, is not depicted as a Herculean figure, nor does he shown signs of strain in bearing the earth on his shoulders.

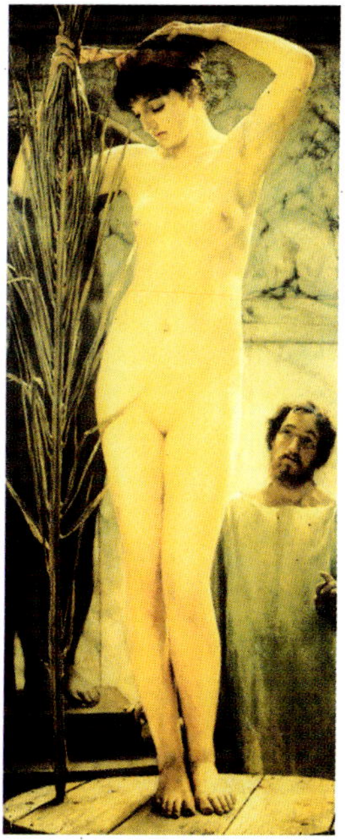

The Sculptor's Model

Lawrence Alma-Tadema

(Dronrijp, Friesland, 1836 –Wiesbaden, 1912)

- 1877
- oil on canvas
- 77 x 33 cm
- private collection

The feelings that this canvas depicts the sculptor as having towards his model seem to involve a mixture of admiration and desire; again, it is the myth of Pygmalion and Galatea. The idealized forms of the model bathed in golden light involve an overall flattening of tones.

The Minotaur

George Frederick Watts
(London, 1817–1904)

- 1877–86
- oil on canvas
- 117 x 93 cm
- Tate Gallery, London

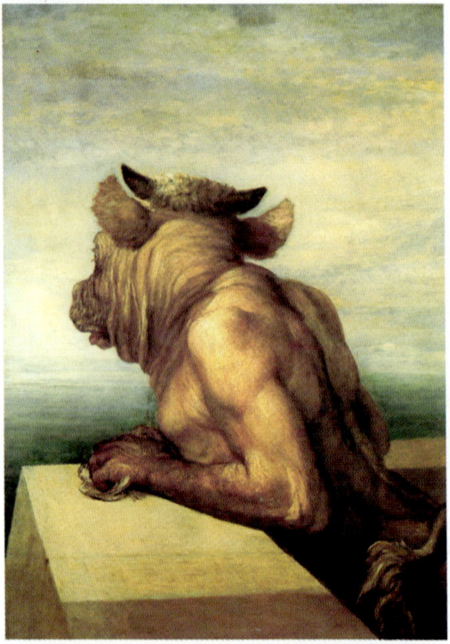

Depicted here, gazing out longingly from the labyrinth from which he cannot escape, the Minotaur crushes in his left hand a songbird, symbol of life and liberty. Its nude torso is exceptionally powerful, as befits a bull-man, while the evocative light it is bathed in calls to mind the beast's lost humanity.

Pornocrates

Félicien Rops
(Namur, 1833–Essonnes, 1898)

- 1878
- watercolors, pastel and wash
- 69 x 45 cm
- Communauté Française de Belgique, on loan to Musée Félicien Rops, Namur

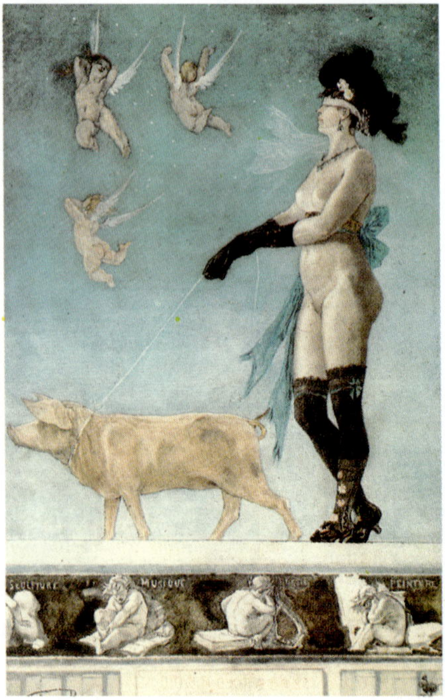

This painting, an allegory of pornography as woman, includes a pig and fleeing cherubs. The woman is blindfolded. Stance and clothing both display and enhance her erogenous zones to full advantage.

In this scene of the temptation of St. Anthony, an erotic nude figure has displaced Christ from the Cross and is attempting to win his surrender.

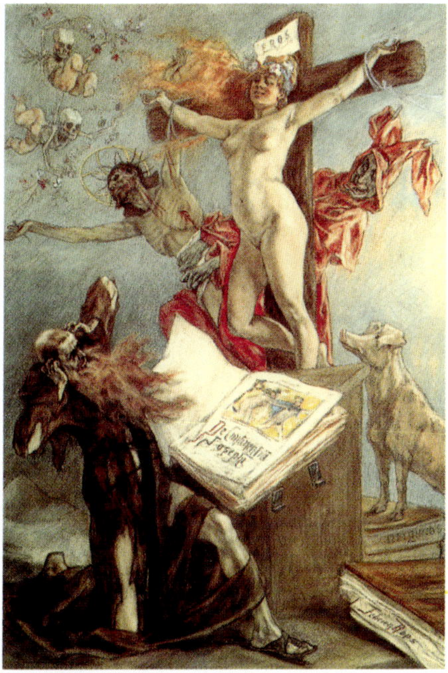

The Temptation of St. Anthony

Félicien Rops
(Namur, 1833–Essonnes, 1898)

- 1878
- colored pencil on paper
- 73.8 x 54.3 cm
- Bibliothèque Royale Albert I, Cabinet des Estampes, Brussels

The painting is a fine example of Falero's best work. The woman's physical beauty is if anything heightened by her expression of wistful contemplation that seems to contain a look at once knowing and not without a touch of bitterness.

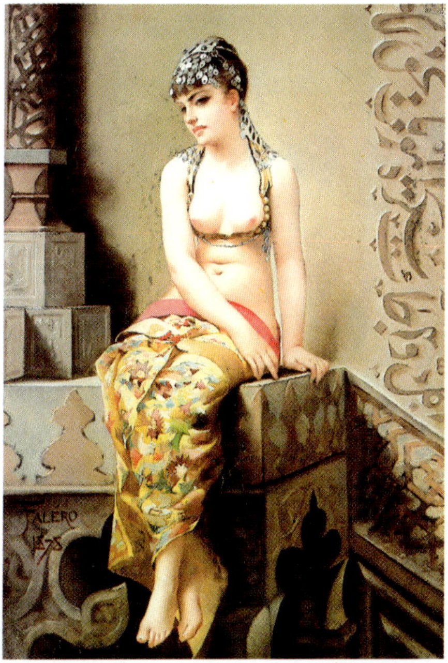

The Sorceress

Luis Ricardo Falero
(Granada, 1851–London, 1896)

- 1878
- oil on canvas
- 30 x 23 cm
- Prince Naguib Hassan Abdallah Collection

Slave Market, Constantinople

Stanislas von Chlebowski
(Pohutynce, 1835–Poznan, 1884)

- 1879
- oil on canvas
- 93 x 72 cm
- Galerie Berko, Knokke-le-Zoute and Paris

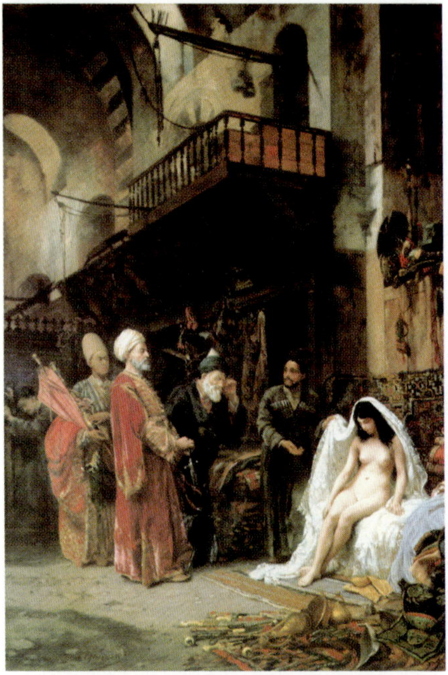

A Circassian trading in high-quality slaves displays one of his women to a rich Turk. The magnate's arrogance and power, the woman's vulnerability and the trader's unashamed self-interest are given fine expression in this canvas.

Woman Defending Herself from Eros

Adolphe-William Bouguereau
(La Rochelle, 1825–1905)

- oil on canvas
- 79.5 x 55 cm
- The J. Paul Getty Museum, Malibu

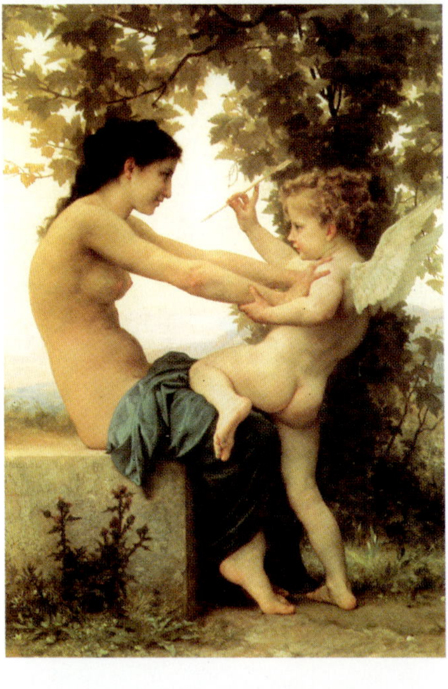

The nude figure here is reminiscent of depictions of Venus disarming her son or playing with him, her well-defined profile of a distinctly Classical turn, whereby one should bear in mind how the air of a work of ancient Greece can lent an enigmatic air to a composition.

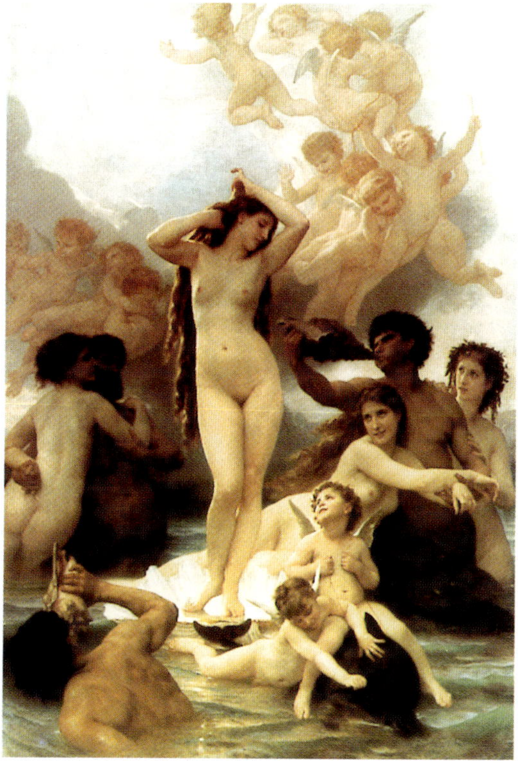

This painter staunchly defended Classicism and artistic orthodoxy. At the time of the completion of this work, he had been a professor at the Ecole des Beaux-Arts for four years and a member of the Académie Française for three. Ostensibly depicting a mythological theme, he gives us an elegant group of male and female nudes with Venus at their center. The work's eroticism and levity was much to the liking of the public at that time. Drawing on a wide variety of Classical forms and modes, the artist manages to produce a graceful, light and lyrical whole. Yet, given the date of the painting, it is clear that its style is completely outdated. It was this that the Academy and the Impressionists most attacked him for.

The Birth of Venus

Adolphe-William Bouguereau

(La Rochelle, 1825–1905)

- 1879
- oil on canvas
- 300 x 215 cm
- Musée d'Orsay, Paris

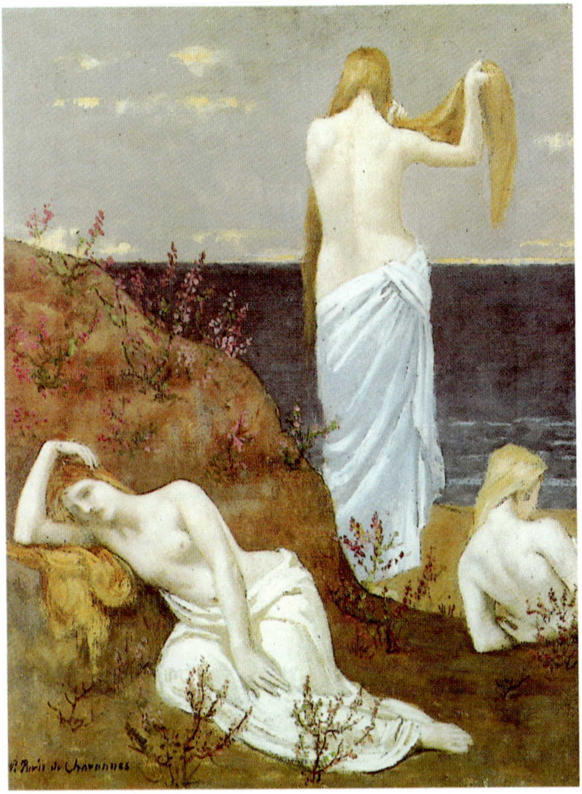

Women by the Sea

Pierre Puvis de Chavannes
(Lyon, 1824–Paris, 1898)

- 1879
- oil on canvas
- 205 x 154 cm
- Musée d'Orsay, Paris

Puvis de Chavannes generally specialized in large murals. This Symbolist Neoclassical painting is one of the very few works that he executed on an easel. It nonetheless bears certain resemblances to a fresco, as, for example, the nearly imperceptible brushwork, light colors, raised horizon, large foreground figures and simplified composition. Indeed, the work as a whole is more decorative than descriptive. The static figures, which are somewhat ethereal, Hellenistic and stylized, combine with the warm tones of the earth, the purple sea and the sky to lend the painting a dream-like quality. The sensuality of these figures is rather cool and distant, their poses mannered. The whole is so meticulously studied as to be rather artificial.

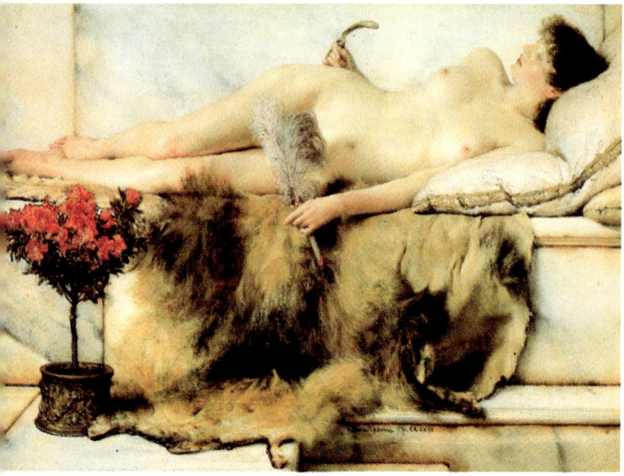

In the Tepidarium

Lawrence Alma-Tadema
(Dronrijp, Friesland, 1836 –Wiesbaden, 1912)

- 1881
- oil on panel
- 24 x 33 cm
- Lady Lever Art Gallery, Port Sunlight

An exotic or historical context often underlines the piquancy of a scene. The tepidarium allows for classical architecture that recalls an exotic past. The woman in this particular scene is of incontestable beauty, and is depicted resting on a white marble bench covered with the skin of an animal.

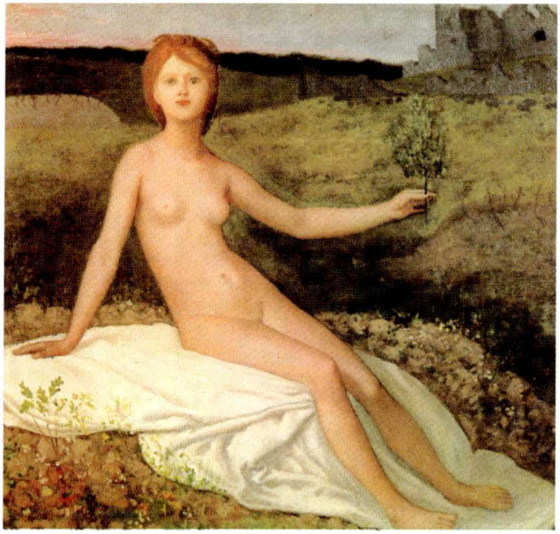

Hope

Pierre Puvis de Chavannes
(Lyon, 1824–Paris 1898)

- ca. 1872
- oil on canvas
- 70.7 x 82 cm
- Musée d'Orsay, Paris

This woman, with her innocent nudity, lends a touch of humanity to the ruins and uncultivated fields around her. This style of anatomical representation breaks slightly with classical academicism, although there is a constructive rigor in form, proportion and gesture.

The Perseus Series: The Death of Medusa

Edward Burne-Jones
(Birmingham 1833 –London 1898)

- 1884/85
- gouache
- 152.5 x 156.5 cm
- Southampton City Art Gallery

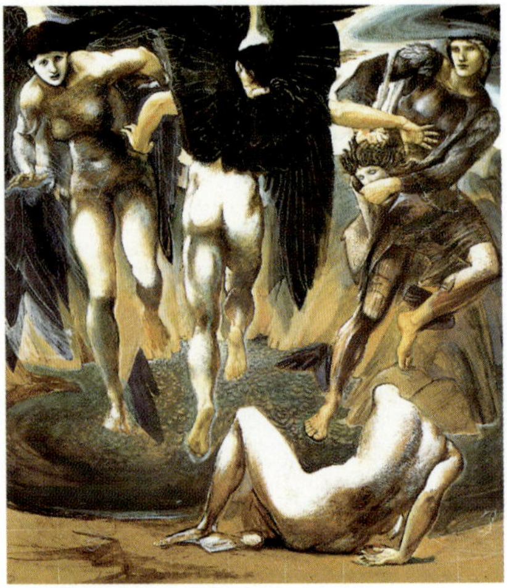

Medusa was heavily pregnant with twins—conceived after meeting Poseidon in a temple dedicated to the goddess Athena. The latter seeks revenge and sends Perseus to cut off Medusa's head. The sensuality of the bodies, however, cannot diminish the brutality and dynamism of this scene.

The Tree of Forgiveness

Edward Burne-Jones
(Birmingham, 1833– London, 1898)

- 1881/82
- oil on canvas
- 180 x 111 cm
- National Museums and Galleries on Merseyside, Liverpool

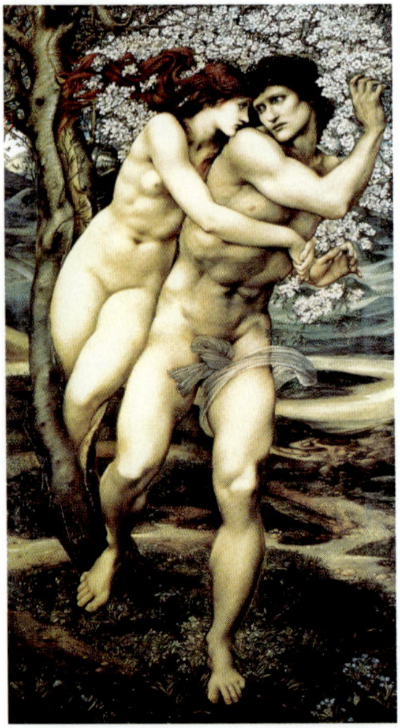

This painting depicts the reunion of Demophon and Phyllis who is emerging from a blossoming almond tree into a new life. She forgives her lover for deserting her. The powerful bodies and their dominance underline the sensual significance of the work. The angle of the two figures—especially that of Phyllis—emphasize the eroticism of the scene.

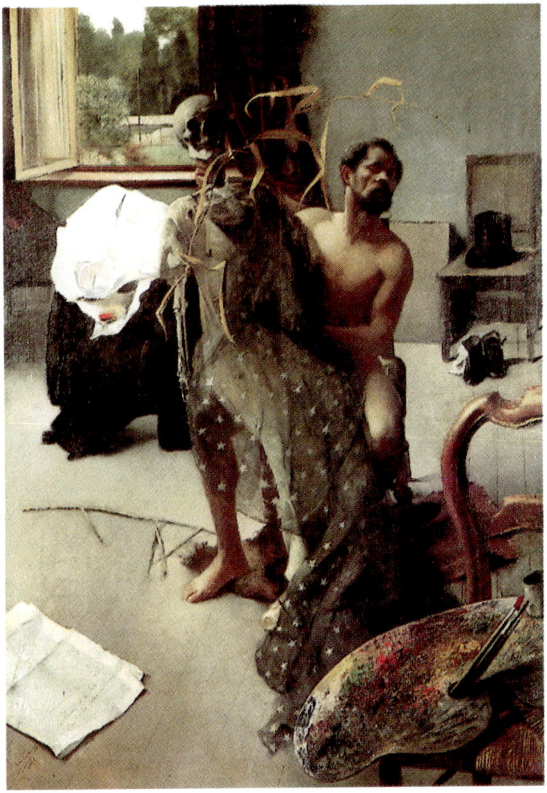

ronic and macabre, this painting depicts a mise-en-scène n which the painter is involved in a sort of grotesque dance. Sitting as if he were a musician playing the cello, he holds a skull and a hanger draped with satin and tulle, evoking a dressed skeleton. The nude exhibits the most severe realsm, with a magnificent study of light, which enters the room from the window in the background. The nude appears in the middle ground and only part of it is well lit. This called for the artist to render a subtle half-light, with numerous hues. The nude's flesh tones are superb, possibly owing to the great economy of means with which they have been rendered and to the fascinating play of light and shadow.

The Studio

Frédéric Léon
(1856–1940)

- 1882
- oil on canvas
- 158 x 117 cm
- Musée d'Ixelles, Brussels

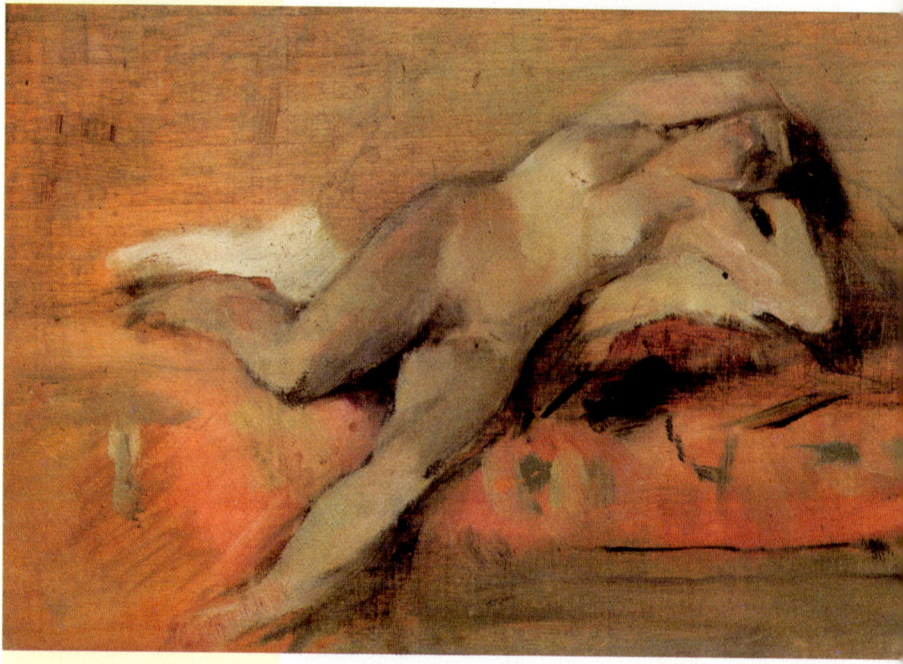

Nude Woman on a Divan

Henri de Toulouse-Lautrec
(Albi, 1864–Malromé, 1901)

- 1882
- oil on panel
- 16.5 x 23.8 cm
- Musée Toulouse-Lautrec, Albi

Despite the youth of the artist when he painted this work, he had clearly already distanced himself from the academic tradition, opting instead for a style of his own, both in conception and technique. This nude attests to the artist's keen interest in the human body. Indeed, Toulouse-Lautrec himself would later say: “only the figure exists; landscape is an accessory.” Here, he depicts a female nude in a pose that is technically difficult to render, leaning back and apparently sleeping. This impression is created by her relaxed aspect, the tenuous lines of her body and her total abandon. The setting serves as a background. Despite the schematic nature of the painting, the artist has depicted the body naturalistically, and the study of light attests to the young painter's extraordinary skill. The artist seems to have captured the nude while in motion rather than in a pose.

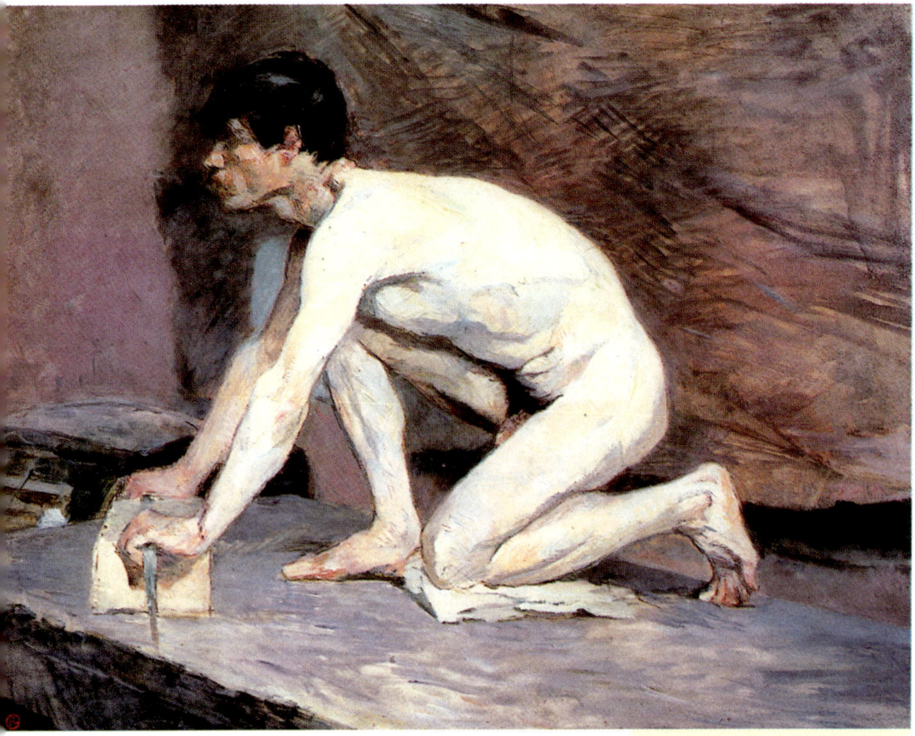

This painting is probably the first executed by Toulouse-Lautrec at the studio of Léon Bonnat, a painter who had studied with Degas at the Villa Medici in Rome and whose style was a synthesis of realistic and academic modes. Although the figure of a young man is shown performing a specific task, it seems to be more a pretense for the artist to represent a nude in a classical pose than anything else. Here, Toulouse-Lautrec shows himself to be a master drafts-man, yet he still seems to be somewhat inhibited and uncomfortable with academic painting. When the work was finished, his instructor criticized it, discouraging the artist. Nonetheless, years later, Toulouse-Lautrec admitted that the reprimand had pushed him to progress.

Study of a Male Nude

Henri de Toulouse-Lautrec

(Albi, 1864–Malromé, 1901)

- 1882
- oil on canvas
- 65 x 79 cm
- The Forbes Magazine Collection, New York

The Sacred Forest of the Arts and Muses

Pierre Puvis de Chavannes
(Lyon, 1824–Paris, 1898)

- 1883
- oil on canvas
- Musée des Beaux-Arts, Lyon

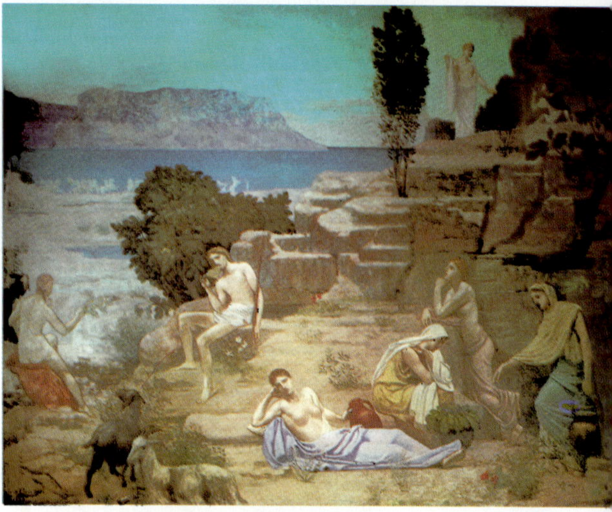

Designed to decorate the Palais des Arts in Lyon, this work presents an evocative, symbolic landscape, with diverse figures as if they were in a wilderness or desert. The figures are all sculpturesque, in rather affected poses, and the overall atmosphere of the painting is cool.

The Waves

Arnold Böcklin
(Basel, 1827–Fiesole, 1901)

- 1883
- oil on canvas
- 180.3 x 237.5 cm
- Alte Pinakothek, Munich

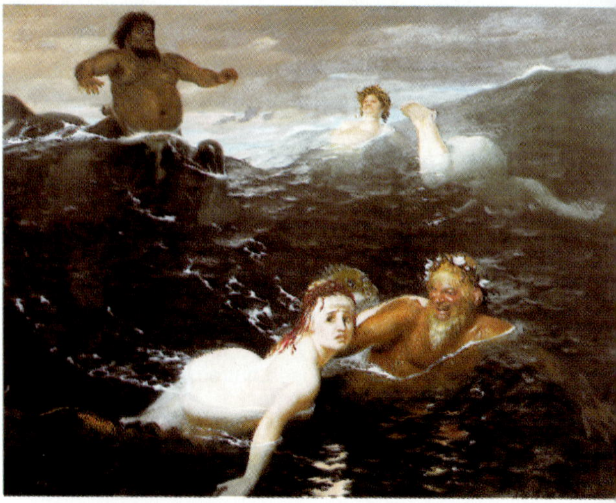

The nudes contrast with the saturated, dark tones of the sea: the tritons have coppery skin, whereas the nymphs are a sensual white of nearly transparent brilliance.

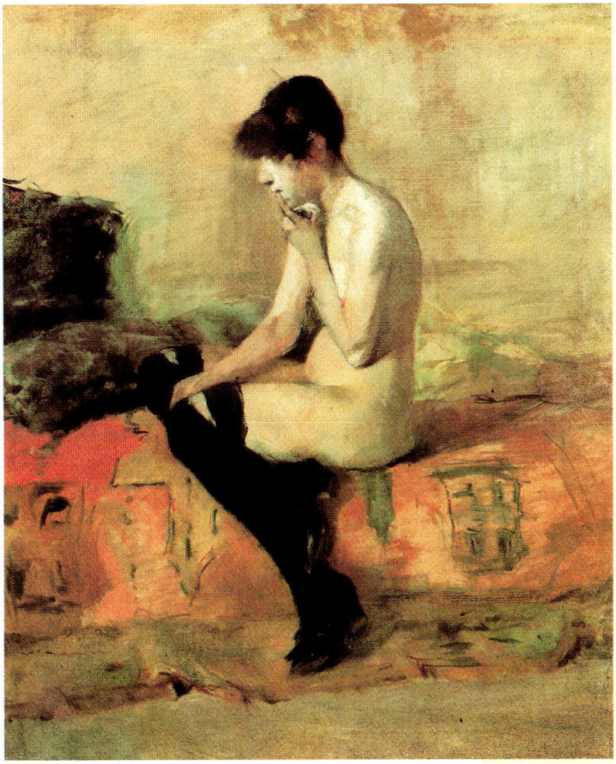

The woman in this painting is shown in profile, wearing only shoes and stockings and sitting on a bed sucking her fingertip with an expression of both concentration and mischief. Although she appears somewhat naive, the figure exhibits unmistakably erotic features: the act of sucking her fingertips, the nipple appearing above her left arm, the bushy hair covering her eyes. These are details that were to recur frequently in later works of the artist, in which his aim was clearly to provoke. Nonetheless, he portrays this woman with great dignity. Remarkable is his exquisite treatment of light, which pervades the entire room, concentrating on the upper body of the figure. Curiously, Toulouse-Lautrec's painterly handling of the woman is gentle, which is quite rare, for he usually rendered his figures with a strong, indeed, almost aggressive line, which became a hallmark of the artist's work.

Woman Sitting on a Divan

Henri de Toulouse-Lautrec

(Albi, 1864–Malromé, 1901)

- 1883
- oil on canvas
- 55 x 46 cm
- Musée Toulouse-Lautrec, Albi

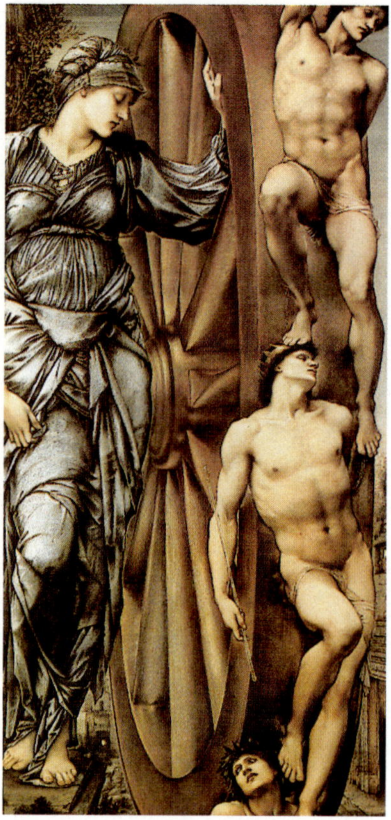

The Wheel of Fortune

Edward Burne-Jones
(Birmingham, 1833
–London, 1898)

- 1883
- oil on canvas
- 200 x 100 cm
- Musée d'Orsay, Paris

This scene shows the goddess Fortune spinning a giant wheel to which three male figures are bound. They are almost completely nude, save the tiny veils that cover their genitalia. Fortune offers herself to the man she most desires. The painter has executed and modeled the figures with painstaking detail; the bodies are exceedingly beautiful and sensual, with remarkable foreshortening, which creates a sense of movement, despite the fact that they are constrained by their bonds. Imaginative and sensitive, this extraordinary draftsman presents idealized and mysterious figures, evoking concepts and forms from the past.

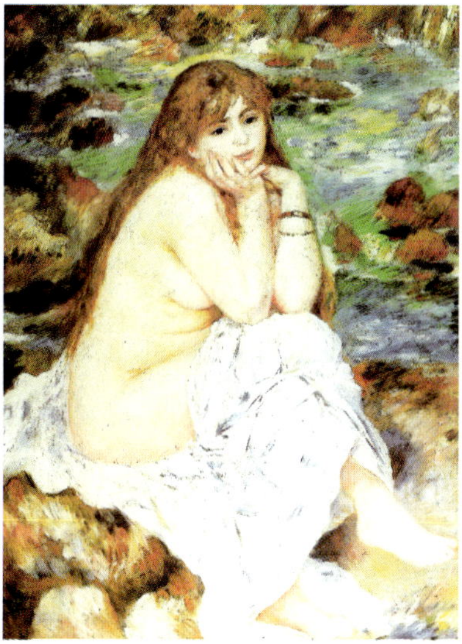

Seated Bather

Pierre-August Renoir
(Limoges, 1841–Cagnes-sur-Mer, 1919)

- 1883
- oil on canvas
- 121 x 91 cm
- Fogg Art Museum, Harvard University, Cambridge, MA. Bequest of Maurice Wertheim

We see a young, relaxed woman with an air of tenderness and candor. Her body is modeled in a narrow range of colors, so that the folds of her flesh generate a voluptuous three-dimensionality. Renoir's characteristic fascination with color and light are evident in this work.

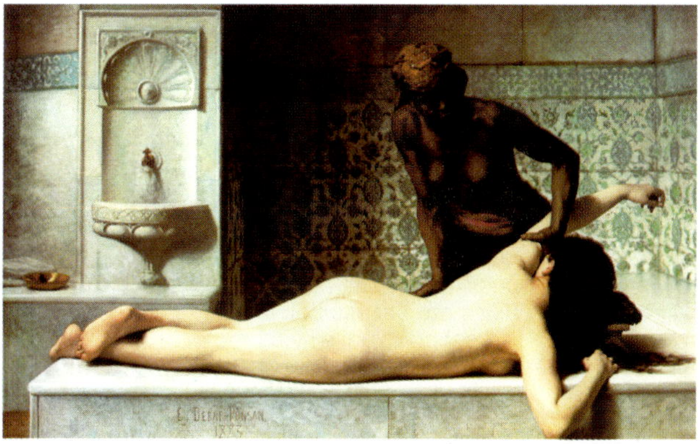

Massage in the Hammam

Édouard Debat-Ponsan
(Toulouse, 1847–Paris, 1913)

- 1883
- oil on canvas
- 127 x 210 cm
- Musée des Augustins, Toulouse

A relaxed female figure, substantial and shapely, executed with superb surface-modeling that brings out its depth and volume. The painting was exhibited at the 1883 Salon. Apart from any more obvious factors, the contrasting skin color of the two women creates an almost palpable sensuality.

The Master

Jean-Joseph Benjamin Constant
(Saint-Omer, 1827–Paris, 1877)

- 1884
- oil on canvas
- 114 x 195 cm
- Musée des Beaux-Arts, Pau

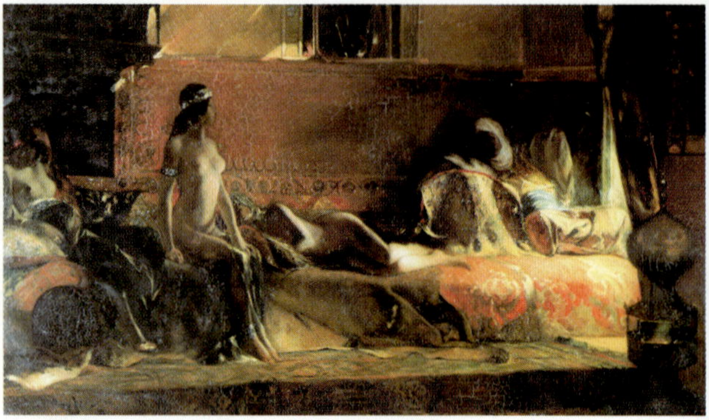

This interior and its decorations have been very atmospherically rendered, color, line and treatment of lighting all being pressed into the service of stimulating the viewer's senses.

Bathers

Adolphe-William Bouguereau
(La Rochelle, 1825–1905)

- 1884
- oil on canvas
- 200 x 124 cm
- The Art Institute of Chicago

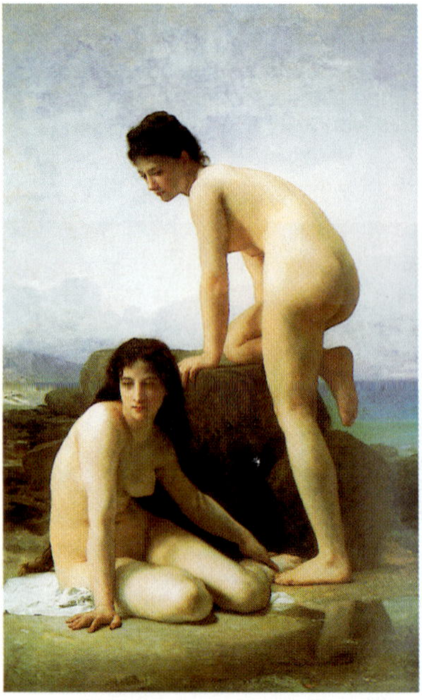

This composition is balanced, the nudes well-modeled, their forms slender and well-proportioned, indicating a good knowledge of human anatomy. While the faces are nearly identical, they are nevertheless expressive.

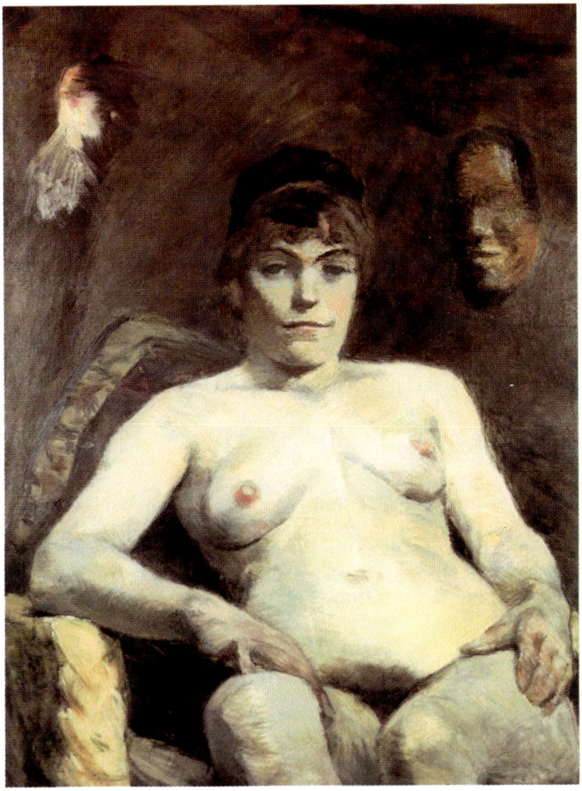

The woman in this painting was a prostitute in Montmartre who, along with many others, went to Place Pigalle every morning to offer herself as a model to artists in order to earn some money. In this work, Toulouse-Lautrec presents a non-idealized naked woman in a dignified manner. She seems so close that the viewer has the impression of almost being able to touch her. The woman is sure of herself, exposing her body unabashedly, with an almost defiant air, which is underscored by the vigorous brushwork and her steady gaze. Her genitals are covered by thick hair and given a prominent position in the painting. This is a hard, naked eroticism with no idealization whatsoever. The significance of the two masks in the top corners of the painting remains a matter of debate among art historians.

Marie

Henri de Toulouse-Lautrec

(Albi, 1864–Malromé, 1901)

- 1884
- oil on canvas
- 79 x 64 cm
- Von der Heydt Museum, Wuppertal

Woman Kneeling after Her Bath

Edgar Degas
(Paris, 1834–1917)

- 1884
- pastel on paper
- 50 x 50 cm
- Hermitage, St. Petersburg

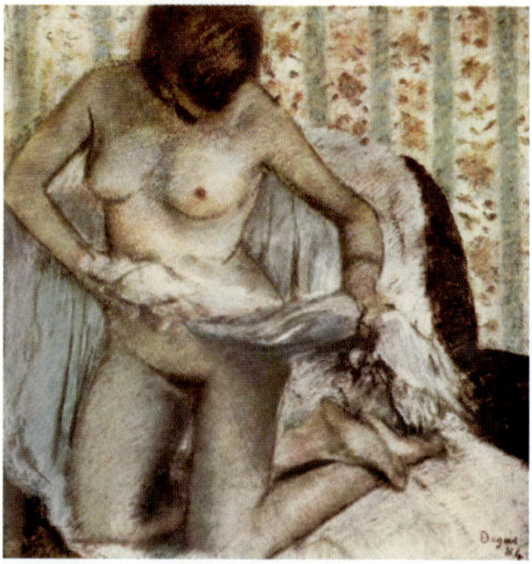

Here, the artist plays with a tenuous light that casts shadows, providing a suitably intimate atmosphere while harmoniously blending the figure into its environment. The vertical stripes on the wallpaper offset the soft curves of the figure's body and the position of her arms.

Triptych of the Hesperides

Hans von Marées
(Elberfeld, Westphalia, 1837–Rome, 1887)

- 1884–85
- panel
- 175 x 88.5 cm
- Neue Pinakothek, Munich

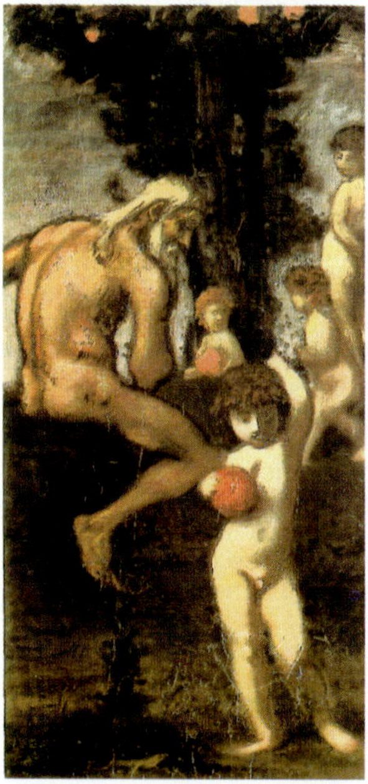

In this scene, various naked figures are depicted next to an apple tree. The pose and execution of the male figure with long, white hair and a beard betray the artist's use of classical models. The stylized bodies of the children, two of whom hold an enormous apple in their hands, have been rendered with a perfect balance of light and shade, a technique that the painter used throughout the entire painting. The color scheme and the dark background provide a sense of mystery, which enhances the figures, who are shown vigilant and intent upon preventing the theft of the apples.

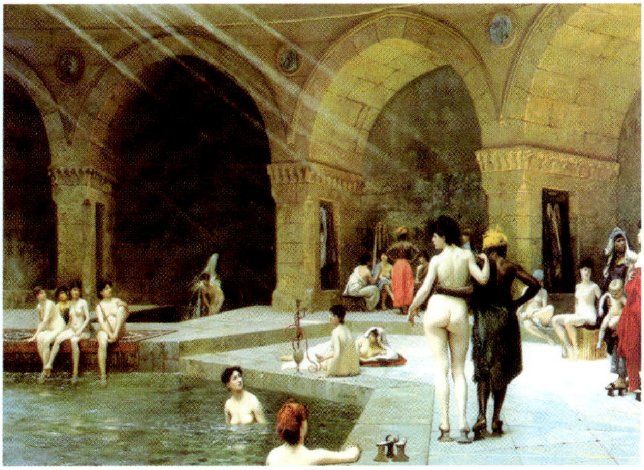

Swimming Pool at Brousse

Jean-Léon Gérôme

(Vesoul, 1824–Paris, 1904)

- 1885
- oil on canvas
- 70 x 96.5 cm
- private collection

Slender, well-modeled figures and interesting details, such as shoes, a hookah pipe and colored servants, help to create atmosphere in this intimate and attractively presented scene.

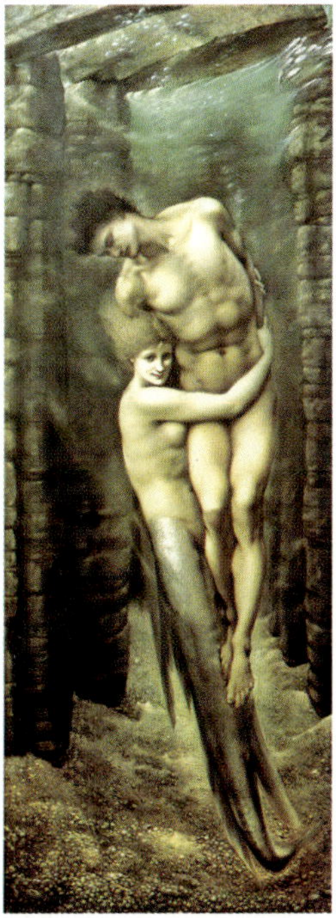

The Depths of the Sea

Edward Burne-Jones

(Birmingham, 1833 –London, 1898)

- 1886
- oil on canvas
- 197 x 75 cm
- private collection

The work depicts a mermaid having ensnared a mortal. The painter has portrayed the figures as well-modeled and relatively slender although not without muscularity. The format is singular.

Nude Woman Combing Her Hair

Edgar Degas
(Paris, 1834–1917)

- ca. 1886
- pastel on cardboard
- 58 x 52 cm
- Hermitage, St. Petersburg

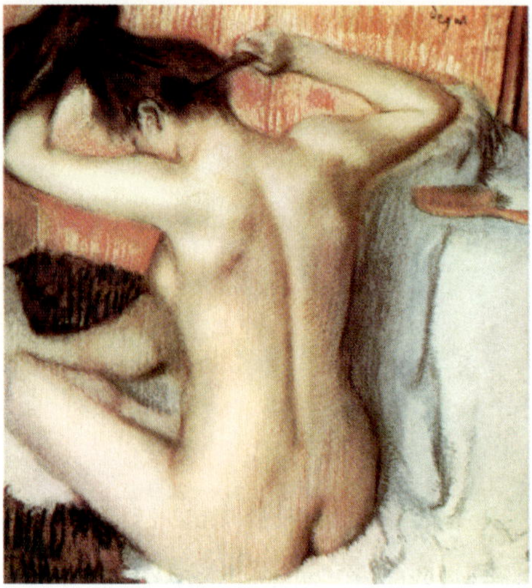

The woman has impeccably smooth skin and her body is modeled in masterly fashion. To frame the scene, the painter has devised a background consisting of large, variegated color fields against which the figure stands out in all its tender sensuality and refined splendor.

Study for The Models

Georges Seurat
(Paris, 1859–1891)

- early 1887
- oil on panel
- 25 x 16 cm
- Musée d'Orsay, Paris

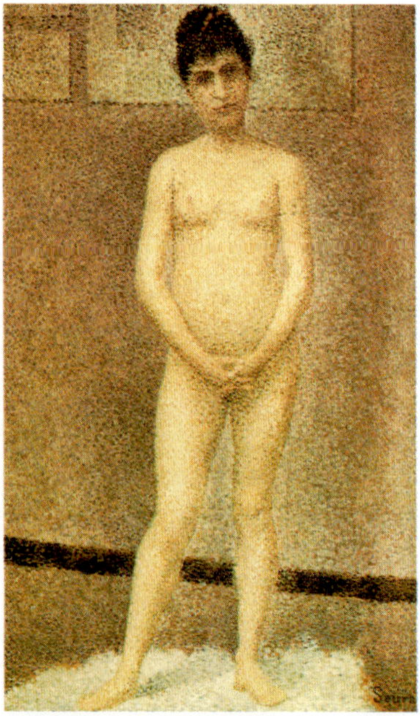

The woman stands in a natural, unsophisticated pose, with tenuous contours, and is not especially attractive. Using light ool ors, the artist has managed to present a body of refined sensuality, with delicate forms and well-resolved volumes, in which everything seems measured, down to the minutest detail. Seurat's interest in form and his singular color technique enabled him to achieve painstakingly-rendered, expressive images, to which this painting attests.

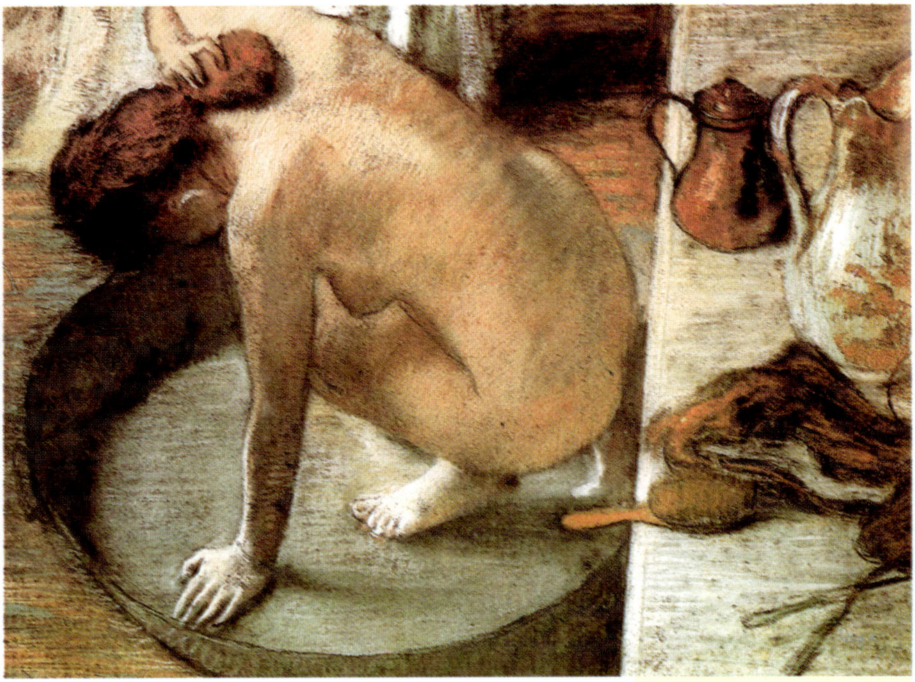

Woman Bathing in a Shallow Tub

Edgar Degas
(Paris, 1834–1917)

- 1886
- pastel on paper
- 60 x 83 cm
- Musée d'Orsay, Paris

Taking ordinary women for his models, Degas was able to capture pose, background, lighting and other details with consummate skill, so that his works invariably appear fresh and spontaneous. His compositions frequently seem to be viewed through the eyes of a voyeur, which might explain in part the erotic charge often inherent in his candid images. Degas himself affirmed that his method afforded him numerous compositional possibilities that his studio work did not. Moreover, pastel both suited impromptu sketches, as well as heightening the sensual and mysterious air of these works. Degas was clearly striving to give academic nudes greater dramatic interest by locating them in a context, thus demonstrating that everyday life can be an inexhaustible source of motifs.

Nude Woman

Vincent van Gogh
(Zundert, 1853–Auvers-sur-Oise, near Paris, 1890)

- 1887
- oil on canvas
- 24 x 41 cm
- Collection S. van Devener Wassemaar

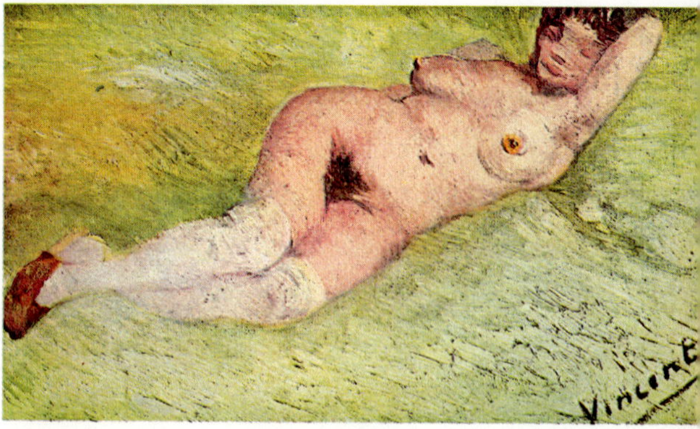

Although the woman is not very attractive—the model is probably one of the many prostitutes who offered themselves to artists as models in return for money—Van Gogh's characteristic curves and lively brushwork achieve an image of great expressive force. The most notable feature of this scene is the woman's face, executed with only a few brushstrokes.

Istar

Fernand Khnopff
(Grembergen, East Flanders, 1858–Brussels, 1921)

- 1888
- drawing on paper
- 16.5 x 7 cm
- private collection

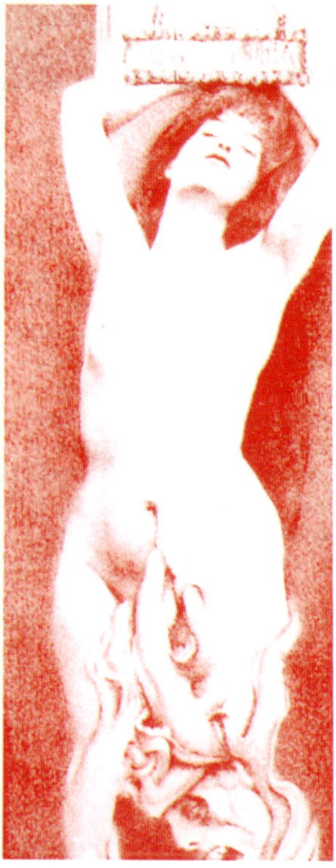

The advent of photography brought with it certain changes in the representation of nude figures, first and foremost an increase in attention to realistic detail, as can be seen in this drawing. Contrasts play a big role in the drawing, while the traditional treatment of academic tonal evaluation is entirely absent.

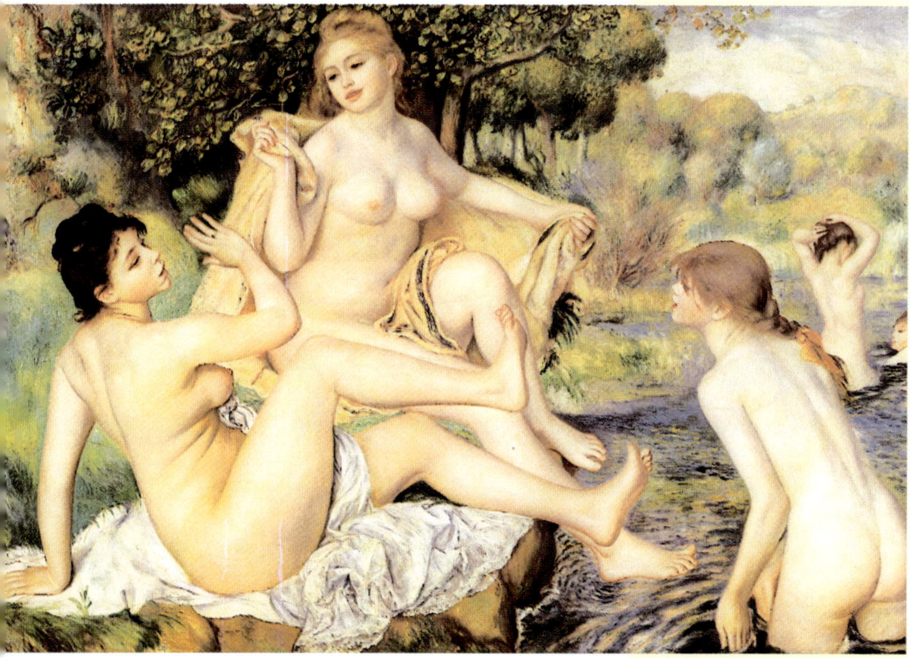

This painting utilizes a theme that was common in 19th-century art, that of bathers. The dynamic, almost monumental composition combines academic Classicism with Romanticism. Judging by the relatively static nature of the figures, it would seem that the artist painted each separately, combining them later in a rather awkward, poorly-integrated scene. Yet the figures are perfectly executed, with voluptuous, firm bodies. Renoir has employed a harmonious, all-pervasive color scheme that lends coherence to the whole.

Bathers

Pierre-August Renoir
(Limoges, 1841–Cagnes-sur-Mer, 1919)

- 1887
- oil on canvas
- 115 x 170 cm
- Philadelphia Museum of Art. Mr. and Mrs. Carroll S. Tyson Collection

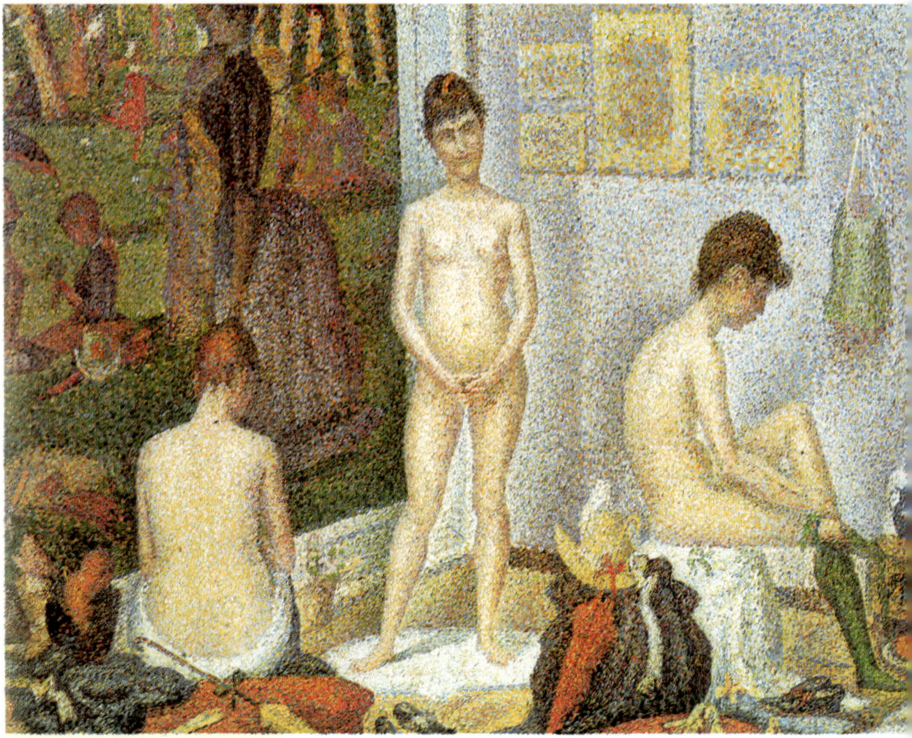

The Models

Georges Seurat

(Paris, 1859–1891)

- 1888
- oil on canvas
- 39.4 x 48.7 cm
- Heinz Berggruen Collection, Paris

Seurat studied Michel-Eugène Chevreul's theory of simultaneous color contrasts and applied it to his painting, giving rise to pointillism. He employed the technique in the present painting, for which he had made preliminary studies of each figure. The scene is inviting: women are shown in a room, dressing. The figures have been skilfully modeled, and illuminated and shaded areas resolved, using warm or cold and dark or light points of colour to achieve a superb visual effect with well-defined contours and accurately-rendered forms. Seurat covered the left wall in the painting with a work he had executed two years before, Sunday Afternoon on the Island of La Grande Jatte.

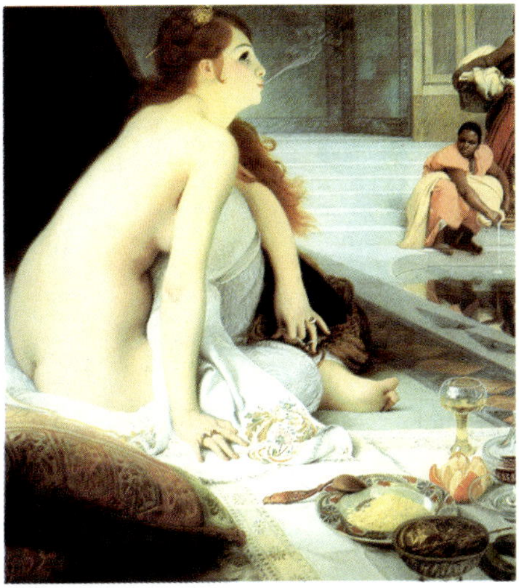

The White Slave

Jean Lecomte du Nouy
(Paris, 1842–1923)

- 1888
- oil on canvas
- 149.5 x 118.3 cm
- Musée des Beaux-Arts, Nantes

The laundry women in the background, one of them wringing out a sheet or table cloth, and the jet of smoke captured issuing from the slave's mouth, even the way she holds her cigarette, create a wonderful snapshot-like quality.

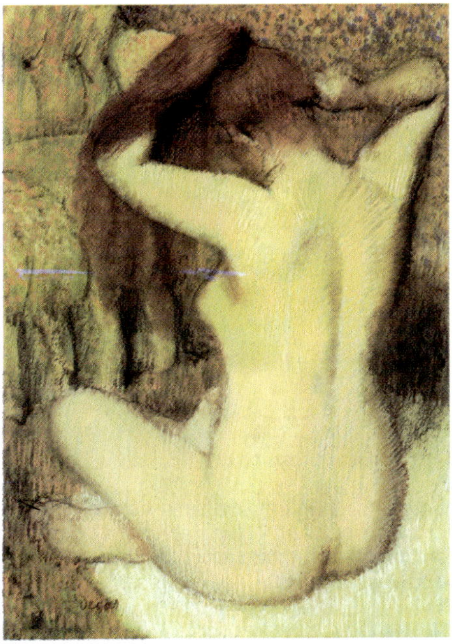

Nude Woman Combing Her Hair

Edgar Degas
(Paris, 1834–1917)

- 1888
- pastel on paper
- 61.3 x 46 cm
- Metropolitan Museum of Art, New York

Donated by Mr. and Mrs. Nate B. Spingold (1956)

In this pastel, the figure occupies almost the entire picture plane, scarcely leaving room for the background, which is largely abstract. Subtly modeled in a narrow range of colors, the woman's soft, smooth skin is bathed in golden light.

La Toilette

Henri de Toulouse-Lautrec
(Albi, 1864–Malromé, 1901)

- 1889
- oil on cardboard
- 64 x 52 cm
- Musée d'Orsay, Paris

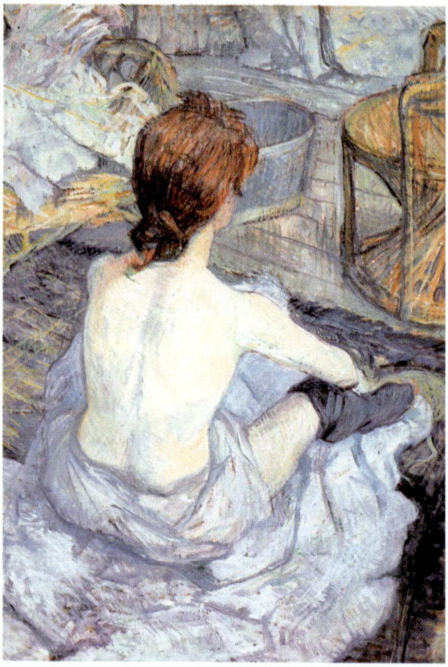

The artist demonstrates his peculiar style and complete mastery of draftsmanship in confident, steady strokes and in a perfect treatment of color, the whole enveloped in an air of chromatic softness and harmony. It is surprising that such a meticulously rendered figure is depicted in a somewhat disorderly setting.

The Steam Bath

Jean-Léon Gérôme
(Vésoul, 1824–Paris, 1904)

- 1889
- oil on canvas
- 73 x 101 cm
- Richard Green Galleries, London

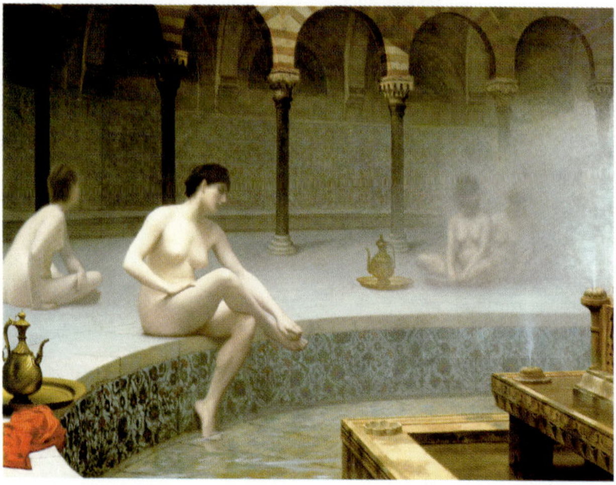

Four female figures are seen here in the exotic setting of a Turkish bath. Their alabaster skin colors show just sufficient tonal modulations to give the bodies depth and volume.

Nöck, a water spirit in Germanic mythology, lures humans with his music and then kills them. The execution of the nude is Classicizing in tendency, its sensuality accentuated by the abandon of its pose as well as the way the reeds caress the thighs.

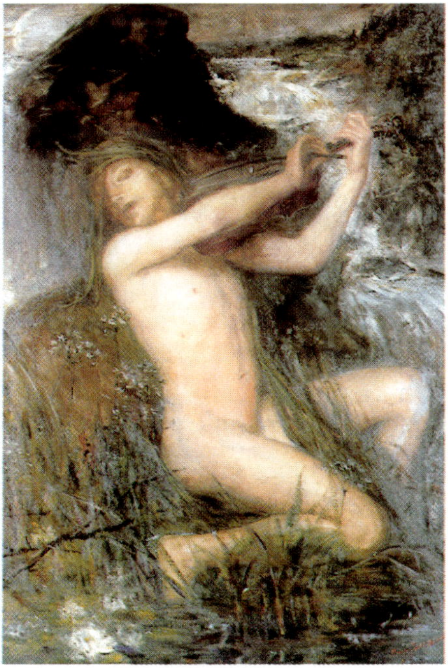

Nöck, the Water Spirit

Ernst Josephson
(1851–1906)

- ca. 1890
- oil on canvas
- 144 x 114 cm
- Nationalmuseum, Stockholm

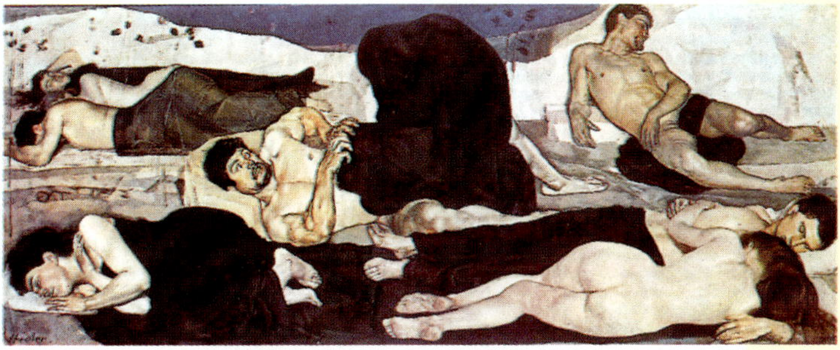

Hodler's mature work had a markedly symbolist flavour. Here, he confines himself to depicting human beings at night: rest, love, dreams, insomnia; everything is presented in an atmosphere of intimacy where black predominates.

Night

Ferdinand Hodler
(Bern, 1853–Geneva, 1918)

- 1890
- oil on canvas
- Kunstmuseum, Bern

Woman Drying Her Back

Edgar Degas
(Paris, 1834–1917)

- ca. 1890
- pastel and wash with charcoal and varnish on cardboard
- 82.5 x 72 cm
- Hermitage, St. Petersburg

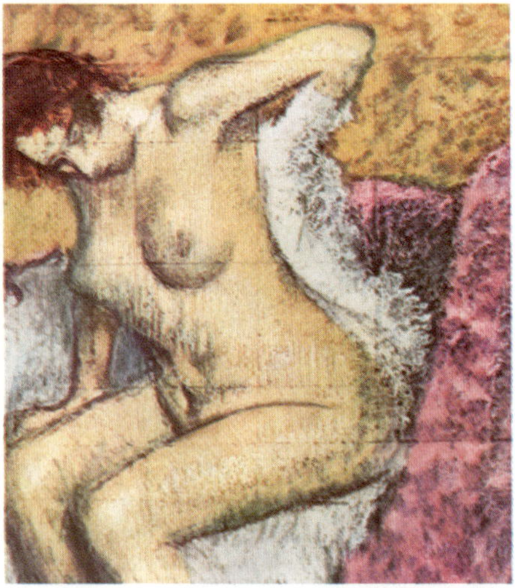

This work is schematic, with elements that remain distinct and are not blended in to the whole. The pose suggests movement and the pastel colors create an unusual atmosphere consisting of variegated color fields that form a background against which the figure's various body parts stand out. The woman is not in a relaxed pose, making a cumbersome gesture with her arm, her back rigid and torso upright and slightly inclined.

Pygmalion and Galatea

Jean-Léon Gérôme
(Vésoul, 1824–Paris, 1904)

- 1890
- oil on panel
- 88.9 x 68.6 cm
- Metropolitan Museum of Art, New York

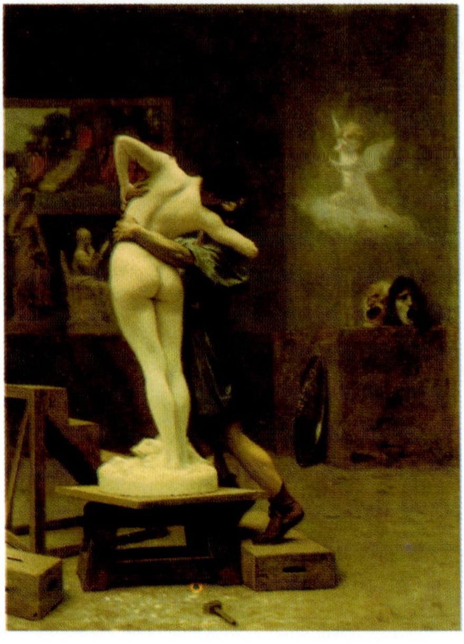

The nude shows signs of coming to life; her skin is shown being transformed from cold, white marble to soft, sensuous skin. The figures are rendered with near photographic precision. Indeed, as photography had recently been invented, photographs were used by the preponderance of artists of the time.

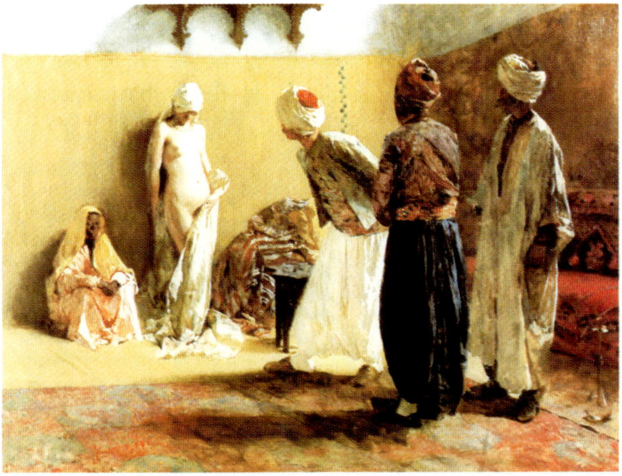

Examining a Slave

Ettore Cercone
(Messina, 1859–Sorrento, 1896)

- 1890
- oil on canvas
- 54 x 77.3 cm
- private collection

The naked woman depicted here is being subjected to a humilating examination by her Arab masters before being incorporated into their harem.

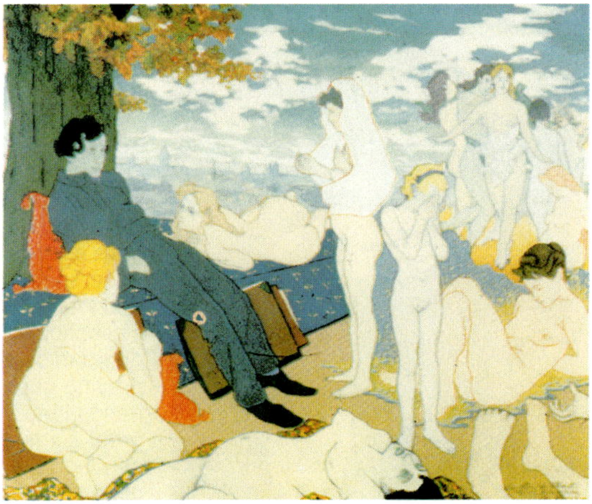

The Flowers of Evil

Charles Maurin
(1856–1914)

- 1891
- oil on canvas
- 81 x 100 cm
- Musée d'Art et d'Industrie, Saint-Étienne

The nudes in this painting are linear and rendered in tonally-pure colors that evoke posters of the art nouveau movement. The figures are drawn with clear attention to sexual details of anatomy and have an unambiguously erotic intent.

La Toilette

Mary Cassatt
(Pittsburgh, 1844–Mesnil-Théribus, Oise, 1926)

- 1891
- etching
- 38 x 26.8 cm
- Bibliothèque Nationale, Paris

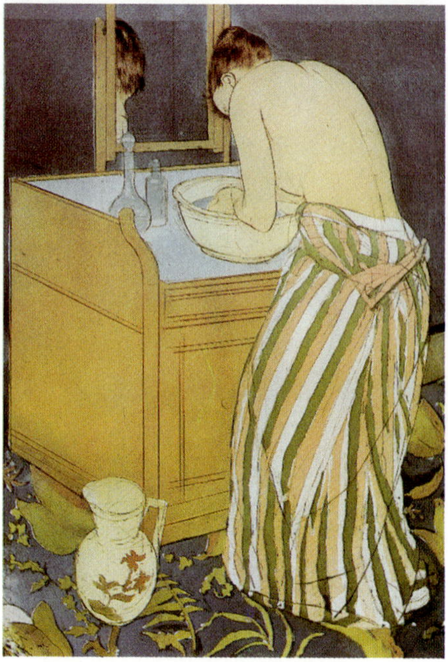

In this straightforward composition, the artist has captured the woman's character and gestures without idealizing them, offering us an image of an ordinary woman in an ordinary setting. Line, subdued color scheme and incorporation of incidental details make this work particularly sensitive and delicate.

Communication with the Beyond

Ferdinand Hodler
(Bern, 1853–Geneva, 1918)

- 1892
- oil on canvas
- 159 x 97 cm
- Öffentliche Kunstsammlung Basel, Kunstmuseum, Basel

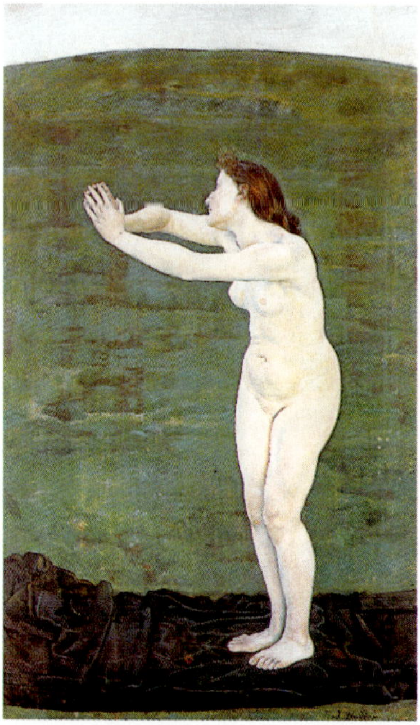

The model, Augustine Dupin, with whom the painter had a child, Hector, is rendered here as a foreshortened figure. Her hips and knees, the slight inclination of her back and particularly the praying gesture of her hands lend the figure great spirituality, although the mystical pose differs from that of more traditional praying figures, as though captured in dance. The pallid nude forms a striking contrast to the intense background of oxidation green.

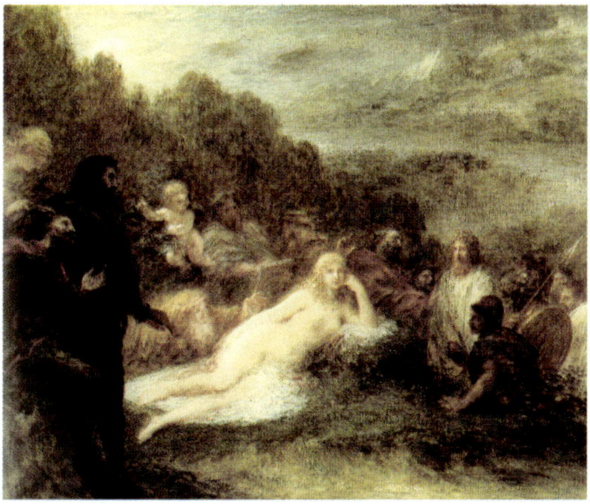

Helen

Henri-Théodore Fantin-Latour
(Grenoble, 1836–Buré, Normandy, 1904)

- 1892
- oil on canvas
- 78 x 105 cm
- Musée du Petit Palais, Paris

Helen, here, is depicted as a rather ethereal figure in an ethereal and atmospheric setting. Surrounded by men, she personifies the art and power of feminine seductiveness.

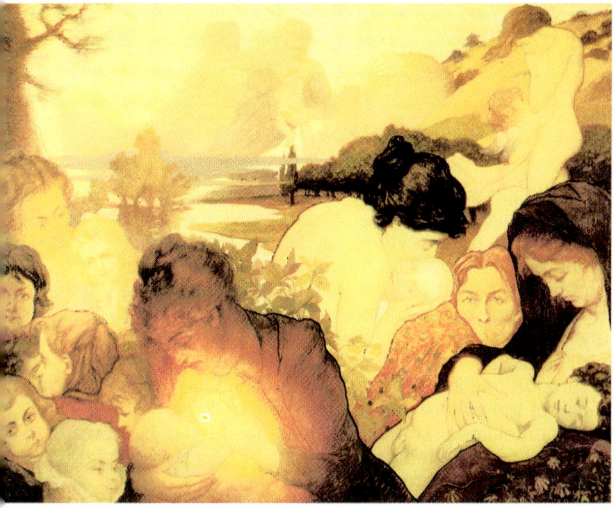

Motherhood

Charles Maurin
(Le Puy, 1856–Grasse, 1913)

- 1893
- oil on canvas
- 80 x 100 cm
- Musée Crozatier, Le Puy

The complexions of the three nudes are exceptionally striking in this allegory of maternity, blending as they do with the golden atmosphere that imbues the entire work. The figures are not intended to be erotic, although they are distinctly sensual. The presence of nude children also sees to it that the viewer's mind does not wander too far.

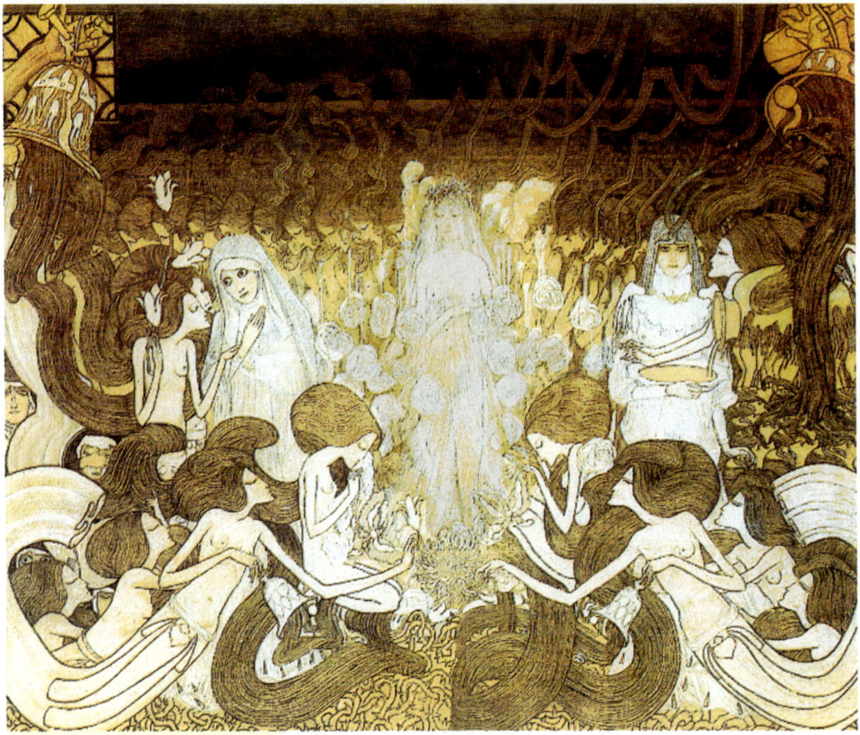

The Three Brides

Jan Toorop (Johannes Theodorus Toorop)
(Poerworedjo, Java, 1858–The Hague, 1928)

- 1893
- black pencil and colored ink on paper
- 78 x 98 cm
- Rijksmuseum Kröller-Müller, Otterlo

This allegorical work contains elements of Symbolism and Art Nouveau. Its organic, decorative forms, recalling plant motifs, recur rhythmically across the entire surface of the painting, creating a number of visual textures around the central figures. The nudes evoke figures in Egyptian art. The nude torsos reveal small breasts, which are subtly suggested by single lines. The long, languid arms resemble reeds undulating in the breeze, while the disproportionately large masses of loose hair occupy much of the picture plane, engendering flowing ornamental lines. The three brides each have their own personality and attributes. In this highly stylized painting, graphic elements predominate.

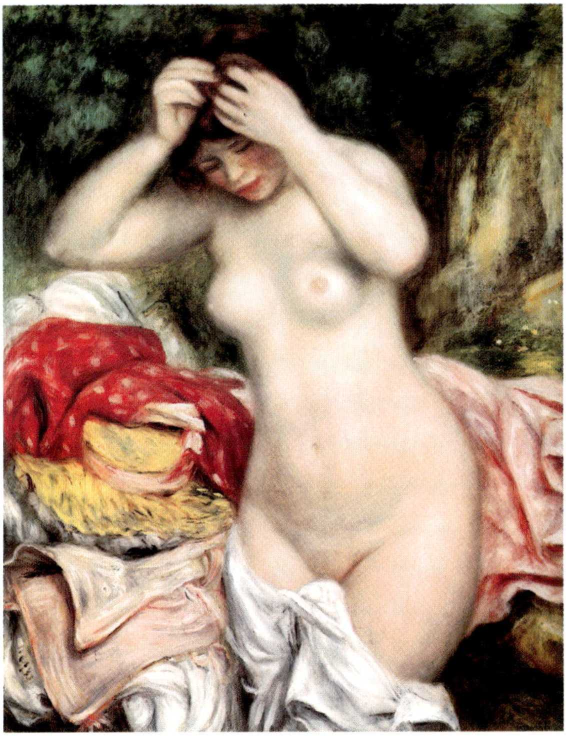

This painting presents the figure of a young, comely woman with well-defined contours, sinuous lines and voluptuous volumes, in which geometrical shapes combine to form a delicate compositional balance. The soft, smooth quality of the skin, the rosy pink of the flushed cheeks and the reddish-brown color of the hair are achieved with a broad palette of subtle tones. The woman's pose, with her hands on her head, serves to exaggerate her forms and heighten her sensuality. The background is rendered in an intense green, recalling the forest at Pont-Aven, where Renoir sojourned in August of 1893. As is typical of the artist, he depicts the figure with a variety of other elements: a straw hat, multi-colored dresses that enliven the scene and some fabric—full of folds and evoking movement—covering the woman's genitals.

Bather Combing Her Hair

Pierre-Auguste Renoir

(Limoges, 1841–Cagnes-sur -Mer, 1919)

- 1893
- oil on canvas
- 92 x 74 cm
- National Gallery of Art, Chester Dale Collection, Washington, D.C.

Sin

Franz von Stuck
(Tettenweis, Bavaria, 1863 –Munich, 1928)

- 1893
- oil on canvas
- 95 x 59.7 cm
- Neue Pinakothek, Munich

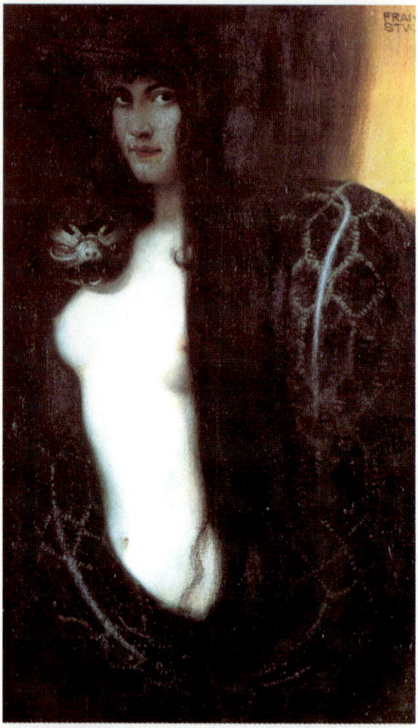

This nude figure personifies sin, or, we might surmise, perversion. It successfully sets up a psychological relationship between viewer and model, whose captivating gaze is perhaps, nevertheless, a touch deficient in anything that we might call genuinely subversive or disturbing. The painterly treatment of the figure is of a generally classicizing tendency.

Hit

Frederic Leighton
(Scarborough, 1830 –London, 1896)

- 1893
- oil on canvas
- 75 x 56 cm
- Roy Miles Gallery, London

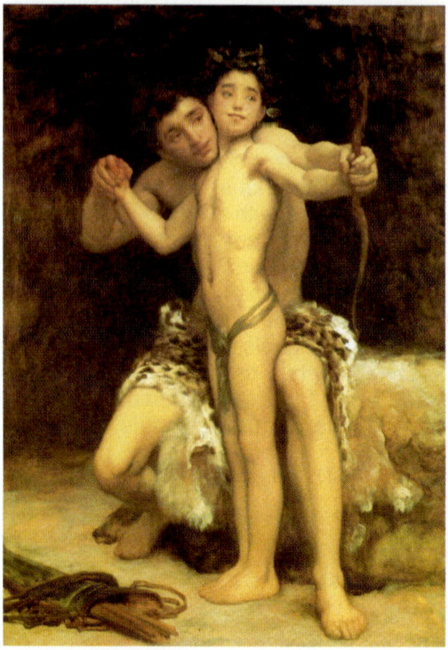

The canvas is anecdotal, yet its merits lie more in the tiny details. The advent of photography may have been responsible for this increased interest in realism—in "capturing the instant". The two subjects here stand out against a dark background, the highlights over their bodies creating depth.

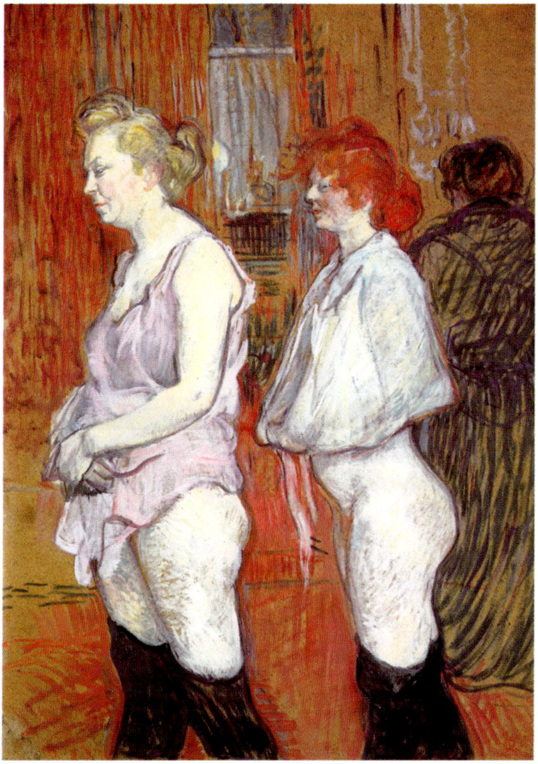

Prostitution was tolerated in Toulouse-Lautrec's day, but prostitutes had to be registered and every week were made to undergo a medical examination in order to prevent the spread of venereal diseases, a justifiable concern at the time. In this scene, prostitutes are shown holding up their dresses while waiting to be examined. Although an important means of control, such examinations were the cause of much concern among prostitutes, since they could lead them to lose their jobs and be admitted to the hospital forthright. The face of the blonde-haired figure says it all, accurately capturing the mood of the moment. The skill with which the artist rendered her slouching shoulders and resigned expression is truly extraordinary. On the far right, with her back to the viewer, stands the Madame; she and the room form a background of the artist's characteristically long, vigorous brushstrokes, executed with relatively dark colors, against which the pale figures stand out as the painting's protagonists.

Rue des Moulins

Henri de Toulouse-Lautrec

(Albi, 1864–Malromé, 1901)

- 1894
- oil on cardboard on wood
- 83.5 x 61.4 cm
- National Gallery of Art, Chester Dale Collection, Washington, D.C.

Female Angel with Halo

Louis Welden Hawkins
(Esslingen, 1849–Paris, 1910)

- 1894
- oil on canvas
- 61 x 50 cm
- private collection, Paris

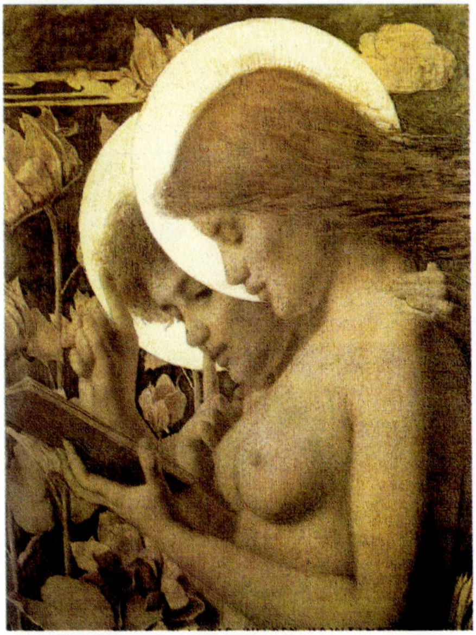

Nude portrait and angel merge in this oil painting. The young girl's shapely figure and the Scripture she and her companion are reading combine against an ornamental background of plants.

Woman Putting on a Stocking

Henri de Toulouse-Lautrec
(Albi, 1864–Malromé, 1901)

- 1894
- oil on cardboard
- 61.5 x 44.5 cm
- Musée Toulouse-Lautrec, Albi

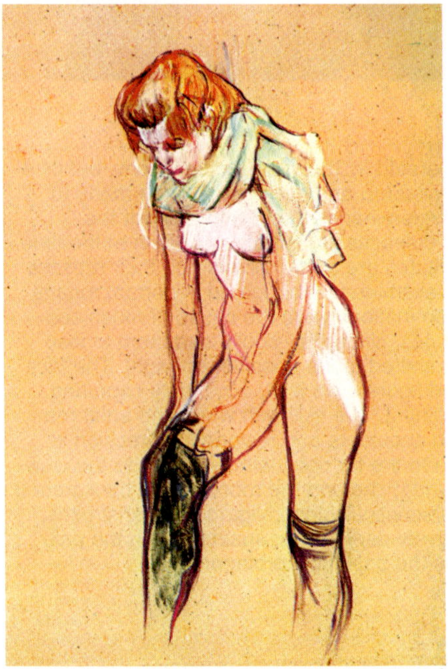

The provocative nature of the image is defused by the remarkable naturalism with which Toulouse-Lautrec renders it. If the artist had any aim in mind with this sketch, it was to take an image of a marginalized world as his theme. Perhaps this is why the painter was always able to count on the collaboration of prostitutes.

At Juno's behest, Semele asked Jupiter to display himself to her in his full splendor, as a result of which she was consumed by the heat of his brilliance. The lifeless nude figure of Semele is depicted here in a sensual pose with attractive forms.

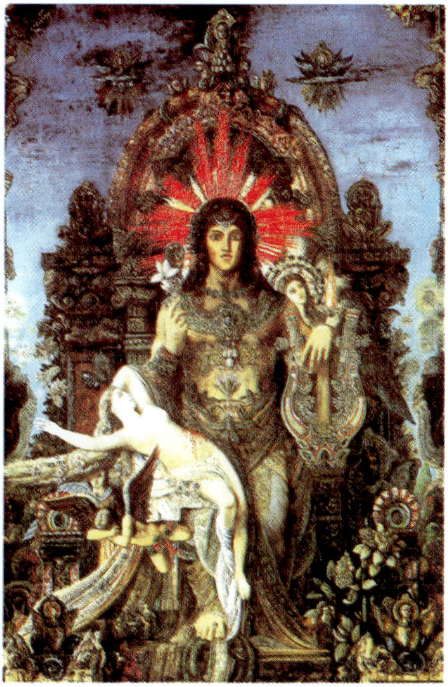

Jupiter and Semele

Gustave Moreau
(Paris, 1826–1898)

- 1894–96
- oil on canvas
- 213 x 118 cm
- Musée Gustave Moreau, Paris

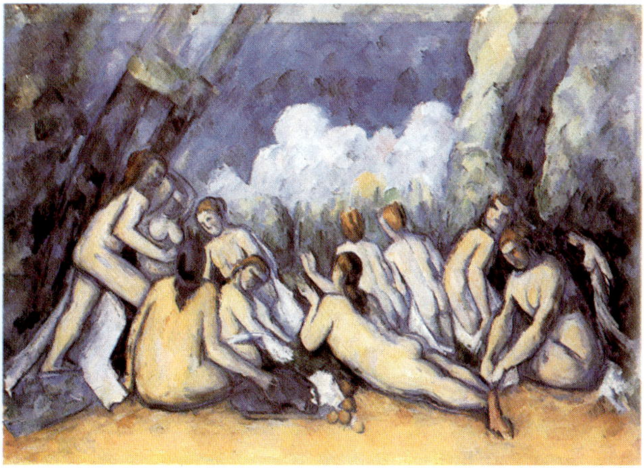

The female nudes appear to have been caught in motion, in the manner of a snapshot. They are drawn with schematic contours and a few cursory brushstrokes, which define their volumes. Eschewing anecdotal details, the artist is primarily concerned with the line, which is rendered here with formal harmony and virtuosity, and is accompanied by a remarkable color scheme.

The Large Bathers

Paul Cézanne
(Aix-en-Provence, 1839–1906)

- 1900–1906
- oil on canvas
- 127.2 x 196.1 cm
- National Gallery, London

Moorish Baths

Jean-Léon Gérôme

(Vésoul, 1824–Paris, 1904)

- ca. 1895
- oil on canvas
- Museum of Fine Arts, Boston

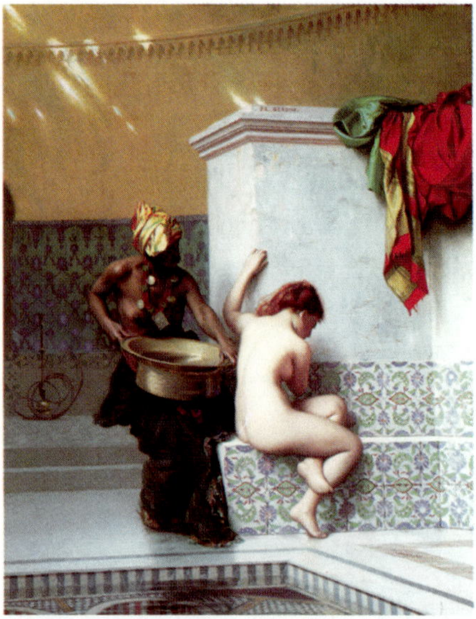

Caucasian women were highly sought-after as slaves. Here, we see a new slave, thoroughly distraught, who is about to be presented to the Arab lord.

Women at the Baths

Jean-Léon Gérôme

(Vésoul, 1824–Paris, 1904)

- ca. 1895
- oil on canvas
- Musée Georges Garret, Vésoul

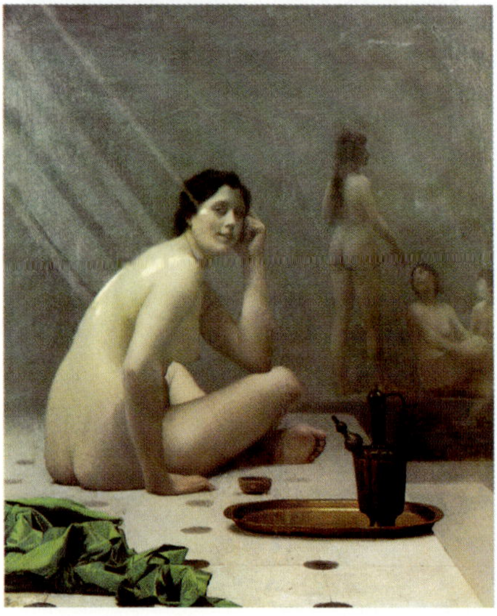

The women depicted here are in a Turkish bath. Noteworthy is the way the steam in the atmosphere has been conveyed, serving to soften both forms and colours. The result is a work of tender lyricism.

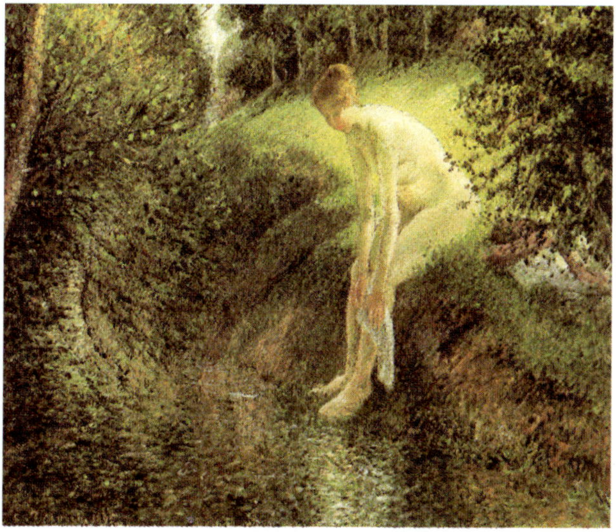

Bather in the Forest

Camille Pissarro
(St. Thomas, Virgin Islands, Antilles, 1830–Paris, 1903)

- 1895
- oil on canvas
- 60.3 x 73 cm
- Metropolitan Museum of Art, New York

Bequeathed by Mrs. H.O. Havermeyer, 1929, from the H.O. Havermeyer Collection

The figure in this painting appears in the brightest spot in the painting. The lightest area of her skin, which is modeled with a limited range of colors, constitutes the figure's back, which stands out against the luminous yellow field behind her. The saturated dark green of the tree on the right provides a striking contrast to the field, lending movement and depth to the composition.

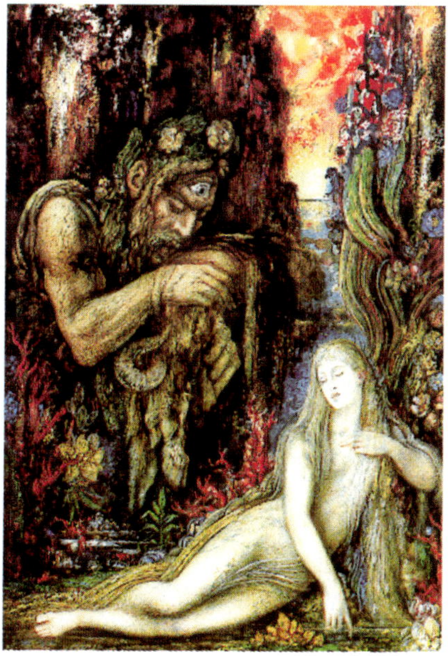

Spurned by Galatea in favour of her true love, Acis, Polyphemus killed the latter by crushing him under a rock. Galatea's delicate, attractive figure is displayed to full advantage here, despite Moreau's tendency to downplay his figures by an over-use of extravagant decoration.

Galatea

Gustav Moreau
(Paris, 1826–1898)

- ca. 1896
- watercolor and wash on paper
- 45 x 34 cm
- Thyssen-Bornemisza Collection, Lugano

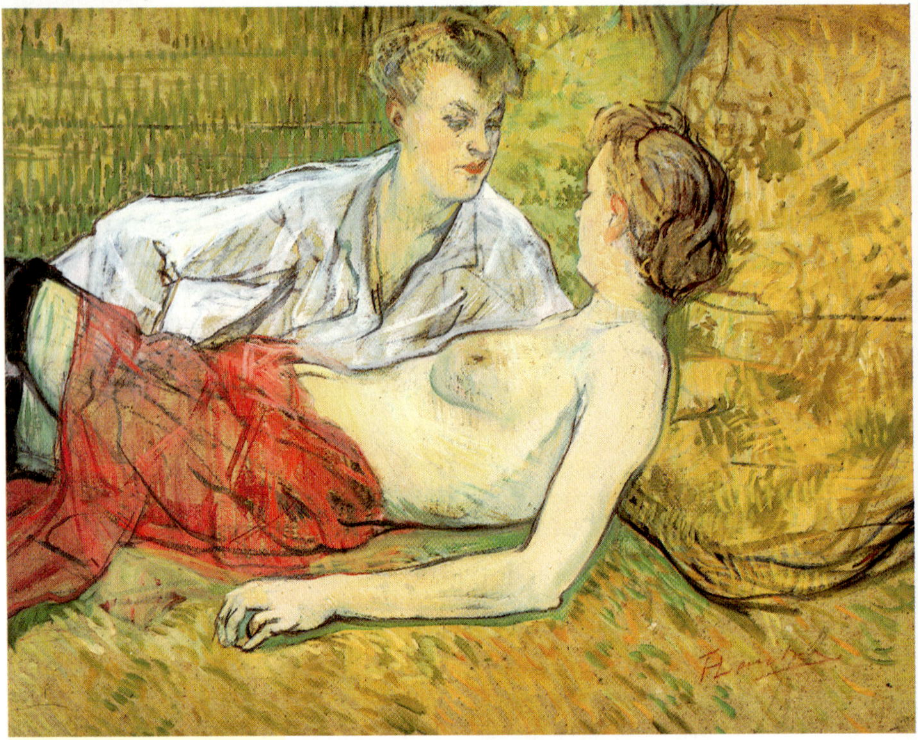

Two friends

Henri de Toulouse-Lautrec
(Albi, 1864–Malromé, 1901)

- 1895
- oil on cardboard
- 64.5 x 84 cm
- E.G. Bürhle Foundation, Switzerland

That lesbian love was a recurrent theme in the artist's oeuvre has been attributed to the influence of his familiarity with the erotic Japanese prints of Utamaro. Yet he had no need to resort to them for inspiration, for he had first-hand experience of this; indeed, it formed part of his everyday life. Only a painter who is intimately acquainted with his subject matter is capable of rendering it with such expressiveness, so much painstaking detail and creativity. This scene shows two young women on a bed; one of them, in the foreground, is shown with her chest bare and her legs open, passively receiving the intimate caresses of her lover, whose masculinity is conveyed by her face and shirt. The painter has rendered the scene in such a naturalistic, dignified manner that it is evident that his aim was not to provoke, but merely to paint two people making love in an intimate setting.

Life Class for Women

Paul Duthoit
(1856–1921)

- 1896
- oil on canvas
- 120 x 104 cm
- Musée des Beaux-Arts, Pau

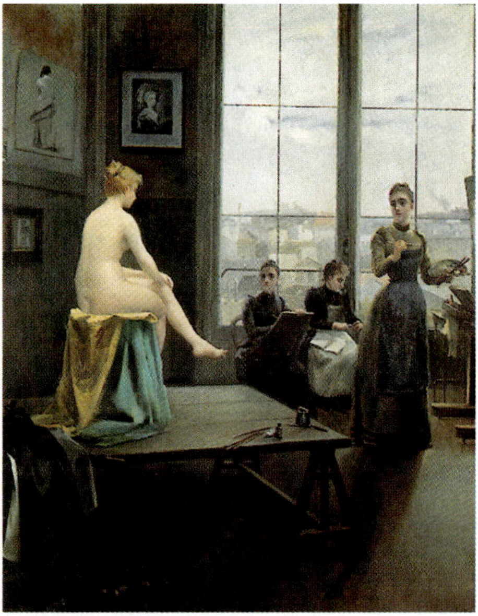

The focal point of the work is the naked female model, which, well illuminated, stands out against the dark walls of the room, which is rendered in saturated gray tones to create a sense of back lighting. This practice of setting a brightly illuminated figure against a dark background can be traced back to the Renaissance.

Te Vaá

Paul Gauguin
(Paris, 1848–Atuona, Hiva Oa, Marquesas Islands, 1903)

- 1896
- oil on canvas
- 96 x 130 cm
- Hermitage, St. Petersburg

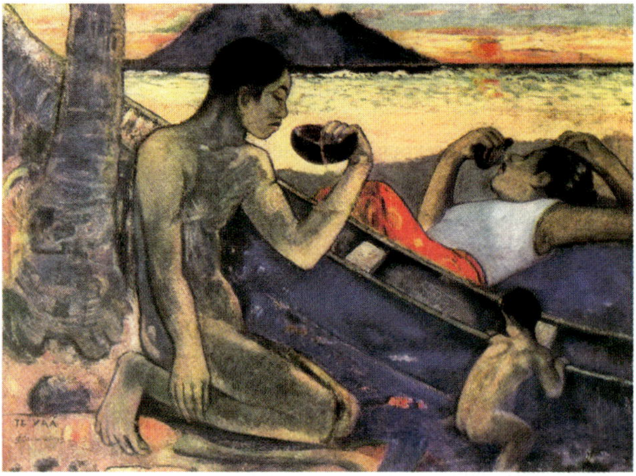

This composition is remarkable for the way the boat's outline divides the picture in two, diagonally. The top half, which features a landscape with a golden sea and a volcano in the background, is a dreamlike if sober image, which is underscored by the woman shown in a deep sleep. In the bottom half, a naked fisherman and his son are shown at work on terra firma, conveying the harsh reality of everyday life. One unusual aspect of the painting is the robust fisherman's profile, which recalls that of ancient Egyptian figures.

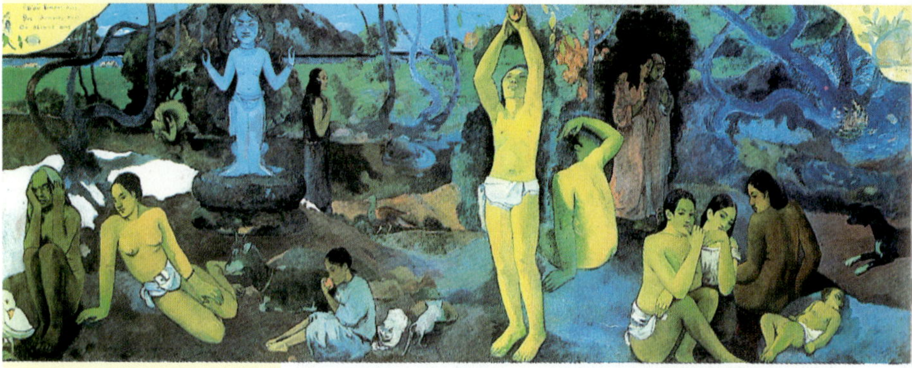

Where Do We Come From? What Are We? Where Are We Going?

Paul Gauguin
(Paris, 1848–Atuona, Hiva Oa, Marquesas Islands, 1903)

- 1897
- oil on canvas
- 139 x 374.5 cm
- Museum of Fine Arts, Boston, MA, Tompkins Collection

This canvas is monumental and steeped in symbolism; indeed, it is a reflection of life. On the right, a newborn infant symbolizes the beginning of life; on the left, an elderly woman represents the end. In the center, appear several young Polynesian nudes, which stand for naiveté, youth and life, and whose colors stand out against a background of deep blues and greens. Everything concerned with life is included here: the monstrous-looking animal symbolizes evolution; the monumental figure resembling an idol, culture and religion; the people in ordinary attire and the girl eating, everyday life; the landscape and the animals, nature; the people conversing, society, to mention just a few. The work's highly complex iconography, its composition and chromatic treatment bear witness to Gauguin's genius.

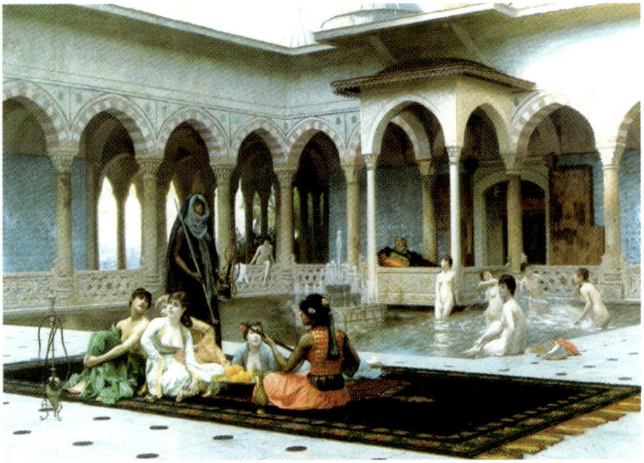

Courtyard at the Turkish Baths

Jean-Léon Gérôme

(Vésoul, 1824–Paris, 1904)

- ca. 1898
- oil on canvas
- 80 x 102 cm
- private collection

The women playing in the water, the seated figure playing an instrument while others listen—such details are frozen here, as in a snapshot. The brightly-colored dresses of the women in the foreground contrast pleasingly with the cool architecture as also with the marmoreal bodies of those in the pool.

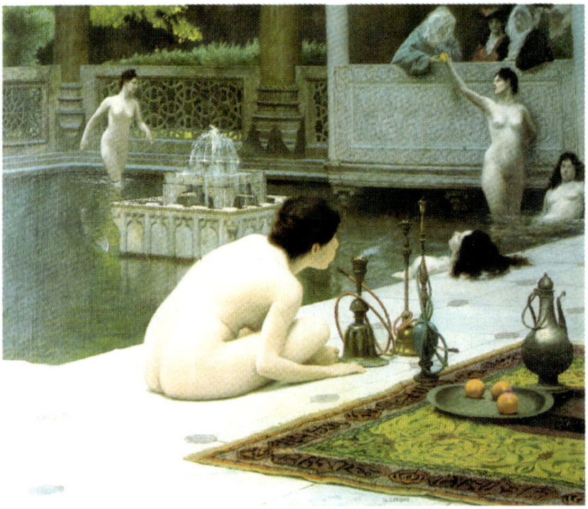

Lighting the Water-pipe

Jean-Léon Gérôme

(Vésoul, 1824–Paris, 1904)

- ca. 1898
- oil on canvas
- 54.6 x 66 cm
- Ghassan Shaker Collection, Gallery Keops, Geneva

Three of the marmoreal female figures here are not only delicately sensual but sculptural as well. Against them, the fruit, carpet, coffee pot and pipes, the two half-submerged women and the women in the booth, all establish a set of contrasts fraught with gentle tension.

Female Nude

Paul Cézanne
(Aix-en-Provence, 1839–1906)

- 1898–99
- oil on canvas
- 92.7 x 71 cm
- private collection, USA

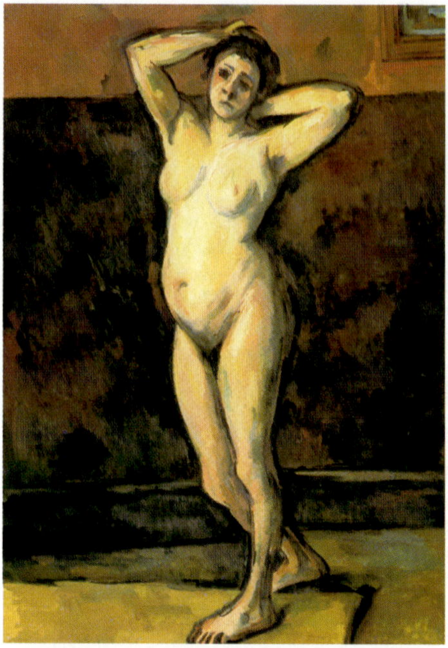

Cézanne is on record as having said it embarrassed him to work with nude women. Here, the artist has depicted a "normal" woman, sensual, but no especial beauty. Amongst other things, the painting is a wonderful study of light and color.

Maternity or Women at the Sea Shore

Paul Gauguin
(Paris, 1848–Atuona, Hiva Oa, Marquesas Islands, 1903)

- 1899
- oil on canvas
- 95.5 x 73.5 cm
- Hermitage, St. Petersburg

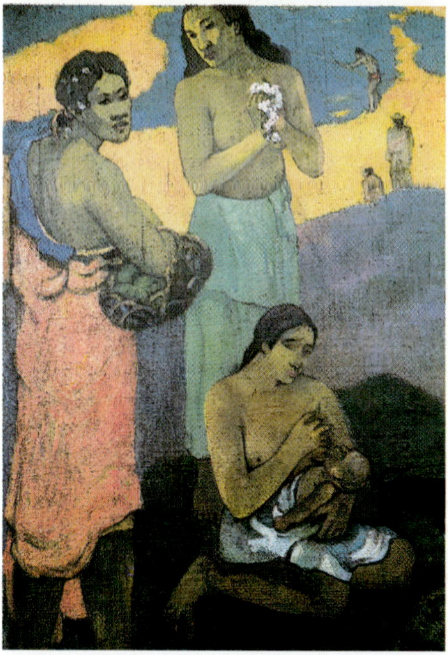

Gauguin, who would have encountered such scenes frequently in Polynesia, painted this work in honor of maternity. While filled with mystery and allure, the scene displays a rich symphony of colors in the background, with broad patches of turquoise, orange, violet and dark green.

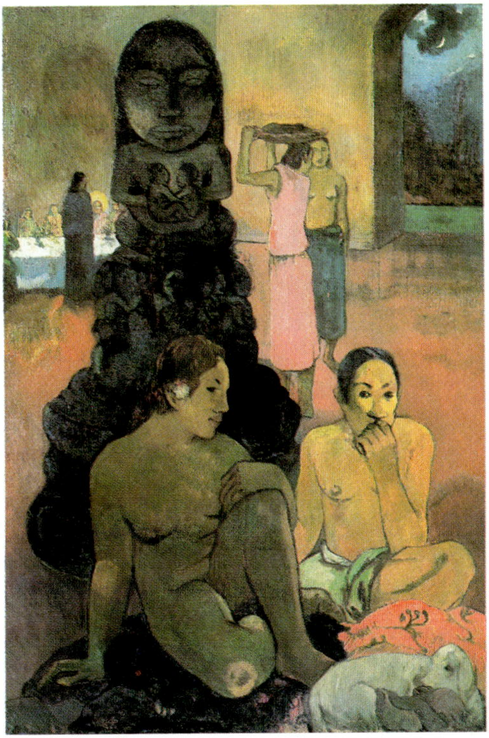

With its straight and curved lines, the architecture forms both the frame and the scenery of this painting. In the foreground appear two women, rendered in different colors. Behind them stands a statue of Buddha accompanied by a myriad symbolic figures. In the background, Jesus and his apostles joined together at the Last Supper evokes Christianity. In the middle ground, two women are shown engaging in a conversation. The artist employs his characteristic techniques of outlining the figures, combining dense and harmonious colors and evoking a mysterious atmosphere, suitable to the enigmatic nature of the work: two skin colors, two women conversing, two religions. Perhaps this is a plea for Christians to consider other religions, to respect and assimilate all they can from them. All works by Gauguin leave the viewer with questions.

The Great Buddha

Paul Gauguin
(Paris, 1848–Atuona, Hiva Oa, Marquesas Islands, 1903)

- 1899
- oil on canvas
- 134 x 95 cm
- Pushkin Museum, Moscow

Bathers

Paul Cézanne
(Aix-en-Provence, 1839–1906)

- 1899–1904
- oil on canvas
- 51.3 x 61.7 cm
- The Art Institute of Chicago, Chicago, IL, Amy McCormick Memorial Collection

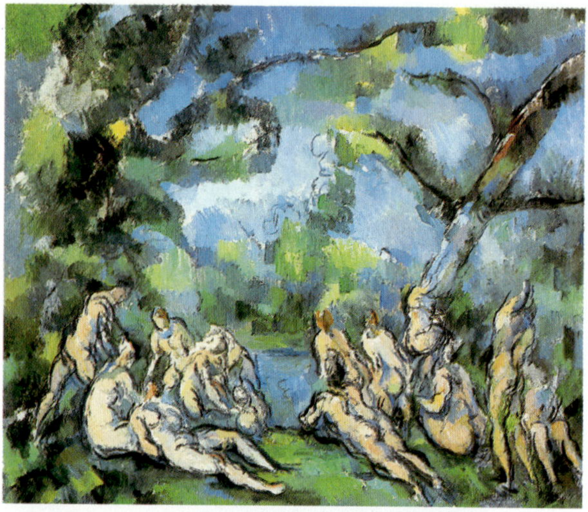

This idyllic scene, with luxuriant vegetation, is drawn against a luminous, blue sky and framed by two large trees. Between the two groups of female nudes in the foreground, the river in which they have been bathing can be seen. The unfinished appearance of the canvas lends it dynamism and freshness.

Nymphs at Dusk

Joan Brull i Vinyoles
(Barcelona, 1863–1912)

- ca. 1899
- oil on canvas
- 249.5 x 350 cm
- Museo de Bellas Artes, Olot, Gerona

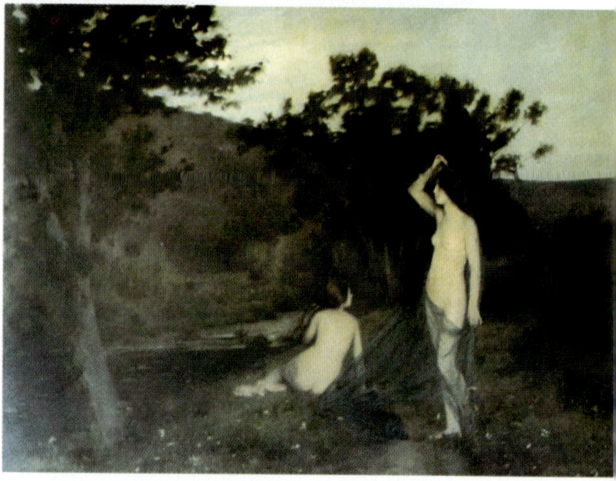

In a dream-like vision enhanced by the painting's ethereal and atmospheric qualities, the artist has depicted two stylized nude figures, their skin smooth and delicate. The poses are perhaps a fraction academic.

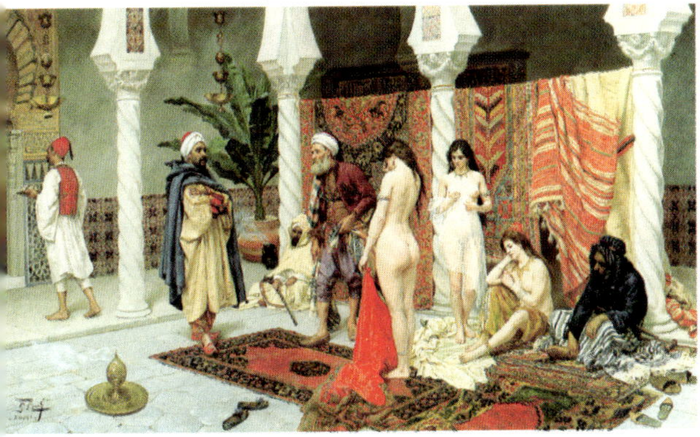

A Buyer Examining Slaves

Giulio Rosati
(Rome, 1858–1917)

- ca. 1900
- oil on canvas
- 61 x 104 cm
- private collection

Young women not infrequently left the Caucasus and traveled to the Orient in the hope of becoming concubines of powerful men, which would enable them to live without any further material worries. In an exotic and colorful setting, a wealthy individual examines several young women.

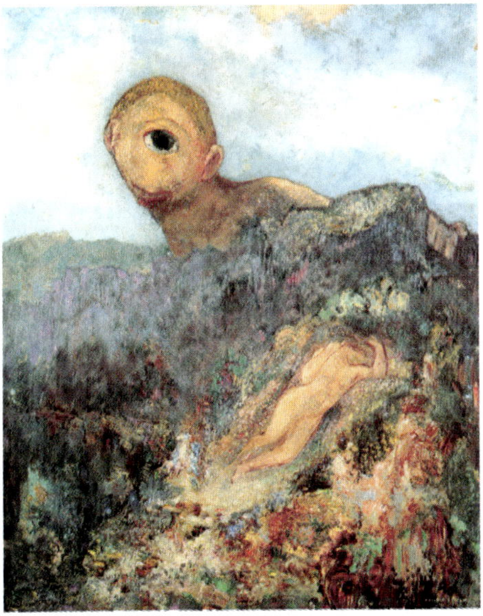

The Cyclops

Odilon Redon
(Bordeaux, 1840–Paris, 1916)

- 1900
- oil on canvas
- 64 x 51 cm
- Rijksmuseum Kröller -Müller, Otterloo

The canvas is a modern rendering of the theme of Polyphemus' love for Galatea. The illuminated female form is, as it were, bedded on a myriad of colors, and while all classical tonal evaluation is absent, the figure nevertheless approaches a certain academic status through its handling of highlights.

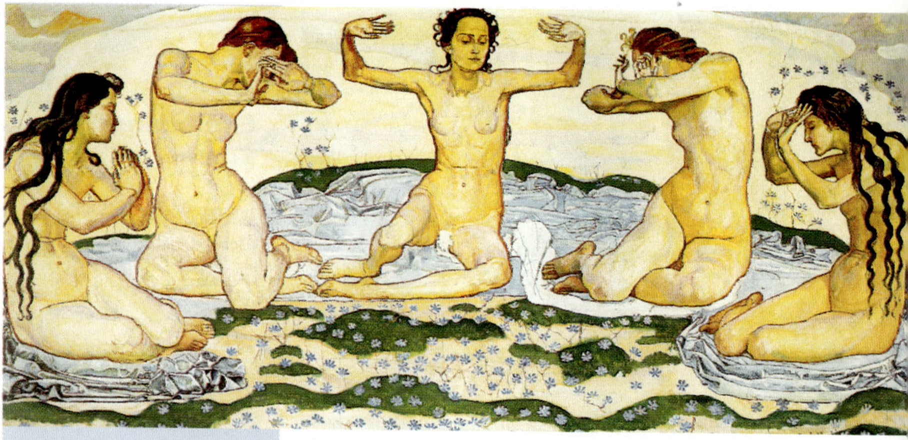

Day

Ferdinand Hodler
(Bern, 1853–Geneva, 1918)

- 1900
- oil on canvas
- 160 x 340 cm
- Kunstmuseum, Bern

The forms, musculature and other details of the bodies have been executed with delicate and subtle tones, eschewing stark contrasts. The canvas breathes vitality and joy, despite the fact that the figures are thin and earnest-looking. A celebration of light and filled with poetry, this work has a basic color scheme that fulfills the requirements of such an idealist image.

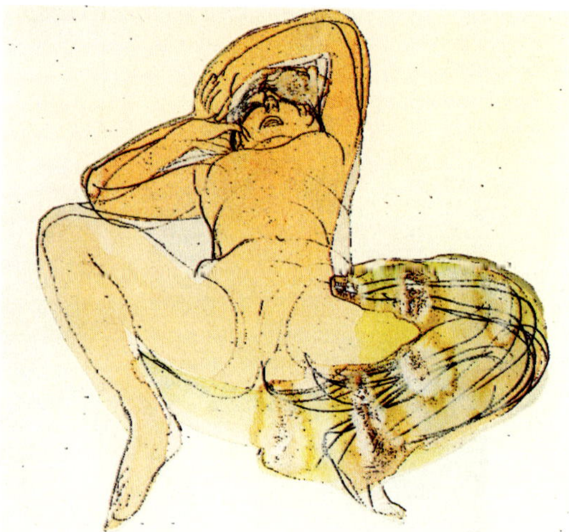

Young Woman Reclining with Her Legs Apart

Auguste Rodin
(Paris, 1840–Meudon, 1917)

- ca. 1900
- graphite and watercolor
- 22.5 x 23.7 cm
- Musée Rodin, Paris

The artist demonstrates a skillful painterly handling of the figure as well as his cleverness in conceiving the figure's pose, with a foreshortening that, rather than simply making the figure recede into the background, brings it closer to the viewer. Four frenetic, loose lines not only delineate the figure, but also set the tone of painting.

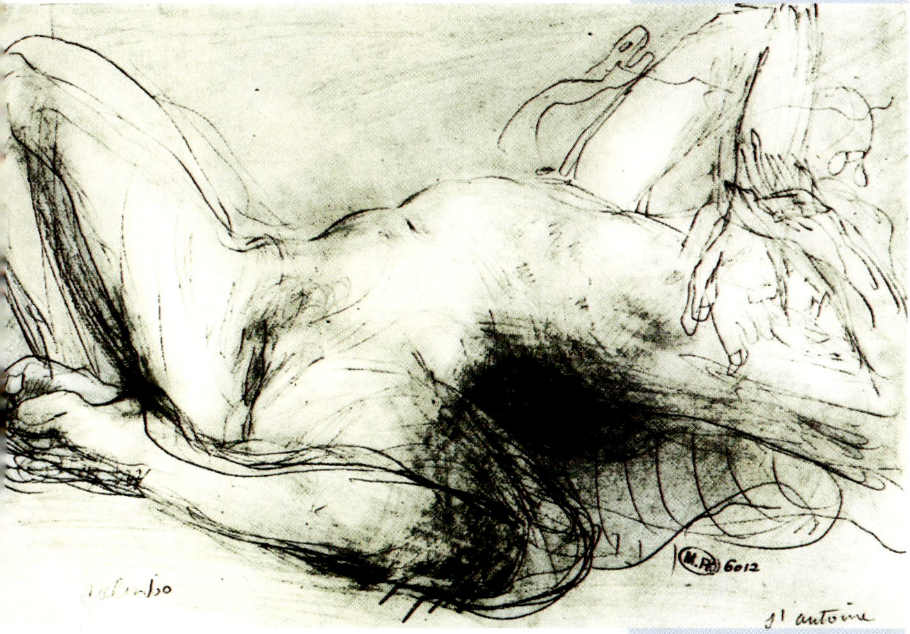

Salammbô

Auguste Rodin
(Paris, 1840–Meudon, 1917)

- ca. 1900
- pencil and stump on buff-colored paper
- 20.4 x 31 cm
- Musée Rodin, Paris

Salammbô, an ancient Phoenician divinity that enjoyed a large following in Tyre and Syria, was the subject of Gustave Flaubert's eponymous novel (1862). The title of the present drawing has, however, little to do with the god. Here, Rodin depicts a female nude lying on her back in a receding diagonal, with her legs spread apart and revealing her pubis to the spectator. The model's striking, contorted pose is achieved by technically superb foreshortening, which the artist executes with bravura. The woman's body is a consummate marriage of forms and volume; the study of light and shadow is achieved by means of stumping. With this technically perfect work, which is loosely and cursorily rendered, Rodin clearly sought to provoke the viewer.

Sleep

Ferdinand Hodler
(Bern, 1853–Geneva, 1918)

- 1903
- watercolors
- 90 x 65 cm
- private collection

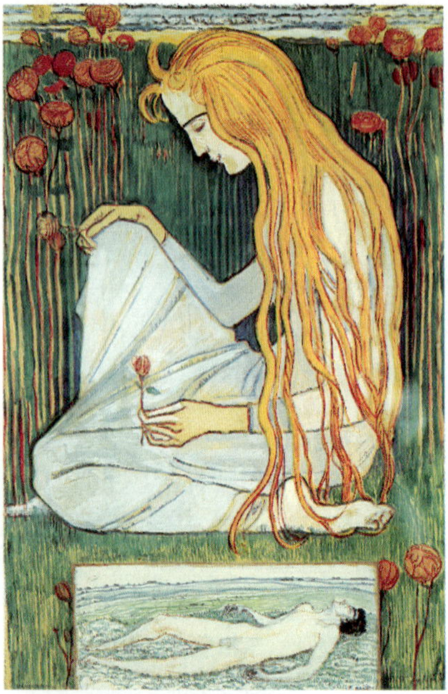

The naked male figure depicted at the bottom of this painting is to be interpreted as opening his mind to his dreams, represented by a woman holding a phallic symbol in the shape of a flower. The execution of the nude figure is sinuous, and line predominates over color.

Hope

Gustav Klimt
(Vienna, 1862–1918)

- 1903
- oil on canvas
- 181 x 67 cm
- National Gallery of Canada, Ottawa

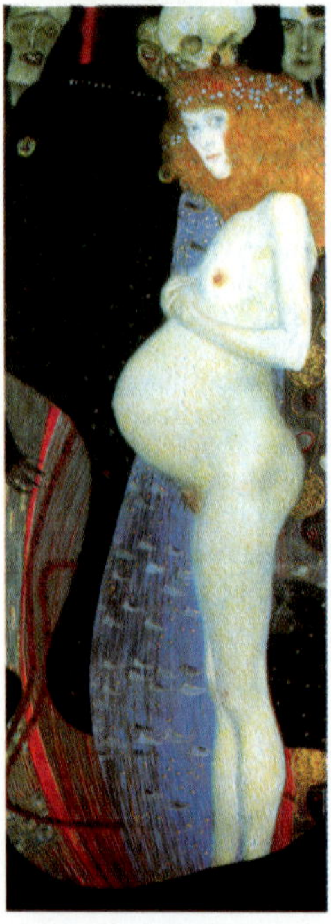

This depiction of a pregnant woman features dramatic interest in a number of ways, not least in the artist's mobilizing an entire range of symbols in the background. Color symbolism is also important, and while the figure's red hair by no means symbolizes purity, the woman comes across as being both highly sensual and of a spiritual quality.

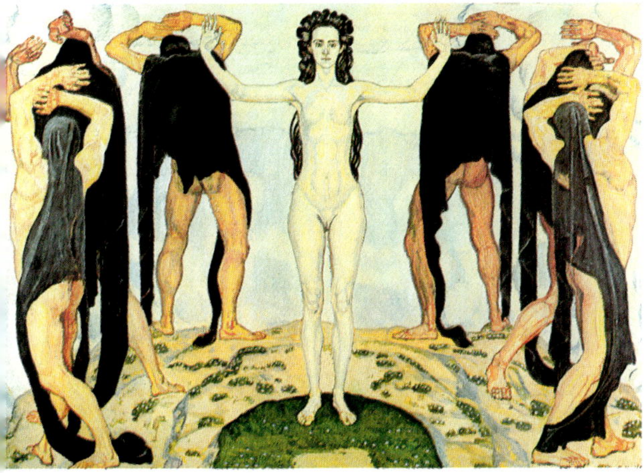

The Truth II

Ferdinand Hodler
(Bern, 1853–Geneva, 1918)

- 1903
- oil on canvas
- 207 x 293 cm
- Kunsthaus, Zurich

The idealization of the female figure in this painting breaks with earlier ideals: apart from the hips, the body is exceptionally slender, and angular, and the vulva is displayed as a prominent anatomical part.

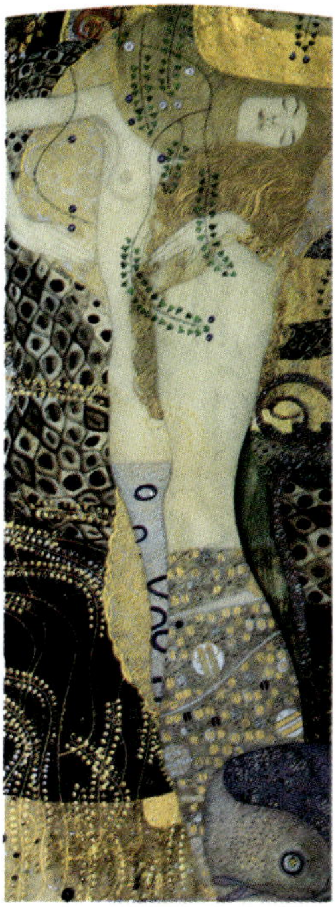

Water Serpents (Women Friends) I

Gustav Klimt
(Vienna, 1862–1918)

- 1904–07
- gold leaf and watercolor
- 50 x 20 cm
- Österreichische Galerie, Belvedere, Vienna

Two stylized figures are shown lying together in a loving embrace on a luxuriously-patterned, gilded cloth. While such subjects were—and are—unacceptable to certain sections of society, the painter has treated it here with exquisite dignity, so that the canvas breathes poetry. The bodily outlines, long hair, facial expressions, and details such as the small breast that can be seen between the two bodies, all convey great sensuality. In addition to technical qualities, such as its plasticity, the work conveys an audacious message of protest that was doubtless warmly received by advocates of free love.

The Three Ages of Life

Gustav Klimt
(Vienna, 1862–1918)

- 1905
- oil on canvas
- 180 x 180 cm
- Galleria Nazionale d'Arte Moderna, Rome

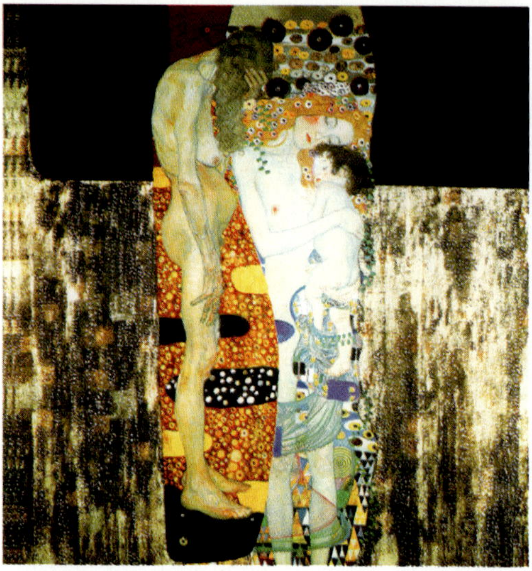

This artist's works frequently involve a refined universe of intrigue in which tragedy and eroticism combine, true to the ideals of the Vienna Secession. This work seems to transmit one of life's tragedies: the way innocence and tenderness can end in despair

Danaë

Gustav Klimt
(Vienna, 1862–1918)

- 1907/08
- oil on canvas
- 77 x 83 cm
- Dichand collection, Vienna

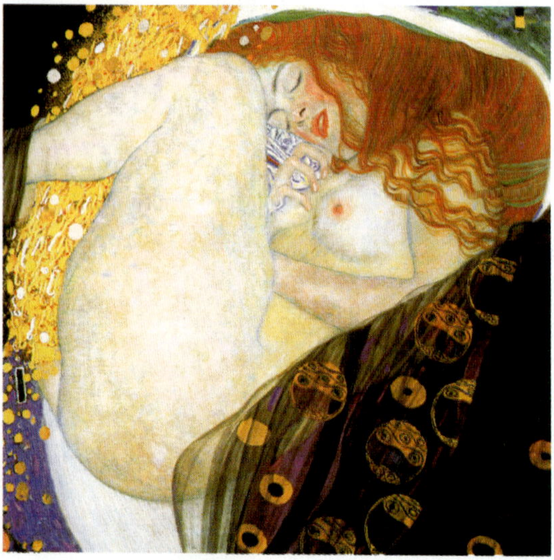

A work that is at once sensual and tender. Klimt's use of warm colors, standing out against the black of the garment and the background, is just one way in which he incorporates tension in this piece.

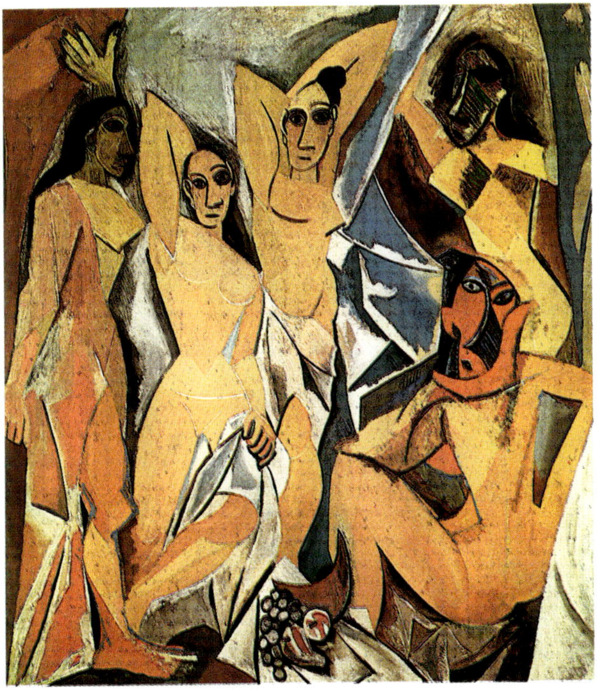

Les Demoiselles d'Avignon

Pablo Ruíz Picasso
(Malaga, 1881–Mougrins, Provence, 1973)

- 1906–7
- oil on canvas
- 244 x 234 cm
- The Museum of Modern Art, New York

This work depicts five women who worked in a brothel on Avinyó Street in Barcelona. Some of the figures' faces have been substituted by masks, and their bodies are fraught with emotional tension. This is in part achieved by presenting various body parts laterally and frontally within a two-dimensional space. Such distortions also determine the figures' relationship to the surrounding space. The nudes are portrayed with great freedom and fluency, and most of the poses are classical: the figure on the far left, shown frontally and laterally, recalls those in Egyptian art; the ones in the center evoke Iberian sculpture; and the two on the right, with their violent contortions, resemble figures in African art. The aggressive lines and the flagrant disregard of any conventional idea of beauty represent a violent revolt against traditional painting. This work is not only a crucial achievement in Picasso's personal development, but, as the herald of Cubism, is also the single most important landmark in the development of contemporary painting.

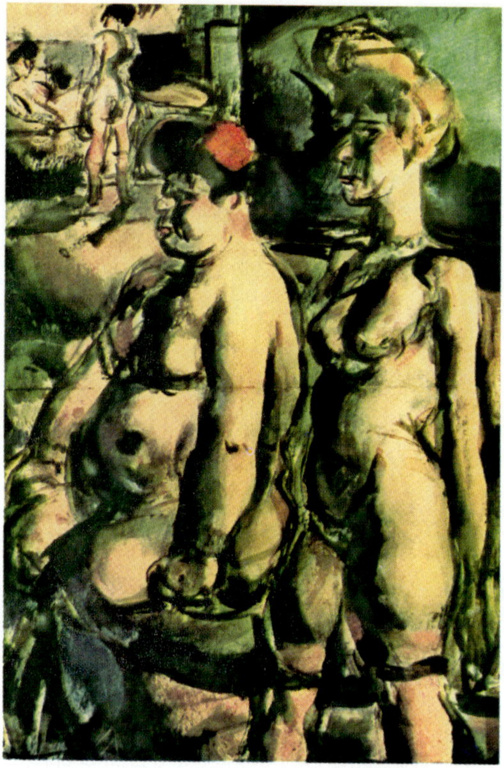

Women

Georges Rouault
(Paris, 1871–1958)

- 1907
- tempera and pastel on paper
- 97 x 65 cm
- Hermitage, St. Petersburg

Set in a brothel, this scene shows two female nudes in the foreground, exhibiting very different body types, waiting for their clients, and two other naked women, in the background, who are engaged in a conversation. The work is a harrowing study of the people and atmosphere of this milieu. The forms and palette vividly convey the degradation, loneliness, tedium, stultification and unhappiness of the prostitutes. It is a depressing, desolate view of the world. Despite this, Rouault treats the scene with respect, for there is not one sign of criticism or mockery of the figures. Indeed, the painting, seems, instead to condemn the society that turns a blind eye to such a sordid existence.

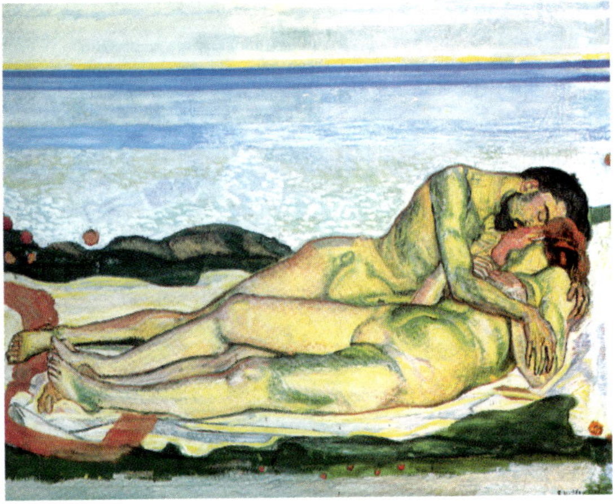

Love

Ferdinand Hodler
(Bern, 1853–Geneva, 1918)

- 1907–08
- oil on canvas
- 145 x 175 cm
- private collection, Switzerland

Under light one might be forgiven for calling magical, these lovers have abandoned themselves to the gentle pleasure of sleep. Hodler's approach to the nude is varied: he uses a wide range of not always harmonious colours—reds, yellows, greens—as well as embodying significant avant-garde influences of a Post-Impressionist nature.

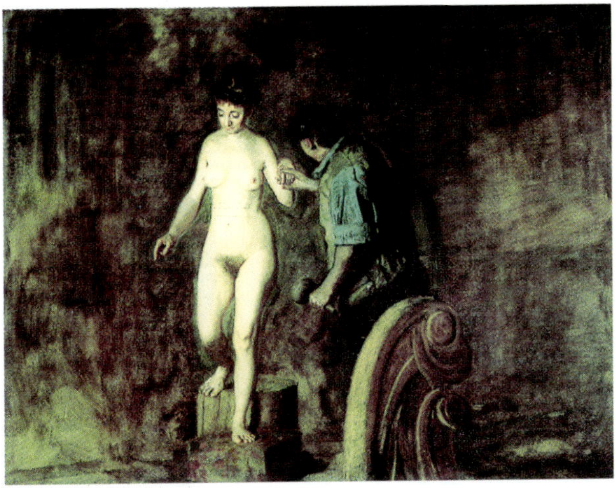

William Rush and His Model

Thomas Eakins
(Philadelphia, 1844–1916)

- 1907–8
- oil on canvas
- 89.5 x 120 cm
- Academy of Arts, Honolulu, Hawaii

The nude is a combination of delicacy, femininity and refined sensuality, enhanced by the touching way in which the artist respectfully holds her hand. Certain areas of the woman's body are brightly illuminated, evoking an almost innocent image. Although certain technical means are duly employed by Eakins to emphasize the theatrical quality of the painting, the work exhibits a high degree of realism.

Nude Woman Reclining

Auguste Rodin
(Paris, 1840–Meudon, 1917)

- graphite pencil and watercolor on paper
- 21.5 x 26 cm
- Musée Rodin, Paris

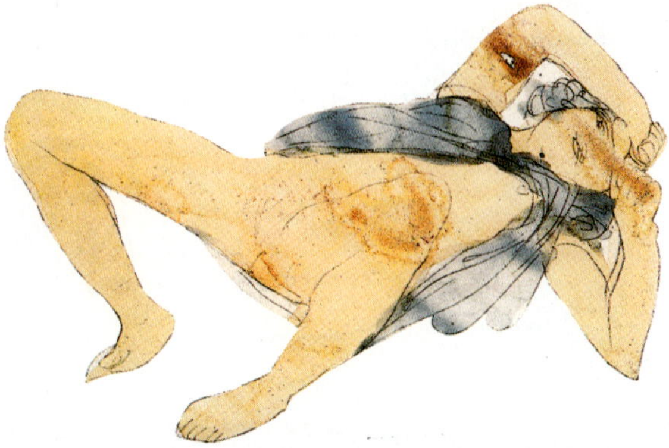

This nude, dramatically foreshortened and outlined with a single line, is shown in an intimate scene, reclining and deep in sleep. In what seems to be an ode to freedom, the figure is shown in a relaxed, uninhibited pose with her naked body in full view, leaving aside all modesty and conventionality. The pale colors of the skin, hair and clothes heighten the sensuality and tension of the scene.

Boy Nude on a Patterned Blanket

Egon Schiele
(Tulln, 1890–Vienna, 1918)

- 1908
- pencil, gouache, metal powder, Chinese ink on paper
- 23.8 x 31.5 cm
- Leopold Museum, Vienna

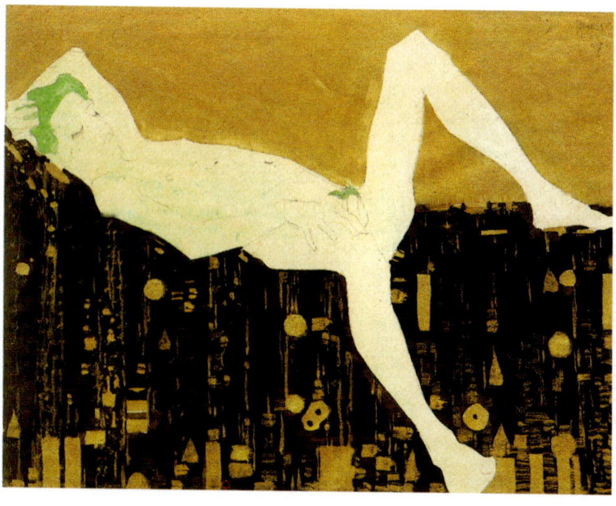

The figure is depicted with smooth skin and is outlined against a solid background. Here, the artist demonstrates his interest in the human body, which he invariably depicts in a provocative fashion: the sleeping boy displays his body unabashedly, indeed, in a most narcissistic manner. There is no concealing the artist's intention to create an erotic image.

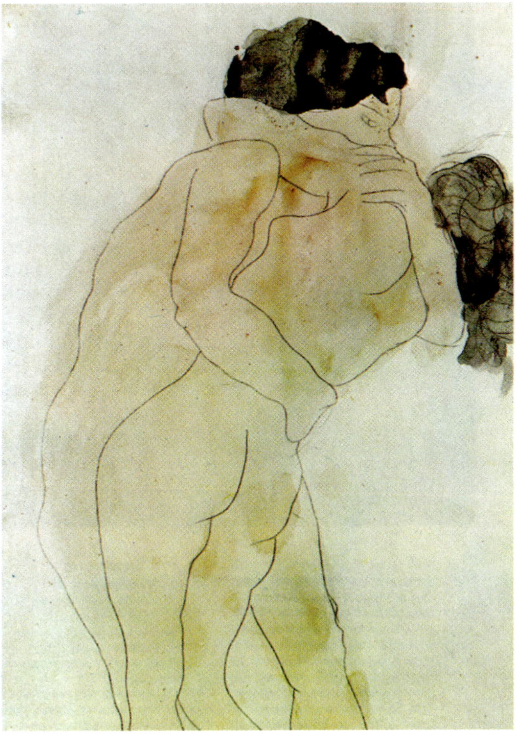

In spite of the simplicity of this composition, it is of high artistic value, for it conveys so much by so few means: the impeccable delineation of the lines, the slender bodies, a highly dramatic, theatrical scene, highly differentiated bodies, a balance of lines and color, the exalted embrace of two lovers, and the extraordinary composition. With a fine, steady line, Rodin draws such expressive anatomical outlines that he has no need to provide volumes or modeling. The lovers' pose and the curvature of their bodies convey the ardent passion of the moment. The light areas of watercolor look more like wash, and refrain from following the contours of the figures' bodies. The painting is a vivid image of eroticism, which is enhanced by its great delicacy and superb draftsmanship.

The Kiss

Auguste Rodin
(Paris, 1840–Meudon, 1917)

- ca. 1910
- watercolor and graphite pencil
- 33.2 x 28.7 cm
- The Ashmolean Museum, Oxford

The Favorite Pastime

Lawrence Alma-Tadema

(Dronrijp, Frisia, 1836 –Wiesbaden, Germany, 1912)

- 1909
- oil on panel
- 66 x 45.1 cm
- Tate Gallery, London

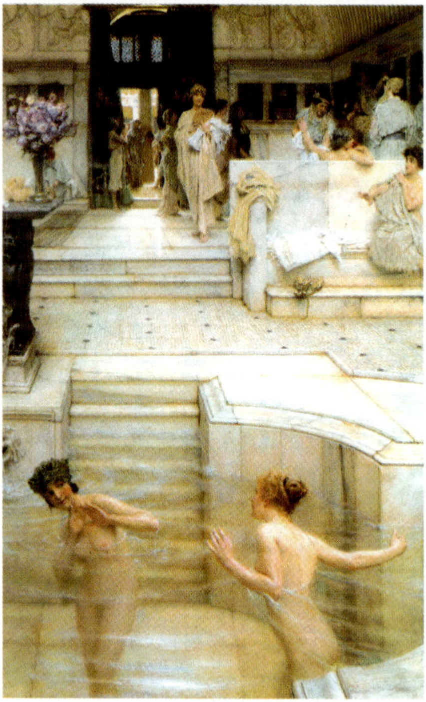

The seductive gestures and near-sculptural poses are notable. The painting is a vivid example of the realist technique of this artist who, heir to Romanticism and admirer of ancient cultures, has a penchant for anecdote and everyday scenes.

Bather Drying Her Foot

Pierre-Auguste Renoir

(Limoges, 1841–Cagnes-sur-Mer, 1919)

- 1910–11
- oil on canvas
- 84 x 65 cm
- Museo de Arte, São Paolo

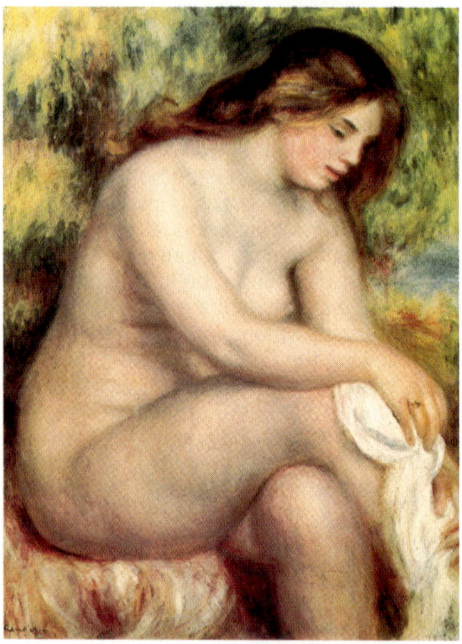

Here, the woman's body is skillfully rendered with a uniform and delicate palette, down to the minutest detail. The play of pastels and intense colors, light and shade, model the skin and define the volumes. The result is a work of great delicacy and sensuality, which is enhanced by the figure's candid facial expression and long brown hair.

The body depicted in this work is of a gaunt, decrepit, grotesque man in a bold pose—at least that is what the viewer gathers from the some of the painting's details, such as the deformed shape of the buttocks, knees and feet, as well as the figure's unshapely profile.

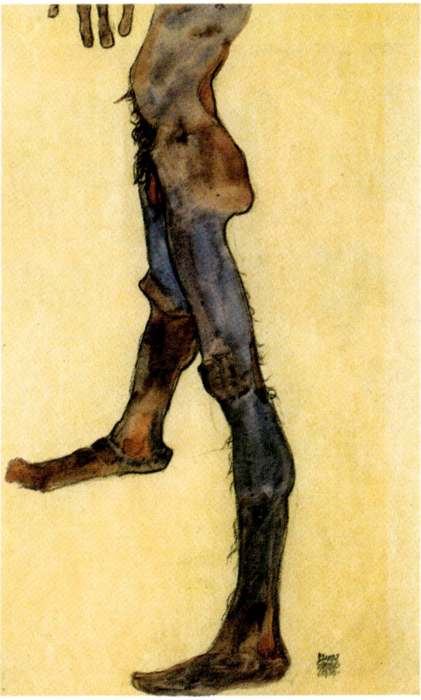

Half Body of Male Nude

Egon Schiele
(Tulln, 1890–Vienna, 1918)

- 1910
- black chalk and body color on paper
- 44.8 x 27.9 cm
- Leopold Museum, Vienna

Several notable details include the unsteady white band that outlines the figure, recalling an aura; the figure's exaggerated features; the elongation of the torso, which lends the figure greater expressive force; the extraordinary drawing of the head and neck.

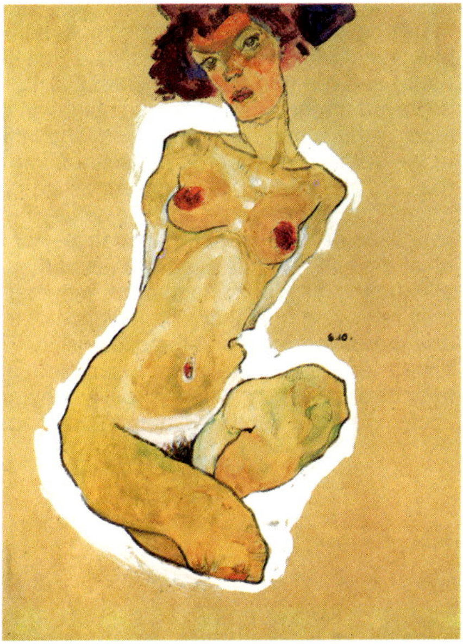

Crouching Female Nude

Egon Schiele
(Tulln, 1890–Vienna, 1918)

- 1910
- black chalk, body color and opaque white on paper
- 44.4 x 31 cm
- Leopold Museum, Vienna

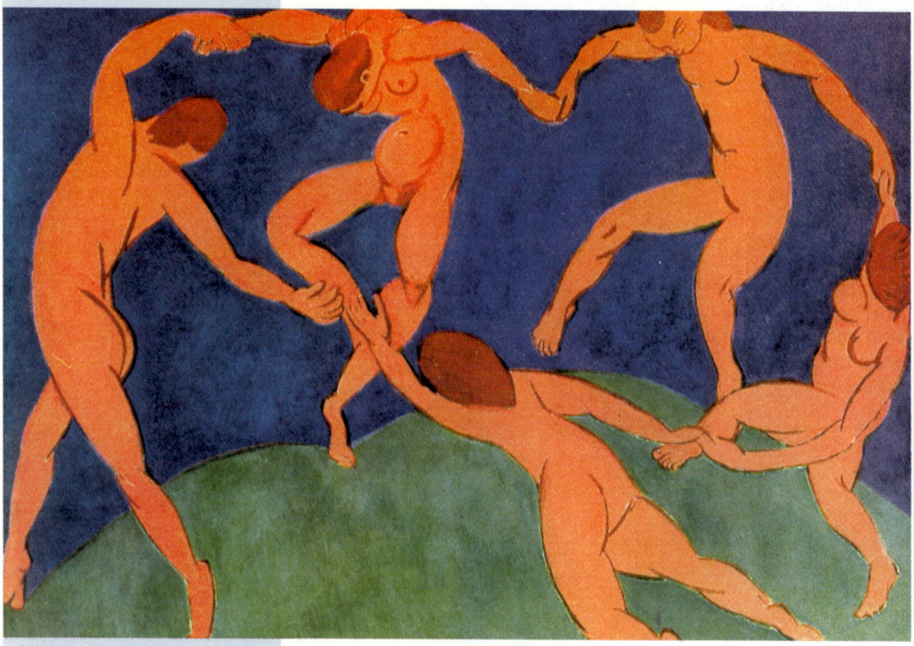

The Dance

Henri Matisse
(Le Cateau, Picardy, 1869–Nice, 1954)

- 1910
- oil on canvas
- 260 x 391 cm
- Hermitage, St. Petersburg

In this painting, Henri Matisse composed a beautiful symphony in three symbolic colors: blue (the sky), green (the earth) and red (the dancing figures). A harmonic balance is achieved through this daring combination of intense colors, lending the scene great vividness. The individual elements of the scene are rendered as abstract forms. Even the five dancers, with their fluid lines suggesting movement, are not an attempt to express a specific dance, but rather an evocation of the very notion of dance. For this reason, the artist did not make detailed studies of the figures. Instead, although clearly feminine in form, with their rhythmic lines, they represent humanity. The balance of the color masses and the cohesiveness of the composition make the figures appear as if they were about to jump out of the frame in their dancing frenzy, when in reality they are dancing in a circle, around a central point in the composition.

Eros

Egon Schiele
(Tulln, 1890–Vienna, 1918)

- 1911
- gouache, watercolors and black pencil on paper
- 55.9 x 45.7 cm
- private collection, Melbourne

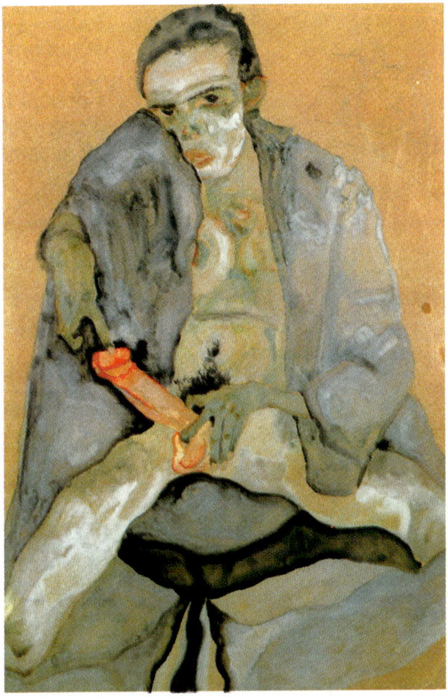

The sexually-obsessed painter is shown taking pleasure in the contemplation and satisfaction of himself, which theoretically, at least, excludes the possibility of his sharing his feelings with anyone else. The painting, however, undermines that one-sided aspect in its unashamed provocation.

Girl with the Lower Part of Her Body Naked

Egon Schiele
(Tulln, 1890–Vienna, 1918)

- 1911
- pencil, watercolor and gouache on paper
- 54 x 35.6 cm
- Leopold Museum, Vienna

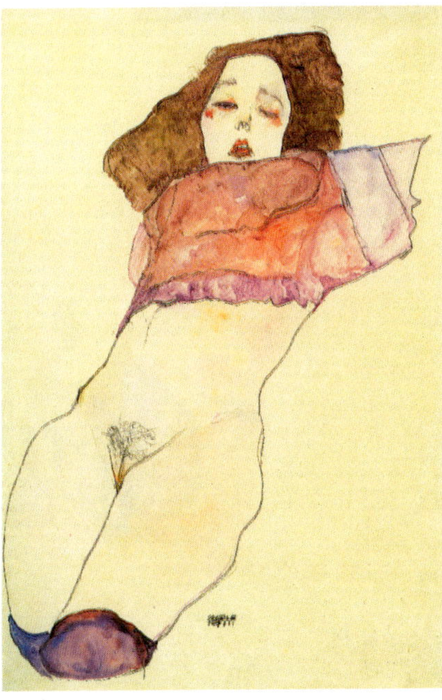

The drawing is technically flawless, with light but steady lines and small yet telling details. The colors, though numerous, are harmoniously balanced. The darker tones of the hair and dress serve to frame the parts of the body that the painter wished to emphasize.

The Birth of Venus

Odilon Redon
(Bordeaux, 1840–Paris, 1916)

- 1912
- oil on canvas
- 143.4 x 62.2 cm
- private collection

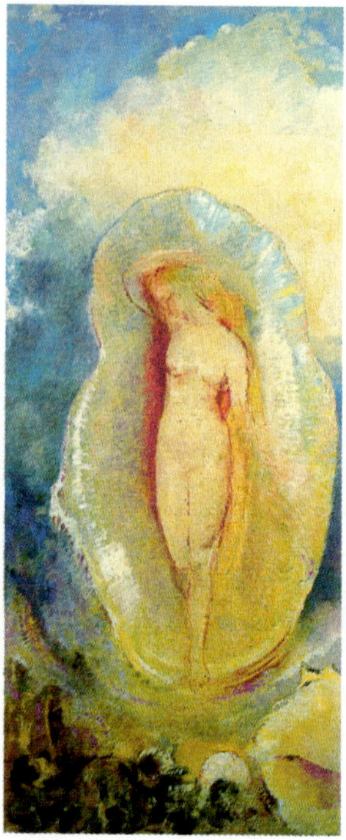

Redon seems, here, to depict Venus emerging from a vulva-like seashell. Modeling is absent from his treatment of her figure, yet the generous if simple lines tracing her form are enough to attain their effect.

Crouching Female Nude, Bending Forward

Egon Schiele
(Tulln, 1890–Vienna, 1918)

- 1912
- pencil, watercolor and gouache on paper
- 37.5 x 28.9 cm
- Leopold Museum, Vienna

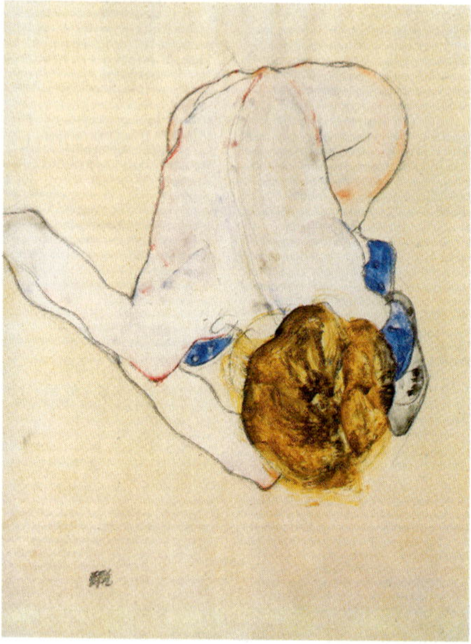

The fact that the body is devoid of straight lines lends it a sense of movement, heightening the expressiveness of the image. In a dazzling display of technique, Schiele gives form to both the contours and the figure's volumes, all with just a few steady strokes of the pencil.

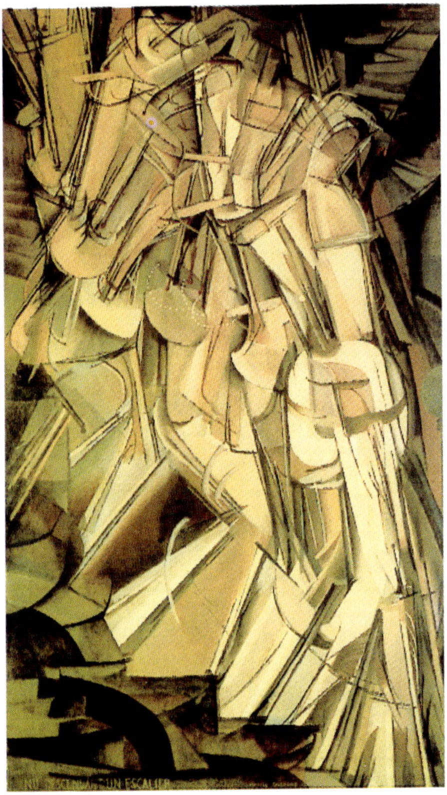

Nude Descending a Staircase, No. 2

Marcel Duchamp
(Blainville, 1887–Neuilly, 1968)

- 1912
- oil on canvas
- 146 x 89 cm
- Philadelphia Museum of Art, Philadelphia, PA

Breaking with all previous painterly traditions, this work presented a new approach to painting, drawing a decisive line between pure creativity and personal taste. The strength of this nude lies in its Futuristic and Cubist composition. The well-proportioned, anthropomorphic figure consists of elementary schematic forms that are superimposed and repeated, engendering a rhythmic flow of movement. This painting, which represents the first sequences of anthropometric motion, retains a classical aspect in its conception, even though it appears to break with previous artistic traditions. The golden light and tonal gradations of the figure suggest a basis in classical figurative art, in which abstraction is employed for a specific purpose and is not an end in itself.

Crouching Woman

Egon Schiele
(Tulln, 1890–Vienna, 1918)

- 1914
- pencil on paper
- 46.4 x .6 cm
- Leopold Museum, Vienna

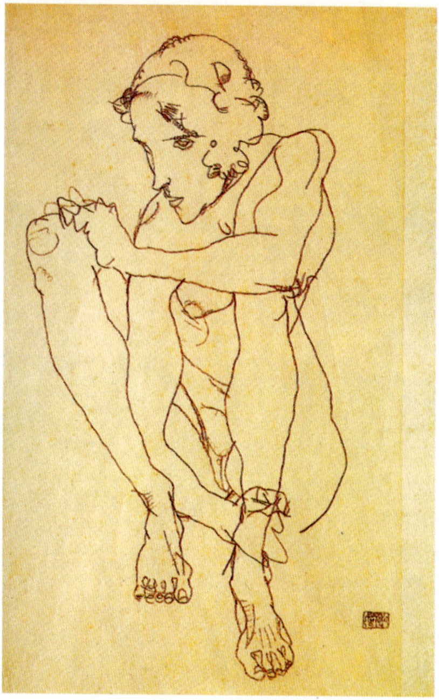

The position of the figure, crouching and with a vacant look in her eyes, evokes a sense of abandonment and helplessness. Her nudity and the exposure of her breasts and genitals underscore her profound anguish and vulnerability.

Two Women Embracing

Egon Schiele
(Tulln, 1890–Vienna, 1918)

- 1914
- pencil, charcoal and gouache on paper
- 48.5 x 26.7 cm
- Leopold Museum, Vienna

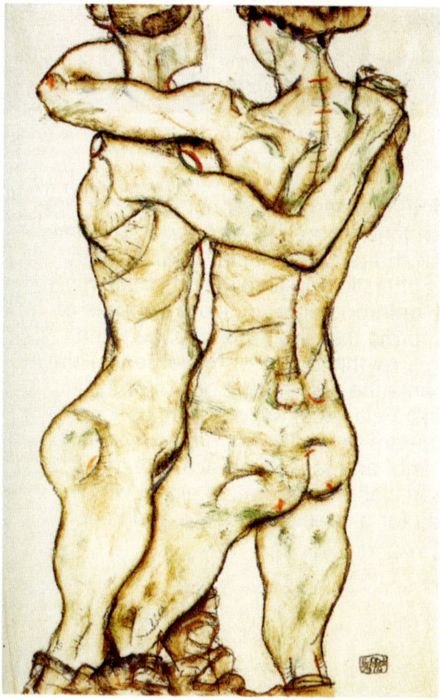

The two women, united in an embrace, with their abdomens touching and one of them putting her leg between those of her companion, represent lovers. The bit of dress that can be seen at the base, as if it has just fallen, lends immediacy to the scene.

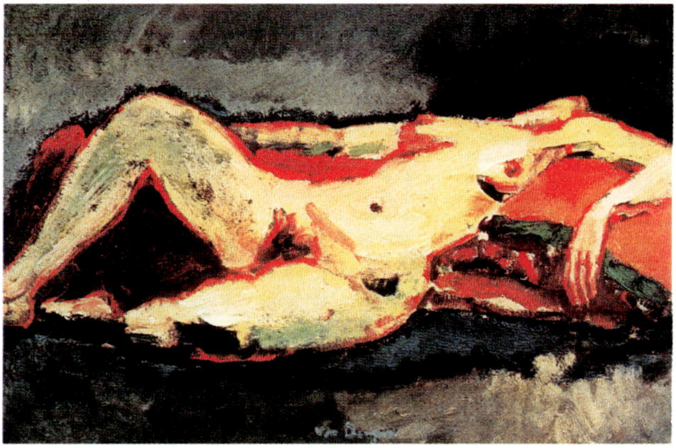

Female Nude

Kees van Dongen
(Delfshaven, 1877–Monte Carlo, 1968)

- ca.1915
- oil on canvas
- private collection

The scene is positively charged with eroticism, which did not sit very well with the bourgeoisie of Paris at the time. With their penchant for delicacy and refinement, they deemed the painting to be excessively crude, almost insolent in tone, on account of the obscene manner in which the subject is presented and its virulent execution.

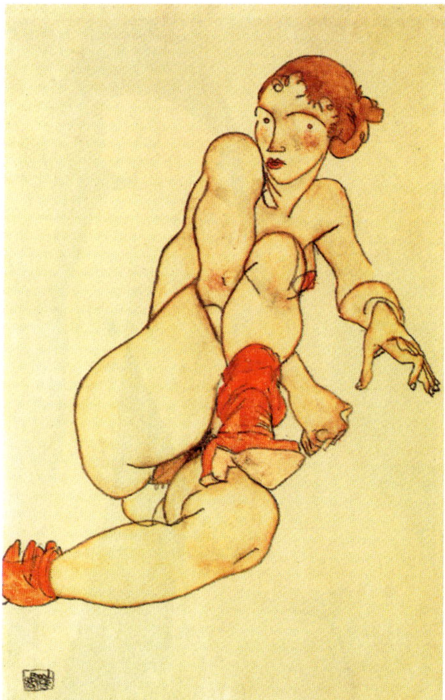

Schiele was a master draftsman with a penchant for placing figures in unusual poses, which he obsessively employs to create compositions that exhibit a lively interplay of line and form. The daring, exaggerated pose of this woman, shown in a diagonal, with her right arm under her right leg, engenders a series of rhythmic lines.

Female Nude with One Leg Raised

Egon Schiele
(Tulln, 1890–Vienna, 1918)

- 1915
- pencil and gouache on paper
- 47.1 x 31.5 cm
- Leopold Museum, Vienna

Reclining Nude Woman

Egon Schiele
(Tulln, 1890–Vienna, 1918)

- 1916
- pencil, watercolor and gouache on paper
- 30.9 x 44.4 cm
- Leopold Museum, Vienna

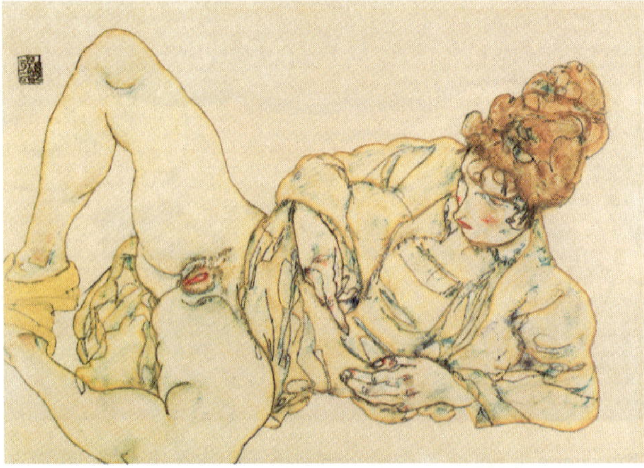

Schiele frequently used his wife as a model, though he would change her face and hairstyle to conceal her identity in his most provocative works. Judging by the number of drawings Schiele devoted to depictions of erotic nudes, the artist had a predilection for presenting the lower half of the body.

Seated Nude

Amedeo Modigliani
(Livorno, 1884–Paris, 1920)

- 1016
- oil on canvas
- 93 x 60 cm
- Courtald Institute Galleries, London

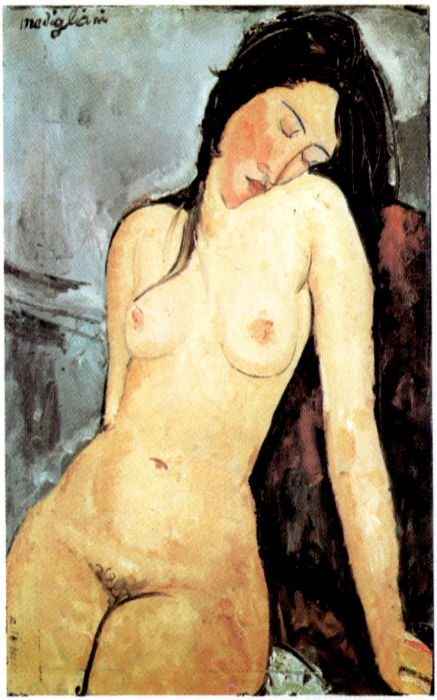

The girl is turned slightly sideways and makes as if to hide her face in a gesture of modesty, which is further suggested by the red face, which forms a stark contrast to the delicate color of the skin, particularly of the upper body.

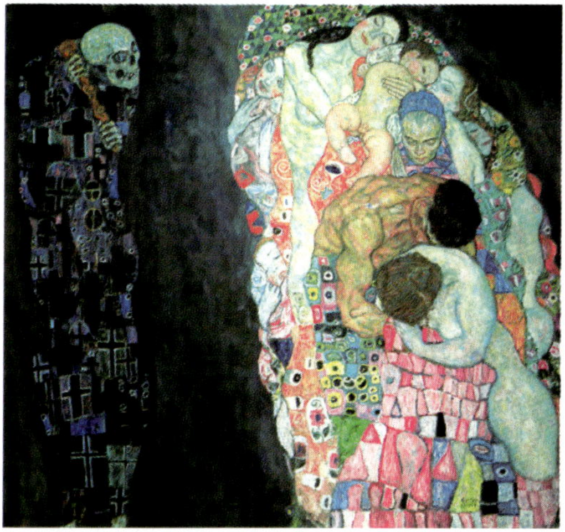

Death and Life

Gustav Klimt
(Vienna, 1862–1918)

- 1916
- oil on canvas
- 178 x 189 cm
- Rudolf Leopold Collection, Vienna

This work contrasts the opposing realities of life and death: Death, represented as a grinning skull in a robe covered in crosses, while Life is shown as an assemblage of partly-quilted bodies sharing love and tenderness.

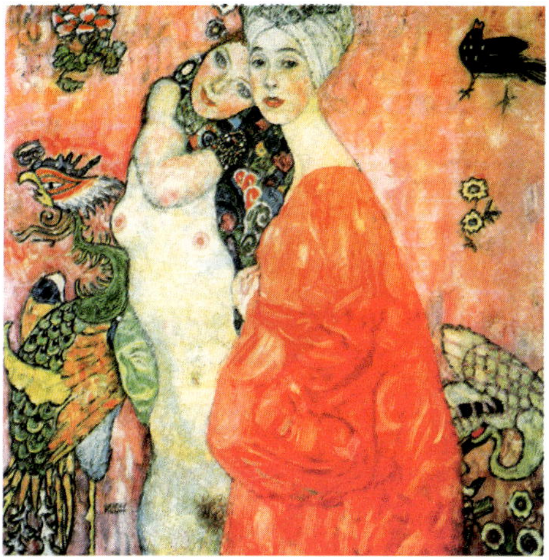

The Women Friends

Gustav Klimt
(Vienna, 1862–1918)

- 1916–17
- oil on canvas
- 99 x 99 cm
- Österreichische Galerie, Belvedere, Vienna

In this canvas, the painter makes play with a wealth of vivid colors, flowers, birds and legendary creatures. The naked woman's sensuality, her pale, delicate skin and tender, smiling expression clash almost with the affable if slightly aloof gaze of her companion. The work is highly suggestive and eloquent. The gaze of the woman in red might also be interpreted as defiance in the face of a repressed and repressive society.

Adam and Eve

Gustav Klimt
(Vienna, 1862–1918)

- 1916–17
- oil on canvas
- 173 x 60 cm
- Österreichische Galerie, Belvedere, Vienna

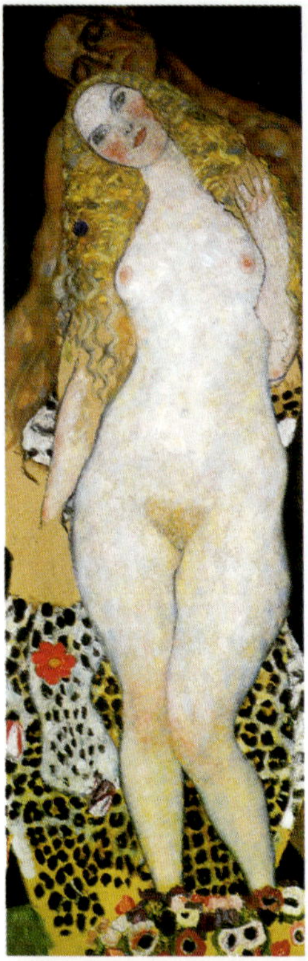

Eve's well-delineated contours map out a rather curiously-shaped, if sensual, body. Standing behind her, Adam is relaxed and serene. The flowers and intense colors express the joy of love.

Nude Lying on Her Left Side

Amedeo Modigliani
(Livorno, 1884–Paris, 1920)

- 1917
- oil on canvas
- 89 x 146 cm
- private collection, Paris

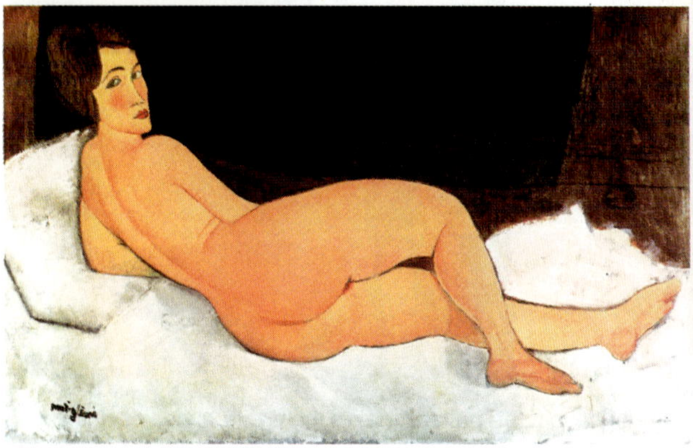

The figure stands out against a background of two basic colors: the deep crimson of the wall and the white of the bed on which the woman is reclining.

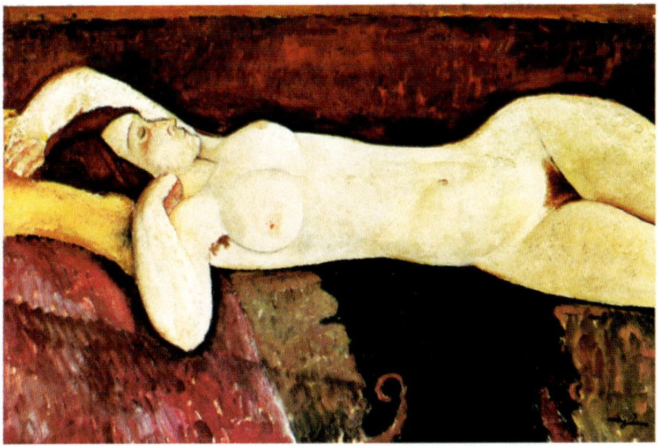

Nude Woman Sleeping

Amedeo Modigliani
(Livorno, 1884–Paris, 1920)

- 1917
- oil on canvas
- 73 x 116 cm
- The Museum of Modern Art, New York

To enhance the eroticism of the image, Modigliani has elongated the woman's torso and exaggerated the forms, making them more seductive. The smooth, soft and luminous skin is clearly defined against the dark, variegated background in which red tones predominate, evoking passion and sexual ecstasy.

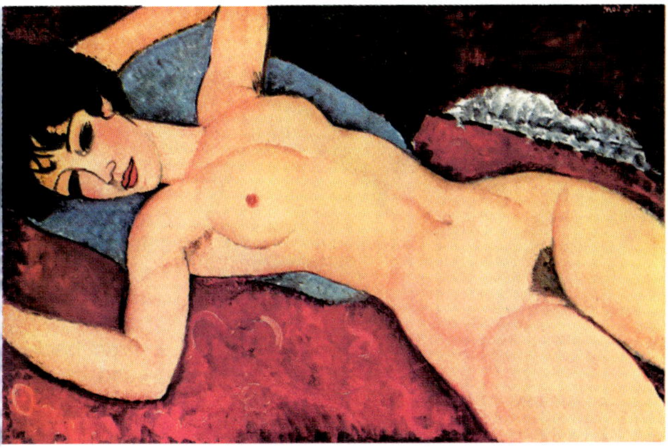

Nude Reclining with Her Arms Apart

Amedeo Modigliani
(Livorno, 1884–Paris, 1920)

- 1917
- oil on canvas
- 60 x 92 cm
- Gianni Mattioli Collection, Milan

The woman is the very embodiment of passion, with her body rendered in warm, intense colors, with luminous skin, rosy cheeks and deep carmine lips. As if that were not enough, the body is presented diagonally in a striking composition, is cut off at the legs to bring it closer to the viewer and is prominent against a background of saturated blues, reds, black and white. The painter was fascinated by this work, which hung in his studio during the last years of his life.

Nude Sitting on a Divan

Amedeo Modigliani
(Livorno, 1884–Paris, 1920)

- 1917
- oil on canvas
- 100 x 65 cm
- private collection, Paris

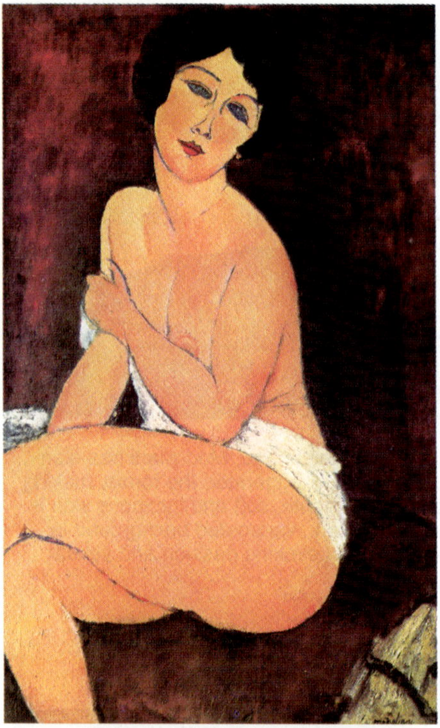

The voluptuousness of this comely, sensual woman is suggested by the folds of skin at her side and the fullness of her buttocks, which she unashamedly reveals to the viewer as she makes a half-hearted attempt to cover her naked body with her arm and a white garment, which serves as a small compositional counterpoint in the scene.

Caryatid

Amedeo Modigliani
(Livorno, 1884–Paris, 1920)

- pastel
- 52.2 x 47.5 cm
- Musée du Petit Palais, Collection Girardin, Paris

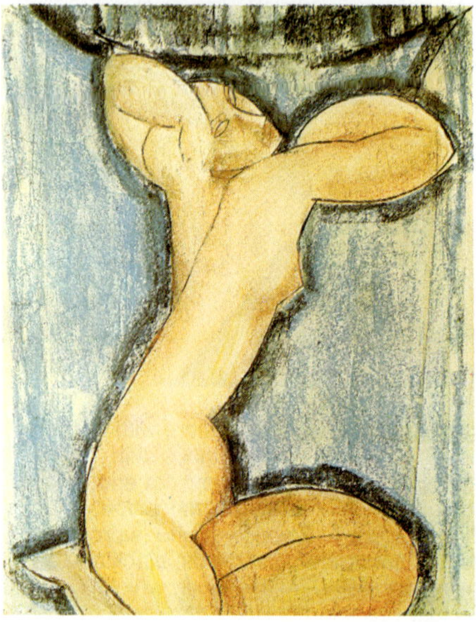

Presenting the nude as the sole subject of the painting, placed before a smooth, abstract background, reveals the artist's interest in idealizing and stylizing the human body. This work recalls a preliminary study and demonstrates Modigliani's aptitude for the sculptural.

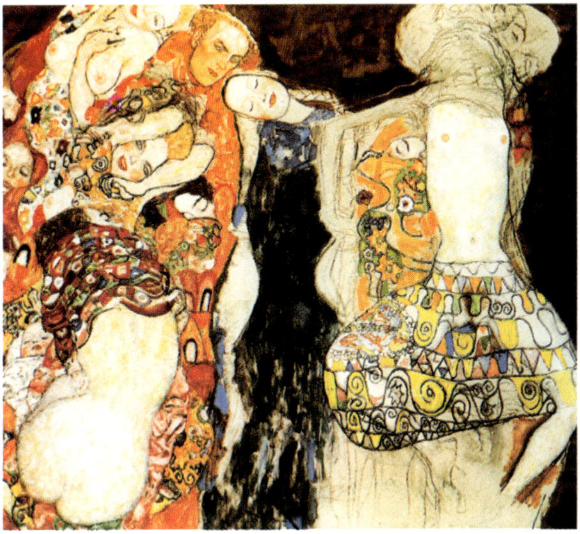

The artist has depicted the same woman in various positions, and in different states of dress or undress, around her male lover, whereby a baby has also been included. The canvas succeeds in giving expression to a wide range of feelings: joy, eroticism, and possibly tragedy as well.

The Bride

Gustav Klimt

(Vienna, 1862–1918)

- 1917–18
- oil on canvas
- 166 x 190 cm
- Österreichische Galerie, Belvedere, Vienna (on loan from a private collection)

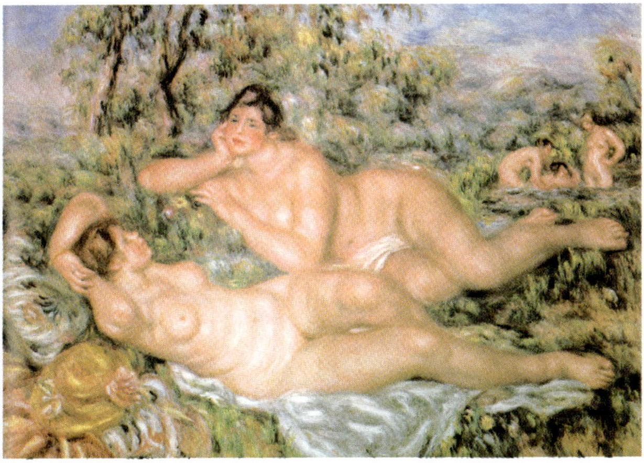

The pink color of their corpulent bodies blends in with the pastel colors of the surrounding landscape. This painting, with its chromatic rhythm and movement, is an ode to nature, poetry, freedom and life itself—a commendable trait of an artist nearing his eightieth birthday.

The Bathers

Pierre-Auguste Renoir

(Limoges, 1841–Cagnes-sur-Mer, 1919)

- 1918–19
- oil on canvas
- 110 x 160 cm
- Musée d'Orsay, Paris

Two Seated Women

Egon Schiele
(Tulln, 1890–Vienna, 1918)

- 1918
- oil on canvas
- 110 x 140.5 cm
- Leopold Museum, Vienna

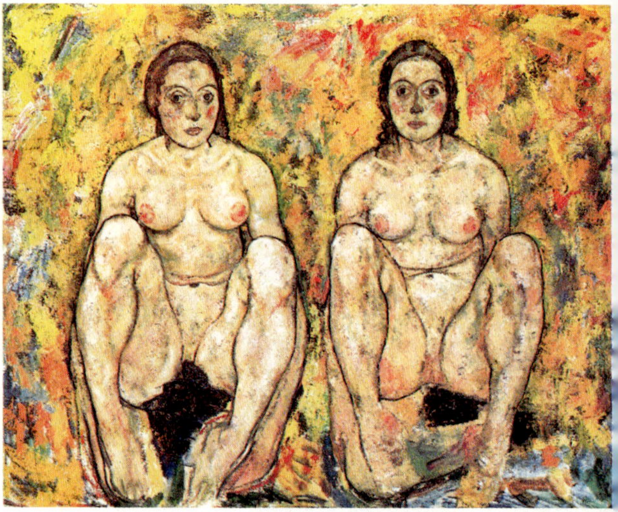

The two female nudes seated next to each other in this work exhibit remarkably similar poses, forms, faces and proportions. This, along with their singular painterly treatment and superb draftsmanship, recalls art of the Middle Ages. Thus presented, the women are shown out of context and are lent a symbolism that is enhanced by the intense colors of the background.

Seated Woman with Her Head Resting on Her Arm

Egon Schiele
(Tulln, 1890–Vienna, 1918)

- 1918
- pencil, charcoal, watercolor and gouache on paper
- 29.7 x 46.2 cm
- Leopold Museum, Vienna

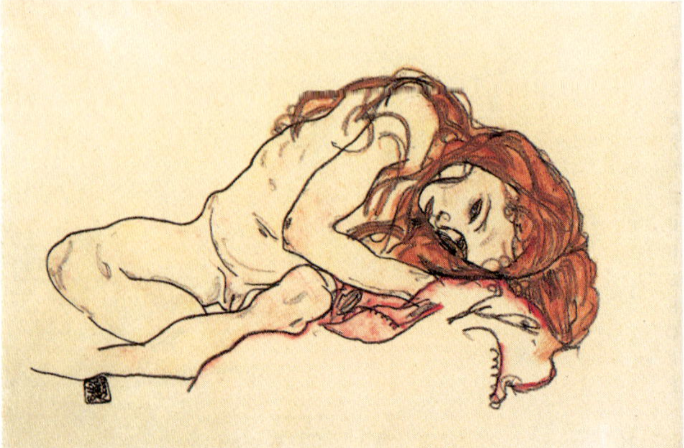

The figure's head represents the focal point, and is consequently the most detailed pictorial element of the drawing. Both the expression of the face and the virtuoso execution of its fine features reveal the artist's indisputable command of his art.

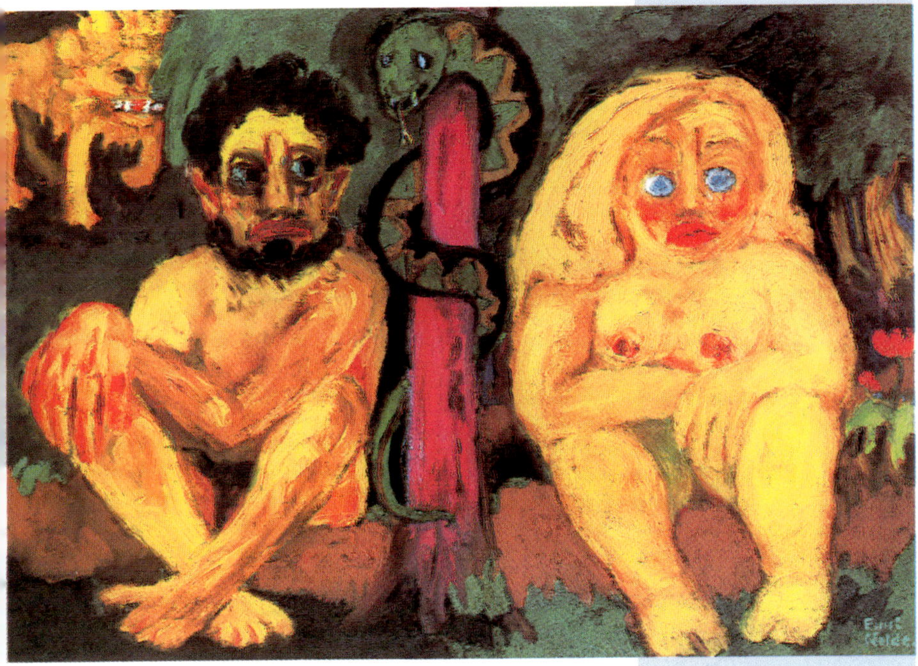

Paradise Lost

Emil Nolde (Emil Hansen)
(Nolde, near Bocholt, Schleswig-Holstein, 1867–Seebüll, near Niebüll, Schleswig-Holstein, 1956)

- 1921
- oil on canvas
- 106.5 x 157 cm
- Nolde Foundation, Seebüll

This painting represents the Fall of man: despite God's warning Eve, allows herself to be tricked by the serpent, accepts the apple, takes a bite and offers it to Adam. The eyes of both figures are open, in the knowledge of their lost innocence and embarrassed by their naked bodies, and now fully aware of the malice that has occurred. In his singular style, Nolde uses intense and vibrant colors, applied in thick impasto, to create a scene of chromatic contrasts. Nolde lamented that often the theme of Adam and Eve was just an excuse to present a civilized nude man and woman, with idealized, erotic bodies. In this painting, however, the crude, corpulent figures convey an unmistakable sense of dejection and hopelessness, Adam symbolizing brute strength and Eve representing the mother of the human race.

Christ on the Cross

Jean Fautrier

(Paris, 1898–Châtenay-Malabry, Île de France, 1964)

- ca. 1925
- oil on canvas
- 155.5 x 90 cm
- Musée National d'Art Moderne, Paris

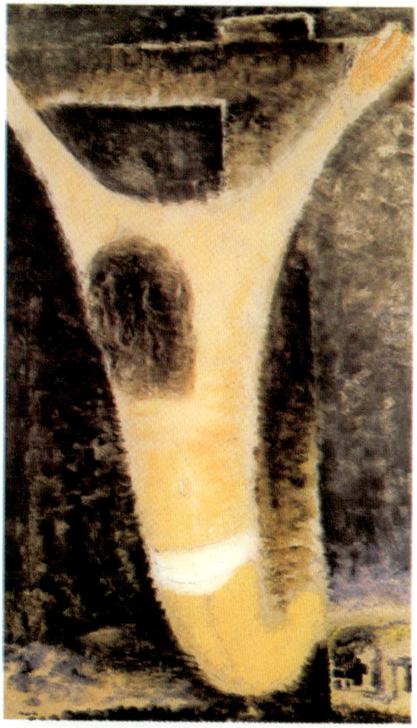

The lines, the dark background, the figure resolved with a field of color punctuated by highlights of definition, the representation of the head—all these elements imbue the painting with an intense profundity, demonstrating the artist's mastery of his art. He does not present but evokes, does not explain but elicits.

Female Nude in Bathtub

Pierre Bonnard

(Fontenay-aux-Roses, Île-de France, 1867–Le Cannet, Provence, 1947)

- ca. 1938
- oil on canvas
- 122 x 151 cm
- The Museum of Modern Art, New York

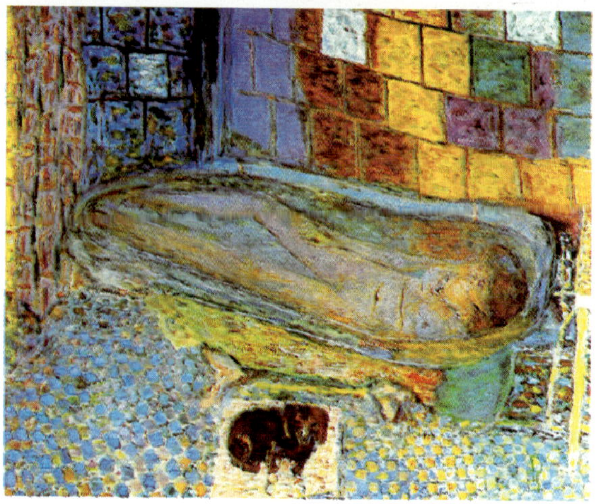

The flesh tones include cold colors that layer and combine with pure, warm tones, creating a symphony of light and color. In this manner, the figure is composed as a whole, the body being outlined with a fine line so as to distinguish it from the background, a technique used by the Nabis and the Fauves.

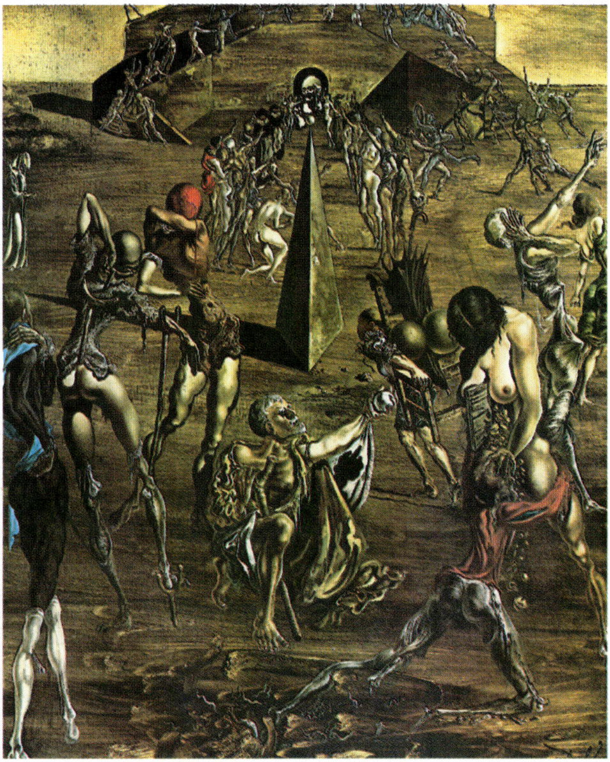

This is an apocalyptic vision of the end of the world, populated with strange figures representing different concepts and situations. All of them appear in a setting that is both dismal and impersonal. Their gestures, expressions and movements lead one to believe that they are waiting for something to happen. With such dramatic tension coupled with an overriding austerity, the artist has taken the surprise, intrigue and disquietude of the scene to an extreme. With a talent for surprising the viewer with his images, despite their utterly unreal nature, the artist presents the figures with countless Surrealist details rendered with great skill. Some of the figures exhibit a morbid sensuality, as if demonstrating what the painter once affirmed: "After eroticism, death is what fascinates me most."

The Resurrection of the Flesh

Salvador Dalí
(Figueres, Catalonia, 1904–1989)

- 1940–45
- oil on canvas
- 90 x 72 cm
- Bruno Pagliai Collection, Mexico and Beverly Hills

The Hands

Paul Delvaux
(Antheit, Liège, 1897 –Veurne, 1994)

- 1941
- oil on canvas
- 110 x 130 cm
- private collection

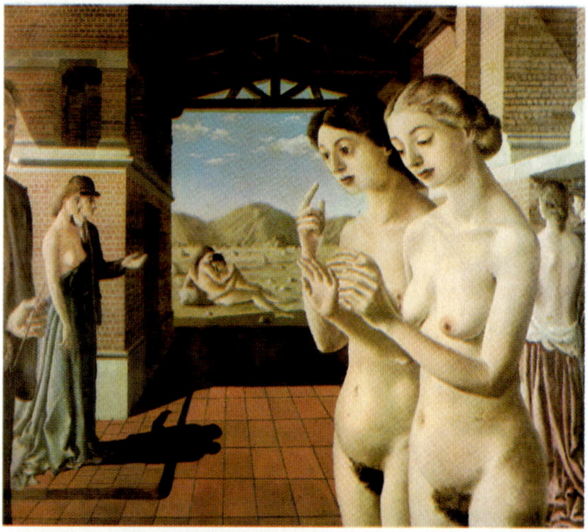

An architectural setting frames the scene, enclosing the statuesque figures in an interior space. Faithful to his Surrealist principles, the painter depicts superbly executed female nudes of exquisite beauty and sensuality, whose lines, flesh tones and volumes are skillfully evoked. Even the couple in the background is rendered with painstaking detail.

Study of a Human Body

Francis Bacon
(Dublin, 1009–Madrid, 1992)

- 1971
- oil on canvas
- 78 x 58 cm
- Sutton Place Heritage

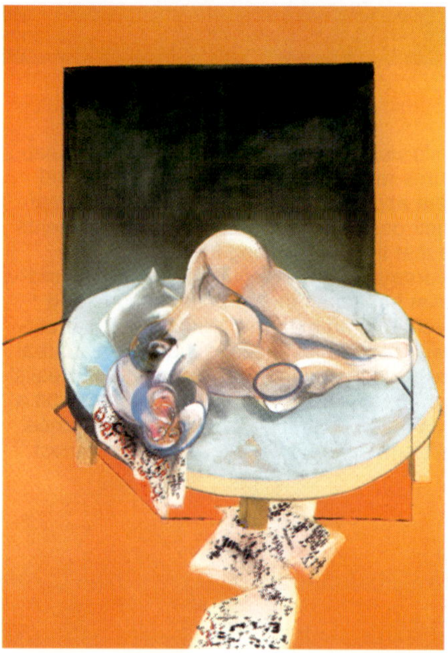

Francis Bacon's penchant for painting triptychs, which he uses to present a narrative in the manner of a storyboard, attest to the artist's desire to portray panoramic views of the absurd world in which his figures find themselves. His existential view of life is tragic.

Salome is depicted here dancing before Herod, while the head of John the Baptist appears to her in a vision. While anatomical details are not especially clear, the figure is nevertheless suggestively erotic through its treatment of skin coloration, parted legs and the brooch at Salome's lower waist.

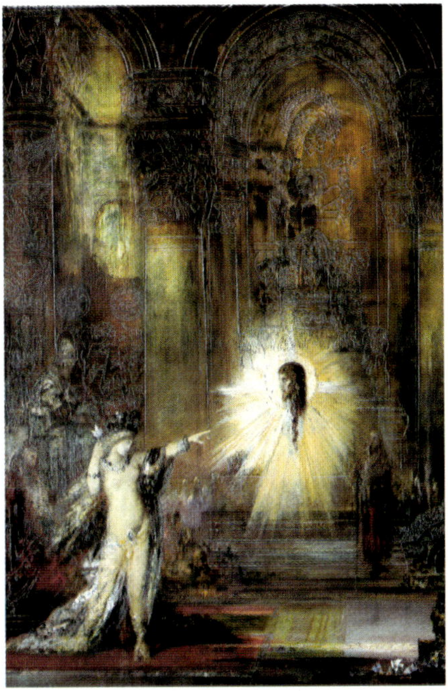

The Vision

Gustave Moreau
(Paris, 1826–1898)

- oil on canvas
- 142 x 103 cm
- Musée Gustave Moreau, Paris

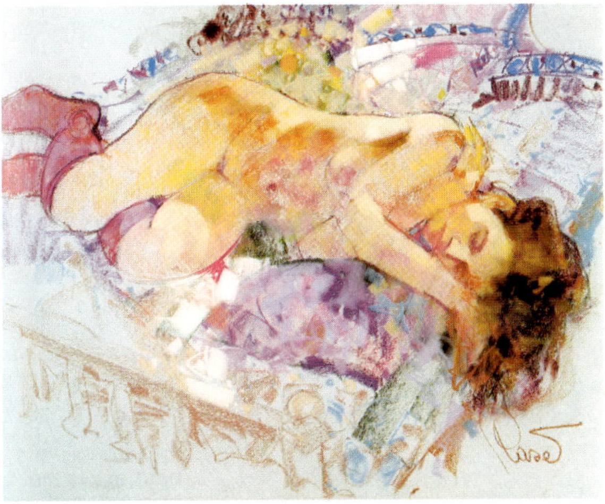

While this female figure, as a whole, certainly dominates the composition, details of line and color and lighting also come into their own and give rise to myriad sensations in the viewer.

Sleeping Female Nude

Joan Raset
(b. Gerona, 1938)

- 1993
- pastel on paper
- 50 x 65 cm
- private collection

Nude

Gloria Muñoz
(b. Barcelona, 1949)

- 1997
- acrylic on canvas
- 150 x 45 cm
- private collection

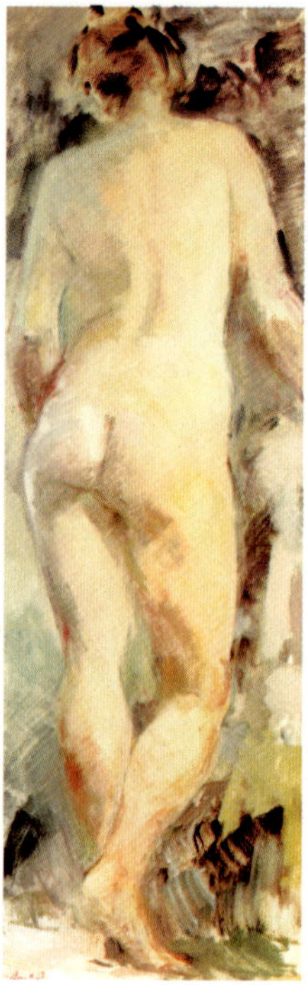

Colour and forceful brushwork are in evidence in this composition, the figure shown in attractive contrapposto.

Nude

Albert Gonzalo i Carbó
(b. Tarragona, 1954)

- 1998
- ink on recycled paper
- 20 x 30.5 cm
- private collection

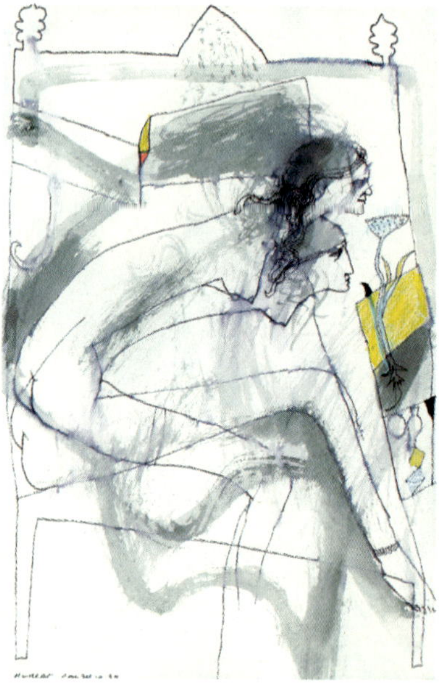

A clear outline here extols the sensuality of this, albeit somewhat androgynous, female figure in the form of a "double exposure".

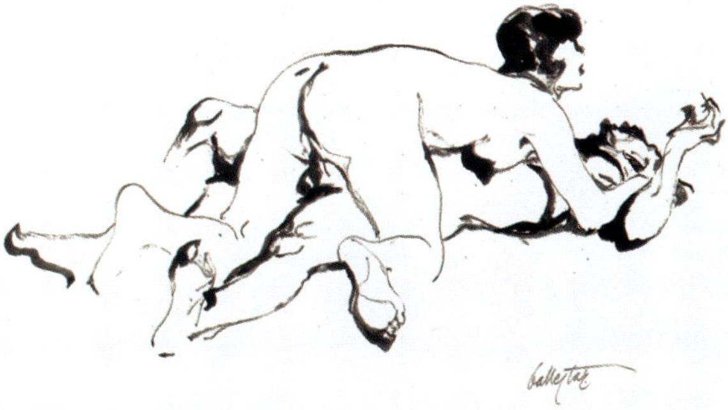

We see, here, highly expressive, forceful bodies, whose forms are well-delineated by their outlines. The artist demonstrates just how much can be depicted and expressed with such minimal means.

Lovers

Vicenç B. Ballestar
(b. Barcelona, 1929)

- 1999
- ink on paper
- 21 x 30 cm
- private collection

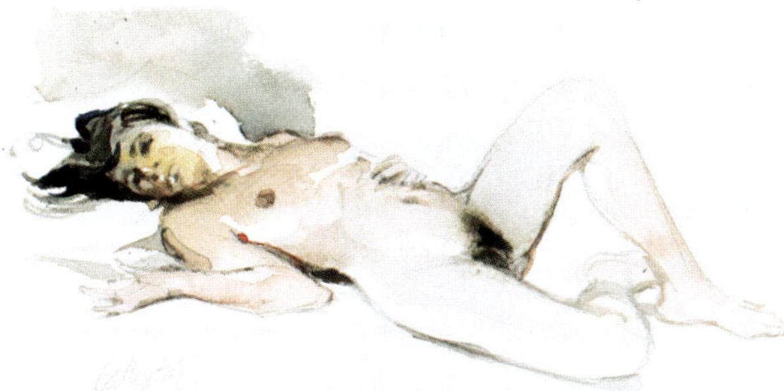

Contrasting ideas come to expression in this masterfully-executed piece: candor and lasciviousness, innocence and provocation, calmness and restlessness. Pose, color-scheme and flawless execution give rise to a dreamy, evanescent and disquieting picture.

The Siesta

Vicenç B. Ballestar
(b. Barcelona, 1929)

- 2000
- watercolor
- 15 x 20 cm
- private collection

Loss

Jesús Teodoro Martín
(b. Barcelona, 1961)

- 1999
- acrylic on canvas
- 130 x 97 cm
- private collection

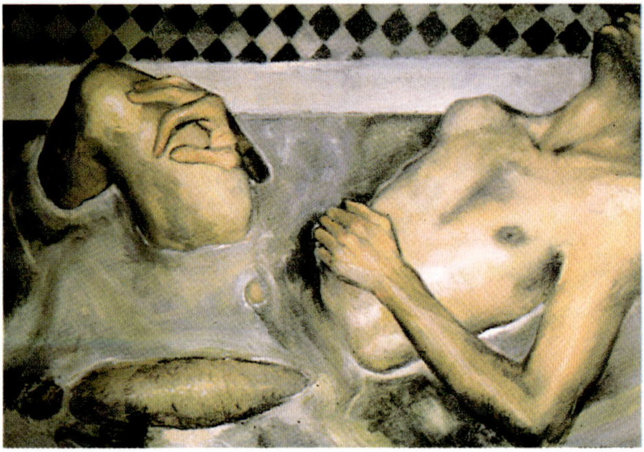

This self-portrait attempts to convert an ostensibly sensual image into an existentialist icon.

Self-Portrait as a Minotaur

Carlos Gomila Camps
(b. Ciutadella, Menorca, 1978)

- 2000
- mixed media on wood
- 200 x 100 cm
- Fondo Patrimonio de la Facultad de Bellas Artes, Universidad Central de Barcelona

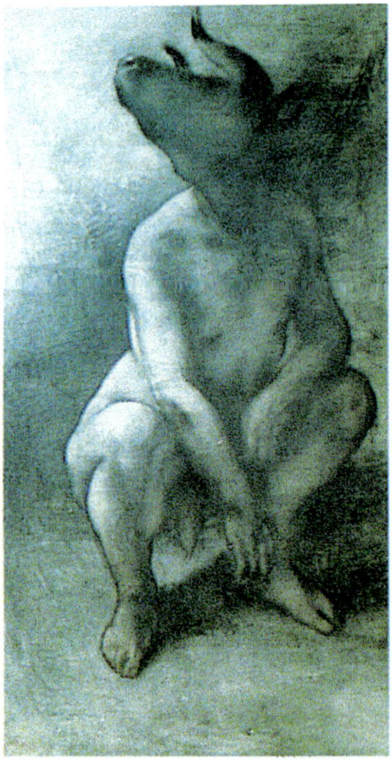

This highly sensual male nude figure with its peculiar realism and grotesque presence can easily provoke a viewer. The way the work establishes bodily fullness and depth is remarkable, to a large extent utilizing bold foreshortening in the limbs as a means of doing so. The handling of light is also a contributory factor.

Index of Artists and Works

A

B

C

D

E

F

H

I

J

M

Q

R

S

T

Contents